REAL ESTATE INVESTOR'S DESKBOOK

ALVIN L. ARNOLD
Member of the New York Bar

WARREN, GORHAM & LAMONT
Boston • New York

WARREN, GORHAM & LAMONT, INC.
210 South Street
Boston, Massachusetts 02111

ISBN 0-88262-732-5

Library of Congress Catalog Card No. 82-70717

PRINTED IN THE UNITED STATES OF AMERICA

To Nancy and our children,
Melissa and Laurence

Preface

The *Real Estate Investor's Deskbook* is a comprehensive guide to all types of real estate transactions and investments. Organized for use as a practical reference, the *Deskbook* presents all the basic information about a specific real estate topic—whether it be forms of ownership, methods of financing, calculating return on investment, or tax consequences of a particular transaction—in one place. It provides developers, investors, brokers, lenders, attorneys, and accountants with clear, straightforward guidance drawn from a practical analysis of the investment considerations related to acquiring, owning, and disposing of real estate. Although designed primarily for the professional with some previous experience in real estate, the *Deskbook* also provides a challenging introduction for the newcomer to this complex and fascinating field.

The *Deskbook* is divided into eleven chapters. The first three chapters deal basically with the analysis that helps an investor to choose and value real estate; the next seven chapters deal with the major real estate transactions and techniques.

Chapter 1, Real Estate as an Investment, discusses the basic considerations related to real estate values and seeks to identify the elements associated with real estate growth, helping the reader to make a wise investment choice.

Chapter 2, Measuring Return on Investment, deals with the various ways—from the simple to the complex—by which return on investment can be calculated and measured. Discussions of financial leverage and tax shelter, two essential elements of profitable real estate investment, are also included here. Thus, this chapter tells the reader how to accurately determine current and future return from a particular real estate property.

Chapter 3, Taxation of Real Estate, sets out the basic federal income tax provisions affecting real estate investment, preparing the investor to meet the tax obligations of various types of real estate arrangements. However, since tax planning is an integral part of the investment process, detailed discussion of some of the important tax rules (e.g., those relating to real estate sales and exchanges, and to leases) are discussed in the appropriate chapters elsewhere in the *Deskbook* and are cross-referenced to Chapter 3.

Chapter 4, Forms of Real Estate Ownership, describes the various ways in which real estate can be owned by an individual or by a group of individuals. In each case, the legal, tax, and business aspects of the particular form of ownership are identified and compared, giving the investor solid information for use in choosing an ownership entity.

The essential and complex subject of real estate financing is covered in three chapters that guide the investor in obtaining the necessary financing for launching a real estate venture. Chapter 5, Sources of Capital; Equity Financing, describes the sources of real estate capital with emphasis on equity financing through syndications and the issuance of real estate securities. Chapter 6, Debt Financing Procedures and Techniques, discusses the entire real estate debt financing cycle, and describes construction and permanent financing as well as a variety of special financing techniques. Chapter 7, Mortgage Insurance and Guarantees; Federal Loans and Grants, discusses the important role of the federal government in real estate finance, as well as the growing role of private mortgage insurance companies.

Chapter 8, Buying, Selling and Exchanging Real Estate, explains the investment, legal, and tax aspects involved in acquiring and disposing of real estate, thus helping the reader to choose the best time and method for buying or selling.

Chapter 9, Leasing Real Estate, discusses all of the key provisions of the lease instrument, which plays such an important role in the real estate field, and also explains leaseholds as investments and as a family-planning technique.

Chapter 10, Operating Real Estate, helps the reader deal with the major questions that arise as a consequence of owning real estate including management, insurance, real property taxation, distressed properties, foreclosure, and bankruptcy.

A lengthy final chapter, Specific Types of Real Estate, discusses the investment attributes of particular types of properties, ranging from undeveloped land to high-rise buildings. Investment topics such as condominium and cooperative conversions, historic preservation, and rehabilitation and modernization of property are also discussed, providing the investor with special insight into these specific properties.

A variety of finding aids make the *Deskbook* a convenient as well as comprehensive reference. A complete table of contents at the front of the volume and individual chapter synopses tell the reader at a glance where to find the major coverage of each real estate topic. Frequent cross-references are a guide to further information on related subjects. In addition, the reader can use the extensive index at the back of the *Deskbook* to quickly locate material on any real estate topic.

Acknowledgments

A volume of this size and scope inevitably reflects the contributions of a considerable number of people, and I thank them all, mentioned and unmentioned. Jack Kusnet has been a constant source of information, ideas, and sound advice, as well as a contributor of portions of the manuscript. Eric Stevenson is primarily responsible for Chapter 7 and has prepared other material as well. James A. Douglas played a considerable role in shaping large portions of the volume. Some material in Chapter 2 and elsewhere has been adapted from text prepared by Charles H. Wurtzebach and Mike E. Miles for our book *Modern Real Estate,* and some sections on financing are the work of Harold Lubell.

Mary Martinez demonstrated how effective a book editor can be in keeping the size of a book manageable without omitting any significant topic. Jo Ann Drew, as she has for all my previous books, worked tirelessly to prepare the manuscript for publication in accordance with her usual high standards. Ellen Newman was a diligent and patient copy editor. Tables at the end of the volume were collected and organized by Nancy Asquith. The book was designed by Dorothy Taishoff.

Alvin L. Arnold

Manhasset, New York
January 1982

Summary of Contents

Contents

1. REAL ESTATE AS AN INVESTMENT

2. MEASURING RETURN ON INVESTMENT

3. TAXATION OF REAL ESTATE

4. FORMS OF REAL ESTATE OWNERSHIP

5. SOURCES OF CAPITAL; EQUITY FINANCING

6. DEBT FINANCING PROCEDURES AND TECHNIQUES

7. MORTGAGE INSURANCE AND GUARANTEES; FEDERAL LOANS AND GRANTS

8. BUYING, SELLING AND EXCHANGING REAL ESTATE

9. LEASING REAL ESTATE

10. OPERATING REAL ESTATE

Depreciation Schedules

[illegible]

Appendixes

1

Real Estate as an Investment

1.01 ELEMENTS OF A GOOD REAL ESTATE INVESTMENT

The value and attractiveness of real estate as an investment is easily established by one simple fact: More great fortunes have been made in real estate than in any other investment field. Three major reasons explain, to a large extent, its continuing appeal:

- From an *investment* point of view, well-located real estate has appreciated at a rate far in excess of the rate of inflation in the United States.
- From a *financing* point of view, real estate can be financed with third-party capital to a far greater extent than any other type of investment.
- From a *tax* point of view, real estate is more advantageous than any other type of investment.

On the other hand, real estate is probably the most complicated type of investment. It can be divided in a myriad of ways and owned through a variety of investment vehicles. In addition, it is likely that hundreds of different financing techniques are currently in use for funding real estate ventures. Once the investment is made, real estate is unique in that it often requires intensive management and is subject to a detailed and complex net of federal tax rules. Finally, real estate is an illiquid type of investment—it is difficult to buy and difficult to sell. These complexities make it essential that a real estate investment be carefully chosen and conscientiously managed for optimum return.

All of the topics set forth above are discussed in the chapters that follow. This introductory chapter identifies the elements of real estate that distinguish it from other types of investments and the features that normally are associated with real estate growth opportunities. It then discusses the various types of interests into which a parcel of real estate can be divided, and concludes with a review of the appraisal process by which judgments about real estate values are made.

[1] Distinguishing Features of Real Estate

The key characteristic of the real estate asset is its association with land; all of the features that distinguish real estate from non-real estate (non-land) assets flow from this fact. The most significant distinguishing features are immobility, unique location, and indestructibility.

[a] Immobility

Real estate is fixed in location and cannot be moved. One consequence of real estate's immobility is that real estate markets, until very recently, were almost completely local markets, or to put it another way, no national market existed for real estate as it did for most manufactured or farm commodities. In the past ten or fifteen years there has been a significant move toward a "national" real estate market, primarily as the result of the increased investment in real estate ownership by pension funds, life insurance companies, and other institutions that formerly limited their real estate activities to mortgage loans. Another important stimulus to the growth of a national market has been the large multi-property real estate syndicates, which raise equity capital from individual investors and purchase a large portfolio of properties (often of a single type, such as apartment buildings) in fifteen or twenty states. Notwithstanding this development, the fact that real estate cannot be moved from place to place means that real estate expertise requires knowledge of individual markets.

[b] Unique Location (Heterogeneity)

Associated with the immobility of land is the fact that every single parcel of real estate in the world has a location that cannot be duplicated. Thus, every parcel of real estate is unique or heterogeneous (one of a kind). By comparison, commodities such as grain or coal (or identifiable subtypes), or intangibles such as shares of stock in General Motors Corporation, are exactly alike and are called fungibles; they have the quality of fungibility, meaning that it makes no difference to a purchaser whether he gets a particular lot so long as the quantity is as agreed.

An important consequence of the uniqueness of every parcel of real estate is the economic feature of scarcity. Since every location is unique, only one parcel (or perhaps a very few) can satisfy the location requirement of a particular property use. And location is considered to be the single most important key to the value of a parcel of real estate. One site, because of its relationship to places of employment, shopping, transportation, schools, and even the properties immediately surrounding it, can command a much higher price than land with similar physical or topographical features but with a different location. So even though no absolute shortage of land exists in the United States, or is ever likely to, land for a particular purpose at a particular time and place may be quite scarce—and it is this scarcity that gives real estate its value.

[c] Indestructibility

Another significant distinguishing feature of real estate is that, both as an economic asset and as the object of legal interest, land is viewed as indestructible.

Land may be mined, eroded, flooded, or desolated; nevertheless, the designated location on the earth's surface remains forever. Since the value of a parcel of land relates primarily to its location, and since this location is indestructible, land is generally excellent loan security; thus, investors in real estate have always been able to obtain very large loans in relation to the value of the property (termed the "loan-to-value ratio"). One of the major reasons for the large fortunes made in real estate in the past has been the financial leverage created by real estate financing. (This process is described at 2.03[6].) While it is true that financial leverage is much more difficult to achieve in today's high-interest-rate market, it remains one of the important attractions of real estate investing.

While improvements and additions to land are not indestructible in the sense that land itself is, they normally have long useful lives, often measured in quarter or half centuries. (Indeed, structures are used today that were built at the time of the American Revolution.) This relative immunity of well-maintained structures to physical deterioration leads to an interesting phenomenon: Buildings rarely fall down, but rather are torn down because a new use will make the site more productive and hence more valuable. (This is discussed in greater detail at 1.03.)

[2] Identifying Real Estate Opportunities

[a] Location as Key to Value

The most common explanation given for the stability of real estate value and its growth potential is that only so much land exists in the country and, therefore, values have no direction to go but up. In other words, the formula is: A fixed supply of land meeting a rising demand equals rising values. But this is much too broad a statement since only about 20 percent of the United States is developed real estate; 80 percent consists of farms, ranches, timberland and pastureland, forests, and other undeveloped space. Nevertheless, the concept of a limited supply of land is the key to understanding the growth in real estate values. It is a limited supply of certain kinds of real estate that is important; to determine the kinds of real estate, the source of economic value in real estate must be discussed briefly.

As noted above, value in real estate is a function primarily of the location of the real estate. Or, as in the endlessly told real estate joke, "Value in real estate depends on three things—location, location, and location." Location, in its economic sense, always implies a relationship between (1) the use to which the particular real estate is put and (2) its related uses. The related uses for a homeowner are proximity to schools, shopping, recreation and, if possible, place of employment; for a shopping center or a retail store, it is more important that the location be near a large residential area. An office building tenant wants to be near public transportation for use by its employees and near meeting places for clients and customers; young, single employees want to be near shopping, restaurants, and other single people. In other words, location is always evaluated in terms of the proposed use of the particular land and related uses. In general, well-located land is land that is part of an urban area, that is, an area in which people are concentrated and in which there is a complex interaction among residential, commercial, and industrial uses.

The formula concerning the stability of real estate value set forth above can then be restated as follows: A limited supply of well-located land for urban uses meeting a rising demand for such land equals rising values. And this indeed is the underlying reason why some real estate values have risen sharply in past years, other real estate remains stable but shows no growth, while yet other real estate has shown a decline in value.

One important exception exists to the rule that real estate value is a function of location. Land sometimes may have inherent qualities or defects that affect value regardless of location. A gold mine is valuable no matter where it is found (provided, of course, the gold can be sold for more than the cost of mining it). Land with spectacular scenery and with an ideal climate may become an international resort even though (and sometimes because) it is far off the beaten track.

On the other hand, and more important, land may have negative qualities that prevent its use despite an excellent location. Almost every large urban area has land that cannot be improved, for such reasons as marshy soil, difficult topography, risk of flooding, and vulnerability to unpleasant odors because of the prevailing winds from nearby industrial plants. Developers often will avoid land with these negative defects in favor of other land with less desirable location but where construction is cheaper or negative factors are not present.

However, land with negative qualities can still become enormously valuable if its location is desirable enough. A classic example is the New Jersey meadowland just across the Hudson River from New York City. Marshy soil and complex questions concerning legal title prevented the development of the land until fairly recently. But its location was so desirable as the New York metropolitan area continued to grow that development finally began. Perhaps an even more dramatic example is Las Vegas, Nevada; not only did the land there have negative qualities because it was on desert, but the location seemed to have no value whatsoever. It was only when the gambling casinos were built that the location gained value and the negative features of the land were overlooked. (It would perhaps be more accurate to say that any location in the state of Nevada had value, since gambling was legal there; the locational value thus overcame the negative defects of the land.) Miami Beach is yet another example of originally undesirable land that became valuable as a resort area.

[b] Factors Creating Demand for Real Estate

If the value of real estate relates to its location, and if location in turn is related to real estate uses, the real estate investor should be particularly interested in those factors that create a demand for real estate uses in a particular locale. Demand for real estate generally can be viewed under three separate headings: population changes, the increase in leisure time and discretionary income, and the movements of industry and trade.

[i] Population Changes. Ultimately, all real estate demand is related to people. People use real estate for living, working, recreation, and for every other human activity. So the overall demand for real estate in the United States can be clarified by seeking the answers to these questions:

- Is population growing, stable, or declining?
- What population shifts are occurring?

- What is the classification of the population by age groups (population profile)?

Population Growth. The 1980 census showed approximately 222 million Americans. By 1990, the projections are that about 244 million people are likely to inhabit the country. While an increase of about 10 percent is not unduly large, an actual rise in number of individuals of about 22 million is very large.

What does this mean for real estate? If in fact 22 million more Americans will be living in this country during the 1980s, our store of "built-up" real estate will have to increase to meet their demands for housing, schooling, employment and recreation. If for any reason that population growth is much greater than is now anticipated, real estate prices would be likely to outpace the price level in general, perhaps by a substantial amount. Indeed, it might be impossible to satisfy the demand for improved real estate because of shortages of labor and materials. On the other hand, if growth leveled off, high vacancy rates and postponed development would put many real estate firms under great pressure. If in the course of the next half century zero population growth is experienced in this country, real estate will become essentially a "replacement industry." Of course, projections that far ahead must be considered purely speculative.

Population Shifts. Americans are the most mobile people in the world. It is one of the greatest virtues of our free-enterprise democracy that people are psychologically, economically, and legally free to move from place to place. (Indeed, the right to travel and settle in a different state is a constitutionally protected right.) And while major population movements are not of great interest to the neighborhood real estate investor, large institutional investors with diversified portfolios follow population movements with a great deal of interest because—once again—real estate values ultimately depend on the demand for real estate uses.

At the present time, two very significant population movements are taking place in the United States. The first major movement is the shift from the North and Midwest to the South and West. This is in part the "move to the sun" that is causing a large increase in population in the southern rim of the United States. In recent years, for example, 85 percent of total population growth occurred in the twenty-nine southern and western states that make up the Sun Belt. The fastest-growing individual states in the next decade (all admittedly from small population bases) are projected to be Nevada, Wyoming, Colorado, Arizona, and Utah.

The second major population movement is from the large cities to the outer suburbs and rural counties. This may reflect reversal of a trend that goes back to 1940, when a rapid outpouring of people from rural areas coincided with the beginning of the U.S. defense effort in World War II. It continued apace in the 1950s as farms were consolidated and as cities with a shortage of workers welcomed rural populations. From 1940 to 1960, a net average of more than one million people per year left the farms (although not all moved to metropolitan cities), and a majority of nonmetropolitan counties declined in population despite high birth rates. By the mid-1960s, this massive movement had virtually reached a halt, although this was not apparent until some years later.

Then, beginning in 1970, the trend began to reverse. For the first time in this century, nonmetropolitan areas began growing at a faster rate than metropolitan areas. It is true that, to a large degree, counties immediately adjacent to metropolitan areas have experienced growth (indicating that urban sprawl is simply continuing). However, nonadjacent counties have also been growing—and growing more rapidly than metropolitan counties. The three factors that seem to be most important in encouraging the growth of rural areas have been:

- Decentralization of manufacturing
- Growth of resort and retirement communities
- Growth of college towns, both because of the growth of the college population and because many nonacademic people are attracted to the amenities in such communities

While the first of these population movements—movement to different regions of the country—is of interest primarily to very large investment groups, the second instance—movement within a single region or from the central-city core to outlying areas—is an important consideration to local investors as well. Those who speculate in undeveloped land, in particular, are alert to patterns of population growth from and around cities.

Population Profile. The final way to look at population figures is to construct a population profile, which is a classification of the population by age group. Since different age groups indicate fairly well-defined differences in their need for improved real estate, a shifting population profile gives us some idea of the changing demand for real estate in the years ahead. Table 1.1 below shows the population profile for the United States at the beginning of each of three decades: 1970, 1980, and 1990 (projected).

To illustrate how the population profile affects real estate, consider the 20–29-year age group in Table 1.1. The group included 31 million people in 1970, jumped to 40 million in 1980 and will decline slightly to 38 million by 1990. (These projections, of course, are fairly accurate since this age group already has been born.) Why the big jump between 1970 and 1980? Because this age group

TABLE 1.1 Population Profile of the United States

	(in millions)			*Percent Change*	*Percent Change*
Population	*1970*	*1980*	*1990*	*1970-1980*	*1980-1990*
Under 5 years	17.1	16.0	19.4	−6.4%	21.3%
5–14 years	40.7	33.9	35.8	−16.7	5.6
15–19 years	19.3	20.6	16.8	6.7	−18.4
20–29 years	30.9	39.8	38.1	28.8	−4.3
30–39 years	22.7	31.3	40.2	37.9	28.4
40–49 years	24.1	22.7	31.2	−5.8	37.4
50–59 years	21.2	23.1	21.8	9.0	−5.6
60–64 years	8.7	9.8	10.4	12.6	6.1
65 years and over	20.1	24.9	29.8	23.9	19.7
Total	204.8	222.2	243.5	8.5%	9.6%

reflects the baby boom that occurred after World War II, particularly in the five-year period from 1955 to 1960. Since it is this age group that normally forms most new households, they constitute the main demand for apartment units and first-time houses. Consequently, it has not been surprising that the decade of the 1970s was very strong for residential building. (The demand has been primarily for private homes rather than rental units because the rapid inflation in the decade made owning real estate a very desirable inflation hedge.) During the decade of the 1980s, this age group will not grow and so will not generate any increased demand (although the 30–39-year age group, also important in home-buying, will increase substantially in numbers in this coming decade).

Consider next the very sharp growth in the 65-year-and-over group throughout the entire twenty-year period shown in Table 1.1. The number of senior citizens increased by 24 percent in the first decade and will increase by 20 percent in the second. This is one reason why real estate developers anticipate a sharply rising demand for retirement communities and congregate-housing facilities (i.e., with central dining rooms), as well as for medical and nursing facilities. And to the extent members of this age group live in their own homes, the demand will be for small and compact housing units near public transportation, with easy access to shopping and recreational facilities.

[ii] Increase in Leisure Time and Discretionary Income. Many factors are creating a demand for real estate in connection with nonwork activities. People have more leisure time than ever before because of the declining workweek, longer vacations, earlier retirement, and longer life expectancy. These factors in combination mean that a larger percentage than ever before of the total "man-hours" of our population can be spent in activities other than earning a living.

In addition to having more time, people have more money than ever before. The main factor creating a higher discretionary income is the growth in our national productivity. This means not only higher salaries and wages for our working population but also increased retirement benefits, from social security and from private retirement plans, for the nonworking population. This interaction of increasing discretionary time and discretionary income has created an explosion in such real estate-related areas as retirement communities, vacation homes, resort areas, motels, nursing homes and a host of others.

One interesting feature of the demand for such uses is that it encompasses real estate in widely diversified locations, many of them far from urban centers. Retirement and vacation homes in Florida and the Southwest are examples. And, of course, resorts very often have appeal just because of their remoteness. So in the context of leisure time and retirement uses, well-located land may be anywhere —a point to be remembered by raw-land speculators.

[iii] Movements of Industry and Trade. The three decades following World War II saw one of the major social and economic upheavals in our history. This involved the dispersion of retail areas from downtown "main streets" (called central business districts (CBDs)) to shopping centers in the suburbs. The dispersion resulted from the mass migration of population from the in-city areas to suburban areas; the migration in turn was made possible by the automobile, which became a middle-class necessity.

The growth of the shopping center had an immediate and disastrous effect on real estate values in most CBDs. Many small towns throughout the country have not recovered to this day from the loss of retail business. Stores remain empty or, where conversion has been possible, have become a self-service laundry, real estate broker's office, discount store, or local telephone or government service facility, none of which pays rentals equal to those of prosperous retailers of former days. Nothing better illustrates the need for investors to be aware constantly of changing conditions than the tremendous loss suffered by many people in blue-chip "main street" real estate values.

In recent years, this dispersion has slowed down, at least in the near-in suburbs where population growth has moderated. On the other hand, many opportunities for retailing operations are opening up in relatively rural areas that are now experiencing a population upturn. In addition, the large cities, particularly in the Northeast, are once again becoming popular as high costs of energy, new construction, municipal services, and so forth render it more economical for many people to live in already built-up areas. This in turn has resulted in a revival of some (but no means all) of the central business districts that were severely depressed ten or fifteen years ago.

Another significant pattern of movement relates to the decentralization of industrial and commercial operations. Manufacturing, particularly of the light industrial kind, has located in "industrial parks" as well as at free-standing locations outside the city limits but near highways offering quick access to the city. More recently, office buildings are being constructed in the suburbs as more and more people seek to avoid long commuting times from suburban homes. Finally, we have seen a proliferation of every kind of roadside and drive-in establishment, in many cases extending far out into the outer suburbs. All of these demands for real estate—commercial, industrial, retailing and service operations, on top of the basic residential demand—indicate that suburban real estate values will very likely continue to rise.

[3] Seven Tests for a Real Estate Investment

No test or series of tests can assure an investor that a particular transaction will prove to be profitable. The tests set out below, however, are valuable for two reasons. First, they help an investor clarify his objectives to prevent him switching from one approach to another, never obtaining the benefit that comes from consistently and logically following any single investment goal. As golf players say, an investor must learn to "keep an eye on the ball," the "ball" being that investment objective best suited to one's economic position, and emotional and psychological makeup; this determines one's ability to assume risks and to live with a particular investment.

The second reason for including these tests is that they help investors avoid obvious errors when buying real estate. These errors, usually (but not always) made by neophytes in real estate, undoubtedly account for most investment losses. A carefully thought-out and researched investment based on the seven tests described below, while it might not produce the anticipated gain over the projected holding period, is much less likely to suffer a severe diminution in value than an investment made on impulse.

[a] Test 1: Secure and High Income

The value of any real estate investment arises from its future flow of income. This is the single most important rule of real estate investing. While other types of investments—works of art, gems, gold, antiques, and the like—may have value without regard to future flow of income, value and income in real estate investing are two sides of the same coin. Even investments in raw land derive their value from anticipated future use and future income. So the first test for a good real estate investment is: Does it produce secure and high income? By asking that question, we are correctly implying that the value of a piece of real estate must be based on the income that can be derived from it. Another way of expressing this idea is by saying that the investment is really a "flow of income." From this point of view, an apartment house is not looked upon as a building on a piece of real estate but rather as an economic asset that will produce a continuing flow of income (rents) for the foreseeable future. The value of this concept is that it emphasizes the alternatives open to an investor; that is, he should never visualize himself only as the owner of a particular kind of real estate, but as an investor with capital that can be invested in whatever area promises the greatest income return.

A corollary to the "flow of income" concept is that we are always talking about future income. What is past cannot benefit us today or tomorrow. We are interested in the past record only as an indication of what we can expect in the future. A parcel of raw land producing no income today, but with great potential for future income, may well be worth more than a dilapidated building in an undesirable neighborhood producing rental income today that can vanish at any time because people refuse to live in the building or in the neighborhood.

There are two features to the future flow of income that can be anticipated from property. The first is the stability of the flow; that is, how certain can we be of receiving it? The second feature is the trend of the income; that is, to what degree can we anticipate that future income will grow? In past years, notably up until World War II, the emphasis in measuring income has always been on the stability rather than the trend. Investors were not accustomed to thinking of a continually growing economy; they were quite satisfied if they could be assured that future income would be at least as good as the present income.

Nowadays, the opposite is true. Not only does every investor expect to see his own investment grow each year, but he expects the national economy to do the same. The new point of view results from the explosive growth in the American economy since 1945. To some degree, particularly in recent years, this merely has been inflationary growth, but in very large part it has represented true growth arising from increasing population and higher productivity by the labor force. As a result of the "growth complex," a very small amount of present income, or even its complete absence, is very often overlooked where there is a reason to expect a sharply increasing trend of income in the future. It is obvious that this approach carries dangers with it, for it means that merely a leveling off, without any actual decline, in the income from an investment can result in a sharply reduced value.

[b] Test 2: Growth of Capital

The second test for a good real estate investment is whether or not the value of the investment will grow over the years. We can conveniently divide this test into two separate portions, that relating to true growth and that relating to inflationary growth.

☐ *True growth.* Since the value of an income-producing real estate investment is directly related to the trend of its income, it should come as no surprise that growth of value will occur when the income flow increases year by year. If investors are willing to pay ten times income, for instance, a present income of $1,000 has a value of $10,000. If the income can be expected to grow at the rate of 5 percent per year, then the value of the investment should also grow at the rate of 5 percent per year. For example, at the end of five years, the income may have grown from $1,000 to $1,250 per year. The capital value should then have risen to $12,500.

Of course, things are never this simple. While as a general rule and over the longer term the above statement—that growth of capital will follow growth of income—is true, a number of factors may upset the relationship over the short term.

The most common of these short-term factors can be combined under the general heading of "investor psychology." If, for some reason, real estate suddenly appears to be a less desirable investment than other fields, for example, common stock, funds will flow from real estate into the stock market, and values for real estate will decline across the board (i.e., the lessened demand for real estate will reduce the price that buyers of real estate have to pay). It must be said that this has not happened to any significant degree in recent years; indeed, the reverse has been the case. As more and more investors become educated to the long-term values in real estate, real estate values have tended to rise rather than decline. The danger in this type of trend is that it ultimately pushes prices to the point when continued buying can only be justified under the "greater fool theory" of investment. A person following this theory admits the foolishness of buying at what is obviously too high a price, but anticipates that in time a greater fool will be available to whom the investment can be sold at a profit. Inevitably, at some point prices will reverse so suddenly that speculators and late buyers will be in no position to protect themselves. It is a game of musical chairs in which the losses can be severe.

☐ *Inflationary growth.* During the past two decades, the United States has suffered through the worst and longest period of inflation in our history. Inflation describes a relationship between actual objects (such as real estate) on the one hand and cash on the other, whereas true growth as just described discusses the relationship between the values of different objects (e.g., between real estate and common stocks). When inflation is rampant, the investor's first concern is to determine if an object of investment is at least increasing in value as fast as the rate of inflation. If it is, the investor is not suffering an erosion of capital, though he may not be making a profit.

In terms of the two tests just discussed (secure and high income, and growth of capital), real estate will be a good inflation hedge so long as (1) its income increases as fast or faster than the inflation rate and (2) the value placed on that income remains at least the same as before.

In general, real estate has been an outstanding inflation hedge during the past twenty years. The major reason is that real estate rentals have increased at least as fast, and often faster, than the inflation rate. A notable exception, however, has been apartment buildings where fears of rent control and the predominance of small landlords (who often have a personal relationship or friendship with tenants) has kept a lid on rent increases. Other types of income properties, such as office buildings, shopping centers and hospitality facilities, have shown very sharp increases in value, although temporary periods of oversupply have interrupted this growth.

Residential housing has been a special case. Home values, of course, do not depend upon rental income but upon the relative bargaining position of buyers and sellers. For several reasons, including the tax advantages of ownership, the shortage of available rental units, and a "bandwagon" psychology, home prices have in fact risen very sharply during this inflationary period. This trend may now be coming to an end as very high home-mortgage interest rates severely reduce the ability of prospective home purchasers to pay carrying costs.

The important point to be made about inflationary growth is that, while real estate may indeed prove to be an effective hedge, no one should actually invest in real estate merely to offset inflation. The risks of real estate investment are sufficiently great so that an acquisition is only warranted when true growth (as distinguished from inflationary growth) can be projected.

[c] Test 3: Minimum Risk of Loss of Capital

The first two investment objectives discussed were positive ones; they were the attainment of secure income and capital growth. This next investment objective is best stated in a negative form: It is to minimize the risk of loss of capital. As many investors have learned, to their sorrow, anything that goes up in price can come down, and when it does, the descent is apt to be more rapid than the ascent. There are essentially two ways to reduce the chance of loss in any investment portfolio: (1) maintaining a high level of "quality"; and (2) diversifying investments.

☐ *High quality (e.g., secure and rising income)*. "Quality" is merely a way of expressing the likelihood that an investment will not suffer a sharp decline in price and thus the term by itself is not an answer to the question of how to minimize loss. "Quality" really means the probability of continuing (and rising) income from an investment regardless of general economic conditions. The more likely it is that an investment will continue to produce income, the greater its quality. Thus, apartment buildings are generally considered more secure than office buildings because, when suffering economic distress, office building tenants are more likely to give up their offices than apartment renters are to give up their residences. On the other hand, office buildings offer greater growth potential; hence the old real estate saying, "you sleep better with apartment houses and eat better with office buildings." On the other end of the scale, business-type properties, such as bowling alleys, tennis courts, motels, and vacation resorts, will suffer far more in a general economic recession or depression than more traditional real estate investments.

☐ *Diversification or divisibility of investment.* The quality of an investment is always a matter of opinion and no one can be absolutely sure that any given investment will not suffer serious price declines during a general economic recession or because of defects or weaknesses in the particular property. Very conservative investors, therefore, will take the further step of diversifying their investments so that the decline of value of any one of them will have only a limited effect on the entire portfolio.

While diversification is quite easily obtainable with common stocks, it is generally harder to come by in real estate investments because of the larger size of the investment units. One rather special way to obtain real estate diversification is to buy shares of one or more real estate investment trusts or real estate corporations, but this is obviously something quite different from a direct personal investment and exposes the investor to risks largely outside his control. Another possible answer for a real estate investor is to form a syndicate with a number of other like-minded persons and use the pool of funds to buy a portfolio of several properties. The fact remains that diversification is difficult to achieve in real estate, and it is the main reason why a prospective investor must be extremely careful to investigate every facet of a particular property before he buys.

[d] Test 4: Favorable Tax Treatment of Income and Gains

Real estate offers the investor very substantial advantages over common stocks and many other forms of property. (The tax aspects of real estate are covered in detail in Chapter 3.) Here is a brief list:

☐ *Investment real estate creates capital gains but ordinary loss.* When real estate is held for business use or investment, gain on a sale is taxable at the favorable capital gains rate, but any loss from the sale of such real estate can be deducted against ordinary income and therefore reduces income tax liability at the full rate.

☐ *Real estate operating and repair costs are deductible against ordinary income.* An investor is entitled to deduct each year from his gross income received from real estate the costs of operating the real estate, including normal repairs and maintenance. This might not seem to be much of a tax advantage since the deduction is for monies actually expended by the investor. But very often repair and maintenance costs have the effect of prolonging the life of the property or of increasing the value of the property. The result is that an investor often can put money in the property for the purpose of keeping the property in efficient operating condition while taking a deduction for such expenditure against his ordinary income; then he can get his money back in the form of capital gain when he sells the property.

☐ *The real estate depreciation deduction creates a "tax shelter."* We discuss the concept of "tax shelter" in real estate in some depth in 3.02[1]. In brief, the use of the depreciation deduction in real estate (where the property suffers no actual loss of value because of good maintenance and rising values) gives an investor what is in effect additional deductions against his ordinary income.

☐ *Investment real estate can be exchanged tax-free for other real estate.* An increasingly important concept in real estate investment is the tax-free exchange whereby investment real estate can be swapped for other investment real estate (subject to certain limitations) without paying any tax on the accumulated gain. This permits an investor to pyramid his properties without ever paying a tax on the gain until the ultimate end of the cycle when the final property is sold for cash.

In other words, Uncle Sam becomes your partner by putting up a part of the money, without asking any return.

[e] Test 5: Ability to Finance and Create Upside Leverage

Until very recently, when interest rates soared to new heights, the greatest single advantage of real estate investment lay in the ease and the extent to which it could be financed with borrowed funds at moderate interest rates. As a result, investors usually were able to create upside leverage—a condition in which the investor could earn more on the borrowed funds than he had to pay in interest, thus making a profit on someone else's capital. (Leverage is explained in some detail in 2.03[6].) No other form of investment could compare to real estate in this respect. And since for a person of modest means the way to a fortune always requires the use of borrowed funds, the leverage potential in real estate was probably its most attractive feature.

The situation today is somewhat different. In most cases, very high interest rates make it impossible to achieve upside leverage. Indeed, third-party financing often results in the opposite condition of downside leverage, whereby the borrower must pay out more for the use of money than he can earn from investing the funds. However, the present situation is likely to prove abnormal. Interest rates at some point are likely to decline, perhaps substantially, which would permit real estate investors once again to benefit from upside leverage for good quality properties.

Even in today's market, financing remains an advantage of real estate investing. The reason is that financing has become so integral a part of the real estate investment process that buyers, lenders, and sellers have worked out a variety of "creative financing" techniques that permit buyers to achieve some, if not all, of the benefits of third-party financing. (This subject is discussed in great detail in Chapter 6.)

[f] Test 6: Liquidity

Liquidity is the ability to convert an investment into cash quickly, at a price close to its true value. Cash represents 100 percent liquidity. The opposite of a liquid asset is a frozen asset, that is, one that cannot readily be turned into cash without heavy loss. Liquidity, in the sense that we use it, requires a speedy sale and conversion into cash or its equivalent at a price close to the fair value of the property.

Real estate is the classic example of an illiquid investment. First of all, a seller cannot assume that merely because there is a demand for real estate, his particular property will find an immediate buyer. Every parcel of land in the world is unique because each has its own distinct location. And every building and improvement in real estate is unique too—because of the way it looks and has been maintained, and for a dozen other reasons. So the right buyer must be found for each seller, and this inevitably takes some time.

In addition, even when a seller is found, real estate cannot be sold simply or quickly. A contract of sale must be drawn up, financing must be arranged, the legal title in the seller must be examined by the buyer's attorneys, and various other steps must occur, the whole process usually consuming up to thirty or sixty days at the very least.

It is true that in times of great distress, when sellers are forced to liquidate (i.e., make liquid) their real estate holdings, buyers may be willing to snap them up, but only because the price is well below that which would generally be considered a fair price. Such sales, therefore, do not meet our definition of liquidity, which requires both a speedy sale and one close to fair value. It must be admitted that the illiquidity of real estate is one of the greatest disadvantages. It means that a buyer, once having bought, is locked in to his investment for some period of time and may eventually have to sell at a substantial loss if it turns out that he made a mistake. Because of this illiquidity, and the difficulty (previously discussed) of achieving diversification, real estate demands the most careful analysis before a decision to buy is reached.

There is another view of liquidity, however, that should be noted. The illiquidity of real estate may have certain advantages. First of all, as has just been said, it puts pressure on the investor to make a very careful preliminary examination and so may prevent the "shoot from the hip" type of purchase that is frequent in the stock market. Second, during times of panic, when pressure to sell becomes very great, the absence of a market for real estate can be a positive advantage because it prevents a sale at a time that, in retrospect, may be the worst time to sell. During the great stock market crash of 1929, fortunes were wiped out in a matter of hours as plunging prices created a panic that caused many investors to dump their holdings on the market for whatever they could bring. Many stock market investors, looking back, regretted their decision to sell during a moment of panic.

On the other hand, real estate investors, unable to sell at all in many cases during the ensuing depression of the 1930s because no buyers were available, were forced to retain their holdings. This turned out to their advantage as the years passed, and real estate prices once again began to climb and eventually reached prices far above those preceding the depression. Of course, many real estate investors were forced to liquidate to pay off loans or satisfy their immediate needs. For these persons, illiquidity was a great disadvantage. But for those who owned their real estate outright, and who were fortunate enough to have sufficient income to see them through the depression years, illiquidity may have been a blessing. Hopefully, we shall never see another great depression again, but we shall undoubtedly see periods of decline and near-panic, during which time, in retrospect, the decision not to sell usually will turn out to have been the correct decision.

Finally, it may be said that illiquidity is an aid to the greatest virtue in investing, that of patience. The great fortunes in real estate (and in the stock market) have been made by holding rather than selling investments. This does not mean a blind unwillingness to sell a particular investment at any time or at any price; it does mean that constant trading, buying, and selling under the impetus of rumors and gossip and a desire to make a quick dollar are usually the sure path to loss.

[g] Test 7: Ease of Management

An important consideration in any investment is the amount of time the investor will have to spend supervising it. Many people make the error of treating the entire return from an investment as profit without considering any portion of it as salary or wages for their time and effort. Those who would never think of working for someone else without pay act as if the hours devoted to their own investments are not worthy of compensation. Properly speaking, the time spent following one's own investments should return a sum of money at least equal to the amount one could earn working at a job for someone else. Of course, in some special cases, as where a person collects rare coins or old books as a hobby as well as an investment, time spent can be considered leisure time as well as working time. But certainly in the case of real estate, management is a major factor, and indeed, it is probably the single greatest disadvantage of investing in real estate rather than other forms of property. An investor owning a number of different properties, each with several tenants and each having its own problems of maintenance, repairs, taxes, etc., easily can spend all of his time managing his portfolio. Even a single property, such as an apartment building having a large number of tenants on short-term leases, can be a full-time job. On the other hand, investing in undeveloped land with the aim of sitting tight in the expectation of rising values will require relatively little management.

There is an alternative to personal supervision of real estate. Professional management generally is available anywhere in the country for a fee, which generally is in terms of a percentage of the gross income (i.e., income before deducting any expenses). For example, a medium-size apartment house may be managed for a fee of approximately 5 percent of the gross rental income. For this, the owner is released from all management and leasing duties (sometimes the manager is entitled to a small additional fee for each lease he negotiates). While this solves the management problem, it significantly reduces the yield to the investor.

1.02 LAND VOLUME, DESCRIPTION, AND MEASUREMENT

[1] Volume of Land in the United States

The total volume of land in the United States is equal to approximately 2.25 billion acres. An acre is 43,560 square feet, or 4,840 square yards. A parcel of land 210 feet by 207 feet is approximately one acre, and there are 640 acres in a square mile. A one-family house in an urban area can be put up on as small a site as one-eighth acre; a large shopping center might take up 100 acres or more. With several billion acres available, there has never been nor is there ever likely to be an absolute shortage of land. However, as already noted, well-located land definitely is in short supply in many places.

In terms of ownership, the federal government owns 33 percent of the total acreage in the fifty states. (Since a large portion of this land is located in Alaska and other remote areas, the value of federal land is much less than 33 percent of the total.) State and local governments own another 3 percent, and American Indians own 2 percent. Another 3 percent is classified as urban, that is, developed or imminently developable land. This leaves 59 percent of the total acreage as privately owned rural land. (Two ways of distinguishing developable from rural land is whether the land has access to a highway and whether it is within commuting distance of an urban area.)

[2] Land Description and Measurement

The precise description and measurement of a parcel of land is obviously of critical importance, particularly in large urban areas where every inch of land has value.

Land typically is described by surface measurements, with the property rights extending downward like an inverted cone to the center of the earth and upwards "to the heavens." (See Table 1.2 below.) Surface measurements are usually by one of two means: metes and bounds or government survey.

TABLE 1.2 Table of Land Measures

LINEAR

9.92 inches = 1 link	66 feet = 1 chain
25 links = 16.5 feet, or 1 rod	5,280 feet = 1 mile
16.5 feet = 1 rod	1,760 yards = 1 mile
5.5 yards = 1 rod	320 rods = 1 mile
4 rods = 100 links	80 chains = 1 mile
100 links = 1 chain	

SQUARE

30.25 square yards = 1 square rod	4,840 square yards = 1 acre
1 square rod = 272.25 square feet	640 acres = 1 square mile
16 square rods = 1 square chain	1 section = 1 square mile
1 square chain = 4,356 square feet	1 township = 36 square miles, or 6 miles square

AN ACRE IS:

43,560 square feet	330 feet × 132 feet
165 feet × 264 feet	160 square rods
198 feet × 220 feet	208 feet 8.5 inches square, or 208.71033 feet square
5,280 feet × 8.25 feet	Any rectangular tract, the product of the length and width of which totals 43,560 square feet
2,640 feet × 16.50 feet	
1,320 feet × 33 feet	
660 feet × 66 feet	

CONVERSION TO METRIC MEASURES:

1 inch = 2.540 centimeters	1 square inch = 6.5416 square centimeters
1 foot = 0.3048 meter	1 square foot = 0.0929 square meter
1 yard = 0.9144 meter	1 square yard = 0.836 square meter
1 rod = 5.0292 meters	1 acre = 0.4047 hectare
1 mile = 1.609 kilometers	1 square mile = 2.590 square kilometers

CONVERSION FROM METRIC MEASURES:

1 millimeter = 0.0394 inch	1 square centimeter = 0.155 square inch
1 centimeter = 0.3937 inch	1 square meter = 1.196 square yards
1 meter = 3.2808 feet, or 1.0936 yards	1 hectare (10,000 meters) = 2.471 acres
1 kilometer = 0.6213 mile	1 square kilometer = 0.386 square mile

☐ *Metes and bounds.* By this method, certain boundary points are measured by physical features or markers called monuments—for example, the bed of a brook or "the old oak tree." Boundaries are then drawn by lines connecting these monuments, which are described by degrees of latitude and longitude called bearings.

This type of land measurement is common in the eastern states. In the case of developed areas, the monuments usually are public streets or highways. In the case of a subdivision or built-up area, where a plat (a plan or chart of an area) has been recorded, specific parcels of property within the plat may be identified by lot and block.

☐ *Government survey.* The government (or rectangular) survey is the typical method of measurement in the western United States. A grid is imposed on a map of the land, with the north and south lines called meridians and the east and west lines called parallels. A single square in the grid, known as a tract, is 24 miles square and is composed of 16 townships. A township is 6 miles square (36 square miles) and is made up of 36 sections. Each section is one mile square and is divided for platting purposes, as shown in Fig. 1.1.

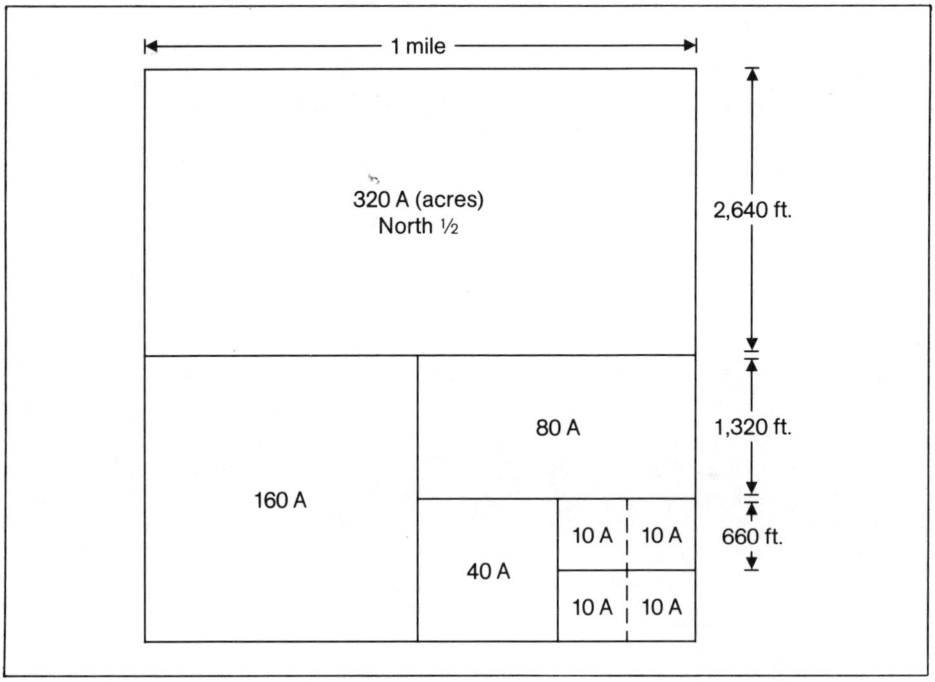

Fig. 1.1 A section of land (640 acres)

The map or description that shows the precise boundaries of land is called a survey. A survey may also show slope (topography), the precise location of any improvements on the site as well as the location of any easements, rights of way, encroachments by adjacent structures, and other physical features of the site. Surveyors, real estate professionals trained in the science of land measurement, prepare surveys.

1.03 TYPES OF REAL ESTATE INTERESTS

In the preceding discussion of the elements that make up a good real estate investment, a parcel of real estate and its ownership were assumed to be single and indivisible. In fact, quite the opposite is the case. Not only can real estate be divided up into several types of physical interests, but the concept of ownership may embrace a variety of legal interests. The fact that investments are available in a multitude of forms is one of the reasons for the attractiveness of real estate. Because each combination of legal and physical interest represents a different balance of risk and reward, an investment position can be tailored to a particular investor's requirements. As a result, capital can be attracted from virtually every type of investment interest, whether institutional, individual, long-term or short-term. The division of real estate into a number of interests is often called the pineapple technique, because each interest can be viewed as a separate slice of the entire real estate parcel with its accompanying rights, privileges, and risks.

[1] Physical Interests in Real Estate

The first thing to be examined is the real estate itself. Real estate consists of land plus whatever grows on the land, or is permanently attached to the land. But, in addition, real estate includes all of the space above and below the surface of the earth.

Ownership of land thus includes:

- Above-surface space (i.e., air space) extending from the surface of the earth to an infinite point in space
- Subsurface space within an area circumscribed by lines drawn from the surface boundaries of the land to the center of the earth (the space forming an inverted cone)

So a parcel of real estate really consists of three different physical levels: (1) surface; (2) subsurface; and (3) air space. Each of these may be utilized or occupied separately from the others. For example, *X* may start out by "owning" Blackacre, a parcel of real estate, and then may transfer to *Y* ownership of the space beneath the surface of Blackacre (i.e., the subsurface rights) and then may transfer to *Z* ownership of the space above the surface of Blackacre (i.e., the air space).

[a] Subsurface Rights

Subsurface rights normally involve the right to remove minerals, such as coal, oil, or gas, or to put something in the ground, such as a pipeline. The general rule is that the owner of land may remove anything from it, subject to governmental regulation with respect to zoning and mining practices (such as laws that bar strip mining). In addition, common law recognizes that a landowner may excavate land, but not to the point of depriving adjacent property of its natural support (which might cause buildings on those properties to collapse).

[b] Air Space

The basic rationale for building up always has been that it permits more intense development of sites having "100 percent location" in a city. The major reason why air-space projects were never heavily utilized in the past is that continued suburban expansion meant that numerous new business districts kept springing up. But the era of expansion is over. Extremely high development and financing costs, and the end of the era of cheap energy, mean that developers are turning their attention back to the center once again. And the increasing use of a new device, transferable development rights, is providing a tool for the most efficient use of air space.

Air space may refer to either air space above the very parcel to be developed, or air space over adjoining parcels. The simplest utilization of air space occurs whenever a special-purpose building, such as a post office, which is traditionally only one or several stories in height, is made part of a taller building with the upper stories available for other uses. (The first example of this use was the U.S. Post Office on upper Third Avenue in New York City.) This type of mixed use permits the maximum utilization of land. Other examples of such use involve putting apartment units above a school or constructing an office building over a garage.

The most common variation of this approach is to put a structure over a surface use that requires only a right of way. Typical examples are railroad tracks and highways; the essential problem in these situations is to find ways to support the weight of the building on columns that can be placed so as not to interfere with the surface use. Other problems involve excessive noise, fumes, and other disturbances. For example, the occupants of lower floors in buildings put up over highways may find that vehicle emission fumes make the space uninhabitable.

Using Transferable Development Rights. The major new development in the air-space field has been the increasing use of transferable development rights (TDRs). In essence, a TDR simply permits the owner of one parcel to benefit in some way from undeveloped air space over another parcel. The roots of the TDR concept lie in the common-law right of one property owner to buy the air space over adjacent property—for example, in order to assure that light and air will not be blocked in reaching a building on his site. From this, two logical steps followed.

1. The first was that the air space over an adjacent structure, instead of merely being kept undeveloped, could be utilized to permit a "piggyback" structure. Thus, a building could be put up on Parcel *A* with the upper portion projecting into adjoining air space, at whatever height was necessary to permit a continuation of the existing use of Parcel *B*. This approach requires changes in zoning laws, but these often have been forthcoming. One attractive use of this device is to permit the preservation of historic structures (normally, not very tall) while at the same time permitting more intense development of the site.

2. The next step involved transferring air-space rights between buildings that were not adjacent to one another. The theory was that so long as total development in a given area did not exceed that permitted by the zoning law, it made no difference whether one particular structure exceeded height or density limitations. While in theory this seems reasonable enough, many professionals fear that this will lead

to far greater development in downtown areas than can be tolerated. Consequently, cities such as New York are approaching the use of TDRs with a great deal of caution.

[2] Legal Interests in Real Estate

In Anglo-American law, real estate ownership is most often viewed as consisting of a "bundle of rights." This includes the rights of possession, control, enjoyment, and disposition:

- The *right of possession* refers to occupancy and includes the right to keep out all others.
- The *right of control* deals with the right to physically alter the property.
- The *right of enjoyment* protects the current owner from interference by past owners or others.
- The *right of disposition* permits conveyance of all or part of one's bundle of rights to others.

All these rights are subject to limitation or restriction by governmental action. They also are subject to restrictions created or agreed to by prior owners that are binding on their successors. For example, owners in a residential community may desire that no parcel of land shall be used in the future for a commercial enterprise. Provided they comply with the legal rules, they can restrict future use of the land within reasonable limits.

The bundle of rights that constitute real estate ownership can be divided in a surprising number of ways. In general, these rights can be classified into three major categories: (1) ownership (freehold) rights; (2) possessory (leasehold) rights; and (3) nonpossessory interests in real estate.

[a] Freehold Estates

Freehold (ownership) estates represent the highest quality of rights associated with real property under our legal system. In general, the holder of such an estate may exercise the full bundle of rights that relate to real property, subject always to overriding public policy as expressed in statute law, court decisions, and governmental regulation. The freehold category includes three significant types of estates: (1) fee simple; (2) defeasible fees; and (3) life estates.

[i] Fee Simple Absolute. The most straightforward estate in land is known as the fee simple absolute or fee simple, and is often referred to simply as a fee. Fee simple ownership represents the most complete form of private-property ownership recognized by our law. A fee simple interest creates an absolute and complete right of ownership for an unlimited duration of time with an unconditional right of disposition and use (i.e., the complete bundle of rights). Consequently, fee simple ownership is the most preferred interest in land.

[ii] Defeasible Fees. A special kind of freehold interest, seen only infrequently today, is the defeasible fee. In plain terms, this is a fee simple interest subject to certain conditions which, if not met, will cause the owner to lose the property. The origin of defeasible fees goes back to the early English common law when land was virtually the sole significant source of wealth. By tying up land with defeasible fees (and other devices), large landholders sought to insure that the land would remain in certain uses or within the family for generations to come—which, in fact, has been the case. This is the reason why some English peers today still hold vast acreages in the United Kingdom.

Two kinds of defeasible fees are fee simple determinable and fee on condition subsequent.

☐ *Fee simple determinable.* This is fee simple ownership that automatically will terminate and revert back to the grantor (original fee holder) or the grantor's heirs on the happening of a stated condition. Such a fee is usually expressed by a conveyance "to *X* and *X*'s heirs *so long as they use the property for* Y *purpose.*" The restrictive condition associated with a fee simple determinable interest essentially limits the right of control and subsequent disposition of the real estate.

An actual example a few years ago involved land that had been conveyed to the local municipality "so long as the land is used as a railroad station." Presumably, the grantor wished to provide a desirable site for the local commuter railroad line and wanted to insure that the land would not be used for any other purpose. With changing times, the railroad discontinued service to the community, and the municipality sought to sell the land. At that point, about ninety years after the grant, the heirs of the original grantor were able to regain the land on the basis that the condition of use was no longer met.

☐ *Fee on condition subsequent.* Just as with a fee simple determinable, a fee on condition subsequent creates an ownership interest that can be lost on the happening of a stated event or condition. The typical phrasing in a conveyance of such a fee would be "to *X* and *X*'s heirs *on the condition that they use the property for* Y *purpose.*"

As in the case of a fee simple determinable, it is clear from such a conveyance that the bundle of rights associated with fee ownership is limited. What is the difference between these two types of defeasible fees? In essence, it is a matter of the precise manner whereby title can be lost by the owner who fails to comply with the condition. The grantor of a fee simple determinable automatically regains ownership on the stated event, whereas the grantor of a fee on condition subsequent must initiate action to recover ownership.

Even though defeasible fees may still be created, they are extremely unusual and regarded with disfavor by the courts because they are restraints on alienability. They limit the transferability of real estate, since one would be reluctant to buy a defeasible fee because of the risk of forfeiture if the condition to title were ever violated.

Why do courts care about the free transferability of real estate? The answer is that the economic as well as the social development of the country would be hindered if many parcels of real estate were tied up with ancient restrictions that prevented the most productive use of the property in today's world. Consider the parcel of real estate, referred to above, that could only be used as a railroad station even though no railroad continued to serve the community.

[iii] Life Estates. The life estate is an extremely common form of freehold estate. In a life estate, the grantor conveys the fee simple interest to a grantee (usually a spouse or other family member) for a period measured by the lifetime of the grantee (or sometimes by the life of a third party). After the measuring lifetime has expired, title to the property automatically will go to another person specified by the grantor.

This subsequent interest is called a remainder (because it is what remains after the life interest expires) and the person who ultimately will receive it is called the remainderman. The person holding the life estate is the life tenant, a term that can be confusing since it has nothing to do with a lease. The life tenant may treat the property in all respects as an owner in fee simple would, subject only to two restrictions:

☐ *The life tenant must maintain the property in reasonably good condition in order to protect the interests of the remainderman.* For example, an apartment building cannot be permitted to deteriorate to the point where it becomes uninhabitable. Any act or omission by the life tenant which does permanent injury to the property, or unreasonably changes its character or value constitutes waste and may be enjoined (prohibited) by a court following legal action by the remainderman.

☐ *The life tenant may convey his or her interest to a third party but can convey no more than such interest.* Thus, if Husband dies, leaving Wife a life estate with a remainder to Son, she may sell only her life estate. Since the duration of her estate is completely unknown and could end tomorrow, it is not likely that anyone would buy such an estate. This is why life estates are normally not used in commercial transactions.

Life estates were the first form of social security. When a landowner died in feudal England, his wife automatically received a one-third interest in all of his real estate whether or not such an interest was specifically conveyed to her by will. In this way, the community was assured that widows would not become a burden on the community. The life estate in feudal England was known as the dower interest and the widow holding such interest was known as a dowager, a term that has come to mean an elderly lady of means. (Under certain circumstances, a widower also had certain rights in his wife's estate; this was known as the right of curtesy.)

The rights of dower and curtesy have been abolished in the United States; most states have substituted for it a statutory interest or statutory share. This statutory interest consists of the right by the surviving spouse to claim an interest in the deceased spouse's estate, even though the spouse was "cut out of the will." For example, in New York State the surviving spouse is entitled to receive a one-third interest in all of the property (real and personal) owned by the deceased at his or her death. However, the surviving spouse must elect either the statutory share or the legacy (if any) provided in the decedent's will. (A statutory share does not extend to property legitimately transferred by the decedent during his or her lifetime; thus, it is still possible for a surviving spouse to end up with nothing.)

In certain states, such as Florida, the ancient right of dower survives in the somewhat different form of a homestead right. By this right, a surviving spouse is entitled to a life estate in the couple's residence if title was held by the deceased spouse at his or her death, and regardless of any other disposition provided for by will.

[b] Leasehold Estates

Whereas a freehold interest conveys ownership, a leasehold estate conveys possession. A leasehold interest is created by a lease, which is usually in writing but is sometimes oral. A lease is a unique form of instrument because it is both a conveyance (i.e., it transfers the right to possession of real estate) and a contract (i.e., it creates rights and duties between the landlord and the tenant).

A primary feature of leasehold interests is that they are for a definite term. Consequently, it is convenient to categorize leasehold interests according to their duration. The four categories are:

- Estate for years
- Estate from period to period
- Estate at will
- Estate at sufferance

At this point, an important observation about leasehold interests should be made. When a leasehold interest is created, it represents a current separation of the bundle of rights that makes up ownership of real estate. The separation is into a fee interest (the interest of the landlord, also called the lessor) and a leasehold interest (the interest of the tenant, also called the lessee).

Therefore, whenever a transaction involves a leasehold, it means that a double interest exists in the property. The tenant has the right to possession of the property, subject to the terms of the lease and for the duration specified in the lease. The landlord retains all of the other ownership rights plus the right to regain possession when the lease expires (the right of reversion).

[i] Estate for Years. By far the most common type of leasehold interest is the estate for years. This type includes all leases with a fixed term—whether a residential lease for one year or a ground lease for ninety-nine years. An estate for years will expire automatically at the end of the period designated, at which time the tenant's right of possession ends and possession reverts to the landlord. The lease, however, may grant renewal options to the tenant which, if properly exercised, will continue the leasehold for another designated term.

[ii] Estate From Period to Period. This type of leasehold estate, also very common, is most often used for residential and small commercial properties. It is created whenever the lease specifies the amount of rent for a designated period but does not state a specified term for the lease.

For example, if a lease provides that rent shall be paid at the rate of $100 per month, a month-to-month tenancy is created. The tenant is entitled to possession and is obligated to pay rent until either landlord or tenant gives notice of intention to terminate the lease. The time of such notice and the form in which it must be given are usually determined by statute (e.g., either party may terminate the lease on thirty days written notice, delivered personally or sent by certified mail to the other). Since this type of estate cannot assure the tenant of possession for any lengthy period, it is not normally used where a tenant, such as a retailer, must spend substantial sums to prepare the premises for use.

[iii] Estate at Will. An estate at will (or tenancy at will) is created by an oral agreement between landlord and tenant to the effect that the tenant may occupy the premises so long as it is convenient for both parties. Estates at will can create problems for both parties since no written instrument specifies the amount of rent or the rights or responsibilities of either party.

[iv] Estate at Sufferance. This rather unusual form of leasehold estate exists when a leasehold interest, whether for years, period to period, or at will, expires or terminates without the tenant vacating the property. In other words, the tenant continues to hold the premises at the sufferance of the landlord; hence, another term for this estate is a holdover tenancy.

In theory, such a tenant may be dispossessed at any time by the landlord. However, as in the case of an estate by will, a prior period of notice may have to be given by the landlord.

[c] Nonpossessory Interests

Nonpossessory interests in real estate include rights to use real estate that do not extend to actual possession (leasehold interest) or ownership (freehold interest). The three common types of nonpossessory interests are easements, profits, and licenses.

[i] Easements. An easement is an interest in real estate that gives the holder the right to use, but not to possess, the real estate. A common form of an easement is a right of way, that is, the right to cross over the land of another. Another is the electric utility or telephone easement, which permits a utility company to place poles at designated points on the land and run wires between them. Since an easement involves some restriction or limitation of the right of ownership, land subject to an easement is said to be burdened with an easement, and, to some extent, its value may be diminished.

There are several types of easements, generally distinguished by the manner in which they are created:

☐ *Express easement.* An express easement is created by a writing executed by the owner of the property subject to the easement. The writing may be called a grant of easement or similar title.

☐ *Easement appurtenant.* Consider two plots of land adjacent to one another. The deed, or document of title, to lot *A* gives its owner the right to cross over lot *B* in order to reach a public highway. In this situation, ownership of *A* (called the dominant tenement) includes as one of the bundle of rights of ownership an easement appurtenant (i.e., an easement that accompanies ownership). *B,* which is burdened by the right of way, is the servient tenement; it is subject to an obligation that may or may not reduce its value in any significant way, depending on the location of the right of way and the use to which *B* is being put.

An easement appurtenant, being a part of the bundle of rights of ownership, is not a personal right but attaches to the land (the legal phrase is "runs with the land") and so is conveyed to subsequent owners of the dominant tenement.

A final distinction in the easement appurtenant is that between an affirmative or negative easement. An affirmative easement permits the owner of the dominant tenement to use the servient tenement in a particular way or for a particular purpose, for example, to cross over it to reach a public highway. A negative easement prohibits the owner of the servient tenement from using the land in a certain way that would disturb or interfere with the use of the dominant tenement. For example, the owner of the servient tenement may be prohibited from putting up a structure above a certain height because it would interfere with the light and air reaching a building on the dominant tenement. Such a light and air easement is a negative easement appurtenant.

☐ *Easement in gross.* Real estate may be subject to an easement that is unconnected with any other parcel of land, that is, an easement that is personal to the one benefiting from it. For example, most properties are subject to electric utility and telephone easements, which permit the utility companies to place electric light or telephone poles at designated points on the land and run wires across the land. More significant types of commercial easements in gross are railroad and pipeline rights of way. If such rights of way run along the boundary of a property, they may pose no significant problems. However, if the grant of such easement is broadly written or fails to specify the location of the easement, they may prevent development of the land. The solution in such cases is to obtain a deed of release of easement from the easement holder.

☐ *Implied easement.* Such an easement arises when the owner of a tract of land subjects one part of the tract to an easement (such as a right of way) that benefits the other part and then conveys one or both parts of the tract to other parties so that divided ownership results. In such case, common law holds that an implied easement arises in favor of the dominant tenement and burdens the servient tenement.

☐ *Easement by necessity.* This is a special form of implied easement and arises when the owner of a tract subdivides or separates a part of the tract so that the severed part has no access to the outside world except across the balance of the tract. Under such circumstances and in order to permit the productive use of the isolated land, common law implies the right of way across the grantor's land to a public highway. Some states provide by statute that the owner of land lacking access to a public way may petition the courts to have a "cartway" condemned for his use. Again, the purpose is to encourage the development and use of land for the benefit of society in general.

☐ *Easement by prescription.* This type of easement arises when a stranger (i.e., one without ownership or possessory right) makes use of land for a prescribed period of time (e.g., ten years) and does so openly and without pretense of having the true owner's consent. Under such circumstances, the use that was originally adverse (against the interest of the owner) may ripen into an easement that is recognized by law. This is similar to the process of acquiring title to land by adverse possession. An example of a prescriptive easement would be extended use by one neighbor of another neighbor's driveway, with the first neighbor openly claiming the "right" to such use.

[ii] Profits. A profit in land (technically known as a "profit à prendre") is the right to take a portion of the soil or timber or remove subsurface minerals, oil, or gas in land owned by someone else. A profit represents an interest in real property and it must be in writing. The distinction between a profit and an easement is that the latter merely permits use of the property, while the former involves a removal of part of the land. A profit also is to be distinguished from a gas and oil or mineral lease. These require the lessee to pay a royalty to the landowner calculated on the amount of natural resource taken.

[iii] License. A license is the right to go on land owned by another for a specific purpose. A license in most cases is merely a revocable privilege granted by the owner to another and does not represent an interest in real estate. Almost everyone frequently is a licensee. Whenever a ticket is purchased to attend a sports or other event in a stadium or hall, the individual is purchasing a license. Similarly, if the privilege of hunting or fishing on the lands of another is given, whether or not for a consideration, the hunter or fisherman is a licensee.

1.04 APPRAISAL OF REAL ESTATE

[1] The Concept of Value

An appraisal is an estimate of value. More specifically, an appraisal is an opinion of value for an adequately described property, as of a specified date, supported by relevant data and based upon an analysis of the factors influencing value. Anyone may have an opinion of value and, to that extent, anyone can make an appraisal. But obviously, the reliability of an appraisal depends on the competence, integrity, and experience of the appraiser.

When a real estate investor retains a professional appraiser to render an opinion of value about a parcel of property, the investor is interested in a particular kind of value—market value. Market value is defined as

> the highest price estimated in terms of money which a property will bring if exposed for sale in the open market allowing a reasonable time to find a purchaser who buys with knowledge of all the uses to which it is adapted and for which it is capable of being used.

Real estate appraisers traditionally utilize three approaches to determining market value: (1) the market data approach; (2) the cost approach; and (3) the income approach. Each of these is described briefly in the sections that follow. Underlying all of these approaches are some basic economic concepts that underlie the idea of "value." Understanding these concepts can give an investor some insight into the rationale of the three appraisal methods.

Here are ten of these concepts:

1. *Substitution.* When two parcels of property have the same utility (usefulness), the property available at the lower price will sell first. This common-sense statement has important implications. For example, in the cost approach, the con-

cept of substitution explains why a buyer would not pay more for improved real estate than the cost to the buyer to acquire a site and construct an improvement of equal utility.

2. *Anticipation.* Here again, the concept embodies a self-evident point of view—an estimate of value always should be based upon future anticipation rather than past performance. Past financial history may be important evidence of future trends, but can never be a substitute for a judgment about the future. This concept is especially applicable when the income approach to value is being used, since here an estimate of future income is capitalized to obtain value.

3. *Change.* In one sense, this concept is merely a specific application of the concept of anticipation. The emphasis here is on the inevitability of change and the need to identify trends that will affect a particular parcel of property. For example, the concept of regression says that the value of a superior property in a neighborhood will be adversely affected by surrounding inferior properties. The concept of progression states the reverse: that an inferior property will benefit by its location in the superior neighborhood. An investor who can identify a very early trend toward neighborhood improvement, and so make bargain purchases of property, is successfully using the concept of change.

4. *Competition and excess profit.* The concept expresses the idea that in a relatively unregulated market, abnormal profits cannot be expected to continue indefinitely into the future. Put another way, unless monopoly profit is protected by unique location, government regulation, or some other factor, competition will be generated that, in time, will reduce the abnormal profit to a normal range.

When the purchaser of a shopping center capitalizes overage rentals at a rate lower than that used for fixed rentals because it is anticipated that competition from another center will reduce overage rents, this is an application of the concept of competition.

5. *Increasing and decreasing returns.* This concept says that in any given case, a certain optimum combination exists of land, labor, capital, and entrepreneurship. If any one of these four factors of production is increasingly applied, diminishing returns eventually will be experienced.

For example, an outlying site may be capable of returning a small cash flow if improved with a one-story retail store. If the owner were to invest additional capital and construct a ten-story office building, the chances are that his return would disappear and be replaced by a negative cash flow. Demand for space in the new building would be insufficient to produce sufficient rental income to match the increased costs of operation. In other words, diminishing returns result from increased capital investment. The determination of just the right combination of factors to produce maximum income from a parcel of property is one of the most difficult jobs of the real estate appraiser or analyst.

6. *Contribution.* This is an application of the concept just discussed. The concept of contribution says that changes in an existing improvement can only be justified in a financial sense if the increase in cash flow represents a fair return on the additional investment.

For example, an office building investor must decide whether to replace manned elevators with automatic ones. Offsetting the initial capital investment will be lower operating expenses due to a smaller payroll. The question is whether the additional cash flow represents a satisfactory return on the new investment. If higher rents can be charged because the automatic elevators are quicker and more efficient, this factor also must be considered. This process illustrates the concept of contribution.

7. *Surplus productivity.* Of the four factors of production, land is the last to be paid. It plays a passive role and a return must first be paid to the other three factors (capital, labor, and entrepreneurship) in order to bring about utilization of the land. Consequently, the return to land is surplus productivity, in the sense that it is the residual return.

This concept is often important in analyzing many small business operations. Consider the case of a couple who operate a fast-food restaurant. They purchase the land, construct the improvement, and work seven days a week. At the end of the year, they realize a good profit. But what is earning a return?

☐ They must first pay themselves salaries for their labor, as well as some return for the entrepreneurial risk assumed.

☐ A portion of the profit represents a return *of* investment (equivalent to depreciation of the improvements), and an additional portion represents a return *on* the investment in the improvements.

☐ The balance, if anything is left, represents a return on the capital invested in the land. It may turn out that there is no surplus productivity and that the land is, in fact, earning no return at all.

8. *Conformity.* Experience has shown that maximum value accrues to a parcel of land when a reasonable degree of physical and economic homogeneity is present in an area. The concept of conformity reflects that economic and psychological benefits arise from the grouping of similar activities. Zoning laws are a partial recognition of this concept.

9. *Supply and demand.* This is the basic economic logic that lies behind pricing. In a wholly free economy, the interaction of supply and demand would be the sole determinant of price and, hence, of value. In our partially free and partially regulated economy, the law of supply and demand is only one factor, although a crucial one, in setting prices.

10. *Highest-and-best use.* This is the most quoted concept in real estate valuation. Its essence is that vacant land is to be valued on the basis of the use that is likely to produce the greatest return in the foreseeable future. The highest-and-best use of land is likely to change over time. An outlying site suitable only for a one-story retail store today may be able to support increasingly larger structures as urban expansion takes place.

The highest-and-best-use concept also applies to developed land, but here an additional factor applies. That extra factor is the cost of demolishing the existing improvement. The highest-and-best use of vacant land might be a twenty-story office building. But if the land already is improved with a ten-story structure, the cost of demolishing it must be added to the investment equation; the result may be that the highest-and-best use (from the point of view of return on investment) remains the present use.

[2] The Appraisal Process

An overview of the entire appraisal process helps an investor understand how a professional appraiser reaches his opinion of value. It also illustrates the basic analytic process that any experienced investor will go through when looking at and evaluating properties.

The formal appraisal process consists of six steps as illustrated in Fig. 1.2:

1. Definition of the problem and the objective
2. Preliminary survey and appraisal plan
3. Data collection and analysis
4. Application of the three appraisal approaches
5. Reconciliation of the three estimates of value
6. Final estimate of value

[a] Definition of the Problem and the Objective

Defining the appraisal problem involves four items that collectively set the stage for the actual appraisal:

☐ *The particular parcel of real estate must be identified,* using one of the forms of legal description previously discussed.

☐ *Then, the particular legal rights or estates to be appraised must be identified.* Is the appraiser to value a fee interest, a life estate, or a long-term leasehold?

☐ *The date of valuation also is important,* since an appraisal describes and values real estate as of a precise moment in time. This is a particularly crucial factor in condemnation proceedings, since the land taken is valued as of the date of taking.

☐ *Finally, a clear understanding must exist both as to the purpose of the appraisal and the type of value sought.* It has been indicated here that market value is normally the standard of value, but, on occasion, the issue may be the rental value of property, the liquidation value of a business, etc.

[b] Preliminary Survey and Appraisal Plan

The preliminary survey and appraisal plan constitute the logistics of the appraisal process. The appraiser defines the data that will be needed and the sources of that data. Based on this information, personnel needs are estimated, a time schedule established, and, in a more complex appraisal, a formal flow chart of the activities is prepared.

[c] Data Collection and Analysis

All relevant data affecting a property are considered in a sound appraisal. The pool of information generally will fall into two categories: (1) that relating to the environment in which the particular property is located (market analysis), and (2) that relating to the property itself (site analysis).

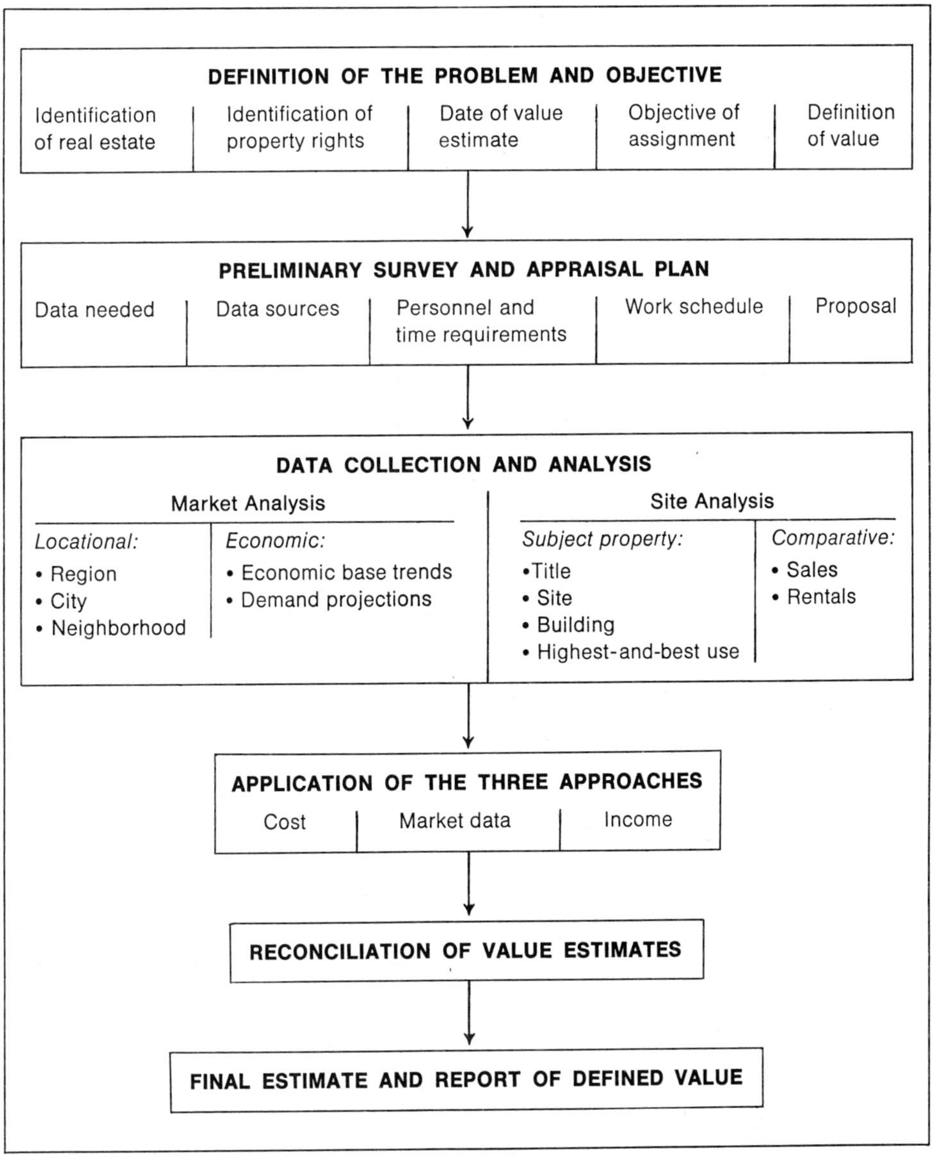

Fig. 1.2 The appraisal process

☐ *Market analysis.* In the first category social, economic, and political characteristics of the region, city, and neighborhood are included. Applying the principle of anticipation, the appraiser will concentrate on the identification of trends that are expected to continue in the future. A continuing question will be how data about the past relates to a projection of the expected economic life of a particular property.

☐ *Site analysis.* The second category of data involves the property itself. The physical site is inspected and the improvements are examined to determine the extent of depreciation and the ability of the improvement to carry out its present or intended use. The highest-and-best use of the property is ascertained.

In the case of vacant land, the appraiser is free to consider any reasonably potential use. In the case of property already improved, the appraiser must be instructed as to whether the property is to be evaluated in terms of its existing improvement or whether a demolition would be considered if an alternate use were more desirable.

The appraiser also will seek complete financial and operating information about the property, as well as comparative market information. "Comparables" are used in all three approaches to value. Depending on the nature of the subject property, comparable property information includes sales data, rental rates, and operating expense figures as well as physical and locational characteristics of properties used in the comparison process.

[d] Applying the Three Appraisal Approaches

It should now be apparent that property appraisal is an art, not a science. An estimate of value is never spoken of as a scientific fact, but rather as an opinion.

Because of this, an appraiser normally will not follow a single path toward a value conclusion. Over the years, three separate approaches have been developed: (1) the cost method; (2) the market data (or market comparison) method; and (3) the capitalization of income method.

The essence of each method is the following:

1. *The cost approach* relies on the principle of substitution. It says that one should pay no more for an existing building than an amount equal to the cost of replacement.

2. *The market data approach* also relies on the principle of substitution, saying that a property is worth approximately the same as another property offering similar utility (a similar stream of benefits).

3. *The income approach* states the value of property is the present worth of future cash flows that the property is expected to generate (e.g., a property is worth X times its annual net or gross operating income).

[e] Reconciling Estimates of Value

The fifth step in the appraisal process involves a reconciliation of the value estimates derived from the three different approaches to value. The reconciliation is not an average of the three results. Depending on the nature of the property and the objective of the appraisal, one approach will appear to be more appropriate than another. Experienced appraisers will meld the results of the three approaches.

[f] Final Estimate of Value

The end of the appraisal process is an estimate of value of the property as of a particular date. Normally, the professional appraiser will write a formal appraisal report setting forth the six steps just described. This report is the justification and evidence of the final opinion of value rendered by the appraiser.

[3] The Market Data Approach

Of the three basic approaches to value, the market data (or market comparison) approach is most easily grasped by the newcomer to real estate because it is related to the comparison shopping done when purchasing a new automobile, a new suit, or products in the local supermarket.

The theory of comparable sales analysis is based on the assumption that the market value of a property (the subject property) bears a close relationship to the prices of similar properties that have recently changed hands. Since no one property is exactly like another and since the passage of time affects values (including the value of the dollar), the goal is to find properties that resemble the subject property as closely as possible and then to make appropriate adjustments to reflect whatever differences exist (including those relating to the time and terms of sale).

It is apparent that the market data approach lends itself best to situations where very similar properties are bought and sold on a relatively frequent basis. Single-family dwellings and raw land often represent such markets, and it is with such properties that the market data approach is most successful.

A straightforward outline of the steps involved in the market data approach is as follows:

1. Comparable properties that recently have traded hands are located.
2. The key features or characteristics of the subject and the comparable properties are identified.
3. The sales price of each comparable property is "adjusted" to reflect the differences between the comparable property and the subject property. (In effect, the price the purchaser of the comparable property would have paid for the subject property is estimated, considering the differences between them.)
4. A judgment about the market value of the subject property is reached through a consolidation process, which weighs the adjusted prices of the comparable properties.

[a] Finding Comparables

The first step in applying the market data approach is finding comparable properties. The reliability of the market data approach is a direct function of the comparable sales used in the analysis.

Example: Suppose *A* is seeking to value a three-bedroom, two-bath, all-brick home at 411 Yorktown Street. *A* discovers that five other three-bedroom, two-bath, all-brick homes on similar lots located on Yorktown have sold in the past three months for $47,500. It is not hard to come to the conclusion that the value of the subject property is very close to $47,500. On the other hand, a ranch house, located in Montana, with twelve bedrooms and one bath, which is 30 miles from the nearest house, is more difficult to evaluate by the market data approach.

Not surprisingly, nearly all appraisals fall somewhere between these two extremes. The task of the appraiser or analyst is to find similar properties, whose sales terms can be verified, to use as comparables in judging the market value of the subject property. In choosing comparables, the appraiser must have a clear idea in mind of what constitutes an acceptable comparable. In addition, the characteristics of the comparable that differ from the subject property must be identifiable and they must be of a kind that can be "priced" with a reasonable degree of certainty. Under normal circumstances, it is desirable that four to seven comparable properties be located.

Remember that property differences can be either positive or negative. That is, each comparable property normally will have some features that make it worth more than the subject property and have some deficiencies that make it worth less.

[b] Identifying Value Characteristics

The appraiser or analyst must next identify the key characteristics of the subject and the comparable properties that determine its value. On this basis, the appraiser will determine which properties are comparable to the subject and then check the comparables for additional characteristics that affect their value. These characteristics can be divided into two broad classifications: (1) property characteristics; and (2) nonproperty characteristics.

1. *Property characteristics.* The property characteristics are essentially physical items. The significant ones are location, size of the land parcel, size of constructed space, type of construction, and quality of construction. The terrain of the site, the design, age, and condition of the improvement, and the interior configuration, are also relevant items. In the case of a residence, consideration should be given to such outdoor amenities as tennis courts and swimming pools as well as for special features of the house, such as fireplaces, elaborate interior features, or any other major element of difference between the subject property and the comparable property.

2. *Nonproperty characteristics.* In addition to physical characteristics, certain nonproperty characteristics are important in utilizing the market data approach. Key nonproperty characteristics include

☐ *Verified sales price.* Since the market approach adjusts comparable selling prices to make them similar to the subject, this method relies heavily on a verified sales price. In most cases, verification is based on information provided by real estate brokers and other appraisers.

☐ *Date of sale.* The elapsed time since a comparable property has been sold may be important if either the national or local economy has been experiencing significant inflation. In recent years, rapid inflation has created a situation where elapsed time of as little as six months has pushed the current market value of the comparable property several percent above its sales price.

☐ *Financing terms.* Since real property is usually purchased with the use of borrowed funds, the financing terms are particularly important. A property with unusually attractive financing will command a better price than an identical property without such financing.

Consider again the example of the home on Yorktown Road. If the subject home was financed with a 7 percent interest-rate loan that could be assumed (taken over) by a new purchaser despite much higher current rates, while the comparable homes had 11 percent loans of equivalent amounts, then the prices of the latter properties would have to be adjusted to reflect the less advantageous financing.

☐ *Unusual conditions of sale.* Finally, any special conditions of sale must be taken into account. This is particularly important in sales that are not at arm's length (i.e., sales between persons who are not strangers to one another, as by a father to a daughter or between business associates).

For example, if a condition of one particular sale was that the seller could continue to use the property for six months without payment of any rent or if the property was to be repaired by the seller subsequent to the sale, then these items must be accounted for in the adjustment process.

[c] Adjusting Prices of Comparables

The next step is to adjust the prices of the comparable properties to reflect the differences between each of them and the subject property. Where the comparable property lacks an element of value possessed by the subject property, then the value of that particular element is added to the sales price of the comparable. Where the comparable has a feature that is not present in the subject property, the value of the feature is subtracted from the sales price of the comparable.

By this process, the subject property is given a value (vis-à-vis each comparable) so that, in theory at least, the person who bought the comparable property would have been willing to buy the subject property at the given value.

The actual adjustments can be made by a unit of comparison (e.g., an adjustment per square foot), dollar adjustments (e.g., a lump-sum adjustment for a fireplace or central air conditioning), or a percentage adjustment. The percentage adjustment is particularly useful in handling differences in location. For example, a property on one street may be 2 to 5 percent more valuable than property on another street that has less prestige, ease of access, or some other particular attribute.

[d] Reaching a Correlation of Value

The final step in the market data approach is to reach an opinion of value for the subject property based upon the adjusted sales prices of all the comparables. Most professional appraisers eliminate any sales prices that vary widely from the others in the group. They do so on the assumption that some element of comparison has been missed or that these particular properties have unique features that make them inappropriate to be used as comparables.

The remaining adjusted sales prices are evaluated and correlated to produce a final indication of market value of the subject property. In the correlation process, the appraiser may give more emphasis to those properties that most closely resemble the subject property.

[4] The Cost Approach

The cost approach to value states that the worth of a property is roughly equal to the cost of reproducing the property minus a figure that approximates the amount of value of the property that has been "used up" in the course of its life (i.e., a figure representing its lessened productivity). In short, a property is worth its reproduction cost minus accrued depreciation. By comparison, the market data approach states that the worth of a property is equal to the price an informed purchaser would pay for it; the income approach says that the worth of a property is equal to the present value of the anticipated stream of future benefits.

While the definition of the cost approach given in the previous paragraph is not controversial in a theoretical sense, the application of this method can be very controversial indeed. Some of the controversies are indicated in the course of this chapter. Several of the ten principles of value set forth in 1.04[1] are involved in the cost approach, particularly the principles of anticipation, substitution, change, increasing and decreasing returns, and highest-and-best use.

Four steps are involved in the cost approach to value:

1. An estimate is made of the cost to reproduce the existing improvements.
2. An estimate is made of the dollar amount of accrued depreciation that has occurred during the life of the improvements. The accrued depreciation is deducted from reproduction costs to show the depreciated cost of the improvements.
3. The estimated value of the land (site value) is arrived at using the market data approach.
4. An opinion of value is arrived at by adding the site value to the depreciated cost of the improvements.

[a] Reproduction and Replacement Cost

An important distinction exists between reproduction cost and replacement cost. Reproduction cost refers to the cost at today's prices to build an exact replica of the structure being valued. Reproduction cost assumes that the same quantity and quality of material and labor is utilized as when the structure actually was built. In short, reproduction denotes the same structure in replica. By comparison, replacement cost denotes the cost of replacing an existing building with one of equal utility although the same materials or the same design may not be used, reflecting changes in technology, design, building techniques, and cost.

Although it might appear that replacement cost should be used in the cost approach to value, the concept of "reproduction cost new" represents the true theoretical foundation for the cost approach because it relates directly to the accrued depreciation that is estimated in the next step in the process. Consequently, most of the discussion that follows is designed to estimate reproduction cost new. While this estimate of reproduction cost must reflect *all* ingredients of cost to the typical purchaser, there are several alternative methods of cost estimation. Generally, an appraiser or analyst will either use one of these methods or use one of several published construction cost services.

☐ *Trade breakdown or builder's method.* The trade breakdown or builder's method of estimating reproduction cost most nearly represents the thinking of residential building contractors and can readily be understood by both appraiser and investor. The method does require a knowledge of the major components of the structure. (Certainly, a working knowledge of structural components is fundamental to the entire appraisal process.)

In the trade breakdown or builder's method:

- Direct costs (labor, materials, equipment, and subcontractor's fees) are added to
- Indirect costs (financing charges, selling costs, insurance premiums, permit and license fees, surveys costs, architectural and legal fees, and builder's profit and overhead) to arrive at
- Estimated reproduction cost new of the improvements on the site.

☐ *Quantity survey method.* A more elaborate approach to estimating reproduction cost involves a complete building cost estimate by a contractor involved in the particular kind of construction in the area. The quantity survey method requires a complete itemization of all prices for materials, equipment, and labor, plus a complete list of all overhead items plus profit. The cost of such an estimate, however, normally exceeds that which an investor or purchaser is willing to pay, and so this method is not used frequently.

☐ *Comparative unit method.* A much more simplified approach is the comparative unit method. Here, an estimate of reproduction cost per square foot is derived by dividing the total known cost of similar structures by the total square footage of those structures. The resulting standard or comparative unit of cost is then applied to the subject property. This approach is acceptable only for preliminary or cursory appraisals rather than in-depth analyses.

☐ *Construction cost services.* Published cost services provide estimates of reproduction cost for typical structures and are useful time-saving devices. These services also provide localized indices to take into consideration varying costs throughout the country. One such cost service is the Dodge Cost Calculator, published by McGraw-Hill. The services identify the costs of the major components of structures and provide adjustments for inflation and for different geographic areas of the country.

[b] Estimating Accrued Depreciation

The concept of depreciation is pervasive in real estate. It is meant here as an appraisal or valuation concept, and it is met again in later chapters as an accounting concept and then as a tax concept. As used here, depreciation refers to reduction in the value of buildings or improvements as a result of physical, functional, or economic factors.

Accrued depreciation is a measure of the loss in utility of the subject property in its present condition, from all forms of depreciation, as compared with its condition as a totally new improvement representing the highest-and-best use of the site. To the extent that improved real estate loses utility (i.e., suffers depreciation), it has suffered a decline in value from its reproduction cost new. Therefore, after the accrued depreciation suffered by an improved parcel of real estate is eliminated, the amount of such depreciation is subtracted from reproduction cost new to arrive at the present depreciated cost of the improvements.

The appraisal process recognizes three different types of depreciation: (1) physical depreciation; (2) functional depreciation (functional obsolescence); and (3) economic or locational depreciation (economic obsolescence).

[i] Physical Depreciation. Physical depreciation is the kind of "using up" of an improvement that is easiest to understand. It is the loss of value suffered by improvements resulting from wear and tear, disintegration, and the action of the elements. All man-made improvements suffer physical depreciation, although it may be very gradual, particularly in the early years of use.

□ *Curable physical depreciation.* Physical depreciation may either be curable or incurable. Curable physical depreciation is also known as deferred maintenance, because the primary cause of such depreciation is the failure of the owner to maintain the property on an ongoing basis. Such depreciation is called curable because the cost of eliminating or correcting it is less than or equal to the value that will be added to the property as a result. Most items of "normal" maintenance come under this heading.

Examples of curable physical depreciation include replacing broken windows, painting the exterior and interior of the house, and cleaning and making minor replacements to the furnace. In all of these cases, the cost to cure is relatively small and is undoubtedly justified (in an economic sense).

□ *Incurable physical depreciation.* The other type of physical depreciation is that which is incurable. The term incurable does not refer to the impossibility of curing the defect, since virtually any physical defect can be repaired or replaced, but to the lack of economic justification in doing so. Physical depreciation is considered incurable if the cost to cure or correct the physical defect is greater than the value that will be added to the property as a result. For example, it would be illogical to replace a five-year-old roof that was capable of lasting another ten years. However, the five-year-old roof is less valuable than a brand new roof.

[ii] Functional Depreciation (Functional Obsolescence). Functional depreciation is the loss of value suffered by real estate because buildings or improvements do not provide the same utility, or do so less efficiently, than would a new structure. Functional depreciation represents the impact of changes in building technology and consumer tastes and preferences on the value of improvements.

Another term for such depreciation is obsolescence. Just as with physical depreciation, functional obsolescence may either be curable or incurable. And again, the use of these terms does not refer to the absolute ability to cure but rather to the economic justification.

☐ *Curable functional obsolescence.* A good example of this is a modern kitchen in a residence. Many individuals will not buy an old house with a kitchen that has not been modernized or will reduce their offer by the cost of a new kitchen. Consequently, the owner of a house who installs a new kitchen might well anticipate recouping the investment upon sale. Other examples of curable functional depreciation include lack of air conditioning in office or commercial space, and outmoded store fronts.

The amount of curable functional depreciation from which a property suffers is equal to

The cost to cure
minus
Physical depreciation previously deducted

The reason for this second step is that, in the appraisal process, the physical depreciation of the particular component has already been deducted. In order to avoid double counting, this depreciation factor must be netted out from the computations. Note that if replacement cost rather than reproduction cost is used, functional obsolescence may be neglected. However, the result will not be as precise.

☐ *Incurable functional obsolescence.* Incurable functional obsolescence is, again, a measure of the reduced ability of a structure, or one of its components, to perform with the same utility as when new. The cost of curing or correcting the defect, however, is more than the value increment that would result. Consequently, the depreciation is deemed incurable.

For example, a four-story private residence that might otherwise be suitable for a multitenant building has a large, winding staircase which, in a modern structure, would be replaced by an elevator. The cost of installing one, however, is not justified by the value added to the property. An office building built many years ago with high ceilings and wide corridors, which offers amenities that cannot be provided today because of high costs, is another example of incurable obsolescence. The owner of such a building probably would decide against lowering the ceilings and narrowing the corridors in order to create more rental space because the additional rental income would not represent a satisfactory return on the additional investment that would be required. Note that in both of these cases, the presence of incurable depreciation does not mean that the property is not a good investment. It may well be so, provided the price reflects the depreciation, which acts to reduce the future flow of income.

To approximate the amount of incurable functional obsolescence, the appraiser or analyst most often relies on the income approach to value. An estimate is made of the lower rent that the improvement will command due to the incurable depreciation, and this rent loss is capitalized by a process that is explained in the discussion dealing with the income approach to value. (See 1.04[5] and 2.06.)

[iii] Economic or Locational Depreciation. The final form of depreciation is termed "economic" or "locational depreciation" (sometimes known as economic obsolescence). It is a measure of the diminished utility, and hence diminished value, of improved real estate due to negative environmental forces in the surrounding area. It directly reflects the importance of the spatial element (location) in real estate valuation.

Note the significant difference between this type of depreciation and the other two. In the case of physical and functional depreciation, the loss of value arose from the condition of the subject property itself, whereas in economic depreciation, the loss of utility arises because of the relationship of the subject property to its surroundings. It is obvious that economic or locational depreciation is almost always incurable since the property owner is not in a position to control conditions external to the property.

As in the case of the other types of incurable obsolescence, economic loss is approximated by setting a value on (capitalizing) the lessened rent that can be anticipated because of the negative economic factors. For example, a zoning change may permit commercial or industrial uses in a formerly residential neighborhood, with the result that an apartment building must drop its rentals to attract tenants.

[iv] Determining Depreciated Cost. After completion of the two initial steps in the cost approach, the total accrued depreciation arising from all three types of depreciation is added up and that figure is subtracted from reproduction cost new. The resulting figure is the present depreciated cost of the improvements on the land.

The problem of valuing the land, which so far has not been considered, remains to be solved.

[c] Valuing the Site

Since the cost approach cannot be used to value land, one of two other methods is utilized. The most common method is the market data approach, which is discussed in 1.04[3]. In other words, the appraiser or analyst asks the question, "What have comparable undeveloped parcels of property sold for in this approximate location in the recent past?" It is also possible to use a variation of the income approach to value, called the land residual approach. Essentially, it involves dividing the projected cash flows from a completed structure between the building to be constructed and the land. Then, the income stream attributable to the land is capitalized to obtain a valuation for the site.

It should be more and more evident that the three approaches to value are closely interrelated, and all deal with identical data, similar logic, and, in many cases, the same mechanics.

[d] Opinion of Value

The opinion of value is the fourth and final step in the cost approach. In the second step, accrued depreciation is subtracted from reproduction cost new to yield the present depreciated cost of the improvements. Now the value of the site is added, which is determined in accordance with one of the methods just described, to arrive at an estimate of value for the entire parcel.

The cost approach to value is most reliable when a property is relatively new, and accurate estimates of construction costs can be made. Further, a newly improved property will normally have suffered less depreciation, particularly of the functional and economic types, which are the most difficult to measure.

[5] The Income Approach

The key to understanding the income approach to valuing real estate lies in understanding the relationship between a stream of income and value. In essence, an investor who buys real estate (or stocks, bonds, or other income-producing property) really is buying a future flow of income, that is, a future stream of benefits. If this is so, it follows that the present value of a parcel of property can be ascertained by

- Determining the amount, certainty, and length of time of such future flow of income.
- Placing a dollar valuation on the future flow of income—by, as appraisers say, applying an appropriate capitalization rate.

The process can be stated more precisely as follows: $V = NOI/R$, where

The market value (V) of property
equals
Its stabilized net operating income (NOI)
divided by
An appropriate market capitalization rate (R)

While the logic of using the income approach for appraising income-producing property is impeccable, a great deal of talent and experience is required in estimating stabilized net operating income (NOI). This is the "true" earning capacity of the property uninfluenced by extraordinary or nonrecurring factors. In addition, there are several subtleties involved in deriving the appropriate capitalization rate.

Since the income approach plays a major role in the investment analysis of a property, only a brief summary of this approach is given here. (This subject is discussed in detail in Chapter 2.)

[a] Determining Net Operating Income

Net operating income is defined as the balance of cash remaining after deducting the operating expenses of a property from the gross income generated by the property. (See 2.02[1] for detailed explanation of how NOI is derived.)

[b] Deriving a Capitalization Rate

Having arrived at a stabilized NOI figure for the property in question, the appraiser has accomplished the first step in applying the income approach to value. The second step is calculating the appropriate capitalization rate. Capitalization is the process of converting a future income stream into a present value. The capitalization rate is the percentage by which the future income stream is divided to arrive at a single figure that represents present value. For example, a capitalization rate of 10 percent applied to an annual income of $1,000 gives a capital value of $10,000 ($1,000 ÷ 0.10 = $10,000).

Capitalization rates vary among particular types of investments and from one period of time to another. Higher capitalization rates (expressed as a percentage) are utilized when NOI is more speculative or when abnormal inflation is anticipated. The converse is also true. Lower capitalization rates are utilized for projects generating a more secure NOI or when significant inflation is not anticipated.

Important factors in choosing a capitalization rate include:

- Type of property (e.g., apartment building, office building, etc.)
- Location (in the main business district, a few feet may make one location better than another)
- Age (the older the building, the less future income can be derived from it in its present state)
- Quality of the tenancies (e.g., a long-term lease usually means more secure NOI than a short-term lease)

(See 2.06[3] and 2.06[4] for a more detailed discussion of how a capitalization, or discount, rate is derived.)

2

Measuring Return on Investment

2.01 INTRODUCTION

The major objective of investors, in real estate or otherwise, is to maximize wealth. Thus, in looking at a prospective investment, they are primarily interested in the bottom line or the return on investment (ROI). In basic terms, investors want to

- Part with as little cash as possible as slowly as possible.
- Recoup the investment as quickly as possible.
- Receive the largest amount of gain in the shortest possible time.

As is apparent from this definition, the two key concepts in discussing ROI are those of cash and time. This chapter analyzes these two concepts, shows the various ways in which an investor can arrive at a figure that can properly be called the ROI, and compares the various methods of measuring return, discussing the advantages and disadvantages of each. A separate section briefly discusses an important subject not often touched upon—risk analysis. It is not sufficient to know only the projected return on an investment; the investor must make some estimate of the risk attached to the investment (i.e., the possibility of receiving less than the projected return or, indeed, of losing all or part of the cash investment). Finally, this chapter concludes with a detailed example showing how ROI is determined using the internal rate of return (IRR), the method most often used in today's marketplace.

A word should be said at this point about the relationship between ROI and investment value, which are opposite sides of the same coin. For example, an investor offered the opportunity of putting up $10,000 in cash to participate in a real estate investment will calculate the ROI in order to answer the question, Is the ROI high enough to justify the investment? On the other hand, a purchaser negotiating for the acquisition of a property will ask, What rate of return should I use in calculating the investment value of the property (i.e., the price I am willing to pay)? In both instances, future returns must be projected; however, in the first example the investor is faced with a "go/no-go" decision since he has been offered a fixed price, while in the second case the price is subject to negotiation. (Future returns are described in detail in 2.02.)

In this discussion the emphasis lies primarily on the first of these two questions; that is, how is ROI determined when a fixed price is assumed? An investor trying to determine the proper price to offer for a property will use the same guidelines.

The concept of investment value given above should be contrasted with the concept of fair market value as derived through an appraisal. The appraised (fair market) value of the property represents the most likely price the property can command in the open market, according to the judgment of an experienced appraiser. Such a market value thus is based upon the requirements of a "typical" investor. (See 1.04[1].)

By comparison, investment value may be thought of as the maximum offering price a particular purchaser will pay in light of his own investment, tax, and other requirements.

A final word should be said about the presence of nonpecuniary returns from real estate. Such returns—what might be termed "psychic income"—include such intangible factors as self-esteem, ego fulfillment, and a sense of security that some derive from the ownership of physical property. Obviously, such nonpecuniary elements cannot be measured precisely, but are present whenever a price is paid for property that is substantially above what is justified by the property's investment value. (A good example might be the willingness of a foreign investor to pay an above-market price for land in the United States because it represents a secure haven for his capital, as well as a potential refuge, in the event that he finds it necessary to leave his homeland.)

2.02 TYPES OF REAL ESTATE RETURN

When a real estate investment is contemplated, the investor's first job is to make a projection, over the estimated period of ownership, of the returns that may be received. A real estate investment can produce one or more of the following four returns:

1. *Cash flow*. This is the spendable cash generated each year after all operating expenses and debt-service payments have been deducted from gross revenues from the property.

2. *Tax savings*. Tax savings will be achieved to the extent that tax deductions (e.g., for depreciation) exceed actual cash outlays. The excess deductions can

be applied to offset (shelter) income from the property that otherwise would be taxable as well as taxable income from other sources.

3. *Equity buildup.* The real estate investor views mortgage amortization or loan reduction as a cash outlay (i.e., as an expense) for purposes of calculating cash flow. But since the amortization reduces the principal balance of the mortgage, it actually increases the investor's equity position in the property. Since this is a form of return to the investor, it must be included in the computation of return on investment (ROI).

4. *Appreciation in value.* If the value of the property appreciates (or is projected to appreciate during the period of ownership), then obviously the investor's equity position will increase and this should be reflected in the calculation of ROI.

Each of these types of return will now be discussed.

[1] Cash Flow

Cash flow from a real estate investment is the spendable cash left over from gross revenues after

- Payment of all operating expenses and provision for replacement reserves (the remaining balance at this point is net operating income).
- Payment of debt service (principal plus interest) on any outstanding mortgages (the balance remaining is cash flow).

Cash flow is a current return in the sense that the investor actually receives cash on a monthly, quarterly, or annual basis.

Cash-flow projections for a real estate investment by a syndicate or other investment group are often developed with great precision for the entire anticipated life of the investment. Of course, the accuracy of these projections is another matter altogether; it is obviously impossible to estimate precisely the changes that will occur over a period of years in such elements as rent levels, cost of heating fuel, and other operating expenses. The real question for the investor is whether the assumptions underlying the cash-flow projections are reasonable in light of present economic conditions. They should neither be unduly conservative nor wildly optimistic, although the former is certainly to be preferred to the latter.

The derivation of a cash-flow figure for a particular parcel of real estate can be best understood by looking separately at each of the two elements used in the calculation of cash flow.

[a] Formula for Net Operating Income

One of the most frequently used terms in real estate financial analysis is net operating income (NOI). This is defined as the balance of cash remaining after deducting the operating expenses of a property from the gross income generated by the property.

There are two important points to remember in determining NOI:

- Debt service on any existing or projected mortgages is ignored, since NOI is intended to demonstrate the earning capacity of the real estate exclusive of any financing.
- Depreciation deductions and any other purely bookkeeping deductions are ignored; only cash expenses for operating the property are considered.

[i] Effective Gross Income. Perhaps the most important items to the investor are the gross rental income (GRI) presently generated by the property and its derivation, effective gross income (EGI). Table 2.1 below illustrates the relationship between these two items.

TABLE 2.1 Derivation of Effective Gross Income and Net Operating Income

Gross (scheduled) rental income (GRI)
minus
Vacancy and collection allowance
equals
Adjusted rental income
plus
Other income
equals
Effective gross income (EGI)
minus
Operating expenses and replacement reserves
equals
Net operating income (NOI)

☐ *Gross rental income.* This figure, also known as scheduled rental income, equals the rental that would be generated if the building were 100 percent occupied at rents equal to those set forth on the rent schedule of the building (which lists each unit and the rent to be charged).

It is important, however, that the investor or his representative read every lease to determine the existence of any rent concessions. These may include such elements as future free-rent months; step-down rentals to take effect during the lease term; renewal options at either the same or lower rental; agreements to alter or improve the unit or to replace such capital items as refrigerators, ranges, and carpeting. To the extent that any such rent concessions exist, they diminish the indicated rental flow. The investor should also determine the reason for such rent concessions. If they were made when the building was first constructed in order to shorten the rent-up period, or during a period of temporary overcapacity in the neighborhood, it is likely that they do not affect the validity of the rent schedule as it will affect future leases. On the other hand, if there is evidence that the present owner made such concessions as a means of "milking" the property, either to line his own pockets or avoid a negative cash flow, this is obviously a sign of danger. Sometimes a landlord will give a "sweetheart lease" (one at below-market rent) to a family member or close friend. Such a lease should either be terminated or the loss of rental should be fully reflected in the purchase price.

An investor should ask the present owner if there are any side agreements with tenants providing for future rent concessions (sometimes in consideration of payment of advance rentals by the tenant). The investor's attorney should also ensure that the contract of sale contains a specific representation by the seller that all leases are bona fide and that no such side agreements exist. In addition, a cautious investor will ask tenants to execute so-called estoppel letters, in which the tenants are asked to represent the accuracy of their present leases; these representations will then bar the tenants from making claims to the contrary in the future. Tenants cannot, of course, be compelled to execute such letters, but often a desire to establish a good relationship with the new landlord is sufficient incentive.

It is important that one further step be taken in connection with the analysis of the rental schedule. The investor should determine how existing rentals (called contract rentals) relate to the current rental value of the apartment units (called the economic rentals). If contract rental is higher than economic rental (indicating that there is an oversupply of space on the market, or that the neighborhood is declining), the investor must scale down the projections of future rental flow. In the opposite case, where economic rental is higher than contract rental, the investor can anticipate raising rentals as current leases expire. (Presumably, the seller has also anticipated this and has increased the purchase price accordingly.) Of course, the comparison of rentals is not an automatic procedure; it often requires the services of a marketing expert.

☐ *Vacancy and collection allowance.* The investor will want to determine which units are vacant and whether such vacancies are due to a deficiency or inadequacy that will make it difficult to rent them in the future, or whether this is merely a normal operating experience. In addition, there should be included in this figure a provision for lost rents due to turnover or to unpaid rentals. Even in a building that is 100 percent occupied, a certain amount of lost rent may occur as units become vacant, since it may require one or more months to rerent the premises. Thus the degree of turnover in the building is important even though the vacancy rate itself may be very low. It may be appropriate to increase this vacancy allowance somewhat if a large number of existing leases are due to expire in the near future and if the investor believes that market conditions will not be strong.

☐ *Adjusted rental income.* This figure represents the scheduled income minus the vacancy and collection allowance.

☐ *Other income.* An apartment building, for example, may generate income from a number of sources apart from the rental of units. These include laundry room equipment; coin-operated vending machines for cigarettes, milk, snacks, and other similar products; garage fees from nonresidents; fees for use of certain amenities (such as tennis courts). These in total may add up to a substantial sum; therefore, the prospective purchaser should both verify current income and consider the extent to which such income might be boosted in the future.

☐ *Effective gross income.* This represents the bottom line for income. It should be pointed out that a purchaser is not buying current income, but a future flow of income. So while the investor should make every effort to confirm and verify the actual current income from the property, he should constantly be aware that there is no guarantee the income will continue at that level in the future. A conservative investor will base his offering price on the current figure (if verified) or possibly a lower one if there are good reasons for believing that the rent flow may diminish. He normally will not be willing to pay to any significant degree for potential increases in gross income since this normally is too speculative to rely upon.

[ii] Operating Expenses. Operating costs for apartment buildings can be divided into two basic categories: (1) operating expenses; and (2) replacement reserves. In analyzing the expenses for an existing building, the investor has two objectives. The first is to verify the actual expenses of the building under its present ownership. The second is to make such adjustments as appear necessary in order to keep the building running at top efficiency and to reflect foreseeable changes due to adjustments in the tax rate, cost increases due to inflation or other reasons, and any different management practices that the investor would institute. The following is a list of the expenses incurred in a typical apartment house:

☐ *Real estate taxes.* This, along with maintenance and repair, is considered one of the most sensitive expense items (i.e., most susceptible to sharp future increases). A particular problem with real estate taxes is that sale of the property may invite reassessment by the local tax authority; in addition, a new owner who is not a resident of the municipality may find he is treated with less consideration than the former owner (the so-called out-of-town risk). Investors in California real estate should be aware that passage of Proposition 13, which puts a lid on real estate taxes as a percentage of market value, permits taxes to rise to full market value whenever real estate is sold. Consequently, apartment buildings in that state may be subject to sharp increases in real estate taxes following a sale. An investor should always investigate the possibility of similar legislation in other states or municipalities, as well as any custom not to assess properties at current market value unless they are sold. Of course, any limit on property taxes will benefit the new investor once he is over the hurdle of the initial reassessment.

When calculating the current tax, the investor should be sure to use the latest tax rate. Property taxes are normally paid in arrears, and the tax rate for the current year is sometimes not set until late in the year. Consequently, the offering statement or expense statement may show real estate taxes utilizing the past-year rate and so be inaccurate.

On the positive side, the investor should consider the possibility of obtaining a reduced assessment, which would lower the tax paid. While this certainly should not be counted on, it is a possibility where assessments for comparable property seem to be significantly lower and it appears that the current manager of the property may have overlooked the opportunity to appeal previous assessments.

☐ *Personal property tax.* Some municipalities impose a personal property tax, which would apply to furniture in furnished units, furnishings in the lobbies and other common areas, and certain other large equipment that may be designated as personal rather than real property.

☐ *Payroll.* This item covers employees of the building owner who work at the property itself (as distinguished from a property management firm or independent contractors who work pursuant to service agreements). Thus, it may include a janitor, building superintendent, or resident manager. If an individual or union employment contract is in effect, it should, of course, be read. If the prospective purchaser intends to hire or discharge employees (e.g., because he has a resident manager at a nearby property who can handle the new property also), then suitable adjustment should be made in the prospective expense statement.

☐ *Payroll taxes and fringe benefits.* This figure is often overlooked in an analysis. It includes workmen's compensation and unemployment and withholding taxes. Provisions should be made for vacation pay and sick pay, where appropriate. One rule of thumb: Use 15 percent of total wages paid for this item. An important point not to be overlooked is whether any employee is given a rent-free apartment. If so, and if the rent for the apartment is included in the gross operating income figure, an equivalent deduction must be made here.

☐ *Professional management.* An outside management firm probably would not be required for a small apartment building; however, for larger apartment projects, professional management often is well worth the 4 to 6 percent of gross rental income that may be charged. A good manager can bring to bear years of experience and professional training to keep costs in line, reduce turnover, and maintain rents at the highest possible level.

☐ *Maintenance and repair (M&R).* This is one of the more sensitive items in the expense analysis. This is so because the amount of money actually spent for M&R is almost completely within the control of the owner. In order to maximize his cash flow, he may keep M&R expenses to an absolute minimum, even to the point where the long-term value of the property is threatened. (This is the condition known as deferred maintenance.) Or the present owner may have cut back on M&R only for the current year in order to make the property appear more profitable and hence worth a higher price. Less serious, but also to be aware of, is an owner who has spent the necessary funds for M&R but instead of including them in his expense statement has capitalized them in his capital account. It then appears to the prospective purchaser that the property is indeed a good buy since it is not only in excellent operating condition but its M&R costs are also (apparently) very low. (It should be noted that on his tax return the owner may show a higher figure for M&R than he does on his own books, since this increases his operating expenses and consequently either reduces taxable income or increases his taxable loss.)

Because of the questions that may arise from the M&R expense account, most experienced investors will have developed their own rules of thumb; for example, M&R expense should run 3 to 5 percent of gross operating income, depending upon the property's age and present condition.

☐ *Property insurance.* Because the types of property coverage vary widely, and because rates differ among different companies and for different investors (depending upon how many properties may be covered), the current owner's figure may be of little value. The prospective purchaser should retain an insurance broker or consultant to determine the approximate cost of insurance premiums.

☐ *Water and sewage charges.* These charges may be based both on meter readings and frontage charges, and the investor should be sure they have not been overlooked.

☐ *Gas, electric, and fuel oil.* In any part of a country where building heat must be provided by the landlord, the cost of doing so must be determined with care because of the sharp rises of the past few years. Gas and electricity may be metered directly to the tenants; or they may be paid by the landlord who then allocates the cost among the tenants; or they may be paid by the landlord and included in the fixed rental. In the first two cases, these costs are of no direct concern to the landlord; in the last situation, however, they may have a significant impact on cash flow if utility costs rise sharply during the term of a lease. A prospective purchaser faced with the third type of situation must make appropriate adjustment, at least until leases can be changed to provide for a pass-through of increased utility costs.

☐ *Maintenance contracts.* Normally, outside concerns will handle refuse removal, elevator maintenance, and exterminator service. In addition, service contracts may cover air conditioning, swimming pools, and landscaping. Such contracts frequently permit termination on thirty-day notice so that different firms may be retained by the new owner. In any event, the costs for such services must be considered.

☐ *Licenses and permits.* The municipality may require such items as a business license, permit to operate the elevator, or permit for the swimming pool. These should be identified and the costs ascertained.

☐ *Supplies.* This covers the costs of cleaning, and office supplies required in the course of the year.

☐ *Common-area expenses.* If the project has a swimming pool or other amenities, any special costs for operating and maintaining such facilities should be identified.

☐ *Office expenses and telephone.* These may be minimal if the owner intends to operate from his own home, or divides the cost of an office over several properties. However, it is worthwhile to identify the various costs involved, which should include the cost of an office secretary, dues to local organizations, subscriptions to professional magazines, and telephone costs.

☐ *Advertising.* If there are few vacancies and demand for apartments is high, this may be nonexistent. In other cases, the expenses that may be incurred include maintaining an outdoor sign, preparing a leasing brochure, and placing classified advertisements in newspapers.

☐ *Accounting and legal fees.* Normally, some accounting expense will be incurred, whether the accountant is retained on a monthly basis or only to prepare tax returns. Legal expense obviously will vary with the experience of the particular building; an attorney may be retained to prepare leases or to handle an occasional eviction.

[iii] Reserve for Replacements. One item in the operating expense schedule that deserves special consideration is that covering reserves for replacement. The term "reserve" is used here in its literal sense; that is, it implies that during the fiscal year covered by the schedule, the specified amount of funds have actually been set aside (presumably in a savings account or other interest-bearing form) so that sufficient cash will be available to replace short-lived items. These reserves differ from other operating expenses for the obvious reason that they are not actually expended but are put aside; thus, they represent a "cushion" that can be utilized if there is an emergency need for cash. By the same token, during periods when cash flow is under pressure, deposits into these reserves can be curtailed.

The seller frequently will not include in his expense schedule a reserve for replacement, since from his point of view he does not anticipate turning over actual cash reserves to the purchaser. However, the investor should ask to see any such schedule (or prepare his own), since these reserves should definitely be included when calculating the NOI from the property. In essence, this item reflects, more or less accurately, the actual depreciation that has been incurred by those items for which reserves are set up.

A number of different ways of setting up replacement reserves can be utilized, and depending upon the one chosen, NOI will be higher or lower. Thus the type of reserve may become a negotiating point between buyer and seller. Tables 2.2 and 2.3 illustrate two different approaches. The tables list twelve items of personal property or building components for which reserves might be set up in a large apartment complex. In Table 2.2 below, the annual reserve amount is calculated by dividing the item cost by the years of useful life of the item. It is assumed that the interest on the money put aside each year will approximate the annual increase in cost of the items to be replaced. A prospective buyer who uses this type of

TABLE 2.2 Reserves for Replacement*

Item	*Life of Item (years)*	*Number of Items*	*Individual Cost per Item*	*Annual Reserve Amount*
Stoves	15	200	$ 250	$ 3,333.33
Refrigerators	15	200	250	3,333.33
Carpets	8	200	600	15,000.00
Drapes	7	200	175	5,000.00
Fixtures	15	for 200 units	100	1,333.33
Air-conditioning and heating units	20	200	700	7,000.00
Recreation equipment	20	major equipment	3,500	175.00
Paving	10	1	10,500	1,050.00
Roof	20	1	12,000	600.00
Exterior painting	5	1	3,500	700.00
Major plumbing	20	1	7,500	375.00
Major electrical	20	1	7,500	375.00
		Total reserves for replacement per year		$38,274.99

* Owners are often reluctant to use this kind of schedule to calculate replacement costs because the figures are so high and no allowance is made for the use of refinance money.

SOURCE: Daniel G. Carless, Tucson, Arizona

schedule, however, will meet with vigorous objection from the seller, since the large reserve will significantly affect the net operating income and, consequently, the value of the project. The seller will argue that the new owner is likely to refinance a mortgage within ten years or so after acquisition and he should anticipate using some of the refinancing proceeds for the replacement of major items.

To the seller, Table 2.3 presents a much more realistic way of providing for replacement reserves, since it looks ahead only for the next ten years and provides for replacement of only those items whose useful lives will terminate during that period. As you can see, the annual reserves under the second approach are much lower than under the first, and so have a much smaller impact on NOI and (via the capitalization method) the value of the property. This approach may well be accepted by the buyer, who should remember, however, that it would be advisable to put a certain percentage of the refinancing proceeds into replacements rather than have it available for other purposes.

TABLE 2.3 Reserves for Replacement Over Next Ten Years*

Item	*Number per Year to Be Replaced*	*Individual Cost per Item*	*Annual Reserve Amount*
Stoves	4	$ 250	$ 1,000.00
Refrigerators	4	250	1,000.00
Carpets	4	600	2,400.00
Drapes	4	175	700.00
Fixtures	4	100	400.00
Air-conditioning and heating units	4	700	2,800.00
Recreational equipment	2 major pieces of equipment over next 10 years	2,500	250.00
Paving	1 in year 5	10,500	2,100.00
Roof	½ in year 7	12,000	1,714.29
Exterior painting	1 in year 5	3,500	700.00
Major plumbing	½ in year 7	7,500	1,071.43
Major electrical	½ in year 8	7,500	937.50
	Total reserves for replacement per year		$15,073.22

* This schedule produces a lower figure for replacement costs. The time period has been limited and refinance money will pay for major replacements.

SOURCE: Daniel G. Carless, Tucson, Arizona

A rough rule of thumb says that reserves for replacement should approximate 3 percent of the gross rental income. As always, an older building with major deferred maintenance will require much larger reserves than a new structure.

A distinction should be made between a replacement reserve (discussed above) and a contingency reserve, which is a reserve set up at the time of purchase to handle any unforeseen events. Whereas a replacement reserve can be calculated with some precision, the contingency reserve is no more than an educated guess. A triple net leaseback to the Bank of America probably would not require a contingency reserve; a management-intensive property, such as a student residence, might require a fairly large reserve to take care of unexpected problems (e.g., a tenant spray-painting his motorcycle in the bathroom) that necessitate a complete redecoration. Obviously, discretion must be used since it is not economically feasible to provide for every contingency. It is not prudent to provide a reserve sufficient to repair damage resulting from a catastrophe; for example, in California, very few owners insure against earthquake damage because of prohibitive costs. The possibility of such an occurrence is a business risk, and a new investment decision would have to be made in the event of such a catastrophe.

[b] Formula for Cash Flow

If an investor had paid all cash for a property so that no debt service need be paid on a mortgage, NOI would be the same as cash flow. Indeed, the concept of cash flow as being equal to net operating income is important when an investor is interested in comparing the returns from two properties. Since it is extremely unlikely that any two properties will have exactly the same financing terms, the investor will want to eliminate the distortions that result from using different financing.

In order to achieve this, the investor will assume that the total investment in each property is put up by the investor (100 percent equity) so that the NOI is equal to the cash flow. In that event, the return from the property can be found by dividing NOI by the total investment. For example, if the total investment in the property is $100,000 and the NOI is $10,000, the return is 10 percent. This type of return is called the free-and-clear return because it is the total return from the property that can be kept by the investor free and clear of any claims by lenders. However, free-and-clear return will only be a true measure of the investor's actual return if he in fact pays all cash for the property so that no debt-service payments need be subtracted from NOI.

As we know, however, it is extremely rare for an investor not to utilize third-party financing in the ownership of real estate. And when financing is used, the debt service that must be paid on any outstanding mortgage debt must be subtracted from NOI in order to show the true cash flow from the property.

When an investor is analyzing the return on property he seeks to acquire, it is obvious that he should not use the debt service on the existing mortgage unless he fully intends to take over the mortgage if the property is acquired. In most cases, the new buyer's financing will be different from the existing financing—either because a new mortgage is added to the existing mortgage or because the existing mortgage will be paid off and completely new financing arranged.

Suppose an investor intends to acquire a property and projects a twenty-five-year holding period before resale. He intends to finance the purchase with a twenty-five-year constant payment self-liquidating mortgage with an original principal amount of $100,000. Assume the annual debt service is 12 percent ($12,000). In this simple case, the investor subtracts $12,000 from NOI to arrive at the amount of cash actually available to him, the figure known as cash flow.

Suppose the mortgage provides for a step-up of interest rates every five years.

If the increased interest is to be paid by increasing the debt service (instead of by extending the term of the mortgage), then cash flow will decline whenever the interest rate rises. If the interest rate rises are set in advance, the projections can be made precisely; if the interest rate increases are unknown, the increased debt service must be estimated.

Yet another possibility exists. After five or ten years, the investor may refinance his mortgage (i.e., pay it off with the proceeds of a new mortgage). Since it is impossible to know whether such refinancing will be desirable or on what terms new financing will be available, the effects on future cash flow cannot be projected with any accuracy.

A point that was made earlier concerning the treatment of loan amortization (debt reduction) as an expense to be deducted before calculating cash flow should be emphasized. If a business firm makes a loan and agrees to repay the loan in periodic installments, the repayments will not be deducted from gross revenues in arriving at net profit (although the interest will be deducted). The fact that the real estate investor does deduct loan amortization is one of the reasons that real estate accounting is confusing to those entering real estate for the first time. Why should the real estate investor treat loan reduction as an expense in calculating cash flow? There seem to be two reasons:

1. Real estate is rarely acquired without some form of long-term financing, which is to be repaid in relatively equal amounts over many years. Consequently, it is convenient (and conservative) for the investor to regard the periodic debt service as an expense of the property, similar to payroll or real estate taxes.

2. The real estate investor does not take a deduction for depreciation in calculating his cash flow, and the treatment of loan repayment as an operating expense can be viewed as a substitute for the depreciation deduction, which at best can only be approximated. (However, if an investor treats as a portion of his return the equity buildup from loan amortization, which assumes that he can sell the property for at least the price at which he acquired it, this second reason for treating loan amortization as an expense has no validity.)

The important point to note is that real estate investors are very much cash-oriented; cash flow, which is the key measure of actual cash return, reflects *only* cash transactions (thus ignoring depreciation, a paper deduction) as well as *all* cash payments (including loan amortization, which ordinarily is not viewed as an expense, as well as replacement reserves, which are not tax deductible).

[2] Tax Savings

To many real estate investors, the tax benefits from an investment often are just as important as the annual cash flow. Tax savings are achieved whenever a taxpayer may take a tax deduction for a "paper expense" (i.e., an expenditure that is not matched by an actual outlay of cash or diminution in value of the property). Thus the deduction for interest paid on a mortgage loan does not create any tax shelter since the deduction is exactly matched by an outlay of cash to the lender (or, as tax people say, the deduction and the outlay are a "wash"). On the other hand, the deduction for depreciation does create tax shelter because (1) no actual outlay of cash is involved; and (2) the property—one assumes—does not actually lose any value due to any of the various types of depreciation, physical, functional, or economic.

An important point to be made about tax savings from real estate is that the savings do not result from an actual avoidance of income tax. Sooner or later, a tax must be paid. However, tax savings are realized through

- Deferring payment of tax from the present to some future date, thus enabling the investor to have the use of the funds in the interim (in effect, an interest-free loan from the government).
- Conversion of ordinary income to capital gain so that the taxpayer ends up paying a smaller tax than he would otherwise have paid. This results from the fact that 60 percent of a long-term capital gain is not subject to tax. Thus, an investor in the highest tax bracket (50 percent) who would have to pay a tax of 50 cents from every dollar of ordinary income in his top bracket need pay only 20 cents of any long-term capital gain (50 percent of the 40 percent taxable portion).

We have already pointed out that in preparing a cash-flow statement, the investor ignores any deduction for depreciation (because it is a bookkeeping entry only and does not involve any cash transfer). Therefore, the investor must prepare a separate taxable profit or loss statement to determine his tax savings. The tax statement will differ from the cash-flow statement in two respects:

- The tax statement will include tax deductions that do not reflect actual cash outlays (e.g., depreciation).
- The tax statement will exclude cash outlays that are not tax deductible (e.g., loan amortization, which is merely a transfer of principal from the borrower to the lender).

Put another way, the tax statement converts cash flow into taxable income or loss. If the result is positive (taxable income), the investor must pay an income tax and this will be a negative return to him for that period. On the other hand, a taxable loss will create tax savings to the investor (the precise amount depending on his tax bracket). In this case, his overall return from the investment will be increased. If the tax statement shows neither taxable income nor loss, then the investor's tax position has created neither a gain nor a loss and his total return from the investment will be derived solely from the other three types of returns (cash flow, equity buildup, and appreciation in value).

[a] Cash Flow Sheltered by Tax Losses

Table 2.4 below illustrates how an office building investment can generate a positive cash flow (dollars in the owner's pocket) and at the same time show a taxable loss. The implication of a taxable loss is twofold: (1) since the property is not showing a taxable gain, all of the cash flow from the property itself is received tax-free; and (2) the tax loss itself may be used to offset other income of the investor and the tax savings so achieved is added to the cash flow from the investment itself. In the specific example given here, the investor receives a positive cash flow in the first year of $6,500 and, in addition, generates a tax loss of $40,360 which, assuming he is in the 50 percent bracket, gives him an additional benefit of $20,180 (one-half the tax loss). Thus his total return is $26,680, which represents a 13.34 percent return on his cash investment of $200,000.

Table 2.4 is divided into three sections (with Section C being shown in two different ways). Section A (Investment Terms) sets forth the manner in which the total purchase price is paid. In this example the investor puts 20 percent cash down, and raises the balance of the price through two mortgages. The first mortgage, at a very favorable 14 percent interest rate in today's market, probably would be granted only on the condition that the investor give the mortgagee an equity participation (a share in cash flow). In this example the equity participa-

TABLE 2.4 Office Building Investment

A. *Investment Terms:*		
Purchase price		$1,000,000
First-mortgage loan (14% interest; 15% constant; 20 years)	$650,000	
Second-mortgage loan (14% interest; no amortization)	150,000	
Cash down	200,000	
B. *First-Year Cash-Flow Statement:*		
Gross income	$220,000	
Vacancy—5%	11,000	
Effective gross income	$209,000	
Operating expenses	84,000	
Net operating income		$ 125,000
Debt service—first mortgage	$ 97,500	
—second mortgage	21,000	
Less: Total debt payments		118,500
Cash flow		$ 6,500
C. *First-Year Tax (Profit and Loss) Statement:*		
Net operating income		$ 125,000
Interest on first mortgage	$ 91,000	
Interest on second mortgage	21,000	
Less: Total interest		$ 112,000
Depreciation (on $800,000 building cost)		53,360
Taxable profit (loss)		($40,360)
Or, Another Way to Derive Taxable Profit (Loss)		
C. *First-Year Tax (Profit and Loss) Statement:*		
Cash flow		$ 6,500
Add back: First-mortgage amortization		6,500
Total		$ 13,000
Deduct: Depreciation		53,360
Taxable profit (loss)		($40,360)

tion is ignored for the sake of simplicity. The second-mortgage loan, also at a favorable interest return and calling for no amortization, is likely to be available only as a purchase-money mortgage (i.e., taken back by the seller) as an inducement to the buyer to purchase the property. Normally, such a loan will mature in a fairly short time (e.g., five years); thus, the purchaser must face the problem of arranging new financing at that time. Normally the purchaser assumes that the increased cash flow from the property will permit him to refinance both the first and second mortgages on more desirable terms. However, this is not assured and represents one of the significant risks in real estate investing under today's high-interest-rate conditions.

Section B of Table 2.4 (First-Year Cash-Flow Statement) shows that at the end of the first year the investor will receive a cash flow of $6,500. This figure is developed in two steps. First NOI is computed. This represents gross rental income (assuming 100 percent occupancy), which is then reduced by (1) a vacancy allowance based on the forecast of actual occupancy; and (2) operating expenses. Then the debt service on the two mortgages is deducted from NOI. What remains is the cash flow, or dollars available to the investor at the end of the year.

Section C (First-Year Tax (Profit and Loss) Statement) begins with the same NOI figure as in Section B. However, since loan amortization is not a tax deduction, only the interest payments on the two mortgages may be deducted. (The difference between the interest deductions in Section C and the debt service in Section B is $6,500, which is the amortization on the first mortgage during the year; there is no amortization on the second mortgage.) In addition to the interest deduction, the investor may take a depreciation deduction on the building. Since this is a non-cash outlay, no depreciation deduction has been taken above in Section B. We assume that $800,000 of the $1 million purchase price is allocated to the building. Using straight-line depreciation with a fifteen-year recovery period as permitted by the new tax law, the investor may deduct $53,360 on his tax return. The combined deductions for interest and depreciation result in a taxable loss of $40,360, which represents a tax savings of $20,180 to an investor in the 50 percent bracket. Another way to compute the taxable loss is to begin with the cash-flow figure in Section B and then to add back the first-mortgage amortization (a nondeductible expense) and deduct the depreciation (a non-cash deduction). This is shown in the alternate Section C of Table 2.4.

[3] Equity Buildup (Loan Amortization)

Loan amortization is the periodic repayment of the principal amount of a loan. A business person (as distinguished from a real estate investor) treats loans and loan repayments as entirely separate from the profit and loss statement. In other words, when a business makes a loan, the loan is entered on the books as a liability and any loan repayments go to reduce that liability—the repayments are never treated as operating expenses of the business. (Interest payments, however, are treated as current expenses.)

The real estate investor looks at loans in a different way. While he recognizes that a mortgage loan is a liability, he treats both interest payments and loan amortization as a current expense. The investor does this even though the money paid toward loan reduction actually increases the investor's equity in the property. As a result, and assuming that the property eventually is sold at a price at least equal to its original cost, the investor will receive an additional gain at that time due to the fact that the mortgage loan will have been partially repaid. This additional gain is what is referred to as equity buildup.

It should be obvious that in the event the property is sold for less than its original cost, all or part of this equity buildup will never, in fact, be realized. For this reason, the return from equity buildup is always a speculative return since it is impossible to know the price for which the property will ultimately be sold. On the other hand, it is not appropriate to disregard the equity buildup, since on the basis of trends in the past several decades it is extremely unlikely that a prime piece of real property will end up being resold at less than its original cost. As a result, most investors will include the amount of equity buildup (which can be precisely calculated whenever the terms of the mortgage loan are known) in calculating return on investment.

[4] Appreciation in Value

Of the four types of possible returns to a real estate investor, appreciation in value clearly is the most speculative. Cash flow and tax savings are realized annually. Equity buildup is also realized annually in the sense that the principal amount of the outstanding mortgage is being reduced (although it is true that the investor will actually realize the gain only if the property is eventually sold for a price at least equal to its original cost). By comparison, appreciation in value is purely a "paper" calculation.

Nevertheless, it seems clear that calculations of ROI more and more will consider the factor of future appreciation. There are several reasons for this:

☐ First, the growth of open-end real estate investment funds (particularly the commingled funds offered by life insurance companies and commercial banks) requires that an annual valuation be placed upon properties in the fund in order that participants may either withdraw or contribute additional funds. As a result, these funds prepare an annual statement based upon current appraisals of owned real estate. The following is a statement from the annual report of one of the largest commingled funds setting forth the method by which annual valuation is determined:

> The purpose of an appraisal is to estimate the fair market value of a property as of a specific date. Fair market value has been defined by the courts as the highest price in terms of money which a property will bring if exposed to the open market, allowing a reasonable time to find a purchaser who buys with knowledge of all the uses to which it is adapted and for which it is capable of being used. This estimate of fair market value generally is a correlation of three approaches, all of which require the exercise of subjective judgment. The three approaches are: (1) current cost of reproducing a property less deterioration and functional and economic obsolescence; (2) capitalization of the property's net earning power; and (3) value indicated by recent sales of comparable properties in the market. In the correlation of these three approaches, the one most

heavily relied upon is the one generally recognized for the type of property in the market.

☐ Second, current prices more and more reflect the (assumed) inevitability of future increases in value of property in order to keep pace with inflation. In other words, investors, whether they like it or not, are forced to consider appreciation as a form of return if they wish to be competitive in the marketplace. In slang terms, investors today often buy "on the come"; that is, they will accept extremely low cash-flow, tax saving, and equity buildup returns in order to benefit from what they see as certain rises in prices over the long term. Obviously, this creates a much more speculative and volatile market than previously existed when current cash-flow return was the dominant consideration. But it is one of the consequences of continuing inflation.

What in fact has been the experience of real estate in the past with regard to changes in value? Until quite recently, no serious attempts had been made to measure real estate appreciation on a regular basis in the way that the various stock market averages measure changes in value of common stocks. But as the importance of this type of return increases, efforts are being made to measure appreciation over various periods. One of the most ambitious efforts to construct the kind of Dow Jones Average for investment real estate is being conducted by John McMahan, president of McMahan Associates, San Francisco, and a professor at the Stanford University Graduate School of Business.

The results of McMahan's efforts are shown in Table 2.5 below. The key figures are those for real return (i.e., adjusted for inflation); they indicate that investment-quality real estate showed an annual return better than 10 percent for the twenty-eight-year period ending in 1978. By comparison, common stock equities showed an annual return of just under 8 percent for the twenty-eight-year period and a negative annual return of almost 2 percent for the ten years ending in 1979. Fixed-income investments (i.e., bonds) showed a negative real return for the entire period.

TABLE 2.5 Return of Assets Classes

Assets	*Total Return*	*Real Return*	*Standard Deviation*
1951-1978			
Equities	11.44%	7.77%	18.29
Fixed income	3.45	(.22)	6.65
Real estate*	13.92	10.25	3.83
1969-1979			
Equities	4.80	(1.90)	18.40
Fixed income	6.15	(.55)	8.81
Real estate*	17.97	11.27	1.51

* Investment grade.

SOURCE: McMahan Associates; R. Ibbotson & R. Sinquefeld, *Stocks, Bonds, Bills & Inflation* (1977)

[a] How Returns Were Calculated

Data for the McMahan study came primarily from the American Council of Life Insurance, which keeps detailed records on properties financed by life companies. McMahan points out that the appraisals on these loans are a good indication of the price performance of the properties over periods of time. The study also used data from the Marshall Valuation Service, a nationally recognized appraisal firm.

The data were broken down into property type and location. The study itself was limited to "the investment grade portion," which McMahan describes as including office buildings, shopping centers, and industrial properties. These properties are the ones most likely to be purchased by pension funds, which is the audience to which the study was directed.

Not only did real estate provide a superior return to equities and fixed-income investments, but it also reduced overall portfolio volatility; that is, price fluctuations were less extreme. This is shown by the figures for the standard deviation; as indicated in the accompanying table, the standard deviation was much lower for real estate than for the other types of investments.

2.03 TRADITIONAL METHODS OF MEASURING RETURN ON INVESTMENT

As recently as fifteen or twenty years ago, real estate investing was primarily the domain of individuals and small syndicates who acquired properties in their own community and held them for relatively long periods of time. Although some national investment organizations played important roles—particularly large life insurance companies and public corporations holding real estate portfolios—these definitely were in the minority. In short, real estate investment had not yet become "institutionalized." Investment decisions were made by local investors and brokers more on the basis of long experience and an almost intuitive sense of value than upon a detailed analysis of the numbers and worked-out projections of future return.

One consequence of this was that return on investment (ROI) was computed in relatively simple ways; in particular, return calculations took no regard of the time value of money (i.e., the concept that a dollar received today is more valuable than a dollar to be received in the future). (This is discussed in detail in 2.06; the traditional measures of return to be discussed in this section treat future dollars as having the same value as present dollars.)

Despite the fact that professional real estate analysts now use almost exclusively the ROI technique described in 2.06 through 2.09, the traditional methods remain of interest for the following reasons:

1. They offer a simple method to compare one investment to another; this is particularly true for the first method of return discussed below, "free-and-clear return."

2. The cash-flow return, the one most commonly used in real estate, tells the number of dollars that will be in an investor's pocket at the end of each year during the holding period (assuming, of course, that projections used in the

analysis turn out to be accurate). This quantitative measure is useful even when the time value of money is ignored.

3. Finally, all of these methods do offer a relatively quick and simple way of determining future return, and so can be used as a preliminary method of weeding out obviously undesirable offerings and permitting the investor to concentrate his attention, and make his detailed analyses, on the most promising ones.

[1] Free-and-Clear Return

Free-and-clear return is derived by dividing NOI by total investment in the property (i.e., the sum of equity plus all mortgages on the property). Table 2.7 below shows a simple computation of free-and-clear return, based on the total investment (price) in Table 2.6. Net operating income, as already noted above,

TABLE 2.6 Total Investment: Apartment Building

Price (total investment)	$1,000,000
Less: First loan (9.5%; 30 years)	650,000
Less: Second loan (8%; interest only)	150,000
Cash (equity) required	$ 200,000

TABLE 2.7 Free-and-Clear Return

Gross rental income (GRI)		$175,000
Less: Vacancy and credit loss (5%)		8,800
Effective gross income (EGI)		$166,200
Less: Operating expenses	$60,000	
Less: Replacement reserves	7,000	67,000
Net operating income (NOI)		$ 99,200
Total investment (Table 2.6)		$1,000,000
Free-and-clear return		9.92%

is the income remaining after operating expenses are deducted from gross rental income. Since the return is on the total investment in the property, no debt service is subtracted from net operating income. In other words, free-and-clear return assumes that an investor puts up 100 percent cash and does not use any financing. Thus, its most appropriate use is to compare one property to another because it eliminates the distortions arising from different financing terms.

For example, suppose an investor is considering two apartment buildings. One has a free-and-clear return of 10 percent and one has a free-and-clear return of 12 percent. The difference in return can be explained in one of several ways:

- The building offering the higher return has a less secure flow of income (e.g., it is in a declining neighborhood) and so a higher return must be offered to attract purchasers.

- The building offering the higher return will need substantial rehabilitation in the near future and the additional investment required will lower the return.
- The two buildings are in fact of equal risk and quality and, therefore, one is overpriced compared to the other.

As this example shows, comparing free-and-clear returns points the way for further investigation by the buyer. On the other hand, free-and-clear return is not useful in showing the true return to the buyer (unless, of course, he indeed intends to put up 100 percent cash and not use any financing). For purposes of estimating the actual return, the investor must use one of the other three traditional returns discussed in the paragraphs that follow.

[2] Cash-Flow (Cash-on-Cash) Return

Cash-flow return, the most frequently used format in real estate, is derived by dividing cash flow by equity.

Cash flow represents NOI minus debt service (i.e., interest and loan amortization) on mortgages to which the property is subject (or to which the property will be subject under the assumptions made). Table 2.8 below shows the cash-flow return on the investment described in Table 2.6.

TABLE 2.8 Cash-Flow Return

Net operating income (Table 2.7)		$99,200
Debt service on first mortgage (10.08%)	$65,500	
Debt service on second mortgage	12,000	
Total debt service		77,500
Cash flow		$21,700
Equity investment (Table 2.6)		$200,000
Cash-flow return		10.85%

Since the cash-flow return of 10.85 percent is higher than the free-and-clear return of 9.92 percent (Table 2.7), the financing creates upside leverage; that is, the total debt of $800,000 (first plus second mortgages) costs the investor a debt service of $77,500, or 9.69 percent. But these funds earn the investor a return of 9.92 percent (the free-and-clear return), or $79,400. The favorable spread of $1,900 annually raises the cash-flow return above the free-and-clear return. (For a discussion of leverage, see 2.03[6].)

[3] Cash-Flow Return Plus Tax Savings

The most obvious omission when calculating the cash-flow return is the tax loss of $16,500 for the current year (see Table 2.9). Since the tax loss has value to any investor who pays income tax, it should be included in the return calculation. Assuming an investor is in the 50 percent bracket, the tax savings is $8,250.

TABLE 2.9 Taxable Income (Loss) Statement (Year 1)

Net operating income (Table 2.7)		$99,200
Interest on first mortgage (9.5%)	$61,700	
Interest on second mortgage (8.0%)	12,000	73,700
Remaining income		$25,500
Depreciation (building plus personal property)		42,000
Taxable profit (loss)		($16,500)
Tax savings (50% bracket)		($8,250)

The calculation then becomes:

$$\frac{\text{Cash flow} + \text{tax savings}}{\text{equity}} = \text{ROI}$$

or

$$\frac{\$29{,}950\ (\$21{,}700 + \$8{,}250)}{\$200{,}000} = 14.97\%$$

[4] Cash-Flow Return Plus Tax Savings Plus Equity Buildup

Most investors who are other than short-term holders and expect to retain the property for more than one or two years will now take a further step. They will add to their return the equity buildup that results from the annual mortgage amortization (loan reduction). Of course, the investor actually will realize this equity buildup

- Only when he sells the property, and then
- Only if he can sell for at least his initial acquisition cost.

Nevertheless, in a period when real estate values have risen very sharply, this is normally a minimum expectation.

Of course, the investor can only view loan amortization as additional profit when he has previously subtracted loan amortization as an expense in arriving at cash flow. In other words, the two are a "wash"; that is, they cancel each other out. Why not then ignore loan amortization as an expense, thereby making it unnecessary to add it back to cash flow when calculating overall return? The reason is twofold. First, the calculation of cash flow is so traditional in the real estate industry that it is not likely to be abandoned. Second, many conservative investors will not add equity buildup back into the return calculation, preferring to use the more conservative standard of cash flow (or cash flow plus tax savings).

Nevertheless, our calculation recognizes equity buildup, which in the example amounts to $3,800 in the first year (the difference between first-mortgage debt service of $65,500 in Table 2.8 and first-mortgage interest of $61,700 in Table 2.9). (Another way to calculate first-year equity buildup is to take the difference between the debt-service constant of 10.08 percent and the interest of 9.5 percent, which equals 0.58 percent, and multiply this by the loan principal of $650,000. The result is $3,770.)

When adding equity buildup, the return on investment becomes:

$$\frac{\text{Cash flow} + \text{tax savings} + \text{equity buildup}}{\text{equity}} = \text{ROI}$$

or

$$\frac{\$33{,}750\ (\$21{,}700 + \$8{,}250 + \$3{,}800)}{\$200{,}000} = 16.87\%$$

[5] Cash-Flow Return Plus Tax Savings Plus Equity Buildup Plus Appreciation

Finally, some investors include the anticipated appreciation in the property's value in their annual return calculation. Obviously, this is by far the most speculative portion of the return. Indeed, because of the difficulty in predicting changes in value over short periods of time, this element of return would seem to be justified only when a long-term holding is assumed so that long-term trends can be used to project future value.

In our example, assume an annual appreciation of 2 percent, or $20,000 per year. (Actually, the annual appreciation would grow very slightly each year as a result of compounding, but this is far too precise a measure in an admittedly speculative projection.) Then, the return calculation becomes:

$$\frac{\text{Cash flow} + \text{tax savings} + \text{equity buildup} + \text{appreciation}}{\text{equity}} = \text{ROI}$$

or

$$\frac{\$53{,}750\ (\$21{,}700 + \$8{,}250 + \$3{,}800 + \$20{,}000)}{\$200{,}000} = 26.87\%$$

[6] Leverage in Real Estate Investing

The use of borrowed funds in real estate investing is so common a practice that we often take for granted our understanding of the relationship between mortgage debt and ROI, and between debt service and NOI. In fact, many investors do not realize precisely how leverage (the use of borrowed funds) works and, in particular, the distinction between financial leverage and operating leverage.

[a] Understanding Financial Leverage

Financial leverage expresses the spread between:

☐ Debt-service percentage, known as the constant (annual payment of loan principal and interest as a percentage of the original loan); and

☐ Free-and-clear return (NOI as a percentage of total investment—equity plus debt—in the property). Financial leverage can be positive or negative. Positive (upside) leverage exists when the debt-service percentage is less than the free-and-clear return. The investor is borrowing funds at a cost less than the return from the property he is buying with these funds. In other words, he is making a profit on the lender's money. In the opposite situation, where the debt-service percentage is more than the free-and-clear return, negative (downside) leverage occurs; the investor is paying more for funds than he is earning from their use.

Example: An investor acquires a $1 million property with an NOI of $100,000. The property thus has a free-and-clear return of 10 percent. The investor puts up $250,000 in cash and borrows $750,000 at 10.5 percent interest, with level payments fully amortizing the loan after thirty-one years. The debt service (10.92 percent annual constant) would be $81,900. This would leave $18,100 of cash flow, or a cash-on-cash return of 7.24 percent on the $250,000 cash investment. This is a case of negative financial leverage; the free-and-clear return is less than the debt service on the loan. In other words, the investor is borrowing money at a cost of 10.92 percent to invest in property returning only 10 percent. The more he borrows, the greater the downside leverage, as Table 2.10 shows.

TABLE 2.10 Changing Financial Leverage *

Loan Ratio	*Loan Amount*	*Debt Service*	*Equity*	*Cash Flow*	*Cash-on-Cash Return*
70%	$700,000	$76,440	$300,000	$23,560	$7.85
75	750,000	81,900	250,000	18,100	7.24
80	800,000	87,360	200,000	12,640	6.32
85	850,000	92,820	150,000	7,180	4.79
90	900,000	98,280	100,000	1,720	1.72

* These figures are based on (1) a property valued at $1 million with annual NOI of $100,000 (10 percent free-and-clear return); and (2) financing by a thirty-one-year fully amortized mortgage at 10.5 percent interest, 10.92 percent constant.

In the case of positive leverage, the opposite would be the case. The higher the loan-to-value ratio, the higher the cash-on-cash return. Some twenty years ago investors would never consider a deal involving negative leverage; today it is common because of rising real estate prices and mortgage interest rates.

[b] Curing Negative Financial Leverage

As we have seen, positive financial leverage exists only when the cash-on-cash return exceeds the free-and-clear return (both expressed as percentages). In the example used above, one of two things would have to happen to convert the financial leverage from negative to positive:

☐ First, the interest rate could be lowered sufficiently to drop the debt-service constant below 10 percent (which is the free-and-clear return). For example, if the interest were 9 percent instead of 10.5 percent, the annual debt service on a 75 percent fully amortized thirty-one-year loan would be $72,000 (9.60 percent constant), leaving a residual net operating income of $28,000 as a cash-on-cash return on $250,000 equity, or just over 11 percent. This is a return higher than the free-and-clear return and hence shows positive leverage.

☐ Second, a standing (interest only) 9.5 percent loan would achieve positive leverage. Interest would amount to $71,250 on the loan, leaving a residual of $28,750 as a cash-on-cash return on the $250,000 equity, or 11.5 percent.

[c] Understanding Operating Leverage

Whereas financial leverage deals with a changing debt-service amount and its effect on cash flow, operating leverage operates in terms of changing net operating income and its relationship to a fixed debt service. Given a fixed loan cost (although even with a variable-rate mortgage, debt service changes little), any increase in net operating income is passed through directly to the owner, including the additional income generated by the portion of the property owned as a result of the borrowed funds. Conversely, any decrease in net operating income is borne entirely by the owner, since his debt service must be paid in any event.

Using the same example as above, in which a $1 million property is subject to a thirty-one-year $750,000 loan at 10.5 percent interest, 10.92 percent constant, Table 2.11 illustrates the power of operating leverage both on the upside and the downside as net operating income changes.

TABLE 2.11 Changing Operating Leverage

Debt Service	*Net Operating Income*	*Cash Return to Owner*	*Cash Percentage Return on $250,000*
$81,900	$100,000	$ 18,100	7.24% [1]
81,900	120,000	38,100	15.24
81,900	140,000	58,100	23.24
81,900	180,000	98,100	39.24
81,900	200,000	118,100	47.24
81,900	80,000	(1,900)	—0— [2]

[1] Negative financial leverage.
[2] Negative cash flow.

Note that a 20 percent increase in NOI (from $100,000 to $120,000) more than doubles the cash-on-cash return, while a doubling of NOI to $200,000 increases the cash-on-cash return more than six times. On the other hand, whereas an NOI of $100,000 creates negative financial leverage (although a positive cash flow of $18,100), a 20 percent decline in NOI to $80,000 creates a negative cash flow to the owner, since debt service then exceeds cash flow. Thus is illustrated the power of operating leverage and the resulting positional advantage or disadvantage to the equity owner.

[d] How to Develop Operating Leverage

How do you develop positive operating leverage? It can be done in one or both of two ways:

- Increase gross operating income (or at least hold it constant while expenses decline).
- Reduce expenses (or at least hold them constant while income rises).

Using the example above, assume an owner buys a sixty-unit apartment house for $1 million, $750,000 of which comes from a loan. If the owner's equity paid for fifteen units while the mortgage loan paid for forty-five units, then the owner in effect is guaranteeing debt service on the forty-five units financed by the lender in consideration of which the owner is entitled to keep any cash flow from those forty-five units in excess of the debt service. If a modest rent increase of $10 per month per unit is imposed, both annual NOI and cash flow increase by $7,200 ($600 × 12). The owner, in other words, keeps the entire increase, not merely the increase on the fifteen units paid for with his own money.

This illustrates one of the reasons many lenders now ask for a participation in any increases in gross income over a certain level. In an inflationary era, the lender views a portion of the increased income as a reflection of rising inflation (rather than operating efficiency) and requires a share of that to prevent erosion of its loan capital. A borrower who agrees to such a provision should be sure that the percentage to be paid to the lender, plus the inevitable increases in operating expenses that will accompany increased income, does not eliminate operating leverage altogether and so switch the positional advantage of the investment to the lender.

A lender who makes a loan on terms that initially create negative financial leverage and also asks for a participation that eliminates or substantially reduces operating leverage is short-sighted in denying an incentive to the owner to properly manage the investment. By the same token, the investor who accepts such terms is creating a situation that will be difficult to handle.

[e] Advantages and Disadvantages of Leverage

Of course, leverage may be good, bad, or neutral depending upon the circumstances of the particular transaction. Consider the following propositions:

☐ *High leverage should be avoided because it creates too much risk.* First of all, the degree of leverage (i.e., the ratio of debt to equity) that can be tolerated depends upon the reliability of the expected NOI. A triple net leaseback in which General Motors is the tenant creates a very high degree of confidence that rental income will be constant, and so reduces the downside risk in operating leverage; consequently, a high level of financial leverage can be accepted. On the other hand, a motel in a seasonal resort area can have widely fluctuating operating income, so that a lower degree of financial leverage is appropriate.

☐ *High financial leverage makes property easier to sell.* This is obviously true when the property has a high degree of positive leverage, since the buyer is getting a higher return than an all-cash payment would yield. But it may also be true for a property with negative financial leverage. Such a property is likely to be bought only by a speculator or operator who has great confidence in his ability to increase NOI. In such a case, the ultimate return will be higher if the property already has financing (since the debt service will remain unchanged) than if the property has no mortgage and is being sold for all cash (since the buyer is unlikely to be able to arrange financing under these circumstances).

This latter point also explains why investors today are often willing to buy leveraged property with a negative carry (i.e., suffering from negative financial leverage). Having confidence that operating leverage will move in their favor as rents increase, they are willing to accept negative financial leverage in order to put a minimum of cash in the property (or alternatively, to spread a given amount of cash among several leveraged properties).

An opposite example is that of government-subsidized housing, which is highly leveraged and where the confidence in future income flows generally is low. This type of high leverage should be confined to high-income individuals who, at the very worst, will receive value from tax deferral. In other words, their tax bracket gives them a positional advantage in this type of investment.

When thinking about leverage, the investor's object always should be to obtain a positional advantage. An investor may be willing to accept a negative financial leverage for a stronger operating leverage, or vice versa; however, one who must give away both positional advantages in order to make a deal is well advised to look elsewhere.

2.04 ACCOUNTING RETURN ANALYSIS

[1] Understanding Accounting Return Analysis

The various techniques for measuring return on investment (ROI) run the gamut from rough rules of thumb to the intricate calculations involved in the internal rate of return; somewhere in the middle lies accounting return analysis. It has the virtue of being relatively simple, while at the same time recognizing all revenues and expenses from the investment; its main defect is its failure to reflect the time value of money (the fact that a dollar to be received in the future is worth less than a dollar today). However, where an investment holding period is expected to be relatively short, or for the purpose of a preliminary "winnowing out" of alternatives, the accounting return analysis can play a role.

[a] Six Steps in Accounting Return Analysis

In the accounting return method, the investor makes the following computations:

1. *Total annual benefit from investment.* This figure is the total of the cash flow plus the tax savings (or minus the tax loss) for each year of ownership (the investor, of course, must assume a given period of ownership).

2. *Total benefits during ownership.* The total annual benefit is then multiplied by the number of years of projected ownership.

3. *Net proceeds of sale.* The investor then projects a selling price, subtracts all sales expenses plus the taxes on any gain, and arrives at net sales proceeds.

TABLE 2.12 Cash-Flow Statement (70-Unit Apartment Project)

	Year 1	*Year 2*	*Year 3*	*Year 4*	*Year 5*	*Year 6*	*Year 7*		*Totals*
Total scheduled income	$175,000	185,500	191,100	196,800	202,700	208,800	215,000	(see note 1)	$1,374,900
Vacancy	$8,800	9,300	9,600	14,200	10,100	12,500	10,800	(see note 4)	$75,300
Effective gross income	$166,200	176,200	181,500	182,600	192,600	196,300	204,200		$1,299,600
Operating expenses	$35,000	36,400	37,900	39,400	40,900	42,600	46,300	(see note 2)	$278,500
Real estate taxes	$28,000	30,200	32,700	35,300	38,100	41,100	44,400	(see note 3)	$249,800
Net operating income	$103,200	109,600	110,900	107,900	113,600	112,600	113,500		$771,300
Debt service—first	$68,200	68,200	68,200	68,200	68,200	68,200	68,200		$477,400
Debt service—second	$15,000	15,000	15,000	15,000	15,000	15,000	15,000		$105,000
Reserves	$8,000	8,000	8,000	8,000	8,000	8,000	8,000		$56,000
Cash flow	$12,000	18,400	19,700	16,700	22,400	21,400	22,300		$132,900

[1] Income increases at 3 percent per year compounded except 6 percent in year 2.
[2] Expenses increase at 4 percent per year compounded plus an additional $2,000 in year 7.
[3] Real estate taxes increase 8 percent per year.
[4] Vacancy is 5 percent in all but the fourth (7.2%) and sixth years (6%).

4. *Net dollar return.* The initial cash investment (equity) is then subtracted from the total return (the totals of (2) and (3)).

5. *Average annual dollar return.* The net dollar return is divided by the number of years of ownership to give average annual dollar return.

6. *Average annual percentage return.* The average annual dollar return is divided by the equity investment to give average annual percentage return.

[b] An Illustration of Accounting Return Analysis

Table 2.12 shows the annual cash flow for a seventy-unit apartment project during an assumed seven-year period of ownership.

Table 2.13 presents the combined annual cash flow (column 4) with annual tax savings for a 50 percent tax bracket investor (column 3) to show total annual benefit (column 5). (Due to lack of space, the computation of annual tax savings is not shown.) Table 2.13 shows the total cash and tax benefits before sale as

TABLE 2.13 Combined Return Statement

	Operating Proceeds				
Year	*(1)* *You Contribute*	*(2)* *You Realize Tax Losses (or Profits)*	*(3)* *You Save (Column 2 × 50% Tax Bracket)*	*(4)* *Cash Flow (See Cash-Flow Statement)*	*(5)* *Total Benefit (Cols. 3 and 4)*
1	$200,000	$27,600	$13,800	$12,000	$ 25,800
2		6,500	3,200	18,400	21,600
3		4,200	2,100	19,700	21,800
4		6,300	3,200	16,700	19,900
5		1,800	900	22,400	23,300
6		1,300	600	21,400	22,000
7		(1,800)	(900)	22,300	21,400
		Total tax and cash benefits before sale			$155,800

SALE PROCEEDS

Cash proceeds	$375,000
Less: Tax payable	(113,500)
Net sale effect	$261,500

Total tax and cash benefits after sale (total return) $417,300

TABLE 2.14 Accounting Return Statement

1. Total return (from Table 2.13)	$417,300
2. Less: Initial cash investment	200,000
3. Net dollar return	$217,300
4. Average annual dollar return ($217,300 ÷ 7 years)	$31,000
5. Average annual % return (accounting return) (line 4 ÷ line 2)	15.5%

$155,800. A sale for $375,000 is then assumed (representing annual appreciation of 2 percent) to produce net proceeds of $261,500, or total benefits of $417,300. In other words, this figure represents the total cash that the investor will realize after seven years of ownership.

Table 2.14 illustrates steps 4, 5, and 6 in the accounting return analysis. Step 4 shows the net dollar return to the investor at $217,300. This becomes an average annual dollar return of $31,000, or an average percentage return of 15.5 percent on the initial equity of $200,000.

[2] Limitation of Accounting Return Analysis

As already noted, the major limitation of accounting return analysis is its failure to consider the time value of money. A simple illustration shows this. Table 2.15 compares two investments, each of which involves an initial cash payment of $3,000 and an ultimate total return of $6,000. Thus the accounting return is 25 percent for each, but it is obvious that alternative *B* is the preferable one because more than half the total return is realized in the first three years as compared to a zero return for that period for alternative *A*.

TABLE 2.15 Accounting Return

AS A DECISION-MAKING TOOL

	Alternative A	*Alternative B*
Cash investment	$3,000	$3,000
Net returns:		
Year 1	0	$1,400
Year 2	0	1,200
Year 3	0	1,100
Year 4	$6,000	$2,300
Total return	$6,000	$6,000

FOR ALTERNATIVES *A* AND *B*

$6,000	Total return
3,000	Cash investment
$3,000	Net return

4)3,000 = $750 average annual $ return

3,000)750 = 25% average annual % return

Consequently, accounting return analysis must be used with caution and is most appropriate when cash inflows from comparable investments follow approximately the same schedule.

2.05 PAY-BACK ANALYSIS

Pay-back analysis of a real estate investment addresses itself to the question, How soon will I be out of the investment? or When will I have my investment dollars back? In other words, the pay-back method calculates the period of time required for the investor to recoup his initial investment through a combination of cash flow and tax savings. This method was an early attempt to allow for the time value of money and, to that extent, represents an advance over the early rules of thumb and accounting return analysis. However, the complete lack of refinement in the system makes it almost valueless in most situations.

There is one occasion, however, when pay-back analysis can be used, that is, when an investment is a wholly speculative one and no realistic projections can be made of cash inflows or tax savings beyond the first two or three years. An oil and gas investment is a good example, since the investor often relies primarily on tax savings in the early years to recoup his investment, whereas future gains depend upon the success in drilling. In such an event, the investor may justifiably ask himself how long it will take to recoup his investment and be "out whole," with any subsequent cash flow or tax savings to be viewed as gain.

Example: Assume an investor is offered three alternatives, each requiring an initial investment of $3,000. Projected returns (cash flow plus tax savings) for the initial four years of each investment can be projected with some certainty, and these are listed in the "annual" column of Table 2.16. The "cumulative" column shows the total received by the investor for the entire holding period to date. It is thus clear that the investor will be paid back his initial investment after two years for Investment *A*, after three years (plus some gain) for Investment *B*, and after four years (plus some gain) for Investment *C*. This does convey some useful information to the investor, but it has told him nothing about the total expected profit and when that is anticipated.

TABLE 2.16 Computation of Pay-Back Periods for Three Investment Alternatives

	Investment A		*Investment B*		*Investment C*	
Year	*Annual*	*Cumulative*	*Annual*	*Cumulative*	*Annual*	*Cumulative*
1	$1,500	$1,500	$ 800	$ 800	—0—	—0—
2	1,500	3,000	1,700	2,500	—0—	—0—
3			1,600	4,100	—0—	—0—
4					$6,000	$6,000
Pay-back period	2 years		3 years		4 years	

Rank ordering of alternatives: *Investment A* (2-year pay-back)
Investment B (3-year pay-back)
Investment C (4-year pay-back)

2.06 DISCOUNTED CASH-FLOW ANALYSIS

The beginning of this chapter points out that the two elements in measuring return on investment are "cash" and "time"; that is, the investor is interested not only in how much money he will receive, but how soon he will receive it.

Until this point in our analysis, only the amount of cash inflows, not the time of receipt, has been considered. Theories that consider the time of receipt as a factor affecting return on investment (ROI) all come under the general rubric "discounted cash-flow (DCF) analysis." The individual methods discussed in the following sections of this chapter include:

- Net present value (NPV) analysis
- Internal rate of return (IRR) analysis
- Reinvestment rate (RIR) analysis (also called adjusted IRR)

Remember, all these methods are included in the broad category of discounted cash-flow analysis because all of them, in one way or another, give effect to the time factor in valuing a return to be received sometime in the future.

Before proceeding to a discussion of each of these separate methods, the basic concepts underlying DCF analysis must be set forth.

[1] Present Value Theory

The key idea underlying discounted cash-flow analysis is the "present value" concept. This concept states simply that a dollar received today is more valuable than a dollar to be received in the future. A dollar received in the future is less valuable for three reasons:

1. *Inflation.* Inflation represents a reduction in the value of the dollar. When price levels rise, more dollars are required to purchase the same amount of goods and services than is previously required. Consequently, during an inflationary period, a dollar to be received in the future is worth less than a present dollar (i.e., the present value of the future dollar is diminished). In other words, the further ahead in time a dollar is anticipated to be received, the less the present value of that dollar because of the expectation of inflation.

2. *Opportunity cost.* A dollar in hand today can immediately be invested and earn interest. (It also can be spent to satisfy some immediate desire; however, in our discussion we assume the dollar is intended for investment rather than consumption.) If the dollar is not to be received for one year, the interest that could have been earned must be foregone. The foregone interest represents the opportunity cost associated with the receipt of a dollar in the future rather than today. Consequently, today's value (present value) of the dollar to be received in one year is diminished by the amount of the opportunity cost. Again, the further in the future the dollar is to be received, the greater the opportunity cost (because the longer period of time a present dollar could have earned interest).

3. *Risk.* If a dollar is to be received in the future, there always exists some possibility that the dollar will not in fact be repaid. The existence of risk thus diminishes the present value of the future dollar; the diminution depends upon the extent of assumed risk. (A discussion about risk is contained in 2.10.)

Given the fact that a future dollar is worth less than the present dollar, how is the difference in value to be determined? The determination is done by means of discounting.

[2] Compound Interest and the Discounting Process

Discounting can best be understood by beginning with a discussion of compound interest. Interest itself is payment for the use of money. Compound interest is no more than interest on interest, and the calculations involved in compounding are very straightforward. Suppose a savings association pays interest at the rate of 5 percent, with the interest calculated once each year. Then a dollar invested (deposited) in a savings account yields $1.05 at the end of the year. It therefore may be said that on the day it is deposited the dollar's future value in one year is equal to

Its present value ($1)
plus
The interest rate times the present value ($0.05)

To this point, simple interest has been described. However, in the second year of the deposit, 5 percent interest would be paid not merely on the $1 original deposit but also on the 5 cents earned as interest during the first year. Thus, the interest earned in the second year would amount to 0.0525 cents ($1.05 × 0.05 = 0.0525), or one-quarter cent more than the first year. This is an example of compound interest.

As a matter of practice, savings institutions have for many years compounded interest semiannually or quarterly, thus raising the annual interest rate by a small fraction. More recently, banks in areas where competition for funds is very great have been compounding interest daily. The result of this is that an annual interest rate of 7.75 percent will actually pay 8.17 percent at the end of a full year, assuming the funds remain in the account during the entire period.

When interest is to be compounded, the amount of interest to be earned over a period of time can be calculated by painstakingly computing the interest at the end of every interest period (whether daily, monthly, quarterly, or otherwise) on the balance outstanding at that time. Another way to calculate the future value is to present the process mathematically:

> The future or compound value is equal to the present value times one plus the interest rate raised to a power equal to the number of periods which the money is left in the savings account, or $FV = PV(1 + R)^n$.

The easiest way to calculate compound value is to use a compound value table. Table 2.17, for example, shows the value of $1 compounded annually for years ranging from one through thirty at annual interest rates ranging from one percent through 20 percent. For example, $1 held for ten years at an annual interest rate of 5 percent will grow to $1.629. Thus, to determine the growth of any amount larger than $1, it is necessary only to multiply the principal amount by 1.629.

Once the concept of compounding interest is understood, an investor has no trouble seeing the limitations of such a method as the accounting return analysis. Table 2.18 shows how $10,000 will grow at a 15 percent rate of return, compounded annually, over different time periods. The table also shows the average annual return (column 5), which is the return that would be shown through the use of accounting return analysis. Thus at the end of five years, the initial sum, compounded at 15 percent annually, has grown to $20,110, or an average annual re-

TABLE 2.17 Value of $1 of Investment Compounded Annually

Year	*1%*	*3%*	*5%*	*10%*	*15%*	*20%*
1	$1.010	$1.030	$1.050	$ 1.100	$ 1.150	$ 1.200
2	1.020	1.061	1.102	1.210	1.322	1.440
3	1.030	1.093	1.159	1.331	1.521	1.728
4	1.041	1.126	1.216	1.464	1.749	2.074
5	1.051	1.159	1.276	1.610	2.011	2.488
6	1.062	1.194	1.340	1.772	2.313	2.986
7	1.072	1.230	1.407	1.949	2.660	3.583
8	1.083	1.267	1.477	2.144	3.059	4.300
9	1.094	1.305	1.551	2.358	3.518	5.160
10	1.105	1.344	1.629	2.594	4.046	6.192
15	1.161	1.558	2.079	4.177	8.137	15.407
20	1.220	1.806	2.653	6.728	16.367	38.338
25	1.282	2.094	3.386	10.835	32.919	95.396
30	1.348	2.427	4.322	17.440	66.212	237.376

turn of 20 percent. Obviously, the true annual return is only 15 percent. After thirty years, the average annual return is 217 percent, a figure that bears no relationship at all to the true annual return of 15 percent. It is the failure to recognize the effect of compounding that yields the larger return under accounting return analysis (i.e., the entire annual return is deemed to be earned by the original investment, instead of being allocated between original investment and accumulated interest).

[a] Discounting

Discounting is simply the inverse of compounding. In discounting, the future value is known, as is the interest rate and the term; the problem is to find the

TABLE 2.18 The Power of Compound Interest

Using the compound interest table at a 15 percent rate of return and a $10,000 investment, given different periods of time, the following dollar returns occur:

(1) End of Year	*(2)* Total Dollar Return	*(3)* Net Dollar Return	*(4)* Average Annual Dollar Return	*(5)* Average Annual Return
1	$ 11,500	$ 1,500	$ 1,500	15%
5	20,110	10,110	2,022	20
10	40,460	30,460	2,707	27
20	163,670	153,670	7,684	77
30	662,120	652,120	21,737	217

present value. Suppose a business associate promises to pay an investor $10,000 in one lump sum at the end of ten years. The question is, What would the investor pay the associate today (present value) for that promise? The answer is a function of the discount rate and how long the investor must wait for the payment. Here, too, a formula is available for calculating the present value of a single payment to be received in the future; it is an algebraic rearrangement of the compounding formula:

$$PV = FV \div (1 + r)^n$$

Table 2.19 suggests that if the discount rate were 9 percent the investor would pay a business associate $4,224.11 today for that promise. Stated another way, with a 9 percent discount rate the investor would be indifferent to receiving $4,224.11 today, or the right to receive $10,000 ten years from today. Also, since discounting is the inverse of compounding, it can be seen that if $4,224.11 were deposited today earning 9 percent interest, the compound value would be $10,000 in ten years.

TABLE 2.19 Discounting (Present Value) Example

What is the value today of the right to receive $10,000 at the end of ten years assuming a 9 percent annual discount rate?

I. Hand computation:

$$PV = \frac{FV}{(1+r)^n} = \frac{\$10{,}000}{(1+.09)^{10}} = \frac{\$10{,}000}{2.3673637} = \$4{,}224.11$$

II. From the Compound Interest and Annuity Table (Table 2.22):
   a. Annual *PV* factor (10 years at 9%) (column 4) = 0.422411
   b. Future value = $10,000
   c. Present value: $10,000 × 0.422411 = $4,224.11

The compounding and discounting formulas can be expanded to handle a series of payments or receipts as easily as a single payment or receipt. The examples in Tables 2.20 and 2.21 present the future value of a series of payments (compound annuity) and the present value of a series of receipts (discounted annuity), as calculated using the annual annuity factor, as found in Table 2.22.

[3] How to Select an Appropriate Discount Rate

Until this point in our discussion, it has generally been assumed that an investor has the choice between acquiring a real estate investment at a fixed price or not acquiring the investment at all. In other words, the price of the investment is not negotiable. Thus the investor starts with a fixed price, projects the total return from the property over its life, and then calculates an ROI by applying one of the various methods already discussed.

TABLE 2.20 Future Value of an Annuity

How much will $500 set aside each year accumulate to in seven years if during the interim the funds can be invested at 9 percent compounded annually?

Amount of the annuity	$500
Term	7 years
Interest rate	9%
Annual annuity factor (from column 2, Table 2.22)	9.200435
Future value of the annuity ($500 × 9.200435)	$4,600.22

TABLE 2.21 Present Value of an Annuity

What is the value today of receiving $500 a year for seven years if the annual discount rate is 9 percent annual compounding?

Amount of the annuity	$500
Term	7 years
Discount rate	9%
Annual annuity factor (from column 5, Table 2.22)	5.032953
Present value of annuity ($500 × 5.032953)	$2,516.48

In reality, most situations do not involve a fixed acquisition price; the investor is in a position to negotiate price. Consequently, he must have some standards or guidelines for determining what his ROI should be. This section discusses possible standards and guidelines.

If this discussion had appeared earlier in the chapter, we would talk about choosing an appropriate annual return. But since the concept of "discounted cash value" (DCF) has been introduced, the more technical term "discount rate" may be used. In other words, on the assumption that certain specified cash inflows (from cash flow, tax savings, and eventual resale) are to be received according to a projected schedule, what discount rate (i.e., what annual percentage return) should be used in order to discount those cash flows to their present value (i.e., the price an investor would be willing to pay today for the investment)?

Certainly, no precise method or generally accepted approach is used for deriving a discount rate, but the following process identifies the elements to be considered and shows how a meaningful rate of return can be derived:

☐ *Real return.* First, the analyst must estimate the required real return (i.e., the premium the investor wants for deferred consumption). This figure can be estimated from historical data by comparing rates of return on government securities with rates of inflation over long periods of time. Various researchers have estimated that this number is between 2 and 3 percent.

☐ *Inflation rate.* An estimate of the expected rate of inflation over the holding period is then made by subtracting the real return from the current yield on government bonds. An investor who expects to hold an asset for ten years can look at the yield on ten-year government bonds (which are assumed to be free of any risks other than risks associated with inflation) and provide a way to estimate the market's expectations regarding inflation. The current total bond yield less the 2 to 3 percent real return is a composite of investor expectations about inflation over a ten-year period.

TABLE 2.22 Annual Compound Interest and Annuity (9.00%)

YEAR	Amount Of 1	Amount Of 1 Per Period	Sinking Fund Payment	Present Worth Of 1	Present Worth Of 1 Per Period	Periodic Payment To Amortize 1	Constant Annual Percent	Total Interest	Annual Add On Rate	PERIOD
	What a single $1 deposit grows to in the future. The deposit is made at the beginning of the first period.	What a series of $1 deposits grow to in the future. A deposit is made at the end of each period.	The amount to be deposited at the end of each period that grows to $1 in the future.	What $1 to be paid in the future is worth today. Value today of a single payment tomorrow.	What $1 to be paid at the end of each period is worth today. Value today of a series of payments tomorrow.	The mortgage payment to amortize a loan of $1. An annuity certain, payable at the end of each period worth $1 today.	The annual payment, including interest and principal, to amortize completely a loan of $100.	The total interest paid over the term on a loan of $1. The loan is amortized by regular periodic payments.	The average annual interest rate on a loan that is completely amortized by regular periodic payments.	
	$S = (1+i)^n$	$S_{\overline{n}\vert} = \frac{(1+i)^n - 1}{i}$	$\frac{1}{S_{\overline{n}\vert}} = \frac{i}{(1+i)^n - 1}$	$V^n = \frac{1}{(1+i)^n}$	$A_{\overline{n}\vert} \frac{1-V^n}{i}$	$\frac{1}{A_{\overline{n}\vert}} = \frac{i}{1-V^n}$				
1	1.090 000	1.000 000	1.000 000 0000	0.917 431	0.917 431	1.090 000 0000	109.00	0.090 000	9.00	1
2	1.188 100	2.090 000	0.478 468 8995	0.841 680	1.759 111	0.568 468 8995	56.85	0.136 938	6.85	2
3	1.295 029	3.278 100	0.305 054 7573	0.772 183	2.531 295	0.395 054 7573	39.51	0.185 164	6.17	3
4	1.411 582	4.573 129	0.218 668 6621	0.708 425	3.239 720	0.308 668 6621	30.87	0.234 675	5.87	4
5	1.538 624	5.984 711	0.167 092 4570	0.649 931	3.889 651	0.257 092 4570	25.71	0.285 462	5.71	5
6	1.677 100	7.523 335	0.132 919 7833	0.596 267	4.485 919	0.222 919 7833	22.30	0.337 519	5.63	6
7	1.828 039	9.200 435	0.108 690 5168	0.547 034	5.032 953	0.198 690 5168	19.87	0.390 834	5.58	7
8	1.992 563	11.028 474	0.090 674 3778	0.501 866	5.534 819	0.180 674 3778	18.07	0.445 395	5.57	8
9	2.171 893	13.021 036	0.076 798 8021	0.460 428	5.995 247	0.166 79[illegible] 8021	16.68	0.501 189	5.57	9
10	2.367 364	15.192 930	0.065 820 0899	0.422 411	6.417 658	0.155 820 0899	15.59	0.558 201	5.58	10
11	2.580 426	17.560 293	0.056 946 6567	0.387 533	6.805 191	0.146 946 6567	14.70	0.616 413	5.60	11
12	2.812 665	20.140 720	0.049 650 6585	0.355 535	7.160 725	0.139 650 6585	13.97	0.675 808	5.63	12
13	3.065 805	22.953 385	0.043 556 5597	0.326 179	7.486 904	0.133 566 5597	13.36	0.736 365	5.66	13
14	3.341 727	26.019 189	0.038 433 1730	0.299 246	7.786 150	0.128 433 1730	12.85	0.798 064	5.70	14
15	3.642 482	29.360 916	0.034 058 8827	0.274 538	8.060 688	0.124 058 8827	12.41	0.860 883	5.74	15
16	3.970 306	33.003 399	0.030 299 9097	0.251 870	8.312 558	0.120 299 9097	12.03	0.924 799	5.78	16
17	4.327 633	36.973 705	0.027 046 2485	0.231 073	8.543 631	0.117 046 2485	11.71	0.989 786	5.82	17
18	4.717 120	41.301 338	0.024 212 2907	0.211 994	8.755 625	0.114 212 2907	11.43	1.055 821	5.87	18
19	5.141 661	46.018 458	0.021 730 4107	0.194 490	8.950 115	0.111 730 4107	11.18	1.122 878	5.91	19
20	5.604 411	51.160 120	0.019 546 4750	0.178 431	9.128 546	0.109 546 4750	10.96	1.190 930	5.95	20
21	6.108 808	56.764 530	0.017 616 6348	0.163 698	9.292 244	0.107 616 6348	10.77	1.259 949	6.00	21
22	6.658 600	62.873 338	0.015 904 9930	0.150 182	9.442 425	0.105 904 9930	10.60	1.329 910	6.05	22
23	7.257 874	69.531 939	0.014 381 8800	0.137 781	9.580 207	0.104 381 8800	10.44	1.400 783	6.09	23
24	7.911 083	76.789 813	0.013 022 5607	0.126 405	9.706 612	0.103 022 5607	10.31	1.472 541	6.14	24
25	8.623 081	84.700 896	0.011 806 2505	0.115 968	9.822 580	0.101 806 2505	10.19	1.545 156	6.18	25
26	9.399 158	93.323 977	0.010 715 3599	0.106 393	9.928 972	0.100 715 3599	10.08	1.618 599	6.23	26
27	10.245 082	102.723 135	0.009 734 9054	0.097 608	10.026 580	0.099 734 9054	9.98	1.692 842	6.27	27
28	11.167 140	112.968 217	0.008 852 0473	0.089 548	10.116 128	0.098 852 0473	9.89	1.767 957	6.31	28
29	12.172 182	124.135 356	0.008 055 7226	0.082 155	10.198 283	0.098 055 7226	9.81	1.843 616	6.36	29
30	13.267 678	136.307 539	0.007 336 3514	0.075 371	10.273 654	0.097 336 3514	9.74	1.920 091	6.40	30
31	14.461 770	149.575 217	0.006 685 5995	0.069 148	10.342 802	0.096 685 5995	9.67	1.997 254	6.44	31
32	15.763 329	164.036 987	0.006 096 1861	0.063 438	10.406 240	0.096 096 1861	9.61	2.075 078	6.48	32
33	17.182 028	179.800 315	0.005 561 7255	0.058 200	10.464 441	0.095 561 7255	9.56	2.153 537	6.53	33
34	18.728 411	196.982 344	0.005 076 5971	0.053 395	10.517 835	0.095 076 5971	9.51	2.232 604	6.57	34
35	20.413 968	215.710 755	0.004 635 8375	0.048 986	10.566 821	0.094 635 8375	9.47	2.312 254	6.61	35
36	22.251 225	236.124 723	0.004 235 0500	0.044 941	10.611 763	0.094 235 0500	9.43	2.392 462	6.65	36
37	24.253 835	258.375 948	0.003 870 3293	0.041 231	10.652 993	0.093 870 3293	9.39	2.473 202	6.68	37
38	26.436 680	282.629 783	0.003 538 1975	0.037 826	10.690 820	0.093 538 1975	9.36	2.554 452	6.72	38
39	28.815 982	309.066 463	0.003 235 5500	0.034 703	10.725 523	0.093 235 5500	9.33	2.636 186	6.76	39
40	31.409 420	337.882 445	0.002 959 6092	0.031 838	10.757 360	0.092 959 6092	9.30	2.718 384	6.80	40
41	34.236 268	369.291 865	0.002 707 8853	0.029 209	10.786 569	0.092 707 8853	9.28	2.801 023	6.83	41
42	37.317 532	403.528 133	0.002 478 1420	0.026 797	10.813 366	0.092 478 1420	9.25	2.884 082	6.87	42
43	40.676 110	440.845 665	0.002 268 3675	0.024 584	10.837 950	0.092 268 3675	9.23	2.967 540	6.90	43
44	44.336 960	481.521 775	0.002 076 7493	0.002 555	10.860 505	0.092 076 7493	9.21	3.051 377	6.93	44
45	48.327 286	525.858 734	0.001 901 6514	0.020 692	10.881 197	0.091 901 6514	9.20	3.135 574	6.97	45
46	52.676 742	574.186 021	0.001 741 5959	0.018 984	10.900 181	0.091 741 5959	9.18	3.220 113	7.00	46
47	57.417 649	626.862 762	0.001 595 2455	0.017 416	10.917 597	0.091 595 2455	9.16	3.304 977	7.03	47
48	62.585 237	684.280 411	0.001 461 3892	0.015 978	10.933 575	0.091 461 3892	9.15	3.390 147	7.06	48
49	68.217 908	746.865 648	0.001 338 9289	0.014 659	10.948 234	0.091 338 9289	9.14	3.475 608	7.09	49
50	74.357 520	815.083 556	0.001 226 8681	0.013 449	10.961 683	0.091 226 8681	9.13	3.561 343	7.12	50

☐ *Average risk premium.* This can be established by looking at the difference between the returns over long periods of time on common stock and the returns on risk-free government securities over the same period of time. A number of studies have estimated this difference at 4 to 5 percent.

☐ *Adjusted risk premium.* The average risk premium must then be adjusted for the relative riskiness of the particular project. This adjustment is subjective, but can be realistically estimated by an analyst who knows the property, the local market, the financial leverage, and the type of investment vehicle to be used as well as the liquidity needs and personal considerations of the investor. It is possible to make meaningful adjustments to the average risk premium and develop a risk premium appropriate for the particular investment.

☐ *Before-tax return.* The real return plus the inflation premium plus the adjusted risk premium give the required rate of return before personal income taxes. Normally, however, real estate investment analysis is conducted on an after-tax basis.

☐ *After-tax return.* The after-tax required rate of return can be derived from the pre-tax rate of return using the formula: After-tax required rate of return is equal to one minus the tax rate times the before-tax required rate of return. (The tax rate is a weighted average of the ordinary and capital gains rates projected for the investor.) Calculation of a rate of return for a specific real estate investment is illustrated in Table 2.23.

TABLE 2.23 Calculation of After-Tax Required Rate of Return

An office building investment opportunity is being evaluated. The investor's expected holding period is ten years. The building is well-built, well-located, and fully leased. The loan is 60 percent of the purchase price and offers reasonable terms. The investment is not highly liquid and offers no particular nonpecuniary benefits to the investor. The investor is in the 50 percent tax bracket and historically about 20 percent of his income is capital gains.

I. Real return—2% (from historical data)

II. Inflation premium—7% (government securities maturing in 10 years are yielding 9%)

III. Risk premium—3% (average of 4%; less 2% for fully leased property in a good market; plus one percent for illiquidity)

IV. Before-tax rate of return (BTR) = 12%

V. After-tax rate of return (ATR) = 6.72%

$ATR = BTR\ (1 - T)$

T = marginal tax rate × percentage of ordinary income + 40% marginal tax rate × percentage capital gains

$T = 50\% \times 80\% + 40\% \times 50\% \times 20\% = 44\%$

$ATR = 12\%\ (1 - 44\%) = 12\%\ (56\%) = 6.72\%$

Investments can be valued by discounting before-tax cash flow at the before-tax discount rate. However, this approach has two disadvantages: (1) it does not incorporate the unique tax situation of the particular investor, and (2) it overvalues investments with below-average tax-shelter potential and undervalues assets with above-average tax-shelter potential.

[4] Other Approaches to Deriving a Discount Rate

The elements just described are the ones that go into the determination of a required investment rate. As a practical matter, however, an investor may find that he relies on two other approaches in determining the discount rate to be applied when judging a prospective real estate investment: the cost-of-capital approach and the alternative investment rate approach.

[a] Cost-of-Capital Approach

This approach is appropriate for business firms or investment organizations that raise all or a substantial part of their capital (equity or debt) from outside sources. The logical question to be asked by such a company is whether the prospective investment will return at least as much as the cost to raise the firm's capital. The rate actually is a composite rate that reflects the cost to the firm of capital from its different sources. Suppose, for example, a company's capital structure shapes up as follows: debt ($100,000 at 12 percent annually), and stockholders' equity ($300,000 figured at 8 percent annually). Under these circumstances, the cost of capital would be figured as a weighted average as follows:

(1) $\$100,000 \times 0.12 = \$12,000$

(2) $\$300,000 \times 0.08 = \$24,000$

(3) $36,000 (required return) $\div$ $400,000 (total capital) = 0.09 or a 9% cost-of-capital rate

The calculation of the cost of capital of even a moderate-sized firm is, of course, a great deal more complex than the above. In the first place, there will probably be more than two sources of capital, and each source will carry with it different terms and conditions. In the second place, determining the cost of stockholders' equity can be a tricky business even in a relatively simple situation. While a discussion of the intricacies of determining the cost of capital to a corporation is beyond the scope of this chapter, it is important for us to see how the cost-of-capital rate, once determined, is used in a DCF analysis. For example, if the cost-of-capital rate is 12 percent, the company will discount all its investment proposals at a 12 percent rate. Thus, the company will use the 12 percent column from the present value table to determine the present dollar value of future returns. If the total present dollar value of the future returns exceeds the present dollar value of the investment, the proposal is considered profitable and, other considerations aside, the firm should invest.

[b] Alternate Investment Rate Approach

An individual investor using his own funds will not use the cost-of-capital approach; the easiest way to determine a discount rate in judging return from a prospective real estate investment is to ascertain what the alternatives are. In effect, the investor should determine what rate of return can be derived from investments other than the one under consideration that are (1) available at the present time; (2) are of a similar nature; and (3) present comparable risks. If there are no such alternate investments, then the investor should compare the prospective investment with alternatives of greater or less risk, making an appropriate modification in the discount rate to reflect the different degrees of risk.

[5] Discounted Cash-Flow Analysis Favors Real Estate

DCF analyses offer real estate investors and their professional advisers and consultants the most accurate method of analyzing an investment available today. It also offers the additional benefit that it is capable of being understood and used to advantage by anyone willing to take the time to follow the basically simple explanation and guide set forth in the preceding pages.

While there may be good marketing reasons for not using DCF analytical techniques in other industries, no such reasons exist in real estate. For example, when the traditional methods of computing returns are applied to long-term security and insurance investments, those methods generally make the investment returns appear higher and the investments appear more attractive than when DCF analysis is used.

Unlike the securities and insurance industries, however, the real estate community has every reason to use DCF analysis. Income-producing real estate is a dynamic investment that produces substantial cash flow and tax savings continuously throughout the life of the investment. Since DCF analysis recognizes that dollars received in the earlier years of an investment are more valuable than those received in later years, when DCF analysis is employed, real estate as an investment medium will generally compare very favorably with other investment mediums. Sophisticated analysts have for a long while generally agreed that real estate offers the investor the best opportunity to maximize his wealth over the long haul. DCF analysis techniques now afford the real estate community a method for clearly demonstrating that fact.

DCF analysis is a viable and straightforward alternative to the traditional methods for computing return on investment. It furnishes us with an accurate tool that overcomes all the disadvantages inherent in the traditional methods of analysis. It takes into account all the net benefits generated over an investment's entire life. It is responsive to differences in the timing of returns. Last, and perhaps most important, DCF analysis is consistent and, therefore, can be used in making meaningful comparisons between investment alternatives.

2.07 NET PRESENT VALUE

Discounted cash-flow (DCF) analysis includes a number of different methods. The one illustrated here is the net present value (NPV) method. Under this method, the investor begins by choosing a return objective. For example, suppose an investor decides, after studying the market and the range of alternative investments, to invest in a very speculative investment provided a return of 10 percent a year is possible. The cost of acquisition is $3,000, to be paid all at once at the time of purchase. Projections show that the investor should receive an after-tax return of $1,500 after the first year and returns of $1,000 after each of the second and third years. At the end of year 3, the investment is expected to have zero value.

Table 2.24 illustrates how to determine if the annual return is at least 10 percent. The left-hand side of the table (outflow) shows the initial $3,000 investment; these dollars are valued fully since they must be paid right away. Consequently, as Table 2.24 shows, the total present value investment is $3,000.

TABLE 2.24 Net Present Value (NPV)

	Investment (Outflow)			*Returns (Inflow)*		
Year	*(1) Investment*	*(2) Present Value Factors at 10%*	*(3) Present Value of Investment (cols. 1 & 2)*	*(4) After-Tax Dollar Return*	*(5) Present Value Factor @ 10%*	*(6) Present Value of Return (cols. 4 & 5)*
0	$3,000	1.000	$3,000	0	1.000	0
1				$1,500	.909	$1,374
2				1,000	.826	826
3				1,000	.751	751
Total present value investment			$3,000	Total present value return		$2,941

Total present value of returns	$2,941
Less: Total present value of investment	3,000
Net present value	($ 59)

The right-hand side of the table (inflow) shows the three annual after-tax returns. To make these future dollars comparable to the present dollars being invested, they must be discounted to their present value. The discount factor (.909) in the case of the first-year return of $1,500 is derived from a present value table that says: "$1,500 to be received a year from now must be discounted by a factor of .909 to give its present value, assuming that it represents a return of 10 percent." As Table 2.24 shows, the present value is $1,364. A similar procedure is followed to determine the present value of the after-tax returns in years 2 and 3. Since the time spread is greater, the discount factor is lower, because the assumed annual return of 10 percent has a compounding effect.

The total present value return of the future inflows is $2,941, or just about the same as the present value of the investment of $3,000. Since the computation is based on the assumption of a 10 percent return, we can say that, in fact, the investor in this example will be receiving 10 percent a year on his investment.

The net present value method has the outstanding virtue of enabling the investor to compare alternatives in which inflows and outflows differ widely in their timing. Of course, selection of the appropriate discount rate is of vital importance. The discount rate (i.e., the investor's expected rate of return) from each investment alternative will depend upon several considerations. The most important of these is the degree of risk assumed; others include the degree of liquidity in the investment and the burden of management. Ultimately, the essence of good investing in any field is the ability to make sound judgments about these factors in alternative investments.

2.08 INTERNAL RATE OF RETURN

We have just discussed a method of measuring return on investment that takes into consideration the time value of money. That method, the net present value (NPV) technique, seeks only to determine a "go" or "no go" decision. In other words, the investor determines only whether the return on investment (ROI) from the projected investment meets the required return. By comparison, the internal rate of return (IRR) seeks to determine the exact ROI from the projected investment. (Another difference exists between NPV and IRR, and this relates to the reinvestment of cash inflows received during the time the investment is owned.)

Most investors have heard about IRR but are hesitant to use it because they believe that it requires a high degree of mathematical expertise. This is not the case at all. As with most complicated ideas, IRR is based on some fairly simple principles; once understood, they enable any investor, with the use of prepared mathematical tables, to reach quite precise results.

[1] Internal Rate of Return as Compound Interest in Reverse

The internal rate of return is usually defined as "that rate of return which equates the present value of future benefits with the present value of the investment outlays." While this may sound complicated, it is merely another way of stating the effect of compound interest. In fact, IRR may be viewed simply as compound interest in reverse (i.e., compound interest worked backwards in time) or discounting.

It may be well to note at this point that, while IRR analysis can be used accurately and effectively without the help of sophisticated tools such as electronic calculators and computers, these tools can be quite helpful in working out the necessary computations. Once we understand how IRR analysis works and gain proficiency in its use, computerized systems take the "busy work" off our hands. They also permit an investor to closely and thoroughly analyze an investment on the basis of different sets of assumptions and projections in order to make a well-informed determination of how the investment will fare under different sets of circumstances. This type of computerized analysis is commonly referred to as sensitivity analysis. It represents one of the most important benefits bestowed on investors by the computer. (This is further discussed in 2.10[3].)

In discussing IRR, this section concentrates on the basic concepts underlying the method to provide a working knowledge of how to use it to analyze investment opportunities that arise.

The IRR method involves the following steps:

(1) Listing of the date of each separate investment outlay (e.g., equity contributions)
(2) Listing of the date of each anticipated future benefit (e.g., estimated future cash flows, tax savings, resale proceeds)
(3) Choice of an estimated rate of return expected from the investment (in order to start the process of calculation)
(4) Using the estimated rate of return, calculation of the present value of each investment outlay, and future benefit. If (as is likely) these present values do not equal each other using the estimated rate of return, further calculations with different rates of return gradually narrow down the differences in present values until an equalization point is reached.

[a] An Example of Internal Rate of Return

Table 2.25 illustrates a proposed investment with a four-year life. Investment outlays are to be made at the end of the present year (year 0) and year 1, while

TABLE 2.25 Present Value of Proposed Investment

A. *20% Present Value Factor*	*Year*	*Investment*	*Present Value Investment*	*Income*	*Present Value Income*
1.000	0	$1,000	$1,000		
.833	1	2,000	1,666	$ 800	$ 666
.694	2			1,700	1,180
.579	3			1,600	926
.482	4			1,000	482
			$2,666		$3,254

B. *40% Present Value Factor*	*Year*	*Investment*	*Present Value Investment*	*Income*	*Present Value Income*
1.000	0	$1,000	$1,000		
.714	1	2,000	1,428	$ 800	$ 571
.510	2			1,700	814
.364	3			1,600	582
.260	4			1,000	260
			$2,428		$2,227

C. *35% Present Value Factor*	*Year*	*Investment*	*Present Value Investment*	*Income*	*Present Value Income*
1.000	0	$1,000	$1,000		
.741	1	2,000	1,482	$ 800	$ 593
.510	2			1,700	867
.406	3			1,600	650
.301	4			1,000	301
			$2,482		$2,411

benefits are to be received at the end of years 1 through 4. The question is, What is the annual return to the investor over the entire holding period?

In order to do a trial-and-error calculation (step 3 above), the investor needs only a table listing the present value of $1. An excerpt of such a table (Table 2.26) shows that if money in hand today could earn 20 percent annually, a dollar to be received one year from today has a present value of 0.833 cents. Put another way, 0.833 cents invested today at 20 percent annually will grow to $1 in one year. As we know, this process of calculating present value is known as discounting.

TABLE 2.26 Present Value of $1

Year	*1%*	*3%*	*5%*	*8%*	*10%*	*12%*	*15%*	*20%*	*25%*	*30%*	*35%*	*40%*
1	.990	.971	.952	.926	.909	.893	.870	.833	.800	.769	.741	.714
2	.980	.943	.907	.857	.826	.797	.756	.694	.640	.592	.510	.479
3	.971	.915	.864	.794	.751	.712	.658	.579	.512	.455	.406	.364
4	.961	.888	.823	.735	.683	.636	.572	.482	.410	.350	.301	.260
5	.951	.863	.784	.681	.621	.567	.497	.402	.328	.269	.223	.186
6	.942	.837	.746	.630	.564	.507	.432	.335	.262	.207	.165	.133
7	.933	.813	.711	.584	.513	.452	.376	.279	.210	.159	.122	.095
8	.923	.789	.677	.540	.467	.404	.327	.233	.168	.123	.091	.068
9	.914	.766	.645	.500	.424	.361	.284	.194	.134	.094	.067	.048
10	.905	.744	.614	.463	.386	.322	.247	.162	.107	.073	.050	.035
15	.861	.642	.481	.315	.239	.183	.123	.065	.035	.020	.011	.006
20	.820	.554	.377	.214	.149	.104	.061	.026	.012	.005	.002	.001
25	.780	.478	.295	.146	.092	.059	.030	.010	.004	.001	.001	.001
30	.742	.412	.231	.099	.057	.033	.015	.004	.001	.000	.000	.000

In our example, the investor estimates that the rate of return is 20 percent and thus will take the present value factors from the 20 percent column in the table. On that basis, Section A of Table 2.25 indicates that the present value of the investment outlays in years 0 and 1 is $2,666, while the present value of the future benefits in years 1 through 4 amounts to $3,254.

Since the present value of the investment is substantially less than the present value of the income, the IRR is more than 20 percent. Section B of Table 2.25 indicates the present value of an investment using a 40 percent value factor.

Now the present value of the investment is more than the present value of the income, so a 40 percent IRR is too high. By interpolation, we can see that we have narrowed the difference by about 75 percent. This would suggest lowering the present value factor to 35 percent, as shown in Section C of Table 2.25.

Since the present values of investment and the incomes as shown in Section C of Table 2.25 are relatively close, we may conclude that the correct IRR is 35 percent. Further refinement is probably not justified nor more usable.

[b] The Rationale of Internal Rate of Return

The example just given shows how to use the IRR method. But why should the equalization of present values produce the rate of return for the investment? The answer will be more clearly understood if the total investment is viewed as a number of separate investments, each equal to the present value of each item of future income.

Thus in Section C of Table 2.25, the present value of the total investment is $2,482. Of this, $593 is invested for one year (see "present value income" column), at the end of which it is repaid together with $207 in profit (a return of 35 percent) or a total of $800 (see "income" column).

A second slice of the original investment, amounting to $867, is invested for two years. It is repaid with a profit of $833 (a 35 percent annual return) of a total of $1,700, and so on, for the remaining portions of $650 and $301.

Put another way, IRR is a device for breaking down income increments into (1) a return of capital; and (2) a profit element in such a way that each income increment produces the same return (35 percent annually, in our example), which then constitutes the return on the total investment.

In more technical terms, IRR permits the investor to determine the discount rate that converts the total of future income receipts into the present value of the investment outlays. That discount rate is the rate of return on the investment.

In our example, one complicating factor exists: A portion of the investment outlay is not made at once, but at the end of year 1. In order to make that value consistent with all the others, it, too, must be discounted back to the beginning of the investment. Realistically, applying a 35 percent discount rate to this figure may not be justified. Consequently, a more complex form of IRR permits the use of a different discount rate in this situation.

[c] Reinvestment of Income

Readers may be aware of one omission in IRR—the question of the reinvestment of income received during the investment holding period. From the explanation given above, it should be clear that when IRR is used to compare different investments, no assumption is made about the return that can be earned by reinvesting revenues received by the investor during the period that he holds the investment.

> *Example:* Assume that two alternative investments each yield an IRR of 12 percent, but one yields most of its revenues in early years and the other yields most of its revenues in later years. Which is better for the investor? The answer depends upon the rate of return expected on the reinvestment of the revenues received. Only when revenues can be reinvested at the computed IRR (i.e., 12 percent) will the two alternatives result in equal total dollar accumulation at the end of the holding periods of both alternatives.

There are ways to change the IRR formula to consider this reinvestment factor.

[2] Comparing Internal Rate of Return and Net Present Value

If all the assumptions that enter into NPV and IRR analyses are the same, the same "go" or "no go" determination should be made regardless of which analysis is used. However, there often is a difference between the two methods in the implicit assumptions that are made—specifically with respect to the reinvestment of benefits earned.

As just noted, IRR analysis makes no implicit assumption that the returns generated by the investment are reinvested at the internal rate for the life of the investment. In NPV analysis, on the other hand, the returns generated by the investment are taken to be reinvested at an assumed rate for the life of the investment. The difference between the implicit assumptions made in NPV and in IRR analysis can lead to important differences in the computations over a period of time where there is a substantial difference in any one or more of the following:

- Timing of the cash invested and/or the returns
- Amount of cash invested
- Length of the life of the investment

However, IRR analysis does have the following advantages:

- IRR analysis provides a clear ranking of investments according to percentage return.
- IRR analysis is mathematically simpler to adjust for risk considerations than is NPV analysis.

In theory, NPV analysis may offer a sounder approach than IRR analysis, since it does not assume a reinvestment rate equal to the rate of return produced by the investment. However, to make it work properly, the choice of the required investment rate must be accurate. As we have already pointed out, choosing the proper rate can be quite difficult. For most real estate investors, it usually is an educated guess at best. If the rate chosen is not an accurate one, the NPV analysis can wind up giving the investor results that are wide of the mark.

2.09 REINVESTMENT RATE

The advantages of net present value (NPV) and internal rate of return (IRR) analyses can be combined by using reinvestment rate (RIR) approach, frequently called the adjusted IRR approach. The RIR approach enables us to deal with the problem of comparing several investments having different investment lives. In order to show how RIR analysis works, consider two investments. One (Investment *A*) has a life of ten years; the other (Investment *B*) has a life of four years.

[1] Example of Reinvestment Rate Approach

Investment A. Investment *A* requires a $10,000 cash investment. The investor will not withdraw any funds during the entire ten-year life of the investment. At the end of ten years, he will cash in his investment for $38,100. His tax on the gain will be $7,025, leaving him with an after-tax return of $31,075.

Using the IRR formula, the $10,000 investment is divided by the $31,075 after-tax return to determine the present value factor (PVF), which is 0.322. A PVF of 0.322 on the ten-year line is in the 12 percent column of the Present Value of $1 Table (Table 2.26). Hence, the IRR for this investment is 12 percent.

Investment B. Investment *B* has a four-year life. The amount of the investment is $10,000 and the after-tax returns are as follows:

Year	*After-Tax Return*
1	$ 2,000
2	2,000
3	2,700
4	14,000

The IRR for this investment is determined according to the trial-and-error method described, page 2-44, and equals 25 percent. (See Table 2.27, which shows that the present value of the future returns ($10,002) is equal to the initial investment ($10,000).)

Assume that Investments *A* and *B* are mutually exclusive (i.e., the investor cannot invest in *B* and subsequently invest in *A*) and that the only other investment available is Investment *C*. Investment *C* has a 5 percent after-tax yield, requires no minimum investment, and will remain available throughout the ten-year period.

At first glance, it appears that Investment *B* is more desirable than Investment *A*. Investment *B* offers a 25 percent return while Investment *A* offers a return of only 12 percent. However, if we choose Investment *B* over Investment *A* without considering Investment *C* with its 5 percent after-tax yield, we would not get a realistic picture of how wealth can be maximized over the ten-year period.

In order to determine the relative desirability of Investments *A* and *B*, we must determine how reinvesting the after-tax returns received during the ten-year period at the alternate investment rate (5 percent in this case) would work out. Table 2.28 assumes that the $2,000 after-tax return received from Investment *B* at the end of the first year is invested for the remaining nine years of the ten-year period at the alternative after-tax investment rate of 5 percent. To find the total value of the first year's return after it has been received and reinvested in Investment *C* for the remaining nine years, we use a compound interest table and multiply the $2,000 after-tax return by the factor located in the ninth-year row under the 5 percent column. (1.551 × $2,000 = $3,102.) (See Table 2.17, page 2-34.) A similar calculation is then made for each of the returns from Investment *B*. For example, the $2,000 second-year after-tax return is invested in Investment *C* at 5 percent for eight years. The total values of each year's return at the end of the full ten-year period are then added together. This gives us a value for Investment *B* (assuming reinvestment of proceeds in Investment *C*) of $28,615 at the end of ten years. (See Table 2.28.)

This total of $28,615 at the end of ten years is then compared with the initial investment of $10,000 to determine the adjusted rate of return. The $10,000 investment divided by the $28,615 return equals a factor of 0.350.

$$\$10{,}000 \div \$28{,}615 = 0.350$$

Looking along the ten-year row in Table 2.26, Present Value of $1, we see that the factor 0.350 lies about midway between 10 and 12 percent. Hence, the

TABLE 2.27 Investment *B* (Unadjusted IRR)

Amount of investment: $10,000

Year	*Benefit*	*Present Value Factor 25%*	*Present Dollar Value*
1	$ 2,000	0.800	$ 1,600
2	2,000	0.640	1,280
3	2,700	0.512	1,382
4	14,000	0.410	5,740
		Total present value	$10,002

TABLE 2.28 Investment *B* (IRR Adjusted for Assumed Reinvestment in Investment *C*)

Assumed reinvestment rate in Investment *C* (RIR): 5%
Investment returns carried through year: 10

Year	*Benefit*	*Compound Interest Factor Through Year 10*	*Value at End of Year 10*
1	$ 2,000	1.551	$ 3,102
2	2,000	1.477	2,954
3	2,700	1.407	3,799
4	14,000	1.340	18,760
5			
6			
7			
8			
9			
10			
		Total value at end of year 10	$28,615

return is approximately 11 percent. This is less than the return on Investment *A* and therefore Investment *A* is the more desirable of the two in terms of wealth creation over a ten-year period. It should be noted here that if a higher reinvestment rate had been available to the investor in Investment *A*, the investment decision might have turned out otherwise. It is also well to note that the point at which the RIR must be in order to make Investments *A* and *B* equally desirable to the investor is 6.3 percent. If the RIR is 6.3 percent, the investor, other things being equal, is indifferent as to a choice between the two investments. If the RIR is less than 6.3 percent, the investor will choose Investment *A*. If the RIR is more than 6.3 percent, Investment *B* is more advantageous. Since the RIR in this example is 5 percent, the choice is Investment *A*.

[2] Evaluation of Reinvestment Rate Analysis

As is the case with NPV analysis, the major hurdle with the RIR approach is the difficulty in selecting a realistic rate. As we have already seen, different rates call for different investment decisions. Proponents of the NPV and the RIR approaches criticize the IRR approach because it makes no assumption that the RIR is the same as the IRR. Proponents of the IRR approach claim that the return on an investment may well be as accurate an indication of the available investment alternatives as we can find for a given investor.

Many sophisticated real estate analysts, consultants, and brokers favor the IRR approach. They point out, for example, that the IRR approach is relatively simple to use and that it does not require the selection of a cost-of-capital rate or an alternate investment rate. Given the current level of sophistication in the field of real estate investment analysis, the knowledgeability of the investing public, and the amount of information available to real estate brokers, consultants, and analysts with responsibility to their clients' situations and investment goals, IRR analysis is, it seems, the approach favored by many.

On the other hand, the RIR and the NPV approaches are peculiarly appropriate in both the corporate and the academic worlds. In a corporate setup, there is a wealth of information that can be made available to a consultant or analyst. In the academic world, if the information is not available, assumptions can be made for illustrative purposes.

In the day-to-day real estate world, even where the required expertise is available, the information needed to determine a proper RIR for a particular investor is quite difficult and time-consuming to obtain. To attempt to do so for, say, some 1,000 investors in a public fund would be quite impractical. It would likewise prove futile to ask the average investor to select a realistic RIR for himself. An investor who, for example, chooses a low RIR under the mistaken notion that it is conservative could be very seriously misled.

The real estate consultant or analyst should, whenever circumstances permit, subject the investment alternatives open to clients to sensitivity analysis, using all three approaches we have discussed. Then, if significant differences appear, the analyst should select a realistic RIR and use the RIR approach.

The way the current real estate world operates, the IRR approach is probably the most practical, useful, and reliable. The tendency in the modern real estate world is for more and more practitioners to have a greater understanding of the entire area of discounted cash-flow analysis and to use its techniques with greater frequency and skill than formerly. The RIR approach can certainly be expected to be used with greater accuracy and frequency in the future.

2.10 RISK ANALYSIS

[1] Types of Risk

Risk is the possibility of suffering adverse consequences resulting from an investment. In this context, there are several types of risk:

- Business
- Financial
- Purchasing power
- Liquidity
- Risk as variance

[a] Business Risk

Business risk reflects the possible unsuccessful operation of the particular project. Business risk is determined by (1) the type of project; (2) its management; and (3) the particular market in which it is located. All of these affect the expected operating cash flows from the project.

The possibility that these cash flows will not be sufficient to justify the investment represents the degree of business risk associated with the investment. A regional shopping center fully rented under long-term net leases to triple-A tenants has a lower business risk than a raw-land investment that anticipates construction of a motel some time in the future.

From a practical point of view, business risk is centered in two major areas. The first is management. Fixing and collecting rents, maintaining and repairing, and controlling operating expenses are key variables in the management area. Market changes represent the other area involving business risk. New competition, changes in local demographic characteristics, new roads bypassing a project, and new employers entering the market all affect the business risk associated with a particular project.

[b] Financial Risk

Financial risk reflects uncertainty about the residual equity return as the result of the use of debt financing. The use of debt increases the variability of the return to equity. This increased variability or uncertainty is the financial risk associated with a particular investment.

Put another way, financial risk is the potential inability of the project's net operating income (NOI) to cover the required debt service. Such an event is more likely to occur when a high proportion of the purchase price is financed with debt. The less debt that is used in the capital structure, the lower the financial risk.

[c] Purchasing-Power Risk

Purchasing-power risk reflects the fact that inflation may cause the investor to be paid back with less valuable dollars. The expectation of inflation is incorporated in the discount rate, but future rates of inflation may be underestimated. The possibility of higher inflation than was incorporated in the discount rate is the purchasing-power risk associated with the investment. In general, purchasing-power risk affects all investors equally and does not vary from project to project.

[d] Liquidity Risk

Liquidity risk relates to the conversion of the investment to cash at some future date. An investor wants to be able to sell quickly and without substantially discounting the price below fair market value. The liquidity risk associated with a particular investment is the risk that a quick sale will not be possible or that a significant price reduction will be required to achieve a quick sale.

Real estate is generally considered an illiquid asset, not easily convertible to cash without sacrificing price. Consequently, liquidity risk tends to be high for real estate investments. This liquidity risk leads to a need for balance in an investor's portfolio. For example, the investor probably should include in the portfolio some highly liquid assets, such as government bonds.

[e] Risk as Variance

The four types of risk just mentioned can be collectively measured and quantified by estimating the variance of the expected equity cash flow. The more variance the investor expects in the equity portion of the return generated by the property, the greater the risk associated with receiving that cash flow.

Many times investors will estimate the cash flow under varying circumstances in order to analyze the sensitivity of the project's rate of return to changes in rental receipts, vacancy, and operating expenses. Sensitivity analysis is an appealing method for estimating risk in the real estate field, since changes frequently occur in the elements that affect cash flow. (See 2.10[3].)

[2] The Risk-Return Relationship

In investment analysis, risk is incorporated in the discount rate used as an estimate of the required rate of return. Recall that the required rate of return involves (1) a real return; (2) an inflation premium; and (3) a risk premium. Thus, risk and return are positively correlated; an investor seeks to maximize return for given levels of risk or minimize risk for given levels of return. The investor expects more compensation if there is a greater chance of adverse financial consequences; that is, the investor wants more return if there is more risk. Investors, in other words, are "risk-averse."

However, even with no risk, the investor requires a certain minimum return. This minimum return represents the real return and inflation premium portion of the required rate of return. Government bonds are generally considered to be risk-free and are used as an indication of the return required when there is no risk associated with the receipt of expected cash flows. Beyond this risk-free rate, risk and return are positively correlated. (See Fig. 2.1.)

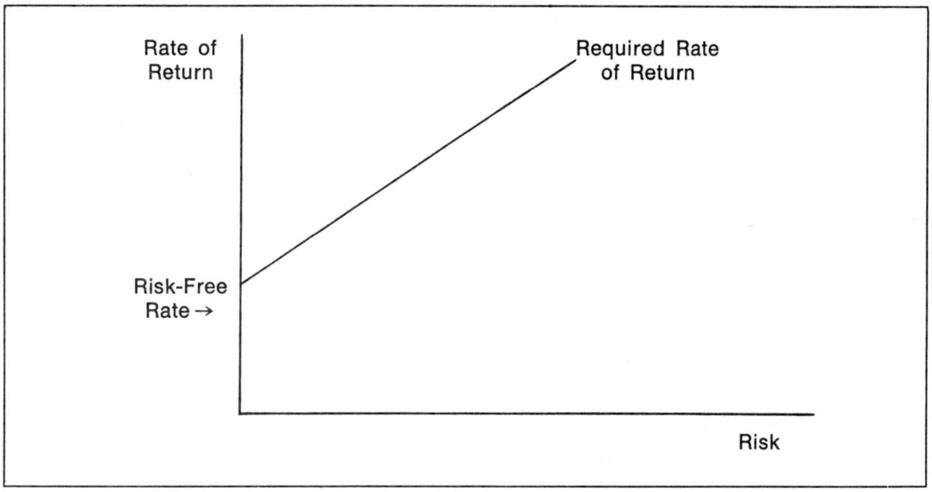

Fig. 2.1 The risk-return relationship

Risk Aversion. The concept of risk aversion is usually proved by using the theory of the diminishing marginal utility of money. Given the situation of an investor who has a risky and a riskless alternative, the riskless alternative might be preferred even though a greater return is possible if the risky alternative is chosen. Assume a riskless government bond paying a certain 8 percent and a riskier apartment house with equal likelihood (50-50) of either a 10 or 6 percent return. Both investments have the same expected dollar return, but the expected utility of the investor might be less in the case of the risky alternative. (The term "utility of the investor" refers to the value of the money to the investor. Simply put, one additional dollar is valued differently by a millionaire and a pauper.)

While most investors are assumed to be risk-averse, there are also risk-seekers in the world; many developers may belong to this group. They are risk-seekers, love action, and will take less than a "fair gamble" for the possibility of becoming very wealthy.

[3] Using Sensitivity Analysis When Projecting Cash Flow

The first section of this chapter discussed cash flow and how to project it over the life of a real estate investment. We stressed the point that any analysis of future return depends as much or more on the accuracy of projected cash flow (as well as of tax savings and other forms of return) as on the particular method of analysis used. In other words, Investment *A*, with a lower projected return on investment (ROI) but carrying much less risk of unpleasant surprises, may prove to be a much better investment over the years than Investment *B*, which initially promises a higher ROI but ends up a disappointment because projected returns were not in fact realized.

The preceding portion has discussed the subject of risk generally. At this point, we turn our attention to a technique known as sensitivity analysis, which enables an investor to measure the impact on his projected ROI of changes in any one of his key projections. The term "sensitivity analysis" derives from the purpose of the exercise, which is to determine how sensitive the ROI is to a change in any one particular element of the projected cash flow, such as rent or occupancy rate.

We will consider the position of an investor who has been offered the opportunity of purchasing the equity in an apartment complex of moderate size. The principles that will be demonstrated, however, are applicable to any type of real estate venture. The investor (whether an individual or an institution) has been approached by the developer with a proposal that the investor commit now, in consideration of an attractive price, to purchase the equity in the project upon completion of construction and the issuance of permanent financing. The pertinent facts are as follows:

- The proposed development consists of a 200-unit suburban garden apartment project.
- Control of the intended site has been secured, and a firm construction bid has been obtained.
- Construction and permanent financing are available, the latter for 75 percent of the project cost at 9 percent for thirty years.
- The total cost of the project will be $3.6 million, including the value of the

land, developer's profit, architectural and other fees, and all other expenses. Accordingly, the loan will be for $2.7 million, carrying annual amortization payments of $263,000.

- The required equity investment is $900,000.

To provide a convenient starting point, it will also be assumed:

- The developer has provided a pro forma operating statement indicating that the apartments will rent at an average of $255 per month, that operating expenses will average $200,000 annually, and, hence, that occupancy at the 95 percent level will produce gross income of $581,000 and net operating income of $381,000 per year.
- On the basis of the pro forma statement, the equity (cash-flow) return would be $118,000, or 13.2 percent before taxes (NOI of $381,000 minus $263,000 in debt service).

This would appear to be an interesting proposal to many investors, even after lowering the return to, say, 12 percent to compensate for the optimism of the developer.

However, modest additional market research (available from any reliable consulting firm if the investor does not have in-house capability) may supply the investor with information that would greatly alter his opinion of the project.

Sensitivity Analysis. Table 2.29 demonstrates the effect of small changes in average rentals on the rate of return to the equity buyer. For each $10 difference in average rental rate achieved, the rate of return to the equity holder changes by about 2.5 percentage points or by $22,800 annually. Thus, a change of less than 4 percent in the estimated average rent of $255 will produce a change of more than 19 percent in the NOI before income taxes.

TABLE 2.29 Effect of Changes in Average Rentals on Income and Return on Equity

Average Rental Rate	*Gross Income*[1]	*Cash Flow*[2]	*Equity Return*
$275	$627,000	$164,000	18.2
265	604,200	141,200	15.7
255	581,400	118,400	13.2
245	558,600	95,600	10.6
235	535,800	72,800	8.1

[1] Assumes 95 percent occupancy.
[2] Assumes $200,000 annual operating expenses and $263,000 debt service.

The net income and, hence, the rate of return is also quite sensitive to the average occupancy rate. As can be seen in Table 2.30, a 2 percentage point change in the rate, say from the forecast 95 percent to an experienced 93 percent, would decrease net income by $12,200 annually—a loss of 10.3 percent in this instance.

TABLE 2.30 Effect of Changes in Average Occupancy on Income and Return on Equity

Average Occupancy Rate	*Gross Income*[1]	*Cash Flow*[2]	*Equity Return*
99%	$605,900	$142,900	15.9
97	593,600	130,600	14.5
95	581,400	118,400	13.2
93	569,200	106,200	11.8
91	556,900	93,900	10.4

[1] Assumes average rent of $255.
[2] Assumes $200,000 annual operating expenses and $263,000 debt service.

TABLE 2.31 Gross and Net Income for Various Combinations of Monthly Rent and Occupancy Rates ($000)

Occupancy Rate	*Average Monthly Rent*				
	$275	*$265*	*$255*	*$245*	*$235*
99%	$653.4	$629.6	$605.9	$582.1	$558.4
	190.4	166.6	142.9	119.1	95.4
97	640.2	616.9	593.6	570.4	547.1
	177.2	153.9	130.6	107.4	84.1
95	627.0	604.2	581.4	558.6	535.8
	164.0	141.2	118.4	95.6	72.8
93	613.8	591.5	569.2	546.8	524.5
	150.8	128.5	106.2	83.8	61.5
91	600.6	578.8	556.9	535.1	513.2
	137.6	115.8	93.9	72.1	50.2

TABLE 2.32 Rate of Return for Various Combinations of Monthly Rent and Occupancy Rates ($000)

Occupancy Rate	*Average Monthly Rent*				
	$275	*$265*	*$255*	*$245*	*$235*
99%	21.2%	18.5%	15.9%	13.2%	10.6%
97	19.7	17.1	14.5	11.9	9.3
95	18.2	15.7	13.2	10.6	8.1
93	16.8	14.3	11.8	9.3	6.8
91	15.3	12.9	10.4	8.0	5.6

The rate of return to equity would, in the example given, fall by 1.4 percentage points.

The preceding tables have treated changes in two key variables independently. Such changes can obviously occur jointly with cumulative effects. Tables 2.31 and 2.32 indicate the results of this happening. If, for example, occupancy averaged 93 percent instead of the estimated 95 percent, and apartment rentals averaged $245 rather than $255 (Table 2.31), the net effect would be to reduce net income from $118,400 to $83,800 annually, a decline of more than 29 percent. Under these circumstances, the equity return would not be the predicted 13.2 percent, but rather 9.3 percent (Table 2.32).

The third key variable in the model presented is the level of operating expenses. Table 2.33 shows that a change of 5 percent in expenses means a change of $10,000 in net income or of approximately 1.1 percentage points in the equity return.

Changes in operating expenses can, of course, be combined with other changes. For example, Table 2.32 shows that if experienced rent and occupancy rates were $245 per month and 93 percent respectively, the realized equity return would be 9.3 percent. If in this situation experienced operating expenses were 5 percent above the forecast, the equity return would decline to approximately 8.2 percent, down 1.2 percent.

TABLE 2.33 Effect of Changes in Operating Expenses on Net Income and Rate of Return on Equity

Operating Expenses	*Net Income*[1]	*Rate of Return*
$180,000	$138,400	15.4
190,000	128,400	14.3
200,000	118,400	13.2
210,000	108,400	12.0
220,000	98,400	10.9

[1] Assumes average monthly rent of $255 and average occupancy of 95 percent.

The variables in this example are the proper subjects of market analysis. Of course, the intuitive estimates of market variables made by some highly skilled individuals are often very accurate. But the average investor may find that an investment for professional and systematic analysis of the "sensitive" factors may yield enormous returns.

3

Taxation of Real Estate

3.01 GROSS INCOME AND OPERATING EXPENSES

[1] In General

[a] How to Determine

The basic formula for determining taxable income from a real estate investment or business is the same as for any other investment or business; that is, (1) gross income is determined, from which (2) all allowable deductions are taken, leaving (3) taxable income. Gross income from real estate normally is either gross rental income (where the property is leased to others) or gross sales or gross receipts (where the property is operated by the owner as a business, as in the case of a recreational facility, motel, fast-food outlet, or the like).

Allowable deductions can be divided into two general categories. The first includes all ordinary and necessary expenses incurred in connection with a trade or business, or in connection with property held for the production of rents; the second includes deductions covered by specific provisions of the Internal Revenue Code, for example, deductions for interest, taxes, losses and bad debts, and depreciation. This section discusses operating expenses generally; all of the special deductions are discussed in detail later in the chapter.

The general rules authorizing the deduction of ordinary and necessary expenses apply to real estate operations in much the same manner as they apply in other business areas. The deductions are authorized by Code Sections 162(a) and 212 (the first covering trade or business expenses and the second covering nontrade or nonbusiness expenses attributable to property held for the production of rents). These expenses include such routine items as wages, fuel, management fees, insurance premiums, and legal and accounting fees. Furthermore, such ordinary and necessary expenses may be deducted in connection with a building devoted to rental purposes even though the building produces no income in the taxable year in question.[1]

[b] Maintaining Books and Records

Whatever the type of business or investment, the taxpayer should be careful to maintain sufficient records of his operations so that he can justify statements made in tax returns. At the very minimum, the following records should be maintained for a real estate business or investment:

---

1 Reg. § 1.212-1(b).

☐ *Company checkbook.* All business or investment receipts and expenditures should be funneled through one account. Personal expenditures should be handled separately. Checkbooks and bank statements should be reconciled each month.

☐ *Cash-receipts journal.* This is a record of all receipts, including checks. It provides the information necessary to determine the gross income from the operation.

☐ *Cash-disbursement journal.* This records all amounts paid out in connection with the business or investment. Normally payment should be made by check, but if paid in cash an appropriate notation should be made or a receipt should be obtained.

☐ *Sales-and-purchase journal.* A taxpayer on the cash basis of accounting will not need more than the two journals already described. Even if the taxpayer is on the accrual basis, the above journals may be sufficient but will require some adjustment at the end of the year. Accrual-basis taxpayers may prefer to maintain a sales journal and a purchase journal in addition to the cash journals to show when sales were made and expenses incurred.

☐ *Payroll register.* This is a record of all wages and salaries paid, including such payments as unemployment insurance, social security withholding, and payroll taxes.

☐ *Additional records.* Whenever the business or investment involves fixed assets, as real estate does, separate records should be kept showing the original cost basis of the assets plus subsequent adjustments as a result of such factors as depreciation deductions and capital improvements.

[2] Preinvestment and Start-Up Expenses

[a] Trade or Business

Preinvestment and start-up expenses relating to an active trade or business (e.g., owning a rental project) may be amortized, at the taxpayer's election, over a period of not less than sixty months beginning with the commencement of the business (although the expenses themselves may be incurred prior to the actual commencement of the business).[2]

Start-up expenditures are any amount paid or incurred in connection with investigating the creation or acquisition of an active trade or business, or with creating an active trade or business. Further, the costs must be of a type that would be allowable as a business deduction if paid or incurred in connection with the expansion of an existing trade or business.

Examples of eligible investigatory expenses, incurred in reviewing a prospective business prior to reaching a final decision to acquire or enter that business, include costs for analysis or survey of potential markets, products, labor supply, and

---

[2] I.R.C. § 195.

transportation facilities. Eligible start-up costs incurred after the decision to establish a business and prior to the time the business begins include advertising, salaries and wages paid to employees who are being trained (as well as to their instructors), travel and other expenses incurred in lining up prospective distributors, suppliers or customers, and salaries and fees paid or incurred for executives, consultants, and for similar professional services.

Certain expenditures are ineligible for the sixty-month amortization allowance by the requirement that they be of a type allowable under Section 162 if paid or incurred in connection with an expansion. These include amounts paid or incurred in connection with the sale of stock, securities or partnership interests, e.g., securities registration expenses, and underwriters' commissions. Start-up costs also do not include amounts paid or incurred for the acquisition cost of a trade or business, which would be capitalized as its basis, or amounts for property to be held for sale or for property that may be depreciated or amortized based on a useful life, including expenses incident to a lease and leasehold improvements. Finally, corporate or partnership organizational expenses that may be amortized under Sections 248 or 709 are covered by those provisions rather than Section 195.

Other elements in the use of Section 195 include:

(1) An active trade or business is one that meets the definition of Section 162, as opposed to Section 212 relating to an investment activity.

(2) The taxpayer must have an equity interest in the business and must actively participate in its management. Thus, investigatory expenses attributable to the acquisition of corporate stock generally will not be eligible for amortization. However, if in substance a transaction is the acquisition of the assets of a trade or business, the investigatory expenses will be amortizable even though one of the steps in the transaction involved the acquisition of stock of a corporation that is later liquidated. For example, a corporate taxpayer will be considered to have acquired the trade or business assets of an acquired corporation, rather than having made a portfolio investment in stock, if the acquired corporation becomes a member of an affiliated group that includes the taxpayer, and a consolidated return is filed. Where a partnership interest is acquired, the taxpayer could be considered to have acquired an active interest if the taxpayer actively participates in the management of the trade or business.

[b] Investment (Nontrade or Business) Activity

As noted in the preceding section, Section 195, permitting a sixty-month amortization of preinvestment and start-up expenses, applies only to an active trade or business. If an investor incurs such expenses in connection with a proposed investment that is not a trade or business, the deductibility of the expenses requires an interpretation of Section 165(a), which allows as a deduction any loss incurred in a trade or business, or incurred in a transaction entered into for profit. In a revenue ruling[3] amplifying a 1957 ruling, the IRS now states its interpretation of the law as follows:

[3] Rev. Rul. 77-254, 1977-2 C.B. 63.

> Expenses incurred in the course of a search for, or preliminary investigation of, a business or investment include those expenses related to the decisions whether to enter a transaction and which transaction to enter. Such expenses are personal and nondeductible.
>
> Expenses that are related to an attempt to acquire a specific business or investment are capital in nature and may be amortized as part of the asset's cost if the attempted acquisition is successful. If unsuccessful, these expenses are immediately deductible.

[i] Deducting Brokerage Fees. One of the more significant preinvestment expenses in connection with a real estate acquisition is the brokerage fee. Here is how such fees probably would be treated in three possible investment situations:

☐ *Property not acquired.* If a specific property is evaluated and then not purchased, expenses in connection therewith are deductible as losses under Section 165 of the Internal Revenue Code.[4]

A corporate investor clearly is entitled to the loss deduction; an individual investor must make a further distinction between expenses in connection with a specific property (deductible if the property is not purchased) and general-search expenses, which are personal and nondeductible.

☐ *Property acquired.* Where the property evaluated is in fact acquired, brokerage fees are treated as a cost of acquiring the property and must be capitalized, with deductibility not permitted in the year of acquisition.[5]

☐ *Properties both rejected and acquired.* Most commonly, an investor or investment group will consider several properties, rejecting some before acquiring others. It is here that some advance planning may create a front-end deduction that might not otherwise be available. If evaluation expenses, including brokerage commissions, are lumped together, it is likely that the IRS might require that they be treated as part of the costs of the acquired properties. However, if the broker evaluating properties is directed to keep detailed records of his efforts, ultimate payment to him may be allocated among all of the properties evaluated, whether or not ultimately acquired. That portion of the fee for rejected properties would then be taken as a front-end deduction.

The deductibility of the rejection fee would be further supported if the investment group obligated itself to pay the broker a specified fee even if no properties at all were acquired.

[3] Home-Office Expenses

The Tax Reform Act of 1976 [6] limited home-office deductions, greatly restricting such deductions for anyone who is not self-employed. However, under Code Section 280A, any real estate executive or investor who can show that part

---

[4] See Rev. Rul. 74-102, 1974-1 C.B. 70; Rev. Rul. 77-254, note 3, supra.

[5] Reg. § 1.263-2.

[6] Pub. L. No. 94-455, 90 Stat. 1520, 26 U.S.C.A. §§ 1 et seq.

of his activities qualifies as a separate or sideline business conducted at home may be able to meet the new requirements.

The tax law now handles the home-office problem by establishing an exclusive-use test and an overall deduction limit. The exclusive-use test prohibits a taxpayer from deducting any expenses attributable to the business use of his home except where a portion of the home is used both exclusively and on a regular basis for one of the following three business purposes:

- Used as the taxpayer's principal place of business
- Used as a place of business by clients or customers in meeting or dealing with the taxpayer in the normal course of his trade or business
- Used in connection with his trade or business in the case of a separate structure not attached to the dwelling.

For employees, an additional requirement is imposed: The business use of the home must be for the convenience of the employer. As amended in 1981, Section 280A makes clear that a taxpayer may have more than one principal place of business. (See 3.01[3][c].)

The second part of the new law places an overall limit on home-office deductions. Under the limitation, the amount of deductions that may be claimed for the business use of the home cannot exceed the gross income generated by the business activity minus business expenses otherwise deductible (e.g., the portion of mortgage interest and real estate taxes allocable to the space used as an office).

These new rules will knock out office-at-home deductions for most executives and professionals who take work home for evening or weekend labors. But for those who do in fact conduct their businesses from home, or who have some sort of separate business "on the side" such as real estate management or brokerage, it appears that deductions are still available. These individuals should lay the groundwork for claiming deductions by setting aside a separate room or area as the principal place of business for their sideline, and they should be prepared to show that they use it exclusively and on a regular basis for their businesses. (This is discussed in detail in 3.01[3][c].)

[a] How to Compute Office-at-Home Deductions

Table 3.1 below shows how the IRS calculates the office-at-home deduction. The cost of such indirect expenses as electricity, gas, telephone, and trash removal must be allocated between the personal and business use of the home. The IRS does not say how the allocation should be determined; however, one possibility is to submeter electrical appliances that use any significant amount of power and so identify the costs attributable to the business portion of the home.

[b] Example of Home-Office Deductions

Suppose two individuals use 20 percent of their homes as their principal place of business. Mr. *A* has $30,000 in gross income from his business and Mr. *B* $1,200. Gross income for purposes of this computation means net profits excluding the deductions for business use of the homes. Mr. *A* and Mr. *B* have

TABLE 3.1 Calculation of Expenses Allocable to Business Portion of Income

Indirect Expenses Otherwise Deductible	*Total*	*Personal Deduction on Schedule A*	*Business Portions (20%)*
Real estate taxes	$2,000	$1,600	$ 400
Mortgage interest	3,000	2,400	600
Taxes and interest allocable to business portion			$1,000

Remainder of Indirect Expenses	*Total*	*Personal Nondeductible*	*Business Portions (20%)*
Lights	$ 600	$ 480	$ 120
Heat	1,600	1,280	320
Insurance	200	160	40
Painting—outside	2,400	1,920	480
Roof repairs	400	320	80
Depreciation	2,000	1,600	400
Indirect expenses allocable to business portion			$1,440

Direct Expenses	*Business Portions (100%)*
Repairs to business portion	$400
Total direct and indirect expenses allocable to business portion	$1,840

TABLE 3.2 Computation of Overall Deduction Limitation

	Mr. A	*Mr. B*
Gross income (excluding home-office deduction)	$30,000	$1,200
Less: Interest and taxes attributable to business portions and deductible in any event	1,000	1,000
Balance of income	$29,000	$200
Total of indirect and direct business expenses	$1,840	$1,840
Amount deductible (lesser of balance of income or total business expenses	$1,840	$200

the expenses shown in Table 3.1. Computation of their overall deduction limitation is shown in Table 3.2.

[c] Real Estate Office at Home Ruled Deductible

A decision by the Tax Court shows when home-office expenses are deductible.[7] Dr. Curphey was a full-time employee of a hospital. During the tax year in question, he also owned and managed six rental properties: three condominiums, two town houses, and a single-family house. He lived in a two-bedroom condominium and used one bedroom exclusively and regularly as an office for bookkeeping and other activities related to the management of his rental properties. The room was furnished with a desk, a bookcase, a filing cabinet, calculators, and a code-a-phone answering service. There was no television, sofa, or bed in the room and he did not allow guests to stay there. The closet in the room was used to store items related to the rental properties, such as furnishings and signs.

The doctor purchased the rental properties to provide a source of income for his retirement. In the tax year in question he did not do well: His gross rental income was $24,760 but he had a net loss of $23,043 and a negative cash flow of $6,242. The Internal Revenue Service challenged the deduction of depreciation and other expenses for the second bedroom. It claimed the doctor's rental activities did not constitute a "business." Second, even if it did, IRS said his place of business was the hospital, not the second bedroom of his condominium. The doctor won against the IRS on both counts.

Whether rental activities constitute a "business" for purposes of Section 280A of the Internal Revenue Code, as opposed to mere investment activities, is a question of fact. The Tax Court found that Dr. Curphey's personal management activities were sufficiently systematic and continuous to place him in the business of real estate rental.

The IRS argued that if a taxpayer is in more than one business, as was the case here, home-office expenses are deductible only if the home office is the principal place of business. Based on time spent and income earned, the IRS argued that the hospital was the principal office. The Tax Court disposed of this argument by holding that a taxpayer may have more than one principal place of business if he engages in more than one trade or business. Accordingly, since it was not argued that the rental properties themselves were his principal place of business for the real estate activities, the second bedroom qualified. (This portion of the decision has been made part of Section 280A, as noted in 3.01[3].)

3.02 REAL ESTATE DEPRECIATION AND RECAPTURE

[1] Depreciation as Tax Shelter

From the very beginning, the federal internal revenue law has been a tax on income rather than on gross revenue, which is why the tax is commonly referred to as an income tax. An income tax system requires a set of rules to determine just what is taxable income, that is, the portion of gross income or gross revenues

---

[7] Edwin R. Curphey v. Comm'r, 73 T.C. 766 (1980).

that will be subject to tax. For example, all monies spent for ordinary and necessary expenses in connection with a business or investment are not considered taxable income. (This is discussed in detail in 3.01.) Other cash outlays such as interest payments, real estate taxes, repairs and losses (all discussed elsewhere in this chapter) are also excluded from taxable income.

In addition to these cash outlays, the federal tax laws have always recognized that a portion of the gross income from a business or investment transaction represents the recoupment of capital invested in "wasting assets," that is, assets that gradually lose value over a period of time due to use, wear and tear, or the action of the elements. All physical assets of a business or investment, with the exception of land, are considered depreciable assets. Land, however, has a permanent life since it is a portion of the earth itself (even though soil or mineral elements in the land may be despoiled or removed).

The concept that taxable income should not include that portion of gross income that represents the "using up" of depreciable assets is given effect by permitting owners of investment or business assets to take an annual deduction for depreciation. Over the years the depreciation deduction has been modified in various ways—usually to reflect the fact that inflation was pushing the cost of replacement property far above the cost of the original property being depreciated.

For example, if a piece of equipment had a useful life of fifteen years and an original cost of $15,000, the owner could deduct $1,000 a year on his tax return as depreciation. At the end of fifteen years, when the equipment was used up, the taxpayer would have recouped $15,000 (the original cost) so that he could buy a new piece of equipment. (Salvage value is ignored in this example.) But if the new equipment cost far more, the taxpayer would have been forced to invest his own money or borrow money in order to replace the used-up asset. To reduce the need for this, the Internal Revenue Code was amended over the years to speed the process of cost recovery through methods of accelerated depreciation and other techniques.

The speedup of depreciation write-offs culminated in the Economic Recovery Tax Act of 1981 (ERTA),[8] when the traditional system of depreciation deductions was replaced by a new system known as the Accelerated Cost Recovery System (ACRS). (In the interest of simplicity the term depreciation will continue to be used in the discussion that follows.) The new system, which applies to both real and personal property (but, as always, excludes land itself) is discussed in this section as it applies to real estate and in 3.03 as it applies to personal property. The new system comes close to being a replacement-cost system since it looks to the future need to replace existing equipment rather than back to the original cost of existing equipment. In the case of real estate, as will be seen, the ACRS will in many cases provide a much greater degree of tax shelter than was available under the former system.

[a] How Depreciation Creates Tax Shelter

Before discussing the details of the new accelerated cost recovery system, a few words must be said about the unique effect of depreciation deductions on

[8] Pub. L. No. 97-34, 95 Stat. 172, 26 U.S.C. § 128.

real estate investment. Buildings and improvements clearly are wasting assets, and therefore are a proper subject for cost recovery. In practice, however, well-located and well-maintained real property often has a useful life far longer than the fifteen years fixed by ACRS. Thus, the cumulative depreciation deductions taken by a property owner often (1) bear little or no relationship to the true economic decline in the value of the property; and (2) will rarely be used to create a cash reserve to purchase replacement property at the end of the fifteen-year recovery period or, indeed, within any foreseeable period. (One type of property to which this statement may not apply is an industrial plant or factory where technological change as well as other forms of depreciation may require replacement within a measurable period.)

As a result of the fact that a property owner may take depreciation deductions far in excess of the actual decline in economic value of the property, a tax shelter is created. In other words, the property owner may take a tax deduction that is matched neither by a cash outlay nor by any diminution in value of the property. Thus, a portion of gross income that is properly taxable income is sheltered from tax. (Actually, the tax is merely deferred until a future date, when the property is sold; this point is discussed in detail in 3.02[5].) Furthermore, the tax shelter created by depreciation deductions is made even more effective because of the way in which real estate is financed.

[b] Cost Recovery and Borrowed Capital

Thus far we have proceeded on the assumption that the capital investment in real estate has actually been made by the investor; that is, a $1 million building represents a cash investment by the owner of that amount. Rarely, however, is real estate purchased for all cash. Because of the fixed, immovable, enduring, and insurable quality of real estate, the major portion of its cost usually can be financed. Regardless of the extent to which a real estate acquisition is financed by third-party lenders, however, the basis for depreciation write-offs is the full cost of the asset, ignoring the actual cash investment by the owner. In other words, the owner gets a full depreciation deduction whether or not he pays for the property in cash, and whether or not he is personally liable for the loan used to finance the property; that is, it makes no difference if the mortgage debt is recourse debt or nonrecourse debt. Note that this rule applies only to depreciable real estate and not to personal property. In the case of the latter, the at-risk rules limit the depreciable basis of the property to the amount as to which the owner is actually at risk (e.g., cash invested plus loans for which the owner is personally liable). (See 3.09[3].)

The justification for allowing an owner to depreciate the entire cost without regard to the amount of third-party debt is that eventually the owner will have to amortize the debt obligation and thereby complete his investment in the property. In actual practice, of course, real estate mortgages are usually amortized at a very slow pace during the early years of ownership, whereas depreciation deductions are much greater, particularly if accelerated methods are used. The owner, therefore, may be able to generate depreciation write-offs that far exceed his cash investment—sometimes as much as 4 or 5 dollars of depreciation for every one dollar of cash investment.

[c] Summarizing Depreciation as a Tax Shelter

The simple depreciation deduction, when applied to real estate, can be viewed in two different ways:

Theory	*Practice*
The deduction compensates the taxpayer for the depreciation of his wasting assets over 15 years.	The value of the depreciable assets is frequently declining at a much slower rate than 15 years (if not actually increasing).
The deduction anticipates that the taxpayer will set up a replacement reserve to be utilized on retirement of the assets.	Depreciation creates untaxed cash flow that can be used by the taxpayer for other purposes than replacing the property.
Depreciation allows the taxpayer to recoup his cash investment through tax deductions.	The taxpayer can take deductions on an amount which may far exceed his actual investment in the property.

For an example of how a positive cash flow can be sheltered by tax (or "paper") losses, see 2.02[2][a].

[2] Accelerated Cost Recovery System

The new Accelerated Cost Recovery System (ACRS) will apply to property placed in service after 1980 (i.e., beginning January 1, 1981). Generally, the recovery period for depreciable real property is fifteen years. The only significant exceptions to this are theme park structures and residential manufactured homes, which are considered ten-year personal property. The fifteen-year life compares to present IRS guideline lives for real property that range from forty to sixty years (although in many cases shorter lives are justified under a facts-and-circumstances approach).

Instead of using the prescribed fifteen-year recovery period, taxpayers may elect a thirty-five- or forty-five-year extended recovery period. A substantial improvement is treated as a separate building for this election. The election of the fifteen-, thirty-five-, or forty-five-year recovery method will be made on a property-by-property basis and, once made, is revocable only with consent of the IRS.

The fifteen-year recovery period does not apply in the following cases:

- Property that must be amortized (e.g., leasehold improvements and low-income rehabilitation expenditures)
- Real property used predominantly outside the United States, which must be recovered over a period of thirty-five years. For such foreign real estate, the annual write-offs must be based upon a 150 percent declining-balance method with a switch to the straight-line method at such time as will maximize the deduction. IRS is to issue a table showing the annual deductions.

[a] Component Depreciation Eliminated

Under the component method of depreciation, each item of equipment or identifiable building component is depreciated separately, based on its own useful life. Since various components of a building will wear out more rapidly than the basic structure, component depreciation has the effect of speeding up cost recovery and so has been a popular technique. Under the new law, component depreciation may no longer be used; instead, the building must be treated as a single unit (composite depreciation).

However, for purposes of making the election to use either (1) an optional (thirty-five- or forty-five-year) recovery period or (2) accelerated depreciation, a substantial improvement of a building is treated as a separate building. For example, the taxpayer may use a fifteen-year period for a substantial improvement even if the rest of the building is depreciable over a thirty-five- or forty-five-year period. Also, the taxpayer may use an accelerated method even if the straight-line method were used for the rest of the building.

An improvement is a substantial improvement if:

- Over a two-year period the improvement cost is at least equal to 25 percent of the adjusted basis of the building (disregarding adjustments for depreciation or amortization) as of the beginning of that two-year period; and
- The improvement is made at least three years after the building was placed in service.

A special rule allows a taxpayer to elect a new recovery period and a depreciation method for the first component placed in service after 1980 on a building owned before 1981, whether or not it is a substantial improvement.

Numerous components placed in service over a twenty-four-month period may in the aggregate exceed the 25 percent basis requirement. When the total exceeds 25 percent, the prior year's income tax return can be amended to reflect the more favorable alternative. Careful timing of the placement in service of components can enable a real estate investor to qualify for fast write-offs, additions, or replacements made after January 1, 1981 to pre-1981 real estate.

[b] Initial- and Final-Year Depreciation

The amount of the depreciation deduction for the initial year of property ownership depends upon the number of months the property is in service during that year. For example, if property is used for five months during the initial year, five-twelfths of the full first-year percentage would apply. And when property is sold, the seller must similarly prorate the annual depreciation deduction to reflect the number of months the property was held by the seller.

[c] Anti-Churning Rules

The new law contains some complex provisions intended to prevent a taxpayer from bringing pre-1981 real estate within the new ACRS in order to benefit from the fifteen-year recovery period. In essence, real property will not be eligible for the fifteen-year recovery period if:

- The taxpayer or someone related to the taxpayer owned the property at any time during 1980; or

- The property is transferred after 1980 and is then leased back to someone who owned the property in 1980 (or a related person); or
- The property is acquired in a tax-free exchange or other transaction that does not involve the recognition of tax in return for property the taxpayer (or a related person) owned in 1980.

[3] Methods of Depreciation

There are two depreciation methods available to the real estate investor under the ACRS system: (1) straight-line depreciation, and (2) accelerated depreciation. (See Table 3.3.)

[a] Straight-Line Depreciation

A taxpayer may elect to use straight-line depreciation either with the regular fifteen-year recovery period or for the optional recovery period of thirty-five or forty-five years. The election is made on a property-by-property basis and is revocable only with the consent of the IRS.

Under the straight-line method, an equal amount is deducted each year over the life of the property.

> *Example 1:* An investor acquires real estate for $100,000 in 1981. Twenty percent, or $20,000, is allocated to nondepreciable land; 80 percent, or $80,000, is allocated to depreciable improvements. The taxpayer elects the fifteen-year recovery period. Thus, the investor is entitled to deduct 6.67 percent of $80,000 ($5,336) each year during the initial fifteen years of ownership, at the end of which time the investor will have recouped, tax-free, the $80,000 investment in the improvements. (The investor's tax basis is reduced by a similar amount.)
>
> The annual deduction offsets taxable income of the investor (whether the taxable income arises from the real property itself apart from the depreciation deduction, or from an outside source). Further, the deduction is available regardless of how much or how little equity the investor puts up and whether or not he is personally liable on the mortgage securing the loan.

The use of straight-line depreciation illustrates all three of the elements of a tax shelter: (1) deferral of taxes; (2) benefits from leveraging; and (3) conversion of ordinary income to capital gain. This can be illustrated by continuing the example to the point where the property is sold by the investor.

> *Example 2:* Assume the investor sells the real estate after ten years, during which time he took total depreciation deductions of $53,360 (6.67 percent per year × 10 years × $80,000). If he is in the 50 percent bracket, this represents total tax savings of $26,680. At the end of ten years, he sells the property for $100,000, his original cost. His basis for tax purposes is $46,640 (cost of $100,000 − $53,360 of cumulative depreciation deductions). Thus his gain is $53,360—exactly the amount of cumulative depreciation, since the property was sold at a price equal to its original cost. Assuming the property

TABLE 3.3 Depreciation and Recapture of Post-1980 Real Estate[1]

Property Type	*Recovery Period (Years)*	*Depreciation Method*	*Recapture*[4]
Residential	15	SL [2] or 175% DB [3]	No Excess depreciation
	35	SL	No
	45	SL	No
Nonresidential	15	SL or 175% DB [3]	No All depreciation
	35	SL	No
	45	SL	No
Subsidized housing	15	SL or 200% DB [3]	No Excess depreciation phased out[5]
	35	SL	No
	45	SL	No

1 Real estate outside the United States is depreciated over 35 years using the 150% declining-balance method.
2 SL = straight-line depreciation.
3 175% DB or 200% DB = 175% or 200% declining-balance method with a switch to the SL method at such time as will maximize the deduction.
4 Depreciation on any real estate (except subsidized housing) held for less than 12 months is subject to 100% recapture. For subsidized housing held less than 12 months, recapture is limited to depreciation in excess of straight-line.
5 Recapture of excess depreciation phased out at rate of one percent for each month over 100, with no recapture after 200 months (16 years 8 months).

is a capital asset in his hands, only 40 percent of this long-term gain is subject to tax, or $21,344. The amount of tax thus is $10,672 (50 percent of the 40 percent taxable portion of the gain).

Net result: The use of straight-line depreciation (combined with resale of the property at a price equal to its original cost) has enabled the investor to

☐ Defer until the sale of the property a total of $10,672 in tax payments, which otherwise would have been due in equal amounts during the ten years of ownership.

☐ Convert ordinary income of $53,360 (which would have been taxable to him over the ten-year period had he not utilized depreciation deductions) to capital gain of $53,360, thus realizing a savings of $16,008 (30 percent of the gain, which is the amount saved by paying a 20 percent capital gains rate instead of a 50 percent ordinary income rate).

☐ Achieve this tax saving on an equity investment of $20,000, assuming that 80 percent of the total investment of $100,000 was represented by borrowed funds.

The use of straight-line depreciation remains the major advantage of real estate investing for the reasons shown above, and with the shortened recovery period to fifteen years under the new law, the tax benefit is greater than ever before.

[b] Accelerated Depreciation

The second method of depreciation available under ACRS is accelerated depreciation. However, accelerated depreciation may be used only in connection with a fifteen-year recovery period. If the taxpayer elects either the thirty-five- or forty-five-year optional period, straight-line depreciation must be used.

A taxpayer electing accelerated depreciation must use either the 175 percent declining-balance method or (for subsidized housing projects) the 200 percent declining-balance method. ERTA eliminates the distinction between residential and nonresidential real estate for purposes of depreciation, both now being eligible for the 175 percent declining-balance method; however, the distinction remains important with respect to the recapture of depreciation. The new law eliminates the use of the following types of accelerated depreciation that were formerly available: 125 percent declining-balance method; 150 percent declining-balance method (except for foreign real estate); and sum-of-the-years' digits. The new law also eliminates the distinction between new and used property. (These continue to apply to real estate placed in service prior to 1981; see Table 3.4.)

TABLE 3.4 Depreciation of Real Estate Owned Prior to 1981

Depreciation Method	*Applicable to*
• 200% declining-balance	• New residential housing
• Sum-of-the-years' digits	• New residential housing
• 150% declining-balance	• All new property, commercial and industrial
• 125% declining-balance	• Used residential rental housing with useful life of at least twenty years
• Straight-line	• All new or used property
• Straight-line using sixty-month useful life	• Low-income rental housing rehabilitation expenditures (subject to dollar limitations)

[i] 175 Percent Declining-Balance Method of Depreciation. This method of accelerated depreciation, as noted above, may be used for either residential or nonresidential property provided that a fifteen-year recovery period is used. It allows a rate of depreciation equal to one and three-quarters of the straight-line rate. However, the rate is not applied to the original cost basis each year (as is the case with straight-line depreciation), but instead is applied to the declining balance (i.e., cost minus accumulated depreciation for prior taxable years). Since the depreciation base is reduced to reflect prior depreciation, the amount claimed as a depreciation deduction is greater in earlier years and declines in each succeeding year of the fifteen-year recovery period.

The new law authorizes the IRS to provide a table to be used in connection with the 175 percent declining-balance method, which will incorporate a switch to the straight-line method at such time as will maximize the deduction. (See Table 3.5.)

[ii] 200 Percent Declining-Balance Method of Depreciation. This method of depreciation may be used for subsidized low-income housing. (Under former law, it was available for all new residential housing.) Commonly referred to as double declining-balance (DDB) this method allows a rate of depreciation equal to twice the straight-line rate. As with 175 percent declining-balance, the rate is not applied to the original cost basis each year but is applied to the declining balance. The IRS table showing annual write-offs using DDB, with a switch to the straight-line method at such time as will maximize the deduction, is at Table 3.6 below. Low-income housing for the purpose of DDB depreciation is property described in Sections 1250(a)(1)(B)(i)–1250(a)(1)(B)(iv) of the Internal Revenue Code and includes

- Housing financed under Sections 221(d)(3) or 236 of the National Housing Act or under similar state or local laws; or
- Housing eligible for the sixty-month write-off of rehabilitation expenditures; or
- Housing occupied by families subsidized under Section 8 of the United States Housing Act of 1937 or under similar laws; or
- Housing financed under Section 515 of the Housing Act of 1949.

[iii] How to Use Tables 3.5–3.6. In any declining-balance method of depreciation, the annual depreciation write-off is taken on the original cost minus all prior depreciation taken. Thus, the amount of write-off will decline for each successive twelve-month period. The new law provides that each twelve-month period shall be measured beginning with the month the property is first placed in service. So if property is placed in service in May 1982, then the first twelve-month write-off of 12 percent of original cost (the result of using 175 percent depreciation over fifteen years) will be allocated as follows: 8/12 to 1982 and 4/12 to 1983, with the balance of the 1983 write-off based on the second-year rate of 175 percent depreciation.

The accompanying tables reflect this new rule and show the annual depreciation deduction according to the month in the first year the property is placed in service.

> *Example 1:* Real estate that is not low-income housing is placed in service in January. The annual depreciation deductions (as a percentage of unadjusted basis) are shown in column 1 of Table 3.5. So if the total cost of the property was $100,000, with $20,000 allocated to land and $80,000 to depreciable buildings, the depreciation write-off in the first year is 12 percent of $80,000, or $9,600. For the second year the depreciation write-off is 10 percent of

TABLE 3.5 ACRS Cost Recovery Tables for Real Estate
All Real Estate (Except Low-Income Housing)

(175% Declining-Balance Depreciation With Switch to Straight-Line Depreciation)

If the recovery year is:	*The applicable percentage is:* *											
	1	*2*	*3*	*4*	*5*	*6*	*7*	*8*	*9*	*10*	*11*	*12*
1	12	11	10	9	8	7	6	5	4	3	2	1
2	10	10	11	11	11	11	11	11	11	11	11	12
3	9	9	9	9	10	10	10	10	10	10	10	10
4	8	8	8	8	8	8	9	9	9	9	9	9
5	7	7	7	7	7	7	8	8	8	8	8	8
6	6	6	6	6	7	7	7	7	7	7	7	7
7	6	6	6	6	6	6	6	6	6	6	6	6
8	6	6	6	6	6	6	5	6	6	6	6	6
9	6	6	6	6	5	6	5	5	5	6	6	6
10	5	6	5	6	5	5	5	5	5	5	6	5
11	5	5	5	5	5	5	5	5	5	5	5	5
12	5	5	5	5	5	5	5	5	5	5	5	5
13	5	5	5	5	5	5	5	5	5	5	5	5
14	5	5	5	5	5	5	5	5	5	5	5	5
15	5	5	5	5	5	5	5	5	5	5	5	5
16	—	—	1	1	2	2	3	3	4	4	4	5

* Use the column for the month in the first year the property is placed in service.

TABLE 3.6 Low-Income Housing

(200% Declining-Balance Depreciation With Switch to Straight-Line Depreciation)

If the recovery year is:	*The applicable percentage is:* *											
	1	*2*	*3*	*4*	*5*	*6*	*7*	*8*	*9*	*10*	*11*	*12*
1	13	12	11	10	9	8	7	6	4	3	2	1
2	12	12	12	12	12	12	12	13	13	13	13	13
3	10	10	10	10	11	11	11	11	11	11	11	11
4	9	9	9	9	9	9	9	9	10	10	10	10
5	8	8	8	8	8	8	8	8	8	8	8	9
6	7	7	7	7	7	7	7	7	7	7	7	7
7	6	6	6	6	6	6	6	6	6	6	6	6
8	5	5	5	5	5	5	5	5	5	5	6	6
9	5	5	5	5	5	5	5	5	5	5	5	5
10	5	5	5	5	5	5	5	5	5	5	5	5
11	4	5	5	5	5	5	5	5	5	5	5	5
12	4	4	4	5	4	5	5	5	5	5	5	5
13	4	4	4	4	4	4	5	4	5	5	5	5
14	4	4	4	4	4	4	4	4	4	5	4	4
15	4	4	4	4	4	4	4	4	4	4	4	4
16	—	—	1	1	2	2	2	3	3	3	4	4

* Use the column for the month in the first year the property is placed in service.

Note: These tables do not apply for short taxable years of less than 12 months.

$80,000, or $8,000. In the first five years the total write-offs equal 46 percent of original cost, or $36,800.

Example 2: Assume the same property is placed in service in May (the fifth month). The annual depreciation deductions are then shown under column 5 in Table 3.5. The first-year depreciation would equal 8 percent of the $80,000 original basis, or $6,400. The second-year write-off would be 11 percent of $80,000 or $8,800. At the end of the fifth calendar year (four years and eight months of actual ownership), total depreciation write-offs equal 44 percent of original basis, or $35,200. Because the property was placed in service so late in the first year, depreciation deductions will overflow into the sixteenth calendar year of ownership.

[4] Allocating Costs Between Land and Improvements

In order to maximize depreciation write-offs, a property owner seeks to allocate as much acquisition cost as possible to depreciable buildings and improvements and as little as possible to nondepreciable land. Under the tax regulations, when depreciable and nondepreciable properties are acquired together for a lump sum (as is usually the case with real estate), the acquisition cost must be allocated on the basis of the respective values of the two portions. The regulations, however, do not describe how the values are to be ascertained. As a practical matter, a taxpayer attacks the question of cost allocation in two stages. The first is to identify those elements that properly are land and those that can be considered man-made improvements; the second is to allocate values to these elements.

[a] How to Depreciate Land Improvements

In most cases, the distinction is obvious between nondepreciable land and depreciable improvements. But what about such improvements to land as grading, filling, roads, and landscaping? These may be depreciable if they are directly "associated with" construction of a building. The key distinction is between (1) preliminary land improvement costs that make the land permanently suitable for any type of structure; and (2) excavating, grading, and other development costs that make the land suitable only for a particular building. The first category of cost is not depreciable, but the second often is.[9]

IRS has ruled that land preparation costs are depreciable if the work on the land must be replaced contemporaneously with the related depreciable asset. For example, a developer puts up an office building or other improvement and spends a substantial amount of money in landscaping, including the cost of topsoil, seeding, clearing, grading, and planting of perennial shrubbery and ornamental trees immediately adjacent to the property. To the extent that the landscaping will have to be removed in the event the building is demolished, the cost of such work is depreciable. However, the cost of landscaping that would not necessarily have to be replaced if the building were to be replaced is not deductible, but rather is part of the cost of the land.[10]

---

[9] See Rudolph Invest. Corp. v. Comm'r, T.C. Memo 1972-129.

[10] Rev. Rul. 74-265, 1974-1 C.B. 56.

Under special tax provisions applicable to farmers, certain expenditures for man-made improvements to land may either be deducted when made or amortized over a specified period of time. These include soil and water conservation expenditures (Code Section 175); fertilizer, etc. (Code Section 180); and the cost of clearing land for farming (Code Section 182).

[b] How to Allocate Costs

The second approach for a property owner seeking to maximize depreciation deductions is to allocate as much of the original cost as possible to the depreciable improvements. In the case of new construction, a careful earmarking of costs is the most appropriate method. When improved property is purchased, the percentage of the purchase price to be allocated to various elements can be done by professional appraisal. However, this involves an extra cost that the purchaser may wish to avoid.

A simple approach, and one that may prove more favorable to the taxpayer, is to make an allocation that is consistent with the relative values placed on land and building by the local tax assessor. (The overall value for assessment purposes may not be relevant in determining the value of the property for depreciation purposes; however, the percentage of value allocated to land and improvements by the tax assessor may be accepted by IRS, particularly if the municipality does not have different tax rates for land and for improvements.)

In one noteworthy case, a taxpayer purchased old property for $300,000 and allocated $50,000 to the land and $250,000 to the building. IRS virtually reversed the figures, allocating $234,000 to the land and $66,000 to the building. In the Tax Court, the taxpayer showed that his allocation was based on two premises. First, his allocation was consistent with the relative values placed on land and building by the local tax assessor. Second, his allocation of $250,000 to the building was consistent with the value of the income the building was capable of generating. The Tax Court totally agreed with the taxpayer's approach, placing considerable weight on the taxpayer's own testimony because he was intimately familiar with the area in which the property was located.[11]

Another example shows how proving the highest-and-best use for the land in question can knock down the amount allocated to the land. The Platts purchased several parcels in Portland, Oregon, with improvements consisting principally of buildings used for low-rent housing. However, the property was located in an industrial zone and nearby industrial property was very valuable. The Platts made their land-to-building cost allocation by appraising the land as residential property. The Internal Revenue Service, asserting the Platts' use of the property for residential rental purposes was "economic foolishness," claimed it should be appraised at its much higher value as industrial property. The Service went on to claim that the Platts obviously intended to exploit the property for industrial use and that they were masquerading as residential rental developers. The Platts, on the other hand, persuasively argued that the character of their land made it unsuitable for industrial development.

[11] Offshore Operations Trust v. Comm'r, T.C. Memo 1973-212.

The court found the IRS position "precariously constructed by means of speculation and conjecture." The Platts' highest-and-best use argument was accepted and their allocation sustained.[12]

[5] Recapture of Depreciation

The three objectives of a tax shelter are to (1) defer tax to a future date; (2) create deductions from investments financed with borrowed funds; and (3) convert ordinary income into capital gain. The concept of recapture of depreciation deals with the third objective; the purpose of recapture is to prevent the conversion of ordinary income into capital gain. It does this by providing that, in certain cases, any gain on sale attributable to the reduction in the seller's basis due to depreciation deductions taken during ownership is to be treated as ordinary income, not capital gain. Note that depreciation recapture has no effect whatsoever on gain attributable to the true appreciation in the value of the property while held by the seller.

Table 3.3 shows the recapture rules for property covered by the new accelerated cost recovery system, and Table 3.7 compares the old and new recapture rules. The new rules may be summarized briefly as follows (for real estate held at least twelve months):

☐ The treatment of residential real property is unchanged (i.e., if accelerated depreciation is used, excess depreciation is recaptured upon sale).

☐ The treatment of nonresidential real property is unchanged if straight-line depreciation is used (i.e., no recapture will occur).

☐ The treatment of nonresidential real property is changed if accelerated depreciation is used. Gain on the sale of such property is treated as ordinary income to the extent of all depreciation taken (not merely depreciation in excess of straight-line).

In determining whether real estate is used for a residential or nonresidential purpose, it is reasonable to assume the same rules will apply as were formerly used to distinguish residential and nonresidential property for purposes of allowable depreciation methods (which differed depending on the property use under former law). Under these rules, residential rental property includes single- and multiple-family housing, apartments, and similar structures used to provide living accommodations on a rental basis. A building or other structure will qualify as residential rental property if 80 percent or more of the gross rental income from the building or structure is rental income from dwelling units. Hotels, motels, inns, or other similar establishments are not treated as dwelling units if more than one-half of the units are used on a transient basis.

[6] Choosing a Depreciation Method

The choice of straight-line or accelerated depreciation is complicated by an additional factor not yet mentioned—the treatment of excess depreciation as a

---

[12] Platt v. United States, 75-1 U.S.T.C. ¶ 9216.

TABLE 3.7 Comparison of Old and New Recapture Rules

Type of Property	*Property of Depreciation on Non-ACRS Real Estate*	*Property of Depreciation on ACRS Real Estate*
All residential and nonresidential real estate, without exception, if held for less than twelve months	All depreciation, including straight-line	Same
All residential and nonresidential real estate except subsidized housing projects, if held for more than twelve months	All depreciation in excess of straight-line	Same for residential; for nonresidential, *all* depreciation is recaptured
Subsidized housing projects, if held between twelve and 100 months	All depreciation in excess of straight-line	Same
Subsidized housing, if held more than 100 months	Recapture of excess depreciation phased out at rate of one percent for each month over 100, with no recapture after 200 months (16 years 8 months)	Same

tax preference item for purposes of the add-on minimum tax. In essence, a taxpayer must pay a 15 percent tax on any tax preference income that exceeds $10,000 or one-half of his regular tax, whichever is greater. A total of nine tax preference items create tax preference income; by far the most important of these for real estate investors is accelerated depreciation actually taken that is in excess of straight-line ("excess depreciation"). (See 3.11[1].)

If it were not for the potential minimum tax liability, it would clearly be advantageous to use accelerated depreciation for residential real property. Although the excess depreciation would be recaptured upon sale (so that no conversion from ordinary income to capital gain occurs with respect to such depreciation), its use does permit a deferral of income tax until the time of sale and, to that extent, enables the investor to use funds interest-free that otherwise would go to pay taxes. However, if the investor envisages the possibility of a 15 percent minimum tax during some or all of the years when accelerated depreciation will be taken, then a careful calculation must be made to determine if using accelerated depreciation still makes sense.

When it comes to nonresidential property, however, a double penalty is payable if accelerated depreciation is chosen. The first is the potential minimum tax liability just discussed. The second is the recapture of all depreciation upon sale, not merely excess depreciation. In other words, the owner of nonresidential property, in order to obtain the benefit of accelerated depreciation (which is the deferral of tax to a future date on the income offset by the excess depreciation) must

- See gain attributable to straight-line depreciation converted to ordinary income upon resale.
- Possibly pay a minimum tax of 15 percent during some or all of the years in which excess depreciation is taken.

In one respect, the new law has lessened the burden to a taxpayer of having tax preference income. Under the prior law, a taxpayer's preference income reduced on a dollar-for-dollar basis the amount of his earned income that was eligible for the maximum tax rate of 50 percent. This provision has been repealed because no income—whether earned or unearned—will now be taxed at a higher rate than 50 percent.

Example: The owner of residential property with a depreciable basis of $1 million holds the property for five years, during which time he uses accelerated depreciation. His annual deductions, and the deductions that would have been taken if straight-line depreciation had been used, are as follows:

Accelerated	*Straight-Line*	*Excess*
$120,000	$ 66,600	$ 53,400
$100,000	66,600	33,400
90,000	66,600	23,400
80,000	66,600	13,400
70,000	66,600	3,400
$460,000	$333,000	$127,000

Assume the taxpayer's regular tax is not in excess of $20,000 (since most of his income is sheltered by the depreciation write-offs). His exemption for preference income then will be $10,000 each year. The minimum tax of 15 percent on the balance of preference income (i.e., excess depreciation) will result in a minimum tax in each of the five years as follows:

Year	*Minimum Taxes*
1	$ 6,510
2	3,510
3	2,010
4	510
5	0
	$12,540

So for a total minimum tax cost of $12,540, the investor is able to defer tax on the ordinary income sheltered by the excess depreciation until the property is sold. Thus, the investor can defer tax on $53,400 for four years, on $33,400 for three years, and so forth (except for the final year's excess depreciation when no deferral occurs because the property is sold). Except for taxpayers in very low tax brackets, use of accelerated depreciation would be worthwhile.

However, if the property had been nonresidential, the opposite conclusion is likely to be reached, since the owner must not only pay minimum taxes of $12,540 but also will see an additional $333,000 of gain (i.e., that attributable to straight-line depreciation) converted from capital gain to ordinary income upon sale. The additional tax on sale alone is likely to be far greater than the savings achieved by deferring taxes through use of accelerated depreciation. Generally, the longer nonresidential property is held, the more likely that accelerated depreciation will prove worthwhile.

[7] Calculating Corporate Earnings and Profits

In calculating its taxable income, a corporation is subject to the same depreciation rules as an individual taxpayer, as set forth above. But when it comes to the question of whether a corporate distribution to its shareholders is taxable as a dividend, or is instead a return of capital, a different rule applies. The rule is that such distributions are taxable as dividends only to the extent the distribution is out of current or accumulated earnings and profits of the corporation. In determining what are earnings and profits, a corporation under present law must use straight-line depreciation over the useful life of the property (whether or not it uses an accelerated method in determining the corporation's taxable income). In short, a corporation using accelerated depreciation may have no taxable income (and so may pay no corporate income tax); nevertheless, because it must use straight-line depreciation in computing earnings and profits, some or all of its distributions to its shareholders may be taxable to them as dividends.

Under ERTA 1981 the rule relating to the use of straight-line depreciation in computing earnings and profits is unchanged. However, the recovery period (i.e., useful life) of the property being depreciated will be in accordance with the following, in which the first three classes refer to personal property, and the last refers to real property:

Extended Recovery Period

Property	*Years*
3-year	5
5-year	12
10-year	25
15-year	35

If the corporate taxpayer elects to use one of the longer recovery periods as described above in the discussion of depreciation, then such longer period must be used to compute earnings and profits.

The effect of this new rule will be to permit a larger amount of corporate distributions to be tax-free to shareholders and, to that extent, will make corporate ownership of real estate more attractive than in the past.

3.03 PERSONAL PROPERTY DEPRECIATION AND RECAPTURE

[1] Accelerated Cost Recovery System

The real estate investor and professional each has a reason to be familiar with the rules of personal property depreciation. The investor usually must allocate a portion of the purchase price for an income property to items of personal property (e.g., furniture and fixtures for the public areas, maintenance equipment). The real estate professional normally will maintain office equipment, an automobile or other vehicles, and other business property that is eligible for depreciation. Builders, of course, frequently will have large investments in depreciable property.

The accelerated cost recovery system (ACRS) places all personal property into one of four recovery periods (unlike real estate, which is subject to a single fifteen-year life). Each of the four recovery periods may be extended into longer periods at the election of the taxpayer. (See Table 3.8.) There are two important points to note about the recovery periods:

- Virtually all types of business property are eligible either for the three-year or five-year recovery period.
- Mobile homes, and theme and amusement parks are treated as personal property eligible for a ten-year recovery period.

[a] Methods of Depreciation

Declining-balance depreciation (discussed in detail in 3.02[3][b]) can be used for all personal property placed in service in 1981 and thereafter. However, the rate of depreciation will rise in three stages until it reaches the maximum

TABLE 3.8 Personal Property Recovery Periods

Regular Period of Depreciation	*Optional Periods*	*Examples*
3 years	5 or 12 years	Autos, light-duty trucks, personal property with ADR midpoint of 4 years or less
5 years	12 or 25 years	Most other equipment, single-purpose agricultural structures, petroleum storage facilities
10 years	25 or 35 years	Mobile homes, real property with ADR midpoint life of 12.5 years or less, such as theme and amusement parks
15 years	35 or 45 years	Public utility property with an ADR midpoint life exceeding 25 years

ADR = Asset depreciation range

of 200 percent in years after 1985. For each stage, IRS has prepared tables showing the annual deduction, with each table providing for a switch to either straight-line depreciation or to the sum-of-the-years'-digits method to maximize the deduction. (See Table 3.9, which shows the methods of depreciation and Table 3.10,

TABLE 3.9 Methods of Personal Property Depreciation

Year Property Placed in Service	*Prescribed Method*
1981–1984	150% declining balance with switch to straight-line
1985	175% declining balance with switch to sum-of-the-years'-digits
After 1985	200% declining balance with switch to sum-of-the-years'-digits

which reproduces the statutory tables showing write-offs for property placed in service between 1981 and 1984.) The statute also contains tables for property placed in service in 1985 and thereafter, which are not reproduced here.

A taxpayer may elect to use straight-line depreciation instead of the accelerated method, but in that case he must utilize the regular recovery period for that type of property and may not elect one of the optional periods.

[b] Anti-Churning Rules

Just as in the case of real property, the new law sets forth rules to prevent a taxpayer from using the new short recovery periods for personal property placed in use prior to January 1, 1981, and also to prevent a taxpayer from using the

TABLE 3.10 For Property Placed in Service, 1981-1984

	The applicable percentage for the class of property is:		
If the recovery year is:	*3-year*	*5-year*	*10-year*
1	25	15	8
2	38	22	14
3	37	21	12
4		21	10
5		21	10
6			10
7			9
8			9
9			9
10			9

increased recovery percentages available after 1984 and after 1985 for property not first placed in use in those years.

Note that personal property is eligible both for the fast write-off under ACRS and for the new investment tax credit. (See 3.05.) Thus, personal property with a three-year life is eligible for a 6 percent investment credit in addition to ACRS depreciation, and personal property with a five-, ten-, or fifteen-year life is eligible for a 10 percent investment credit in addition to ACRS depreciation.

All personal property of a similar class (i.e., eligible for the same recovery period) and placed in service in the same tax year must be treated the same by the taxpayer; that is, he cannot elect an extended recovery period for a part of such property and use the regular recovery period for the balance of the property. However, different elections may be made for each separate class of personal property, and for property in the same class that is placed in service in different tax years.

The ACRS makes no distinction between new and used property, and any salvage value is ignored.

[2] Recapture of Depreciation

The new law does not change the prior rule that any gain on the disposition of personal property is treated as ordinary income rather than capital gain to the extent of prior depreciation taken (i.e., all depreciation is recaptured upon sale).

[3] First-Year Expense Deduction

Under former law (Code Section 179), purchasers of tangible personal property used in business (but not for the production of income) could take bonus first-year depreciation equal to 20 percent of the cost of the property. The new law repeals the existing provision and replaces it with a new Section 179 that gives the taxpayer an election to deduct immediately as an expense the cost of new or used personal property up to:

- $5,000 per year in 1982 and 1983
- $7,500 per year in 1984 and 1985
- $10,000 per year in years after 1985

Note that although the new provision is effective for property placed in service after January 1, 1981 and thereafter, the first deduction may be taken for property acquired in 1982. Thus, neither the new expense deduction nor the prior bonus depreciation is allowed for property placed in service in 1981 (or tax years beginning in 1981).

All taxpayers other than trusts, estates, and certain noncorporate lessors are eligible for the first-year expense deduction. The new expense deduction does not apply to land or buildings; however, it does apply to personal property used in connection with a real estate operation. Examples would include individual-room air conditioners, refrigerators, stoves, and lobby furniture.

When Section 179 property is disposed of, the first-year expense deduction is treated as a depreciation deduction for purposes of recapture. Thus, any gain recognized on the disposition of Section 179 property will be treated as ordinary income to the extent of (1) the amount of the first-year expense deduction; and (2) the accrued depreciation claimed during the ownership period.

A partner in a partnership may claim the first-year expense deduction on his allocable share of qualifying property purchased by the partnership. Both the partnership and each single partner are subject to the annual dollar limitation; in other words, the partnership is treated as a single entity for purposes of the expense deduction and so may take only a single deduction up to the ceiling permitted each year. That deduction may then be allocated among the various partners. For example, in 1982 a partnership with five partners may take the maximum deduction of $5,000 with each partner receiving an allocable portion of that deduction.

If a first-year expense deduction is taken, the property cost eligible for the investment tax credit is reduced by the amount of such deduction.

3.04 TAX BENEFITS FOR REAL ESTATE REHABILITATION

[1] Rehabilitation Tax Credit

[a] In General

Prior to 1978, buildings and their structural components were not eligible for any investment tax credit. In order to provide an incentive to rehabilitate and modernize existing buildings, Congress granted investment credits for such expenditures in the Revenue Act of 1978.[13] In essence, rehabilitation expenses for a nonresidential building at least twenty years old became eligible for the 10 percent investment tax credit plus an additional energy credit. If the rehabilitation was of a certified historic structure, the taxpayer was given an election of either the 10 percent investment credit or a sixty-month amortization of the rehabilitation expenditures.

The new law substitutes a three-tier investment credit for both the 10 percent investment credit and the sixty-month amortization. The new credit is:

- 15 percent for nonresidential structures between thirty–thirty-nine years old
- 20 percent for nonresidential structures at least forty years old
- 25 percent for certified historic structures, whether residential or nonresidential

The new rules are, in some respects, more restrictive than the former ones; this is because buildings between twenty–twenty-nine years of age no longer are eligible for a credit, and because an energy credit may not be taken in addition to the rehabilitation credit. In some respects, however, the new rules are more liberal; the amount of the credit is now increased substantially, from 10 percent to a range of 15 to 25 percent. In addition, the credit now extends to residential properties (provided they are certified historic structures) whereas the former credit applied to nonresidential buildings only.

---

[13] Pub. L. No. 95-600, 92 Stat. 2763, 26 U.S.C.A. § 1.

[i] Combining Credit With Depreciation Write-Offs. The combination of the rehabilitation credit with the faster write-off permitted under the accelerated cost recovery system (ACRS) is capable of generating extremely large write-offs during the early years of ownership. This is true despite the following two limitations:

☐ *Straight-line depreciation.* The rehabilitation credit is available only if the investor elects to use straight-line depreciation with respect to the rehabilitation expenditures. (Formerly, the investor could use accelerated depreciation.) However, this probably will make little difference, particularly in the case of nonresidential properties, since the use of accelerated depreciation now carries the penalty of full recapture upon resale.

☐ *Reduction of basis.* When the rehabilitation credit is taken, the basis of the property must be reduced by the amount of the credit (except for certified historic structures). Formerly, the basis of the property was not reduced, which means that depreciation write-offs will be slightly lower than otherwise; this effect will be more than offset by the new fifteen-year recovery period.

[ii] Planning a Rehabilitation. The new law limits the investment credit to a "substantial rehabilitation"; this is one in which the rehabilitation expenses during a two-year period are at least $5,000 and exceed the adjusted basis of the property as of the beginning of the period.

However, an investor may substitute a five-year period for the two-year period (thus permitting the required expenditure to be made over a much longer period) if:

- Written plans and specifications exist for the entire rehabilitation process; and
- There is a "reasonable expectation" that the entire rehabilitation will be completed.

It is not clear whether the adjusted basis of the property at the beginning of the rehabilitation period refers to the adjusted basis of the improvements only or of the improvements plus land. If the latter, the floor for eligible rehabilitation expenditures can be reduced substantially by leasing rather than purchasing the land under the buildings.

Treasury regulations under the former rehabilitation credit presumably will continue to apply to the extent that they do not conflict with the new law. Significant points covered by these provisions include the following:

☐ *Buildings eligible for credit.* Eligible buildings include factories, warehouses, office buildings, hotels, and retail and wholesale stores. Buildings used for residential purposes, such as apartments, are not eligible for the credit unless they are certified historic structures. The status of an eligible building is determined on the basis of its use when placed in service after the rehabilitation. For example, if an apartment building (not a historic structure) is rehabilitated for use as an office building, it is eligible for the credit.

☐ *External walls.* At least 75 percent of the external walls must be retained in order for the expenditures to qualify as a rehabilitation. However, existing walls can be resurfaced by applying new siding or a facade, or reinforced, and still permit the rehabilitation to qualify for the credit.

☐ *Rehabilitation of only a part of the building.* Where only a part of a building is rehabilitated, the rehabilitation expenditures will qualify for the credit if the part of the building that is rehabilitated constitutes a major portion of the building. Whether or not a portion constitutes a major portion depends on factors such as volume, floor space, and functional differences between the rehabilitated and unrehabilitated parts of the building. For example, where a substantial part of a building is used for retail stores and another part is used for warehousing, each part constitutes a major portion of the building for purposes of these provisions.

☐ *Definition of qualified rehabilitation expenditures.* The type of expenditures that qualify for the credit are interior or exterior renovation, or restoration expenditures that materially extend the useful life of the building or significantly upgrade its usefulness. For example, expenditures for replacement of plumbing, electrical wiring, flooring, permanent interior partitions in walls, and heating or air-conditioning systems qualify when they are incurred in connection with a rehabilitation that materially extends the useful life of a building and significantly upgrades its usefulness. However, in order to exclude minor repairs or improvements, the expenditures must be of the type that would be capitalized rather than expensed, and be incurred with respect to property with a useful life of at least five years.

☐ *Cost of acquiring or enlarging an existing building.* The cost of acquiring or enlarging an existing building is not considered a qualified rehabilitation expenditure, nor are costs incurred in connection with certain facilities, such as parking lots, that are related to an existing building. If in the course of a qualifying rehabilitation the floor space of an existing building is increased by reason of interior remodeling, such increased floor will not constitute an enlargement of the building.

[iii] Other New Provisions; Effective Date. Under the new rules, a lessee may qualify for the rehabilitation credit if the remaining term of the lease at completion of the rehabilitation (without regard to any renewal period) is at least fifteen years.

An owner may now claim the investment credit for rehabilitation expenditures to property leased to a tax-exempt organization or governmental unit (as to uses after July 29, 1980).

The new law applies to expenditures incurred after December 31, 1981. The old law continues to apply to rehabilitations begun prior to 1982 that qualify under the old law but not under the new law (e.g., rehabilitation of a twenty-year-old building). If a rehabilitation does qualify under the new law, expenditures incurred prior to 1982 qualify for a 10 percent credit, while expenditures incurred thereafter receive the higher credit (15, 20, or 25 percent). For a certified historic structure the election between the 10 percent credit or the sixty-month amortization applies to any pre-1982 expenditures, but only the 25 percent credit is available for expenditures in 1982 and thereafter.

[b] Historic Structure Rehabilitations

As noted above, rehabilitations of historic structures are eligible for a 25 percent investment credit. Such rehabilitations must meet two requirements:

☐ *Certified historic structure.* The building itself must be a certified historic structure, which is defined as a depreciable structure that is:

- Listed individually in the National Register of Historic Places; or
- Located in registered historic districts if the structure is certified as contributing to the significance of the district.

Registered historic districts include those on the National Register and those that are state or locally designated, if the ordinance or law authorizing or creating the district and the district itself are certified.

☐ *Certified rehabilitation.* The rehabilitation must be certified by the Secretary of the Interior as being consistent with the historic character of the property or the district.

The new 25 percent investment credit undoubtedly will be a powerful incentive to historic structure rehabilitations. In addition, persons who demolish a historic structure rather than preserve it will also lose the right to deduct demolition costs. (See 3.09[1][a]; historic structures are discussed in 11.16.)

[c] Impact of Tax Credit Plus Depreciation

The new rehabilitation tax credit can have an enormous impact on an investment return because the credit is (1) taken up front and so reduces the equity required; and (2) a dollar-for-dollar offset against taxes, not merely a deduction. In addition, the combination of the rehabilitation credit and the new fifteen-year recovery period can produce very large deductions as compared to former law, as is shown by this hypothetical case.

[i] Example of Rehabilitation With Tax Credit Plus Depreciation. In January 1981, a taxpayer purchases a fifty-year-old nonresidential building for $1.2 million. Beginning in January 1982, he restores it, spending $2 million, and places the improvements in service in January 1983. He elects to use straight-line depreciation over a fifteen-year period. The following tax consequences will result:

☐ *1981–1982 depreciation write-offs.* Assume that of the $1.2 million cost, $200,000 is allocated to nondepreciable land and $1 million to the depreciable structure. Under straight-line depreciation, the annual depreciation deduction in 1981 and 1982 will be $66,667.

☐ *Rehabilitation tax credit.* In 1983 the taxpayer is entitled to a 20 percent tax credit of the $2 million rehabilitation cost, or $400,000.

☐ *1983 and subsequent depreciation.* In 1983 the depreciable basis of the building is increased by $1.6 million (the $2 million rehabilitation cost minus the $400,000 credit). So in 1983 and thereafter the annual depreciation deduction, using straight-line depreciation, will be $173,334.

As Table 3.11 below shows, over the first three years a 50 percent taxpayer realizes savings of $260,000 over and above that realized under former law. Note that the 15 percent minimum tax on preference income will not apply to the investment under the new law because straight-line depreciation is used.

TABLE 3.11 Rehabilitation Tax Benefits Under ERTA

Depreciation 1981–1982 (6.67% annually on $1 million)	$133,334
Depreciation 1983 (6.67% on $2.6 million)	173,334
Total (3 years)	$306,668
Tax savings (50% tax bracket)	$153,334
Rehabilitation credit 1983 (20% of $2 million)	400,000
Total tax savings (3 years)	$553,334
Total 3-year tax savings under former law (40-year life; 150% depreciation; 15% minimum tax)	291,666
Increased tax savings	$261,668

[ii] Calculating Return on Investment. The magnitude of the tax savings shown in Table 3.11 can be appreciated even more by showing how such tax savings affect the return on investment even in today's high-interest-rate environment. Assume that at the completion of the rehabilitation, the fair market value of the property was $3.5 million, approximately 10 percent above the total investment in land and building of $3.2 million. (See Table 3.12.) The investor obtains a first mortgage of $2.45 million (70 percent of value) at 14 percent interest and 15 percent constant. Assume also that the property throws off a net operating income exactly equal to the debt service of $367,500. This would require a free-and-clear return of 10.5 percent, which would seem to be a minimum expectation. As a result, zero cash flow is realized. However, the large deductions for interest and depreciation will yield a taxable loss of $148,500 for the first year the rehabilitated property is in service. For an investor in the 50 percent bracket, this represents a 38 percent after-tax return on his net investment of $197,000 (after tax savings in years 1-3). Since straight-line depreciation is used and amortization begins at one percent, the annual loss will decline very slowly during the fifteen-year recovery period. On the other hand, net operating income should increase in future years, creating a positive cash flow. And if interest rates decline so that the first mortgage can be refinanced, it is possible that the investor can mortgage out in a few years.

[2] Amortization of Low-Income-Housing Rehabilitation Costs

As a stimulus to efforts to rehabilitate low-income rental housing, the Tax Reform Act of 1969 [14] added a new provision,[15] which permitted rehabilitation

[14] Pub. L. No. 91-172, 83 Stat. 487, 26 U.S.C.A. § 6050.

[15] I.R.C. § 167(k).

TABLE 3.12 Rehabilitation Property Investment

Total investment (land plus building)		$3,200,000
First mortgage (70% of $3.5 million; 14% interest; 15% constant)		$2,450,000
Equity required		750,000
Less: Tax savings (3 years) (from Table 3.11)		553,000
Net equity		$ 197,000
Cash Flow:		
Net operating income (10.5%)		$367,500
Less: Debt service		367,500
Cash flow (—)		$ 0
Tax Gain (Loss):		
Net operating income		$367,500
Deduct interest	$343,000	
Deduct depreciation	173,000	
Total deductions		516,000
Net loss		($148,500)
Tax savings (50% bracket)		$74,250
Return on $197,000 investment		38%

expenditures for such property to be written off over a sixty-month period. This provision will expire on December 31, 1983. ERTA 1981 raised the ceiling for such expenditures from $20,000 to $40,000 in certain cases. (See 3.04[2][b].) If the sixty-month write-off is used, it is in lieu of any otherwise allowable depreciation or amortization for the same expenditures. The cost of the building itself, however, as well as any expenditures that do not qualify for the sixty-month write-off, can be depreciated under the usual rules.

[a] Definition of Terms

☐ *Low-income rental housing.* Property eligible for the sixty-month write-off must consist of dwelling units held for rental to individuals and families of low or moderate income, as determined by the IRS in a manner consistent with the Leased Housing Program under Section 8 of the United States Housing Act of 1937.[16] Pursuant to this authority, IRS regulations described in great detail the rental policies that must be followed by the rehabilitated project. Living accommodations may not include a unit in a hotel or motel or similar establishment in which more than one-half of the units are used on a transient basis.

☐ *Rehabilitation expenditures.* The term "rehabilitation expenditures" means amounts chargeable to capital account relating to property or additions or im-

[16] As amended by Pub. L. No. 93-383, 88 Stat. 1633, 42 U.S.C. § 3535.

provements to property (or related facilities) with a useful life of five years or more. Rehabilitation expenditures do not include the cost of acquisition of low-income buildings or mortgage interest relating to such acquisition.

To qualify for the election, the expenditures must be incurred or paid before January 1, 1984; costs under a binding contract entered into before that date will qualify for the short-term write-off even though the money is actually spent later.

[b] Limitation on Expenditures

Rehabilitation expenses for any particular year do not qualify for the sixty-month write-off unless two tests are met:

☐ *$20,000 ($40,000) test.* No more than $20,000 of qualifying expenditures with respect to any dwelling unit may be written off the sixty-month period. Any excess is added to the basis of the structure and is depreciated under the usual rules. ERTA 1981 leaves this rule unchanged and adds an alternative ceiling of $40,000 per dwelling unit if:

- The rehabilitation is part of a program under which tenants who demonstrate home-ownership responsibilities may purchase their units at a price that limits the seller's profit; and
- The tenants occupy the units as their principal residence. (This provision applies to amount paid or incurred in 1981 and thereafter.)

☐ *$3,000 test.* No rehabilitation expenditures may qualify for the sixty-month write-off unless in two consecutive years the sum of such expenditures with respect to any dwelling unit equals $3,000.

> *Example:* In 1981, *L* incurs $1,200 of rehabilitation expenditures for a dwelling unit in a low-income housing project. The expenditures do not qualify for the sixty-month write-off since they are less than $3,000. In 1982 *L* spends an additional $1,500 for the same unit. Since the two-year total is $2,700—still less than $3,000—the expenditures do not qualify for the special write-off. In 1983, *L* completes the rehabilitation, putting in an additional $14,000. *L* may elect in 1983 to write off over sixty months the $1,500 in expenditures in 1982 and the $14,000 in expenditures in 1983 (since these together do not exceed the $20,000 ceiling).

No limit is imposed on the number of separate units that may be rehabilitated under this provision. Thus, if a taxpayer incurs the maximum amount of qualified expenditures ($20,000) for each of 100 units, the total of $2 million may be deducted over the sixty-month period.

3.05 INVESTMENT AND ENERGY TAX CREDITS

[1] Investment Tax Credit

[a] In General

The regular investment tax credit (as distinguished from the rehabilitation tax credit, discussed in 3.04[1]) is intended to be an incentive for capital expenditures by businessmen and investors. To qualify for the investment credit, the property acquired by the taxpayer must be Section 38 property—in essence, tangible personal property used in a trade or business. (Types of Section 38 property that might be purchased by real estate investors and so be eligible for the investment credit are listed below.) However, the law prohibits the credit from applying to property used predominantly for permanent lodgings, or used outside the United States. Furthermore, no investment credit is available if the property has a useful life of less than three years.

[i] Amount of Investment Credit. Under former law, the amount of the regular investment credit (expressed as a percentage of the acquisition cost) was as follows:

Estimated Useful Life (Years)	*Credit (%)*
3-4	3.33
5-6	6.66
7 or more	10

Under the new law, the amount of the investment credit for the four depreciation classes of personal property is as follows:

Recovery Period (Years)	*Credit (%)*
3	6
5, 10, and 15	10

(See 3.03[1] for a description of the types of property in each depreciation class.)

Example: Property qualifying for the investment credit is purchased for $10,000 in 1981. It has a three-year life for purposes of depreciation. Thus, a credit of $600 (6 percent of $10,000) may be used to offset $600 of tax otherwise payable on 1981 taxable income.

[ii] Other Investment Credit Rules

☐ *Used property.* The present ceiling of $100,000 of used property eligible for the investment credit will be increased to $125,000 in 1981 and to $150,000 in 1985. (There is no ceiling on the amount of new property eligible for the credit.)

☐ *Carryover of credit.* The investment credit may be used to offset the first $25,000 of tax liability plus (beginning in 1982) 90 percent of any tax in excess of $25,000. Any unused investment credits under present law may be carried back three years and forward seven years. Under the new law both the carryback and carryforward periods are extended to fifteen years. Remaining unchanged is the present law that any such carryovers may be used first against a current year's tax limit, before the current year's credit is applied. (This makes the carryover privilege more valuable since carryover credits are less likely to remain unused.)

[iii] Recapture of credit. Under present law, the investment credit is recomputed (and so a portion recaptured) on early disposition of property as if the actual useful life of the property had been used to determine the amount of credit.

Under the new law, the credit is recomputed on early disposition by allowing a 2 percent credit for each year the property actually is held. In other words, if five-, ten-, or fifteen-year property is actually held for at least five years, no recapture occurs (five years times 2 percent annual credit equals the 10 percent credit originally taken). Three-year property would have to be held for at least three years to avoid recapture.

Table 3.13 below shows the amount of investment credit recaptured each year.

TABLE 3.13 Recapture of Investment Tax Credit

	The recapture percentage is:	
If the recovery property ceases to be Section 38 property within:	*For 15-year 10-year and 5-year property*	*For 3-year property*
(i) One full year after placed in service	100%	100%
(ii) One full year after the close of the period described in clause (i)	80	66
(iii) One full year after the close of the period described in clause (ii)	60	33
(iv) One full year after the close of the period described in clause (iii)	40	—0—
(v) One full year after the close of the period described in clause (iv)	20	—0—

[iv] At-Risk Rules Now Apply. The new law has extended the at-risk rules to limit loss deductions on personal property financed with nonrecourse debt (see 3.09[3]) to the investment tax credit as well. The investment tax credit at-risk limitation applies to the same types of taxpayers and activities as does the at-risk limitation applicable to losses. Thus, it applies to individuals, Subchapter S corporations, and other closely held corporations.

In general, a taxpayer is not considered to be at risk with respect to any portion of an investment represented by nonrecourse financing. Thus, if business equipment that cost $100,000 was purchased for $20,000 cash with the balance represented by credit extended by the seller, then a 10 percent investment tax credit would be calculated on the $20,000 cash investment only (and it would make no difference whether the credit extended by the seller was unsecured or was secured by the business equipment being sold).

However, the new law contains a significant loophole to the at-risk rule. The full investment tax credit can be taken if the taxpayer is at least 20 percent at risk on the investment (either through cash investment or a recourse loan), and if the balance of the cost is financed by nonrecourse notes from qualified lenders (e.g., banks and savings associations, insurance companies, and most other third-party lenders in the business of making loans). The new at-risk rules for the investment tax credit apply to property placed in service after February 18, 1981. Inasmuch as real estate activities are not subject to the at-risk limitation, the rehabilitation tax credit is also not subject to the limitation.

[b] How to Maximize Credits for Real Estate

As noted above, the investment credit is available only for tangible personal property, as defined by Section 38 of the Internal Revenue Code. Real estate investors, however, often fail to realize how large a proportion of their investment in real estate may properly be apportioned to Section 38 property. According to Marshall & Stevens, Inc., a national appraisal firm, the following percentage of assets frequently qualified for the investment tax credit:

Type of Building	*Qualifying Assets*
Shopping center	5 to 10%
Office building	10 to 20
Light manufacturing plant	20 to 35
Heavy manufacturing plant	30 to 60
Research center	35 to 70
Processing plant	40 to 100

Many firms depend on nontechnical personnel to properly classify assets as real estate or personal property. Probably the best way is to have on-the-spot engineering inspections to identify property eligible for the investment credit.

For new construction, once the individual components have been identified, the next job is to segregate total construction costs into the various components. The steps involved are as follows:

- Identifying actual component costs where available
- Analyzing each subcontract in order to allocate costs to their respective components
- Prorating all indirect costs to the various components

The second step is often the most difficult because subcontractors often are unable or unwilling to break down their cost. However, lending appraisal and accounting skills should enable the real estate owner to come up with figures that can be supported in an IRS examination and that will give the owner the maximum credit available.

CHECKLIST FOR THE AVAILABILITY OF THE INVESTMENT CREDIT

	Qualifies for Credit?		
Description of Property	*Yes*	*No*	*Uncertain*
1. Storage bins and farm silos	X		
2. Fences used in connection with raising livestock	X		
3. Water wells to provide water for raising poultry and livestock	X		
4. Paved barnyards	X		
5. Trailer park electrical hookups, plumbing hookups, and water wells		X	
6. Electrical, plumbing, and sprinkler systems in a factory		X	
7. Special electrical and plumbing installations for specific machinery	X		
8. Outdoor lighting for parking lots		X	
9. Wall-to-wall carpeting attached to wood strips by hooks	X		
10. Wall-to-wall carpeting glued to floor	X		
11. Sprinkler system in building		X	
12. Special fire extinguisher to protect against fire at location of hazardous item of equipment	X		
13. Expenditures for dismantling, transporting, and installing used Section 38 property	X		
14. Movable office partitions	X		
15. Ski chair-lift towers and loading ramps			X
16. Amusement park rides	X		
17. Grading and ramps for amusement park rides			X
18. Aircraft hanger		X	
19. Paving around aircraft hanger	X		
20. Costs of excavating and grading paved areas		X	
21. Orchard of citrus trees	X		
22. Leased propane-gas storage tanks, water heaters, and water softeners	X		
23. Computer, including software cost that is not separately stated	X		
24. Roadways in manufacturing complex used by trucks transporting materials and finished products	X		
25. Parking lot for employees and visitors		X	
26. Canopies over loading or storage docks		X	
27. Raised floor for installation of computer equipment in factory	X		
28. Movable trailers used as on-site construction offices	X		
29. Trailer mounted on permanent concrete block foundation		X	

Description of Property	Qualifies for Credit? Yes	No	Uncertain
30. Furniture leased by taxpayer to tenants of apartment buildings		X	
31. Automotive equipment used for performing maintenance services in apartment complex		X	
32. "Butler building" for raw material storage		X	
33. Lighting to illuminate the exterior of a building	X		
34. Identity signs and "logo" symbols on retail establishments and restaurants	X		
35. Outdoor advertising billboards			X
36. Elevators in apartment buildings		X	
37. Elevators and escalators in other types of buildings	X		

[2] Energy Tax Credits

The Energy Tax Act of 1978, as amended in 1980,[17] created two energy tax credits—one for business property and one for residential property—to encourage persons to invest in energy-saving devices.

[a] Business Energy Credit

Business firms may claim a tax credit (in the amount specified below) for certain energy-saving equipment placed in service between October 1, 1978 and January 1, 1983 (except for solar- or wind-energy property, for which the credit is available until January 1, 1986.) The energy credit is in addition to the regular investment credit. The equipment must be of a kind eligible for depreciation or amortization and must have the useful life of three years or more.

The property eligible for the credit must be one of the following: [18]

- Alternative energy property (10 percent energy credit)
- Solar- or wind-energy property (15 percent energy credit)
- Specifically defined energy property (10 percent energy credit)
- Recycling equipment (10 percent energy credit)

A property owner should ask the seller whether the equipment has been certified by the Secretary of the Treasury before purchasing equipment that is believed to qualify for a tax credit. Under Internal Revenue Service proposed regulations, manufacturers can obtain IRS certification that their product meets the statutory requirements necessary to qualify for the credit. Lenders might also be interested in determining whether the property has been certified by the Treasury as qualifying for the tax credit.

---

17 Pub. L. No. 95-618, 92 Stat. 3174, 19 U.S.C.A. § 1202.

18 Some specialized types of equipment are omitted from this list.

The law permits state and local governments to issue tax-exempt bonds to finance the construction of (1) solid-waste-disposal facilities; (2) steam-generating facilities; (3) hydroelectric-generating facilities; and (4) solar-wind-, or geothermal-energy projects. However, there are various limits on the amount of such bonds that may be issued and there are regulations governing the type of government guarantees to be provided bond holders.

[b] Residential Energy Credit

To encourage homeowners and tenants to conserve energy by insulating their residences and installing solar devices and other sources of renewable energy, Section 44C provides a credit for specified expenditures serving these objectives. The credit is allowed for two types of expenditures: (1) qualified energy-conservation expenditures—for insulation and other energy-conserving components such as storm windows, thermostats, and improved furnace ignition systems—for which the credit is 15 percent of the first $2,000 of qualifying expenditures; and (2) qualified renewable-energy-source expenditures—for such heating and cooling devices as solar, geothermal, and wind systems—for which the credit is 40 percent of the first $10,000 of qualifying expenditures.

Expenditures of both types qualify only if the affected dwelling is located in the United States and is used by the taxpayer as his principal residence; prior expenditures on the same residence for which the taxpayer was allowed a credit reduce the dollar amount qualifying for the credit in later years. An additional condition, applicable only to conservation expenditures, is that construction of the dwelling must have been substantially completed before April 20, 1977. Without this limitation, Section 44C would provide an incentive for the construction of poorly insulated houses, since the purchaser could then qualify for a subsidy by rectifying the deficiency. As amended in 1980, Section 44C (1) allows credits to two or more persons with separate principal residences who share the expense of joint qualifying energy-conservation or renewable-energy-source installations serving both premises; and (2) precludes "double dipping" by claims for credits for installations financed with subsidized government loans or nontaxable government grants.

The credit for a taxable year cannot exceed the taxpayer's tax liability (reduced by most other credits) and is not refundable, but unused credits can be carried forward to later taxable years.

3.06 DEDUCTION FOR INTEREST

[1] In General

The deduction available to the owner of real estate for interest paid on mortgage loans, or other debt incurred in connection with the property, is fully deductible whether or not the real estate is held in connection with the taxpayer's trade or business, or for the production of rental income, or for personal use (such as a residence). In either of the first two cases, the taxpayer normally will choose to deduct interest as a trade or business expense under Code Section 162 or as a rental property expense under Code Section 212. By doing so, these expenses become deductions from gross income and thus may be used even though the taxpayer takes the standard deduction. On the other hand, interest on property used for personal use must be deducted from adjusted gross income, and thus is available only when the taxpayer does not use the standard deduction.

Even if the taxpayer does itemize his deductions, he will benefit by taking interest deductions for trade, business, or rental property from gross income (rather than as an itemized expense from adjusted gross income); by doing so, his adjusted gross income is reduced for the purpose of computing the "floor" for his medical-expense deduction, which is calculated by taking 3 percent of the adjusted gross income figure. In addition, in those rare cases where a taxpayer is liable for the alternative minimum tax, he will seek to have his itemized deductions kept as low as possible, since a preference item for computing the alternative minimum tax is the excess of certain itemized deductions over 60 percent of adjusted gross income.

For interest to be deductible, it must be paid on "true" indebtedness. The debt must be valid and enforceable, and it must be that of the taxpayer. Generally, in real estate transactions interest is specifically stated as such. However, even where interest is disguised as something different (to avoid the state usury laws, for example), it is still interest if it is paid as compensation for the use or forbearance of money.

On home-mortgage loans (e.g., Veterans Administration or Federal Housing Authority loans), a portion of each payment consists of deductible interest. However, on many home-mortgage loans, an initial loan fee is assessed, usually at the rate of 0.5 to 2 percent of the amount of the loan. This is deductible in full by the borrower, if he can show that it is a financing fee incurred solely for the use of money as contrasted with a service fee being paid for performance of a service. In that regard, Revenue Ruling 72-315 [19] may help. In this ruling, the IRS changed its previous position that finance and service charges by retail stores could not be deducted unless the amount of interest was specifically determined by the payor. Now, the Service will permit the full finance charge to be deducted without the paying taxpayer showing that what he paid for was "interest."

Prepaid interest deductions, at one time a popular form of front-end deduction, were dispatched completely by the Tax Reform Act of 1976 (TRA 1976).[20] Cash-basis taxpayers must now deduct prepaid interest ratably over the period of a loan, regardless of when the interest actually is paid—thus conforming to the present rule for interest prepayments by an accrual-method taxpayer. The new rule covers all types of taxpayers and includes interest paid for personal, business, or investment purposes. It also applies to prepaid interest on a wraparound mortgage.

In general, points (additional interest charges paid when a loan is closed) must also be deducted ratably over the term of the loan. The one exception to this rule is that points paid by a cash-method taxpayer on a mortgage covering his principal residence may be deducted entirely in the year paid, provided that the practice of charging points is customary in the locality and the number of points charged the taxpayer does not exceed the normal amount.

---

[19] 1972-1 C.B. 49.

[20] Pub. L. No. 94-455, 90 Stat. 1520, 26 U.S.C.A. §§ 1 et seq.

[2] Construction Period Interest (and Taxes)

Before 1976, amounts paid for interest and taxes attributable to the construction of real property were currently deductible (unless the taxpayer elected to capitalize these items as carrying charges, which he would do to the extent that he lacked current income against which to offset the deductions). TRA 1976 requires that such interest and taxes be capitalized and amortized over a ten-year period.[21] The first year of the period is the year in which the taxes or interest are paid or incurred; subsequent amortization begins in the year in which the property is placed in service or available for sale.

The TRA 1976 excluded from the new rule construction of personal residences and vacation homes. In addition, the rule was to be applicable to low-income housing beginning in 1988; however, the Economic Recovery Tax Act of 1981[22] permanently exempted low-income housing from the rule. Thus, construction period interest and taxes in connection with personal residences, vacation homes, and low-income housing is immediately deductible by the property owner. Furthermore, Section 189 applies only to individuals, Subchapter S corporations, and personal holding companies, but not to other corporations, trusts, or estates.

The TRA 1976 set up transitional or phase-in rules for nonresidential and residential real estate, shown in Table 3.14 below.

TABLE 3.14 Phase-In Schedule for Capitalization Rule

If construction period interest and taxes are paid or accrued in the indicated taxable year, the percentage of such amount allowable for deduction in each amortization year is as follows:

Nonresidential Real Property	*Residential Real Property*	*Annual Amortization Percent Allowable*
Taxable Year Beginning		
1976 *	1978	25%
1977	1979	20
1978	1980	16 2/3
1979	1981	14 2/7
1980	1982	12 1/2
1981	1983	11 1/9
after 1981	after 1983	10

* Special rule permits deduction of 50 percent in 1976 and amortization of remaining 50 percent over three years.

The application of the transitional rules and the phase-in of the amortization period can be illustrated by the following example. Assume that $120,000 of interest and taxes are paid or incurred in 1980 with respect to the construction of residential real estate and that the property is ready to be placed in service in

[21] I.R.C. § 189.

[22] Pub. L. No. 97-34, 95 Stat. 172, 26 U.S.C. § 128.

1982. The $120,000 must be capitalized, but a deduction for taxable year 1980 is to be allowed for $20,000 (1/6 of the amount capitalized). The remaining $100,000 (i.e., 5/6 of the total) is to be deducted ratably over a five-year period beginning in 1982 (the year in which the property is placed in service). Thus, $20,000 is to be allowed as a deduction for taxable year 1982.

When determining which interest and tax payments must be capitalized, which may be expensed, and for which an immediate deduction is available, the following questions must be considered:

☐ *When does construction begin?* Until construction actually begins, interest and taxes are deductible. The IRS regulations (promulgated under the depreciation provisions of the Internal Revenue Code) provide that construction is deemed to commence when physical work begins; thus, land assemblage and soil testing are preconstruction activities, and interest and taxes paid or incurred during that period are deductible.

☐ *What constitutes construction?* Probably adding to an existing building would be considered to amount to construction for purposes of the TRA 1976 capitalization rule. In that case, there would have to be an allocation of interest and taxes between the new addition (not deductible) and the existing improvement (deductible).

☐ *What will be the allocation of general borrowing?* A developer may have obtained unsecured loans, the proceeds of which he uses in his overall business, or he may have obtained loans secured by blanket mortgages (i.e., those covering several properties). In most cases, there will be problems of allocating the amount of interest paid or incurred between new construction (not deductible) and existing buildings (deductible).

[3] Effect of Tax-Exempt Investments

Real estate investors who also own tax-exempt securities must be particularly careful to avoid a relatively little-known rule that might result in their loss of the deduction for interest paid. The Internal Revenue Code specifically denies a tax deduction for interest on a debt if the indebtedness is incurred or continued to purchase or carry tax-exempt securities.[23] The courts generally say that this rule does not bar interest deductions *merely* because a taxpayer happens to own or buy tax-exempt securities. The debt must be incurred or continued for the purpose of buying or carrying "exempts"; that is, a sufficiently direct relationship must exist between the borrowing and the exempts. IRS, however, despite lip service to these principles, has applied its own guidelines to challenge interest deductions in cases where the relationship does not seem to be direct at all.[24]

[a] IRS Rules

A person who owns tax-exempt securities, and who incurs a debt of a personal (non-investment) nature, such as a mortgage to buy or improve his residence, en-

---

[23] I.R.C. § 265(2).

[24] Rev. Proc. 72-18, 1972-1 C.B. 740, as clarified by Rev. Proc. 74-8, 1974-1 C.B. 419.

counters no problems. But if he uses the loan for any investment, the borrowing is "presumed" to be for the purpose of carrying the exempts, because he could have sold them instead of borrowing for the new investment. The fact that selling the bonds would mean a large loss is not considered to be important by the IRS. This is the thrust—and the toughest part—of the rules for individual investors. Here are a few other points to note:

☐ The presumption of the direct relationship between the borrowing and the exempts (i.e., where there is, in fact, no direct link between the two) will not apply if the exempts are not more than 2 percent of the investment portfolio (including real estate investments) plus business assets, all valued at cost or other tax basis, rather than at market value.

☐ The above presumption will not apply if the loan is used in an actively conducted business (except for dealers in tax-exempts, who have special rules), unless the taxpayer could reasonably have foreseen, when buying the exempts, that it would be necessary to borrow to meet the regular needs of the business.

☐ Partners are treated as holding the exempts and incurring the debts of the partnership in proportion to their respective capital interests, and the partnership purpose for incurring indebtedness will be attributed to the general partners.

How much is disallowed? To the extent that there is a direct link between the borrowing and the exempts (e.g., using the exempts as collateral or tracing their purchase to the loan proceeds), the entire interest deduction will be knocked out. In the more typical situation without a direct tie-in, such as where a person owning municipals free and clear later borrows to make taxable investments, the IRS disallows the interest expense in the ratio that the average amount of exempts for the year bears to total assets (less "untainted" debt), with all valuations at cost or tax basis, rather than at market value.

For example, suppose *A* owned $100,000 in municipals, and all other assets, less the home mortgage, had cost $400,000. If *A* borrows $50,000 at 7 percent to invest in real estate, one-fifth ($700) of the $3,500 interest deduction would be lost because the exempts are one-fifth of total assets less the untainted home mortgage. On the other hand, if *A* borrowed the $50,000 to purchase a home, none of the interest deduction would be lost.

[b] Rules Can Also Apply to Home Loans

While this is generally true, in certain circumstances IRS may contend that someone who takes out a mortgage on his residence and who owns tax-exempts is borrowing to continue to carry tax-exempts, thus making the mortgage interest nondeductible. For example, in *Mariorenzi v. Comm'r,*[25] taxpayer had a new family residence built, which was fully paid for out of his current earnings. Shortly thereafter, Mr. Mariorenzi obtained a mortgage loan on his new home, even though he still had ample funds in his checking and savings accounts; at about the same time, he was buying tax-exempts. IRS asserted that the loan was incurred to

[25] T.C. Memo 1973-141.

enable him to continue to carry and make new investments in tax-exempts. Accordingly, the Service disallowed interest deductions attributable to the mortgage loan. In upholding IRS, the Tax Court found a "sufficiently direct relationship" between the incurring of the debt and the purchasing or carrying of tax-exempt securities. The Tax Court indicated that there would be no disallowance if a taxpayer who already had a mortgaged home occasionally bought exempt securities.

[c] Shopping Center Holding Tax-Exempts

Another situation in which there generally is no disallowance is where a taxpayer who holds tax-exempts borrows to meet the reasonable needs of its business. But if borrowing generates excess funds, then there can be some disallowance, as happened in *Indian Trail Trading Post, Inc. v. Comm'r,*[26] where the borrower owned a shopping center. Part of the borrowed funds was used to repay an earlier loan, but since the borrowing generated cash in excess of current business needs, Indian Trail also invested some of the proceeds in tax-exempts. This investment was continued for a substantial time. While Indian Trail claimed an interest deduction with respect to the entire debt, the Tax Court denied the portion attributable to the tax-exempts. Not only were the proceeds of the borrowing directly traceable to the purchase of tax-exempts, but the facts indicated that the debt was "continued" for the proscribed purpose.

[d] Recent Case Provides Guidance

More recently, a taxpayer was successful in the Tax Court in defeating an IRS attempt to associate investments in tax-exempts with loans to pay taxes. The taxpayer, Mrs. Norris, owned almost three million shares of Texaco stock, from which she made substantial gifts to her family; in connection with these gifts, she had to pay gift taxes of nearly $16 million. Mrs. Norris took out bank loans in excess of $5 million in order to pay the taxes. At the same time, Mrs. Norris had an "agency account" managed for her by the bank making the loans; she had no control over the account, since it was managed on a discretionary basis by the bank's investment department. During the same period in which Mrs. Norris was borrowing funds from the bank, the investment advisers were purchasing in excess of $2 million in tax-exempt securities. IRS sought to deny Mrs. Norris the tax deductions for the interest paid on the substantial loans she had taken out, but the Tax Court ruled that under these facts, there was no showing of a "purposive connection" or a "sufficiently direct relationship" between the taxpayer's indebtedness and her ownership of tax-exempt obligations.[27]

[4] Investment Interest Limitation

Real estate investors rightly view tax-deductible interest payments on debts connected with real property as one of the key advantages of owning real estate. However, a limitation on such deductions was introduced by the Tax Reform Act

---

[26] 503 F.2d 102 (6th Cir. 1974).
[27] Estate of Norris, T.C. Memo 1981-368.

of 1969,[28] called the limitation on excess investment interest.[29] The essential purpose of the limitation is to restrict the amount of the interest deduction to the amount of investment income the taxpayer receives in the same year; interest on loans to carry property that generates little current income, but has potential of producing future capital gains, is not deductible until the gains are in fact realized. Thus, income and expense are to be matched; this is a principal object of tax reform.

Investment interest is defined as interest paid or accrued on debt incurred to purchase or carry property held for investment. Note that interest deductions on all forms of investments are subject to the rule; it is not merely loans on real estate that are affected.

Investment interest may be deducted only to the extent of

- An initial exemption of $10,000 ($5,000 for married persons filing separately).
- Net investment income from dividends, interest, rents, royalties, net short-term capital gain from investment property, and Sections 1245 and 1250 gain less investment expenses.
- Actual cash losses incurred in connection with property subject to a net lease.

Interest deductions disallowed under these rules are subject to an unlimited carryover and may be deducted in future years (subject to the applicable limitation each year).

The limit on the interest deduction operates only in the case of taxpayers other than corporations—that is, individuals, partners, shareholders of Subchapter S corporations, and trusts. In addition, trusts are not entitled to the initial $10,000 exemption, so this form of real estate ownership will be under a slight disadvantage in this respect.

> *Example:* Assume that in 1981 a taxpayer who has paid $50,000 in interest charges on loans to carry a portfolio of stocks and a net leased property receives $15,000 in dividend income and $15,000 in net lease rentals, for a total of $30,000. After adding to this net investment income the initial exemption of $10,000, the taxpayer has excess investment interest of $10,000 ($50,000 minus $40,000). This $10,000 is carried forward to future years.

[a] What Is Investment Real Property?

The limitation on excess investment interest applies only to investment real property. For purposes of this term, real estate may be classified as follows:

☐ *Real estate for personal use.* This is not investment real estate, and interest on loans used to carry such property is not subject to any limitation under this rule.

☐ *Trade or business property.* The limitation has no application to most rental property (for example, an apartment building or office building owned and

[28] Pub. L. No. 91-172, 83 Stat. 487, 26 U.S.C.A. § 6050.
[29] I.R.C. § 163(d).

operated by the taxpayer). Such property is considered trade or business property rather than investment property.

☐ *Net leased property.* This type of investment is probably the most significant type of real estate affected by the limitation. In general, property will be considered subject to a net lease if business deductions with respect to the leased property are less than 15 percent of the rental income from the property. Business deductions do not include ground rents or expenses for which the taxpayer is reimbursed by the lessee.

☐ *Undeveloped land.* Another type of property that ordinarily will be deemed investment real estate is raw land held for speculation. Thus, interest on loans used to finance such land may be subject to the excess interest limitation. An investor who acquires land and intends to erect commercial property may have a difficult time proving it is not investment property as long as it remains undeveloped. However, if a history of maintaining an inventory of such property for development can be shown, the investor may be able to classify it as trade or business property.

3.07 DEDUCTION FOR PROPERTY TAXES

A taxpayer may deduct state, local, and foreign real property taxes;[30] the deduction is permitted whether or not the property involved is business, investment, or personal-use property. However, only taxes paid on trade or business property, or property held for the production of rents may be deducted from gross income (rather than from adjusted gross income), which permits the deduction to be used even though the taxpayer uses the standard deduction. (See 3.06[1].)

A taxpayer may also deduct state and local personal property taxes, whether or not such taxes are incurred in a business or income-producing activity. However, other state and local taxes, such as mortgage recording and transfer taxes, are deductible only if incurred in carrying on a trade or business, or in connection with property held for production of income.

Real property taxes are taxes imposed on interests in real property and levied for the general public welfare. Thus, a sewerage service charge based on usage by a property owner is not deductible as a tax (although it may be deductible as a business expense). Taxes generally are deductible only by the person upon whom the taxes are imposed or, if imposed upon property, by the owner of the property. Thus, on a separate return, no deduction is allowed for a husband paying tax on property owned by his wife. If a lease provides that the tenant shall pay real estate taxes on the property, the tenant cannot deduct the amount paid as taxes since they are not his taxes. However, if the rent is a deductible item (because the property is used in a trade or business, or for the production of income), he can deduct the taxes as an additional rental payment. The landlord is entitled to take the deduction for taxes paid (but he must offset against this the income received as additional rental from the tenant).

---

[30] I.R.C. § 164.

If two persons own property as joint tenants or tenants by the entirety, each may deduct the taxes that each person pays. If one pays more than his share, even up to the full amount, that person may take a deduction equal to the amount paid. (This same rule applies to payments of interest on a mortgage on property held in concurrent ownership.)

[1] Special Assessments

Part or all of the cost of municipal improvements that increase the value of properties adjacent to the improvement may be assessed against those properties. Such a special assessment is not deductible because of the fact that it tends to increase the value of the property. Such special assessments must be capitalized and treated as part of the cost of the property, and will then be taken into account in determining gain or loss on disposition.

[2] Construction Period Taxes

Section 189 of the Internal Revenue Code requires certain real estate taxes (and interest on debt) paid during construction to be capitalized rather than deducted at once. (See 3.06[2].)

3.08 DEDUCTION FOR REPAIRS

[1] In General

When real estate is in need of some major repair, the owner naturally considers all the options. The funds for the costly repair will be spent in a single year, but there may not be any offsetting tax benefits until some time later. The IRS-approved method for handling large repair bills to income-producing real estate usually denies an immediate deduction for the entire amount.

According to Treasury regulations, repairs in the nature of replacements, to the extent that they arrest deterioration and appreciably prolong the life of the property, must be capitalized and deducted ratably over the property's remaining useful life. Only the cost of incidental repairs that neither materially add to the value of the property nor prolong its useful life, but just keep it in an efficient operating condition, may be deducted as an expense.[31] And, again, the regulations state that the cost of making permanent improvements is not deductible.[32]

These regulations are the theoretical rules governing IRS policy in a given instance as to whether a repair must be capitalized or expensed. However, as a practical matter, the Service is much more apt to hold that any large expenditure is an item that should be capitalized. This may seem logical, but it is not always correct.

In all such instances, the facts surrounding the undertaking of the work are very important. A renovation may be a deductible repair under some circumstances, and a capital replacement in others. Nevertheless, some types of work typify repairs rather than replacements. These include repainting the outside and

---

[31] Reg. § 1.162-4.

[32] Reg. § 1.162-11(b).

inside of a building, mending leaks, plastering, and repairing gutters. But the cost of a new roof, a general lighting improvement in the building, and strengthening walls are capital expenditures.

Extensive reconditioning of a building right after it is purchased does not necessarily indicate capital expenditures. Such work still could be repairs; but, here too, the facts are very important. For example, if a purchaser takes over liability on an existing contract for repairs and reconditioning, he probably can take an immediate deduction. On the other hand, general reconditioning to make property suitable for the purchaser's purpose has been held to be a capital expenditure, even though part of the work, standing alone, might be considered to be repairs.

Real estate owners should know that segregation (and immediate deductibility) of repair expenses has been accepted by IRS in some cases.

In one case, a corporation leased a plant for an initial period of fifteen years with an option to renew the lease for three five-year periods. The lease agreement provided that the lessee was to take good care of the premises and to keep it in good order and condition, making all necessary repairs. "Repairs" were to include replacement or renewals.

About three years after the company occupied the building, the roof began to leak. Repairs were made, but other leaks developed. A roofing expert determined that the most economical way to fix the roof was to replace the asphalt, gravel, and perlite with a wood-framed, copper-covered roof-expansion joint and then to cover the entire roof with fiberboard insulation and an asphalt and gravel top. The cost would be $20,791.

The company had the work done, then deducted the entire cost on its tax return. IRS disallowed the deduction, ruling the cost should properly have been capitalized and depreciated over the remaining term of the lease. But the Tax Court disagreed and permitted the full deduction.

The corporation's only purpose in having the work done, said the court, was to prevent leakage and keep the property in operating condition, not to prolong its useful life, increase its value, or make it adaptable to another use. There was no replacement or substitution of the roof. Inserting an expansion joint was a structural change, but this was the most economical way to repair the roof and keep the building in operating condition. Also, the work did not materially add to the value of the property within the meaning of the Regulations. When the property was leased, the roof did not leak; the repair restored it to that condition.[33]

Anyone who is contemplating or has recently made any costly repairs should reconsider full deductibility in light of *Oberman*. If the repair basically restores the property to its original condition and is not an improvement or addition that adds to the life of the property, this case provides strong authority for a full deduction.

[2] How to Fractionalize Large Expenditures

[a] Reconditioning or Improvement

A key point often overlooked by investors is that, just as a forest is made up of individual trees, so an extensive plan of improvement or reconditioning may

[33] Oberman Mfg. Co. v. Comm'r, 47 T.C. 471 (1967).

quite properly be regarded as a series of separate repairs. The idea, then, is to try to fractionalize any extensive job by breaking it down into its component parts, doing each part separately and independently, preferably over a series of years.

Example: In one case involving a dilapidated building, to meet the needs of tenants, Mr. Cobleigh, the new owner, employed a contractor to perform various jobs, including painting, roof patching, installing a new glass brick front and new tile, and replacing screen doors and gutters. Cobleigh claimed the work was a series of small repair jobs, not contemplated as an overall plan. But in a trial before the Tax Court, the evidence showed that the oral agreement with the contractor contemplated that he would perform all the work as part of an overall plan to recondition the dilapidated building into an efficient business structure. Consequently, the court ruled that the entire amount was a capital expenditure, even though part of the expenditure was for work that ordinarily could be characterized as "repairs" when taken separately.[34]

[b] Fractionalizing a Remodeling Job

Just as "fixing up" property can be fractionalized, so can the process of "breaking down" improvements in the course of remodeling. Normally, a landlord's remodeling costs are treated as capital expenditures. Even if remodeling involves destruction of a portion of the structure, no demolition loss is allowed if the demolition is required as a condition of getting a new lease.

But consider the following situation: Mr. Gorman agreed to knock down a wall of his building and add a new structure to obtain F.W. Woolworth Co. as a tenant. The wall contained a decorative logotype of the previous tenant, constructed by Mr. Gorman under the requirements of the prior lease. Gorman claimed (1) a demolition loss for the portion of his building destroyed in the remodeling process; and (2) an ordinary loss deduction for "extraordinary obsolescence" of the specially made wall. His theory was that the special wall was abandoned when its useful life was suddenly terminated by the needs of the new tenant. The Tax Court rejected the first deduction but allowed the second.[35]

As the *Cobleigh* case shows, the landlord's treatment of the work on his own records can wipe out a repair deduction that might otherwise be available. Whenever extensive work is undertaken, careful analysis may show that the work can properly be accounted for as a number of separate jobs. If, however, the work truly constitutes a general and integrated improvement program, no repair deduction will be available.

[3] Repair vs. Casualty Deduction

Assume a business property is damaged by a fire or other casualty, and the damage is repaired immediately. Should the tax return deduct the damage as a loss, or the repair cost as a business expense? The choice can be significant.

---

[34] Clair H. Cobleigh v. Comm'r, T.C. Memo 1956-261.
[35] Gerald R. Gorman v. Comm'r, T.C. Memo 1974-18.

Casualty-loss deductions are limited to the lesser of (1) the difference between the fair market value of the property before and after the casualty; or (2) the adjusted basis of the property. On the other hand, a business-expense deduction for repairs need only be ordinary and necessary to be fully deductible, assuming it escapes characterization as a capital expenditure. Moreover, a loss is deductible only when "sustained." If at the end of the year there is a possibility of recovery, through insurance or otherwise, the loss is not "sustained." There is no such constraint on the deduction of business expenses.

In a recent case, a company's machinery and equipment were extensively damaged by a flood. In the Tax Court, the Internal Revenue Service argued that the owner's loss was not "sustained" because the owner was litigating a claim for recovery against its insurance company. But the owner had claimed its repair cost as an ordinary and necessary business expense and the Tax Court allowed the deduction in full.[36]

When casualty-damaged business property is repaired and the loss does not exceed the repair cost, the business-expense deduction route should be chosen if a there is a possibility of recovery. This approach will not work, however, if the IRS can successfully characterize the repair cost as a capital expenditure.

3.09 DEDUCTION FOR LOSSES

Losses discussed fall into two categories: (1) losses incurred in a trade or business, or in a transaction entered into for profit; and (2) theft or casualty losses. (Sale or disposition losses are discussed at 8.03[2].)

[1] Business or Transaction Losses

Generally speaking, a taxpayer who incurs operating losses (operating expenses in excess of gross income) from a trade or business (including the holding of property for rental purposes) or from a transaction entered into for profit is entitled to an ordinary loss deduction; that is, the loss may be used to offset other income of the taxpayer. Two special types of losses particularly applicable to real estate are demolition and abandonment losses; each of these is discussed separately below. The special rules affecting "hobby losses," which may restrict the use of a loss deduction otherwise available, is also discussed.

[a] Demolition Losses

Demolition of a building can result in one of the following:

- An immediate loss deduction
- Depreciation or amortization deductions over a period of years
- An increase in the basis of the underlying land, which increases loss or reduces gain on its ultimate disposition

Each treatment stems from the intent of the owner at the time of acquisition or from contractual obligations to third parties.

---

[36] R.R. Hensler, Inc. v. Comm'r, 73 T.C. 168 (1979).

Assume that Owner (*O*) bought land and a building in 1961 and used them in business for the past ten years. The building has an adjusted basis (usually, cost plus any additions less depreciation) of $100,000. *O* decides to demolish the building and erect a new office building for his business on the same site. *O* is entitled to deduct the entire $100,000 basis as a loss upon demolition (plus the net cost of demolition less any net proceeds from the demolition).

This is obviously the most preferred tax treatment, since the owner gets an immediate full deduction.

Now assume that instead of using the present site *O* buys other land with an old building for $100,000, demolishes the old building, and constructs a new one in its place. Here, *O* gets no immediate deduction at all; however, the basis for the land would be the full $100,000 he paid, increased by the cost of demolition of the old building.

What *O*'s intention was at the time the site was acquired explains the big difference in tax treatment on similar facts. The amount that can be deducted as a demolition loss under Code Section 165 and the conditions giving rise to a deduction are spelled out in Reg. § 1.165-3. These rules indicate that the key to the deduction is that the owner not have an intention to demolish at the time he acquires the building. Otherwise, as shown above, the entire cost of demolition must be allocated to the land.

[i] Partial Demolition. Suppose that after ten years of use Owner (*O*) decides to demolish only part of the building. This could occur either where he intended to replace this part with a more modern one or where he intended to leave the land vacant for additional parking space. In either case, he would be entitled to an immediate deduction equal to the unrecovered basis of the demolished portion (again increased by the demolition cost and reduced by any proceeds of demolition).[37]

Depreciation Deductions. A middle ground between immediate deductibility and full capitalization occurs where the owner has the intent to demolish at the time of purchase of the land and building, but also intends to rent it out or use it for a period prior to demolition.

Suppose *O* buys land and building for $100,000, and at the time of purchase intends to demolish within four years and to rent during the interim period. Assuming that the value of the net rent for the building for the four years is $18,000, the taxpayer would allocate $82,000 ($100,000 – 18,000) to the land and depreciate the $18,000 over the four-year rental period, taking a $4,500 deduction each year.

Now, suppose that instead of waiting four years to knock down the old building, as originally intended, the owner does so after only two years. The undepreciated portion, $9,000, could then be deducted as a loss in the year of demolition.

[ii] Guideline to Intentions. As indicated, the key to the deduction is an absence of intent to demolish at the time of acquisition. Intent is gleaned from

---

[37] See Wm. S. Gilman v. Comm'r, 72 T.C. 730 (1979).

the particular facts and circumstances. There are no set rules. However, IRS does have some guidelines, which can serve as useful planning guides.

These factors show an intent to demolish at the time of acquisition:

- A short delay between the date of acquisition and the date of demolition
- Evidence of prohibitive remodeling costs determined at the time of acquisition
- Existence of municipal regulations at the time of acquisition, which would prohibit the continued use of the building for profit purposes
- Unsuitability of the buildings for the taxpayer's trade or business at the time of acquisition
- Inability at the time of acquisition to realize a reasonable income from the buildings

The following factors show an intent to demolish after acquisition:

- Substantial improvement of the buildings immediately after their acquisition
- Prolonged use of the buildings for business purposes after their acquisition
- Suitability of the buildings for investment purposes at the time of acquisition
- Substantial change in economic or business conditions after the date of acquisition
- Loss of useful value occurring after the date of acquisition
- Substantial damage to the buildings occurring after their acquisition
- Discovery of latent structural defects in the buildings after their acquisition
- Decline in the taxpayer's business after the date of acquisition
- Condemnation of the property by municipal authorities after the date of acquisition
- Inability after acquisition to obtain building material necessary for the improvement of the property

[iii] Demolition of Historic Structures. A special rule applies to any demolition of a certified historic structure, or of any other structure in a registered historic district, unless it is certified by the Secretary of the Interior not to be of historic significance. In such case, no deduction may be taken by the owner for (1) the amount expended for the demolition itself; or (2) any loss sustained on account of the demolition (i.e., the owner's remaining tax basis in the building). Instead, such amounts and such losses must be treated as additional land costs and will be recaptured only when the property is disposed of by the owner.

[b] Abandonment Losses

As already noted, a taxpayer who incurs operating losses from a trade or business or from a transaction entered into for profit may deduct those losses in arriving at taxable income. If the taxpayer abandons the trade or business or for-profit transaction, the losses resulting from that abandonment normally will constitute operating losses. These will include not only the expenses incurred in the year in question (to the extent that they exceed any income for the year) but also the value of assets that must be abandoned along with the business or transaction venture. (Expenses incurred in the course of investigating a proposed venture or in deciding whether to enter the venture may or may not be deductible if the taxpayer decides not to proceed; see 3.01[2][b].)

In the case of real estate ventures, abandonment losses may result either from (1) abandonment of a proposed project; or (2) abandonment of an existing structure. In the case where a proposed project is abandoned before construction is complete, the developer will deduct so-called intangible property, which may include such items as legal, financing, architectural, and engineering fees and costs. The tax regulations provide that a deductible loss is incurred when intangible property suffers a "sudden termination of usefulness," where the business or transaction is discontinued or where the property is "permanently discarded from use." [38] Thus, if the project is permanently abandoned, the entire intangible cost sunk into it can be written off for tax purposes.

No deduction is, however, available unless the project is actually and permanently abandoned and is not merely postponed; to show that a project has been permanently abandoned, some overt act usually is necessary. A mere showing of a "partial" abandonment may not be sufficient to ensure that the loss deduction sticks. For example, it is difficult to prove an abandonment of architectural plans if some of them are retained to be used for a future project. And where a second architect is employed to draw new plans for a job after the original architect's plans have proved too costly, no abandonment loss may be allowed for the cost of the original plans if any part of those plans is incorporated into the job.[39]

The exact type of overt act that should be performed to establish complete and permanent abandonment depends on the circumstances of each case. Under some circumstances, it may be sufficient to permit an option to purchase land to expire or, perhaps, to sell land; under other circumstances, a physical destruction of architectural or engineering plans and specifications may be necessary. To make sure of the deduction, examine the circumstances and perform whatever overt act is necessary to make an unequivocal showing of a complete and permanent abandonment of the proposed construction.

In one case, the owner of raw land incurred $100,000 in rezoning expenses as an abandonment loss. Generally, such expenses are not currently deductible, but are treated as capital expenditures, to be added to the owner's investment in the land. But in this case, the developer decided not to proceed with a proposed department store when the rezoning request was denied. The Tax Court, in permitting the developer to deduct the expenses and abandonment loss, applied a practical test. It said that the adverse zoning ruling brought the entire project to an abrupt end because it foreclosed future commercial development of the area. Thus, the expenditure of $100,000 by the developer created nothing of any continuing value to him.[40]

When it comes to the abandonment of an existing structure, the problem is sometimes more difficult. The question of whether an abandonment has occurred depends on whether the owner has shown an irrevocable intention never to use

---

[38] Reg. § 1.165-2(a).

[39] Robert B. Haspel v. Comm'r, 62 T.C. 59 (1974).

[40] Chevy Chase Land Co. v. Comm'r, 72 T.C. 481 (1979).

the property again or to sell or otherwise dispose of it. Whereas personal property may be destroyed as evidence of such intention, it is not possible to destroy land itself. A property owner who demolished a building could take a demolition loss but normally the costs of such demolition do not warrant such action. (See 3.09[1][a].)

A case decided by the Tax Court shows how one owner was successful in abandoning a building (while keeping the land). The owner was a partnership that owned a building that was leased to the federal government for a short period. When the lease ended, the partnership considered restoring the building to its former use as a hotel. But it was considered not to be economically feasible, nor was it considered worthwhile to demolish the building and devote the land to another use. So the partnership decided to abandon the building in order to be able to take an ordinary loss deduction. This is what the partnership did:

- The building was locked and boarded up.
- A barricade was placed around the building for protection against falling masonry and stones.
- Utilities were terminated, although a standby fee to maintain utility connections was paid.
- Maintenance was discontinued.
- Action was taken to terminate insurance coverage, except for fire protection.

The IRS contended that the partnership had not abandoned the hotel because it retained title to the building, held the land for sale, which would have entailed selling the building as well, paid standby utility fees, asked police to investigate theft of building fixtures, kept fire insurance, and paid property taxes without indicating that the amounts were solely for the land.

At the trial one of the partners, who was very experienced in real estate, testified that financing to reopen the hotel was impossible to obtain and abandonment was the only course.

The Tax Court ruled that this testimony, plus the actions of the partnership, showed an intention to abandon, and the court permitted the abandonment loss deduction.[41]

Several cases, more than fifty years ago, permitted abandonment losses in connection with special-purpose buildings where evidence showed that conversion to another use would have been too costly. The *Hanover* case, however, dealt with a general-purpose building and should be an appropriate precedent for the abandonment of buildings in blighted neighborhoods where rehabilitation or conversion is not economically justified.

Note that a special problem exists when property is subject to a mortgage. In that case, it may be impossible for the owner to abandon it in a tax sense and create an ordinary loss. The reason is that the owner, in such case, is considered to have yielded the property to the lender and this probably will be construed as a disposition creating a capital loss instead of an abandonment creating an ordinary loss.

---

[41] Hanover v. Comm'r, T.C. Memo 1979-332.

Charitable Foundations. In an even more unusual approach, Mr. Pearsall, owner of forty-seven low-income rental units in Richmond, Virginia, was determined to get rid of the properties after he was labeled a slumlord. However, he did not wish to abandon them and he could not find any local organizations to accept his donation of the properties. So he formed his own tax-exempt charitable foundation, to which he contributed the buildings while retaining the land, and claimed a charitable deduction of $60,000. IRS argued that the property that Pearsall contributed to his foundation was worthless, so that no charitable deduction was allowable. While the Tax Court agreed it was unlikely a "willing buyer" could be found for the property, the court nevertheless thought the buildings had value. Based on the income they produced, the court allowed a deduction of $25,000.[42]

[c] Hobby-Loss Limitations

A special provision of the Internal Revenue Code[43] bars the deduction of losses from a business or transaction unless the taxpayer can establish that the business or operation was carried on with the intention of making a profit. In other words, if the activity was merely a hobby (although the statute does not use that term), then expenses and losses in connection with the hobby are personal and nondeductible (except that they are deductible to the extent of income from the hobby).

If an expense is deductible in any event such as taxes, interest, or casualty losses, then they remain deductible even though they are incurred in connection with a hobby. However, these already-deductible expenses reduce the amount of hobby income against which otherwise nondeductible hobby expenses can be offset. (Special rules exist for vacation homes that are rented out for a portion of the year; see 11.11[3][e].)

How is a hobby distinguished from a business operation or transaction entered into for profit? One of two tests is used:

1. An activity is presumed not to be a hobby if it results in a profit in two out of five consecutive years. This is a presumption only and IRS may seek to overturn it by appropriate evidence.
2. Even if the activity does not produce profits in two out of five years, the activity nevertheless may be considered a business if the taxpayer can establish a profit-seeking intention.

Real estate investors are particularly susceptible to the hobby-loss limitation because an investor may be willing to "eat" a string of losses in the course of building up a clientele or in anticipation of selling at a profit sometime in the future. Nevertheless, the taxpayer may be able to establish that his motive was to seek a profit. In one case, an investor who had incurred twelve consecutive annual losses from operating a ski lodge was able to convince the Tax Court that this was a business, not a hobby, so that the losses were fully deductible. The investor, a successful executive, operated the lodge in addition to his main job.

---

42 Pearsall v. Comm'r, T.C. Memo 1977-230.
43 I.R.C. § 183.

The latter gave him sufficient income so that he could absorb the long years of losses. Nevertheless, the Tax Court found he was in business for a profit, based on these important factors:

☐ Taxpayer operated the lodge in a businesslike manner; excellent records were maintained.

☐ The purchase, construction, and financing of the lodge resulted from careful planning. Its operation was directed toward obtaining sufficient revenue to realize a profit. The losses resulted not from lack of attention or ability by the taxpayer, but were due to changes in the local economy.

☐ Most important, the lodge was never used for the taxpayer's personal enjoyment. When he and his family went to the area to ski, they stayed at another facility where they rented a room on an annual basis. The only time they stayed at the lodge was when they were working on it.

On this basis, the court found that the taxpayer was deriving no personal pleasure or gratification from operating the lodge; therefore, it was a business.[44]

The mere fact that a house is rented to a relative of the owner does not preclude the owner from treating the transaction as one made for profit, so long as (1) a fair rental is charged; and (2) the house is the principal residence of the tenant.

[i] Impact of New Accelerated Cost Recovery System. Real estate investors who anticipate that losses may be challenged by IRS as arising from a hobby and therefore will be nondeductible should carefully consider the impact of the new fifteen-year recovery period available under the Accelerated Cost Recovery System. The additional depreciation write-offs will make it less likely that a business or investment will be able to satisfy the two-out-of-five-years profit test under Section 183. Under such circumstances, an investor may decide to utilize straight-line depreciation under one of the optional extended recovery periods available for real estate (either thirty-five years or forty-five years).

[2] Theft or Casualty Losses

All property owners are allowed deductions for casualty losses. These are losses of property arising from "fire, storm, shipwreck or other casualty, or from theft." Deduction is allowed for the full amount of each casualty or theft loss in connection with a trade or business or rental property; in the case of other property, however, the first $100 of loss each year is nondeductible.

There has been little controversy over the meaning of the terms "fire" and "storm." The phrase "other casualty" has generated most of the controversy in this area. The IRS position is that the loss must have resulted from a sudden, unexpected, identifiable, and proven event of an unusual nature, such as an accident, mishap, or sudden invasion by a hostile agency. However, a casualty-loss

---

[44] Allen v. Comm'r, 72 T.C. 28 (1979).

deduction will not be lost merely because the loss was foreseeable or because of the taxpayer's own negligence (unless it is willful).

No deduction is allowed to the extent the loss is compensated for by insurance. Moreover, if a claim for reimbursement exists as to which there is a reasonable prospect of recovery, the loss is not sustained until it can be ascertained with reasonable certainty whether such reimbursement will be received. Despite denial of liability for damages, a reasonable prospect for recovery exists if, in a qualified attorney's opinion, the taxpayer's claim is likely to be upheld.[45]

[a] Measuring Personal Casualty Loss

Only rarely is the amount of the casualty-loss deduction equal to the cost of the property destroyed. The deductible amount is the lesser of either (1) an amount equal to the fair market value of the property immediately before the casualty, reduced by the fair market value of the property immediately after the casualty; or (2) the adjusted basis of the property for determining loss from a sale or other disposition.[46] The regulations suggest that fair market value before and after the casualty should be determined by "competent appraisal." Doubtlessly recognizing the impracticability of this procedure in many instances, the regulations also provide that the cost of repairs essential to restore the property to its prior condition, if reasonable, may be accepted as evidence of the amount of loss in value.

Any decrease in value resulting from potential buyer resistance attributable to apprehension concerning recurrence of a similar casualty cannot be taken into account in measuring the damage to property. If it is established that buyer resistance is short-lived, the portion of the decline in market value attributable to buyer resistance can be measured by the interest on the proceeds that would be realized at the end of the period of buyer resistance.[47]

The rules governing the amount of a casualty-loss deduction may be illustrated by an example. Suppose that a taxpayer's house, which cost $30,000 exclusive of land, is completely destroyed by fire. Immediately before the fire, the house and land had a fair market value of $56,000. Fire insurance proceeds amounted to $20,000. The deductible loss would be determined as follows:

Value of property immediately before casualty	$56,000
Less: Value of property immediately after casualty (land)	20,000
Value of property actually destroyed	$36,000
Loss to be taken into account (Lesser of amount of property actually destroyed ($36,000) or its adjusted basis ($30,000))	$30,000
Less: Insurance received and $100 floor	20,100
Deduction allowable	$ 9,900

45 Fort Howard Paper Co. v. Comm'r, T.C. Memo 1977-422.

46 Reg. § 1.165-7(b).

47 See Charles C. Cantrell v. Comm'r, T.C. Memo 1978-237.

When household contents are destroyed by fire, the measure of loss generally is replacement value less depreciation. Proof of acquisition cost (basis) is not essential, at least where the facts indicate that the basis of the damaged personal property equals or exceeds its diminution in value.[48] Where a home was destroyed by fire, the Tax Court has accepted an inventory listing costs prepared from memory as some evidence of the cost of its contents.[49]

The Treasury has published the following table (Table 3.15, below), which shows the tax consequences of casualty losses under a variety of circumstances, disregarding the $100 floor. It should be observed that the basis of damaged property is reduced by the amount of the loss deduction and any insurance recovery.

TABLE 3.15 Tax Consequences of Casualty Losses

(a) Value Before Disaster	*(b)* Value After Disaster	*(c)* Loss in Value, (a) minus (b)	*(d)* Cost or Other Basis	*(e)* Insurance or Other Compensation Received or Recoverable	*(f)* Allowable Casualty Loss Deduction, Lesser of (c) or (d) Minus (e)	*(g)* Taxable Gain, (e) Minus (d)	*(h)* Remaining Tax Basis, (d) Plus (g) Minus Sum of (e) and (f)
$15,000	$11,000	$ 4,000	$10,000	$ 3,000	$ 1,000	—	$6,000
15,000	3,000	12,000	10,000	—	10,000	—	—
5,000	2,000	3,000	10,000	3,000	—	—	7,000
15,000	1,000	14,000	10,000	3,000	7,000	—	—
19,000	10,000	9,000	5,000	8,000	—	$3,000	—
18,000	—	18,000	10,000	12,000	—	2,000	—

[b] Measuring Business Casualty Loss

As with a personal casualty loss, the general rule for determining the amount of a business casualty loss is that it is limited to the lesser of the difference between the fair market value of the property before and after the casualty, or the adjusted basis of the property. However, if business property is totally destroyed by a casualty and if the fair market value of the property immediately before the casualty is less than its adjusted basis, then the adjusted basis is the amount of the loss. In other words, if adjusted basis is higher than value at the time of the casualty, the amount of the loss is the adjusted basis. This rule often may favor a taxpayer whose property has declined in value over a taxpayer whose property has increased in value.

Another important difference in the method of computation of personal and business loss deductions may restrict the business loss. The difference occurs when the property consists of more than one component, typically the case with

---

48 John R. Pfalzgraf, Jr. v. Comm'r, 67 T.C. 784 (1977).

49 Daniel B. Kenerly v. Comm'r, T.C. Memo 1975-139.

real estate consisting of land and building. In the case of personal casualty losses, both components are regarded as a single unit and their basis is aggregated for the purpose of determining the amount of the loss. But in the case of business casualty losses, the components are separated and the basis for each separate component is determined. Then, if the casualty affects only one component, only the basis of that component goes into the computation. For example, if a fire completely destroys a building but does not harm the land, the basis of the building alone is taken into account.[50]

[3] At-Risk Limitation

The Tax Reform Act of 1976 (TRA 1976)[51] introduced a new at-risk concept into the Internal Revenue Code. Essentially, the at-risk rule limits the amount of any loss that may be deducted by an investor to the amount of capital that he actually has at risk.

The amount a taxpayer is deemed to have at risk includes:

- Cash and the basis of other property the taxpayer contributes
- Any funds borrowed for use in the activity to the extent the taxpayer is personally liable to repay the debt
- The net fair market value of the taxpayer's other assets, which secure nonrecourse borrowing

However, if the taxpayer is protected from a loss on borrowed funds through guarantees, stop-loss agreements, repurchase agreements, or the like, such borrowing is not included as at risk.

Any loss not deductible in any year because it is in excess of the amount by which the taxpayer is at risk is carried forward and may be used in a subsequent year during which it does not exceed the amount at risk.

The Revenue Act of 1978 (RA 1978)[52] added a provision for the recapture of previously allowed losses if the amount at risk is reduced below zero. The amount recaptured is limited to the excess of losses previously allowed over any amounts previously recaptured (in connection with the particular activity). Reduction of the at-risk amount can occur by one of the following methods:

- Distributions to the taxpayer
- Changes in the status of debt from recourse to nonrecourse
- Commencement of a guaranty or other similar arrangement that affects the risk of loss
- Other means

The TRA 1976 introduced two at-risk rules. One dealt with four specific activities (farming, oil and gas, motion-picture films, and personal property leasing) and covered all types of taxpayers except regular corporations. The second applied only to partnerships and covered any activity engaged in by the partnership. The RA 1978 expands the at-risk rules and combines them into a single

---

50 Ray F. Keefer v. Comm'r, 63 T.C. 596 (1977).
51 Pub. L. No. 94-455, 90 Stat. 1520, 26 U.S.C.A. §§ 1 et seq.
52 Pub. L. No. 95-600, 92 Stat. 2763, 26 U.S.C.A. §§ 1 et seq.

rule. By the expanded provision, all activities except real estate are subject to the at-risk rule when carried on by all types of taxpayers, with the specific exception of corporations that are other than Subchapter S corporations, personal holding companies, or (newly added by the RA 1978) close corporations in which five or fewer individuals own more than 50 percent of the stock. In view of this extension of the rule, the rule relating to partnerships has been repealed as unnecessary.

Obviously, this extension of the at-risk limitation to all other investments has increased the attractiveness of real estate as an investment.

3.10 CHARITABLE CONTRIBUTIONS FOR CONSERVATION PURPOSES

A special provision of the Internal Revenue Code[53] permits the owner of real property to take a tax deduction when he makes a contribution of certain types of real estate interests for conservation purposes. This type of contribution is of particular interest to many real estate owners because a substantial deduction may be obtained even though the donor does not give up any present use of the property. At the same time, the donor is furthering the goals of conservation or historic preservation.

The tax rules covering this type of charitable contribution are complicated and have gone through a number of changes since 1969, with the latest coming in 1980. The rules set forth below apply to transfers made after December 17, 1980 (and, for certain types of transfers, may be effective for earlier years as well).

[1] Property Interests Eligible for Deduction

A charitable contribution by an owner of his entire interest in real property has always qualified for a deduction, assuming the other rules pertaining to charitable contributions were met. In addition, certain types of partial interest now also qualify for the deduction. These include:

- A remainder interest in a personal residence or farm
- An undivided portion of a taxpayer's entire interest in real property
- Certain interests that originally had to be made in trust, but that now may be made without a trust
- Certain partial interests made "exclusively for conservation purposes"

The balance of the discussion relates to the last category just named, that is, partial interests exclusively for conservation purposes. Such partial interests now include:

- Any remainder interest in real property
- A restriction granted in perpetuity on the use that may be made of the real property, including restrictions that may be created by a lease, a preservation easement, or a restrictive covenant

53 I.R.C. § 170(f).

- The taxpayer's entire interest in real property other than his interest in subsurface oil, gas or other minerals, and the right of access to such minerals.

[2] Definition of Conservation Purposes

A charitable contribution of a real property interest will be deemed made for a conservation purpose if it has one of the following four objectives:

1. The preservation of land areas for outdoor recreation, or for the education of the general public.
2. The preservation of a natural environmental system, such as a fish, wildlife, or plant habitat.
3. The preservation of open space (including farm land and forest land) where such preservation will yield a significant public benefit either in the form of scenic enjoyment for the general public, or because it is pursuant to a clear government conservation policy.
4. The preservation of historically important land areas or certified historic structures.

The contribution of an interest in real property must not only be for conservation purposes but must be exclusively for such purpose. This requires that the interest be granted in perpetuity, as already noted, and must be capable of legal enforcement to insure that the interest retained by the donor cannot be used in ways inconsistent with the conservation purposes.

For example, the exclusivity requirement is not met whenever the present (donor's) use of the property either (1) can diminish the conservation values that are sought to be protected; or (2) may be destructive of other significant conservation interests. When the donor has retained a mineral interest in the property, the requirement that the conservation interest be in perpetuity would not be satisfied if any method of mining or extraction of the mineral interest is permitted that is inconsistent with the conservation purposes.

[3] Qualified Organizations

The contribution of a partial interest for conservation purposes creates a deduction only if the recipient is a government or a publicly supported charity (or certain other charities controlled by either of the foregoing).

[4] Valuing the Contribution

The amount of the charitable contribution for conservation purposes is the fair market value of the property interest conveyed to the recipient. The general rule for determining the fair market value of a conservation interest is that such value is

The fair market value of the property unrestricted
minus
The fair market value of the property restricted

Such "before and after" value normally must be established by a competent appraisal, which will consider the selling price of other properties burdened with comparable restrictions (to the extent such sales can be ascertained).

> *Example:* The "before and after" approach can be illustrated as follows: An investor owns ten acres of farmland that could have been sold for $2,000 per acre, assuming it could have been devoted to its highest-and-best use (one-family houses). The investor grants an open-space easement to the community, agreeing that no development will take place on the land. Land in the general area restricted to farm use has a fair market value of $1,500 per acre. Thus, the value of the open-space easement is $5,000 (10 times $500) since the land subject to the easement can now be used only for farming.[54]

Note that the donor in this example obtains a deduction equal to the current fair market value of the interest given up even though he need not pay any capital gains tax on the appreciation in the value of the property prior to the charitable contribution. Suppose the farmland in the example had cost the owner $200 per acre ($2,000 total). Had the owner sold the open-space easement for $500 per acre ($5,000 total) and then given the cash proceeds to charity, a capital gains tax on the $3,000 realized on the sale of the easement would have to be paid first. This tax is avoided by a direct grant of the easement.

[5] Donating a Preservation Easement

One of the most popular forms of charitable contributions for conservation purposes is the preservation easement, which is illustrated in the example above. An easement is a special kind of interest in land. Unlike a fee or leasehold interest, it is nonpossessory; that is, the holder of the easement is only entitled to some benefit from the land. This benefit may arise either from using the land in a particular way (such as having a right-of-way to cross it) or by having the owner of the land refrain from some activity or use.

A preservation easement concerns nonuse or nonaction by the owner of the land. Examples include

☐ *Scenic or open-space easement.* Here, the landowner agrees that he will not improve the land (or change existing improvements) to interfere with views of or across the particular site. The purpose, in other words, is to protect the visual amenities of the location.

☐ *Facade easement.* Here, the owner agrees that the exterior physical features of a building will not be changed; the purpose is to preserve buildings having historical or architectural importance. Thus, a syndicate may acquire a historic building with the intention of donating the exterior to the community while renovating the interior to be used as residential or office space. The effect is to reduce the front-end outlay by the tax saving generated by the charitable contribution.[55]

---

[54] Rev. Rul. 73-339, 1973-2 C.B. 68; Rev. Rul. 76-376, 1976-2 C.B. 68.

[55] See Rev. Rul. 75-358, 1975-2 C.B. 76; Rev. Rul. 75-373, 1975-2 C.B. 77.

☐ *Building easement.* The owner of a building of historic or architectural importance may agree to make no changes to any part of the building, interior or exterior.

In all of these situations, the landowner, having given up one or more rights with respect to the land, has incurred some loss of economic value. It is this loss of value that represents the charitable contribution and that may qualify as a tax deduction.

3.11 MINIMUM TAXES AND REAL ESTATE

The purpose of the add-on minimum tax and the alternative minimum tax is to insure that everyone, individuals and corporations alike, pays at least some income tax, even though all income comes from tax-sheltered or tax-favored sources. (However, even here an exception exists. Interest on tax-exempt state and municipal bonds is subject to neither minimum tax. Thus, a taxpayer who invests solely in tax-exempts will pay no income tax.)

As their names indicate, the two minimum taxes are mutually exclusive; that is, a taxpayer never pays both of them. Instead, he pays the greater of (1) his regular tax liability plus the add-on minimum tax; or (2) the alternative minimum tax.

For real estate investors, the essential difference between the two minimum taxes is that the add-on minimum tax is imposed on excess depreciation, whereas the alternative minimum tax is based upon the untaxed portion of long-term capital gains.

[1] Add-On Minimum Tax

The add-on minimum tax applies to all taxpayers, whether individuals, corporations, or other legal entity. The add-on minimum tax is payable in addition to the taxpayer's regular income tax (hence the name). The tax is imposed on items of tax preference (defined below); the rate of tax is 15 percent of the total of tax preference items in excess of the greater of $10,000 or (1) one-half of regular income taxes in the case of noncorporate taxpayers; or (2) the full amount of regular income taxes in the case of regular corporations.

Tax preference items for the add-on minimum tax include the following:

- Excess depreciation for real estate (see below)
- Excess depreciation for leased personal property (see below)
- Excess amortization for certified pollution-control facilities
- Excess amortization for railroad rolling stocks
- Excess market value over option price under qualified stock options
- Excess percentage depletion of mineral property
- Certain reserves for bad debts by financial institutions
- Excess amortization of child-care facilities
- Excess intangible drilling costs on oil and gas wells

[a] Excess Depreciation of Real Estate

Excess depreciation is defined as the amount of depreciation write-off using an accelerated method that exceeds what is allowable using the straight-line method. Prior to the Economic Recovery Tax Act of 1981 (ERTA 1981),[56] both accelerated and straight-line depreciation were calculated on the basis of the useful life of the property. As a result of the new fifteen-year recovery period introduced by ERTA 1981, both are now determined on the basis of such fifteen-year life.

Example: Assume a taxpayer has $35,000 of excess depreciation deductions (i.e., deductions in excess of straight-line depreciation) and has no other tax preference income. In calculating the add-on minimum tax, the taxpayer is entitled to an exemption of $10,000 or one-half his regular tax payment, whichever is greater. Assume the exemption is $10,000; then $25,000 of excess depreciation would be subject to the add-on minimum tax of 15 percent, which would mean a tax of $3,750 would be payable in addition to the taxpayer's regular tax.

[b] Excess Depreciation for Leased Personal Property

Excess depreciation on leased personal property is an item of tax preference for taxpayers other than corporations (but including Subchapter S corporations). As in the case of real property, excess depreciation is the difference between accelerated and straight-line depreciation. However, unlike the case of real property, the four depreciation recovery periods for personal property are stretched out for purposes of determining straight-line depreciation in connection with the add-on minimum tax. The following chart shows the stretched-out recovery periods:

Property Class	*Recovery Period*
3-year	5 years
5-year	8 years
10-year	15 years

The major problem for real estate investors in connection with the minimum tax is the interplay between it and the benefits from deferring tax by the use of accelerated depreciation. (See 3.02[6].) Note that under former law, tax preference income reduced on a dollar-for-dollar basis the amount of personal-service taxable income that was eligible for the maximum tax rate of 50 percent. This provision has been repealed for 1982 and thereafter, since no income will now be taxed at a higher rate than 50 percent.

[2] Alternative Minimum Tax

The add-on minimum tax was a creation of the Tax Reform Act of 1969,[57] an alternative minimum tax was created for individuals, but not for corporations,

---

[56] Pub. L. No. 97-34, 95 Stat. 172, 26 U.S.C. § 128.

[57] Pub. L. No. 91-172, 83 Stat. 487, 26 U.S.C.A. § 6050.

by the Revenue Act of 1978.[58] ERTA 1981 reduced the top rate of the alternative minimum tax from 25 percent to 20 percent. The alternative minimum tax is payable only if it is in excess of the regular tax liability plus the add-on minimum tax. In other words, no taxpayer pays both a minimum and an alternative minimum tax. The latter tax will be payable only in unusual cases, notably when a taxpayer has a very large long-term capital gain and virtually no other taxable income (see the example below).

The alternative minimum tax is imposed upon the following types of income:

- Taxable income as computed in the usual fashion
- The excluded portion (60 percent) of long-term capital gains realized in the taxable year (but excluding gain on sale of a residence)
- Excess itemized deductions

The amount of excess itemized deductions is the excess of (1) itemized deductions taken by the taxpayer for the taxable year other than those for state and local taxes, medical expenses, and casualty losses; over (2) 60 percent of adjusted gross income as reduced by the above three items.

The alternative-minimum-tax rate is as follows:

AMT Income	*Tax Rate*
Up to $20,000	No AMT
$20,000 to $60,000	10%
$60,000 and above	20%

In effect, the alternative minimum tax is a new method of taxing capital gains. If we ignore the item of excess itemized deductions (likely to be significant only in rare cases), alternative-minimum-tax income essentially is 100 percent of long-term capital gains (i.e., the 40 percent that constitutes regular taxable income and the 60 percent that is excluded in computing taxable income), and then such income is subjected to a tax of up to 20 percent. Since the first $100,000 of alternative-minimum-tax income is taxed at less than 20 percent, it becomes apparent that it would take a significant amount of net long-term gains in a year before the effective rate approached 20 percent.

> *Example:* Owner (*O*) in 1982 has $100,000 taxable income (including taxable portion of capital gain), plus $10,000 of excess depreciation (accelerated over straight-line), plus $50,000 of untaxed long-term gain. *O* does not pay a 15 percent minimum tax (because the $10,000 minimum-tax deduction offsets the excess depreciation tax preference). In calculating the alternative minimum tax, *O* adds taxable income ($100,000) to untaxed gain ($50,000) for a total of $150,000. The $20,000 exemption reduces this to $130,000, on which the alternative tax would be $22,000 (10 percent on $40,000 plus 20 percent on the balance of $90,000). Since this is less than the regular tax liability on *O*'s $100,000 of taxable income, no alternative minimum tax is payable.

---

[58] Pub. L. No. 95-600, 92 Stat. 2763, 26 U.S.C.A. § 1.

4

Forms of Real Estate Ownership

4.01 OVERVIEW OF THE OWNERSHIP DECISION

[1] Types of Ownership in General

A discussion of the forms of real estate ownership really covers two related, but separate, subjects:

- First, the nature of the owning entity, that is, whether title to the property is in the name of an individual, partnership, corporation, or trust.
- Second, the number of entities that share in the ownership of the property, that is, whether ownership is held by a single entity or shared among two or more individuals, partnerships, corporations, or trusts.

Multiple ownership is known technically as concurrent ownership. The three types of concurrent ownership—tenancy in common, joint tenancy, and tenancy by the entirety—almost always involve individuals only.

The above listing of types of concurrent ownership does not include syndicates, since this term refers to all forms of group ownership (whether the group participates via a single ownership entity, such as a partnership, or holds title in some form of concurrent ownership). Real estate syndication is discussed in detail in 5.03[2].

[2] Tax Considerations

When choosing an ownership form, investors should consider both tax and nontax factors. The four general categories of entities described above (individuals, partnerships, corporations, and trusts) as well as the concept of concurrent ownership, are all recognized by the Internal Revenue Code and are generally treated as described below:

☐ When property is concurrently owned, each owner is taxed as to his pro rata share as if that owner had title to the entire property.

☐ Individual owners lump the income and loss from real estate together with their other items of income and loss.

☐ Partnerships, whether general, limited, or joint ventures, are not taxable entities, but are merely tax conduits; taxable gain and loss is passed through directly to individual partners, who then treat these items as if they were individual owners of the property.

☐ Corporations are taxable entities separate from their participants and report profits separately (i.e., a double tax is imposed, once on the corporate level and once on the shareholder level when income is distributed as dividends). Although an entity such as a partnership may not be organized as a corporation, in certain cases it may nevertheless be treated as an "association taxable as a corporation." (See 4.03[5][a].) Subchapter S corporations, however, are treated as if they were partnerships. (See 4.04[2].)

Trusts, as well as the estates of decedents, are taxable entities separate from their participants and report profits separately (except that real estate investment trusts are subject to special tax rules, as is discussed in 5.02[8][e]).

In general, tax considerations in choice of an ownership entity can be summed up as follows:

☐ Whether, and the extent to which, the entity in which the property is held or the venture is conducted may be ignored for tax purposes and the deductions, expenses, and losses generated can be passed on directly to the participants, thereby sheltering their income from the venture as well as from other sources;

☐ Whether the income generated will be subjected to being taxed twice, once to the entity and once when distributed to the participants;

☐ The availability of favorable capital gains treatment on a sale, distribution, or liquidation of an interest in the entity, or on a sale or other disposition of the real estate itself; and

☐ The burden that will be placed on an investor's estate by having to pay estate taxes on an interest in an entity that may be difficult to turn into cash.

See Table 4.1 for a comparison of income tax consequences of three common forms of ownership.

TABLE 4.1 Comparison of Income Tax Consequences of Various Forms of Ownership

	Partnership	*Corporation*	*Subchapter S Corporation*
Amount of equity	Same.	Same.	Same.
Taxation of entity	Entity not taxed; each partner reflects his pro rata share of partnership income or loss whether or not actually distributed.	Entity pays tax on its income; stockholders pay additional tax on corporate dividend distributions.	Same as partnership.
Taxation of investor	Partner taxed on own share of partnership taxable income; excess cash distributions reduce basis of partnership interest; after basis is recovered fully, excess cash distributions are taxed as capital gains.	Shareholders taxed on dividend distributions to the extent they derive from accumulated or current earnings and profits; distributions in excess of earnings and profits reduce shareholder's basis in corporate stockholding; after basis is recovered fully, distributions in excess of earnings and profits are taxed as capital gains.	Shareholder taxed on pro rata share of corporate income; excess cash distributions reduce basis of stock; after basis recovered, distributions taxed as capital gains.
Depreciation	Ordinary depreciation helps determine income or loss at partnership level, and thus may shelter partner's unrelated income. Additional first-year depreciation is separately computed and each partner	Depreciation deductible at corporate level only; thus, shareholder's unrelated income cannot be sheltered. In addition, full tax benefit of depreciation write-off can sometimes be lost. Net	Depreciation deductions help determine income or loss at corporate level, and thus may shelter shareholder's unrelated income.

	Partnership	*Corporation*	*Subchapter S Corporation*
	picks up a share of the partnership's write-off for this item as his own, thus possibly sheltering unrelated income.	operating loss carrybacks and carryforwards and flexibility of depreciation methods help ease the problem.	
Investment tax credit	Each partner may pick up his share of the partnership's investment credit to reduce tax liability on unrelated income; carrybacks and carryforwards further aid the sheltering of unrelated income.	Investment credit may reduce tax at corporate level only; absence of corporate profitability may endanger any tax benefit from investment credit; investment credit carrybacks and carryforwards lessen this likelihood.	Each shareholder may pick up his proportionate share of corporate investment credit to reduce tax liability on unrelated income; carrybacks and carryforwards further aid the sheltering of unrelated income.
Capital gains and losses	Capital gains or losses are passed through to individual partners and combined with other capital items; resulting net capital gain or loss subject to usual individual income tax treatment. Each partner may pick up his share of partnership losses to shelter unrelated income; losses picked up by a partner reduce his basis for partnership interest; carrybacks and carryforwards may further enhance the sheltering of unrelated income.	Corporation cannot pass through capital gains or losses as such to shareholders. Special 28 percent corporate rate of taxation on net capital gains benefits only corporations taxed at 46 percent bracket. Shareholder distributions resulting from capital gains are subject to ordinary taxation. Losses are not passed through to shareholders; they may provide tax benefit by being carried back or forward to offset other year's income.	Subchapter S corporations can pass through capital gains or losses to shareholders; combined with other shareholder capital gains or losses, the resulting net capital gain or loss is subject to usual individual income tax treatment. Losses are passed through to stockholders to shelter unrelated income; each stockholder's loss is limited to the total of his basis for his stock and any corporate indebtedness to him. Losses passed through to a

(continued)

TABLE 4.1 Comparison of Income Tax Consequences of Various Forms of Ownership *(continued)*

	Partnership	*Corporation*	*Subchapter S Corporation*
			stockholder reduce his basis in his corporate stock. The usual carryback and carryforward rules at the stockholder's level provide additional tax shelter.
Taxable year	Generally limited to taxable year of all its principal partners.	Choice.	Choice.
Limited liability	Usually, general partners liable for partnership obligations; limited partners usually enjoy limited liability.	Generally, shareholders not liable for corporate debts; exceptions may arise for certain classes of liability (wages, taxes, etc.) or for corporate obligations where formalities of corporate operation are disregarded.	Same as ordinary corporation.
Compensation arrangements (including qualified pension and profit-sharing, accident and health, group-term life, medical reimbursements, death benefits, stock option and other fringe benefits)	Partner who is not employee does not qualify; limited to self-employed pension and profit-sharing plan.	Stockholder-employee qualifies; amount of benefit must be reasonable when considered with salary.	Stockholder-employee qualifies; limitations similar to partnership rather than corporations.

	Partnership	*Corporation*	*Subchapter S Corporation*
Tax rate	Taxed at partner level; Individual rate brackets reduced to 15 brackets for joint returns and 16 for single taxpayers.	*Taxable Income* — *Tax Rate* $0 to $25,000 — 17% $25,000 to $50,000 — 20 $50,000 to $75,000 — 30 $75,000 to $100,000 — 40 Over $100,000 — 46 Alternative capital gains rate is 28 percent.	Taxed generally at shareholder level. Individual rate brackets reduced to 15 brackets for joint returns and 16 brackets for single taxpayers.
Flexibility	No limitations.	Construction-phase realty corporations may be delayed in undertaking new projects by possible inability to use fully depreciation or other net operating loss deductions until a later time of greater corporate profitability. Careful planning with depreciation strategies and carrybacks or carryforwards may help, although with less current tax shelter than in other business forms.	Failure to keep passive income at less than 20% of gross receipts or to meet other requirements will result in loss of Subchapter S status and, possibly, severe income tax consequences.

[3] Business, Legal, and Other Practical Considerations

No one can afford to ignore tax considerations in selecting a form of ownership for real estate holdings or ventures. However, to focus solely on taxes and overlook business, legal, and other practical considerations can lead to disaster. If the chosen form of ownership serves to avoid or minimize taxes but also makes it difficult to operate profitably, or to dispose of the interests, the price paid for tax savings is too high.

The important nontax considerations that should be taken into account in selecting and organizing the entity include:

- Cost of formation
- Number of people and type of management needed to run the real estate activities
- Degree of flexibility required to conduct the activities
- Extent and probability of exposure to liability
- Ease of transferability of interests
- Ease of transferability of the real estate
- Expected duration of the venture
- Possibility of obtaining fringe benefits

4.02 INDIVIDUAL OWNERSHIP (SOLE PROPRIETORSHIP)

[1] Common Uses and Advantages

Individual ownership of real estate is most often found in connection with (1) residential property; and (2) relatively small-scale real estate and business enterprises. The major advantage of individual ownership is its simplicity, but once an enterprise reaches a certain size, the need to raise additional capital or the potential liabilities generally make it more desirable to use one of the artificial entities, such as a corporation or partnership. The basic tax advantage of individual ownership, as compared to corporate ownership, is that the income and profits are taxed once only or, alternatively, losses are available to be offset against outside income. If the property or enterprise generates net income, the individual owner adds it to his other income and pays a single tax on the total. If the property or enterprise generates taxable losses, these act as a tax shelter to reduce the owner's other taxable income.

Even when a partnership would normally be indicated, individual ownership may be coupled with a management agreement instead. Under this type of arrangement, a real estate developer or manager may agree to participate in a real estate venture and take his return in the form of a development or management fee (possibly contingent on the gain or income from the venture) rather than acquire an interest as a partner.

A summary of the important tax features of individual ownership or sole proprietorship is as follows:

- All the tax attributes of the proprietor are directly reflected on his individual income tax return.
- Net income from the proprietorship is taxed to the investor at ordinary income tax rates.

- Depreciation deductions from the proprietorship may be used by the investor to offset income from other unrelated sources. Carrybacks and carryforwards can be used and can further aid the sheltering of unrelated income.
- The investor may use the investment credit from the proprietorship to reduce his tax liability on unrelated income. Carrybacks and carryforwards are available.
- The investor combines his capital gains and losses from the proprietorship with his other capital gains and losses, and the resulting net capital gain or loss is subject to the usual income tax treatment.
- The investor can use his net operating loss from the proprietorship to offset his income from unrelated sources; carrybacks and carryforwards are available.

[2] Use by Married Individuals in Non-Community-Property States

Individual ownership of real estate by a married person, in most of the United States, is subject to no specific right or interest on the part of the owner's spouse. The rights of dower and curtesy, created by the English common law to give the spouse of a decedent certain rights in any real estate owned at death, have been abolished in the United States. It is true that virtually every state does provide for a spouse's statutory right to share in the estate of a decedent, but this right to share does not relate specifically to real property. Thus a married individual may freely dispose of property during his or her lifetime and, in addition, may make any disposition of the real property upon death, subject only to the general right of the surviving spouse to a specified share of the total estate. However, in the eight states that follow the laws of community property, a different rule applies.

[3] Use by Married Individuals in Community-Property States

The type of ownership known as community property derives from Spanish or French law and is now recognized by statute in eight states: Arizona, California, Idaho, Louisiana, Nevada, New Mexico, Texas, and Washington. In these states, each spouse is an equal co-owner of all the property acquired during the existence of the marriage as a result of the joint efforts of the spouses, and there is a presumption that all the property of a husband and wife is community property. However, the spouses can, by mutual consent, convert community property into the separate property of either spouse. Property is not considered community property if it was owned by either spouse before the marriage, or acquired by either spouse during the marriage by gift, inheritance, or will. In addition, community property statutes sometimes provide that one-half the earnings of either spouse during the existence of the marriage belongs to the other spouse, and this rule has been the basis of some celebrated proceedings between both married and unmarried couples in recent years.

Upon the death of a spouse leaving no will, the surviving spouse may or may not take all of the community property, depending upon the statute of the particular state. Divorce ordinarily destroys the community-property status and, pending a divorce, separation agreements involving property settlements and reservations with respect to the future earnings of one or both spouses usually are made.

4.03 PARTNERSHIPS AND JOINT VENTURES

Partnerships are the most commonly used form of unincorporated business organization involving more than one individual; their popularity is particularly evident in the case of real estate operations.[1] A partnership is a form of business organization in which two or more persons are associated as co-owners in a continuing relationship for the purpose of carrying on a common enterprise or business for profit. An agreement of partnership (also called articles of partnership) defines the rights and obligations of each partner and sets forth how profits and losses are to be shared. There are two types of partnerships: general partnerships (including joint ventures) and limited partnerships.

In many cases, the investor in real estate is faced with a decision between the partnership and corporate forms of ownership. Thus, the discussion of partnerships and corporations that follows makes frequent comparisons of their advantages and disadvantages.

[1] Advantages and Disadvantages

The reason for the popularity of the partnership entity is twofold. First, it allows the participants to maintain two of the key advantages of holding real estate individually:

☐ *The right to deduct taxable losses from the property against the investor's other income.* The partnership form permits this because, unlike a corporation, the partnership itself is not subject to tax but serves as a conduit through which the tax consequences of a particular project are passed through to the individual partners.

☐ *The right to compute taxable losses such as depreciation on the total cost of the property.* This is possible even though the investor's equity is only a small portion of the total and is achieved by the nonrecourse-liability rule. Although a partner, including a limited partner, can deduct losses only to the extent of his basis (cost) of the partnership interest, the share of those liabilities of the partnership for which no partner is personally liable (nonrecourse liability) may be included in the basis.

Second, not only does the partnership give the individual the same tax advantages as individual ownership, but it offers two additional advantages (the second applies only in the case of limited partnerships):

☐ *The opportunity for several investors to pool their equity capital.* In this way it is possible to acquire larger and higher priced properties, which are usually not only of better quality, but are also more easily financed.

☐ *In the case of limited partnerships, the insulation of the limited partners (who are passive investors) from liability for debts or claims against the partnership beyond the investors' actual equity.* By comparison, an individual investor, in

---

[1] Unless otherwise indicated in the discussion that follows, the term "partnership" includes joint ventures, since the latter are merely a special form of general partnership.

theory at least, may be liable to the extent of his entire assets for mortgages, assuming they are recourse loans, or for injury or damage resulting from the use of the property and not covered by insurance.

Offsetting the major tax advantages of the partnership form are several potential disadvantages, including:

☐ *Lack of centralized management.* In a corporation, management decisions are made by a board of directors elected by the shareholders; however, some major decisions, such as selling all of the assets of the corporation, must be approved by a majority or more of the shareholders. This system thus operates much more efficiently than if all the shareholders had to be consulted on each matter. By comparison, a general partnership requires the approval of a majority or all of the partners before any decision can be reached. A limited partnership offers a solution to the problem of management since only the general partner or partners (usually a small number) make all of the management decisions; thus, the management structure of a limited partnership closely approximates a corporation.

☐ *Duration of existence.* Whereas a corporation may provide for a perpetual existence, a partnership must be created for a specific term of years. However, since this term can be ninety-nine years or more, no significant difference between the two forms of organization exists in this respect.

☐ *Transfers of interests.* Perhaps the most significant objection to the partnership form is the relative difficulty in transferring interests as compared to the ease of transferring shares of stock in a corporation. A share of stock may be transferred merely by endorsing the certificate and does not require the approval of the board of directors of the corporation. (In special cases, as where a stock trust is created, the approval of third parties may be required for a transfer of stock.) On the other hand, the substitution of a new partner for an existing partner normally requires the approval of the other partners (in a general partnership) or of the general partners (in a limited partnership). However, a partner does not need his partner's consent to transfer his rights to share in the profits of the partnership; this may be done without actually substituting another partner in his place.

As a practical matter, transferability of interests in local ventures is not likely to be a significant problem. In these ventures, the individuals are known to one another and normally are prepared to retain their interests during the entire holding period of the property. In the event that one of them finds it necessary to liquidate his interests, the normal practice would be for the remaining partners to take up this interest or to mutually agree upon a new partner. However, in the case of the large national real estate partnerships, the lack of easy transferability does represent a disadvantage compared with a public corporation traded on a stock exchange or in the over-the-counter market. To some degree, the transferability problem is alleviated by some syndicators who stand ready to buy back limited partnership interests at a figure to be set by an appraisal of the underlying property; in other cases, the syndicator may maintain a list of interested outside investors who are prepared to buy interests of existing partners.

[2] Considerations in Setting Up a Partnership

[a] Guide for Determining Whether or Not a Partnership Exists

It is possible for a partnership to exist without the knowledge or the intention of the partners; on the other hand, investors may believe they are in partnership when in fact they are not. Under the Uniform Partnership Act (UPA), which is the model statute for general partnerships, the following rules aid in determining whether a partnership exists:

- ☐ Persons who are not partners with respect to each other are not partners as to third persons except where, by their conduct, they have led others to believe that they are partners and to rely on that belief to their disadvantage so as to create a partnership by estoppel.
- ☐ The mere existence of joint or part ownership of property does not establish that a partnership exists, regardless of whether or not the co-owners share the profits made by the use of the property.
- ☐ The sharing of gross returns from property does not, in and of itself, establish the existence of a partnership, regardless of whether or not the persons sharing the returns have a joint or common right or interest in the property from which the returns are derived.
- ☐ Proof that an individual shares in the profits of a business is prima facie evidence that he is a partner in the business, unless he receives the profits as payment of (1) a debt (installment or otherwise); (2) wages; (3) rent; (4) an annuity paid on behalf of a deceased partner; (5) interest on a loan (even though the amount of the payment varies with the profits of the business); or (6) consideration for the sale of the goodwill of a business or other property by installments or otherwise.

[b] Checklist of Considerations

☐ *Choice of name.* While a partnership can choose any name under which to conduct its operations, its name should not be too similar to that of another business organization. Where the participants' individual names are used as the partnership name, whether or not the partnership name will continue to be used after the death or retirement of a partner and whether or not it is permissible to do so under local law must be considered.

☐ *Registration of name.* In some states, a partnership name must be registered with a public agency or officer, for example, a county clerk or secretary of state.

☐ *Nature of business.* The nature of the partnership business must be clearly spelled out.

☐ *Permits and licenses.* The partnership agreement should provide that it is not to become effective unless and until required licenses or permits are procured.

☐ *Partners' contributions.* These may be in the form of property, cash, or services or of any combination of these. In addition to making a capital contribution to the partnership, a partner may make a loan or sell property to the partnership either for cash or on the installment basis. In each instance, the legal, tax, and accounting consequences to the partner and the partnership must be examined and dealt with.

Where property is contributed, the partners' right to reconcile the tax bases and accounting values of the contributed property in order to prevent distortions should be taken into account.

☐ *Duration of partnership.* The parties may agree to a definite term or the partnership may continue at will. A partner may terminate his relations with the partnership even though he does so in breach of the partnership agreement. Although this may result in an action for damages against him by the remaining partners, the partnership would still be dissolved. The partnership agreement may provide for liquidated damages in such event.

If the partnership agreement specifies a fixed term, the parties may continue the business beyond that term as a partnership at will or they may extend the term or enter into a new partnership agreement.

☐ *Partnership profits and losses.* The members of a partnership share in the partnership income and profits. While partnership losses are also, as a rule, shared among the partners, this is not always the case.

Where the partners share both profits and losses, they are usually shared in the same proportion. However, the partners may agree that different kinds of partnership income shall be distributed among the partners in different proportions. Whatever the arrangement may be, it should be carefully set out in the partnership agreement.

A partnership is not an entity separate from its members for income tax purposes. Each partner is taxed on his share of the partnership income and profits and is entitled to deduct his share of the partnership losses. The partnership files only an information return, not an income tax return such as an individual or corporation would file.

☐ *Compensation of partner for services to partnership.* In the absence of an express provision in the partnership agreement to the contrary, a partner usually is not entitled to compensation for his services to the partnership. If a partner is entitled to and does receive compensation for his services from the partnership, this is a deductible business expenditure of the partnership.

☐ *Payments to retired partner or estate heir of deceased partner.* Payments made to a retired partner or to the estate or heir of a deceased partner may represent that partner's capital interest, his pro rata interest in unrealized receivables and fees, his share of the potential gain or loss on partnership inventory, or mutual insurance among the partners.

☐ *Withdrawal of capital.* Where it is anticipated that the partnership will accumulate a substantial amount of money, the partners should be permitted to withdraw a sufficient sum to meet their income tax obligations. The partnership agreement should clearly spell out the parties' understanding with respect to the partners' rights in this regard.

☐ *Management of partnership affairs.* All partners have an equal voice with respect to the management and conduct of the business affairs of a general partnership, unless they agree otherwise. The partnership agreement should clearly state each partner's rights and duties and the extent to which the partners are authorized to bind the partnership by their contracts.

In the absence of an agreement to the contrary, the assignee of a partnership interest does not have a voice in the management of the partnership affairs during the continuance of the partnership.

☐ *Accounting.* The partnership agreement should require all partners to account to the partnership with respect to all matters affecting the partnership.

☐ *Partnership property.* Property acquired with partnership funds is partnership property, unless an intention to the contrary is clearly established.

☐ *Partner's death or withdrawal.* The partnership agreement may provide for the continuation of the business after the death or withdrawal of a general partner. While such provision may, along with other corporate attributes, give the partnership the tax status of a corporation so that its income is subject to a tax at the entity level and also at the investor level, in the absence of such a provision the partnership will be required to wind up its affairs upon a partner's death or withdrawal from the partnership.

☐ *Indemnification of partner.* The partnership may be required to indemnify each partner for payments made, and personal liabilities reasonably incurred, in the ordinary and necessary course of the partnership business.

☐ *Family members.* Partnership interests can be given to family members so as to spread income over several low-bracket taxpayers, but this is feasible only where capital is a substantial income-producing factor in the partnership. (See 4.03[7].)

[3] General Partnerships

[a] Definition and Advantages

A general partnership, as the name indicates, is a partnership consisting solely of general partners; there are no limited partners. Thus, all of the partners are entitled to an equal voice in partnership affairs, although this may be subject to some limitation by specific provision in the partnership agreement. Each participant is assured of a right to join in the management of the investment; thus, this type of ownership vehicle is most suitable for a relatively small and intimate group of investors who are confident of their ability to work well together. A general partnership requires no formal legal action or charter from the state in order to function. Once organized, however, a general partnership must operate in accordance with legal rules that in most states follow the model of UPA.

Flexibility is a distinct advantage of general partnerships. However, it underscores the importance of operating with a well-drafted partnership agreement that clearly defines the terms used and the rights and obligations of the parties. "Net profits" or "proceeds from sales or refinancing," for example, are terms that may be subject to different meanings. These and all the material terms used should be clearly defined so that no ambiguity exists and costly disputes can be avoided.

The partnership agreement can be so drafted as to mold the rights and responsibilities of each partner to fit his goals and areas of expertise. While each partner may retain a veto power over partnership decisions, voting rights may be allocated among the partners as they agree, and the responsibility for management may be delegated to one or some of the partners.

The partnership agreement may also provide that some partners are to receive the return of their investment in part or in whole before distributions are to be made to the other partners. The partners may also enter into indemnification agreements among themselves. Furthermore, the partnership agreement can be modified and amended from time to time by agreement of the partners.

As a formal matter, a partnership may have to file and record in a public office a certificate disclosing the names and addresses of the partners. This certificate must be amended as the partners change. If an assignee of a partner is not admitted as a partner, he probably does not have to be added to the certificate.

[b] Basic Disadvantages

The major disadvantage of the general partnership is that each partner is personally liable for the partnership debts; that is, all of the partner's assets may be reached by a creditor of the partnership in the event that the partnership assets are not sufficient. For this reason the general partnership is normally used only by a small group of investors who are known to each other. Other important disadvantages include:

☐ *Authority of individual partners to bind the partnership.* Those who deal with a general partnership have the right to assume that each partner has broad authority to bind the partnership, provided the transaction is within the scope of the partnership's business and apparently relates to that business. Since each partner is jointly and severally liable for the partnership's obligations, a partner may find himself in the unenviable position of having to dig into his own pocket to pay an obligation that was incurred by another partner apparently on behalf of the partnership.

☐ *Limited transferability.* Basically, UPA permits a partner to assign his share of the profits from a partnership, but the assignee does not have the right to participate in the management or administration of the partnership's business.

☐ *Possibility of dissolution.* Under UPA, dissolution of a partnership can occur without any violation of the partnership agreement

- At the end of a specified term.
- On the completion of a specified undertaking.
- At the will of any partner (in the absence of an agreement otherwise providing).
- At the consent of all the partners who have neither assigned nor encumbered their interest.
- On the expulsion of a partner pursuant to the terms of the partnership agreement.

In addition, any partner may cause the partnership to be dissolved for a breach of the partnership agreement. Dissolution may also be caused by the death or bankruptcy of a partner, court order, an event making the partnership business illegal, or if it becomes unlawful for the members to carry on the business as a partnership. A court may decree the dissolution of a partnership because of the mental incompetence of a partner, the wrongful conduct of a partner, or if the partnership business can only be carried on at a loss.

The occurrence of an event of dissolution does not necessarily require that the partnership's real estate operations must be terminated. The partnership agreement can provide for the continuation of the business without the deceased, incompetent, or bankrupt partner.

☐ *Less privacy and anonymity.* Generally, a partnership offers less privacy, anonymity, and confidentiality than does a trust or corporation. The requirement of filing a certificate (and sometimes publishing it) forces disclosure of the identity of the owners; in a partnership owning rental properties, for example, this could be a significant annoyance. In a partnership, any partner may inspect the books; however, in a corporation, the identity of the stockholders and the contents of the business records rarely have to be disclosed, even to stockholders.

[4] Limited Partnerships

If, as we have already observed, the partnership form of ownership is a favored form of ownership for income-producing real estate, then the limited partnership form of ownership is the favored type of partnership organization. A limited partnership makes it possible for a real estate professional to combine the financial resources of passive investors with his own skills in an organization that allows flexibility of operation, limited liability for his investors, and the tax benefits of the pass-through of taxable income, gain and losses, to his investors.

Under the Uniform Limited Partnership Act (ULPA), a limited partnership is one formed by two or more persons, having as members one or more general partners and one or more limited partners. While the general partner or partners manage the affairs of the partnership and are personally liable for the debts and obligations of the partnership, the limited partners, who are the passive investors, are not bound by the partnership debts and obligations.

A limited partnership is a hybrid between a corporation and a general partnership. It is similar to a corporation in that a limited partner's exposure, like that of a corporate shareholder, is limited to his equity investment, and his status as a limited partner does not give him the right to control or actively participate in the affairs of the partnership. The general partners' role and functions, on the other hand, are analogous to the role and functions of the directors and officers of a corporation.

Just as a corporation must file a certificate of incorporation with the appropriate state agency, a limited partnership, upon formation, must file a certificate of limited partnership with the appropriate state authority. A limited partnership certificate must contain the names and residences of both the general and the limited partners and also the pertinent provisions of the partnership agreement. The certificate must be amended whenever necessary to reflect the current status of the partnership. Moreover, as discussed in the next section, if a limited partnership too closely resembles a corporation, it will be taxed as if it were, indeed, a corporation.

In other respects, a limited partnership more closely resembles a general partnership than it does a corporation. For the most part, the rights and liabilities of the general partners in a limited partnership are similar to those of a partner in a general partnership. Additionally, a limited partnership has the same problems of continuity of existence and transferability of interest as a general partnership.

While it is possible for one person to be, at the same time, both a general and a limited partner in the same partnership, such a person will be in the same position as other general partners except that, in respect to contributions, this partner will be treated the same as the other limited partners.

[a] Status of General Partner and Limitations on Authority

A general partner in a limited partnership manages the partnership affairs, can bind the partnership by his acts and conduct, and can be held personally liable for the partnership obligations. However, under ULPA the general partner has no authority to

- Do any act in contravention of the limited partnership certificate.
- Do any act that would make it impossible to carry on the ordinary business of the partnership.
- Confess a judgment against the partnership.
- Possess partnership property or assign rights in specific partnership property for other than a partnership purpose.
- Admit a person into the partnership as a general partner.
- Admit a person into the partnership as a limited partner unless the right to do so is given to him in the partnership certificate.
- Continue the partnership business upon the death, retirement, or insanity of another general partner, unless the right to do so is given him in the certificate.

A general partner may be given authority to perform any of the above acts by the written consent of all of the limited partners. And all the limited partners may ratify such an act once performed by a general partner.

[b] Status of Limited Partners and Extent of Limitation of Liability for Partnership Debts

All the limited partners stand on equal footing vis-à-vis each other as to the return of their contributions, their right to income, and any other partnership matter, unless there is an agreement providing for priority as to such items. Such priority provisions must be stated in the partnership certificate.

Generally, a limited partner cannot bind the partnership by his acts nor is he liable to partnership creditors; however, this does not mean that he is completely free from obligations arising out of the partnership. For example, he is liable to the partnership for the contributions he has agreed to make to the partnership and for any breach of the partnership agreement by him. Also, he may be held liable to the partnership for a sum equal to the amount he has received plus interest as a return of his capital contribution where necessary to discharge the partnership's liabilities to creditors who extended credit to it or whose claims arose before his contribution was returned to him.

Under ULPA a limited partner may, without incurring the liability of a general partner, (1) be given the right to inspect the partnership books at the partnership's place of business; (2) be kept abreast, and receive an accounting, of partnership affairs; (3) have the partnership dissolved and wound up by a court decree; (4) share in partnership profits and income; and (5) receive the return of his contributions. Likewise, a limited partner does not incur the liability of a general partner although he has the right to elect or remove the general partner or partners, a voice in determining whether the partnership agreement should be amended, whether substantially all of the partnership assets should be sold, and whether the partnership should be terminated or continued.

On the other hand, the more rights that are granted to the limited partners, the greater the probability that they will be deemed to have the liability of general partners in regard to third persons. Certainly, if a so-called limited partner takes an active role in the day-to-day affairs or management of the partnership, he will, at least as to outsiders, be subject to the liability of a general partner.

[c] Loans by Limited Partners to Partnership

Under ULPA a limited partner may make a loan to, and transact business with, the partnership. Under a literal interpretation of the terms of ULPA, however, a limited partner cannot receive or hold any partnership property as collateral security for his loan, since this would be a fraud on the partnership creditors.

A mortgage given to a limited partner by a partnership as security for his loan to a partnership is valid as to the other members of the partnership. However, a third-party creditor has a superior claim to the mortgaged property if the partnership does not have other sufficient assets to meet the obligation.

Some jurisdictions do not follow a literal interpretation of ULPA with respect to the effect of secured loans made by limited partners to the partnership. In these jurisdictions, the receipt of a mortgage or other collateral security by a limited partner for his loan to the partnership is a fraud on partnership creditors only if, at the time the loan is made, the partnership assets are insufficient to discharge the debts owed by the partnership to outsiders.

[d] Effect of Limited Partner's Death or Incompetence

The death or incompetence of a limited partner does not result in the dissolution of the partnership. The personal representative of a deceased limited partner has all his rights for the purpose of settling his estate, including the right to constitute an assignee of the limited partnership interest as a substituted limited partner. The estate also remains liable for the decedent's liabilities as a limited partner.

[e] Assignment of Limited Partner's Interest and Effect Thereof

A limited partner's interest may be assigned. The assignee may be designated as a substituted limited partner, in which event he has all the rights and liabilities of his assignor; if he is not so designated, his rights are limited to receiving the profits, income, or return of contributions to which his assignor would otherwise be entitled.

All the remaining members of the partnership may grant to the assignee of a limited partnership interest the rights of a substituted limited partner, or this designation may be conferred on the assignee by his assignor if he is so empowered by the partnership certificate. To consummate his status as a substituted limited partner, the certificate must be amended to reflect this fact. The assignor is not released from any liability he may owe to the partnership by the substitution of his assignee as a limited partner.

[5] Qualifying as a Partnership for Tax Purposes

[a] How to Distinguish a Partnership From a Corporation

In our discussion, we have assumed that the tax-shelter vehicle called a partnership in fact qualifies as a partnership under the Internal Revenue Code and Treasury Regulations. However, merely organizing an entity in partnership form does not assure that it will be treated as a partnership under the Code. IRS has the authority, in proper cases, to deem an entity in partnership form to be in fact an "association" that is taxable as a corporation. In this event, of course, all of the partnership benefits, including the pass-through of losses, is lost.

The present rule for determining if a limited partnership will be treated as such has been in effect for many years. The rule is stated as a negative: So long as the partnership meets no more than two of the four tests listed below, it will be treated as a partnership. The rule was phrased in negative terms because it developed at a time when IRS was fighting a trend by doctors and other professional groups to seek treatment as corporations rather than partnerships. Thus, the IRS emphasis when the regulation was first written was to establish tests that had to be met in order to qualify as a corporation for tax purposes. Today, of course, the emphasis is just the opposite—partnerships want to *avoid* meeting the tests for corporations. The tax rule, however, remains as originally written.

☐ *Continuity of life* (*Test 1*). The absence of continuity of life of the entity points to a partnership, not a corporation. Since it is easy for a syndicate to provide that death, insanity, or retirement of a general partner terminates the partnership, this test normally is not met by the typical syndicate and consequently points toward partnership treatment.

☐ *Centralized management* (*Test 2*). The essence of a limited partnership syndicate is that the general partner will in fact manage the partnership (and, indeed, he must if the limited partners are to retain the limited liability they require). At the same time, the majority ownership normally is in the limited partners. This means management is centralized. Thus, this test, which points toward treatment as a corportion, is met by the real estate syndicate.

If the general partner has a minimum 20 percent interest in the partnership, then, despite his management of the partnership, management is not centralized and this test is not met; that is, it points toward partnership treatment. But the general partner rarely has this substantial an interest.

☐ *Limited liability* (*Test 3*). This test is not met—and, hence, partnership treatment is indicated—if the general partner (1) has personal liability for the nonrecourse debts of the partnership; and (2) has substantial assets. The latter requirement insures that neither a dummy corporation nor an individual without assets (one who is judgment-proof) can be made the general partner in order to give the appearance, without the reality, of unlimited liability. Since most syndicates are set up with a general partner having substantial assets, this test normally will not be met; that is, partnership treatment will be indicated.

A corporate general partner of a syndicate must meet special safe-harbor rules, which are discussed in detail below.

☐ *Free transferability of interests* (*Test 4*). Free transferability does not exist—and, hence, partnership treatment is indicated—if a limited partner requires consent by the general partner to transfer his interest to a substitute limited partner. This provision is common in many syndicate agreements.

Free transferability also should not exist if a partner can assign only his right to share in the profits of the venture and not his right to participate in the management of the partnership. And transferability does not exist if, under state law, the transfer of a partner's interest in the partnership results in the dissolution of the partnership and the formation of a new partnership.

There can be a modified form of transferability of interest under which each partner can transfer his interest in the partnership to an outsider only after offering it to the other partners at fair market value. This modified form of transferability will probably be given less significance as a corporate characteristic than full transferability.

Since many syndications will fail to meet Tests 1, 3, and 4, partnership treatment—the pass-through of gains and losses—can reasonably be assured under present rules.

There have been some indications that the Service is considering revising these regulations to make it much more difficult to qualify as a partnership. For example, IRS might require that a partnership meet no more than one of the four tests in order to avoid being taxed as an association. This would make it increasingly difficult, if not impossible, for many limited partnerships to qualify.

[b] Difficulties in Obtaining Advance Rulings From IRS

At one time it was a relatively simple matter for a real estate syndicate to obtain an advance ruling from the IRS that the syndicate would qualify as a partnership. However, the major thrust of the IRS attack on tax-shelter syndicates has been via a series of administrative rulings that set forth a policy against giving advance rulings unless certain specific requirements are met by the applicant—requirements which, in essence, impose limitations on the degree of tax shelter that can be obtained. The two most significant rulings are those relating to the safe-harbor rules for corporate general partners and the tax-avoidance guidelines for partnerships in general.

[i] The Safe-Harbor Rules for Corporate General Partners. When a corporation, rather than an individual, is the general partner of the syndicate, specific requirements have been set forth by IRS in connection with the limited-liability test (Test 3 above). In order for the partnership to fail to meet the test of limited liability—that is, to be treated as a partnership for purposes of this test—the corporate general partner must meet two requirements: the net worth requirement and the ownership requirement.[2] It should be noted that there is no specific statutory sanction for these rules.

☐ *Net worth requirement.* If the total contributions to the partnership are less than $2.5 million, then at all times during the life of the partnership, the corporate general partner must have net assets equal to 15 percent of the total contributions or $250,000, whichever is the lesser. If the total contributions are $2.5 million or more, the corporate general partner must have net assets equal to 10 percent of total contributions.

☐ *Ownership requirements.* The limited partners in the partnership cannot own, directly or indirectly, more than 20 percent of the stock of the sole corporate general partner.

Suppose there are several corporate general partners, not just one? Then, for purposes of the net worth requirement, the assets of the corporate general partners can be combined. However, the ownership requirement is applied individually to each corporation; that is, if the limited partners own more than 20 percent of the stock of any one corporate general partner, the syndicate is deemed to have general liability, and so, for purposes of the limited-liability test, it is deemed a corporation, not a partnership.

[ii] The Tax-Avoidance Guidelines for Limited Partnerships. Under present law, if the purpose of a transaction is tax avoidance, the transaction may be set aside for federal tax purposes, with the result that the taxpayer will not receive the deductions resulting from the transaction to which he would otherwise be entitled. As a result, the IRS generally will not issue a ruling letter with respect to any transaction where there is a serious question whether or not the principal purpose of the transaction is tax avoidance.

In Revenue Procedure 74-17 [3] IRS set forth guidelines it will apply in determining whether the formation of a limited partnership is for the principal purpose of reducing federal taxes. If the requirements of the revenue procedure are not satisfied, no ruling letter will be issued. However, the taxpayer is still free to argue, either with an IRS agent or before a court, that he is entitled to the deductions claimed in connection with the partnership.

The IRS guidelines contained in Revenue Procedure 74-17 are as follows:

- All of the general partners, in the aggregate, must have at least one percent interest in each material item of partnership income, gain, loss, deduction, or credit.
- The aggregate deduction of the limited partners during the first two years of the partnership's operations cannot exceed the amount of the equity investment in the partnership.

---

[2] Rev. Proc. 72-13, 1972-1 C.B. 42.

[3] Rev. Proc. 74-17, 1974-1 C.B. 438, T.I.R. 1290, issued May 3, 1974.

- No creditor who makes a nonrecourse loan to the partnership may acquire, as a result of making the loan, any direct or indirect interest in the profits, capital, or property of the limited partnership, other than as a secured creditor.

[iii] Information and Documents Required to Obtain Advance Ruling by IRS. Revenue Procedure 75-16 [4] sets forth a checklist of the information and documents that the IRS requires for advance rulings for both general and limited partnerships. Included in this checklist are the following:

- ☐ An outline or highlighted copy of all promotional material used to sell interests, including statements concerning the probable tax consequences of the arrangement and the effect of the requested ruling on such tax consequences.
- ☐ A statement indicating whether there will be any shift in the proportion of the profit-and-loss sharing ratio during the course of operations. If there is such a shift, details of the shift and the business reasons for it will be included.
- ☐ A statement as to whether the amount of any negative capital account balance of a general or limited partner will be paid by the partner to the partnership on its dissolution, liquidation, or termination.
- ☐ A net worth representation as to the general partner(s), accompanied by supporting financial data including, for example, audited balance sheets or unaudited balance sheets with a representation that they have been prepared in accordance with generally accepted accounting principles.
- ☐ A detailed description of all benefits that creditors may receive from the partnership, such as conversion or exchange rights, recourse rights against other property, or benefits that accrue to neighboring property owned by the creditors because of loans to the partnership.

[c] Possibility-of-Profit Test

The net effect of the IRS rulings of the past few years is that a real estate syndicate can be organized as a limited partnership and be taxed as such provided that the endeavor is not seen as one having as its principal object the avoidance or evasion of taxes. In turn, tax avoidance or evasion is likely to be found where there is virtually no possibility of economic profit (as distinguished from tax savings) as a result of the investment.

On the other hand, the fact that the limited partners receive no current cash flow from the investment, but merely utilize tax losses created by the property, will not by itself justify avoiding the tax-shelter transaction so long as the possibility of economic profit over the life of the investment remains possible.

[6] Taxation of Partnerships and Partners

Partnerships have distinct advantages over corporations with respect to federal income taxation. These advantages are accentuated where the partnership

---

[4] Rev. Proc. 75-16, 1975-1 C.B. 676.

venture is a real estate enterprise, since the very substantial tax deductions that real estate generates (e.g., depreciation, interest, maintenance, and repair) are passed through directly to the partners and serve as a tax shelter for them.

For federal income tax purposes, a partnership is a mere conduit. In itself, a partnership is not an income taxpayer. It merely computes its taxable income, gain or loss, and then each partner reports his share of that income, gain or loss, on his own income tax return.

Each partner picks up his share of partnership taxable gains and losses. Partnership income or loss is allocable to each partner for the portion of the year in which he is a member of the partnership. A partner's share of income or loss may be allocated on a daily basis, or the partnership year may be divided into two or more segments and the partnership income or loss in each segment divided among those who were partners during that segment.

The partners pick up the profits and losses of the partnership as ordinary income or losses or as capital gains or losses, depending on their nature when realized by the partnership. Each shares in the depreciation deductions and the taxable losses generated by the partnership property, and each partner can use these items as tax write-offs to shelter both his income from the partnership and his unrelated income.

Any cash distributions to partners in excess of taxable income reduce the bases of their partnership interests. If a partner's tax basis has already been reduced to zero, such distributions are treated as capital gains.

Usually, the tax deductions that are generated by a real estate enterprise and are passed through to the partners are greatest during the early stages of the venture. These include depreciation, loan commitment fees, interest and points, real estate transfer taxes, sales or use taxes, and management fees. A partner may also take a deduction on his individual return for his share of the partnership's investment credit.

While the amount of partnership losses a partner may deduct on his tax return is limited to his basis in his partnership interest, that basis is increased by his share of partnership liabilities. And, in this regard, for a nonrecourse mortgage liability, all the partners share in the liability in the same proportion as they share in profits. In addition, carrybacks and carryforwards may further enhance a partner's opportunities to shelter income not only from the partnership but also from unrelated sources.

Since a partnership interest is personal property even though the partnership is a real estate partnership, some states do not impose an estate tax on the interest of a nondomiciliary decedent even though the partnership's real property is located in that state.

[a] Tax Consequences of Contributions by Partners to Partnership

A partner who contributes property or money to the partnership realizes no taxable gain or loss as a result of his contribution. If the property is appreciated property, he may be credited with its current value, but the partnership's basis for the property is the same as the contributing partner's basis. Consequently, the partnership may be able to take only relatively low depreciation deductions for the property. The tax disadvantage to those partners who contributed cash rather than property to the partnership may be somewhat rectified by allocating a larger depreciation deduction to those who contributed cash than to those who contributed appreciated property.

For example, a partner may transfer real estate, or he may transfer a contract or option to purchase real estate to the partnership in exchange for his partnership interest and realize no taxable gain or loss as a result of the transaction. Since his adjusted basis for the property carries over to the partnership, where the property has appreciated in value while it was held by him so that its fair market value exceeds the partnership's basis for the property, there is a built-in taxable profit that must be accounted for when the property is sold. If the partnership sells the property shortly after it acquires it for a price equal to the value of the partnership interest that it transferred to the contributing partner in exchange for the property, the partnership will show a taxable gain in an amount equal to the excess of the price over the basis.

Conversely, if the contributing partner's adjusted basis exceeds the fair market value of the property at the time of the transfer to the partnership, there is a built-in taxable loss in the exchange. A sale by the partnership at the same price it paid for the property will enable the noncontributing partners to take a tax loss, even though they suffered no real economic loss from the transaction. Under these circumstances the partnership agreement may provide for a special allocation, taking into account the built-in profit or loss.

Where a partner contributes property in exchange for his partnership interest, the exchange may have an immediate tax impact on the partner. If the property that he exchanged for his partnership interest is subject to encumbrances that are assumed by the partnership, his basis in his partnership interest is reduced by an amount equal to the assumed indebtedness. Should this result in a reduction in basis to below zero, the partner will have a taxable gain. When the partnership interest is worth more than the property's fair market value, the excess may be deemed compensation for services performed by him for the partnership and may constitute ordinary income.

Beyond a partner's tax basis for his partnership interest, he cannot deduct his share of partnership losses. He can, however, boost his tax basis by making a capital contribution before the end of the year.

[b] Taxation of Syndicator's Interest in the Partnership

In the typical syndicate-partnership, the syndicator obtains control of the desired property before he forms the investment group. Control may be obtained by outright purchase, by a contract to purchase, or with an option. The syndicator then forms a partnership and contacts investors; the syndicator contributes the property, contract, or option, and the investors contribute cash.

The syndicator may receive his reward for putting the deal together in several ways. If he is paid a sum in cash, it is immediately taxable to him as ordinary income; thus, this form of compensation is normally not used. Instead, the syndicator receives an interest in the syndicate, which may be taxed in one of two ways:

- If the syndicate interest is given to the syndicator in exchange for his services in putting the transaction together, the value of the interest is taxable to him at once as ordinary income.

- If the interest is given to the syndicator in exchange for the property, contract, or option contributed by him, then the exchange is tax-free and the syndicator need pay no immediate tax. (The value of the syndicator's interest cannot exceed the value of the property contributed by him.)

An Atlanta developer, D.N. Stafford, attempted to put these principles to work. He negotiated on his own behalf with an insurance company for the development of a hotel property. As a result of these negotiations, he and the insurance company entered into a letter of intent, expressing the insurance company's intention to give him a ground lease for the hotel property and a mortgage commitment, both on favorable terms. After acquiring the letter of intent, Stafford sought out investors and set up a limited partnership to construct, own, and operate the property. Twenty limited partnership units were sold for $100,000 each, two of which were purchased by Stafford, and a twenty-first unit was issued to Stafford, the sole general partner, in exchange for his transfer of the letter of intent to the partnership.

According to IRS, Stafford's receipt of the twenty-first unit produced taxable income in the amount of $100,000 for services rendered. Stafford, on the other hand, claimed that he had transferred property to the partnership in exchange for an interest in the partnership, and that no gain was recognized on the exchange. Considering the dispute to be whether Stafford had transferred property or services for the interest, the district court upheld Stafford's claim. It found that the letter of intent regarding the lease agreement and mortgage commitment was a species of property, and that it had substantial value.

But finding that there was a real issue of fact as to what Stafford actually transferred for the unit, the Court of Appeals for the Fifth Circuit reversed and remanded for further proceedings. It held that the district court improperly granted Stafford's motion for a summary judgment since there was some evidence that he received the unit for his services in putting the deal together for the investors and for services to be rendered. And, in a footnote, the court pointedly questioned whether a nonbinding letter of intent was "property" for purposes of Section 721 of the Code.[5]

Had the letter of intent matured into a signed lease and mortgage commitment that were contributed to the partnership upon its formation, Stafford's gain would have been tax-free—assuming (1) that the property transferred had a value at least equal to the value of the interest received; and (2) that he acquired the lease and mortgage commitment himself and not on behalf of the investment group.

[c] Special or Disproportionate Allocations of Partnership Income, Profits, and Losses

While the partnership agreement may make special or disproportionate allocations of items of taxable income, profits, losses, and deductions among the partners, these special allocations are effective only if they have substantial economic effect. If they do not have substantial economic effect, the allocation of each individual item of income, profits, losses, and deductions must be computed on the

[5] Stafford v. United States, 80-1 U.S.T.C. ¶ 9218 (5th Cir. 1980).

same basis as the partner's interest in the partnership as a whole. This, in summary, is the rule under the Tax Reform Act of 1976 [6] (TRA 1976). Although the TRA 1976 rule applies to partnership taxable years beginning after December 31, 1975, a special or disproportionate allocation of items of partnership income, profits, deductions, or losses always was barred if its principal purpose was tax avoidance or evasion. Thus, even before the TRA 1976, IRS considered the following in determining whether a special or disproportionate allocation was valid or whether it was made for the primary purpose of tax avoidance or evasion:

- Aside from the tax consequences, is there a substantial economic effect on the dollar amount that the partner will receive from the partnership's profit or losses?
- Is there a business purpose for the allocation?
- Are related items subject to the same allocation?
- Is the allocation for a limited duration of time?
- Was the allocation made only after its amount was ascertainable or could reasonably be estimated?

Whether there is a real economic effect on the partner who receives the special allocation determines whether it will pass muster with IRS. IRS will not, for example, permit one partner to receive the benefit of all of the partnership's tax deductible items if that partner, regardless of whether there are profits or losses, will receive distributions from the partnership as if no special allocation had been made.

Nevertheless, the ability of a partnership to make these allocations is an attractive feature. A partner in a high tax bracket, with no other tax shelters, is often willing to reduce his share of the proceeds of the sale of the property in exchange for receiving a larger allocation of deductible items from the partnership.

[d] Determining the Tax Basis of a Partnership Interest

To understand the tax treatment that results from a partnership interest, it is necessary to know the manner in which a partner's tax basis is determined. As we have already indicated, the initial basis is the price paid for the partnership interest. If real estate or other property was transferred to the partnership in exchange for the partnership interest, the partner's initial basis in his partnership interest is the same as the basis he had for the property immediately before the transfer. That basis is increased by a pro rata share of partnership liabilities and income, regardless of whether the income is taxable. The basis is decreased by a distribution of partnership property or losses, or by a reduction of partnership obligations.

> *Example:* Assume that a partner paid $100,000 for a 50 percent interest in the partnership and that the partnership purchased real estate for $800,000 ($200,000 cash + a $600,000 mortgage loan). The partner's basis would be $400,000 (purchase price for interest + 1/2 of the partnership's liability on the mortgage loan). When the venture reaches the point at which $100,000 has been taken for depreciation and the principal amount due on the mortgage

[6] Pub. L. No. 94-455, 90 Stat. 1520, 26 U.S.C.A. §§ 1 et seq.

has been reduced by $20,000, the partner's basis is reduced to $340,000 ($400,000 – pro rata share of depreciation ($50,000) and pro rata share of mortgage reduction ($10,000)).

[e] Sale or Exchange of Partnership Interests

When a partner sells or exchanges his interest in the partnership, a capital gain or loss is realized, measured by the difference between the amount realized from the transaction and the adjusted basis of the partnership interest, except to the extent that the proceeds of the transaction are attributable to his pro rata share of unrealized receivables or substantially appreciated inventory items.

Where the transaction requires the recognition of ordinary income or loss as to some of the proceeds, the amount realized is reduced by the amount attributable to unrealized receivables and substantially appreciated inventory items, and the adjusted basis of the transferred partner's interest is reduced by the portion of the basis attributable to such unrealized receivables and substantially appreciated inventory items.

The initial basis of a partnership interest acquired by contribution is the sum of the amount of money contributed plus the contributor's adjusted basis in any property contributed. Where the partnership interest is acquired in connection with the performance of services, the initial basis of the interest includes the amount of taxable income realized by the performer in connection with the receipt of the interest.

A partner's initial basis for his partnership interest is increased by his distributive share of (1) partnership taxable income; (2) partnership tax-exempt income; and (3) excess of partnership deductions for depletion over the basis of the partnership property subject to depletion. The adjusted basis of a partner who makes additional contributions is increased by the amount of cash contributed on his adjusted basis for any property contributed.

A partner's basis for his partnership interest is decreased—but not below zero—by the amount of cash distributed to him plus the basis to him of any property distributed by the partnership, the amount of his depletion deductions for oil and gas wells, and his distinctive share of partnership losses and nondeductible expenditures of the partnership not properly chargeable to capital account.

[f] Investment Organization and Selling Fees

Substantial fees are often incurred in organizing a partnership and marketing partnership interests. For tax purposes, these fees are divided into two categories: (1) syndication fees, and (2) organization costs. Syndication fees are permanently capitalized and never deducted by the partnership. They reduce the gain or increase the loss of each partner upon his disposition of the partnership interest. As defined by the TRA 1976 Committee Reports[7] syndication fees are all expenditures connected with issuing and marketing the partnership interests, such as sales commissions, professional fees in developing the prospectus or offering, and printing costs.

---

[7] I.R.C. § 709.

Organization costs include all costs related to the formation of the partnership, such as legal fees to prepare the partnership agreement; legal fees to draft the offering itself are not included. All expenditures allocated to organization costs are to be amortized over a period of no less than sixty months. In accounting for these expenditures, an aggressive approach is best used, with detailed invoices or other records to support cost allocations. In a typical situation, substantially more costs are allocated to syndication fees than organization costs.

[g] Comparison of a Land Lease and a Partnership

In some situations, a land-lease arrangement may be wiser than a partnership arrangement. If an investor owns a parcel of land that he wants to develop and does not want to sell it outright and thus incur the large capital gains tax, the first option contemplated is usually creation of a partnership. However, if the investor becomes a general partner and the development should prove unsuccessful, he will be liable for partnership debts. In this case, a better solution might be to lease the land to a developer. Assuming that the ground rental reflects current market conditions and the lessee does not have an option to purchase at a "bargain price," the IRS will not challenge the transaction as a disguised sale with a purchase-money mortgage and, therefore, no tax problem will arise. In this way, the lessor can obtain all of a partner's advantages while avoiding some of the problems inherent in the partnership form of ownership.

The following points should be considered when making a decision between a partnership and land-lease arrangement:

☐ *A lessor can obtain the same benefits as a partner.*

- The major advantage of a partnership position is the right to participate in profits and property appreciation. To a large degree, a lessor can achieve the same end by having the rent step up in accordance with a cost-of-living index or to include a participation in gross income realized by the lessee.
- A partner (whether limited or general) may have a priority right to share in the cash flow. A lessor, however, always has priority over the cash flow retained by the lessee.

☐ *A lessor has certain advantages over a partner.*

- If the project ran into trouble, the landowner-partner might have to cure all defaults to protect his position and, in any event, he would remain a partner. The landowner-lessor might still have to cure a default on a mortgage (to which he had subordinated his fee) to take possession of the property, but he would then no longer be liable for any other expenses of the partnership.
- Administering a land lease is much less management-intensive than participating in a partnership (although it is true that as a limited partner, the landowner could avoid any management responsibility).
- The landowner as lessor retains complete control over disposition of the land (subject to the lease), whereas in a partnership he would have to obtain the consent of his partner. For example, the landowner could mort-

gage the fee subject to the leasehold interest and so obtain cash while at the same time retaining ownership of the land.

☐ *A partnership has certain advantages over a lease.*

- The landowner-lessor will not participate in any appreciation of the improvements, as will a partner. (However, the land probably will appreciate at the same rate, at least if the rental is not fixed.)
- The landowner as lessor cannot benefit from any tax shelter arising from depreciation of the improvements. This can be a significant factor but presumably would be taken into consideration when arriving at a fair rental. The additional depreciation that the developer receives (because of not having to share it) has value to him and should be reflected in the rental.
- The landowner as lessor will have no voice in the management of the property; however, this may be an advantage rather than a disadvantage.

The developer may be quite willing to utilize a land lease rather than a partnership, provided he is able to obtain the same financing. This can easily be achieved if the lessor is willing to subordinate his fee interest to a development mortgage.

[7] Family Partnerships

A family partnership—that is, one in which the partners are members of a single family unit—enables a high-bracket taxpayer to shift income to family members in lower tax brackets. It is particularly appropriate for use by real estate investors because capital investment rather than personal services must be the primary factor producing income. The ideal situation for creation of a family partnership occurs when the taxpayer owns property generating taxable income with potential for substantial price appreciation in the future.

[a] Example of Potential Benefits

For example, assume a mother of two children (ages 7 and 9) is in the 50 percent tax bracket. She purchases a rental property for $1 million ($50,000 in cash, plus a $950,000 mortgage). Title to the property is taken by a partnership in which the mother has a 50 percent interest and in which each child has a 25 percent interest. The value of the interest transferred to each child is $12,500 (or a total of $25,000 for both children, 50 percent of the equity in the property). We further assume

- No gift tax is payable on the transfer.
- The property generates taxable income of $10,000 per year ($100,000 after 10 years).
- The property is sold for $1.25 million after 10 years (producing capital gain of $700,000).

Based on these assumptions, the savings achieved after ten years would be as shown in Table 4.2.

TABLE 4.2 Savings After Ten Years

	Income Taxes	*Tax on Gain*[2]
No partnership created:		
Taxes payable (50%)	$50,000	
Sale by mother		$125,600
Family partnership created:		
Taxes payable (mother 50% & children 20%)		
Estate value (mother)	35,000[1]	99,200
Savings as a result of family partnership	$15,000	$ 26,400

[1] 50% of $50,000, plus 20% of $50,000 = $35,000.
[2] Assume no other income.

It should be noted that the income shifted to the children is not available to the mother for her own purposes and indeed cannot be used to discharge her legal obligation of support of her children. Precisely what this obligation amounts to varies from state to state.

[b] Requirements of a Family Partnership

In order for family members to be regarded, for tax purposes, as partners in a family partnership, three requirements must be met:

☐ *Capital interest.* The family member must have a capital interest in the partnership, that is, an equity in the partnership assets. It makes no difference how the interest is derived (i.e., the interest can be created by gift). Among other things, a partnership equity requires that there be a right to share upon a dissolution of the partnership. The mere right to participate in earnings and profits does not represent a capital interest.

☐ *Capital as a material income-producing factor.* A family partnership as a tax-shifting technique cannot be used when partnership income arises primarily from the rendition of services, since the family members normally are not in a position to do the necessary work. Thus, a family partnership is feasible only where a substantial portion of the income is derived from the investment of partnership capital. Real estate, of course, meets this requirement very well.

☐ *Partnership reality.* The partnership must be a real entity, with the family members actually treated as owners of interest in the business. Factors indicating that the family member is not a true owner are discussed in the following paragraphs. However, in the absence of those factors, the new partner will be treated as an owner for tax purposes, even though she does not participate in the business (whether as a general or limited partner).

[c] Pitfalls to Avoid in Setting Up the Partnership

As just noted, a family member must actually own an interest in the partnership in order for income to be legitimately shifted to him. Some things that IRS looks for to show that no true ownership interest exists are the following:

☐ *Control over distribution of income.* Suppose the donor (e.g., mother) retains control by one method or another of income that, according to the partnership books, has been distributed to the donees of partnership interests (the children). That will be taken as an indication that no true ownership interests were intended. On the other hand, actual distributions to family partners of a major portion of the partnership income points toward true ownership.

☐ *Restraints on right to withdraw.* If the family members are true partners, they must be entitled to liquidate their interest in the partnership when they wish.

☐ *Control of related assets.* Sometimes the donor of the partnership interests has indirect control of other assets central to the partnership's operation; such indirect control may be through a separate business or another partnership. For purposes of testing whether the family members have a true ownership interest, such indirect control by the donor will be judged as though the donor had direct ownership.

☐ *Unusual management powers.* In the case of a general partnership, the family members' substantial participation in management is strong evidence of a true ownership interest. However, this factor will not be relevant in the case of a limited partnership, where the family members are barred from management by the nature of the entity.

[d] Use of a Limited Partnership

As noted, the problem of management participation by family partners is eliminated when a limited partnership is used, as is commonly done when real estate is owned. When a family member is a limited partner, these specific requirements must be met in order for the limited partner to be treated as a true owner:

- The limited partner must be able to assign his partnership interest.
- His rights with respect to the investment must not be limited to the right to an accounting or to withdrawal from the partnership.
- A written agreement must exist stating that the general partner does not have unusual discretion in making income distributions to limited partners.
- The limited partner must become subject to liability as a general partner if he participates in management.

[e] Allocating Partnership Income

A final but important rule relating to family partnerships involves the allocation of profits and losses. The two rules peculiar to family partnerships are (1) reasonable compensation must be paid for services rendered to the partnership by the donor, even if such compensation is not required in the partnership agreement; and (2) partnership income must be allocated in proportion to capital interest.

If these rules are not followed, the partnership will still be valid, but IRS may reallocate profits and losses among the partners.

[f] Gift of Partnership Interest to Minor

Family members who are minors can be partners in their own names if they are competent to manage their own property and participate in partnership activities. If this competence is lacking, the interest for a minor child can be transferred to a trust or a guardian. Since a guardian is subject to judicial supervision and may have to make periodic accountings to the court, this approach is more burdensome than a trust but may be the only alternative in states that do not allow a trust to be a partner.

If a minor's interest is transferred to a trust, the best approach is to set up an irrevocable trust with an independent trustee so that any potential conflicts of interest are avoided.

The tax questions, both in the creation of a family partnership and in the gift of an interest to a minor, are complex and require the use of professional tax advisers.

In the type of situation visualized here (i.e., ownership of an income property), the alternative of a Subchapter S corporation is barred by the rule that such a corporation cannot have more than 20 percent of its income from passive sources such as rent. However, in another situation such as construction, a Subchapter S corporation can achieve the same results with less risk than a family partnership.

[8] Joint Ventures

Joint ventures have become a commonplace feature in real estate. They reflect a fundamental and long-term shift in the relationship between builders and developers on the one hand, and those providing land or cash on the other. Until just a few years ago, the builder-developer was the one exercising primary control over new construction. With land and capital relatively plentiful and inflation not significant, it was the entrepreneurial element that was in demand. At the same time, a stable economic picture enabled the builder-developer to obtain funding on relatively favorable and fixed terms, while the relative ease of development enabled him to buy and warehouse land until it was needed.

All that has changed. While entrepreneurial ability is still a critical element for real estate success, money and land are much harder to obtain, and due to the prospects of continuing inflation, the money and land contributors want to share in the profits of a project. As a result, joint venturing is replacing outright land selling and straight mortgage financing. Indeed, some observers foresee a time in the not-too-distant future when builders and developers will be hired hands, working for large institutions and receiving a fee and possibly a share in profits. Just as likely, the large building firms will themselves become large enough (as some are already) to provide much of the financing for today's immense developments.

Whatever the long-range picture turns out to be, joint ventures have become one of the most significant ways of bringing the entrepreneur together with those who supply the money and land.

[a] Legal and Tax Aspects

The term "joint venture," like the term "syndicate," does not have specific legal significance. A joint venture essentially is the coming together of a small number of persons to carry on a particular transaction, rather than a series of transactions or a continuing business. The particular form of ownership used can be a general or limited partnership, regular or Subchapter S corporation, real estate investment trust or tenancy in common.

There is no doubt, however, that the general partnership is the most common form of entity used for a joint venture. Indeed, if a venture is not clearly identified as a corporation or other type of vehicle, most courts probably will consider the venture to be identical with a general partnership.[8]

A relationship may be deemed to be a joint venture for tax purposes even though the parties do not intend such a characterization. Two cases decided by the Tax Court show how this issue may arise.

☐ *Employee or joint venturer?* In the first case, an investor named Ralph Jensen located a parcel of land that he thought was ripe for development, and approached a partnership with a proposal to enter into a joint venture. A letter agreement referring to a joint venture was signed. The partnership paid Jensen a fee for his development efforts for about six months; then they entered into a formal employment agreement, which recited that no joint venture existed. This was done to protect the partnership against potential liens on the property. Subsequently, when the employment agreement was terminated and Jensen was paid off, he dissociated himself from the partnership.

The issue was whether the cash received by Jensen was to settle his employment contract (which would make it ordinary income) or to purchase his share of the joint venture (which would make it capital gain). The Tax Court said that a joint venture had originally been set up, and it remained so despite the employment agreement. So Jensen won.[9]

☐ *Customer or joint venturer?* In the second case, taxpayers were partners in a partnership and also shareholders in a corporation. The partnership would acquire land and sell it at a profit to the corporation that would develop it. The idea was to split the total gain into two parts. One part, from the appreciation in the value of the land, would be taxed to the partnership as capital gain, while the other part, from building and selling homes, would be ordinary income to the corporation.

The IRS challenged the arrangement, saying that the corporation was not a customer but was a joint venturer with the partnership. The Tax Court agreed. Although the developers were careful, on paper, to separate the activities of the partnership and the corporation, their efforts were so closely related that they

[8] See Madison Nat'l Bank v. Newrath, 261 Md. 321, 275 A.2d 495 (1971).

[9] Ralph T. Jensen v. Comm'r, T.C.M. 1980-335.

must be regarded as a single entity. Supporting this view was the fact that the partnership sold land to the corporation on easy terms; no interest was actually charged, and repayment was scheduled over several years as the land was expected to be developed and resold. In essence, all the risk of nondevelopment fell on the partnership.[10]

[b] Organizing the Joint Venture

The participants in a joint venture usually have roughly equal bargaining power because they are relatively few in number and each makes an important contribution to the success of the venture. By comparison, control in a public syndicate almost always is in the hands of the syndicator, since it is the syndicator who deals with a large number of investors, each putting in a relatively small amount of money and usually without experience in real estate. So the joint venture agreement is a matter of negotiation, often vigorous.

The following are the key issues that must be solved in the typical joint-venture arrangement.

☐ *Choice of legal form.* In general, the legal form will be general partnership, limited partnership, corporation, or joint-venture agreement (closely analogous to the general partnership).

The limited partnership and corporation offer limited liability to the money partner, but the former restricts the partner's management participation and the latter may have tax disadvantages. On the other hand, both the general partnership and joint venture permit great flexibility in management but increase the potential liabilities of the parties.

The two most commonly used solutions are:

- Money partner forms a small subsidiary corporation to act as a general partner (with liability consequently limited to the assets of the subsidiary).
- Financing partner remains a silent limited partner after setting up as many controls and checkpoints in the joint-venture agreement as he can get the developer to agree to.

An objection to the use of a subsidiary corporation as a general partner is that it may negate most or all of the tax advantages the financial partner expects to gain. In addition, combining the use of the subsidiary with direct cash investment as a limited partner creates the risk that the subsidiary may be deemed merely the instrument of the limited partner, who will lose his insulation from liability for partnership debt.

☐ *Roles played by the venturers.* Put quite simply, one or more parties usually provide the financing while one or more parties provide the expertise. But role definition is often more complex: Various types of expertise are often needed, and the money partners often want to participate in the management of the venture. So a specific listing of roles is valuable and will also aid in the proper choice of legal form, as discussed above.

---

[10] G. Cappuccilli v. Comm'r, T.C.M. 1980-347.

☐ *Capital requirements.* The agreement should spell out specifically the total capital requirements, the obligation of each venturer, and the time of payments. Investors will prefer staged advances, since this not only increases their return (because not all the cash need be put up at once) but also gives them greater control. The agreement should consider such questions as (1) Must the investor or developer make additional capital contributions if there are budget overruns? (2) Is there a ceiling on such calls? and (3) Must the developer guarantee the budget, that is, be solely responsible for unexpected cash demands?

☐ *Making financial arrangements support the goal of the venture.* Money fuels the joint venture; it should be spent in a way that moves the venture in the right direction. If the goal in the venture is net profit, compensation should not be tied to a percentage of gross assets or gross revenues, since these might then be stressed to the detriment of profit.

The same consideration applies to the risk of loss. The money partner—the person who stands to lose cash—is usually more concerned about risk than the expert, who stands to lose only his time and skill; thus, the latter may be much more inclined to enter into high-risk situations with high-profit potential. There is also the chance that the money partner may turn out to be too conservative. Therefore, the parties should make some effort to agree in advance on the degree of risk that will be tolerated.

☐ *Budgeting.* In joint ventures, budgeting is most important. The developer in a joint venture cannot operate in the same way that he would independently. The investor wants to see early in the venture a detailed cash-flow projection that shows money going in and money going out. The budget should be revised from time to time as conditions change, and as much notice of changes in the financial plan as is possible should be given. It is better to give the investor bad news as it occurs and to explain all the choices than to surprise the investor after the project has been lost.

☐ *Compatibility of the parties.* Compatibility is just as important in a joint venture as in a marriage. In particular, one party may be much more inclined than the other to walk away from a failing project. While compatibility cannot be agreed to in a contract, the parties should be aware of its importance.

☐ *Assessing the risks involved.* While the subject of risk has already been mentioned, it is worth stressing that the parties should try to have a common understanding of the risks involved and, in a general way, what action should be taken if certain risks materialize.

☐ *Capital, profits, and losses.* Two key questions for the parties to decide are how to raise additional capital if it becomes necessary and how to distribute profits and losses. Agreements on additional capital contributions vary widely, of course. Since it is clear that more capital may be needed, it is necessary to decide who should be the first to come forth with the additional capital; the money partner is usually the one, since that is his role in the venture. However, the money partner may insist that any additional contributions shall be returned to him before any other distribution of cash is made to the venturers; the additional contributions may be termed a loan and carry a specific interest return, rather than be an equity contribution.

☐ *Distribution of cash flow.* A basic question to be decided is whether the developer should receive most or all of the cash flow until the permanent loan has been funded, or whether the money partner is the first to receive all the cash until his capital is recouped. One view is that the developer should always be entitled to a significant share of the cash flow at all stages of a venture.

Cash-flow distribution is a completely separate matter from distribution of tax losses to create tax shelter. Customarily, the allocation of these losses among the venturers is different from the allocation of cash.

The developer should pay special attention to a requirement that there be a timely distribution of cash flow. Otherwise, years may pass before all outstanding obligations are paid or the final stage of the transaction is reached. This is likely to be much harder on the developer than on the financial partner. The developer also must consider whether to put up any initial cash or additional capital if it is needed later on. A cash-shy developer will not want this obligation; on the other hand, some developers may want to put up cash to increase their final return.

☐ *Developer's other activities.* Several questions to be decided are whether the investor is to have a right of first refusal on other ventures that the developer may do, and whether the developer is to be limited in other activities that he may undertake while the one project is in the works. The investor will not want the developer to build an office building across the street from the one to be put up by the joint venture. If the joint-venture office building is a success, it must be decided whether the developer can then build across the street.

☐ *Arrangements for settling disputes.* Disputes will inevitably arise and the agreement should make some provision for resolving them. Sometimes bringing in a third party is appropriate; at other times, the only solution is to break up the venture. A classic means of doing so is to allow one party to name a price at which he is willing to either buy or sell; the other partner then has to make the decision as to which option to take. This may work quite well when both parties have similar motivations and resources, but obviously this is not always the case; variations of this procedure may therefore be necessary.

☐ *Provision for withdrawal of a partner.* The final issue to be solved is the situation where one partner is unable or unwilling to finish the venture. Typically, this is covered by a buy-sell provision permitting the remaining partner to buy out the defaulter at the latter's cost. Since a venture is entered into based on the expertise and affinity of the partners, the agreement normally will bar transferability to other parties except under strict conditions.

[c] Financing Arrangements in Joint Ventures

The basic theme of the joint venture is that the money partner, as to all or a part of his investment, assumes the same risk of loss as the developer. By comparison, all of the other financing techniques give the money source (i.e., lender) a prior claim to income and to assets in the event of loss.

Here are brief examples of three popular joint-venture approaches to financing:

☐ *Imputed equity approach.* Here, the money partner puts up the entire cost and gives the developer a partnership interest equal to the increase in market value as a result of the construction. For example, consider the case in which a project costs $8 million and has a market value of $10 million upon completion. The money partner puts up the full $8 million cost and the developer is considered to have contributed $2 million (the imputed equity). Cash flow is then split 80-20 between the partners. When the property is financed with an outside lender, the first $6 million of refinancing proceeds goes to the money partner (reducing his investment to $2 million) and the balance, if any, of refinancing proceeds is split 50-50. Thereafter, the two partners are equal and share cash flow equally.

☐ *First mortgage plus equity.* In a variation on the above, the money partner provides a $6 million first mortgage (75 percent of cost) at a rate slightly below current market. In consideration of this, the money partner gets a 50 percent share of the remaining $4 million market value for $2 million. Thus, the developer once again is left with a $2 million interest while having mortgaged out. The two partners are 50-50 in equity interest but the money partner, of course, has a prior claim to the extent of its $6 million mortgage.

☐ *Convertible mortgage.* Here, the lender extends a first mortgage at a maximum loan-to-value ratio at a below-market interest rate. In exchange, the lender is given the option of converting the debt into equity at fixed times in the future. One way is to permit the lender to convert annual amortization into equity; however, since amortization is so low in the early years, this may not be sufficient inducement. Alternatively, fixed percentages of the outstanding loan may be converted to equity at the end of five, ten, or more years. The developer gains an advantage by receiving close to 100 percent financing at a favorable rate, and during the early years of the loan retains virtually all the depreciation write-offs and cash flow in excess of debt service. Depending upon how the equity is to be valued when acquired by the lender (often at some discount from then-market value), the developer also keeps a large portion of future appreciation.

[d] Classification of Joint-Venture Interests as Securities

Generally, an interest in a real estate joint venture is not considered a security under federal and state securities laws, but there is always danger that the person putting together the venture (a developer or real estate professional) may exercise so much control or management power that the courts may decide that the security laws do apply.

The United States Court of Appeals for the Fifth Circuit has spelled out three different situations where an interest in a joint venture may be a security in *Williamson v. Tucker,*[11] which involved a series of transactions. In each transaction, undivided interests in a parcel of undeveloped land were transferred to a

---

[11] Williamson v. Tucker, [Current Binder] CCH Fed. Sec. L. Rep. ¶ 97,724 (5th Cir. 1980).

joint venture. In each venture, the purchasers put up the purchase price in the form of promissory notes to buy the property.

Each of the joint ventures had approximately fifteen venturers. In each case, Godwin Investments (the promoter) had signed a contract to purchase an interest in the property. Godwin then attracted potential investors to participate in a joint venture through materials describing the investment potential of the proposed venture. The materials also touted the management expertise of Godwin Investments and included the following language: "Our firm aggressively pursues all zoning and proper land-planning efforts to assure the maximum profit potential of each investment."

Despite the representations of Godwin Investment's management duties and capabilities, the participants in each joint venture retained substantial control of the venture in the agreement that they signed. Each joint-venture agreement required the unanimous consent of the venturers to

- Confess a judgment.
- Make, execute, or deliver any bond, mortgage, deed of trust, or guarantee.
- Borrow money in the joint venture's name or use joint-venture property as collateral.
- Amend the agreement to modify the rights of the venturers.

Several years after entering into joint-venture agreements, four of the venturers filed suit to rescind the agreements they had signed, cancel the notes they had executed, and recover the amounts they had already paid on the notes. The plaintiffs argued, among other claims, that their interests in the joint ventures amounted to an "investment contract," and therefore a "security," under the 1933 and 1934 Acts.[12] A district court rejected this argument and dismissed the case for lack of subject matter jurisdiction.

The Fifth Circuit noted that the U.S. Supreme Court[13] defined the term "investment contract" as follows: "An investment contract for purposes of the Securities Act means a contract, transaction or scheme whereby a person invests his money in a common enterprise and is led to expect profits solely from the efforts of a promoter or a third party."

The Fifth Circuit observed that the *Howey* test requires satisfaction of three distinct elements: (1) an investment of money, in (2) a common enterprise, (3) on an expectation of profits to be derived solely from the efforts of others.

In examining the third element of the *Howey* test, the court pointed out that the word "solely" should not be interpreted in the most literal sense. In the court's view, there are the following three instances in which interests in a general partnership or joint venture can be designated as a security even though the partners or venturers retain some nominal control:

☐ *Limited distribution of power.* A security may exist if an agreement among the parties leaves so little power in the hands of the partner or venturer that the arrangement in fact distributes power as would a limited partnership.

---

[12] Securities Act of 1933, 48 Stat. 74, 15 U.S.C.A. §§ 77a–77aa; Securities and Exchange Act of 1934, 48 Stat. 881, 15 U.S.C.A. § 77b–77e.

[13] SEC v. W.J. Howey Co., 328 U.S. 293, rehearing denied 329 U.S. 819 (1946).

☐ *Inexperience.* A security may exist if the partner or venturer is so inexperienced and unknowledgeable in business affairs as to be incapable of intelligently exercising partnership or venture powers.

☐ *Dependence on management.* A security may exist if the partner or venturer is so dependent on some unique entrepreneurial or managerial ability of the promoter or manager as to be unable to replace the manager of the enterprise or otherwise exercise meaningful partnership or venture powers.

The Fifth Circuit observed that the plaintiffs would have a hard time fitting into any of these categories, but remanded the case to allow them to develop a fuller record before the district court. The Fifth Circuit acknowledged that the plaintiffs were executives with prior experience in real estate investments. In addition, the joint-venture agreements gave the plaintiffs significant control powers. Nonetheless, the court noted that the plaintiffs may have been dependent on the promoter's management expertise to plan uses for the property and to arrange for the necessary zoning changes. In the court's view, the plaintiffs were entitled to an opportunity to expand upon the dependency issue in their efforts to demonstrate the existence of an "investment contract."

For a general discussion of real estate securities, see 5.03[3].

4.04 CORPORATIONS

[1] Corporations in General

A corporation is a separate legal entity—an artificial person—created in accordance with the laws of a particular state; the federal government does not have the power to create business corporations. Its charter may provide that it shall have a perpetual life, and it establishes its operation through a board of directors elected by the shareholders. However, for business and tax purposes the corporation is an entity entirely distinct from its stockholders. Thus, the major advantage of, and original purpose for, the corporate form was to limit each shareholder's liability to the amount of his capital investment; a secondary purpose was to make shareholder interests freely transferable by means of assignable corporate shares.

The major disadvantage in using a corporation to own real estate is that the corporation is recognized as an independent entity for tax purposes. Thus, tax losses from corporately owned real estate may not be passed through to the individual shareholders, but may be utilized only by the corporation itself; since it may not have any other income against which the losses may be offset, the losses may be of no use. On the other hand, if the corporate real estate produces net income, a problem of double taxation must be faced. The corporation first must pay a corporate income tax on its net income; then, to the extent the income is distributed in the form of dividends, the shareholders must pay a personal income tax on such income. In the case of a small, closely held corporation (known as a close corporation), the problem of double taxation often can be avoided by distributing corporate income to the shareholders in the form of salaries or other compensation; in this situation, the corporation may deduct the cost of such salaries and thus reduce its own income, although the shareholder-employees will be taxed on the income they receive.

[a] Legal Consequences of Corporate Form of Ownership

A checklist of the basic legal and economic incidents and consequences of operating under the corporate form of ownership follows:

☐ *A corporation*

- Can hold and deal in property in its own name.
- Can sue and be sued in its own name.
- Has only those powers and can engage in only those activities that are within the scope of the powers expressly or impliedly granted to it under its state charter or certificate of incorporation.
- Continues to exist until it is dissolved by law, unless a statute limits its duration (see below).
- Can raise capital by the sale of new shares, bonds, debentures, or other securities.
- Can, apart from its shareholders, seek out sources of credit and borrow funds. And, in a closely held corporation the corporate shares can be used as collateral for a corporate loan.

☐ *Corporate shareholders*

- Are not, merely by reason of being shareholders, personally liable for corporate debts and liabilities; each shareholder has at stake only the amount of his capital contribution (see below).
- Can, as a rule, freely sell or otherwise transfer their shares, in the absence of a provision to the contrary.
- Are not responsible for the management of the corporation or of the venture conducted by the corporation.

☐ *Corporate directors*

- Are the repository of the central authority of the corporation. The board of directors manages the affairs of the corporation and acts according to the vote of a majority of its members.
- Must account to and are responsible to their stockholders for their acts or conduct that is outside the scope of their charter powers or that is otherwise improper or unlawful.

☐ *Corporate officers*

- Can exercise only such authority as is delegated to them under the corporate charter or certificate of incorporation and bylaws.
- Can bind the corporation by their acts or conduct that is within the scope of their actual or apparent authority.
- Are answerable to the board of directors and must account to the board for their activities.

[b] Tax Consequences of Corporate Form of Ownership

A corporation is a legal entity that exists separate and apart from its stockholders. It is also a separate taxable entity for income tax as well as property tax purposes. Thus, corporate income is taxable first to the corporation when it is received or accrued and again to the shareholders when it is distributed to them in the form of dividends. What's more, unlike a partnership, a corporation does not pass through to its shareholders the tax benefits that flow from its ownership of real estate such as depreciation deductions, interest deductions, and property tax deductions, nor does it pass through to its shareholders the taxable losses its operations generate.

On the other hand, while corporate income is subject to double taxation as outlined above, corporations are subject to income tax rates that are always below those of a sole proprietorship or an individual investor. (See Table 4.3 below.)

TABLE 4.3 Corporate Income Tax Rates

Taxable Income	*1982 Individual* *	*1982 Corporation*	*1983 Individual*	*1983 Corporation*
$ 0–25,000	up to 29%	16%	up to 26%	15%
25–50,000	up to 44%	19%	up to 40%	18%
50–75,000	up to 49%	30%	up to 44%	30%
75–100,000	up to 50%	40%	up to 48%	40%
100,000 plus	up to 50%	46%	up to 50%	46%

* Filing a joint return.

To the extent that corporate income can be paid out in salaries to the principals, the double tax is avoided since the amount paid out as salary is deductible as a business expense. In addition, a corporation can accumulate income (up to a point) that can ultimately be passed through to the principals as a capital gain when the corporation is liquidated or when the shareholders sell their shares at prices that reflect the earnings that have been accumulated.

Important tax factors to consider in choosing corporate form of ownership are:

☐ Principals, as officer-stockholders or as employee-stockholders, can have a tax-favored retirement or pension plan set up for them.

☐ Principals can be paid a salary for which the corporation can take a tax deduction as an ordinary business expense.

☐ The compensation paid to a principal as a corporate officer or employee is subject to withholding and social security taxes.

☐ While a shareholder can assign his shares as he sees fit in the absence of restrictions imposed by agreement, corporate charter, or otherwise, he cannot assign earnings separate from the shares.

☐ Corporate income is taxable to the corporation and not to the shareholders until it is distributed to them in the form of dividends.

☐ Income accumulated in the corporation is not taxable to the shareholders, but there is a penalty tax if the purpose of the accumulation is to avoid the corporate surtax and the accumulation is greater than is permissible.

☐ A corporation can use a loss generated by a real estate investment to offset income from its other properties, or it can carry over the loss to offset future income. The corporate loss may produce tax shelter for the individual stockholders if the corporation is eligible to, and does, elect Subchapter S status. (See 4.04[2].)

☐ Anyone considering using a corporation for an operation that will produce passive income such as rents or royalties should consider the possibility of the corporation becoming a personal holding company subject to a penalty tax imposed on undistributed personal holding company income.

☐ A dealer is one who holds real estate for sale to customers in the regular course of his business and is taxed at ordinary income rates on his profits. When he buys real estate for investment purposes, he may be able to separate his investment property from his other property and receive capital gain treatment on a subsequent resale of his investment property. If the dealer is a corporation, investment property might be acquired and held in the individual form; and if the dealer is an individual, investment property might be acquired and held in a corporation.

☐ An investor can sell a tract of land to a corporation, which can then sell the individual lots, houses, or condominium units. The sale to the corporation will result in a capital gain to the investor. While the corporation will be a dealer, only the profit added to the property by the corporation's efforts will be taxed as ordinary income to the corporation. To be effective, the incorporation should not be tax-free since this would prevent the investor from realizing a capital gain at the time of the transfer to the corporation with the result that the entire gain would be ordinary income to the corporation and to the shareholders when distributed by the corporation. To avoid a tax-free incorporation the investor can take back cash from the corporation, or the short-term obligations of an already operating corporation, or issue at least 21 percent of the corporate stock to an outsider.

☐ Low-bracket taxpayers can manage the real estate and be paid salaries by the corporation for their services. The salaries can account for a substantial portion of the corporate income and thus reduce the corporate tax burden. The salaries would be taxed at ordinary income rates but only at the taxpayers' low tax brackets. What's more, the corporation would be entitled to deduct the amounts it paid as salaries from its gross income provided the salaries are reasonable and are paid for actual services rendered to the corporation.

☐ Where the principals want to leave a corporate business by selling their shares or liquidating the corporation, they can wind up with ordinary income rather than a capital gain if the corporation has held the property for less than three years. However, this so-called collapsible corporation rule can be avoided where almost all the corporate property is depreciable property used in the corporation's trade or business, provided no owners of a substantial amount of corporate shares are dealers in real estate.

☐ Corporations are, of course, subject to various state and local taxes, which are deductible on its federal income tax return.

☐ Death benefits of up to $5,000 can be received tax-free by a stockholder-employee's beneficiaries.

[2] Subchapter S Corporations

As noted in the preceding section, the corporate form of doing business often does not lend itself to real estate investments. On the one hand, corporate ownership of real estate generating taxable losses prevents the losses from being passed through to the shareholders for use by them to offset outside income. On the other hand, corporate ownership of real estate generating taxable income imposes a double tax on the income, once at the corporate level and once at the shareholder level (to the extent the income is distributed in the form of dividends).

However, an exception to these rules for corporate ownership applies in the case of Subchapter S corporations (so called because they were created by that particular subchapter of the Internal Revenue Code). In general, Subchapter S corporations combine the best features of corporate ownership and of partnership ownership. They are corporations for the purpose of insulating their shareholders from personal liability for corporate obligations, and the use of stock certificates makes transfer of ownership a simple matter; at the same time, they are not independent tax entities and, just as a partnership, are able to pass through to the shareholders the profits and losses from operations (subject however to the limitation described below). However, there is a major impediment to the use of the Subchapter S corporation used in lieu of partnerships: The Subchapter S corporation is intended for active business operations and cannot be used whenever passive-investment income amounts to more than 20 percent of its gross receipts in any year. This sharply limits the use of such corporations in real estate operations to companies in which there is some form of active business operation. Nevertheless, when the passive-investment requirement can be satisfied, a Subchapter S corporation can be an advantageous form of investment for real estate.

[a] Limitation on Pass-Through of Losses

We have already seen that one of the principal tax-shelter benefits obtained under the partnership tax provisions is that the adjusted basis of an individual partner in his partnership interest not only includes his cash investment, but also a pro rata share of any nonrecourse liability of the partnership. By contrast, the adjusted basis of the shareholders of a Subchapter S corporation in their stock includes their investment in the stock and any loans they may have made to the corporation, but, most significantly, does not include any portion of the corporation's liabilities. In the case of both the Subchapter S corporation shareholder and the limited partner, it is the adjusted basis in partnership interest or stock that serves as the upper limit on the amount of loss that may be deducted by the shareholder (partner) in a given year. Thus, in comparison to the limited partner, the Subchapter S corporation shareholder is severely limited in terms of the amount of losses and, therefore, tax shelter available.

[b] Passive Investments vs. Business Operations

As already stated, a Subchapter S corporation may not be used for any year in which the corporation has passive-investment income greater than 20 percent of its gross receipts for the year. Passive investment income is defined as "gross receipts derived from royalties, rents, dividends, interest, annuities and sales or exchanges of stocks or securities." The key issue here for real estate investors is the definition of rents. Certain types of real estate operations are clearly not affected by this 20 percent rule. For example, a real estate management company or brokerage firm may be organized as a Subchapter S corporation, since neither measures its gross receipts in the form of rentals. Thus, a real estate investor who has a substantial portfolio of buildings and who also conducts his own management or brokerage services may create separate Subchapter S corporations to perform these services, possibly giving stock to family members as a way of distributing profits among family members.

In addition, certain types of real estate investments that primarily generate rental income may nevertheless be able to comply with the 20 percent requirement. This will occur if "significant services" are rendered by the corporation (landlord) primarily for the convenience of the tenants or those using the real estate. For example, hotels, motels, boarding houses, apartment hotels, and tourist homes may often be held in Subchapter S ownership if such services as maid service and meals are provided to guests or tenants. On the other hand, services customarily rendered in connection with the rental of rooms or space only, such as supplying heat and light, cleaning public areas of the building, and trash collection, are not the type of significant services that prevent the income received by the landlord from being rental income. Operation of an automobile parking lot, where the cars are parked by an attendant, is eligible for Subchapter S corporation since the gross receipts are not considered rentals.

In general, a corporation engaged in the rental of real property on a long-term basis cannot utilize Subchapter S treatment.

[c] Other Requirements for Subchapter S Treatment

In addition to the requirement that no more than 20 percent of its gross receipts may be passive-investment income, a Subchapter S corporation must meet the following requirements:

- ☐ The number of stockholders may not exceed twenty-five; however, a husband and wife are counted as one shareholder regardless of the manner in which they hold their stock.

- ☐ All shareholders must be individuals, estates, or certain types of voting trusts. A testamentary trust can be a shareholder but only for sixty days after shares are transferred to it as a result of the death of a decedent. No nonresident alien may be a shareholder.

- ☐ The corporation may have only one class of issued stock.

- ☐ The corporation must not derive more than 80 percent of its gross receipts from sources outside the United States.

☐ The corporation must elect Subchapter S treatment, which must be done either during the previous year or during the first seventy-five days of the taxable year for which the election is made. (By being able to wait until two and one-half months of the year has passed before deciding whether to elect Subchapter S status, investors are in a much better position to determine if losses will be generated during that year that they will wish to pass through to themselves directly.)

4.05 TRUSTS

The trust form is the one least commonly used of the three institutional forms of real estate ownership (the other two being, of course, the corporation and the partnership). The great advantage of the real estate trust, which it shares with the partnership, is its ability to act as a conduit for tax purposes and avoid the double tax resulting from use of the corporate form. But trusts are unpopular because of the very narrow line that separates a true trust from an association, which is taxable as a corporation under the Internal Revenue Code.

The use of a trust as an ownership vehicle for real estate for a group of investors (known as a business trust to differentiate it from the personal trust used in family and estate planning), had its origin in Massachusetts at a time when corporations in that state were limited in their powers to hold and deal with real estate. For this reason, the term "Massachusetts trust" is often applied to the business trust. Although the restrictions in Massachusetts (and elsewhere) on corporations have long since been removed, business trusts still are occasionally used, for reasons discussed below. (A special form of the business trust is the real estate investment trust, which is a creature of the Internal Revenue Code and is discussed in detail in 5.02[8].)

[1] How a Trust Operates

A trust is a legal relationship in which (1) a trustee holds legal title to property (real estate or otherwise) with the responsibility of administering it and distributing the income for the benefit of (2) a beneficiary holding beneficial (equitable) title. It normally is created by a written agreement, and so is called an express trust. In some very special cases, a trust may be created by implication or by operation of law. The person creating the trust is called the trustor or settlor, and often the same person also is a beneficiary.

In a business trust, which is frequently called a land trust, the owner of real estate transfers title to property to a trustee, such as a trust company. Some of the possible benefits are:

- Ownership is simplified, especially where several owners are involved. By creating the trust, only one legal owner results—the trustee. If any of the beneficiaries of the trust are affected in any way, such as having a judgment entered against them or being divorced, the title to the property is not affected.
- Transfers of title to subsequent buyers is made easier. The trustee, as legal owner, is the only one that need execute the contract and deed; the sales proceeds are then divided up among the various owners in accordance with their beneficial interests.

These benefits generally can be achieved by use of a partnership as well, but in some parts of the country it is the custom to utilize a trust instead.

Whether a trust will be treated as an association depends upon the application of the same tests as in the case of a partnership. (See 4.03[5][a].)

[2] Personal Trusts

Trusts are a common means of holding property for the benefit of members of a family, particularly the spouse or children of a decedent. A trust may be set up by will (a testamentary trust) or may be set up during the lifetime of the settlor (an inter-vivos trust; that is, one between living persons). It is an extremely flexible instrument and for that reason is one of the most frequently used vehicles for controlling personal wealth, which today is more often in the form of securities than real estate.

Personal trusts, basically set up to protect and conserve property rather than to operate a business, are not normally subject to being taxed as an association.

4.06 CONCURRENT OWNERSHIP

There are three forms of concurrent (multiple) ownership in which real estate can be held:

- Tenancy in common
- Joint tenancy
- Tenancy by the entirety

In addition, as noted in 4.02[3], eight states recognize the special form of concurrent ownership known as community property.

[1] Tenancy in Common

Tenancy in common is the most frequently used form of concurrent ownership. In most states, it occurs when real property is transferred to two or more persons without express language creating one of the other types of concurrent ownership. For example, a tenancy in common is created by either of the following two conveyances: (1) "to *A* and *B*" or (2) "to *A* and *B* as tenants in common."

When two or more persons hold as tenants in common (and incidentally, the term "tenants" as used here is unrelated to a lease or leasehold interest), each has an undivided interest in the entire property to the extent of his ownership share. For example, each of three tenants in common would own a one-third undivided share in the entire property rather than each owning a specified one-third portion of the property. While normally each co-tenant has the same share as his co-tenants, this need not necessarily be the case; one of three co-tenants may own a 40 percent undivided share with each of the others owning 30 percent shares.

Each co-tenant may sell, mortgage, or give away his interest during his life or transmit it at death, just as if he owned the entire property in single ownership (with the consent of all of the co-tenants). When there is a transfer of the interest of one co-tenant, the new owner becomes a tenant in common with the remaining owners.

Each tenant's right to possession of the property is subject to the rights of the co-tenants. Each has the right to an accounting of rents and profits (when the property produces income) and each is entitled to a contribution and reimbursement by the others of monies expended by him for necessary maintenance and repair and for the payment by him of taxes, insurance premiums, and other claims against the property.

Since each tenant in common owns an undivided interest in the property, difficult problems may arise when the tenants disagree among themselves and wish to go their separate ways. Any tenant in common is entitled to begin a legal proceeding (called an action for partition). If the property cannot be equitably divided, the court will order it to be sold, with the proceeds to be divided among the co-tenants according to their interests.

Tenancy in common is usually considered a viable form of ownership only for a small project with very few investors. The property may not be sold, mortgaged, or even leased without the consent of all the co-tenants. However, in the absence of an agreement to the contrary, each co-tenant can transfer his interest, as already noted.

Each tenant in common reports income, gain or loss, from the property according to his own share of ownership. In terms of gift taxation, liability arises from the gift of an interest in a tenancy in common or if one tenant in common pays more than his share of costs (without being reimbursed).

The interest of a deceased tenant in common is taxed as part of his estate according to its value on the date of death or on the optional valuation date. The heirs acquire the interest of a deceased tenant in common at a basis for income tax purposes equal to the value used for estate tax purposes.

[2] Joint Tenancy

A joint tenancy is the same as a tenancy in common—with one very significant difference. The difference is the right of survivorship, which means that if any one joint tenant dies, his interest automatically passes in equal shares to the remaining joint tenants. For example, if *A* and *B* are joint tenants of property and *A* dies, title to his one-half undivided share automatically goes to *B,* who thereby becomes the sole owner of the property. If three joint tenants had owned the property and one died, each of the two survivors would take one-half of the deceased joint tenant's interests.

Because of the unusual survivorship feature of joint tenancies, this type of ownership can be created only by express language in a conveyance, for example, "John Jones and Mary Jones, as joint tenants with right of survivorship and not as tenants in common." A conveyance merely to "John Jones and Mary Jones" normally will create a tenancy in common rather than a joint tenancy.

Joint tenancy is preferred to tenancy in common because the survivorship feature provides that the property will pass upon the death of the owner without the need for a will or a probate proceeding. Thus, no public record will exist of the transfer of such property and this is an attractive feature to many wealthy persons. In addition, except for unusual circumstances, creditors of the deceased joint tenant cannot reach property that has passed into the surviving joint tenant's hands.

The rules for taxing jointly owned property under the federal estate tax have undergone a number of changes in recent years. Under the Economic Recovery Tax Act of 1981,[14] the rules for taxing jointly owned property now are as follows:

(1) When the joint owners are not married to each other, jointly owned property is included in the estate of the first joint owner to die except to the extent that it can be shown that the survivor provided all or part of the consideration for acquiring the property. If all (or part of) the property is taxed in the estate of the first co-tenant to die, the property (or the part) will acquire a stepped-up basis equal to its value at that time. If the property has appreciated, the effect of this rule is that at the cost of an estate tax paid by the decedent's estate, the survivor avoids capital gains tax on the pre-death appreciation. Whether the exchange is worthwhile depends on the amount of appreciation and applicable tax rates.

(2) When the joint tenants are married to each other, the estate of the first spouse to die will include one half of the value of the property regardless of which spouse furnished the consideration. That half of the property will achieve a "stepped-up" basis at that time. In light of the new unlimited marital deduction, it would be preferable from a tax point of view for the spouse who dies first to own the entire interest in the property (instead of having joint ownership). In this way, the decedent could leave the full interest in the property to the surviving spouse with a stepped-up basis while at the same time incurring no estate tax because of the unlimited marital deduction. If the surviving spouse held the property until he or she died, then an estate tax would be payable if the value of the estate exceeded the exemption (which will rise in a series of steps to $600,000 in 1987).

While a joint tenant cannot devise his interest by will (since it passes automatically on his death), he can sell or give away his interest during his lifetime. If he does so, the new owner becomes a tenant in common (not a joint tenant) with the remaining owners. This results because the early English common law, which was very conceptual, conceived of a joint tenancy as a merger of four unities: interest, time, title, and possession. The time requirement means that all of the joint tenancies must be established at the same time. Thus, if one joint tenant later transfers his interest to another, the unity of time is broken and the new owner becomes a tenant in common.

Because of the survivorship feature, the joint tenancy is normally used only among family members or among members of a closely related group.

A joint tenant is required to report his proportionate part of the gross income from property he owns measured by his interest in the property. Similarly, he is entitled to deduct his proportionate part of expenses attributable to the property. However, unlike tenants in common, if one joint tenant pays expenses in excess of his proportionate share, he may deduct the full amount of such expenses. Gain or loss on the sale of jointly held property is allocated among joint tenants in proportion to their interests.

[3] Tenancy by the Entirety

A tenancy by the entirety is a joint tenancy between husband and wife. The tenancy carries with it the same right of survivorship as a joint tenancy so that,

---

[14] Pub. L. No. 97-34, 95 Stat. 172, 26 U.S.C. § 128.

upon the death of either spouse, the survivor takes the entire estate. Unlike a joint tenancy, however, neither spouse can convey any part of the property during their joint lives unless the other spouse joins in the conveyance. Thus, tenancy by the entirety (like the ancient right of dower) acts to protect the rights of a surviving spouse in property owned during the marriage. In most states recognizing the tenancy by the entirety, any conveyance to a husband and wife is presumed to be to them as tenants by the entirety unless the title is specifically indicated to be otherwise. For example, a conveyance to "*A* and his wife, *B*" will, in these states, create the tenancy by the entirety, whereas a conveyance to "*A* and *B* as tenants in common and not as tenants by the entirety" will create a tenancy in common.

Property held under tenancy by the entirety is not subject to levy by creditors of only one of the owners. In the event the owners are divorced, the tenancy is destroyed and the divorced spouses become tenants in common. Just as in the case of a joint tenancy, upon the death of a tenant by the entirety, one-half the value of the property is included in his or her estate.

Where the spouses choose to file separate instead of joint returns, each tenant by the entirety reports his or her own share of the income, gain or loss, from the property on his or her separate return.

5

Sources of Capital; Equity Financing

5.01 INTRODUCTION

In talking of financing, the overriding consideration to be borne in mind today is the increasing lack of distinction between debt and equity. It is only during periods of relative price stability that lenders are willing to provide financing on traditional fixed-interest terms. In the inflationary environment existing in the United States for the past two decades, any provider of capital must be concerned with protecting the capital against erosion, and this can only be done by some form of participation that permits the lender's return to move upward, in dollar terms, as the purchasing power of the dollar declines.

At the same time, there is an important distinction between debt and equity, which may be simply stated as follows: The provider of debt capital insists (1) on a prior claim to income (in the form of debt service); and (2) on a prior claim on assets (in the event of default). In exchange for this, the lender agrees to take a relatively fixed return. By comparison, the provider of equity is willing to take a subordinate claim to income and assets in exchange for the sole or major claim to profits once they have passed the level where debt-service requirements of the lender are met. In other words, the equity investor holds the residual or operating position; he receives what is left over (but all of it after fixed claims are met); but he must absorb all loss to the extent of his equity interest before the debt position suffers loss.

The material in this chapter is divided into two parts:

- Sources of capital (5.02) discusses private and institutional providers of both debt and equity capital.
- Equity financing (5.03) discusses how equity capital is raised, subject to federal and state laws affecting the issuance of securities. (Debt financing is discussed in Chapter 6.)

5.02 SOURCES OF REAL ESTATE CAPITAL

Capital is the lifeblood of the real estate industry. Unlike the operator of a small business that may be started at home with virtually no cash investment, the owner or developer of real estate must have capital, often a substantial amount, with which to begin an enterprise. This is because land itself—being permanent and indestructible—always costs money to acquire, and because any improvements put on land, usually built to last for many years, also are expensive. Consequently, very early in the consideration of any investment the investor must decide where the money will come from.

A wide variety of financing sources are available to the real estate industry. They range from the individual who has a few thousand dollars that he is prepared to put into a real estate deal to a large life insurance company or pension fund that represents many billions of dollars in capital. Each of these financial sources has limitations and advantages and it is important that the investor and his professional associates are aware of all of them. At each stage of the investing process—acquisition, development, or operational—a particular form of financing and a particular financial source may be most appropriate. Furthermore, depending upon the stage of the economic cycle and how tight the money market is, one type of lender may be more suitable or available than another.

As already pointed out, the most significant trend in real estate financing today is the disappearing line between straight debt and straight equity. More and more, traditional lending institutions are showing an interest in straight-equity investment or financing with equity participations. On the other hand, private individuals who traditionally were the primary source of equity capital are putting more of their funds into such debt instruments as the Government National Mortgage Association (GNMA) and conventional mortgage-backed securities (see 6.17[6]), which offer a higher interest return than other debt investments available to individuals. Consequently, in the following discussion of financial sources, no strict division is made between lenders and investors; each type of financial source may be one or another depending upon the circumstances.

[1] Noninstitutional (Private) Investors

Private investors, either acting individually or in a group (syndicate), represent the primary source of equity capital for real estate investment. Their role in equity investments is discussed in detail in 5.03, which describes the various ways of "packaging" equity investment in real estate.

Insofar as private investors provide debt capital, they do so in one of two ways: (1) By depositing money in such intermediary institutions as savings banks, and savings and loan associations (discussed separately below), or in mortgage-backed securities or other investments available in the secondary mortgage market (see 6.17); or (2) by dealing directly with borrowers.

[a] Purchase-Money Mortgages

The most important way in which individual investors directly provide real estate debt financing is through purchase-money mortgage financing. This type of mortgage is one that is taken by a seller from a buyer in lieu of purchase money; that is, the seller helps finance the purchase. The technique of purchase-money financing is discussed in 6.12. This leaves for discussion here the role of the private investor in providing debt financing as a third party (i.e., not as a seller).

In some parts of the country, particularly when money is tight, third-party individual lending plays an important role in providing residential mortgages. In the typical case, the purchaser of a home takes over an existing first mortgage but lacks the necessary funds to pay the balance of the purchase price in cash. If the seller of the home is unwilling to take back a purchase-money second mortgage, the purchaser must seek outside financing, which generally will not be forthcoming from institutional sources. In such a case, the real estate broker or a local mortgage company may have a list of individuals willing to provide a second mortgage. (Real estate brokers who are able to maintain a "stable" of private lenders often can realize a significant source of additional income by charging a commission for arranging third-party loans.)

Private investors who make second-mortgage loans often do so for a limited term of five to ten years, at the prevailing rate for second mortgages, which usually is several points above the first-mortgage rate. Since a private lender normally is interested in maximizing his return, he may be willing to extend a standing (non-amortized) mortgage, particularly when the term is short. The second mortgage will usually allow prepayment at any time without penalty, permitting the borrower to refinance if and when interest rates drop and a new first mortgage can be obtained on the home.

A private lender who engages in this type of lending must be sure to have familiarity with the usury laws of the particular state in order to avoid the risk of litigation and the possibility of loss of income (or even of principal) in the event that the borrower is charged a usurious rate.

[b] Secondary Market in Purchase-Money Mortgages

Another way by which private individuals invest in residential mortgages is by acquiring them in the secondary-mortgage market. For example, the seller of a home takes back a purchase-money mortgage and, not wanting to hold it until maturity, offers it for sale. This can be done by notifying a real estate or mortgage broker who keeps lists of interested individuals, or through the use of classified ads; interested individuals can then purchase the "takeback paper." The price is usually at a substantial discount from the face amount of the mortgage in order to provide the buyer of the paper with a competitive return.

For example, in the current market, the seller of the home may have taken back a purchase-money mortgage in the amount of $10,000 carrying an interest rate of 10 percent per year. Assuming the mortgage calls for no amortization, the home-buyer must then pay $1,000 a year as interest. An individual investor purchasing this mortgage in the open market might be willing to pay only $7,000, even though the mortgage has a face value of $10,000. The interest yield then becomes 14 percent ($1,000 annual interest on $7,000 investment); since the mortgage is likely to be paid off in full at maturity, the buyer of the mortgage will also realize a substantial annual gain at that time, that is, a $3,000 gain on the $7,000 investment.

[2] Life Insurance Companies

Life insurance companies (LICs) are among the largest financial institutions in the world. Their primary function is to provide financial security to their policy holders through life insurance. The premiums collected by the companies are used largely to maintain reserves from which benefits are paid; these reserves constitute enormous capital pools that must be invested for long periods of time. Since the inflows of funds (from premium payments) can be predicted with great accuracy in advance, and since fund outflows (upon the death of individual policy holders) can also be estimated with great accuracy, the LICs are in a position both (1) to commit several years in advance to provide loan funds to borrowers; and (2) to make long-term loans.

Since an LIC's obligations usually are measured in fixed dollars (e.g., the face amount of a life insurance policy), the LIC in theory need not be unduly concerned about the depreciation of the dollar through inflation. As a result, LICs always have been a major source of fixed-interest mortgages for both residential and income properties. However, this point of view has gradually been changing as a result of the sustained period of high inflation in the United States. To maintain their markets, LICs have been forced to offer a variety of indexed or variable insurance and annuity plans, which give the insured or beneficiary some hope of hedging against inflation. These plans mean that the LIC cannot be sure in advance of the number of dollars that will be needed when the plans or policies mature. Thus, the LIC must itself seek an inflation hedge and this means loans carrying variable interest rates, equity participations, or early call provisions. (See 6.03[1].)

Life insurance companies are not restricted in the types of loans they may make, as are, for example, savings banks and savings and loan associations. Hence, LICs will decrease their mortgage lending at times when interest rates on bonds and business loans are at a significant premium over mortgage rates. This normally will happen during periods of tight money or rampant inflation because mortgage rates (due to usury ceilings and other causes) tend to be "stickier" than bond rates and do not rise as quickly. It follows that LICs are a good source of mortgage loans at a time when bond interest rates are in a period of decline; since the LICs have a steady inflow of funds, they must place those funds continually and so will be more receptive to mortgage loans when general market rates are lower. A borrower holding an existing loan from an LIC who anticipates the need to refinance also will seek to do so at a time when the general interest rate level is low, both because the refinancing may be made at a more favorable rate and because the LIC will have the funds for a new loan at that time.

LIC mortgage loans generally fall into three groups:

- One- to four-family residential
- Income or commercial properties
- Farm and special-purpose properties

☐ *Residential loans.* Until the relatively recent past, LICs were a primary source of residential mortgage loans. But as interest rates rose due to inflation and residential mortgage rates failed to keep pace because of usury ceilings in many states, the LICs gradually moved away from the residential mortgage market. (Their place has been taken primarily by GNMA and conventional mortgage-backed securities, which are sold to institutions and wealthy investors.) To the extent LICs continue to do residential mortgage lending, wide geographic diversification is achieved through a branch-office system or through a correspondent relationship with local mortgage companies.

☐ *Income or commercial loans.* The most important financing role of the LICs today is in income and commercial properties, including office buildings, apartment houses, shopping centers, and all forms of retail and industrial properties. In recent years, the LICs have shown a definite preference for properties that have built-in inflation hedges, such as hotels and motels, which can raise their rates as frequently as necessary to keep pace with inflation. In addition, most income properties permit the use of variable-interest or equity-participation loans, which now are favored by LICs.

☐ *Farm and special-purpose property loans.* Farm loans and loans for special-purpose properties such as fast-food restaurants, hospitals, industrial plants, and other properties not easily convertible to another use are made by LICs on a case-by-case basis. One significant development in LIC lending has been the growth of construction loans by LICs. Traditionally, construction financing has been the province of commercial banks. One reason for this is that construction financing is a specialized form of lending, requiring a staff trained in understanding how to supervise the construction process; another is that construction loans normally do not have a term of more than two years and, as indicated above, the LICs have a much longer time frame. Nevertheless, the LICs, facing increasing competition in the long-term end of the market and experiencing increasing cash inflows as a result of the growth of pension-fund assets under their management, have shown increasing interest in construction lending, particularly when the construction loan is packaged together with the permanent loan. The advantages to the borrower in dealing with an LIC for a construction loan include:

- *Fixed cost.* Unlike commercial banks whose cost of funds are tied to the short-term money market and whose loans must be geared to a fluctuating prime rate, LICs can lend at fixed rates, usually one to two points above the rate for the permanent commitment. This gives the borrower the distinct advantage of being able to project his cost of money accurately, providing that construction progresses on schedule.
- *Lower expenses.* When a package loan is utilized, the permanent lender and the construction lender are one entity. Thus the borrower can effect cost savings in a number of areas. Only one fee need be paid for the lender's legal costs, an engineering inspection, and origination and appraisal.
- *Time saving.* A significant saving in time (as well as in additional costs) arises from the need to make only a single presentation in connection with the loan application. In addition, no time need be spent on negotiating a take-out or buy-sell agreement between the permanent and construction lender.

[3] Commercial Banks

Commercial banks (CBs) are the largest type of financial intermediary in the American financial system. Under the dual banking system utilized in the U.S., CBs are regulated either by federal or state government agencies. Federally chartered CBs are required to belong to the Federal Reserve System and to the Federal Deposit Insurance Corporation; state-chartered banks may join if they wish. Traditionally, the primary sources of funds for CBs are demand deposits (checking accounts); to a lesser degree, their funds come from savings deposits and time certificates of deposit (CDs). Consequently, CB assets are concentrated at the short-term end of the lending spectrum, consisting primarily of loans to businesses for operations and receivables financing. A significant portion of assets are in consumer loans, primarily automobile and personal loans.

In the area of real estate, CBs are dominant in construction lending, since this is a form of short-term financing that the banks are equipped to handle. (The techniques of construction lending are discussed in 6.07.) However, CBs also do a significant amount of permanent-mortgage lending, both for residences and income properties. Federal and state regulations limit real estate loans to a certain percentage of bank assets and also impose ceilings on loan-to-value ratios. Overall, mortgage loans make up only about 15 percent of most CB portfolios (a notable exception being Hawaiian CBs, where mortgage loans dominate the portfolio). It should be mentioned, however, that short-term construction and land-development loans are not counted as real estate loans for regulatory purposes. Commercial banks are also very significant holders of farm debt, accounting for perhaps one-fourth of the nation's total farm debt, which includes loans for farm real estate as well as for farm operations.

Three special types of loans made by commercial banks that deserve special mention are:

☐ *Home-improvement loans.* About half the total loans for home-improvement purposes are made by CBs. These loans usually are made as conventional installment loans rather than real estate loans. Interest rates tend to run somewhat higher than for long-term mortgages (and about the same as for automobile loans), and run for five to seven years. A special form of home-improvement loan is the Federal Housing Administration (FHA) Title I guaranteed loan; this is further discussed in 7.01[7].

☐ *Second-mortgage loans.* Commercial banks may devote a limited portion of their funds to second-mortgage loans. In the past, CBs generally did not encourage such loans but the recent sharp rise in the value of residential properties (creating for the typical homeowner a substantial equity in his home) plus the increased competition for loans has brought about a change in the attitude of most banks. Generally, a bank will make a second-mortgage loan in an amount equal to 50 to 75 percent of the equity value (i.e., the difference between the outstanding first mortgage and the current appraised value of the home).

☐ *Mortgage-warehousing loans.* Mortgage bankers frequently finance their loan originations with a line of credit from a commercial bank. From the bank's point of view, these loans are treated as mortgage-inventory or mortgage-warehousing loans (i.e., business loans secured by the mortgages being originated by the mortgage banker).

Commercial banks, because of their close relationship to the community and their need for continuing source of loan demand, place a good deal of emphasis on a continuing customer relationship. Consequently, an investor or developer is well advised to maintain a checking account and savings account with a local CB, as well as negotiate personal loans when needed. By doing this, the investor can be assured of consideration when the time comes to negotiate a construction loan or long-term mortgage loan.

[4] Savings and Loan Associations

Savings and loan associations (S&Ls) are the primary source of financing for one- to four-family homes. Consequently, even though their total assets are far less than those of commercial banks, the mortgage portfolios of S&Ls are very close in size to those of the CBs. Savings associations generate loan capital from large numbers of individual savings accounts and certificates of deposit. Since these types of accounts tend to be fairly stable (and in the case of certificates of deposit, may not be withdrawn prior to maturity without payment of a penalty), S&Ls are in a much better position to "loan long" than CBs, and indeed, are required to devote the principal portion of their deposits to long-term home mortgages.

As of January 1, 1981, the Depository Institutions Deregulation and Monetary Control Act of 1980[1] has allowed S&Ls for the first time to offer checking accounts, unsecured loans for automobiles and other merchandise, lines of credit, and full-service credit cards. The checking accounts take the form of NOW (negotiable orders of withdrawal) accounts. Under these accounts, which may be offered by both CBs and S&Ls, the depositor earns interest on checking account balances. The effect of these changes will be to make S&Ls much more similar to CBs than ever before. The reason for the change was the inability of S&Ls to maintain their deposit inflows under a system that prevented them from raising interest rates in line with the interest rates of competing institutions (notably the money-market funds).

Most S&Ls today are of the mutual (nonstock) type although a good number are shareholder-owned and operated for profit. The number of S&Ls has been declining steadily for the past ten years and totaled 4,621 in 1980. Savings and loan associations are subject to a dual system of chartering and regulation, just as are commercial banks. State associations are chartered under state statutes and are supervised and examined by state banking departments. Federal associations are chartered under the Home Owners' Loan Act of 1933 [2] and are subject to regulation by the Federal Home Loan Bank Board (FHLBB).

The real estate loan portfolio of a typical S&L is made up of three types of loans:

☐ *Home-purchase loans.* This constitutes by far the largest group of loans, aggregating more than 60 percent of total S&L loans. These loans are used by the borrower to purchase a new or existing home; the amount of down payment required varies anywhere from 5 to 25 percent of the purchase price, depending on regulatory limitations, the amount of funds the S&L has available, and the credit standing of the borrower. Loan terms may be for twenty or more years, again on the basis of a number of factors, including the age of the structure.

---

1 Pub. L. No. 96-221, 94 Stat. 132, 12 U.S.C.A. §§ 4a et seq.

2 48 Stat. 128, 12 U.S.C.A. §§ 1461–1468.

☐ *New-home construction loans.* Savings and loan associations do a degree of construction financing, generally for new private homes, but also for apartment buildings and other income properties. At times when loan demand is relatively slack, S&Ls seek out construction financing as one way to employ idle funds and also to gain the inside track in acquiring the long-term mortgages that will be sought by the final owners.

☐ *Home-improvement loans.* This type of loan is made to enable a property owner to repair, remodel, or add to an existing home; they have grown substantially in amount in recent years and S&Ls are a major source of such financing. Home-improvement loans either may be made on an unsecured (personal loan) basis or secured by a mortgage or other collateral. The FHA has a home-loan insurance program under which lenders are guaranteed repayment in exchange for limiting the amount of interest charged. (See 7.01[7].)

[5] Savings-and-Loan Service Corporations

Since 1964, federal S&Ls have been authorized to create service corporations. A service corporation is a one percent subsidiary of one or more federal S&Ls. Its function is to engage in activities that are prohibited to its parents.

For example, it may originate, buy, sell, and service real estate loans and participations, and may undertake brokering and warehousing loans and even 100 percent loans on the collateral of first (and sometimes second) liens.

As part of a project to develop housing, a service corporation may acquire, hold, and rent unimproved property, engage in housing developments, and perform all related maintenance, management, and rental services; in addition, it can joint venture.

[6] Mutual Savings Banks

Mutual savings banks (MSBs) originally developed to encourage thrift among working people in the 19th century. At that time, the primary population centers were in the eastern part of the country and it is in the eighteen Northeastern and Middle Atlantic states that the 460 or so MSBs are concentrated. (Of all MSBs, 74 percent are located in New York, Connecticut, and Massachusetts.) Outside of this region, MSBs exist in only two other states—Oregon and Washington. Population growth in other parts of the country coincided with the development of the S&L, which, patterned after the MSB, is now the predominant form of thrift institution.

Mutual savings banks are regulated in ways similar to the S&Ls (except that there are no federally chartered MSBs). The term "mutual" indicates that the bank is owned and operated by its depositors and is managed by a board of trustees; that is, it is a nonprofit institution. Savings and loan associations, by comparison, may be either mutual or stock, that is, owned either by depositors or by shareholders. The association that speaks for MSBs is the National Association of Mutual Savings Banks (NAMSB), headquartered in New York City.

While MSBs have authority to invest in a variety of investment instruments, from common stocks to bonds and personal loans, the bulk of their investments are in long-term residential mortgages. Total mortgage investments (including GNMA securities) were approximately two-thirds of all MSB assets in recent years. As with the S&Ls, MSBs have been subject to a high degree of disintermediation during periods of high interest rates and have been forced to rely on a variety of new deposit instruments, such as six-month CDs, in order to maintain deposit levels. There seems little doubt that in future years the trend will be toward a greater percentage of variable-interest-rate loans that, by increasing interest income to the lending bank, will permit it to raise interest levels on deposits so that large outflows of funds do not result.

Mutual savings banks are regulated by the state in which they are located as to maximum loan-to-value ratios, the maximum percentage of assets that may be invested in mortgages, and the maximum interest rates that may be charged.

One of the more serious problems facing the industry is more than $25 billion in home mortgages that yield 8 percent or less. These mortgages comprise about one-third of the industry's total mortgage portfolio. For numerous institutions the average return on the total loan portfolio is little more than 8 percent. This is especially true of MSBs in such states as New York, where laws governing their operation have only recently been eased. Under recent legislation, however, they now can offer the same array of consumer services as federally chartered thrift institutions.

At the same time, the cost of funds to savings banks—as well as to all depository institutions—has skyrocketed. Between 30 percent and 40 percent of the total deposit base of the industry now resides in high-yielding six-month money-market certificates (MMCs), whose interest rates are tied to Treasury bill rates.

[7] Credit Unions

A sometimes-ignored source of financing for real estate is the credit union system. There are more than 23,000 credit unions (CUs) in the United States with assets approximating $50 billion. However, only about one in every five CUs has real estate loans, the vast majority of these for single-family homes. Credit unions also provide significant financing for home improvement and for the purchase of mobile homes. As with other types of institutions, credit unions are either federally or state-chartered; state-chartered CUs generally have much more liberal lending powers in the area of real estate than do federal CUs. The association for the industry is the Credit Union National Association (CUNA).

[8] Real Estate Investment Trusts

A real estate investment trust (REIT) is to real estate what a mutual fund is to common stock. It is a vehicle that pools the capital of a large number of individual investors and then either invests the capital in the ownership of real estate (equity trust) or lends the capital to real estate borrowers on the security of mortgages (mortgage trust).

Real estate investment trusts were first authorized in 1960 by an amendment to the Internal Revenue Code; they are creatures of the tax law and must comply with specified conditions in order to retain their special tax status. This special status enables a REIT to distribute its income to its shareholders without the REIT itself paying any federal income tax. Thus, the double tax normally payable on corporate distributions (by the corporation and its shareholders) is avoided. An equity REIT, in addition, can utilize depreciation deductions to shelter what would otherwise be taxable income to its shareholders.

While most existing REITs have been organized by banks, insurance companies, and financial conglomerates, there is no obstacle to a local real estate company or investment group creating a REIT for their own purposes; these purposes are to earn advisory fees for managing the REIT's properties or to create a source of financing.

Although the organization of a real estate investment trust is far more involved than the creation of a limited partnership, the REIT form offers some very definite advantages to the professional real estate person or firm. First of all, its tax benefits are clearly defined and are far less likely to be attacked than the tax position of a limited partnership. Second, the shares of a REIT are easily transferable and, indeed, may be traded on a public market if the REIT is sufficiently large. This feature of liquidity is a valuable one for investors, who like the assurance that they are in a position to cash in if their circumstances require. Finally, the relationship between the adviser and the REIT is more of an arm's-length relationship than is that between a general partner and his limited partners. Consequently, the adviser is in a better position to utilize the REIT for financing or other purposes than is a general partner.

On the other hand, a REIT cannot pass through losses as can a limited partnership and so is inappropriate where tax shelter is the major goal of investors.

[a] Benefits Offered to Small Investors

Real estate investment trusts do provide small investors with the following benefits:

- The prospect of realizing annual income (partly or wholly tax sheltered and likely to grow over time) as well as the prospect of long-term capital gain from the appreciation of properties owned by the REIT
- The ability to minimize risk by participating in a portfolio of properties rather than in a single property
- The ability to sell or transfer shares with a minimum of difficulty
- The availability of professional management by outside advisers
- The benefits of centralized management, limited liability, and continuity of life (since the term of the REIT may be perpetual)

[b] Operation of Real Estate Investment Trusts

For the real estate professional or local business firm, the incentive for organizing a REIT lies in two potential benefits:

- The receipt of advisory fees for managing the REIT
- The use of the REIT as a source of financing or as a customer for the adviser's own business

☐ *Advisory fees.* A REIT is run directly by a board of directors or board of trustees, depending on whether it is utilizing the corporate or trust form. The board is responsible for raising capital for the trust (both equity and debt); for setting investment policy; and for approving recommendations of an outside adviser. The reason why an outside adviser is almost always used is that REITs are obliged by the tax law to be passive investors; that is, they themselves are not permitted to engage in the trade or business of real estate.

For his services in managing the properties of a REIT, the adviser is paid an annual fee equal to

- A percentage of the total assets of the REIT, or
- A percentage of the income and gains realized by the REIT during the year.

Sometimes, the fee is a combination of both (e.g., one percent of the assets of the trust plus an incentive fee of 10 percent of all income above an amount representing an 8 percent return on shareholders' equity).

Generally speaking, advisory fees are not subject to government-imposed ceilings (with some exceptions; for example, restrictions are imposed by the Midwest Securities Commissioners Association). As a result of the debacle suffered by many trusts following the 1974-1975 real estate recession, many trusts sharply curtailed fees paid to advisers (or very small fees became payable because of the absence of earnings or the diminished asset base). However, so long as a REIT is profitable and growing, there seems to be no reason why the advisers should not be properly rewarded for their efforts.

☐ *Use of a REIT for financing or as a customer.* A second primary motive for organizing a REIT is to utilize it either (1) as a source of financing for projects to be developed or operated by the adviser; or (2) as a customer for services to be provided by the adviser.

Perhaps the best example is a local bank that can anticipate receiving from a REIT that it advises, in addition to advisory fees, the following:

- Deposits of temporarily uninvested REIT funds
- Income and fees from loans to the REIT
- Fees from serving as transfer agent, registrar, and dividend agent

and which can sell to the REIT mortgages originated by the bank, thus generating funds for new bank loans.

For nonbank advisers, REITs can offer financing and a market for the adviser's products or services. For example, in the case of a mortgage banker acting as adviser, the REIT can supply short-term financing for the origination of loans (the warehousing function) as well as provide a market for the sale of mortgage packages—both needs of the mortgage banker. Developers can also benefit from taking on the role of REIT adviser. Since REITs are generally under no restrictions as to the type of loans or investments they can make, the REIT can provide construction financing as well as long-term second or wraparound loans. In addition, REITs can enter into a sale-leaseback arrangement with the developer. Other real estate firms can also benefit from the adviser position, since the REIT will require the same services as any other professional investor, including insurance brokerage, property management, and property brokerage, all of which carry fees for the adviser.

☐ *Conflicts of interest.* Any REIT adviser that uses the REIT as a financing source or as a customer automatically is involved in a conflict of interest (i.e., the adviser is serving its own interests as well as that of the REIT). The mere existence of a conflict of interest is not an impropriety (unless it is specifically prohibited by local law). However, the adviser must be careful that it does not favor its own interests over that of the REIT; if it does and litigation ensues, it may be required to turn over any profits it has made to the REIT.

The best rule to follow in any conflict of interest situation is full disclosure to the REIT shareholders. There is nothing wrong and, indeed, it may be beneficial for the REIT to utilize the services of its own adviser and pay the customary fees for such services, but all concerned should be fully aware of what is happening.

[c] Ways in Which Real Estate Investment Trusts Can Expand

Real estate investment trusts are generally thought of as nongrowth entities; that is, their asset base cannot expand through internal growth because all of their profits must be distributed to shareholders instead of being reinvested. If this were so, advisory fees would also be unable to grow, being calculated as a percentage of assets or annual income. However, there are several ways in which REITs can grow:

☐ Although a REIT must distribute 95 percent of its taxable income, it can retain the remaining 5 percent of taxable income and, more significantly, all cash flow generated by depreciation deductions.

☐ The REIT may reduce taxable income by an appropriate loss reserve, thus permitting the retention of additional cash.

☐ As the REIT's properties appreciate in value, mortgages may be refinanced to produce new cash not required to be distributed.

☐ The REIT may issue new stock at a price above that of book value (the process known as equity leveraging) or debt obligations at a cost lower than that which the REIT can earn on the money (the traditional form of debt leveraging). Equity leveraging generally will be limited to REITs traded publicly while debt leveraging normally is utilized by mortgage trusts.

[d] Business and Legal Considerations

In contemplating the formation of a REIT, the following points should be considered:

☐ *Size.* While a REIT can be capitalized in any amount, it is generally considered that a capitalization of $10 million is the minimum if the primary motive of the organizers is to receive advisory fees.

☐ *Initial capital.* An advantage to the REIT is that the organizers themselves need put in virtually no capital, except that needed for the preliminary organizational expense. And such expense can be recouped from the REIT if the offering is successful.

☐ *Open- and closed-end.* An open-end fund stands ready to redeem its shares at any time at a price equal to current fair market value. Most mutual stock funds are of this type. By comparison, a closed-end fund will not redeem its shares, which means that share prices may move above or below the current full market value of the fund's assets. Virtually all REITs are closed-end funds because of the difficulty of valuing real estate each day in order to set a price for share redemption. However, a REIT may be open-end if a satisfactory method of valuation can be worked out.

☐ *Federal securities laws.* A REIT offering is subject to the same SEC rules and is eligible for the same exemptions as any other offering of stock. Since a trust must have at least 100 owners, it cannot qualify for the private-offering exemption but it might qualify as a wholly intrastate offering.

☐ *State securities laws.* A REIT also is subject to the securities laws of the state in which it is organized and this frequently will require a registration of the offering.

☐ *Investment Company Act.* While most REITs do not fall within the definition of an investment company contained in the Investment Company Act of 1940,[3] it is possible that a particular REIT may require registration under that Act.

[e] Tax Rules Applicable to Real Estate Investment Trusts

In order to achieve the special status that permits them to pass through gains and income without paying tax, REITs must comply strictly with the rules set forth in Sections 856-858 of the Internal Revenue Code. These rules are of two types: those relating to the organization and operation of the REIT, and those relating to its assets and income.

☐ *Rules relating to structure and operation.* In its organization and operation, a REIT must

- Be managed by one or more trustees (if set up as a trust) or directors (if set up as a corporation). The trustees or directors themselves may be individuals or corporations.
- Issue transferable shares of beneficial interest to the owners of the REIT.
- Not hold any property primarily for sale to customers in the ordinary course of trade or business (although an amendment has been proposed in Congress to remove this restriction).
- Not be more than 50 percent owned by five or fewer individuals (otherwise the REIT could be used to avoid personal holding company rules).
- Have at least 100 or more persons own shares of beneficial interest. These persons may include individuals, partnerships, corporations, trusts, and estates.

☐ *Rules relating to assets and income.* In respect to its assets and income, a qualifying REIT must meet the following conditions:

---

[3] 54 Stat. 789, 15 U.S.C.A. §§ 80a-1–80a-52.

- At least 95 percent of the REIT's gross income must be derived from rents, dividends, interest, gain from the sale of stock, and real property (including mortgages).
- At least 75 percent of the REIT's gross income must be derived from rents, mortgage interest, gain from the sale of real property (including mortgages), and dividends and gains from shares of other qualified REITs.
- Less than 30 percent of the REIT's gross income may be derived from the sale of real estate held for less than four years and from the sale of securities held for less than six months.
- The REIT must distribute at least 95 percent of its taxable income to its shareholders each year.
- At least 75 percent of the REIT's total assets must consist of real estate assets, cash, and government securities.

If a REIT fails to comply with any of these requirements, it becomes taxable on its income as if it were a regular business corporation.

[f] Use of Real Estate Investment Trusts in Stock Pairings

A number of businesses with large real estate assets have recently come up with a novel way to cut taxes on the corporate level. In essence, the real estate is split off into a separate REIT, which can distribute income free of tax at the corporate level. Here are some of the tax considerations that should be borne in mind when a company considers this approach.

A stock pairing splits a corporation into two separate entities, each entity owned by the same group of stockholders. The shares of the two entities are paired for trading purposes so that shares of one entity may not be sold independently of the other (hence the name "stapled stock," which is also used to describe this approach).

Business operations are conducted by one of the paired companies while the other, organized as a REIT, owns all the real estate used by the operating company. The operating company pays rent to the REIT for the use of the real estate; the REIT in turn distributes the rent to shareholders without paying a tax on the corporate level. Accordingly, substantial tax savings are achieved while the operating entity continues to engage in active management and development activities prohibited to a REIT. The reason for the requirement that the shares of both companies be traded together is to minimize any questions that might arise concerning possible conflicts of interest between the two companies.

Pairings are complex operations, and the various legal and tax considerations must be carefully thought out. The Internal Revenue Service (IRS) has ruled that a pairing operation involves a taxable distribution to the shareholders. This distribution normally will be taxable to the shareholders in accordance with the general rules applicable to dividends. (A REIT may not qualify under Section 355 of the Internal Revenue Code for a tax-free spin-off since a REIT, due to its passive nature, cannot engage in an active trade or business—one of the requirements under that section.)

There are a number of disadvantages of stock pairing with a REIT that should be considered. Some of these are:

☐ Pairing may involve a taxable distribution to REIT shareholders as mentioned previously. In some circumstances it could be prohibitive.

☐ The Internal Revenue Service has ruled that each entity must have separate officers and employees; however, they apparently could have common boards of directors.

☐ If the paired entity acts as a lessee, an individual shareholder would be required to own less than a 10 percent interest in the paired stock due to statutory limitations applicable to REITs.

☐ The IRS has authority under Section 482 of the Code to reallocate rentals paid by the operating entity to the REIT and to allocate other income and deductions between the related entities.

☐ Administrative expenses of maintaining the separate entities and ensuring REIT compliance would be increased.

☐ Because the stock is paired, the entities may not be free to borrow, raise capital, or engage in other transactions individually without affecting the paired entity.

☐ Any further acquisitions by the paired companies would probably not be tax-free.

Although the pros and cons of stock pairing must be evaluated very carefully, it appears that there may well be some real estate-intensive companies for which stock pairing involving a REIT may warrant consideration and could have some decided advantages.

[9] Pension Funds

A pension fund holds assets that are to be used for the payment of pensions to corporate or government employees, union members, and other groups. They represent the newest and most rapidly growing of the financial intermediaries, with total assets now totaling in excess of $500 billion and expected to reach $1 trillion by 1985. Pension funds were virtually unregulated until 1974 when Congress passed the Employee Retirement Income Security Act (ERISA).[4] This statute regulates investments made by pension and profit-sharing plans and imposes standards of conduct on fiduciaries who operate or are in any way involved with such funds. The asset and liability structure of pension funds is somewhat similar to that of life insurance companies in that the inflow of funds is continuous and stable and payment obligations are actuarially determinable; that is, accurate predictions can be made of the payments that must be made in future years. Consequently, pension funds would seem to be a logical source of long-term real estate loans.

In fact, pension fund assets have been concentrated in common stocks, bonds and short-term money-market obligations. Only about 2 percent of pension fund assets are currently invested either in mortgages or real estate equities, but this

[4] Pub. L. No. 93-406, 88 Stat. 829, 898, 29 U.S.C.A. § 1001.

percentage is likely to grow substantially in future years and eventually may reach as much as 10 percent of total pension fund assets. One reason for the increase is the ERISA requirement that a pension fund diversify its investments, which has been taken to mean that some portion of assets should be put into real estate. Until recently, many pension fund fiduciaries lacked familiarity with real estate investments, but this is gradually changing.

To the extent that pension funds have invested in real estate, they heretofore have operated primarily through commingled funds operated by commercial banks and life insurance companies. However, the trend is now toward direct equity investments by pension funds, sometimes operating as joint ventures.

[a] Pension Fund Real Estate and the Employee Retirement Income Security Act

Real estate (and other) investments by a pension fund must be made in the context of three primary restraints on the fiduciary. These are:

☐ *Adherence to instrument.* Fiduciaries must act solely in the interest of the participants and beneficiaries, and must adhere to the plan documents, except where these conflict with ERISA itself.

☐ *Prudent-man rule.* Fiduciaries must act as a prudent man would act in handling his own investments. The Department of Labor will not rule on the meaning of "prudent"; consequently, common-law precedents will be important in interpreting the term.

☐ *Diversification.* ERISA sets up as an affirmative requirement that investments be diversified, absent a showing that concentration of assets is desirable for the particular fund.

So long as the investment meets the three requirements mentioned above, ERISA does not prohibit any kind of real estate investment, except

- Transactions between a fund and a party in interest (e.g., a lease between a fund and a real estate broker who is acting for the fund); and
- Self-dealing transactions by a fiduciary.

In addition, acquisition by a pension fund of employer real property is prohibited, except that up to 10 percent of a fund's assets may be invested in qualifying employer real property.

Qualifying employer real property is real property that meets five conditions:

- It is sold by the employer to the fund and leased back to the employer
- The real estate involves a substantial number of separate parcels
- The parcels are dispersed geographically
- The parcels are not special purpose (e.g., an industrial plant)
- The investment is otherwise prudent

The following is a checklist for equity and debt transactions by pension funds under ERISA. It should be of value not only to real estate professionals who act for pension funds, but also to investors and others seeking to sell real estate to a pension fund.

☐ *Factors to be considered in equity transactions:*
- Plan needs and objectives
- Diversification
- Location, stability, and growth potential of property
- Price (there must be evidence of market shopping by the fund)
- Comparable sales
- Independent appraisals
- Property uses
- Required investment in light of fund's need for liquidity
- Available financing
- Rate of return
- Cash-flow and long-term capital growth
- Degree of risk
- Comparable investment opportunities

☐ *Factors to be considered in debt transactions:*
- All factors under "Factors to be considered in equity transactions," above
- Financial strength of borrower (emphasized by Department of Labor)
- Financial statements of borrower
- Personal guarantee or additional collateral
- Availability of, and comparison with, outside financing

As pension funds become more involved with, and experienced in, real estate investments, they will have a substantial impact on price structures, financing approaches (including the no-financing all-cash approach), and appraisal techniques. Pension fund purchases in part may well be responsible for the drop in capitalization rates (rise in prices) that the market in prime properties is now experiencing.

[b] Tax Aspects of Pension Fund Investments

Pension funds are exempt from federal income taxes. However, if they generate business income, then that income is subject to tax at ordinary income rates. Business income is that arising from the regular operation of a trade or business. The reason for this exception to the pension funds' tax-exempt status is to prevent unfair competition with businesses that are forced to pay normal taxes. The tax on such income is known as the unrelated business income tax (UBIT) because it covers business income unrelated to the primary purpose of the tax-exempt organization.

Until 1981, a pension fund that bought real estate that was in part financed by a mortgage had to treat a portion of the income from the real estate as unrelated business income and pay a tax on it. The theory was that to the extent the pension fund was using borrowed money rather than its own cash, it could unfairly compete with other purchases of real estate if the rental income generated from use of the borrowed funds was tax-free.

As a result of this rule, pension funds almost always limited their real estate investments to all-cash deals. In today's high-interest-rate market, this often makes sense (since traditional mortgage financing often creates downside rather than upside leverage). Nevertheless, the barrier to leveraged purchases unquestionably has kept some pension fund capital from going into real estate.

The tax law was changed at the end of 1980 to permit qualified pension and profit-sharing plans to invest in certain debt-financed real estate without becoming subject to the unrelated business income tax; the new law does not extend to charitable foundations or college endowment funds.

For a leveraged real estate investment to be tax-exempt under the UBIT, it must meet the following requirements:

☐ *No contingent price.* The price of the real estate must be fixed in amount at the date of purchase.

☐ *No kickers.* The price of the property (or the amount or timing of any payment) must not be dependent upon future revenues, income, or profits from the property.

☐ *No sale-leaseback.* The property may not be leased to the seller or to anyone related to the seller.

☐ *No disqualified persons.* The property may not be purchased from or leased to disqualified persons, that is, people who, because of their relationship to the employer sponsoring the pension plan, are prohibited from engaging in certain transactions.

☐ *No "sweetheart loan."* The financing used by the pension fund must not take the form of a nonrecourse purchase-money mortgage that is either junior financing or that carries a below-market interest rate.

Some pension fund managers may have hesitated to invest in leveraged real estate not only because of the potential tax burden but because such investments might not have been considered prudent. The exemption created by the new law implicitly approves debt-financed real estate as a prudent investment for fiduciaries such as pension funds.

Even when a proposed real estate investment may subject a pension fund to UBIT, the fund may be well advised to go ahead. There are two reasons for this recommendation. First, to the extent that depreciation deductions from the real estate shelter rental income, the pension fund will receive no taxable income that is subject to the unrelated business income tax. For example, if the real estate in question produces zero taxable income, no UBIT will be payable during the period of ownership. Second, although a portion of any capital gain on resale will be subject to tax, the pension fund can utilize the 60 percent long-term capital gain deduction before determining the tax. Thus the total UBIT exposure for the pension fund is likely to be minimal. And offsetting the potential tax exposure is the increased diversification made possible by the use of debt, as well as the upside leverage that may be achieved.

[c] Examples of Pension Fund Financing

Most discussions of pension fund investing in real estate emphasize the need for the pension fund to take a conservative posture. But this does not mean that imaginative approaches are completely ruled out. The following examples illustrate some less conventional real estate investments of pension funds.

☐ *Straight second mortgage.* Real estate professionals know that second mortgages are not necessarily high-risk loans. In one case, a pension fund took a second mortgage on a large, well-located office building subject to a first mortgage that could not be prepaid. The pension fund was able to obtain a high interest rate plus a bonus payment at the termination of the mortgage so that the total return comfortably exceeded current returns on first-mortgage loans.

The property owner was happy to pay the premium return because he did not have to renegotiate the first mortgage and was able to avoid a wraparound financing that would normally have been required by a private lender. (In a wraparound, the new lender benefits from the lower interest rate on the existing first mortgage since the wraparound rate applies to the total loan. This is not so when a straight second mortgage is used.)

☐ *Convertible mortgage.* In another case the owner of an office park in an industrial complex needed additional equity funds. The pension fund adviser suggested a convertible second mortgage carrying an interest rate 50 percent below the existing first mortgage and requiring no amortization. After ten years, the second mortgage is convertible into a predetermined percentage of the equity.

The pension fund thus maintains a protected (mortgage) position for ten years, albeit at a below-market return, but can anticipate a much higher return from an ownership position when the mortgage is converted. The property owner obtains the additional equity without a taxable sale and without the need to share the profits for the initial ten-year period.

☐ *Land sale plus leasehold financing.* Yet another approach is one that has been a favorite of institutional lenders in the past. This combines a purchase of land by the pension fund with a simultaneous leaseback to the developer, with a mortgage on the developer's leasehold. In substance, purchase of the land fills the equity gap and permits the developer to keep his equity requirements to a manageable level.

As pension funds (and their advisers) develop more expertise in real estate, they are likely to follow the investment patterns of the large life insurance companies and other institutional investors/lenders. This pattern is helping the differences between equity and debt investments to become less distinct.

[10] Commingled Real Estate Funds

The commingled funds operated by commercial banks and life insurance companies are real estate mutual funds for institutional investors. This approach to real estate investing is especially popular with the pension funds, which often lack the staff and know-how to invest in real estate on their own. Presently there are about twenty commingled funds on the market, the best known of which are Prudential Life's PRISA, Equitable Life's Separate Account No. 8, and First Chicago's Fund F. Most of them have generated annual net yields ranging between 8 and 15 percent, including unrealized appreciation.

Here are guidelines that are helpful in judging a commingled fund:

☐ *Staff depth.* One of the main reasons for a pension fund or other institution to join a commingled fund is to obtain the benefits of an experienced staff. Commingled funds may be staffed with former loan officers who have been trained to spot bad deals rather than recognize those with good potential. Thus, it is often wise to speak to the people dealing in acquisitions (rather than the people who are selling the fund) to find out their experience.

☐ *Portfolio risk.* The major reason for buying real estate today is to obtain an inflation hedge, not to get current income. The easiest way to show inflation protection is to buy multitenant properties with short lease terms (like apartment houses or small-tenant office buildings). In these properties, rents can move up quickly. But the other side of the picture is that if a market becomes overbuilt or an economic recession occurs, vacancies can quickly build up (witness the experience of the REITs in 1973-1974). Inflation protection is a more sophisticated concept than it first appears. So a fund's portfolio properties should be assessed in terms of average lease length and tenant credit rating.

☐ *Volatility in some markets.* In addition to the risks of overbuilding and economic recession, some types of real estate investments have become extremely volatile; that is, the risk exists that large amounts of capital will rush in and then rush out, causing prices to roller-coaster even though basic economic conditions do not change very much. This may be happening in certain parts of the commercial real estate market, as both institutional and foreign money compete for the same type of property. To the extent that real estate becomes a game of "fashions," price moves could imitate those of the growth stocks of recent years. In this type of market, nimble trading—another word for speculation—is the key to success; few institutional investors want to get caught in that type of game. When judging a fund, therefore, it is advisable to ask for a breakdown of properties by market value and ask the fund managers who the buyers would be if properties had to be sold.

☐ *Lack of liquidity.* It is taken for granted that real estate is an illiquid type of investment, and so participants in a commingled fund cannot expect cash immediately. But a fund could place 10 percent or so of its assets in liquid securities to provide a cushion in the event some investors needed cash quickly. Alternatively, the fund should hold some properties that can be sold quickly to avoid the need for distress sales if cash has to be raised.

☐ *Distribution of income.* In addition to being illiquid, some funds also distribute no income. While an investor may be willing to forgo income, it should do so only in exchange for a good opportunity for increased appreciation of property values.

[11] Foreign Investors

Real estate is benefiting from an overall increase in foreign investment here, brought on by changing conditions in other countries, ranging from increased socialization to outright military dictatorship. The United States is attractive to foreign investors because of its relative political stability, less dangerous inflation, and fewer legal restrictions on foreign investment.

For a number of reasons, much of the foreign capital flowing into the United States is attracted to real estate. Most investors are familiar with land investment in their own countries where it may reflect the most dependable form of investment. In addition, U.S. real estate has several features that make it particularly suitable as compared to property elsewhere. First of all, large amounts of property are available for purchase at prices perceived to be quite low when compared with other countries. This country also has an established and predictable legal framework for real estate ownership, and nonrecourse mortgage financing (i.e., without personal liability) is available, generally on more attractive terms than in other countries. This permits leveraging, a feature not lost on the foreign investor. In addition, the ownership of real estate can be transferred relatively easily. Americans may think of real estate as an illiquid investment, but it is much more liquid here than in other countries. Another advantage is that experienced property managers are available in most sections of the United States to handle post-acquisition problems, and relatively few restrictions are imposed on property use compared with other countries. Finally, a reasonable likelihood exists that investments will appreciate in value.

Most of the funds are now coming out of Europe, particularly from Italy and Great Britain where socialistic pressures are greatest. Canadian and Mexican investment capital also flows in as these governments tighten controls on the private ownership of property. Some funds are coming from Asia and Latin America where private property has been expropriated or forced into flight by military conquest. Highly publicized Arab investment, however, has been relatively limited thus far.

Many foreign investors are wealthy individuals, but an increasing proportion are foreign institutions, banks, corporations, and pension funds. In some cases, these institutions—particularly banks—are "fronting" for individual investors who prefer to work anonymously.

[a] Choice of Real Estate and Management Considerations

Most foreign investors look for existing commercial and industrial property in or near major U.S. cities. Raw land or development situations are not generally attractive because of the risks involved and the difficulty of overseeing the many facets of development activity. Residential properties are also frequently avoided because of continuing management problems and the possible threat of tenant strikes or rent control.

Shopping centers and office buildings are the most favored form of investment for foreigners, particularly if a large percentage of the space is anchored by triple-A tenants. Industrial buildings with similar high-quality credit tenants may also be considered, although they do not have the "image" quality of shopping centers and office buildings.

The following are representative of the guidelines followed by many foreign investors in choosing U.S. property:

☐ They avoid properties subject to long-term leases since the latter reduce the sensitivity of the rental income to inflation. They always seek to tie rentals to sales increases or to an index such as the Consumer Price Index.

☐ They seek the best locations and are probably more selective in this respect than most American investors. They also want buildings of top quality that are likely to resist obsolescence and so maintain their ability to generate rental income in a competitive market.

☐ They regard our high loan-to-value ratios (75 percent or more) as the best protection against inflation, since it means that most of the investment in the property is serviced with a fixed payment; thus, any increases in net income go directly to the equity investor. They are not concerned with the downside leverage in today's market because they believe prices and rental income will increase.

Foreign investors analyze real estate on a minimum ten-year projection of revenue and expenses. They will recalculate cash flows for each succeeding year on the assumption that expiring leases can be renewed at higher rentals and also to reflect increases in operating costs. Their overall goal on an after-tax basis is at least a 10 percent discounted rate of return; with the right property, this may mean they will take an initial cash-flow return of as little as 4 percent with the expectation of a rising return over the projected holding period.

A problem facing foreign investors is the management of property after it has been acquired. This can be particularly difficult if the property is located in areas where professional management firms are not available. One possible solution is to have the seller or broker assume the management role. This also tends to increase the investor's confidence that the seller or broker will stand behind the property, not just collect the sales proceeds or commission and disappear from the picture.

Americans seeking to interest foreign investors in U.S. real estate should be aware of certain marketing pitfalls. Regardless of whether land is improved or unimproved, brokers and property owners wishing to sell to foreigners are strongly advised not to go to foreign countries expecting to find eager investors waiting in line to buy projects that U.S. investors have rejected. Many foreigners have been badly burned in the past by American real-property hucksters and will not be taken again so easily. Most of these investors, particularly Europeans, are quite sophisticated and are looking for the same quality of investment as their American counterparts.

The more productive approach is to:

- Fully understand what the foreign investor is looking for.
- Offer properties meeting these criteria, in a format understandable to the foreign investor.
- Obtain all of the facts and present them honestly.
- Be prepared to stand behind the property once it has been acquired.

In this manner, a level of confidence is built with the foreign investor that will ultimately lead to a profitable long-term relationship.

[b] U.S. Laws Affecting Foreign Investments

In the United States, each state is allowed to regulate foreign ownership of real estate. Thus, to understand U.S. policy, one must examine the laws of each of the fifty states. One-half of the states do not significantly restrict foreign ownership of land; however, the states vary widely in their regulations, ranging from no restrictions to total prohibition. A General Accounting Office classification of states according to restrictions is shown in Table 5.1.

TABLE 5.1 Classification of States According to Number and Types of Restrictions on Alien Ownership of U.S. Farmland

Category	*States*
No restrictions on alien ownership of U.S. farmland	25
Restrictions on alien ownership of U.S. farmland	25
Types of state restrictions:*	
(a) Minor restrictions	6
(b) Restrictions on acquisitions of state property	4
(c) Restrictions on inherited land	9
(d) Restrictions on size of landholdings or on duration of ownership	11
(e) General prohibition or major restrictions on nonresident alien ownership of land	9

* The sum of states in categories (a) through (e) totals more than twenty-five because states often fall into more than one category.

These classifications[5] show that twenty-five states had laws that restricted alien ownership of U.S. farmland. Some of these state laws had several types of restrictions on alien land ownership.

The nine most restrictive states are Connecticut, Indiana, Kentucky, Minnesota, Mississippi, Missouri, Nebraska, New Hampshire, and Oklahoma. For the most part, nonresident aliens cannot own land in these states, although exceptions can be made in some instances. In Connecticut, nonresident aliens may own real estate for quarrying or mining; in Indiana, nonresident aliens may inherit real estate, but must dispose of it within five years; in Minnesota, nonresident aliens may hold land obtained by inheritance or which has been acquired prior to the 1977 law; in Missouri, they may continue to hold agricultural land if owned prior to the 1978 law and other real estate may be held without restriction; in Nebraska, aliens may own real estate within municipal boundaries and within three miles of the boundaries; nonresident aliens in Oklahoma who inherit or acquire real estate by foreclosure must dispose of the property in five years.

Five states limit the amount of land that aliens can own. Iowa, Missouri, Pennsylvania, South Carolina, and Wisconsin limit area from 5 acres to 500,000 acres.

[5] Based upon state laws of May 1978.

Illinois, Indiana, Kentucky, Mississippi, Nebraska, and Oklahoma limit the amount of time aliens can own land. Most of these states require aliens to sell their land within five years.

[c] Tax Rules for Foreign Investments in U.S. Real Estate

Congress passed the Foreign Investment in Real Property Tax Act of 1980 (FIRPA),[6] which completely changes the rules for taxing foreign investors in U.S. real estate. Basically, the new law seeks to put real estate investments in the U.S. by nonresident aliens and foreign corporations on a par, taxwise, with domestic investments.

A nonresident alien individual or a foreign corporation carrying on a trade or business in the United States always has been taxed on the income from the trade or business, just as is a U.S. resident. However, prior to FIRPA, the foreigner who disposed of U.S. real property unconnected with a trade or business was not taxed; the effect of FIRPA is to eliminate this distinction. Consequently, gain or loss from a real property disposition by a foreign owner is now subject to the same tax rules and rates that apply to U.S. taxpayers. A special rule is provided where a U.S. taxpayer might have had to pay the alternative minimum tax (AMT). Instead of paying the AMT, nonresident aliens are subject to tax at a minimum rate of 20 percent (if that tax would produce a tax higher than the one under the regular method).

Note that FIRPA does not:

- Impose any limitations on the ownership of U.S. real estate by foreigners.
- Impose any withholding requirement on the sales proceeds received by a foreign seller.
- Have any effect on nondispositive transactions.

However, the new law does impose a requirement concerning information returns.

[i] United States Real Property Interests. The tax imposed by the 1980 law applies to any disposition by a foreign investor of a United States real property interest (USRPI). The statutory definition of USRPI is very broad and includes

☐ *Direct ownership of U.S. real estate,* including fee and leasehold interests, options to acquire real estate, and furnishings and other personal property associated with the use of real property. While fixed-interest mortgages are not included in the definition, it is not clear whether participating mortgages are included. This may be clarified when the Treasury issues its Regulations.

☐ *Indirect ownership of U.S. real estate* (i.e., real property interests held by a partnership, trust, or estate). By a "look-through" approach, U.S. real property interest held by a partnership, trust, or estate is treated as owned proportionately by the partners or beneficiaries. The consideration received for a disposition of an interest in these entities, to the extent attributable to U.S. real property interests, is treated as an amount received from the sale or exchange in the United States of

---

[6] Pub. L. No. 96-499, 94 Stat. 2682, 26 U.S.C.A. § 861.

such property. A similar approach is applied in the case of U.S. real property holding corporations, discussed below.

Since the United States has treaties with many foreign nations concerning tax treatment of their citizens, the new law provides that, if a conflict exists between a treaty and the provisions of the new law, the treaty will control as to any gain recognized by a foreign investor before January 1, 1985. After that time, FIRPA will apply.

[ii] U.S. Real Property Holding Corporations. Foreign investors frequently hold U.S. real estate by means of a domestic U.S. corporation. Since the corporation may own other assets as well, the new law applies only to what it calls U.S. real property holding corporations (RPHC). An RPHC is a domestic corporation in which the market value of its U.S. real property interests is 50 percent or more of its total assets. (However, any assets that are non-real estate or are nontrade or business assets are excluded in the calculation. This is to prevent the corporation from avoiding taxation under the new law by pumping up its assets with non-real estate investment holdings.)

In determining whether a domestic corporation is a U.S. real property holding corporation, two special rules apply. Briefly, the first says that if the corporation owns 50 percent or more of the stock of one or more corporations that own U.S. real estate, the first corporation is deemed to own a pro rata share of such real estate. The second is that in applying the 50-percent-of-assets rule, IRS can look back five years prior to the time when the real property is disposed of. This means that a sale of an interest in a domestic corporation may be taxed even though at the time of the disposition the owning corporation no longer is an RPHC.

There are three sets of circumstances under which no tax will be imposed on the sale of an interest in an RPHC:

- The first is when the interest disposed of is that of a creditor of the corporation. However, the interest must be solely as a creditor; presumably an interest such as a convertible mortgage or debt linked with an option would not qualify.
- A limited exemption exists for any stock regularly traded on an established securities market. Such stock is not subject to tax under FIRPA if its owner held 5 percent or less of such class of stock.
- A sale of stock is exempt from tax under FIRPA if the corporation has already disposed of all of its U.S. real property interests and if the proper tax were paid on any dispositions that were subject to FIRPA.

[iii] Foreign Corporations Owning U.S. Real Estate. The new law treats foreign corporations in a completely different way than domestic corporations. As we have seen, when a domestic corporation is classified as an RPHC, any transfers of stock or other interests in the corporation are subject to tax. By comparison, one who holds shares or another kind of interest in a foreign corporation is not subject to tax when he disposes of it. Instead, the new law imposes a tax on distributions of U.S. real property interests from foreign corporations. The object is to create a more easily enforceable mechanism for taxing gains of foreign corporations.

The new law says that whenever a foreign corporation distributes a U.S. real property interest to its stockholders (whether in liquidation or otherwise), then the corporation must recognize gain on the distribution as if the corporation had sold the real property at its fair market value. For example, suppose a foreign corporation with foreign investors buys U.S. real estate. After several years, the property appreciates sharply in value; the foreign investor then sells shares in the foreign corporation to an American investor. The foreign investor has no tax obligation to the United States; however, if the American investor subsequently has the corporation distribute the real estate to him, the corporation will be liable for a tax based on the full appreciation in the value of the real property since its original acquisition. This means that at the time the U.S. owner purchases the stock in the foreign corporation, he should discount the price to reflect the future tax that will be payable as a result of the appreciation in value of the corporate real estate as of the time the stock is purchased.

American purchasers of stock in foreign corporations owning U.S. real estate who are unaware of this provision may pay an excessive price for the stock if the price is not discounted to reflect the future tax liability. On the other hand, so long as the U.S. purchaser is content to leave the real property in the foreign corporation, no tax will be payable.

5.03 EQUITY FINANCING

[1] In General

This section discusses the subject of raising equity capital for the acquisition or development of real estate. As already noted, the line between equity and debt financing is becoming less distinct each year, as traditional debt sources seek equity participations as a hedge against inflation. Nevertheless, a basic distinction continues to exist between the two types of investment, which involves the risk of loss. The equity investor assumes the primary risk of loss since his is the residual interest in the property; that is, other claims must be satisfied before he realizes a return on or a return of his capital. By contrast, debt capital represents a priority interest as against the equity position (although there may be various levels of priorities among lenders themselves). Of course, a lender is also exposed to the risk of loss, but he will incur a loss only after the equity position has been entirely wiped out.

A person may be both an equity investor and a lender in the same piece of property; alternatively, the same participation in a property may carry both equity and debt aspects (as when a mortgage loan includes a contingent share in future profits).

Whereas debt capital can normally be classified in a variety of ways (see the list of topics in 6.01) equity investments generally carry the same priorities and have the same time factor; that is, they usually last for the life of the investment. It is true that a form of preferred equity may exist, similar to preferred stock in a corporation, but this is not usual. Thus, in discussing equity investments, the important question is not so much that of priority of interest and time of investment as the various ways in which equities may be "packaged."

The two major ways in which equity investments in real estate can be packaged are (1) joint ventures; and (2) real estate syndications. Equity investments via joint ventures usually involve large institutional investors; a discussion of this subject is found at 4.03[8]. This section discusses the real estate syndicate, which is becoming the primary method of raising equity capital for real estate from individual investors. The question of when syndicate offerings constitute real estate securities, requiring registration under federal or state statutes, is discussed separately.

[2] Real Estate Syndication

Real estate syndicates—groups of investors who pool their capital for investment in real estate—are experiencing a sustained boom that seems likely to continue for years into the future. The basic rationale for the syndicate vehicle is that investing in even a single parcel of real estate requires substantial capital; by comparison, the investor in securities can buy as little as one bond or one share of common stock. Normally, the syndicate is a limited partnership because this vehicle combines the limited liability of a corporation with the pass-through of losses for tax purposes. However, a syndicate may take any other form of ownership, such as a corporation or a tenancy in common.

[a] Historical Development of Real Estate Syndication

A bit of historical perspective will show how far the syndication process has come. The first syndication phase began in the 1920s, when mortgage bonds were a popular investment totaling, by some estimates, $10 billion. In effect, the debt side of a property's balance sheet was chopped up and sold in small units. The seemingly secure bonds, which, of course, ranked ahead of the equity position, were in fact often highly speculative. The face amounts of the bonds frequently were unreasonably high in light of the underlying property value; as a result, the properties could not generate enough cash flow to meet the debt service. The excessive loans were made possible by fraudulent appraisals that permitted exorbitant front-end fees to the bond promoters. The depression of the 1930s was the final crusher, forcing many properties into default. In a final twist of the screw, so-called protective bondholder committees were formed by the very promoters who had originally sold the bonds, ostensibly to represent the interests of the bondholders. In fact, the committees were a front to enable the promoters to purchase the bonds at a small fraction of their face value. In this way, the promoters regained ownership of the property at an extremely low price.

More than twenty years elapsed before the public ventured into the real estate arena once again. In the 1950s and early 1960s, group ownership appeared in its second phase. This time the emphasis was on dividing up the equity in a property by means of limited partnership interests, which offered a way to avoid the double taxation that applied to corporate ownership of real estate. Many of the early syndicates were outstandingly successful, due largely to the fact that real estate prices were then low and excellent values could be obtained. Perhaps the outstanding example of the large public syndication of the period was the Empire State Building syndication by Lawrence Wien and his associates. A total of $26 million was raised from investors who were guaranteed a 9 percent annual cash return.

Unfortunately, as competition heated up among syndicators, higher and higher cash yields were promised to investors at the same time as competition for properties drove up their prices. The result was predictable: A number of syndications failed to meet their anticipated returns. A major reaction occurred; but despite the well-publicized problem syndicates, the vast majority of investor dollars were in sound ventures.

A third phase of real estate syndication, which is still present in today's market, began in the early 1970s with raw-land syndicates in California. The movement rapidly spread to develop properties, particularly housing projects, which offered the greatest possibility of tax shelter to high-income investors. The most significant feature of this current phase of real estate syndication has been the development of large, multiproperty syndications (some sponsored by large Wall Street brokerage firms) which raise many millions of dollars by selling units priced as low as $5,000 per share. But accompanying this growth of large public syndicates has been the development of private syndication groups (kept small enough to avoid the need to register under federal and state securities statutes) in which the individual shares are priced much higher, often $50,000 a share or more.

The discussion of real estate syndication that follows is intended to focus attention on the key issues that must be resolved by a syndicator and the techniques that can be utilized by prospective investors in evaluating a proposed investment.

[b] Organizing Real Estate Syndicates

[i] Raising the Necessary Capital. The first question for the syndicate to decide is how much equity shall be raised, in what manner it will be contributed, and the nature of outside financing that will be sought. Decisions on these questions will depend very much upon the size and type of properties that can be acquired. In essence, equity can be raised in one of two ways:

☐ *Immediate cash payment.* The members of the syndicate can agree to put up specified amounts of cash at once. The amounts, of course, may vary and normally each investor will have a share in the investment in proportion to his equity contribution (except for the syndicator who normally receives a share for his efforts in putting the deal together).

☐ *Staged payments.* The alternative is to have payments made in stages over a period of time. While in some cases the syndicate group may prefer to wait until all of the money has been contributed before acquiring a property, other alternatives are available:

- Immediate purchase of a property for a low down payment and a large purchase-money mortgage with substantial amortization payments keyed to future equity contributions
- Purchase of an option on the desired property, with option payments to be credited against the purchase price
- Lease of the desired property with a right to purchase at a future date when all the equity has been contributed

The syndicate should also decide at the outset its policy as to whether outside debt should be utilized. Here again, there are several alternatives:

☐ *All-cash investments.* Extremely conservative investors may prefer to follow an all-cash investing policy. This, of course, precludes any upside leveraging from outside financing and also limits the type of properties to be acquired to the amount of the equity capital to be raised. However, this policy also substantially cuts risks since the major overhead cost of mortgaged real estate is the debt service on the loan. Alternatively, the investors may agree to financing that (1) does not exceed a designated loan-to-value ratio; (2) is self-liquidating (as distinguished from a balloon or standing loan); and (3) meets any other conditions specified by the investors.

☐ *Recourse versus nonrecourse financing.* Real estate remains the only major investment area not subject to the new at-risk restrictions of the Internal Revenue Code. In other words, real estate investors may take as their basis for computing depreciation deductions not only their actual cash investment but also their pro rata share of a nonrecourse mortgage (i.e., one as to which no investor has personal liability). Although no specific proposals have been made to eliminate this favored treatment of real estate, it remains a possibility for the future. To the extent that such a future tax change would be retroactive, or would apply to future mortgages taken out on the syndicate property, the syndicate members should decide whether and under what conditions they would be willing to assume personal liability on a mortgage loan in order to preserve depreciation write-offs.

[ii] Single vs. Multiclass Syndicate. Closely allied to the question of how cash is to be raised is the question of how benefits are to be distributed. In the simple form of syndicate, no distinction exists between investors; each receives his pro rata share of cash flow and taxable income and loss. However, investors very often want different benefits; some prefer cash to tax write-offs, while others prefer a lower but secure return to a higher and riskier one. And within broad limits, a syndicate may satisfy the aims of different groups by using the "pineapple technique" pioneered by William Zeckendorf years ago. At least three different approaches can be distinguished:

☐ *Allocation of benefits.* Here, two or more classes of interests in the same syndicate are offered to investors. For example, investors contributing 50 percent of the equity may be entitled to a preferential cash-flow position, e.g., a 5 percent return before any other funds are distributed. The other class, also contributing 50 percent of the equity, then receives the next 5 (or other) percent of cash flow, plus either additional cash flow or tax benefits over and above those received by the first group. Subsequent cash flow is then divided on an agreed-upon ratio. Alternatively, the syndicate may sell subordinated debentures, that is, debt obligations senior to the equity interests but junior to all other debts such as mortgages. Interest on the debentures must be paid before any distributions to the equity interests; the debentures may also be convertible into equity at a specified price, or at stepped-up prices over a period of years.

Any disproportionate allocation of tax benefits to different investors in the same syndicate raises complex tax questions not touched upon here.

☐ *The land/building split.* Another method that has been used for some time is to create two legal interests in the property, a fee and a long-term leasehold. Two syndicates are then organized. One syndicate purchases the land, while the other purchases the building and leases the land from the first syndicate for a ground rental of, say, 10 to 12 percent per year. The landowning syndicate is attractive to investors interested in a relatively high and secure cash flow (but which is fully taxable), while the building-owning syndicate offers a riskier and perhaps lower cash flow but one that may be fully tax-sheltered.

A further variation is to organize a third syndicate to sublease the land and lease the building from the second syndicate, paying either a fixed or a percentage rental. In this "sandwich-lease" situation, the major risk is taken by the third (sublease) syndicate which has the operating position, but it also stands to gain the most from the future success of the property. The second (prime lease) syndicate has both depreciation write-offs and a cash-flow return that depends, however, on the operating ability of the sublessee, while the first (fee) syndicate has the most secure position but the least tax shelter and the least possibility of future gain.

☐ *The equity/loan split.* This approach is similar in some respects to the land/building approach, but, instead of a division of *ownership* between two syndicates, one syndicate, made up of the cash-flow investors, makes a subordinated loan to the second syndicate, which is comprised of the investors seeking tax benefits, and which owns the entire property. The first syndicate, instead of receiving a ground rental, receives loan interest. The loan is subordinated to a first, and possibly a second, mortgage on the property. This approach is subject to one limitation to which the land/building approach is not, that is, the need to comply with the applicable usury ceiling.

[c] Liquidity for Syndicate Interests

An important issue in organizing a real estate syndicate is whether investors will be able to cash in their interest on relatively short notice at a price having some reasonable relationship to its true value.

There are four ways that a syndicate may provide for liquidation of syndicate interests:

☐ *Repurchase guarantee.* The syndicator himself or some other financially responsible entity may guarantee repurchase for a set price for a certain period of time. Such repurchase agreements usually are for a limited period, perhaps starting one year after the formation of the syndicate and then running for up to twenty-four months. The repurchase price often is equal to the original investment together with, in some cases, interest at 6 or 7 percent.

☐ *Repurchase fund.* Sometimes, a cash fund is created by raising initial capital in excess of that required to purchase the syndicate property or by withholding a certain portion of the cash flow from the property.

☐ *Repurchase by syndicate.* The partnership agreement may impose upon the remaining partners the obligation to pay for a withdrawing partner's interest over a period of time.

To the extent this may require the remaining partners to pay in additional cash equity, this alternative may prove unacceptable to investors who want to limit their cash investment or who fear a snowball effect if a number of partners withdraw.

☐ *Repurchase financing.* The syndicator may be able to arrange in advance with a bank for a loan on the syndicate interest for a portion of its value (usually between 50 and 80 percent). Since such syndicate interests normally are not acceptable collateral, the syndicator may have to enter into a put agreement with the bank. This requires the syndicator to purchase the syndicate share from the bank in the event of a default on the loan.

Of course, setting the resale price of the interest is another matter entirely. Guaranteeing resale at the initial purchase price (as in the first alternative above) is feasible only for resales during a limited period. Usually, the resale price must be based on a formula. In one syndicate, the resale price is equal to cash assets held by the syndicate plus 60 percent of the appraised value of the land, and minus all liabilities (including mortgages) of the syndicate.

[d] Blind Pool vs. Specified Property Offerings

Is the specified property syndicate—which identifies in the offering statement the precise properties to be acquired—the safer road for the real estate investor to travel? Or should he prefer the blind pool—where properties are sought after the cash has been raised? Which is better for the syndicator himself?

Those favoring specified property offerings argue that the more data available about the syndicate's properties the better. The following points explain and support this view:

☐ *Availability of projections.* Prior knowledge of purchase prices, types of property, location, financing terms, and operating history enables the investor to make some judgment about the prospects of the syndicate. The investor can examine the operating record and (in states that permit them) future projections of operating costs, taxes, and income. In blind pools, he must rely on industry or rule-of-thumb guidelines or the track record of the sponsor.

☐ *Careful preparation.* A sponsor of specified properties is forced to think through all the details of the acquisitions in advance of the offering. There is less risk of material items being overlooked, and possible problem areas being uncovered.

☐ *Effect of state regulations.* In a number of states, regulations governing qualification and distribution of real estate securities favor specified property offerings. Unspecified property programs are generally more strictly regulated with regard to minimum capitalization, sponsor experience, description of investment objectives, and prediction of future returns.

☐ *Less pressure to purchase.* Specified property programs are not subject to the pressures experienced by blind-pool sponsors who may feel compelled to act quickly to find projects in which to invest funds in hand, in order to realize tax deductions projected or promised for the current year.

Some experts believe that blind pools are a better bet for the investor for the following reasons:

☐ *Cash on hand.* A syndicator with cash available can negotiate better price, terms, and yield. The chances are greater that a seller can be tempted to accept a low offer if the buyer is able to close immediately.

☐ *Yield on reserves.* With interest rates at high levels, the blind-pool sponsor need not feel compelled to invest all his cash at once. A respectable return can be realized by investments in short-term money instruments.

☐ *Diversification.* A blind-pool program is more likely to invest in a number of properties than is a specified property offering. One reason for this may be the difficulty faced by the latter's sponsor in tying up several properties (with purchase contingent upon the raising of funds) prior to the actual offering. The blind pool thereby offers greater diversification of risk. The investors in a partnership that buys interest in multiple properties have a much better chance of approximating a true or average return than those in a partnership holding only one or two properties.

☐ *Economies of scale.* A blind-pool syndication, also because it tends to be a multiproperty operation, can reduce per-property costs for the benefit of the investor. In two important areas—property management and professional administration of funds—it is more efficient to run a multiproperty program than operate a single property.

☐ *Liquidity.* A large blind-pool syndication with a substantial number of investors often can make a trading market in its shares and therefore provide better liquidity than a specified property program.

[e] Safeguarding the Syndicate Investment

At this point, having raised the necessary funds and decided on the organization of the syndicate, the investors are prepared to acquire one or more properties. In many cases, particularly where the syndicator is an experienced professional, the terms of purchase will be no different than in any arm's-length transaction. However, promoters of large public syndications often seek some guarantee by the seller (particularly in the case of new construction) that the property, for an initial period of time, will meet specified goals. In this way, the promoter has reasonable assurance that his projected distributions actually can be made during this period. Naturally, the seller will offer a guarantee only in exchange for a higher purchase price or perhaps a management contract covering the period of the guarantee; the seller in effect risks only the loss of the additional profit or management fee. Despite this, guarantees often are of value to the syndicate since they are some assurance that the seller will exercise his best efforts to operate the property (and complete it on time in the case of new construction).

In general, there are three methods to involve the seller-developer on a continuing basis:

☐ *Guarantee against negative cash flow.* Here, the seller guarantees that he will provide cash to offset a negative cash flow from the property for an initial period of time, frequently one to three years. This is intended to eliminate the risk that slow rent-up or unexpected start-up costs will generate an initial cash loss. These cash advances by the seller may or may not be repayable from future cash flow.

Example: A public syndicate entered into the following arrangement with the developer of a new apartment project. The developer was obligated to make loans to the syndicate equal to any negative cash flow for any month during the initial forty-two months after the syndicate took title. The loan was to bear interest at one percent above the prime rate and was repayable only if there was a positive cash flow for the total period of forty-two months. If during that entire period there was a negative cash flow, the loan was to be forgiven by the developer.

☐ *Minimum cash-flow guarantee.* The most favorable type of guarantee is one that requires the seller to put up cash if the project fails to produce a positive cash flow of a specific amount. Here again, the guarantee normally is for a relatively short period of time immediately following the closing of title. Alternatively, the seller may guarantee only that sufficient cash will be generated to pay the syndicate investors a minimum return (e.g., 6 percent) on their cash investment, with any excess cash flow to be divided between seller and syndicate in a predetermined proportion.

Example: A contract for the sale to a syndicate of a garden apartment complex involves a guarantee by the seller of a fixed cash amount plus a percentage of net operating cash flow for the initial twenty months of operation, with the balance of any net operating cash flow to be kept by the seller.

☐ *Gross rental and occupancy guarantees.* Not quite as good for the outside investors is a guarantee by the seller that the project will generate gross rental income of a fixed amount or will reach a fixed occupancy level. While this eliminates the risk of delayed rent-up, it does not meet the risk that initial operating expenses will be larger than anticipated.

Example: An apartment project to be purchased by a syndicate had a projected gross rent roll of $325,000. If this level was not reached by a designated date, $25,000 of the purchase price was to be refunded to the syndicate. In addition, the management fee of 5 percent a year to be paid to the seller was to be deferred if necessary in order to achieve a specified cash flow figure.

An alternative to having the seller make payments to the syndicate, or defer his management fee, if cash flow or occupancy levels are not reached is to have the syndicate pay for the property in stages, with the final stage dependent upon the achievement of the specified cash flow or occupancy level. The obvious advantage of this method to the syndicate is that it is a self-enforcing process. In addition, the equity need not be provided all at once, so helping to solve the first problem (raising equity) discussed in this section. Finally, the percentage yield to the cash investors is increased during the time when the full equity has not been paid.

[f] Evaluating a Syndicate Prior to Investment

Although the general advantages of real estate syndication can easily be spelled out, the acid test for the investor is actually to participate in a successful, rather than an unsuccessful, syndicate. Unfortunately, the elements that contribute to a successful investment in real estate are usually not ascertainable from reading financial statements. The key elements include such factors as location of the property, its physical condition, whether it is sited in a rising, stable or declining area, and the competency of management. Ideally, an investor in a real estate syndicate should visit and inspect each property that makes up the syndicate portfolio, as well as inspect the books and records of the property. Since this is normally not possible, the prospective investor must fall back on guidelines that are available from the offering statement or from a personal conversation with the syndicator.

Here are the major guidelines that a prospective investor in a real estate syndicate should follow:

☐ *Management.* This is the most important consideration. Every SEC-registered offering has a table showing the results of properties that have gone full cycle and have been sold (or foreclosed). This should be carefully reviewed. Successful syndicate management means the ability to operate properties on a day-to-day basis. Reliance upon outside property managers will severely diminish the chances of ultimate success.

☐ *Compensation.* General partners of real estate syndicates usually receive three types of compensation: front-end, operational, and rear-end. Some experts feel that front-end compensation (including securities and brokerage commissions) should not aggregate more than a brokerage commission in a private transaction. On this basis, front-end fees should run 5 to 6 percent of the total value of the property purchased.

During the operational stage of the syndicate, the general partner will take from 10 to 15 percent of the cash distributed to the limited partners (often subordinated to a specified return to the latter). A general partner that actually manages the property will also take a property management fee of 3 to 5 percent of gross revenues of the partnership.

Finally, upon disposition of a property, the general partner normally participates in the proceeds in two ways: a commission for arranging a sale and a share of the profits. Both of these should be subordinated to payment to the limited partners of their total remaining investment, plus a reasonable return.

☐ *Conflicts of interest.* The SEC requires all potential conflicts to be listed in the offering statement, no matter how implausible. So, it is important to read the list carefully to discern if the general partner really will be subject to conflicting pressures. One significant conflict is a syndicator that is also the developer of the property being purchased. In effect, the same party is buying and selling. Other conflicts of interest that invite trouble are those (1) giving the syndicator a commission on reinvestment of monies from property sales (which encourages churning); and (2) involving and dealing between the syndicator and related parties (e.g., a lending institution or real estate investment trust).

☐ *Syndicator's experience.* As is true whenever the investor is not a professional, the reputation of the seller or promoter is the best assurance of future performance. Many offering statements now contain a history of past offerings by the promoter. If the history is unavailable or if it does not show the cash flow and tax benefits realized, the promoter should be happy to provide these details on request. Investors should not hesitate to check out the syndicator with their accountant, attorney, and bank.

☐ *Cost of acquisition.* When a specific property is identified in the offering, some effort should be made to determine its true market value. The following two criteria should be used:

- Determine whether the property has recently changed hands and at what price. Your object is to find out whether the promoter himself (or an affiliate) purchased the property in the recent past at a price substantially lower than that to be paid by the syndicate. While such "flipping" is not illegal, it obviously gives rise to the suspicion that the syndicate is buying at an inflated price.
- Capitalize the indicated cash-flow return. If the projected cash flow is, say, $50,000 and the investor wants (or believes the current market calls for) a return of 8 percent on cash invested, the cash invested should not exceed $625,000 ($50,000 divided by 8 percent). Obviously, this is a mechanical formula and can merely indicate the possibility of an inflated price.

☐ *Property financing.* Rarely is it the case that a syndicate buys property for cash over an existing long-term self-liquidating mortgage. More often, one of the following three scenarios exists:

- *New construction.* While a construction loan commitment may have been obtained, there may or may not be assurances of permanent financing. If there are none, additional risk attaches to the venture.

- *Balloon mortgage.* Balloon mortgages, which are becoming more common in all forms of real estate transactions, have always been a staple of real estate syndicates. For example, a loan with a ten-year term may have a thirty-year amortization schedule. In this way, lower debt service (often necessary to enable the syndicate to pay a cash return) is combined with reduced risk for the lender (who can get out in ten years if the loan risk increases). The problem for the investor is, can it reasonably be assumed that refinancing can be accomplished when the balloon loan matures? It may be impossible to make an informed judgment, which means that an additional element of risk is added.

- *Wraparound loan.* A wraparound loan may be a legitimate financing device whereby the seller wraps a purchase-money second mortgage around existing financing. Or it may be a means whereby the seller is permitted to realize an inordinately high profit in exchange for accepting only a low cash payment (again, in order to enable the syndicate to show a positive cash flow). In this situation, the syndicate is trading off future appreciation (in the form of a too-high sales price) in exchange for a low initial cash investment. This often is a very unwise trade-off, since, if the appreciation fails to materialize, the property may be lost through default.

An additional risk with a wraparound mortgage that inflates the purchase price is that the IRS may disallow interest and depreciation deductions on that portion of the purchase price it deems unreasonable.

[g] Promoter Compensation and Participation

Syndicate promoters normally take their compensation not in the form of cash fees but as participation interests in the syndicate itself. Sometimes, both the promoter and the outside investor fail to appreciate the difficulties in defining exactly what the participation will include. Subtle changes in wording can have dramatic effects on how the flow of benefits will be allocated between the two groups. Here are some general guidelines for use in analyzing a participation interest in any particular syndication.

☐ *Determining on what assets the participation interest is based.* The participation interest, as noted above, normally is a form of compensation to the promoter for (1) packaging the investment; (2) forming the partnership; and (3) sometimes, for rendering continuing services to the partnership, such as handling its books and records. The participation interest may be computed with respect to one or more of the following:

- Assets of the partnership
- Income from operations of the partnership
- Cash flow from property sales or mortgage refinancing by the partnership

☐ *Participation in partnership assets.* The partnership agreement may provide that the general partner will receive a partnership interest even though he makes no cash investment. For example, a general partner wishing to retain a 20 percent ownership in the syndicate would capitalize the partnership at $125,000 and raise $100,000 in cash from limited partners with the understanding that the additional $25,000 in partnership interests was being assigned to him in recognition of his promotional efforts. Thereafter, the general partner would receive his share of any partnership distribution (although his share might be subordinate to the shares of the limited partners).

☐ *Participation in partnership's income from operations.* The promoter's participation in the continuing income expected during the life of the syndication should be defined with great precision. Use of such terms as return to the partners, operating income, cash flow, or the like all leave open unanswered questions. Essentially, the agreement must make clear what items are to be deducted from the gross cash flow before the promoter's interest is to be computed. Deductions may include:

- Depreciation (which may or may not be computed by the method used on the partnership's tax returns);
- Allowance for reserves (e.g., replacement and contingency reserves);
- Mortgage amortization;
- The tax liability calculated for a limited partner in a specified tax bracket;
- Cash available for distribution but not actually distributed.

☐ *Participation in refinancing and sales proceeds.* When the promoter is entitled to participate in the proceeds from sale or refinancing of a partnership, there are also a large number of variables that can have a substantial impact on the amount the promoter actually will receive. Any or all of the following may be deductible from gross sales proceeds before the promoter's interest is calculated:

- Closing costs and real estate sales commissions
- Purchase price (i.e., the promoter shares only in the profit)
- Mortgage (either initial mortgage or balance at time of sale)
- Initial equity investment (i.e., cash investors first recoup their entire equity from sales proceeds)
- Tax liability on sale calculated at some specified rate

Similarly, any or all of the following may be deductible from refinancing proceeds before the promoter's share is calculated:

- Initial mortgage balance (i.e., promoter shares only in the proceeds from the new debt)
- The mortgage balance at time of refinancing

☐ *Subordination of promoter's participation.* The partnership agreement also will specify whether the promoter's participation is to be equally with the limited partners or whether it is to be subordinate in some manner. Frequently, the participation is made subordinate to receipt by the limited partners of one of the following:

- A specified return on their investment
- The return of their investment
- Both of the above

Whenever the general partner's interest is subordinate to receipt by the limited partners of their initial investment, there normally is no question about "cumulative rights." That is, no matter how many years it takes, the limited partners are entitled to receive back all they put in before the general partner receives anything. However, when the limited partners have a prior right to receive a fixed return on their investment (e.g., 6 percent a year), it should be clear whether this priority is cumulative. For example, if in year 1, no 6 percent distribution is made, must the limited partners receive 12 percent in year 2 (two years' cumulative returns) before the general partner can receive anything?

[h] Example of a Complex Syndication

The following is an example of a complex (double) syndication that illustrates one way in which equity and debt interests can be combined in a single investment. The example has these major components:

- The use of tax-exempt financing for a racquetball facility
- Upside leveraging of the return to the lending syndicate by the use of subordinated financing
- A sale-leaseback of the facility between the equity syndicate and an operating company

☐ *First offering: Equity partnership.* Four different entities are involved in the syndication; they are identified in Fig. 5.1, which also shows the key relationships among them.

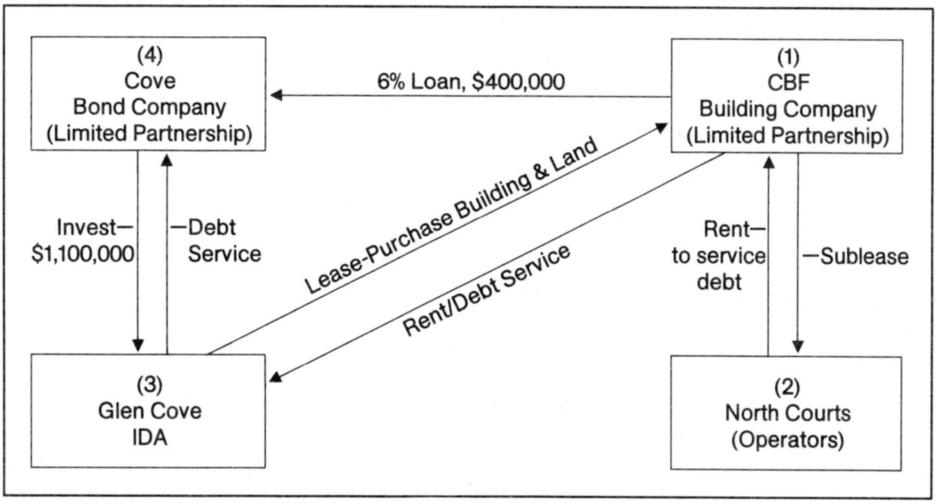

Fig. 5.1 Diagram of a transaction

CBF Building Co. (Entity No. 1), a limited partnership, is raising a total of $440,000 in equity capital. As is described below, the bulk of these funds will be used for a loan to the financing partnership in order to leverage the return to its investors. Capital contributions to CBF will be made in five stages, the first upon subscription and the balance in annual installments.

The partnership objective is primarily long-term appreciation of the real estate which the partnership will own free and clear after twenty years, and secondarily cash flow and tax benefits. (As shown in Table 5.2, a 70 percent tax bracket investor may hope to recoup his investment within four years.)

CBF will develop a 16-court racquetball and physical fitness center in Glen Cove, N.Y. The facility is located on 1¾ acres of land and will comprise just over 20,000 square feet on each of two floors. An important element in the design of the facility, in the opinion of the general partner, is the relative ease with which a portion or the entire building may be converted to alternative uses (e.g., office space) in the event racquetball revenues should fail to meet projections.

☐ *Sublease by equity partnership.* The racquetball facility will not be operated by CBF Building Co. but will be leased to North Courts (Entity No. 2). (The lease is actually a sublease because, as is discussed below, the financing of

TABLE 5.2 CBF Building Company Project Investment Summary for One Unit Paid in Installments

				70% Bracket Taxpayer		
Year	*Capital Payments*	*Cash Distr.*	*Share of Tax Loss/ (Gain)*	*Tax Recovery*[1]	*Yearly Gain*[2]	*Cum. Gain*
1979	($ 6,000)	$ 701	$11,650	$12,650	$13,350	$13,350
1980	(10,500)	2,755	20,600	14,400	17,150	30,500
1981	(10,500)	2,721	10,300	7,200	9,900	40,400
1982	(10,500)	2,782	7,300	5,100	7,900	48,300
1983	(6,500)	2,735	5,000	3,500	7,250	55,550
1984		2,662	2,300	1,600	4,250	59,800
1985		5,607	(700)	(500)	5,100	64,900
1986		7,459	(2,300)	(1,600)	5,850	70,750
1987		7,934	(3,800)	(2,650)	5,300	76,050
1988		8,409	(5,100)	(3,550)	4,850	80,900
Totals	($44,000)	$43,765	$45,250			$80,900

[1] Includes $4,500 investment tax credit in 1979.
[2] Total of cash distribution and tax recovery.

the syndicate involves a sale-leaseback to the Glen Cove Industrial Development Agency.) North Courts, the operator, is a corporation owned by the syndicator. The sublease will be for fifty-nine months at a base rent of approximately $225,000 per year plus overage rental equal to 10 percent of gross revenues in excess of $400,000 per year. From this rental, CBF will be obligated to maintain the facility at an estimated cost of $35,000 to $45,000 per year.

☐ *Financing the racquetball facility.* At this point in our analysis, the equity partnership CBF is raising $440,000 in capital for a racquetball facility and has arranged a sublease with an operating firm that will pay an annual rental to yield the equity partnership approximately $185,000 a year ($225,000 rental minus about $40,000 in expenses). But how will the facility be financed?

The total cost of the land and structure is estimated at $1.65 million. Of this, CBF will obtain $1.45 million from the Glen Cove Industrial Development Agency (Entity No. 3). CBF will obtain these funds by selling the completed facility to the IDA and simultaneously leasing it back for twenty years. The annual rental will be $190,000, equal to the debt service that IDA must pay on the revenue bonds it issues to raise the funds to purchase the facility. At the end of twenty years, CBF has an option to purchase the facility for the purely nominal amount of $10.

The balance of the cost ($200,000) primarily represents the unpaid portion of the land cost and will be assumed by CBF and repaid over a twenty-year period.

☐ *Second offering: Financing partnership.* The Glen Cove IDA is a public benefit corporation of New York State that is authorized to issue tax-exempt revenue bonds for the purpose of financing recreation projects (among others). For this transaction, the Glen Cove IDA will issue a total of $1.45 million in fifteen-year industrial revenue bonds carrying an 11 percent interest rate.

In today's market, such bonds, even paying 11 percent tax-free, might be difficult to market to institutional investors. Consequently, another limited partnership is being organized to purchase the bulk of the revenue bonds. This entity is Cove Bond Co. (Entity No. 4). It will purchase $1.1 million of the revenue bonds (with the balance of $350,000 of the bonds to be purchased by the syndicator or other persons not involved in the transaction). Cove Bond Co. will raise the capital necessary to purchase the $1.1 million in revenue bonds by

- Issuing $725,000 in limited partnership interests (of which $25,000 will be used for front-end expense).
- Borrowing $400,000 at 6 percent interest from CBF Building Co.

The $400,000, 6 percent loan from CBF Building Co. is a nonrecourse loan to be amortized over fifteen years through level monthly payments of $3,375 (10.1 percent annual constant). Since Cove will use the money to purchase revenue bonds on which an annual constant of 13.6 percent will be paid (to amortize the bonds in fifteen years), Cove benefits from upside leverage and its partners will receive an annual return of 12.75 percent (plus amortization).

CBF is willing to make the favorable loan to Cove since this enables CBF to achieve virtually 100 percent financing of the racquetball facility. The interest received by CBF on the $400,000 loan, when added to the net rental revenues from the sublessee North Courts, is projected to produce the cash return to CBF Partners shown in Table 5.2.

An additional "sweetener" to the Cove investors is an option for Cove to acquire a 10 percent partnership interest in CBF Building Co. at a price of $70,000 (payable in IDA revenue bonds) after fourteen years.

☐ *Summing up the offering.* The syndicator here has created two offerings, each of interest to a different type of investor, and has tied them together through tax-exempt financing:

- The equity partnership, CBF, will be attractive to investors seeking long-term appreciation rather than present income; because of the very desirable financing, these investors can hope to recoup their entire investment within the first few years of operations.
- The financing partnership, Cove, is aimed at investors interested in high current income who are willing to recoup their cash investment gradually over the life of the loan (fifteen years in this case). By channeling the financing through an industrial development agency, the return is made tax-free. In addition, if the operation is successful, they will have an option to participate in the equity in future years.

This type of recreational facility obviously carries substantial risks. However, if the operation is successful (either in its original form or as a result of a conversion), the rewards to investors could be substantial.

[3] Real Estate Securities

When the federal government first began regulating securities in the 1930s, the purpose was to eliminate serious abuses in the stock and bond markets. Few people, if any at all, considered that real estate transactions were covered by the two key statutes, the Securities Act of 1933 and the Securities Exchange Act of 1934.[7] However, those Acts both contained a "sleeper"—the definition of the term "security" included an investment contract. More than a decade later, the U.S. Supreme Court ruled that an investment contract could include the sale of land even though bond and stock certificates were not used to evidence ownership.[8] Since that time, the SEC has continuously, and generally successfully, sought to expand its jurisdiction over real estate dealings.

The following discussion outlines the various tests used by the courts to determine when a real estate offering falls into the investment-contract category and explains the exemptions from registration that are available.

[a] When Real Estate Offerings Are Securities

[i] The Howey Test of an Investment Contract. In the *Howey* case, the Supreme Court said an investment contract would exist when these four elements were present:

- A person invests his money
- In a common enterprise, and
- Is led to expect profits
- Solely from the efforts of a promoter or a third party.

Although the first element of the test talks in terms of investing money, the investment need not be cash. Furnishing property or services will do. What must be invested is something tangible and definable in return for which the investor gets an interest substantially resembling a security.

The common-enterprise element is closely allied with the efforts-of-others concept. Generally speaking, where the courts find the efforts of others involved, they have little problem in finding a common enterprise as well. The key to whether the profits come solely through the efforts of others lies in determining if the developer or the third party makes the entrepreneurial or managerial efforts that will make or break the enterprise. The word "solely" is not to be taken literally; the purchaser can exert some effort on his own behalf without changing the investment-contract nature of the deal. The efforts of the developer or the third party, on the other hand, must be more than minimal: An agreement to build roads in a subdivision or to perform day-to-day management of a mobile-home park is insufficient to meet this criterion, for example. But a specific contractual promise to make those substantial improvements that determine the value of the purchaser's investment will be scrutinized carefully by the courts. The promotional materials of the developer play an important role in this scrutiny; mere puffery will not create

---

[7] Securities Act of 1933, 48 Stat. 74, 15 U.S.C.A. §§ 77a–77aa; Securities Exchange Act of 1934, 48 Stat. 881, 15 U.S.C.A. §§ 77b–77e.

[8] SEC v. W.J. Howey Co., 328 U.S. 293, rehearing denied 329 U.S. 819 (1946).

the kind of contractual promise that will turn a deal into an investment contract.

The common enterprise need only be between the investor and the promoter. The investor need not have anything to do with any other investors.

The expectation of profits is also an integral part of the *Howey* test. Courts have held that the profit motive must be the primary reason for the purchase. This means not only that purchaser motivation must be closely examined, but also that, as with the common-enterprise/efforts-of-others element, promotional materials play a role. If the possibility of profit is not mentioned to the purchaser, it can hardly have been his primary reason for buying. And what profits are not can be as significant as what profits are. Tax benefits from cooperative ownership are not profits for this purpose. Nor are savings based on the fact that state-subsidized cooperatives cost less than other housing, nor are reductions in tenants' monthly charges because of income produced by commercial facilities or capital appreciation of shares in a privately owned cooperative. To the extent that these benefits are profits, they are only incidental to the desire to obtain housing. The profit motive is not primary, and the *Howey* test is not met by them.

[ii] The Risk-Capital Test. A second approach to the investment contract question is the risk-capital test. This has been developed by state courts in applying state securities laws. The risk-capital test has been used in some federal cases as well, but the Supreme Court has not as yet adopted it.

Basically, under the risk-capital approach, a transaction is an investment contract whenever

- The purchaser invests initial value in an enterprise.
- A portion of such value is subjected to the risks of the enterprise.
- The developer/seller has represented that some substantial benefit will result to the purchaser from his investment.
- The purchaser has no right to exercise practical control over the managerial decisions of the enterprise.

Unlike the *Howey* test, this approach looks to the expectation of a substantial benefit rather than to a profit motive. (For example, a California case held that purchase of a country club membership amounted to an investment contract.) This broader approach seeks to protect investors whenever a promoter attempts to raise venture capital, whether on a promise of profit or not.

The question arises whether, under either test, risk is a necessary element of the operation invested in. In the *Howey* case, the Supreme Court said that "it is immaterial whether the enterprise is speculative or non-speculative." But some of the later cases in lower federal courts and state courts have turned on the question of whether the particular enterprise was risky or not.

[iii] Consequence of Security Finding. Naturally, the major consequence of finding a security is the need to conform to the requirements of the 1933 and 1934 Acts,[9] calling for registration, prospectus delivery and broker-dealer registration. Certain statutory exemptions to these rules are available depending on the

---

[9] See note 7, supra.

circumstances. (See 5.03[2][b].) Securities sales also have the disadvantage to the developer of subjecting him to liabilities for fraud whether or not registration is required.

[iv] Specific Real Estate Transactions as Investment Contracts. The SEC over the years has issued guidelines for determining whether specific types of real estate offerings are subject to federal securities laws. These guidelines as well as pertinent court decisions are summarized briefly in the following paragraphs.

☐ *Condominiums.* An SEC release[10] lists the guidelines applicable to offers and sales of condominiums or units in a real estate development. Any of the following factors indicate that a security is being offered:

- Rental arrangements with emphasis on economic benefits to the purchaser and the managerial efforts of a promoter
- Rental pools, even if voluntary
- Rental arrangements under which the purchaser must hold his unit available for rental for any part of the year or is otherwise materially restricted in his occupancy

However, the sales of units will not be considered securities merely because the developers continue their affiliation under maintenance agreements or where income from commercial facilities used to offset common area expenses is not a primary income source for the individual owners.

It is still uncertain whether time-sharing resort condominium sales are securities sales. It would appear that the answer is no where the members do not share in profits generated by the resort operation.

☐ *Cooperatives.* Under SEC Rule 235, cooperative sales are exempt from regulation if

- The cooperative corporation is exclusively engaged in providing housing.
- Its securities are issued and transferred only with the sale or lease of housing units.
- The aggregate offering price of its securities is less than $300,000 for any given twelve-month period.
- The price of its securities is based on selling price to members or on par value.

Where there are commercial facilities associated with a cooperative, no securities problem exists as long as the income therefrom only offsets common charges, and the operation is merely incidental to the project.

☐ *Real estate syndicates.* Syndicate interests are usually considered securities. The SEC position has been that limited partnership interests and interests in joint or profit-sharing real estate ventures are investment contracts. The courts are quick to spot a syndication only thinly disguised as a general partnership. For example, three promoters offered general partnership interests in a partnership

---

[10] SEC Release No. 5347 (Jan. 4, 1973).

to buy and lease back a motel (to the promoters). The promoters put up no capital. The court ruled that the interests of the cash investors were securities.

☐ *Entire real estate partnership.* In a case in which a purchaser bought a mobile-home partnership, the court pointed out while limited partnership interests are always securities, purchase of an entire partnership has none of the elements necessary for a security.

☐ *Loan commitments.* Permanent and construction loan commitments are commercial transactions in nature rather than investment. There is no common enterprise in the investment sense.

☐ *Promissory notes.* These are decided on a case-by-case basis, since notes are securities "unless the context otherwise requires" under the statutory definition. To a large degree, the *Howey* and risk-capital tests are applied in these cases.

☐ *Mortgage loan participations.* Even though the underlying loan is not a security, participation in the loan may be if the tests for an investment contract are met—again, a case-by-case determination.

☐ *Sale-leaseback arrangements.* Where the rent paid to the owner is based on the varying amounts for which the lessee is able to sublease the property, a security exists. Where fixed rentals are involved, and no variables enter the picture, there is no security involved.

☐ *Sale-repurchase arrangements.* The SEC has stated that such arrangements are "not entirely free from doubt." An example would be condominiums sold as principal residences subject to repurchase on specific nonassignable terms. In a non-real estate case, the sale of medallions subject to repurchase at the original price plus 10 percent was held to be the sale of a security.

☐ *Rebate arrangements.* Opposite determinations were made by the SEC in two specific instances:

- No security sale where buyers of undeveloped real estate from a closely held company were to receive rebates from profits the company made in the year of purchase, but were not to share in losses.
- Sale of security where full purchase price of land to be rebated if value had not quadrupled in twelve years.

☐ *Undeveloped residential subdivision lots.* As noted in the discussion of the *Howey* test, the question of the existence of an investment contract is dependent on the presence of an expectation of profit solely from the efforts of others. Given undeveloped lots, the answer turns on the degree to which the developers have made contractual promises to do the improvement of the lots themselves.

[b] Exemption of Real Estate Offerings From Registration

There are several important exemptions available for real estate offerings that involve a relatively small dollar amount, or are made to a limited number of investors or are confined to a narrow geographic area. The principal federal exemptions are:

- The private placement exemption in Section 4(2) of the 1933 Act[11] and Rule 146 thereunder.
- The intrastate offering exemption under Section 3(a)(11) of the 1933 Act and Rule 147 thereunder.
- The small offering exemptions, including Regulation A and Rules 240 and 242 of the SEC.
- The accredited investors exemption.

[i] Private Placement Exemption

Section 4(2). The private placement exemption, Section 4(2), of the Securities Act of 1933, applies to transactions by an issuer not involving any public offering. The theory of this exemption is that registration and disclosure are not necessary for sophisticated investors who have access to the information required in a registration statement and who can fend for themselves.

In determining whether the private placement exemption is available, the following four factors are important:

- *Number of offerees.* The exemption must be met with respect to all offerees, and the issuee should keep records of the offers made.
- *Sophistication of the offerees.* The issuer must be able to show that it took precautions only to make offers to sophisticated investors.
- *Size and manner of the offering.* If the issuer can show that the offering is small and made directly to the offerees, his chance of obtaining the exemption is greater.
- *Relationship of offerers to issuer.* All offerees should have the kind of relationship with the offeree that would insure their access to the kind of information contained in a registration statement.

Rule 146. Because of uncertainty about whether or not the requirements of Section 4(2) are satisfied, the SEC issued Rule 146, which provides a so-called safe harbor. This means that if the issuer complies with all the requirements of the rule, he will be entitled to a private placement exemption. (It is still possible, however, for an issuer to fail to satisfy the requirements of the rule and still be entitled to an exemption under Section 4(2).) All of the conditions of Rule 146 must be complied with, and the issuer has the burden of proof with respect to compliance. Another important point is that compliance with Rule 146 exempts only the issuer from the registration requirements of the federal securities law; he is still subject to the antifraud provisions.

The requirements of Rule 146 are as follows:

☐ *Number of purchasers.* The issuer must have reasonable grounds to believe that there are no more than 35 purchasers. Not included in computing this number are certain purchasers such as relatives, corporations owned by the pur-

[11] See note 7, supra.

chaser or his relatives, or any purchaser who buys for cash in a single payment an interest worth $150,000 or more.

☐ *Advertising.* General advertising and solicitation, including newspaper advertising and mass mailings, are prohibited.

☐ *Nature of offerees.* The issuer must reasonably believe that each offeree is sophisticated enough in financial and business matters to evaluate the risks and merits of the investment and that the offeree can bear the economic risk of the investment. Slightly different requirements must be met with respect to the actual purchasers. It is permissible for an offeree to rely on a representative as an aid in evaluating the investment, but the representative must be independent of the issuer.

☐ *Information requirement.* The information that the issuer must provide to an offeree concerning a private offering is basically the same kind of material information that would be presented in a registration statement pursuant to the Securities Act of 1933.

In addition, the issuer must disclose to the offeree in writing prior to the sale that the purchaser of the securities must bear the economic risk of ownership of the securities for an indefinite period of time, because the securities are not registered pursuant to the Securities Act and cannot be resold unless registered or subject to an exemption from registration. Also, limitations on transfer of the securities must be disclosed in writing prior to the sale.

☐ *Limitations on transfers.* The limitations on transfer of securities by the original purchaser are to prevent resale of the securities in transactions that may constitute a public distribution. The issuer must exercise reasonable care to insure that the original purchasers are not purchasing for resale to the public. Reasonable care includes the following:

- Reasonable inquiry to establish that the purchaser is acquiring the shares for his own account
- Placing the legend on the certificate giving notice that the securities are not registered and that there are restrictions on transfer
- Issuing stop-transfer instructions to the transfer agent or placing such instructions on the appropriate records of the issuer
- Obtaining a written agreement from the purchaser that the securities will not be sold without registration pursuant to the Securities Act unless an exemption is available

All offers and sales that are part of an offering must meet all of the conditions of Rule 146 in order to qualify for the exemption. In determining whether offers and sales should be regarded as part of a larger offering, and thus integrated, the following factors will be considered:

- Whether the offerings are part of a single plan of financing
- Whether the offerings involve issuance of the same class of security
- Whether the offers are made at or about the same time
- Whether the same type of consideration is to be received
- Whether the offerings are made for the same general purpose

[ii] Intrastate Offering Exemption

Section 3(a)(11) of the Securities Act. The intrastate offering exemption (Section 3(a)(11) of the 1933 Securities Act) applies to essentially local offerings to finance local businesses. The exemption is applied even though the U.S. mails or other instruments of interstate commerce are used in the distribution. However, the exemption applies only to distributions that are genuinely local in nature. Both the SEC and the courts are likely to construe the exemption narrowly in order to carry out the purpose of the law to protect the investing public.

Strict construction of the intrastate exemption literally means that a single sale or a single offer to one nonresident will destroy the exemption with respect to all parts of the issue.

Rule 147. Just as with the private offering exemption, the SEC promulgated a special rule, Rule 147, which sets out a specific set of requirements to be followed to obtain the exemption. Complying with Rule 147 is not the only way of obtaining the exemption, but it is certainly the safest.

Basically, the issuer must show all of the following under Rule 147:

☐ The issuer is a resident of, and doing business in, the state in which all offers and sales are made. The requirement of doing business is satisfied only by the performance of substantial operational activities. In addition, the issuer must have at least 80 percent of its assets within the state, must derive at least 80 percent of its gross revenues from within the state, and must also use within the state at least 80 percent of the proceeds derived from the offering.

☐ No part of the issue will be offered or sold to persons who are nonresidents or resold by the original purchasers to persons who are not residents of the state for at least nine months from the date of the last sale of the offering. Residence means the person's principal residence, that is, the dwelling place where the person is most frequently present with the intention of making it his home. (Once the sale has been completed, however, the purchaser is free to move where he wishes.)

☐ The issuer has taken the required precautions (which he can document) against interstate distribution.

What is an issue? For the exemption to be available, all securities that are part of the issue must be sold within one state. In this context, the word "issue" is defined in accordance with the same factors listed above concerning a separate offering under Rule 146.

[iii] Small Offering Exemptions

Regulation A. Under Section 3(b) of the 1933 Securities Act, security issues are exempt from registration requirements when the aggregate amount offered does not exceed $1.5 million. SEC Regulation A sets forth the rules to obtain this exemption.

Strictly speaking, Regulation A does not permit the issuer to completely avoid all federal registration requirements. The issuer must still file what is known as a "notification" that the exemption is being claimed as well as a short-form registration statement. A further advantage of Regulation A is the absence of restrictions on the number, sophistication, or residence either of offerees or of purchasers. The one restriction is the $1.5 million ceiling within a twelve-month period, which is computed with some flexibility.

The $1.5 million limit is computed annually, regardless of whether the offerings are continuous or part of an overall program. Thus, it may be possible to break down an offering into several Regulation A offerings so that, on an annual basis, the ceiling is not exceeded.

If an offering is in excess of $100,000, a circular containing information required by the SEC must be furnished to each offeree prior to or concurrently with the making of a written offer and prior to sale.

Rule 240. An issuer who wishes to make a small offering but cannot meet the requirements of Regulation A may qualify for an exemption under SEC Rule 240. Rule 240 is clearly designed to exempt the small, nonprofessional company from the registration requirements of the 1933 Act. To qualify under Rule 240, an issuer cannot have more than 100 holders in all of its affiliated business ventures, and the sales or offerings proposed, combined with all the sales of the preceding twelve months, cannot exceed $100,000. Thus, a maximum of $100,000 may be syndicated every year. The 100 security-holder limitation is applied at the time the issuer relies on the exemption.

Unlike Regulation A, which requires filing before the exempt offering is made, Rule 240 allows the issuer to sell up to $100,000 worth of securities without filing with the SEC. However, before exceeding the $100,000 limit, the issuer must file with the regional SEC office. The disclosure requirements are not as involved as those under the registration requirements of Section 5 of the 1933 Act. As is also true under Regulation A, Rule 240 contains no investor-sophistication regulations, although advertising through general media distributors is prohibited.

Because of its restrictions on the number of holders—which includes officers, developers, and full-time employees in the 100 limitation—as well as the low ceiling of $100,000, the Rule 240 exemption is rarely valuable to the professional real estate syndicator. Without going into any greater detail, it should be noted that the use of Rule 240 for the real estate industry may be additionally burdensome because of a prohibition against paying any commission for soliciting prospective buyers. Unless the SEC allows the salesperson to collect the usual commission for the sale of the real estate as opposed to the sale of a security interest, the issuer may find that it cannot use Rule 240 even for a small syndicate. If Rule 240 is used, salespersons would have to receive a flat salary without a bonus or commission; this is particularly unappealing in an industry such as real estate.

Rule 242. SEC Rule 242 exempts from the registration requirements of the 1933 Securities Act offerings of up to $2 million provided the offerees are:

- Institutional-type purchasers (up to any number)
- Purchasers of at least $100,000 of securities (up to any number)
- The issuer's executive officers or directors
- Up to 35 other purchasers

If all of the offerees fall within the first three listed above (called accredited persons), then no specific information need be furnished to them by the issuer. On the other hand, if the offerees include any other purchasers (up to the 35 permitted), then all purchasers have to be furnished with the same kind of information as is specified in Part I of Form S-18. In addition, the issuer must make available to any nonaccredited person who makes a written request any written information that the issuer gave to any accredited person. No general advertising or solicitation is permitted under Rule 242.

Rule 242 securities have the same status as those to which Section 4(2) applies. Consequently, they are not "free" securities and cannot be resold without registration or an available exemption.

The issuer must file a notice with the SEC Office of Small Business Policy within ten days after completion of the issue. Amended notices with changed facts, if any, must be filed every six months until the completion of the issue.

[iv] Accredited Investor's Exemption. Section 4(6) of the Securities Act exempts from the registration requirements of the Act sales or offers to accredited investors. The offering price of the issue is limited to $5 million, and advertising and public solicitation are prohibited. In addition, an appropriate notice must be filed with the SEC.

Accredited investors is defined to mean banks, insurance companies, registered investment companies, registered business development companies, small business investment companies licensed by the SBA, employee benefit plans, and certain individual retirement accounts. An individual is not considered an accredited investor, and, for this reason, the exemption is not practicable for most offerings by a real estate limited partnership.

6

Debt Financing Procedures and Techniques

6.01 OVERVIEW OF REAL ESTATE FINANCING CYCLE

The role of debt financing in real estate is pervasive, from the moment a parcel of real estate is considered for acquisition or development through the entire period of ownership. Until the historically high interest rates of recent years, it was virtually unthinkable to consider a real estate investment without also considering how to finance it with third-party funds. Nowadays, the level of interest rates has caused a significant increase in the degree of all-cash investing. This is so because very high interest rates sometimes result in a situation in which there is either: (1) downside leverage (where the cash-flow return to the investor is lower than the free-and-clear return generated by the property); or, even worse, (2) negative carry (where the carrying costs of the financing exceed the net operating income from the property, requiring the investor to pay the difference out of his own pocket). (Both of these situations are discussed in detail at 2.03[6].)

Nevertheless, most real estate continues to be financed through the use of third-party debt and this chapter discusses the various elements and techniques involved in debt financing.

A convenient method of classifying real estate loans is according to the stage of development during which the loan is made, creating a sequence of loans that begins with the acquisition of raw land and ends with a fully developed property that produces income for the investor. The following review of this sequence

- Demonstrates the importance of financing at every stage of the real estate process.
- Indicates how different sources of financing specialize in lending at particular stages.
- Illustrates how loans at each stage are tailored, in their terms and interest rates, to reflect the particular risks at each stage.

[1] Land Acquisition

The first step in the development of an office building, shopping center, or other project is acquisition of the land by the developer. The most common financing problem at this stage is the absence of institutional lenders. Institutions generally consider risk to be in inverse proportion to the cash flow from the property, since they consider the primary source of loan repayment to be the property itself. Since raw land generates no cash flow, loans to finance its acquisition are considered the most risky and frequently are avoided altogether or limited to a small percentage of an institution's loans, either as a matter of legal restriction or internal policy. A more important source of financing for land acquisition is the private mortgage firm, which is not subject to regulation and is willing to assume the extra risk in return for the higher interest received. Yet another significant source of financing is a purchase-money mortgage taken back by the seller of the land; here, the financing is extended because the seller often has no alternative if a buyer is to be found.

Raw-land loans are generally for short terms such as five years, and often are standing—no loan amortization is required. While periodic interest usually must be paid, interest sometimes is accrued, thus imposing no cash drain at all on the developer until the completed project begins to produce cash flow.

Since land acquisition financing is relatively unavailable and costly, the developer often must have recourse to equity financing. One obvious source is the developer's own assets; another frequent approach is to raise cash by a sale of interests to outside investors in a limited partnership in which the developer is the general partner. The developer may avoid the need for any significant financing by entering into a joint venture with the landowner from whom he had planned to purchase the property; the landowner contributes the land and the developer contributes expertise and whatever small amount of cash is needed for preliminary expenses. Yet another approach is to acquire the land under a long-term ground lease, an arrangement in which the obligation to pay a continuing ground rental for the term of the lease, which may run ninety-nine years or more, is substituted for a large initial capital outlay.

[2] Land Development

Land development refers to the process of preparing raw land for the construction of improvements. The process includes grading of land where necessary, obtaining rezoning if required, and the installation of sewers, streets, and sidewalks. Although developed land (in the sense used here) creates no more cash flow than does raw land, it is nevertheless one step closer to the ultimate use and thus is somewhat easier to finance. Indeed, development loans are often lumped together with construction financing (which is discussed in 6.01[3]) to form a category known as construction and development (C&D) loans. In addition, the sources of financing used for land acquisition are frequently used for land development as well.

[3] Construction

Real estate construction finance is a specialized process in which the commercial banks play a dominant role. At one time, real estate investment trusts

(REITs) were a major factor in the construction-lending field, but this is no longer true. The funds provided by the construction loan are used to pay for construction materials, labor, overhead, and related costs. The real estate is the collateral for the loan (which thus takes the form of a mortgage); sometimes the developer is required to post additional collateral such as other real estate, securities, or possibly third-party guarantees.

Construction loans usually run from six months to two years and, unlike other forms of real estate finance, the actual loan funds are disbursed in stages (or draws) as construction proceeds. For example, 20 percent of the loan might be drawn down when the foundation is laid, the next 20 percent when the walls are put up, and so forth. In this way, the construction lender is assured that construction funds are being used only for the intended purpose, and that in the event of a default the value of the property will have been increased, it is hoped, in an amount equal to the construction loan disbursements. Construction lending is considered hazardous because construction itself is the riskiest form of real estate activity, subject to numerous natural, economic, and political risks. Therefore, the lender's return on construction loans is at the high end of the interest range. Typically, the borrower (developer) pays an initial loan fee of one or 2 percent of the loan plus an interest rate on funds drawn down that is several points above the prime rate. Interest is accrued only on funds actually advanced and normally is paid when the principal is due, that is, when construction is complete.

The anticipated source of repayment of the construction loan is the permanent loan. The short-term construction lender, in an effort to avoid a situation in which permanent financing will not become available upon completion of construction, usually protects itself by requiring the developer to obtain a permanent loan commitment as a condition to obtaining the construction loan. The commitment is an agreement by another lender, such as a savings association, to make the permanent loan provided the building is constructed in accordance with its plans and specifications. This permanent loan commitment is known as a take-out commitment because it is the means whereby the construction lender will be taken out of the transaction when construction is completed. Sometimes, if the builder has exceptional financial strength, a construction loan will be made without the assurance of a takeout; this type of construction loan is known as an open-end loan.

[4] Ownership and Use

The final stage in the real estate cycle begins when the property is placed in service. At this stage, a lender can anticipate a long period of cash flow from the property to service a loan and so it is at this point that a long-term (permanent) loan can be obtained. As noted above, in most cases a lender will already be committed to making the permanent loan; the developer need only provide to the permanent lender evidence of completion and the loan is disbursed, with most or all of it being used to pay off the construction lender.

Sometimes the permanent loan commitment will require not only that the improvements be completed but also that a minimum rental level be achieved before the full amount of the permanent loan is funded or disbursed. Such a rental achievement requirement might provide that upon completion of the improvement, 50 percent of the permanent loan will be disbursed, with the balance of the permanent loan to be disbursed once 80 percent of the building is rented. A loan containing this type of clause is called a floor-to-ceiling loan because it is disbursed in two stages. The purpose of the clause is to assure the lender that sufficient cash flow is forthcoming to service the loan before the entire amount is disbursed.

Suppose the construction lender has insisted on a permanent (take-out) loan commitment equal to the full amount of the construction loan. If the best the developer can do is obtain a floor-to-ceiling loan (with the ceiling amount equal to the construction financing), a gap will exist if only the floor amount of the permanent loan is funded at the completion of construction. To close this gap, the developer must obtain a second loan commitment to provide gap financing. By this commitment, another lender agrees to provide a permanent second mortgage in the event the full amount of the permanent first mortgage is not advanced when construction is completed.

Permanent financing of a newly completed real estate project is likely to go through a number of modifications over the life of the project. The possibilities include:

☐ *Liquidation.* The loan may be gradually amortized during its term, eventually being liquidated in its entirety, at which point the owner's equity interest will equal the full market value of the property. This is likely to happen only in the case of single-family homes, since with most investment real estate, owners desire a fairly high level of debt financing both to minimize their own cash investment and, where possible, to create desirable financial leverage.

☐ *Refinancing.* Prior to the maturity of the original mortgage, the owner may renegotiate its terms with the original lender, increase the loan amount, or pay off the existing mortgage and obtain a new mortgage. All of these are known as loan refinancing. In general, refinancing is done for one of three reasons: (1) to increase the property's sale potential by making the financing more attractive to a buyer; (2) to generate tax-free cash for the owner by increasing the existing debt; or (3) to decrease the existing debt so as to reduce the monthly debt service and so increase the cash flow to the owner.

☐ *Prepayment.* In many cases, the owner of the property will sell it before the existing mortgage has been paid off. In such event, the lender may call the loan or the new owner may wish to pay off the existing mortgage and arrange new financing.

6.02 PERMANENT (LONG-TERM) FINANCING

[1] In General

The key distinction between real estate and most other forms of investment is the extent to which real estate can be financed on a long-term basis with outside capital. In virtually no other form of financing can the investor expect to put up as little as 20 or 30 percent of the capital while obtaining up to 70 or 80 percent from a third-party source for a term that may run as long as thirty years. The reason for the availability of long-term financing for real estate is its unique nature as security. Real estate is immobile and insofar as the land is concerned, indestructible, while the improvements are normally long-lived. In addition, real estate prices are far less volatile than those of common stocks or other investments; consequently, a lender can be reasonably sure, if he has exercised care in his loan underwriting, that the market value of the real estate securing the loan will remain high at least during the term of the loan. Finally, well-chosen real estate has shown sustained growth potential and consequently offers even further assurance that loans will be repaid.

The extreme inflation of the past ten years has shaken, but not destroyed, these basic principles that underlie permanent financing for real estate. The effect of the inflation has been twofold. First of all, the sharp rise in interest rates has sharply reduced the extent to which an investor can achieve upside leveraging with real estate financing. (For a discussion of leveraging, see 2.03[6].) As a consequence, a far smaller "cushion" of security exists for the lender since even a small decline in net operating income from the property can create a negative cash flow for the investor, which increases the likelihood of a default under the loan. The second major effect of inflation has been the erosion of the purchasing power of the dollar, which means, from the lender's point of view, that long-term fixed-rate lending is likely to produce no true return (and indeed, an actual loss) over the term of the loan.

Consequently, lenders are using a number of different approaches, including the modification of loan terms, to insure a true return on the loan. One trend is to favor loans on properties that are better able to keep pace with inflation—shopping centers, hospitality facilities, and the like. In such cases, the lender is in a better position to insist on a participation in the owner's increasing cash flow.

In all types of loans, call provisions are being inserted into loan agreements with increasing regularity; they allow the lender to call for payment of the debt prior to the scheduled amortization rate. Loans are being called in as short a time as ten years or upon the happening of a specified event, such as sale of the property. Another item gaining importance is the indexing of long-term commitments, thus tying them at the time funds are being disbursed to some scale that keeps abreast of inflation. Still another approach is rate review with an adjustment every five years or so. Some lenders foresee the average term of a mortgage (not necessarily the amortization period) being shortened to five to ten years, which could lead landlords to index rentals.

Despite the great changes in long-term financing patterns in the past ten years, financing available for real estate remains the single most important factor enabling real estate investors to achieve higher returns than would be possible in alternative forms of investment.

[a] Real Estate Borrower's Objectives

The borrower's objective in seeking permanent financing for a parcel of income-producing real estate is to maximize the return on investment. To this end, the borrower seeks high loan-to-value ratio loans at the lowest possible financing cost. Secondary (junior) financing is to be avoided if possible, because it normally must be repaid in a fairly short time (raising problems of refinancing) and also calls for a higher interest rate because of the extra risk involved. The borrower also wishes to avoid any participation by the lender in the projected return from the property. In short, a borrower favors pure debt financing extending over a long term with low amortization (loan reduction) prior to maturity. These objectives are consistent with the borrower's desire to minimize his cash investments, maximize yield and cash flow, and take advantage of continuing inflation by amortizing debt with continually cheaper currency. Finally, the borrower will want to avoid personal liability if at all possible. To this end, the borrower will seek to use separate corporate entities or subsidiaries, dummy corporations, nonrecourse loans and other exculpatory (liability-insulating) devices.

A second tier of objectives for the borrower includes a loan commitment from the lender on the best possible terms before the actual closing of the loan; a liberal prepayment provision to permit refinancing by the borrower if the occasion arises; and financial terms structured to permit the borrower to achieve the most desirable tax consequences and benefits.

[b] Real Estate Lender's Objectives

The basic objectives of the real estate lender are apt to be quite different from, although not necessarily directly opposed to, those of the borrower. Many lenders, for example, see eye-to-eye with the borrower about the desirability of high-ratio, long-term loans with low amortization on high-quality real estate, since the security for the loan cannot be faulted and the lender has minimum cash turnover, which reduces its overhead and out-of-pocket expense. But the lender is faced with two problems. First, there may be statutory or regulatory restraints (e.g., usury ceilings and limitations on loan-to-value ratios or on dollar amounts), which prohibit a loan that both lender and borrower wish to make. The second problem the lender faces is continuing inflation, which can threaten an intolerable degree of capital erosion for "locked-in" loans. Consequently, the lender wants to devise a means of self-protection. Fixed high-interest rates build a measure of inflation protection into the loan. The lender then will want to preserve the protection by stiff prepayment provisions, or by barring prepayment absolutely. Faster loan amortization or the use of balloon loans (which, in effect, permit the lender to reconsider his decision before the loan is fully amortized) are other alternatives. Finally, the prospect of continuing high rates of inflation has motivated many lenders to seek one of the various forms of equity participation as an inflation hedge.

A final and crucial consideration for the lender is that the loan be adequately secured by the real estate or other collateral to be financed. To some degree, continuing inflation provides a measure of safety in this respect since real estate values are likely to rise about as fast as the general price indices. In addition, the lender will want to be satisfied that the property's value is based upon a sound appraisal and that the flow of income from the property (the primary source for the debt service) will not be threatened by incompetent management or by fraudulent practices that milk the property.

[2] How a Lender Evaluates a Loan

The mortgage lender can be viewed as a special kind of real estate investor, one having a claim that is senior to the claim of the equity investor. As an investor, the lender seeks to earn a rate of return that is the total of three elements:

- Rate representing the real return (i.e., compensation for the use of funds)
- Rate reflecting an inflation premium (i.e., compensation for the declining value of the dollar)
- Rate representing the risk premium (i.e., compensation for the possibility that the loan may not be repaid on time or at all)

The "real return" required by lenders, that is, the rate of interest reflecting compensation for the funds advanced, can be estimated by comparing, over the past two decades, the relationship between (1) the return on Treasury bonds and (2) the rate of inflation. Since Treasury bonds are deemed to be risk-free (the federal government always can print new money to pay its debts), the interest return on Treasury bonds is made up of only two of the above elements: real return and inflation premium. By subtracting the actual rate of inflation from the total rate of return on Treasury bonds, the real return can be determined. Generally, the difference between these two rates has been 2 to 3 percent annually, and this is considered to be the amount of the real return sought by investors.

Because the real return is considered to be constant, changes in the level of interest rates (including those on real estate loans) from one period to another are the result of changes in the other two factors.

The second element in the rate of return—the inflation premium—will move up and down in accordance with inflationary trends in the economy and generally will affect all types of loans in the same way. For example, when inflation increases, the interest rate on all twenty-year loans (whether on real estate or otherwise) will increase approximately to the same extent.

The risk premium, on the other hand, is a function of the safety and liquidity of the particular loan. The better the collateral (the higher the quality of the real property asset) and the wealthier the borrower (assuming personal liability on the note), the lower will be the risk premium demanded by the lender. Mortgage underwriting essentially is the process whereby a lender analyzes a loan to determine the degree of risk involved, that is, the likelihood that interest and principal payments on the loan will not be made promptly or that the loan eventually may not be repaid. The interest rate charged will rise and/or the loan-to-value ratio will decline as the perceived risk of the loan increases.

Mortgage underwriting decisions generally are made on the basis of a set of guidelines that the lender has designed for use in evaluating individual mortgage loan applications. These generally can be classified into two types of tests: (1) Do the quality of the property and the borrower's reputation and track record meet the lender's requirements? and (2) What is the value of the property (for purposes of applying a loan-to-value ratio); or alternatively, What is the net operating income from the property (for the purpose of determining the debt-coverage ratio)?

[a] Property Quality and Borrower Reputation: Residential Properties

When evaluating property quality and borrower reputation, a fundamental distinction exists between a residential mortgage and an income-property mortgage. In the first, as distinguished from the second, no income is being produced by the property and the loan will be serviced out of the income of the borrower (homeowner). Thus, in residential-loan underwriting primary emphasis is placed on the borrower's ability to repay the loan, whereas in income-property lending, the real estate itself is the primary security. The residential lender will concentrate upon the following three areas in reaching a decision about the borrower's credit standing:

☐ *Ability to pay.* A borrower's financial capacity is evaluated by examining the quality and quantity of income available to meet debt-service requirements. Quality of income refers to the stability of the income stream—how likely it is that the borrower will become unemployed or lose the assets that provide him with income. Certain kinds of employment, such as professional work and government employment are very stable, while other jobs, such as commission salespersons (such as real estate brokers), seasonal workers, and self-employed business persons, are much less certain.

A more difficult question arises when a borrower has more than one source of income. At one time, the income provided by a working wife was discounted by lenders because of the possibility that the wife might leave her job to bear children. However, this latter consideration has been made irrelevant by passage of the Equal Credit Opportunity Act (ECOA).[1] ECOA prohibits a lender from discounting the quality of income because of the borrower's age, sex, national origin, marital status, race, color, religion, or the fact that the borrower's income is derived from welfare or public assistance payments.

☐ *Income ratios.* Income ratios are used by lenders to express the borrower's ability to make the loan's monthly payments. Income ratios express in percentage terms how much of the borrower's monthly income must be devoted to debt service if the requested loan is granted. The debt service is assumed to include payments covering principal amortization, interest, taxes, and insurance premiums, and so is referred to as PITI (an acronym made up of the first letters of each word). The ratios are used as guidelines only and do not constitute the sole basis for evaluating a loan application.

When a conventional (non-Federal Housing Administration or non-Veterans Administration) home mortgage is being sought, lenders concentrate on two income ratios in their underwriting process. The first income ratio, which is now in a state of transition, holds that the monthly PITI payment may not exceed 25 or 30 percent of the monthly gross income. The second income ratio requires that PITI *plus* monthly installment payments covering other debts (e.g., automobile, credit cards) should not exceed one-third of the monthly gross income.

With respect to FHA-insured mortgage loans, underwriting guidelines emphasize two income ratios; these are referred to as the 35 percent rule and the 50 percent rule. The 35 percent rule stipulates that total housing expense (PITI plus monthly utilities and maintenance) should not exceed 35 percent of net effective income, that is, gross income less federal income taxes, or what is more generally known as take-home pay. The 50 percent rule states that total monthly obligations should not exceed 50 percent of net effective income. Total monthly obligations include total housing expense plus installment payments on other debt obligations plus withholding for state income taxes plus social security (F.I.C.A.) payments.

---

[1] Pub. L. No. 93-495, 88 Stat. 1521, 15 U.S.C.A. §§ 1691–1691e (1974).

☐ *Credit analysis.* The final element to be examined is the borrower's credit standing or reputation. The question here is whether the credit history of the applicant raises any question about the applicant's commitment to discharge his obligations. The lender, with the applicant's permission, will contact a credit bureau for a credit report. The report lists the status of the applicant's various credit accounts, both past and present. The type of each account (open, installment, or revolving) and source of credit (bank, credit card, department store) will be listed. The applicant's customary payment pattern will be rated on a scale that ranges from "pays as agreed" to "turned over to a collection agency."

[b] Property Quality and Borrower Reputation: Income Properties

In the case of income properties, the lender looks to the cash flow from the property to service the loan and therefore the primary security for the loan is the property itself. In the case of prime properties, the property alone will be sufficient security for the loan, and the borrower, if he wishes, may obtain an exculpatory clause in the mortgage freeing him from any personal liability on the note; this is known as nonrecourse financing. On the other hand, where the property is of lesser quality or does not generate a cash flow (e.g., raw land), then the borrower normally must assume personal liability on the mortgage and, in addition, may be required to provide other collateral in the form of stocks and bonds or other assets, or guarantees by third parties; this is known as recourse financing.

[c] Determining Property Value and Debt-Coverage Ratio for Commercial Loans

An institutional lender considering a commercial real estate loan usually starts out with fairly fixed guidelines for loan-to-value ratio, loan term, and interest rate. For example, for a prime property having net operating income (NOI) of $4.5 million, a lender might offer a 75 percent loan-to-value ratio, a term of thirty years, and a 13 percent interest rate. The problem, then, is to determine the value of the property. A lender will use one or both of two methods: band of investment and debt-service coverage.

☐ *Band-of-investment method.* The lender seeks to derive a capitalization rate which, when applied to the NOI from the property, will show fair market value. The band-of-investment method (so-called because it assumes a band or spectrum of investment positions in the property being valued) derives a capitalization rate by blending the investment returns sought by the equity and mortgage positions.

The calculation below shows the capitalization rate derived by this method when a 75 percent loan-to-value ratio mortgage is made at a 13.29 percent constant (13 percent at thirty years) and where the equity position requires a 9 percent return.

Band-of-Investment Method

Equity share (25%) × equity yield (9%) =	2.25%
Mortgage share (75%) × debt constant (13.29%)	9.97
Derived capitalization rate	= 12.22%

Applying the 12.22 percent capitalization rate to an assumed NOI of $4.5 million gives a value of $36.8 million. A mortgage equal to 75 percent of value thus would provide $27.6 million of the needed $30 million cost; the balance of $2.4 million would have to be provided by the developer, another equity source, or some form of subordinated financing.

☐ *Debt-service-coverage approach.* Here, the loan is determined by the ability of the property to pay it back. The coverage factor for a prime property might be 1.25 to 1.3 times the mortgage payment. In other words, the NOI should be at least 25 percent greater than the annual debt service required for the mortgage.

In our example, the NOI is projected at $4.5 million. Dividing that by a coverage factor of 1.25 gives a figure of $3.6 million—the maximum amount that should be devoted to debt service. Since the lender requires a debt service of 13.29 percent, the maximum loan would be $27.1 million (multiplying this by 13.29 percent gives an annual debt service of $3.6 million).

It is apparent that the two methods both support a loan of approximately the same amount ($27.6 or 27.1 million). If the actual loan were $27.5 million, the debt-service requirement would be $3.65 million (13.29 percent of the loan). This would give the developer a cash flow of $850,000 on an investment of $2.5 million, or a return of 34 percent—quite desirable, provided the developer can raise the necessary equity.

[3] What Lenders Want in Leases

When providing permanent loan financing for commercial properties such as office buildings, shopping centers, and warehouses, lenders look not only to the real estate itself as security but also to the credit of major tenants. This holds true in the appraisal of the property as well as in the underwriting of the loan. The developer who can produce executed leases with creditworthy tenants is much more likely to obtain a satisfactory mortgage loan commitment than the developer who asks a lender for a commitment to lend on unleased real estate on a purely speculative basis.

Since the leases are so important to the lender, the developer who contemplates permanent mortgage financing must give careful consideration to the terms and conditions in leases that lenders generally look for. This presents a difficulty. Lenders have idiosyncrasies peculiar to their own lending policies, and all lenders do not have exactly the same requirements. At the time of negotiations with the first prospective tenants—and sometimes even until much later—the developer is probably not certain of the identity of the permanent lender. Nevertheless, he must try to anticipate what that unidentified lender will want. He is faced with a dilemma: Which comes first, the leases or the commitment? No leases may mean no commitment. But if in his negotiations he is not successful in anticipating the lender's requirements, the developer may find himself with fully negotiated and executed leases that are unacceptable to the lender.

Amending the lease is a possibility, of course, but obtaining the amendment of an executed lease is a difficult task and the developer may be compelled to grant concessions to the tenant in order to secure his approval. Yet another possibility is a preliminary lease review by the lender. But lenders for the most part are unwilling or unable to devote time to detailed examination of leases until their commitment has been unconditionally accepted by the borrower. Even after acceptance of the commitment, lenders are most reluctant to review leases in draft form, primarily because they lack the personnel required for the time-consuming—hence costly—examination of specific leases. However, most lenders are willing to examine and approve in advance the basic form of lease that the developer proposes to use. Therefore, a developer who has a standard lease form should submit it to his lender for review and approval at the earliest possible time.

The following is a brief consideration of some of the provisions and conditions of leases that lenders regard as particularly important.

[a] Inflation Hedges: Net Leases and Escalation Clauses

Until recently, lenders customarily paid little or no attention to the inclusion in leases of provisions requiring the tenant to pay a share of real estate taxes and operating expenses. Now, because of the energy shortage with its consequent sharp increases in electric and fuel costs, continually rising real estate taxes (due at least in part to the financial problems of some municipalities), and much higher wage and salary costs, lenders require that landlords be protected against inflation in virtually all leases, even those for comparatively short terms. From the lender's viewpoint, this protection is necessary to preserve the income stream, which assures repayment of the mortgage debt.

Such protection can be afforded by a net lease, under which the tenant is obligated to pay all (in the case of a single-tenancy property) or his pro rata share (in the case of a multiple-tenancy property) of the real estate taxes and operating expenses of the property, except possibly exterior and structural repairs.

The required protection can also be provided by means of an escalation clause requiring the tenant to pay as additional rent all, or his pro rata share of, increases in real estate taxes and operating expenses. The escalation clause should be operative after the first lease year, also known as the base year. In the case of a retail tenant, the lender will not object if the tenant has the right to offset escalation payments against percentage rent. Rent adjustments that are tied to a cost-of-living or consumer price index are not really satisfactory because fluctuations in the index may bear no relationship to increases in real estate taxes and operating expenses for a particular parcel of real estate. While lenders are not as concerned with the terms and conditions of residential leases, they now generally require that all newly constructed apartment units be separately metered and that tenants occupying such units pay all electric costs.

[b] Subordination of Lease to Mortgage

Most standard lease forms provide that the lease shall be subordinate to all mortgages and underlying ground leases affecting the property. In the states in which a deed of trust is the customary security instrument, subordinate leases are automatically terminated upon foreclosure by the lender. In some states where a mortgage is used, it is clear that a subordinate lease is terminated upon foreclosure only if the tenant is named as a party defendant in the foreclosure action. In other mortgage states, a foreclosure automatically terminates subordinate leases, whether or not the tenant is named. In a few mortgage jurisdictions, the state of the law is not clear.

Normally the lender, who attributes value to particular leases in the appraisal of the security and the underwriting of the loan, wants those leases to survive any foreclosure. So while some developers still believe that lenders want leases to be subordinate to mortgages, the reverse is actually the case, except possibly in those jurisdictions in which the mortgagee can preserve a subordinate lease by not naming the tenant as a defendant in the foreclosure action. Even in such jurisdictions, first mortgagees object to leases being subordinate to all mortgages because of the possibility that a foreclosing second mortgagee may terminate a desirable lease by naming the tenant as a defendant in the suit. Accordingly, as a general proposition, most leases should not be subordinate.

As a practical matter, a knowledgeable tenant will seek to assure the right to continued occupancy after foreclosure of a mortgage either by (1) requiring that the lease be recorded prior to the mortgage, which effectively prevents subordination, provided that the lease has no provision expressly providing subordination to future mortgages; or (2) inclusion of a nondisturbance agreement under which the mortgagee agrees to accept the tenant after foreclosure. This is often acceptable to the lender, but the priority of a lease containing terms that are onerous to the landlord, and particularly of a lease at a below-market rental, is another matter entirely, and the lender will want such a lease to be subordinate to the lien of its mortgage.

[c] Condemnation of the Property

Any provision that entitles a tenant to share in a condemnation award, except an award for trade fixtures, relocation expenses, or the like, is objectionable. In the event of a partial or total taking under the power of eminent domain, the award in condemnation replaces, as security for the loan, the real estate that has been taken. The lender must have the right to apply the award as he sees fit, either in repayment of the loan or toward the costs of restoration, to insure that the loan remains adequately secured.

There is no question that a tenant should have the right to terminate the lease if a taking of a substantial portion of the premises renders the use of the untaken portion impractical or economically unsound. What constitutes a substantial taking depends upon the circumstances. For example, a taking of a remote corner of the parking area in a shopping center that has ample parking might not be substantial, whereas a taking of a smaller percentage of the parking area in a center with already tight parking would probably be substantial, particularly if the portion taken were adjacent to or close to the tenant's store. Similarly, a tenant should be entitled to a reduction in rent on the basis of some reasonable formula in the event of a partial taking of premises that are exclusively occupied by that tenant.

[d] Fire Damage to the Property

In general, the same considerations that pertain to a taking under eminent domain and to the application of a condemnation award pertain also to damage or destruction by fire or other insured casualty and to the use of insurance proceeds. However, since the premises can be fully restored after a fire or other insured casualty (which is not the case in the event of a taking in condemnation), the position is stronger, at least from the tenant's point of view, for application of insurance proceeds toward payment of the costs of restoration rather than toward reduction of the mortgage debt.

Of course, if the lender agrees to permit the proceeds to be used for restoration, it must be assured that the tenant will reoccupy the premises for the remainder of the lease term. As a corollary, the unexpired portion of the term should be a meaningful period of time. The lender is going to be reluctant to unconditionally agree in advance that insurance proceeds must be used to restore when the lease may have only three years or less before it expires at the time of restoration.

In addition, the lender will insist upon safeguards designed to insure that the proceeds of a casualty or condemnation will be properly used for restoration. These include the following requirements:

- The deposit of the proceeds with the mortgagee
- There be no default under the terms of the mortgage
- The buildings and improvements as restored will be of substantially the same character and of at least equal value to those that were damaged or destroyed
- The periodic disbursement of the proceeds shall not exceed 90 percent of the value of the work performed and shall be conditioned upon the receipt of satisfactory architect's certificates
- Evidence that the mortgagor has sufficient funds, in addition to the condemnation award or insurance proceeds, to assure the completion of the work
- Protection against mechanic's and materialmen's liens, which might gain priority over the lender's mortgage

A tenant is unquestionably entitled to a total or partial abatement of rent for the period and to the extent that the premises are rendered untenantable. Any lender who is disturbed by this can protect himself by requiring his borrower to carry rent insurance. Abatement provisions should bear some reasonable ratio to the deprivation suffered by the tenant. A tenant should be entitled to terminate his lease if the premises are destroyed or materially damaged and not restored within a reasonable period of time. What constitutes a reasonable period of time depends upon the circumstances. In general, a lender would probably regard any period of less than six months as unreasonably short.

[e] Rental Offsets

The developer may sometimes have to grant tenants rental concessions to induce them to take space in his property. Such concessions may take the form of below-market rents for the initial term of the lease, or a period of time at the beginning of the lease term that is either rent-free or at a reduced rent. The developer may also assume the tenant's rental obligation for the unexpired term of a lease of space in other property. Lenders recognize that such concessions facilitate the renting up of a property and may well prove to be a benefit in the long run. However, developers should likewise recognize that such concessions reduce the cash flow that is generated by the property and that, if significant, they may adversely affect both the lender's appraisal and underwriting.

Very often a lease will give the tenant the right to cure defaults on the part of his landlord and to offset the costs of curing against future rents. Examples of such defaults are the following:

- Default in the payment of an indebtedness secured by a mortgage or other lien that has priority over the lease
- Failure to repair the property
- Failure to correct building violations

With respect to the first example, the right of offset should be specifically restricted to those liens that have priority over the lease and actually threaten the tenant's right of continued occupancy. The right of offset with respect to repairs that the landlord has failed to make or violations that the landlord has failed to correct should be conditioned upon reasonable prior notice to the landlord and the lender of the default. An exception may be made in the case of emergency repairs, where the giving of notice would be impractical.

6.03 PAYING INTEREST AND REPAYING LOAN PRINCIPAL

The methods used by lenders in evaluating loans to residential or income-property borrowers have already been discussed (see 6.02[2]), including how a lender determines an interest rate as well as the maximum loan amount on a particular property. In addition, a lender usually has a fairly standard policy concerning the term of a mortgage loan. Consequently, once a lender has indicated the willingness to make a loan, the two important questions remaining to be negotiated are the extent to which (1) the interest rate will vary over the loan term or be supplemented by an equity participation (see 6.03[1]); and (2) the loan will be amortized prior to maturity, and the precise form of such amortization (see 6.03[2]). Also discussed in this section is the extent to which usury laws limit the amount of interest that can be charged.

[1] Interest Rates and Equity Participations

[a] Fixed-Interest Rates

The amount of interest the borrower will pay over the life of the loan is obviously of major importance. Given a fixed loan amount, the higher the interest rate, the smaller the amount of total debt service that will go towards loan amortization (prepayment). Given a fixed rate of amortization demanded by the lender, the higher the interest rate, the longer must be the term of the loan or the smaller the total amount of the loan.

The simplest approach to setting the interest return to the lender is to fix a level rate of interest for the entire term of the loan. This was almost uniformly done in the case of real estate loans prior to the major inflationary outbreak of the past fifteen years. However, because of the rise of market interest rates to record levels, many lenders will not agree to fixed-interest rates on long-term mortgages as their sole return. A fixed rate creates the risk to the lender that if inflation continues the loan amount may be virtually wiped out in terms of purchasing power by the time the loan matures. For the borrower, current interest rates are so high that they often preclude the possibility of any positive cash flow during the early years of ownership; the borrower must hope for continued inflation in order to create a positive cash flow at some point in the future. For these reasons, the long-term fixed-rate mortgage is considered by many to be obsolete; however, this may prove to be a premature judgment. When interest rates decline (as they have always done in the past following periods of inflation), the pressure on institutional lenders to put funds to work may bring back the fixed-rate loan.

[b] Alternatives to Fixed-Interest Rates

For the present, however, the fixed-rate loan has been substantially superseded by variable-rate or equity-participation loans. In the variable-rate loan, the interest rate is tied to an outside standard, for example, the prime rate on loans to business borrowers or the interest cost of new AA utility bonds. Variable-rate loans are customary for residential loans. Under the equity-participation approach, the return to the lender (over and above a fixed minimum rate) is tied in some way to the operation of the property itself, with the lender typically receiving a share of future increases in gross or net income. These are commonly used in income-property loans.

[i] Equity Participation Techniques. Equity participations or equity "kickers" give the lender a share in the profits from the enterprise without any associated risk of loss. The borrower will grant the participation in order to obtain a loan carrying a fixed-interest rate low enough to permit the borrower to realize some positive cash flow from the outset. The lender, on the other hand, is willing to pair a fixed-interest rate with an equity participation in order to obtain a hedge against continued inflation.

Following is a list of the various forms of equity participations that may be entered into. It should be noted that it is difficult to draw a line between an equity participation by a lender and a true equity (as opposed to a debt) interest in the property. The distinguishing feature used here is whether or not the lender assumes a risk of loss as to any part of his investment that parallels the risk of loss assumed by the borrower. In an equity participation, the lender does not assume a risk of loss; he merely risks not receiving an extra return via the participation, while in a true equity relationship, the lender-partners' risk of loss is the same as that of the other investors.

☐ *Interest participations.* Extra interest as percentage of *gross income* may be calculated as follows:

- Without limitation
- Above a minimum gross income figure
- Up to a fixed ceiling of interest or maximum gross income
- With step-up or step-down percentages
- After a fixed return to the developer

Extra interest as percentage of *net profit* (with variations as listed above).

Extra interest as percentage of *overages* (percentage rentals) is most commonly used in shopping center loans.

☐ *"Rental" participations.* The lender enters into a sale-leaseback with the developer; his return is in the form of rent rather than interest. (Sometimes a leasehold mortgage is also part of the picture.) One advantage of the lease is that usury problems are avoided.

Extra rental may be a percentage of *gross income* (with variations as listed above), a percentage of *net profit* (with variations as listed above), or it may be based on the following:

- Fixed step-ups
- Reappraisals of the land at periodic intervals
- Cost-of-living or similar index changes

☐ *"Profit" participations.* Here the lender comes closest to being a true partner or joint venturer with the developer. Indeed, in some cases the lender may cross the line from equity participation to partnership. This may create serious problems of liability to third parties, and such arrangements always should be checked by local counsel.

A typical example is that of a large life insurance company, which entered into a joint venture with a developer. The company put up $10 million in cash and the developer provided the know-how. A shopping center was constructed, throwing off net operating income of $1.2 million. The lender then received a straight-interest return of 9 percent on its $10 million investment, or $900,000. The developer then received a designated percentage of the excess, 40 percent of $300,000, or $120,000. The balance of $180,000 was split between the two parties, with the lender receiving 60 percent and the developer 40 percent.

☐ *Special types of participations.* One special type is sale and installment repurchase. The participation is built into the repurchase price as a contingent payment based on any of the variations described in the bulleted items of "Interest Participations." Another special type is participation in refinancing. Whether the lender's participation is via interest on a mortgage, rental under a lease, or repurchase price under a sale-buyback, the lender may be entitled to a share of any refinancing proceeds (i.e., excess of new mortgage loan over old one). Such proceeds represent mainly appreciated value of the investment. Other types are participation in gain on any resale within the designated period, and an option to purchase an interest in the developer's real estate, stock, or partnership.

When equity participations or kickers are used, the following guides should be observed:

☐ *Favor high turnover properties.* Kickers work best when the gross income for the property involved is not held down by long-term leases. Thus, apartment projects and motels are suitable because short-term leases in the one and the absence of fixed rates in the other enable gross income to keep pace with inflation. On the other hand, a property subject to a long-term lease with no step-up in rentals will throw off no additional return to the participating lender.

☐ *Require estimated payments in advance.* The lender should not wait until annual financial statements are prepared to receive its participating share. Some lenders seek monthly estimated payments, which are then adjusted up or down at the end of the year. This makes the pill less bitter for the developer and reduces the risk that figures will be misrepresented. It may also be a good idea to require quarterly profit and loss statements.

☐ *Provide continuous supervision.* A company with a large number of participation agreements should have someone following developments in the properties covered on a full-time basis.

☐ *Determine usury.* Equity participations by lenders raise a legal issue that remains unanswered in most jurisdictions; it is whether the fruits of such participation are deemed additional interest in determining if usury has been exacted. Pending a definitive ruling in the lender's jurisdiction, equity participations should possibly be limited to the following situations:

- The lender uses a subsidiary to acquire the equity interest.
- The applicable usury law imposes a ceiling that permits the participation, even where it is deemed interest.
- The transaction comes under an exemption to the usury statute (as where the borrower is a corporation).

[2] Debt-Service Arrangements

[a] In General

The question of debt service is often of crucial importance to the borrower since the debt service has the first claim (except for real estate taxes) on the cash flow from the property and normally represents the largest single claim on the cash flow. As we have seen, the lender will look to the net operating income of the property to determine the maximum amount of debt service that the property can safely carry.

At a given rate of interest and a given rate of amortization, the amount of debt service will determine the maximum amount of the loan the lender is willing to grant. To the extent that the borrower can reduce the fixed-interest rate (perhaps by substituting an equity participation), the same amount of debt service would then permit a larger loan. (See 6.03[1].) Alternatively, by reducing the rate of amortization, the borrower is able to obtain a larger loan for the same amount of debt service.

[i] Types of Loan Amortization. In terms of the amount of the loan that will be paid off prior to the loan's maturity, real estate mortgages fall into three categories:

- No amortization (standing) loans
- Partially amortized (balloon) loans
- Fully amortized (self-liquidating) loans

☐ *Standing loan.* A standing loan calls for no amortization during its term; the entire principal becomes due on maturity. Prior to the depression of the 1930s, most real estate loans took this form, normally having a term of five years and being renewed (rolled over) at the end of each five-year period. When the depression struck and banks were unable or unwilling to roll over the loans, borrowers had no alternative but to default. This was one reason for the extremity of the real estate collapse. Then, beginning in 1934 when the Federal Housing Administration introduced the amortized home loan, amortized loans became the rule; nevertheless, standing loans continue to be used in some income-loan situations.

From the borrower's point of view, standing loans have one significant advantage. Since no part of the cash flow need be set aside for loan reduction, the residual cash flow to the borrower from the property is increased. (Alternatively, the same amount of debt service can support a larger loan since the entire debt service is applied to interest.) Lenders are sometimes willing to offer these loans when the property represents outstanding security or when the borrower has an excellent credit rating and assumes personal liability for the loan. The disadvantage of a standing loan is that the borrower may be unable to pay the full principal when the loan matures, either because the property has deteriorated, business conditions have changed, or the borrower has overextended himself.

☐ *Balloon loan.* A partially amortized or balloon loan calls for some but not complete repayment of principal during the loan term. At maturity, the borrower will have a substantial sum (balloon) still to be repaid. A balloon loan represents a compromise between a standing loan, which maximizes cash flow to the borrower but increases the risk of nonpayment, and a fully amortized loan, with the opposite result. In a typical loan situation, a borrower may apply for a mortgage loan in a specified amount for a specified term (e.g., twenty-five years), with the loan to be fully amortized over its life. The loan request is based upon the maximum amount of annual debt service that can be paid while still permitting the borrower to realize a residual cash flow from the property in an amount sufficient to warrant the investment. The lender may agree to the amount of annual debt service but still be unwilling to grant a loan for the requested length of time. The lender may be concerned that in twenty-five years the property will decline in value or the loan may otherwise unfold to the lender's disadvantage. In this situation, the parties may agree that the loan will have a ten- or fifteen-year maturity, with periodic debt service on a twenty-five-year amortization basis. Consequently, at maturity (at the end of ten or fifteen years), a substantial balloon will remain. At this point the lender may decide to renew the loan or, if his original fears turn out to be justified, to insist on full repayment in which case the borrower must seek refinancing elsewhere.

☐ *Self-liquidating loan.* A self-liquidating or fully amortized loan is invariably the type of financing used for residential mortgages in the United States. In this type of payment, most or all of the periodic payments are in amounts slightly larger than the interest due at that time. The excess amount goes toward reduction of the loan so that, at the time the loan matures, the entire principal has been repaid. As time goes by, the borrower is building up additional equity in the property and the lender is obtaining an additional "cushion" against loss in the event of a default. (The lender's cushion grows only when the market value of the property remains stable or increases, and not if the market value decreases.)

Although home prices have risen inexorably over the years, requiring larger mortgages and higher monthly payments, the full amortization concept has not been abandoned. Instead, new home-buyers have been accommodated by extension of the mortgage term to thirty-five or more years. In addition, the introduction of alternative mortgage instruments (see 6.03[2][b]) provides different payment patterns to ease the burden during the early years of home-ownership.

[ii] Manner of Paying Amortization. Even after the borrower and lender agree upon the interest rate to be paid and the extent to which the loan will be amortized prior to maturity, they must agree on the precise schedule of payments to be made on the loan. The choice is between a constant-payment schedule (with payments remaining unchanged over the life of the loan) and a variable-payment schedule (one that varies in some manner during the loan term). A loan may be constant payment or variable payment regardless of the type of amortization utilized; however, the use of either type of payment is best understood if viewed in the context of the various types of amortization loans.

☐ *Self-liquidating loan.* In the case of a self-liquidating (fully amortized) loan, the debt service almost always takes the form of a constant periodic payment. The payment is first applied to satisfy the interest that has become due on the loan since the last installment and is then applied to principal repayment (amortization). As the loan is gradually reduced, the portion of each successive payment required to discharge the accrued interest declines and consequently the portion applied to the reduction of principal rises. In other words, under a constant payment self-liquidating loan, amortization begins at a very low rate but increases as the years go by while interest payments are large in the early years and decline in later years.

☐ *Balloon loan.* In the case of balloon loans, variable payments are common. Frequently the borrower pays a fixed percentage of amortization with each payment, plus interest on the outstanding balance. The interest payment decreases slightly each time while the amortization payment remains constant; the net result is that each payment is slightly less than the previous one. Borrowers may prefer this arrangement because, over a period of time, their net cash flow from the property will grow instead of remaining level. However, they have to make a balloon payment when the loan matures.

Where a project is expected to take several years before it reaches its maximum potential, the lender may agree to an arrangment calling for very low amortization payments during the early years and higher amortization payments as the property becomes more profitable. Since the increased sums paid as amortization very often exceed the decline in interest payments, the net effect is that the periodic payments increase over time. The benefit to the borrower, of course, is that he is given some breathing space during the early years. There are infinite variations to this approach, which can be tailored to the particular needs of the borrower.

Table 6.1 below illustrates this type of variable-payment loan, assuming a \$100,000 debt with 8 percent interest, no amortization for five years and 10 percent amortization commencing in the sixth year. (Interest is paid annually, at the end of the year, on the amount of the outstanding loan.)

TABLE 6.1 Variable-Payment Loan

Year	*Principal*	*Interest*	*Total Payment*	*Unpaid Balance*
1	$ 0	$8,000	$ 8,000	$100,000
2	0	8,000	8,000	100,000
		(same through Year 5)		
6	10,000	8,000	18,000	90,000
7	10,000	7,200	17,200	80,000
8	10,000	6,400	16,400	70,000
		(same through Year 15)		

☐ *Reverse interest.* Another example of a variable-payment loan is the reverse-interest loan. This calls for fixed installment payments of principal (i.e., amortization), plus accrued interest on the amount paid on each installment. (In the usual case, of course, interest is paid on the entire outstanding principal at the time of each payment.) With this approach, interest payments increase with each installment even when principal payments remain constant; accrued interest is greater due to the passage of more time since the sale. If the loan is not paid off before maturity, the seller will still receive the same amount as if the mortgage were paid by the usual method. A buyer may prefer a reverse-interest loan for two reasons:

- It shifts most of the tax deductions for interest to later years when presumably the buyer will be in a higher tax bracket. The buyer, to postpone the deduction, must use the cash basis, not accrual basis, for reporting income.
- Assuming principal payments are constant, installment payments will start low and grow larger, which the buyer may prefer if he anticipates higher future income.

Table 6.2 below illustrates a reverse-interest loan.

TABLE 6.2 Reverse-Interest Loan

($50,000 loan; 8% interest; 5 years)

Year	*Principal*	*Interest*	*Total Payment*	*Unpaid Balance*
1	$10,000	$ 800	$10,800	$40,000
2	10,000	1,600	11,600	30,000
3	10,000	2,400	12,400	20,000
4	10,000	3,200	13,200	10,000
5	10,000	4,000	14,000	0
	$50,000	$12,000	$62,000	

[b] Special Residential Loan Programs

As is indicated in the preceding sections, there is virtually no limit to the number of ways that a mortgage loan can be structured with respect to its four basic elements: principal amount (loan-to-value ratio); interest rate; monthly payments; and loan term. In commercial loan transactions involving relatively sophisticated borrowers, the variations in any of these elements of the loan are made on a case-by-case basis. But when home mortgages are involved, the situation is different.

Home mortgages are subject to fairly strict regulation both on the federal and state levels. The reason for this is twofold. First, home borrowers are generally unsophisticated in negotiating large loans, and federal and state regulations are intended to protect them from overextending themselves or from being committed to unconscionable terms. Second, most of the funds for home mortgages come from thrift institutions, which have been given certain advantages in the capital markets and under the tax laws because they are the primary source of home financing. To be sure that the thrift institutions carry out this obligation, federal and state regulators impose requirements on the home-mortgage loans they make.

After years of inflation, it became obvious that thrift institutions could no longer make mortgage loans at rates substantially below free-market interest rates. This was due to the fact that their source of funds—savings deposits—were being depleted as individuals began switching their funds to higher-yielding instruments (the process known as disintermediation). As a consequence, and over vigorous protest by many consumer groups, federal and state regulators have gradually approved a series of new mortgage forms intended to force the borrower to absorb some of the burdens of inflation by paying higher interest rates.

This process culminated in 1981 when all federally chartered thrift institutions and commercial banks were given almost complete freedom to tie mortgage payments to market interest rates.

With respect to thrift institutions, the Federal Home Loan Bank Board permitted interest rates to be pegged to almost any public index of interest rates, with the lender having the right to raise or lower monthly payments or adjust the loan principal to reflect interest changes. (Existing mortgages, however, were not affected.) The only limit on the use of a standard for determining interest rate changes is that the standard be "readily verifiable by the borrower and beyond the control of the lender."

With regard to commercial banks, the Comptroller of the Currency has signed adjustable-rate mortgage (ARM) regulations that would permit interest rate rises of one percent each six months with no limit on adjustments over the life of the loan, as well as a choice of three different indexes: the six-month Treasury bill rate; the yield on Treasury securities adjusted to a constant maturity of three years; or the Bank Board's average mortgage rate on previously occupied homes.

The new freedom for lenders means that if inflation continues in the future, homeowners no longer will be able to count on the kind of financial leverage they have benefited from in the past. Housing, in other words, will lose some of its preferred investment status and, to that extent, home prices may rise less rapidly or even plateau for lengthy periods of time. On the other hand, the financing "faucet" for new homeowners will not be subject to sudden shutoffs as in the past and this should lead to a more stable construction picture.

Following is a summary of the most popular alternative mortgage instruments that are presently in use. All of them have one essential objective: to transfer some of the risk of continually rising interest rates from the lender to the borrower.

[i] Variable-Rate Mortgage. The simplest form of alternative mortgage instrument, and one that is used frequently in commercial as well as residential mortgage transactions, is the variable-rate mortgage (VRM). It offers lenders the ability to vary interest rates over the loan term to keep pace with the lender's cost of money. The basic issue in a VRM is the standard to be used in determining interest-rate movements. State regulations may prohibit the interest rate from rising more than a fixed amount within a specified period (e.g., each year) and may or may not place a maximum on the total interest-rate increase over the life of the loan. Whereas the lender is given the option to raise interest rates if permitted by the standard, it is obliged to lower interest rates when the standard declines.

If the interest rate is increased, the borrower may be given the option of increasing the monthly payment, and so keeping the term unchanged, or of extending the term and keeping the monthly payment constant. If the latter option is chosen, the cash-flow position of the lending institution is unchanged although its profit margin is increased.

Many lending institutions give the borrower the option of choosing a VRM at an initial interest rate slightly below the current market rate, or a standard fixed-interest mortgage at the current market. In addition, a lender is much more inclined to permit a subsequent purchaser of the home to assume a VRM than to assume a standard fixed-rate mortgage.

[ii] Graduated-Payment Mortgage. A graduated-payment mortgage (GPM) is one in which payments begin at a lower level than under a standard mortgage and step up in a series of fixed raises over the first few years. Unlike a VRM, the interest rate for a GPM remains the same throughout the loan term. As a result, the monthly payments in the early years of the mortgage are less than the interest due on the mortgage so the unpaid interest is added to principal (capitalized). The mortgage loan is fully amortized over its life; in order to achieve this, the final level of payments is somewhat above that which would be paid under a constant-payment mortgage.

Under a GPM, the borrower usually may choose one of several alternatives. For example, payments may increase at the following rates:

- 2.5 percent each year for the first five years and then level off for the balance of the term
- 5 percent each year for the initial five years and then level off
- 7.5 percent each year for the first five years and then level off
- 2 percent each year for the initial ten years and then level off

The major disadvantage of a GPM loan is that the borrower will pay substantially more interest (because of much slower amortization) than under a conventional loan. A further disadvantage is that if the home is resold before monthly payments have "caught up" with those under a conventional loan, the mortgage principal will have grown, thus giving the owner a smaller equity for his next house than he had originally.

[iii] Graduated-Payment Adjustable Mortgage. The graduated-payment adjustable mortgage (GPAM) combines the VRM and the GPM. Just as with the GPM, the GPAM offers a lower monthly payment for an initial period of years, after which loan payments level off at a higher rate, which is sufficient to amortize the loan over its term. Additionally, however, interest rates can move up or down (as in the case of a VRM) in line with market conditions.

The GPAM is still in the formative stage. Because of its complexity, it is unlikely to be as popular as either the GPM, which is more favorable to borrowers since it provides for a fixed-interest rate or the VRM, which in theory at least is neutral as between borrowers and lenders.

[iv] Price-Level Adjusted Mortgage. The price-level adjusted mortgage (PLAM) is a unique mortgage plan in which the loan principal, rather than the interest rate, is variable. The interest rate applicable is the true interest rate, that is, the rate that would be changed in the absence of inflation, a rate that might be as low as 4 percent. The monthly debt service on the mortgage is based on this real interest rate and at the end of each year the outstanding mortgage balance is adjusted by an inflation factor; that is, the loan principal is increased sufficiently so that it represents the same purchasing power as did the original loan principal.

A PLAM is the most effective of all alternative mortgage instruments in lowering the initial monthly payment. The monthly payments under a PLAM will increase at the same rate that the general price level increases. The borrower is therefore assuming a risk that if inflation increases much more rapidly than does the borrower's income, he may be unable to keep up with the increasing monthly payments.

[v] Shared-Appreciation Mortgage. The shared-appreciation mortgage (SAM) is a variation of the equity-participation technique long used by commercial property lenders. The borrower is given a below-market interest rate (and, consequently, below-normal amortization payments) for an initial period (e.g., ten years). In exchange, the borrower gives the lender a share of the appreciation in the home's value after the stipulated period or upon resale, whichever comes first. If the home is not sold within the stipulated period the borrower must pay the lender a lump sum, as contingent interest, equal to the lender's share of the appreciation as determined by an appraisal. Under the most usual arrangement, lenders provide funds at a rate one-third lower than the prevailing mortgage rate (e.g., 9.5 percent instead of 14 percent) and receive one-third of the profits when the house is sold.

In order to protect the borrower against the chance of having to pay a large sum of cash representing the lender's share of the appreciation at the end of the stipulated period, the lender usually guarantees to refinance with a new long-term mortgage at that time (at then-current interest rates).

From the point of view of both borrower and lender, the SAM is a much more speculative type of financing than any of the other alternative mortgage instruments. This is because the variable factor is not the interest rate or the monthly payment but the change in value of the underlying property. If housing appreciation continues at the 9 percent annual rate of recent years, the value of the house will double after eight years, perhaps making it impossible for the homeowner to continue to own the house when the mortgage is refinanced; on the other hand, the lender will have received a high total return. If housing prices remain stable or increase very slowly, the homeowner will benefit while the lender receives a substandard return.

[vi] Flexible Loan Insurance Program. The flexible loan insurance program (FLIP) loan is a graduated-payment mortgage that has been developed to overcome the negative amortization aspect of the GPM (i.e., the fact that the GPM loan increases rather than decreases in amount during the initial period). The FLIP loan is also known as the pledged-account mortgage (PAM) because it utilizes a pledged savings account to achieve graduated payments for the home-buyer with level payments for the lender.

The essence of the FLIP mortgage program is the use of the home-buyer's down payment to create an interest-bearing savings account that is pledged as additional security for the mortgage loan. The account also serves as a source of supplemental payments for the borrower during the first few years of the loan. In other words, each month the lender withdraws an amount from the savings account that, when added to the borrower's reduced payment, equals the normal mortgage payment under a conventional loan. As the borrower's payments increase, the supplemental payments decrease; the account usually is entirely used up after about five years.

Private mortgage insurance can be used to cover the top 20 or 25 percent of the loan against a possible default by the borrower, thus keeping the lender's exposure on a FLIP loan within traditional limits. To date, FLIP has been approved for state-chartered lenders in at least twenty-seven states. FLIP loans are conventional loans rather than Federal Housing Administration (FHA) or Veterans Administration (VA) loans.

[vii] Reverse-Annuity Mortgage. A reverse-annuity mortgage (RAM) is designed to overcome the escalating expense of maintaining home ownership—particularly among fixed-income retirees—by enabling them to use the equity in their home as supplemental monthly income while retaining ownership.

Senior citizen homeowners often face the problem of insufficient income to meet their basic living expenses. Generally, they own their own home free and clear, but usually the only way they can utilize the equity in their home is to sell it and move to other housing. By using a RAM, they can convert the equity in their home into a stream of income while continuing to live in the house.

A wide variety of RAMs are possible. The simplest version is a rising-debt RAM in which a lender contracts to pay an annuity to the borrower, thus generating rising indebtedness over time. The accumulated indebtedness is payable upon sale of the property, death of the borrower, or at some specified date, whichever comes first.

Assuming that a homeowner has paid for (or has almost completed payments on) the home, the lender appraises the home and makes a RAM loan based on a percentage of the current value. The loan is paid to the borrower in the form of an annuity—a regular schedule of monthly payments for the life of the loan. At the end of the term, the total loan funds have been disbursed. But during the entire term, the borrower still owns, lives in, and maintains the home.

Should the borrower die during the term of the loan, the estate is liable for the obligation. As with the traditional loan, the lender is protected by the equity in the home and by its probable appreciation in value. Risk is further lessened by the fact that the borrower retains substantial equity in the property and receives regular RAM payments to help maintain it. Additionally, at the end of the RAM term, the lender could reappraise the property and, assuming it had appreciated in value, fund another RAM loan. A portion of the proceeds would be used to repay the existing loan and the balance would be used for additional financing.

As an example, assume that a husband and wife, both age 65, own their $58,000 home free and clear, and that they obtain a ten-year rising debt RAM for $45,000 at a 9 percent interest rate. The lender would send them a check for $226.45 per month for ten years. At the end of the ten years the couple would have received a total of $27,173.40, and would owe the lender a total of $45,000. The interest owed to the lender would be $17,826.57, or $148.55 per month for the ten-year period, as summarized in Table 6.3.

TABLE 6.3 Reverse-Annuity Mortgage

($45,000 loan, 9% interest, 10 years)

Year	*Payments to Borrower*	*Interest Owed*	*Total Balance*
1	$ 2,717.34	$ 244.56	$ 2,961.90
2	2,717.34	755.69	6,190.38
3	2,717.34	1,557.39	9,709.42
4	2,717.34	2,675.80	13,545.17
5	2,717.34	4,139.42	17,726.14
6	2,717.34	5,979.34	22,283.40
7	2,717.34	8,229.40	27,250.80
8	2,717.34	10,926.54	32,665.28
9	2,717.34	14,110.97	38,567.06
10	2,717.34	17,826.57	45,000.00
	$27,173.43		

Assuming that the home did not change in value during the ten-year period, the remaining equity in the $58,000 RAM example would be $13,000. At this point, the couple could sell the home, pay off the lender, and retain the remaining $13,000 equity. If the couple passed away before the end of the ten-year period, the proceeds of the estate would be used to repay the outstanding balance of the loan. In either case, the couple would have lived in the home while simultaneously reducing their equity.

Another version of the RAM combines a rising-debt loan with a deferred life-annuity policy purchased from a life insurance company. A partial disbursement of the loan proceeds would purchase the annuity, deferring lifetime payments to the annuitant to some future date. The balance of the loan is paid monthly to the borrower until the annuity payments from the life insurance company begin. This modification of a rising-debt RAM defers payment of the loan until estate settlement, protecting the borrower against principal repayment of the loan until death while shifting the time-uncertain annuity payments to the life insurance company.

[3] Usury

[a] In General

Usury is interest charged to a borrower for the use of money in excess of a maximum rate permitted by law. The penalty for a usurious transaction will mean loss of all or a portion of the interest on the loan and, in some states, loss of the principal as well.

The essential elements of usury are

- An agreement to lend money or its equivalent, or an agreement to forbear the repayment of money for a period of time. This latter agreement is encountered when a lender extends the maturity of an existing loan in consideration of additional interest.
- A rate of interest on the loan higher than allowed by state statute or, in some cases (e.g., California or Tennessee), higher than a limitation contained in the state constitution.
- An intention to charge a usurious rate of interest. Usually this intent is manifest from a written document that evidences the rate of interest being charged.

Every loan application brought to an institutional lender is examined to determine whether the loan requested by the borrower may be usurious. Often this is a difficult problem; usury laws differ from state to state and have thus generated a complex patchwork of interpretations with significant variations.

[i] Factors Indicating Usury. There are certain factors that a lender should be aware of in determining whether or not a loan is usurious. These are

- The legal rate of interest in the state where the property is located.
- Transactions exempt from the statute (e.g., corporate borrowers).
- The penalties for charging in excess of the legal rate of interest.

Most national lenders, such as large insurance companies, maintain digests of the basic ingredients of the law in each state, and they diligently seek to maintain these digests up to date. Nevertheless, there are occasions when complex questions involving usury require an opinion from an attorney located in a particular state.

[ii] Exemptions to Usury Ceilings. Most states have special laws governing interest rates on consumer installment loans, which exempt such loans from general usury limitations. A significant exemption in the mortgage field is the FHA-insured loan; in some states the same exemption applies to VA loans.

Continuing inflation since 1945 has resulted in a reevaluation of traditional concepts of usury. A burgeoning economy must be fueled with expanded industrial facilities, office buildings, apartment dwellings, and shopping centers. Usury laws that do not keep pace with inflation and accompanying higher interest rates tend to restrict the availability of financing for borrowers subject to usury ceilings.

The past decade has seen the beginning of an era of expanding exemptions to usury laws in order to permit development, while retaining protection for the consumer. The trend is evidenced in the following areas:

- More than forty states and the District of Columbia now provide that loans to corporations have some form of exemption from usury ceilings.
- A number of states exempt business-purpose loans. These may be defined negatively as nonpersonal loans.
- Some states provide for exemption for loans made to business entities, such as partnerships, limited partnerships, joint ventures, and real estate investment trusts.
- More than sixteen states have exemptions for loans above a certain amount, ranging from $5,000 to $500,000. Sometimes, these exclusions must be combined with one of the exemptions listed above.

Under some types of alternative mortgage instruments discussed in the previous section (e.g., VRMs and RRMs), interest rates might conceivably rise above the state usury ceiling. Under the PLAM, a court might argue that the adjustment in principal amounts is the equivalent to a rise in interest. To avoid possible usury problems, Congress passed the Federal Preemption of State Usury Laws on Residential Mortgages.[2] This provides that:

- All state usury provisions, whether by statute or state constitution, are inapplicable to residential first mortgages, first-lien loans to finance a cooperative, or a first lien on a manufactured house, provided
- The loan is made by a federally chartered bank or savings association, or a lender whose loans are eligible for purchase by the Federal National Mortgage Association, Government National Mortgage Association, or the Federal Home Loan Mortgage Corporation, or by any other lender whose accounts are federally insured or who is a member of the Federal Reserve or Federal Home Loan Bank Systems.

This federal preemption can be superseded by a state law enacted prior to April 1, 1983.

[iii] Penalties for Usury Violations. The penalties imposed upon a lender for charging an amount in excess of the lawful rate of interest vary almost as much as the usury laws themselves.

Procedurally, usury is a defense to the enforcement of the obligation by the lender. Therefore, if a lender instituted proceedings to foreclose a mortgage held as security for a usurious loan, the mortgagor could raise the defense of usury and subject the lender to the penalties prescribed by law (as well as the adverse

---

[2] Title V of the Depository Institutions Deregulation and Monetary Control Act of 1980, Pub. L. No. 96-221, 94 Stat. 132, 12 U.S.C.A. §§ 4a et seq.

notoriety that accompanies the defenses). It is the law in all states that the mortgagor cannot waive the defense of usury because such waiver clearly violates the intent of the usury statute.

In some states the penalty for exacting usury is the loss of all interest in excess of the legal rate; in other states, the lender faces the loss of principal and interest; and in California, the lender is confronted with the possibility of criminal prosecution for a felony.

It is important to bear in mind that, generally, the borrower seeking a loan on real estate in Albany, Chicago, Des Moines, or Milwaukee cannot pay a higher interest rate than is permitted by the state in which the property is located.

However, one legal nuance is worthy of mention, while also noting that the law is complex and counsel's advice is advisable in each case. Where a loan may be usurious in one state and lawful in another, it may be possible to have the loan governed by the statute that permits the desired rate of interest. For example, *A* seeks a permanent loan from a New York lender in the amount of $5 million on an office building in Los Angeles. The interest rate in California is constitutionally set at 10 percent. In New York there is no interest limitation on loans in excess of $250,000. Therefore, if the loan can be regarded as a New York loan, it would not be usurious. Factors involved in determining whether it is a California or New York loan include the following:

- The location of the property
- The state in which the loan was negotiated
- Where the loan was closed
- The residence of the borrower
- Where payments are to be made

Again, the law concerning the choice of jurisdiction governing the legality of the interest rate is complex and requires a careful review of the relevant case decisions.

In addition to examining the general usury statutes, the lender must also consider possible penal statutes (so-called loan-shark laws), which make it a crime to charge interest above a certain rate. Usually, this rate is substantially higher than the rate permitted by the general usury statutes.

[iv] What Is Interest? One of the lender's greatest problems arises in determining exactly what constitutes interest. For example, high rates have promoted several forms of lenders' participations in the borrowers' profits, which may or may not be regarded as interest. If the participation is regarded as interest and elevates the rate above the legal limit, the participation may be of little real value to the lender.

Sometimes the lender's participation takes the form of receipt of a portion of the proceeds of refinancing or resale. Since the event of refinancing or resale is within the control of the mortgagor, it is not regarded as contingent interest.

In a very tight mortgage market a developer may offer an ownership position for a very modest consideration as an inducement to a lender for making a loan. The lender must consider the possibility in some states that a court will regard the actual value of the ownership portion as additional consideration for the loan and construe it as interest. If so, the next concern for the lender is whether the interest would be added to the interest payable in the first year or spread over the term of the loan. In the former case, the risk of usury may be very substantial.

A special case in determining whether the consideration or money received by the lender is interest is the sale-leaseback. In the sale-leaseback transaction the characterization of rent as interest can render the transaction usurious. Ordinarily, of course, rent is not interest on a debt. However, it is not unknown for a sale-leaseback to be determined by a court to be a disguised loan. If the sale price of the property is substantially less than its market value, the suspicion arises that title was conveyed as security for a loan and the deed was really a mortgage. Repurchase options in particular tend to render a sale-leaseback suspect. If the amount of the rent is then viewed as interest on the sale price and exceeds the maximum permitted by usury laws, the entire transaction can be determined to be a usurious loan.

There are other consequences that may seriously impair the value of a sale-leaseback transaction that is deemed a loan. Most important to the developer is that the Internal Revenue Service may regard the rental as an interest payment so that only the portion of the rent that can be justified as interest is deductible. From the lender's point of view, if the transaction is a mortgage and not a lease, the lender must foreclose the mortgage instead of evicting the tenant, which is a more expensive and time-consuming procedure.

[b] Items That May Be Regarded as Interest

The most frequently asked question about usury laws is whether or not they cover certain items in a loan transaction that are not labeled as interest. The following is a checklist of the specific costs that may be questioned and the rule that is most generally followed.

☐ *Fees and charges.* The lender's out-of-pocket expenses, when reasonable and actually incurred, are not deemed interest for usury purposes. However, a lender may not seek reimbursement for a part of its general overhead expenses of carrying on business.

☐ *Discounts.* If the lender charges a discount (i.e., points) and someone other than the borrower pays it, no usury problem arises. For example, a seller may reduce his price or the broker may reduce his commission to pay the discount. Beware, however, of two pitfalls: The first is that the court will look to the substance of the transaction to determine that the one paying the discount is, in fact, independent of the borrower. The second is that the lender may be charged with notice of the true facts even though it was ignorant of them. In short, the lender must be a policeman in the transaction.

It follows from the above that discounted loans, where the borrower pays interest in advance through a deduction from principal, may be usurious where the effective, as contrasted with the stated, rate of interest exceeds the legal maximum.

☐ *Commitment fees.* The best statement of the rule probably is the New York Banking Department regulation, which permits as a noninterest charge a reasonable fee for the legally enforceable commitment by the lender to reserve funds for future disbursement to the borrower. The term "legally enforceable" may or may not permit the commitment to be conditioned upon various factors (e.g., appraisal, title examination, etc.).

☐ *Prepayment premiums and late charges.* Prepayment premiums and late charges generally are not deemed interest for usury purposes. The courts use two rationales:

- A prepayment or a late charge is in effect paid at the option of the borrower, and therefore is not interest.
- Such charges, if prorated over the life of the loan, do not result in a usurious interest rate.

Of course, when stated interest is the maximum amount, the second defense is not available to the lender.

☐ *FHA and fire insurance premiums.* Neither of these payments should be deemed interest for usury purposes, since even though they are required by the lender, the money ultimately is paid to a third party.

☐ *Advance interest.* Many states permit taking interest in advance in case of monthly, quarterly, or semiannual interest payments, where the interest is on balances actually outstanding. But where not authorized by statute, this can be a dangerous practice. If the lender begins to charge "phantom interest" (i.e., interest is paid on the first of the month but is computed on the balance as of the end of the month), this definitely creates the risk of usury if the stated interest is already at the usury ceiling.

☐ *Escrows and other retained monies.* A lender properly can withhold sums from borrowers in the form of escrows, provided a true escrow is involved and the funds are not used by the lender for profit. On the other hand, when a lender withholds part of the loan proceeds and keeps the retained portion in its funds generally available for investment (e.g., a compensating balance), New York has held that interest for usury purposes is determined by applying the contract rate of interest to the balance actually advanced to the borrower.

☐ *Extensions of matured obligations.* Fees and charges in connection with the extension of time for payment of a matured note (with or without an additional loan) will be judged under the same rules as set forth above. However, even if they are deemed usurious, it will only be with respect to the extension of the loan, and will not affect the validity of the original obligation.

If in consideration of the extension, a new interest rate is imposed, the usury ceiling in effect at the time of the extension is the determining law, not the ceiling in effect when the loan was first made.

☐ *Extension of unmatured obligations.* The extension or modification of an unmatured note presents a more difficult problem. Suppose, for example, the usury ceiling is 8 percent. The borrower has an existing loan of $1,000 at 6 percent interest and asks for an additional $200. The lender is willing to advance an additional $200 at 8 percent, provided that the 6 percent rate on the original loan is also increased to 8 percent. Technically, the borrower is not paying over the 8 percent ceiling on either amount, but for the small amount of new money, the borrower actually is paying a much higher than ceiling rate. A similar problem arises in the case of the wraparound second mortgage.

In the absence of a clear-cut decision in a state, this must be deemed a dangerous exposure of the lender to the usury penalty. However, if the lender substantially modifies the terms of the original loan (in favor of the borrower), then the increase in rate is probably acceptable.

☐ *Purchase-money mortgages.* The purchase-money mortgage extended by the seller of real estate to help the buyer finance his purchase is, in some states, not subject to the usury ceiling. The reason is that the parties, by simple manipulation of the principal amount, can always set the interest at or below the ceiling. A rule so easily evaded is really no rule at all.

☐ *Using a 360-day year.* Sometimes a note provides for interest calculations on the basis of a 360-day year. Unless authorized by statute, this can create a usury problem where the stated interest rate is at the ceiling.

☐ *Waiver of rights under mortgage.* A charge imposed by the lender for its waiver of a right under the mortgage cannot make the loan usurious, unless the borrower can show the charge was part of a scheme to defraud. In one case, the mortgage gave the lender the right to accelerate the maturity of the loan if the property were sold. The borrower was forced, for compelling reasons, to sell and in order to keep the $320,000 loan alive, had to pay $15,000 to the lender. It was held that there was no usury in this instance.

6.04 MORTGAGE LENDING PROCESS

[1] Mortgage Loan Application

A loan application is the formal request for a loan made by a borrower to a lender. In its simplest form, such as a personal or automobile loan, the application may consist of a single page with details about the applicant's employment, credit standing, and financial assets. Real estate loan applications normally are far more extensive and frequently are referred to as the loan "package" because of the number of documents involved.

The following is a list of documents and data that make up a loan application for construction or permanent financing:

- Specific project description and plan of development.
- Nature of requested loan. This includes the amount of loan, requested interest rate, funding schedule (if all of the funds are not to be advanced at once), method of repayment, form of amortization, and prepayment privilege.
- Identification of interim lender. If the application is for a permanent loan, the lender will want to be in touch with the party making the interim or construction loan.
- Borrower's financial statement. This shows both the borrower's assets and his anticipated cash flow from other projects, since this is backup security for the requested loan.

- Borrower's background, experience, and current projects. Experience is a crucial factor in the lender's evaluation. In addition, the borrower's present commitments evidence not only his management capability but also whether he may become overextended.
- Pro forma financial statements. Detailed statements concerning the proposed project include an income-expense schedule (or sales schedule in the case of a sales project), and a list of committed or prospective tenants.
- Leases and letters of intent. Leases already executed, and letters of intent by prospective tenants (even though they are not binding) are included.
- Appraisal or feasibility studies. In the case of an existing property, an appraisal by an independent consultant is necessary. In the case of new development, a feasibility study indicates that the proposed project can be justified on economic grounds.
- Market study. In the case of new construction, a market study indicates that there is an existing demand (or demand will exist when the project is completed) for the new space.
- Survey and legal description of the site.
- Aerial photographs of the site.
- Rendering. This shows the completed project and is frequently provided by the architect.
- Existing zoning. This either indicates that the proposed use complies with existing zoning or that rezoning must be sought.
- Purchase price or projected cost breakdown. In the case of an existing property, the agreed-upon price, and in the case of new construction, the cost of the land and the projected costs of construction should be shown.
- Building plans and specifications.

[2] Mortgage Loan Commitment

[a] In General

Mortgage loan commitments are as essential to the financing of real estate as contracts of sale are to the selling of real estate. A mortgage loan commitment is a contract between a prospective creditor and debtor under which the debtor agrees to borrow a sum of money from the creditor and the creditor agrees to lend such sum to the debtor. It customarily arises as a consequence of an application for mortgage loan financing by an owner, purchaser, or developer. The application is an offer by the prospective debtor to borrow a specified amount of money upon stated terms and conditions, and the commitment is the lender's acceptance of the offer. Both application and commitment should set forth the amount, rate of interest, maturity, and other basic terms and conditions of the proposed loan. If the terms and conditions set forth in the commitment vary materially from those set forth in the application, the commitment constitutes a counteroffer that must be accepted by the borrower before a contract arises.

The commitment defines the terms and conditions of the loan. The subsequent loan documents are to a commitment what the deed is to a contract of sale. Unlike a contract of sale of real property, a commitment cannot be specifically enforced, but the party who breaches the commitment is liable in damages. Therefore, commitments should be treated with the same regard accorded any other binding contract.

[i] The Essential Conditions of a Commitment. Commitments are issued by savings banks for loans on single-family residences, by commercial banks and real estate investment trusts for construction loans of all kinds, and by life insurance companies for permanent financing on office, apartment, retail, and other income-producing properties. While the substance of a commitment varies considerably with the purpose and type of property, the following elements should be contained in all commitments:

- Agreement by the lender to lend a specific amount
- Designation of the party to whom the loan will be made (name of mortgagor or identity of borrowing entity)
- Terms of the loan including rate of interest and maturity
- Method of repayment (e.g., constant monthly installments, interest only, etc.)
- Prepayment privilege, if any
- Description of the security. (A legally satisfactory description, such as metes and bounds, is not essential; the description need only adequately identify the mortgaged property. If the lender requires a lien on personal property, it should be included in the description of the security.)

The above elements of the commitment reflect the essential business considerations of both lender and borrower—the heart of the loan transaction.

[ii] Commitment Fees. Before seriously entertaining an application for a mortgage loan, an institutional lender must appraise the property, evaluate the borrower's integrity and financial responsibility, and also determine the economic feasibility of the real estate as security for the proposed loan. These tasks involve expenses that call for payment of an application fee by the borrower. Such fee is usually expressed as a fractional percentage of the loan and is paid simultaneously with the submission of the application. In some cases, the application fee is also regarded as the consideration paid by the borrower for the issuance of the commitment. An application fee should be distinguished from a commitment fee, which is in the nature of a security deposit to protect the lender against the uncertainties of the money market since a borrower may go elsewhere for his loan if interest rates soften. The amount of the security deposit or commitment fee constitutes a designation of the monetary damages that the lender will sustain in the event of the borrower's breach of the commitment.

In the ordinary mortgage loan transaction, actual damages are uncertain and difficult to ascertain because of the vagaries of the money market and the complexities of attributing a precise cost to the lender for holding funds available for the loan and for the post-commitment processing of the loan. Therefore, an arbitrary commitment fee expressed in the form of a percentage of the loan is usually employed. Although arbitrarily fixed, such fee should represent a reasonable estimate of the loss to the lender in the event of the borrower's failure to honor the commitment. Commitment fees of at least 2 percent of the face amount of the loan are most common.

Sometimes, in an effort to hedge his bet, a prospective borrower anticipating more favorable rates or terms in the future secures a standby commitment from a lender. Such a commitment obligates the lender to make the loan but does not obligate the borrower to take down the loan. Fees for this commitment are frequently geared to the period of time during which the commitment remains outstanding. This form of commitment usually constitutes a developer's last resort in the event he is unable to secure more favorable financing elsewhere and is generally obtained by him solely because his construction lender requires some type of firm takeout. (See 6.04[2][d].)

[b] Construction Loan Commitment

The function of the construction loan commitment letter is to set forth in writing the terms of the loan and the conditions that must be met before any funds are advanced. The letter normally will be signed by the lender, by the borrower, and by any parties guaranteeing the loan. The commitment letter should include all of the following:

☐ *Description of loan.* This includes the amount, term, interest rate, right of prepayment, service, or loan fees.

☐ *First and second liens.* The mortgage or deed of trust securing the construction loan must be a first lien (or in the case of a leasehold mortgage, subject only to the ground rental). Normally, secondary financing is forbidden as this may overextend the developer and increase the risk of a default.

☐ *Recordation.* Normally, all of the key documents should be recorded.

☐ *No assignment.* The lender will not want the borrower to assign the commitment without the lender's consent, since the borrower's reputation and credit standing are key factors in the decision to make the loan.

☐ *Evidence of title.* The state of the property's title must be satisfactory to the borrower and, in most cases, title insurance must be provided.

☐ *Plans and specifications.* Improvements must be constructed substantially in accordance with the plans and specifications that the lender has relied upon in making the commitment.

☐ *Compliance with zoning requirements.* The improvements must conform to existing zoning and building code requirements (and the issuance of a building permit will not be conclusive evidence of such conformity).

☐ *Assignment of leases.* The lender must make collateral assignments of leases as they are entered into.

☐ *Permanent mortgage commitment.* The developer must remain in compliance with the conditions set forth in the permanent mortgage commitment, which normally has been issued prior to the construction loan commitment. (See 6.04[2][c].)

☐ *Insurance.* The developer must comply with specified insurance requirements.

☐ *Loan holdback.* The final portion of the construction loan (10 to 15 percent) will not be disbursed until final completion, which may be evidenced by an architect's certificate or a permanent certificate of occupancy.

☐ *Progress payments.* These are conditions to be met before each construction loan disbursement is made.

☐ *Payments to general contractor.* Construction loan disbursements may be made either to the general contractor when he presents waivers of liens by the subcontractors, or directly to the subcontractors.

☐ *Interest computation.* It should be clear whether interest is to be charged only on amounts disbursed or by some other manner of reckoning.

☐ *Usury ceiling.* Where the interest rate will exceed the state's usury ceiling applicable to loans to individuals, a corporation may execute the note and mortgage and then assign the funds to the individual owner. In a state where the usury ceiling applies even to corporations if the corporation is merely a facade and the ultimate borrower is an individual, the borrower may be required to covenant in the commitment that the corporation is the legal and equitable owner of the property and has no present intention to convey title to an individual. This could substantially reduce the viability of the project because of the loss of soft money.

☐ *Acceptance of commitment.* The borrower normally must accept the commitment within a fixed period, so that the lender may minimize tying up its funds.

[c] Take-Out Commitment

Since construction loans are short-term loans, the source of repayment (upon completion of the building) must always be the permanent financing. Three approaches for dealing with repayment are:

☐ *Open-end commitments.* The construction loan is given without any assurance that permanent financing will be available when the building is finished. In tight-money periods, builders prefer this as it gives them the opportunity to benefit from lower interest rates in the future. However, only the financially strongest builders can hope for open-end commitments.

☐ *Commitment with guarantee.* A lender may waive a firm take-out commitment if the builder can offer a guarantee of repayment of the construction loan, and back it with his own collateral or that of friends and associates. This, too, normally is unavailable except for top-rated builders.

☐ *Permanent take-out commitment.* By far the most common procedure is for the construction lender, before committing himself to the construction loan, to require a written commitment by a recognized lender (a "bankable" commitment) that upon completion of the building, a permanent mortgage loan will be made.

[i] Checklist for the Permanent Loan Takeout. The value of the take-out commitment to the construction lender varies directly with the number of conditions to which the takeout is subject. These conditions fall into two categories:

(1) those that can be satisfied when the construction loan is closed (or that, at least, are subject to the control of the construction lender); and (2) those wholly beyond the control of the construction lender.

Obviously, the latter are the ones that must be carefully scrutinized and that require either the amendment of the permanent commitment, or the assumption by the construction lender of a calculated business risk.

Examples of conditions that require careful review include the following:

☐ *Appraisal of the building on completion.* If the permanent lender conditions his loan on a certification upon completion of no material adverse change in the original appraisal, the construction loan is put at risk. The construction lender should seek an amendment that the improvements were completed substantially in accordance with the original plans and specifications.

☐ *Certification of completion by third party.* Even when the condition merely is that the building is completed in accordance with the plans and specifications, the permanent lender may want a person other than the original architects or engineers (who presumably have been approved by the construction lender) to do the certifying. This, too, puts the matter beyond the construction lender's control.

☐ *Property undamaged at closing.* This condition invites controversy when the permanent lender does not want to go through with the loan. A possible compromise would be to permit the permanent lender to back out only if the damage exceeds a certain figure and is not restored within a fixed period.

☐ *Estoppel certificate from tenants.* Normally, the leases require the tenants to deliver such certificates, but the construction lender should seek to qualify this requirement if possible.

☐ *Satisfactory title or other state of facts.* Any subjective standard is objectionable to the construction lender who wants, above all, a clear-cut obligation to buy his loan. Objective standards always should be sought.

☐ *Approval of all major leases.* Usually the construction lender will want to approve (and have the permanent lender approve) major leases before the first construction advance. Where this is not possible, lease standards should be agreed upon by the two lenders.

[ii] Special Take-Out Techniques. Take-out techniques include 100 percent financing with umbrella takeout and a construction loan with built-in takeout.

☐ *100 percent financing with umbrella takeout.* The umbrella takeout offers an institutional lender an opportunity to come in early on a new development and provide 100 percent financing for the builder. It involves a three-step financing pattern. First, the lender buys the land and leases it back under a long-term ground lease. Then it provides the developer with construction financing, which will be converted into an intermediate-term leasehold mortgage when the property is completed. Finally, the developer gets a permanent takeout from the lender on terms somewhat above the current market but not as onerous as in a standby commitment. The developer in this way achieves virtually 100 percent financing.

In return for coming in at the earliest stage of development and providing all the financing, the lender may look for benefits such as

- A minimum ground rental.
- A ground rent "kicker" based on a percentage of the increase in gross rental income over the initial projections.
- A share of the benefits that will accrue when the leasehold mortgage is refinanced with a third party. The refinancing normally will occur when the project is completed and has a demonstrated cash flow, and probably will be on better terms than the initial mortgage.

☐ *Construction loan with built-in takeout.* Another variation is the combination construction-permanent loan. Here, the borrower at the very outset pays a front-end fee of 3 to 4 percent of the construction loan. After two years, he has a right to convert the construction loan into a permanent loan of up to ten years, with all of the project's cash flow to be devoted to debt service. An unusual feature is a step-up prepayment penalty (instead of the customary step-down). Thus, the construction loan is prepayable without penalty during the first two years. When it becomes a permanent loan, the penalty starts off at 4 percent and increases at one percent a year to a maximum of 10 percent. The reason for the step-up penalty is that the lender prefers a short-term rather than a long-term position and so wants to be reimbursed for postponing maturity.

[iii] Protecting the Permanent Lender. The take-out commitment is likely to set the interest rate for the loan around current levels. Suppose the interest rate drops several points during the construction period? The developer will obviously prefer to find another permanent lender who will provide funds at the lower rate. The construction lender, of course, does not care where the take-out funds come from, which means that the original permanent lender will be the one at a disadvantage if rates drop. Therefore, the permanent lender must protect himself against the borrower breaking the loan commitment. There are three approaches that the permanent lender can take in order to protect himself:

- Legal action against the borrower
- Nonrefundable deposits by borrower
- Buy-sell agreements

☐ *Legal action against borrower.* The two possible legal remedies for a lender suing a borrower for breaking a loan commitment are (1) specific performance; and (2) money damages. Specific performance means the court will order the borrower to perform the contract with the lender (i.e., enter into the permanent loan). This remedy is available only when money damages are considered to be inadequate. However, since a lender's damage would be measurable in money terms, specific performance would not be granted.

While in theory, at least, a permanent lender could sue a borrower for damages for a broken commitment, there seem to be no actual instances of such lawsuits. The main reason seems to be the reluctance of lenders to start litigation as a matter of public relations and reputation; another reason is the difficulty that might exist in determining what actual loss the lender suffers, although the loss would seem to be the difference between the interest the lender would receive on a new loan and the interest it would have been entitled to on the broken commitment. (But a borrower can enforce a commitment against the lender.)

☐ *Nonrefundable deposits by borrower.* A second approach used by permanent lenders is to require the developer to pay an advance commitment fee of perhaps 2 or 3 percent of the loan amount, which sum is forfeited if the borrower fails to go through with the loan. These deposits have been fully supported by the law over the years as appropriate compensation to the lender for breach commitments.

However, these fees are not likely to be substantial enough to deter borrowers from seeking loans elsewhere if interest rates are dropping rapidly. And to the lender, the forfeited fees usually do not make up for the loss of the loan.

☐ *Using buy-sell agreements.* The third approach, used more frequently in recent years, is the buy-sell agreement among developer, construction lender, and permanent lender. In essence, a buy-sell agreement obligates the construction lender as well as the borrower to go through with the permanent loan commitment once the building is completed. The typical buy-sell agreement provides that the

- Construction lender will not accept any payment by the borrower that does not come from funds provided by the permanent lender.
- Permanent lender will be given notice of any defaults under the construction loan, which faults the latter may cure if it wishes.
- Permanent lender has the right to purchase the loan despite any existing defaults by the borrower.
- Construction lender will be informed of any defaults by the borrower under the permanent loan commitment, so that the construction lender can cure the default if it wishes.

Even with a buy-sell agreement, the permanent lender cannot be assured that the borrower and construction lender may not make a separate arrangement. A practical solution that makes the buy-sell agreement self-enforcing is the use of convertible or combination documentation.

In this approach, both the construction and permanent mortgages and related instruments are incorporated into one set of loan documents. At the time of the permanent-loan closing, the construction lender merely assigns the loan documents to the permanent lender and no new documents need be executed by the borrower. Of course, this requires careful coordination by the two lenders at the time the original loan commitment is made, but it does provide the greatest protection for the permanent lender.

[iv] Purchase Commitments. There is a growing trend toward the use of a take-out purchase commitment as security for the construction lender. In this approach, a purchaser replaces the lender in the role of assuring the construction lender that upon completion, funds will be forthcoming to pay off the construction loan. The major impetus for this new trend is the declining cash-flow return on prime properties; as a result, institutions and other investors are willing to commit to purchase prior to completion in order to obtain a slightly higher return. The builder, on his part, is often happy to go along because the purchase commitment, being for the entire cost of the project (plus the builder's profit), will often support a higher construction loan and consequently reduce the builder's front-end equity requirement.

Most of the provisions in a purchase takeout will be the same as those in a loan takeout, since the rationale and function of the two commitments are essentially the same. But there are some subtle differences. The following areas merit special attention when a purchase, rather than a loan, commitment is being used:

☐ *Variations in construction.* Even though a take-out lender normally has the right to approve any changes in the plans and specifications for the building, the lender often is quite lax in enforcing this right. Since debt service on the permanent loan normally will run comfortably below projected operating income, small changes in construction that may affect cash flow are not significant. But the purchaser is in a different position. Any marginal changes in income come directly out of his pocket. Therefore, he is sure to exercise his right to approve changes throughout the construction period.

☐ *Rental achievement clause.* Commonly, the permanent lender will fund only a percentage (e.g., 80 percent) of the total loan upon completion, with the balance due when specified occupancy levels have been achieved. A similar achievement clause may be incorporated into a purchase contract as protection for the buyer. The gap between floor and ceiling price might equal the builder's profit or it might be somewhat higher. In a loan situation, if the higher occupancy level is never achieved, the builder simply pays debt service on the outstanding loan. But in a purchase contract, the parties must determine if the balance of the purchase price is to be waived entirely, reduced in amount, or paid on a deferred basis.

☐ *Buy-sell agreement.* In a loan situation, the permanent lender often insists that he, the construction lender, and the builder enter into a three-party buy-sell agreement. The purpose is that the builder (in the event long-term interest rates fall during the construction period) cannot switch to another permanent lender. The construction lender is a party because he is in a position to assign the construction loan to the permanent lender when the building is completed. Obviously, this relationship does not exist in the case of a purchase, since the construction lender cannot assign to the purchaser the title documents covering the property. However, the take-out purchaser is in a position to protect himself by imposing a firm obligation on the builder to sell upon completion (an obligation that presumably can be enforced by the remedy of specific performance).

☐ *Substituted builder.* A related problem involves the possibility that the original builder may run into trouble and be replaced by another. The take-out lender normally is not unduly concerned with this situation since its security will be the completed building. A long-term purchaser, however, may be relying upon the expertise and reputation of a particular developer and may be unwilling to consummate the purchase if another is substituted. In this case, the construction lender's takeout may be subject to a condition (i.e., that the original developer will complete the project) that may not be acceptable to him. This must then be worked out in negotiations.

[d] Standby Commitment

The standby loan is really a commitment to make a loan in the future in the event that the borrower cannot arrange financing from other sources. For example, a builder completes his acquisition of a site for a high-rise apartment building just at the time when mortgage rates seem to be peaking out. If he delays construction, the carrying charges on the land may cause him to exceed his budget by a substantial amount. On the other hand, he cannot arrange construction financing unless he has a commitment by a lender to issue a permanent first mortgage at the completion of the building. Such a permanent commitment will, of course, be made at the current high interest rates. Even when the commitment is not legally binding on the builder, he will not want to risk damaging his reputation by reneging on the commitment if interest rates turn down at the time the building is ready for occupancy. His alternative is to use the standby commitment, in which it is understood that the builder reserves the right to go elsewhere if he can.

Standby loans are usually made by noninstitutional lenders. It is important for the borrower to deal with a lender whose commitment will be "bankable," that is to say, the reputation of the lender must be such that a construction loan will be forthcoming on the strength of it.

Basically there are three types of standbys:

☐ *The first-mortgage standby,* written to take out a construction lender upon completion of a project.

☐ *A (second-mortgage) floor-to-ceiling gap standby,* covering the amount of money between the floor guarantee in a take-out loan and the loan to be advanced upon attainment of a specified rent roll. A floor-to-ceiling loan commits the lender to make a fixed minimum loan upon the completion of the building, with additional increments of the loan to be made as and when certain levels of occupancy are reached. Thus, the minimum loan (or "floor") might be 50 percent of the maximum loan, with an additional 10 percent to be available when 60 percent of the building is rented and an additional 10 percent for each additional occupancy of 10 percent, up to the maximum loan at 100 percent occupancy. Normally, the additional loan increments are available only for a fixed period of time after completion—e.g., one year. The purpose of the standby commitment in connection with a floor-to-ceiling loan is to assure the builder (and the construction lender) that sufficient funds will be available to repay the construction loan even if only the minimum amount of the permanent loan is forthcoming.

☐ *Standbys issued to take out commercial banks* that are financing land to be developed, or to take out a lender that has made a second mortgage to a valued account.

[i] Reasons for Using Standby Commitment. There are three basic circumstances under which a borrower who is developing real property will use a standby commitment:

- Interest rates are high and the borrower believes rates will be lower when the project is completed, at which time permanent financing will be cheaper.
- Interest rates are declining; the borrower wants protection against rates

shooting up again and also wants to retain the option of getting permanent financing at lower rates if the declining trend continues.

- The developer believes that the real estate market is strengthening, that his project will be an immediate success, and that on the strength of his initial operating statements he will be able to obtain better permanent financing after the building is up than prior to the completion of construction.

Many experts take the position that under the first two circumstances, the reasons given for using a standby commitment are essentially speculations and do not justify the cost of a standby commitment. The third reason may justify a standby if the underlying expectations of improvement appear to be well grounded.

[ii] Cost of Standby Commitments and Loans. Standbys usually run for eighteen to twenty-four months. In exchange, the lender receives an immediate fee in the range of 2 to 3 percent per year. Frequently, the builder has the right to extend the loan for six months or a year, with an additional fee of 1.5 percent for each six-month extension.

If the lender is asked to fund his commitment, the terms are usually steep. Loan-to-value ratio generally equals 75 percent of appraised value and the lender generally will ask for most or all of the following:

- Initial bonus payment of two to five points
- Interest rate 2 to 3 percent over prime
- Term of up to ten years, frequently with amortization based on a fifteen-year or longer payout (i.e., a balloon loan)
- Participation in gross rental
- Personal guarantees

The major advantage for the lender is that he can earn substantial fees without advancing any funds. He may also have the opportunity to buy a share in the property, when the long-term financing is obtained from other sources, or to make either long- or short-term first mortgages after the completion of the project.

The lender will look for sound basic qualities in the deal and evaluate the developer's track record, integrity, financial strength, and backing. The intention of both the developer and the standby lender is that the commitment will never be funded. However, if the opposite turns out to be the case, the standby lender must have the resources available to back up his financial commitment and the authority to do so under applicable laws.

[iii] Sophisticated Standby Financing Techniques. Standby financing can be used in a variety of ways. Here are two actual examples (the interest rates do not necessarily reflect current market rates):

☐ *The instant wraparound standby commitment.* A 357-unit high-rise apartment is under construction by a partnership seeking tax shelter. The project is 30 percent complete, financed so far on the builder's own line of credit, and the total estimated cost is $9.5 million. Since the partnership may want to convert to a condominium in five or so years, it does not wish to be tied down to a permanent loan commitment.

The builder sought a standby from XYZ Insurance Co. as a takeout for a construction loan. Capitalizing the net rental income at 9.5 percent, XYZ valued the completed structure at $9 million and granted an eighteen-month standby commitment for an $8.5 million, ten-year loan. The loan would be payable interest only (10.5 percent) for the first thirty months, then interest only (11⅛ percent) for the next eighteen months, and then the same interest, plus amortization on a thirty-year schedule for the balance of the term. The loan, if funded, would be prepayable at a one percent premium after one year. The standby fee was 1.75 percent.

Since XYZ would not want to make the entire loan if the commitment was funded, it obtained a commitment from a savings bank to take down a senior participation of $6.75 million at 9.5 percent interest, rising to 10.5 percent interest, plus amortization after thirty months. Thus, the loan would be a wraparound, with XYZ holding the junior position. XYZ would service the loan.

Both XYZ and the bank would be satisfied if the standby was funded. XYZ would

- Have received a standby fee.
- Receive a servicing fee during the mortgage term.
- Have leveraged its 11⅛ percent interest rate as a result of the wraparound (e.g., it puts up $1 million on which it receives 11⅛ percent; in addition, it keeps the spread between the 11⅛ percent paid by the borrower and 9.5 percent received by the savings bank on the $6.75 million balance of the loan).

The savings bank, in turn, has diversified out of its usual lending area, has a senior position and a good return on a sound loan, and will have an inside track on the permanent financing at a later date.

☐ *The deferred interest standby.* Another example involves an office building on which XYZ Co. granted a $2.4 million standby at a fee of 1.5 percent per year. If funded, the loan would be at prime, plus 4 percent. The standby features an unusual deferred interest provision. If prime plus 4 percent is more than 11.5 percent, interest charges in excess of 11.5 percent may be deferred until the prime declines below 7.5 percent (thus bringing the interest rate below 11.5 percent). At that point, the deferred interest is paid off by continuing the 11.5 percent rate.

If the deferred interest is not fully repaid at maturity, it is due at that time, constituting a floating balloon payment.

[3] Mortgage or Deed of Trust

A loan made to finance the acquisition or construction of real estate is almost always secured by the real estate itself. (Sometimes, the loan is also secured by other collateral; see 6.04[4].) A real estate-secured loan is called either a mortgage or a deed of trust (trust deed), depending on the particular state in which the transaction occurs. The mortgage form is used most frequently in the eastern United States, while the deed of trust is more common in the western states. (Some states permit both to be used, although as a matter of practice, one form usually is predominant.) The function of both the mortgage and the deed of trust is exactly the same—to provide real estate as security for a loan. However, the way in which each carries out the function is somewhat different. The important differences between the two types of instruments are: (1) the parties to the instrument and (2) the foreclosure procedure upon a loan default. These distinctions will be made in the section describing the specific provisions of the mortgage agreement. In the discussion that follows, the term "mortgage" includes "deed of trust" unless otherwise indicated.

A mortgage is a legal instrument setting forth the various obligations of the lender and the borrower, both with respect to the loan and with respect to the real estate, which acts as security. Since real estate law is a matter of state rather than federal concern, the rules concerning the execution of a mortgage and the consequences of a default may differ considerably from place to place. There has been some standardization of mortgage documents as a result of the development of secondary-mortgage-market programs that involve the purchase and sale of mortgages on a national basis. The most significant development in this area has been the standard mortgage documents developed by the Federal Home Loan Mortgage Corporation in conjunction with the Federal National Mortgage Association. Even in these documents, provision is made for variations required by differing state laws.

When a mortgage has been executed its holder has a security interest in the real estate; that is, he has no right to possess or use the real estate by virtue of the mortgage; the mortgage merely creates a lien (claim) on the real estate to secure the repayment of a debt. Immediately after the mortgage has been executed and delivered to the lender, he should have it recorded in the local land-records office. By doing this, the lender gives notice to the world of his lien on the real estate and so retains priority over subsequent purchasers or claimants. It is not until the debt has been repaid that the lien is cancelled or discharged.

The following items describe the major provisions of the mortgage agreement, explaining differences between the mortgage and deed of trust where appropriate.

☐ *Parties.* The mortgage is a two-party instrument between the borrower (mortgagor) and the lender (mortgagee). When a deed of trust is used, three parties are involved: the borrower (trustor); a third party, usually a trust company (trustee); and the lender (beneficiary). In effect, title to the trust deed is split into legal title and equitable title. Whereas under a mortgage, the mortgagee holds both kinds of title, in a deed of trust, the legal title is held by a trustee who acts on behalf of the lender who owns the equitable title. The trustee will transfer the security instrument back to the borrower when the debt has been repaid or, alternatively, will act to protect the lender in the event of a default under the terms of the trust deed. It is in this latter connection that the deed of trust differs significantly from the mortgage.

☐ *Loan amount and repayment.* This provision sets forth the amount of the loan and the manner in which it will be repaid.

☐ *Interest.* The rate of interest and the manner in which interest is to be paid are recorded in this provision.

☐ *Description of property.* The real property that is to secure the loan must be precisely described; the same description normally is used as in a contract of sale. Sometimes, several properties will secure the loan, the instrument then being known as a blanket mortgage. If the mortgagor's interest in the real estate is other than that of a fee simple, the exact nature of the interest should be spelled out. The most common type of interest that can be mortgaged, apart from a fee simple, is a leasehold, and the mortgage is then known as a leasehold mortgage. (See 6.11.)

☐ *Priority of mortgage.* It is possible for an owner to execute several mortgages on the same piece of property, each securing a debt to a different lender. So long as the owner makes all loan payments when due, no questions of priority will arise. But if the owner defaults under one or more of the loans and a foreclosure action is brought, the problem of distributing the cash proceeds from the foreclosure sale must be solved. The rule is that proceeds of a foreclosure sale are used to discharge mortgages in order of their priority or seniority. In the absence of any agreement among the lenders themselves, the priority of the mortgages is determined by the date of execution and recordation. The mortgage first executed and recorded is the first or senior mortgage; all others are junior loans, being designated as the second mortgage, third mortgage, and so on. Exceptions to this order of priority will occur when

- Two or more lenders agree that their mortgages will have equal priority; or
- One lender voluntarily yields a senior position for one more junior (called subordinating the loan).

Of these two approaches, subordination is much more common than the co-equal approach. Subordination typically occurs when a developer buys raw land and the seller takes back a purchase-money mortgage. The developer, knowing that construction financing can be obtained only in the form of a first mortgage, will want a provision in the purchase-money mortgage that it will become subordinate to a construction loan when the latter is obtained. The seller usually agrees to this, that is, to convert his first mortgage into a second mortgage, since otherwise construction financing will be unavailable and the buyer will not purchase the land in the first place.

☐ *Release provision.* This provides that, upon payment of a specific sum to the mortgagee, the lien of the mortgage shall be removed from a specifically described portion of the mortgaged premises. This clause is most commonly used when the mortgagor, a developer planning to construct one-family homes, obtains a construction loan on the entire tract. As individual homes are sold, they must be freed from the lien of the construction loan so that the purchaser can arrange permanent financing (which will only be extended in the form of a first mortgage). (See 6.06[3].)

☐ *Prepayment.* Mortgage loan prepayment provisions are always important to the borrower. A borrower who can refinance his loan at the right time can substantially increase his cash flow or even his yield. He may, for example, be able to increase the amount of his financing, reduce his debt service, or decrease the amount of the interest rate. Where the mortgage calls for a variable interest rate, the importance of the prepayment provision is increased.

A mortgage loan is a contract between borrower and lender. The rights of the parties are determined by the written terms of the agreement, subject, of course, to judicial and legislative rules. In the absence of a prepayment provision in the loan agreement, the borrower has no right to prepay the loan. The borrower cannot force a prepayment under the guise of a default.

While the borrower will always want a right to prepay, the lending institution prefers to withhold the prepayment option, since the borrower normally will exercise the option only under circumstances unfavorable to the lender. The issue resolves itself to how much the borrower is willing to pay for the option of relieving himself of a loan obligation at a time of his choice.

Five major considerations enter into a prepayment clause. Each party should determine in advance the order of priority of these considerations.

☐ *Initial no-prepayment period.* Frequently, the lender insists that the loan remain on its books for a minimum period of time during which no prepayment will be allowed either with or without a penalty. This permits the lender to recoup at least a portion of its overhead in making the loan. It also discourages shopping around by borrowers for better terms.

Sometimes lenders permit prepayment at any time, if the prepayment is made in connection with a resale of the property or a demolition of existing improvements. On the other hand, to prevent raids on their portfolios, many lenders frequently insist on a longer waiting period if the purpose of the prepayment is to refinance with another institution.

☐ *Prepayment penalty or premium.* The charge imposed by the lender for the privilege of prepayment is not treated as an interest charge and so is beyond the reach of virtually all state usury statutes. The reason is that the charge is payable only in connection with the borrower's exercise of an option given him by the lender.

In theory, a prepayment premium may vary depending on the purpose of the prepayment, but this arrangement is less common than differing waiting periods as noted above.

Penalties may be stepped up or stepped down. The latter is more common. For example, a prepayment clause may provide that no prepayment is permitted for the initial three years of the loan, and that the penalty for prepayment in the fourth year is to be 5 percent and is to decline by .5 percent a year thereafter until it reaches one percent, at which point no further decline occurs. Obviously, the theory behind the step-down is that the longer the loan is outstanding the greater is the amount of the lender's front-end expense that is recouped by normal interest payments.

Many lenders are willing to waive any prepayment penalty if the borrower takes out a new mortgage with the same lender. It is rare, however, for this to be included in the written agreement; the waiver remains within the lender's discretion.

☐ *Dates when prepayment may be made.* It contributes to the smooth operation of the lender's loan department to have prepayments made only on specified dates, but the borrower may find this requirement creates problems for him. If the borrower is selling or refinancing the property, the loan normally must be repaid on the date of loan or title closing, no earlier and no later. On the one hand, the property must be free of liens on the closing date. On the other hand, the borrower does not have the funds to repay the loan before that date. An alternative to payments only on installment dates is to arrange for a minimum period of notice before any prepayment.

☐ *Notice of prepayment.* When notice of prepayment is required, the loan instrument should make clear what the notice should contain and the manner in which notice should be given.

If the borrower is bound by his notice, his failure to prepay would constitute a default under the mortgage, giving rise to remedies set forth in the instrument.

☐ *Partial prepayments.* Partial prepayments of the mortgage debt give rise to special considerations because the mortgage relation will continue. The borrower may wish to reduce the debt for investment reasons. The reduction in interest payments may represent a better return to the borrower than is available to him by investing his excess funds elsewhere, or he may wish to reduce his monthly payments. The lender frequently is willing to accept small prepayments, notwithstanding the loss of some interest income, as a matter of good public relations and because the loan risk is reduced as the loan-to-value ratio declines.

The first four considerations discussed earlier are as applicable to partial as to full prepayments. Normally, residential mortgagees permit partial prepayments (e.g., 20 percent of the original loan principal) to be made without penalty at any time during the mortgage term.

☐ *Acceleration provisions.* An acceleration clause is one that provides, in the event of a breach of the loan agreement by the borrower, for the advancement of the date on which the entire balance of the mortgage loan is due. In other words, the mortgagee is given the option to notify the mortgagor that the entire balance of the loan with interest is immediately due and payable. If payment is not forthcoming, the mortgagee may proceed to its remedies under the mortgage. A mortgagee will include in the acceleration clause acts or conduct by the mortgagor that are not traditionally defaults but that the lender does not wish to occur. Two typical examples are sale of the mortgaged property to a third party (the due-on-sale clause) and creation of any additional liens against the mortgaged property by the borrower, e.g., a second mortgage (the due-on-encumbrance clause). A variety of other acts or conduct by the mortgagor may trigger an acceleration clause.

☐ *Due-on-sale acceleration clause.* The lender's argument in favor of a clause accelerating the mortgage debt in the event of a sale by the borrower is that the lender made the loan in part on the credit and reputation of the borrower and so should have the option to review its position in the event of a sale. The borrower's answer is twofold: (1) if the mortgage contains an exculpatory clause, or if the borrower has not signed a note and is not personally liable for the debt, the credit standing of a new mortgagor is irrelevant; and (2) even where the mortgagor is personally liable for the debt, the lender should be permitted to call the loan only when there is reason to believe an increase in risk has occurred because of a sale or transfer of the property.

The following are possible compromise clauses that can be used singly or in combination to resolve the conflict:

- *Require transferee to meet standards.* To protect the lender's legitimate interest in having a creditworthy borrower, the mortgage may provide that the lender may accelerate the loan only when the new owner of the property is not reasonably satisfactory to the lender or fails to meet its normal credit standards.

- *Original borrower to remain liable.* The lender may be willing to permit a transfer of the property on condition that the original borrower remain liable for the loan. Since transfers of real property often are made subject to the mortgage, the borrower may have no objection to this provision.

If the borrower initially is not personally liable for the mortgage debt, chances are that he will not be willing to assume personal liability when he transfers the property. However, he may be willing to do so in order to consummate a favorable sale, or if the amortization of the mortgage obligation or the appreciation in the value of the property has proceeded to a point at which he feels amply protected.

- *Recast mortgage.* In lieu of an option to accelerate the entire loan, the lender may be willing to recast the loan to provide for a shorter term or an increased debt service, either with or without any interest rate increase. In addition, a partial one-time amortization payment might be required to reduce the outstanding loan amount. By these means, the security of the loan can be increased.

- *Permitted transfers.* Either alone or in conjunction with any of the foregoing, an acceleration clause should permit certain transfers without the lender having the option to call the loan or change any of its terms. The following should normally be exempt: (1) transfers to another entity controlled by the borrower; and (2) transfers resulting from his death, from operation of law, or from a merger or acquisition (if certain financial standards are met).

☐ *Due-on-encumbrance clause.* The considerations affecting the second main type of acceleration clause—that permitting the lender to accelerate the entire loan if any lien (e.g., a second mortgage) is placed against the property—are somewhat different from those affecting the due-on-sale clause. The lender's position is that any additional financing weakens his security because the additional debt service reduces the cushion, that is, the income from the property above the debt service on the first mortgage. (In the case of a residential mortgage, the additional financing lessens the credit status of the borrower.) In addition, to the extent that the owner is able to reduce his equity investment to a very low figure by the use of secondary financing (so-called milking), his incentive to maintain the property is reduced. The borrower, while recognizing the validity of this argument, may seek to limit the due-on-encumbrance clause in the following ways:

☐ *Acceleration only on threat of foreclosure.* Borrowers may seek to change the wording of the due-on-encumbrance clause to provide that the loan may be accelerated only when the creation of the encumbrance, or subsequent events (e.g., a default under the second mortgage), would unreasonably impair the security of the first lender.

- *Permitted encumbrances.* The borrower may seek to except from the due-on-encumbrance clause secondary loans meeting specified requirements. For example:

  (1) Any secondary loan which, together with the first loan, does not exceed a fixed loan-to-value ratio, such as 80 percent of the then market value of the property (thus assuring the original mortgagee that a sufficient equity cushion remains to protect the first lender's security);

  (2) Any secondary loan made by an institutional lender, or by a lender approved by the original mortgagee, which approval shall not be withheld unreasonably.

☐ *Real estate taxes and insurance premiums.* The mortgagor agrees to pay real estate taxes promptly and also to insure the property against fire and other risks and to pay the premiums on such insurance when they come due. It is customary in the case of home mortgages, and frequent in the case of many income mortgages, for the borrower to be required to pay to the lender each month approximately one-twelfth of the annual amount necessary to pay real estate taxes and insurance premiums. Then, the lender makes the payments directly to the taxing authority or insurance company when bills are rendered. Such payments are known as escrow payments. In recent years, many savings institutions have begun to pay interest on such escrow deposits as a result of pressure by consumer groups which, in some states, has resulted in legislation compelling the payment of interest.

☐ *Condition of property.* The borrower is obligated to maintain the property in good repair, not to demolish any improvements without the permission of the lender, and in general, not to permit the occurrence of waste, that is, acts or omissions by the owner of real estate that injures it to the detriment of the mortgage lender that relies on the property as security.

☐ *Default.* A default under a mortgage occurs whenever the mortgagor fails to live up to a promise or discharge an obligation specified in the mortgage or in the promissory note. The mortgage instrument normally specifies a number of events of default, the most important of which include failure to pay interest and principal when due; failure to pay real estate taxes and insurance premiums; and failure to keep the property in good repair. In virtually all cases, the mortgagor is given a period of time within which to cure the default (e.g., ten days in the case of a failure to pay interest and principal when due).

In the event a default occurs and is not cured by the mortgagor within the permissible period, the mortgagee normally has the right to accelerate the payment of the entire loan principal (see above) and upon failure of the mortgagor to pay the amount due, the mortgagee may proceed to its other remedies, including foreclosure of the property.

☐ *Foreclosure.* Foreclosure is the legal process by which a mortgagee may have property sold at a public sale in order to raise cash to pay off a debt due the mortgagee. Two types of foreclosure are common in the United States. Foreclosure by action and sale is associated with the mortgage, while a foreclosure by power of sale is associated with the deed of trust. It is in connection with foreclosure that the two types of instruments most significantly differ.

In a foreclosure by action and sale, the mortgagee must commence a court action seeking a decree of foreclosure and an order for a sale of the real estate upon notice to the mortgagor and to the public. Assuming that the court finds that a default has indeed occurred it will issue an execution (an order to the local sheriff or other appropriate official to take possession of the property and sell it at public sale). At the foreclosure sale, the property is sold to the highest bidder. The proceeds of the sale are applied first to the payment of the unpaid mortgage debt plus unpaid interest and court costs, and second to the mortgagor (or any junior creditors). In many states, the mortgagor has an equity of redemption, which gives the mortgagor a specified period of time following the foreclosure action to pay off the debt plus unpaid interest and recover the property. If such an equity of redemption exists, the property cannot be sold until the equity period expires.

The other method of foreclosure is foreclosure by power of sale. When the security instrument is a deed of trust, it may provide that upon a default by the mortgagor, the trustee may sell the property covered by the deed of trust without the need of commencing a legal action and obtaining a court order. However, the sale carried out by the trustee will be valid only if adequate notice has been given to the mortgagor and to the public generally so that there is a reasonable opportunity for the trustee to realize the true market value of the property.

[4] Personal Liability and Other Security

Very often a mortgage lender is unwilling to rely solely on the real estate as security for its loan. In certain transactions it is customary for the lender to insist that the borrower assume personal liability or that personal property (by a chattel mortgage) serve as additional security.

Two typical cases are the following:

- An apartment or motel loan, where a lien on all furnishings, furniture, and fixtures used in the operation of the property is vital
- A construction loan, where the personal liability of the builder is a universal requirement

In other instances the speculative nature of the loan may be such that additional security becomes highly desirable, if not necessary. The speculative element may arise for any number of reasons including the

- "Pioneering" aspect of the improvements, as in the case of the first suburban office park in a particular area.
- Intention of the developer to charge rents at a higher rate than have been proved in the marketplace.
- Inexperience or financial weakness of the mortgagor with respect to the size and type of the project for which he is seeking the loan.

[a] Borrower's Personal Liability

Mortgage loans are frequently made without any liability on the part of the mortgagor for repayment of the indebtedness (nonrecourse financing). For the protection of its investment, the mortgagee under these circumstances can look only to the real property and the rents and other income that it produces.

As a practical matter, in many jurisdictions the personal obligation of the mortgagor to repay the debt may be of little value. In some states the mortgagee often finds that he has a dilemma when there is a default. If he seeks first to sue the mortgagor on the personal covenant to pay the debt that is continued in the note, he may, under the theory of election of remedies, lose any right to reach the real estate subsequently through foreclosure. On the other hand, the mortgagee who forecloses first and then endeavors to enforce a deficiency judgment against the debtor may encounter other problems. In a number of states the amount of the deficiency judgment is not fixed by the difference between the highest bid at foreclosure and the outstanding indebtedness, but rather by the difference between the value of the security, as determined by an independent appraiser, and the amount of the unpaid debt. Experience has shown that the appraiser will rarely find that the value of the security is less than the unpaid debt.

Another difficulty exists in many states in which the security instrument is a deed of trust instead of a mortgage. A foreclosure by trustee's sale may preclude any deficiency judgment. The undesirable alternative is the longer and more expensive route of a judicial foreclosure which, as an additional detriment, may give the debtor a considerable period during which he may redeem the foreclosed property.

Personal liability may be limited in time. For example, a lender may require personal liability until the real estate has achieved a stated rental level or until the loan balance has been reduced to a stated amount. If there is more than one mortgagor, liability may be joint and several (with each mortgagor individually liable for the total debt) or merely joint (with each mortgagor liable only for a fixed percentage of the debt).

[b] Third-Party Guarantees

A guarantee of the mortgagor's indebtedness by a third party is a viable alternative or addition to the personal liability of the mortgagor. It is not subject to most of the problems previously mentioned, which dilute the value of the mortgagor's own liability. It is most commonly obtained with respect to a loan made to a corporation where the lender requires

- A guarantee of corporate debt by one or more of the corporation's stockholders; or
- A guarantee of the debt of a wholly owned subsidiary corporation by its parent.

A guarantee by a corporation of the indebtedness of a third party is enforceable only if it serves some sound business purpose of the corporation. Thus, the corporate guarantee of the obligation of a stockholder is invalid.

Lenders require that any guarantee of a mortgage debt be absolute and unconditional. Therefore, the guarantee should not be subject to any right of offset and should not be affected by any failure to give notice of default or by any waiver or indulgence granted by the lender to the mortgagor.

An interesting problem arises when a loan is made to a subsidiary of a foreign corporation. Here, the lender must be sure that the guarantee is enforceable in the homeland of the parent corporation and will require an opinion from foreign counsel.

Convenience Lease. The convenience lease can be considered as a special type of third-party guarantee that is relatively new to mortgage financing. It is generally a long-term lease to a creditworthy tenant and is entered into without any intention that the tenant actually occupy the leased space; insead, the purpose is to assure the lender of an adequate income stream in the event of a mortgage default. A convenience lease may be subject to partial or total termination by the lessee before the end of the lease term upon certain conditions:

- When the loan balance is reduced to a stated amount
- When a stated leasing level of tenants in actual occupancy has been achieved
- Pro rata, as parts of the demised premises are leased to others for actual occupancy

A corporation's power to enter into a convenience lease as lessee is subject to the same disability as its power to guarantee. The question of whether a corporate convenience lease should properly be noted in the corporation's financial statements is beyond the scope of this text.

[c] Escrows for Completion

Many permanent mortgage loans on new construction are closed before the improvements have been fully completed. The unfinished work is usually not substantial, but the cost to complete may still represent a material sum of money, particularly in connection with a large project. The incomplete work may involve paving of parking lots or new streets, and the installation of swimming pools, tennis courts, and other recreational facilities in an apartment development, or finishing of unleased retail or office space in a shopping center or office building.

While the lender may be willing to advance the full amount of its loan prior to full completion, it will require assurance that funds will be available to pay the costs of completion. Escrows serve many purposes and have been readily adapted to furnish this assurance to the mortgagee.

The estimate of cost to complete should be made most carefully by the lender. A shortage in the funds escrowed for completion can result in a loan-to-value ratio that is less than was contemplated by the lender. The amounts per square foot required to complete retail, general office, or medical office space for tenant occupancy vary greatly. Because of the difficulties involved in estimating costs, the lender as a practical matter should, in any event, require full completion of 50 to 60 percent of all rentable space, irrespective of the amount escrowed.

The escrowed funds should be held by a third party in order that possible construction loan and usury problems be avoided. Where the amount of the escrow is substantial, the lender may agree to its investment in an interest-bearing account, certificates of deposit, or government obligations that are not likely to fluctuate materially in price. The escrow agreement should provide for the release of funds on a stated basis as work is completed. There should be a specific date for completion of all work. If all work is not completed by that date, all monies remaining in the escrow should be payable to the mortgagee to be applied in reduction of the debt. In the event of a mortgage default during the term of the escrow, all funds then in the escrow should also be immediately payable to the mortgagee and applied in reduction of the debt.

[d] Collateral Security

The term "collateral" is a broad one. It includes a lien on any property, either real or personal, the use of which is necessary or convenient to the continued operation or enjoyment of the primary security. For example, a lender may require as additional security a lien on the total energy plant that furnishes electricity to an apartment development.

Collateral security also extends to liens on additional property not related to the operation of the primary security. In this situation, the sole purpose of the additional lien is to provide further security for the lender. Such unrelated collateral can be given subject to release upon the achievement of a leasing level or reduction of the loan balance on the same basis as the release of personal liability, a guarantee, or a convenience lease. Generally the collateralization of a loan is derived through a second mortgage or a similar arrangement. In its simplest form the collateral security consists of a second mortgage on additional property. In a more complex form the collateralization may be based upon cross-defaults, or cross-collateralization. Both of these situations involve two or more mortgage loans with the same mortgagor.

In the case of cross-defaults, the documents evidencing and securing each loan provide that any default with respect to one loan shall also constitute a default on the other loan. In theory such provisions should be a strong inducement to a borrower to use the excess income from an economically viable property to carry the mortgage on a property that is in distress. As a practical matter, however, the mortgagor may be able to bid in the good property upon foreclosure and leave the lender holding the bag with the poorer security.

Under cross-collateralization, each loan is secured by a mortgage, which constitutes a first lien on one property and a second lien on the other property. Such arrangement overcomes the deficiency inherent in the cross-default. Since each loan is secured by a blanket mortgage, the borrower's equity in both properties is at risk in the event of a default on either loan.

Collateral security can take many other forms. A lien on personal property is desirable whenever such property is significant in the operation of the real estate. In connection with a motel or hotel loan, an assignment of accounts receivable should be considered because of the extended use of credit cards in connection with the operation of these properties.

[5] Mortgage Loan Closing

The commercial mortgage loan closing is a complicated transaction. It requires the coordinated efforts of the principals and specialists like attorneys, accountants, architects, engineers, surveyors, and title insurers. All the participants must understand their respective responsibilities and the time limits within which they must perform. Each should have read and should be familiar with those portions of the mortgage loan commitment that involve his particular function.

[a] Construction Loan Problems

The borrower should submit to the lender at the earliest possible time the required final plans and specifications, soils reports, and specialized engineering inspection reports. Both may be dismayed to discover at a late date that construction that is already in place is not acceptable to the lender's architect. At best, the correction of construction deficiencies is costly; at worst, the elimination of deficiencies may be impossible, and the mortgage commitment may have to be terminated. If interest rates have risen in the interim or if the developer is firmly committed to temporary construction financing, his loss can be substantial.

A positive benefit of early submission of plans and specifications is that an experienced lender's architect can recommend or require changes that result in a better final product.

The closing of a permanent mortgage loan on new construction is always conditioned upon full and satisfactory completion of the improvements. The lender will ultimately require a certificate of occupancy and a certificate of completion from the inspecting and/or supervising architects. Lenders also usually require that the completed property be inspected by one of its employees. To avoid delays in closing a mortgage loan, the lender should be notified as soon as the property is ready so that this inspection may be incorporated into the inspector's other assignments. If the borrower cannot comply fully with completion requirements (for example, he can supply only a temporary or partial certificate of occupancy prior to the closing or he is able to obtain only a qualified certificate from the supervising architect), he should notify the lender's attorney so that the latter may assess the legal consequences.

Many loan commitments require the borrower to establish an escrow to cover the estimated costs of incomplete tenant improvements or on-site improvements like paving or landscaping. If the commitment does not set forth a precise formula for computation of the escrow, the borrower should require the lender to designate the precise sum as soon as possible in order to avoid negotiations over the amount at the time of closing.

[b] Problems With Leasing Requirements

Most commercial mortgage loans are conditioned upon occupancy by tenants (often specifically named in the commitment) acceptable to the lender under leases with terms and conditions that are satisfactory to the lender. A borrower who discovers at closing that the leases are unacceptable to the lender finds that amendment of existing leases is difficult if not impossible, particularly when tenants are already in occupancy. But except in unusual cases, lenders' attorneys are reluctant to examine leases before the lender's unconditional acceptance of the loan commitment. The borrower should submit to the lender the final drafts of major tenant leases, as well as a standard form of a lease for use with smaller tenants as soon as possible after the lender makes the loan commitment and before the leases are actually executed. When the borrower submits standard form leases that include revisions, such revisions should take the form of riders or actual changes in the lease text rather than by interlineation. Since these techniques enable the changes to be readily identified, they expedite the lender's review.

If a lease must be executed before the prospective lender can review it, the lease should include a provision substantially like the following:

> Tenant agrees to execute and deliver to Landlord within a reasonable period of time any modification of this Lease required or requested by the holder or potential holder of a mortgage on the demised premises provided such modifications do not (1) materially increase Tenant's obligations or liabilities pursuant to this Lease or (2) decrease Tenant's rights under the Lease.

Lenders require that the tenant's acceptance of occupancy be evidenced by an estoppel executed by the tenant shortly before the date of the closing of the loan. Borrowers should start accumulating required estoppels at least thirty days prior to the closing. If the estoppel is conditioned (for example, acceptance of occupancy may be subject to a punch-list for unfinished work), the lender should be immediately advised.

The lender's commitment for an apartment project is usually conditioned upon a level of rental achievement rather than upon specific tenant leases. The borrower should submit to the lender before closing an affidavit or a certified rent-roll as evidence that the project has achieved the required rent level. Many lenders will verify actual occupancy when they make their preclosing inspection of the completed project.

[c] Preclosing

A commercial mortgage loan should be preclosed; nothing delays a closing more and causes more anxiety than the need to negotiate the terms and conditions of loan documents on the day of the closing. All documents that are to be delivered at the closing should have been drafted and approved by all parties prior to the closing; the prior approval of documents saves time and expense and avoids inconvenience. Such documents normally include the following:

- Note
- Mortgage or deed of trust
- Conditional assignment of rents and/or assignment of lessor's interest in leases
- Uniform Commercial Code financing statement
- Opinions of counsel
- Escrow agreement for unfinished work, if any

The fact that the substance of attorney's opinions is a matter of considerable negotiation may come as a surprise to the layman. Nevertheless, if closing delays are to be avoided, a draft of any opinion required of the borrower's attorney should be submitted to lender's counsel before the closing.

[d] Title Problems

The title insurance company is an indispensable party to virtually every mortgage loan closing. The title insurer's preliminary report on title (sometimes designated a title certificate or title binder) should be submitted to the lender at an early date. It should be accompanied by an indication as to what title exceptions will be disposed of prior to the closing and by copies of all instruments, such as easements or restrictive covenants, that will appear as exceptions to title in the title insurance policy when it is issued. Copies of lien waivers, affidavits, and other papers required by the title insurer at closing should be submitted to it for advance approval. If the lender requires the borrower to obtain affirmative insurance or special policy endorsements to protect it against possible problems of usury, zoning violations, or other contingencies, the borrower should investigate the availability of such affirmative insurance or endorsement as soon as possible. If they are not available, the lender must have time to consider possible alternatives.

The borrower should order a survey that complies with commitment requirements as soon as it is feasible to do so. Weather conditions or a heavy work load may prevent a surveyor from acting immediately on the request. Copies of the survey should be furnished to the lender and title insurer as soon as they are available. The borrower's attorney should examine it carefully for deficiencies or inaccuracies. The failure of a survey to show abutting streets and easements affecting the proposed security is a recurring cause of closing delays.

[e] Miscellaneous Problems

The following are a few of the many additional areas in which problems that delay closings are often encountered.

☐ The borrower should submit to the lender evidence of required hazard insurance, with a mortgagee endorsement attachment, before the closing. Most lenders' attorneys have neither the expertise nor the authority to approve such evidence at the closing.

☐ If a chattel mortgage is required by the lender, the borrower should submit a certified inventory of the chattels for prior approval. In addition, the borrower should furnish evidence prior to the closing of its interest in the chattels and of any liens on the chattels that will not be satisfied out of the loan proceeds.

☐ The borrower should clear in advance all requirements for matters such as street dedication or compliance with environmental protection laws and regulations and should furnish the lender prior to closing with such evidence of dedication or compliance as it may require.

☐ If easements are necessary for the proposed use of the property or to permit the property to constitute an independent and self-sufficient parcel of real estate, copies of the instruments that created or will create such easements should be submitted to lender's counsel for prior approval.

☐ In the case of a leasehold mortgage, it is, of course, critical that a copy of any proposed ground lease or an executed copy of any existing ground lease be submitted to the lender for approval at the earliest possible time.

Borrower and lender should not consider fixing a firm loan closing date until they are satisfied that all preclosing requirements have been met, bearing in mind that the borrower may need time for document execution and that the lender may need some lead time to adjust his cash-flow requirements and arrange for an orderly transfer of the loan proceeds.

6.05 LOAN REFINANCING

[1] In General

Whenever interest rates decline, owners of leveraged real estate are given an opportunity to refinance existing mortgages. Under what circumstances is refinancing desirable? The following discussion offers some background as well as some guidelines for action if the opportunity arises.

In the broad sense, refinancing involves any change in the financing of a property. Thus it includes the following:

- Paying off an existing loan with the proceeds of a new one
- Changing the terms of (recasting) an existing loan
- Obtaining additional financing while leaving the present loan unchanged

An investor normally will refinance in order to obtain one of four objectives. These are:

☐ *Realize tax-free cash.* To the extent that the total loan after the refinancing exceeds the loan prior to it, the owner realizes tax-free cash. The cash is tax-free because a loan transaction does not trigger realized gain as would a sale or other disposition of the property. If the total debt after the refinancing equals the original loan amount when the property was acquired, the investor has recouped the loan amortization he paid during the period of ownership. To the extent that the new debt exceeds the original financing, the investor is reducing his original equity in the real estate.

☐ *Reduce the interest cost.* Refinancing to take advantage of lower interest rates obviously is beneficial. Of course, the prepayment penalty on the original loan plus the cost of obtaining the new loan must not be so great as to wipe out the discounted (present) value of the interest savings realized through the refinancing.

☐ *Increase cash flow.* Refinancing may reduce the debt service payable by the investor and so increase his cash flow. This is most commonly achieved by extending the maturity of the original loan or by obtaining new financing with a longer loan term. Even if the interest rate and loan amounts remain unchanged, the periodic debt service will be lower.

Obviously, these objectives sometimes conflict. Pulling out tax-free cash means an increase in total financing, which will increase the debt service (unless a combination of lower interest and longer loan terms offsets it). And increasing the outstanding debt through refinancing often leads to overfinancing and so increases the risk of default.

☐ *Make property more salable.* A final objective of refinancing is to obtain the highest possible mortgage prior to putting the property on the market. This may make an eventual sale much easier since (1) the seller avoids the risk that financing may be unavailable at that time; and (2) the sale need not be delayed pending the buyer's obtaining a loan. And if the refinancing can be done today at an interest rate lower than is being paid on the existing mortgage, the future buyer benefits doubly—higher mortgage at lower interest.

But suppose refinancing is possible only at a higher interest rate and a higher constant payment. It may still be worth refinancing.

[2] Refinancing in Anticipation of Resale

In most cases, refinancing today (even if interest rates drop two or three points) will mean substituting a higher interest rate and constant payment for those on the existing mortgage. Is it still worthwhile to refinance in anticipation of a sale? It may well be, because of the increased leverage created for the new owner.

> *Example:* An owner offers for sale at $1 million an apartment house with a net operating income (NOI) of $100,000. Thus the free-and-clear return (return on total investment in the property) is 10 percent. The property is subject to a first mortgage that originally was $500,000 and calls for annual payments of $45,000 (9 percent of the original loan). However, since it has now been amortized to $300,000, the constant now represents 15 percent of the current loan ($45,000 on $300,000).

The seller has three ways of selling the property:

☐ *Sell for all cash.* The mortgagee would be delighted to accept prepayment of its low-interest loan. But a buyer can hardly be expected to put down $1 million in cash.

☐ *Sell the property subject to the existing mortgage.* But this means the buyer must put up $700,000—still a large amount of cash—for a return of only $55,000, or 8 percent ($100,000 NOI minus $45,000 debt service). Assume the buyer anticipates that rents can be increased in the near future so that the cash flow jumps to $75,000. Even then, the cash-flow return is still just under 11 percent ($75,000 on equity of $700,000).

☐ *Refinance the loan now.* Assume the seller can obtain a new first mortgage of $700,000 carrying a constant of 12 percent ($84,000 a year). This reduces the equity required of a buyer to $300,000. The cash flow initially is only $16,000, or 5 percent ($100,000 NOI minus $84,000 debt service). But if the cash flow increases by $20,000 to $36,000, the return is 12 percent, higher than under any of the other alternatives.

In short, the refinancing makes the property more salable to an investor by

- Raising the cash-flow yield from 11 to 12 percent.
- Reducing the cash required by $400,000.
- Increasing the tax shelter, since a larger portion of the debt service is deductible interest.

All this even though the interest rate is up by several percentage points.

6.06 LAND ACQUISITION AND DEVELOPMENT FINANCING

[1] Financing Land Acquisition

The most common feature of land acquisition financing is the absence of institutional lenders. Such lenders generally prefer to limit their financing either to (1) developed properties generating a cash flow that can be used to service the mortgage; or (2) properties in the process of development that promise a cash flow in the near future. Since raw land generates no cash flow, loans to finance its acquisition are considered the most risky and frequently are avoided altogether by institutional lenders or are limited to a small percentage of their loan portfolios, either as a matter of legal restriction or internal policy.

As a result, persons seeking to acquire raw land must look elsewhere. Five possible sources or techniques for financing land acquisition are the following:

☐ *Purchase-money mortgage.* The most frequent form of financing raw land is by a purchase-money mortgage taken back by the seller. The purchaser normally seeks a standing (no amortization) loan or one with delayed amortization payments. If the purchaser intends to develop the land in the future (rather than merely hold it for resale), it is vital that the seller agree to subordinate his first mortgage to a later construction loan, otherwise construction financing will not be obtainable. (For a detailed discussion of purchase-money mortgages, see 6.12.)

☐ *Purchase option.* With this approach, a speculator or developer can tie up large tracts of land at a minimum cost. Speculative options must be sufficiently long-term to enable the intended market for the land to develop before the option period expires. (For a detailed discussion of options, see 8.01.)

☐ *Long-term lease plus option.* A variation of the preceding approach is to enter into a lease with the owner that contains an option to purchase the property at any time during the lease term. There are two possible advantages for the prospective purchaser as compared to the straight option. Payments under a lease will be deemed rent and consequently will be fully deductible by the tenant at the time paid. In the case of an option, payments are not deductible until and unless the option expires without being exercised. The second advantage is that a default of paying rent will not result in an automatic loss of the investment since some form of legal proceeding will have to be instituted by the landlord. By comparison, failure to make an option payment when due will cause an immediate termination of all rights under the option.

☐ *Joint venture.* A third approach is a joint venture with the seller or with a third party. The partner may be a true partner, sharing all losses and gains in a determined proportion, or he may take a position somewhat between an equity owner and a lender (i.e., his interest may be superior to that of the operating partner but subordinate to any outside financing that might be obtainable).

☐ *Interim land loans.* Some private loan companies, as well as individual lenders, specialize in short-term (one- to three-year) loans on vacant land. Interest rates are likely to be in the same range as second mortgages on developed properties. This type of loan, which normally does not require amortization during its term, gives the speculator or developer time to wait for a market to develop for the land or for improvements on the land. Such interim loans normally will not exceed 50 percent of the appraised value of the land. Just as in the case of purchase-money mortgages, such third-party loans should contain a provision subordinating the loan to construction financing (assuming the borrower contemplates the possibility of construction during the interim loan term). If the lender objects, a possible compromise is to permit the borrower to substitute other collateral, for example, securities, certificates of deposit, or other real estate. If other real estate is to be substituted, the lender normally will insist upon the right to approve the specific real estate to insure that its value is at least equal to the released property.

[2] Three-Party Financing of Land Acquisition

The credit of a secondary lender often permits a raw-land developer to obtain a loan from an institutional lender that such lender otherwise would not be able or willing to make. The institutional lender, before entering such a transaction, must be satisfied with either the credit and responsibility of the secondary lender, or collateral provided by the secondary lender to support its extension of credit.

[a] Standard Forms

A secondary lender's credit can support a loan in one of three ways:

- *Absolute guarantee,* by which the secondary lender guarantees repayment of the loan to the primary lender.
- *Absolute purchase* (or "put"), under which the secondary lender agrees to buy the loan from the primary lender if a default by the borrower occurs.
- *Take-out commitment,* whereby the secondary lender will agree to buy the loan from the primary lender at or prior to a specified time on certain terms and conditions.

While the primary lender may find any of the three forms acceptable, secondary lenders generally do not give absolute guarantees or puts because (1) they might lose control over the loan; and (2) it is more difficult to structure the conditions under which their obligation to purchase the loan would come into play. Consequently, the third form (the take-out commitment) is the form most frequently used.

[b] Take-Out Commitment

When the primary and secondary lenders negotiate a take-out commitment, the basic issue is how much of the risk of the loan is shifted from the prime lender to the secondary lender (issuer of the takeout). Specifically, the following points must be dealt with:

☐ At what point will the takeout become effective, i.e., when must the issuer take over the loan? This can occur either at maturity or in the event of any default during the term of the loan.

☐ Which lender has the risk of carrying the loan while it is outstanding? For example, which of the two lenders is responsible for unpaid real estate taxes on the property?

☐ Under what circumstances is the issuer of the takeout excused from performing? For example, must he purchase the loan in the event the borrower becomes bankrupt or the property is condemned? Is the issuer excused from performing if the primary lender defaults on its obligations under the loan, e.g., if it fails to notify the issuer of an event of default or improperly releases a guarantor or collateral put up by the borrower?

☐ Must the developer improve the property before the take-out obligation arises? Sometimes the secondary lender can make his obligation contingent on some physical development of the property, e.g., construction of streets and sewers, or upon a rezoning of the property.

☐ The secondary lender will want to be sure that the title insurance policy in favor of the primary lender is assignable when the takeout becomes effective. Otherwise no protection exists against risks arising before the takeout occurs.

The criteria for issuing a take-out commitment should be exactly the same as for making the loan in the first instance. Therefore, the secondary lender will evaluate the developer's financial strength, experience, responsibility, and equity in the transaction; and (2) appraise the land in terms of proposed development and consider alternative uses of the land if the loan is defaulted.

In addition, the secondary lender will seek security for its take-out commitment just as it would seek security for an actual loan. Security (either of the loan by the primary lender or of the take-out commitment by the secondary lender) may, for example, include the following:

- Personal guarantee of the developer
- Mortgage or deed of trust on the land being financed
- Mortgage or deed of trust on other property owned by the developer

[3] Financing Land Development

Land development refers to the process of preparing raw land for the construction of improvements. The process includes grading of land where necessary, obtaining rezoning if required, and the installation of utilities, sewers, streets, and sidewalks. Although developed land (in the sense used here) creates no more cash flow than does raw land, it is nevertheless one step closer to the ultimate use and thus is somewhat easier to finance. Most development loans represent a first lien on the property, they are short-term in nature, and the interest charged is usually tied to commercial banks' prime lending rate (3 to 4 points above prime).

Development loans are usually made separately from construction loans when the raw land must be subdivided into smaller tracts or lots. The proceeds are dispersed in draws as the development progresses. The lender will allow release of specified tracts (lots) from the overall mortgage as development proceeds and the individual lots are sold to builders. When tracts or lots are released, the borrower must make a payment to the lender in exchange for the release. This release price, as it is called, is generally 10 to 20 percent greater than the proportional principal and interest associated with the released tract. This insures the lender of repayment with the sale of the choice lots and defers the developer's receipt of most of the profit until the development has been nearly sold out.

For example, if a developer finances ten lots with a loan of $100,000 with accrued interest of $10,000 to be payable at the maturity of the loan, the proportional amount of debt plus interest per lot would be $11,000. Assuming a release price of 20 percent per lot, it would be necessary for the developer to pay the lender $12,200 whenever a lot was sold and was removed from the lien of the mortgage. As a result, the entire loan of $110,000, including accrued interest, would be virtually paid off after the sale of the ninth lot (9 × $12,200 = $109,800). In effect, the developer is forced to defer all or most of his profit until sale of the final lots but in view of the prior claim of the lender, this is not unreasonable.

6.07 CONSTRUCTION FINANCING

[1] Characteristics of Construction Financing

Third-party financing plays a crucial role in the construction of improvements on land, just as it does in the ownership of real property. It is rare indeed for a real estate developer or builder to utilize his own funds in new construction. (The exception to this rule is the construction done by companies putting up industrial properties for their own use.)

Construction financing is significantly different from long-term financing. A construction loan may be defined as a short-term loan intended to provide most or all of the funds necessary to construct improvements on real estate that is secured by a first mortgage on the property and that is intended to be fully repaid upon completion of construction. The unique features of a construction loan are due to (1) the nature of the construction process as well as (2) the risks involved in a construction project, whether natural, economic, or political. The key features of a construction loan are:

☐ *Short-term.* The term of the loan normally matches the expected construction period, six months to three years. Since most construction lenders specialize in this type of financing and do not wish to hold long-term loans, they normally wish the loan to be repaid in full when construction is completed. Sometimes, however, they will agree to continue to hold the loan; in effect, it is converted into a permanent loan.

☐ *Staged disbursements.* Unlike a permanent loan, under which all of the funds are advanced at the time the loan documents are executed, a construction loan is disbursed in a series of payments, matching the stages of construction. In this way, the borrower need not pay interest on money until it is needed, while the lender reduces its risk since the amount of the outstanding loan is more or less matched by the value of the construction in place.

☐ *Repayment.* Since the property is generating no cash flow, and the loan is being disbursed in stages, no amortization occurs during the life of the loan; instead, the entire loan is repaid at maturity. Normally, the repayment comes from the proceeds of long-term financing, although sometimes it is made from the proceeds of an all-cash sale to an outside investor.

☐ *Loan-to-value ratio.* In general, the amount of the construction loan is intended to equal all or most of the total construction costs (i.e., the developer's investment is primarily in the land itself). However, the loan-to-construction cost ratio will be less than 100 percent if the borrower cannot provide adequate security or a take-out commitment equal to the full construction cost (see next paragraph).

☐ *Security.* Although the construction lender acquires a first mortgage on the land and the construction in place, its primary assurance of repayment is the existence of a take-out commitment by a permanent lender (or sometimes by an equity purchaser), which requires the lender (or purchaser) to fund (provide cash under) its commitment upon the completion of construction. (This is discussed in more detail in 6.07[3].) In addition, the construction lender may require the developer to provide additional collateral in the form of mortgages on other real estate or otherwise.

Because of the risk involved in construction financing, the loans return a high yield to the lender. This yield is normally substantially higher than the nominal (face) interest rate on the loan, which results primarily from the fact that an initial front-end fee is normally charged on the full amount of the loan, even though the loan will be disbursed in stages.

For example, assume a one-year construction loan for $200,000 at an interest rate of 15 percent plus a front-end fee of three points (percent). Assume further that the average amount of the outstanding loan during the year is 50 percent (because it is disbursed in stages). The yield would then be calculated as follows:

$100,000 (50% of loan) × 15% =	$15,000
$200,000 × 3% fee	6,000
Total return	$21,000
Yield = $21,000/100,000	21%

[2] Sources of Construction Financing

The sources for construction loans may vary to some degree depending on the stage in the economic cycle and on the particular type of property to be financed. But in general, the main sources of construction loans are in the order listed below. The importance of the source lies primarily in the type of documentation required and the relationship (insofar as the lender is concerned) between the construction loan and the permanent loan. Some construction lenders (such as commercial banks) have no desire at all to hold the permanent loan and require strong assurances of a source of repayment when construction is completed. On the other hand, a savings and loan association or life insurance company may make a construction loan primarily for the purpose of gaining the inside track in obtaining the permanent loan, which is its primary interest.

☐ *Commercial banks.* The commercial banking system historically has provided most of the construction financing in the United States. The major reason for their primary role is that commercial banks are short-term lenders (since their assets are also short-term, being primarily in the form of demand deposits). And since construction financing requires a special expertise, it would not be easy for another financing source to replace the commercial banks. As already noted, the commercial bank normally requires assurance that funds will be available at the completion of construction to take out the bank. (This subject is discussed further in 6.07[4].)

☐ *Life insurance companies.* Traditionally, life insurance companies were interested primarily in permanent loans since their liability base (policy reserves, pension funds, etc.) is not subject to sudden withdrawals. However, in recent years, life insurance companies have played a much larger role in construction lending, primarily because their cash inflows have increased at a rate far greater than anticipated. This has been primarily due to the tremendous growth in pension funds and profit-sharing plans, many of which are managed by the life insurance companies. These companies have been seeking additional outlets for loans. Construction financing is of interest to them not only because it is a new source of investment but because it permits them to offer financing "packages" that combine construction financing with the permanent loan. The benefits to a developer of such a package loan are that (1) the life insurance company may offer fixed-rate construction financing since they are not subject to sharp changes in their cost of funds; (2) financing expenses are cut since only one loan negotiation is required; (3) far less time is required to negotiate the combined construction-permanent loan package; and (4) the developer is no longer subject to the risk that delayed construction will result in loss of the permanent loan commitment (which normally has an expiration date).

☐ *Real estate investment trusts.* Real estate investment trusts (REITs) were an extremely important source of construction financing (as well as of development financing) in the early 1970s. But too-hasty expansion and lack of experience led many REITs into making large numbers of bad loans that resulted in a very severe shakeout in the mid-1970s. Now, after several years of retrenchment, the REITs are once again doing some construction lending. One advantage of dealing with REITs is that they are subject to virtually no regulation with respect to the type of loan they may make, whereas both commercial banks and thrift institutions are subject to state and federal regulation.

☐ *Thrift institutions.* Both savings and loan associations and mutual savings banks have always done a certain amount of construction lending, usually, however, only in the locale where the particular institution is located. However, the major reason for construction financing by thrift institutions is as a means of acquiring permanent home loans that will be made when construction is completed.

☐ *Pension funds.* So far, pension funds have played an extremely small role in construction financing. The reason is that the risks in such financing are much greater than in other types of real estate investments and pension funds, being fiduciaries, are under an obligation to invest prudently. In addition, most pension funds have had no opportunity to develop an expertise in construction lending.

☐ *Mortgage bankers.* These firms may often provide construction financing as a means toward obtaining permanent loans that then will be packaged and sold to the mortgage bankers' correspondents, normally the large life insurance companies. The mortgage banking firms themselves raise the necessary capital by borrowing from local commercial banks, usually under a line of credit. The construction mortgages are then given to the bank as collateral for the loan (the process known as warehousing).

[3] Risks in Construction Financing

When evaluating a proposed construction loan, the lender must be very aware of the types of risks it is assuming and the extent to which it can protect itself against such risks. Essentially, two types of risks exist in connection with a new project: (1) contruction risks; and (2) economic risks.

☐ *Construction risks.* These are risks that may prevent completion of the improvements in accordance with the plans and specifications. This type of risk is always assumed by the construction lender (as distinguished from the permanent take-out lender) because the take-out commitment is always conditioned upon completion of the building in accordance with the plans and specifications. Construction risks include the following:

- Labor problems, including strikes, and labor shortages
- Extreme weather conditions causing construction delays
- Increase in construction costs beyond that anticipated in the construction budget
- Errors in preparing the construction budget or the plans and specifications that cause higher-than-anticipated costs
- Poor management of the construction process
- Misappropriation of construction funds by the developer or others
- Insolvency of the developer

If one or more of these risks materialize, the consequences will be either that the project will not be completed on time (which may permit the permanent lender to cancel the take-out commitment) or that construction costs will be substantially above budget, requiring the introduction of additional capital by the construction lender, the developer or some other party. The construction lender can protect itself against these risks by

- Satisfying itself as to the competence and reputation of the general contractor and major subcontractors.
- Requiring the posting of a payment, performance, or completion bond.
- Adequately supervising the construction process so that difficulties are identified very early.

☐ *Economic risks.* Economic risks are those involving the possibility that the completed project cannot be sold or rented in accordance with projections, with a resulting loss to the developer. These risks may or may not be assumed by the construction lender, depending on the nature of the take-out commitment. (See 6.04[2].) If the take-out commitment requires the permanent lender to fund its loan upon completion of the project, then the permanent lender assumes any economic risks involving rentup or sale of the completed property. However, if the take-out commitment has a rental achievement clause, requiring a specified percentage of the space to be under lease, or (as in the case of a condominium) requiring a certain number of units to be presold before the permanent lender is required to finance any single mortgage, then it is the construction lender who assumes much of the economic risk.

Economic risks include the following:

- Market changes, such as a sudden oversupply of space, that result in inadequate demand
- Improper pricing of the newly constructed space, with the result that rentals or sales are made at a loss or prices and rentals are not competitive
- Poor design or construction defects that create instant obsolescence
- Changes in the neighborhood (economic and social depreciation)

There is little that either the construction lender or permanent lender can do to protect against economic risks apart from making a careful feasibility study prior to making the loan commitment.

[4] Negotiating the Construction Loan

Having set forth the basic characteristics of construction financing and described the sources of such financing and the risks involved, we turn our attention to negotiating an actual construction mortgage. The key steps in the process include the following:

- Property analysis by lender (see 6.07[4][a])
- Loan analysis by lender (see 6.07[4][b])
- Loan commitment (see 6.04[2][b])

[a] Property Analysis by Lender

In the broad sense, there are two areas of consideration for the lender in any mortgage application: the property and the borrower. After thorough analysis of all the facts involving each, a lending institution makes its decision as to what sort of a mortgage it is willing and able to grant in light of its lending policy.

The lender requires the following information about the property:

☐ *An area property map* indicating its location relative to the rest of the community. The borrower is entitled to highlight those influences that tend to stabilize or increase value.

☐ *A site plan* to see how much land is being offered, the shape of the site, and the location of the building and other improvements to be located on the plot.

☐ *Plans and specifications* that will indicate how many square feet there are and what the room arrangement will be, and will give data on the installations for air conditioning and plumbing. Are exterior walls wood construction or masonry? Are curtain walls dry wall or paneled? What will the building look like from the exterior? What are the elevations?

☐ *A proposed rent-roll and operating statements,* which will indicate the names of the proposed tenants, the amount of space each will occupy, and some information on the lease or leases—dollar amount of rent, term and special provisions such as responsibility for taxes, insurance, repairs, utilities, and other operating costs. This information is the backbone of any commercial presentation, since the economic feasibility of the project and its ability to support the long-term mortgage must be determined.

☐ *Cost of the project,* including a breakdown that will indicate the costs of raw land, land improvements, and building construction; equipment and furnishing costs; architectural and loan fees; interest charges; overhead; and legal fees. While most of the anticipated expenditures cannot be supported by firm contracts at the application stage, they must be by the time of commitment. In many instances, the first draw is conditioned upon approval of such contracts.

In addition, the applicant sooner or later is likely to find it necessary to produce the following:

☐ *Zoning.* A letter from the local zoning board indicating that the proposed building meets local ordinances, or, it if does not, how the developer proposes to solve the problem.

☐ *City planning.* A letter from the architect indicating the provision for parking spaces and for elevators in the building, as well as the requirements under city regulations.

☐ *Utilities.* Letters from utility companies indicating that such utilities as gas, electricity, water, and sewer facilities are presently available as required.

☐ *Soil conditions.* Soil conditions can affect total construction costs by up to 30 percent. So the application should be accompanied by a letter from a structural engineer with pertinent information.

☐ *Plans and specifications.* The applicant should be prepared to provide floor plans and specifications detailed enough to indicate type of construction and level of quality intended. In addition, a budget based on one of the better-known construction cost indices, with adjustments for local conditions, should be drawn up.

☐ *Environmental impact study.* A project that requires approval of an environmental impact study by the Environmental Protection Agency must be reasonably sure of such approval before a loan will be approved.

☐ *Energy.* Energy often is a critical consideration, particularly since the economic life of a new building will extend well into the next century. An estimate of annual energy cost as calculated by competent professionals is very desirable.

[b] Loan Analysis by Lender

A lender having no previous experience with a developer will put together a loan dossier in order to reach an informed opinion about the developer's experience and reputation. Into the dossier will go reports and information supplied by banks, credit bureaus, builders, architects, lawyers, contractors, materialmen, insurance companies, and others who have had dealings with the applicant. From the lender's point of view, the dossier should support the conclusion that the developer is capable of building the project, based upon his past record, his relations with his subcontractors, and his financial record.

The construction lender will expect to see a current balance sheet of the developer. Since real estate traditionally is a "cash-short" industry, a developer's balance sheet typically will show his net worth, consisting primarily of directly owned real estate, stock ownership in real estate corporations, mortgages, and other debt instruments. Working capital typically will be a small percentage of total assets. In order to corroborate the net worth figure, the lender may wish to study the individual real estate investments in detail. In brief, a thorough analysis by the construction lender very nearly amounts to a reappraisal of all of the developer's properties. One point of particular interest to the lender will be the net cash flow from the other properties of the developer, since these probably represent the source of much of the equity that the developer will put into the new project.

The primary interest of the construction lender is in determining that the developer will have sufficient funds (construction loan plus other cash) to complete the construction project. If an examination of the developer's financial statements does not show where the cash over and above the construction loan has its source, it usually will turn out that one of the following is the case:

- The developer's estimate of the cost of construction is less than the figure independently arrived at by the lender.
- The developer, by means of holdbacks, is withholding a portion of the monies that will be due his subcontractors and materialmen, with the intention of paying them out of the proceeds of the permanent loan or from sale of the property upon completion.
- A portion of the work and material is being paid for by the developer's promissory notes or by the conveyance of ownership interest in the project.

☐ *Checking construction costs.* The lender generally works with standard cost figures. The developer may have used actual figures where he has already entered into firm contracts. Sometimes the developer may act as his own general contractor or may do a portion of the work himself; in that case, the developer's lower cost of construction may be due to making no provision for his own profit. The lender may not be willing to accept the lower figure since, if the lender must ever complete the job upon the developer's default, the work the developer intended to do himself will have to be relet at a cost that will include a margin for profit and hence increase the total cost.

☐ *Guarantees.* A developer usually wants the construction loan to be made to a corporation formed solely for the purpose of holding title to the real property and having no other assets (a so-called shell, or one-shot, corporation). This insulates the developer from various liabilities that may arise during the course of construction. However, the lender usually insists that the developer personally guarantee the project's completion, by the required date, according to the approved plans, and free of liens. The developer's guarantee amounts to a pledge of his personal assets to the lender, and to this extent, the shell corporation does not insulate him from liability.

☐ *Bonds.* Except in the case of very strong developers, the lender may well insist that the developer obtain a performance bond and a labor and material payments bond. Such bonds involve four parties: The bond is in favor of the developer (owner) and the lender, and it is signed by the general contractor as principal and by an insurance company as surety (that is, as the one who is insuring the contractor's obligations). Taken together, these bonds insure that funds will be available to complete construction and pay all amounts for labor and materials.

☐ *Appraisals.* The lender will not be satisfied with mere assurances that the project will be completed. He will also wish to have an appraisal of the completed project, with projections of gross income and expenses, and with a projected value for the property based upon a capitalization rate, all to be determined by an experienced appraiser. Occasionally, a developer will submit an appraisal with his application, and if the appraiser's qualifications are satisfactory to the lender, this appraisal will be sufficient. On the other hand, on a large project or where no appraisal is submitted initially, the lender will make its own arrangements for an appraisal. (The borrower pays the appraisal fee.)

Because the appraisal of real estate is an art, not a science, the lender (and the developer, too) should examine the appraisal report closely to be sure that assumptions are not unrealistic and that the reasoning of the appraiser is supported by experience. This is particularly true in the case of new projects, where there is no actual operating history.

[c] Construction Loan Commitment

The loan negotiation process will end, if the loan is approved, with a commitment letter. (See 6.04[2].)

[5] Loan Closing; Building Loan Agreement

The closing of a construction loan, as well as the type of documents executed, follow very closely the procedure already described for permanent mortgage loans. (See 6.04[5].) One instrument that is unique to the construction loan is the building loan agreement (sometimes called the construction loan agreement). Its function is to pull together in one place all of the obligations of both developer and lender, as well as to prevent future problems arising from conflicting provisions in the subordinate documents (the mortgage, construction note, and guarantee of completion).

Some of the matters covered by the building loan agreement include:

☐ *Loan entitlement clause.* Some developers, after having executed the building loan agreement, fail to take down construction advances and instead shop around for short-term credit, which may be extended to them on more favorable terms on the security of the building loan agreement. To avoid this practice, construction lenders are inserting a clause in the loan agreement requiring the developer to pay interest on the amount of loan proceeds to which he would have been entitled (on the basis of the completed construction), whether or not the loan advance is actually made.

☐ *Requests for advance.* The loan agreement frequently will contain a statement that any request for advance by the developer constitutes an affirmation that all of the representations and warranties made at the time the agreement was executed remain true and correct unless the developer says otherwise. Thus, the developer must be very careful to review these representations at the time of each advance.

☐ *Loan advances.* Construction lenders are moving away from the method of making advances in accordance with a fixed schedule. Instead, they are often using a line budget approach, with advances being made on an item-by-item basis in accordance with the amount of construction completed.

☐ *Utility services.* As a result of utility shortages and no-growth moratoria in many communities, lenders are becoming concerned about the availability of utility services to a new project. Consequently, the borrower will be required to represent that all utility services needed for the project are available at the project boundaries.

[6] Loan Disbursement Process

Payments by a construction lender are normally made in stages as the work progresses. In this way, the lender is assured that the funds are actually used as intended; in addition, the construction in place increases the value of the real estate and so provides additional security for the construction loan. Normally, payouts are authorized by the general contractor, who is responsible for overseeing the work. However, payouts go directly to the subcontractor doing the work so that no question can arise about his receipt of the funds.

At least once a month, and preferably more often, the lender may inspect the progress of construction to make sure that work is being done as specified. Such inspections often are performed by a professional engineer or similarly qualified person, known as the draw inspector (because he authorizes the payment of construction funds, known as draws). The draw inspector performs the following functions:

- He makes a complete analysis of the plans and specifications at the time the proposal is submitted to the lender for approval. The inspector should determine whether the plans adequately define the amount of work needed to complete the project and if the estimated costs are valid. Frequently, the developer allocates insufficient funds for construction because of overly optimistic estimates of costs.
- Once work begins, the inspector makes periodic visits to the site to insure that work on the project is of proper quality and that nothing necessary for the completion and proper operation of the building is omitted.
- He keeps track of the pace of construction since slow progress will cause interest rates to increase and other costs to rise due to inflation. In either case, there may be inadequate funds to finish the job.

- When the construction lender advances a portion of the loan, the inspector must insure that the payment does not exceed the value of work-in-place plus the value of any stored material. (Typically, a specified percentage, usually 5 to 10 percent, is deducted from the appraised value of the work-in-place and stored materials. This provides a cushion of protection against errors in authorized payments.)
- Finally, the draw inspector must be alert to any attempts on the part of the developer to divert the construction funds to other projects.

6.08 SHORT-TERM AND INTERIM FINANCING

An interim mortgage provides short-term (usually one- to three-year) financing to an investor who is unwilling or unable to obtain a permanent loan at the time new construction is completed or existing property is acquired. Interim financing can be used for both newly completed buildings and existing projects. For example, the developer of a new building may believe that more desirable long-term financing will be available several years later, when the building is fully rented and has become "seasoned." Consequently, he takes out a three-year interim loan in order to pay off the construction loan. He anticipates refinancing the interim loan with a long-term mortgage when the former becomes payable. Since the interim loan is bridging the gap between the construction loan and the permanent loan, it is often known as a "bridge" loan.

Similarly, an investor who buys an office or commercial building, intending to convert it into a condominium or rental project, will seek interim financing to provide the funds necessary for conversion and renovation. When the work is completed, the interim loan will be replaced by a permanent loan (if a rental project is the result) or will be paid off from the proceeds of the sale of condominium units. Interim loans normally are first-mortgage loans. They cannot be fully amortizing loans because the term is so short; they either are standing loans (usually) or may require some partial amortization during the loan term.

A special form of interim financing is accomplished by way of a second-mortgage loan. This type of financing is used where the investor cannot or does not wish to pay off the existing first-mortgage obligation. Normally, interim second mortgages carry an interest rate of 5 percent or more above prime, but at times the spread may be narrowed so as to make interim second mortgages relatively more attractive. (See 6.09.)

[1] When to Use Interim Financing for New Construction

Most often, interim loans are used in newly completed projects. The loan funds are used to take out (repay) the construction lender, and the investor then is in a position to operate the property for several years before committing himself to permanent financing. Here are some situations that may call for interim financing:

☐ *Temporary oversupply.* When occupancy in a new building becomes available at a time when vacancy rates are high, the developer may have to sit through a period of several years with large blocks of empty space. Consequently, a permanent loan may be either unavailable or available only at premium rates and a low loan-to-value ratio.

☐ *Accelerating demand.* A contrasting situation is one in which rents are expected to rise sharply in the next few years; interim financing may enable the developer to obtain a much larger loan by waiting.

☐ *Temporarily unfavorable conditions.* Sometimes a condition peculiar to the particular project dims the short-term outlook. For example, negotiations with a major tenant may be stalled when the permanent takeout is being sought. Here, an interim loan takeout (often in the form of a standby takeout) gives the developer breathing space.

☐ *Leases dependent upon completion.* Sometimes it is much easier to rent completed or partially completed projects than to obtain leases on blueprints alone. If the permanent financing is dependent upon signed leases, the developer again may be better off with an interim loan takeout to secure the construction lender.

☐ *Multiphase projects.* Shopping centers, industrial parks, and office complexes often are built in phases. As a result, permanent financing for the entire project may be unavailable at the outset; if several lenders are used, complicated legal arrangements must be set up. Interim permanent loans for each phase can provide financing until the entire project is completed.

☐ *Condominium projects.* Here, the condominium developer expects to pay off the construction loan from the proceeds of the sales of individual units. This may put the developer under pressure to meet a deadline, and it can be avoided by interim financing.

☐ *Personal liability.* For a number of reasons, including the lack of operating history for the project, a permanent lender may want the developer to assume personal liability. By signing an interim note, the developer limits his exposure to the period before he can refinance a nonrecourse loan.

[2] When to Use Interim Financing for Existing Projects

Intermediate-term financing may also play a role in financing and refinancing existing income properties. Here are some examples where it might be used:

☐ *Superior management.* When an existing income property is acquired, the buyer may have to arrange immediate purchase-money financing. If he is convinced that better management will substantially increase the cash flow from the property, an interim loan will enable him to refinance in a few years on substantially better terms.

☐ *Refinancing prior to loan maturity.* An investor, requiring funds, may want to pull cash out of a property by refinancing. But if the existing mortgage is not prepayable, or if its low rate makes prepayment undesirable, an interim second mortgage (often in the form of a wraparound mortgage) can bridge the period until the original mortgage matures.

☐ *Refinancing when original mortgage matures.* In the opposite situation, the existing mortgage may mature at a time when a new permanent loan cannot be made on advantageous terms because major leases with short terms remaining have not yet been renewed, or for any of the reasons given above. Interim financing can bridge this uncertain period.

☐ *Substantial renovation required.* Interim financing is also useful when a buyer acquires property requiring substantial renovation. The buyer, in effect, is in the same situation as the builder of a new building. He cannot obtain a permanent loan that reflects the full value of the building until the renovation is completed. And in order to do the renovation, he needs short-term money.

[3] Negotiating the Interim Loan

While lenders often try to make interim loans and mortgages callable (by them), the borrower should try to get a definite term for the loan, even if only for a year. In a bad market, time is always on the borrower's side, provided he has bargained for an adequate amount. A two- to three-year term is the minimum desirable since it may take that long for rates to decline. The most prevalent term is apt to be in the three- to five-year range. The borrower may want to keep the term short because the fees charged by the lender are based on the duration of the loan. The best loan is one that can be paid off after a short lock-in period on reasonable notice to the lender, and on payment of a reasonable penalty.

Prepayment privileges under an interim loan vary. Many loans are made without lock-ins. When the lender insists on a lock-in, it may be up to one-half of the loan term, with a minimum period of six months.

For prime properties, interest rates on interim first-mortgage loans can vary from one percent above the permanent-loan rate to the permanent-loan rate itself. For higher-risk situations, the interest rate may be 1.5 percent or more above the rate for prime real estate loans.

[4] Examples of Short-Term Financing

The following examples illustrate two specific types of short-term financing:

☐ *Bridge loan with partial releases.* An investor acquires a town house project with 474 units, constructed in 1969. The entire purchase price of $8 million is financed with a four-year intermediate loan by a major credit company. The loan provides for partial releases should the property be converted to condominiums. In this way, individual unit owners are in a position to obtain their own first-mortgage financing. In the absence of such a partial release provision, the investor would have to renegotiate loan terms at the time it decided to convert the project.

Except where the lender has complete confidence in the investor, the lender will hesitate to grant a partial release privilege unless a number of conditions are met, particularly relating to presales. The reason is that a conversion that is only partially successful will leave the project as half condominium and half rental, which is not a desirable situation.

☐ *Intermediate-term wraparound loan.* An apartment project was subject to a $3.9 million first mortgage at 9.25 percent. Prepayment prior to 1983 would require a very large penalty. The investor was able to arrange a $6.2 million wraparound loan (providing the investor with $2.3 million of new money) at a 9.75 percent interest rate with a thirty-year amortization schedule and a seven-year term. By wrapping its loan around the existing first mortgage carrying a half-point lower interest rate, the lender was able to leverage its return. As a result, the investor was able to obtain the new loan at prevailing interest rates while saving a substantial prepayment penalty.

The investor, of course, is anticipating that interest rates will be no higher in seven years than at present since at that time the wraparound loan must be refinanced. If rates are lower after 1983, the entire loan can be refinanced since the first mortgage can be prepaid.

6.09 JUNIOR FINANCING

Junior (second, third, or subsequent) mortgages frequently are thought of as highly speculative paper, offered only by distressed property owners to lenders who seek to squeeze out exorbitant rates of interest. In fact, a junior mortgage can represent a very sound investment, well secured by existing cash flow, and beneficial both to the borrower and to the lender. Junior mortgages are of particular interest in the type of economic climate that prevails today—relatively high first-mortgage rates but with prospects for lower rates in the future, which makes it desirable for property owners to retain financing flexibility. The following examples help to demonstrate the role of junior financing:

☐ *Interim loan prior to refinancing.* A frequent use of interim loans is to permit a delay in refinancing. An owner of investment property amortizes his low-interest permanent loan down to 50 percent or less of current market value. Needing cash, he can refinance at today's rates but thinks rates will be lower in six months to three years. It is cheaper for him to raise cash by a high-interest second mortgage for 20 or 30 percent of the property's market value than to refinance the first mortgage and pay a higher interest rate on the entire loan. As added protection (in case long-term rates rise rather than fall), he may be able to obtain the right, at a price, to renew the second mortgage for an additional term or even a right to convert it into a long-term amortized loan.

A related situation is one involving a permanent loan that bars prepayment. An owner needing immediate cash then is forced to resort to secondary financing.

☐ *Interim loan for reconversion or rehabilitation.* With new construction costs rising so rapidly, many investors are finding it profitable to convert or rehabilitate existing structures. New long-term financing normally is not available until the work is completed. If the building carries a present first mortgage, financing the renovation or rehabilitation can be done by a short-term second mortgage. In effect, this is secondary construction financing and normally will require security (such as guarantees) apart from the property itself.

☐ *Long-term amortized loan.* Both of the above examples involve short-term standing loans. Sometimes an investor can obtain a relatively long-term (ten-year) second mortgage calling for some amortization, with a balloon at maturity. Such long-term loans normally can be made only on high-quality properties and, of course, at relatively high interest rates. A special example of this approach is the wraparound loan. (See 6.10.)

☐ *Purchase-money financing.* Of course, the most common type of junior financing is the purchase-money mortgage. The seller frequently is willing to take a subordinate position because (1) he otherwise could not sell the property; and (2) a repossession in the event of default gives him back his original property in addition to whatever portion of the purchase price he retains.

Of more interest is the role of purchase-money second mortgages in real estate syndications; often, they make possible additional cash flow to permit higher distributions to the members of the syndicate. The seller is compensated by receiving a purchase price above the true market value of the property.

Such purchase-money financing usually matures fairly quickly. Since the syndicate agreement normally makes no provision for raising additional equity, the new owners must hope that appreciation of the property will permit refinancing the first mortgage to throw off enough cash to pay the second at maturity. In the past, this often has turned out to be a forlorn hope.

[1] Sources of Second Mortgages

Second-mortgage financing can be obtained from both institutional and noninstitutional sources. Usually, loans from these sources are relatively short-term (three to five years), will carry either a fixed-interest rate substantially above that for first-mortgage loans or have a floating-rate basis that is three to four points over prime, and contain relatively liberal prepayment conditions.

Institutional second mortgages may be available from life insurance companies, from wholly owned subsidiaries of such companies that can operate outside of insurance industry regulations, pension funds, commercial banks, and thrift institutions. The latter two have recently begun to emphasize residential second mortgages as a means to enable homeowners to pull out a portion of the appreciated value in the form of tax-free loan proceeds. In general, institutional second mortgages (as compared to noninstitutional loans) will carry somewhat lower rates and be for somewhat longer terms. However, prepayment privileges are likely to be less generous and loan-to-value ratios may be lower due to regulatory restrictions.

Most second-mortgage financing comes from such noninstitutional sources as real estate investment trusts, commercial finance companies, and mortgage companies. Because they are not subject to regulation, these sources may be willing to provide junior financing which, when combined with the first mortgage, equals 85 percent of appraised value. By comparison, institutional sources very often are limited to a combined 75 percent ratio.

A frequent rule of thumb utilized by a second lender is "five times the bottom line." In other words, the amount of junior financing available on a given property is equal to the cash flow remaining after first-mortgage debt service multiplied by five.

[2] Junior-Mortgage Checklist

Drafting a second mortgage is a lawyer's job. But nonlawyers should also have an understanding of the key provisions in the mortgage document that can minimize the risk.

☐ *To what is the mortgage subordinate?* A junior mortgage may be subordinate to specific existing mortgages, but only to the present outstanding balance of such mortgages; to specific existing mortgages and future extensions, replacements, or renewals thereof, but with specified dollar amounts; or to any mortgages, present or future, that the borrower may wish to put on the property.

Clearly, the secondary lender should seek to restrict the subordination as much as possible: The greater the subordination, the greater the risk. To a very large degree, the particular circumstances of the loan will indicate the extent of subordination required.

A common technique is to permit the borrower to refinance the existing senior lien in a higher amount (to reflect increased value of the property), but a part or all of the excess funds from refinancing must be used to reduce the balance of the second mortgage.

☐ *Changing senior-mortgage payments.* The second mortgage frequently provides that there can be no reduction or omission of installment payments on the first mortgage. The reason is that a property owner under pressure may seek to postpone first-mortgage payments in order to conserve cash. Since the first mortgage is not being amortized as quickly as anticipated, the secondary lender is under increased risk that in event of default, the property will not be sufficient to pay off his debt. In addition, the lender wants to avoid being tied to a losing property. As soon as trouble is indicated, quick action is often best, at least from the lender's point of view.

☐ *Escrows of first-mortgage payments.* To insure that debt service on the senior mortgage is actually paid, the second mortgage may require the property owner to deposit first-mortgage payments in escrow with the secondary lender, who in turn pays them to the senior lender.

☐ *Notice of defaults under senior loan.* An important provision in the second mortgage requires the owner to notify the secondary lender immediately of any notice of default sent by the senior lender. An even better protection for the secondary lender is to have the first lender himself agree to send such notices, but this usually cannot be obtained.

☐ *Right to cure first-mortgage defaults.* In addition to receiving notice of defaults, the secondary lender wants the right to satisfy defaults under the first mortgage and add any costs or expenses incurred to the balance under the second loan, together with interest.

☐ *First-mortgage default triggers secondary default.* Finally, the second mortgage should provide that a default under the first mortgage is also a default under the second mortgage, or accelerates the maturity of the second loan. This will permit the secondary lender to take steps immediately to protect himself, including the calling of other security that may have been given in addition to the second mortgage.

☐ *Additional security.* As just mentioned, the secondary lender often insists on security in addition to the second mortgage itself, in view of the increased risks involved in junior financing. The additional security can include personal guarantees by the borrower or his associates; assignment of leases and rents from the property (if the senior lender has not obtained the assignment, it can give the secondary lender an important advantage); subordination of claims by other creditors of the borrower (for example, those about to receive partial payment from the proceeds of the secondary loan); and pledge of stock or other collateral, whether of the borrowing company or otherwise.

6.10 WRAPAROUND FINANCING

The wraparound mortgage is a second mortgage that, instead of being wholly independent of the first loan, wraps around it. That is, the borrower pays debt service on the entire wraparound loan to the second-mortgage lender, who then pays the first lender his share.

Wraparound loans have become an integral part of real estate financing. One reason is that in the past few years of record-high interest rates, most first mortgages were made with lock-in clauses, preventing prepayment during an initial period as long as ten years, with substantial prepayment penalties thereafter. Consequently, traditional refinancing, involving paying off the existing first mortgage with the proceeds from a new loan, is not available to many property owners.

The other traditional alternative—a straight second mortgage—is often not feasible because institutional lenders cannot or do not wish to make such loans. The wraparound approach, while providing the same high return as a second mortgage, does offer some additional protection to the new lender and does not carry the stigma (if such can still be said to exist) of making second-mortgage loans.

[1] Advantages to Second Lender

The essential advantages to the second lender (over a straight second mortgage) are:

☐ The higher interest rate paid by the borrower covers the entire wraparound loan, not merely the new cash advanced. Consequently, the second lender's return is leveraged, sometimes very substantially, whenever the wraparound interest rate exceeds the rate on the underlying loan. (In other words, the second lender ends up getting as much or more as he would through a straight second mortgage even though the nominal rate on the wraparound loan is much lower.)

☐ Since the second lender acts as a conduit in servicing the first mortgage, he is in a position to insure that payments are in fact being made promptly on the senior lien. By comparison, in a straight second mortgage the second lender may not be aware of defaults under the first mortgage that could result in a foreclosure, wiping out the second mortgagee's position.

☐ It is a method of lawfully avoiding usury limitations (at least under court decisions rendered to date). The second lender may be barred by the applicable usury law from charging the lender's desired rate on the new money being advanced. By having the borrower pay a single interest rate on the combined loan (which rate is higher than the rate on the existing first mortgage), the lender receives the desired return on the new money without violating the usury ceiling.

[2] Benefits to the Borrower

From the borrower's point of view, the wraparound loan is attractive when he desires to convert into cash some of the appreciated value of his property and he finds that

- He cannot refinance with his present mortgagee because the latter demands too high an interest rate on a new loan; and
- He cannot refinance with another lender because the mortgage bars prepayment.

In such an event, the borrower might be willing to make a straight second mortgage, but, as noted above, many institutional lenders are unwilling to do so, particularly for a long term. In such an event, the wraparound loan provides the solution.

[3] Sources of Wraparound Loans

Any unregulated lender can make wraparound loans without restriction (except that the lender will be subject to the same usury rules as anyone else). Among institutional lenders, the following are the main sources of wraparound loans:

☐ *Life insurance companies.* Since such companies are subject to state regulation, the rules will vary depending upon the home state of the company. In New York, for example, wraparound loans are treated as second mortgages and are therefore subject to the so-called basket provision, which permits a life insurance company to invest up to 5 percent of its assets in subordinate investments. In general, life insurance companies are a good source of wraparound loans, particularly for longer terms.

☐ *Savings institutions.* Mutual savings banks (all of which are state-chartered) and state-chartered savings and loan associations are subject to the rules of their particular jurisdiction. Federally chartered savings associations are subject to regulation by the Federal Home Loan Bank Board (FHLBB). The present rule allows a wraparound mortgage to qualify as a first lien on property if the investment itself qualifies (e.g., up to a 75 percent loan-to-value ratio for commercial property and up to 85 percent for residential). Since federal savings and loan associations can put only 20 percent of their assets into commercial properties, with the balance going into residential properties, they are a better source of loans for apartment buildings than for other types of investments.

☐ *Real estate investment trusts.* Real estate investment trusts (REITs) may make wraparound loans. A problem is that a REIT must distribute at least 95 percent of its taxable income either in the year earned or the subsequent year. Because (as is noted below) a wraparound lender often realizes taxable income without receiving an equivalent amount of cash flow, a REIT can sometimes be caught in a squeeze. The REIT can avoid the problem by either

- Utilizing noncash deductions (such as depreciation from owned property) to reduce total taxable income; or
- Paying out cash from reserves until the wraparound mortgage matures.

☐ *Pension funds.* Pension funds are not specifically barred from wraparound loans. They are subject to the well-known prudent-man rule, but this would not seem to bar wraparound loans as a matter of course.

[4] Legal Considerations for the Lender

No legal complications (except one noted below) exist for the borrower under a wraparound loan; he is liable to pay the full debt service on both the old and new money whether the format is a wraparound or a combination of straight first and second mortgages. The lender, however, must be alert to potential problems. One, already mentioned, is that a court may declare that for purposes of determining usury, it is the lender's return, rather than the borrower's payment, that counts. Two other potential problems are:

☐ *Prepayment of first mortgage.* The new lender must be sure the borrower has no right to prepay the first mortgage, since this would significantly reduce the yield that makes the wraparound attractive to the new lender.

☐ *Payment of debt service.* As already noted, one of the benefits to the wraparound lender is that it actually receives the debt service for the first mortgage and thus can be sure the first mortgagee is not in default. But there is a problem here too. If the new lender is not obligated to make the payments on the first mortgage, the voluntary nature of the payments by the new lender may prevent it from being subrogated to the rights of the first lender in the event of a default under the first mortgage. If such right of subrogation does not exist, the new lender's payments to the first mortgagee may become subordinate to intervening liens by third parties.

On the other hand, lenders dislike the idea that they may have to pay debt service on the first mortgage even after the borrower has defaulted on the wraparound loan. One possible solution is to make the second lender's obligation to pay debt service on the first mortgage terminate upon any default by the borrower under the wraparound loan.

Note that the borrower has a concern here also. He wants to be sure that the second lender in fact does make the payments on the first mortgage. So it is in the borrower's interest to have the wraparound loan specifically obligate the new lender to pay the debt service on the original loan. And both borrower and new lender should seek to have the first mortgage provide that if any default occurs under the first mortgage, both will be notified and given the opportunity to cure the default.

[5] The Economics of Wraparounds

Wraparound mortgage analysis can be highly complex. The reason is that the three distinct components of wraparound loans (dollars, term of the loan, and amortization) create an almost unlimited number of possible combinations. Specifically,

- The wrap may involve additional dollars or no new dollars.
- The term of the wrap loan can be shorter, longer, or simultaneous with that of the underlying loan.
- Amortization (repayment) of the new funds can occur during all or any portion of the term of the wrap loan.

In most cases, a wraparound loan will involve additional dollars being advanced by the new lender. In the example that follows, the wraparound loan also has a longer term than the underlying loan and will be amortized throughout its life.

> *Example:* Assume the owner of a commercial property obtained a $2.5 million loan in 1970 at an 8.5 percent interest rate, 9.7 percent constant, for twenty-five years. (See Table 6.4, Section A.) At the end of eight years, he wishes to refinance and so pull out (as tax-free loan proceeds) some of the appreciated value of the property.

He arranges a wraparound loan for $3 million at 9 percent interest, 9.7 percent constant for thirty years. As shown in Table 6.4, Section B, the borrower receives $831,400 of new money; this costs him an additional $48,100 a year in debt service plus an additional thirteen years of debt-service payments (because the loan term has been extended).

Consider the position of the new lender. As Table 6.4, Section C, shows, the interest return on the new money is 10.4 percent ($87,100 in annual interest on new money advanced of $831,400). However, the actual cash received by the new lender in the first year is only $48,100, or a cash yield of 5.7 percent. The difference of $39,000 represents interest accrued by the new lender, which will not be received until the underlying loan is paid off.

Table 6.4, Section D, shows what happens in the second year of the wrap loan. Note that while the underlying loan has been reduced in amount (because of the amortization payments in year 1), the balance (representing the new loan) has increased by $39,000—the amount of accrued *interest* from year 1. As a result, both the interest yield and the cash yield decline slightly, as they will continue to do until the underlying loan is fully repaid.

In short, the wraparound (new) lender is saying to the borrower, "If you will permit me to realize an above-market interest rate by utilizing a wraparound loan, then I agree that a portion of the annual interest can be accrued until the first mortgage has been repaid, at which time the entire debt service will be payable to me." This creates additional risk for the new lender since it is increasing its investment in an aging property; it also may create problems of cash flow (as noted above for REITs) since more taxable income is being earned than cash flow is being received.

TABLE 6.4 Wraparound Financing: Interest and Cash Return on New Money

A. Original loan: $2.5 million; 8.5%; 25 years made in 1970

1979 balance	$2,168,600
Debt service per year	$241,550

B. New wraparound loan: $3 million; 9%; 30 years

New funds advanced	$831,400
Annual debt service	$289,650
Increased debt service	$48,100

C. Year 1 (Year 9 of the underlying loan) ($000)

	Amount	*Cash Payment*	*Interest*	*Principal*
Wrap loan	$3,000.0	$289.7	$269.1	$20.6
Underlying	2,168.6	241.6	182.0	59.6
New money	831.4	48.1	87.1	(39.0)

Interest yield on new money	10.4%
Cash yield on new money	5.7%

D. Year 2 (Year 10 of the underlying loan) ($000)

	Amount	*Cash Payment*	*Interest*	*Principal*
Wrap loan	$2,979.5	$289.7	$267.2	$22.5
Underlying	2,109.0	241.6	176.7	64.9
New money (plus accrued interest)	870.5	48.1	90.5	(42.4)

Interest yield on new money	10.3%
Cash yield on new money	5.5%

6.11 LEASEHOLD FINANCING

[1] In General

Leasehold mortgage financing is a special form of junior or secondary financing. The developer or investor leases the property from its owner and then mortgages his leasehold interest. The interest of the leasehold lender is subordinate to the interest of the fee owner (lessor of the property). The fee owner, of course, may agree to subordinate his interest, but in that case, the leasehold mortgage becomes the equivalent of a fee mortgage.

The leasehold mortgage is of relatively recent origin, having come into general use only after World War II. Developers (and investors) have three motivations for using leasehold financing:

☐ *Landowner will not sell.* Much high-priced land is held by families or trusts that will never sell because they regard land as the best protection against continued inflation and because tremendous capital gains taxes would be payable. Consequently, a developer may have no choice but to take a long-term lease and raise his financing via a leasehold loan.

☐ *Less equity required.* Even when the landowner will consider a sale, the developer may not be able to afford to buy. By leasing, he eliminates the need for any equity outlay for land. In addition, tax-deductible ground rent is substituted for debt service on a mortgage that otherwise would be used to finance the land purchase; such debt service would be deductible only to the extent it represented interest.

☐ *Higher financing obtainable.* Finally, a developer or investor who owns the land to begin with may decide to split it into fee and leasehold in order to increase the potential financing. (See below.)

[a] Sources of Leasehold Financing

A leasehold mortgage is a form of junior financing because the lender's claim is subordinate to the landowner's right to receive the ground rental; that is, the lender

- Takes the risk that a default by the lessee may result in a termination of the lease, thus wiping out the lender's security.
- Assumes the obligation, in the event the lender takes over the property, of paying rent to the landowner.

Nevertheless, mortgage lenders have little hesitancy about making leasehold mortgages on prime properties (usually at an interest rate from one-quarter to one-half percent above a comparable fee mortgage). Experience has shown that, with a properly drawn ground lease to protect the lender, there is little significant added risk. The major leasehold lenders are insurance companies and the larger commercial and savings banks; these normally are subject to statutory limits on the types of leasehold loans they may make.

For example, the New York Insurance Law requires that the unexpired term of the ground lease be not less than twenty-one years, including options to renew that the lender itself can exercise. In addition, the leasehold loan must be fully amortized by the time 80 percent of the lease term has expired. (Thus, if a developer negotiates a thirty-year ground lease, a New York institutional lender is limited to a twenty-four-year self-amortizing loan.)

An additional complication would arise if the landowner mortgaged his fee interest. If he then defaulted under the fee mortgage, that lender might wipe out the leasehold in foreclosing against the fee, thus eliminating the leasehold lender's security. Consequently, most institutional lenders are barred from making a loan in this situation.

A developer or investor who is contemplating leasehold financing must be aware of—and prepared to satisfy—the lender's special concerns in this type of loan. The lender's concerns fall into two categories: economic risk and legal risk.

[b] Economic Risk in Leasehold Financing

In any mortgage loan, the lender takes the risk that the income property supporting the loan may throw off insufficient net operating income to service the loan. In the case of a leasehold, a major additional item of expense to the lessee is, of course, the ground rental.

Consequently, the lender may be uncomfortable with the economic risk created by

☐ Ground rentals that step up in fixed amounts and could eliminate much of the lessee's operating income during the lease term.

☐ Ground rentals that are subject to other adjustments not related to land values. For example, if the ground rent is to increase in accordance with changes in the Consumer Price Index, rentals could rise sharply even though the lessee is unable to raise his income from the property (i.e., from subleases to the occupancy tenants).

☐ Any other provisions in the ground lease (e.g., requiring the lessee to provide additional insurance coverage at the lessor's demand) that could sharply increase the lessee's costs.

[c] Legal Risks in Leasehold Financing

Legal risks fall into two categories:

- Risk arising from provisions in the ground lease that may result in a termination of the lease
- Risk arising from lease provisions that restrict the lessee's freedom to use the leased premises for the maximum production of income

☐ *Lease termination risks.* Two types exist:

- *Termination by default.* If the lessee fails to pay rent or otherwise perform his lease obligations, the lessor may be entitled to terminate the lease, thus wiping out the lender's security. To protect itself, the leasehold lender normally insists that the lease provide that the lender must be given notice of any defaults by the lessee, must have the opportunity to cure such defaults, and if for any reason the lease is terminated, the lender is entitled to a new lease in its own name upon curing of any defaults.

- *Failure to renew.* The other type of termination risk is the failure to exercise a renewal option given in the lease. Even when the lease term is longer than the mortgage term (the usual case), the mortgagee may insist upon the right to exercise the renewal option because if it takes over the lease, addition of the renewal term may make the leasehold more salable.

☐ *Leasehold usage risks.* These risks may arise from any lease provisions that restrict the use of the leasehold by the lessee (or by the lender, if it takes over). To reduce or eliminate these risks, the lender normally will require that the lease provide that

- The lessee may mortgage, assign, or sublet the leased premises.
- The use of the land is unrestricted.
- A condemnation award or insurance proceed will be used to restore the premises.

A smart developer or investor will seek to have these provisions put into the ground lease, when originally negotiated, to minimize the need to amend the lease at a later time when leasehold financing is sought.

Example of Leasehold Financing. As noted above, a developer or investor may deliberately split a fee simple interest into a separate fee and leasehold in order to increase the amount of financing that can be obtained. Tables 6.5 and 6.6 show how the increased financing is obtained. In Table 6.5, a single interest in fee simple exists. The property owner is able to obtain a 75 percent first mortgage at 9.75 percent constant. Since the free-and-clear return (i.e., the net operating income as a percentage of total investment) is 10 percent, only very slight upside leverage exists and the cash-flow return is 10.7 percent.

TABLE 6.5 First Mortgage

Total investment (i.e., value)	$7,390,000
Less: Mortgage (75%)	5,540,000
Equity	$1,850,000
Net operating income	$739,000
Less: Debt service (8.5% interest, 9.75% constant)	540,150
Cash flow	$198,850
Cash-flow return (cash flow as percentage of equity)	10.7%

In Table 6.6, the property owner has created separate fee and leasehold interests and mortgaged each one. As a result, his total equity requirement is reduced by $190,000 even though the investor retains complete ownership as before (only now his ownership is via separate fee and leasehold interests). The cost to the investor is merely a fractional decline in the cash-flow return (from 10.7 percent to 10.5 percent). Note that the fee mortgage in Table 6.6 carries a somewhat lower constant than that in Table 6.5. The reason is that it is somewhat more secure than the mortgage in Table 6.5 because only a portion of the cash flow is needed to service the Table 6.6 mortgage. Thus there is a cushion (consisting of the balance of the cash flow) that protects the Table 6.6 mortgagee in the event of a decline in cash flow. The leasehold mortgage, because there is a slightly higher risk than a fee mortgage, has an interest rate one-quarter percent higher than the fee mortgage in Table 6.6.

For another example of leasehold financing, see 6.15[1].

TABLE 6.6 Fee Mortgage and Leasehold Mortgage

Total investment		$7,390,000
Fee mortgage	$ 800,000	
Leasehold mortgage	4,930,000	
Less: Total financing		5,730,000
Equity		$1,660,000
Net operating income		$739,000
Debt service, fee mortgage (8.5% interest, 9% constant)	$72,000	
Debt service, leasehold mortgage (8.75% interest, 10% constant)	493,000	
Less: Total debt service		565,000
Cash flow		$174,000
Cash-flow return		10.5%

[2] Subleasehold Financing

A more complex form of leasehold financing involves use of a sublease. This arrangement permits two first mortgages to be made in addition to the groundlease and thus increases the leverage to the investor. The following steps are used to accomplish this type of financing:

1. The fee owner leases the property (and conveys title to the improvements) to prime tenant. Prime tenant actually is a dummy, having no function except to create a leasehold interest.

2. Prime tenant subleases to subtenant, which is the actual operating position. The subrental is equal to the sum of the ground rental plus the debt service that prime tenant will pay on the leasehold mortgage it will execute in Step 4 below.

3. Subtenant enters into space leases (actually sub-subleases), which generate the actual rental income from the property.

4. Prime tenant mortgages the leasehold to institution *A*; this leasehold mortgage is subordinate both to the fee interest and to the subleasehold.

5. Subtenant mortgages the subleasehold to institution *B* (the subleasehold mortgage).

At the outset, note that both institutions *A* and *B* have first mortgages, one on the leasehold and one on the subleasehold. This avoids any violation of regulations prohibiting second mortgages. Institution *A* is willing to subordinate its mortgage to the fee since it is permitted to make leasehold mortgages and because the value of the leasehold supports the loan (see below for the reason for subordination to the subleasehold). In estimating the value of the leasehold, institution *A* reasons as follows:

- So long as the sublease is not in default, the subrental is sufficient to pay the debt service on the leasehold mortgage.
- If the sublease is in default, the leasehold interest can reach the space rentals direct and thus be able to continue servicing the leasehold mortgage.

So institution *A* values the leasehold as if there were no sublease. Result: It gives a 75 percent mortgage on the combined value of the leasehold and the subleasehold.

Institution *B*, on the other hand, has its mortgage secured only by the subleasehold and thus only the value of the subleasehold can be considered. Since the subrental is limited to the ground rental plus the amount necessary to service the leasehold mortgage (which represents 75 percent of the total value of the leasehold and subleasehold), the remaining income to the sublease, when capitalized, should represent the balance of the 25 percent value of the two leaseholds. So institution *B*, giving a 75 percent loan on the value of the subleasehold, is loaning approximately 18 percent of the total value of the two leaseholds (i.e., 75 percent of 25 percent). This means that subtenant and prime tenant (really the same party) are obtaining 93 percent financing.

Should institution *B* worry that the prime tenant could default under the leasehold mortgage, permitting institution *A* to foreclose and wipe out the subleasehold? No, because institution *A* has agreed to subordinate its leasehold mortgage to the subleasehold. If a foreclosure of the prime lease occurs, the subleasehold would continue.

It is easy to see how the creation of a separate leasehold and subleasehold permits two simultaneous first mortgages. What is not so easy to see is how the same property can support a 75 percent loan in one case, and a 93 percent loan in another. The answer is this: In the latter case, institution *B* is taking on a much greater economic risk than it normally would because the subleasehold mortgage is secured by the most exposed portion of the income stream. When space rentals are collected, the ground rental must be paid first, then the leasehold rental, and only the excess belongs to the subleasehold. The impact of any decline in rental income will fall fully on the sublease position. A decline of 25 percent in rental income would wipe out the subleasehold and the subleasehold mortgage with it.

In the actual case described above, institution *B* apparently was able to secure an appraisal sufficient to justify the high-risk loan.

6.12 PURCHASE-MONEY FINANCING

[1] In General

In a purchase-money transaction, the seller accepts, in lieu of cash, the buyer's note for the unpaid price secured by a mortgage on the property being sold. Not only does this provide immediate financing for the buyer, but it also creates a simultaneous investment for the seller secured by property with which he is intimately familiar. In addition, the return to the seller (interest on the mortgage) is often higher than he would otherwise obtain in a savings bank or other investment.

The specific terms of the mortgage can be varied in a great many ways to make the deal attractive to both parties. Here are the major considerations:

☐ *Loan-to-value ratio.* Obviously, the seller will want the buyer to put in as much cash as possible (usually, a minimum of 10 percent); otherwise, the buyer may consider himself more of a tenant than an owner.

☐ *Interest rate.* This normally will reflect the bargaining strengths of the parties. A seller particularly anxious to dispose of property will agree to charge a below-market interest rate; an equally anxious buyer may be willing to pay a premium rate. In some states, e.g., New York, interest rates on purchase-money mortgages are not subject to usury ceilings, and this will make them more attractive to sellers.

☐ *Term of the mortgage.* Here, there may be a problem, since the seller often is not willing to wait twenty or twenty-five years for his money, while the buyer cannot afford the high monthly payments that a short-term (five- to ten-year) mortgage would require. One solution is the balloon mortgage, with monthly payments geared to a twenty-year (or more) schedule but with the loan to mature in ten or fewer years. Consequently, at maturity there will be a large unpaid balance (the balloon).

☐ *Prepayment.* There often is both a right and duty to prepay. The buyer usually has the right to prepay at any time without penalty if he can arrange better institutional financing when money becomes easier. The seller may insist that the buyer must refinance whenever an institutional loan becomes available at or below a certain interest rate, and pay off the purchase-money mortgage balance at that time.

☐ *Right to assign.* Suppose the buyer resells in a few years? Can he sell subject to the purchase-money mortgage (i.e., transfer it without the present seller's consent)? If the seller's consent is necessary, must he give it if the new buyer meets reasonable credit standards? Or can the present seller absolutely insist that his mortgage be paid off on a subsequent resale? This is a matter to be negotiated between the parties.

To this point, we have assumed that a purchase-money mortgage takes the place of an institutional first mortgage. But just as common is the situation where the seller has an existing first mortgage that he can transfer to the buyer but the latter cannot make up in cash the difference between the existing mortgage and the sales price. Here, a purchase-money second mortgage can be used to fill the gap.

> *Example:* Assume a selling price of $50,000, subject to an existing $25,000 first mortgage. The seller may be willing to take back a purchase-money second mortgage for $12,500 with the buyer putting up $12,500 in cash. The term of such a second mortgage usually is shorter than if the mortgage was the senior lien, not only because there is more risk in a second mortgage, but because the amount is smaller and can be paid off over a shorter period.

Another major use of the purchase-money second mortgage is to permit a transaction to be closed on terms satisfactory to both buyer and seller. It has often been used by syndicators when acquiring properties for syndication. A standing or low-interest purchase-money mortgage makes it possible to produce a cash flow from the property high enough so that, after the syndicator's share, enough remains for the other investors to make the deal attractive.

Example: A syndicator has been negotiating with the owner of an office building in a prime commercial area. The property is subject to an existing first mortgage for $1.2 million and has a net cash flow of $45,000 after expenses and debt service. After hard bargaining, the parties remain $100,000 apart, the owner asking $1.8 million, the buyer offering $1.7 million. At the buyer's price, he must put up $500,000 cash, on which the $45,000 cash flow would return 9 percent. Any more cash invested would mean the property "won't show"—that is, the return will be inadequate to permit syndication.

At this point, the use of a purchase-money second mortgage is proposed. If the seller would take a much smaller down payment, say, $150,000 in cash, the purchaser is willing to pay $1.85 million for the property, or $50,000 more than the original asking price. The gap of $500,000 between the lower down payment and the higher purchase price will be covered by a ten-year standing purchase-money second mortgage with interest at 6 percent.

As the following tables indicate, the property now "shows" the return has risen sharply.

TABLE 6.7 Seller's Original Proposal

Purchase price	$1,800,000
Less: Existing mortgage	1,200,000
Cash required	$ 600,000
Cash flow	$45,000
Return on $600,000 cash investment	7.5%

TABLE 6.8 Purchase-Money (PM) Mortgage Proposal

Purchase price		$1,850,000
Less: Existing mortgage	$1,200,000	
PM mortgage	500,000	1,700,000
Cash required		$ 150,000
Cash flow before PM mortgage interest		$45,000
Less: 6% on PM mortgage		30,000
Revised cash flow		$15,000
Return on $150,000 cash investment		10%

The 6 percent interest rate appears a bargain, but the seller is receiving an additional $50,000 in purchase price. If necessary, the seller can be offered an escalation (step-up) interest rate. Alternatively, the no-amortization period can be reduced. All of these matters are for negotiation. Of course, the mortgage will have to be paid off within ten years, but the buyer makes this type of deal on the assumption that rising values will enable him to pay the mortgage out of future appreciation.

So far, we have considered only the financing consequences of using a purchase-money mortgage. What about the tax effects? Based on our example:

☐ *For the buyer,* the purchase-money mortgage produces an additional interest deduction each year of $30,000. Assuming the buyer is in the 50 percent bracket, this is worth $15,000 in tax savings.

☐ *For the seller,* since the purchase-money mortgage is a standing mortgage —payable all at once at the end of its term—the capital gains tax on this portion of the gain is deferred for ten years.

[2] Trading Purchase-Money Paper

Paper money, as we use the term here, refers to purchase-money notes taken back by a seller in place of cash. Purchase-money financing has always been important in real estate. In times such as these, when interest rates are high and lenders have turned more conservative and are imposing stricter requirements for loans, sellers often find that the only way a sale can be made (particularly in the case of raw land or speculative properties) is by taking back a substantial purchase-money note.

However, once having received the note, the seller should not regard himself as locked into a fixed-return investment until the note is paid off. Smart brokers and lenders know how to utilize paper money to get the most mileage both for the equity investor and for the person (or retirement fund) that is income-oriented.

[a] Trading Paper Money

To understand how this technique operates, consider the following example:

Example: Johnson sold his motel in 1974 for $520,000, with $75,000 down and with the purchaser taking over an existing $295,000 first mortgage. The balance of $150,000 was represented by a contract for deed (a form of land contract), payable over seventeen years at an 8.5 percent interest rate.

When approached by a broker, Johnson offered to sell the contract for deed at a discounted price of $88,000 to yield 14.5 percent, the discount reflecting the somewhat risky nature of the security as well as current interest rates. The broker had as a client a retirement trust which, among other assets, had $57,000 in cash and a $31,000 first trust deed earning 8 percent and maturing in nine years. The trust being tax-exempt, it was interested only in before-tax yields.

The broker swapped Johnson's contract for deed for the retirement trust's first trust note and cash. Both the note and contract interest were assigned with recourse; that is, each assignor remained personally liable in the event of a default in payments. *The results:* Johnson converted long-term paper with a below-average yield into $50,000 in cash, plus a note due to mature eight years earlier than the contract interest given up. True, he discounted his own paper very substantially but the amount of the discount probably represented a profit he would not have realized on the original motel sale had he insisted on all cash.

The retirement trust almost doubled the yield on the paper they held and also made a profitable investment of their excess cash.

[b] Buying With Paper Money

Consider another case. Suppose an investment has turned out very well, enabling the investor to sell at a profit of $50,000 after a few years. The gain is represented entirely by a purchase-money second mortgage, calling for 8 percent annual interest for five years, after which the entire principal amount will become due. The investor is reporting gain under the installment method.

At this point, there is an annual income of $4,000 a year, fully taxable as ordinary income, representing the mortgage interest. The investor probably cannot sell the mortgage for cash except at an unacceptable discount; in addition, the sale would trigger a capital gains tax on the entire installment sale profit.

One possibility is to use the purchase-money paper as a down payment on a new property. Suppose the investor finds property that can be purchased for $150,000 with $30,000 down. The investor could offer the seller the $50,000 purchase-money mortgage for the down payment, in effect giving it to him at a 40 percent discount. However, this would still constitute a disposition of the paper for tax purposes, triggering payment of the entire remaining capital gains tax on the original sale.

[c] Borrowing on Paper Money

A further alternative is to use the purchase-money note as collateral for a loan. For example, an investor might be able to borrow $30,000 at 12 percent interest for five years, pledging the $50,000 note as security. Since his interest income on the mortgage is $4,000 a year and the interest cost of the new loan is $3,600 per year, he continues to receive an annual income of $400 on the mortgage. And the $30,000 loan can be used as down payment on new property, which we will assume costs $150,000, has an annual cash flow of 8 percent, and has excellent prospects of appreciating at a rate of 3 percent a year.

Table 6.9 illustrates the investor's position before and after acquiring the new property.

By this simple device of using a purchase-money mortgage as collateral for a loan, the investor has turned a financial disadvantage (i.e., the receipt of "paper" instead of cash when he sold his property) into an advantage (he raised cash without having to pay an immediate tax on his profit on the sale). As a result, he was able to add to his net spendable income of $28,000 an annual equity buildup of $2,400 (through mortgage amortization on the new property) and a projected appreciation of $4,500 a year. His net equity income, in total, will rise from $2,800 to $9,700 a year if everything works out as planned.

TABLE 6.9 How Investor Fares Before and After Acquiring New Property

	Before Acquisition		*After Acquisition*	
Net interest from mortgage	$4,000		$ 400	
Cash flow (8% of $30,000)	0		2,400	
Income tax @ 30%	1,200		0 *	
Net spendable income		$2,800		$2,800
Principal buildup (amortization)		0		2,400
Growth		0		4,500
Net equity income		$2,800		$9,700

* By acquiring depreciable real estate, the investor is able to generate cash flow without having to pay any current income tax.

6.13 TAX-EXEMPT FINANCING

[1] In General

Tax-exempt financing has become a major source of funds for commercial real estate development.[3] The rates for tax-exempt bonds generally are 2 to 2.5 percentage points less than conventional financing. Thus, if current mortgage rates for conventional loans are in the 12.5 to 13 percent range, the rates for industrial development bonds (IDBs) would be in the 10.5 to 11 percent range.

Here is an example of the benefits achieved from an issue of industrial development bonds (sometimes called industrial revenue bonds or IRBs).

Assume a project qualifies for a conventional loan of $1 million at 12.75 percent with a twenty-eight-year amortization schedule. The annual constant (payment of principal and interest) is .1313. However, under a tax-exempt with a rate of 10.75 percent for twenty-five years, the constant is .1155. Thus, the annual payment differences are as follows:

	Conventional	*Tax-Exempt*
Amount	$1,000,000	$1,000,000
Constant	× .1313	× .1155
Annual payment	$131,300	$115,500

The differential between these two examples is approximately $15,800. Since most conventional long-term loans have no prepayment for the first ten years of the loan, approximately $158,000 is saved in that period. Or, in other words, approximately $15,800 per annum in additional cash flow after debt service is produced.

[3] Its use in residential construction was sharply restricted by the Mortgage Subsidy Bond Tax Act of 1980, Pub. L. No. 96-499, 94 Stat. 2599, 42 U.S.C.A. § 1753.

[a] How Tax Exemption Is Created

Tax-exempt financing encompasses all debt obligations (notes, bonds, and mortgages) issued by a state or municipality (or one of their authorized agencies). No federal income tax need be paid by the recipient of interest paid by the state or municipality on such obligations.

The basis for the tax exemption is our federal structure, which recognizes both the national government and the state governments as being sovereign. Thus, the obligations issued by one type of government are not taxable by the other. However, this tax exemption exists only so long as an obligation is issued for a public purpose. A Supreme Court decision in 1875 interpreted the meaning of "public purpose" to exclude public financing of private projects. However, following the Great Depression of the 1930s, some states, beginning with Mississippi in 1936, revived the idea of industrial bond financing, and this time, the courts were much more liberal in defining what a public purpose was.

Today twenty-three states permit the issuance of general obligation bonds (supported by the issuer's full faith and credit) while forty-eight states permit revenue bonds (which are secured only from the revenues of the particular project). About half the states limit tax-exempt financing to industrial purposes, while the other half permit commercial purposes as well.

The justification for all industrial financing—that is, the public purpose—is to encourage industrial or commercial development and so increase employment opportunities in the particular locality.

[b] Federal Limits on Tax-Exempt Issues

As tax-exempt financing spread, the federal government began to count up its tax losses. So, in 1968 Congress added Section 103 to the Internal Revenue Code. This created the concept of the industrial development bond, which is defined as any publicly issued bond or other obligation where there is a clearly identifiable private interest, such as an industrial plant financed with the proceeds of the bond issue. Interest paid by the state or municipality on such bonds is taxable unless the bond falls within one of the exemptions set forth in Section 103. These exemptions are based either on the size or the purpose of the bond issue. Interest is exempt on

- Issues of $1 million or less.
- Issues up to $10 million if the private firm benefiting from the issue agrees to a six-year capital expenditure program (and this limit is raised to $20 million if the financing is in connection with an Urban Development Action Grant program).
- Any bond issue, without dollar limit, to finance any of six specified purposes: (1) residential property; (2) sports facilities; (3) convention or trade show facilities; (4) airports, docks, mass commuting facilities, or parking facilities; (5) air- or water-pollution-control facilities; (6) facilities for the furnishing of water. (Over one-half of tax-exempt financing in recent years has gone for pollution-control facilities.)

[c] How to Set Up Tax-Exempt Financing

By means of a tax-exempt bond, note, or mortgage, a state or municipal government agrees to provide inexpensive financing in order to attract industry or commerce to a particular locale. The proceeds of the public financing are used to acquire and improve land for a particular user (industrial plant, warehouse, etc.).

The property may be net-leased to the user, with rental payments equal to the debt service on the tax-exempt issue. At the end of the lease term, the user is permitted to purchase the property for a nominal sum, say, $100. Alternatively, the state or municipal government may sell the land to the user under a long-term installment contract, with installment payments used to service the debt.

In either case, the user obtains a facility through the use of public financing and, because of the tax-exempt feature, incurs a much lower overall cost for starting up operations. While most tax-exempt financing has gone for industrial purposes, much has been used for commercial or retail uses. For example, tax-free financing has been used to construct hamburger outlets for McDonald's, retail stores for K-Mart Corp., as well as for racquetball clubs, bowling alleys, restaurants, and shopping centers.

A business firm or developer interested in tax-exempt financing in a particular locale must first identify the local development authority, which may be known as an economic development authority, community improvement corporation, or industrial development authority. Then the enabling statute of the municipality or state must be examined to see if the particular use is eligible for public financing.

[d] Using a Mortgage Instead of a Bond

While most tax-exempt financing takes the form of a bond issue, with the bonds sold to institutional or private investors, increasing use is being made of the tax-exempt loan or mortgage, with the funds being provided by a bank or other institutional lender. These transactions are identical with normal loan or mortgage financing, except that the interest received by the lender is tax-exempt and consequently a lower interest rate is charged. The borrower is technically the state or municipal government; in fact, the debt service on the mortgage will come from rents or installment payments made by the user of the facility.

[2] Tax-Increment Financing

Tax-increment financing (TIF) is likely to become more important in the next few years as federal financing programs for real estate are decreased or eliminated. TIF is to public financing what the mortgage is to private financing—in both cases, funds are advanced for new construction with repayment (debt service) projected from the income produced by the new project.

In TIF financing, a municipality floats a tax-exempt bond issue, with interest and principal payments on the bonds to be paid out of the additional (incremental) taxes to be generated from a real estate project built with the borrowed funds.

In effect, TIF creates a public and private partnership through which the municipality and the developer share the risk of a new or redevelopment project.

Tax-increment financing may be used only when the particular state has authorized this type of financing. (The only federal involvement concerns Internal Revenue Code requirements for exempting the interest from federal income tax.) The TIF program began in 1947 in Minnesota, but did not become popular until the 1960s when it was used in connection with urban renewal. Of the thirty-seven states that now have TIF laws, over 75 percent only authorized the program since 1975. In many states, TIF is used solely or primarily for industrial and commercial redevelopment, and for public works, such as parking and sewage plants. Since no uniform pattern for TIF law exists, a developer must read the state statute carefully before seeking to utilize TIF.

Example: Wisconsin's TIF law permits a municipality to include up to 5 percent of its total assessed valuation in a TIF district. The city of Madison, with about a $2 billion tax base, thus has about $100 million available as TIF venture capital. It is using $1.4 million of that to provide financing for a lakefront condominium project on a 2.2-acre site of an old brewery. Before floating the bond issue, the city council was required by state law to declare the site at least 25 percent blighted and to approve the project plan by a three-fourths vote. The bonds took the form of general obligation bonds (since that time, Wisconsin has switched to a type of revenue bond for TIF).

The city used the $1.43 million raised through the bond issue to write down the land costs, to clear the site of old buildings, and to adapt the site from industrial to residential use. Construction financing was then provided by nine local lenders, formed into the Madison Downtown Consortium. And the consortium also agreed to provide end loans at 13.5 percent interest, but this commitment was never funded because buyers of the condominiums were able to obtain their own financing.

6.14 NONMORTGAGE FINANCING

[1] Land Contracts

In parts of the United States, a substantial portion of residential real estate is sold by means of land contracts (also called contracts for deed or conditional sales contracts). Under this type of agreement, a small down payment, frequently 10 percent or less, is made by the buyer with the balance of the purchase price payable in installments over a period of years. Until all or most of the purchase price is paid, the seller retains title and gives the purchaser possession only. (By contrast, when a mortgage or deed of trust is used, legal title passes to the buyer.)

The advantage to the seller in the use of land contracts is that in the event the buyer defaults in making the installment payments, the seller may declare the contract forfeited and recover possession of the property much more quickly than under a foreclosure proceeding, which would be required in the case of a mortgage. And unless the state in which the property is located has legislated to the contrary, the seller may keep all of the payments made by the buyer prior to the default even though the total paid may far exceed the rental value of the property during the period of possession.

The interest of the seller, known as a vendor's interest, is a marketable investment in states where land contracts are popular. Normally, the sale is at a discount ranging from 10 to 30 percent of face value, thus substantially increasing the purchaser's yield to maturity. This yield will be further increased whenever a contract is paid off by the property buyer prior to maturity.

[2] Commercial Term Loans

Specialized properties, such as industrial plants, normally are considered overimproved if they are offered on the market for an alternative use (i.e., a use other than the original one). Consequently, the prudent lender, when appraising such a property as mortgage collateral, must do so on the lower value basis of a possible alternative use, and the potential borrower may discover that the collateral will not support needed borrowings.

A strong company could solve this problem by seeking a "credit" loan, based solely on its balance sheet and earnings history. But many good companies may find that they are unqualified for long-term unsecured loans. The requisites for such borrowing may be a relatively high credit rating, a strong earnings picture sufficient to pay off both interest and amortization with ease, and various desirable balance-sheet ratios.

Commercial or industrial firms who cannot be considered credit firms may find solutions for their borrowing problems in intermediate-term commercial loans. This type of loan, which should be amortized in ten to fifteen years, may be structured in a number of ways. In all likelihood, it will be a hybrid financial package, based on the collateral of real property, of machinery and equipment, and on a cautious corporate cash-flow analysis.

As an example of the use of a commercial term loan by a specialized borrower, consider the case history of a soft-drink company, ABC Bottling Corp. High sugar prices had eroded recent after-tax income, as well as the company's rating. Nevertheless, the company believed that its problems were behind it, and it was determined to build a new bottling plant. The estimated cost of the improvement was $4,445,000, to be built on land acquired for $625,000, for a total cost of $5,070,000.

The original lender's appraiser rightly concluded that it could value the proposed property only on the basis of its earnings under alternative use. However, after assuming liberal rentals for the office space and for the production facility as a warehouse, the capitalized value of the proposed property reached $3,875,000. An 80 percent loan would yield ABC Bottling only $3,100,000, less than two-thirds of the $5 million loan sought.

The mortgage banker servicing ABC Bottling decided that he could design a loan from an intermediate-term commercial lender for the full $5 million.

[a] Cash-Flow Analysis

The first requisite for an intermediate-term commercial loan is a payments structure that can be serviced by a conservative forecast of the borrower's cash flow. It must be remembered that interest payments are made from pretax income, whereas amortization must be derived from post-tax cash flow. Prudent

TABLE 6.10 Ten-Year Depreciated Collateral Value and Loan Balance Schedule

ABC BOTTLING CORPORATION
($000)

Year-End	*Improvements (20-Year Life)*	*Land*	*Total Real Estate*	*Total Machinery and Equipment**	*Aggregate Collateral Value*	*Loan Balance*	*Loan/ Collateral Ratio*
0	$3,250	$625	$3,875	$2,200	$6,075	$5,000	82.3%
1	3,087	625	3,712	1,945	5,657	4,667	82.5
2	2,925	625	3,550	1,690	5,240	4,333	82.7
3	2,762	625	3,387	1,435	4,822	4,000	83.0
4	2,600	625	3,225	1,180	4,405	3,667	83.2
5	2,437	625	3,062	925	3,987	3,333	83.6
6	2,275	625	2,900	740	3,640	3,000	82.4
7	2,112	625	2,737	555	3,292	2,667	81.0
8	1,950	625	2,575	370	2,945	2,334	79.3
9	1,787	625	2,412	185	2,597	2,001	77.1
10	1,625	625	2,250	0	2,250	1,668	74.1

* Machinery and equipment to be depreciated over 5- and 10-year lives.

lending policy requires that post-tax cash amount to at least 150 percent of the annual obligation for principal retirement. The analysis persuaded the potential lender that while the recent earnings record of ABC Bottling indicated that it could not support a ten-year repayment schedule ($500,000 per year), it could support a fifteen-year loan ($333,333 per year).

The mechanics of this analysis are summarized below. For each of five preceding years, the lender must determine:

(A) Pre-tax earnings	+
(B) Less: Interest on proposed $5 million loan	−
(C) Yields: Pre-tax pro forma income	+
(D) Less: Taxes at 50 percent	−
(E) Yields: Net pro forma income	+
(F) Plus: Depreciation and noncash charges	+
(G) Yields: Cash flow available to repay principal loan	×

For ABC Bottling Corp., Line (G), Cash Flow, showed the following results:

($ thousands)

1970	*1971*	*1972*	*1973*	*1974*
765	810	835	690	485

[b] Analyzing the Collateral

However, $485,000 is barely 150 percent of the amortization requirement of $333,333 per year. Despite the borrower's forecasts, prudence dictated an analysis of long-term collateral available to support the loan.

The lender was initially willing to undertake the same $3 million mortgage offered by the conventional mortgage lender since this amounts to 80 percent of the economic value of the new construction. An additional collateral package amounting to at least $2.2 million, consisting of machinery, equipment, and rolling stock, was then assembled to support the additional $2 million sought.

Since different depreciation rates applied to the various elements contained within the collateral, the lender created a total depreciation schedule, in order to compare, year by year, the outstanding value of the loan with the balance of aggregate collateral value. A ten-year summary of this analysis is given in Table 6.10.

The relatively high loan-to-collateral ratios accepted by the lender for the term of the loan reflect its belief in the creditworthiness of the borrower. The bottling company, believing that improved earnings would enable it to negotiate more favorable loans in the future, was able to include in the loan agreement a prepayment program that permitted refinancing at a 4 percent premium in the third year and at no cost by year 7.

Given the current unwillingness of the traditional suppliers of commercial mortgages to make long-term commitments, mortgage bankers and brokers who design reasonable intermediate-term packages may open new opportunities for both borrowers and lenders.

[3] Corporate Financing Techniques

As indicated in the preceding section, new avenues of financing for real estate can open up if the borrower considers his overall situation. For example, here are three short- or intermediate-term corporate financing techniques that sometimes can be used for particular types of real estate, notably fast-food outlets and restaurants, which are as much businesses as they are real estate operations.

☐ *Current line of credit.* A current line of credit normally runs for one year, subject to reconfirmation if the borrower's annual financial statement is satisfactory. Normally it is unsecured and takes the form of thirty-, sixty-, or ninety-day notes, which are automatically rolled over within each one-year period (although the lender has no legal obligation to do so). The notes usually carry a floating interest rate, that is, a rate that moves with the market. They may or may not involve a compensating balance requirement (under which the borrower must maintain a minimum balance on deposit at all times).

The basic advantage of a current line of credit is its simplicity; funds can be obtained merely by a telephone call. However, this extremely short-term credit normally should be used solely to replenish working capital for another short-term use. Food-service operations may use this type of credit to finance equipment acquisitions.

☐ *Revolving credit.* Revolving credit ("revolver") is financing under a formal loan agreement that runs anywhere from fifteen months to five years, although three years is the norm. The lender obligates itself to provide cash on demand, up to the limit set in the agreement. The borrower pays interest only on the money actually advanced, plus a commitment fee for the balance of the credit.

For example, if a revolving credit were for $5 million and the borrower took down $2 million, he would pay interest on that amount and a commitment fee on the $3 million that the lender is obligated to provide upon demand. The borrower may repay and reborrow funds at any time without penalty.

The major advantage of revolving credit is its flexibility; this makes it tailored to a situation where a borrower has to meet obligations on a schedule that cannot be determined in advance, such as, for labor and materials during a construction project. Another advantage is that it is treated as a long-term liability on the balance sheet, and so satisfies the principle of matching liabilities and assets.

The major disadvantage of a revolving credit is the overall interest cost. The interest rate normally floats with the market, and if market rates rise sharply, the borrower may be placed in a cash-flow squeeze with little chance of refinancing.

☐ *Intermediate-term loans.* An intermediate-term loan, with its five- to seven-year life and requirement for amortization, comes closest to standard real estate financing. Amortization may either be a constant self-liquidating format (e.g., 20 percent a year for a five-year loan) or with a balloon payment at maturity (e.g., 10 percent a year for four years and 60 percent at maturity). The interest rate may be floating or fixed, although lenders are likely to avoid fixed-interest loans in a market such as the current one. The loan is evidenced by a term loan agreement that may be as detailed as a mortgage.

Intermediate-term loans, because of their relatively long life, are classified as long-term liabilities and so are appropriate for the financing of long-term assets.

When negotiating any one of these loans, it is important for borrowers to determine the compensating balance requirement since this has an important effect on the true interest rate. For example, an 11.75 percent loan requiring the borrower to maintain a balance in his account equal to 10 percent of the loan actually yields an additional 1.33 percent to the lender, or a total interest cost to the borrower of just over 13 percent.

Since the loans just described normally are unsecured, only companies with strong financial statements can hope to obtain them. These types of financing are appropriate for companies experiencing rapid growth which can anticipate rising cash flows to service the debt.

[4] Letters of Credit

A letter of credit is an agreement in writing by a bank or other lender, made at the request of a customer, that the lender will honor drafts or other demands for payment by third parties, in accordance with the conditions set forth in the agreement. The letter of credit transaction thus involves three parties:

- The *beneficiary,* the person to whom the letter is given so that he will extend credit to

- The *account party,* the person whose obligation is backed by the letter of credit, which is written by
- The *issuer,* a bank or other lender, which undertakes to pay a fixed amount on a certain date in accordance with the conditions of the letter

This is not quite as simple as it sounds. The beneficiary will not accept a letter of credit unless it is equivalent to cash or securities—that is, the letter cannot be hedged with conditions and the credit of the issuer must be unquestioned. For example, a tenant delivers a letter of credit as security under a lease. If the tenant defaults, the landlord wants to be able to convert the letter into cash virtually upon demand. He will not be willing to have payment be conditioned upon proof that a default actually has occurred or any other procedures. In brief, the landlord wishes to be in the same position as if he held cash.

Here are three situations in which letters of credit can play a role:

☐ A long-term lease is about to be executed, and the tenant must put up a substantial security deposit, to be held by the landlord during the term of the lease.

☐ A lender is about to issue a one- or two-year mortgage commitment and wants a substantial good-faith deposit, to be forfeited if the commitment is not exercised.

☐ A builder about to sign a construction contract must put up security that the job will be completed.

In all of these situations, the party having to give the assurance could put up cash. But cash is always expensive and sometimes unavailable. So a number of substitutions for cash are used whenever the obligation is in the nature of a standby or a guarantee. Deposit of negotiable securities is one alternative. An even better one, because it involves the transfer of credit, is use of a letter of credit.

[a] Advantages of the Letter of Credit

To the account party (the borrower), the obvious advantage of a letter of credit is that he need not use his own assets, or pay interest on borrowed funds. His only cost is a relatively small annual fee paid to the issuer. Of course, the account party must have a very high credit rating, or otherwise provide acceptable collateral, in order to obtain the letter of credit.

The advantage to the issuer (lender) is that he collects a fee for an intangible, for example, his credit rating. In most cases, the lender never advances any actual funds. (If funds are advanced, the account party will be charged normal interest.) In addition, the lender's obligations under letters of credit need not be reported as liabilities in its financial statements.

[b] Guidelines for Letters of Credit

Letters of credit are legal instruments and normally will be drafted by legal counsel. But all parties should be aware of some general considerations:

☐ The beneficiary must be sure that the letter of credit is wholly independent of the underlying agreement (lease, mortgage commitment, or contract of sale). As in the case of the lease security deposit discussed above, the beneficiary wants to be able to collect under the letter of credit easily and quickly.

☐ The issuer should take steps to insure that it will not have to pay under the letter of credit until the conditions that trigger the payment actually have occurred.

6.15 HIGH-RATIO FINANCING TECHNIQUES

[1] Component (Split) Financing

The ability to leverage a small equity position by means of high-ratio financing is a prime attraction offered by real estate investments. One of the most popular techniques for achieving leverage is component, or split, financing. The name derives from the fact that in this approach, the land and the improvements are placed under different ownership, and each is financed separately. As a result, the investor is able to achieve one or both of two objectives: (1) reducing the equity requirement; and (2) creating upside financial leverage.

TABLE 6.11 Proposed Project

Projected cost (land + structure)	$3,000,000
Projected value upon completion	$3,600,000
Projected net operating income (NOI)	$540,000
Free and clear return:	
On cost	18%
On value	15%

In discussing the various high-ratio techniques, we will assume a proposed project as set forth in Table 6.11. This could be a newly constructed project, a conversion, or a rehabilitation. Whatever the particular approach, the assumption is made that fairly soon after acquisition, the fair market value of the property has risen 20 percent over original cost. Since long-term financing is based on current market values rather than cost, this gives the investor some leeway in putting together a viable financing package.

[a] Conventional First-Mortgage Loan

If the developer or investor in the project was fortunate, he might be able to obtain a conventional first mortgage for $2.7 million (75 percent of value and 90 percent of cost) at 15 percent interest, 15.36 percent constant for twenty-five years, callable by the lender (i.e., subject to higher interest) after five years. Table 6.12 shows that the required equity then is $300,000 on which the cash-flow

TABLE 6.12 First-Mortgage Loan

Cost of project	$3,000,000
Less: Mortgage (75% of $3.6 million value)	2,700,000
Equity required	$ 300,000
Equity based on $3.6 million value upon completion	$900,000
Net operating income	$540,000
Less: Debt service (15.36% of loan)	415,000
Cash flow	$125,000
Cash-flow return:	
On cost equity of $300,000	41.6%
On value equity of $900,000	13.9%

return is 41.6 percent. If the current value of the property is considered, the equity is $900,000 and the cash-flow return is 13.9 percent.

The investor undoubtedly will assume that future increases in the interest rate (when the loan is negotiated) will be met by increased cash flow; the same would be true if the loan had a fixed interest rate for its entire term but the lender was to receive a share of future rent increases. The 42 percent return on the actual equity, if fully tax sheltered, represents an excellent return and is justified by the risks involved in new construction or rehabilitation.

Nevertheless, the developer is forced to raise $300,000 in equity. Can this amount be reduced?

[b] Fee Mortgage and Leasehold Mortgage

Probably the original creative-financing technique is for the owner to carve a leasehold out of the fee interest while keeping ownership of both fee and leasehold. He then arranges for two separate mortgages, one on each interest. Assume the value of the land is $800,000. The ground rental is set at 15 percent, or $120,000. (In this example, the fee is unsubordinated to the leasehold mortgage (i.e., is not subject to foreclosure by the leasehold mortgagee if a default occurs under that loan).) Thus the ground rental is the first claim on the cash flow generated by the project and is the most secure "slice" of income. Consequently, the ground rental can support a very high mortgage (90 percent of value, in this example), and the developer can obtain a fee mortgage of $720,000 at 14 percent interest for twenty-five years. (The slightly lower interest rate than the 15 percent in the first example reflects the lesser degree of risk.)

Subtracting the land value of $800,000 from the total value of $3.6 million leaves $2.8 million as the value of the leasehold. A 75 percent leasehold mortgage amounts to $2.1 million. Since this is slightly riskier than the fee mortgage, the interest rate might be 16 percent for twenty-five years. Total financing from both mortgages amounts to $2.82 million or $120,000 more than under a straight first mortgage. Thus the equity requirement is reduced from $300,000 to $180,000. The cash-flow return on this equity rises from 42 percent to 52 percent because of the additional upside leverage—more money is being borrowed at a debt service lower than the 18 percent free-and-clear return from the property. (On the other hand, the cash-flow return on value equity declines from 14 to 12 percent because more money is being borrowed at a higher cost than the 15 percent free-and-clear return on the value equity.)

[c] Land Sale-Leaseback and Leasehold Mortgage

Suppose the developer wants to reduce his equity requirement even further. Instead of mortgaging the fee for 90 percent of its value, he can sell it for 100 percent, lease it back for a long term and then put a building on it. Thus, as Table 6.14 shows, he raises an additional $80,000 and need put up only $100,000 in equity. The fee is not subordinated to the leasehold mortgage and so has first claim for the ground rent on the net operating income.

In addition, the fee owner (not the developer) is entitled to future appreciation in the value of the land. Hence a ground rental of 12 percent is acceptable—sharply lower than the 14.4 percent constant on the fee mortgage in Table 6.13. So the cash flow return on the cost equity rises to 102 percent; the return on value equity also rises because the low ground rental means that upside leverage is achieved for the equity as well.

TABLE 6.13 Fee Mortgage; Leasehold Mortgage

Cost of project		$3,000,000
Less: Fee mortgage (90% of $800,000 land value)		720,000
Remaining cost		$2,280,000
Less: Leasehold mortgage (75% of $2.8 million leasehold value)		2,100,000
Equity required		$ 180,000
Equity based on $3.6 million value		$780,000
Net operating income		$540,000
Debt service:		
Fee mortgage (14.4% constant)	$104,000	
Leasehold mortgage (16.3% constant)	342,000	
Less: Total debt service		446,000
Cash flow		$ 94,000
Cash-flow return:		
On cost equity of $180,000		52.0%
On value equity of $780,000		12.1%

[d] Subordinated Land Sale-Leaseback and Leasehold Mortgage

With the next step, the developer finally "mortgages out" and need put up no equity at all. By offering the land purchaser a higher ground rental on the leaseback (13 percent versus 12 percent in Table 6.14), the developer obtains his agreement to subordinate his fee interest to the mortgage—i.e., make the fee addi-

TABLE 6.14 Land Sale-Leaseback; Leasehold Mortgage

Cost of project	$3,000,000
Less: Land sale (100% of value)	800,000
Remaining cost	$2,200,000
Less: Leasehold mortgage (75% of $2.8 million leasehold value)	2,100,000
Equity required	$ 100,000
Equity based on leasehold value	$700,000
Net operating income	$540,000
Less: Ground rental (12% of land value)	96,000
Balance of NOI	$444,000
Less: Debt service on leasehold mortgage (16.3% constant)	342,000
Cash flow	$102,000
Cash-flow return:	
On cost equity of $100,000	102.0%
On value equity of $700,000	14.6%

tional security for the loan. As a result, the mortgage is treated as one on a fee (not a leasehold). The interest rate drops to 15 percent and the loan amount rises to $2.7 million since the loan is 75 percent of the entire project value. The increase of $600,000 in loan proceeds (compared to the situation shown in Table 6.14) eliminates the final $100,000 of required equity and also gives the developer $500,000 in cash. (In addition, the developer retains his equity in the leasehold; assuming its value at $2.8 million and a mortgage of $2.7 million, this value equity is $100,000.)

TABLE 6.15 Subordinated Land Sale-Leaseback Leasehold Mortgage

Cost of project	$3,000,000
Less: Fee mortgage (75% of $3.6 million value)	2,700,000
Subordinated land sale (100% of value)	800,000
Equity required	$ 0
Cash proceeds (from increase in project value)	$500,000
Net operating income	$540,000
Less: Debt service (15.36% of loan)	415,000
Ground rental (13% of land value)	104,000
Cash flow	$ 21,000
Cash-flow return:	
On cost equity of $0	Infinite
On value equity of $100,000 (in leasehold)	21%

Note that in both this and the previous example, the developer realizes taxable gain from the sale of the land; for the sake of simplicity, the taxes due are ignored in the calculations.

[e] Sale-Leaseback of Entire Property

In the final step in this sequence of increased outside financing, the developer can sell the entire property (land plus structure), realize cash proceeds equal to the increase in value of $600,000, and then take a leaseback of the property for a long term subject to a ground rental. Of course, the gain is subject to tax. Assuming a fixed ground rental of 14 percent of the market value of the property, Table 6.16 shows a cash-flow return of $36,000 to the developer on zero equity.

TABLE 6.16 Sale-Leaseback of Entire Property

Price (market value)	$3,600,000
Equity required	$0
Cash proceeds (increase in project value)	$600,000
Net operating income	$540,000
Less: Rental (14% of value)	504,000
Cash flow to developer	$ 36,000
Cash-flow return	Infinite

The sale-leaseback requires the developer to give up all rights to the appreciation in value of the property. In addition, it is unlikely that the purchaser-lessor actually would accept a fixed ground rental for the term of the lease. Instead, the rental would probably be subject to periodic increases based on reappraisals of the property, or the lessor would be entitled to a share of all cash flow above a fixed amount.

[f] Sale Plus Installment Buyback

The major disadvantage of the sale-leaseback approach is that the developer gives up all depreciation write-offs as well as all future appreciation in the value of the property. By using a sale plus installment buyback instead, the developer can keep the depreciation write-offs as well as some portion of future appreciation.

As Table 6.17 shows, the first claim on the net operating income of $540,000 is the annual installment payment under the repurchase contract. In order to permit the developer to realize a cash flow at once, the installment payments in this example are set at 14 percent of value, or $504,000 annually. This permits the developer to realize a $36,000 cash flow. The installment payments are comparable to debt service under a mortgage; the bulk of the early payments will represent interest on the unpaid purchase price and only a small amount will represent payment of principal. If under current market conditions, the 14 percent payment

TABLE 6.17 Sale and Installment Buyback

Sale price (market value)	$3,600,000
Equity required	$0
Cash proceeds over cost to developer (increase in project value)	600,000
Net operating income	$540,000
Less: Installment payments (14% initially)	504,000
Cash flow to developer	$ 36,000
Cash-flow return	Infinite

is too low, the parties have two alternatives. One is to raise the payment to 15 percent of value (thus absorbing the entire cash flow) so that the developer's cash-flow return will come only from future growth in NOI. Another is for the installment payments to step up periodically during the repayment term, thus permitting the developer to pay the obligation out of anticipated increases in NOI.

In addition to the fixed installment payments, the purchaser may insist on a contingent payment equal to a percentage of the increases in NOI. The contingent payment is considered as additional interest and compensates the purchaser for his loss of future appreciation, which he would keep if he leased rather than sold the property back to the developer.

We noted above that the advantage of this technique to the developer is that he can keep the depreciation write-offs from the property. This results from the fact that in an installment sale, title to the property is divided between the parties. The purchaser obtains legal title but the developer retains equitable title, which is sufficient to support his claim to the depreciation write-offs. However, it is important that this type of transaction be supervised by an experienced tax professional to be sure that the tax consequences are not unexpected ones.

[2] Junior Financing

High-ratio financing through a combination of first and second mortgages is the most common method of achieving high leverage and minimum equity. While the subject of junior financing has already been discussed at 6.09 and the subject of wraparound financing has been discussed at 6.10, the following examples relating to the transaction described in 6.15[1] illustrate how these approaches work in a particular case. Note that these examples differ from those in 6.15[1] in that the property interest is not split into several components. Instead, the financing is divided into first and second mortgages.

[a] First- Plus Second-Mortgage Financing

A developer in trouble who requires short-term funds regardless of cost can use the traditional high-leverage approach of secondary financing. The amount of such financing will depend on the interest rate demanded and the amount of "cushion" required by the secondary lender (i.e., cash flow remaining after deducting debt service on both mortgages). Table 6.18 shows a possible financing package in our hypothetical case.

TABLE 6.18 First and Second Mortgages

Cost of project		$3,000,000
Less: First mortgage (75% of $3.6 million value; 15% interest)		2,700,000
Second mortgage (balance of cost)		300,000
Equity required		$ 0
Equity of developer based on $3.6 million value		$600,000
Net operating income		$540,000
First-mortgage debt service (15.36% of loan)	$415,000	
Second-mortgage interest (18%)	54,000	
Less: Total debt service		469,000
Cash flow		$ 71,000
Cash-flow return:		
On cost equity		Infinite
On value equity of $600,000		11.8%

In our example, a standing second mortgage carrying an 18 percent interest rate permits the developer to mortgage out and realize a 12 percent return on his value equity of $600,000. The excess cash flow (over the total debt service) is 1.3 times the interest on the second mortgage, providing the second lender with some cushion against a decline in NOI. Note that the developer could pay substantially higher interest on the second mortgage and still realize a positive cash flow so long as no amortization was required.

[b] First Mortgage Plus Wraparound Loan

The wraparound loan is a more sophisticated version of the second mortgage described in the previous example. As Table 6.19 shows, the developer can raise the same additional sum of $300,000 but (we assume) at an interest cost of only 15.5 percent as against 18 percent for the straight second mortgage. At the same time, the wraparound lender realizes an effective interest return in excess of 20 percent a year because it is able to leverage on the slightly lower interest rate paid to the first mortgagee.

In terms of cash flow, the developer realizes only $64,000 in our wraparound loan example, as against $71,000 with a straight second mortgage. The reason is that despite the lower interest rate, the amortization requirement increases the debt service on the new loan. On the other hand, we have assumed that the wrap-

TABLE 6.19 First and Wraparound Mortgages

Lender *B* makes wraparound loan . . .	$3,000,000, 15.5% interest 25 years (15.86% constant)
Around Lender *A*'s first-mortgage loan . . .	$2,700,000, 15% interest 25 years (15.36% constant)
Additional money from wrap (enabling developer to mortgage out)	$300,000
Net operating income	$540,000
Debt service on wrap loan	476,000
Cash flow	$ 64,000
Cash-flow return:	
On cost equity	Infinite
On value equity of $600,000	10.7%

Note: Lender *B* collects $476,000 annually and pays $415,000 to Lender *A*. The balance of $61,000 pays Lender *B* debt service of 20.33% on the $300,000 additional investment. This gives *B* an effective interest return in excess of 20% annually.

around lender will be willing to make a twenty-five-year loan, equal in term to the first mortgage; by comparison, the standing second mortgage in Table 6.17 is normally not available for more than a few years. Thus, although the developer realizes a slightly lower cash-flow return with the wraparound, his financing is set for twenty-five years ahead.

[3] Bondable Net (High-Credit) Lease

In the conventional mortgage situation, the key element of security is the real estate itself. However, in a 100 percent financing situation such as a high-credit lease, the lender looks primarily to the credit of the tenant who leases all or virtually all of the premises on a net basis. The tenant normally must be a corporation with a credit rating in the top three grades. In effect, the lease is treated as a bond; hence the name bondable net lease. Typical tenants might include a major variety chain, food chain or public utility.

A long-term lease also may be bondable when the tenant is a municipality or other governmental agency that has its rental obligations backed by an acceptable taxing authority. Another type of tenant, becoming more frequent in this era of conglomerates, is the joint-venture corporation, formed for a special project by two or more public corporations. While the subsidiary may have no credit rating of its own, a guarantee by the parents will make the lease eligible for 100 percent financing.

A bondable lease must contain the following indispensable provisions:

☐ *Rent and term.* During the initial term of the lease (which must at least be equal to the loan term), rent payments must be sufficient to pay debt service on the loan, without any possibility of reduction or cancellation.

☐ *Net lease.* The lease must be absolutely net, meaning that the tenant must pay all operating charges (including real estate taxes, payroll, maintenance and repairs but excluding debt service on the loan).

☐ *Insurance.* All insurable risks must be recovered in an amount equal to 100 percent of replacement cost. If certain risks are uninsurable (e.g., hurricane damage) the landlord must be protected under the buy-out provision (see below).

☐ *Buy-out by tenants.* The lease may provide for its cancellation by the tenant in the event of extreme circumstances, e.g., total condemnation or condemnation of a major part of the premises, or total destruction by an uninsured risk. But in such event, the landlord must have an option to sell the premises to the tenant at a price equal to the unpaid balance of the loan.

☐ *Assignment to lender.* As security for its loan, the lender will require the landlord to assign the lease as collateral security for the loan. Under such assignment, the tenant may pay rent directly to the landlord only so long as the tenant receives no notice from the lender to do otherwise. Upon any indication of a default by the landlord under the lease or the loan, the lender may protect itself by requiring rental payments to be made directly to it.

☐ *Priority over mortgage.* While the lender also will require a first mortgage on the real estate, the mortgage must be subordinated to the lease. This assures the lender that, in the event it forecloses the mortgage, the lease, which is the primary security, will not terminate. A mortgage, it should be noted, may be necessary to satisfy the legal requirements of a real estate loan by the lender.

This type of loan, being more similar to a corporate bond issue than a real estate mortgage, normally is not made with savings institutions. More likely, lenders are pension funds, life insurance companies and substantial private investors. Interest rates on these loans will run about one percent below standard mortgage rates.

While 100 percent financing reduces any equity investment by the borrower, it normally denies him any significant cash flow during the life of the loan. This is so because rental income (relatively low because of the high credit standing of the tenant) is not likely to exceed the total debt service by very much.

On the other hand, 100 percent financing can create very large depreciation deductions representing substantial tax savings to high-income landlords. This, indeed, is often the primary attraction of this type of transaction.

6.16 ABC FINANCING

ABC deals—so called because three parties simultaneously are involved as buyer, seller, and lessee—originally developed as a financing technique in oil and gas investments. The technique then was adopted for a particular type of real estate transaction—one where the buyer cared nothing for current cash flow but was interested only in appreciation of the property over a long holding period. More recently, a variation of the ABC deal, which might be called the AB deal, has offered real estate syndicates the opportunity to sharply increase front-end write-offs as a percentage of cash invested. While neither ABC nor AB arrangements are entirely free from the risk of IRS challenge, they have a good chance of surviving if the role of each party can be shown to have economic justification.

The following paragraphs describe how ABC financing and its variation work. These transactions always should be carried out under the supervision of professional counsel who are familiar with the legal and tax aspects.

[1] Investing With a Standard Mortgage

Let us begin by describing a typical transaction for which ABC financing may be suitable. Suppose *A* is buying an income property from *B* and is seeking financing from *C*. Negotiations have reached the stage described in Table 6.20.

TABLE 6.20 Standard Financing on Income Property

Purchase price	$1,000,000
First mortgage (25 years)	$750,000
Equity investment	$250,000
Net operating income (NOI)	$82,500
Annual debt service (11% constant)	82,500
Cash flow	$ 0

While it is unusual for all of the operating income to be used to service the loan, it is not unheard of where the property is subject to a net lease with a top credit. In our example, the buyer *A* (perhaps a foreigner anxious to invest capital in U.S. real estate) is uninterested in current income and plans to hold the property "permanent." He looks ahead twenty-five years, when the mortgage will be fully amortized and he can anticipate the figures in Table 6.21.

At the end of twenty-five years, *A* owns the property free and clear for a total cost of $375,000, having received no income during the period. Since the

TABLE 6.21 Taxable Income and Total Equity—25 Years

Net operating income (NOI)		$2,062,500
Interest deductions (total debt service—$750,000 loan amortization)	$1,312,500	
Depreciation (straight-line 40-year life, $800,000 allocated to improvements	500,000	
Taxable income		$250,000
Tax (50% of taxable income) (viewed as additional equity)		$125,000
Original equity		250,000
Total equity		$375,000

value of the property might have multiplied five times or more, this is not a bad result for someone not seeking current income.

[2] Use of ABC Financing

Now, consider this alternative method of financing the property just described. Instead of having *A* buy the property from *B* outright with financing of $750,000 provided by *C*, the parties execute these transfers:

- *B* sells a twenty-five-year leasehold to *C* for $750,000; no rent is to be due during the lease term.
- *B* then sells the fee interest (subject to the leasehold) to *A* for $250,000.

The financial and tax consequences to the parties are:

☐ *B* receives $1 million for the property, just as in the original transaction. It is true that any gain attributed to the $750,000 received from the leasehold will be ordinary income (because advance rental), but we will assume that *B*'s tax position makes this irrelevant.

☐ Just as before, *C* puts up $750,000 and receives over a period of twenty-five years the entire NOI from the property. *C* is able to recoup its $750,000 tax-free (treating it here as leasehold amortization instead of loan amortization). The excess is rental (instead of interest) income.

☐ Just as before, *A* puts up $250,000 initially, receives no return for twenty-five years, and then owns the property free and unencumbered of either mortgage or lease. Unlike the original transaction, however, *A* receives no taxable income during the period and so saves $125,000 in taxes.

In essence, the ABC financing "carves out" a leasehold from the fee. The leasehold is sold to *C*, the financing party, with the proceeds to *B*, the seller, taking the place of the $750,000 mortgage in the original transaction. By comparison, in the original transaction *A*, the buyer, received as income and then paid over to *C* as loan amortization a total of $750,000. *A* was able to offset $500,000 of depreciation against this, but that left $250,000 of taxable income, which cost *A* $125,000 in taxes. Through use of a carve-out, the financing party, *C*, pays out and then recoups its $750,000 out of NOI without *A* acting as a conduit.

If the differences between the original and ABC transactions were formal only and lacked economic substance, IRS might very well claim that the ABC lease was really a mortgage and so deny to *A* the benefits flowing from the ABC arrangement. However, a good argument can be made that *C*, the financing party, has changed its position with respect both to its security and return in the ABC situation.

☐ First of all, *A* as lessor (in the ABC situation) has no personal liability to *C* for the $750,000, whereas *A* as borrower might have been required to sign a note. (Of course, no difference would exist if *A* would have been able to obtain nonrecourse financing.)

☐ More significantly, *C* as lessee has only the twenty-five-year leasehold as security for its investment, whereas *C* as lender would have had the security of the entire fee. While it is true that a top credit occupancy tenant makes the risk very small, it exists nevertheless.

☐ Finally, *C* as lender could never receive anything more than the agreed interest return whereas *C* as lessee could receive more (or less) depending on the net operating income during the twenty-five-year period. Only where the occupancy tenant paid an absolutely fixed and unchanging net rental would *C*'s cash flow be certain for the entire lease period.

It is apparent that in ABC financing, the lender comes close to and may cross the line separating lending and investment. And, indeed, the more the lender becomes an investor, the stronger the argument that true economic substance is involved in the form of the transaction.

What happens to the depreciation in the ABC transaction? In the original transaction, *A* had a basis of $1 million ($800,000 depreciable) of which $500,000 was written off after twenty-five years. In the ABC arrangement, his basis is $250,000 ($200,000 depreciable). Since the lessee (*C*) did not construct the improvements, *A* presumably could begin to depreciate his investment at once, which would mean that $125,000 (using a forty-year life) could be written off during the initial twenty-five years.

How to Use the AB Variation. The carve-out technique just described can also be used in a two-party transaction, with the seller reserving an income interest so as to permit the buyer to put up less initial cash.

For example, a syndicate is purchasing an existing income property with no operating history. The purchase price is $200,000 cash over an $800,000 mortgage. For the sake of simplicity, assume the first year's payment on the mortgage is $80,000, representing 10 percent interest and no amortization. To induce the syndicate to buy, the seller is willing to give a guarantee against negative cash flow during the first year; that is, he guarantees that the property will have an NOI of at least $80,000, sufficient to service the mortgage. First-year depreciation is $30,000.

In this situation, the syndicate has invested $200,000 cash and anticipates in the first year no cash flow (since $80,000 income is offset by $80,000 interest) and a tax loss of $30,000 (the depreciation deduction) equal to 15 percent of the $200,000 equity.

Suppose, instead of the foregoing, the contract of sale reserved in the seller an income interest in the property for the first year (worth $80,000, the anticipated NOI).

Then, instead of paying $200,000 cash over the mortgage, the syndicate pays $120,000 cash and agrees to pay the first-year debt service (e.g., $80,000 in interest). Although the dollars remain exactly the same (a $200,000 cash outlay by the syndicate), the syndicate generates $110,000 of first-year deductions (depreciation plus interest paid), equal to 55 percent of the equity. This is achieved by eliminating the syndicate as a conduit for the NOI, which goes directly to the seller.

There appears to be sufficient economic substance to the transaction to answer an IRS challenge.

- First, the syndicate is receiving additional security since if the property fails to achieve its projected return, the syndicate need not call upon the seller to make up the difference; instead, the seller is automatically out of pocket.

- Second, the seller, instead of collecting $80,000 at the closing, is obliged to realize it over the first year of operation.

IRS may nevertheless seek to impute the income to the buying syndicate, claiming in substance that it paid the full $200,000 in cash. The real issue involves which party is at risk as to the $80,000 of first-year income. If properly set up, it is the seller who would seem to be at risk in a carve-out situation, and so no imputation of income to the syndicate is justified. Another tax test used by IRS—who generates the income—also supports the carve-out technique since it is the seller who is managing the property and creating the income.

Finally, it seems clear that the buyer is entitled to the depreciation deduction because (with the exception of the first year's income) it is entitled to the operating income plus any gain on sale.

The income reservation in the seller is in effect a one-year leaseback. However, the transaction should not be set up as a lease because IRS may then argue that the buyer has given the seller a lease on favorable terms from which it can be inferred that the buyer is really paying more for the property than appears.

6.17 SECONDARY MORTGAGE MARKET

[1] In General

There are many ways for financial institutions to raise the money necessary to invest in mortgages. Savings and loan associations, savings banks, and commercial banks, for example, rely on deposits and the sale of savings certificates. Life insurance companies obtain their money from policy premiums, and they sometimes borrow from banks on a short-term basis. The Federal Land Bank, which makes mortgage loans to farmers, sells bonds to the public. The U.S. Treasury sells bonds and notes to raise money for the U.S. Farmers Home Administration to make direct mortgage loans for housing in rural areas.

Another way to raise money for mortgage investment is to sell mortgages or to sell securities that are secured by mortgages. This buying and selling of mortgages, or of securities based on mortgages, is generally called the secondary mortgage market.

[2] Private Transactions

More than half the secondary market in mortgages (as distinct from mortgage securities) is conducted between private lending institutions, such as banks and mortgage bankers, without any participation by a government agency or a quasi-public corporation. On the other hand, the mortgage securities market in housing is dominated by securities with a government guarantee. However, a secondary market in conventional mortgage loan securities is developing (see 6.17[6].)

A typical secondary-market transaction between private parties might take place as follows. A mortgage banking firm in Maryland expects to commit $3 million in mortgage loans during the next ninety days at a rate approximating 15 percent, adding a fee to it of 1 point (one percent of the mortgage amount). This firm has worked with a Chicago savings and loan association that often has more money than it needs for mortgages it originates directly. The mortgage firm calls the savings and loan association, which agrees that at the time the mortgages close it will provide the $3 million needed if it receives 13.5 percent profit, plus 2 points. When the mortgages are made and the funds disbursed, they are transferred to the Chicago savings and loan association, but the Maryland firm retains servicing. For the payment of interest, the savings and loan association receives 13.5 percent, and the balance (assuming the mortgage loan is over 13.25 percent) is paid to the Maryland mortgage firm, part of which compensates the firm for servicing.

Many of the private transactions in the secondary market are negotiated directly between the principals. Many others, however, are arranged through the secondary-marketing efforts of the larger mortgage insurance companies (discussed in Chapter 7). Verex and MGIC, two large and competitive mortgage insurance companies with headquarters in Wisconsin, are particularly active in offering nationwide telephone assistance for secondary-market sales.

The largest single component of the secondary market is that consisting of single-family mortgages, which are grouped together into "pools." Frequently, a savings institution will issue a commitment to purchase mortgages from a mortgage banker at a future date, the mortgage banker paying a fee for the commitment. To a much smaller extent are mortgage loans on income-producing properties, such as office buildings and shopping centers, bought and sold on the secondary market, since these usually are held by the original lenders as long-term investments. Property-improvement loans are not usually sold in the private secondary mortgage market.

Some long-term lenders occasionally sell participations in commercial and industrial mortgage loans. Unlike participation between lenders at the time a loan is made, which is a common occurrence, the sale of a participation after a loan is closed is much less frequent. It may happen, for example, when a life insurance company makes a loan that is to be repaid in part by standard installments of interest and principal and in part by a share of the equity return. The company will sell the loan portion to a pension fund, which prefers to invest in long-term loans at fixed-interest rates, and keep the equity portion for its own portfolio.

Some financial institutions sell mortgage bonds for a fixed term, such as ten years, at a fixed-interest rate and secured by mortgages held by the institution. They are a debt of the issuing institution, not a sale of the mortgages.

All the transactions involving the sale of mortgages of single-family homes are influenced by the secondary-market operations of three organizations, nicknamed Ginnie Mae, Fannie Mae, and Freddy Mac.

[3] Government National Mortgage Association

[a] In General

The Government National Mortgage Association, known as GNMA or Ginnie Mae, guarantees securities that are based on mortgages; the securities are often called "Ginnie Maes." GNMA is a federal agency, structured like a corporation without stock or stockholders, and located within the U.S. Department of Housing and Urban Development (HUD).

The mortgage-backed securities program of GNMA was established in 1970 to increase liquidity in the secondary market and to attract new sources of financing, such as pension funds, for residential loans. The program works as follows:

A mortgage banker or a financial institution makes a number of one- to four-family mortgage loans that are insured by the Federal Housing Administration (FHA), guaranteed by the Veterans Administration (VA), or insured by the Farmers Home Administration. The lender then packages a group of these mortgages that have similar characteristics (term, interest rate, type of insurance or guarantee), although they need not be in the same location or even the same state. When this group or "pool" of mortgages is assembled, the lender may issue securities itself or it may transfer the mortgage loans to a securities dealer, who will then become the issuer of the securities.

The company assembling the mortgages must be approved by the Federal Housing Administration, and the issuer of the securities must be approved by GNMA. The issuer must meet certain financial asset requirements; this protects buyers of the securities from the possibility that the issuer will not comply with the terms of the prospectus.

The pool of mortgages is assigned as security to GNMA. The actual mortgage documents are held by a custodian, usually a bank. Custodian accounts are established to hold debt-service payments and escrows for property taxes and mortgage insurance. The securities are almost always of a type called "modified pass-through." This means that the investor receives a monthly check for his proportionate share of principal and interest, whether or not the principal and interest has been actually collected by the mortgagee from the mortgagors. In addition, the principal on each prepaid mortgage is passed through to the investors.

The federal government, through GNMA, guarantees to the buyer of the securities the timely payment of principal and interest. The buyer of Ginnie Maes thus has a double federal guarantee: the mortgages themselves are insured or guaranteed; and the timely payment of principal and interest is also guaranteed.

The investor in Ginnie Maes determines his yield not only by the interest rate but by the expectations of the time that the mortgages will remain unpaid. For the purposes of calculating comparisons, the GNMA form of prospectus for Ginnie Maes uses a table that usually shows that the average mortgage will be prepaid in twelve years.

[b] Ginnie Mae Futures

The Chicago Board of Trade maintains a market for future delivery of GNMA securities. A futures contract is an agreement to make or take delivery of a specified amount of Ginnie Maes at a specified time.

In the pricing of GNMA futures contracts, the interest rate shown is 8 percent. Since the actual interest rate on the underlying mortgages is almost always higher than 8 percent, the securities are sold at a discount. Thus a certificate at 8 percent (face amount) to yield 14 percent would be priced at a discount of about 34 percent, or, stated another way, the standard $100,000 certificate sold in the futures market would be priced at $66,000 assuming a current market interest rate of 14 percent. The assumption used for yield purposes is that the mortgages will be prepaid in twelve years.

Separate prices are quoted for futures for delivery in each of three-month intervals over a period of three years. This is useful for borrowers and lenders as a way to hedge commitments to sell or purchase mortgage money in the future. For example, if a mortgage banker commits himself to sell future mortgages at today's rates believing that interest rates will increase, he may also purchase a futures contract at today's rates as a hedge. Then, if his assumption was wrong and interest rates go down, the value of the futures contract will go up (the discount is less), and the mortgage banker or builder has protected himself.

[c] The Options Exchange

The Chicago Board Options Exchange also offers a market for puts and calls in Ginnie Maes. A put is an option to sell and a call is an option to buy. Options have terms of three, six, nine, twelve, or fifteen months. The units traded are those listed on the futures exchange, that is, units of $100,000 priced for comparison purposes assuming an interest rate of 8 percent.

The difference between the options exchange and the futures exchange is that the futures exchange requires delivery of the Ginnie Maes from seller to buyer whereas in the options exchange, delivery of the securities is optional. The buyer of a call option pays a fee and may exercise that option any time prior to its expiration or may allow the option to lapse unused.

[d] Various Types of Ginnie Mae Securities

Although securities backed by level-payment single-family mortgages represent by far the largest part of GNMA's pools, there are other types of Ginnie Maes:

- Securities based upon pools of graduated-payment mortgages, insured under section 245 by the FHA. (See 7.01[3][b].)
- Mobile-home loans, insured by the FHA or guaranteed by the VA. (See 7.01[6].)
- Project loans (FHA-insured) on multifamily rental apartments. Usually no more than one FHA-insured project is put into a "pool."
- Construction loan mortgages on projects. Often a construction loan may be combined in a securities offering with a project long-term mortgage loan.
- Tax-exempt securities on housing projects with Section 8 assistance. (See 7.03[4][b].)
- Hospital loans with mortgages insured under FHA Section 242.

GNMA securities play the largest role in the secondary market for housing. Between 1970 and mid-1981, approximately $125 billion of mortgage-backed securities have been sold.

GNMA's role in providing assistance for low- and moderate-income housing is discussed at 7.03[4][b]. The taxpayer-supported Special Assistance Function, as it is known, is a procedure by which GNMA purchases multifamily FHA-insured loans at a below-market interest rate and sells them to investors. The mortgages for subsidized housing have been made at a 7.5 percent interest rate, and the mortgages sold at deep discount. This program ended in 1982.

[4] Federal National Mortgage Association

[a] In General

The Federal National Mortgage Association (FNMA), known as Fannie Mae, is the largest purchaser of mortgages in the secondary market. These mortgages are originated by mortgage companies, banks, savings and loan associations, and credit unions, and they may be either conventional mortgages or FHA-insured or VA-guaranteed mortgages. Mortgage bankers are the primary sellers to FNMA. In 1980, FNMA purchased $8.1 billion of mortgages, almost all on one- to four-family houses.

FNMA started as a government agency in the 1930s, but in 1968, its secondary-market functions were separated from its special assistance role for subsidized housing. The secondary-market role was placed in a congressionally chartered private corporation, which thereupon issued stock to the public and soon listed its stock on the New York Stock Exchange. FNMA, nevertheless, retains a close tie to the federal government. Five of its fifteen directors are appointed by the President of the United States, while the other ten are elected by the stockholders. FNMA pays federal taxes, but is exempt from state and local taxes, except property taxes. Its obligations (debentures and notes) are issued through the Federal Reserve Bank and are considered federal agency securities, even though these obligations are not federally guaranteed. The law requires the directors and officers of FNMA to set the corporation's policies in close coordination with the Secretary of HUD.

FNMA borrows by issuing both short-term and long-term obligations. The short-term discount notes are sold at a price below the face amount due at maturity; short-term interest notes are sold at par with all interest due at maturity. FNMA sells long-term debentures, which are similar to corporate bonds. The extent of this borrowing can be seen from the fact that, in 1980, FNMA borrowed $29 billion, of which $23 billion was to refinance expiring obligations and $6 billion to finance new mortgage purchases.

[b] Free-Market-System Auction

FNMA's principal method of purchasing mortgages on one- to four-family houses from mortgage bankers and financial institutions is the free-market-system auction. Every other Monday, FNMA holds two auctions, one for the purchase of government-insured or guaranteed mortgages and the other for conventional mortgages. The seller specifies the price at which he will sell, and he has a choice of selling competitively or noncompetitively. For a competitive bid, he telephones with his price and the amount of mortgages to be sold. On the next day, FNMA announces how much it will purchase and it selects those offers that produce the largest yield to FNMA. For a noncompetitive bid, a seller specifies how much he will sell at the weighted average yield of all competitive bids accepted in the Monday auction.

Although the terms "purchase" and "sale" are used, FNMA actually issues a commitment to purchase, with delivery to be made in four months. This is an optional delivery for the seller; it is, for the seller, a standby commitment, for which he pays a fee, but under which during that four months, the seller has no obligation to deliver if prices change in his favor. FNMA, on the other hand, is bound to purchase any mortgages accepted by it.

The vast majority of commitments by FNMA are for four months but there is also an FNMA auction for twelve-month commitments. The twelve-month commitment, for which a larger fee is paid, is often used by new-home builders so that they will have mortgage money available for buyers after construction. FNMA commits the funds but no interest rate is specified. In 1981, FNMA introduced a one-month commitment, but the seller of mortgages must deliver. Unlike the four-month and twelve-month commitment, the seller cannot renege if it finds a better price for mortgages before the delivery date.

[c] Types of Mortgages Purchased

FNMA purchases FHA and VA mortgages up to the legal limit on the size of each single-family mortgage under FHA, currently $93,750 for FHA mortgages. It purchases conventional mortgages in a maximum amount for a single-family house of $107,000. Both limits normally increase each year.

Conventional mortgages eligible for purchase may be loans with a loan-to-value ratio of 80 percent or less. If the loan-to-value ratio is more than 80 percent but not more than 95 percent, then the loan must carry private mortgage insurance for the amount above the 75 percent loan-to-value ratio. Mortgage terms may not exceed thirty years. Higher mortgage limits are permitted in Alaska, Guam, and Hawaii.

A variety of programs have been developed by FNMA for single-family mortgage purchases. It is the primary market for FHA-insured graduated-payment mortgages. It is offering to purchase adjustable-rate mortgages of almost any kind that lenders wish to offer as long as the rate changes are based on recognizable and approved indices, such as six-month Treasury bill certificates.

FNMA has one plan to buy mortgages where the rate of interest during the first years of the mortgage has been lowered through the payment of an amount of money, similar to a fee, to the lender. This "buy down" program requires the buyer or seller to put money into an escrow fund, which the lender then draws upon to increase its yield. The mortgage interest rate for the buyer may be reduced as much as 3 percent. The program is similar to a graduated-payment plan for conventional mortgages.

FNMA developed a Refinance/Resales program as a consequence of the rise in interest rates in the late 1970s and 1980s. Because FNMA holds a large number of low-yielding long-term mortgages and has to borrow primarily on the short-term market where interest rates are high, FNMA is in a financially difficult period. Furthermore, few people now pay off an FHA or VA mortgage when a house is sold, because the mortgage is assumable and the interest rates are low on the older mortgages. Buyers of houses can combine an assumable first mortgage with a second mortgage or a wraparound mortgage, and still pay less than would be required for a new first mortgage of the same amount.

In order to rid itself of its low-yielding mortgages and to discourage assumptions, FNMA offers to purchase a new mortgage at a below-market interest rate if the property already has an existing mortgage, either insured, guaranteed or conventional, which is part of FNMA's mortgage portfolio. That portfolio contained in mid-1981 about $51 billion in single-family mortgages.

The interest rate offered in the Refinance/Resales program reflects the size of the mortgage to be paid off, the interest rate on that mortgage, and the amount of the new mortgage desired. An owner may refinance up to 90 percent of the value of the house, and a new buyer may finance up to 95 percent of the value, with the maximum limits discussed above. The Refinance/Resales interest rate is comparable but slightly below the rate that one might obtain on a wraparound mortgage.

[d] Other Purchase Programs

FNMA is the primary buyer for government-insured multifamily housing mortgages and for mortgages on nursing homes, hospitals, group medical practice facilities, and Title X loans (acquisition and development of large-scale planned complexes of single-family homes). It offers a market for mobile-home loans. A market is being developed by FNMA for second-mortgage loans.

Conventional FHA and VA mortgages on condominium units will be purchased by FNMA. In order to expedite the purchase of condominium unit mortgages, FNMA established a procedure whereby it reviews and approves the legal and management arrangements of condominium houses or apartments. The developer of a condominium may obtain commitments from FNMA anywhere from twelve months to forty-eight months in advance, depending on the time it takes to build or renovate. The interest rate on these mortgages is adjusted annually and an annual fee is charged.

Special programs have been designed to encourage lending in older urban areas. Lenders may assemble pools of conventional mortgages in these areas, in the same way that they would assemble FHA or VA mortgages for Ginnie Maes, and then FNMA will purchase a participating interest in the conventional mortgage pool, ranging from 60 to 80 percent of the pool's value. The amount invested by FNMA must be reinvested by the lenders in other mortgages in older urban areas.

Another program for urban lending commits FNMA to purchase rehabilitation loans on one- to four-family houses. These loans must be secured by mortgages.

FNMA lends money on one-year terms to commercial banks and to other financial institutions for construction loans or rehabilitation loans in urban areas. The short-term loans are secured by residential mortgages; when a lending pattern has been established, the financial institution has a line of credit with FNMA for urban loans.

[5] The Mortgage Corporation

[a] In General

The Mortgage Corporation is directed by the Federal Home Loan Bank Board, thus its initials are FHLMC, for Federal Home Loan Mortgage Corporation, but it is known either by its name as the Mortgage Corporation or by the nickname Freddy Mac. Unlike FNMA, it is not privately owned; its stock is nonvoting and is held by the twelve Federal Home Loan Banks. It does operate, within the offices of the Bank Board, as a public corporation that finances itself by its fees and not with taxpayers' money.

Whereas FNMA primarily borrows to purchase mortgages, Freddy Mac sells its mortgages in the form of securities. To acquire the mortgages that it will later sell, Freddy Mac uses a procedure somewhat similar to that of FNMA. On Tuesdays of each week, sellers, which are primarily savings and loan associations, offer mortgages to Freddy Mac and the next day Freddy Mac accepts the offers with the highest yields. If a seller's bid is accepted, delivery of the mortgages is mandatory. Freddy Mac's option program is quite separate from its program in the secondary market.

The seller may offer Freddy Mac a pool of whole loans or it may offer a participation in a pool of mortgages, the participation being anywhere from 50 percent to 95 percent of the loan package.

In addition to this program of mandatory delivery of mortgages, Freddy Mac offers two types of forward commitments for which the sellers pay fees. In one program, delivery of the mortgages is optional for 120 days, and, if the seller chooses during those 120 days, he may extend the time for actual delivery to a maximum of six months. In the second program, the seller pays for an option to deliver mortgages anytime within an eight-month period.

[b] Types of Mortgages Purchased

Freddy Mac purchases conventional loans of the same kind as purchased by Fannie Mae. The maximum amount of a conventional single-family loan is $107,000 in 1982. If the loan-to-value ratio is over 80 percent, private mortgage insurance is required. Payments on the mortgages must begin not later than sixty-two days after disbursement of funds, and the terms of the mortgages must be between ten and thirty years. Freddy Mac also purchases condominium unit mortgages.

Freddy Mac purchases adjustable-rate mortgages of two kinds: those with interest rates which go up or down without limit, and those with the interest rate adjustable upward or downward not more than two percentage points a year. Unlike Fannie Mae, Freddy Mac will not purchase loans where the amount owed or the length of the term will be increased or extended if the interest rate increases.

In 1981, Freddy Mac began the purchase of home-improvement loans. Each loan must be secured by a lien on the property being improved. The loan term must be either five, ten, or fifteen years, unless the amount of the loan exceeds $30,000, in which case it may be a twenty-year loan. The loan must be amortized over its term, and the loan, when added to other secured financing on the property, should not exceed 90 percent of the property's estimated market value. The loan must be closed and disbursed when sold to Freddy Mac, and the improvements financed by the loan must be completed prior to delivery. Freddy Mac does not buy the whole loan, but an 80 percent participation. The seller retains the servicing plus 20 percent of the loan.

Freddy Mac also purchases multifamily housing loans. Whereas Ginnie Mae puts a multifamily loan into a separate pool, Freddy Mac includes multifamily loans with single-family loans as security for its participation certificates.

[c] Participation Certificates

To raise money for mortgage purchases, Freddy Mac sells the mortgages it purchases in the form of securities. It assembles a large group of single-family and multifamily mortgages into one pool, and then issues mortgage participation certificates. The buyers of the certificates receive the interest collected and their pro-rata share of principal payments received. These certificates are unlike Ginnie Maes in that (1) the mortgages are not federally guaranteed, although most of them carry private mortgage insurance for the top portion of the loan; (2) there is no federal guarantee of the pool of mortgages, and (3) the pool of mortgages is assembled by Freddy Mac whereas any approved mortgagee can assemble a pool of Ginnie Maes.

The yield on participation certificates is based on the yield of the mortgages and on the experience of Freddy Mac, which shows that the weighted average life of a conventional mortgage on a single-family house in its portfolio is between six and eight years.

Although Participation Certificates dominate Freddy Mac's sales program, Freddy Mac also sells guaranteed mortgage certificates. These are similar to bonds because the payment of principal is guaranteed: the buyer receives principal payments at the time specified, or receives the actual payment of principal, whichever is greater. Unlike the participation certificates, which are real estate assets in the investor's portfolio, the guaranteed mortgage certificate is a debt obligation of Freddy Mac.

[6] Conventional Mortgage-Backed Securities

In 1977, First Federal Savings and Loan of Chicago and Bank of America in California successfully imitated the principles of Ginnie Maes by issuing pass-through securities backed by conventional mortgages. Each mortgage in the pool was of a standard type and covered by private mortgage loan insurance if the loan-to-value ratio exceeded 80 percent. In addition, the pool of mortgages itself was partially insured by a private mortgage insurance corporation.

Until interest rates became so high that pools of existing mortgages had to be substantially discounted, the conventional pass-through security appeared to be a major secondary marketing tool for the 1980s. A number of financial institutions followed the pattern of the early conventional mortgage pools, and may soon start to prepare pools of adjustable-rate mortgages.

The pass-through certificate issued by the lender is, like a GNMA certificate, a sale of assets rather than a debt obligation. There is no recourse against the issuer if a mortgage in the pool goes into default. As with Ginnie Maes, buyers receive interest and income in a specified amount each month, regardless of whether the lender has actually received the payment from the borrower. These conventional mortgage pass-through certificates may be placed privately or sold to the public.

When an issue is sold to the public, and often when it is placed privately, the issuer has the issue rated by Standard & Poor, Inc., an investment rating service. It seeks to have the securities rated AA, which is a good bond quality, making the issue of suitable quality for pension funds.

Standard & Poor fixes its rating based in large part upon its analysis of the capability of the parties assembling and selling the issue. It requires a strong private mortgage insurance company for the guarantee of a portion of the pool; usually the top 5 percent is insured, meaning that if the investor suffers any losses (due, for example, to extensive foreclosures), then a private mortgage insurance company pays those losses up to an amount equal to 5 percent of the principal value of the total securities. Standard & Poor also requires all-risk hazard insurance, a form of policy that covers floods and earthquakes and other catastrophes that may not be covered in the homeowner's insurance policy.

[7] Secondary Mortgage Outlook

The secondary market is changing as quickly as the methods used to finance real estate. A secondary market in second-mortgage loans is in the process of development by private corporations; life insurance companies have made tentative plans to provide a secondary market for home-improvement loans in urban areas; adjustable-rate mortgages will soon be packaged and sold in the form of securities; mobile-home loans will be developed with adjustable rates as soon as a secondary market in those loans becomes feasible.

Finally, the development of the computer as a method for financial institutions to exchange information quickly is of major importance to the secondary mortgage market. Today, unlike ten years ago, many mortgage lenders use computer service to obtain daily statistics on mortgage rates, securities prices, and the availability of mortgage securities. Soon, even the smallest lender will have a computer capable of providing this information.

7

Mortgage Insurance and Guarantees; Federal Loans and Grants

7.01 MORTGAGE INSURANCE AND GUARANTEES FOR SINGLE-FAMILY AND MANUFACTURED HOMES

[1] Introduction

Although a loan to buy or build real estate is secured by a mortgage, the lender may require that the mortgage be insured or guaranteed in order to protect the lender against losses due to default in mortgage payments. Moreover, an insured or guaranteed loan may be sold on the secondary market. (See 6.17.) Private mortgage insurance companies offer insurance for single-family home mortgage loans; the federal government offers insurance or guarantees for home loans depending upon the type of program.

This section covers insurance and guarantees for houses with one to four units. Since the vast majority of one- to four-family houses are single-family houses, that term will be used. Insurance and guarantees for multifamily buildings (having five or more units) are discussed in 7.02. Section 7.03 is devoted to nonrural housing loans where the interest rate is subsidized or subsidies are provided to the tenants. Finally, the variety of loans available for farmers and others in rural areas is so extensive that Section 7.04 is devoted to that subject.

[2] History

Mortgage insurance in the United States began in 1934 when the federal government offered 100 percent insurance of mortgages on residential properties. The insured loan had to be repaid by equal monthly payments and be fully amortized over the term of the loan. The borrower paid a premium for the mortgage insurance of one half of one percent of the principal balance remaining on the mortgage each year. The Federal Housing Administration (FHA), which administered the program, initially established insurance programs for mortgages on single-family houses and on multifamily apartments.

During the Second World War, the federal government developed a guarantee program for mortgages in order to permit a veteran to buy a house without a down payment. This guarantee, administered by the Veterans Administration (VA), does not cover the entire loan but does cover a substantial portion of it. There is no premium or fee paid by the borrower for the VA guarantee; the expenses of the program are paid by the taxpayer.

In the late 1950s and early 1960s, several private companies began offering private mortgage insurance (PMI). The PMI company would usually insure 20 percent or 25 percent of the mortgage. PMI companies offered somewhat lower rates than the FHA because the insurance coverage was less, no property inspection was required, and the type of property insured was usually in the more affluent neighborhoods. One important reason for the growth in popularity of PMI was that decisions on whether or not to provide insurance were usually given in twenty-four hours, whereas approval of insurance by the FHA required an inspection by the FHA, which often involved delays of days or weeks because of a shortage of FHA appraisers. In the late 1970s and early 1980s, more PMI was sold than FHA insurance on single-family houses; however, the total number of houses insured by the FHA and guaranteed by the VA each year has, with one exception, annually surpassed the number of houses with mortgages privately insured.

[3] Single-Family Programs of the Federal Housing Administration

Insurance programs of the FHA are generally known by the section of the National Housing Act that authorizes the particular program. For example, the basic FHA insurance program is known as the 203(b) program.

[a] Section 203(b)

☐ *Maximum mortgage.* To qualify for insurance, the Section 203(b) mortgage may not exceed 97 percent of the first $25,000 of the price, plus 95 percent of the price over $25,000. Total financing may not exceed 97 percent of the estimated value of the house. A veteran may obtain 100 percent financing. There are also maximum mortgage amounts: $67,500 for a single-family house, $76,000 for a two-family house, $92,000 for a three-family house, and $107,000 for a four-family house. These maximum limits may be increased in high-cost areas by the Secretary of HUD to the lesser of (1) 133 percent of those specified maximums; or (2) 95 percent of the median one-family-house price in the area, as determined by the HUD Secretary. For two-, three-, and four-family houses, the percentage increases.

☐ *Interest rate.* The Secretary of HUD establishes a maximum or ceiling interest rate that may be paid for residential mortgages. This rate, called the FHA ceiling rate, is usually a little below the interest rate on similar term uninsured mortgages that financial institutions are charging at the particular time. Therefore, when a financial institution makes an FHA-insured mortgage it will demand a fee (in effect, a discount of the mortgage amount) so that its return or yield from the insured mortgage will be approximately equal to its return or yield from an uninsured mortgage.

The FHA does not allow the borrower to pay more than one point as a service fee for obtaining an FHA-insured loan. Consequently, the fee that the lender requires must be paid by the seller. For example, suppose that the market rate of interest is 14.5 percent, but the FHA ceiling rate is 14 percent. The amount of the fee that the lender will require will depend in part on the lender's expectations of the time in which the mortgage will be held. The lender might consider three points (or 3 percent) to be sufficient payment to compensate for the one half of one percent difference between the FHA rate and the market rate. If the mortgage were $60,000, 3 percent of $60,000 would be $1,800—the amount that the seller would have to pay the lender.

☐ *The term of the loan, assumption, and prepayments.* The FHA-insured mortgage may not have a term of more than thirty years or less than ten years, unless the FHA specifically approves a term of longer than thirty years but not more than thirty-five years, to enable a lower-income buyer to purchase. Any FHA-insured mortgage may be assumed without penalty, and there is no penalty for prepayment of the mortgage.

☐ *Buyer's expenses.* In addition to the down payment, the buyer must usually pay one point to the lender for the processing of the mortgage. If the buyer is purchasing a newly constructed home, he may be required to pay 2.5 points to cover the cost of inspections and partial disbursements during construction. The buyer must pay the mortgage insurance premium of one half of one percent of the outstanding principal balance each year.

☐ *Procedures.* Either the seller or the buyer may have an FHA inspection of the house to be sold; this determines whether the house meets FHA's Minimum Property Standards. An appraisal is also made of the property. The application for the loan and the FHA insurance is given to a lender such as a mortgage banking firm or a financial institution that has been approved by the FHA; the lender then submits standard documents to the local FHA office for approval. When approved, the loan is insured and is effective as of the date of the closing of the sale. The lender may then keep the loan or sell it, service the loan or sell the servicing to some other company.

[b] Section 245—the Graduated-Payment Mortgage

This FHA insurance program insures mortgages that permit lower monthly payments by the borrower during the first few years of the mortgage term. In the first year of the mortgage, the borrower defers a portion of the interest payment and the lender adds the deferred interest to the principal loaned. Each year the monthly payments increase, usually until the sixth year of the mortgage when the level of monthly payment remains steady for the remainder of the mortgage term. This technique enables the buyer to pay $100 a month less (on a larger FHA-insured mortgage) than he would pay if the mortgage were a level-payment mortgage under Section 203(b).

There are two types of graduated-payment mortgages (GPMs). One limits the loan to 97 percent of the appraised value, so the initial loan must have a lower loan-to-value ratio to permit the increase in loan principal, due to deferred interest, without exceeding the 97 percent figure. Anyone is eligible for such a loan, and there are five variations in payment schedules allowed. The second type of GPM permits the loan to increase to 113 percent of the original amount.

The initial experience with GPMs in early 1980 proved that lenders wanted a higher rate of interest on these mortgages because, in part, the complexity of bookkeeping made the mortgages difficult to understand. Consequently, the FHA ceiling interest rate is one half of one percent higher for GPMs than it is for other single-family mortgages. The other terms of the GPM are similar to those of Section 203(b) mortgages.

The GPMs are limited in the number that may be insured in any one year. As an administrative matter, the FHA has been limiting the second type of GPM to those who have not owned a house during the previous three years.

[c] Condominium and Cooperative Housing Units

The FHA insures mortgages on condominium residential units (town houses or apartments) under Section 234(c). The rules follow the Section 203(b) program, but the maximum amount of mortgage is between $67,500 and $74,900 (in 1981) depending upon the area. For cooperative units, the FHA may insure the mortgage on the unit itself under Section 213, or it may insure the shares owned by a member of the cooperative housing unit under Section 203n.

[d] Home Mortgage Insurance in Older Declining Neighborhoods

Many mortgage applications for single-family mortgages under one of the FHA programs described elsewhere in this section would normally not be acceptable risks because the neighborhood's property values appear to be declining. However, unlike a private mortgage insurance company, the FHA is willing to risk granting insurance when to deny it might hasten the decline of the neighborhood. When this determination has been made the FHA insures this mortgage in a special risk insurance fund that traditionally has had more losses than are compensated for by the mortgage insurance premiums. The taxpayers replenish the special fund when needed.

The existence of the special fund does not mean that normal underwriting standards will be overlooked. The credit of the borrower and the condition of the house are as important in this program as in the others.

The major program under the special risk fund is Section 223(e) for homes in older declining neighborhoods. Another program provides insurance for subsidized houses. (See 7.03[3][a].)

[e] Home Mortgage Insurance for Low- and Moderate-Income Families

This program (Section 221(d)(2)) is designed to aid lower-income families to purchase low-cost housing. The maximum mortgage limits are substantially below those of Section 203(b). These mortgages, riskier than those under Section 203(b), are covered by a third insurance fund, called the general insurance fund. Households displaced by government action (such as renewal) have a particular opportunity to obtain loans under this section, but this is not a subsidy program.

[4] Veterans Administration Guarantees for Single-Family Homes

Whereas the FHA insurance program covers single-family and multifamily housing, home improvements, manufactured housing, and health facilities, the VA program covers only single-family residential mortgages and manufactured housing and lots. The purpose of the VA program is to help the veteran by requiring little or no down payment for a home purchase. Under the FHA insurance program, usually at least 5 percent of the purchase price must be paid by the buyer at closing; under the VA program, the veteran may borrow all but the closing costs.

[a] Who Is a Veteran?

A veteran must have served ninety days on active service unless a service-incurred disability prevented him from serving that length of time. For World

War II veterans, the ninety days must be between September 16, 1940 and July 25, 1947; for Korean War veterans, the time served must be between June 27, 1950 and January 31, 1955; for Vietnam veterans, the service must be between August 5, 1964 and May 7, 1975.

Alternatively, any veteran who served on active duty 181 days or more, any part of which was after January 31, 1955 and before September 8, 1981 (and the discharge was not dishonorable) is eligible. After September 7, 1981 two years of service is required. Current servicemen are also eligible if they have already served for two years on active duty.

Surviving spouses of persons who died as a result of military service are eligible.

The entitlement (a veteran's right to use VA guarantees) may be used only once, but if the loan is paid in full, then application may be made to restore eligibility.

[b] Extent of Veterans Administration Guarantees

The VA does not insure mortgages, but rather guarantees a specific amount of the loan. Because it is not insurance, the borrower does not have to pay an insurance premium. The cost of the guarantee and the costs of administering the VA program are paid by the government.

The guarantee may not exceed 60 percent of the loan amount or $27,500, whichever is less. If, for example, a $70,000 loan guaranteed by the VA went into default and was sold at a foreclosure sale, resulting in a $30,000 loss for the lender, the VA would pay $27,500 of that loss and the lender would lose the remaining $2,500.

There is no maximum amount of loan for a VA guarantee. The Federal National Mortgage Association, however, makes it a practice to buy on the secondary market only those VA mortgages that are less than four times the guarantee. Four times the guarantee maximum of $27,500 equals $110,000; many mortgage bankers will not make a VA loan in excess of that amount.

[c] Procedure

The procedure for obtaining a VA guarantee is quite similar to obtaining FHA insurance, but the lender works with the local office of the Veterans Administration rather than the U.S. Department of Housing and Urban Development (HUD). Upon request, the VA will appraise the house and present the owner with a Certificate of Reasonable Value. The loan may not exceed that value or the purchase price, whichever is less.

The interest rate on VA mortgages is the same as the FHA ceiling interest rate. If the lender requires a fee in order to bring the yield on the mortgage to market rates, that fee is paid by the seller of the property.

[5] Private Mortgage Insurance of Single-Family Homes

There are fourteen private mortgage insurance companies licensed to do business, several of which are licensed in every one of the United States. Since 1957, when the first mortgage insurance company began operation, the industry has grown so that in 1981 its assets total more than $1.5 billion.

[a] Extent of Insurance Coverage

Private mortgage insurance is often used for conventional mortgage loans (loans not insured or guaranteed by the government). The insurance companies offer policies that cover the top 20 percent of a mortgage loan that does not have a loan-to-value ratio in excess of 90 percent. If the loan-to-value ratio is over 90 percent, then the insurance covers the top 25 percent.

By "top 20 percent," the mortgage insurance company means that it will pay up to 20 percent of the claim when the lender retains the property. Any additional loss, or any profit from resale, is the loss or profit of the lender. Alternatively, the mortgage insurance company has the option to pay the entire claim and take title to the property.

A claim would normally consist of the principal balance due on the mortgage, the accumulated unpaid interest, attorney's fees (within a limit), any property taxes or property insurance that has been paid by the lender, and any necessary costs to preserve the property. Where there has been a foreclosure, the costs of the foreclosure would be covered. For example, if the claim totaled $50,000, the private mortgage insurance company would either pay the lender the full $50,000 and take title to the house, or pay the lender $10,000 (assuming 20 percent was covered) and let the lender keep the property.

[b] Premium for Insurance

The premium for private mortgage insurance is paid by the buyer of the house and depends upon whether the coverage is 20 percent or 25 percent. The types of programs and the premiums vary among the companies. Usually the first-year premium is higher and is paid at the time of closing. A typical premium charge might be one percent of the mortgage amount for the first year if coverage were 25 percent, and then one quarter of one percent for each of the next ten years. Single-premium plans are offered by most companies, offering coverage for anywhere from five to fifteen years. The average term of a mortgage insurance policy has been about eight years.

[c] Wraparound Mortgage Insurance

Because FHA and VA mortgages are assumable by new buyers, those buyers frequently arrange secondary or wraparound mortgages (see 6.10) in order to obtain additional funds over and above the first mortgage. The Federal Home Loan Bank Board has ruled that federal savings and loan associations may make wraparound mortgages, and those mortgages will normally be considered first liens where (1) the underlying mortgage is an FHA or VA mortgage; and (2) mortgage insurance from an established mortgage insurance company covers the entire loan balance above the first mortgage. Consequently, several mortgage insurance companies are offering insurance on wraparound mortgages, but there is insufficient evidence as yet to tell whether wraparounds will be a major factor in home financing.

[d] Procedures to Obtain Insurance

Institutional lenders often make arrangements with one or more mortgage insurance companies so that the lender will understand the underwriting requirements of the insurance company, and the company will be certain that the institution is adequately financed and competent to initiate mortgage loans. When a home-buyer seeks a mortgage that must be insured, the lender inspects the house and prepares the application for insurance. Once the mortgage insurance company has the application in proper form, it normally approves or disapproves the insurance within twenty-four hours. The insurance policy is issued to be effective as of the date of closing.

[6] Insurance or Guarantees for Mortgages of Manufactured Housing

The term "manufactured homes" or "manufactured housing" replaced "mobile homes" or "mobile housing" in the housing laws as of December 1980. One reason for the change is that these modular houses, which are manufactured in factories in accordance with national standards, are usually mobile for but a few hours of their existence: the trip to and from the dealer's lot to the prepared site. Once the manufactured home is on its permanent site, it does not move again.

Manufactured housing now means more than mobile homes. Some manufactured housing is built in factories in accordance with state or local building codes and is then transported to a building site; it includes shell homes, panelized homes, and modular homes. Although part of the house is factory built, part is constructed on the site. If this type of housing meets the necessary codes for building single-family houses, it can obtain long-term mortgages in the same manner as site-built housing.

The majority of manufactured housing, however, is what is commonly known as mobile homes. These are homes that are built in factories and contain all the structural components; they include a wheeled chassis. When the home is moved to the site, it is necessary only to anchor it and attach it to the utility systems and waste-disposal systems. Approximately one quarter of the single-family market consists of this type of manufactured housing.

Most manufactured-housing sales are financed by banks, finance companies, and savings and loan associations. Private mortgage insurance of manufactured-housing loans has been available from one company, but it is not often used.

The VA guarantees a large number of manufactured-housing loans. Its guarantee, available to qualified veterans, covers 50 percent of the loan. The VA appraises the manufactured housing and its site. The maximum loan is $20,000 for a single-wide home (usually 12 feet wide and 60 feet long) and also $20,000 for a double-wide (24 feet wide and 60 feet long).

The FHA insures mobile-home loans in nearly the same way that it insures home-improvement loans. The FHA does not inspect or appraise the mobile home; instead, the FHA agrees with the lender that it will provide 90 percent insurance on each mobile-home loan made by that lender. The lender risks the remaining 10 percent of the loan. If there is a foreclosure and loss, the FHA pays 90 percent of that loss and the lender pays 10 percent of it.

The FHA will insure a single-wide mobile-home loan up to a maximum amount of $22,500 for twenty years. It will insure a double-wide mobile home up to $35,000 for a maximum term of twenty-three years. The minimum down payment is 5 percent of the first $3,000 of the purchase price and 10 percent of the amount in excess of $3,000. The buyer of the home must have an acceptable site for it.

Both the FHA and the VA have insurance or guarantee programs for sites of manufactured housing, or for combination loans with both site and mobile home as part of the same loan.

Mobile-home loans (or manufactured-housing loans) from the VA or FHA may be sold on the secondary market in the form of government-backed securities. (See Chapter 6.)

[7] Insurance for Home-Improvement Loans

The largest number of loans under any federal housing program are made under a U.S. program known as the Title I [1] Property Improvement Loan Insurance Program, which has been in existence since 1935. It is unlike other HUD programs because the government does not review individual loans at the time of approval.

Approved lenders, which include almost all banks, savings and loan associations, credit unions, and many finance companies, enter into a contract of insurance with HUD. The lender originates and services all home-improvement loans under Title I. The lender pays HUD an insurance premium of one half of one percent of the net proceeds of the loan. If there is a default the lender calls upon the U.S. Government to pay 90 percent of the losses.

Unlike other FHA insurance programs, property-improvement loans cannot be used for purchase of property or for refinancing. Loan decisions are based on the creditworthiness of the borrowers as determined by the lenders.

There are four types of loans available. The most important is the loan for repair, improvement, or alteration of a single-family house. Other types cover improvements in multifamily structures, garages or service buildings, or buildings for agricultural purposes. The maximum loan for a single-family house is $17,500 and the maximum term is fifteen years. The interest rate is set from time to time by HUD; it is comparable to market-rate interest for uninsured intermediate-term loans. No points or discounts may be charged.

7.02 MORTGAGE INSURANCE AND GUARANTEES FOR INCOME-PRODUCING PROPERTY

[1] Federal Mortgage Insurance for Rental Housing

In 1934, when the Federal Housing Administration (FHA) started to provide insurance for mortgage loans for single-family housing, it also initiated insurance on mortgage loans for multifamily housing, which can be defined as rental housing with more than four residential units. Apartment buildings insured with federal mortgage insurance were never as popular as apartment buildings financed with conventional mortgages. However, in particular areas, only FHA-insured loans

---

[1] National Housing Act, 49 Stat. 1246, 12 U.S.C. § 371 (1934).

were available to developers. When the government began to subsidize multifamily housing on an extensive basis in the 1960s, the subsidies could be applied only to FHA mortgages. These subsidies and rent supplements are described in 7.03.

FHA insurance programs are customarily identified by the section of the National Housing Act [2] that authorizes the program. The basic insurance program for apartments is Section 207.

[a] Section 207

A builder or developer of an apartment project may obtain FHA insurance of the mortgage for 90 percent of the estimated value of the apartment. In order to limit the insurance program to apartment buildings designed for the moderate-income family, there are maximum cost limits depending upon the number of bedrooms. The maximum is $19,500 for a residential unit without a bedroom (called an efficiency apartment); $21,600 for a one-bedroom unit; and $25,800, $31,800, and $36,000 for units with two, three and four or more bedrooms, respectively. These limits apply to costs attributable only to the dwelling use and not to exterior land improvements. The dollar limitations may be increased for high-rise buildings with elevators. Whether or not the building is a high-rise, the FHA may allow cost limitations to increase by as much as 75 percent in high-cost geographical areas; in special cases, the increase can be 90 percent. Up to 20 percent more may be added to meet the costs of installing a solar-energy system.

The term of the FHA-insured mortgage under Section 207 is forty years. The interest rate is set by HUD and is not necessarily the same interest rate ceiling established for single-family mortgages.

[b] Section 221(d)(4)—Rental Apartments

To the extent that any apartment buildings are being built today with FHA insurance, developers usually obtain financing with mortgage insurance under Section 221(d)(4) of the National Housing Act.

The mortgage insurance under Section 221(d)(4) for new construction covers 90 percent of the estimate of the replacement cost when improvements are completed. The maximum mortgage amounts per unit are similar but not identical to the limits under the Section 207 program. They may be increased by the FHA in high-cost areas by 75 percent, and, in approved cases, by 90 percent.

One reason that builders use Section 221(d)(4) rather than Section 207 is that they can invest a smaller amount of their own money in the project. If there is an identity of interest between the builder and the sponsor of the project (i.e., both are owners and in partnership), an amount that may be equal to 10 percent of the construction cost can be credited against the expected equity investment of the sponsor. This provision may reduce the actual cash required as an investment in the apartment building to as little as 2 percent or 3 percent of the total cost.

The rents for Section 221(d)(4) apartments, as for other FHA-insured apartments, are reviewed periodically to see that they are suitable for moderate-income

---

[2] Id.

families. Section 221(d)(4) apartments are often built with Section 8 subsidies (discussed in 7.03).

[c] Project Loans for Condominium Apartments

Another loan program that is almost identical to the Section 207 program is Section 234(d), which insures mortgages for developers of multifamily buildings when the units in the buildings will be sold as condominiums. The mortgage provisions permit the release of part of the project mortgage in order to permit first liens on sale of the individual units in that condominium.

[d] Nonprofit Sponsors

For many years, particularly in the 1960s, nonprofit organizations were the sponsors of multifamily housing projects. As a rule, nonprofit sponsors could obtain 100 percent financing for the buildings. Section 221(d)(3) covers the role of nonprofit sponsors in multifamily apartments, but, because of the difficulties many nonprofit organizations had with management of housing, the use of this section has been limited in recent years.

[e] Programs for the Elderly

Section 231 provides a mortgage insurance program for housing for the elderly and handicapped. Sponsors may be profit or nonprofit, and the program resembles that of the moderate-income Section 221(d)(4) housing. This Section 231 should not be confused with the more popular Section 202 program (described in 7.03), which authorizes direct loans from the government to build housing for the elderly.

[f] Refinancing Conventionally Financed Apartments

A large number of conventionally financed apartment buildings are in need of moderate repairs and are not producing any profit for the owners. Rents cannot be increased enough to cover the escalating cost of utilities, while old loans, with high debt-service requirements, are nearing the end of their terms. The Section 223(f) program was designed to permit refinancing of conventional mortgages with longer-term FHA-insured loans. In order to permit sufficient refinancing to cover repairs and to lower the debt service due to the extension of term, FHA insurance seemed to be the best solution. One difficulty, however, is that the program could be enormously expensive to the government; thus, the future of many older apartment buildings is uncertain.

At the present time, Section 223(f) is tightly restricted. It covers refinancing of conventional mortgages provided that the property is retained as a rental property for at least twenty years; it is targeted to rental apartment buildings with less than 100 units in older declining areas; the repairs are limited to 15 percent of the mortgage amount; and the funds available for the program are extremely limited.

[g] Processing an Application for Mortgage Insurance

To obtain FHA insurance on a rental housing project to be constructed, the developer submits an application to the local office of HUD for a site and market appraisal, called a SAMA letter. The HUD office determines the need for the project, establishes the rents that should be obtainable in that area for that building, appraises the site's value with the expected improvements, and advises on other matters, such as the availability of transportation and the zoning issues.

In some cases, the developer, after receiving the SAMA letter, submits schematic drawings and outline specifications. HUD establishes the costs, checks the operating projections, reviews the builder's qualifications, and establishes a mortgage amount. At that point, HUD issues a conditional commitment.

Some developers go directly from the receipt of the SAMA letter to a firm-commitment stage. For a firm commitment, the developer must submit the construction contract and final architectural plans, a revised application for mortgage insurance, and other documents. HUD issues a commitment to insure the project at a specified rate for a specified amount. The cost to the developer is $3 per thousand dollars of mortgage. There are also fees to be paid for HUD inspections.

[2] Federal Mortgage Insurance for Health Facilities

[a] Hospitals

The FHA will insure up to 90 percent of the mortgage loan for construction or substantial rehabilitation of a hospital. The mortgage term is twenty-five years, and the interest rate is the FHA ceiling rate for multifamily projects. The hospital may be a proprietary hospital or a nonprofit hospital. The state in which the hospital is located must certify that there is a need for a hospital of that size and type in that area.

[b] Nursing-Home and Intermediate-Care Facilities

The permanent mortgage for a nursing home may be insured by the FHA in an amount not to exceed 90 percent of its estimated value; this amount may include the fixed equipment to be used in the operation of the nursing home. An increase in the amount of the mortgage can often be obtained when there are operating losses during the first two years of operation. The term of the mortgage may not exceed forty years.

Intermediate-care facilities are also included. As with a nursing home, an intermediate-care facility must provide continuous care by trained personnel. Each facility must have twenty or more patients.

[c] Group-Practice Facilities

The FHA will insure 90 percent of the mortgage on a group-practice facility, which is a facility in which a group practicing medicine, osteopathy, dentistry, podiatry, or optometry provides preventative, diagnostic, and treatment services to ambulatory patients. The facility does not include beds or any provision for extended care. The term of the loan may not exceed twenty-five years. The owner of the facility must be a nonprofit organization, but tenants may be a profit-motivated group. The group must show that a comparable mortgage would not have been available without FHA insurance.

[3] Federal Mortgage Insurance for Land Development and Mobile-Home Parks

Title X of the National Housing Act authorizes mortgage insurance for land acquisition and development for large-scale developments of single-family homes. The amount of the insured mortgage is determined by a complicated formula, but the average loan may be 85 percent of the acquisition and development costs. The loan may not exceed ten years. The application and commitment fees for the mortgage insurance are $4.50 for each $1,000 of mortgage amount. In addition, the inspection fee of $5 per thousand must be paid. Developers with less than 100 lots to develop will not use this insurance program because of its complexity and cost.

FHA mortgage insurance also covers the acquisition and development of mobile-home parks. The program is included under Section 207, which also covers mortgage insurance for apartment buildings. The maximum mortgage is $9,000 for each lot to be rented to a mobile-home owner.

[4] Programs of the Small Business Administration

The Small Business Administration (SBA) makes direct loans to assist small business, and it guarantees the loans to small business made by financial institutions. Its program of guaranteed loans is far larger than that of direct loans.

SBA loan programs are by no means confined to real estate; they cover equipment loans, operating loans, loans for receivables, and other purposes. All must go to small businesses, which are defined in a variety of ways, depending upon such matters as the number of employees in the business and its gross annual receipts.

The maximum loan guarantee for the SBA is $500,000 and is increased periodically. The SBA will have a much lower ceiling on guaranteed loan authority in 1982 than it has had in recent years. It is possible that the SBA will also reduce the portion of loan guaranteed from 90 percent to 70 percent for certain larger loans. Assuming that today's 90 percent guarantee by the SBA will continue to apply to most SBA loans, there is an active secondary market for the guaranteed portion of those loans.

When an SBA loan is used for purchase or construction of facilities, the maximum term is twenty years; other SBA loans have a maximum of ten years. The interest rate is negotiated between borrower and lender, but is subject to a maximum imposed from time to time by the SBA. Variable-rate loans are permissible, but there is a guarantee fee of one percent.

A number of loans that may be used for real estate are available for particular purposes to

- Small businesses to repair or replace real estate damaged or destroyed by a disaster such as a fire or flood. Disaster loans are usually direct loans.

- Small businesses to help them comply with environmental, safety, or health laws and regulations.
- Small businesses that have suffered economic injury due to a factor beyond the business' control, such as the closing of a nearby military base.
- Small businesses engaged in the solar-energy business to help acquire or construct plant or equipment.

Local-development-company loans, guaranteed by the SBA, are used primarily for long-term financing of business real estate. A local development company is either profit or nonprofit and it is composed of twenty-five or more residents or businesses within a small specified geographical area, such as a small town or a neighborhood within a city. A local development company is authorized to borrow money, guaranteed by the SBA, which it in turn lends to small businesses within the area. For example, the local development company may enter into an agreement to buy certain stores in a particular urban neighborhood, then lease those stores to small businesses. It could borrow up to $500,000 for each store purchased and leased. Alternatively, it might lend up to $500,000 to each small business in that neighborhood that agreed to repair, rehabilitate, and improve its premises. As another example, a local development company could build a shopping center in a small town, lending money to each small business in that center to lease or buy its store. The term of each loan may not be longer than twenty-five years. The money is obtained from financial institutions and guaranteed 90 percent by the SBA.

[5] Other Federal Loan Guarantee Programs

[a] Geothermal Loan Guarantees

The Department of Energy is attempting to accelerate the development of geothermal resources. It will guarantee loans up to 75 percent of total project costs, which includes land and buildings. No one loan may exceed $100 million, and the maximum term is thirty years.

[b] Overseas Housing Guarantee Program

The Department of State's Agency for International Development studies low-cost housing needs of certain developing countries and arranges for the country to apply in the United States for a U.S.-guaranteed housing loan. The principal and interest are 100 percent guaranteed; the lender need not see the housing development project. The average loan is approximately $15 million. The borrower pays the market rate of interest for a thirty-year loan, as a rule, plus a one percent guarantee fee at closing and one half of one percent each year thereafter.

[6] Private Mortgage Insurance for Income-Producing Property

Private mortgage insurance for income-producing property (called commercial loan insurance) provides protection against unexpected mortgage losses by insuring the top 10 percent to 20 percent of a loan or mortgage. If, for example, a lender normally would grant an 80 percent loan-to-value mortgage, use of a commercial loan insurance policy that insured 15 percent of that loan would reduce the risk on the property to the equivalent of a 68 percent loan-to-value mortgage. In private residential financing, mortgage insurance is almost always required. In contrast, experience over the past decade suggests that commercial loan insurance has not become a common element in financing. Nonetheless, one should be aware of this form of insurance because it occasionally permits a borrower to secure financing that would otherwise not be available. For the entrepreneur or the creative real estate developer, commercial loan insurance may prove crucial in financing a new type of project with little or no proven record of profitability.

[a] Protection Afforded and Costs

Standard commercial loan insurance covers only permanent self-amortizing loans and does not cover construction or other interim financing. In insuring 10, 15 or, less frequently, 20 percent of a loan, the standard policy reserves to the insurer three alternatives when the loan goes into default and the insured enters a claim: It may pay the lesser of (1) 15 percent (for example) of the original amount of the loan; (2) 15 percent of the outstanding balance of the loan plus all other insured claims; or (3) it may pay the unpaid balance of the loan and other claims in exchange for marketable title to the property. Under the second and third alternatives, such insurable losses usually include legal costs incurred in foreclosure, taxes, and insurance advanced by the lender, and costs of maintaining and restoring the property, as well as unpaid principal and interest. Experience suggests that 15 percent of the sum of such claims and the outstanding balance rarely, if ever, is less than 15 percent of the original balance, so that the first and third alternatives are the more likely courses of action.

Costs of the insurance varies with some lenders tailoring cost to meet their perception of the risks on an individual project. Typical costs often include a small commitment fee, a first year's premium, and a much smaller premium for the following years. One insurer offering a separate policy for apartment buildings charges one quarter of one percent as a commitment fee, 60 percent of which is credited toward the policy premium; one percent premium for the first year; one half of one percent of the outstanding balance thereafter, with an optional single premium for five years coverage of 2.5 percent.

Because the lender and the commercial loan insurer have a mutual interest in the insured loan, the insurer will generally rely for underwriting purposes on the documents submitted by the borrower. In addition to the loan application, the insurance application will usually require copies of the financial statements of the borrower, current appraisals, and other typical lending exhibits. While more and more lenders are coming to evaluate a project on which a loan is sought from the viewpoint of the equity owner, the insurer in insuring the marginal income from the property is particularly sensitive to income flow and may often require a feasibility study or study of alternative uses, if not required by the lender itself.

Under a standard policy, the insured may present claims to the insurer only after it has obtained marketable title following a foreclosure of its equivalent. Nonetheless, although not provided for specifically in the policy, a useful side benefit, especially for the lender with little experience in or capacity for property management, is the insurer's willingness to deploy its expertise in curing default and preventing foreclosure.

A number of terms in the policy are worth noting. Prior written consent of the insurer is required for any modification in the terms of the loan; thus, if the insurance is to continue, the insurer is perforce a party to any workout that would modify the loan. Similarly, the project must be completed according to the plans and specifications approved by the insurer. Given the likelihood that some modifications in plans will become necessary in a large project during the course of construction, careful attention should be paid to this provision and the insurer's approval sought for changes in plans and specifications.

The policy typically requires that the insurer be notified of any default in payment within fifteen days and be provided with monthly status reports on the default. After two months default, the policy requires the insured to take legal action to have income or rents from the property paid to itself or to a receiver; foreclosure or its equivalent must be initiated after a default of three months. These schedules may be modified, however, by agreement between insurer and insured; again, the policy makes the insurance company a party to any workout.

[b] Uses and Benefits

Commercial loan insurance is based upon the notion of shared risk; the lender reduces but by no means eliminates his exposure on an insured property. The insurance will be most useful, in theory, where insurer and lender have differing capacities for evaluating the project and thus differing evaluations of risk. Beyond that, it is difficult to generalize about situations in which commercial loan insurance may be helpful. But several situations taken from actual examples and all variations on the theme of uncertainty and differing perceptions of risk may be cited:

(1) Where a project is built for a specialized purpose and the alternatives are lower economic uses, the insurance can fill the gap between the value of the property employed in the two different functions. Here, even with a solid borrower and project, the uncertainty and risk for the lender is heightened by the greater loss incurred upon conversion to the lower use. Often, the difference in value between alternative uses will be greater than the maximum 15 to 20 percent coverage, however, and insurers, like lenders, are less than enthusiastic about commitment to highly specialized and hard-to-convert properties.

(2) Where the prospects for a project are sound but the borrower will not accept personal liability on the loan, thereby reducing the potential funds available to rescue a distressed property, insurance has in some cases made the nonrecourse debt acceptable to a lender.

(3) Loan insurance is most frequently helpful where there is an inability on the part of the lender to assess certain risks confidently, due to its inexperience with a type of project or to the borrower's inexperience. For example, one savings and loan institution undertook its first financing of a motel project with loan insurance. In that case, the borrower's lack of experience in the construction of budget motels added another element of uncertainty. As typically happens, however, once the first project proved successful, later financing was completed without resort to insurance.

(4) Similarly, where an institution's lending activities are usually confined to one geographic area, loan insurance may be helpful in persuading it to accept a loan outside of that area.

Interviews with lenders and insurers suggest that most uses of loan insurance involve relatively small deals (for apartment buildings the average loan insured in one area was $1 million), smaller lenders, frequently a lender's or borrower's first venture into a specialized area, and more often a savings and loan than a commercial bank. The insurance is generally not necessary or desirable for the large, relatively standard office building, industrial park, or shopping center loans, which form the bread-and-butter loans in the portfolios of large lenders. But commercial loan insurance serves a vital function in the development of the McDonalds of tomorrow by assisting in the financing of innovative real estate projects such as budget motels, mini-warehouses, skateboard rinks, and similar projects properly adjudged marginal by the prudent lender.

7.03 DIRECT FEDERAL LOANS, GRANTS, AND SUBSIDIES

[1] Introduction

The previous two sections discussed federal guarantees and insurance for real estate loans; this section considers direct loans made by the federal government to real estate developers and owners, grants made to local communities for housing or economic development, and subsidies for housing low- and moderate-income families. Because direct loans are the principal way of financing real estate in rural areas, a separate section (7.04) is devoted to this type of financing.

[2] Direct Loans for Housing

[a] Housing for the Elderly and Handicapped

Although there is a federal guaranteed loan program for housing for the elderly and handicapped (Section 231), the most extensive program for housing for the elderly over the past twenty years has been the Section 202 program for direct loans from the government to the housing sponsor. The loans are made at an interest rate equal to the average rate paid on federal obligations during the previous year, a rate below the market mortgage-interest rate. The term of the loan may be for fifty years.

The borrower must be a private nonprofit sponsor with experience with the problems of the elderly. Labor unions and social service organizations have often been the sponsors of such housing. At least 20 percent of the units must be reserved for tenants who require Section 8 assistance (discussed in 7.03[4][a]).

[b] Housing Rehabilitation Loans

The federal government has loaned money directly to homeowners and apartment building owners at a subsidized interest rate (usually 3 percent) for repairs of existing housing. The program, called the Section 312 program, has been administered by selected cities for targeting in urban areas in particular need of rehabilitation. This loan program is to be discontinued after 1981, but similar programs will be available from cities that use their Community Development Block Grant funds for this purpose.

[3] Subsidized Home-Ownership

[a] Interest-Rate Subsidies

Section 235 of the National Housing Act [3] was extensively used during the late 1960s and early 1970s to provide interest-rate subsidies so that low- and moderate-income families could purchase houses. The program was discontinued in 1973. A revised program was initiated in 1977 to enable eligible families to purchase new homes with a mortgage where the interest rate has been reduced to as little as 4 percent. The eligible family of four, for example, must not have income higher than 95 percent of the median income in the area.

The sales price of the house must not exceed 125 percent of the mortgage limit. That limit is $47,500 in high-cost areas, unless the family has five or more members, in which case it is $55,000. For lower-cost areas, the limit is $40,000.

The homeowner must pay 20 percent of his income for the monthly mortgage payments. The federal government pays the lender the difference between the homeowner's payments and the mortgage payments, as long as the interest rate does not fall below 4 percent.

Because the buyer is receiving such a substantial subsidy, recapture provisions come into effect when the owner sells the house, refinances the house, fails to make mortgage payments for at least three months, or rents the house to others for a year or more. In any of these events, the federal government recaptures the lesser of (1) subsidy payments actually made; or (2) 50 percent of the net appreciation of the property. If the house is sold to another family eligible under the program, the recapture provisions are not operative.

No new loan applications were accepted after March 31, 1982.

[b] Homesteading

The federal government transfers a limited number of houses without charge to counties or municipalities. Approximately seventy cities are participating in the homesteading program; each participating city agrees to use its own funds, or funds from its Community Development Block Grant, to help buyers of these houses repair them. The houses are usually those that the federal government has obtained in foreclosure or assignment, and often the houses are in poor shape.

The cities receiving the houses in their jurisdictions transfer the houses by a lottery, an auction, or sell them to persons who agree to live in them and to rehabilitate them.

[4] Subsidies for Rent Payments

[a] Section 8

By far the largest subsidy, involving government expenses of billions of dollars each year, is the Section 8 [4] program. The subsidy payments are made directly

---

[3] 49 Stat. 1246, 12 U.S.C. § 371 (1934).

[4] U.S. Housing Act of 1937, as amended by Pub. L. No. 93-383, 88 Stat. 633, 42 U.S.C. § 3535.

to landlords to cover the difference between what a low- or moderate-income family can pay in rent and the amount of rent that may be charged for the rental unit, whether it be an apartment, a house, or a mobile home. The U.S. Department of Housing and Urban Development (HUD) determines annually what the fair market rents ought to be in each particular area of the country, for both newly constructed housing and existing housing.

Those eligible to receive the benefits of a subsidized rental unit are families whose income must not exceed 80 percent of the median income in the particular area. Special priority for some of the available rental units is given to "very low-income families" whose income is 50 percent or less of the median income in the area. Somewhat different income rules apply for elderly and handicapped persons.

In 1982, approximately 140,000 units of housing will be subsidized for the first time with Section 8 subsidies; less than half of the units will be new construction. Approximately a million units have already been subsidized under this program.

The program subsidizes existing housing, housing that has been moderately rehabilitated, substantially rehabilitated and new housing—with somewhat different rules for each category. For existing housing, allocations of subsidy funds are given by HUD to local public-housing authorities, which determine the eligible applicants. As a rule, an eligible family that has a certificate of eligibility is allowed to find its own housing in the marketplace, a rental unit where the owner will agree to the subsidy conditions.

For new construction, the owner will generally build an apartment project with FHA mortgage insurance, often under Section 221(d)(4). He enters at the same time into a contract with HUD to receive Section 8 subsidies for as few as 20 percent of the apartment units or as many as 100 percent.

The eligible family may pay anywhere from 15 percent to 30 percent of its income for rent, depending upon the size of the family and its income. The balance of the fair market rent is paid by HUD. One of the reasons that the Section 8 program is popular with landlords is that it permits an automatic increase in rents, and thus in subsidy, with the annual increase in housing costs in the area. Vacant units, moreover, will be covered by the subsidy for a brief period of time.

In any area, at least 30 percent of the Section 8 subsidy allocation must be for very low-income families.

[b] Special Financing Program for Section 8 Projects

The subsidies for Section 8 rental payments would be even higher than they are if new construction for Section 8 projects were required to pay the FHA ceiling interest rate for apartments. To assist Section 8, the government developed the Tandem Plan for apartments that are to be built with 100 percent-subsidized Section 8 units. For example, the Government National Mortgage Association (GNMA), an agency of the U.S. Government (see 6.15), agrees to commit mortgage money at 7.5 percent. GNMA originally sold that 7.5 percent forty-year mortgage to the Federal National Mortgage Association (FNMA) at market interest rates and paid the difference from taxpayers' funds. This arrangement between GNMA and FNMA led to the designation "Tandem Plan." Today GNMA sells the mortgages at auction at a deep discount.

The Tandem Plan has proved very expensive when mortgage rates have been in the double digits; it will be modified or discontinued in 1982.

Tax-exempt financing has been one way to finance Section 8 projects at nearly 3 percent below the FHA ceiling interest rate. One way that this is done is by having the lender make an FHA-insured loan on the housing project before the interest rate is determined. The lender issues securities guaranteed by the GNMA. These securities are then purchased by a public authority with the legal power to issue tax-exempt bonds. This authority then contracts with an investment firm that places the authority's tax-exempt bonds or securities in the amount of the purchase price of the mortgage with a private investor or investors. Because the mortgage is FHA-insured and the securities based on that mortgage are federally guaranteed, the tax-exempt issue has an AAA rating (the best) from Standard & Poor's, an investment rating service that rates municipal bonds.

Tax-exempt bond issues are usually issued by public housing authorities. Some of the housing mortgages are not FHA-insured, but are guaranteed by the state agency.

[5] Public Housing

Public housing is designed to meet the housing needs of persons who have the lowest income, generally below what is needed to obtain housing assisted by Section 8. Approximately 4,500 public-housing authorities build or manage housing units.

The housing is built with tax-exempt financing. The federal government acts as agent for the local-housing authorities in raising funds for public housing. The security for the tax-exempt notes is the federal guarantee and the annual contributions contract under which the federal government agrees to pay building costs for local public-housing projects. In the past several years, the federal government has been issuing short-term notes for this purpose, with terms of ninety days to one year. The annual volume of these tax-exempt notes is about $10 billion a year, most of which is used to refinance existing obligations.

[6] Miscellaneous Programs

A variety of other programs that are financed and administered by HUD deserve mention but not explanation because they are relatively small programs or are no longer active:

- Since many federally insured housing projects are in financial difficulty, the government offers a flexible subsidy program to help them become profitable again.
- HUD has undertaken a public-housing modernization program, and it also provides operating subsidies for certain public-housing systems.
- Many apartments financed under Section 236 still receive subsidies so that the interest rate on these mortgages is reduced to as little as one percent. The program took no new applications after 1973. Rent supplements that are additional payments to landlords for low- and moderate-income families are gradually being replaced by Section 8 payments.

- HUD continues to support certain existing new communities, a program that now takes no new applications.

[7] Grants and Loans for Economic and Community Development

[a] Community Development Block Grants

Nearly $4 billion a year is given by the federal government to municipalities in Community Development Block Grants. The major portion goes to approximately 700 cities by a formula, called an entitlement, which is based on the extent to which the municipality is impoverished, the age of its housing, the extent to which it has grown or failed to grow, and other factors in relation to its population. Most of the balance of funds goes to smaller communities that compete for specific grants. The funds granted must principally benefit low- and moderate-income families or aid in the elimination of slums and blight or meet urgent community needs. The cities use these funds for housing rehabilitation, construction of public facilities, acquisition of public property, water and sewer facilities, or for social services or economic development.

[b] Urban Development Action Grants

Approximately 300 cities with populations of 50,000 or more are designated "distressed," as are 10,000 smaller cities, villages, and towns. Distress is measured by such factors as the extent of poverty, amount of unemployment, age of the housing, and lack of growth in population. The 300 larger cities compete for grants, and the 10,000 smaller cities compete separately for grants. In addition, certain nondistressed cities with impoverished areas called pockets of poverty can compete for grants to be made in those "pockets."

The purpose of these urban development action grants (UDAG) is to assist distressed cities (and a few urban counties) that require increased public assistance and private investment to alleviate physical and economic deterioration. Private investment is the key to receipt of a UDAG. The grant given to the city for a project must be accompanied by private investment in an amount that is usually about five times the amount of the grant.

The grants go to the cities, which either use the funds themselves for the particular project—for example, by building a municipal parking garage for an adjacent hotel—or lend the money on beneficial terms to the developer. Successful applications, which may be for shopping centers, office buildings, hotels, industrial parks, factory expansion, or other construction, are measured in part by the number of jobs that are created or retained. Approximately $500 million is given in grants each year; a grant may be any size.

[c] Section 108 Loan Guarantees

A city that receives an annual amount of money under the Community Development Block Grant program may pledge up to three times that annual grant as security for a loan. If it does, the federal government then guarantees the loan. In 1980 and 1981, the loans have been made by the Federal Financing Bank, part of the U.S. Treasury, at the interest rate that U.S. obligations of intermediate term were selling for.

The money borrowed by the city may be used only for acquisition of real property or rehabilitation of property owned or acquired by the city. The loan may cover related expenses such as land clearance, relocation, and development of utilities, but it may not be used for construction of new buildings.

The usual pattern is for a private developer to plan an industrial park, a shopping center, or housing project. The city, desiring this development as a means of economic improvement, borrows money to buy the land under the development, the loan being repayable in a relatively short time. The developer then purchases the land from the city when the loan expires, perhaps in five years. In the meantime, the developer has been leasing the land, and the lease payments pay the interest on the loan.

The amount of total loan guarantees is restricted to $250 million. Administration proposals for 1983 would eliminate the program.

7.04 REAL ESTATE FINANCING IN RURAL AREAS

[1] Introduction

Banks, savings and loan associations, and credit unions all make real estate loans in rural areas, but the availability of mortgage money is frequently limited. One reason is that financial institutions in rural areas do not have sufficient assets to make large loans, and the urban financial institutions, such as large banks, life insurance companies, and pension funds, are seldom willing to lend money in areas of the countryside with which they are unfamiliar. Consequently, one government agency, the Farmers Home Administration, and one quasi-public system of lending institutions, the Farm Credit System, have increasingly played a major role in rural real estate financing.

The Farmers Home Administration, abbreviated FmHA and not to be confused with the FHA (Federal Housing Administration), is an agency within the U.S. Department of Agriculture. It has nearly 1500 branch offices throughout the nation. A predecessor agency began making farm loans in the 1930s; FmHA was created in 1949 and began making housing loans to farmers in that year. Its housing loan programs were extended to nonfarmers in rural areas in 1961.

Unlike the mortgage programs of the FHA or the Veterans Administration (VA), only a small proportion of FmHA loans are made by private financial institutions and guaranteed by FmHA. The majority are loans made directly by FmHA to the borrower.

The real estate programs of FmHA may be divided into three main groupings: housing programs, programs for farmers, and community-facility programs. Each will be discussed in this section. A fourth category, the business and industry programs of FmHA, will accept no new loan applications after 1981. During 1982, it is expected that many of the FmHA programs will be reduced in size, and, possibly, the community-facilities program may be eliminated.

The Farm Credit System, unlike FmHA, is really not part of the federal administration, but consists of financial institutions owned by their borrowers and operating on a not-for-profit basis. The components of the System that make real estate loans are the twelve federal Land Banks, which operate through approximately 500 local federal Land Bank Associations. The Land Banks were created in 1916 as part of the federal government, but the law provided that their stock would be acquired by the Land Bank Associations through stock subscriptions of the borrowers from those Associations. Since 1947, each federal Land Bank Association has been owned by its stockholders, who are farmers, growers, or ranchers, and who are borrowers from the Banks. Both Banks and Associations are chartered by the federal government and subject to supervision by the Farm Credit Administration, which is part of the Department of Agriculture. Federal Land Banks do not lend government funds, nor are their loans guaranteed by the government.

The federal Land Banks, like FmHA, make housing loans and loans to farmers. This section will first outline the FmHA programs.

[2] Housing Loans of the Farmers Home Administration

[a] Location

The FmHA housing programs operate in open-country areas and in towns with populations no larger than 10,000 people. Towns that have more than 10,000 people but less than 20,000 and are outside standard metropolitan statistical areas (SMSAs) will qualify if there is a serious lack of mortgage credit in the town. FmHA publishes a list of these rural localities having more than 10,000 and less than 20,000 people.

[b] Single-Family Homes

An FmHA home-ownership loan may be used to buy, construct, relocate, improve, or rehabilitate a dwelling and any related facility (such as a garage) for use by the borrower as his residence.

Like FHA housing programs, FmHA housing programs are known by numbers, the home-ownership program being Section 502.[5] There are a variety of types of Section 502 loans, the type being dependent on the income of the borrower.

FmHA uses three types of income appraisal for its housing programs: above-moderate income, moderate income, and low income. Limits on income for each of the three categories vary from state to state.

To determine income, FmHA takes the income of the borrower plus that of all adults who live with the borrower. Then 5 percent of that amount is deducted plus an additional $300 for each dependent child. A borrower seeking a home mortgage must be a person who does not own an adequate dwelling and who is a citizen of the United States.

☐ *Above-moderate-income families.* FmHA will guarantee a loan from a financial institution. If it is a direct loan, it is made on the same terms as an FHA home-ownership loan under Section 203(b): The borrower pays the FHA ceiling interest rate and a mortgage insurance premium of one half of one percent of the

---

[5] Housing Act of 1949, Pub. L. No. 81-171, 63 Stat. 432, 42 U.S.C. § 1471.

outstanding principal balance. The amount that may be borrowed is 97 percent of the first $25,000 of the mortgage loan and 95 percent of the balance. The term of the loan is thirty-three years, whereas the FHA loan term is thirty years.

The guaranteed loan is a 90 percent guarantee of a mortgage loan from a financial institution. The borrower pays a one-time fee of one percent for this guarantee. The interest rate and the term of the loan (not to exceed thirty-three years) is negotiated between borrower and lender.

There is no ceiling on the amount of the mortgage, but the program is not designed for expensive houses. As a general rule, a house financed with an FmHA loan will not exceed 1400 square feet in size. This program is not operating in 1982.

☐ *Moderate-income families.* If there is no interest credit involved, FmHA will loan money to a moderate-income family at the rate that FmHA uses to borrow money from the U.S. Treasury. This rate, approximately equal to the long-term Treasury bond rate, is usually about 3 percent below the market interest rate for mortgages. No down payment is required.

☐ *Lower-income families.* For those families whose adjusted annual income is less than an amount specified, FmHA will provide interest credits. The family must spend 20 percent of its adjusted income on principal and interest for its housing and must pay real property taxes plus insurance. For example, a family with an adjusted annual income of $10,000 could pay $2,000 a year towards its mortgage. Suppose that the borrowing rate for FmHA is 12 percent, and the house that the low-income family wishes to buy costs $40,000.

The annual payment for a 12 percent, thirty-three-year mortgage of $40,000 (assuming monthly payment) is $4,848. The family can pay only $2,000, so the subsidy is $2,848 a year.

The law does not permit the subsidy from FmHA to bring the interest rate on the mortgage below one percent annually. The interest credit is reviewed periodically. If the borrower's income goes up, the amount he pays monthly goes up and the subsidy decreases.

This subsidy is subject to recapture when the house is sold or refinanced. The family that received the interest credit must repay that amount (without interest) if they receive money from a sale or refinancing. For example, if the subsidy for $2,848 a year has been paid for five years, the borrower will owe FmHA $14,240 when the house is sold. However, this obligation is secured by the real estate loan. If the borrower makes less than $14,240 on the sale, the profit is turned over to FmHA but there is no obligation for the borrower to pay the amount still owing.

[c] Rental Housing

Section 515 of the Housing Act of 1949 [6] authorizes FmHA to make mortgage loans on multifamily housing for low- and moderate-income residents of rural areas. The apartment may be owned by a nonprofit applicant or a limited profit applicant. If it is a limited profit applicant, the cash-flow return on the equity

---

[6] Id.

invested must not be more than 8 percent annually. A limited profit borrower will often have invested not more than 10 percent of the total cost, and will of course be receiving the tax benefits from owning an apartment.

The rental apartments must generally be garden apartments and the units must be very modest in size. As a guideline, a one-bedroom apartment must be about 600 square feet, and a four-bedroom apartment must not be more than about 1,200 square feet.

The borrower receives a direct loan from FmHA at the interest rate at which FmHA borrows, the rough equivalent to Treasury bond rates for long-term obligations. Some or all of the tenants will be low- or moderate-income persons eligible to have a part of their rent paid by FmHA to the landlord. The low-income tenant will be paying about 30 percent of his income.

For example, suppose a low-income tenant with an adjusted gross income of $6,000 a year is able to pay only $1,800 a year in rent. Suppose, however, the rent for the unit is $250 a month or $3,000 a year. FmHA pays the $1,200 difference directly to the owner.

Although FmHA has this rental assistance program, it is also possible for the owner to obtain Section 8 rental assistance from the Department of Housing and Urban Development (HUD). (See 7.03[4][a].) In 1981, about 10,000 units of housing in rural areas were assisted with Section 8, but there are far fewer Section 8 assistance funds planned for 1982 and 1983. Section 8 cannot be combined with rental assistance from FmHA.

The term of the loan to build apartments is fifty years.

[d] Congregate Housing

Congregate housing offers such social services as meals, transportation, and some housekeeping services. It is designed to provide a semi-independent lifestyle for the elderly or handicapped. It does not include facilities for those needing medical treatment or institutional care. FmHA has been conducting a demonstration program to test whether congregate housing should be financed under the Section 515 rental housing program.

Loans to nonprofit organizations or governmental agencies can cover 100 percent of the cost; loans to profit-making organizations cover 95 percent of the cost. In most cases, congregate housing must be built with assurance that grant funds from other federal programs will be available to help pay for social services.

[e] Farm-Labor Housing

A farm owner, an association of farmers, a municipality, or a nonprofit organization may build housing for farm laborers. FmHA will lend money for the mortgage at one percent interest over a term of thirty-three years. The housing would not contain more than fifty units and must be modest in cost. The loan may cover all the costs, including land, construction, water and sewage facilities, and basic household furnishings. The units must not be used by anyone other than domestic farm laborers and their families.

[f] Housing Repairs

A homeowner may obtain an FmHA loan to repair or improve his house. The term of the loan may be as long as twenty-five years. The loan amount must be less than $7,000.

The interest rate is at the Treasury rate unless the borrower is a homeowner of very low income and the repairs are needed to make the house safe or to remove health hazards. In that case, the interest rate will be as low as one percent, and the maximum loan will be $7,500 for a twenty-year term.

The elderly may receive a combination of grants and loans in order to repair their homes. If a very low-income elderly person needs $7,000 for essential home repairs, but can afford to pay the debt service on only $3,000, then the grant will be for $4,000.

Weatherization loans will be made for five-year terms at the same interest rate as the Section 502 program. The local utility or rural electric cooperative will administer this program.

[g] Self-Help Housing

If a group of families agree to work together to build their own homes, they may receive financing and technical assistance from FmHA. A nonprofit organization may borrow money at a below-market interest rate to develop housing sites for self-help housing projects. Then FmHA makes grants to nonprofit groups to pay for technical assistance required in order to build their own houses. The technical assistance staff provides basic instruction in construction.

[3] Farmers' Loans From the Farmers Home Administration

Rural housing loans are made in eligible areas regardless of whether or not the homeowner or building developer is a farmer. FmHA also has a number of programs restricted to farmers and ranchers. The borrowers must be unable to obtain credit on reasonable terms from other sources. Most of the programs are designed to help with family-size farms. There is a particular effort to help young people finance a start in farming.

[a] Emergency Disaster Loans

A program that loaned more than $3 billion in 1981 is the FmHA emergency disaster loan program. To be eligible, the farm or ranch to receive the loan must be in a county that has been designated a disaster area, perhaps as the result of a flood, a severe drought, or an earthquake. The President of the United States designates the area a major disaster, the Secretary of Agriculture has the power to designate a smaller disaster, and the State Director for FmHA may designate a disaster when not more than twenty-five farmers are affected.

The applicant for an emergency disaster loan must be an established farm operator, either an owner or a tenant, who was operating the farm at the time of the disaster. The applicant must be a U.S. citizen and unable to obtain suitable credit elsewhere. There is no requirement that the applicant be the owner of a small-size farm; even the largest agricultural owners are eligible.

Disaster loans are divided into three categories: (1) loans to cover actual losses suffered due to the disaster; (2) loans to meet annual production expenses and other essential needs to enable prompt recovery; and (3) loans to help the farmer achieve a sound farming operation comparable to what it was before the disaster. As a rule, only part of a disaster loan will be used for real estate, such as restoring or replacing damaged buildings or buying new buildings to replace old ones.

Loans to cover actual losses are at an interest rate of 8 percent, and the maximum loan may not exceed 80 percent of the amount lost. Loans to cover major adjustment losses (not actual losses) are made at the Treasury rate of borrowing and are now limited to not more than $500,000 per borrower.

The term of a disaster loan for real estate may not exceed thirty years unless the FmHA allows a longer period under exceptional circumstances. In ten years, FmHA will review the real estate loans made at subsidized rates and, if the borrower is able to obtain financing at reasonable market rates, he will be asked to repay the disaster loan.

Between late 1978 and 1982, FmHA made billions of dollars of loans to farmers and ranchers who suffered economic hardship because of a general lack of farm credit. This program, called the Economic Emergency Loan program, ended in late 1981.

[b] Farm-Ownership Loans

FmHA makes loans directly to farmers to buy land, construct, repair or improve buildings, improve farmland, develop water facilities, and establish farm-based business enterprises to supplement farming income.

FmHA may lend up to 100 percent of the value of the completed real estate or its cost, whichever is less, so there is no down payment required. There is a ceiling of $200,000 for direct loans for farm ownership. The borrower pays the interest rate paid by FmHA for its borrowing from the U.S. Treasury.

An alternative to a direct loan is a guaranteed loan for the same purpose, which may not be more than $300,000. FmHA guarantees 90 percent of the loan amount; the financial institution risks 10 percent of the loan. The borrower pays a one percent fee for the guarantee. The interest rate is negotiated between borrower and lender.

A limited-resource farmer may borrow money at 5 percent for a farm ownership loan. A limited-resource farmer or rancher is one who, because of limited resources such as lack of equipment, land, adequate financing, or sufficient background in farming, needs a lower interest rate in order to succeed. After the first three years of a loan to a limited-resource farmer, the loan is examined every two years to determine if the farmer is able to obtain the money instead from private financial institutions at market interest rates. If so, he is expected to pay off the 5 percent loan and obtain financing from private sources.

[c] Special-Purpose Loans

The terms available for farm ownership loans are available for a variety of farm-related loan programs. Farm operating loans are a major lending program, but do not usually involve real estate. The real estate loan programs, like the ownership programs, limit the borrower to $200,000 for a direct loan and $300,000 for a guaranteed loan. Interest rates are at FmHA borrowing rates, except for limited-resource farmers, who may borrow at 5 percent. The loan programs include:

☐ *Soil and water loans.* These loans may be used to drill wells, improve water supply systems for irrigation, level land, and install erosion protection.

☐ *Recreation loans.* The farmer may use part of his farm for a commercial fishing pond, a campground, a tennis camp or golf course, or other recreational purpose.

☐ *Nonfarm enterprises on farm property.* Loans may be obtained for property that will supplement the farming income, such as setting up a service station, building a roadside vegetable stand, having facilities to board animals, or a lawnmower repair and rental shop.

☐ *Aquaculture.* Loans will be given to help with commercial production of plants and animals in water under controlled conditions.

[d] Association Loans

FmHA will make direct loans at its borrowing rate to associations of farmers and ranchers. An association may be as small as three members or as large as necessary, but it must have the legal capacity to borrow as follows:

- Irrigation and drainage associations may borrow to develop community irrigation, drainage, and other soil- and water-conservation facilities. There is no limit on the size of loan.
- Grazing associations may borrow to acquire and develop grazing land for the livestock of association members. No one loan may exceed $4 million.

[4] Community-Facility Programs of Farmers Home Administration

The community-facility programs consist of programs for water and waste disposal, watershed and flood protection, and for community facilities. A fourth group of programs for resource and conservation development ended in late 1981.

[a] Loans and Grants for Water and Waste Disposal

FmHA will make direct loans for water facilities or for waste-disposal facilities in rural areas with populations of less than 10,000 people. Loans may be made for terms of forty years at 12.25 percent.

The loan applicant must be a state, county, village, or other public authority, or it may be a nonprofit organization. There is no limit on the loan amount. FmHA will determine if the utility service charges or tax payments will be sufficient to repay principal and interest on the loan.

When a community is small and its population consists of lower-income families, FmHA may provide a grant in connection with its loan. Grants are seldom given to areas with more than 5,000 people.

[b] Watershed and Flood Protection

Interest rates on FmHA direct loans for watershed and flood protection are set below the borrowing rate but above the 5 percent level, and are at 8.6 percent as of mid-1981. The term of the loan is not to exceed fifty years, with interest only payable during the first ten years. The area for the loan must be rural, with less than 10,000 people. A watershed loan is made in conjunction with financial support from the Soil Conservation Service of the Department of Agriculture. The borrower must be a state, county, village, or other public authority, or it may be a nonprofit organization.

[c] Community Facilities

FmHA loans to community facilities may be made in rural areas with less than 20,000 population. There is no maximum for any one loan, but there is a statutory ceiling of $250 million for all community-facility loans made in one year. The borrower must be, as with all other loans of this type, either a public agency or a nonprofit organization. Loans may run for as long as forty years, and the interest rate is 12.25 percent.

Usually the FmHA loan will supplement other loans and donations. For example, an FmHA loan has assisted in the construction of a library where the primary funds came from donations and municipal funds. The loan program has assisted airports, firehouses, health-care centers, educational facilities, industrial parks, utilities, and public rights of way. Loans were at 5 percent until October 1981.

[5] Business and Industrial Loans of Farmers Home Administration

The business and industrial loan program of FmHA is accepting no further applications and will be terminated in 1982. This was a guaranteed loan program, which operated in towns and cities of less than 50,000 population. In 1981, $652 million in loans were guaranteed, including loans for alcohol-fuel facilities. In 1980, the level of loan guarantees equaled approximately $1 billion.

[6] Real Estate Loans From the Federal Land Banks

[a] Purpose of the Loans

The Land Banks make long-term loans for such activities as housing, building or buying farms, buying or improving farm property, and agricultural warehouses. In addition to Land Banks, there are federal Intermediate Credit Banks, which purchase the loans of Production Credit Associations: operating loans, intermediate-term loans, and marketing loans. The Production Credit Association may make a short-term loan, such as a construction loan, for real estate.

A third part of the Farm Credit System is the Bank for Cooperatives, which operates through twelve district banks. It makes loans to eligible cooperatives of farmers, ranchers, commercial fishermen, and to cooperatives engaged in marketing, processing, or storing agricultural products; purchasing, manufacturing, or distributing supplies to farmers; or providing business services to farmers, including cooperatives for rural electric, telephone, or other utility services. Some of these loans are real estate loans, but made by the Banks for Cooperatives rather than the federal Land Bank.

[b] Eligible Borrowers

The federal Land Banks make real estate loans with terms ranging from five to forty years, secured by first mortgages. The eligible borrowers are farmers or ranchers, defined as those owning agricultural land or engaged in the production of agricultural products on a full- or part-time basis. Corporations and partnerships qualify if they meet certain tests regarding ownership by farmers, growers, or ranchers and a percentage of the income results from production of agricultural products. A farm-related business may also be a borrower if it furnishes custom-type services performed on the farm and directly related to farm-operating needs.

Loans may also be made to rural residents, regardless of whether or not they are farmers, provided that the purpose is a first mortgage on a house or mobile home. A rural area is open country, primarily agricultural in character, which may include towns or villages with not more than 2,500 people. The area may not be adjacent to a large population center.

[c] Terms of Loans

The interest rate is set by the Land Banks from time to time, but has always been below the market rate of interest for real estate loans from other financial institutions. In mid-1981, for example, the real estate lending rate for Land Banks was 13 percent as compared with 16 percent for similar loans by other financial institutions.

The amount of the loan is not to exceed 85 percent of the appraised value of the real estate. The term of the loan is normally comparable to terms offered by FmHA but they do not exceed forty years. There is no maximum loan limit. Loans may be prepaid without penalty at any time.

[d] Ownership by Borrowers

When a farmer borrows from a federal Land Bank through a federal Land Bank Association, he purchases stock in the Association in proportion to the amount of the loan. If the borrower is not a farmer, grower, or rancher, he purchases a nonvoting participation certificate. The stock and participation certificates help capitalize the Association, which then buys stock or participation certificates in the Land Bank. Net earnings of the Land Banks may be passed back to the Associations, which may pass dividends on to their members. When a loan is paid in full, the stock or the participation certificate purchased is retired at par value.

8

Buying, Selling and Exchanging Real Estate

8.01 HOW TO USE PURCHASE OPTIONS

[1] In General

An option to purchase real estate is a right granted for a valuable consideration to buy a specified property for a specified price and within a specified period of time. The optionee is the party to whom the right is granted; the optionor is the party who grants the right. The option period (i.e., the duration of the option) is the period designated in the contract granting the option during which the optionee has the right to decide whether or not he will exercise the option and purchase the property.

Options to purchase property offer an extremely important technique for real estate investors and developers. They create leverage and conserve cash, since the optionee (i.e., option holder) is in a position to control large parcels of property for a relatively small cash outlay.

An option to purchase land permits the optionee to tie up land until he decides whether or not to buy. For example, an investor may be aware of the likelihood that a piece of property will be used for a new highway, shopping center, or other development. He therefore obtains options on surrounding land that are good until the time when he expects that his information will be confirmed. If he is wrong and the development does not materialize, he suffers only the loss of his option price; if he is right, he is in a position to make a bargain purchase of the property. Similarly, an investor may take a long-term option, running for several years, in expectation of a change in economic conditions or the like.

Options are important in the land assemblage process. For example, a developer who wishes to acquire contiguous parcels and who is only interested in an all-or-nothing acquisition can use options rather than straight purchases in order to reduce his risk in the event that he cannot acquire all the land he needs.

Another purpose of an option is to permit the holder to speculate in property on a very small cash outlay, by buying and selling the option itself. For example, a speculator pays $1,000 for a six-month option to buy real estate at a price of $50,000. Before the option period expires, the value of the real estate rises to $60,000. The optionee can sell his option to a third party for $10,000, enabling the latter to acquire the property at a price equal to its current value of $60,000 ($10,000 for the option plus $50,000 option price paid to the owner of the real estate). The optionee, in such an instance, makes a $9,000 profit on his $1,000 investment.

[a] Forms of Options

Forms of options include

☐ *Fixed option.* This is the simplest form of option, entitling the optionee to buy the property at a fixed price during the option period.

☐ *Step-up option.* This type of arrangement is used in long-term options; the purchase price of the property increases by steps periodically throughout the option period. In the case of a renewable option, the step-up will frequently occur at the time of renewal.

☐ *Rolling option.* These options are most commonly used by subdividers of raw land. The option covers several contiguous tracts. The developer buys and subdivides one tract and, if it proves profitable, he can then acquire the next tract. Thus, the option "rolls" from one tract to another. Usually, the price steps up as each tract is acquired, thus permitting the landowner to share in the increased value of the property as it is built up. In addition, the landowner spreads his gain over a period of years and so is not required to report it at once.

☐ *Full-credit option.* Here, the price for the option is fully credited against the purchase price of the property, if the option is exercised.

☐ *Declining-credit option.* As an inducement to the optionee, the percentage of the option price that may be credited against the purchase price of the property declines as time goes by.

[b] Tax Treatment

As to the federal income tax treatment of options, if the property being optioned is a capital asset in the hands of the optionor, he is not taxed on the receipt of the option payments. Instead, his tax on these amounts is deferred until the option is exercised or expires. If the option is exercised, the option payments then become part of the sale proceeds and serve to increase the capital gain or reduce the capital loss. If the option expires, the payments retained are then taxed as ordinary income. In effect, the seller avoids paying tax entirely during the option period, and gets a capital gain (or a reduced capital loss) if the option is exercised; if the option is not exercised, the option payments are retained by him and he pays an ordinary income tax on those payments.

An optionee who sells or assigns his option on property that would be a capital asset in his hands should be in a position to achieve favorable long-term capital gain treatment for the transaction, provided he retains the option for a sufficient length of time to qualify for such treatment before he sells or assigns it. On the other hand, if he exercises the option and purchases the property and subsequently sells the property, he may wind up with a short-term capital gain, unless he has held the property for the required length of time before selling it.

(Note that where the option contains a provision against its assignment to another or if there is a question as to the optionee's right to assign the option, the optionor's written consent to the assignment should be obtained.)

[c] Other Option Alternatives

An option can exist even though it may be called by another name. Examples include

☐ *Contract with liquidated damages.* The purchaser may sign a contract of sale calling for a small down payment and a liquidated-damages clause, which limits the seller's remedy to the down payment in the event of the buyer's default in failing to close. Since the buyer may walk away without liability during the contract period, he in effect holds an option.

☐ *Large purchase-money mortgage.* Another way is for the purchaser to acquire the property for a small cash payment and a large purchase-money mortgage that contains an exculpatory clause, limiting the seller's remedy to repossession of the land in the event of the buyer's default. Here again, the buyer in effect holds an option. If the mortgage permits release of individual lots or tracts as they are sold off by the purchaser, the transaction is the equivalent of a rolling option.

☐ *Lease with option to purchase.* Yet another alternative to the option is the lease with option to purchase. This may make sense when the property is throwing off some income that will offset all or a large part of the periodic rental payments to be made during the lease term.

[d] Limitations

As compared to the contract or purchase-money mortgage, options do have some limitations. These limitations derive from the fact that the holder of an option does not have any legal or equitable interest in the property, as does an owner or contract vendee. Consequently,

- The purchase price is not reduced if improvements on the property are damaged or destroyed.
- The optionee has no standing to seek a zoning change.
- The optionee is not protected against subsequent encumbrances or liens on the property during the option period.
- Time is of the essence under an option (i.e., it expires on the date specified).

All of these limitations can be overcome by specific provisions in the option agreement, but this is not always agreeable to the optionor.

[2] How Option Can Improve Seller's Tax Position

As just noted, an option can often take the form of a nonrecourse purchase-money mortgage. Using an option can create much better tax consequences for the seller, since ordinary income can be converted into capital gain.

For example, suppose a buyer (*B*) is interested in acquiring a tract of undeveloped land from a Seller (*S*) and offers an above-market price provided *S* will take back a purchase-money mortgage equal to 100 percent of the sales price, with interest only to be paid for a period of years and the entire principal due at maturity. The mortgage will be nonrecourse (*B* having no personal liability on the note).

In economic substance, this arrangement is the same as an option. If *B* decides he does not want to keep the property, he simply defaults in his payments and *S* takes the property back, keeping the interest payments but having no further claim against *B*.

Suppose the transaction was actually recast as an option. The price for the option could be paid periodically and set at an amount equal to the interest that otherwise would have been charged on a purchase-money mortgage. The option payments would be credited against the purchase price if the option were exercised.

(As noted below, this strengthens the argument that a true option exists.) The property purchase price would be pegged at the same amount as the principal of the purchase-money mortgage plus interest payable during the term. (The credit for the option payments offsets the portion of the price attributable to interest. Thus, the property price is exactly the same under the mortgage or option approach.)

Under the purchase-money mortgage arrangement, *S* must treat the interest received as ordinary income. However, under the option arrangement (and assuming the property is a capital asset in *S*'s hands), the situation is different. *S* need not report the option payments as income at the time received. Any tax on these amounts is deferred until the option is exercised by *B* or expires. If the option is exercised, the payments then become capital gains. If the option is dropped, the payments retained by *S* are taxed as ordinary income (but of course he keeps the property as well).

In 1977, the Tax Court upheld this approach against strong IRS objections, and in 1980 the IRS acquiesced in the decision.[1] The facts in the case were as follows.

Koch granted a prospective purchaser an option to purchase large land holdings in Florida for $11 million. The option was to continue for five years provided an option payment was made each quarter equal to 1.5 percent of the purchase price (6 percent per year). Koch did not report the option payments as income during the years when the option was outstanding.

IRS made the following three arguments, all rejected by the Tax Court:

- Since the payments were a percentage of the option price, they really were interest (just as if a purchase-money mortgage had been created). But there was, in fact, no debt so there could be no interest.
- The transaction was actually a series of three-month options, and as each option expired, the option fee became income. But, in fact, a five-year option had specifically been entered into.
- Since the option payments could not be credited against the purchase price (if the option was exercised), the payments were immediate income. But since the seller could easily have raised the purchase price if the option payments were to be offset against the price, this factor was not significant. (Note that in our example above it was assumed that the option payments would be credited against the purchase price.)

There is, of course, another aspect to consider. If a sale with purchase-money mortgage is converted to an option, the buyer loses a tax deduction for interest paid on a mortgage. Instead, the option payments become part of his cost for the property (if he exercises the option) or a capital loss if he does not.

Suppose the property is presently producing income. This technique can still be used if the option is combined with a lease having a term equal to the period of the option. However, IRS could argue that the combined option-lease arrangement amounts to an immediate conveyance.

Another approach for income property is to adjust the payments to be made

---

[1] Carl E. Koch v. Comm'r, 67 T.C. 71 (1977), acq. 1980-1 C.B. 71.

under the option or upon acquisition of the property to reflect income kept by the seller during the option period.

[3] How Option Can Improve Buyer's Tax Position

Suppose the parties want to give the buyer the maximum tax break in this type of transaction. Can it be set up to do so? The answer is yes. If a long-term option is divided into a series of one-year (rollover) options, the expiration of each will give the optionee (buyer) an immediate loss deduction against ordinary income while at the same time preserving his right to acquire the property any time during the total option period. A case decided by the Tax Court shows how this technique works.

The optionee and the owner of a building negotiated a deal under which the optionee was to pay $350,000 to acquire a ten-year option to purchase the building for $2 million. The $350,000 was paid in the year the option agreement was signed. However, instead of setting up a single option that could be exercised at any time during the ten-year period, the parties provided for ten separate one-year options. They carefully documented the separateness of each option: The options were numbered sequentially, each had its own effective date, expiration date, and exercise price, and a schedule set forth the declining portions of the $350,000 refundable if an option was exercised after year 1, year 2, and so on. When an option lapsed, the cost of that option could neither be refunded nor credited against the purchase price.

When the first option lapsed after the expiration of year 1, the optionee claimed a loss of $35,000. The IRS disallowed the deduction. It maintained that, in substance, the optionee had purchased a single ten-year option for $350,000 and had to wait until the ten-year period expired before a loss deduction could be claimed.

The Tax Court found, however, that the carefully drafted agreement of the parties provided for ten separate options. In its view, the substance of the deal conformed with its form. Thus, the optionee was entitled to an immediate deduction of $35,000.[2]

There's a tax kicker here that the court did not rule upon. If one of the options is exercised in a later year, it appears that losses from option lapses in prior years are unaffected. This means that use of a series of separate options may permit avoidance of the rule that the entire cost of an option must be added to basis when the optionee exercises the option.

From the optionor-seller's viewpoint, separate options may be undesirable. The optionor must pick up ordinary income as each option lapses rather than at the end of the entire option period.

8.02 PURCHASE AND SALE OF REAL ESTATE

[1] When to Sell Real Estate

Many investors are reluctant to squarely face the question, Should I sell my real estate? One reason is that much depends on unpredictable future events,

---

[2] Paul D. Dunlap v. Comm'r, 74 T.C. 1377 (1980).

such as inflation trends and interest rates. Another is that a wrong decision can come back to haunt an investor while one can often live comfortably with indecision.

Unfortunately, ignoring a decision can be costly. Real estate is a dynamic investment, affected constantly by changes in the overall economy, the property's own transitions, and considerations personal to the investor. Appreciation in value, built up carefully over many years, can disappear quickly under adverse circumstances. Return on investment (ROI), seemingly at a very desirable level, can, in fact, be much lower than it appears in an absolute sense (as equity grows through appreciation and loan amortization) as well as in a relative sense (as returns from alternative investments rise).

The following are the financial considerations that should concern a real estate property owner who thinks about selling.

[a] Declining Return on Investment

The three factors affecting the return on a leveraged investment are as follows:

- Changes in the property's market value
- Gradual loan amortization
- Changes in net operating income (NOI)

While changes in NOI will be immediately noted by the investor, the impact of the other two factors may not be. The reduction in the outstanding loan is accompanied by an equivalent buildup in equity, so that the cash-flow return declines even though net operating income remains the same. And if the property is appreciating in value, the return on net market value (equity marked up to reflect appreciation) also declines as a result.

Tables 8.1 and 8.2 illustrate the relationships between appreciation, loan amortization, and ROI. Table 8.1 illustrates how loan amortization reduces ROI where the property simultaneously is increasing in value. ROI is cut from 10 percent to just over 5 percent even though cash flow more than doubles in the interim.

Table 8.2 relates future appreciation to equity growing as a result both of loan amortization and earlier appreciation. (Net operating income is ignored in this table.) The table demonstrates, given the stated assumptions, that at the end of the first five years, the compounded annual return on the original investment is almost 24 percent. During the second five-year period, the compounded annual return is cut to under 14 percent.

Alternatives. In both situations just described, the investor is experiencing declining financial leverage because of appreciation and loan amortization. He has four alternatives:

1. Refinance, which enables him to pull out tax-free cash and so releverage the property. Much depends, however, upon the cost of refinancing and the higher interest rate that must be paid. In substance, the investor should refinance only if the return on the newly generated funds exceeds the additional amount required to service the new mortgage.

TABLE 8.1 Appreciation, Loan Amortization, and ROI

	When Acquired	*Today*
Fair market value	$100,000	$180,000
Less: Loan balance	75,000	65,000
Equity	$ 25,000	$115,000
Cash flow	$2,500	$6,000
ROI	10%	5.2%

TABLE 8.2 Loan Amortization and Property Appreciation

	Year 1	*Year 5*	*Year 10*
Purchase price (or value)	$800,000	$1,080,000 [1]	$1,458,000 [2]
Less: Mortgage (30 years, 9.75% interest)	(640,000)	(617,000)	(580,000)
Equity (or net market value)	$160,000	$463,000	$878,000
Appreciation return	—	23.7% [3]	13.6% [4]

1 Increase in value based on loan amortization and 7% annual appreciation from original purchase of $800,000 (compounding ignored).
2 Increase in value based on loan amortization and 7% annual appreciation from value of $1,080,000 in year 5.
3 Compounded annual return on original investment of $160,000.
4 Compounded annual return on net market value of $463,000 in year 5.

2. Sell, which will generate a large amount of cash for new investment, but it will be at the cost of a capital gains tax on the realized gain.

3. Exchange, which substitutes new real estate for the present holding without any tax liability. It is not easy, however, to find the right parcel for exchange.

4. Do nothing, which may be the right choice at a time when interest rates may be peaking, at least where the property continues to show good potential for appreciation.

[b] Declining Tax Shelter

The second major financial reason for considering a sale (or other disposition) is declining tax shelter, which results from the interaction between loan amortization, interest deductions, and depreciation write-offs. Depreciation charges, which reduce taxable income but have no effect on cash flow, either remain level or decline as time passes. If straight-line composite depreciation is used, write-offs will be level each year. But if either accelerated or component depreciation is used, write-offs will decline over time. Thus, taxable income either will remain unaffected or will rise as a result of depreciation charges. With a constant-payment loan, debt service is unchanged and also has no effect on cash flow over time. However, as nondeductible loan amortization rises and deductible interest charges decline, taxable income increases.

As a result of this interaction, cash flow that was originally received by the investor tax-free gradually becomes subject to tax. The point is finally reached where taxable income exceeds cash flow (sometimes called the tipping point). The owner must pay tax on an amount larger than his cash flow; in effect, the cash flow from the property is being taxed at a rate higher than the top rate on the investor's other income.

Table 8.3 illustrates this effect. Declining depreciation write-offs and rising amortization result in a 35 percent decline over five years in the amount of taxable loss (which is available to shelter cash flow and other income of the investor).

TABLE 8.3 How Loan Repayment Reduces Net Available Tax Shelter

	Year 1	*Year 3*	*Year 5*
Total depreciation available[1]	$32,000	$28,864	$26,048
Less: Loan principal payment[2]	(6,304)	(7,655)	(9,293)
Net available tax shelter[3]	$25,696	$21,209	$16,755
Net loss[4]	—	—	35%

[1] Based on $800,000 purchase, 80% improvements depreciated over 25 years, 125% declining-balance method.
[2] Based on original loan of $640,000, amortized over 25 years at 9.75% interest.
[3] Net tax shelter available to offset cash flow.
[4] Over the first 5 years of ownership there is a 35% reduction in net tax shelter available to offset cash flow. This loss becomes more severe with each year of continued ownership.

The special considerations that apply to an investment made primarily for tax shelter are discussed at 8.02[2].

[c] Former Guidelines May Not Apply

Years ago, when accelerated depreciation methods were in general use, and before depreciation recapture had been conceived, income properties were usually "flipped" back and forth every seven or ten years. This resulted from the sharp drop-off in annual write-offs—and consequent loss of tax shelter—after that period of ownership. In addition, the entire profit on sale (including that arising from the lower tax basis as a result of depreciation write-offs) was taxed at capital gain rates. This permitted the conversion of ordinary income into capital gain, and so was a further encouragement to early resale.

However, all that is past. All depreciation in excess of straight-line is recaptured upon sale (with the exception of subsidized housing) so that gain attributable to depreciation write-offs during ownership is taxed as ordinary income. As a result, the incentives to a short-term sale have been reduced.

Nevertheless, the basic principle that tax shelter declines over time still applies since rising amortization reduces annual interest charges, while the use of accelerated depreciation, which is still very popular, will cause depreciation write-offs to decline. So, a decision to refinance, which increases the proportion of interest costs to total debt service, or sell must still be faced, although generally after more years of ownership than was true formerly. (Note that for properties first placed in use in 1981 and thereafter, the new fifteen-year recovery period is used instead of depreciation over the useful life of the property. In addition, only composite (and not component) depreciation may be used.)

[d] Personal Reasons for Selling Real Estate

The owner of an income property may decide to sell for one of several of the following important reasons other than the internal economics of the property:

☐ *End managerial role.* Among all investments, income-producing real estate imposes the greatest managerial burden on its owner (unless the entire burden is assumed by an outside management firm, which involves a cost many owners are unwilling to incur). At some point in his life, the real estate owner may decide the time has come to take a more passive investment role.

☐ *Move to new location.* Americans are the most mobile people on earth. A real estate investor moving a considerable distance cannot easily continue to supervise income property and so may wish to sell or exchange it for property at his new location.

☐ *Changing neighborhood.* Even though a building's "financials" still look good, the careful owner may begin to note signs of deterioration in the neighborhood. Since this type of economic depreciation is incurable by any one owner, it often constitutes a signal to sell.

☐ *"Milked" property.* Sometimes an owner will permit his building to become rundown or fail to keep it competitive with newer buildings. This may be due to negligence, to the owner's tight financial position, or to a deliberate "milking" of the property. While this type of depreciation (physical or functional) is often curable, the owner may lack the sufficient funds or the incentive to do so. Consequently, a sale may be the only alternative.

☐ *Opportune sale (or new investment).* Finally, an offer to buy the property at a top-dollar price may be too attractive for the owner to turn down. This may be the case when a foreign investor, seeking protection of his capital, is willing to accept a sub-par return on investment in order to acquire desirable U.S. real estate. Alternatively, the property owner may find an investment opportunity in another area that he deems too good to miss and that may justify an immediate sale of his real estate.

[2] When To Dispose of a Real Estate Tax Shelter

The problem of when to sell can be a particularly intricate one for a limited partner in a real estate syndication set up primarily to generate tax-shelter benefits, since in this type of investment, a contingent tax liability exists from the outset and grows increasingly larger for a substantial number of years.

Here is a basic outline of the key considerations in determining when to dispose of a tax-shelter investment (either the property itself or a limited partnership interest in the owning syndicate).

[a] Alternatives Open to the Investor

In most real estate syndicates in which tax benefits form the backbone of the investment, the transaction is usually structured to provide a sound return even assuming the project is given away at the end of the projected holding period (usually twenty to twenty-five years), although it is usually reasonable to expect the project to have some residual value at that time.

The long-term future of the underlying real estate is often difficult to predict, but the future of the investment is somewhat more clear. The tax deductions taken in the early years generate a contingent tax liability that must eventually either be paid or provided for. As the investment ages (particularly in the second ten years of the holding period), planning for the optimum disposition of the interest becomes more and more important to the investor.

A good first step is to evaluate the real estate itself. Then, depending upon this evaluation, consider the possibilities of one of the following:

- A sale of the project by the syndicate for a cash profit
- A sale of the investor's own interest for a cash profit
- Having the investor's own interest pass to his estate

[b] Evaluating the Real Estate: Distressed Property

The contingent tax liability of the investor can be triggered only by a transfer of ownership, either of the entire project (via a sale or foreclosure) or of the investor's own interest. The first point to establish is whether or not the limited partners as a group will have control over sale of the project. Most partnership agreements provide that a majority in interest of the limited partners must approve a voluntary sale before it can take effect. On the other hand, a foreclosure of the mortgage—over which the limited partners have no control—will have the same tax consequences as a sale for $1.

So, assuming that the limited partners as a group can control any voluntary sale, the key issue at any given time is whether the project is likely to be foreclosed; that is, is it in financial difficulty? If it is, the investor should investigate further, since foreclosures often are avoidable, and even if inevitable, knowledge of when a foreclosure will take place allows an investor a measure of tax planning of his other interests to soften the blow.

Foreclosures are most likely to be avoidable when the long-term potential of the project is strong and where the problems arise from short-term causes. In such cases, because the debt service is fixed, inflation may restore the bottom-line performance of the troubled property. Also, many lenders, including the Department of Housing and Urban Development (HUD), are unlikely to foreclose unless they see no other alternative. In every case of a troubled project, investors should seriously investigate the possibilities of doing a workout, since the other parties (including the lenders) often will prove cooperative.

[c] Evaluating the Real Estate: A Sound Property

Assuming that the property owned by a syndicate is in sound financial condition, investors should consider the potential residual value of the property to a new buyer. This value will usually reflect either of two alternatives:

- Continued operation as a rental property
- Conversion to some other use (e.g., condominiums)

The potential as a rental property will depend principally on the underlying cash flow from the property. History indicates that real estate markets run in cycles of about eight to ten years, but throughout the cycle the price that buyers will pay is usually a function of the net cash flow before debt service from a property. (This is analogous to the stock market, which also runs in cycles, as measured by a price-earnings ratio.) If a property is showing a positive cash flow (a cash surplus above its mortgage) and can be expected to continue to do so, the potential to sell is probably good.

The second possibility is sale to a buyer interested in using the property for some other purpose. The current hot market is condominium conversion. A condominium developer is not interested in the rental strength of an apartment project; he cares about the replacement cost and amenity package (as well as the feasibility of converting the particular project into condominiums). Thus, townhouses are more desirable than garden apartments, and high-rent properties are usually better candidates than low-rent ones. How long the current condominium boom will continue is anyone's guess, but it seems reasonable to expect that a property with a high replacement cost that is well-maintained will be attractive as a conversion prospect.

If investors in a limited partnership become convinced that the project is unlikely to be lost through foreclosure and that it will continue to maintain a sound physical and operational structure, they can anticipate a future sale of the property that will produce significant dollars.

[d] Guidelines for Selling the Property

Assume the property has some residual value that would be recognized on a sale. When is the optimum time to sell, and what should the syndicate do in order to realize the optimum price? The first thing to realize is that ordinarily a first-user apartment property should be held for approximately half the life of its mortgage because the property normally will generate tax benefits for the investors for at least that long. Further, as time passes and tax (primarily depreciation) deductions are taken, the size of the contingent tax liability is likely to grow, and it will take some time for a property to sufficiently appreciate in value to pay the contingent tax liability and still give the investors a reasonable after-tax return.

After about twenty years, however, the value of the ongoing tax shelter begins to dwindle. Around that time, there normally is a period of about five to eight years when the investors are relatively indifferent about the tax benefits they are receiving. During that "window" period, their predominant concern is to find an attractive offer. Because this period corresponds to the length of time of a typical real estate cycle, it seems reasonable to expect that some time during that period, an attractive offer will be received.

However, the size of the contingent tax liability often is a determining factor. For example, if an investor had a contingent tax liability of $15,000 (assuming a $1 sale price), and was offered a price that would net him $20,000 (after paying taxes on the cash received but before counting the impact of the existing tax liability), his net on the transaction would be only $5,000. If the investor believed he could obtain the same price next year, he would be well advised to hold on to the investment provided one year's benefits exceeded the loss time value of the sale price. In this example, one year's time value of money might be $400 ($5,000 × 8 percent). Hence, if one year's ownership benefits exceeded $400, the investor would do better to hold than he would be to sell for the $20,000 net sale price. (The following is a formula for this purpose.)

Formula for Determining When to Hold for Another Year. Assuming that the project has a fixed sale price (*SP*) measured in dollars above the mortgage, produces annual ongoing deductions (*Di* per year), and carries a total contingent tax liability (*T*), the optimal time to sell occurs when the value of receiving one year's tax benefits is less than the net cost of one year's delay in receiving the after-tax sale proceeds. Using an 8 percent discount rate, this equation can be written as:

$$.08 \times (SP - T) = Di$$

which rearranges to

$$.08 \times SP = Di + (.08 \times T)$$

Since *Di* is positive for the first twenty or so years (declining a bit each year), and *T* is almost always positive and almost always increasing, it usually makes sense to sell during the early years only if *SP* (the gross sale price above the mortgage) is large, or when both *Di* and *T* are small (as in the case of a recently acquired second-user project, for instance). This is the underlying reason why second-user projects are much more apt to change hands than first-user, shelter-oriented projects.

Attractive offers do not just happen, however; they must be solicited. This is the responsibility of the general partner. A general partner's benefits in one of these transactions usually consist mainly of the upfront development fee payable plus a share in the residual proceeds; most of the benefits of the holding period usually flow to the limited partners. This gives the general partner a very strong incentive to sell the project, if he can find an offer that will be attractive to the limited partners. One would therefore expect that the general partner would be constantly on the lookout for attractive sale offers and that eventually he would succeed in obtaining an offer that is sufficiently attractive, on an after-tax basis, to persuade the limited partners to accept it.

Assuming that a good offer is received, the general partner would transmit it to the limited partners, asking them to vote whether or not they wish to sell the project. Here the limited partners would need the services of a professional to prepare analyses of the after-tax consequences of the sale and projections of the future tax benefits or costs of continuing ownership of the project.

[e] Guidelines for Selling an Interest in the Partnership

Assuming that the potential sale of the project does not materialize, or that an investor wishes to dispose of his interest when there is no sale offer on the table, the possibility of selling the interest to a high-bracket taxpayer should be considered. The reason that resales of interests are frequently good deals for both parties is that the new investor can receive a step-up in basis (under Section 754 of the Code) equal in size to the amount of the contingent taxable gain of the old investor. This new basis is depreciable by the new investor, allowing him to redepreciate (as a second user) the deductions taken by the first investor as a first user. The difference in benefit can be substantial, and the old investor can realize a significant cash price for his interest.

A few practical guidelines may help to determine if selling an interest in a shelter-oriented syndication is desirable. If an investor is in the same tax bracket as he was when he acquired the investment, and if he expects to continue to be in that bracket, he probably should not pursue this route. If, however, the interest was acquired pursuant to a side transaction after the original syndication, the investor may be holding an asset that he cannot use to fullest advantage. If (for whatever reason) the realization of the contingent tax liability would not cost the investor very many dollars, it might make sense to dispose of the interest at that time.

In other words, it probably takes some change in circumstance to make selling the interest likely to be a good idea. In order to find out, an investor must determine: (1) what the tax consequences of triggering the contingent liability would be; and (2) what price the interest could bring in the market place. The determination of value is not simple. However, a fairly accurate approximation method is available (see following).

Valuing a Partnership Interest. The approximate cash sales price of an interest in a tax-shelter partnership can be estimated as follows: The next four years of after-tax benefits from depreciation (i.e., the annual depreciation times the assumed tax rate of the buyer), plus ten times the average expected annual cash flow, plus one tenth of the step-up in basis under Section 754 (the negative capital account of the seller), minus the future equity payments remaining to be made to the partnership. This formula assumes that the sales price will be paid in installments over a period of four or five years, since an installment sale will produce a much higher price than a one-shot payment.

Bear in mind that if the investor acquired his interest in a private placement—as is usually the case—he represented that he had no intent to distribute his interest and agreed not to sell it unless he complied with federal securities laws and the securities laws of his home state. Hence, the investor will have to review any such sale with an attorney, and may have to provide the partnership with a legal opinion as to such compliance.

[f] Transferring an Interest to an Estate or by Gift

In the event that the interest has little value or that the investor decides he wishes to continue ownership indefinitely, it is reasonable to make plans for the treatment of the interest in the owner's estate. Disposition of an interest upon death is given very favorable treatment under the federal income tax laws. Basically, death is treated as a sale of the interest to the estate (thus making the estate eligible for the Section 754 step-up in basis), but neither the decedent nor the estate must pay recapture or capital gains taxes upon the transfer (but estate tax must be paid). In effect, the existing contingent tax liability is forgiven.

In the view of most tax specialists, an outright gift of an interest may trigger tax liabilities comparable to a sale; hence, an investor should not make such a transfer without reviewing it with a lawyer or accountant; even in the case of a transfer to a trust whose income is taxed to the investor, a review of the matter with his advisers is necessary.

[g] Conclusions

In attempting to plan for the disposition of an equity interest in a shelter-oriented real estate partnership, the real estate should be evaluated first. Then, if there is a danger of foreclosure, the investor should take steps to protect his interests. If there is little danger of foreclosure, a decision to either continue to hold the interest and use the tax benefits, or sell the interest to a new high-bracket investor should be made. The potential of the underlying real estate, either as a rental property or for some other use should be evaluated and appropriate plans made for the disposition of the interest into an estate if it is not terminated via a sale of the project.

[3] Negotiating Techniques

[a] In General

Negotiating an agreement is an art, not a science. Successful negotiators are those who combine a good deal of experience with a sound understanding of human nature. Still, one can set down a number of rules for negotiating that should prove valuable to the beginner. For example, here are some general rules for any type of negotiation:

☐ One should try not to negotiate when feeling poorly or at a time when very emotionally involved in the particular subject matter. Negotiating is a strenuous activity and one who is not in top form is likely to miss admissions by the other side or give up concessions without meaning to do so.

☐ If acting for an institution or organization, try to establish a personal relationship with the other party. Individuals tend to give greater weight to commitments made to individuals than to those made to institutions.

☐ Keep negotiations going as long as possible (assuming there is room for improvement in the negotiations). The longer negotiations go on, the likelier that additional concessions will be made, because of the investment of time and effort.

☐ Start off with minor issues, and leave the make-or-break issues to the last. At the very beginning of a negotiation, a crucial issue may create a stalemate because neither side has yet accepted the need for concessions.

☐ Always be prepared to yield on some points (or put another way, start negotiating with some demands you really do not expect to achieve). No one is willing to concede on every issue and unless each side has achieved enough to "save face," the negotiations are not likely to succeed.

[b] Eight Real Estate Negotiating Techniques

Here are some of the frequently used techniques in real estate negotiations, and the defenses that may be used against them.

[i] Offense: "Take It or Leave It!" A popular opening offensive ploy is for a seller to rush the investor. "Time is critical" or "This property is too hot to sit on" are common ploys. Sometimes a seller will begin a negotiating session by explaining how he cannot afford to put the property "on ice" while the investor undertakes an in-depth analysis. Another is the ploy based on threat: "If you don't have enough confidence to move on it right now, I have other prospects who will."

Defense. As a first line of defense, the investor should point out that any real estate transaction, whether it is a small residential property or a multimillion dollar acquisition, takes time to consummate. He should explain that he will not be put in the uncomfortable position of fearing that he might make a mistake, and further explain that he will move to complete his analysis with all deliberate speed, but intends to be thorough. If this is not satisfactory, he can suggest that negotiations terminate.

Most often, this retort will take wind out of the seller's sails. Also, it will set an important tone for future negotiations: The investor will not be bulldozed. At worst, it will end negotiations early on, precluding a waste of valuable time.

[ii] Offense: "I've Got A Secret!" To increase the sales appeal of a property and offset contrary arguments, a seller might spring a surprise by entering new information in a direct comment such as, "You might not be aware of the fact that the property is now 100 percent occupied," or "I just got a call from that new tenant we've been negotiating with and he is definitely going in." This is clearly an aggressive offensive ploy injected to shake an investor's confidence and intimidate him.

Defense. Assuming the comments are true—and the investor is aware of the facts—the best retort would be to point out to the seller that he is fully aware of the facts and is not surprised. Example retort: "If I didn't think the property had the potential, I wouldn't have been interested in purchasing it in the first place." Another response is, "I've already considered these factors." However, if the investor was not aware of these new developments, he must neutralize the statement with, "That doesn't surprise me at all."

[iii] Offense: "The Denial." "Did I say that?" Or, "I never said that!"

Defense. Quite often during negotiations, statements are made by the other side that, although seemingly unimportant, are actually key concessions. Consequently, the investor should take copious notes on everything said during the negotiations. In addition to being helpful in identifying statements made by the other party, the notes provide valid recall at the proper moment and can be used to prove points or point out inconsistencies. This is especially important if concessions have been made as a result of something the other side has said and he "conveniently" forgets later on. The emotional strain of a negotiating session often causes people to overstate the situation, but only to their disadvantage if one is prepared to point out inconsistencies.

[iv] Offense: The "Laundry List." Many times the other side will start out a session by enumerating in detail all the problems with current price and terms. He is attemping to inundate the investor by laboring over each point, and keeping him on the defensive.

Defense. By enumerating all of his points and problems and seeking to negotiate on a point-by-point basis, the other party is actually setting himself up for a very effective defensive strategy. The investor should note those points with which he is in agreement and separate them from those points with which he disagrees. This strategy does the following:

- One can see all the problems at one time without stating a position, and has the opportunity to reevaluate a strategy.
- One can quickly conclude how reasonable the other side will be during the balance of the negotiations by the points he enumerates and the manner in which he states them.
- One is able to analyze where trade-offs and other compromises can be made.

[v] Offense: "The Crisis." The other party may create a crisis, artificial or real, in order to force the investor into making a critical decision. Usually, these are the types of decisions that bear greater weight than others. For example, "My accountants have just informed me that there are tax liabilities I hadn't considered, so I have to restructure the deal to make it more worthwhile."

Defense. While it is possible to acquire a sharp ability to instantly differentiate the important from the unimportant, it is often necessary to reserve the right to recess and reflect on any point that is critical. Do not be pressured into completing a negotiating session within a set time limit.

On the other hand, if the investor has fully researched the subject matter being negotiated, the ability to make a quick decision on relatively unimportant points will demonstrate his "good faith" attitude. This can be helpful in trading off the time necessary to consider heavier decisions.

[vi] Offense: "The Bully." A negotiating session is often a highly emotional experience. Be prepared to see the other party become abusive by yelling or overreacting in a variety of ways. This may be done by an individual who is either overwrought with problems unrelated to the current transaction or who purposely uses this tactic to bully.

Defense. Defuse the tension that has been created. The only productive approach is for the investor to immediately point out that he is not accustomed to nor will he conduct negotiations in an atmosphere of this kind. Also, if time is needed to recess, use of this offense by the other side will provide a perfect opportunity. Should the inappropriate behavior continue, an end to negotiations should be suggested.

More often than not, the other party will regain his composure, providing the investor with new control over the direction of the discussions.

[vii] Offense: The "Ultimatum." "Unless you do this, we have no deal!"

Defense. The investor not only can counter the ultimatum, he can use it to seize an opportunity to back the other party into a corner. The seller should be told, "Are you saying to me that unless I accept your position (explain the position as stated), we have no deal?" When the aggressor hears his proposition "played back," he usually backs off, giving the investor an accurate measure of his total strength. Alternatively, if the ultimatum was meant, the investor has a clear-cut, well-defined position to evaluate, and also knows how important the point is to him. Hence, if he feels he can give in, he should take advantage of the opportunity by attempting to gain some key concessions of his own.

[viii] Offense: The "Missing Party." "I can't make a decision on this because my partner (the board of directors, the committee, etc.) is not present and I need to consult with him or them on this." Or, "I don't think my partners are going to go along with this."

Defense. When this situation arises, the investor should make it clear that he will not continue negotiations unless the "missing party" is produced or the seller can immediately confirm that he only has veto power, not the right to counternegotiate. By limiting the "missing parties' " right of counternegotiation, the investor eliminates the possibility of having a "firm" deal negotiated further.

As is apparent, a resourceful negotiator can often turn a defensive position into a winning strategy. The old adage, "the best offense is a good defense," does indeed have value in any negotiating atmosphere.

[4] Key Elements in the Sales Contract

The contract of sale (also known as a sales contract, agreement of sale, and by a variety of other names) is the key instrument executed when real estate is purchased and sold. The contract states the conditions under which the property will be transferred and the rights and duties of each party during the contract period.

Once having signed the contract, a party is legally bound by it unless the other party consents to a change. While the contract of sale does not itself transfer title—this being the function of the deed—it is extremely rare for a commercial real estate transaction to be consummated without a written contract.

A contract is essentially an exchange of promises or an exchange of a promise (by one party) for performance of an act (by the other party). All contracts—

whether for transfers of real estate, brokerage services or any other purpose—can be classified in certain ways and have certain essential elements:

☐ *Mutual agreement.* A contract requires a "meeting of the minds" by the parties concerning the substance of the agreement. This mutual agreement is normally manifested by the procedure of offer and acceptance.

An offer is a statement by one party of willingness to enter into a contractual arrangement. An offer must (1) be definite and certain; (2) define the precise subject matter of the proposed contract; and (3) be communicated by the offeror (the one making the offer) to the offeree (the recipient of the offer).

Once an offer has been received by the offeree, it remains open and capable of being accepted until (1) it expires by its own terms; (2) the offeree rejects it; or (3) the offeror revokes it. An offer also can be canceled by the destruction of the subject matter (as where a building is destroyed by fire) or by circumstances that make the proposed contract illegal.

Acceptance of an offer occurs when the offeree, by word or deed, clearly manifests his intention to accept. The acceptance must (1) be positive and unequivocal; (2) conform precisely to the terms of the offer; and (3) be communicated to the offeror within the permissible time period.

An offeree may neither accept nor reject an offer but instead may make a counteroffer. Then, it is up to the original offeror to decide to accept, reject, or make yet another counteroffer. And so the procedure will continue until a final rejection or acceptance has taken place.

☐ *Reality of assent.* The assent of a party is real when it is given freely and with full knowledge of the circumstances affecting the agreement. When assent is not freely given, the contract may be invalid (i.e., not binding), depending upon the cause. Four such causes are fraud, mistake, duress, and undue influence.

Fraud is the intentional misrepresentation of a material fact in order to induce another to part with something of value. It clearly indicates an absence of real assent by the defrauded party. To constitute fraud, there must be a misrepresentation of a fact, not merely an opinion (so-called puffing). The misrepresentation also must be material (i.e., significant or substantial), and it must be made with the intention that the other party rely on it to his detriment.

Mistake may or may not be a ground for holding a contract invalid. Mistakes of law (i.e., not understanding the legal consequences of an action) normally are not enough to excuse someone from complying with a contract. Mistakes of fact (e.g., how much acreage is included in a parcel of land) may or may not justify a cancellation (rescission) of a contract, depending upon how material the mistake is and whether the other party should have realized a mistake was being made.

Duress is the obtaining of consent by the use of force.

Undue influence is the use of improper or excessive persuasion by one in a confidential relationship to another.

☐ *Legal capacity to contract.* A valid contract also requires that each party have the legal capacity to enter into a contractual relationship. Legal capacity means the ability to reason and understand the significance of an agreement.

Minors (children under the age of eighteen or twenty-one, depending upon the particular state) generally lack legal capacity to enter into a contract except for contracts for necessaries (e.g., contracts or purchases of food, medicine, clothing). Essential housing is usually considered a necessity as well, and so a minor may be held liable for the reasonable value of residential property occupied by the minor. If the contract is not for a necessity, the minor has the right to disaffirm the contract on reaching majority. This type of contract is called voidable because it is considered to be valid until the minor takes steps to disaffirm his obligations.

Insane, incompetent, and at times intoxicated persons are not legally competent to enter into a contract. Until fairly recently, married women often lacked the right to own real estate as well as to exercise other legal rights. But by enactment of laws protecting married women's rights in virtually all states, these common law disabilities have been eliminated so that a married woman now occupies the same legal status as her husband.

☐ *Consideration.* Consideration for a promise or for performance is that which is given in exchange for it. The concept of consideration is fundamental to the Anglo-American idea of a contractual relationship. Except in rare instances, a promise unsupported by consideration from the other party cannot be enforced.

In general terms, consideration can include anything that constitutes a benefit to the promisor (the one making a promise) or a detriment to the promisee (the one to whom the promise is made). If *A* promises to pay *B* $10, that is consideration because *B* benefits. If *A* promises to refrain from doing something that is otherwise a matter of right (such as putting a building of more than six stories on his land), that also is consideration. It is important to note that the law does not look to the adequacy of the consideration but merely whether consideration was actually bargained for. Thus, past consideration (payment for an obligation already owed) cannot be consideration for a new contract. Similarly, illusory promises are not good consideration.

☐ *Legality of the transaction.* A contract will be enforceable only if the purpose is legal. A contract to buy or sell real property for an illegal purpose (e.g., gambling in a state that bars this activity) would be void and unenforceable.

☐ *Contract in writing.* A final requirement for certain types of contracts is that they must be in writing in order to be enforceable. This requirement originally was imposed by an English statute, the Statute of Frauds, enacted in 1677. Its purpose was to prevent many fraudulent claims that were based on alleged oral promises or agreements. All American states have statutes modeled after the original Statute of Frauds, and they are known by that name. For the purposes here, the two significant types of agreements to which statutes of frauds apply are as follows:

- All contracts for the sale and purchase of real estate
- All leases of real estate for a term exceeding a specified period (more than one year in most states)

Note that the Statute of Frauds will be satisfied so long as the person against whom the contract is sought to be enforced has signed it. It is not necessary that the person seeking to enforce the contract has signed it.

Generally, the writing must contain the following information:

- The identity of the parties
- The identification of the subject matter of the contract
- The consideration

The writing need not be designated a contract. Any written memorandum will suffice to satisfy the statute, provided it contains the requisite information.

With this general background in mind, the major provisions in a typical real estate contract are now reviewed.

[a] Description of Premises

A contract for the purchase and sale of real estate should accurately describe the real property to be conveyed and also the personal property to be included in the conveyance. The description may be by street address, full legal description, reference to a public map, by plat attached to documents or schedules, or by some combination of these. Regardless of the method used, however, unless the description furnishes the means of determining with reasonable certainty the property intended to be conveyed, the contract is unenforceable.

Sources for the description of real estate include current surveys, copies of the seller's warranty deed or title policy, and current title reports or binders. If a current, accurate description is not available or if the parties contemplate that a survey will be made before the closing, it is advisable to provide that the description that will be used at the closing will be based on the survey.

The description of the property furnished by the seller should not be accepted blindly by the purchaser. Thus, for example, where the property is identified in the contract by more than one description, the seller's representation that only one tract of land is described should not be relied on by the purchaser. Instead, a representation of contiguity should be required. Also, if rights of access or other rights affecting adjoining property are important to the use and enjoyment of the property being purchased, those rights should be specifically included. Where appropriate, clauses may be included to cover such items as air rights, rights in adjoining streets, strips and gores, and leaseholds.

Where the contract states that the purchaser is buying a specified number of acres "more or less" and it is important to the purchaser to acquire at least a specified number of acres, he should insist on the right to terminate the contract if the property is found to have less than the required acreage.

A contract for the sale of land frequently includes a so-called Mother Hubbard clause to the effect that the description includes all the property owned by the seller at the location or, where appropriate, that it includes all real property owned by the seller in the particular city or county.

[b] Purchase Price

The purchase price for the property must be clearly specified or it must be so stated that it can be readily ascertained by an arithmetical calculation based on clear instructions set forth in the contract.

[i] Adjustment of Purchase Price. Where the total amount of the purchase price may be affected by various factors, the contract should specifically state what they are and the exact manner and extent to which they will affect the price. If the purchase price is to be adjusted according to the number of acres or the total area actually conveyed, the contract should state that the total number of acres or square feet are to be determined by a survey and how much shall be paid for each square foot or acre. Generally, where the purchase price is set by an area formula, the portion payable in cash is normally stated as a percentage of the total price rather than as a dollar amount.

[ii] Allocation of Price Among Different Portions of Tract. Some parts of a tract of land may be more valuable than others as, for example, where different zoning classifications apply to different parts of the tract or where part of the land is not usable. Under these circumstances, the purchaser should consider having the price allocated among different portions of the tract according to their relative values for the purpose of determining the tax basis of each portion. The determination of the cost of portions of land on the basis of the fair market value of each portion has been approved by the Tax Court as has also been the allocation of cost according to front footage, release prices, tentative sales prices, and assessed valuation.

[iii] Allocation of Price Between Land and Buildings. An important technique for maximizing depreciation deductions consists of allocating as much of the cost of acquiring property as possible to the depreciable buildings and improvements on the property and as little as possible to nondepreciable land.

The Treasury Regulations require that when nondepreciable and depreciable properties, such as land and buildings or improvements, are acquired together for a lump sum, the acquisition cost must be allocated on the basis of the respective values of the land and the buildings or other improvements on the land. The Treasury Regulations do not state how the respective values are to be ascertained. One way is to use a professional appraisal; other ways are to base the allocation on the relative values placed on the land and buildings by the local tax assessor or on the taxpayer's own information resulting from his personal familiarity with the area in which the property is located. Still another method is for the taxpayer to evaluate the buildings situated on the land from the investment point of view by capitalizing its cash flow. This may produce a particularly favorable allocation in the case of a building which, although old, is a very profitable one.

The contract should specify how payment of the purchase price shall be made, any down payments or earnest money payments that are required, and the method, medium, and time of payment.

The trend of modern decisions is to move away from treating time as being of the essence of a real estate contract except where the parties indicate their intention that it be so treated. For this reason, the seller may want to include an express provision in the contract that time of payment is of the essence of the contract. Payment may take the form of cash, check subject to collection, the purchaser's note or bond, or any other method or medium of payment.

The contract may, of course, call for payment of the purchase price in installments. (See 8.02[4][f].)

[c] Down Payment and Escrows

Under the terms of the contract of sale, the purchaser will generally be called upon to deposit a sum of money or other thing of value—for example, a down payment or earnest money—as a good-faith token and as security for the performance of his part of the contract. Usually, the deposit will be held in escrow during the period between the signing of the contract and the closing of title. Similarly, where the contract imposes obligations not only on the purchaser but also on the seller, and the seller's obligations are of such a nature that his default would cause substantial damages to the purchaser, the seller may be required to make an escrow deposit as security for his performance. This may occur, for example, where the seller is required to complete improvements on the property by a specified time and according to given plans and specifications, or to arrange for financing, or to bring in specified tenants in order to provide a specified amount of rental income, by the time the contract closes.

An escrow deposit may take many forms, and may be composed of cash or other thing of value such as, for example, a promissory note, draft, or letter of credit. The consideration for the sale, a sum representing liquidated damages, the sales agreement itself, the deed to the property (pending a determination of the marketability of title) may all be placed in escrow. If the deposit is a down payment or earnest money, the amount is credited against the purchase price and paid over to the seller at the closing, unless the purchaser has committed a breach of contract. Likewise, in the case of a deposit by the seller, the deposit is returned to him at the closing in the absence of a breach or default by him.

While the seller is frequently given the right to designate the escrow agent, this is not always true. It is important, however, that the escrow agent be a well-recognized, independent, and responsible entity such as an attorney, a title company, a bank, or an escrow company. The escrow agent should be given explicit and detailed instructions agreed to by the parties concerning his custody and disposition of the fund, documents or other things of value entrusted to his care. He stands in the position of a fiduciary bound to act according to the dictates of the escrow arrangement. His duties should be strictly ministered, limited to the safekeeping of the fund in a separate, properly identified, interest-bearing account and paying over the fund or delivering the documents at the proper time and place to the proper person when required to do so under the terms of the escrow arrangement.

The parties may want to enter into an agreement with the escrow agent that is separate from their sales agreement or that refers to the sales agreement and incorporates its provisions by reference. Since an acknowledgment at the end of the sales agreement by the escrow agent should serve to legally bind the escrow agent, the use of a separate escrow agreement generally only serves the purposes of clarity and explicitness and probably is unnecessary where the original contract between the buyer and seller is sufficiently explicit. A separate escrow agreement may provide that the escrow agent act as directed by both of the parties or it may refer back to the terms of the original agreement between the seller and purchaser. In any event, the parties should make sure that the escrow agent accepts the terms of the contract between the parties and agrees to be bound by its provisions. This acceptance is necessary to avoid unnecessary litigation, which may ensue when a nondefaulting party discovers upon making demand on the escrow agent for disbursement of the deposit to him that escrow agent will not release the deposit unless the consent of both parties is first obtained. Thus, it is well to obtain the agreement of the escrow agent at the outset to be bound by the terms of the sales contract.

Where the contract requires the purchaser to make the deposit as security for his performance, the seller may insist on a provision declaring that the sum placed in escrow shall constitute liquidated damages if the purchaser subsequently defaults or breaches the contract. The purchaser may concede the provision but insist on provisions that allow for specified contingencies excusing default or delay in performance by him or permitting him to cure a default. In addition, the purchaser may ask for a provision under which, in the event that the seller defaults in the performance of his part of the contract, the purchaser shall be entitled to the return of the escrow fund or, in the alternative, specific performance by the seller of the contract.

The parties should agree in advance as to how the charges by the escrow agent shall be paid. If the escrow agent is to serve without charge, this should clearly appear.

It should be noted that the mere deposit of money or other thing of value in escrow as security for the performance of the terms of a contract of sale, like any other security deposit, is not a taxable event and no income tax consequences flow therefrom. However, interest or other earnings generated by the deposit is taxable as ordinary income to the person entitled to such interest or earnings.

Deposits Pending Escrow Closings. Real estate, in some areas of the country, is customarily sold through a procedure known as an escrow closing under which the purchaser and seller do not meet face to face to exchange documents and consideration. Instead, the purchaser deposits the agreed purchase price with the escrow agent and such other documents as are required and the seller deposits the executed deed to the property and related documents with the escrow agent. Likewise, if financing by a lender is to be provided, the mortgage or deed of trust and its related instruments are also deposited with the escrow agent. The escrow agent consummates the transaction when it receives all the necessary instruments and cash and title passes to the purchaser. Between the time when a document, cash, or other thing of value is deposited with the escrow agent and the time when the transaction is consummated, the items deposited are considered to be in escrow.

[d] Existing Mortgages

A contract for the sale of real property may expressly provide that the sale is made subject to an existing mortgage (or deed of trust). Under such a provision, the parties understand that the mortgage will not be satisfied by the seller by the time the closing takes place and title is transferred to the purchaser. Instead, the parties expect that the purchaser will, following the transfer of title to him, make the principal and interest payments as they fall due under the mortgage obligation.

A purchaser who takes subject to an existing mortgage on the property should be aware that the property is subject to being foreclosed or sold if there is a default in the payment of the debt service called for by the mortgage obligation. However, since he is not personally liable for the mortgage obligation, he cannot be held personally responsible for the deficiency if the proceeds of the foreclosure sale are not sufficient to satisfy the balance due under the mortgage obligation plus interest and costs. Instead, the mortgagee must look to the original seller (the mortgagor) to recoup the deficiency, assuming that the mortgage obligation is a recourse obligation, that is, one under which the mortgagor or borrower is personally responsible for the mortgage indebtedness.

A contract for the sale of real estate may call for the purchaser to assume an existing mortgage or mortgages rather than merely taking title subject to the mortgage or mortgages. Where the purchaser assumes a mortgage on the property, he undertakes personal liability for payment of the existing mortgage indebtedness. If the seller was personally liable to the mortgagee for the mortgage obligation before the sale, he remains personally liable after the sale even though the purchaser assumes the mortgage, unless the assumption of the mortgage obligation by the purchaser is accompanied by a novation (new contract). Thus, if the holder of the mortgage agrees to substitute the personal liability of the purchaser for that of the seller (in other words, if the mortgage holder agrees to a novation), the seller is released from any future obligation to repay the mortgage indebtedness. On the other hand, if the mortgage holder refuses to permit a novation, the seller remains personally liable and, in most jurisdictions, the purchaser is also personally liable to the mortgage holder. If the seller becomes liable to pay any part of the mortgage debt, he is entitled to reimbursement from the purchaser since, as between them, the purchaser is primarily liable.

Where interest rates are rising and the existing mortgage on the property is subject to a favorable interest rate, the purchaser may want to include a provision in the contract to the effect that the existing indebtedness will be taken over by him. There is, however, a danger that the seller may prepay the mortgage indebtedness at or before the closing; the seller might find it desirable to do this where the purchase price is payable partly in cash and partly by the purchaser's assumption of a first-mortgage note bearing a favorable interest rate on the property and, in addition, by the purchaser's execution of a junior-mortgage obligation, in the seller's favor, which bears a higher interest rate than the obligation secured by the existing first mortgage. Under these circumstances, the seller has an incentive to prepay the first-mortgage obligation before the closing and to evidence the entire indebtedness by the junior-mortgage obligation, which carries a higher interest rate. For this reason, the purchaser might want the contract to provide that the unpaid balance of the first-mortgage indebtedness will not be less or more than a specified sum at the closing. In addition, the purchaser will also want assurance that the existing indebtedness will be current and not in default at the time of the closing.

In a tight-money, high-interest-rate and inflationary economy, the seller will be interested in the continued existence of a mortgage on the property if the mortgage balance is still relatively large and a substantial portion of the mortgage term remains, since he can offer prospective purchasers a property with low-interest-rate financing. In addition, he can save any prepayment penalty the mortgage obligation provides for if the purchaser is permitted to take over the mortgage. (The purchaser, for his part, may wish to include a provision in the contract giving him the right to a credit for the amount of the prepayment penalty.)

It should be noted, however, that many mortgages carry a due-on-sale clause under which the mortgagee may accelerate the mortgage debt so that it becomes immediately payable in the event that the property is sold by the mortgagor. If such payment is not forthcoming and the sale takes place or, possibly, on the signing of a sales contract a default occurs, the mortgagee may proceed to its remedies under the mortgage. (Due-on-sale clauses became popular at a time when interest rates began their rapid rise and lenders were anxious to close out existing mortgages at low interest rates in order to earn a higher return on the funds.) There is, however, authority to the effect that if the risk undertaken by the lender-mortgagee is not increased by the sale, he cannot take advantage of the clause and call the entire balance of the loan due and payable.

Estoppel Certificates. Where, at the time the contract is entered into, there is a mortgage on the property, the purchaser should request a duly executed estoppel certificate, statement, or letter from the mortgagee that states all the current particulars with respect to the mortgage, including the interest rate, the balance due, that there has been no default under the mortgage, and so forth. The party executing the estoppel certificate, statement, or letter cannot later claim that the facts stated are different since the statement was issued with the intention that it be relied on by the purchaser, and the purchaser bought the property in reliance on it.

[e] Third-Party Financing

Frequently, a contract for the sale of real property contemplates that a mortgage loan from a source other than the seller will be necessary to finance the transaction. For this reason, the contract is made contingent on, or subject to, the purchaser's procurement of a mortgage loan or a mortgage loan commitment meeting specified requirements as to amount, interest rate, duration or term, and so forth, from a third-party lender such as an institutional lender. Where there is an existing mortgage on the property, the purchaser may be given the option of either assuming the existing mortgage or obtaining outside financing. Under these circumstances, it is important to know whether the existing mortgage contains a due-on-sale clause giving the mortgagee the right to accelerate the balance due.

The parties may agree on limiting the time within which the purchaser must procure the loan or loan commitment and, in addition, the purchaser may be required to make a bona fide loan application and to proceed diligently with respect thereto. The parties may agree that the purchaser's procurement of the loan or loan commitment within the required time and containing the required terms shall be a condition precedent to the obligation of either party to perform, or that the purchaser's failure to obtain the required mortgage loan or loan commitment within the allotted time may be ground for rescission or cancellation of the contract. For example, the seller may be given the option to cancel the contract or apply, on the purchaser's behalf, for a mortgage loan on the property that meets the contract requirements. Or the contract may give the seller the option to provide the purchaser with financing in the form of a purchase-money mortgage where the purchaser is unable to obtain financing elsewhere. (This type of provision might, for example, be used in a tight-money, high-interest-rate economy.)

The contract should provide for a refund to the purchaser of the sums paid by him to the seller where the contract is canceled for failure to obtain the necessary financing within the required time; if the seller is entitled to his costs, the contract should clearly state exactly what he is entitled to.

[f] Purchase-Money Financing

Frequently, the seller is willing to help finance the transaction by extending a purchase-money loan to the buyer secured by a mortgage (or deed of trust) on the property. The loan may take the form of a first-mortgage loan where there is no mortgage on the property at the time of the transaction or where the existing mortgage loan is paid off at that time and no outside financing is obtained. Under these circumstances, the purchase-money loan usually will be in an amount equal to the difference between the purchaser's cash investment and the purchase price of the property. More frequently, however, a purchase-money mortgage will be a second or junior mortgage, since it will be subordinate to the existing or a new mortgage loan on the property made by an outside lender. Under these circumstances, the purchase-money loan will be used to fill the gap between the purchase price of the property and the aggregate of the purchaser's cash investment and the proceeds of the existing outside-mortgage loan.

Sellers frequently enter into purchase-money financing arrangements with their buyers when money is tight and interest rates are high. In this way, they are enabled to make sales they might otherwise be unable to make. In addition, the loan generates interest income for them.

Where the parties anticipate that they will enter into a purchase-money mortgage loan arrangement, the sale contract should reflect that fact and should specify that it is contingent on the execution of a purchase-money obligation (e.g., promissory note or notes, or bond) and a mortgage (or deed of trust) securing that obligation in favor of the seller, and it should set forth all the material details of the mortgage (or deed of trust) and the obligation that it secures, including the amount of the note or bond, the loan term, the amount of periodic debt service (including interest and amortization), the interest rate, and the amount of the balloon payment (if any). The parties may, of course, agree and the sale contract may provide that the purchase-money mortgage (or deed of trust) loan shall be a standing, rather than an amortized, loan and, if the parties so agree, the contract may provide for a standing mortgage loan for a specified period of time under which the purchaser is given the right to prepay the principal or to extend the term by making periodic amortization payments.

If the purchase-money mortgage is to be junior to an existing mortgage on the property, the contract should so state; and if it is to be subordinate to a new mortgage on the property in favor of an institutional lender, the contract should clearly state that fact. In addition, the contract may provide that the purchase-money mortgage is to be consolidated with an existing mortgage on the property. The contract should further state whether the purchase-money mortgage is to be a recourse or a no-recourse obligation, that is, whether the purchaser is to be personally liable for the loan or whether the seller's sole remedy in case of default is to proceed against the property.

Where the purchaser wants to have portions of the property released from the mortgage lien as payments are made, the contract may provide for a release schedule or establish a formula under which the property is released according to the percentage of the mortgage burden borne by each affected parcel.

In entering into a purchase-money mortgage for depreciable property, the purchaser may want to inflate the purchase price by entering into a long-term standing mortgage loan with the seller for a large face amount under which he assumes no personal liability for the debt. The idea is for him to allocate a large part of the inflated price to the depreciable buildings and improvements and base his depreciation deductions on the inflated amount. However, the Internal Revenue Service reviews transactions involving purported purchases of depreciable property where it appears that the transactions may have been designed to create or inflate depreciation deductions and will disallow unwarranted deductions. An inflated purchase price linked with no-recourse financing and a minimal down payment may even be viewed as precluding the bona fide investment in property that is necessary to support depreciation deductions and also as precluding the existence of the bona fide debt or obligation that is required to support interest deductions.

As for the seller's position, an inflated purchase-money mortgage may serve to convert interest income that is taxable at unfavorable ordinary income rates into a capital gain. This can be accomplished by his trading a lower interest rate on the purchase-money mortgage obligation in return for a higher price for the property and a correspondingly greater amount for the mortgage loan. The down payment remains the same and the interest rate is reduced to a point at which the reduction of the seller's interest income is roughly matched by the increase in the purchase price, which is treated as a capital gain, thus increasing the seller's capital gain and reducing his ordinary income from the transaction. As for the purchaser, he loses some of his interest payment deductions but he increases his depreciation deductions. The amount he actually pays for the property remains approximately the same.

A deflated purchase-money mortgage loan may be desirable where the seller is in a low tax bracket and the buyer is in a high tax bracket. Here, the seller would trade a lower purchase price for a higher interest rate on the purchase-money mortgage obligation. The reduction in the purchase price can be approximately equal to the increase in interest payments. The seller receives more interest income and less capital gain; the buyer pays less in the form of nondeductible amortization payments and more in the form of deductible interest payments.

Both inflated and deflated purchase-money mortgages must be entered into with great caution and with the advice and assistance of skilled income tax counsel. (See 7.02[6].)

[g] Surveys

The purchaser will want to be given, within a specified number of days after the execution of the agreement, a current survey of the property prepared by a licensed surveyor.

The contract should set out the requirements of a satisfactory survey. Depending upon the circumstances, these may include that the survey be prepared by a registered professional surveyor who is acceptable to the purchaser and also to the title company; that the survey be completed and delivered within a specified time; that the survey describe the property by metes and bounds and show the gross number of acres as well as the number of "net acres"; that it locate all existing easements, rights-of-way, alleys, streets, and roads; that it show any encroachments upon the property; that it contain the surveyor's certification; that it show all dedicated public streets that provide access to the property and whether such access is paved to the property lines; and that it show the location of any necessary easements.

In the case of a contract under which the price to be paid by the purchaser is to be determined on an "area basis," a properly prepared survey will determine the exact price to be paid. A properly prepared survey will also provide or determine the exact description of the property to be used in the closing documents. In addition, it will also provide both the purchaser and the title insurance company with vital information concerning the existence and location of all easements, streets, improvements, encroachments, and other matters which may adversely affect title.

[h] Title and Title Insurance

The parties to a contract for the sale of real estate should be aware and make provision for the possibility that the seller may be unable to convey title to the property or to some part of the property on the closing date in accordance with provisions of their agreement. If this should occur, the seller, of course, will not want to be liable to respond in damages to the purchaser or to cure the defects of title regardless of the cost to him. The purchaser, for his part, will want assurance that the seller will be obligated to convey good title when the closing date arrives. Within this framework, the parties may agree that the purchaser shall either accept, without abatement of the purchase price, such title as the seller can convey, or terminate the agreement and receive a refund of his earnest money deposit; that if the purchaser does elect to accept the seller's defective title, there will be an abatement of the purchase price based on a predetermined formula; or that the seller shall be required to remove, at his own expense, any and all defects of title that are subject to removal, regardless of the cost.

A contract that specifies that a marketable title is required refers to a title that is free from liens or encumbrances except those specifically set forth in the contract, discloses no serious defects, does not depend for its validity on doubtful questions of law or fact, and will not expose the purchaser to the hazard of litigation or embarrass him in the peaceful enjoyment of the property. In addition, title should be such as a reasonably well-informed and prudent person acting on business principles with full knowledge of the facts and their legal significance will be willing to accept with the assurance that he, in turn, will be able to sell or mortgage the property at fair value.

The following matters have been ruled to render title unmarketable: (1) a reasonable hazard of litigation; (2) title acquired by adverse possession; (3) an outstanding right in a third person that interferes with the use or transfer of the property or subjects the property to an obligation, leases, liens of any tax assessment or water charge; (4) outstanding dower interests; (5) debts of decedents or a reasonable possibility of their existence; (6) easements; and (7) outstanding mineral and oil rights.

Regardless of the agreement reached by the parties with respect to defects of title, the purchaser will want to include a provision that if the seller's inability to convey good title results from his own acts or omissions he will be considered to be in default under the contract and will continue to be liable to the purchaser for damages resulting therefrom.

The seller may object to being required to convey a marketable title and insist that the furnishing of a title insurance policy should be sufficient to satisfy all title requirements. On the other hand, the purchaser will want to insist on obtaining a marketable title; indeed, the owner's title insurance policy form that is used in some states does not insure marketability, but only insures against title being vested otherwise than as stated in the policy; against any defect or lien or encumbrance on title; and against any lack of a right of access to and from the property.

The contract may not only be made contingent on the seller's ability to convey good and marketable title to the purchaser; it may further provide that marketability will be conclusively established only if the purchaser can obtain, from an accredited title insurance company, a title policy that is standard for the area.

The purchaser may also want the option of accepting such title as the seller is able to convey or rejecting title where the seller is unable to convey good and marketable title. In addition, the contract may provide that the seller must cure such defects as can be cured by the payment of money.

The seller, for his part, may want the right to adjourn the title closing in order to give himself an opportunity to cure such defects of title as may appear or he may want the contract not to obligate him to cure title defects but simply to give him the right to return the purchaser's down payment and be released of all liability under the contract.

The purchaser may want the contract to require that the seller obtain a title commitment from a reputable title insurance company and, further, that the seller rectify defects of title where the condition of the title is unsatisfactory, and that if title defects are not rectified, the purchaser should have the right or option to terminate the contract.

A policy of title insurance does not cure a defective title; it does, however, protect the buyer against loss as a result of defects and encumbrances that are not specifically excepted from the insurance coverage. In this regard, it is important for the purchaser to understand the legal implications of the endorsements to the title insurance policy and the exceptions contained therein.

A title insurance policy insures against loss or damage to the insured by reason of defects, liens, or other encumbrances on his title that are not specifically excepted from, or excluded by, the policy. The policy does not cure a defective title; if the defect is such as to render the title unmarketable, title insurance will not render the title marketable. Instead, the title remains unmarketable and subsequent purchasers who may be unable or unwilling to obtain title insurance can continue to object to the defective title. In most states, a title company has no duty to point out title defects and encumbrances to the purchaser. Instead, its only duty is to protect the purchaser against loss as a result of defects and encumbrances.

To different degrees, all title policies cover losses or costs arising from defects disclosed by the public records; defects not disclosed by the public records; the costs of defending title against attack, whether justified or not; and mistakes of the title examiner, whether errors, omissions, or mistakes of judgment.

Defects disclosed by the public records include liens, restrictive covenants, breaks in the chain of title, and faulty acknowledgments. These defects are usually covered unless they are included among the exceptions set forth in the policy. Hidden defects not disclosed by the public records include forgeries, fraudulent representations of marital status, minority or mental incapacity, mistaken identity, and loss of title by adverse possession. Hidden defects are generally insured against when (1) surveys, inspections, affidavits, and similar requirements are met; and (2) the printed-form exceptions relating to hidden defects are deleted.

Standard Title Policy Forms. The basic title insurance policy forms now used by the vast majority of companies throughout the United States are the American Land Title Association (ALTA) standard forms. However, a few states (e.g., Texas and New York) require that other forms be used.

Basically, every policy of title insurance contains a description of the property; the name of the insured; the amount of loss insured against; the extent of coverage; the exclusions from coverage; the general exceptions; and conditions and stipulations.

There are two forms of ALTA's owner's policies: Form A-1970 is a nonmarketable form and Form B-1970 insures marketability of title. The essential difference between the two forms is that Form B does not except from coverage damages resulting from a refusal to purchase, lease, or lend money on the property by reason of defects of title, and Form A does make that exception. Form B is available wherever ALTA forms are used, and is the form customarily issued. In a few states (e.g., Florida, Indiana, and Illinois), however, Form A is predominantly used.

The ALTA form insuring the mortgagee is Loan Policy No. 1970. Finally, a single-form ALTA policy that includes both the owner's and mortgagee's policies is also available.

The ALTA Form B owner's title insurance policy insures (1) against loss or damage, not exceeding the face amount of the policy, incurred because title to the property is vested other than as stated in the policy; (2) that there is a defect in, or encumbrance on, the title that the policy does not specifically except from coverage; (3) the purchaser cannot gain access to the property; or (4) title is unmarketable.

On the other hand, the Texas form of title insurance only "guarantees" that the insured has good and "indefeasible" title to the property.

In addition to the normal risks covered under the standard title policy forms, various types of affirmative insurance usually can be obtained by endorsement of the title policy by the company. These endorsements can be extremely important to a purchaser, particularly if he is acquiring improved property or if he plans to improve the property himself. For example, in ALTA states, the purchaser can obtain endorsements that insure (1) that the property is in a specified zoning classification permitting certain uses (or, in the case of completed buildings, the improvements are not in violation of existing zoning ordinances); (2) the property, if it consists of more than one tract, is a contiguous tract; (3) a right of access exists to a specific street or easement; (4) existing restrictive covenants have not been violated and there is no possibility of forfeiture or reversion; (5) existing restrictive covenants do not prohibit a specific use; and (6) easements and rights-of-way that physically affect the property are of a specified width and location, do not interfere with the use of existing improvements, and are appurtenances to the property.

In some states, however, affirmative insurance by endorsement covering matters not specified in the owner's policy is not available.

Standard title insurance policy forms set forth risks of loss that the policy does not insure against. Thus, the ALTA forms of owner's title insurance policies (Forms A-1970 and B-1970) contain a Schedule B. This schedule sets forth printed and typed exceptions from coverage (none of which may be shown by the public records) matters that would be revealed by a survey; claims of parties in possession; easements; mechanic's and materialman's liens imposed by law; taxes or special assessments that are not shown by the public records.

Title companies in ALTA states generally have wide latitude in including additional exceptions to the extent they think advisable. But the purchaser may be able to negotiate with the title company to have the exceptions deleted from his policy. In states other than ALTA states, exceptions must strictly comply with the basic manual of rules prescribed by the state boards of insurance.

[i] Building and Zoning Regulations

Anyone purchasing a piece of real estate must be aware of the zoning ordinances and requirements that apply to the property. Regardless of whether he expects to use the property "as is" and for the same purposes for which it is being used at the time of the sale, or whether he expects to place new improvements on the property and use it for other purposes, unless he studies the local zoning ordinances and requirements and inserts appropriate protective provisions in the contract of sale, he may suffer severe losses. If he is to avoid purchasing property that he cannot use or develop for the purposes or in the manner contemplated or if he is to avoid incurring severe fines and penalties because of zoning violations or being compelled to remove all or part of the existing improvements, he must take appropriate measures to protect himself.

A purchaser who is acquiring property subject to unsuitable zoning regulations should insist on having the contract of sale conditioned on obtaining the required zoning change or accommodation (e.g., zoning variance, rezoning). A contract so conditioned should clearly state who shall be required to make the necessary application, maintain the necessary proceedings, the time frame within which the necessary steps will be taken and contemplated, who shall bear the cost, and the rights of the parties in the event the zoning change or accommodation cannot be obtained. As a general rule, the purchaser will want the option to rescind the contract and have his down payment or earnest money returned to him if the zoning change or accommodation cannot be obtained.

The income tax treatment of the costs incurred in obtaining a zoning variance or change in respect of income-producing or business property depends on which party incurs the cost and on whether or not the sale is consummated. Costs reasonably incurred by the purchaser become part of the purchaser's tax basis in the property and can be written off by him over the life of the property. Costs reasonably incurred by the seller become part of the cost of the sale and are deductible by him. If the zoning proceeding is unsuccessful and the sale is not consummated, the costs are deductible business expenses for the purchaser or seller, depending upon which of them is required to bear the costs.

In addition, the purchaser must also be concerned with building violations, that is, violations of regulations adopted by local governmental entities concerning the construction, design, quality, use, occupancy, and maintenance of buildings and structures located within their jurisdictional confines.

Most local governmental entities have, in addition to general building codes, adopted specialized codes for plumbing, electrical systems, and other structural requirements.

The purchaser should be aware of all these regulations and whether the existing structures on the property violate any of them and negotiate the terms of the contract accordingly.

[j] Licenses, Permits, and Certificates of Occupancy

Where it is essential for the use of a building or structure located on the premises and included in the sale that a certificate of occupancy be procured for it, the parties should include in their contract suitable provisions concerning the matter. In this regard, certificates of occupancy are issued by local governmental authorities such as county or municipal building departments or other municipal agencies to indicate that the buildings or structures to which they apply comply with building code requirements and are ready and fit for occupancy. Certificates of occupancy may be required both for residential and nonresidential structures.

Frequently, the use to which the purchaser expects to put the property requires either that a license or permit be issued by a governmental agency authorizing the particular use or activity or, where such a license or permit has already been issued, that it be transferred to the purchaser. Success in obtaining a license or in obtaining the transfer of an existing license may be essential to the right of the purchaser to conduct or continue the conduct of a business enterprise located thereon. For this reason, contracts for the sale of real estate frequently contain provisions concerning the seller's duty to keep necessary licenses or permits (e.g. liquor license) in force and cooperate with the purchaser in obtaining the transfer of a license or permit to him. This is particularly true where the sale of the real estate includes a going business located on the premises.

[k] Condition of Premises; Violations

Where the purchaser is willing to buy the property "as is," the seller should make sure that the contract clearly shows that the property is being sold without any representations or warranties by him as to its condition. It is dangerous for the seller to assume that if he makes no express representations or warranties in the contract, he undertakes no liability for the condition of the property since he may find that representations and warranties may be implied by a court from the circumstances of the sale or the nature of the property. For this reason, the seller should press for a contract provision specifically stating that the seller is not making any representations or warranties of any kind or character, whether express or implied, and in addition, he should obtain from the purchaser an acknowledgment or representation that he is not relying on any such representations or warranties by the seller.

If, on the other hand, the purchaser is not buying the property "as is," and insists on including in the contract representations and warranties by the seller as to the condition of the property, the seller should insert a provision disclaiming representations and warranties by him other than those expressly set forth in the agreement.

A cautious purchaser may insist not only on having the seller expressly warrant the condition of the property, but also on a provision giving him the right to inspect the property and rescind or cancel the contract if the condition of the property proves to be unsatisfactory or not as warranted or represented by the seller. It is always prudent for the purchaser to inspect the property and make suitable tests with the aid and advice of experts in order to obtain a clear picture of the physical conditions that exist on the property.

A prudent purchaser of property on which there are existing leases and tenancies will want the seller to disclose in the contract just what leases and tenancies exist and the service and repair arrangements between the seller and the tenants under their leases or other contracts; he will want to require the seller to continue to perform according to those arrangements until title passes. The seller, for his part, will not want to be responsible for repairs or maintenance, or for performing any acts that are the obligation of the tenants under existing leases, and will want the purchaser to take title subject to any failure of performance by tenants.

In addition, a cautious purchaser should obtain all relevant data concerning the seller's employees engaged in the operation and maintenance of the premises.

Where the purchaser is given the right to enter upon the premises and inspect the property before title is transferred to him, the seller should insist on the right to be indemnified or held harmless by the purchaser against any and all losses, damages or claims arising out of the purchaser's entry and activities on the premises. The seller should also require that the tests the purchaser conducts in the course of the inspection are at the purchaser's sole cost and expense.

The particular physical conditions that exist on a piece of property or to which the property is subject and that may cause concern to a purchaser depend upon the use to which the purchaser expects to put the property. Undesirable physical conditions against which purchasers want to protect themselves cover a wide range and include proneness to flooding, height of the water table, inadequate load-bearing quality of the soil, incomplete or otherwise defective buildings or other improvements, faulty building systems and equipment, and so forth. Frequently, the possibility of termite infestation or damage poses a serious problem and the purchaser may want the seller to warrant that the building is free from such infestation or damage. Often, the contract will give the purchaser the right to cancel on discovering the existence of an undesirable condition warranted against by the seller.

The seller may be held liable to a third person injured as a result of dangerous or defective conditions existing on the property shortly after the purchaser takes title if the dangerous or defective condition existed before title was transferred, the condition was not disclosed to the purchaser so that the purchaser had no knowledge or notice of it, the seller actively concealed the condition, or the purchaser has not yet had a reasonable time to discover and remedy the condition. Of course, the purchaser may assume the risk of defective and dangerous conditions and of responsibility for injuries to third persons caused thereby.

Unless he is purchasing the property "as is," the purchaser should require provisions in the contract offering him protection against defective conditions existing on the property resulting in administrative or court orders or notices of violations by local governmental authorities mandating the correction of such conditions in order to comply with statutory or regulatory standards. The purchaser should require the contract to protect him against such orders and notices of violations that are in effect at the time the contract is entered into, during the contract period, and until the time when the contract closes and title passes to him. What's more, in order to safeguard himself, the purchaser should also require the seller to furnish him with such authorizations as may be necessary to permit him to search the records of the local agencies for violations filed against the property.

The protective provisions may take several different forms. Thus, for example, the seller may be required to cure the violations or remedy the offending conditions before the closing or to deposit a sum of money in escrow as security against his performance of the necessary work within a specified period of time after the closing.

The seller, for his part, may want the contract to afford him the option to cancel the contract and return the purchaser's down payment or earnest money if the cost of remedying the offending conditions or curing the violations exceeds a specified amount. In addition, the seller will want to be exonerated from any obligation to cure violations, etc., imposed against any of the tenants on the premises.

[l] Fixtures and Personal Property

A contract for the sale of real estate that contemplates that personal property installed at, or used in connection with, the real property will be transferred to the purchaser along with the real property should identify the personal property to be so transferred as clearly as possible. Frequently, a schedule itemizing the personal property, fixtures, equipment, and so forth is attached to the contract and incorporated therein by reference. Where the sale includes real property and a going business located thereon, the sale may include such items as good will, the registered fictitious name under which the business is conducted, licenses or permits, trade fixtures, and furnishings. In addition to an itemization of the articles of personal property that go with the sale, the purchaser may want the seller to warrant and represent that he owns title to those articles free and clear of all liens and encumbrances or that he will be entitled to a credit against the purchase price for sums remaining unpaid under the obligations secured by those liens and encumbrances.

Each of the parties will want to allocate the purchase price between the real and personal property so as to obtain the best tax results for himself, and will consider such matters as depreciation, depreciation recapture, and the investment credit. However, depending on the situation of the parties, each can be expected to accommodate the other's needs in order to consummate the transaction.

[m] Sale of Going Business

Frequently, the parties to a contract for the sale of real estate are buying and selling more than a parcel of real property with the buildings and improvements situated on it. Instead, the major purpose of the transaction is the purchase and sale of a going business enterprise that is being conducted on the premises. Consequently, the parties must agree not only on the terms and protective provisions they require when building and selling a parcel of real estate, but also on the terms and provisions they require for the purchase and sale of the enterprise that is conducted on the property. Thus, for example, their contract should, in addition to the usual provisions of a real estate sales contract, deal with such matters as the management and operation of the business during the period between the contract date and the closing of title, the right to enter into contracts on behalf of the enterprise during that period, the purchaser's right to inspect the property and obtain information concerning the conduct and management of the business, liability for obligations relating to the business, the goodwill of the business and the right to use the business name, collective bargaining contracts with employees, books, and records, accounts receivable, furniture, equipment, and trade fixtures. In addition, the purchaser may want a provision in the contract prohibiting the seller from interfering with, and competing against, the enterprise.

With respect to the federal income tax consequences of the sale of a going business, the sale proceeds must be allocated to the various assets of the business, and capital gain or loss and ordinary income or loss computed accordingly. The allocation must be made among all the assets sold according to their respective relative values (according to the ratio of the value of each asset to the sum total of the values of all the assets sold). Even though the parties expressly allocate the price among the different assets, the Internal Revenue Service may make a reallocation according to the realities of the transaction.

[n] Existing Leases and Tenancies

The purchaser under a contract for the sale of improved property which is subject to multiple leases and tenancies should insist on the right to examine the leases and require the seller to make representations and warranties concerning the status and details of each lease and tenancy, including the term of the lease or tenancy, renewal and other options, rents and other charges, the amount of rent which has been prepaid or is in arrears, the amount of security deposits, and whether any utilities are furnished in return for the rent charged. In addition, the purchaser should also require representations and warranties of the seller that none of the leases has been modified, altered, or amended, that no tenant has the right to cancel or terminate his lease, that all scheduled leases are in full force and effect, that no tenant has any interest in the property other than a leasehold possessory interest, that the seller has complied with all his obligations under each lease and that no work remains incomplete, that no lease has been assigned or otherwise encumbered, that there are no brokerage or leasing commissions due except those disclosed in the contract, and that there are no management, service, supply or maintenance contracts applicable to the premises, except those disclosed in the contract.

The seller, for his part, may insist on the right to take action in the event of tenant defaults that occur before the closing date.

The purchaser, in order to protect himself against unprofitable leases, may insist on a provision under which the seller agrees not to lease vacant space after the execution of the contract and before the closing without the purchaser's written consent. If such a provision is included, however, the seller should insist on a provision for payment to him at the closing of a sum equal to the rent he would have received if consent had not been withheld by the purchaser.

Once title to the property passes to the purchaser, he stands in the same relation to the tenants on the premises as the seller. Since he stands in the shoes of his predecessor, he is bound by, and enjoys the benefits of, all the terms and conditions of the leases and tenancies to the same extent as his predecessor.

[i] Current and Past-Due Rentals. The seller should require a provision calling for the adjustment of current rentals and the apportionment of rentals due under percentage leases and rent escalation clauses.

The contract should identify the period for which the seller is to be entitled to receive rental payments made by tenants and the seller may want the purchaser to agree to collect the funds as his agent or trustee and make prompt remittance of those funds to him. On the other hand, the purchaser may want to assign the right to collect past-due rentals to the seller and relieve himself of the burden.

[ii] Tenants' Security Deposits. The purchaser will want to include a provision setting forth the details of all the tenant security deposits and for the transfer to him of the security deposits when the contract closes. The seller, for his part, will want the purchaser to agree to indemnify him, to the extent of the funds transferred, against any claims which may be made against him by the tenants or those who own the deposits. In addition, the seller may want the right to apply security deposits to tenant defaults before the closing, provided this is permitted by local law.

[o] Possession of Premises

The contract should clearly set out the date when possession of the property is to be delivered by the seller to the purchaser. In most jurisdictions, the purchaser has no right to possession before title closes and the deed is delivered to him, unless the contract provides otherwise. The parties may, however, enter into an arrangement under which the purchaser is entitled to immediate possession of the property once the contract is executed and he is also entitled to retain possession until he defaults in making the payments required of him or commits some other breach of contract. The seller, under this type of arrangement, will want the contract to clearly spell out the conditions on which the purchaser's right to retain possession depend and also the seller's rights in the event of a default or breach of contract by the purchaser.

Where the contract requires the seller to deliver possession of the property to the purchaser on or before a specified date, the purchaser may want to include a provision for liquidated damages where the seller fails to deliver possession to him by the date specified. The contract may also provide that the purchase price shall be reduced by a fixed amount for each day that possession is withheld from the purchaser after the date set for delivery and, further, for an escrow deposit to be made by the seller to cover such reductions of the purchase price.

Where the purchaser is to take possession before the closing or before legal title is transferred to him or, on the other hand, where the seller is to remain in possession after the closing or after title is transferred to the purchaser, the relation that exists between the parties during the term of such possession must be clearly spelled out in the light of both the legal and tax consequences to the parties. If, for example, a landlord-tenant relation exists between them, summary proceedings to evict the occupying party may be available. However, since, in some states, summary proceedings may be available even in the absence of a landlord-tenant relation, state law should be checked. From the point of view of income tax consequences, if a landlord-tenant relation is established, the payments made for the use and occupancy of the premises will be treated as rent and, therefore, as ordinary income to the recipient and as an ordinary business deduction for the payer. If a different relation is established, different tax consequences may follow. Where, for example, provision is made for reduction of the purchase price if the seller remains in possession after the time he agrees to surrender possession, such reduction serves to reduce the seller's capital gain on the sale and the purchaser's basis for the property.

Generally, the purchaser will want the right to actual possession free and clear of leases, tenancies and occupancies other than those clearly set forth in the contract. If the seller is permitted to remain on the premises after title passes to the purchaser, the purchaser will want a provision requiring the seller to deliver the premises in the condition in which they are at the time of the closing or the contract date.

[p] Damage, Destruction, or Condemnation of Property

A contract for the sale of real estate should provide for the contingency that all or part of the property may be taken in the exercise of the power of eminent domain or may be damaged or destroyed by fire or other casualty during the period between the time when the contract is entered into and the time when the closing takes place and title is transferred to the purchaser. Frequently, the contract will provide that if all or a substantial portion of the property is taken or destroyed before the closing occurs, the transaction is to be canceled, and the parties returned to their original position; that is, the seller is not entitled to enforce the contract and the purchaser is entitled to the return of his down payment or earnest money. This result would follow, in any event, in a jurisdiction that has adopted the Uniform Vendor and Purchaser Risk Act or a similar statute. However, this rule does not apply in some jurisdictions and, in those jurisdictions, the risk of loss from damage caused by fire, flood, hurricane, erosion and the like, as well as from the exercise of the power of eminent domain, passes to the purchaser on execution of the contract.

Suppose only a portion of the property is taken in the exercise of the power of eminent domain or is destroyed by fire or other casualty and the portion taken or destroyed is not substantial in comparison to the size of the entire property. The contract should provide for this contingency and set forth the rights of the parties if the contingency occurs. Thus, the parties should reach a meeting of the minds with respect to such matters as the right to rescind the contract, the right to a reduction of the purchase price and the amount of the reduction, what shall constitute a substantial taking or destruction authorizing the cancellation of the contract, and what shall constitute an insubstantial taking or destruction.

Contracts for the sale of real estate generally place all risk of loss by reason of condemnation before the closing and transfer of title on the seller and give the purchaser the right to cancel, on notice to the seller, where all or part of the property becomes subjected to a bona fide threat of condemnation before the transfer of title to him. On the other hand, the contract may contemplate that the purchaser will take possession of the property before title is transferred to him as, for example, where the purchase price is to be paid in installments, the purchaser goes into possession once the contract is executed, and legal title does not pass to the purchaser until the full purchase price with interest is paid. The seller, under such a contract, will want the contract to require the purchaser to give him notice of the institution of a condemnation proceeding against the property and the right to participate in the proceeding or in negotiations with the condemning authority in lieu of condemnation.

For a discussion of the tax consequences of destruction or condemnation of property, see 8.04[4].

[q] Casualty and Liability Insurance

The contract should include provisions concerning the obligations of the parties to provide insurance coverage with respect to the property and the disposition of the proceeds of insurance policies in the event that such proceeds become payable. The purchaser will want to be provided with a schedule of all the insurance policies carried for the property and, as a rule, such a schedule will be attached to, and made part of, the contract by reference. In addition, the purchaser will want the contract to require the seller to pay the premiums and comply with all notices and requests of the insurance carriers until the closing is held and title is transferred to him.

Once the contract is entered into by the parties, the purchaser has an insurable interest in the property; the seller retains his insurable interest until such time as title passes to the purchaser and the seller is divested of his interest. While each of them has the right to insure himself against loss during such time as each has an interest in the property, neither the purchaser nor the seller is required to insure the property for the other's benefit unless the contract so provides. However, the parties may, for example, agree that the purchaser shall maintain insurance for the property for the seller's protection until such time as the contract is fully performed and the buyer takes title to the property. Indeed, a provision so requiring frequently appears in contracts under which the purchaser takes possession of the property once the contract is executed, but does not obtain legal title until he has made full payment of the purchase price with interest and has performed all the other terms and conditions of the contract.

The major types of insurance coverage that real estate people deal with (in addition to title insurance, which is treated in 8.02[4][h]) are casualty (e.g., fire and extended coverage) insurance and liability insurance. Extended coverage insurance protects the insured against a wide range of risks in addition to fire damage, including, among others, wind, storm, hail, explosion, civil commotion, riot, sprinkler leakage, motor vehicle, and aircraft. Liability insurance covers the insured against loss by reason of being answerable to third persons who are injured as a result of dangerous or defective conditions existing on the premises. The seller will, for example, want the purchaser to provide liability insurance for his benefit where the purchaser will be in possession and operate the property for a period of time during which the seller still has legal title to the property.

The contract, in addition to fixing responsibility for the procurement and maintenance of insurance coverage, should also deal with the disposition of insurance proceeds. For example, the contract may require that fire and extended coverage insurance proceeds be used to reduce the purchase-money mortgage on the property or, on the other hand, to restore the damaged property to its original condition (where the purchaser is in possession but legal title still rests in the seller and the seller has an interest in preserving the property).

Sums paid for insurance coverage with respect to investment, income-producing, or business property are deductible as ordinary business expenses, provided they are reasonable and necessary.

Where property is damaged or destroyed as a result of a risk that is covered by a fire and extended coverage insurance policy, there is an involuntary conversion of the property into the cash proceeds of the policy, and any loss resulting from the conversion is recognized for tax purposes. However, gain is not recognized if the requirements for nonrecognition imposed by the Internal Revenue Code are complied with. (See 8.04[4].)

[r] Representations and Warranties

Contracts for the purchase and sale of real estate usually contain provisions concerning warranties and representations by the seller as to material elements of the transaction. In addition, the purchaser may be called on to make representations or warranties to the seller. A warranty may be distinguished from a representation in that a warranty is a promise that is given contemporaneously with, and as part of, the contract, while a representation is of an existing fact and usually precedes and induces the contract. In the case of a breach of warranty, the contract remains binding, but the opposite party may sue for damages by reason of the breach. On a false material representation, however, the opposite party may elect to avoid the contract and recover the entire price paid or he may affirm the contract and sue for damages.

Representations and warranties may be expressed or implied. For this reason, the contract may include provisions that the seller (or both the seller and the purchaser) makes no representations or warranties, whether express or implied, and that the purchaser is not relying on any representations or warranties made by the seller (or that neither party is relying on representations or warranties made by the other). Alternatively, the contract may state that no representations or warranties are being made or relied on other than those expressly stated in the contract as being made.

The specific representations and warranties that the parties will want to insist on depend on the situation of the parties, and the nature of the transaction and the property. However, basic representations and warranties, such as the marketability of title or that no condemnation proceeding is pending, should be considered to be fundamental in any contract for the sale of real estate.

[s] Indemnification of Parties

Careful draftsmen will frequently include indemnification provisions in a contract for the sale and purchase of real estate under which the party whose responsibility it is to meet certain obligations with respect to the subject property agrees to indemnify and hold the other party harmless against claims or demands based on those obligations. Thus, for example, the purchaser may require that the seller be obligated to protect him against claims, liens, or encumbrances asserted for work performed or services furnished at the premises before the closing, and the seller may require similar protection with respect to post-closing claims; and both parties may agree to appropriate indemnification provisions under which each is required to defend and hold the other harmless for losses suffered as a result of debts, liens, and encumbrances incurred with respect to the property, depending on whether the obligation was waived before or after the closing.

[t] Assignment of Contract

In the absence of a specific provision in the contract to the contrary, either party may assign his interest to another, unless the contract calls for a performance that depends on the particular qualifications of the original contracting party. For example, a contract to sell real estate where the purchaser is to pay the entire consideration in cash at the closing does not depend on the characteristics of the particular purchaser, since cash paid by one purchaser is as good as cash paid by another. But, if the purchase price is to be represented in substantial part by the purchaser's note and purchase-money mortgage, with the purchaser assuming personal liability, the seller, even in the absence of any provision in the contract, may be in a position to bar assignment.

To avoid any question as to the right to assign, the seller frequently will provide in the contract that there may be no assignment or that an assignment may be made only to specified assignees (e.g., a relative of the purchaser or a corporation in which the purchaser holds a specified percentage of stock). Another reason for a seller to bar assignability is to prevent the buyer from seeking to sell his contract interest at a profit to himself before the closing date—a practice called "trading on the equity." The seller may object to this practice either because the real estate is cheapened by being "shopped around" or because the seller wishes to be in a position to insist on a share of any profit if the speculative buyer is able to find a new purchaser before the closing date.

If the purchaser insists on having the right to assign the contract to another before the closing and the seller consents thereto, the contract can give the buyer either an unlimited right to assign or the right to assign to a specified entity. In either case, the buyer will want a provision discharging him from all his obligations under the contract once it is assigned. As for the seller, he will want provisions entitling him to receive prompt notice of an assignment and also a provision that the assignee is fully bound by the contract.

[u] Breach of Contract

Once a valid and enforceable contract for the sale and purchase of real estate is breached by one of the parties, the other party is entitled to maintain an action to recover damages resulting from the breach. This is true in the case of any contract and it is no less true in the case of a real estate contract. What's more, since real estate is considered to be unique, mere money damages may not adequately compensate the injured party where a real estate contract is breached. For this reason, a purchaser of real estate may seek equitable relief such as specific performance where the seller fails or refuses to consummate the transaction and convey to him according to their agreement. On the other hand, in the case of a default or breach of contract by the purchaser, an award of money damages usually is sufficient to compensate the seller, since the seller usually can resell the property. All this is true without any special provisions in the contract setting out what shall constitute a default or breach and the rights and remedies resulting therefrom. Nevertheless, the parties to a contract for the sale and purchase of real estate commonly include in their agreement provisions dealing with the rights and remedies of the opposite party where one of the parties is guilty of a default or breach of their agreement.

Real estate sale contracts frequently provide that if the purchaser defaults in the performance of his part of the agreement, his earnest money deposit will serve as liquidated money damages. As a practical matter, this type of provision converts the contract into a kind of option, since the earnest money payment can be viewed as an option payment that ties up the property for the purchaser until a specified time when he must choose whether or not to exercise the option and purchase the property. In drafting a liquidated damage provision, the draftsman must be aware that the amount set must be reasonable and that an agreement to pay a fixed lump sum as liquidated damages by reason of a breach of an inconsequential nature may be unenforceable because it is unreasonable. To avoid an inference of unconscionableness, the contract should state that the parties have agreed on the sum specified as liquidated damages as constituting a reasonable forecast of the probable actual loss resulting from the breach. In addition, the "difficulty, inconvenience, and uncertainty of ascertaining actual damages" may be stated in the contract and be helpful in this regard.

[v] Brokerage Commissions

A contract for the sale and purchase of real estate should identify the broker who brought the parties together, the party who is to be responsible for the payment of the brokerage commission, and the amount, time, and manner in which payment is to be made. Where no broker has participated in the transaction, the contract should include a representation by each of the parties to the other that no broker was involved and that if any claim for broker's commissions or fees is ever made as a result of any contract or commitments made by such party with respect to the property, he will indemnify the other party against any loss or expense suffered as a result of the claim.

Generally speaking, the seller will be responsible for the payment of brokerage commissions and, where the parties so agree, the contract should contain a provision to that effect. Assuming the seller is responsible for the brokerage commission, he will want to provide that the commission will not be payable unless and until the contract is closed and that, if the contract is not closed for any reason, including failure of title or the default of either party, the commission will not be considered to have been earned and will not be due or payable. (Note that there is authority to the effect that a brokerage commission "payable at closing" is payable even if a closing does not occur as a result of the seller's default, if the broker has performed all his obligations and has procured a ready, willing, and able purchaser.) The parties may, of course, agree that the purchaser is to pay the broker's commission and deduct the amount paid from the purchase price, in which case that agreement should be clearly spelled out in the contract.

As far as the broker himself is concerned, he should avoid fixing his commission according to a schedule of fees suggested by a local real estate board or similar trade association. Instead, he should negotiate for and set a specific sum as his fee or commission for each transaction in which he is involved; he should not rely on a "uniform," "customary," or "suggested" fee, since such reliance may violate federal or state antitrust or price-fixing laws.

[w] Recording the Contract

In order to be in a position to claim priority over rights of third persons intervening between the date the agreement is entered into and the deed is filed of record, the purchaser may prepare, execute, and file of record a short form, notice, or memorandum of the purchase agreement. Once the document is properly filed of record according to the statutory requirements of the jurisdiction in which the property is situated, this constitutes notice to "all the world" of the existence of the agreement and the purchaser's rights thereunder. Furthermore, by filing a notice instead of a copy of an entire contract, the purchase price and other details of the contract that the parties do not want to publish to the world are not revealed.

[x] Notice, Approval, and Consent

The contract provisions with respect to the giving of notice by each party to the other should make it clear whether notice must be in writing, when the deadline for giving notice occurs, and what shall constitute sufficient notice. Provisions that state that notice shall be deemed to have been given and received when a properly addressed, certified, or registered letter is deposited in the U.S. mails with the postage prepaid is not unfair to either party, since it operates to the benefit of both. However, since the mails may be delayed, the parties may provide that written notice shall be deemed to be given and received not when the letter is deposited in the mails, but within a specified time after it is so deposited.

The contract may also require that the written consent or approval of a party or his attorney be obtained with respect to designated matters and, further, that the party whose right it is to consent or approve will not withhold his consent or approval arbitrarily.

[y] Arbitration

The parties to a contract for the sale of real estate frequently provide for the submission to arbitration of claims or disputes between them that arise out of their contract. The contract may, for example, provide for the submission to arbitration of all claims or disputes arising thereunder between the parties or for the submission of claims or disputes with respect to designated matters.

The contract may set forth in greater or lesser detail the machinery by which arbitration is to be initiated, the method of appointing the arbitrators, the number of arbitrators, and the conclusive and binding nature of their determination. Where the contract imposes the requirement, disputes or claims that come within the requirement cannot be litigated in the courts in the first instance.

While arbitration offers a speedier and less costly way of resolving disputes between the parties than recourse to the courts, ultimate recourse to the courts cannot be prohibited, since an appeal can be taken from a judgment entered on the basis of an arbitration award.

[z] Construction of Contract

The contract may provide rules for its interpretation as a guide to discovering and giving effect to the intention of the parties. These rules may be so framed as to be applicable throughout the contract or to specific portions thereof and the parties may express their intentions that different rules of construction shall be applicable to different parts of the contract. Provisions contained in the contract concerning how the parties want their contract to be construed and given effect can be very helpful where doubt or ambiguity might otherwise appear and as an aid to the court if litigation ensues, since the courts will honor the parties' intentions as expressed in these rules whenever possible.

The contract may stipulate that the law of a particular state shall govern the construction, operation, effect and enforceability of the contract and all questions concerning the marketability of title. In addition, the contract may recite that it contains the entire agreement between the parties with respect to the transaction and there are no other terms, provisions, understandings, covenants, statements, or conditions with respect to the transaction, whether oral or written and whether contemporaneous with, or prior to, the execution of the contract. In other words, the contract may expressly state that it sets forth the complete agreement between the parties with respect to the matter. The purpose of this type of provision is to avoid the possibility that a course of dealings between the parties or that communications, statements, or understandings between them, whether oral or in the form of written correspondence, will be read into this written contract.

In general, a contract is entire and, therefore, not severable if it consists of a number of parts that may be considered as parts of one whole. If, however, each part may be considered to amount to a distinct contract entered into at one time and stated in the same instrument, the contract is severable. Thus, if the consideration for the contract is single and entire, the contract is not severable even though the contract deals with a number of distinct and independent matters. If, however, the consideration is capable of being allocated among the different parts of the contract, the contract is severable.

Where the parties expressly state that their contract is severable and that the invalidity of one part shall not impair the validity of the remainder, this amounts to an expression of the intentions of the parties that their contract shall be construed to be valid and enforceable to the extent that it is possible to do so.

[aa] Execution and Acknowledgment

An instrument such as a contract for the sale of real estate may be said to be executed when it is signed by the parties or when it is signed and acknowledged by the parties. The acknowledgment will take the form of a declaration or certificate taken before a notary public, commissioner of deeds, or other attesting officer stating that the parties appeared before him and signed the document as a voluntary act.

It is generally advisable for the contract to state the date when each of the parties signed and also to state that whenever the term "the date hereof" is employed in the contract, that date will be the last date of execution by the parties. Usually, a contract for the sale and purchase of real estate will impose time deadlines on both parties with respect to such matters as, for example, delivery of title commitments and surveys, satisfaction of conditions, and closing. Frequently, these time deadlines are determined to be a specified number of days after "the date hereof." Since the parties often do not execute the contract on the same day and since the time lapse between the signings may be significant, the above provision is an advisable one.

[5] Real Estate Closings

The closing of a contract for the sale and purchase of real estate usually takes the form of a final meeting of the parties at which the instruments necessary for conveying title to the premises and the personal property on or used in connection with the premises are executed and delivered by the seller to the buyer and the consideration for the sale passes from the buyer to the seller. It is at this meeting that the final documents are signed and delivered, expenses are apportioned, income from the property is prorated, and all closing adjustments are made.

In some parts of the country, however, the closing of a real estate transaction does not take place at a meeting held between the buyer and the seller. Instead, the purchaser deposits with an escrow agent the agreed purchase price and such other documents as may be required, while the seller deposits with the escrow agent the executed deed to the property and related documents. In addition, if financing by a lender is to be provided, the mortgage or deed of trust and its related instruments are also deposited with the escrow agent. When the agent has received all of the necessary documents and cash, it will consummate the transaction and title will pass to the purchaser. Between the time that a document or cash is deposited with the escrow agent and the transaction is consummated, the items deposited are considered to be "in escrow."

Documentation Required at the Closing; Recordation. When the parties meet face-to-face to close the transaction, the seller brings the deed to the property, and any documentary stamps that may be required will be attached to the deed at that time or immediately before recordation. The seller will also have with him any leases that pertain to the property. He will also bring the insurance policies covering the property (e.g., fire and extended coverage), and any certificates of occupancy, electrical inspection, elevator inspection, approval or inspection by the fire underwriters, and the plumbing department of the city (if such is required).

The seller will also bring with him receipted bills for real estate taxes, water and sewer charges, and any other items as to which adjustments will be made at the closing. He may also bring a contract with the labor union representing the building employees.

In addition, the seller will have a bill of sale covering personalty ready for delivery to the buyer and, if there is a building service contract, the seller will deliver that as well and also the keys to the buildings.

At the closing, the buyer will be ready to deliver a certified check for the approximate amount that will be due from him. While the adjustments are often approximated in advance of closing, they are computed accurately and finally, and often paid by check executed at the closing.

If the buyer is a corporation, a copy of the corporate resolution authorizing the purchase may be required. Likewise, if the seller is a corporation, a resolution authorizing sale may also be required.

The seller, for his part, will want to obtain an owner's estoppel certificate from the purchaser if a purchase-money mortgage or deed of trust is to be assigned at the time title closes.

Where the property is subject to a ground lease, the contract should provide for an assignment of the seller's interest in the ground lease to the purchaser and should also contain a provision whereby the purchaser assumes the seller's obligations under the ground lease.

As already indicated, the adjustments are made at the closing; and the deed, any mortgages, release of mortgages or other liens, the check or checks for the purchase price and the adjustments, and any other documents are turned over to the attorneys for the parties or to the title insurance company to be held until the deed and other documents are recorded. Recordation normally takes place as soon as possible after the closing, frequently on the same day.

Time and Manner of Closing. Normally, the parties should include in their contract a provision stating the date and place of closing, the documents to be transferred, and whether or not time shall be construed as of the essence of the contract.

The contract may provide for a contingent closing date and may give either party the right to adjourn and extend the closing date on giving timely notice to the other party. In addition, the acceleration of the closing date may also be provided for. As already indicated, the closing may be held through the use of an escrow agent rather than at a meeting of the parties and their attorneys. Thus, the contract may specify an escrow agent through whom the transaction is to be completed and to whom the appropriate documents evidencing the transfer of title are to be delivered. In addition, the contract may set forth specific escrow instructions for the closing and the additional documents to be delivered that relate to the particular type of property being conveyed.

The contract should provide for the execution and delivery of a deed in recordable form conveying title to the property and should state the type of deed required, that is, whether the deed shall be a full covenant and warranty deed, a bargain and sale deed, and so forth.

Adjustments and Closing Statement. Normally, the parties expect to adjust and apportion, at the closing, charges against, and income accruing from, the property. For example, if the seller has paid real estate taxes for the year in advance and sells the property during the course of the year, he is entitled to a credit to reflect that portion of the tax payment made by him that will accrue to the benefit of the purchaser (i.e., that covers the portion of the year during which the purchaser will be the owner). If, on the other hand, the seller has not yet paid real estate taxes for the current year, he is charged with that portion of tax attributable to the part of the year during which he owned the property. Other items that may require adjustment include payment of insurance premiums and utility costs, escrow accounts with mortgagees, and the value of heating fuel and supplies stored at the property. In the case of rental income properties, rent must also be adjusted.

Adjustments also include modification of the purchase price itself to take into consideration changes in the bargain. For example, if the property includes more or less acreage than specified in the contract, the parties may agree (or the contract may specifically provide) that the purchase price be adjusted by a given price per acre.

The seller's or the purchaser's attorney, or the broker who brought about the transaction, may prepare at, or immediately after the closing, a closing statement setting forth the total dollar amounts received by or credited to the purchaser.

Some state laws require the use of closing statements; other states make their use optional with the parties. (With respect to real estate mortgage closings, in contrast to real estate title closings, federal and state laws require the preparation of closing statements in connection with real estate mortgages made to individuals in transactions within their purview.)

Transfer Taxes and Stamp Tax. Transfer taxes are taxes levied by state or local governments on transfers of property or interests in property. The tax may take the form of a documentary stamp tax requiring revenue stamps to be affixed to deeds, conveyances, or other documents transferring title to, or interests in, property.

Included among transfer taxes are those imposed not only on conveyances of real estate by deed, but also those imposed on transfers of securities (such as stocks and bonds) and such taxes as inheritance and estate taxes. Here, however, we are concerned only with taxes imposed on the conveyance of real estate.

A documentary stamp tax is one imposed on written instruments, the payment of which is represented by stamps affixed or impressed on the instrument. Formerly, the federal government imposed a documentary stamp tax on, among other documents, real estate deeds and mortgage obligations. When the federal government repealed its tax on these instruments, transfer taxes were imposed by various states and even some local governmental entities.

A contract for the purchase and sale of real estate should clearly state whether the purchaser or the seller, or both, shall be responsible for the payment of the transfer (or documentary stamp) taxes that may be imposed on the conveyance. Where the seller is required to pay the transfer tax, the amount so paid by him is part of the cost of selling the property and is deductible by him from the total amount received by him in determining his gain from the sale. Where the purchaser is required to pay the tax, the amount paid by him becomes part of the cost of the property to him and, therefore, increases the tax basis of the property.

[6] Deeds

A deed to real property is a written instrument by which title to the property is conveyed by the owner (the grantor) to another (the grantee). A deed is not valid as between the grantor and the grantee unless it is delivered to and accepted by or on behalf of the grantee and it also meets the following requirements.

The grantor must be identified and he must be a competent adult. Where there is more than one grantor, each grantor must be capable of conveying his interest in the property. There must also be a definite and identifiable grantee. While there must be a valid consideration that is set forth in the deed, the actual consideration need not be so set forth and a nominal consideration may be stated. Where, however, a trustee is the grantor named in the deed, the deed must state the actual consideration for the conveyance.

A deed must contain language (e.g., "grant and convey") that shows that the property is being conveyed and the property conveyed must be sufficiently described to identify it. The description may take the form of a metes-and-bounds description or any other description, provided the property is sufficiently identified.

A deed must be signed by the grantor and, under the statutes of some states, the signature must be witnessed or notarized, or both. Generally, a deed must be delivered by the grantor to the grantee and, unless delivered, it is invalid and ineffective to transfer title. The grantee must be in existence at the time the deed is delivered. Thus, a deed delivered to a corporation before it comes into existence is void. Once a deed is delivered by the grantor to the grantee and accepted by the grantee, title passes. Delivery must be made during the lifetime of both the grantor and the grantee; if the grantor dies before delivery is made, title is not conveyed. (However, under the Torrens System of registering title to property, the registration of the deed and not the delivery of the deed conveys the title.) As regards rights of third parties, a deed usually is not effective unless it is recorded or registered according to the statutory requirements of the jurisdiction.

Deeds are of several different types; the key distinction among them is related to the precise responsibilities that the grantor assumes in connection with the conveyance. These responsibilities are called warranties. A warranty combines a representation that a certain state of facts is true and the responsibility to make good any damages if the facts turn out to be otherwise.

☐ *General warranty deed.* This deed includes the broadest warranties by the grantor and so would be most preferred by the grantee. While the precise warranties in such a deed depend upon the law of the particular state, a warranty deed usually contains four basic covenants:

- The covenant of seisin, by which the grantor represents he in fact owns the property
- The covenant of the right to convey
- The covenant against encumbrances, i.e., a representation that no claims exist against the property other than those specified in the deed or contract
- The covenant of quiet enjoyment, by which the grantor represents that no person with a superior right to the property can interfere with the grantee's use or possession of the property

In some states, these covenants are actually spelled out in the deed; in others, the use of certain language in the deed is taken to imply the existence of these covenants.

☐ *Special warranty deed.* This is exactly the same as a general warranty deed with one important distinction. The grantor will be liable for breach of his warranty only if the cause arose through the grantor's own act or during his period of ownership. The grantor thus disclaims any responsibility for defects that arose before he became the owner.

☐ *Bargain and sale deed.* This type of deed conveys title to property just as effectively as either kind of warranty deed but contains no covenants (or in some cases, merely a covenant against the grantor's acts). Thus it is also known as a deed without covenants. The term "bargain and sale" can be traced back to the early common law of England, when this type of conveyance was used to avoid certain legal complications that ensued if a warranty deed was used.

☐ *Quitclaim deed.* While this deed, too, can effectively convey title, it is normally used as a means of surrendering a claim to property that may or may not be valid. In effect, the grantor under a quitclaim deed says "I don't know if I own this property, but if I do, I convey to you whatever rights I may have." This type of deed often is used to correct an error made in an earlier conveyance.

In addition to the categories just distinguished, deeds are often known by the name or authority of the person executing them. Thus, an executor's deed is made by the executor of an estate (and the grantee is put on notice that he must be sure of the executor's authority to make the conveyance). A sheriff's deed conveys property sold at a sheriff's sale following foreclosure proceedings, while a tax deed follows a forced sale for failure to pay real estate taxes. The term "judicial deed" is often used to describe any deed from a sale resulting from a judicial proceeding. Most of these deeds are without covenants but this is not invariably so.

Under the doctrine of merger by deed, the purchaser's acceptance of the seller's deed is prima facie completion of the contract and all stipulations made therein. Thereafter, the purchaser's rights are based solely on the warranties, if any, contained in the deed. For this reason, the purchaser may want to include a provision for the survival of all representations and warranties after the closing. The parties may also, of course, include in the deed warranties and restrictions agreed to by them. Accordingly, merger by deed may constitute a trap either for a seller or purchaser who, having bargained for some right in the contract, loses that right on acceptance of the deed because the contract does not provide for the survival of the right, or the deed does not set forth the right.

The parties may include in their contract a provision that is merely declaratory of the doctrine of merger by deed or one that serves to modify the effect of the doctrine on the rights and obligations of the parties.

8.03 TAX ASPECTS OF REAL ESTATE SALES

[1] Calculating Gain or Loss

When real estate is sold or disposed of, the seller will realize gain or loss. The amount of gain or loss is computed by subtracting from the amount realized the seller's basis in the property. The amount realized is the money plus the fair market value of any property received by the seller in exchange for the property given up. (The amount realized also includes the amount of any purchase-money mortgage taken back by the seller as well as the amount of any existing mortgage taken over by the buyer.) The amount realized is reduced by selling expenses such as advertising, commissions, and legal fees relating to the disposition.

Once having determined the amount realized from the sale, the seller deducts the adjusted basis of the property in order to determine the amount of gain or loss. The adjusted basis of property is the original basis adjusted for any capital additions or capital recoveries. Original basis is the cost or other basis of the property on the date it was acquired by the seller.

Capital additions include the cost of capital improvements and betterments made by the seller to the property. These expenditures must be distinguished from expenses for the ordinary repair and maintenance of the property. Capital additions are added to the basis of the property; by comparison, repairs and maintenance costs may be deducted from income each year if the property is used in a trade or business or for the production of income.

Capital recoveries are those items that must be deducted from original basis, with the result that the realized gain to the seller is increased (or the realized loss is decreased) when the property is sold. Capital recoveries include items such as depreciation, amortization, and depletion. The reason such capital recoveries are deducted from basis is that they already have been reflected on prior tax returns of the seller as an offset to income.

> *Example:* Mrs. Smith purchased property for $50,000 and takes cumulative depreciation deductions of $10,000 during ownership. She then sells the property for $60,000. The amount realized from the sale (assuming no selling expenses) is $60,000. Mrs. Smith's original basis is $50,000. However, her adjusted basis is $40,000 since she has already recouped $10,000 of her original cost via depreciation deductions taken during ownership. Thus, her realized gain is $20,000.

Some special rules for determining basis are as follows:

☐ *Lump-sum purchases.* When several properties are acquired in a lump-sum purchase, it is necessary to allocate the total cost among the individual parcels. The cost is allocated on the basis of the fair market values of the individual properties acquired.

☐ *Conversion to business property.* When property held for personal use is converted to income-producing use (as when a personal residence is converted to rental use), the basis for loss is the lesser of the adjusted basis or the fair market value of the property at the time of conversion. The basis for gain is the adjusted basis at the time of conversion. After the property is converted, both its loss and gain basis are adjusted for any depreciation taken after the conversion.

The purpose of these rules, which apply to both real estate and personal property, is to prevent the taxpayer from converting personal-use assets that have declined in value to business use in order to sell the asset and recognize a business loss (or from using the higher basis to obtain greater depreciation deductions).

Example: Mrs. Jones purchased a residence for $50,000, in which she lived for five years. At that time, the value of the property has declined to $40,000 and Mrs. Jones converts it into a rental unit. Since the $40,000 fair market value is lower than the $50,000 adjusted basis, depreciation must be based on the $40,000 value (which in turn, of course, must be allocated between land and building). If the property is subsequently sold for $55,000, the adjusted basis is $40,000 minus any depreciation deductions. If the property is sold for $35,000, the adjusted basis again is $40,000 minus depreciation deductions.

☐ *Acquired from decedent.* Property acquired from a decedent takes a basis that is equal to the value placed upon the property for purposes of the federal estate tax. The general rule is that the basis of property is the fair market value of the property at the date of the decedent's death. Property acquired from a decedent includes property acquired by bequest, devise, or inheritance.

As a result of this rule, any appreciation in value during the time the property was held by the decedent escapes income tax completely. There is a step-up in basis to the fair market value. Conversely, any decline in value is not available as a deductible loss.

Example: Peter acquired land in 1942 for $4,500. Peter leaves the land to Alfred upon his death in 1979. The value of the land on Peter's death is $38,000. Alfred's basis in the land will be $38,000. The increase in value will not be subject to income tax. If the land had declined in value, the resulting loss in basis would not be deductible.

The holding period on property inherited from a decedent is considered to be long-term regardless of the actual period held.

☐ *Acquired by gift.* In case of property acquired by gift, the basis of the property for the purpose of determining gain is the donor's adjusted basis or the adjusted basis of the last preceding owner by whom it was not acquired by gift. The basis for determining loss is the lower of the basis for gain or the fair market value of the property on the date of the gift.

Example: Mary was given property that has an adjusted basis of $10,000 at the date of gift. The fair market value of the property on that date is $9,000. Mary later sells the property for $11,200. She would report a gain of $1,200 ($11,200 selling price – $10,000 adjusted basis). However, if Mary sells the property for $8,000, the fair market value on the date of the gift would be the basis since it is lower than the donor's adjusted basis. Mary would have a realized loss of $1,000 ($9,000 basis for loss – $8,000 amount realized).

The preceding rules can result in situations where neither gain nor loss is realized by a donee. If Mary sells the property for $9,400, there would be neither a gain nor a loss. The basis for determining loss is $9,000, which creates no loss; the basis for gain is $10,000, but no gain is realized.

The rules prevent the donee from benefiting from a decline in value while the donor held the property. However, the rules result in the donor being able to shift the burden of tax on a gain to the donee.

The holding period of property acquired by gift is also two-pronged. If the property is sold at a gain, the holding period begins on the date the property was acquired by the donor. Where the donee uses fair market value as the basis, the holding period begins on the date of the gift.

The basis for depreciation, amortization, or depletion is the donor's adjusted basis regardless of whether the fair market value of the property is greater or less than the donor's adjusted basis at the time of the gift.

Where a gift is made within three years of death, the gift is included in the donor's gross estate upon death at its then value. If the donee retains the property until the donor's death, the donee may use the estate rules for determining basis; if the property is disposed of before the death of the donor, the gift rules are applied.

Realization vs. Recognition of Gain or Loss. All of the discussion to this point has involved the calculation of realized gain or loss when property is disposed of. However, there is an important distinction between realization of gain and recognition of gain. Realization is an economic fact that occurs when property is sold or disposed of. Recognition means that the gain or loss is taken into account in determining the seller's tax obligation. Realized gain is recognized gain except in these three circumstances:

- When the seller disposes of the property via a tax-free exchange. (See 8.04[1] and 8.04[2].)
- When the seller of a residential property is eligible for the special tax-free treatment for such sales. (See 8.04[3].)
- When the owner of the property disposes of it as a result of an involuntary conversion. (See 8.04[4].)

[2] Capital Gains and Losses

[a] In General

Whenever the seller of real estate realizes gain or loss, he must not only calculate the amount of gain or loss (as discussed in the preceding section) but must also determine the character of such gain or loss, i.e., whether capital gain (or capital loss) or ordinary income (or ordinary loss).

In this regard, real property falls into one of three classes for purposes of determining whether the gain or loss is capital or ordinary—that is, (1) a capital asset; (2) a so-called Section 1231 asset; or (3) an ordinary asset.

Generally, any real estate held for investment or used as a personal residence is a capital asset. (Undeveloped land held for appreciation in value is the most common example of investment real estate that is a capital asset.) If real estate held as a capital asset is owned for more than twelve months and is sold at a gain, the gain on its sale is taxable as a capital gain. However, while losses from investment real estate are deductible as capital losses, no loss, whether capital or ordinary, may be taken on the sale of a personal residence.

Section 1231 assets include depreciable property used in a trade or business, provided the property has been held for more than twelve months. Generally, the owner of income-producing real estate (e.g., an apartment house or office building) is considered to be using the property for trade or business, and if such property is sold at a gain, it is capital asset and the gain is a capital gain. If the property is sold at a loss, the property is not a capital asset and the loss is an ordinary loss and is fully deductible against ordinary income.

All real estate assets other than capital assets and Section 1231 assets are ordinary assets. Such assets are called "dealer" property; real property, held by a person engaged in the business of buying and selling real estate and for whom real estate is inventory, is dealer property. (Note that depreciable property that is used in a trade or business and held for less than one year is an ordinary asset.) Sale of such ordinary assets give rise to either an ordinary gain or an ordinary loss of real estate. (See 8.03[2][b].)

To compute net capital gain or loss on a sale, the taxpayer first offsets long-term capital gains and losses to arrive at net long-term gain or loss; then he offsets short-term capital gains and losses to arrive at net short-term gain or loss; then the short-term and long-term figures offset each other, resulting in a single amount that is net long-term capital gain; or net long-term capital loss; or net short-term capital gain; or net short-term capital loss.

Short-term capital gains are taxable as ordinary income. Up to $3,000 of short-term capital losses may be fully offset against ordinary income; any excess short-term capital loss may be carried over indefinitely to future years. With respect to long-term capital gains and losses recognized by an individual taxpayer, 60 percent of net long-term capital gain is excluded from income before applying regular tax rates, so that only 40 percent of long-term gain is subject to the regular tax.

Since the maximum tax rate in 1982 and thereafter is 50 percent, this means that the maximum tax or realized long-term capital gain is 20 percent (50 percent tax of 40 percent taxable portion of realized gain).

The 60 percent portion of long-term gain that is not subject to regular income tax is a tax-preference item for purposes of the alternative minimum tax. (See 3.11[2].)

An investor realizing a net long-term capital loss may continue to offset 50 percent of such loss against ordinary income (up to $3,000 a year, with any excess carried over to future years), even though only 40 percent of long-term capital gain is subject to tax.

[b] Real Estate Dealers

Real estate is "dealer property," the sale of which yields ordinary income or ordinary loss, if (1) it is held primarily for sale, and (2) the sale is to customers in the ordinary course of the seller's trade or business. In addition, depreciable property used in a trade or business and sold or disposed of within one year of acquisition is also considered dealer property. While an objective rule for distinguishing a dealer from an investor that will apply in all cases cannot be set forth, the courts have, over a long period of years, developed a number of important factors to be considered in determining the question.

The following checklist sets out in summary form guidelines for making the distinctions that have been culled from the cases. While these guidelines are quite broad and permit different results in situations that appear to be essentially similar, if not identical, they are still helpful, since they point to the important factors that will be given weight by IRS and the courts in reaching a determination in a particular case.

☐ *Purpose of acquisition.* The seller's purpose (whether for long-term investment or short-term resale) in acquiring the property.

☐ *Actual use.* The purpose for which the seller actually used the property.

☐ *Holding period.* The length of the holding period.

☐ *Replacement.* Whether the property was promptly replaced with similar property (as it would be in the case of a dealer's inventory).

☐ *Segregation.* Segregation of the investment property from business or dealer property on the owner's books.

☐ *Activity.* The extent of promotional or developmental activity inasmuch as dealers, not investors, promote and develop their holdings.

☐ *Intention.* Whether the owner's intent at the time of the sale was the liquidation of an investment rather than a turnover of inventory.

☐ *Frequency of sales of similar properties.* The frequency of sales of the particular type of property sold (more sales tend to indicate a business rather than an investment).

☐ *Source of gain.* Whether the gain realized was due to development activities of the owner or was long-term appreciation.

☐ *Manner of disposition.* The manner in which the property was sold.

☐ *Purpose of holding at time of disposition.* The purpose for which the property was held at the time of the sale.

One of the factors considered by the courts in reaching a determination is the owner's segregation of his dealer property from his investment property. The Tax Court recognizes that the owner's segregation of his properties into investment and dealer on a sale is ordinary income or capital gain. The segregation, by itself, is not conclusive; and the surrounding circumstances must substantiate the reality of the segregation. However, in a marginal case, the segregation may serve to clinch capital gains treatment.

[c] When Subdivision Creates Capital Gain

It is a basic principle of real estate that a large tract of land will bring far more if sold as separate lots rather than in one piece. The trouble is that the process of subdividing the tract almost always makes the owner a *dealer* in real estate (see 7.03[2][b]), which means that his entire profit will be taxed as ordinary income rather than at the more favorable capital gains rates. The higher tax may cancel out most or all of the additional profit.

But there is a way out provided by the tax law that should be known to every investor. This provision (I.R.C. § 1237) was put into the law for the deliberate purpose of enabling true investors (as distinguished from full-time dealers) to dispose of property that they otherwise would have difficulty in selling, without penalizing them by treating them as dealers.

In order to qualify under this special section of the law, an investor must meet the following requirements:

- He must own the property for at least five years (unless he inherited it, in which event one year is enough).
- He did not acquire the property for the purpose of development.
- He does not hold any other property as a dealer in the year that he sells lots in this property.
- He did not make any substantial improvements that sharply enhanced the value of the parcels sold.

Once he qualifies for this special treatment, the investor can sell the first five lots and still realize capital gain, even though he actively participated in making the sale. In the year that the investor sells the sixth lot, everything sold in that year (even the first five lots if they also are sold in the same year) and thereafter gives him ordinary income up to 5 percent of the selling price; the rest of his profit is capital gain.

Example: Suppose *A* owns a tract of land and subdivides it into ten units, all of which are sold in the same year. Since the sixth lot was sold in the same year as the first five, the initial exemption for five lots does not apply. The tax would be as follows:

- The basis (cost) for each of the ten units is $10,000.
- *A* sells each unit for $30,000.

Selling price	$300,000
Less: Basis	100,000
Gain	$200,000
Less: Gain subject to dealer treatment (5% of the selling price)	15,000
Capital gain	$185,000

Special rules govern the treatment of selling expenses, which somewhat complicates the results.

[d] How Section 1231 Minimizes Taxes

Section 1231 of the Internal Revenue Code is, in essence, a taxpayer-relief provision that allows the seller of business property to achieve maximum tax deductibility from its sale at a loss, while allowing a favorable capital gains rate on sales producing gain. Section 1231 is important to every taxpayer who sells real property at a gain. But the investor who should be particularly alert to this section is the one who contemplates several sales in a single year, some of which may give rise to gains and some of which to losses. By properly manipulating the timing of the sales, he may be able to have the gains taxed as capital gains and the losses deductible as ordinary losses, rather than having the losses offset the gains and thus losing the benefit of the section.

[i] Section 1231 Assets Defined. For property (real or otherwise) to qualify under Section 1231, it must meet three requirements:

- It must be used in a trade or business.
- It must be of a character that is subject to the allowance for depreciation.
- It must have been held by the taxpayer for more than one year.

In addition, the property may not be held by the taxpayer primarily for sale to customers in the ordinary course of his trade or business; that is, it cannot be dealer property.

Where real property is concerned, it is not necessary that the property be subject to depreciation; thus, a parking lot or other vacant realty that contains no depreciable improvement would still qualify as trade or business property if it was actively utilized for income-producing purposes.

The phrase "used in the trade or business" is not otherwise defined in the Internal Revenue Code and has been left to interpretation by the IRS and the Tax Court. The Tax Court has found that the rental of a single-family residence constitutes the operation of a trade or business even if the taxpayer is not otherwise engaged in the business of renting property for a livelihood. A leasehold of land and improvements used in the business of a taxpayer who is not a dealer in leases is Section 1231 property, assuming it is held for more than the necessary holding period.

It would seem that the courts and the IRS have usually given the broadest interpretation to the phrase "used in the trade or business"; it therefore encompasses the bulk of the real estate that most investors and operators are concerned with—rental realty, both commercial and residential (such realty being utilized in the business of producing rental income), and realty directly employed in the operation of any other type of business, such as factories, lofts, and special-purpose structures.

[ii] How Section 1231 Works. The statutory rule for determining the nature of gain or loss from Section 1231 property can be paraphrased as follows: If, during the taxable year, gains from the sale of Section 1231 property exceed losses from the sale of such property, all such gains and losses are capital gains and losses. If the losses exceed the gains, the gains and losses are ordinary gains and losses.

It is clear from the rule that if a taxpayer has only Section 1231 gains during the year, the gains will be designated as capital gains. It is likewise clear that a taxpayer having only Section 1231 losses can treat them as ordinary losses, thus deducting them in full against ordinary income. The difficulty arises in the case of multiple dispositions in the same year, some of which produce gains and some losses. In such a case, the taxpayer must compare the aggregate of his 1231 losses with the aggregate of his 1231 gains.

☐ *Gains larger than losses.* If the gains are larger in amount, all the gains and losses will be capital gains and losses. This means that the losses take on the unfavorable status of capital losses and must be used to offset capital gains (which are taxed at a maximum 20 percent rate for individuals and 28 percent for corporations), rather than being used as a deduction against ordinary income (which is taxed at up to a 50 percent rate for individuals and 46 percent rate for corporations). In other words, the capital losses to an individual are worth only a maximum of 20 cents on the dollar, whereas ordinary losses are worth up to 50 cents on the dollar. On the other hand, any net 1231 gain will be taxed as capital gain.

☐ *Losses greater than gains.* If the taxpayer's losses for the year are greater than his gains, all the gains and losses will be ordinary gains and losses. Thus, while losses become deductible in full against ordinary income, the gains take on the unfavorable status of ordinary gains and must be offset by the ordinary losses.

It can be seen that Section 1231 generally helps the taxpayer since, when losses exceed gains, they are ordinary losses, and, when gains exceed losses, they are capital gains. However, the effect of Section 1231 can be viewed another way: When both gains and losses occur in the same year, the smaller of the two receives unfavorable tax treatment. When the gains are smaller in amount, they become ordinary gains and when the losses are smaller in amount, they become capital losses. Is there a way to make all gains capital gains and all losses ordinary losses?

[iii] What to Do. The best and surest way to derive maximum advantage from Section 1231 is to have all 1231 gains fall in one tax year and all 1231 losses in another. Each will thereby receive favored tax treatment under the rule. It may often be impractical to structure such timing with capital assets such as stocks and securities, especially in a volatile market situation. But it is usually much easier to control the timing in the case of real estate sales. Most taxpayers do not have many dispositions of Section 1231 realty in a single year. Even in a period when distress selling is common, it is usually possible to arrange for great flexibility in title closing dates. For example, if a taxpayer plans the disposition of two Section 1231 assets at year-end, and one will produce a gain and the other a loss, he should make an all-out effort to postpone one of the sales until the following year. One closing on December 31 and the other on January 2 will do the trick even though they are only two days apart.

The dollar value of such a saving can be illustrated by the following example. Assume a calendar-year corporate taxpayer with two office buildings placed on the market in the latter part of the year. One sale is estimated to produce a $200,000 gain, the other a $100,000 loss. There are no other dispositions of 1231 assets. The taxpayer has unlimited ordinary taxable income from other sources. If both properties are placed under contract and sold before year-end, the tax treatment would be as set forth in Table 8.4.

Now assume that the corporation, mindful of the workings of Section 1231, separates its transactions into two taxable years—the loss sale occurs on December 31 and the gain disposition on January 2 of the following year, as shown in Table 8.5.

The sale in one year resulted in the loss transaction being capital in nature; thus the $100,000 loss was used inefficientlv to offset capital gain income. When

TABLE 8.4 Sale in a Single Year

Capital gain income	$200,000
Less: Capital loss offsetting capital gain	(100,000)
Net capital gain	$100,000
Tax on net capital gain (80%)	$20,000
Tax cost of consummating both transactions in a single year	$28,000

the transactions were separated, the loss, because of Section 1231, became an ordinary loss and was utilized to maximum benefit as a deduction against ordinary income, which, in the case of the corporate taxpayer, was taxable at the corporate rate of 46 percent. Although the above example is structured so as to reflect a dramatic money-saving result, the fact is that careful planning with Section 1231 can, in most cases, produce a significant tax saving.

TABLE 8.5 Sale in Separate Years

Loss Transaction:	
Ordinary loss fully deductible	($100,000)
Tax saving achieved at 46% bracket	($46,000)
Gain Transaction:	
Capital gain income	$200,000
Tax on capital gain at 28%	$56,000
Tax cost of consummating both transactions ($56,000 less $46,000)	$10,000
Summary	
Tax cost on sale in one year	$28,000
Tax cost on sale in separate years	10,000
Savings achieved by waiting two days	$18,000

[3] Installment and Contingent Sales

[a] In General

The installment sales method of reporting gain from sales of real estate (and also from casual sales of personal property) is intended to be a "relief provision" for sellers.

Generally, the entire gain on the disposition of property must be reported in the year the property is sold. However, if a significant portion of the price is represented by a purchase-money mortgage or other obligations of the buyer, the seller may receive less cash in the year of sale than the amount of tax, thus placing him in a liquidity bind. The installment method relieves this liquidity problem by permitting the seller to spread the income tax over the period during which payments of the sales price are received by him. Basically, the installment method works as follows: A gross profit percentage is determined at the time of sale and that percentage is applied to all future payments received from the buyer in order to determine the amount of gain to be reported by the seller each year.

Even when a seller is offered the entire purchase price in cash, he may prefer to use the installment sales method and have payments made over a number of years. The reason is that by spreading the gain over several years, the seller avoids bunching the gain in the top tax bracket.

> *Example:* In 1982, Mr. Jones realizes a long-term capital gain of $1 million from the cash sale of real estate. Ignoring all other income and deductions, he must report 40 percent of the gain, or $400,000. His tax (on a joint return) will be approximately $187,449, with about half of the taxable income in the top 50 percent bracket. (The alternative minimum tax will not apply under these facts.) If the sale price were paid in four equal installments, so that Mr. Jones would realize long-term gain of $100,000 in each of four successive years, his total tax would be approximately $112,347 ($37,449 a year × 3), a savings of $75,102, because less of the total gain would be taxed in high brackets. Of course, Mr. Jones incurs an "opportunity cost" because he cannot invest all of the funds immediately; on the other hand, he presumably will charge the buyer interest on the unpaid amounts. However, it is clear that from a tax point of view, Mr. Jones realizes a substantial saving by using the installment method.

Prior to the Installment Sales Revision Act of 1980,[3] a sale qualified for the installment reporting of gain if (1) no more than 30 percent of the total price was received in the year of sale; (2) two or more payments of the purchase price were made in separate years; and (3) the seller affirmatively elected to report his gain according to the installment method. The 1980 Act eliminated the 30 percent requirement and the two-payment rule. Thus, the seller can receive any amount less than 100 percent of the sales price in the year of sale, or can receive no payment in the year of sale, with the entire price to be paid in a subsequent year. In addition, the election requirement has been eliminated; installment reporting automatically applies unless the seller elects not to use it by reporting the entire gain in the year of sale.

[i] What Are Payments Received in Year of Sale? Payments received in the year of sale do not include obligations of the buyer to the seller, including any purchase-money mortgage and the amount of any preexisting mortgage assumed or taken over by the purchaser except to the extent that it exceeds the seller's basis in the property sold. While the purchaser's promissory note or other evidence of his obligation to pay in a later year does not constitute a payment in the year of sale even if the seller discounts the note and receives cash in return in the year of

[3] Pub. L. No. 96-471, 94 Stat. 2247, 26 U.S.C.A. § 1.

sale, there is a payment in the year of sale where the purchaser gives the seller his or a third party's promissory note or other evidence of indebtedness that is due in the year of sale. Likewise, bonds or debentures with interest coupons attached, in registered form, payable on demand, or in some other form calculated to make it possible to trade them readily in an established securities market are payments in the year of sale.

Where the purchaser places a sum of money in escrow, this is not a payment in the year of sale, provided the terms of the escrow place the funds beyond the seller's reach.

All payments received through the close of the year in which the sale occurs are included as payments made in the year of sale. Thus, deposits or other payments under a purchase-money mortgage subsequent to the closing, but before the close of the tax year, are payments received in the year of sale.

Likewise, where the installment sale contract requires that the purchaser assume the seller's liabilities with respect to the property in determining whether the amount by which those liabilities exceed basis, and therefore constitute a payment in the year of sale, liabilities of the seller, such as liens, accrued interest, and taxes, that are assumed and paid in the year of sale by the purchaser must be taken into account. Also included among payments received in the year of sale are the following items, if received or performed before the close of the seller's taxable year in which the closing takes place: cash; the fair market value of other property; seller's obligations discharged by purchaser; and the amount, if any, by which a preexisting mortgage assumed or taken over by the purchaser exceeds the seller's adjusted basis for the real estate.

[ii] Unstated Interest Problem. The problem of unstated interest can be a significant one for an installment seller and can arise whenever any payments due under a deferred-sales contract either carry no interest or carry an unrealistically low rate of interest as determined by the IRS.[4] The effect of unstated interest is that the total sale price will be discounted by the IRS, thereby converting a portion of the price into interest with the result that part of the gain that might otherwise be treated as a capital gain becomes ordinary interest income to the seller. Prior to the 1980 Act, the most important consequence of discounting the sale price to a lower figure was that the amount received by the seller in the year of sale might prove to be in excess of 30 percent of the revised sale price so that the seller would be denied the use of the installment method of reporting his gain. This is no longer a problem.

Under the Treasury Regulations, an interest rate of at least 9 percent must be charged by the seller on the deferred portion of the purchase price. Absent a 9 percent interest rate, IRS will discount the deferred payment by 10 percent.

In one situation, a maximum imputed interest rate of 7 percent is set by statute, notwithstanding the Treasury rate of 10 percent. This situation is one meeting the following three requirements:

1. The sale is of land (not buildings).
2. The sale is between members of the same family.

---

[4] I.R.C. § 483.

3. The total annual sales between the family members does not exceed $500,000. (The regular imputed interest rate applies to any sales above the ceiling.)

[iii] Computation and Reporting of Gain. In determining the ratable share of each installment payment that must be reported as gain when received by the seller, an inclusion ratio must be determined. This ratio is calculated in the year of sale and remains constant as long as payments are received under the installment contract. The ratio is arrived at by dividing the total realized gain by the contract price (i.e., all amounts that will ultimately be received by the seller from the buyer), including all payments that are deemed received for purposes of computing the amount received in the year of sale, as well as the buyer's obligations (e.g., purchase-money mortgage), but not including payments that will be made by the purchaser to third parties. The preexisting mortgage assumed or taken over by the purchaser is therefore excluded from the contract price except to the extent that it exceeds the seller's adjusted basis.

The amount of each payment (including any payment received in the year of sale which must be reported as gain) can be determined by the following formula:

$$\frac{\text{Total gain realized}}{\text{Contract price}} \times \begin{array}{c}\text{Amount received}\\ \text{in any year}\end{array} = \begin{array}{c}\text{Gain to be reported}\\ \text{in any year}\end{array}$$

[iv] Nature of Gain Reported. Gain reported according to the installment method retains the same nature it would have had if the entire gain were reported in the year of sale. Although received in installments by the seller, long-term capital gain retains its character as such and, if the sale would have produced a short-term capital gain or ordinary income, each subsequent payment retains its nature as such.

A sale of real estate may qualify for installment reporting even though part of the capital gain realized will be recaptured as excess depreciation.[5] However, all the gain that is required to be recorded under the installment method will be treated as ordinary income until the full amount of the recaptured depreciation is reported and, thereafter, all payments will be capital gain. In other words, there is no allocation between capital gain and ordinary income; the requirement that the ordinary income element be picked up first in its entirety is imposed by Treasury Regulations. These regulations have been challenged in the case of recapture on personal property but were held valid. Since the recapture provisions are similar for both real and personal property, it appears likely that the real property recapture provisions will also be upheld if challenged.

[b] Guide to Installment Sale Repossessions

An installment sale always creates the risk of a buyer default, at which point the seller must consider a repossession of the property, either through voluntary agreement with the buyer or through foreclosure. What are the tax consequences

[5] I.R.C. § 1250.

when an installment sale transaction ends in a reacquisition by the seller? And what, if anything, can the seller do that makes the most tax sense?

A repossession of real estate under a purchase-money mortgage (that is, by the original seller of the property rather than by a third-party lender) automatically triggers application of a mandatory set of rules set forth in Section 1038 of the Internal Revenue Code. This section applies whether title passed in the original sale or whether the transaction is in the form of a land contract; whether or not there was a gain or loss on the original sale; and whether or not the reacquisition by the seller was voluntary or through foreclosure.

In general, under Section 1038, the seller need not recognize either gain or loss when he repossesses the property; any recognition is postponed until the real estate is resold. However, the section has an exception that may all but swallow the general rule, sometimes even producing a tax on a nonexistent gain. The exception requires the seller to recognize any previously unreported gain on the installment sale to the extent of all cash received prior to the repossession.

On the other hand, while under Section 1038 the installment seller may have to recognize gain, he never can recognize a loss on the repossession (a loss will occur when the fair market value of the property at the time of repossession is less than the seller's basis in the remaining installment obligations that were to have been paid).

Example: Mr. Smith sold property with a basis of $80,000 for a price of $100,000. The buyer paid $10,000 in cash and executed a purchase-money note for $90,000, to be paid in nine annual installments. The seller elected the installment method of reporting (enabling him to spread his tax on his gain over the nine years of installments). The buyer made two annual payments of $10,000 each, then fell upon hard times and walked away from the property. The seller took back the property by a voluntary reconveyance in satisfaction of the remaining debt. At that time, the property was worth $60,000. This reacquisition results in a taxable gain of $14,000, computed as follows in Table 8.6.

The Result. Despite the fact that no money is received by the seller when he takes back the property, he must pay a tax on a "gain" of $14,000. Furthermore, the seller has received back only $90,000 worth of cash and property ($30,000 in cash and property now worth $60,000). Since his original basis was $80,000, his total gain should really be no more than $10,000. Nevertheless, the seller has been forced to report a total gain of $20,000 ($6,000 previously and $14,000 now).

It is true that when the seller finally resells the property, the tax consequences will even out; however, this is little consolation if he now has to dip into his pocket to pay additional taxes.

There are several possible approaches to avoiding the mandatory rules of Section 1038 as they apply to a purchase-money mortgagee who faces the situation just described.

☐ *Transfer the obligation.* The original seller may be able to sell or otherwise transfer the obligation to a third party, in an arm's-length transaction. The

TABLE 8.6 Computation of Taxable Gain

Money previously received in excess of reported gain:		
Money received before reacquisition		$30,000
Less: Gain reported ($30,000 × ($100,000 − $80,000)/$100,000)		6,000
		$24,000
Unreported gain:		
Sales price of property		$100,000
Less: Basis of property	$80,000	
Previously reported gain	6,000	
		86,000
		$ 14,000
Taxable gain (lesser of excess money or unreported gain)		$14,000

third party would then foreclose and acquire the property. Section 1038 should not apply to either the seller or his transferee in this case.

☐ *Transfer mortgage to a controlled subsidiary.* A corporate seller could make a Section 351 transfer of the mortgage to a controlled subsidiary, if the subsidiary is not merely an agent or nominee of the seller. While the subsidiary would carry over the seller's basis, it may be able to avoid Section 1038 effects, since it is not the original seller.

☐ *Pay the buyer off.* If the seller repurchases the property, paying the buyer a consideration in addition to discharging the debt should not involve application of Section 1038 (unless the original contract provided for the payment). However, this payment probably will not work if made after the buyer has already defaulted, or if default is imminent.

It should be noted that if the repossessed real estate has appreciated in value, Section 1038 can be quite beneficial to the repossessing seller since he need not pay a tax on the unrealized appreciation. Indeed, this was the primary reason for putting the section into the Code.

[c] Family Installment Sales

Installment sales can be used as a method of switching income and gain among family members so as to reduce the overall family tax burden. For example, Father owns real estate with a basis of $10,000 and a present fair market value of $100,000. He desires to sell the property for cash but wishes to spread the gain over a period of years to reduce the tax burden. So he makes an installment sale to Son at a price of $100,000, the present market value of the property. Father will thus report gain only as payments are made by Son. Son then sells the property to a third party for all cash. Son realizes no gain on the transaction. Thus, the family unit utilizes the installment method even though the property has been sold outside of the family for all cash.

The Installment Sales Revision Act of 1980 (for transactions made after May 14, 1980), imposes significant restrictions on this type of related-party sale.

☐ *Two-year resale rule.* The most important restriction is the two-year resale rule. This provides that if Father makes an installment sale to Son, and Son then resells the property within two years, Father must recognize his entire gain at the time of such resale no matter how many installment payments remain to be paid by Son. In other words, resale by the related purchaser (Son) triggers recognition of the entire gain on the installment sale by Father.

(In the case of marketable securities, the two-year limit does not apply; if the related buyer resells them at any time during the installment period, the initial seller must report the balance of his gain at once.)

☐ *Cancellation of installment obligations.* If Father makes an installment sale to Son and later cancels the installment payments to be made by Son, the question arises as to whether Father need report the balance of the gain due under the installment sale. Formerly, it was held that the balance of the gain need not be reported. The new law changes that ruling and makes the balance of the gain taxable.

☐ *Bequest of installment obligation.* Suppose Father died before the installment payments were made and the obligations (an asset of the estate) were left to the Son. Formerly, the result would be that the obligation would disappear and the remaining gain would never be taxed. The new law makes the remaining gain taxable.

For purposes of the foregoing rules, related purchasers include not only family members (spouse, child, grandchild, or parent) but also controlled corporations, partnerships, trusts, and estates. Thus the new rule would bar use of the installment method by the owner of a rental project who sells it to a controlled corporation, which in turn converts the units into condominiums and resells them within two years.

☐ *Depreciable property.* Whenever the installment sale is of depreciable property (e.g., improved real estate) and the buyer is seller's spouse or an 80 percent-owned entity, then installment-sale reporting may not be used at all. The reason is that the buyer (spouse or controlled entity) will be able to use a stepped-up basis (the installment-sale price) for depreciation purposes and so the seller is required to report all of his gain at once.

Bypassing Related-Party Rules. If you plan to use an installment sale of real estate in connection with a family transfer and find the related-party rules of the new law to be an obstacle, consider the following:

☐ The brother or sister of a seller is not considered to be a related party so that an installment sale followed by a resale within two years will not trigger the recognition of gain to the original seller.

☐ According to the Senate Finance Committee report, the new law does not affect private annuities, which often can achieve the same end as an installment sale.

☐ Remember that an installment sale to a family member that is not followed by a resale within two years is not affected by the new law and can still achieve certain benefits (e.g., transferring income and future appreciation) from the property to a more lightly taxed family member.

[d] Contingent Sales

The tax treatment of contingent sales has been changed by the Installment Sales Revision Act of 1980. A contingent (or open-end) sale is one in which the price depends on future and uncertain events. For example, the owner of raw land may sell it to a developer under an arrangement calling for the landowner to receive a fixed percentage of the sales proceeds of the developed lots.

Formerly, contingent sales received special tax treatment. A cash-basis seller could treat 100 percent of the installment payments as a return of capital until his entire cost basis had been recouped; all subsequent payments represented gain. By comparison, installment-sale reporting requires the allocation of each installment payment between return of capital and gain. Thus a contingent sale, when it was available, usually was preferred.

The new law provides that contingent sales may now be reported on the installment method; the intent is to limit contingent sale treatment to those rare and extraordinary cases where the fair market value of the purchaser's obligations cannot readily be ascertained.

In order to utilize the installment method, a seller under a contingent sale must make certain assumptions about the sales price, since the installment sale requires a gross-profit ratio to be determined in order that each payment can be allocated between cost and gain. For this purpose, the regulations require a sale to be classified into one of four distinct categories (listed in order of applicability):

- Sales having a stated maximum selling price
- Those lacking a maximum price but having a maximum period over which payments are to be made
- Those having neither of the above
- Those making use of the income-forecast method

☐ *Maximum selling price.* A sale falls into this category whenever the seller, in the year of sale, can calculate the maximum sales proceeds receivable by him. Presumably, a land contract sale would fall within this category. The seller would then calculate his gross profit ratio (gross profit as a percentage of the contract price) and apply this ratio to each payment to determine the income component.

If it later turns out that the seller will end up with less than the maximum sales proceeds, the gross profit ratio is recomputed for all future years. If he has already reported more income than he now expects to receive, he can recognize a loss equal to the difference.

☐ *Fixed-payment period.* Suppose property is sold under an agreement calling for three annual payments equal to a percentage of sales for each year (e.g.,

50 percent of sales in year 1 and 25 percent of sales in years 2 and 3). In that case, the seller can allocate 50 percent of his basis against proceeds for year 1 and 25 percent of basis for each of the following two years.

☐ *No maximum price or fixed period.* A more likely situation for a real estate seller than the one just described is a percentage of sales over whatever period it takes to develop the property. Thus there will be no maximum price nor fixed period of payment. In that case, say the Regulations, the seller's basis is to be recovered ratably over fifteen years. If at the end of that time, the seller has received insufficient proceeds to use up his entire basis, any remaining basis is carried forward annually until future payments are received (or the obligation becomes worthless).

☐ *Income-forecast method.* The final method, which involves a forecast of future income to be received by the seller, is available only for the following types of property: mineral properties; motion-picture films; television films; taped television shows. However, a taxpayer may request a ruling from the IRS regarding the availability of the method to other situations, such as real estate.

8.04 TAX-FREE SALES AND EXCHANGES OF REAL ESTATE

Of all the tax-postponement devices that might be available, certainly the best is a specific Internal Revenue Code provision deferring tax to a future date. And, for real estate, the Code contains four such provisions:

- A provision permitting the tax-free exchange of like-kind investment and trade or business property. (I.R.C. § 1031.)
- A provision permitting a homeowner to sell his present residence and acquire a new one (or exchange homes) without having to recognize and pay tax on any realized gain. (I.R.C. § 1034.)
- A provision permitting an over-55 homeowner to exclude entirely up to $125,000 of the gain realized on the sale of his residence. (I.R.C. § 121.)
- A provision permitting the owner of property that has been involuntarily converted (i.e., destroyed or condemned) to acquire similar or related property without recognizing any realized gain. (I.R.C. § 1033.)

[1] Tax-Free Exchanges of Investment and Business Property

[a] In General

The real estate exchange is a highly versatile and flexible tool for financing real estate and achieving tax savings. Yet, it has never achieved wide popularity in much of the nation. This is partly because setting up a successful exchange often takes much more patience and hard work than arranging a straight purchase and sale, and, partly because many brokers and investors simply do not understand the potentials of the exchange or are frightened off by the intricate footwork that sometimes must take place in order to comply with the strict requirements imposed by the Internal Revenue Code.

The key advantage of a tax-free exchange pursuant to Section 1031 of the Code is that gain realized by one or both of the exchangers need not be recognized (that is, tax need not be paid on the gain) at the time of sale. Instead, the tax is postponed until a future taxable disposition occurs of the newly received property. Thus, a series of exchanges can defer tax indefinitely (and if the property ultimately ends up in the estate of the exchangor and a stepped-up basis is achieved, tax may be avoided permanently). The advantage of this tax postponement is obvious. The investor is enabled to reinvest his full capital into new properties, without any diminution due to tax payments. Uncle Sam, in effect, extends an interest-free loan to the investor, who thus is able to obtain leverage over and above that obtained from regular mortgage financing.

In addition to the tax advantages, an exchange (whether tax-free or not) can be used as a financing tool, since it permits the substitution of real estate for cash. Furthermore, like the two men who exchanged a $50,000 dog for two $25,000 cats, real estate exchanges, by inflating the values on both sides of the transaction, can offer the parties the psychological satisfaction of "getting their price."

The Economic Recovery Tax Act of 1981[6] does not deal specifically with tax-free exchanges. However, since the new Accelerated Cost Recovery System (ACRS) is available only for property placed in service after 1979, it is important to determine whether the undepreciated basis of property received in an exchange after 1979 will be eligible for the new fifteen-year write-off.

Tax-free exchanges can be arranged not only between two parties; three-way and even four-way exchanges are also possible. Thus, suppose that *B* wants to purchase *A*'s property for cash but *A* wants to exchange his property for *C*'s property and *C* wants to sell his property for cash. In this situation, there are three ways in which a three-party exchange can be accomplished:

1. *A* sells to *B* for cash and then buys *C*'s property.
2. *B* buys *C*'s property and exchanges it for *A*'s property.
3. *A* exchanges properties with *C*, who then sells to *B* for cash.

Method (1) is a purchase and sale and not a tax-free exchange. Methods (2) and (3) can both qualify as tax-free exchanges, provided the various steps are performed in the right order.

It is also possible for a tax-free exchange to be arranged by way of a four-party exchange transaction. Thus, an exchange is tax-free to *X* where *X* transfers his property to his attorney as escrowee; the attorney then purchases property from *Z* for cash and then exchanges that property for *X*'s property; then *Y* purchases *X*'s original property from the attorney.

A contract for the exchange of real properties is generally similar to a contract for the sale of real estate except that the exchange contract carries two or more property descriptions and there are two or more separate statements of encumbrances and the values of the properties for purposes of the exchange are stated. Where the properties are being exchanged on an even basis, no cash changes hands and the contract need not make provision for cash or other payment but, where the equities are uneven, one party may be required to pay cash for the difference in value or may be required to pay part of the difference in value in cash and the remainder by way of a purchase-money note or bond and

[6] Pub. L. No. 97-34, 95 Stat. 172, 26 U.S.C. § 128.

mortgage. Under these circumstances, the contract should clearly spell out the arrangement agreed on by the parties.

[i] Requirements to Be Met for Tax-Free Exchange. Section 1031(a) of the Internal Revenue Code provides that no gain or loss on an exchange of real estate is recognized if property held for productive use in a trade or business, or for investment, is exchanged solely for property of a "like kind," to be held for productive use in a trade or business, or for investment. Note that the exchange qualifies for tax-free treatment so long as the properties involved fall into either class. Thus, property held for productive use in a trade or business may be exchanged for property held for investment. Similarly, property held for investment may be exchanged for property held for productive use in a trade or business. However, certain types of property are specifically excluded. For the real estate investor, the major exception covers stock in trade or other property held primarily for sale.

"Primarily for Sale" Defined. Where real estate owners are concerned, the term primarily for sale requires some clarification. Basically, the term is intended to bar "dealers" in real estate (as distinguished from investors and businessmen) from obtaining the benefits of tax-free exchanges. However, it should be borne in mind that whether any particular property is held primarily for sale depends not upon the owner's motives in general, or with respect to his overall property holdings, but rather upon the concrete circumstances surrounding the specific property that is the subject of the exchange. Thus, one who holds real estate as an investor, or in connection with a trade or business, may nevertheless buy a particular parcel with the contemporaneous intent to hold it primarily for resale (whether for cash or as an exchange transaction), that is, he is a "dealer" with respect to that individual parcel.

"Like Kind" Defined. The key concept underlying the Section 1031 tax-free exchange, and one not entirely easy to grasp, is that of "like kind." Only like-kind properties may be exchanged for each other. The concept refers to the nature or character of the real estate, and not to its grade or quality. For example, the extent to which property is improved relates only to grade or quality—not class. So, unimproved real estate may be exchanged for improved real estate. A ranch in New Mexico may be exchanged for an apartment house in New York City—provided both properties have been held as investments or in a trade or business. And, it is clear that unproductive (i.e., non-income-producing) property can be held as an investment, even though the holder only will realize a return on resale.

The Treasury Regulations amplifying Section 1031 state that no gain or loss is recognized if

- A taxpayer exchanges property held for productive use in his trade or business, together with cash, for other property of a like kind for the same use.
- A taxpayer who is not a dealer in real estate exchanges city real estate for a ranch or farm, exchanges a leasehold of a fee with thirty years or more to run for real estate, or exchanges improved real estate for unimproved real estate.

- A taxpayer exchanges investment property and cash for investment property of a like kind.

If there is a substantial difference in the rights created in and to the properties, then they are not of like kind. So, for example:

- A leasehold interest in land and a fee title are not like kind unless the lease has thirty years or more to run.
- An assignment of oil payments and an interest in real estate are not like kind.
- However, an outright and absolute conveyance of a mineral interest in land for a fee title in real estate is an exchange of like-kind properties.

Land Trust Certificates. Land trust certificates cannot qualify for tax-free exchanges. A taxpayer is no longer considered the owner (either in a legal or equitable sense) of real estate that has been transferred to a land trust. His interest is that of a beneficiary, and, under the laws of many states, such an interest is considered to be personal property. So the exchange of an interest in a land trust for real estate would not be a like-kind exchange. In addition, the regulations specifically prohibit the tax-free benefits of Section 1031 from applying to "certificates of trust or beneficial interest."

Only One Party to Exchange Need Seek Tax-Free Benefit. In order for an exchange to come within Section 1031, the property exchanged cannot be held for resale, or as a residence. (Deferment of gain on sale of a residence may be available, however, under Sections 121 and 1034 of the Code.) The test is applied separately to each of the parties to the exchange. Thus, *X* may give *Y* a hotel and receive in exchange farmland to be held by *X* as an investment. *X* has a tax-free exchange. But if *Y*'s intention is to resell the hotel, then the hotel in *Y*'s hands is held for resale. The exchange is a taxable transaction so far as *Y* is concerned, while *X*'s side of the transaction is tax-free.

Exchanges Where Other Property or a Mortgage Is Involved. So far, we have discussed the simplest form of exchange—the exchange of one piece of like-kind real estate for another. But in the real world, this is seldom the case. One or both of the parties usually balances out the exchange with cash or other property (called "boot"), or an existing mortgage on one of the properties is taken over by a party.

When such money or other property (boot) is received by a party, then all or part of his realized gain on the property he is giving up is recognized. The amount of the recognized gain cannot exceed the total of the cash plus the fair market value of the other property *received* by him. (If boot is received by a party who incurs a loss on the property he gives up, then the loss is not recognized.)

> *Example 1: A* (not a dealer) exchanges real estate held for investment purchased many years ago for $5,000 (and that is now worth $8,000), for other real estate (to be held for productive use in trade or business) having a fair market value of $6,000, plus $2,000 in cash. The gain realized by *A* on the

property he is exchanging is $3,000 ($8,000 less $5,000). But the gain is recognized only to the extent of the $2,000 cash received.

It is also important to know *A*'s basis for the property he acquired in the exchange, since the basis will determine gain or loss on any subsequent disposition of the acquired property. *A*'s basis for the new property remains at $5,000—the basis of the old property ($5,000), less the amount of the boot received ($2,000), increased by the amount of gain recognized on the exchange ($2,000).

Example 2: Suppose that *A* (not a dealer), holding real estate held for investment purchased many years ago for $10,000, exchanges it for other real estate to be held for investment that has a fair market value of $9,000, plus an automobile that has a fair market value of $2,000, plus $1,500 in cash, or a total of $12,500. *A* realizes a gain of $2,500 ($12,500 less $10,000), all of which is recognized, since the boot ($3,500—the car plus the cash) exceeds the total realized gain. The basis of the property received by *A* in exchange is the basis of the real estate *A* transfers ($10,000), decreased by the amount of money received ($1,500), and increased by the amount of gain that was recognized ($2,500). This results in a basis for the property received by *A* of $11,000. This basis of $11,000 must then be allocated between the automobile and the real estate received by *A*. The basis of the automobile is its fair market value at the date of the exchange, $2,000, and the basis of the real estate is the remainder, or $9,000.

[b] Boosting Depreciation in a Tax-Free Exchange

Another important advantage that can be secured via a tax-free exchange of real estate is a step-up in the all-important depreciation deduction. Here are three techniques for increasing the depreciation deduction following a tax-free exchange of real estate:

[i] Improving the Land-Building Allocation Ratio. Whenever an investor thinks about depreciating his real estate for tax purposes, his first step is to allocate his cost between the land and the improvements. Naturally, he will want to allocate as much as possible to the depreciable buildings and as little as possible to the nondepreciable land. But the allocation must be made within the context of economic realities. If the property is later exchanged, the investor must carry over his old cost (reduced by depreciation deductions taken during his period of ownership). But he is not bound by the land-building ratio. Consequently, if the new property has the same or a more favorable ratio, the depreciation deductions during the first few years may actually be higher than previously even though the exchange is tax-free.

Example: An investor acquires improved property for $100,000. Of this amount, $20,000 is allocated to the land and $80,000 to the building. Over the years he claims $53,000 in depreciation deductions on the building so that its tax basis is reduced to $27,000. His land and building now have an aggregate basis of $47,000 ($20,000 land cost plus $27,000 adjusted building cost).

Assume the market value of the property is $60,000. Our investor now finds a like-kind property worth $60,000 and makes a tax-free exchange. He carries over his $47,000 basis to the new property. Assume that an appraisal establishes that 80 percent of the value of the new property is allocable to the building and 20 percent to the land (the same as for the old property). Thus, 80 percent of the carry-over basis of $47,000 ($37,600) is the new basis for depreciation deductions, whereas had the investor retained the original property, he would have had only $27,000 remaining in the building's basis for depreciation purposes.[7]

[ii] New Property With Shorter Useful Life. A second way to increase the depreciation deduction by means of a tax-free exchange is to swap one property for another with improvements having a shorter useful life. (This assumes the exchanged property is not eligible for the fifteen-year write-off under ACRS.)

Example: In the situation just discussed, we assumed an investor owned property with a remaining basis of $27,000 attributable to the depreciable improvements. Assuming the building had a remaining useful life of twenty-seven years, and that straight-line depreciation is being used, the investor can take $1,000 a year as a depreciation deduction. If he swaps for a property with a building having a useful life of eighteen years, and the same $27,000 is allocated to the improvements, the annual depreciation deduction jumps to $1,500 a year.

Of course, the investor would not take a building with a shorter useful life in exchange for his present building unless it had other desirable features to offset the reduced future flow of income. We are ignoring these other considerations for the sake of simplicity.

[iii] More Highly Leveraged Property With a Higher Basis. When valuing properties for exchanges, only equities count, not market value. In the example above, the investor owned property free and clear with a market value of $60,000. In that example, he swapped it for another property, free of debt, with a market value of $60,000. But he might as easily have swapped it for a property with double the market value but subject to an existing mortgage of $60,000. The equities would remain equal but the investor would step up his tax basis from $47,000 (the remaining cost basis in the original property) to $107,000 (his original cost basis plus the amount of new debt of $60,000). If 80 percent is allocated to the depreciable improvements, his new basis for depreciation is $85,600 (as compared to the depreciable basis of the original building of $27,000).

[c] How Exchanges Facilitate Property Transfers

In addition to its potential for tax saving, an exchange can be useful as a financial device, or as an additional inducement to a property transfer.

---

[7] See Rev. Rul. 68-36, 1968-1 C.B. 357.

[i] Cash-Poor Buyer. When a prospective buyer does not have enough cash, and cannot get a mortgage, the seller's usual alternatives are to pass up the offer, or extend a large purchase-money mortgage. The latter, however, subjects him to substantially the same financial risks that may have been the very reason why he wanted to sell in the first place. An exchange means he can take other property of the buyer in lieu of taking back a mortgage; it also may increase the likelihood that the seller will get his asking price. That the seller also has no tax on his gain also is appealing (assuming, of course, that the exchange qualifies for tax-free treatment).

[ii] More Than One Mortgage. Because a piece of real property may change hands several times in such exchanges, it may end up subject to several mortgages, since mortgages frequently are used to balance out the equities. Some investors regard this as a burden, since several payments must be made each month or quarter, and the likelihood of inadvertent defaults is increased. But an owner with more than one mortgage may be in a more flexible position, because, if he receives additional cash on subsequent occasions, he can pay off one or more of the mortgages in full, and so reduce his monthly mortgage payments. On the other hand, a partial prepayment on a single large mortgage usually shortens the life of the mortgage, but does not reduce the size of the monthly payments. Also, a mortgagee sometimes is willing to accept prepayment in full at a substantial discount. Several small mortgages increase the possibility of such a windfall.

[iii] Investor Seeks Long-Term Appreciation. A tax-free exchange has appeal for the real estate investor who wants to swap income-producing property for real estate (e.g., raw land) with potential for long-term appreciation. That his depreciation deductions now are low and will not be increased after the exchange makes no difference to him since (if he is seeking raw land) his new investment is non-depreciable. If such an investor exchanges his income-producing property for several parcels of raw land near some area that has good growth potential, he will have put the full amount of his capital (undiminished by taxes) to work in another investment. No tax will be payable until the new property is sold.

[iv] Exchange for More Financeable Property. An investor may be able to make a tax-free exchange for property that is capable of supporting a mortgage with a higher loan-to-value ratio. For example, property that justifies a mortgage not exceeding 60 percent of its value might be exchanged for property on which a lender will extend a 70 percent mortgage. In that case, the exchange will release cash for other uses equal to 10 percent of the value of the property. Or, an investor may hold real estate subject to a mortgage that bars prepayment, or permits it only for a stiff penalty. If the investor requires cash, he might consider a tax-free exchange for similar property capable of being refinanced.

[v] Exchange for More Salable Property. An investor needing cash may be able to exchange difficult-to-sell property for property that can be disposed of for cash more easily. But care is needed in such a cash-out exchange, because, as we have already noted, when there is an intent to resell the acquired property immediately, the tax-free exchange rules do not apply. The investor seeking to cash out would have an immediate taxable gain on the exchange. On the other hand, since the basis of the property acquired by him in the exchange is increased by the amount of recognized gain (and assuming no appreciation in the new property), the aggregate gain on the exchange and the sale will equal the same taxable gain that would have resulted from sale of the old property in the first place.

[2] Tax-Free Exchanges of Residences

The special dispensation given homeowners by Section 1034 is intended to solve a problem that affects a large number of people in a society suffering from continued inflation and consisting of large numbers of highly mobile individuals. As these individuals move from place to place, they may sell and buy homes every few years. In theory, the appreciation in the value of the home sold should enable them to make the higher down payment required for the new house. However, the need to pay a tax each time on the appreciation and value would frustrate this roll-over. Hence Section 1034, which provides that under specified conditions, gain on the sale of a personal residence will not be recognized to the extent that an amount equivalent to the "adjusted sales price" is used in purchasing a new residence. The "adjusted sales price" is the amount realized on the sale reduced by certain expenses for work done on the old residence to assist in its sale. Note that unlike the exchange of income or business properties, which must be an actual swap, the residential exchange may consist of a sale and a reinvestment of the proceeds in a new house, as well as a direct exchange.

The three basic requirements that must be met to defer gain under Code Section 1034 can be summarized as follows:

☐ The homeowner must purchase and use a new residence as his principal residence within twenty-four months before or after he sells his old residence. Alternatively, he may build a new residence as his principal residence. If he does so, he must build and use the new residence within twenty-four months before or two years after he sells his old residence. (These time deadlines are suspended while the taxpayer is on active duty in the armed forces.)

☐ The homeowner must have used his old home as his principal residence and must also use or intend to use his new home as his principal residence.

☐ The homeowner must spend an amount to purchase or build the new home that is at least equal to the amount he received from the sale of the old one. If the new home costs less, a portion of the gain will be taxed.

If a taxpayer meets the three requirements set forth above, tax deferral of the gain on the sale of his residence is mandatory. Section 1034 is not an elective provision. However, where a homeowner is over fifty-five years of age, he may choose between a tax-free rollover under Section 1034 and a tax-free sale under Section 121 or may use both together.

Example: Here is a simplified illustration of how computations under Code Section 1034 can work out. Assume a taxpayer purchased a principal residence for $50,000 some years ago. He sells it for an adjusted sale price of $100,000, realizing a profit of $50,000. Within eighteen months of the sale, he buys a new principal residence for $100,000 or more. Under these circumstances, he need not recognize his $50,000 gain. What's more, he can continue his tax deferral through a chain of buying and selling residences until such time as he fails to purchase a new residence within the required time.

Example showing fix-up and selling expenses of old residences: Assume that a taxpayer owns a principal residence with a basis of $25,000. To make the house more salable, he incurs qualifying fix-up costs in the amount of $500. He sells the house for $45,000, incurring selling expenses in the amount of $2,500. He then purchases a new principal residence for $40,000 and moves in within twenty-four months. The portion of his gain that is taxable is calculated as follows:

a. Sales price of old residence	$45,000
b. Less: Selling expenses	2,500
c. Amount realized on sale	$42,500
d. Less: Basis of old residence	25,000
e. Profit on sale	$17,500
f. Fix-up costs	$ 500
g. Adjusted sales price (line c less line f)	$42,000
h. Less: Cost of new residence	40,000
i. Taxable gain	$ 2,000

In sum, of the total profit of $17,500, the taxpayer has a taxable gain of only $2,000. The remaining $15,500 in profits are not taxed at that time. Rather, the taxpayer's cost basis in his new residence is reduced by that amount, resulting in a cost basis of $25,000.

More than one tax-free rollover within twenty-four months is permitted, provided the homeowner moves from his old principal residence and into his new principal residence for reasons of employment, whether as an employee or as a self-employed person. Otherwise, homeowners are limited to one tax-free rollover every twenty-four months.

[3] Home Trade-In Agreements

Trade-in plans offer a special type of real estate exchange and are frequently used in residential sales. They will qualify as a tax-free exchange if they meet the requirements set forth in the beginning of this section.

Under a trade-in agreement, a homeowner agrees to purchase another home, and the seller, who may be a builder, developer, or broker, agrees to purchase the homeowner's current home at a specified price, provided the home is not sold at that price or more within a specified time. The basic purpose of a trade-in is to free the homeowner's equity in his current residence; usually he reinvests that equity in the down payment for his new home. The problems that confront many would-be home purchasers is one of timing, in that while a homeowner without appreciable savings other than his equity in his current home needs that equity to buy a new home, he cannot sell his current residence without having another residence available for his occupancy. Thus, he must be able to carry out two separate transactions involving nonliquid assets within a short time of each other. By using a trade-in arrangement, the homeowner is assured that his equity will be available to him when he needs it for the purchase of his new home. The broker or the builder who will take the house in trade does so with the intention of reselling it as soon as possible.

Among the different types of home trade-in agreements are:

☐ *Outright trade-in.* The present home is sold outright; the equity is used for a down payment on the new home. The sale of the old and the purchase of the new home are completed simultaneously and the homeowner knows exactly what his current home will bring him. The broker or builder takes title to the old house immediately and it is up to him to resell it. He assumes the risk of repairs and maintenance while he owns the house and the possibility that he will have to accept a price on the resale that is lower than expected. Builders of new homes who are prepared to carry an inventory of homes frequently find outright trade-ins beneficial.

☐ *Conditional trade-in.* Here we have what amounts to a combination of an option agreement on the old and a conditional sale of the new home. While both contracts of sale are executed simultaneously, the contract for the new home is conditioned on resale of the old within a specified period of time. If a resale cannot be made within the time specified, both contracts are canceled. Conditional trade-ins may be attractive to a builder when the market is very slow.

☐ *Guaranteed trade-in.* Under this arrangement, the broker or builder is given a limited time to sell the present home at an agreed-on price. If he sells within that time, he receives the entire broker's commissions. If the house is not sold, the broker or builder buys the house at a price that is somewhat less than the price a third party would have to pay. The broker or builder only assumes a conditional obligation that he frequently is not called on to fulfill. The homeowner is assured of obtaining a minimum price for his current home before he takes title to his new home. If, for one reason or another, the homeowner needs the cash at once, the broker or builder can arrange to advance the guaranteed amount to him at interest, so that the homeowner is in the same position as if the trade-in had been direct.

[4] Tax-Free Gain on Sales of Residences

Special tax treatment is available to taxpayers who are over fifty-five years of age and who sell their principal residence at a gain.[8] Such a taxpayer may exclude from gross income all the gain realized up to a ceiling of $125,000. Code Section 121 applies only if the property has been owned and used by the taxpayer as his principal residence for periods aggregating three years out of the five-year period ending on the date of the sale or exchange.

---

8 I.R.C. § 121.

The taxpayer must make an election to exclude the gain from gross income, and he can make the election only with respect to one such sale during his lifetime. The provisions of the section are also applicable to the sale of stock of a cooperative housing corporation by a tenant stockholder, the sale of a condominium dwelling unit, and the involuntary conversion of property used as a principal residence. The provisions also apply where only a portion of the property sold has been used as the taxpayer's principal residence; but, in that case, the section applies to the amount of the gain attributable to the portion of the property so used.

Generally, a taxpayer cannot tack on the holding and use periods from one residence to another in order to comply with the three-out-of-five-year rule or the five-out-of-eight-year rule except in the case of an involuntarily converted residence (e.g., destruction by fire damage, taking under power of eminent domain) that is replaced under the provisions of Code Section 1033. Where this situation occurs, the period during which the taxpayer used and occupied his old residence may be tacked on to his holding periods for the replacement residence.

Spouses who file a joint return for the year in which they sell their residence and who hold their residence as tenants by the entirety or joint tenants or as community property are treated as a single person for purposes of the $125,000 exclusion of gain. If one of them meets the age, holding, and use requirements for the exclusion, both spouses are deemed to meet those requirements.

The election is a once-in-a-lifetime election, and this includes married as well as single taxpayers. The election does not apply separately to each spouse, but if each of two taxpayers has independently made elections before marriage, there is no recapture of the tax attributable to the gain previously excluded by either spouse.

[i] Combining Tax-Free Gain With Tax-Free Rollover. A taxpayer may avail himself of both Section 121 and Section 1034 (tax-free sale and replacement of principal residences), thereby realizing a substantial tax savings if, as sometimes happens with an older person, he sells an expensive residence and buys a smaller one.

Example of computation showing recognized gain under $125,000 exclusion: A fifty-eight-year-old taxpayer sells his principal residence (a condominium apartment) for $300,000 in 1982. He bought the apartment some thirty years ago, and his basis for the apartment at the time of the sale is $75,000. His selling expenses are $18,750. He elects to take the $125,000 exclusion, and his taxable gain is computed as follows:

Sales price		$300,000
Less: Selling expenses	$18,750	
Basis of residence	75,000	
		93,750
Amount realized		$206,250
Less: Exclusion		125,000
Recognized gain		$ 81,250

Example of computation of recognized gain under both $125,000 exclusion and tax-free rollover: As already indicated, an election to use the $125,000 exclusion does not preclude taking advantage of a tax-free rollover. Thus, if a taxpayer over fifty-five years of age sells his residence and buys another replacement residence within the time required under the provisions of Code Section 1034 (twenty-four months), he may find himself in a position to take advantage of both tax breaks.

Sales price		$300,000
Less: Selling expenses	$ 18,750	
Exclusion	125,000	
		143,750
Revised adjusted selling price		$156,250
Less: Basis of residence		75,000
Recognized gain		$ 81,250

Under the above figures, the seller's entire real gain of $81,250 can be deferred if he purchases a replacement residence that costs him at least $156,250. If he purchases a new residence at a cost between $75,000 (basis of residence sold) and $156,250 (revised adjusted selling price of residence sold), his gain will be computed by subtracting the cost of the new home from $156,250; thus, less than his entire gain of $81,250 will be recognized.

Since resorting to a tax-free rollover may be used more than once but the $125,000 exclusion may be used only once, a homeowner who will realize a relatively small gain may be wiser to select the tax-free rollover (even though a small tax may be payable) and preserve the one-shot tax-free sale for a later date. However, if the homeowner chooses the rollover and takes title in his own name (rather than in the name of his spouse or in joint names) but thereafter dies before selling the new residence, the tax-free privilege will be lost. Consquently, the decision as to which election to make and the manner of taking title to the new residence should be considered carefully.

[ii] Combining Tax-Free Gain With Installment Sale. A taxpayer may combine the exclusion of gain under Section 121 with an installment sale under Section 453. This is illustrated in a 1980 IRS Ruling.[9] This ruling would seem to have been confirmed by the Installment Sales Revision Act of 1980, which made the installment method automatic unless the seller elects not to use it by reporting the entire gain in the year of sale.

Example: Taxpayer sold his house for $300,000, with payments to be made over several years. Since his adjusted basis was $115,000, his total gain was $185,000. He elected to exclude $125,000 of this gain under Section 121 and reported the remaining $60,000 gain by the installment method. Since his taxable gross profit was $60,000 and the sales price was $300,000, the percentage of each installment payment to be treated as taxable gain is 20 percent of the payment (60/300).

Thus, if the $300,000 was to be paid by the purchaser in three annual payments of $100,000, each payment would consist of $20,000 in gain,

[9] Rev. Rul. 80-249, 1980-2 C.B. 166.

$41,666 excludable under Section 121, and $38,333 as a nontaxable return of basis.

[5] Involuntary Conversions

An involuntary conversion of property may occur where property is lost, stolen, destroyed, condemned under the exercise of the power of eminent domain, or sold under a threat of condemnation. Any loss resulting from an involuntary conversion is always recognized, but a gain is not recognized if the requirements of Section 1033 of the Code are met. Under that section, if money received from an involuntary conversion, whether in the form of a condemnation award or insurance proceeds, is invested within the required time in property that is similar or related in service or use to the property that has been converted, the gain on the conversion, at the election of the taxpayer, is immediately taxable only to the extent that the amount received on the conversion exceeds the cost of the new property.

Example: If property with a cost basis of $100,000 is destroyed by fire and the insurance proceeds are $150,000, the total realized gain is $50,000. If the owner invests in other qualifying property within the required time and with a cost of $140,000, gain in the amount of only $10,000 is recognized provided the owner so elects.

In the case of condemnation (as compared to casualty losses), the replacement standard is somewhat more liberal, since the condemnation award may be invested either in similar-or-related-in-use property or in like-kind property. The like-kind test allows for a much broader choice of replacement property than the similar-or-related test. Thus, for example, under the like-kind test a leasehold with at least thirty years remaining can be replaced by a fee, city real estate can be replaced by a farm or a ranch, and unimproved property can be replaced by improved property.

Under the similar-or-related-in-service-or-use test, there is no qualified replacement where the proceeds of unimproved real estate taken in condemnation are invested in improved real estate or where the proceeds of the conversion of real property are applied in reduction of an indebtedness previously incurred in the purchase of a leasehold. However, as already indicated, this strict similar-use test is subject to one important exception: If the involuntary conversion results from the condemnation or threat of condemnation of real property used in a trade or business or held for investment, then the replacement property need qualify only as like-kind property.

A direct purchase of similar-use replacement property is not required. A qualifying replacement is made if the taxpayer purchases stock in the acquisition of control of a corporation owning qualifying replacement property. The term "control" here means the ownership of stock possessing at least 80 percent of the total combined voting power of all classes of stock entitled to vote and at least 80 percent of the total number of shares of all other classes of stock of the corporation, and the formation of a new corporation to acquire replacement property may meet the statutory requirements. However, where replacement only with like-kind property is permitted, the replacement must be direct rather than through the acquisition of corporate control.

In the case of condemned property, the tax-free replacement period is three years; with regard to property lost through a casualty, the replacement period is two years. The period begins to run after the close of the first taxable year in which any part of the gain from the disposition of the converted property is realized. An extension of time can be obtained under certain circumstances.

To qualify for nonrecognition of gain, the qualified replacement property must be purchased within the required time, and this requires that the burdens and benefits of the property must pass to the taxpayer. A mere contract to purchase qualified property coupled with a down payment, placing the deed in escrow until the closing but not actually closing until after the statutory period has expired, is not sufficient.

[a] Effect of Threat of Condemnation

A threat or imminence of condemnation starts the period within which an investment in qualified property can be made. It is important to note that a threat or imminence of condemnation can justify the purchase of qualified replacement property before a condemnation award is made. Also, gain on a sale made under a threat or imminence of condemnation may be reinvested in qualified replacement property tax-free or, if not so reinvested, may be eligible for capital gains treatment if the sale is of Section 1231 property (property used in a trade or business and capital assets held for more than one year).

A sale under a threat of condemnation may be made to the condemning authority or to a third party.

[b] Effect of Failure to Elect Nonrecognition or of Nonqualification for Election

If the taxpayer does not qualify for the nonrecognition election or if he qualifies but nevertheless chooses not to make the election, the gain on the involuntary conversion will be treated either as ordinary income or as capital gain, depending on the circumstances. If gain on an involuntary conversion will be treated as capital gain, long-range tax economy may be better served by an immediate recognition of the gain if the replacement property is depreciable. In such a case, for the price of immediate capital gains tax, the taxpayer gets a larger basis for depreciation deductions, which are offsets against ordinary income. Thus, suppose a building used in the taxpayer's business for over six months is destroyed by fire and that the building has an adjusted basis of $50,000. He receives insurance proceeds of $90,000, which he reinvests within the required time in a new building costing $90,000. If the taxpayer wishes to have the gain recognized, the gain would be subject to a capital gains tax[10] and the basis of the new building would be $90,000. In addition, the new property would be eligible for the fifteen-year write-off under ACRS. On the other hand, if the taxpayer elects nonrecognition, the basis would remain $50,000, with correspondingly small depreciation deductions. The applicability of the recapture-of-depreciation provisions also would have an important bearing on this decision.

---

[10] See I.R.C. § 1231.

[c] Effect of Partial Taking; Treatment of Severance Damages

Frequently, only a part of an owner's property is taken in a condemnation. When this occurs, the remaining property may suffer severance damages as a result of the partial taking. For tax purposes, an award of severance damages is not considered part of the award for the property condemned. Instead, severance damages are treated as damages received for injury to the remaining property. As such, they are treated as a reduction of the basis of the remaining property and are subject to tax only to the extent that they exceed the basis of the retained property.[11] In many cases, this results in the severance damages being received tax-free.

Usually, then, it is to the owner's advantage to have as much of the total award as possible allocated to severance damages. Suppose, for example, that property that is partially condemned has an adjusted basis of $100,000, of which $25,000 is allocable to the condemned portion and $75,000 to the retained portion. The award amounts to $35,000. If the owner can prove that $10,000 represents severance damages, there is no gain on the condemnation, since $25,000 of the award is applied against the adjusted basis of the condemned property ($25,000) and the remaining $10,000 of the award is applied against the adjusted basis of the retained property, reducing its adjusted basis to $65,000 ($75,000 less $10,000). On the other hand, if the owner cannot prove that $10,000 represents severance damages, the $35,000 will be applied in its entirety against the adjusted basis of the property condemned ($25,000), resulting in a $10,000 gain. Assuming that the involuntary conversion does not qualify for nonrecognition treatment, the $10,000 gain will be taxed.

---

[11] Pioneer Real Estate Co., 47 B.T.A. 886 (1942); Rev. Rul. 271, 1953-2 C.B. 36.

9

Leasing Real Estate

9.01 THE LEASE RELATIONSHIP

Under our system of law, real estate ownership is most often viewed as consisting of a "bundle of rights." This bundle includes the rights of (1) possession; (2) control; (3) enjoyment; and (4) disposition. When the owner of property (as landlord) enters into a lease with another party (the tenant), the owner transfers a portion of this bundle of rights to the tenant for a specified period of time (the lease term). Specifically, the tenant

- Obtains the right of possession, or the right of occupancy.
- Obtains the right of enjoyment, i.e., the right to preclude others from interfering with his occupancy.
- May or may not obtain (depending upon the lease terms) a right of control, i.e., the right to physically alter the property.
- May or may not obtain (subject to the lease terms) the right of disposition, i.e., the right to convey the leasehold estate to others.

However, at the expiration of the lease term, all of these rights revert to the landlord, who once again becomes the sole holder of the bundle of rights that make up ownership.

Because leasing involves a continuing relationship between landlord and tenant, the lease agreement often is a detailed and complex document. It must clearly set forth all of the specific rights granted to the tenant as well as all the reciprocal obligations (primarily rent) assumed by the tenant. It must also describe in detail the events of default that may cause a premature termination of the lease. From the point of view of the lease instrument, leases can conveniently be classified into three categories: (1) office and apartment leases; (2) retail leases; and (3) ground and entire-building leases. Sections 9.02 to 9.20 of this chapter discuss the key clauses in each of these types of leases.

Sections 9.21 to 9.25 discuss the leasehold as an investment and financing tool. We have already seen (in 6.15) how the division of property ownership into a fee and a leasehold permits greater financing to be achieved by the developer or owner of the property. In these sections, we discuss in more detail the considerations that induce (1) the developer or owner of property to sell the fee and take back a leasehold either to use it himself or to sublease space to others; and (2) an investor to purchase a fee subject to a leasehold rather than acquiring the fee outright.

9.02 RENT PAYMENTS

The key clause in any lease is that calling for the payment of rent. There are, however, as many different ways of determining rental as there are landlords and tenants. Notwithstanding the great number of rental provisions that appear in leases, most of them fit into one of the following categories:

- Fixed rental for the term of the lease (flat rental)
- Fixed rental with provision for specific increases or decreases (step-up or step-down rental)
- Fixed rental with adjustment for increased real estate taxes or for increased operating expenses, or for both (escalation rental)
- Fixed rental with adjustment to reflect changes in cost of living (cost-of-living rental)
- Fixed rental with adjustment to reflect reappraisals of the property (reappraisal rental)
- Percentage rental

It is not unusual for a lease to include a combination of these rental categories.

[1] Flat Rental

The traditional and least complicated method of setting the rent is to provide in the lease that the rental "will be $........ per annum, payable monthly in advance." This is generally the rental provision preferred by tenants since they then know exactly what their rental obligation will be. In the current inflationary era, the assurance that a major cost will be fixed for a definite period of time is worth a good deal to any businessman, since it reduces the risk that he will be unable to operate at a profit.

But for good reason, most landlords try to avoid fixed rentals since they make the landlord the victim of inflation. When saddled with a fixed rental, the landlord cannot pass on increased operating expenses or real estate taxes. To the extent that the tenant is required to assume the burden of such increased costs (either by paying an additional rental to the landlord or by being responsible for maintaining the property), the landlord's return remains at the same dollar level as when the lease was entered into. And if the tenant is required to pay an additional rental to reflect continuing inflation as well, the landlord's return can be maintained at the same level, in terms of purchasing power, as at the commencement of the lease.

Fixed rentals are still frequently used in short-term residential and commercial leases running from one to three years. But even with some such limited lease terms, landlords often require tenants to accept some form of rent escalation.

[2] Step-Up or Step-Down Rental

A step-up rental provision provides for a fixed rental with specific increases at specified intervals during the term of the lease. This type has the advantage of being simple; there is no need for an elaborate set of definitions or for detailed procedures. Tenants very often are willing to accept such fixed step-ups because they recognize the seemingly inevitable upward trend of costs. The loss of precision in matching the increases to changes in the cost of living or operating costs is believed to be more than offset by the simplicity of the clause.

One other purpose of the step-up rental under a retail or ground lease is to permit a tenant to commence a new business under favorable circumstances. After a period of years, the rental will be stepped up, at which time the parties anticipate that the tenant will be in a position to pay the higher amount. Sometimes, such a step-up rental is combined with a percentage rental. During the early years of the lease, a low fixed rental is set, with the tenant agreeing to pay a percentage rental on any sales in excess of a minimum figure. As the rental is stepped up during the later years of the lease or during renewal terms, the floor under which no percentage rental will be payable on sales is also raised. In effect, percentage rentals are gradually transformed into fixed rentals.

In one specific instance a landlord may agree to a step-down rental. If he is able to obtain favorable mortgage financing for improvements to the property primarily because of the tenant's high credit standing and the tenant can show that when the initial mortgage is paid off the cash flow to the landlord will increase substantially, the landlord may agree to a step-down of the rental at that time.

[3] Escalation Rental

Escalation leases provide for a fixed rental with adjustment for real estate taxes, operating expenses, or very often, for both. Some form of the escalation rental will be found in almost all leases for office, industrial, and commercial space. Leases of retail space will often combine some form of percentage rental with escalation provisions. Obviously, one of the major reasons for escalation rentals is to offset the effect of inflation on the landlord's costs and return on investment.

[a] Real Estate Taxes

Tax-adjustment clauses (also known as tax-escalation clauses and tax-stop clauses) typically are based on the real estate taxes paid by the landlord during the initial year of the lease. If real estate taxes increase in subsequent years, the tenant is required to pay his proportionate share of the increase (or the entire increase, if the tenant occupies the entire building). It should be noted that in some leases, the tenant is required to pay all real estate taxes in addition to the fixed rental. This usually, but not necessarily, is limited to a net-lease situation where the tenant occupies the entire premises, pays all operating expenses, and remits a net rental to the landlord each month.

When the leased property has not yet been constructed at the time the lease is entered into, the base period normally will be the first year during which the property is assessed as fully improved. (If an earlier year is used, the real estate taxes will jump very sharply, and the tenant will be paying substantially more dollars than he anticipated when fixing his percentage of future increases.)

Since it will almost never be true that the fiscal year of the taxing authority and the lease year will be exactly the same, the parties will have to determine if the base year for computing tax increases will be the fiscal year beginning in the first lease year or ending in the first lease year. Normally, since taxes can be expected to rise each year, the tenant will prefer the fiscal year beginning in the first lease year to be the base year, while the landlord will prefer the earlier fiscal year.

If the leased premises are only part of the taxable premises, the tax escalation or adjustment provision should carefully spell out how the tenant's share of the increased real estate taxes is to be determined. Particular care in negotiating and drafting tax escalation or adjustment provisions should be exercised by the tenant if other tenants on the premises are not required to pay their share of increased taxes or if the landlord himself occupies a portion of the premises.

One problem with tax-escalation clauses is that the landlord may become disinterested in contesting any increase in the assessment since the tenants will bear the burden of the increased taxes. In some states the tenant is permitted to challenge an assessment in his own name. In others, the proceeding must be brought in the landlord's name, and, in such a state, the lease provision should authorize the tenant to bring the action or proceeding in the landlord's name. A provision authorizing the tenant to maintain an action to challenge an increased assessment should clearly spell out (1) the exact procedure to be followed; (2) the tenant's right to receive notice of any increase; (3) the landlord's duty to cooperate with the tenant in maintaining the proceeding; (4) who shall be responsible for the payment of legal fees and other costs of the proceeding; and (5) the landlord's right to be given the first opportunity to bring the proceeding or action, assuming the landlord desires the right.

[b] Operating Expenses

Lease provisions requiring the lessee to pay a proportionate share of increases in the operating expenses of the property should spell out, with as much precision as possible, the amount or extent of the tenant's obligation and, in this regard, a specified percentage of operating expenses is frequently used for each tenant; the base year for the calculation of operating expenses usually is the first year, with the tenant being obligated to pay increased operating costs beginning with the second lease year.

The term "operating expenses" should be clearly defined in the lease. The tenant normally will want to limit operating expense to items directly related to the operation of the building (e.g., payroll, insurance premiums, maintenance and repair, and utility services). The landlord, for his part, may want to include such indirect expenses as, for example, management, accounting and legal fees, and advertising costs. Sometimes, a lease will use a single item of expense as a standard for the entire operating costs of the property, as, for example, wages paid to porters.

Where the tenant is one of several tenants in a multitenanted building and rent escalations or adjustments are based on increases in operating costs, the parties must recognize that an allocation of expense increases is necessary and should clarify the following points in the lease:

- The precise ratio of the tenant's space to the entire building space.
- The exact percentage of cost increases the tenant is to pay; this will not necessarily be the same as the tenant's space ratio. In leases of retail properties, for example, more valuable space may be charged with a higher escalation percentage. (An alternative approach is to establish rental ratios, rather than space ratios.)
- If a fixed ratio is established, the lease should state whether the landlord must absorb expenses attributable to vacant space; if the parties agree otherwise, their agreement should be spelled out in the lease.
- Whether the tenant's obligation extends only to the building as it then stands. (Normally, expenses attributable to further additions or improvements will be charged to the occupants of the additional space.)

Where the lease requires the tenant to pay for such utilities as electrical current and water, he will want to make sure that increases in these costs are excluded from the rent escalation provisions of the lease.

A rent escalation or adjustment clause covering operating expenses may use either the so-called pass-through method or the key-wage method. Under the pass-through method, all operating expense increases over the base-year expenses are passed through to the tenants. The key-wage method may be used by landlords who dislike giving tenants operating-expense statements each year. (Among other reasons, these statements can create disputes between the parties.) The key-wage method uses the wage rate of one type of employee, such as elevator operators or porters. In theory, their wage increases will, more or less, keep pace with inflation and with rises in other operating expenses; use of such a wage ratio is simple and rarely gives rise to arguments in its application. Under this method, every percentage (or penny) increase in the hourly wage will be matched by an increase in the tenant's rental per square foot.

The major considerations and areas to cover in negotiating and drafting lease escalation or adjustment provisions based on changes in the cost of operating the property include the following:

- Operating expenses must be carefully defined; as a general rule, the term only covers expenses directly attributable to the property itself and does not include the lessor's administrative salaries and overhead. Whether management fees, advertising, and lease commissions are to be included should be made clear.
- If wage-saving improvements are made, the lessor will want to retain the benefits. For example, if elevators are automated during the lease term, payroll expenses will drop and the landlord will want the right to have the base-year operating expenses adjusted downward.
- The lessee will want a provision requiring the lessor to operate the property efficiently and without incurring unreasonable expenses.
- The parties should agree on the type and content of the financial statement to be rendered by the landlord.
- The lease should state whether annual changes are to be measured on the basis of total operating expenses or on an item-by-item basis. The former method favors the tenant, since declines in some expenses will offset rises in others.
- The lease should state when escalation charges are to be paid by the lessee. Normally, they are paid annually. However, the lessor may want to provide that, in the event of a fuel shortage, increases in fuel costs can be passed along monthly or quarterly.
- The parties should make clear whether downward adjustments as well as upward adjustments are contemplated and also whether there are to be limits to the amount of adjustment.

[4] Cost-of-Living Rental

Lease provisions under which the amount payable to the landlord as rent is subject to being increased or adjusted periodically can be so drafted that increases are triggered by rises in a so-called outside standard (i.e., one that is not directly related to the cost incurred by the landlord in operating the property rather than one that is triggered by actual increases in operating costs). Examples of an outside standard include a specified consumer price index, the prime interest rate, and property reappraisals. Landlords tend to favor an outside standard since, through its use, the landlord stands to be reimbursed for his increased costs and his cash flow as well. In addition, he need not provide his tenants with statements showing his increased costs in order to obtain the increased rent.

[a] Consumer Price Index

By far the most popular of outside standards used in leases is the Consumer Price Index (CPI), published by the Bureau of Labor Statistics of the U.S. Department of Labor. The CPI generally is applied only in leases under which the tenant uses all or most of the building and pays all the operating expenses. In principle, however, the CPI can be used for any type of lease.

In 1978, the U.S. Bureau of Labor Statistics (BLS) introduced two CPIs to replace the old index, which was abandoned that year. Since the CPI now appears in two versions, lessors and lessees will have to agree on which to use.

Essentially, a CPI measures the purchasing power of consumers' dollars by comparing what a sample "market basket" of goods and services costs today with what the same basket cost at an earlier date. Thus, a CPI must use a base year against which subsequent changes are measured. The present base year is 1967 (i.e., 1967 = 100).

Beginning with January 1978, the BLS has been publishing these two indexes:

☐ *Revised CPI for urban wage earners and clerical workers (CPI-W).* This revised version of CPI continues to be based on buying habits of about one half the population. However, it updates the weights assigned to the expenditure groups, such as food, housing, and apparel. The sample of areas where the pricing takes place is updated, as well as the statistical methods used.

☐ *CPI for all urban consumers (CPI-U).* Based on a larger group than CPI-W, this index reflects the buying habits of about 80 percent of the civilian population of the United States. In addition to urban wage earners and clerical workers, CPI-U includes self-employed, professional, white-collar, and other salaried workers as well as retired and unemployed persons.

[b] Other Considerations in Choosing a Standard

In addition to the basic choice as to which index to use, parties to a lease have two other choices to make:

☐ *Geographic area.* The first choice is between the national index and the index for a particular locality. Both the CPI-W and the CPI-U have monthly indexes for the United States and for the five largest metropolitan areas, and also bimonthly indexes for twenty-three other metropolitan areas.

☐ *All items or rent.* Most rent adjustment clauses use the "all items" figure in the CPIs rather than the figure for rent. The figure for rent in the CPIs is for residential rather than commercial rent; there is also a separate figure for home-ownership costs. In general, residential rent increases have not kept pace with the overall increase in the cost of living; consequently, use of the rent item as a standard for rent escalation generally works better for lessees than for lessors.

Whether rent escalation provisions are triggered by the CPI or by some other method as, for example, the prime interest rate, the parties must agree on such matters as the period of time that is to elapse between rent adjustments ("index" adjustments often are made as frequently as once each year); the minimum change in the standard required to trigger an adjustment (index clauses frequently require the index to move a minimum percentage before any rent change is triggered); and a ceiling on rent increases (normally, there is no ceiling on rentals set under the index method because it is typically used in leases with very long terms).

[5] Reappraisal Rentals

The lease may provide for periodic increases in the amount of rent payable by the tenant to the landlord according to reappraised valuations of the property. Thus, for example, net ground leases under which the tenant is to build the improvement frequently tie rent increases to periodic reappraisals of the land. Likewise, a net lease of improved property may also tie rent increases to periodic reappraisals of the property.

In the case of a lease of land where the tenant constructs the improvement, the appraisers may consider the highest-and-best use of the land to be other than its actual use and so may come up with a higher value than its current use would justify. As a result, the tenant would then be paying rent based on a use not available to him unless he demolishes the present structure. The problem becomes more serious if the property has been rezoned to permit more intensive and more profitable uses since the lease was entered into by the parties.

In drafting lease provisions tying rent increases to periodic reappraisals of the property, the parties should clearly spell out (1) when and how often reappraisals or revaluations shall be made; (2) how appraisers are to be chosen; (3) the assumptions on which reappraisals or revaluations are to be made; (4) what shall trigger a rent adjustment; (5) the formula for making the adjustment; and (6) how disputes shall be handled.

[6] Percentage Rentals

Percentage rental provisions are frequently included in commercial leases, that is, in leases where the tenant will operate a business involving the sale of goods or services on the leased premises rather than use the premises for office or industrial purposes or as a personal residence.

These provisions are usually written so that the tenant pays a fixed annual minimum rent plus a percentage rent based on gross sales, gross revenues, or gross receipts in addition to or against the minimum rent. Rarely will the parties agree on a net profit standard, since it creates a great likelihood of disputes as to accounting procedures. In addition, a new profit standard may increase the possibility that the landlord will be deemed to be the tenant's partner, thus creating adverse legal consequences for the landlord.

Even with a gross sales standard, however, a conflict of interest may arise between landlord and tenant, since the landlord may seek to have gross sales maximized even though this may be at the expense of the tenant's net profit.

A percentage rental clause should state how the percentage rent will be computed, and the extent to which the tenant's freedom of action will be limited to protect the landlord's right to receive percentage rent.

Where the percentage rent provision is based on "gross sales," the lease should clearly indicate whether "gross sales" excludes such items as returns and allowances, bad debts, sales taxes, excise taxes, freight and insurance charges, the value of services provided free to customers (e.g., free repairs), and sales made by telephone or otherwise indirectly from the leased premises.

When the tenant's profit margin is substantially the same on all sales, a percentage rental based on sales represents a fixed percentage of operating profit (the crucial percentage for the tenant). However, where a large portion of gross sales is represented by products that produce a low margin of profit, the percentage rental may wipe out the tenant's entire profit from the low-margin goods. One way to solve this problem is to use a split rate, with different percentages applicable to different products.

Where there is an assignment, sublease, or concession by the tenant, assuming this is permitted by the lease, the lease may provide that all sales by the assignee, subtenant, or concessionaire are included in the computations of gross sales (but that the rental paid to the prime tenant is not). If however, the new operation has a different sales mix from that of the original tenant and if the business is a high-margin, low-gross operation, the landlord suffers because he may collect no percentage rentals. If the new business has high sales but low profits, the new operation may be unable to show a profit, which means, in effect, that the prime tenant's right to assign is sharply restricted. One solution is to provide that if an assignment or sublease generates lower percentage rentals than the prime tenant had been paying, the prime tenant will make up the difference in additional rental.

The following are basic types of percentage rental provisions in use in commercial leases:

☐ *Percentage against minimum rental.* The tenant pays a fixed minimum, which is credited against a percentage computed on the total business done by the tenant on the leased premises for the year.

☐ *Minimum rent plus percentage rent.* The tenant pays a minimum plus a percentage of the total proceeds of the business done by the tenant on the leased premises for the year, or only those proceeds above a specified limit. The minimum rent may be a fixed, step-up, or experimental minimum. A step-up minimum provides for graduated increases over the life of the lease or during renewal terms. An experimental minimum may be used for an untried tenant or a new location; under it, a rental step-up is conditioned on the achievement of specified volume levels. (In addition, the percentage may be stepped up or down on a graduated scale as gross sales reach predetermined levels.)

☐ *Percentage with no minimum rent.* Here, the landlord's rental income totally depends on the success of the tenant's business. A landlord should be very careful of this type of provision, since it can prejudice his financing efforts; lenders measure the security of their loan by the minimum rents to be paid to the borrower. Very strong tenants, however, are apt not to agree to a minimum rental where the location is an untried one.

☐ *Ceiling on rental.* In any of the above situations, the landlord may agree to a maximum rental that is not to be exceeded under any circumstances. Usually, however, he will point to the inflationary spiral of the last few years as the best argument against such a ceiling.

The following important protective provisions should be included by the landlord in a percentage rent arrangement:

- The tenant should be obligated to carry on his business on the premises in good faith.
- The lease should require the tenant to be open for business during normal business hours and/or during certain specified hours.
- The tenant should be prohibited from competing with himself within a certain radius of the premises.

- The tenant should carry and display certain merchandise and hire adequate personnel.
- The tenant should make periodic reports of sales volume.
- The landlord should be entitled to inspect the tenant's books and records.
- Assignments or subletting by the tenant without the landlord's consent should be prohibited by most percentage rental agreements.
- Provision should be made for a pro rata adjustment of the base figure above which percentage rentals are payable to reflect a period of reduced volume in sales attributable to unforeseen events such as fires or strikes.
- Recapture of the premises should be provided for if the tenant is unable to generate sufficient volume to pay percentage rentals after a minimum number of years.
- There should be a disclaimer that any partnership, joint venture, or relation other than landlord-tenant exists between the parties because they share the profits from the business conducted on the leased premises.

[7] Tax Considerations

The following rules apply to the deductibility of rental payments for tax purposes:

[a] Rent as Deductible Expense and Taxable Income

As a general rule, rent is deductible to the tenant of commercial property as an ordinary and necessary business expense. To the landlord, it is taxable as ordinary income.

Section 162 of the Internal Revenue Code specifically provides that

> There shall be allowed as a deduction all the necessary expenses paid or incurred during the taxable year in carrying on any trade or business including . . .
>
> (3) Rentals or other payments required to be made as a condition to the continued use or possession, for the purposes of the trade or business, or property to which the taxpayer has not taken or is not taking title or in which he has no equity.

[b] Deduction Limited to Tenant's Legal Liability

The deduction for rent is limited to the amount for which the tenant is liable by the terms of the lease. Thus, if the tenant pays more rent during the course of the year than he is legally liable for, he may not deduct the additional rent. The rule applies irrespective of whether the landlord treats the excess rent payments as advance rentals or security deposits.

> *Example:* If on January 1, a tenant who maintains his books and records on a calendar-year basis enters into a ten-year lease, under which he is required to pay rent of $1,000 per year and immediately pays not only the $1,000 allocable to that year but the entire $10,000 rent for the ten-year period, he

may deduct only the $1,000 allocable to the first year. The remaining $9,000 in deductions must be spread over the remaining nine years of the lease.

[c] Rental Must Not Be Excessive

To be deductible, rent payments need not only be legally due in accordance with the terms of the lease but also must be reasonable. The question of whether rent is unreasonably high usually arises only where the lease agreement is not an arm's-length transaction, for example, when parties are members of the same family or are related corporations. If the Internal Revenue Service deems rental excessive, it will permit a deduction only of a reasonable rental.

There is, however, no absolute bar to a lease agreement between related parties. Thus, a shareholder who owns a building or other property may lease it to a corporation he controls and the reasonable rental of the property may be deducted by the corporation as a business expense. The advantage to the corporation, in such a case, of leasing the property rather than owning it is that it obtains a rental deduction that normally is larger than the depreciation deduction to which the corporation would be entitled as owner of the property. The landlord-shareholder, of course, will report the rental payments as ordinary income and may take the depreciation deduction.

The disallowance of a rental deduction by a corporation on the ground that it is in excess of the fair rental value of the property may result in a further determination that the payments by the corporation were in fact disguised dividends to the shareholder.

[d] Tenant's Obligation to Pay Taxes and Other Expenses

Where a tenant under a lease-imposed obligation must pay taxes, insurance, or other expenses that normally would be borne by the landlord, these payments are considered rent and are deductible by the tenant. The tenant may deduct taxes paid by him even if his lease does not require that he pay the taxes.

9.03 SECURITY DEPOSITS AND ADVANCE RENTALS

Most leases provide for a security deposit to be paid at the time the lease is executed. It is desirable that the lease provision indicate precisely what the security is to cover. For example, the security may be for the failure to pay any rental when due, or for breakage or damage during the term of the lease, or for any damage of the premises at the time the lease terminates, or for any default under any lease covenant. Usually, of course, the security deposit clause is stated in very broad terms.

Sometimes a landlord will agree to waive any security deposit, provided the lease is signed individually (rather than by a corporate dummy) or guaranteed by an individual. A tenant who is very short of working capital may prefer to assume personal liability instead of posting a deposit equal to several months rent.

The lease should provide that any security deposit may be assigned to the new owner in the event the landlord sells the demised premises.

It is important that the lease specify whether a payment is a security deposit or an advance rental. If the payment is a security deposit, the tenant is not entitled to apply it in discharge of the final months rent payments. On the other hand, an advance rental normally may be so used. Since the landlord usually will not have an opportunity to inspect the premises until the lease is terminated, the security deposit gives the landlord greater protection.

From a tax point of view, advance rentals are taxable to the landlord as ordinary income as soon as received. A security deposit, however, is not so taxable to the landlord until applied to remedy defaults in accordance with the terms of the lease. This is true even though the security deposit need not be segregated or held in trust by the landlord, but may be commingled with the landlord's personal funds. (In some jurisdictions, security deposits must be kept in a separate account by law and/or must bear interest in favor of the tenant.)

In most instances, the security deposit or advance rental is a cash payment. However, it may take other forms, such as a deposit of marketable securities, a letter of credit or a surety bond, or even a chattel mortgage or security agreement on the tenant's chattels located on the premises. When marketable securities are used, the tenant is required to post additional security if the securities drop below a minimum market value. Most provisions allowing a tenant to deposit securities in lieu of cash permit the tenant to keep the dividends or interest on the security so long as he is not in default under the lease. Once a default occurs, the income may be kept by the landlord.

9.04 TERM OF LEASE; POSSESSION OF PREMISES

[1] In General

Lease terms may range anywhere from one to twenty or more years. Where the demised premises already are in existence, the customary procedure is to set forth a beginning date and a termination date, as well as to state the length of the lease (in years or months). An investor should be careful that the length of the term and the commencement and termination dates do not create a conflict; otherwise, it may be necessary to have a court interpret the lease.

Where the premises are to be constructed, the very high risk that completion may be delayed usually precludes stating a definite commencement date. Instead, the lease term usually will commence upon the substantial completion of the premises, the issuance of a temporary or permanent certificate of occupancy, or the date upon which the tenant can commence business operations. If the substantial-completion test is used, it is desirable to define the term as precisely as possible.

A ground tenant should negotiate for the longest initial lease term and for as many options to renew or extend as possible. The tenant benefits in several ways from a long-term ground lease. For example, the longer the lease term, the greater the price he should be able to realize on an assignment of his leasehold interest. What's more, even though the price may not be greater, it will be quite difficult for the ground tenant to assign or mortgage the lease, or sublet the premises, at a time when the lease does not have much longer to run.

[2] Right to Possession vs. Actual Possession

In many jurisdictions, the tenant merely is entitled to the right to possession at the commencement of the lease, not actual possession. Thus, if a preceding tenant has not yet vacated the property, the new tenant must take steps to evict him and, in addition, must pay rental to the landlord. It is desirable, from the viewpoint of both landlord and tenant, that the lease deals specifically with the question of actual possession and remedies to which the tenant will be entitled if he does not receive such possession. Four alternatives can be distinguished:

☐ *Tenant has right to possession only.* This is simply a restatement of the common law; that is, the tenant has the right to possession as of the commencement of the lease term, but must take it upon himself to evict any holdover tenants and must pay rent in the meantime.

☐ *Rent abatement.* The compromise position is to provide that if the tenant does not obtain actual possession (through no fault of his own) as of the date of commencement of the lease term, rent shall abate until possession is obtained, but the tenant may not rescind the lease. When the building in which the demised premises are to be located is in the process of construction, the landlord will frequently use this approach rather than using one of the alternatives listed above (e.g., substantial completion or issuance of certificate of occupancy).

☐ *Right to rescind.* The third alternative, by far the least likely, is the clause permitting the tenant to rescind in the event actual possession is not delivered at the commencement of the term or within a reasonable period thereafter.

☐ *Alternative space.* The landlord may offer to provide alternative space to the tenant, if the demised premises are not available at the commencement of the lease term. This may be acceptable to a tenant who does not require a specific location to carry on his business activities, and where the cost of moving his operation is either minimal or where the landlord will agree to pay such cost.

The clause also should make clear whether the landlord or tenant shall be responsible to evict any holdover tenant.

[3] Right of Entry by Tenant Prior to Term

If the premises are in process of construction, or if it is anticipated that the premises will be vacant for some period before the term of the lease commences, the tenant normally will seek the right to enter upon the premises to install fixtures and make such alterations as are contemplated by the lease. The landlord frequently will agree to this without requiring payment of any rental but may insist that all the other terms of the lease (e.g., the tenant to make repairs made necessary by the tenant's negligence) be deemed to apply immediately upon the tenant's entry on the premises.

[4] Obligations Between Execution Date and Commencement of Term

The period of time between the date the lease is executed and the actual commencement of the term may be substantial. During such period, the lease is binding on both parties, but only with respect to those provisions that are not dependent upon the taking of possession by the tenant and the commencement of the term.

[5] Damages for Failure to Deliver Possession

Where a landlord has the obligation to deliver actual possession of the premises and fails to do so, he may be liable to the tenant for damages in the absence of an exculpatory clause in the lease. The usual measure of damages is the difference between the rental provided for in the lease and the fair market rental value of the premises.

In addition to these general damages, a tenant who has been denied occupancy by his landlord may recover such foreseeable expenditures and costs incurred in preparing to enter the premises as losses on expenditures for stock and equipment, moving costs, and the like. Such special damages must be proved.

Profits may be an additional element of damages where it is possible to estimate the profits that would have been earned had the tenant moved in when anticipated. However, where a tenant attempts to recover profits for a new business or enterprise, such claims are usually rejected as being too remote, speculative, and contingent.

Where a tenant is leasing a store that is occupied by another tenant at the time the lease is signed, the new tenant may insist on a clause calling for liquidated damages, that is, damages in a fixed amount in the event actual possession is not available when the lease commences.

9.05 MAINTENANCE AND REPAIR OF PREMISES

[1] In General

Maintenance and repair clauses in leases deserve careful attention by both landlord and tenant because the expense of maintaining and repairing real estate is growing in today's high-priced economy. This expense can make a substantial difference between the effective rental and the contract rental from the property, with the effective rental being higher or lower depending upon which party has the burden. And to the extent that market forces keep rents down, landlords are under increasing pressure to minimize the work they do on leased premises.

The following are the major considerations in drafting a maintenance and repair clause for retail, office, and apartment leases.

[2] Retail Leases

A retail tenant occupying an entire freestanding building normally will enter into a net lease with the landlord, in which case all of the maintenance will be performed and paid for by the tenant. In a multitenant building, however, where portions of the building are not under the tenant's control, there will be a division of responsibility.

☐ *Maintenance by the landlord.* Obligations of the landlord frequently include the following:

- Structural maintenance, that is, that relating to the foundation, the four outer walls, and the roof (but often excluding repair required because of an act or negligence of the tenant)

- Maintenance of the public portions of the building, for example, public halls and stairways, plumbing, wiring, and other building equipment for the general supply of water, heat, air conditioning, gas, and electricity
- Maintenance and repair of a building sprinkler system (but this may be the tenant's responsibility if the need for the system is due to the tenant's use of the premises)
- In a shopping center, maintenance and repair of the common areas, the lighting, drainage and sewer systems, the shopping center sign, all directional signs, lighting that is not part of specific premises, and the parking areas.

☐ *Maintenance by the tenant.* Obligations of the tenant relate generally to all of the space encompassed by the leased premises:

- The store premises themselves
- The sidewalks in front and on the side of the leased premises, including the removal of all snow, ice, and rubbish
- Any portion of the roof that is exclusive to the leased premises
- Tenant's service connections to all utilities
- The storefront, including all window glass
- All maintenance and repair required because of the negligence of the tenant, its employees, or visitors
- Air conditioning and heating to the extent that the system is exclusively within the control of the tenant

A tenant having the obligation to maintain and repair should seek to absolve himself for repairs due to wear and tear and for latent defects. (The one exception is where the tenant himself puts up the building.) Sometimes, the landlord will agree to make all repairs for the first year except those due to tenant's misuse, rather than remain responsible for latent defects during the term of the lease.

[3] Office Leases

The tenant in a multitenancy office building normally expects to be largely free of any maintenance responsibilities. At the same time, it is important to him that the building be well maintained both for the comfort of himself and his employees and to maintain the status of the building in the eyes of visitors. Consequently, the tenant should seek to have the lease impose a specific obligation on the landlord to maintain the building; a tenant in a strong negotiating position may be able to obtain a specific schedule and frequency of cleaning services, including window washing. The cleaning service normally includes the tenant's own premises. Thus, the only exception to the landlord's responsibility is that due to the negligence of the tenant.

[4] Apartment Leases

Under the common law the landlord has no implied duty to maintain or repair leased premises, no matter what their condition at the time of leasing and whether or not the condition is known to the tenant. However, changing judicial attitudes have created in many states an implied warranty of habitability—a court-created obligation on landlords to make housing accommodations fit for use. This implied warranty varies among the states that have adopted it, and the range of remedies is wide, including the right to move out (constructive eviction), the right to refuse to pay rent until defective conditions are corrected, and the right to repair and deduct the cost from the rent.

Here is an example of a maintenance and repair clause for an apartment lease. The landlord agrees to maintain the following minimum standards:

- Effective weather protection
- Plumbing facilities in good working order
- An adequate hot and cold water supply
- Heating (and air conditioning, if furnished) in good working order
- Gas and electrical systems (and appliances, if supplied) in good working order and condition
- Public areas in a clean and safe condition
- Elevators, if any, in good and safe condition

On his part, the tenant agrees to the following:

- Maintain the apartment in a clean and sanitary condition
- Dispose of all rubbish and garbage
- Properly use all appliances and fixtures
- Keep out materials that cause a fire or safety hazard
- Not destroy or damage any part of the building or apartment
- Keep the apartment in good order and repair

[5] Relationship to Other Clauses

The repair and maintenance clause should always be read in conjunction with the lease clauses covering the provision of utility services, the right of the tenant to make alterations, the tenant's obligation to comply with laws, and damage or destruction to the premises. To some extent, obligations of a party under any of these clauses may relate to the maintenance and repair clause.

[6] Tax Considerations

Repair expenditures incurred or made by the party on whom the burden is placed by the lease usually are deductible by him as ordinary and necessary business expenses. However, only expenditures incurred for incidental repairs that do not materially add to the value of the property nor appreciably prolong its life but keep it in an ordinarily efficient operating condition are deductible.

On the other hand, repairs that are in the nature of replacements that arrest deterioration and appreciably prolong the life of the property must be capitalized and depreciated over the property's remaining useful life or charged against the depreciation reserve, if such an account is kept.

Real estate owners frequently fractionalize an extensive job by breaking it down into its component parts and doing each part separately and independently, sometimes over a series of years, rather than keeping it as one job and doing it all at one time. In this way, the amounts that they can deduct as repairs can be increased.

Normally, a landlord's remodeling costs are treated as capital expenditures. And, even if remodeling involves destruction of a portion of the structure, no demolition loss is allowed if the demolition is required as a condition of getting a new lease. However, an ordinary loss deduction for extraordinary obsolescence may be allowed where a specially made wall must be destroyed by a landlord in order to accommodate the needs of a new tenant.

A word should be said concerning the replacement of broken plate glass. Where the lease places the burden on the tenant, the landlord may want to reserve the right to do the necessary work and bill the cost to the tenant as additional rent if the tenant fails or unreasonably delays in making necessary repairs. The tenant, for his part, will want a provision under which glass breakage caused by the landlord's negligence or by any cause included in the landlord's insurance coverage need not be repaired by the tenant.

The cost of maintenance and repair of glass constitutes an ordinary business deduction for the tenant where the tenant is required to make the repairs and for the landlord where the landlord is required to make the repairs. The party who is required, by the terms of the lease, to pay plate-glass insurance premiums is the one who can take the deductions for the premiums.

9.06 ALTERATIONS, IMPROVEMENTS, AND SIGNS

[1] Alterations and Improvements

Commercial and ground leases almost always make provision for initial alterations by the tenant prior to commencing business. In addition, the lease invariably contains a provision with respect to alterations or improvements during the term of the lease. Landlords usually are insistent that the tenant obtain the landlord's consent in advance of making any particular improvements or alterations. The landlord's purpose is twofold:

- To be sure that the particular changes will not be of such extreme design or style, or be so bizarre, that they will reflect adversely upon the building
- To insure that the work is done in a satisfactory manner so that the risk of present or future damage to the property is minimized and the least possible inconvenience is suffered by other tenants

[a] Initial Improvements

The main point to remember in drafting provisions dealing with alterations and improvements is that the more specific the provisions, the less likelihood there is for future disputes. (On the other hand, the tenant will want to retain some flexibility in the event changes become desirable in the course of the work.) In the case of improvements to be made at the commencement of the lease term, there normally is no serious problem about setting forth the changes in detail. The most definitive approach would be to have actual plans and specifications drawn up and initialed by the parties simultaneously with the execution of the lease. Another approach is for the parties to detail the objectives of the tenant in making the changes and to provide more or less definite descriptions of the improvements.

[b] Alterations During Term of the Lease

Unlike the initial alterations, changes that may be desired by the tenant in the future usually cannot be described in great detail since they will depend upon various contingencies. Thus, the tenant may wish to convert storage and warehouse space into selling space, divide the leased premises into fewer or more selling areas, etc. Whether the tenant may make changes in order to devote the leased premises to a different use than at the commencement of the lease will, of course, depend upon a consideration of the use-and-occupancy clause. Provisions dealing with the necessity for the landlord's consent to alterations or improvements during the term of the lease fall into the following three categories:

☐ *No consent required.* This type of clause is most frequently found where the tenant occupies an entire freestanding structure (e.g., a supermarket or department store) under a long-term lease and where the lease rather than the real estate itself is the primary basis for the value of the parcel.

☐ *Consent required.* Where a local credit tenant is one of several in a building, under a short- or medium-term lease, the landlord may refuse to permit any alterations without his prior consent. Sometimes the ambiguous phrase "such consent not to be withheld unreasonably" is added to protect the tenant against a wholly arbitrary refusal by the landlord.

☐ *Consent required for certain alterations.* The final alternative is to classify improvements or alterations into two categories, one requiring consent and one not. The most common line of division is that between structural and nonstructural changes. The latter would permit the tenant to alter display cases, partitioning, fixtures, etc. On the other hand, structural changes conceivably might include an addition to the building that for a variety of reasons may be unacceptable to the landlord. Another method of distinguishing alterations requiring consent from those that do not is to establish a dollar ceiling above which consent will be required.

[c] Key Conditions of Lease

The greater the likelihood that the tenant will make substantial alterations or improvements to the demised premises, the more detailed will be the conditions set forth in the lease with which the tenant must comply. Following is a checklist of the key conditions:

☐ *Laws and regulations.* The tenant normally will be responsible for obtaining building permits, complying with all governmental regulations, and paying the expenses in connection therewith.

☐ *Selection of architect.* A common procedure is for the tenant to have the right to select an architect, subject to the reasonable consent of the landlord.

☐ *Union labor.* Depending on the locality, the lease may require that all labor be union-affiliated.

☐ *Approval of contractors and subcontractors.* The landlord may wish the right to approve the general contractor and subcontractors.

☐ *Mechanic's liens.* The landlord generally will insist that the tenant take steps to insure that no mechanic's liens are filed against the property by contractors or materialmen or, if any lien is filed, that the tenant will remove the same by payment or by bonding within a specified period.

☐ *Payment or performance bond.* The landlord may require the tenant to post a payment, completion, or performance bond, which insures that the contemplated work will be completed notwithstanding nonpayment by the tenant of his bills or default by the contractor or subcontractors.

☐ *Insurance.* To the extent that insurance policies required elsewhere in the lease are not sufficient to protect the landlord or the building from risks or liabilities during the course of alteration, the landlord will require the tenant to provide additional insurance.

[d] Ownership of Improvements or Alterations

A separate lease provision normally will deal with the ownership of installations made by the tenant and the removal of such installations if the tenant is to retain ownership. If the parties contemplate that substantial alterations or improvements may be made during the term of the lease, their ownership or disposition should be clearly dealt with either in the termination clause or the alterations clause. The customary clause provides that such improvements become the property of the landlord. The landlord should require that the improvements become his property immediately upon installation rather than on the termination of the lease. In this way, he can reduce the risk of claims by third parties to an interest in the improvements.

[e] Additional Real Estate Taxes Because of Improvements

If improvements made by the tenant will increase the assessed valuation of the property and so result in a rise in real estate taxes, the usual procedure is for the tenant to be obligated to pay the additional taxes.

[f] Special Considerations Applicable to Ground Leases

A ground tenant under a long-term ground lease will expect to be given wide latitude to make changes, improvements, and additions to the buildings and improvements on the demised premises. He will also expect to have the right to erect new buildings and to demolish existing buildings.

The ground landlord will want to make sure that he will not bear any part of the cost. He will also insist that the tenant be required to replace or restore any building demolished by him so that the new or restored building is equal in value to the demolished building.

9.07 SIGNS

In commercial leases, an important provision is that dealing with the tenant's rights and duties with respect to signs, both inside and outside the demised premises. Normally, the largest or most prestigious tenant will seek to have the largest and most prominent sign. If there are relatively few tenants in the building, each may be given the right to install a roof or roadside sign. Where there are many tenants, most may be limited to a sign immediately over their individual premises, and on show windows and doors.

In order to maintain the prestige and appearance of the building, the landlord generally will insist on the right to regulate the size and style of signs. If the tenant has an established trademark, he should seek a provision in the lease specifically authorizing its use.

Unless the lease specifically provides otherwise, courts have ruled that tenants are entitled to place signs on the outside of buildings at the entrance to their premises. However, they are not permitted to put a sign on the roof of the building unless they have leased the entire premises.

Signs on the roof or exterior walls of the building may fall and damage passersby or property. Thus, the lease normally will require the tenant to maintain adequate insurance against such possibilities. Also, many municipalities must approve in advance any signs overhanging the sidewalks. If such approval is necessary, the lease should require the tenant to obtain it prior to installation of the sign.

When the lease ends, the tenant generally should be required to remove the sign, since it is of no value to the landlord and the cost of removing it may be high.

9.08 USE AND OCCUPANCY

[1] In General

In general, two different kinds of use-and-occupancy clauses can be distinguished. The first, a purpose-and-use clause, is affirmative in nature, spelling out precisely what the space can be used for. Occasionally, the permitted uses will be tied to a competing store, for example, "the premises are to be used for a supermarket that may sell all food and nonfood products that are carried by supermarkets operated by the *X* company in the City of Chicago."

The second type of use-and-occupancy clause is the exclusion clause, which specifies the particular uses prohibited to the tenant. Generally, tenants will prefer the exclusion clause because every activity not specifically prohibited is permissible.

Negotiating the use-and-occupancy provisions of a ground lease should, in the absence of unusual circumstances, pose no insuperable difficulties. The ground tenant will want to make sure that he acquires the right to use and occupy the premises for any and all lawful purposes. He will want that right to extend to any and all portions of the premises. The ground landlord, for his part, may want a portion of the premises to be used initially for a particular purpose, as for example, a shopping center or residential use, possibly because the landlord owns adjacent property that will be affected by such use. In the case of a retail lease, however, negotiating the use-and-occupancy clause may be arduous. Some of the considerations are given below.

[2] Sources of Restrictions on Tenant's Use of the Premises

Frequently, there will be existing restrictions pertaining to use and occupancy to which the premises are subject. Some of them are as follows:

☐ *Zoning restrictions.* In many areas, zoning ordinances restrict the type of commercial operation permitted. It is in the interest of both landlord and tenant to review carefully, before the lease is executed, the applicable zoning ordinance in the light of the intended use of the premises.

When the intended use is prohibited by existing zoning, the lease may be conditioned upon a rezoning. In such case, the lease should spell out clearly whether the landlord or the tenant must process the application and who is to bear the costs incurred. Normally, the rent will not commence until the rezoning has been granted, but this should be clearly set forth in the lease.

If the intended use is permitted by the present zoning ordinance, there remains the possibility that future changes may bar the use. While the tenant probably could terminate the lease under the doctrine of "frustration," it may be desirable to include a provision specifically granting the tenant a right to cancel the lease in such circumstance.

☐ *Covenants and restrictions.* Another source of limitations on the use of the property are covenants and restrictions applicable to the fee interest. A tenant about to execute a long-term lease or a tenant contemplating substantial alterations should satisfy himself, by appropriate title searches, that such covenants and restrictions do not affect his intended use. Alternatively, he may seek a representation from the landlord in the lease to the effect that no such restrictions exist.

☐ *Restrictions in other leases.* Probably the most frequent source of restrictions on the use of demised premises are provisions in other leases entered into by the same landlord. Such restrictions are most common in shopping center leases, where the major department store or supermarket tenants may require the landlord to agree that other stores will not be leased for designated purposes or will not be leased without the specific consent of the major tenant.

[3] Restrictions on Competitive Leasing by Landlord

Another clause related to the use-and-occupancy provision is one restricting the landlord from leasing other premises in the same building or at nearby locations for uses that compete with the intended use by the tenant. Whether the tenant can successfully obtain this clause depends on the strength of his negotiating position. If the landlord does agree, he frequently will insert a condition that if he buys property within the restricted area that already contains competing tenants, such tenants may continue at the same location.

In negotiating this clause, the tenant may be willing to define the permitted uses at the demised premises more strictly in consideration of the agreement by the landlord not to lease adjacent space to competing tenants. Or the definition of prohibited uses by other tenants of the landlord may be more narrow than the definition of permitted uses at the demised premises.

[4] Negotiation of Shopping Center Lease Restrictions

A successful shopping center is a carefully integrated pattern of retail uses. To achieve the desired tenant mix, shopping center developers use three different types of restrictions in their leases.

☐ *Exclusive clause.* Landlord agrees not to lease other premises in the center (or in a specified area) to another tenant for the same purposes as the present lease.

☐ *Trade-area limitation* (*radius clause*). Tenant agrees not to use any other premises within a specified radius of the center for the same purposes as the present lease calls for.

☐ *Use clause.* Tenant agrees to use the premises for only those purposes specified in the lease.

These lease restrictions went virtually unchallenged, until about fifteen years ago when exclusive and radius clauses came under attack as restraints on competition and thus violative of the antitrust laws. Since then, the great majority of court decisions on the subject have tested the lease restrictions against a standard of "reasonableness." Under these decisions, a restriction is judged reasonable depending on the term (in years) of the restriction; the geographic area affected; and the scope and character of the business activity restricted. The courts, in other words, recognize that a legitimate business interest is served by these clauses in many cases.

[a] Exclusive Clause

Since a shopping center landlord can never be certain that an exclusive will not be challenged in court by other tenants, his object should always be to avoid giving them in the first place. A tenant seeking an exclusive may be willing to indemnify the landlord against the consequences of granting the exclusive, but since courts will not enforce an indemnity against an illegal action (in this case, unreasonable restraint of competition), the indemnity may not provide adequate protection.

In large shopping centers (200,000 square feet or more), exclusives normally are not expected by tenants because of the size of the trading area. In these cases, the tenant's assurance of a proper retail mix comes from the track record of the developer.

In a smaller center, however, exclusives still are sought by tenants, and a landlord who grants them should try to limit the exclusive to the most profitable lines of the tenant. The landlord should also recognize that the larger the tenant and the more stores he operates, the more strictly should the exclusive be drawn, since size often is a crucial factor in determining the impact of the exclusive on competition. In addition, instead of banning all competitors of the tenant, the landlord should seek to phrase the limitation to a reasonable number of competitors.

The Federal Trade Commission (FTC) has published a number of consent decrees involving department stores and developers. These decrees indicate that the most vulnerable aspects of lease restrictions intended to benefit tenants are (1) a veto power over other tenants in the center; (2) control of pricing policies of other tenants; (3) floor-space limitations on other tenants; and (4) restricting the location of other tenants.

In addition, in two decrees where the major tenant also was the developer, the developer/major tenant agreed not to request trade-area limitations from other tenants.

[b] Trade-Area Limitations

In the case of a trade-area (radius) restriction, the landlord, rather than the tenant, seeks the protection. The landlord should bear these considerations in mind:

- When all the trade-area limitations in a shopping center have the same mileage radius, it is easier for a court to find them to be arbitrary and capricious (since the market area for various tenants may differ markedly).
- Since the narrower the limitation, the greater the likelihood that a trade-area limitation will be enforced, the landlord should restrict the limitation to a radius within which a second store of the tenant would take significant sales away from the shopping center store.
- A preferable approach might be to have the lease provide that (for purposes of determining percentage rental) gross sales will include sales from other stores of the tenant within a prescribed marketing area.

[c] Use Clauses

These clauses were originally phrased in terms of price (e.g., low-priced or high-priced). The consent decrees between retailers and the FTC make it clear that the FTC regards this type of clause as an attempt to fix prices and therefore in violation of federal antitrust laws. Consequently, merchandise is currently being identified by such terms as "popular," "quality," "high-fashion," and the like.

With merchandising policies undergoing rapid changes in today's marketplace, tenants are more reluctant to accept restrictive-use clauses. Possible approaches are to

- Provide that only a specific amount of the square-foot area of the tenant's premises will be used for specific types of merchandise, thus permitting the tenant to expand his sales mix in the balance of the store.
- Add to a specific business purpose such terms as "amenities," or "similar or compatible merchandise." In view of the generality of the language, these terms may merely induce litigation when disputes arise.

The party (whether landlord or tenant) who actually drafts the restrictive clause should be particularly careful to avoid ambiguity. In interpreting such clauses, courts follow the usual legal rule that any ambiguity is to be interpreted against the person who actually wrote the language.

9.09 ASSIGNMENT OR SUBLEASE BY TENANT

The tenant can assign his leasehold interest to a third person provided the lease does not bar him from doing so or the landlord consents to the assignment. The assignee undertakes to make the tenant's rent payments and perform all of his lease obligations. In a true assignment, as contrasted to a sublease, the assignor (i.e., the original lessee) is freed from all of his obligations under the lease and the assignee (the new tenant) "steps into his shoes." To constitute a sublease rather than an assignment, the lessee must retain a reversionary interest in the remaining lease term. Most leases, whether commercial or residential, forbid assignments and subleases without the written permission or consent of the lessor (although in some cases, assignment is permitted to named or defined persons, for example, members of the lessee's family or a corporation in which the lessee has a specified stock interest).

The essential thrust of an assignment-and-sublease clause in a commercial lease will depend upon the nature of the leasehold. A short-term commercial tenant, who intends to do virtually no improvement or alteration of the premises, normally will be faced with the standard lease clause barring any sublease or assignment without the consent of the landlord. On the other hand, a tenant under a long-term lease who intends to spend perhaps $100,000 or more in altering and improving the premises is in a much stronger position to insist upon some right to sublease or assign in the event the original business cannot be continued, in order to recoup at least a portion of his investment. Of course, in an income-producing leasehold, that is, where the tenant intends to sublet space in order to create income, the right to sublet is a necessary part of the lease.

[1] Variations in the No-Sublease, No-Assignment Clause

While many leases contain simply a flat prohibition against any assignment or sublease by the tenant, there are a number of common variations that give the tenant some flexibility. The most frequently used of these variations is the addition to the language requiring the landlord's consent that "such consent shall not be withheld unreasonably." This is a deliberately ambiguous and vague phrase, since the landlord usually is unwilling to commit himself in advance to any definite consent. On the whole, the courts have deemed the refusal of consent to be reasonable whenever the landlord could point to a difference between the original tenant and the proposed tenant that would lessen the landlord's financial security or affect the reputation or operation of the building.

In addition to the "reasonable consent" clause, the prohibition against subleasing or assigning the lease may be subject to several limited exceptions:

☐ *Subleases to concessionaires.* In many discount operations, the prime tenant actually operates only a portion of the store himself, with the remainder subleased to concessionaires.

☐ *Sublease for similar use.* Sometimes the landlord will agree to a sublease or assignment provided the same use is continued by the new tenant.

☐ *Assignment to affiliated party.* The landlord may agree that an individual tenant or partnership may assign to a corporation in which the individual or the partners hold the controlling interest. Here the transfer is purely a matter of form, and the landlord usually will have no objection. However, the landlord should be sure that subsequent transfers of the corporate stock cannot be made without his consent; otherwise a loophole is created whereby new tenants can be substituted for the original one.

It should be noted that where the tenant is a well-known business name, the lease may not only prohibit assignment or subletting but may affirmatively require the tenant to carry on its business at the demised premises. The landlord's intention is either to be assured that the retail service will be available for other tenants or to benefit from the prestige of the "name" tenant.

[2] Conditions to an Assignment or Sublease

Whenever an assignment or sublease is permitted, the landlord usually will insist upon certain conditions being met. In general, they are as follows:

- The original tenant (in the event of an assignment) must remain liable for all of the obligations under the lease. (Of course, in the case of a sublease, a three-party relationship is created and the prime tenant remains liable in any event.)
- The tenant, at the time of the assignment or sublease, must have fulfilled all his obligations under the lease (and under any other agreements he may have with the landlord).
- An original, executed copy of the sublease or assignment must be delivered to the landlord.

[3] Landlord's Right to Cancel as Alternative to Sublease

During the recent period of rapidly rising rents, landlords found that tenants often were able to sublet the premises at a rental higher than the prime rental, with the prime tenant, of course, keeping the difference. In order to prevent the tenants from reaping what the landlords regarded as "windfall profits," many landlords, in writing new or renewal leases containing a right to sublet, added a clause giving the landlord the right to cancel the lease within a certain number of days after receiving notice from the tenant of his intention to sublease. Thus, the landlord retains the option of re-leasing the premises himself at a higher rental.

[4] Assignments and Subleases Under Ground Leases

The tenant under a ground lease should have the right to assign his leasehold interest. He should also be given the right to sublet all or any part of the leased premises. While the ground landlord may want a provision that his consent to an assignment or sublease will not be unreasonably withheld, this type of provision should be avoided by the ground tenant because, if the ground tenant obtains a mortgage, the lender will insist on an unrestricted right to assign or sublet in the event the tenant defaults and the lender takes over the property. In such event, the lender normally will want to be able to sell the leasehold or sublease it, as quickly as possible.

Under some circumstances, the ground tenant may prefer to sublet the entire premises rather than assign the leasehold interest. Where a prospective new user of the entire premises is not financially strong, the ground tenant will want the protection that a sublease rather than an assignment can give him in case of default. The necessity for gaining the ground landlord's approval of the sublease can be a serious hindrance to negotiations.

In any event, whether the ground tenant ultimately assigns or sublets, because of the difficulties involved in obtaining the ground landlord's consent and the possible extraction of a quid pro quo by the ground landlord each time his consent is required, it is very rare for the ground tenant to agree to a provision requiring the landlord's consent.

9.10 MORTGAGES BY LANDLORD OR TENANT

[1] Landlord (Fee) Mortgages

A lease may be made subordinate to any mortgages (or ground leases) affecting the demised premises, and the tenant may then reserve the right to cure the landlord's default under any such obligations, and recover any expense incurred. The tenant may be required to execute appropriate instruments for the landlord's mortgagee, and the landlord may reserve the option to cancel the lease if the tenant refuses to do so.

Under a lease that is subordinated to a fee mortgage, the rights of the lessee are subject to and limited by the terms of the mortgage and, accordingly, foreclosure of the mortgage loan either automatically terminates the lease or entitles the foreclosing lender, at its option, to terminate the lease depending on the law of the state involved. Where a lease is prior to a mortgage or where the lease is entitled to the benefits of a nondisturbance agreement, however, the lease survives the foreclosure of the mortgage loan.

[2] Tenant (Leasehold) Mortgages

Leases frequently contain provisions prohibiting the lessee from mortgaging his leasehold interest. Sometimes, a lease will provide that the lessee may not mortgage his leasehold interest without the lessor's written consent, instead of absolutely prohibiting such a mortgage. The parties may anticipate that the leasehold interest will be mortgaged by the lessee, for example, where high-ratio financing is sought and the leasehold interest is separated from the fee interest in order that each interest may be mortgaged separately. (See 6.15[1].)

Where the parties contemplate that the tenant will obtain a leasehold mortgage loan, the landlord may agree to subordinate his fee interest to the lien of the leasehold mortgage. This frequently occurs in ground leases, since the tenant is in a much more favorable position to obtain maximum financing if the fee is subordinated. Lenders regard a leasehold mortgage, where the fee is not subordinated to the mortgage, as a form of secondary financing, since a default by the tenant under his lease can result in the cancellation of the lease and the loss of the leasehold interest as security for the loan; and, also, if the tenant defaults under the leasehold mortgage and the mortgagee takes possession of the leasehold, the mortgagee will have to pay rent to the landlord since the rental obligation is superior to the mortgagee's interest. (See 6.11.)

The landlord may, of course, resist subordination of his fee interest, but he may consent to the arrangement because he does not want to lose a deal that in other respects he considers favorable or because he can negotiate a higher ground rental when he agrees to subordinate, since the tenant is then in a better position to create more financial leverage.

9.11 INSURANCE

Although frequently treated as "boilerplate," the insurance clause in a lease is a most important one. All insurance coverage can be divided into two classes: casualty (including consequential loss) insurance, which protects the insured against losses suffered by him personally; and liability insurance, which protects the insured against claims by others who have suffered damages or injury as a result of the insured's acts. Depending on the activities of the tenant, the length of the lease, and the size of the leased premises, the lease will require the tenant to insure the landlord and the leased premises against the various risks involved in operating the tenant's business.

[1] Casualty Insurance

The most common form of insurance the tenant may be required to carry is fire and extended coverage (E.C.). Extended coverage includes a variety of perils that may be just as likely to occur as fire, for example, windstorm and hail, explosion, riot and civil commotion, loss by aircraft and vehicles, smoke, and sprinkler leakage. For a modest additional premium, the tenant may have the landlord named as an additional insured on his own policy.

The building should always be insured against loss in the full amount of the building value. A landlord who permits tenants to reduce insurance to just meet the 80 percent co-insurance limitation makes a serious mistake. The impossibility of fixing the value of the building with precision makes it desirable to have a margin for error so that the landlord will not be self-insured for a portion of the loss. (Indeed, the purpose of the 80 percent co-insurance clause is precisely to create this cushion for the benefit of the insured.)

If a fire or other peril occurs, direct losses suffered by the insured are covered under the casualty policy. However, consequential losses will not be covered. The most common examples of consequential losses are the loss of rental income to a landlord when payments by tenants are abated because of a fire and the loss of profits to a businessman because of his inability to continue his business operations. Special policies have been created to cover such losses, including

- *Rent insurance,* which pays to the landlord amounts equal to the rentals lost because of the suspension of the rent obligation.
- *Business-interruption insurance,* which pays to the businessman all or a portion of profits lost because of interrupted business.
- *Leasehold insurance,* which compensates a tenant for the loss of the leasehold; that is, the measure of the tenant's loss is the difference between the rental he was paying and that which he will have to pay in order to secure alternate space.

The landlord will be interested in only the first of these types of coverage; the tenant may want to obtain the other coverages for his own benefit.

[2] Waiver of Subrogation

Frequently, if the landlord is to provide the fire insurance, the tenant will seek a waiver-of-subrogation clause. In the absence of such a clause, and in the event of a fire resulting from the negligence of the tenant, the landlord's insurer will be subrogated to the landlord's right to sue the tenant for damages. In most cases, an insurance company will agree to waive its right against the tenant if such is requested by its insurer, the landlord. While the likelihood of the tenant being sued is very slight, the protection afforded by a waiver-of-subrogation clause should be sought since it normally involves no cost to the tenant.

[3] Liability Insurance

A tenant will usually have liability coverage for himself, and in many cases the lease requires the tenant to provide such coverage for the landlord also. Although it is unlikely that the landlord would be liable to a third party injured or suffering damage on the premises of the tenant, the landlord customarily wants the protection of liability coverage, and the tenant very often can add the landlord as an additional insured on the tenant's policy for a small additional premium. Usually the liability policy will be either a comprehensive personal-liability policy or owner's, landlord's, and tenant's public-liability policy.

[4] Protective Provisions for the Landlord

The prudent landlord will provide a procedure in the lease to insure that insurance policies not only are obtained but are kept in effect. Thus, the tenant may be required to exhibit the policy to the landlord when the lease commences and thereafter provide copies of paid premium bills on each anniversary of the lease.

[5] Special Considerations Applicable to Ground Leases

The ground tenant will try for lease provisions that obligate him to repair, rebuild, or restore the buildings and improvements only if the damage or destruction results from a cause or casualty covered by insurance. The landlord will want his ground tenant to have that obligation regardless of whether or not the damage or destruction resulted from a cause or casualty covered by insurance. More often than not, the tenant will go along with the landlord's demands in this regard even though he stands to increase his insurance costs if he obtains an all-risk insurance policy that covers any eventuality, including subsidence.

The ground lease should require the insurance proceeds to be held in trust. The choice of the person or entity that will act as trustee depends on the negotiations of the parties. Where the proceeds are to be paid in trust to the mortgage holder, the tenant should insist that his lender's mortgage commitment require the mortgagee to make those proceeds available to him for the purpose of restoring, rebuilding, or repairing. The ground lease should set up the method by which the tenant obtains the proceeds for the stated purposes. Holdback provisions depend upon the negotiations of the parties.

9.12 INDEMNITY OF LANDLORD

An indemnity is an undertaking to shield another person from loss. (A hold-harmless clause, for practical purposes, has the same meaning.) With the possible exception (varying from state to state) of indemnifying another person against his own negligence, indemnity agreements are perfectly legal and enforceable. The party giving an indemnity (called the indemnitor and, typically, a tenant under a lease) should be aware that an indemnity is the equivalent of an insurance policy in that indemnification must be made even though the indemnitor is wholly free from fault. So when a tenant indemnifies the landlord against any loss resulting from use or occupation of the leased premises, the tenant may be liable for losses resulting from fire or other casualty whether or not the tenant was at fault and whether or not the landlord had insured against the risk.

[1] Ways in Which Indemnity Can Be Obtained

In order to limit his exposure, a tenant should seek to limit an indemnity clause in a lease in several ways:

☐ *Tenant's negligence.* The most limited form of indemnity requires the tenant to protect the landlord against loss arising from any negligent acts of the tenant, its employees, or invitees.

☐ *Tenant's acts.* The indemnity may be broadened to include any losses arising from any act of the tenant, its employees, or agents whether or not any negligence occurred.

☐ *All but landlord's acts.* In a net lease, the landlord may insist upon an indemnity against any loss to the landlord arising through the acts of any party other than the landlord himself.

☐ *Complete indemnity.* Under the broadest form of indemnity, the tenant agrees to assume full liability for all loss arising from use of or acts on the leased premises even if due to the negligent acts of the landlord or his employees. As the *Hogeland*[1] case indicates, such an indemnity will be upheld in most states where the landlord's negligence is "passive" rather than "active" or is not "willful negligence."

☐ *Insurance exception.* Regardless of the type of indemnity given, the indemnitor should seek to limit its undertaking to the amount of the uninsured loss. Thus, to the extent that either party has insured against the particular risk, the indemnity would not apply.

If the parties intend that the landlord, rather than the tenant, be responsible for specified losses to third parties at the leased premises, an indemnity in favor of the tenant can be inserted in the lease.

[2] Exculpatory Clause

Under an indemnity clause, a tenant agrees to substitute his liability for that of the landlord in connection with claims by third parties. Under an exculpatory clause, the tenant excuses the landlord's liability to the tenant arising from any act

---

[1] Hogeland v. Sibley, 366 N.E.2d 263 (N.Y. 1977).

of the landlord. Just as in the case of an indemnity, however, a landlord will remain liable for certain types or degrees of negligence notwithstanding an exculpatory clause in the lease.

9.13 DAMAGE OR DESTRUCTION

The parties should provide in their lease for the possibility that the leased premises, building, or shopping center, etc., in which the leased premises are situated may be damaged or destroyed by fire or other casualty or taken in whole or in part in the exercise of the power of eminent domain.

Under the common law and where the lease is silent on the subject, the landlord has no obligation to repair or restore the property, and there is no abatement of rent where premises are damaged or destroyed by fire or other casualty. In many jurisdictions, however, the harsh common-law rule no longer prevails, and in these jurisdictions a lease may be terminated or the tenant's obligation to continue to pay rent may be modified as a result of the destruction of, or severe damage to, the property. In any event, the parties may and should provide in their lease for the contingency and set out the rights and liabilities of the parties should the contingency occur.

Among the important items to cover are the circumstances under which repairs and restorations are to be made, which of the parties shall be obliged to make them, the extent of that obligation, who shall bear the cost, whether the lease may or shall be terminated and at whose option, and whether the rent is to be abated, apportioned, etc. Where the tenant is required to repair the damage, he may want a provision requiring the landlord to contribute to the cost, or he may want the right to use insurance proceeds for that purpose, the right to obtain a lien against the premises, or the right to extend the lease to permit him to amortize his costs. If the landlord has the duty to repair or restore, he may want the option to terminate the lease (e.g., where the cost will exceed a specified amount or at his unfettered election), or he may want the right to extend the term by the length of time required to do the work.

In negotiating and drafting lease provisions concerning the effect of damage to, or destruction of, demised premises resulting from fire or other casualty on the rights of the parties to the lease, the parties and their professional consultants should be aware of the income tax implications of casualty losses. (See 3.09[2].)

9.14 CONDEMNATION

[1] In General

If a lease is silent on the subject of condemnation, the tenant generally will be permitted to recover the value of the leasehold. Generally, the value of the leasehold is the present value of the difference between the contract rental (i.e., the rental to be paid by the tenant over the term of the lease) and the economic rental (i.e., the rental the premises could command in the current market). The landlord then is entitled to receive the value of the fee interest minus the value of the leasehold received by the tenant. Since the setting of such values is a time-consuming and expensive task, it is preferable for the parties to agree upon a formula in the lease agreement.

The landlord generally seeks a clause providing that in the event of condemnation, the lease is terminated, the tenant is liable for no further payments, and the landlord is entitled to the entire condemnation award. Where the tenant has a relatively short-term lease and has made no substantial investment in the premises, such a provision may be satisfactory to both parties. (In any case, the tenant will be entitled to seek an award covering his "trade fixtures.")

[2] Total Condemnation

When the entire property is taken by eminent domain so that no possibility exists of continuing the tenant's business, the simplest provision is that noted above; that is, the lease terminates and the landlord receives the entire award. However, where the tenant has made a substantial investment in alterations or improvements, the tenant will seek to be reimbursed in whole or in part for such investment. The problem is that the tenant's improvements very often will not increase the total value of the parcel, so that it becomes a matter of dividing up the same proceeds, which would be paid in any case. The tenant's argument to the landlord (when negotiating the lease) is that the tenant will be unwilling to make substantial improvements (which, in the likely event that no condemnation occurs, eventually will accrue to the landlord) unless the tenant can recoup part of his investment if the lease terminates earlier than anticipated. A compromise position is to set up an amortization schedule for the improvements (e.g., in a twenty-year lease, the improvements will be amortized at the rate of 5 percent a year), with the tenant to be entitled to receive the unamortized cost of the improvements if condemnation occurs before the lease ends. This basic compromise can be varied in any number of ways.

A second point that should be covered is the date at which the lease will terminate if condemnation occurs. Often, notice of condemnation will be given some considerable time before the building is actually taken by the condemning authority. The landlord, naturally, will want the lease to continue as long as possible. The tenant, who will usually be seeking other quarters, will want to be able to terminate upon giving a minimum period of notice.

[3] Partial Taking

With respect to a partial taking of the premises, the general rule is that if the lease is silent on the subject, the tenant is entitled to compensation for the diminished value of his leasehold interest. The better practice is for the parties to include a specific provision in the lease concerning the effect of a partial condemnation of the premises.

The four issues that generally must be resolved with respect to a partial taking are as follows:

☐ *Cancellation in certain cases.* If the partial taking involves condemnation of more than a designated percentage of the leased premises, the lease may provide for an automatic termination of the lease, or that either landlord or tenant shall have the option to cancel. This is in anticipation of the possibility that such a small portion of the premises will remain that continuing commercial use will not be feasible.

☐ *Restoration of premises.* If the premises require restoration, one party should be designated to do the work. Usually, the cost of restoration will come out of the condemnation proceeds. If the cost may exceed the amount of proceeds, the lease should provide for the manner for raising the additional money.

☐ *Abatement or diminution of rent.* If, as is usual in the case of a partial taking, the tenant has no right to any condemnation proceeds, the tenant will seek to have the rent abated during the period of restoration when he is unable to carry on his business. In addition, he will seek to have a clause providing that the rental following restoration shall be reduced by the same proportion as the leased premises have been reduced by the taking. To the extent that the condemnation proceeds received by the landlord have been used up in restoration, the landlord will resist any diminution of the rent, since his overall investment remains the same.

☐ *Allocation of proceeds.* If condemnation proceeds are to be allocated between landlord and tenant, an appropriate formula should be specified in the lease. Apportionment on a square-foot basis may or may not be equitable. For example, if 10 percent of the demised premises is taken, it does not follow that the tenant will lose 10 percent of his business and thus be entitled to receive 10 percent of the proceeds.

[4] Tax Considerations

The following should be noted with respect to the income tax consequences to the parties where the property is condemned or where it is damaged or destroyed. There may be an involuntary conversion of property by reason of destruction, theft, condemnation, or imminence of condemnation. If a loss results, the loss is recognized for tax purposes, but if a gain results, the gain is not recognized if the requirements of the Internal Revenue Code are complied with. Under the Code, if the money received as a result of the conversion is invested within the proper time in property that is similar or related in service or use to the converted property, the gain on the conversion is recognized only to the extent that the amount received is greater than the cost of the replacement property. And, where an involuntary conversion results from condemnation or the threat or imminence of condemnation, the money (i.e., the proceeds of the condemnation award) may be invested in property that is similar or related in service or use to the old property or in property that is of like kind to that property.

In the case of an involuntary conversion of leased property, the modern approach to determining the suitability of the replacement property for purposes of obtaining nonrecognition of gain is to focus on how the original and the replacement properties are used by the landlord. However, even if both the original and the replacement properties are used by the landlord for rental purposes, the replacement property may not be considered acceptable if the landlord's duties, responsibilities, or functions are materially different with respect to the two properties. For this reason, a hotel has been ruled not to be an acceptable replacement for an office building.

Tenants as well as landlords may be in a position to benefit from the nonrecognition of gain resulting from an involuntary conversion. Thus, where a tenant realizes a gain as a result of a condemnation award because of his leasehold interest in the building that was condemned, he may be entitled to nonrecognition treatment of that gain where he acquires qualified replacement property within the required time.

9.15 DEFAULT BY TENANT

Any act, conduct, or omission on the part of the tenant which, under the terms of the lease permits the landlord at his election to terminate the lease and, in addition or as an alternative, seek damages or other remedies as specified in the lease or by statute, is a default or breach of the lease.

Generally, leases carry a provision listing so-called events of default on tenant's part, which give the landlord the right to cancel upon the occurrence of an event of default.

Leases normally do not contain default clauses against the landlord either because the lease is net (so that the landlord undertakes no obligations to the tenant during the lease term), or because if the landlord breaches any of his obligations under the lease (e.g., his duty to maintain and repair, provide utility service, etc.), the tenant's only remedy is that given to him by law, which is to sue for damages or to construe the landlord's action as amounting to an eviction permitting the tenant to consider the lease terminated.

Defaults by a tenant under a lease normally are classified as (1) failure to pay rent or other money due under the lease; or (2) failure to comply with any other obligations or promises under the lease. In the case of monetary defaults, the lease normally permits the landlord to declare a default after a specified number of days has passed since the due date and without notice to the tenant that the money has not been paid. In the case of other defaults, however, the landlord normally must notify the tenant that a default has, in fact, occurred and give the tenant a specified number of days to cure the default before the lease can be declared terminated.

Leases generally list the bankruptcy of the tenant as an event of default and, in this regard, the relevant provisions of the Bankruptcy Reform Act of 1978 [2] must be considered. Under the Act, a lease clause permitting the landlord to terminate the lease in the event of the tenant's bankruptcy is not enforceable. Instead, the trustee in bankruptcy has the right either to affirm the lease and continue in possession or to terminate it. However, if the tenant was in default under the lease before the bankruptcy, the trustee must cure the default and provide "adequate assurance" that the tenant's obligations will be met in the future. In addition, if the trustee wishes to assign the lease to another party, adequate assurance of future compliance with lease terms must be given, whether or not any prior lease defaults had occurred.

The purpose of the provision is to permit a bankrupt tenant to continue in business if survival seems possible. At the same time, the landlord is assured, at least on paper, that rent will continue to be paid and other defaults corrected.

---

[2] Pub. L. No. 95-598, 92 Stat. 2549, 11 U.S.C.A. §§ 101–151326.

Suppose the landlord goes bankrupt. Can his bankruptcy trustee terminate the lease and force his tenant to vacate? Under the earlier provisions of the Bankruptcy Act, the landlord's trustee in bankruptcy had the right to reject leases, but was subject to the provision that the rejection "does not deprive the lessee of his estate."

No one knows precisely what the last phrase means. Some years ago, when the Penn Central went bankrupt, tenants feared that the trustee would seek to terminate (in effect, renegotiate at higher rentals) some of the long-term leaseholds on Park Avenue in New York City, occupied by large office buildings. This never happened, but the legal uncertainty remained.

The 1978 law seems to eliminate this problem by providing that if the landlord's trustee does disaffirm a lease, the tenant has the option of

- Treating the lease as terminated and vacating the premises; or
- Reaffirming the lease, subject to the condition that it will perform the landlord's covenants (e.g., duty to clean the premises) and deduct the cost of doing so from the rent due.

Suppose the tenant holds a ground lease subject to a leasehold mortgage and seeks to terminate the lease. Will this wipe out the leasehold mortgagee's security (precisely the fear that existed during the Penn Central bankruptcy)? This should not be a problem for a number of reasons. First, leasehold mortgages usually are given only in net-lease situations where the landlord has no obligations and consequently where its trustee in bankruptcy would have no basis for disaffirming the lease. Also, the leasehold mortgage usually contains a clause prohibiting the tenant from canceling without the lender's consent.

Suppose the landlord of a multitenant building defaults. Presumably, each tenant has the right to its own election. This could lead to a complicated situation.

9.16 TERMINATION OF LEASE; SURRENDER OF PREMISES

A written lease for a fixed term automatically terminates at the end of the period specified, without notice being given by either party. A lease that sets no fixed term but provides for rent payments at fixed intervals (typically month to month) usually will require either party to give notice in order to terminate the lease.

[1] Clause Providing for Surrender of Premises by Tenant

Although not necessary, a lease clause providing for surrender of the premises by the tenant on termination of the lease generally is included. The important part of such a clause is that dealing with fixtures or improvements that have been made or installed by the tenant during the lease term. Generally, such fixtures and improvements are handled in one of three ways:

☐ *Must be removed.* The lease may require the tenant to restore the premises to their condition prior to the lease term, except for normal wear and tear; that is, the tenant must remove all of his improvements and fixtures, or be liable for damages if he fails to do so.

☐ *May be removed.* The tenant may be given the right to remove any improvements or fixtures if he wishes to do so; if he fails to do so, they will be deemed abandoned to the landlord, and the tenant will be liable for no damages for failure to remove.

☐ *May not remove.* Where the improvements substantially add to the value of the premises, or where their removal would cause problems to other tenants or otherwise be inconvenient for the landlord, the lease may require the tenant to leave all or certain described fixtures and improvements. (Usually, trade fixtures, which are used by the tenant in connection with his business, are removable by him unless the lease specifies otherwise.)

If the landlord is holding a security deposit, he frequently will provide that such deposit can be used to remedy any defaults by the tenant that occur upon surrender of the premises.

[2] Holdover Tenants

A tenant who remains in possession of the premises beyond the termination of the lease is deemed a holdover. At common law, a holdover could be treated as a renewal of the lease for a term up to one year. In many states, this rule has been abrogated and a holdover is deemed to be a tenant on a monthly basis.

To avoid the confusion that may arise where the tenant is a holdover, the lease should specifically define whether a holdover tenant is deemed a monthly tenant, a yearly tenant, or otherwise.

Where the lease contains a tax-escalation clause, specific provision should be made rendering the tenant liable for increased taxes during his holdover term.

Where it is contemplated that the tenant may sublease the property, he should insist on a provision relieving him from liability resulting from a holdover. In the same clause, the landlord may insist on language prohibiting the principal tenant from subleasing the property beyond the term of the initial lease.

9.17 OPTION TO RENEW

A lease provision dealing with the right to extend or renew on the expiration of the original term should set out just how the election or option must be exercised.

While the right or option to renew is always important, it is of special importance where the tenant is a business or commercial tenant. The success of a retail operation, for example, may result in large part from the location of the business; and even where initially the location was not crucial, moving to another location once a business has become successful is almost always costly in terms of lost business.

In drafting a renewal provision, the following considerations should be covered:

☐ *Renewal term.* The tenant may be given an option for a single renewal term or a series of terms.

☐ *Renewal rental.* Generally, the rental for the renewal term or terms is specified in the lease agreement. Most often, the rental will be stepped up during the renewal term on the theory that the tenant will renew because the business is profitable and so the landlord is entitled to more rent. Sometimes the rent may remain flat during the renewal term.

When the parties are unable or unwilling to agree on a renewal rental at the time the lease is executed, they may provide that the rental is to be fixed at the time of renewal by one or more outside parties. As under all such reappraisal or arbitration clauses, the method of selection of the parties and the standards by which they are to reach their decision should be clearly indicated. A common standard for setting the renewal rental is "the prevailing fair rental for similar property at the time of renewal" or "the highest rental the landlord could secure from other responsible parties at the time of the option."

A third alternative is to provide that the amount of rental during the renewal period will be set by agreement of the parties. The majority rule is that such a renewal provision is void for uncertainty. But some states follow the rule that the court may set a reasonable rental in order to sustain the clause.

☐ *No-fault condition.* Most leases provide that a tenant in default under any provision of the lease cannot exercise an option to renew. Since the general rule is that all lease clauses are independent of one another, the absence of such a condition would permit a tenant in default to exercise an option to renew, an occurrence that would not be to the liking of the landlord.

☐ *Manner of giving notice of renewal.* The tenant normally must give notice of his intention to renew at a designated period of time prior to the end of the initial lease term. The landlord may seek a period as long as a year in advance so that he will have adequate time to find a new tenant if no notice is given; the tenant will prefer to make his decision as near to the lease expiration date as possible.

Occasionally, the lease clause will provide that a renewal will be automatic unless notice to the contrary is delivered to the landlord by the tenant within a specified time prior to the expiration of the initial term. The landlord may favor such a clause because it puts the burden on the tenant to terminate the lease. Sometimes a tenant operating a large number of stores (e.g., a chain supermarket) will prefer the automatic-renewal clause because it eliminates the possibility that renewal notices will not be sent out through oversight or error. In at least one state (New York), the landlord under a lease containing an automatic-renewal clause is obligated by statute to notify the tenant prior to the expiration of the period in which the tenant's notice of intention not to renew must be given. The purpose of the statute, of course, is to favor a tenant who through carelessness or otherwise is not aware of his need to notify the landlord if he wishes the lease to end.

An alternative to automatic renewal is to fix a longer initial term and give the tenant a right to cancel at designated intervals. In this way, the burden of giving notice is shifted from the landlord to the tenant.

9.18 OPTION TO PURCHASE; RIGHT OF FIRST REFUSAL

Under the option to purchase, the tenant has complete freedom to exercise or not to exercise the option during the designated option period. On the other hand, under a right of first refusal, the tenant's right must first be triggered by an offer from a third party to the landlord to purchase the property. Only at that point may the tenant seek to purchase the property by matching the third-party offer. The theory underlying both the option to purchase and the right of first refusal is that the tenant should have some power to retain possession of his business premises. If he anticipates that he will be unable to renew his lease either because the present owner has other plans for the property or because a third party wishes to purchase the property for his own use, the tenant can protect the goodwill he has built up by purchasing the fee interest. However, the clause requires no showing of purpose by the tenant; he can exercise his option or right of first refusal because he believes the property is a good investment or for any other reason.

[1] Option to Purchase

Negotiating an option to purchase is virtually the same as negotiating an actual contract to sell, since the terms set forth in the option clause will be binding on the parties just as would be a contract of sale. Following are some of the considerations that apply in negotiating and drafting the clause:

☐ *Price.* The most desirable procedure is to establish a set price in the option clause. An alternative to a fixed price is a provision for an appraisal at the time the option is exercised. If an appraisal is to be made, the method of selecting the appraisers and the standard by which they are to establish value should be set forth in detail.

☐ *Other details of the sale.* Sometimes the option clause will merely specify that the terms of the contract of sale shall be those that are customary for sales of similar property in the area. This may suffice when the property has no unusual features and where local customs are well-established; on the other hand, the dangers of such a clause are obvious. The elements that should be detailed, if possible, are the following:

- Description of the property
- Purchase price
- Manner of paying the price
- Right of the purchaser to obtain financing
- Method of handling any existing mortgages on the property
- Liens and encumbrances to which the title will be subject
- Period between exercise of the option and the closing date
- Closing procedure, costs, and adjustments
- Form of deed

☐ *When option exercisable.* An option can be exercisable at any time during the lease term, only upon termination of the lease or only during specified periods of the lease. If the lease permits renewal, it should be clear if the option is exercisable during that period.

☐ *How to exercise the option.* Usually, the tenant exercises the option by delivering written notice to the landlord of such exercise.

[2] Right of First Refusal

The right of first refusal or first-option clause is frequently more complex than the purchase option because of the involvement of a third party. Under the first-refusal right, the tenant is permitted to match the offer made by a third party, both in price and other terms of the purchase. Once the tenant matches the offer of the third party, the landlord cannot then refuse to go through with the sale or seek to increase the price by obtaining another offer. If the landlord fails to sell the premises to the third party after the tenant's refusal to match the offer, the right of first refusal probably is not extinguished and will be triggered by any subsequent offer. However, in order to remove any doubt on this point, the clause in the lease should so specifically provide.

In drafting the right of first refusal, the landlord should be careful to exclude from the operation of the clause certain types of transfers. For example, in the normal situation, the parties do not intend that the tenant be given the right of first refusal if an individual landlord transfers property to a corporate entity, or if a corporate landlord transfers property to its shareholders or to a subsidiary or affiliated corporation, or if the property passes by will or intestate succession. This result can be achieved generally by making the first-refusal right applicable only to a sale to an outside party.

Among other provisions of the first-option clause, the manner and form of notice that the landlord is to give to the tenant of a third-party offer should be specified. The time within which the tenant may decide whether or not to meet the offer must be indicated (the time should be sufficient so that the tenant can arrange financing, if necessary).

A question that frequently arises in the interpretation of such clauses is whether the tenant need match only the net offer (after brokerage commissions) of the third party on the theory that a sale by the landlord to the tenant will not involve any brokerage commission. The landlord usually will insist that the tenant must meet the gross purchase price, arguing that the landlord, not the tenant, is entitled to any saving of brokerage commission. (Alternatively, the landlord may in fact be obligated to pay a brokerage commission if the right of first refusal is exercised, either pursuant to a commission agreement in connection with the sale to the third party or in connection with a brokerage agreement made with a leasing broker when the lease was initially entered into.)

Finally, it should be noted that rights of first refusal often make it more difficult for the landlord to sell the property. Purchasers who discover that the property is subject to such a right frequently become disenchanted because of the possibility of delay. In addition, a third party is unwilling to act as a "stalking horse," doing the negotiating for the ultimate benefit of the tenant. Thus, while a right-of-first-refusal clause is often very beneficial to the tenant, it is usually avoided by the landlord wherever possible.

9.19 BROKERAGE COMMISSIONS

A lease should not be executed until the landlord and tenant agree as to whose obligation it is to pay the broker's commission. In most jurisdictions, it is sufficient for a broker to earn his commission if he brings the parties together and they agree as to the material terms of the lease. In the absence of an agreement to the contrary, the landlord would then be liable for the commission. For these reasons, an agreement with the broker setting forth the amount of the commission should be entered into before any material negotiations ensue.

Regardless of whether the landlord or the tenant is responsible for the broker's commission, the following important items should be covered:

- Is the broker entitled to a commission for the initial term only based on the basic or fixed rent, or is he entitled to a commission for the initial term and any extended term or terms?
- Does the party responsible for paying the commission prefer to permit the broker to take a part interest in a joint venture or partnership in place of cash as his commission?
- Is the broker's fee payable if the landlord fails or refuses to execute the lease after it has been put in final form or the landlord fails to satisfy the conditions of the lease that are within the landlord's control?
- Is the broker's fee payable where the tenant fails to execute the lease after it has been put in final form or the tenant fails to satisfy the conditions of the lease that are within the tenant's control?
- What is the amount of the commission and how is it to be paid?
- What happens to any unpaid portion of the fee if the lease is executed and all the conditions are fulfilled but the tenant subsequently defaults under the lease?

9.20 PARKING FACILITIES

In the suburbs and to a large degree in city areas, adequate parking often is crucial to successful retail operation. Consequently, the tenant under a commercial lease should be sure that a clause in the lease specifically deals with parking facilities. If the tenant occupies an entire building, he normally will want the leased premises to include any parking space adjacent to the building. Then the tenant is assured of exclusive use of the space unless the lease specifically provides otherwise.

[1] Use of Parking Facilities by Several Tenants

When the landlord retains possession of parking space that is to be used by several tenants, the tenant may seek to have a separate portion of the lot specifically allocated to him. Since such a practice prevents maximum use of the space, the landlord will usually refuse. The tenant should then satisfy himself that the parking space is adequate for all the tenants. A special consideration relates to the parking of employees' cars. Such parking may be prohibited absolutely, in order to increase the space available for customers, may be permitted only at certain times, or only in those spaces furthest removed from the retail areas.

The lease also should protect the tenant against the possibility that the landlord may construct additional stores that also will have access to the parking space. To the extent they will create excessive congestion in the parking area, the business of all tenants will suffer.

[2] Maintenance and Repair of Parking Facilities

If the leased premises include the parking space, the tenant will usually be responsible for its maintenance and repair. If the parking space is to be used in common, the lease should indicate whether the landlord or the tenants as a group will be responsible for maintenance and repair, and if the landlord is so responsible, whether the tenants have a duty to contribute toward the cost of so doing. The following items should be covered specifically:

- Cleaning
- Snowplowing
- Striping
- Lighting
- Signs
- Police protection
- Traffic signals, if any

9.21 AMORTIZING, SELLING, AND MODIFYING LEASES

A lease, once executed by landlord and tenant, fixes their relationship for the entire term of the agreement. However, this relationship may be altered or terminated by mutual consent at any time. If this occurs, tax consequences will result with respect to any payments that are made at the time of the lease alteration or termination, the tenant's initial lease acquisition, or improvement costs that are being amortized by him. The following is a brief summary of these tax consequences:

[1] Calculation of Cost (Basis) of Lease

A tenant acquiring a leasehold will normally incur certain costs that are not immediately deductible, for example, title policy costs, broker's commission, attorney's fees, appraisal expenses, etc. In addition, the tenant may pay a bonus to the landlord for the lease or may purchase the lease from a prior tenant. With the exception of advance rentals applicable against specific future months, such costs are amortizable by the tenant over the life of the lease. Thus, in a ten-year lease, 10 percent of the acquisition costs would be deductible during each year. (The rule is the same whether the tenant uses the cash or accrual method of accounting.)

Suppose the lease contains an option to renew. In that case, the tenant may still amortize his acquisition cost over the original term, provided that 75 percent of the acquisition costs are allocable to the original lease term. Otherwise, the amortization period includes both the original term and the option period. The allocation, to stand up, probably should be based on the opinion of a qualified appraiser.

Even if 75 percent of the acquisition costs are attributable to the original lease term, the tenant may still have to spread his amortization over the initial plus renewal term if the facts show with reasonable certainty that the lease will be renewed. For example, if the renewal rental steps down very sharply from the initial rental and represents a bargain rate, it is likely that IRS would argue the reasonable certainty of renewal exists.

[2] Depreciation of Improvements Made by Tenant

Improvements made by the tenant to the leased premises do not constitute rent unless the lease specifically makes them such. Consequently, the tenant "owns" the improvements and he may depreciate them over the lease term. Here again, a question arises if the lease contains an option to renew. The Internal Revenue Code provides, as a general rule, that

- The renewal period is to be included in the depreciation period if, when the improvement is made, the remaining term of the lease excluding any renewal period is less than 60 percent of the useful life of the improvements; but
- The renewal period is not to be included (regardless of the 60 percent rule) if the tenant can show that it is more probable than not that the renewal option will not be exercised.

Example: The tenant enters into a ten-year lease with a ten-year renewal option. He immediately constructs an improvement with a twenty-year life. Since the original term is less than 60 percent of the useful life (ten-year term is 50 percent of twenty-year life), the building must be depreciated over the initial plus renewal terms of twenty years. However, if the tenant can establish that he probably will not renew the lease, he can depreciate over ten years.

Regardless of whether the tenant depreciates the improvement, when they revert to the landlord at the end of the lease term, the landlord realizes no income as a result.

[3] Sale or Exchange of Lease

A sale of the lease by the tenant to the landlord is treated as a lease cancellation. Sale by the tenant to a third party will cause the tenant to realize gain or loss, depending upon whether the sale price exceeds or is less than the tenant's basis for the lease.

To a tenant who uses the leased premises to carry on a trade or business or who is in the business of subleasing space for profit, the lease is trade or business property, so Section 1231 of the Code applies, with the result that any gain is capital in nature, with any loss being ordinary and therefore deductible against ordinary income. One who sells a lease of his residence will realize capital gain or capital loss. (However, see 9.21[5] for a discussion of recapture of depreciation.)

If a landlord "sells" a lease without selling his interest in the property (e.g., his fee ownership), the transaction is viewed as merely an assignment of the right to receive rents and the proceeds of the sale are deemed to be a loan to the landlord, who must continue to report the rent as income.

A lease of premises used for productive use in a trade or business can be exchanged in a tax-free transaction for property "of like kind" under Section 1031 of the Code. If the lease term has thirty years or more to run, it can be exchanged tax-free for a fee (ownership) interest.

[4] Lease Cancellation

Lease cancellation can be handled in one of the following ways, with the tax treatment varying with the method of cancellation:

☐ *Payment by landlord to tenant.* If the landlord pays the tenant to cancel the lease, the tenant treats the payments the same as if received from a third party. The landlord treats the payment as a capital expenditure that must be amortized under the following circumstances:

- If the landlord then makes a new lease, over the term of the new lease.
- If the landlord then puts up a new building, over its useful life.
- If the landlord then uses the property himself, over the remaining term of the canceled lease.

☐ *Payment by tenant to landlord.* If the tenant pays the landlord to cancel the lease, the payments are ordinary income to the landlord and (assuming the lease is for business premises) an ordinary business expense to the tenant, and hence immediately deductible.

☐ *No payment.* If the lease is canceled with no payment by either party, there are no tax consequences unless landlord or tenant has a positive basis in the lease. If either does, he may take a tax loss.

[5] Recapture of Tenant Depreciation

As noted above, a tenant who incurs costs in acquiring a lease, or who pays for improvements to the real estate, may be able to amortize his costs over the initial lease term, even though he has one or more options to renew. However, if he later sells or cancels the lease, a part of the payment he receives may be converted from capital gain into ordinary income through the impact of the depreciation-recapture rule of Section 1250 of the Code.

In brief, the rule is this: If the tenant receives a payment for selling or canceling the lease, he must treat as "excess depreciation" the difference between the amortization he actually has taken and the amortization that he would have taken had he included the renewal period. (However, the addition of the renewal period cannot extend the amortization period by more than two thirds.)

> *Example:* A tenant executes a lease for a ten-year term plus a ten-year renewal term. He amortizes costs over the initial term (i.e., at the rate of 10 percent per year). He sells the lease before the end of the initial term. Then he must recalculate his amortization to include the renewal term (but without extending the original term more than two thirds). Since two thirds of ten years is six and two-thirds years, the new amortization period is sixteen and two-thirds years, or an annual rate of 6 percent. The excess depreciation (10 percent a year minus 6 percent a year) is applied to payments the tenant receives to determine how much is ordinary income and how much is capital gain.

[6] Lease Modifications

Suppose a lease is modified during its life with respect to the term, amount of rent, or terms of occupancy? Any of the following modifications may have a tax impact on the parties, of which they should take note in advance.

☐ *Changing the lease term.* Extending a lease term by modifying the lease (rather than by exercising an option to renew) permits the tenant to amortize any outstanding acquisition costs over the newly extended life of the lease. In the more unusual case of a reduced term, the opposite would happen and the tenant would increase his annual amortization to enable him to write off all of his costs over the lease term.

☐ *Changing the rent.* Future changes in rent have no immediate tax effect. A retroactive change (for example, if a mathematical error has been made) that results in additional payments by or reimbursement to the tenant will be additional income or rental expense, as appropriate.

☐ *Changing treatment of leasehold improvements.* Normally, improvements made by the tenant are not income to the landlord, as already noted. The parties might decide partway through the term, however, to treat the fair market value of an improvement as additional rental, in which case the landlord would realize income and the tenant could deduct, as an expense, the undepreciated cost.

A tenant who puts up an improvement paid for with borrowed funds normally is better off taking the depreciation deduction for the improvement rather than negotiating for a rent credit to recoup his equity investment. But if circumstances make the rent credit more valuable to the tenant after the term has begun, he may seek to modify the lease to obtain the rent credit.

☐ *Changing the premises or terms of occupancy.* If the leased premises are reduced from two floors to one floor, the modification is treated as a partial lease cancellation so that payments and unamortized costs attributable to the portion given up will have the tax consequences described for lease cancellations.

[7] Abandonment of Leased Premises

Suppose the tenant vacates the premises before the end of the term and continues to pay rent? He may be able to establish an abandonment loss for the unrecovered cost of any leasehold improvements. One tenant who moved his office to another location and could show that the improvements were not thereafter used by anyone was able to take the loss. Can the landlord claim a loss where the tenant abandons the property and fails to pay a percentage rental (because he is doing no sales at the premises) although continuing to pay the base rental? In one case where the loss was not allowed, the court accepted the theory of the landlord but ruled that the landlord had not established his rent loss with sufficient precision.

9.22 NET LEASES AS INVESTMENTS

To this point in our discussion of leasing, we have concentrated on the terms of the lease instrument itself and the various ways in which the lease apportions rights and obligations between the two parties who share the rights of ownership (in essence, the tenant having the right of immediate possession and the landlord having the right of reversion when the lease terminates).

[1] Circumstances Giving Rise to Net Leases

The two legal interests that are associated with a lease relationship, now to be considered in an investment and financing context, are

- The leasehold interest held by the tenant.
- The fee interest held by the landlord out of which the leasehold has been carved.

In the great majority of leasing relationships, the landlord regards himself as an owner-operator; that is, he is in the business of leasing space and in exchange for rental payments, he undertakes to perform specified obligations—for example, providing heating and air conditioning, cleaning services, security, and the operation of the common areas of the building such as the lobbies and corridors. This type of leasing relationship exists in almost all cases of multitenant occupancy, whether apartment house, office building or retail space. The lease entered into between the landlord and his tenants is known as a gross lease because the rentals paid by the tenant cover not only the ultimate profit kept by the landlord but the operating expenses of the building.

However, in many instances the landlord seeks to disassociate himself entirely from the operating responsibilities of the property. Instead, he prefers to play a purely passive investment role, merely collecting his rent as owner of the fee interest while having another assume all responsibility for operating the property. The lease between such a passive owner-investor and a tenant is known as a net lease because the rental represents only the landlord's profit, with the tenant responsible for all operating expenses (in addition to the net rental). Such a net rental situation generally arises in one of two contexts:

☐ *Sandwich (operating) lease.* In the first situation, a landlord may seek to lease an entire building (or vacant land) to another (the operator), who will then sublease the space in the building to others (occupancy tenants). The operator (so called because he holds the operating position) keeps as his profit the difference between subrentals collected from the occupancy tenants and the net rental paid to the landlord. (This is discussed in more detail in 9.23.)

☐ *Sale-leasebacks.* In the second situation, the user of property (typically, a business firm) sells property used in its trade or business to an investor and simultaneously leases the property back for continued use by the tenant. Again, the landlord-investor receives a net rental and assumes no responsibility for operating the property. The primary motive of the user in such case is to free up capital that can be better used in its primary business. (This is discussed in more detail in 9.24.)

[2] Negotiating a Net Lease

As already noted, where the lease requires the lessee to assume the responsibility of paying the operating expenses of the property and the rent is to be received by the lessor entirely net to him, the rent is called a net rent and the lease is referred to as a net lease. Sometimes a distinction is made between a net lease, a net-net lease, and a net-net-net lease. As these terms are commonly understood, where the distinction is made, under a net lease, the lessee pays all operating expenses but not the real estate taxes; under a net-net lease, the lessee pays the operating expenses and the insurance premiums; and under the net-net-net lease, the lessee pays the operating expenses, the insurance premiums, and the real estate taxes. Under some leases, the lessee is even required to pay the debt service under an existing mortgage on the fee interest as well.

In any event, regardless of the nomenclature used, where a lease is drawn so as to be completely "net" to the landlord, in addition to paying the stipulated rental, the tenant assumes the obligation to pay all charges with respect to the premises including property taxes, insurance, repairs, maintenance, and all other expenditures incurred in the use and operation of the premises.

Where a landlord has a completely net lease with a tenant with a high-credit rating, he gets what virtually amounts to a guaranteed income free of management obligations for the duration of the lease.

Property subject to a net lease can offer an excellent investment opportunity. Thus, for example, an investor may purchase the fee interest in real estate, which is subject to a long-term net lease to a high-quality tenant. Commonly, this type of transaction occurs when a company buys land, erects a building on the land according to its own specifications, and then sells the property to an investor with a simultaneous leaseback to itself so that it can occupy and use the building for its own purposes. Or, a builder may purchase land, erect a building on it to his tenant's specifications, and then sell the property to an investor. In either case, the investor's rental return is protected primarily by the tenant's credit and only secondarily by the real estate itself. In addition to a safe rental income stream, the investor can reasonably anticipate that the real estate will have grown substantially in value by the time the lease will terminate and, indeed, this anticipated gain represents much of the attractiveness of the investment.

The major points that should be covered when drafting net-lease provisions include:

☐ *Repair.* Tenant should be responsible for all costs of repair whether external or internal, structural or nonstructural, ordinary or extraordinary.

☐ *Restoration.* Tenant may be given the right to cancel if the premises are substantially destroyed, but not merely because the tenant's improvement is damaged.

☐ *Improvements and alterations.* Alterations and improvements should be made by the tenant subject to both the landlord's and the mortgagee's consent and the tenant should be required to give security for satisfactory completion of improvements and for restoration of the property to its original condition when the lease terminates.

☐ *Taxes.* All taxes, water charges, etc., should be paid by the tenant, including all assessments, whether recurring or special. Periodic deposits by the tenant to prevent default should also be provided for.

☐ *Mortgage.* In determining the net rental, all obligations imposed by the mortgage on the property should be accounted for. If the property is not mortgaged, provision should be made for including the obligation of a mortgage if one is placed on the property and subordinating the lease to the mortgage. Provision can also be made for the mortgagee to give the tenant a recordable instrument stating that, in case of foreclosure, the tenant will not be joined as a party defendant if he is not in default.

☐ *Insurance.* Insurance policies should be carried in the names of both landlord and tenant and should be paid for by tenant. Rent insurance covering at least one year's rent, taxes, and insurance premiums may be required as well. Where there is a mortgage on the property, loss, if any, should be payable to the extent of the mortgagee's interest and the tenant should be required to provide additional insurance if the mortgagee requires it. In case of loss, the landlord will want the mortgagee to make the proceeds available to restore the premises.

☐ *Condemnation.* In case of a complete taking of mortgaged property, the condemnation award should go first to the mortgagee to the extent of the value of land and improvements, with a fixed sum to the tenant for the value of the leasehold and the improvements. The remainder, if any, should go to the landlord and tenant according to a predetermined formula. In case of a partial taking by public authorities, the lease may require that the tenant bear the cost of restoring the property to a workable unit, with the landlord making the net proceeds of the award available to the extent necessary and to retain the remainder. Reduction in rent, if any, should be based on a reasonable formula based on the productivity to the tenant of the area taken and the area remaining.

☐ *Government regulations.* The tenant should be required to comply with all federal, state, and local laws and regulations presently in effect and subsequently adopted.

Generally, where a tenant is obligated to pay any of the landlord's expenses, those payments are additional rental income to the landlord that is currently taxable to him. As for the tenant, he is entitled to deduct those payments as rent. The landlord, for his part, may be entitled to a corresponding deduction as, for example, where the tenant is obligated to pay the real estate taxes on the property, the payments are additional rent and therefore deductible by the tenant and taxable to the landlord but the amount paid for taxes by the landlord as the owner of the property is deductible by him. The same treatment is given to insurance premiums, interest, and other deductible expenses of the landlord that are paid by the tenant.

Where the lease requires the tenant to make mortgage amortization payments on the landlord's mortgage, these payments are taxable to the landlord as additional rent when they are made and it is immaterial that the landlord is not personally liable under the mortgage. Further, since the payments are amortization payments, the landlord gets no corresponding deduction for them as he would if they were interest payments. As far as the tenant's income tax position is concerned, a tenant under a long-term lease required to make the landlord's mortgage amortization payments has been required to amortize each payment ratably over the life of the lease, the payments being considered advance rent.

Where the lessee pays assessments for improvements as distinguished from real estate taxes, the lessee cannot deduct the amounts paid in the year of payment; instead, he must write the payment off over the life of the lease or the life of the improvement, whichever is shorter.

[3] Subordinated and Unsubordinated Fee Interests

Any discussion of fee and leasehold interests must first note the distinction between subordinated and unsubordinated fee interests.

Whenever a parcel of real estate has been divided into separate fee and leasehold interests, the fee is unsubordinated when it is superior to any mortgage that the tenant places upon his leasehold interest. In other words, if the tenant does obtain a leasehold mortgage and subsequently defaults, the lender may take over the leasehold interest (and become the tenant) but still must pay rent to the fee owner. A fee interest will always be superior to the leasehold interest unless the fee owner takes affirmative action to subordinate his interest.

A subordinated fee interest arises when a fee owner voluntarily takes second position (with respect to priority in event of a default) to a lender who provides a loan to the tenant secured by a mortgage on the real estate. The fee owner commits himself to subordination by entering into a separate subordination agreement with the tenant or by becoming a party to the mortgage as a mortgagor. As already noted, by subordinating the fee, the owner assumes a risk that his interest may be wiped out in the event the tenant defaults under the mortgage. Consequently, the landowner will agree to subordinate only if (1) the extra risk is minimized as much as possible, and (2) he is rewarded adequately for assuming the risk.

[a] Establishing Ground Rents

In the case of a land lease and an unsubordinated fee (i.e., where the fee owner retains priority over the leasehold mortgage), the annual rental customarily has been 6 to 7 percent of the appraised value of the land. The reason for the low rate is that the fee owner will ultimately benefit from the land appreciation during the lease term (and thus differs from the cash lender who will receive back depreciated dollars).

When the fee is subordinated, the landowner is assuming some of the risk of the equity position and so is entitled to a greater return. Current rentals for subordinated fees range anywhere from 9 to 13 percent a year, with the average probably around 11 percent for good-quality properties.

The initial ground rental may be subject to escalation or increase in one of three different ways:

☐ *Land reappraisal.* Many land leases provide for periodic reappraisals of the land (e.g., every five years) which, because rental is expressed as a percentage of land value, will cause rental to move up (or possibly down). The type of reappraisal clause most favorable to the landowner requires the land to be appraised as if it were vacant, that is, as if available for its highest-and-best use (which may not necessarily be the present use).

☐ *Rent escalation.* Between land reappraisals, the rent may be subject to escalation in accordance with an outside standard (e.g., the Consumer Price Index) or an inside standard (e.g., gross revenues received by the lessee from the property).

☐ *Refinancing proceeds.* As years pass, the ratio of the outstanding mortgage loan to the property value will decline as (1) the mortgage is gradually amortized; and (2) the value of the property rises. At some point, the lessee will want to refinance the existing mortgage in order to pull out tax-free cash. The landowner (whose willingness to subordinate was crucial when the original mortgage was obtained) normally will insist that he receive a share of the excess refinancing proceeds, perhaps equal to the proportion of the land value to the total property value.

> *Example:* Land and building together have an initial value of $1 million, supporting a mortgage loan of $700,000. After five years, the mortgage is amortized to $670,000 while the property value rises to $1.2 million. A new 70 percent mortgage (for $840,000) is obtained; thus, $170,000 in tax-free refinancing proceeds are available. The landowner and the lessee may split this 20-80 or in any other agreed proportion.

The lessee frequently obtains an option to purchase the land after a period of years. This most often occurs when the transaction is a sale-leaseback (i.e., when the lessee originally owned the land and entered into a sale-leaseback with an institution in lieu of straight mortgage financing). However, an existing landowner may be willing to grant a purchase option on sufficiently attractive terms.

When the sale-leaseback technique is used, the option purchase price frequently is set so that the land purchaser (institution) receives its money back plus a fixed annual return over and above whatever ground rental has been paid. So long as the option price bears a reasonable relationship to market value, the transaction should escape IRS attack as a disguised mortgage.

[b] Protecting the Subordinated Fee Owner

A landowner, in addition to receiving a fair rental, will want to minimize the risk that the land may be lost due to a default by the lessee under the mortgage. Protective steps include the following:

☐ *Criteria for mortgage.* The landowner may agree to subordinate only to a mortgage made by an institutional (as distinguished from a private or foreign) lender and provided the debt service on the loan does not exceed a designated percentage of projected cash flow (to reduce the risk of a loan default).

☐ *Criteria for refinancing.* Even though the landowner will share in refinancing proceeds, the owner will not want the debt service on the refinanced mortgage to exceed a specified percentage of cash flow.

☐ *Rent guarantee.* If possible, the landowner will seek to have the principals of the lessee guarantee rental payments (at least until gross income from the property reaches a specified level).

☐ *Cross-default clause.* If the lessee defaults under its mortgage loan, it should be required to give notice to the landowner, and such default should also be a default under the lease. In this way, the landowner is in a position to cure the mortgage default in order to prevent loss of the land in a foreclosure.

Where vacant land is involved, the landowner should seek to have the subordination effective only after the completion of construction and at the time the permanent loan is funded. In this way, the landowner avoids the risk that his land will be lost due to defaults by the developer under the construction loan.

9.23 SANDWICH LEASES

[1] In General

In its broadest sense, a sandwich lease is any leasehold interest in real property that is sandwiched between the fee (ownership) interest on one side and a subleasehold (created by occupancy subleases) on the other side. In this situation, the sandwich lease also is an operating lease, since the sandwich lessee (called the prime tenant as distinguished from the subtenants under the subleases) actually manages the property, keeping as his return the excess of the rentals received from the subtenants over the operating expenses plus ground rental paid to the fee owner.

In a more technical sense, however, a sandwich lease describes a situation involving three "investment" positions in the property. The first is that of the fee owner who enters into a net lease with a prime tenant. The prime tenant in turn enters into a sublease with a subtenant who actually manages the property and thus holds the operating position. The subtenant in turn leases out portions of the property under occupancy leases (which thus become sub-subleases).

Sometimes, a sandwich leasehold position merely is a form of secondary financing, with the sandwich (prime) lessee receiving a fixed rent from the sublessee (from which the prime lessee must pay the prime rental to the fee owner, with the balance representing the profit to the prime lessee). In this type of situation, the prime lessee gains no benefit from any future increased profitability of the property and thus is in the position of a mortgage lender; furthermore, its loan position is a secondary one since it is subject to termination for its failure to pay the ground rental to the fee owner. At other times, where the prime lessee can share (via percentage rentals, for example) in the success of the sublessee, the prime lessee may be said to have a true equity position.

An example of a sandwich lease arrangement occurs where an owner leases income property for which the lessee agrees to pay an annual fixed rental. Instead of operating the property itself, the tenant subleases the property to a third party at a higher rental and third party then leases out space to those who will actually use and occupy the space. As a simple illustration, assume that the landlord leases premises to the prime tenant at an annual fixed rental of $10,000. The prime tenant subleases to the subtenant at an annual fixed rental of $12,000 per year. The subtenant, in turn, leases space to the occupancy tenants and assumes all of the cost of operating the building. If the sublesse can realize net operating income of $14,000 a year and pays $12,000 per year to the prime tenant, it keeps $2,000 per year as its profit. The prime tenant, in turn, pays $10,000 to the landlord and keeps $2,000 for itself. If the rental under the sublease is subject to rent escalation or percentage rental clauses, the rental received by the prime tenant may vary, either increasing its profit or causing it a loss.

The position of the three parties varies substantially with respect to risk and possible return. The most secure position is that of the landlord (fee interest) since the landlord has no obligation with respect to the other two parties and is absolutely entitled to receive its fixed rental; and failing to do so, it may terminate the prime lease, which normally also will cause the termination of the sublease. On the other hand, the return to the landlord is fixed.

The prime tenant must pay the fixed rental each year to the landlord or risk loss of its lease. However, for no investment (or a small investment depending on whether it paid the landlord a bonus for the leasehold), it is entitled to receive a cash return equal to the difference between the subrental received and the prime rental paid. However, its failure to pay rent will cause loss of its lease.

The position of the sublessee is the riskiest since it has the burden of a high annual-rent payment and assumes all of the risks involved in operating the property. On the other hand, any additional profit from the property that may arise from higher rentals accrues directly to it.

[2] Case Study of Sandwich Lease

The following example of a syndicated sandwich leasehold is an excellent illustration of the William Zeckendorff "pineapple approach" to slicing a real estate investment into a number of interests in order to attract the widest range of participants.

The Property. George Borak, an experienced real estate investor, wanted to acquire an existing leasehold interest in a six-year-old office building containing over one million square feet of rental space, located in the midtown area of a major city. The key facts about the ground lease were the following:

- The owner of the leasehold interest would sell for $48 million ($18 million cash over a $30 million leasehold mortgage).
- The remaining term of the ground lease was thirty-two years, and renewal options ran for another sixty years.
- The annual ground rent was $800,000 for the initial term; thereafter, the ground rent would be set at a figure equal to 7 percent of the fair market value of the land.

The major tenant of the building was a large corporation that occupied 30 percent of the space. Its lease had fifteen years to run; thereafter, the tenant could renew for two additional fifteen-year terms at specified rentals plus escalation. The balance of the building was occupied by high-credit tenants under leases that would expire at various times during the next ten years.

Just before Mr. Borak entered the picture, the ground lessee had obtained a commitment from a lender for a leasehold mortgage loan of $30 million at 9.25 percent interest, payable at $3.1 million per year (10.3 percent constant). The mortgage would be self-liquidating in twenty-five years, but the lender had the right to call it at the end of the fifteenth year, at which time approximately $20 million would still be due. Since the time of the "call" coincided with the date at which the major tenant's lease came up for renewal, it was obvious that the lender wanted to be able to force payment of the loan if the major tenant departed.

Assuming the loan commitment were to be funded, the leasehold would produce a cash flow of $1.55 million, as shown in Table 9.1.

TABLE 9.1 Cash Flow Before Taxes

Annual rental income		$10,850,000
Less: Annual ground rent (for next 32 years)	$ 800,000	
Annual debt service (first-leasehold mortgage)	3,100,000	
Annual operating expenses, including real estate taxes	5,400,000	
		9,300,000
Net cash flow		$ 1,550,000

The Objectives. Mr. Borak had two objectives. The first was to realize some cash profit at once. The second was to acquire for himself a permanent interest in both the future cash flow from the property and in the proceeds of any future sale or refinancing. Thus, his problem was to raise $19 million (the purchase price of $18 million plus an additional $1 million to cover acquisition costs and his front-end profit) and also to get the contributors of this cash to give him a share in the enterprise. He reviewed several different methods of achieving his goals. The solution he chose involved a second-leasehold mortgage, a syndication of the leasehold, and the creation of an operating sublease position owned by himself. These three steps are described in the following paragraphs:

☐ *Solution step 1: Second-leasehold mortgage.* Mr. Borak was able to obtain $10 million (of the total $19 million required) by a commitment for a second-leasehold mortgage by a savings bank. (When the mortgage was funded, the bank took a $4 million portion and brought in other banks as participants in the balance.) The loan commitment was at 10 percent interest, an attractive rate at the time. Constant annual debt service was 11 percent ($1.1 million per year). The loan would mature in fifteen years, the same time the first-leasehold mortgagee could call its mortgage. At that time, if the loans were called, a balance of $20 million would be due on the first mortgage and a balance of $6.5 million would be due on the second. Thus, $26.5 million would have to be refinanced on a leasehold that could run (with renewal options) for another seventy-seven years. And while it could reasonably be anticipated that the value of the leasehold could easily support the refinancing required (even if the principal tenant did not renew its lease), the second-leasehold mortgagee did assume the risk that it might have to pay off the first-leasehold mortgage and operate the property itself if new financing could not be obtained.

☐ *Solution step 2: Syndication of prime lease.* Mr. Borak then organized a limited partnership and offered shares to highly taxed individual investors who contributed the balance of the $9 million in cash needed to buy the leasehold. These investors were promised an immediate annual cash return of $450,000 (5 percent of their aggregate investment) out of the cash earnings of the property, as shown in Table 9.2.

TABLE 9.2 Syndicate Return

Cash flow after debt service on $30 million first mortgage (from Table 9.1)	$1,550,000
Debt service on $10 million second mortgage	1,100,000
Net cash flow	$ 450,000
Return on $9 million equity	5%

The major attraction to the limited partners, however, would be the projected tax shelter from leasehold amortization write-offs. Mr. Borak's tax counsel advised him that the total cost for the leasehold of $49 million (including the $1 million Mr. Borak was to receive personally) could be amortized over the thirty-two-year remaining life of the initial lease term. (The renewal terms would not have to be included in the amortization period unless renewal of the ground lease by the syndicate appeared likely. Since it was not at all clear whether the major tenant in the building would renew its occupancy lease after fifteen years, renewal of the ground lease was far from certain.)

Amortizing the cost over thirty-two years would create an annual write-off of approximately $1.5 million, or more than three times the annual cash flow. Thus the cash flow would be entirely sheltered from tax; in addition, the limited partners would have a large amount of deep shelter, that is, tax shelter for income from other sources.

Finally, if the syndicate did renew the ground lease and continued to operate the property, there was a good chance that refinancing or sale of the leasehold before its termination would enable the limited partners to realize substantial cash proceeds.

Since a leasehold (as distinguished from a fee) interest in real estate will ultimately expire, no residual value can be anticipated. In this syndicate, the total annual return (cash plus tax benefits) should properly be allocated between a return on investment and a return of investment since there can be no assurance that the leasehold ever could be sold or refinanced.

☐ *Solution step 3: Carving out an operating subleasehold.* Mr. Borak could have stopped here and have been well satisfied. He had raised $49 million ($40 million by two leasehold mortgages and $9 million by syndicating equity interests), out of which he retained $1 million for acquisition costs plus his profit. However, he still wished to participate in the future of what he believed to be an excellent investment. So as an integral part of the syndication, he had the limited partnership that owned the leasehold (which we shall now call the prime tenant) enter into a sublease with himself (becoming the subtenant). No consideration was paid for this sublease; however, the basic annual rental was set at $5.45 million for the initial fifteen years. This sum would enable the prime tenant to pay debt service and ground rental and make the promised 5 percent return to the investors, as shown in Table 9.3.

TABLE 9.3 Prime Rental

Annual ground rent	$ 800,000
Annual first-mortgage debt service	3,100,000
Annual second-mortgage debt service	1,100,000
Annual 5% return to limited partners	450,000
	$5,450,000

At this point, a three-tier investment had been created in the office building, as follows:

- The fee owner (ground lessor) would continue to receive his $800,000 annual ground rental, with eventual escalation, and would receive back an unencumbered fee when the lease ultimately expired.
- The prime tenant (syndicate) was obligated to pay the ground rental plus debt service on two leasehold mortgages, but would receive rental income sufficient to discharge these payments and provide a 5 percent return to investors (plus substantial tax shelter). The prime tenant thus occupied a sandwich position, being placed between the fee owner and the operating position.
- The subtenant (Mr. Borak) held the operating position; that is, he would manage the property and be entitled to keep all cash flow above the rental of $5.45 million paid to the prime tenant. His position was the most highly leveraged, since he would bear the initial brunt of any decline in cash flow but would be entitled to keep all of the increase.

Of course, a fourth level of legal interest also exists, the occupancy leases held by the actual tenants in the building. In legal parlance, they become sub-subtenants. Despite their lowly position, they are the most important ingredient since they produce the rental income from which all else flows.

Case Analysis. Examining Mr. Borak's interest more closely, it can be seen that initially he gains nothing, since net operating income from the office building is just equal to debt service and total rents, as shown in Table 9.4. On the other hand, Mr. Borak paid nothing for his sublease, he has no personal liability for the rent, and the sublease is freely assignable. So Mr. Borak, as an operating subtenant, has carved out of the transaction a call on future profits at no cost to himself.

If he is able to manage the property so that net operating income rises, the entire increase will be his. (In fact, Mr. Borak agreed with the prime tenant to pay as additional rental 50 percent of his operating profits in excess of $400,000 annually.) If the net operating income declines, Mr. Borak can walk away without incurring any liability whatsoever. That would require the prime tenant to take

TABLE 9.4 Sandwich (Prime) Leasehold

Total Investment:	
Equity contributed	$ 9,000,000
First-leasehold mortgage	30,000,000
Second-leasehold mortgage	10,000,000
Total investment	$49,000,000
Net Operating Income From Property:	
Annual rental income	$10,850,000
Annual operating expenses	5,400,000
Net operating income	$ 5,450,000
Income Distribution:	
To fee owner (ground rent)	$ 800,000
To first-leasehold mortgagee	3,100,000
To second-leasehold mortgagee	1,100,000
To prime tenant (net prime rental)	450,000
To subtenant (George Borak)	0
Total income	$5,450,000

over the operating position. If net operating income declines no more than $450,000 (the amount of the prime tenant's annual cash flow), the prime tenant would do no worse than break even. Any further decline would put it into a negative cash-flow position and conceivably cause it to default under the lease, throwing the property back in the hands of the fee owner.

9.24 SALE-LEASEBACKS

[1] In General

In a sale-leaseback, real property is sold to a buyer who simultaneously enters into a long-term lease of the property with the seller. Thus, the seller-lessee remains in possession of the property and pays a net rental to the buyer-lessor, with the seller-lessee responsible for payment of all operating expenses and real estate taxes. In essence, a sale-leaseback is exactly the same as the type of net-lease transactions we have been discussing with the additional feature that the property originally was owned by the lessee who must sell it in order to permit the property to be divided into separate fee and leasehold estates.

Four different types of sale-leaseback transactions can be distinguished:

☐ *Sale-leaseback of land and improvements.* In this most frequent situation, the owner of improved real estate sells it to an investor and simultaneously enters into a long-term net leaseback. Thus, the seller-lessee obtains the burdens and virtually all of the benefits of ownership while, at the same time converting its investment into cash. The most important of the benefits given up are the right to take depreciation deductions and the right to any future appreciation in the value of the property. Normally, the lease will run anywhere from twenty-five to ninety-nine years and contain reappraisal or adjustment rental clauses so that the rental will keep pace with value of money and vary in accordance with some outside standards such as the Consumer Price Index. The seller-lessee may or may not have an option or right of first refusal to repurchase the property in the future.

☐ *Sale-leaseback of land only.* Here, the investor buys the land (but not the building on it) and leases the land back to the seller under a long-term lease calling for the payment of a ground rental. (Alternatively, raw land may be sold and leased back, with the seller-lessee then constructing improvements.) In this situation the seller retains the right to depreciation deductions since it retains title to the improvements.

☐ *Sale-leaseback of improvements only.* Here, the seller-lessee retains title to the land while selling and leasing back an existing building on the land. Normally, the purchaser of the building is interested primarily in depreciation deductions, rather than rental income or long-term appreciation.

☐ *Sale leaseback of land and building to different investors.* In this situation, two separate sales and leasebacks are entered into by the seller, one covering the land and one covering the building.

[2] Sale-Leasebacks by Business Firms

The unique aspects of the sale-leaseback arise in the case of business firms that employ the technique to raise capital and avoid high borrowing costs. This form of sale-leaseback was pioneered by the Safeway Corporation in the 1940s as a means of raising the capital needed to expand its grocery business. In essence, a sale-leaseback permits the business firm to free capital frozen in real estate assets to be used to generate a much higher rate of return in the business itself.

On the other side, sale-leasebacks of retail facilities and industrial properties often are very attractive to real estate investors who can pick up the tax advantages of ownership (particularly depreciation deductions) and at the same time have an assured return under a long-term net lease with a high-credit tenant. In particular, foreign investors like this type of deal because it minimizes risk and the need for personal management.

In deciding whether to sell or to mortgage its real estate in order to raise capital, a corporation must consider the following two nontax and two tax factors:

☐ *Amount and cost of financing.* Since the primary objective of the corporate seller normally is to raise capital, the sale-leaseback has one major advantage over a mortgage. The former provides the corporation with cash equal to 100 percent of the fair market value of the property, whereas the latter normally will not exceed 75 or 80 percent of value. And despite the 100 percent financing, the sale-leaseback does not necessarily carry a higher carrying cost (rent as a percentage of the sales price) as would a mortgage (debt service as a percentage of the loan).

Actually, if either a leaseback or a mortgage can be obtained by the corporation on identical terms, the leaseback almost always is cheaper over its entire life, at least for property not first placed in service by the owner after January 1, 1981 (when the new fifteen-year recovery period is available for real estate). This is due to the fact that the fully deductible rent payments by the seller-lessee under the leaseback give greater tax benefits than would the smaller deductions to it (as mortgagor) for interest and depreciation if a mortgage had been used.

☐ *Residual value.* The other nontax factor to be considered by a business firm in connection with a sale-leaseback is the residual value of the real estate at the end of the lease term. In the case of a leaseback, this residual value belongs to the buyer-lessor, whereas in the case of a mortgage, it belongs to the business firm.

Thus, in any particular case, the comparison between the two financing methods depends upon the anticipated residual value, appropriately discounted to present value, as well as the length of the lease or loan term, existence of renewal options, and type of depreciation available.

☐ *Extent to which property depreciated.* If a sale and leaseback occurs, the former owner (now tenant) of the property loses his depreciation deduction. This loss may be minor, however, if one or more of the following factors is present:

- A large portion of the initial cost of the property has been allocated to nondepreciable land.
- The property was originally acquired at a very low cost so that depreciation deductions, relative to current market value, are very small.
- The property has been fully or nearly fully depreciated due to the passage of time.

☐ *Relation between tax basis and market value.* A second tax factor that often tips the balance for or against a sale-leaseback is the tax consequence to the owner arising from the transaction. When the value of the property is less than its taxable basis (i.e., the property has lost value since its acquisition), the owner will realize a loss on the sale. Assuming the property is used in his trade or business, the loss can be deducted in full against ordinary income. This, obviously, is a favorable tax factor to the seller; he is able to offset current income by realizing a loss while still retaining use of the property.

There are two situations in which the loss realized on the sale is not deductible. First, the loss on a sale to a related person would be disallowed. Related parties are spouses or an individual and a corporation in which the individual owns more than 80 percent of the outstanding stock.[3]

The second exception to loss deductibility is peculiar to the sale-leaseback arrangement. Under Section 1031 of the Code, an exchange of real estate for a lease with a term of thirty years or more will be considered an exchange of like-kind property, with neither gain nor loss realized on the exchange.

In the opposite situation, when the market value of the property sold and leased back exceeds the tax basis to the seller, the excess will be taxable income. It will be long-term capital gain if the property had been held for more than twelve months and if the property was held for investment or used in the seller's trade or business. In other cases, the gain will be short-term (the equivalent of ordinary income).

---

[3] I.R.C. § 1239.

There are two exceptions to the rule allowing the gain to be treated as a capital gain rather than ordinary income. First, a portion of the gain may be converted into ordinary income because of the depreciation-recapture rules under Section 1250 of the Code. These rules vary with the length of time the property was owned, the type of depreciation taken, and the period to which it is attributable (i.e., before or after January 1, 1970).

Second, just as the loss on a sale to a related person would be disallowed, Section 1239 provides that the profit on a sale to related persons is treated as ordinary income.

> *Example:* Merely to illustrate the possibilities, let us assume ABC Corp., near the end of its fiscal year, realizes it will need a large inflow of working capital in the next few months. In addition, it has a large operating loss carryover that will expire in the current fiscal year. ABC Corp. also has owned its business premises for the past twenty years. The building has been fully depreciated for tax purposes so that no further depreciation deductions will be available. The building is worth $250,000 and its rental value is $20,000 a year.
>
> Tax counsel for ABC Corp. comes up with a way to provide working capital and not lose the tax benefits of the expiring loss. He proposes that ABC Corp. sell the building to a third party and lease it back under a long-term net lease. ABC Corp. receives $250,000 in cash, which is largely nontaxable (because a portion of it is offset by the loss carryover and the balance is subject only to long-term capital gains tax). ABC Corp. achieves both its objectives while still retaining use of the premises.

[3] Distinguished From Mortgage for Tax Purposes

Let us assume that a corporation has decided that a sale-leaseback of corporate property is the best way to raise the maximum amount of cash at the least cost. In negotiating the leaseback, the corporation will have the following three objectives:

- Control the property for as long as possible
- Have maximum flexibility in using the property
- Be able to repurchase the property at the lowest possible price at some future time

The purchaser, usually a passive investor, may have no objection to these demands. But the real question is whether IRS will treat the transaction as a mortgage in substance, thus destroying the tax assumptions on which the deal is based.

The Internal Revenue Service studies the terms of the lease with care. If, by virtue of a repurchase option at an attractive price, it appears that the property will revert to the seller-lessee, then the transaction would appear to be a loan rather than a sale. If the initial lease term is for such a long period that the lessee retains the use of the building for its entire economic useful life, then too, the transaction is more like a loan than a sale. Finally, the renewal options on the lease will be examined to determine whether they are true options rather than mere formalities to extending the lease. If the rent during the renewal period is nominal in amount or substantially less than the rent during the initial lease term, the transaction looks more like a mortgage.

Other indications of a loan rather than a true sale and leaseback are:

- Rent that bears little relationship to the actual rental value; or
- Rent that declines over the years and is apparently intended to cover the principal amortization of the building by the buyer-lessor.

[a] The *Lyon* Case

In 1978, the U.S. Supreme Court handed down one of its rare real estate tax decisions. In *Frank Lyon Co. v. United States,*[4] in a 7-2 vote, the court upheld a sale-leaseback transaction that had previously been restructured by the IRS as a straight mortgage.

While the particular facts of the case prevent the decision from offering firm guideposts for sale-leaseback transactions, persons interested in the tax consequences of sale-leasebacks should study the decision carefully for an indication of what the courts look for in determining whether or not the transaction is a sham.

To summarize what has already been said above, a sale-leaseback transaction consists of the sale and simultaneous leaseback of a parcel of real estate, with the lease term usually running for twenty-five or more years and with the rental payments to the buyer-lessor generally on a net basis (so that the seller-lessee pays all of the operating expenses and real estate taxes).

Generally, the prime advantage to the seller-lessee in a sale-leaseback is that it minimizes the cost of raising capital to be employed in its business. On the other side, the advantage to the purchaser-lessor is in the benefits he obtains by being the owner of the real estate rather than a mortgage lender. These benefits include not only the right to the long-term appreciation in the value of the land but also the tax deductions—notably for depreciation—available to him as owner.

As the Supreme Court said in the *Lyon* case, "So long as the lessor retains significant and genuine attributes of the traditional lessor status, the form of the transaction adopted by the parties governs for tax purposes." However, if the sale-leaseback form has no economic substance but is a sham used to disguise a straight financing relationship in order to reach certain tax results, then the form will be ignored.

Facts of the Case. Worthen Bank, in Arkansas, purchased land to build a new bank building. When it discovered that under federal and state banking regulations it would not be permitted to carry the building on its own books, it entered into a sale-leaseback with Lyon Company, a closely held business firm independent of the bank (except that its majority shareholder was on the bank's board).

The transaction was worked out as follows:

- The bank retained ownership of the land, giving Lyon a seventy-five-year ground lease subject to a nominal rental ($50 per year) for the initial twenty-five years and then to much higher rentals for the balance of the term.

---

[4] 435 U.S. 561 (1978).

- Lyon purchased the building from the bank for its cost of $7.5 million, leasing it back to the bank for twenty-five years, subject to renewal options for an additional forty years and subject to repurchase options that could be exercised by the bank three different times during the lease term.
- The $7.5 million investment in the building would consist of a $500,000 equity investment by Lyon plus a $7 million first mortgage by New York Life.

Risks and Benefits of Ownership. The tax issue first arose when IRS audited Lyon's 1969 tax return. IRS ruled that Lyon was not the owner of the building for tax purposes and so (1) had no income or expense as "owner"; and (2) had interest income on the "loan" of $500,000 to the bank. IRS was overruled by the federal district court to which the case was appealed, but the Court of Appeals upheld the IRS contention that Lyon was not the true owner of the building, giving the following reasons:

- Lyon could not profit from its investment by selling its interest to a third party, because the bank had a right of first refusal at a negotiated price, which, said the court, necessarily had to relate to the option price set forth in the lease.
- The purchase option in the lease set a price that would return to Lyon its $500,000 investment plus interest compounded at 6 percent per month, so that Lyon could not benefit from any appreciation in the property's value if the option were exercised; the court concluded such exercise was likely.
- The bank had ultimate control over the disposition of the building as a result of its lease, which, with renewal options, could run for a total of sixty-five years plus the bank's ownership of the land.
- Then rental to be paid by the bank was exactly equal to the debt service on the mortgage and was to be paid by the bank under all circumstances; thus Lyon assumed no real risk and obtained no real economic benefit apart from the tax-shelter benefits (approximately $1.5 million for the first eleven years).

The circuit court held that all of this refutes Lyon's claim to be treated as the true owner of the building.

[b] The *Lazarus* Case

In its argument before the Supreme Court, IRS relied heavily on the earlier case of *Helvering v. Lazarus & Co.*[5] Without going into details of that case, suffice to say that the Supreme Court rejected it as a precedent for this case because *Helvering* involved two parties only, whereas the *Lyon* case involved three parties (the bank, Lyon, and the mortgagee, New York Life) that were related in a particular way; that is, the bank had obligations to its lessor, Lyon, which in turn was obligated as borrower to New York Life. Had the bank itself been the borrower from New York Life and had then entered into a separate transaction with

---

[5] 308 U.S. 252 (1939).

Lyon, the *Helvering* case would have applied and Lyon would have been treated as a lender, not as an owner.

[i] The Risk of Loss. Thus, Lyon was primarily liable on the mortgage debt, not the bank, and Lyon "exposed its very business well-being to this real and substantial risk," the first of two risks that the Court identified.

Further, this liability was present on Lyon's balance sheet "for all the world to see." And so its financial position was substantially affected by the presence of the long-term debt despite the offsetting presence of the building as an asset.

[ii] The Risk of No Return. The second real risk to which the Supreme Court pointed involved the potential return on Lyon's $500,000 investment. The rent payments alone, being exactly equal to the debt service, would generate no return for the twenty-five-year life of the mortgage. Only if the bank exercised its repurchase option would Lyon get its money back plus a 6 percent annual return. If the bank did not repurchase the building but exercised all of its renewal options under the lease, Lyon would again end up, when the lease finally expired, with its money back plus 6 percent annual return. However, if the bank did not exercise either its purchase or renewal options, Lyon might well end up with a loss since it would continue to be obligated to pay ground rent whether or not Lyon was able to find another tenant for the building.

The Supreme Court also noted that the government is not likely to lose any revenue as a result of the form of the transaction. Had it been a straight loan, the bank instead of Lyon would have utilized the "ownership deductions" such as depreciation against its operating income.

In essence, the Court concluded that it is Lyon's capital invested in the building and so it is Lyon that is entitled to depreciation deductions.

The Court went on to list a variety of other factors that gave economic reality to the sale-leaseback transaction. These included the following:

- The regulations that prevented the bank from putting up its own building
- Lyon's legitimate motive to diversify and its independence from the bank
- The reasonableness of the rentals and the option prices
- Lyon's not being engaged generally in the business of financing
- Lyon's potential liability under the ground lease
- The absence of special tax circumstances for one of the parties

Consequently, the *Lyon* case cannot be interpreted as significantly opening the door to sale-leaseback transactions that formerly would have been treated as sham. An investor, developer, or business firm seeking to create a sale-leaseback transaction in the form of *Lyon* should have its professional counsel study this decision with the greatest care. The dissenting opinion, written by Justice Stevens, construes the facts in the case in just the opposite manner from the majority, reaching the conclusion that since the bank has the right to reacquire the building for a price not in excess of the unamortized financing, the bank in economic fact is the owner of the building.

9.25 LEASING AS FAMILY-PLANNING TECHNIQUE

Leasing business property to family members can create significant tax savings for business persons in high-income brackets. The use of a trust-leaseback (or its alternative, the gift-leaseback) is subject to a high risk of challenge by the Internal Revenue Service. Thus, professional counsel should always be consulted when using this approach. However, the Tax Court and the Fifth Circuit Court of Appeals have set forth fairly clear criteria for upholding such leasebacks.[6]

[1] Example of a Trust-Leaseback

The following example demonstrates how a trust-leaseback is set up and the benefits of this technique.

Suppose a real estate professional operates his business from premises he owns free and clear and which has a present market value of $200,000. Assume his annual depreciation deductions are $7,000 and he is in the 50 percent bracket; thus his annual tax saving is $3,500.

Now suppose he creates a trust for the benefit of his children, gifts the real estate to the trust and leases it back for $25,000 a year. The rental payments still stay within the family unit but the parent's tax saving jumps to $12,500 while the net tax cost to his beneficiaries only amounts to $2,700. (See Table 9.5 below.) Thus the net tax benefit is $9,800, almost triple the $3,500 saving when no trust is used.

TABLE 9.5 Trust-Leaseback of $200,000 Property

Rental payments by parent	$25,000
Parent's tax bracket	×.50
Parent's tax benefit	$12,500
Children's gross income	$25,000
Less: Depreciation deduction	7,000
Children's net income	$18,000
Children's tax bracket	×.15
Children's tax	$ 2,700
Net tax benefit to family	$9,800
Tax benefit if no trust	$3,500

[2] Four Legal Tests for a Trust-Leaseback

In order to achieve the benefits of a trust-leaseback, the property owner must pass four fairly well-defined tests:

---

[6] See Lewis H.V. May v. Comm'r, 76 T.C. 7 (1981); Mathews v. Comm'r, 520 F.2d 323 (5th Cir. 1975).

☐ *No retained equity.* The grantor (parent) cannot retain an equity interest in the gifted property (otherwise it is as if the property was never given away). The best way to insure this is to have the property go to someone other than the grantor when the trust ends (e.g., the grantor's spouse or children).

☐ *No control.* In addition, the grantor must not continue to exercise control over the property or the rental income (again, because otherwise it is as if the property was not given away). For example, the grantor should not be able to revoke the trust, use the trust income for his benefit, determine who gets the income, or be able to control the decisions of the trustee.

☐ *Arm's-length transaction.* The lease itself should be in writing and rentals should be reasonable in light of current market conditions.

☐ *Business purpose.* The leaseback (as distinguished from the initial transfer of the property to the trust) must have a bona fide business purpose. This usually is satisfied if in fact the grantor uses the property to carry on his business.

Some courts have imposed an additional requirement for a valid trust-leaseback that ordinarily cannot be met. The requirement is that the initial creation of the trust (in addition to the subsequent leaseback) have a business purpose. Since this ordinarily cannot be shown, taxpayers in these states probably should not utilize this technique.

10

Operating Real Estate

10.01 MANAGING REAL ESTATE

[1] Property-Management Functions

Property management is the name given to the function of providing services to the property user and of maintaining the property and collecting rents to which the owner is entitled. The management function usually is performed by owners themselves in the case of small properties. For larger properties or when owners live at a distance, the function normally is performed by a property manager, either an individual or a management firm.

Property management often can make a significant difference in the net cash flow from income property and consequently is an important variable when analyzing a property. The management contract is the key document defining the relationship between the managing agent and the property owner-principal. By virtue of the contract, the property manager acts as the owner's agent in satisfying the service demands of users (who lease space over time) and in insuring that the users perform their lease obligations, most notably the prompt payment of rent.

The property-management function varies widely in its complexity and in the time demands made of the manager. At one extreme, management of a single-family residence is least time-consuming and complex and is often combined with the real-estate-brokerage function. At the other, property management in a large shopping center or office building is a full-time occupation. In hotels and motels, the service element is critically important, and consequently makes good management even more valuable.

The key functions of a property manager are:

☐ *Rent collection.* The property manager's first function is the collection task. Tenants must pay minimum rent and possibly percentage rents and expense items as provided for in the lease. When tenants do not pay on time, it is the responsibility of the property manager to safeguard the owner's interests and collect revenues in the most expeditious manner possible.

☐ *Tenant relations.* Once rent has been collected, the property manager is responsible for ongoing operations. The first priority is tenant relations; as in any business, it is important to satisfy the customer. The property manager is in a better position to do this if he knows the tenant's general needs and is periodically in personal contact with all of the tenants.

Operating rules will be defined in the lease; however, there are always gray areas in enforcing certain operating rules. For example, in a regional shopping center, how loud can the music be played by a record store? Can a tenant have handbills distributed to shoppers? How late must stores remain open before Christmas? All of the general-management functions are performed as the property manager, working under the basic rules established in the lease, seeks to satisfy all tenants' desires for space over time with certain services.

☐ *Personnel.* Depending upon its size, a property may require one or many employees for purposes of maintenance, security, etc. The property manager is the one to determine employment requirements and recruit prospective employees. In addition, the manager normally will handle employment contracts, supervise the employees and, where necessary, discharge employees who fail to perform satisfactorily.

The management contract must specify who is to pay the resident employees (including the resident manager). In some cases, the resident manager is on the property manager's payroll and is therefore an additional cost to the property manager. In other cases, the resident manager is paid out of the operating cash flows of the project. In the latter case, one would expect a lower level of compensation to the property manager, since fewer expenses would be incurred.

☐ *Maintenance schedules.* The property manager is responsible for establishment of the maintenance schedule. This involves not only custodial services but also, for example, provisions for snow removal in those regions requiring it. In a larger property, one or more engineers will be required for ongoing operation; it is the responsibility of the property manager to ensure that these individuals perform in a consistent and coordinated manner. The property manager is also responsible for inventory control, which includes making certain that cleaning supplies and any other necessary items are available when needed. (Note that in a major hotel, inventory control involves furniture, food, liquor, and so forth.)

☐ *Security.* Security has become an increasingly important function of the property manager. The increase both in personal and property crime has made security precautions a top demand by many tenants, whether residential or commercial. In addition, legislation and court decisions in many states have increased the liability of a landlord for injury or property loss suffered by a tenant resulting from inadequate safety precautions or failure to repair doors, windows, or other points of access into the building or rental units. The property manager must seek to minimize the risk of crime while at the same time keeping operating cost increases under control. (See 10.01[3].)

☐ *Property insurance.* Adequately insuring a property at the minimum cost is an important duty of the property manager. This requires the manager to keep up to date about the many types of insurance coverages available and to recommend appropriate insurers for the property. (This latter function is often performed by an insurance broker who deals with the property manager or directly with the owner.) Finally, the property manager must investigate all accidents or claims for damages and make sure that reports are filed promptly with the insurer. (See 10.02.)

☐ *Payment of expenses; books and records.* The property manager must see to it that operating expenses, real estate taxes, and mortgage payments are made when due. Depending upon the particular arrangement, the manager may be authorized to sign checks or may merely prepare a list of payments for the owner's attention. The manager also will keep financial records of income and outlays and will work with the accountant retained by the owner in the preparation of annual financial statements and tax returns. The manager also will be responsible for preparing reports required by governmental authorities.

☐ *Showing and renting space.* Although marketing real estate is a function distinct from managing it, the two are often combined in the hands of the property manager. This is particularly true in the case of apartment properties where the manager actually on the site (the resident manager) usually shows vacant apartments and handles lease negotiations. Because of the importance of the leasing function and the expertise and special effort required for successful leasing, the manager often receives a leasing commission over and above his regular management fee. The leasing function can be divided into three steps, all or some of which may be performed by the property manager:

- *Set rental levels.* One of the most important functions of the property manager may be to establish a lease schedule that will maximize the rental income over time from the property. To do this, the manager must (1) keep current information on rentals in comparable buildings; (2) tolerate a certain percentage of vacant space (since a fully occupied building may be evidence of unduly low rentals); and (3) vary rentals among the various space units in the building to reflect the relative advantages and disadvantages of each. For example, space on higher floors usually commands a premium over that on middle floors due to a better view.
- *Solicit prospects.* The second step in the leasing process is to advertise space in appropriate media (whether billboards, newspapers, radio, or television) and show space to prospective tenants. This latter function, often performed in a perfunctory way, should more properly be regarded as the the time for an intensive personal selling effort on the part of the leasing agent. To do this properly, the leasing agent must not only be familiar with every detail of the property being shown but also should ascertain the precise needs and desires of the prospect.
- *Negotiate and execute leases.* Finally, the property manager will be involved, to a greater or lesser extent, in the negotiation and execution of the lease. In the case of an apartment project, where standard form leases are used and little negotiation normally occurs, the manager may perform the entire process. On the other hand, a long-term lease of several floors in a major office building will require the efforts of legal counsel and the owner, too. Even here, however, the property manager plays an important preliminary role because of his initial contacts with the tenant.

If the property manager is successful in enforcing rules of operation, does a good job of re-leasing (if this is part of the contract), has effective maintenance and security schedules, does a good job of inventory control, manages employees well, efficiently handles collections, and keeps good accounting records, then he has done all that possibly can be done to assure that the anticipated budget will be achieved—market conditions allowing, he or she should prepare the budget. The owner will receive the expected cash flow, and the property manager will be compensated as specified in the management contract.

[2] Property-Management Agreement

[a] Duties and Obligations of the Manager

Normally, an owner and his property manager enter into a written agreement laying out the obligations of the latter and his compensation. This often is a more complicated document than one would think. The following is a checklist of key considerations:

☐ *Showing and renting space.* If the property manager is to be a leasing agent as well, the management agreement should specify whether he is to do any or all of the following:

- Conduct market surveys to determine rent levels
- Arrange for necessary legal documents to be prepared
- Advertise for tenants
- Screen prospective tenants
- Negotiate and execute leases and renewals

☐ *Maintaining the property.* Items to be covered in connection with the manager's duty to maintain the property include:

- Periodic inspection to determine needed repairs
- Contracting for the performance of large-scale improvement or renovation
- Purchasing supplies, tools, and materials
- Arranging for emergency repairs or work ordered by governmental authorities

☐ *Dealing with other personnel.* Duties of the property manager in this area may include:

- Making periodic surveys to determine employment requirements
- Recruiting prospective employees
- Entering into employment contracts
- Supervising and, when necessary, discharging employees

☐ *Arranging necessary services.* An income property requires a variety of services by outside contractors; these may include garbage removal, cleaning, air conditioning, elevator maintenance, and others. The property manager may have the following obligations:

- Negotiating for services considered necessary
- Verifying the performance and quality of services rendered
- Paying for such services
- Resolving disputes relating to the quality, quantity, or cost of services rendered

☐ *Financial affairs.* The property manager may have some or all of the following duties in connection with fiscal affairs:

- Collecting rent and other revenues
- Paying operating expenses, including real estate taxes and mortgage payments
- Preparing income and expense reports

- Preparing operating budgets and income forecasts
- Preparing reports for governmental authorities
- Retaining accountants or other professionals

☐ *Insuring the property.* Adequately insuring a property at the minimum cost is often a significant function of the property manager. In this area, his duties may include:

- Drawing up a list of necessary insurance coverages
- Selecting insurance companies to provide the coverage
- Investigating accidents or claims for damage
- Filing reports with insurers

[b] Compensating the Property Manager

A property manager's compensation may be in one of two forms: (1) fixed fee or salary; or (2) variable commission or percentage of income. In addition, he may be given fringe benefits and expense reimbursements.

Normally, a fixed fee is paid for services requiring a relatively fixed expenditure of time and where an incentive for extraordinary effort is not necessary. Maintaining the books and records of the property is an example.

On the other hand, a service such as finding new tenants is one that calls for the exercise of discretion and good judgment and may involve intensive efforts. For this type of work, a leasing commission frequently is paid to the manager over and above his fixed fee.

[c] Special Considerations

In addition to the key provisions outlined above, several other questions are of major importance in setting up a management agreement.

☐ *What is the duration of the management agreement?* It is not a good idea to contract for an unspecified period. Stipulate a definite initial period (one or more years), and then continue on a month-to-month basis.

☐ *What employees shall the agent provide?* The number of employees should be stipulated and job descriptions provided for each employee. The manager should be made responsible for the acts and wages of each site employee. All workers who handle money should be bonded.

☐ *What expenditures is the manager authorized to make?* Expenditures should be limited to specified periodic charges, except in case of emergency. This will protect the owner against large expenditures made without his knowledge or consent. The agent might be asked to submit from time to time recommendations for capital expenditures that will correct obsolescence and improve the property.

☐ *What type of advertising and promotion will be undertaken, and who will pay for it?* The agreement should state clearly who is to pay for the various types of advertising. The agent should have a basic obligation to advertise vacancies and display signs.

[3] Increasing Property Security

Crimes connected with real estate take many forms ranging from malicious mischief (such as graffiti) to theft of tenant property and complete destruction of buildings by bombing. The total bill to property owners is staggering, including as it does repair and replacement costs, loss of rentals, and preventive measures.

[a] Preventive Measures

Preventive measures, costly though they may be, often pay for themselves many times over. Such measures include those listed below:

☐ *Building design.* One expert advocates building entries and exits directly on streets (to increase visibility to passing cars and patrolling police), well-lighted and visible lobbies, use of a small hallway rather than long corridors serviced by a bank of elevators with generally a decrease in the amount of public space. Stating that some buildings aid in the victimization of its occupants, the expert also recommends limiting the number of tenants using one entrance to 150 tenants or families and, wherever possible, judicious location of building away from high-crime-rate areas.

☐ *Use of effective locks and key control.* Despite the fact that almost any lock can be picked by a professional, certain types of locks are more secure than others for different types of doors. A mortise lock is best for a metal door; a Segal lock is best for a wood door; and a police-type lock should be used where the frame around the door is weak. Where a bolt-type lock is used, the bolt should be at least one inch long. In apartments or private residences, chains and peepholes are a must for the protection of the occupants.

☐ *Effective police protection.* Police personnel are becoming increasingly aware of the importance of prevention of real estate crimes. For example, having determined that most of these crimes occur between the hours of 5:00 P.M. and 2:00 A.M., many police departments now deploy a larger force during these hours.

☐ *Use of doormen or uniformed guards.* With proper training and deployment, uniformed personnel are an important deterrent to criminals. Although the use of the retired sixty-five-year-old man in uniform is not recommended, an alert guard, familiar with the tenants and their guests and with a good identification system, can do much to prevent crime.

☐ *Use of a security service.* With the increased availability of contractual security comes the problem of how to select the service that will fill the particular need. While price must be a consideration, other factors to be considered include:

- Age, physical condition, and training of guards provided
- Use of firearms by guards who will maintain their standards of skill
- Turnover of personnel
- Supervision of guards (should be daily and unannounced)
- Condition of equipment and uniforms (should be furnished by the service, except for fire-fighting equipment, and maintained in good order and repair)
- Penalty clause for failure of performance of the contract by the service

☐ *Use of mechanical, electrical, or electronic detectors.* These range in price from several hundred dollars to six figures, depending upon the amount of equipment, the installation expense, and the sophistication of the system. Before buying any particular system, the real estate owner must determine his own needs, the effectiveness of the present security system, and how the cost will be absorbed. In some instances he can attract tenants by advertising the effectiveness of his security measures; in other instances the tenant will be willing to bear the cost of additional protection.

☐ *Training of personnel.* Personnel and tenants should assist in securing the building by assuming some responsibility for their immediate area. They should be alerted to question all guests as to their identity and mission, keep valuables out of sight or locked, and speedily report violations of security. Women should be warned against riding in elevators with strangers, to lock all doors when working late, and to be escorted through dark areas and to parking lots. All employees should receive training in procedures to follow in case of bomb scare or riot.

[b] Security Contract Considerations

With the increased need for protection has come a proliferation of firms offering both service and equipment. The real estate owner must be particularly careful to have satisfactory answers to the following questions before signing any contracts:

☐ *Quality*

- Does the product being offered actually give the protection needed?
- Is the system durable and not subject to frequent electrical or mechanical failure? What is its expected life?
- Is the system foolproof? How can it be circumvented? What are its limitations?

☐ *Terms of sale*

- Is the price of the system in proportion to the cost of the equipment? (If a system costs more than two and one-half times the cost of its components, the buyer should be suspicious of overpricing.)
- On what terms is the equipment being sold? Is the contract clearly one for leasing or for outright sale?
- If monthly services are to be performed, is the maintenance charge reasonable? Is the supplier reasonably sure to remain in business?

Maintaining efficient security as crime rates rise will be an increasing responsibility for real estate owners and managers in both residential and commercial properties. The obligation is to protect both the tenants and the property. Determining the amount of protection required and how best to provide it will be a continuing consideration for the person dealing in real estate.

10.02 INSURING REAL ESTATE

[1] Analyzing Property for Insurance Coverage

Insuring real estate adequately is always a vital part of any investment program. During periods of market weakness, existing policies should be reviewed to be sure that no inadvertent violations are occurring; for example, a building remaining vacant after a tenant's default may permit cancellation by the insurance company. This section deals with the major considerations in obtaining adequate insurance coverage for the owner of income property; homeowner insurance is also discussed. As with other technical areas, it is recommended that owners consult with their insurance brokers or other professional advisers before taking specific action.

Insurance policies relating to real estate can be divided into two types: those protecting the owner against loss due to casualty and those protecting the owner against liability to third parties. The first class includes fire and extended coverage and consequential loss coverage such as business interruption insurance and rent insurance. The second class consists of one or more kinds of liability policies.

In order to provide adequate insurance coverage for property, the owner or investor must be aware of the risk to which the property will be exposed. Once he is aware of the nature of the risks involved, the investor or owner can systematically analyze the risk to provide the most extensive coverage consistent with his financial ability.

The following checklist points out the major steps that should be taken by an owner of property in choosing and implementing an insurance coverage plan:

☐ *Step 1: Potential loss identification.* This consists of determining the forms a loss might take and the perils of the loss. To identify the forms a loss might take, one should study financial statements for the property. The profit and loss statement will disclose income sources that would cease in case of loss or damage, and the balance sheet will indicate assets subject to loss or damage, including both real and personal property: buildings, dwellings, buildings under construction, tanks (including those underground), towers, pipes, unimproved land, wharfs, docks, etc. (real property); and furniture, fixtures, improvements, vehicles, fine arts, lawns, shrubbery, valuable records, recreational facilities, data processing equipment, etc. (personal property). Perils include fire, smoke, windstorm, water damage, weight of ice and snow, electrical disturbances, intentional destruction, negligence, obsolescence, condition of the premises, collapse, construction hazards, glass breakage, or rupture and puncture of vessel.

☐ *Step 2: Potential loss measurement.* This involves estimating the maximum size of any loss that might occur. Losses range from small (covered by the owner without disrupting his finances) to important (causing severe financial hardship and possibly requiring borrowing) to critical risks (those that threaten an owner with bankruptcy). This step should be coupled with the first to determine the exposures that could be the most financially damaging. Monitoring for change (explained in step 5) is particularly important here to assure accuracy of measurement. As prices rise, measurement of potential loss should be modified.

☐ *Step 3: Consideration of protection alternatives.* In addition to studying the different kinds of insurance coverage and the various alternatives offered by insurance companies, the property owner should also consider measures that reduce loss probability and loss severity. For example, it may be less expensive in the long run for an owner to make improvements to his building that will reduce the chance and the severity of a fire than to purchase an expensive policy for the existing structure.

☐ *Step 4: Selection and implementation.* If the owner has systematically followed the preceding steps of the checklist, he will be in a position to choose the best insurance coverage for his property.

☐ *Step 5: Monitoring for change.* A conscientious property owner should continually reevaluate his insurance coverage to determine that it is adequate for his needs. In addition, if there is any acquisition of additional property or improvements to the existing property, it is important that these changes be reflected in the insurance coverage.

[2] Casualty Insurance

Casualty insurance includes all types of coverage that protect the insured against loss to his own property or income, or injury to himself, as a result of actions either by himself or by third parties; it is also known as property insurance. By far the most important type of casualty insurance is fire and extended coverage. Other types that protect against direct loss or damage include burglary and theft, personal property floaters (for individuals), vandalism and malicious mischief, automobile collision and comprehensive, boiler and machinery coverage, and a variety of others. Insurance coverage is also available for loss suffered as a consequence of damage or destruction to property—for example, covering loss of rental income. Finally, two special programs of the federal government provide flood and crime insurance at subsidized rates.

[a] Fire and Extended Coverage

Fire insurance covers loss by fire, lightning, and certain types of smoke damage (for example, that caused by a fire whether involving insured property or a neighboring building). Other types of smoke damage, such as the type caused by a defective heating apparatus, are not covered. Most fire insurance policies are written on the basis of actual cash value. This means that if the property is damaged, the insurance company will pay the cost of replacement or repair minus physical depreciation. However, the insured may obtain a replacement-cost endorsement, which (for an additional premium) requires the insurance company to pay the full replacement cost without any deduction for depreciation.

In virtually all cases, the fire policy will include extended coverage, which insures against loss due to windstorm, hurricane, hail, explosion, riot, civil commotion, smoke, and aircraft and land vehicles. Additional extended coverage can be obtained for vandalism and malicious mischief; these can also be written under separate policies. These extra coverages normally involve a relatively small increase in premium.

In the past few years, companies have begun to write "all-risks" coverage, which protects the owner against all losses except those specifically excluded. However, here the extra cost may be substantial.

[b] The Co-Insurance Clause

The purpose of the co-insurance clause is to encourage the property owner to have large amounts of insurance relative to the value of the property. Without co-insurance, owners willing to gamble that they would never suffer more than a partial loss might have only 40 or 50 percent of the value of their property.

Almost without exception, all fire insurance policies in the United States contain co-insurance clauses for 80 percent or 90 percent (or have no co-insurance clause at all). In other words, the insured assumes responsibility for 20 percent or 10 percent (or none) of the loss on the replacement value of his property. Note that the normal measure is replacement rather than market value; a property owner who cuts his insurance because market value has dropped because of vacancies or other reasons may end up underinsured.

> *Example:* Suppose the owner of a building with a replacement cost of $1 million insures it for $800,000 (80 percent co-insurance). In that case, if the owner suffers a total loss, he would in fact receive $800,000. (An insured can never receive more than the face amount of the policy.) Suppose the building is insured for only $600,000. If there is a total loss, the owner will receive only $600,000; his personal loss will double from $200,000 to $400,000. Table 10.1 below summarizes these two coverage possibilities.

TABLE 10.1 Amounts of Coverage for Total Loss

	Adequately Insured	*Inadequately Insured*
Replacement cost	$1,000,000	$1,000,000
Face value of policy	800,000	600,000
Total fire loss	1,000,000	1,000,000
Check to insured	800,000	600,000

It is obvious how underinsuring increases the personal loss when the building is totally destroyed. But in the far more common case of a partial loss, complying with the co-insurance clause means the difference between no personal loss and one that may be significant. This is so because the insurer will pay only that fraction of the loss equal to the proportion the face value of the policy bears to the amount required under the co-insurance clause. Table 10.2 shows how it would work out.

TABLE 10.2 Amounts of Coverage for Partial Loss

	Adequately Insured	*Inadequately Insured*
Replacement cost	$1,000,000	$1,000,000
80 percent co-insurance clause	800,000	800,000
Face value of policy	800,000	600,000
Partial fire loss	400,000	400,000
Check to insured	400,000	300,000

Instead of being fully covered, the underinsured owner suffers a $100,000 out-of-pocket loss even though the face value of his policy exceeded the amount of damage. The reason: Since the owner carried insurance equal to three quarters of the amount required under co-insurance ($600,000 rather than $800,000), the owner only collects 75 percent of the loss.

The following are six steps that should be taken to assure adequate coverage:

☐ *Appraise the property.* Independent appraisers will calculate replacement values for a fairly nominal fee. Some insurance brokers may themselves be sufficiently experienced to give accurate estimates.

☐ *Add a stipulated value or stated value endorsement to the policy.* This should include a provision that the policy value will increase automatically each year to cover cost increases due to inflation. And when an owner is a substantial purchaser of insurance, the insurer may be willing to compromise the stipulated value figure.

☐ *Use lower co-insurance requirements.* If replacement cost makes the insurance premium sky-high, the co-insurance requirement can be dropped below 80 percent. This will increase the premium rate but reduces the total amount of insurance required. The net effect can be a premium reduction.

☐ *Use high loss deductibles.* Some companies offer loss-deductible policies, with the owner paying the first $1,000 or more of each loss. This will reduce the premium.

☐ *In the event of a loss, use a good professional adjuster.* His fee is usually more than paid for by a higher award.

[c] Consequential Loss Coverage

A fire or other peril may cause a loss that does not arise directly from destruction of the property—for example, the loss of rental income after a fire destroys a building, due to the inability of the tenants to operate their businesses. (The one exception to this is the net-leased property where the tenant is not entitled to rent abatement, even though the premises become unusable.) This type of loss is called a consequential loss. The basic types of insurance against consequential losses include

- Business interruption (use and occupancy) insurance, which protects a business owner against the loss of profits due to the inability to carry on business because of casualty to the premises. The policy pays all continuing expenses of the business (including rent if the premises are leased) plus the estimated lost profits based on past experience.
- Delayed profits insurance, covering loss of profits caused by a delay in a project's completion.
- Rent insurance and rental value insurance, covering loss of rental money after a fire or some other insured peril makes a building unusable, protects the landlord against loss of rent income from the date of damage until the building can be restored to "tenantable condition." The landlord is entitled

to receive the gross rental, including all charges assumed by the tenant under the lease, but minus expenses that do not continue during the period of nonuse. If the tenant is obliged to pay a percentage rental based on sales, this, too, will be covered. Sometimes, the lease requires the tenant to pay the premiums on the rent insurance. If the owner himself uses space on the premises, he can obtain rental insurance based upon the rental value of the premises.

- Leasehold insurance, covering a tenant's financial loss due to cancellation of a lease financially advantageous to him (in the sense that the rental on a new lease will be higher).
- Excess rental value insurance, the reverse of leasehold interest insurance, covering a landlord for the difference between the rental paid under a lease canceled by the tenant because of damage to the premises and the present (lower) rental value of the premises.

[d] Flood Insurance

If a real estate investor is planning to buy, build, or improve residential or commercial property, flood insurance must be obtained if it is available, when the property is

- Located in a flood-prone area.
- To be financed with a mortgage from a lender regulated or insured by the federal government.

The Federal Insurance Administration (FIA), a part of the Federal Emergency Management Agency (FEMA), publishes flood-hazard boundary maps, which show flood-prone areas in most communities. A flood-prone area is one where there is a risk of serious flooding at least once every 100 years. The term "base flood" is used by FEMA to describe that level of flooding that has a one percent chance of occurrence in any one year. Over a thirty-year period (the term of a mortgage on a new house), the laws of probability lead to the conclusion that a base flood in a flood-prone area has a 26 percent chance of occurring, about one chance in four. Floods being as unpredictable as they are, it is, of course, quite possible to have several base floods within a few years or to go several centuries without such a flood.

[i] How Communities Become Insurance-Eligible. The process for becoming eligible for flood insurance begins either when the FEMA on its own initiative undertakes a survey of potential flood levels or the community requests FEMA to undertake the survey.

When the FEMA has prepared its flood-hazard boundary map showing the flood-prone areas, the community may enter the first phase of the program, called the emergency program. If, after a year, the community has not applied for the emergency program, then neither federal grants or loans nor loans from federally regulated or insured institutions will be available in the flood-prone area. Almost all communities with flood-prone areas, therefore, do apply unless the area is one in which very little building or refinancing is likely to occur.

The community qualifies for the emergency program by requiring construction or development permits for proposed construction—a requirement already adopted by almost every community. All such permits must be reviewed to assure that the sites are relatively free from flooding. In flood-prone areas, structures must be properly anchored, materials and construction methods should minimize flood damage, and subdivisions should have adequate drainage.

When the community has qualified for the emergency program, subsidized insurance rates are charged for all structures in the flood-prone area.

[ii] Qualifying for the Regular Program. When the emergency program is in effect, FEMA undertakes the preparation of a detailed map (the flood insurance-rate map) of the flood-prone areas in the community. This map shows precisely where the base-flood line is located, that is, where flooding has a one percent chance of occurring each year. A hearing, announced in a local newspaper, is a customary part of the map preparation so that those affected may protest if they believe the map or the determination of flood probability to be in error.

When the rate map is ready, the community must require all new construction or substantial improvements either to be built to specified elevations over the base-flood level or flood-proofed. This is part of a floodplain management program of preventive measures to reduce flood damage.

The availability of the rate map plus the enactment of a floodplain management program qualifies the community for the regular program, instead of the emergency program. When the regular program is in effect, expanded coverage is available and the rates for insurance change.

Approximately 17,000 communities are now in either the emergency or regular program.

[iii] Buying Insurance. Once the investor has learned whether his property is in a flood-prone area and whether flood insurance is available, he can determine rates from the data in Table 10.3.

TABLE 10.3 Flood Insurance

Type of Structure	*Maximum Insurance Available Under Emergency Program*	*Rate per $100 in Emergency Program*	*Maximum Insurance Available Under Regular Program*
Residential single-family	$ 35,000	$.25	$185,000
Other residential	100,000	.25	150,000
Contents, all residential	10,000	.35	60,000
Small business	100,000	.40	250,000
Contents, small business	100,000	.75	300,000
Other nonresidential property	100,000	.40	200,000
Contents, other nonresidential property	100,000	.75	200,000

Whether the community is in the emergency or regular program, the minimum premium is $50, and each claim is subject to a deductible of $200.

> *Example:* If the community is in the emergency program and the house is worth $35,000 or more, $35,000 coverage would cost $87.50 annually. If the community is in the regular program, an additional $150,000 of insurance could be purchased (however, the maximum insurance may not exceed the replacement value of the house). The rate for the additional insurance is the actuarial rate (determined by an evaluation of the potential risk and damage to the insured property).

Replacement cost is paid only under the residential single-family program; for other types of structures, payments are based on the value of the property, not on what it costs to replace it.

Flood insurance, as noted above, must be purchased if it is available and if the property owner seeks financing from a lender insured or regulated by the federal government. The amount of required insurance under the regular program is twice the amount available under the emergency program. For example, a single-family house is eligible for $35,000 coverage under the emergency program; thus, it needs $70,000 coverage under the regular program to be eligible for financing (assuming its value is at least $70,000).

[e] Crime Insurance

The crime insurance program was enacted into law in 1970 to enable businessmen and home and apartment residents to purchase burglary and robbery insurance in those states where it was not otherwise available at affordable rates. Policies currently are sold in twenty-six states, the District of Columbia, Puerto Rico, and the Virgin Islands.

Three fourths of all policies issued under the program have been residential or household policies. The maximum policy coverage is $10,000, with a $50 deductible for each claim.

To be eligible for residential insurance, the residents must meet certain security requirements. For example, outside doors must have either a dead bolt or a self-locking dead latch. The annual premium for a $10,000 policy is $80. Applications are available from insurance agents or brokers and claims may be made either to the insurance agent or directly to a servicing company under contract to the government.

An applicant for commercial crime insurance may obtain robbery insurance, burglary insurance, or both. The maximum coverage for either or for the combination is $15,000. The deductible depends on the gross receipts of the business. For example, if sales exceed $500,000, the deductible is $200. Before a business property qualifies, all doors, doorways, and accessible openings must be adequately protected during nonbusiness hours.

The rates for commercial insurance are based on the class and location of the business. For example, a grocery store with gross receipts between $100,000 and $300,000 annually would pay $180 a year for $1,000 of insurance; for $15,000 of coverage, the annual premium would be $1,035.

Although the federal crime insurance program has generated net losses of $104 million, the federal government has actually incurred no out-of-pocket costs. This is due to the fact that the crime insurance program is combined with the federal riot reinsurance program for accounting purposes. The latter program, enacted in 1968, provided an incentive to the states to create what are known as FAIR plans, an acronym for fair access to insurance requirements.

The states that set up FAIR plans require property insurance companies to provide "essential property insurance" (covering fire, extended coverage, vandalism, and malicious mischief) to residents and business owners unable to obtain coverage in the private market. Insurance companies had been generally unwilling to provide such coverage in areas where urban riots are likely to occur, so the U.S. Government sold riot reinsurance to these companies. Fortunately, the extent of riots and disorders has been considerably less than predicted in the late 1960s, so there has been an accumulation of premium income for riot reinsurance. It is this accumulation which, up till now, has paid for the losses under the federal crime insurance program.

[3] Liability Insurance

The second major class of insurance is liability insurance. Unlike a casualty policy, which protects the real estate owner from loss due to damage to the property itself, a liability policy protects the owner against claims by third parties who have suffered damage or injury due to causes attributable to the real property. Even though the owner rents out all of the space to tenants, the owner may still be liable for acts of negligence to third parties who visit the premises (the extent of liability will vary from state to state). In addition, the landlord may be liable to his tenants for his negligence. Consequently, owners always will carry some form of general liability policy. This will either be an owner's, landlord's, and tenant's liability policy (OLT), which is usually a scheduled policy (i.e., it names the particular properties and risks insured against) or a comprehensive general liability policy, which offers protection on a nonscheduled basis.

Also available are a contracts-liability policy and an owner's and contractor's protective-liability policy.

The contracts-liability policy covers liability arising out of a contract or agreement. A contractor may undertake in an agreement with his principal to hold the principal harmless and indemnify him for any accidents arising out of the work being done. Also, a lessee often agrees to protect the lessor from any consequences arising out of use of the leased property.

The owner's and contractor's protective-liability policy covers an owner or contractor against any liability arising out of work done by another, such as a subcontractor or an independent contractor.

The question of how much liability insurance an owner should have is one of judgment. The owner must carry enough insurance so that he feels adequately protected. In making this decision, an owner should realize that, although pertinent, the size of a building and the number of its tenants are not the only factors to consider. Also important are the age and condition of the building, the past history of accidents, the neighborhood, and the kind of tenants in the building. Accidents always involve the unexpected, and serious accidents can happen in any kind of building.

The owner should also be aware of statutory limitations on recovery of damages for accidents. In most states there is a limit on the amount of damages recoverable for accidental death. However, there is usually no limit placed on recovery for temporary or permanent disability. The owner should be familiar with the trend in jury awards for such accidents in his community, and may want to increase his coverage if these awards are high.

Liability limits in policies are expressed as 50,000/100,000. This means that a single claim by one person is limited to $50,000. If more than one person is injured in a common accident, then each injured person can receive up to $50,000. However, the total paid to all claimants cannot exceed $100,000.

[4] Surety Bonds

A surety bond is a three-party instrument in which an insurance company or another party lends its credit to guarantee another's obligations. They are particularly significant in the construction industry since one of several contingencies might make the contractor unable to finish the job. There are two types of surety bonds:

☐ *Bid bond.* This type of bond is usually required to accompany contractors' bids for public work jobs; sometimes they are also required by private builders. The bid bond guarantees that the winning bidder will enter into the contract and will furnish the prescribed performance bond (and, if required, a payment bond). In case of default by the bidding contractor, the surety (the company issuing the guarantee) is liable for the difference between its principal's bid and the next lowest bid. The bid bond may be written with either a fixed penalty or an open penalty.

☐ *Performance bond.* There are four kinds of performance bonds, including:

- *Construction-contract bond.* This kind of performance bond guarantees the contractor's faithful performance for the construction of a building, and often includes the construction lender as an insured. The construction-contract bond may also be called a completion bond.
- *Labor and material payment bond.* This kind of performance bond guarantees that the contractor will foot all bills for labor and materials. It may be written as a separate policy or as part of the construction-contract bond.
- *Maintenance bond.* This bond guarantees that a contractor's work will not be defective in either workmanship or in materials. It may be written as a separate policy or as part of the construction-contract bond.
- *Supply-contract bond.* This bond guarantees a contract to supply goods or materials.

[5] Homeowners' Insurance

Homeowners' insurance is a multiple-peril insurance policy that provides both property and liability insurance to the owner of a one-family house, condominium, or cooperative apartment or mobile home, or a renter of residential premises.

Homeowners' coverage falls into three basic categories: (1) protection for the dwelling itself; (2) protection for the contents of the dwelling; and (3) protection against liability claims for damages because of bodily injury or property damage.

Most insurance companies offer one or more of six basic types of policies, including a separate policy for mobile homes. These may be briefly described as follows:

☐ *Form HO-1: "Basic" coverage for home and contents.* The basic form covers against loss or damage from fire or lightning, extended coverage perils plus vandalism, malicious mischief, glass breakage, and theft of personal property. Personal liability, medical payments and physical damage to the property of others are also covered. The increased cost of living elsewhere while the home is being repaired after an insured loss is included.

☐ *Form HO-2: "Broad" protection for home and contents plus added coverages.* The broad form gives coverage for the same perils as the basic form—broadening some perils and adding several other important coverages (bursting of steam or hot-water appliances or heating systems, damage by vehicles (including homeowner's) to the dwelling, and water leakage or overflow from plumbing or heating systems). Other additions include freezing (limited to certain types of property), damage from falling objects, building collapse, broader glass breakage, and accidental injury from electrical currents to electrical appliances and fixtures.

☐ *Form HO-3: Special coverage for dwelling, plus the same broad coverage of HO-2 for contents.* This is becoming the most popular form. Together with the broad protection for the contents, it provides all-risk coverage for loss or damage to the building, unless specifically excluded. Some coverages not in HO-2 but in HO-3 include paint spills, water seepage, and damage from overheated appliances.

☐ *Form HO-4: Contents broad form, if a home or apartment is rented.* The contents broad form is similar to form HO-2 and is designed to provide protection for loss of or damage to contents, plus give liability coverage.

☐ *Form HO-5: Comprehensive coverage for home and contents.* For a more expensive home with valuable furnishings, the comprehensive form protects the dwelling and contents against all risk of loss, unless specifically excluded.

☐ *Form HO-6: For a condominium.* Form HO-6 covers personal property plus $1,000 insurance on improvements (such as wall paneling, additional kitchen cabinets, carpeting, etc.) made to the unit at owner's expense. This $1,000 minimum limit can be increased. Most personal property and real property, not covered in the building policy purchased by the owners' association, can be insured under this policy.

Also available is loss assessment coverage to protect against charges levied if there is a building loss or a liability claim that is not fully covered in the association policy.

☐ *Mobile-home form: For a mobile home.* Operating like a HO-2 form, this form protects the mobile home, and the furnishings and personal property in it, against loss or damage from fire and lightning, extended coverage perils, vandalism, collapse, vehicle damage by others, aircraft, accidental rupture of water-heating system, accidental discharge of water, freezing of plumbing or heating system, and weight of ice, snow, and sleet. Personal liability, medical payments and physical damage to the property of others are also covered. In addition, it helps pay additional living expenses if a loss forces insured out of his mobile home.

[6] Homeowners' Warranty Program

An estimated three out of every ten homes built in 1980 were covered by the Homeowners' Warranty (HOW) plan created by the National Association of Home Builders (NAHB). Since 1974, when HOW began, approximately 900,000 homes have been covered under the plan.

[a] The Home-Buyer's Coverage

The purchaser of a new house warranted and insured under the HOW program gets ten-year protection.

In the first year, the house is warranted against all defects in workmanship and materials due to noncompliance with HOW-approved standards. The HOW-approved standards consist of the first written performance standards in the industry. These define the acceptable minimum levels of construction and spell out the building codes that are recognized by the program, such as the Minimum Property Standards of the Department of Housing and Urban Development (HUD).

In the second year of ownership, the builder warranty covers malfunctioning of the major systems, such as heating, plumbing and electrical systems. In both the first and second years, the house is also warranted against major structural defects.

On any claim under the warranty (during the first two years) the builder has the choice of making the repairs himself, employing another firm or firms to do the repairs, or giving the homeowner the money required to have the repairs done.

There is no deductible charged to the homeowner for warranty claims made to the builder during the first and second years. If, however, the builder refuses or is unable to pay the claim, and the HOW Corp., as co-warrantor, pays the claim, a $250 deductible is imposed.

For the third through the tenth year, the program becomes an insurance program rather than a warranty program. The owner can claim damages for major structural defects from the Insurance Company of North America. The builder is notified of the claim and can offer his opinion, or ways to repair damage, but the builder does not pay the claim. There is a deductible of one percent of the purchase price of the house for each claim made by the owner during this period. For example, if the house cost $75,000 and a major structural defect were discovered in the fourth year that cost $2,000 to fix, the homeowner would pay $750 and the insurance company would pay $1,250.

[b] Disagreement Between Owner and Builder

If the buyer and builder disagree on what needs to be done or how much it will cost, either can request use of the dispute settlement procedure established by HOW. HOW has created local councils which, along with HOW's regional offices, administer the program. The HOW local council will attempt to mediate the dispute. If within seven days this attempt is unsuccessful, the dispute will go to the National Academy of Conciliators (NAC), which will assign an arbitrator knowledgeable in the HOW program and in building standards.

If the builder loses the NAC ruling, he is expected to remedy the defect immediately, but he does have an appeal to the NAC office, which may assign another arbitrator or panel of arbitrators to review the case. The builder may not take the case to court.

The homeowner may at any time use the builder rather than go through the dispute-settlement system established by HOW. (Most courts, however, will refuse to hear such a case until the arbitration system has been used.) He may also seek a court reversal of an NAC ruling against him. The advantage to the homeowner of the HOW dispute-settlement system is that it is free and it is prompt. So far, about 12,000 cases have been resolved, most by mutual consent.

[c] Cost and Benefits to the Builder

The builder who wishes to have new houses covered by the HOW program must apply to his local HOW council. He is then screened for his technical qualifications, financial stability, and the quality of his customer service record. The local council will charge an initial service fee for the houses enrolled under the program. The premium is based on the risk in the specific area, just as automobile insurance is. He must enroll all the houses he builds within the jurisdiction of the local council; he cannot include one subdivision but omit coverage for another.

The former rate for this insurance and warranty coverage was $2 per $1,000 of the sales price of the house. The new rate is based on the loss experience in the area and ranges from $2.60 per $1,000 to $3.90 per $1,000. Thus, a builder who was building houses for sale at $75,000 each, with the local premium at $3.25 per $1,000, will pay $243.75 for each house, plus the local council warranty service fee.

There is a quality volume discount on the premiums for a builder who has been in the HOW program for at least three years, has an annual volume of at least $7.5 million, and a loss ratio of below 50 percent.

Compared to the ten-year HOW coverage, the Federal Housing Administration (FHA) and the Veterans Administration (VA) provide the buyers of new FHA- or VA-financed houses with only a one-year warranty against defects in workmanship and/or materials. The builder does not pay any fee for the government warranties, although he pays for inspections. If the builder, however, fails to remedy any defect or pay a reasonable claim, he may be taken off the list of FHA- or VA-approved builders. If that happened, the builder's houses would not be eligible for federally insured or guaranteed mortgages.

10.03 REAL PROPERTY TAXATION

[1] In General

The real property tax varies from locality to locality and may be relatively insignificant in some places, while, in others, it may constitute the single largest real estate operating expense. Property taxes are ad valorem taxes—that is, they are based on value. Consequently, property taxes are based neither on the ability of the property owner to pay nor on the particular benefits received by the owner.

Real estate taxes are determined by applying tax rates to assessed valuations.

The tax rate is set by the legislature or local governing council. It is often expressed in mills (tenths of a cent). For example, a tax rate of 50 mills per $100 is the equivalent of 5 cents per $100 (of assessed valuation). The assessed valuation is the value placed on real (and sometimes personal) property and recorded on the assessment roll of the taxing district. The standard followed in determining assessed valuation, usually specified by law, is the value that would be obtainable for the property in the open market. Assessed valuation may equal 100 percent of such open-market value or a fraction thereof (e.g., 50 percent of full value). Then, the total amount of revenues required to be raised from this source by the taxing district will be divided by the assessed valuation and the result will be the tax rate for the current year.

In 1978, California voters approved Proposition 13, a voter-initiated statute that was a harbinger of a significant "tax revolt" in many parts of the country. Under Proposition 13, California real property taxes were reduced by limiting the maximum property tax rate to one percent of full cash value of real property and by rolling back assessed property values to 1975-1976 levels, subject only to an annual 2 percent increase. Only when ownership of a property changes may the property be reassessed to reflect its current market value. In addition, the legislature was barred from enacting new property taxes while local governments could impose special taxes only if two thirds of the voters approve.

A number of other states have since passed Proposition 13-like measures, and indications are that local governments will continue to be required to fit budgets to available property tax revenues rather than the other way around.

Local governments recognize that the property tax is a land planning tool as well as a means of raising revenue. This is particularly true when the property tax is a significant element of a property's operating expenses and so has a great impact on residual equity cash flows. By giving special property tax relief in such cases, local governments can encourage one land use over another or attract a new industry to the community.

For example, farmers near developing urban areas sometimes find their property taxes rising substantially because of sharp increases in assessed valuations reflecting the market value of their land as development acreage rather than as farmland. As a result, the land sometimes must be sold since it can no longer be used profitably for agricultural purposes. In order to prevent this loss of farmland, some communities follow a practice known as value-in-use assessment. This permits farmland to be assessed at a lower value in order to encourage the continuation of agricultural use.

A growing problem in many communities is the percentage of property exempt from tax liability because it is used for public, charitable, or religious purposes. This problem comes into sharp focus in cities that have economic bases dominated by government employment. If a major educational institution is located in a state's capital, a very large percentage—perhaps as much as half—of the property within the city may be tax-exempt. This means that the city either must set high tax rates or develop other sources of revenue.

If property taxes are high, then property owners in the district are being taxed at a higher rate than owners in other districts. This may contribute to increased development outside the city limits to avoid the high city taxes. The result is an eroding city tax base and future city financing difficulties.

[2] Assessment of Real Property

Assessment is a term often misused and misunderstood. It encompasses the

- Official act of determining the amount of the tax base.
- Official act of discovering, listing, and appraising property. This may be performed by an assessor, a board of review, or a court.
- Valuation placed upon property in the course of such acts, and the entering of same upon the assessment roll.

The assessor is the public officer or member of a public body, elected or appointed, whose duty it is to make the assessment. It is obvious that while the assessor's duties are varied, his major obligation is to appraise or otherwise determine the value of a property in his jurisdiction to serve as a basis for the levying of the ad valorem tax.

Appraisal theories would seem to mandate that an assessment and an appraisal be one and the same. Unfortunately, this is not the case. Basically, an assessment must consider two things: value and uniformity (all property treated alike). Although the concepts of market value are accepted by most taxing jurisdictions as the criteria to be used in determining the tax obligation, the taxpayer may have difficulty in locating (or recognizing) market value on his tax statement. This difficulty may arise even in those states that legally require full-value assessments.

The problem, which tends to cause distortion of the market value concept, arises when the assessment ratio is applied. This usually is a percentage factor applied to the basic valuation. The rationale for such application is generally murky and not infrequently politically motivated. This adjustment produces the "official" value that appears on the tax roll, assessment notices, and tax bills, and is commonly referred to as the assessed value.

Assessed value should bear some directly traceable relationship to market value. However, this is too often not the case. The pressure of a residence-oriented constituency might, for example, result in the lowering of assessment ratios for such properties at the expense of industrial or commercial taxpayers. Although this, when it occurs, is an obvious violation of the uniformity of treatment promised in tax codes, one must be realistic and recognize that it can and does happen. This is upsetting for the assessor, who is attempting to conduct himself responsibly, as well as for the injured taxpayers who are being inequitably assessed.

The importance of the assessed value is its direct relationship to tax dollars through the employment of the tax rate. The tax rate is determined by elected officials, not the assessor, even though his position also may be an elected one. In theory, the tax rate is developed by dividing the needed local budget requirement dollars into the official assessment base, also known as the assessable base. This tax rate is then applied to each property's assessed value to determine the tax bill. If a semiannual or quarterly bill is tendered, this bill is usually only a simple fraction of the whole.

This simplified illustration of the tax rate/tax bill is the method followed by each of the taxing authorities whether it be state, county, city, town or village, school district, or special districts such as fire, hospital, or flood control. Bear in mind that this is not the method used for special assessments for improvements such as sewer or water and streets. Such assessments are not ad valorem taxes.

Assessing is a mass appraisal process that utilizes a check-off system or simple entries on a "field card." Most assessments are completed in minutes rather than the hours, days, or weeks required for appraisals. In the assessment process it is generally assumed that the title to property is fee simple. Real property has come to mean the property itself rather than the rights of ownership, and some forms of real estate are often classified as chattels or personal property.

[3] Protesting an Assessment

In most states, a prescribed method of protesting an assessment has been mandated. Usually the taxpayer's first level of recourse in case of a disagreement is through the assessor, his supervisor, and the assessment office. This is an informal discussion on a one-to-one basis, and most disagreements can be resolved at this point.

The second level of protest is to the taxing district's board of review or its equivalent. In those jurisdictions where multitaxing powers utilize a single assessment, more than one review board may be used, but the findings of one board usually are accepted by the others. At this level, a prescribed format is followed even though legal representation is not mandatory.

The third level of protest is to a state board of equalization or its equivalent. This level is the same in some respects as official courts, and prescribed methods must be followed. This usually requires some formal presentations and the procedures are recorded for the next level of protest, if needed.

The fourth level of protest is to the courts. This requires formal legal proceedings, highly qualified witnesses, documented evidence, and skilled legal representation.

Approximately 10 percent of assessments are protested to the first level each year. This rate is much higher if reassessment has just occurred, and may be lower in a dormant or inactive period. Only about 10 percent of the originally protested assessments go beyond the first level. Of those appeals going to the courts that are adequately prepared, 90 percent are found in favor of the taxpayer.

Standards vary widely from one taxing jurisdiction to another. There are taxing jurisdictions that are known for good, high-quality assessments utilizing a high degree of professionalism, but there are also those that are deemed to be far less than professional. A number of states supervise the assessment process, and one state, Maryland, has total state-assessment authority.

While there are, in effect, annual assessments, these seldom incorporate total annual reassessment programs, which include physical inspection and revaluation. Physical reassessment programs vary by state, with seven- to ten-year intervals not uncommon. Within such intervals, inequities might reasonably justify the protest effort.

Appraisal firms are often called upon to assist clients prior to or during the first level of protest. Often the time limit to file the appeal is less than thirty days, and the dollar amount of the disagreement is unknown at the time this assistance is requested. At this initial stage of a protest, a brief narrative report may be all that is required by a client in order to weigh the equity of an assessment. This report when properly presented should be sufficient for equitable settlement of protests at the first level. It should be brief and concise, and, if practical, should follow the sequence used and understood by the assessor. A lengthy, highly technical report with numerous exhibits and appendices may be rejected merely because of its complexity. On the other hand, too brief or too simplified a report can be ineffective, so it is vital to the success of the appeal that good judgment be exercised in the compilation of the report.

The first step is to make a systematic review of the assessor's work sheets, records, methods and procedures, a brief inspection of the property, and an analysis of available data. From this the appraiser can formulate a broad opinion and be in a position to advise if indeed there is an erroneous assessment, to approximate the degree of error, and to determine in which classification or subclassification of property the error lies. To do this effectively, the appraiser must follow the general property guidelines established by assessors. These usually are:

☐ *Land (highest-and-best use, vacant, and available)*. Caution: This must be considered as a total site, not per unit as originally plotted, acquired, or as may be separately recorded in the land records. The market value concept that the assessor may have used should be examined.

☐ *Land improvements such as fencing, paving, walks, rail spurs, drainage, etc.* These are generally assessed on the cost approach and added to the building value. Caution: These items are subjected to much more severe depreciation considerations. It should be determined what these items contribute to the market value of the package.

☐ *Buildings.* Rarely will the assessment reflect the three approaches to value. The cost approach is the one most favored by assessors. There may be a major area of error in the depreciation allowance, misgrading of the structure, and misuse of cost tables. Often assessors are lacking proper sales data, and the income data, if used at all, are based upon broad tables because of the uniformity required by the system. The courts usually rule that sales data are the best indicator of value. They are more readily understood and are accepted above any other data.

☐ *Personal property.* This may be subclassed into broad-use classes such as machinery and equipment used in manufacturing or processing, office furniture and equipment, motor vehicles, and so forth. Generally, the taxpayer is required to furnish his costs by year of acquisition. To this data, the assessor typically applies inflation indexes before calculating a depreciation allowance. Not uncommon is the use of straight-line depreciation over twenty years to a floor of 25 percent of historical cost, regardless of age. Although this is a simplified version of the method used, it demonstrates that, while uniformity may be accomplished, the market value requirement often is not met. Caution is required in analyzing data pertaining to tools, jigs, fixtures, short-life items such as lift trucks, spare parts and supplies, inventory items, work in process, and raw materials.

Often duplication occurs for machine foundations, power-feed wiring, process piping, etc. The assessor may have included these items in his building assessment. This most commonly occurs when the building valuation is based, at least in part, on indexed historical costs that have included expenditures for these items. Unless the assessor has carefully explored such possibility, or has been made aware of it by the taxpayer, it is most likely that duplication will occur.

Other classes of property are assessed by vastly differing methods, even within one state. These include leaseholds, mineral deposits, shares of stock, bonds, holdings at banks and savings and loans, of banks, utilities, railroads, and pipelines. The taxpayer must become familiar with the methods being used in his taxing jurisdiction if he is to properly interpret his assessment.

At the higher levels of protest a formal market value report is usually required. While this formal report may be prepared prior to selection of legal representation, it has been found that a team-effort approach is much more effective. The appraiser is responsible for the development of the valuation report and can be called upon as an expert witness, while the legal counsel provides for the proper court procedures and is responsible for each facet of the hearing. Most attorneys and courts prefer concise technical reports that are easy to follow. They must be factual and well documented, with sufficient exhibits and appendices. The terminology used in the report, preparation for trial, the taking of depositions, court testimony for rebuttal or cross examination should all be thoroughly reviewed with the attorney and his guidelines should be followed.

While the customary three approaches to value are usually presented, the sales information is the most scrutinized at the higher levels of appeal. This method of valuation apparently is the most easily understood and is considered a better indication of value by the courts. It is most desirable that documentation supporting comparable sales, together with adjustments for regional, state, national and, if applicable, international variances be presented.

With few exceptions, the most negative attitude of the courts is met when only the income-approach method is used. Lack of understanding, past difficulties in presentations, and suspicion of the wide flexibility in the development of capitalization rates have contributed to the lack of confidence in this method.

The courts are generally not receptive to in-house technical reports prepared by an employee, officer, or owner of a property under appeal, or to reports prepared by "professionals" where the fee for services is contingent upon the tax reduction settled upon. They feel, naturally, that such reports may be biased, and often ask for the submission of an additional report prepared by an outsider. The code of ethics of most professional organizations prohibits contingency-fee structures.

It is safe to say that, although protesting to the higher levels of appeal is not really a complicated process, professionalism and good teamwork are the keys to a favorable outcome. The attorney must be adequately prepared, have expert technical witnesses, well-documented evidence, and expertise in presenting the case. The appraiser must prepare all technical data, submit complete documentation systematically arranged, be personally familiar with all the property facts, and be able to convey these facts to the attorney and to the court, verbally and in written form.

10.04 DISTRESSED REAL ESTATE

[1] Early Warning Signs

As a practical matter, a property does not develop problems overnight. To the experienced investor and to the lender that monitors its loan portfolio carefully, signs of trouble can be spotted long before a loan default or bankruptcy becomes imminent. And problems caught early on can be cured, often with minor adjustments rather than major surgery. Remember, even the borrower with the best track record in the world can be hit by outside economic forces or internal difficulties—but neither borrower nor lender can take ameliorative steps until they recognize trouble on the horizon.

The following occurrences are warning signs that a piece of property may be headed for serious trouble:

☐ *Abnormally low operating expenses.* If maintenance and operating costs are much lower than those of comparable buildings, this is a sign of deferred maintenance or distorted financial statements. A good standard for comparison is the annual *Income/Expense Analysis* published by the Institute of Real Estate Management.

☐ *High tenant turnover.* If tenant turnover exceeds 30 percent yearly, a potential buyer should be concerned. This usually indicates tenant unhappiness or poor rental value.

☐ *Late mortgage payments.* The owner's checkbook (if the investor may examine it) will reveal late payments; the lender may or may not be willing to give the investor this information.

☐ *Late operating statements.* Most lenders require periodic statements from borrowers. If the owner's copies indicate these are being filed only after significant delays, this points to poor management (or a disinclination to show results).

☐ *Mistakes in management statements and records.* If tenant records are not up to date, payment discounts are not being taken or other errors are appearing in the owner's reports, poor management is indicated.

☐ *Poor physical condition.* An examination of the property that shows lack of grounds care, evidences of vandalism, etc., not only point to deferred maintenance but a lack of owner interest.

☐ *Lowered property reputation.* Talking to neighboring property owners, merchants, and others can tell an investor a lot about how the building is viewed by those in a position to know.

☐ *High vacancy rate.* Any rate substantially above a 5 percent figure is an obvious signal of possible problems.

[2] Overfinanced Property

If the cause of a property's distress is overfinancing, particularly a burdensome junior mortgage, both the owner and lender are best off seeking a private reorganization of the property's debt structure. In most cases, first mortgagee should avoid foreclosure if possible, but it should not compromise too easily since it invariably holds the strongest negotiating card.

Generally, the institutional lender will be faced with one of two scenarios in a default situation: one in which it is the sole lender, and the second one in which junior lenders are also involved.

[a] Owner and Institutional Lender

When only the two parties are involved, the key question is the ability and honesty of the owner or developer. A good position for the lender to take initially is that interest on the loan will be reduced in consideration of a partial prepayment of the outstanding loan balance (running anywhere from 10 to 40 percent). This relieves the property of some debt-service burden and also reduces the lender's risk. The difficulty is that the owner may lack any other assets that he can use for the prepayment; in such case, the lender must make the hard decision of whether to foreclose (on the theory that the "first loss is the best loss") or seek to work with the owner to financially rehabilitate the property.

[b] Existence of Junior Lenders

The negotiating strategy of the first mortgagee is more complicated when junior lenders are in the picture. Junior lenders can be classified into one of three types:

☐ *Traditional second-mortgage companies.* These firms, usually with adequate cash and credit, are basically real-estate oriented. They loan money on sound properties, and usually will be prepared to foreclose in a default situation, taking over the property and keeping the first mortgage current. In other words, this type of lender will protect the first mortgagee.

☐ *Purchase-money second mortgagees.* The junior lender here is a former owner who sold the property subject to a purchase-money mortgage representing the bulk of his profit on the deal. He is, in short, a paper lender. Such lenders, if they are forced to foreclose, are more likely to try to milk the property for whatever they can than to maintain it as a viable investment. Consequently, they will not protect the first lender if they take over.

☐ *Real estate investment trusts (REITs).* The typical mortgage REIT has no alternative but to take over the property and keep the first mortgage current in order to gain time to recoup its investment. Although it is not interested in managing a real estate portfolio, it cannot afford to permit the first mortgagee to foreclose and possibly wipe out the entire second loan.

Regardless of the type of second lender involved, the first mortgagee should recognize it negotiates from a position of strength. Consider one case where a second mortgagee, earning 11 percent interest, suggested that it and the first lender (holding a 6 percent loan) both forbear to an equal extent. The prime lender, not surprisingly, refused. The whole object of being a first mortgagee and accepting a lower interest rate is to have first claim on earnings and assets. Of course, the prime lender should not be too adamant in its position, otherwise no workout may be possible.

[3] Workouts

[a] In General

Even if a property is in serious trouble, it still may be possible to save it by arranging a "workout" with the lender. Most lenders want to avoid foreclosure or debtor bankruptcy, and in the vast majority of cases are amenable to negotiating a workout. A workout is a plan by which the owner and the lender agree to work together to outlast the crunch and save the property.

The problem with foreclosure is that it is an expensive and time-consuming process, during which the property can deteriorate badly. And if the problem is primarily that the property has been caught up in a general economic downspin, the lender will, by foreclosing, merely take on the owner's problems. In the case of defaulted construction loans, the lender will gain ownership of an incompleted project. Since few half-finished structures ever bring their full pro rata value at a foreclosure sale, the likelihood is that the lender will take a loss. In addition to all this, one lender's foreclosure bid may spark a bid for bankruptcy by other creditors of the borrower. (In one situation, however, foreclosure may be the lender's best choice. This is when construction is in the early stages and the borrower or other parties are good for a money judgment for any deficiency after a foreclosure sale.)

Although workouts invariably mean a higher financial investment than originally planned, they can nevertheless be profitable, as in the case of a stalled construction loan. With construction costs continuing to increase, some bailouts may represent a bargain investment when completed. The questions to ask are whether the economy will remain sound and whether demand—and inflation—will produce sufficient value over a reasonable period of time.

[b] Construction Workouts

Once a workout is proposed, the interested parties must decide what caused the loan default or the construction stoppage, and what is needed to complete the project. To the extent the cause of the trouble is not a monetary one, the developer should be given whatever assistance or advice is needed. But in almost every case there is also a monetary problem, if only because any delay in construction increases overhead and interest charges. So the second step is to investigate possible sources of new funds (either compulsory or voluntary).

Additional funds will come either from investors who already have an interest in the property or from new equity investors seeking bargain deals. When bargaining with "old" investors, the following points should be emphasized:

- They can benefit from increased cash flow generated by future tax losses.
- They can postpone payment of tax on foreclosure gain, thus reserving current use of their cash.

A good place to start looking for new investors is the roster of parties to the workout. Many different people must be considered and involved in any workout, and they may be a prime source of funds. Some simply stand to lose more through foreclosure; some may be legally obligated to put up money. The following entities or individuals should be considered:

- Developer (borrower)
- General contractor
- Bonding company
- Title company
- Supervising architect

- Major tenants
- Contract purchaser
- Developer's unsecured lenders
- Permanent lender

[c] Permanent Loan Workouts

The basic practical solution for a permanent mortgage in distress, aside from the obvious need for more efficient management, is through mortgage relief. This is obtainable through agreement with the mortgagee. Here are some of the possible loan workouts:

☐ *Stretching the loan term.* This approach merely delays the time until the lender recoups his entire principal. However, he receives his full interest (and indeed, more than that originally expected because of the stretch-out). This offers quite limited relief to the borrower since the percentage of the total annual debt service that goes toward amortization is quite small (unless the loan has been outstanding a good many years).

☐ *Interest-only (standing) loan.* This will permit slightly greater relief, but again, loan amortization usually represents only a small number of dollars each year.

☐ *Accruing interest; no cash payments.* Significant relief is obtained when the entire debt service can be temporarily suspended. At the same time, the lender, to avoid recognizing any loss, accrues the income on its books, anticipating that it will all be paid in the future. This may or may not be realistic.

☐ *Reducing interest rate.* Since the bulk of the debt service usually is interest, not amortization, the borrower should concentrate his efforts on reducing interest payments. Interest can be accrued (as just described) or the interest rate can be paid in a substantially reduced amount. A lender may prefer the latter approach because so long as any interest is being paid, the mortgage need not be placed in a non-interest-accruing status on the lender's books.

☐ *Incorporate unpaid interest into principal.* This is a device for the benefit of the lender's books. He refinances the original loan with a new, larger loan; the additional principal is used to pay off the accrued interest on the old loan (merely a paper transaction). So long as the lender can justify the larger loan by the future possibilities for the property, this brings everyone up to date. The new loan may or may not call for immediate debt-service payments.

☐ *Waiver of replacement reserves.* This is granted automatically in most cases. The danger is that this will soon lead to deferred maintenance, which will cause rapid deterioration of the property and a downward spiral that cannot be reversed.

Beyond this point, the only alternatives for the lender are to place the loan in a non-interest-accruing status, taking over the property by a deed in lieu of foreclosure, or foreclosing. These drastic steps, however, will not be taken if the lender believes the present owner can do as well with the property as anyone else.

10.05 FORECLOSURE AND BANKRUPTCY

With some distressed real estate, workouts just will not work—either owner and creditors cannot agree on a procedure, or the salvage methods used are insufficient to stave off disaster. In these cases foreclosure or bankruptcy will result.

[1] Foreclosure

[a] In General

Foreclosure is a legal process by which a mortgagee may take legal action to realize on the security for his loan when the covenants of the mortgage have been breached by the borrower. In effect, by filing or giving notice of the foreclosure action, the lender gives the borrower the option of paying in full and redeeming the pledged property or of forfeiting his right to the property so that it can be sold to satisfy the mortgage debt. The two basic forms of foreclosure are foreclosure by power of sale and statutory foreclosure. Under the first, permitted in most but not all states, the lender need not commence a court proceeding but may, after appropriate notice to the borrower, put up the property for sale at a public auction. Under statutory foreclosure, the foreclosure sale can be conducted only under court supervision and after a foreclosure action has been commenced.

During the foreclosure proceedings, the mortgagee should recommend a qualified managing agent to a court-appointed receiver. The object is to make possible active cooperation between the mortgagee and the building manager, and thus increase the likelihood of presenting the property as a viable investment to potential buyers. Unfortunately, political patronage in many cities may make it difficult for the mortgagee-recommended manager to be appointed.

Prior to the sale, the mortgagee may prepare a sales flyer to be mailed to qualified prospective purchasers. He may even enter into a contract before the foreclosure sale takes place. If a contract is signed, the buyer, at his own request and with the mortgagee's and the receiver's approval, may act as subagent of the managing agent as an inducement to his purchasing the property. Although the lender does not have to bid in at the foreclosure sale, a contract entered into prior to the sale should specify that it is subject to the mortgagee's becoming the successful bidder. Ideally, the closing will be concurrent with the mortgagee's receipt of the referee's deed.

Following the foreclosure sale (at which the lender himself may "bid in" the property if he wishes), the proceeds of sale are applied first to any indebtedness in order of priority (the first mortgage is entirely satisfied, followed by the second mortgage, etc.) and any surplus is paid to the borrower.

The lender who has brought foreclosure frequently will bid on the property to the point where the bid price is equal to the amount of the debt. For him to permit a third party to buy the property for less would mean that he would receive only a portion of the debt owed him. By bidding the property at least up to the amount of his debt, the lender insures that he will receive title to the property if no one is willing to bid a price sufficient to pay off the debt. Once the bid price rises above the debt, however, the lender normally will be happy to have his debt discharged out of the proceeds of the sale.

In the event the lender does not bid up the property to the amount of the debt and it is purchased at a lower price, there will remain a deficiency. Provided the borrower is personally liable for the debt (having signed a promissory note in addition to the mortgage), the mortgagee has a claim against the borrower for the deficiency. If this is uncollectible, the lender is entitled to claim a bad-debt deduction. (In the case of corporate mortgagees, this will always be a business bad debt, which may be fully offset against ordinary income.)

[b] Foreclosure Tax Rules

[i] The Lender's Point of View. Since foreclosures have been relatively uncommon for the past decade, the tax rules affecting bids are generally not familiar to lenders. But it is important to choose the right bid price. This can maximize the deductible loss to the lender, considerably softening the financial blow.

When a mortgagee forecloses and no third party is willing to buy the property at a reasonable price, the mortgagee itself usually will buy the property. When it bids in the property, two tax events occur:

- The mortgagee has a bad-debt deduction equal to the difference between the uncollectible mortgage and the bid price.
- The mortgagee has a gain or loss to the extent the fair market value of the property either exceeds or is less than the bid price.[1]

In other words, for tax purposes the mortgagee wears two hats: Under its creditor hat it may get a bad-debt deduction, and under its purchaser hat it has a gain or loss.

Since there is often no third party interested in purchasing the distressed property, the mortgagee may be in a position to bid it in at almost any price. Good tax planning normally dictates making a low bid, since the smaller the bid price, the larger the bad-debt deduction. But if the bid price is less than fair market value, the excess of fair market value over the bid price produces immediately taxable gain. So the question is, How much can the mortgagee lower the bid price without producing an offsetting taxable gain? Under the Regulations, the bid price is presumed to equal fair market value, "in the absence of clear and convincing proof to the contrary."

[ii] The Owner's Point of View. For the foreclosed owner, too, there is more involved in foreclosure than mere loss of the real estate that secured a loan. When an owner forfeits real property through a mortgage foreclosure, the tax consequence is that the defaulting owner has sold the property for a price equal to the unpaid obligations at the time of disposition. He may therefore realize a theoretical capital gain and be required to pay a real capital gains tax. The Tax Court has held that a forfeiture of real estate resulting from a default in an extended payment contract will be treated similarly, even though in this situation title technically remains in the seller all along.[2]

Not every foreclosed owner will realize this paper gain. But the owner of

---

[1] Reg. § 1.166.6.

[2] White v. Comm'r, T.C. Memo 1974-69.

property that is mortgaged in excess of its adjusted cost basis who loses the property by foreclosure must register a gain to the extent of the excess. This can be particularly troublesome for limited partners in failing syndications who stand not only to lose their investment but to be hit with a substantial tax bill as well.

What if the borrower registers a loss upon foreclosure? A foreclosed owner's loss can be computed as follows. Suppose that a mortgagor purchased property for $100,000, paying $25,000 in cash and giving a purchase-money mortgage of $75,000. Default and foreclosure occur after the mortgagor has made amortization payments of $5,000 and has taken depreciation deductions of $10,000. The net cash proceeds of the foreclosure sale amount to $70,000, just enough to pay the mortgagee in full. The loss is computed in the same general way it would be if the owner sold the property voluntarily.

Original basis for property	$100,000	
Less: Depreciation	10,000	
Adjusted basis for property		$90,000
Less: Net cash proceeds		70,000
Loss of mortgagor		($20,000)

If the net cash proceeds were $75,000, so that the mortgagor received $5,000 in cash, his loss would be reduced to $15,000.

Sometimes, of course, foreclosure proceeds are less than the mortgage debt. Suppose the net cash proceeds were only $60,000 in our example, leaving a $10,000 deficiency. Assuming that the unpaid portion of the debt survives the foreclosure and the mortgagor pays the deficiency, the tax consequences to the mortgagor should be unchanged. The payment of the deficiency is treated, in effect, as part of cost represented by an additional payment to the mortgagee on the mortgage debt.

Original basis for property	$100,000	
Less: Depreciation	10,000	
Adjusted basis for property		$90,000
Less: Net cash proceeds	$ 60,000	
Deficiency payment	10,000	
		70,000
Loss of mortgagor		($20,000)

If there is a loss, a deduction should follow. Unless he had been holding the property "for sale in the ordinary course of business" (or if it was inventory or a Section 1231 asset) the mortgagor will probably be subject to capital loss limitations. So a builder, for instance, who loses the last ten houses in a tract, will probably be eligible for an ordinary income deduction. But the foreclosed owner of raw land will not be. Borrowers should check out the situation with their tax counselors before foreclosure occurs, since they may want to consider an alternative move.

[2] Bankruptcy

There are two kinds of bankruptcy—straight bankruptcy or liquidation, and reorganization. Under straight bankruptcy no attempt is made to save an ailing business. The purpose is to allocate the assets fairly among all creditors and permit an honest debtor to receive a full discharge from any further liability for his debts. More complicated is reorganization, which seeks to reorganize and save the bankrupt's business operation; rehabilitation of the debtor is the final goal.

In order to understand how reorganization works under present law, a brief historical digression is necessary. For forty years prior to October 1, 1979, the federal bankruptcy law provided three ways in which a debtor's business could be reorganized as proceedings—Chapter X proceedings, Chapter XI proceedings, and Chapter XII proceedings.

Chapter X proceedings were available to corporations only and provided for reorganization while the debtor remained in business. Reorganization could not affect secured debts, and bankruptcy under this form of reorganization could be either voluntary or involuntary. Chapter XI proceedings were available to corporations, partnerships, and individuals. This form of reorganization permitted the debtor to retain possession of the property while arranging a plan for payment and dealt only with unsecured debts. Finally, a Chapter XII proceeding was a form of reorganization available only to noncorporate debtors owning real property. When the petition was filed by either the debtor or one of his creditors, all enforcement proceedings against the property were stayed, including foreclosure. Chapter XII also contained a feature particularly disliked by lenders—the so-called cramdown provision. It was the right of the bankruptcy court to pay off a mortgage on the basis of the present market value of the property (usually far less than the outstanding principal due). Because of this, investors in distressed syndicates would use a Chapter XII proceeding to block foreclosure action by a lender following the borrower's default. Often the borrower's real motive in seeking protection of a bankruptcy court was to avoid the tax consequences of a foreclosure recapture of depreciation, which could result in a large tax liability.

The present law, which is known as the Bankruptcy Reform Act of 1978 [3] became effective on October 1, 1979. It was the first comprehensive revision of the federal bankruptcy laws in over forty years, and made some important changes in the rights of lenders, lessees, and lessors in the event of a bankruptcy proceeding affecting real estate. Most important, the present law consolidates Chapters X, XI, and XII into a single chapter governing reorganizations. This consolidation had important effects on the cramdown provisions and the automatic stay previously attractive to debtors under the old law.

[a] The Borrower-Lender Relationship

The two significant elements of a bankruptcy proceeding affecting mortgage lenders are (1) the automatic stay of a separate mortgage foreclosure proceeding; and (2) the cramdown method of reorganizing.

---

[3] Pub. L. No. 95-598, 92 Stat. 2549, 11 U.S.C.A. §§ 101-151326.

[i] Automatic Stay of Foreclosure Action. Under the bankruptcy law, the filing of a petition operates as an automatic stay of any pending proceedings or the enforcement of judgments already obtained. Thus, a mortgagee can neither foreclose his mortgage nor enforce other remedies. The purpose of the stay, obviously, is to decrease the financial pressure on the debtor and to prevent one creditor from pursuing remedies to the detriment of others.

Under the former statute, debtors often used the automatic stay provision to force mortgage lenders into favorable settlements. The new law seeks to end this type of pressure by providing for adequate protection for a creditor who is subject to a stay of a pending action or of remedies for a judgment already obtained. In the case of a mortgage lender, the potential damage from a stay arises from the depreciation in value of the real estate securing the loan.

When a mortgage lender is stayed, the trustee in bankruptcy must provide an adequate protection method. For example:

- The trustee may make periodic cash payments from the bankrupt estate to the mortgagee in an amount equal to the depreciation in value of the real estate securing the loan.
- Alternatively, the trustee may give the mortgagee an additional or replacement lien on other property to the extent of the loss of value of the original security.
- Finally, the trustee may grant the mortgagee an administrative expense priority when it is fairly certain that there are enough assets in the estate to pay administrative expenses.

These methods are not exclusive and the trustee may fashion other means of protection to fit the situation.

This provision is far more favorable to lenders than was prior law. A difficult issue in practice undoubtedly will be to determine how much value a property loses during the course of a stay in a bankruptcy proceeding—in order to determine the degree of protection needed by the lender.

[ii] Cramdown Method of Reorganization. Reorganization plans in bankruptcy can be confirmed (approved) by the court either by (1) the acceptance method; or (2) the cramdown method. The acceptance method means simply that all of the classes of creditors go along with the proposed reorganization. The cramdown method, by comparison, permits the court to confirm a plan despite the rejection of it by one or more classes of creditors. All that is required is that at least one class of creditors approve the plan.

Under Chapter XII of the prior Bankruptcy Act, which covered noncorporate real estate ventures, the use of the cramdown method often meant that a mortgage would be paid off on the basis of the present (distressed value) of the property. The mortgagee, in other words, lost the right given by the mortgage to "bid in" the property at a foreclosure proceeding, acquire title, and hold it until conditions improve. The cramdown provision in the new law appears to be much more favorable to the secured lender.

Basically, a bankruptcy court can cram down a reorganization plan despite the disapproval of a mortgage lender if the court finds that the plan is fair and equitable with respect to that lender. The phrase "fair and equitable" was used in the former law and has been construed by the courts as requiring absolute priority among classes according to their rank. In essence, a plan is fair and equitable with respect to a particular creditor when he will receive full compensation for his claims before any junior creditor receives anything. In addition, a plan is not fair and equitable if a creditor who is senior to the cramdown creditor receives more than 100 percent of the amount of his claim.

The new law contains guidelines for the application of the fair and equitable standard to (1) secured creditors; (2) unsecured creditors; and (3) holders of equity interest. Since a mortgage lender, by definition, is a secured creditor, only the guidelines for secured creditors are outlined below.

☐ *Retain security.* The first way to treat a secured lender fairly and equitably (and thus pave the way for a cramdown by the court) is to permit the secured lender to retain his security interest (mortgage) to the extent of the allowed secured claim (see below) and to give the lender cash payments (1) that are equal to the amount of the allowed secured claim; and (2) that have a present value equal to the value of the collateral for the loan.

☐ *Indubitable equivalent.* The second way for complying with the fair and equitable standard is for the secured lender to be given the indubitable equivalent of his secured claim. Giving the collateral to the lender, or giving him a lien on similar collateral may satisfy this standard. Present cash payments to the lender that amount to less than the allowed secured claim (see below) will not be the indubitable equivalent of the collateral.

☐ *Lien on sale proceeds.* The third alternative for complying with the fair and equitable standard is to permit the sale of the collateral free and clear of the mortgage lien and for the lien to attach to the sale proceeds. Then, the lien on the proceeds must be treated in accordance with either of the above two alternatives.

It is important to emphasize that the new law does not permit the cramming down of a plan against a dissenting mortgage lender by giving the lender equity securities in the reorganized debtor. In other words, a secured lender cannot be bought off with newly issued securities that are speculative at best. This is one way that the new law seeks to preserve the priority of secured interests such as mortgage loans.

Understanding the meaning of "allowed secured claim" is crucial to an understanding of the cramdown method. Suppose a lender gave a $15 million mortgage secured by an $18 million parcel of real estate. Subsequently, the debtor files for bankruptcy at a time when the value of the real estate had dropped to $12 million. If the lender does not go along with a reorganization plan and the court wishes to confirm it by the cramdown method, the amount of the allowed secured claim is either $12 million or $15 million, depending upon the choice of the lender.

- The lender may decide to split his claim into two parts. The secured portion would be $12 million (the current value of the real estate) and the unsecured portion would be $3 million (the excess of the mortgage principal over the current value of the property).

- Alternatively, the lender may elect to be treated as fully secured. In that case the allowed secured claim equals the $15 million debt despite the lower current value of the real estate.

Normally, the lender will elect to be fully secured (the second approach) whenever he believes the real estate has the potential to increase in value. By electing to be fully secured, the lender is in exactly the same position as if he had foreclosed the loan and bid in the property. Thus the new law is designed to prevent the practice found objectionable by lenders under the former Chapter XII proceeding. Then, a debtor could threaten bankruptcy in the event the mortgage lender refused to compromise the amount of the loan, since the debtor could be reasonably sure that in a cramdown proceeding, the lender would end up getting less than the full value of the debt.

[b] The Landlord-Tenant Relationship

The new federal bankruptcy statute, which became effective in 1979, has significantly changed the consequences when a landlord or a tenant becomes bankrupt. Knowing these consequences is important for two reasons: (1) so that during lease negotiations, each party can (to the limited extent possible) include clauses that minimize the adverse effects of the other party's bankruptcy; and (2) so that if a bankruptcy occurs, the other party will be in a position to protect his rights against the trustee in bankruptcy.

As discussed earlier, a bankruptcy proceeding may involve either a liquidation or reorganization of the bankrupt. The discussion that follows applies to both types of proceedings unless otherwise indicated.

[i] Unexpired Leases of Bankrupt Tenants. If a tenant goes bankrupt, his trustee has the power either to reject or to assume (continue) unexpired leases, subject to the court's approval. Lease clauses that automatically terminate the lease or declare the lease in default in the event of the tenant's bankruptcy are now void.

If the trustee assumes the lease, he may ignore lease clauses that bar assignments by the tenant—but if the trustee does assign the lease to another tenant in order to raise cash, the trustee must provide adequate assurance of future performance by the new tenant of the lease obligations.

The effect of these rules is to give the trustee the best of both worlds—the right to terminate leases that impose burdensome liabilities upon the bankrupt tenant and the right to take advantage of favorable leases that benefit the tenant.

If the tenant's trustee rejects an unexpired lease, then the landlord has a claim for damages resulting from the tenant's defaults prior to the bankruptcy.

[ii] Rules for Assumption of Leases by Trustee. When it comes to the trustee's power to assume unexpired leases of the tenant, the Bankruptcy Code spells out certain specific limitations. These are designed to protect the rights of the landlord or other third parties.

The bankrupt tenant commonly is in default under his lease at the time the bankruptcy proceeding begins (nonpayment of rent, for example). In such a case, the trustee may not assume the lease unless he either (1) cures the defaults; or (2) provides adequate assurance that cure will occur promptly. Moreover, the trustee must provide adequate assurance of future performance of the tenant's obligations under the lease before it can be assumed. What constitutes adequate assurance is determined on a case-by-case basis, depending upon the particular facts and equities of the situation.

[iii] Assuming or Assigning Shopping Center Leases. In the special case of a bankrupt tenant in a shopping center, the law contains certain other requirements in addition to those just mentioned. These requirements result from the recognition that a shopping center is a carefully planned enterprise with a particular tenant mix, with the landlord's profit primarily derived from percentage rentals.

Specifically, the trustee may not assume a shopping center lease of a bankrupt tenant unless there is adequate assurance

- Of the source of future rent payments due under the lease.
- That any percentage rent due under the lease will not decline substantially.
- That assumption or assignment of the lease will not substantially breach any related provision in another lease or financing agreement, such as a radius, location, use or exclusivity provision.
- That assumption or assignment of the lease will not substantially disrupt the tenant mix or balance in the center.

If any of these assurances cannot be made, the shopping center landlord may insist that the lease be rejected by the trustee so that the premises may be rented to a new tenant.

[iv] Time Limits for Assumption or Rejection. The bankruptcy law imposes time limits for the trustee to assume or reject a lease. In a liquidation proceeding, the trustee has sixty days to act. The court, however, may extend this time. If the trustee does not act within sixty days (or extended) period, the lease is deemed to be rejected.

In a reorganization proceeding, the sixty-day limit does not apply. Instead, the trustee may assume or reject the lease at any time before confirmation of the reorganization plan, unless the court upon the request of the landlord orders the trustee to make a decision sooner. The landlord must show grounds for requesting an immediate decision.

As just indicated, some time will pass between the filing of a bankruptcy petition and the decision of the trustee to accept or reject the lease. Must the landlord continue to provide services to the tenant until the decision is made? The answer is that the landlord must render services only when the landlord is assured that he will be paid for them.

[v] Unexpired Leases of Bankrupt Landlords. If the landlord goes bankrupt, a two-step process occurs. First, the landlord's trustee has the option of rejecting or assuming the lease. If the lease is a favorable one (in terms of rentals) for the landlord, his trustee normally will assume the lease. However, the trustee must cure any defaults by the landlord under the lease or provide adequate assurance that cure will occur promptly in the future.

If the lease is not favorable to the landlord (usually because the rent is below current market levels), the trustee may reject the lease. However, at that point the second stage of the process comes into play. The tenant then has the choice of either (1) treating the lease as terminated; or (2) remaining in possession of the premises for the balance of the lease term.

If the tenant chooses to remain in possession despite the trustee's rejection of the lease, any damages due to the landlord's failure to perform his obligations under the lease may be offset by the tenant against the rent due. However, the tenant does not have the right to obtain an affirmative judgment against the bankrupt estate for such damages.

The result of this present rule in the bankruptcy law is that a tenant holding a favorable lease may not be evicted because of the landlord's bankruptcy, but the tenant may have to perform the landlord's functions for the balance of the lease term.

11

Specific Types of Real Estate

11.01 UNDEVELOPED LAND

[1] Introduction

Undeveloped (raw) land offers the greatest potential return of any available investment; it carries commensurate risks. The increasing pressure of population growth combined with rising personal incomes, in conjunction with the fixed amount of land available to meet the resulting demand for commercial, recreational, and residential space, has created steadily mounting land values. Discounting those price levels that result solely from an inflated economy, these factors will increase the inherent value of carefully selected undeveloped property many times beyond its present price. At the same time, a new attitude toward growth and a rash of new environmental laws have created new risks for the land speculator.

Although by one measure 80 percent of the nation's land is undeveloped, not every purchase of this raw acreage will result in substantial profits, or even warrant an investment risk. If the location is poor, the investor may find that he has been left in the backwash of progress. If the purchase is ill-timed, the cost of carrying the property can wipe out whatever eventual return is realized. Even if the location and timing are good, a poorly constructed transaction could destroy an otherwise well-conceived plan.

The basic form of raw land is acreage in its natural, unused state. It can be woodland, plainland, desert, mountain, or swamp. Most land in this category has obvious inherent physical defects that make development impractical, although sometimes the application of contemporary technology may overcome them.

Raw land, however, in terms of investment property, need not be real estate that has not been developed for some use; today's farm is tomorrow's residential community and shopping center. It has been suggested that land has low-value and high-value uses ranging roughly as follows: (1) agriculture, ranch, or timberland; (2) recreation or resort property; (3) industrial property; (4) commercial property; and (5) residential property. This classification is not necessarily rigid. For example, the demand for second homes by city dwellers has probably placed some recreation property in a high-value category. Part of the trick in investing is to determine what land presently being put to a low-value use has a high-value potential before this becomes readily apparent to others. In other words, profitable raw-land investing is, almost by definition, speculative.

The application of the low-value/high-value criterion can uncover another source of raw land, this time in an urban setting. Air rights, the vertical plane above existing construction, has become an important commodity in many major cities. Serving no present use, especially when existing above roadways and railroads, which only require a horizontal path, these rights can immediately be put to high-value purposes when occupied by commercial and residential buildings.

[2] Advantages of Land Investment

[a] Low Cost

The attractiveness of an investment in raw land is its low cost when compared to that of developed income-producing property. In the case of the latter, rents or profits are a function of the price, the purchaser's concern being an annual yield on his investment. However, the price of raw land, if properly negotiated, may bear little or no relationship to its ultimate use. Various types of landowners with whom a prospective purchaser will deal are (1) working farmers; (2) gentlemen farmers; (3) estates; (4) lenders who have foreclosed mortgages; (5) government agencies and municipalities; (6) builders and developers; (7) large corporations; and (8) other land speculators. Each of these groups has its own reason for making land available. It may be a desire for retirement income, a need for ready cash, or the bailing out of a defaulted loan. This often will facilitate a purchase at a modest cost, often with favorable financing via a purchase-money mortgage.

[b] High Potential Gain

Closely allied to the relatively inexpensive cost of raw land is the large profit the investment will return if the purchaser's appraisal of the ultimate high-value use of the property proves to be correct. Further, these profits normally can be taken as capital gains and thus be subject to lower income tax rates.

In addition to these advantages, the low cost of undeveloped property permits the purchase of substantial acreage. As a result, a tract held for investment may be divided into smaller units that can be sold at different times. Should the buildup in values be rapid, the original cost may be realized by a partial sale, permitting the retention of the remainder of the property until its highest value is reached, with little risk to the owner.

[c] Diversification of Investment

The low cost of raw land also permits an investor to avoid the concentration of his capital in one make-or-break unit. Purchases of property can be made at several locations, so that if one investment should be improvident, the others can carry the loss and still return a profit. The purchase of urban income property by a person of modest means may not carry this protection. There, the investor must bear the risk of a deteriorating neighborhood or a change in fashion in the location of services, without the financial ability to retreat to new high-value use areas. In the past twenty years many purchasers of city apartment houses and satellite commercial space surrounding large department stores have suffered the consequences of these changes.

[3] Disadvantages of Land Investment

[a] No Current Income

When raw land is not put to use, it generates no income for its owner. Consequently, carrying charges and periodic mortgage payments must be made with the purchaser's own resources. This will to some extent, but not completely, be offset by the deductibility of interest, land taxes, and other charges on the investor's income tax return.

The income produced by raw land being put to a low-value interim use is generally insufficient to do more than cover the carrying charges, if that much; the most the investor can hope for is income large enough to meet mortgage payments or represent a nominal return on invested equity. Additionally, these low-value uses generally require expert or day-to-day supervision that the investor is not equipped to furnish. For example, farmland, which provides a living for the farmer engaged in its cultivation, will give nothing to the investor who has not been trained as an agriculturalist. Tenant farming during the holding period may have other advantages, such as maintenance of the property, but it will not produce an income that would warrant the cost of purchase.

The purchaser of raw land, therefore, has only one source of profit—the increment in the value of the investment. While he is waiting for this, he is forced to pay all or a part of the carrying charges out of his own pocket; purchasers of income-producing property do not have such a problem. The purchaser of raw land, therefore, must rely entirely upon the realization of his appraisal of ultimate value and the period within which it is reached.

It becomes apparent that time is the enemy of any purchaser of underdeveloped land. Even though predictions of the eventual increase in value may have been correct, if it arrives after a lengthy holding period, the cost of carrying the investment will reduce or, in some cases, wipe out the profit. Another factor to bear in mind is that at today's interest rates, money left in a savings bank doubles in about six years, without risk to the depositor. An investment in raw land that nets out at that rate is not worth making; to be worthwhile, the return must be substantially in excess of current money rates.

[b] Difficulty in Financing

The nature of raw land, especially property that is not being used to generate any income, does not make it attractive to institutional lenders. The value of raw land may be difficult to appraise because a lender will not evaluate it on the same basis as the speculator-purchaser. The future growth in value on which the purchaser-borrower relies usually is wholly discounted by the lender who is more interested in rents, which can be applied in the event of a default, and the ease of resale if foreclosure becomes necessary. Of course, a purchaser may be able to obtain funds from institutional lenders on the strength of his own credit, but it is much more advantageous to borrow without the risk of personal recourse.

Mortgage financing may be available for land that is employed in some income-producing activity, even though it is a low-value use. However, the income would have to continue following the purchase and, as has been shown, this may be impossible to guarantee.

This difficulty can be obviated by the willingness of the seller to take back a purchase-money mortgage or to grant options that are exercisable at a time when the purchaser can better determine whether his judgment will prove correct.

[c] Risk of Overpayment

While the primary advantage of the purchase of raw land is its availability at a low cost, the reverse of this proposition should not be overlooked; some undeveloped land may be overpriced. This can happen for several reasons.

First, the standards applicable to the appraisal of developed income-producing property are lacking. There are no buildings with structural soundness to be determined, no rent rolls to capitalize, and often no recent sales of comparable property on which a judgment of value can be based.

Second, the land may already have passed through the hands of several speculators, each more optimistic than the last. A thorough check of land-transfer records and earlier prices should satisfy a prudent purchaser in this regard.

Third, the very fact that a person outside of the community is in the market for acreage can inflate prices. While persons residing in the area may have an excellent idea of the present value of land within it, the outsider who is investing in the possibility of substantial increases may become a "mark."

It therefore is wise to investigate and purchase with as little public notoriety as possible. Employment of a local real estate broker can be of enormous help. He is familiar with the real property in his bailiwick and knows of recent transfers and prices. He is aware of what property is available and the reasons why the owners wish to sell. He can conduct negotiations on a more personal basis than can the purchaser and with a minimum of publicity.

[d] Physical and Legal Defects

Even though property may be located in an area in which growth can be expected, it may have inherent defects that render it unsuitable for development and, hence, for speculative investment. These include features of the terrain such as steep grades, lack of an adequate water supply, drainage problems, and subsoil difficulties, any of which could make development excessively expensive. The careful investor should examine his proposed purchase thoroughly before committing himself and, if indicated, seek the opinion of qualified experts such as soil and structural engineers.

In addition to inherent physical defects, there may be existing legal rights and burdens which, although not incompatible with the use of the land at the time of purchase, may make the transition to a higher-value use difficult or impossible. These would include charges on the land such as prescriptive easements, grants of riparian rights, and adverse possession of portions of the tract. Here, the local broker can be of invaluable assistance; his knowledge of community affairs will enable him to identify problems of this sort that may not be readily discoverable by investigation. It is also essential that the purchaser have an up-to-date survey of the property before purchasing. These two steps will keep the purchaser from making a costly blunder.

[e] Government Regulation

Even if the property measures up in all other respects, local zoning laws, building codes, and related land-use regulations may prevent development of the property. A check of all local laws and regulations is an absolute must for any prospective purchaser. If the zoning laws would make the intended use impossible, the possibilities of obtaining a variance should be investigated. Here, a local attorney and broker will be of great assistance.

Another problem to guard against is that while the prospective purchase may be zoned to permit a higher-value use, surrounding areas may be zoned for uses that would interfere with or diminish development, as in the situation where the investor has determined that the area will be ripe for residential development within a reasonable period and there is land available that is zoned for this purpose. However, property adjacent to the tract is zoned for industrial use, which can create smoke and noise pollution and heavy truck traffic, which would destroy the attractiveness of the proposed residential lots. One solution would be the creation of a buffer zone by leaving part of the land undeveloped. However, this would reduce the profits to be realized on a resale and could make the investment worthless unless the inability to use some of the acreage were reflected in a reduced price paid by the investor. A better solution might be to pass the purchase by and look elsewhere for more suitable land.

A somewhat different risk presents itself when the land is unzoned. While this permits the available land to be employed for its intended purpose, contiguous property can be developed for incompatible uses. Again, one can use a portion of his acreage as a buffer against an unfavorable use of adjoining land. Or, the possibility of zoning the area for higher-value uses might be explored, using the services of local professionals.

Even if the land is already zoned for the purposes intended by an investor, however, the possibility of future upzoning creates a considerable risk. This has become a prevalent practice in many rural communities. In some places upgrading is accomplished not by rezoning but by limiting the number of building permits issued in any one year. Another effective technique is the adoption of an ordinance requiring the construction of a number of different models in any residential development and possibly also providing that the same models cannot be constructed within a certain distance of each other (so-called look-alike ordinances). This may increase building costs to the point that the tract cannot be used in the manner originally intended. It may be possible to protect against this by filing a subdivision map immediately upon purchase and thereby insure the present zoning. But this entails substantial engineering and surveying costs, filing fees, and bond premiums. In addition, real estate taxes will rise because the lots will be assessed individually, thus increasing the carrying charges. The alternative is to hold the tract as raw land and hope that it is not burdened by upzoning or other local requirements during the waiting period.

[4] Patterns of Land Growth

Most speculative land investment occurs near urban areas, since it is there that demand for new development is most likely to occur. Most of our cities and urban areas grow in one or more of the five ways below. An investor able to identify a pattern in the process of unfolding has discovered one of the keys to successful land investment.

☐ *Radial growth.* Many cities grow along straight lines (highways) radiating out from the city, like spokes from a wheel. (Thus, this is also known as the spoke or strip pattern of development.) The focus is the central business district (CBD); as the area grows, homes and businesses are sited along the roads that permit easy access to the center. Ultimately, the strips may join one urban center with another. Examples are Route 41 between Chicago and Milwaukee, and Route 1 from Miami to Fort Lauderdale and north.

☐ *Concentric growth.* Also called the ring pattern, this consists of a series of circles around the CBD. Closer-in circles include industrial zones and lower-class housing, while the outlying areas are the high-income subdivisions. A city combining the radial and concentric patterns will develop in the form of a star, with the spokes leading the way and the circles gradually filling in with development.

☐ *Sector growth.* A pattern evident since very early times is that similar uses concentrate in one area. Thus wholesale-food merchants are in one sector, while light manufacturing, the clothing business, and the secondhand auto dealers each have their own neighborhoods. By concentrating, each industry makes face-to-face dealing more convenient, generates more overall retail traffic, and encourages the development of accessory services. These sectors do not change easily or quickly but they will occasionally, and land values will increase substantially when a higher use (in terms of rents and land prices) replaces a lower use.

☐ *Hop-skip-and-jump growth.* The three growth patterns already discussed would seem to imply that land development is a steady, step-by-step process. Nothing could be further from the truth. The major factor determining land value usually is accessibility, and this means proximity to highways, rail lines, or other transport routes. Thus, land that is close-in "as the crow flies" is not necessarily the most valuable. (Other reasons for high land values, such as topography, or nearness to such natural features as lakes, also have no relationship to close-in land.) As a result, urban growth skips over much land that becomes "dead" land, at least until land prices become so high (and commuting times become so long) that developers seek out bypassed parcels.

☐ *Fan-shaped growth.* It is obvious that geography affects urban growth. Frequently, a river, ocean, or mountain blocks urban growth in one direction; consequently, the path of growth (whether radial or concentric) is in the shape of a fan rather than a circle. Even when a city is on a river that is bridged, the main growth generally clusters on the side with the principal business and financial center. (Two exceptions are Kansas City, Missouri and Kansas City, Kansas.) Because fan-shaped growth usually proceeds faster along the available expansion path, it may offer more rapid increase in land values along its periphery.

11.02 FARMLAND

[1] Introduction

The growing popularity of farmland as a real estate investment is based upon an optimistic outlook for rising farm prices through the end of the century. A turning point seems to have been reached from a period of chronically excessive food supplies (and depressed farm prices) to a period where the balance between food supplies and demand will be more consistently tight than in the past. Indeed, the Economics and Statistics Service of the U.S. Department of Agriculture (USDA) sees a need to encourage production—primarily monetary incentives to help farmers pay for increasing costs of energy, fertilizer, and labor.

Underlying the bullish outlook for farm prices is rising world demand. In 1970, about one out of every five U.S. farm acres grew food for export. By 1980, exports accounted for one out of every 3.5 acres planted, or almost 30 percent of total marketing. And as world population growth continues (although at a slower rate), foreign demand is likely to grow. Further stimulating this demand is the improvement in diets, with more meat, eggs, and milk being consumed.

Farm production outside the United States is likely to grow at a slower rate in the future as more marginal lands are farmed and as rising energy costs hold down maximum yields; therefore, increased supply must come from the United States. We do have the necessary cropland to increase food supplies, but farmers will require real-price increases of one to 3 percent a year in order to increase production.

Overall, USDA projects a gradual but steady gain in farmers' net income. Until 1985, annual growth of 4 to 5 percent is projected, but in the latter half of the decade, net farm income could grow rapidly—perhaps as much as 9.6 percent annually—with mounting export demand, a slowing inflation rate, and higher consumer incomes.

Investors in farmland should be aware that food prices are notoriously volatile and so farm income fluctuates widely. At best, many investors in farmland realize only a small current cash flow because of the effects of downside leverage. The free-and-clear return from most farmland ranges from 6 to 8 percent a year; by comparison, interest rates on farm mortgages run considerably higher, approximating those for commercial mortgages. Therefore, cash flow may be significantly lower than the free-and-clear return, and in some cases, may disappear entirely.

Thus the major incentive for purchasing farmland normally is the expectation of future appreciation.

[2] How to Choose a Farm Investment

In 1935, U.S. farms totaled 7 million; today they number less than 2.5 million. Another half to three-quarter million units may disappear by the year 2000, according to USDA projections. The primary reason will not be urban sprawl but absorption of smaller units by large ones.

This means, of course, that U.S. farm production will become increasingly concentrated among fewer and larger units. At present, according to the USDA, the top one percent of U.S. farms (in terms of acreage) produces about 25 percent of the nation's food. In twenty years, this one percent will account for half of total U.S. output, while the lower 50 percent of our farms (in terms of acreage) will produce less than one percent of America's crops and livestock.

As farms become larger, their capital requirements also grow. Today, a large farm (sales of more than $100,000) requires about $1 million in assets. In twenty years, this capital requirement is likely to double. This is one reason why farm ownership in the United States is likely to become more concentrated in the hands of large corporations or investment groups.

Opportunities for investing in farmland abound, and the investor will have many choices open to him. Before deciding, however, the investor should consider his personal investment goals in the context of the economic, financial, and tax characteristics of farming. Once the decision to invest is made, he must choose among different geographical areas, soil types, commodities, specific sites, the acquiring entity to use, the manner of acquisition, financing arrangements, management and leasing arrangements, and other incidental decisions. These items are discussed below:

☐ *Choice of crops.* Once a specific geographic area is chosen, the investor must decide what crops will be grown. When evaluating land for a specific crop, its suitability for the crop must be realistically considered. As a general rule of thumb, if no one else in the area is growing a particular crop, there is probably a valid reason. Deviations from normal practices in an area should be carefully considered before being implemented.

The following factors should be considered when evaluating a potential crop:

- Climate
- Soil
- Quantity and quality of available water
- Availability of labor
- Availability of processors and markets
- Supply and demand factors
- Production costs

☐ *Choice of property.* Once the investor has chosen a specific geographic area and the crops to be grown, he should seek out properties for sale. Sources of information include real estate brokers, lenders, or lending institutions actively engaged in making loans for farm properties, farmers, farm-management firms, farm suppliers, commodity buyers, accountants, and lawyers. Once a specific property is identified, the investor should make an intensive analysis of the property and the local factors affecting its productivity.

☐ *History of past uses and production.* The investor should study the production and expense figures for the property for as long as the last ten years, if available. In addition, an informal meeting with the individual who has actually farmed the property over an appreciable period can provide important information. For example, certain areas may have undesirable drainage characteristics that are not obvious or there may be a weed-control problem that requires extra expenditures.

☐ *Climate.* The climate in the area must be suitable for the intended crops. The length of the growing season must be sufficient to allow for the maturation of the crops. For example, almonds require from 240 to 250 days without frost while crops such as lettuce, celery, carrots, and radishes require only from 72 to 120 frost-free days. The typical range of temperatures experienced in the area during the growing season and, of more importance, the highest temperature during the growing cycle should be considered. Finally, the investor should determine how late in the growing season frost is normally experienced. For example, with respect to tree fruits and nuts, an entire crop can be lost if a severe frost coincides with the bloom period.

☐ *Precipitation and water supply.* The sources and quantity of water available to the site must be investigated. The annual amount of rainfall and snowfall should be ascertained as well as the times of the year during which the precipitation occurs in substantial amounts. In addition, the quality, quantity, and availability of water from all sources should be determined. The local water-utility company is a good source of information. In many developed farm areas, there is a local, state, or federally funded irrigation district from which information can be obtained. Additional information is usually furnished by local governmental offices, county agricultural personnel, and private well drillers. Some water-utility companies will provide free efficiency testing of water pumps. These tests yield the following information: the pumping efficiency as a percent of full potential, the gallons per minute pumped, the level of the water table, and the drawdown of the water level when the pump is operating.

☐ *Soil and topography.* Does the site offer a soil type that is conducive to growing the crops? The soil survey for the site should provide this and other important information. Soil-survey books are compiled for each county and published by the National Cooperative Soil Survey. The books are the joint effort of the U.S. Department of Agriculture and local agencies such as the agricultural stations of the state university and the U.S. Forest Service. The surveys are available from the local office of the Soil Conservation Service, the state farm adviser, or the county agent's office.

If the soil is suitable for the contemplated crop, the next question is whether the soil will yield marginal, average, or above-average production of the crop. To answer this question, the composition of the soil should be ascertained and the topography of the site evaluated. The following questions should be answered:

- What is the composition of the soil?
- What nutrients are available to the growing plant?
- What farming difficulties are associated with the soil type?
- Are there negative components in the soil (e.g., salt, etc.)?
- What crops are grown in the soil in the area?
- Are the crops grown successfully?
- Does the topography of the land present problems?
- If flood irrigation is contemplated, is the land level enough?

Topographical maps are available for all geographic areas of the country from the U.S. Geological Survey. While these maps are not specifically designed for agricultural usage, they are helpful in indicating the contour of the land and the improvements or landmarks on it.

[3] Sources of Financing

Mortgage loans are the most common way investors finance the purchase of farms. For the most part, long-term farm mortgages are level-payment, fully liquidating loans that run from twenty-five to thirty years. The important sources of these loans are life insurance companies, federal Land Banks, the Farmers Home Administration, farm mortgage companies, agribusiness enterprises, and sellers themselves.

☐ *Life insurance companies.* Many life insurance companies make long-term mortgage loans to finance the purchase of farm properties. Prominent among them are Travelers, Equitable, Connecticut General, John Hancock, Aetna, Metropolitan, Prudential, Northwestern, and Connecticut Mutual. These companies will deal with outside investors as well as farmers. Most loans are first mortgages that run up to 70 or 75 percent of the value of the real estate and improvements for a term of twenty-five to thirty years. The loans are generally nonrecourse (i.e., the personal guarantee of the borrower is usually not required).

☐ *Farm mortgage companies.* A farm mortgage company is a private firm that lends money secured by farm property. These mortgages are, in some cases, financed by the public sale of obligations secured by the underlying farm mortgage, including certificates representing fractional interests in the specific mortgage. Farm mortgage companies also serve as middlemen in the placement and servicing of farm mortgages held by life insurance companies and other lenders located at a distance from the borrower.

☐ *Commercial banks.* First-mortgage loans by commercial banks to finance the purchase of a farm are self-liquidating loans in amounts up to 70 or 75 percent of the appraised value of the property. The interest rates are comparable to mortgage loans for other income or business real estate, and payments of principal and interest are tailored to the borrower's needs; one or two payments per year are usually made. The loans are usually nonrecourse and terms run from fifteen to twenty years.

☐ *Purchase-money mortgages.* Frequently, the seller will finance all or part of the purchase of a farm. The loan sometimes takes the form of a purchase-money junior mortgage for the difference between the first mortgage and the balance of the purchase price. Or the owner may be willing to finance with a first mortgage the entire difference between the down payment and the purchase price. The terms of the loan vary according to the circumstances of the sale. Both the property owner and the purchaser can benefit from this kind of financing. While the purchaser benefits because he can make his equity investment on a piecemeal basis over a substantial period, the owner can benefit from the installment reporting of his gain.

☐ *Business firms engaged in agriculturally oriented enterprises.* Corporations whose business is related to farming are sometimes sources of financing. Food processors, for example, will often make loans for the purchase of land by those who will grow the crops used in their food-processing operations. Farm commodity buyers will also make loans for the purchase of farmland. Generally, the loan will be a self-liquidating constant-payment first mortgage for a period of twenty-five to thirty years, but with a five- to ten-year due-and-payable provision. The interest rate usually reflects the market rate at the time the loan is made.

☐ *Farm Credit System.* The federally supervised Farm Credit System (FCS) is the country's leading supplier of agricultural credit. The lending institutions that make up the FCS are chartered by the U.S. Government. However, none of their funds are government allocated, none of their capital is supplied by the government, and none of their loans are government secured. They are borrower-owned cooperatives supplying credit at cost to their members. The system is owned and operated by the farmers and ranchers it serves.

☐ *Farmers Home Administration.* The Farmers Home Administration (FmHA) is a rural credit agency of the Department of Agriculture. It both makes and guarantees farm-ownership loans to eligible applicants who will operate family-sized farms. Guaranteed loans are made by commercial sources, and the FmHA provides the lender with a guarantee against loss. Direct loans are made by the FmHA from a revolving fund. Repayment and interest terms vary according to the type of loan; the maximum term is forty years, and the interest rate is based on the cost of borrowing by the government. Borrowers with limited resources can qualify for lower interest rates.

☐ *Small Business Administration.* Since 1976 the Small Business Administration (SBA) has made loans for the purchase of farms. Only borrowers who cannot obtain funds from a private lender are eligible. They must also qualify as a small business, which means that annual receipts cannot exceed a certain amount. The SBA can guarantee up to 90 percent or $500,000 (whichever is less) of a bank loan to a small farm.

[4] Farm Operation and Management

An investor who is not himself a full-time farmer must lease his farm to a tenant who will perform all of the farming operations. A variety of lease arrangements offer different risk-reward allocations.

☐ *Share lease.* Under this arrangement, the landowner retains some of the risk of farming and must monitor or supervise his investment. Usually, the lease is for one year with the landowner paying the real estate taxes and half of the variable expenses. The tenant provides the labor and machinery and pays the other half of the variable expenses. The net profit is split evenly. Share leases are generally used for such crops as wheat, corn, and soybeans. The landlord's annual share of profit over a period of years may represent a return ranging from 3 to 6 percent of his investment.

☐ *Cash lease.* The tenant pays a fixed amount for the use of the farm and improvements. He receives all of the income and usually pays all expenses except taxes, insurance, and major building repairs. The landlord has little or no management responsibilities and is assured of a stable income. This leasing arrangement is most desirable for inexperienced or absentee investors.

☐ *Standing rent lease.* Under this arrangement, the tenant pays a fixed quantity of crops or livestock as the standing rent. It operates in much the same way as a cash lease with the exception that the landlord's return will fluctuate with the price of the crop.

The link between the absentee landowner and the farmer is usually a professional farm manager. Such a manager typically will charge fees ranging from 8 to 10 percent of the owner's share of the net income from the farm. The major functions of a farm manager (in conjunction with the person actually farming the land) are the following:

- Determine the optimum timing for each farming operation
- Procure adequate labor
- Contract for timely application of seed, chemicals, and supplies
- Contract for necessary services and utilities
- Care for equipment and improvements
- Implement and oversee capital improvements
- Provide adequate and timely accounting information

[5] Tax Aspects of Farm Investments

The decision to invest in farmland normally will be influenced only slightly, if at all, by tax considerations. Farms offer little tax shelter. However, some special tax provisions (mostly favorable) do apply; they are briefly described below.

☐ *Soil and water conservation.* Farmers can elect to deduct as an expense (rather than capitalize) money spent for soil and water conservation and for the prevention of erosion.[1] The amount deducted in any year cannot exceed 25 percent of the gross income from farming for that year; any excess can be carried over to future years. The election applies to expenses for the treatment or moving of earth on land actually used in farming, either before or during the time the expenditures are made. It does not apply to money spent on depreciable facilities or structures; those items must be capitalized.

The deduction for soil and water conservation is an opportunity to convert ordinary income into capital gain. An investor purchasing a farm can deduct 25 percent of his expense for leveling, grading, clearing brush, building drainage ditches, etc., against ordinary farm income. When the farm is sold, it will bring a higher price because of the improvements, with the gain taxed at capital gain rates.

☐ *Development expenses.* A farmer can elect to deduct or capitalize expenses such as taxes, labor, seed, fertilizer, insurance, interest, etc., during the period of development of a farm. Once the productive state is reached, however, he must deduct these expenses currently. There is no opportunity to deduct currently capital expenditures such as wells, irrigation pipes, drain tile, masonry or concrete tanks, reservoirs or dams, and roads. Capital expenditures in connection with soil and water conservation, as indicated above, is an exception.

☐ *Fertilizer costs.* The cost of fertilizer and lime may be deductible in full in the year paid even though the benefits of the added materials will be realized over a period of years. If the farmer does not elect an immediate deduction, the cost must be amortized over the period of benefits.

☐ *Expenses of clearing land.* Farmers can elect to deduct currently the cost of clearing land if the purpose is to make the land suitable for farming.[2] Clearing land includes such expenses as eradication of trees, stumps, and brush, the treatment or movement of earth, and the diversion of streams and water courses.

The deduction is limited to the lesser of $5,000 or 25 percent of taxable income from a farming business.

☐ *Casualty losses.* Like other taxpayers, farmers can deduct casualty losses resulting from hurricanes, tornadoes, heavy rains, freezing, lightning, floods, storm, drought, cyclone, landslides, avalanches, dust storms, sinking of land, ice pressure, cave-ins, thaws, severe blizzards and cold, and similar natural causes.

Loss of topsoil from slow, continuous erosion and wasting away of land due to natural causes steadily and progressively working on the soil lacks the elements

---

[1] I.R.C. § 175.
[2] I.R.C. § 182.

of suddenness and unexpectedness necessary to qualify as a casualty loss. Consequently, such losses are not deductible. But a loss of topsoil due to windstorm, destruction of grazing grasses by drought, or impairment of soil by silt would be sufficient grounds for claiming the deduction.

☐ *Impact of hobby-loss provisions.* Investors in farmland should be aware of the hobby-loss or "gentlemen farmer" provisions of the Internal Revenue Code.[3] Those provisions apply to farming operations that are not primarily conducted as profit-making enterprises. A taxpayer is presumed to be farming for profit if his gross farming income for at least two out of five consecutive tax years exceeds the deductions attributable to farming activities for those two years (or if he can otherwise establish his profit motive). If a taxpayer is not farming for profit, he cannot deduct farm expenses in excess of farm income. The purpose of these provisions is to discourage agricultural investments with no other purpose than to create tax losses for the investor.

☐ *Deductions by farm syndications.* Section 464 of the Internal Revenue Code limits deductions for certain expenses (e.g., feed, seed, and fertilizer) for farming syndicates (partnerships in which 35 percent of the losses are allocated to the limited partners and are subject to federal or state securities law). The deduction of these items is allowed only for the taxable year in which the supplies are used. In addition, all expenses of such farming syndications incurred before the first year of production must be capitalized.

☐ *Special requirements for farm corporations.* Section 447 of the Tax Reform Act of 1976[4] provides that a farm organized in corporate form, or as a partnership but with a corporate partner, must use accrual-basis accounting and capitalize its preproduction expenses. The purpose of this is to bar the immediate deduction of those items such as soil-tillage and pruning expenses that would be possible if the cash method of accounting were used. The following kinds of farm corporations are excepted:

- Nurseries, sod farms, and tree farms other than those growing fruit and nut trees
- Subchapter S corporations
- Family corporations in which at least 50 percent of the total combined voting power of all classes of stock is owned by one family
- Corporations controlled by two or three families, provided certain stock ownership rules have been met
- Corporations that have not had gross receipts in excess of $1 million for any year beginning after December 31, 1975

11.03 INDUSTRIAL PROPERTY

[1] Introduction

Industrial real estate is an area of investment overlooked by too many investors. Even during a period of temporary economic slowdown, there is a continu-

---

[3] I.R.C. § 183.

[4] Pub. L. No. 94-455, 90 Stat. 1520, 26 U.S.C.A. §§ 1 et seq.

ing demand for new and modern industrial space as companies shift locales to meet new demands or cut costs, and seek more modern improvements in order to increase productivity. Generally speaking, industrial property includes that used for warehousing, wholesaling, distribution, assembly, or manufacturing purposes. These facilities can be classified as either multipurpose or single-purpose. The first type is adaptable to a wide variety of tenants and may be used by one or more tenants at any one time. A single-purpose facility is usually designed to meet the requirements of a specific tenant who will be the sole occupant of the building. Obviously, it will be harder to lease a single-purpose building when it becomes vacant than a multipurpose facility.

Here are five reasons why industrial property is often a better investment than residential or commercial projects:

☐ *Less management responsibility.* While this is not invariably the case, most industrial leases are on a net (or semi-net) basis with the tenants having the responsibility of maintaining the property and paying real estate taxes, insurance, and other operating expenses. Even when the landlord had these duties under a gross lease, the tenants almost always have escalator clauses in the leases requiring them to pay tax, insurance, and other operating expense increases.

☐ *More physical value.* In most industrial properties, up to 90 percent of the structure constitutes the floor, walls, and roof (called the shell) with a minimum amount of initial costs devoted to inside improvements that need constant maintenance. In an apartment house or office building, by comparison, the inside work is much greater. In practical terms, this means that an industrial property tends to suffer less physical and functional depreciation than do other properties.

☐ *Greater appreciation.* Since new industry tends to locate in outlying areas rather than the crowded inner cities, initial land costs are lower. This, combined with the relatively lower construction costs of industrial property, gives the investment a greater chance to increase in value.

☐ *Better lease arrangements.* Industrial leases are longer than most office and apartment leases. They customarily are written at a flat rate, but include an escalation clause based upon changes in operating costs, as already noted. This combination offers the landlord a good balance between a secure rent roll and one that will rise to meet increased inflation.

The bulk of industrial space leased or sold in recent years has been for warehousing and distribution activities (as much as two thirds of total space in some recent years). The next highest use was manufacturing (about 20 percent of total space), and the balance was devoted to research and development. However, research and development utilization is likely to increase in future years as a result of new tax credits available for research and development activities.

A number of factors underlie the present strong market for light industrial and warehouse properties throughout the United States. These include

☐ *Strong demand in prospect.* In the next few years, increasing demand for industrial space will result from the growth in the high-technology and electronic industries, which continue to come up with new breakthroughs (e.g., innovations in word-processing equipment). Other factors pushing up demand will be an expected increase in exports as the dollar stabilizes, as well as increased foreign industrial investment here.

☐ *No current oversupply.* Any increased demand for industrial space will require new construction, since demand and supply presently are about in balance. Demand has fallen off slightly in the past year or so, but this has been matched by a drop-off of supply due to tight financing.

☐ *Improved regulatory climate.* Municipalities, and the public in general, seem to be moderating their insistence on environmental controls, recognizing the need for continued business expansion. Industrial parks, since they are in effect planned business communities, frequently will be preferred over freestanding industrial properties.

[2] Site Selection

Here is a checklist of eleven leading factors for selecting potential sites for later resale or lease to industrial users:

☐ *Size and shape.* One of the clearest changes in plant location over the last few decades has been the general trend toward larger sites—in order to insure adequate space for deliveries, employee parking, and possible future expansion. A spacious site also makes for better plant appearance and provides greater privacy.

☐ *Topography.* The usual preference is for a comparatively level site, with just enough slope to provide good drainage. Some firms, however, may choose a hilltop location because of supposed advantages in appearance and advertising value. In other cases, the type of building preferred by the company may be best adapted to a sloping site.

☐ *Utilities.* Utilities (electric power, water, natural gas, and sewerage) are always an important consideration. While utility rates may represent an important cost variable between communities, they are normally uniform within a community. So the principal difference in utility costs between sites in the same community is in the cost of extending utility lines to the plant site. This can represent a significant element in the total development cost of the site.

☐ *Water supply.* Many industrial plants use large quantities of water in the production process and, of course, all need water for drinking and sanitary purposes. When the former is the case, location near a natural source of water is frequently a necessity, and such characteristics of the water supply as temperature, mineral content, bacterial content, and regularity of flow may be important.

☐ *Flooding.* Whenever flooding is a possibility, it should be a major site consideration. If records of previous floods are available, these should be checked over a long period. If not, long-time residents of the area and newspaper accounts of past floods can often provide useful information.

☐ *Drainage and soil conditions.* Large areas of standing water on a site indicate that subsurface drainage problems can be expected. It is important to avoid the site that is a natural low spot. Soil engineers should be consulted if any doubt exists that soil conditions will permit adequate drainage. Soil structure should be investigated, since that may bear on foundation conditions and the cost of developing the site. Soil structure must receive special attention if a plant will require land with an exceptionally high load-bearing capacity.

☐ *Cost of development.* A prospective user will consider not only the price of the land but also the additional costs of grading, filling, drainage, excavation, foundation construction, building access roads, constructing a railroad siding, providing for water supply and waste disposal, and bringing in other necessary utilities. When all development costs are brought into the comparison, the lowest-priced site sometimes turns out to be the most expensive.

☐ *Location within the community.* As a site factor, location within the community has various facets. One is accessibility—from the standpoints of employees, customers, and salesmen. Roads, traffic conditions, availability of public transportation, and distance from residential areas must be considered. Another facet is advertising value—a location on a main highway or main-line railroad or one from which the plant is visible over a large area may be sought. Still another facet concerns the immediate surroundings. Like a family shopping for a new home, the manufacturing firm looks for attractive surroundings and tries to avoid possible community relations problems.

☐ *Transportation facilities.* Transportation is a significant factor at each major stage of site selection, that is, in the choice of region, community, and specific site. Accessibility of a site to the various modes of local transportation is usually a primary consideration to a user. Thus, if the firm plans to use railroad transportation, it must look into the feasibility and cost of constructing a spur or siding. If it plans to ship by truck, attention must be given to such matters as distance from main highways, type of access roads, roadway requirements within the site, and potential traffic problems.

☐ *Taxes and insurance.* In site selection, tax considerations are usually centered on property tax rates and assessments. As regards property taxes, many companies pay as much attention to long-range stability as to the present level of rates. Fire insurance costs are considered in surveying both communities and sites. In selecting the community, firms are interested primarily in insurance ratings. In evaluating sites, the prospect is usually careful to note all factors likely to affect the insurance classification of the plant.

☐ *Zoning and other legal aspects.* Zoning is a site factor that has often been overlooked in the past. Profiting from the experiences of others, most firms now regard proper zoning as highly essential. A careful check of zoning regulations is desirable for two principal reasons—to avoid litigation and to protect the new plant against incompatible industrial neighbors or other land use. In addition to zoning, other local regulations, such as building codes, laws relating to waste disposal, smoke, and fumes, and restrictions on highway use need to be checked.

[3] Incubator Buildings

An important reason for the vitality of the American economy over the years is the continuing development of all kinds of new businesses. These new operations, however, frequently have a problem in renting space. Being new, their space requirements are uncertain and they do not represent the type of high-quality tenant many landlords desire; being small, they cannot afford to pay top rentals.

The type of building that is most suitable for the needs of new, small businesses is called an incubator building; since it often combines industrial and office space, it is also called a transitional warehouse. It offers an investment opportunity for small real estate syndicates, which can give the necessary management.

The incubator building is invariably a single-story structure, flexible in the ratio of office to warehouse space. Typical tenants might consist of new manufacturing, service, or distribution companies. The optimal size for a project ranges from 70,000 to 100,000 square feet, divided into modules of 2,000 to 4,000 square feet each. Because many of the businesses involve manufacturing or distribution, each unit should have its own outside access or possibly a truck dock.

Each module will have up to 500 square feet of finished office space, including an executive office, reception area, air conditioning, and carpeting. Visitor parking space is provided in front with employee parking in the rear.

Incubator buildings normally are built on the outskirts of major urban areas where land costs are much lower, so access to major highways (and to airports) is important. A location adjacent to an existing industrial park can be a valuable plus. Finally, these buildings often are close to the residential areas where the tenants live.

As with any development, initial studies must be made to determine the feasibility of the project. Among the major concerns in determining feasibility are these:

- The number of small tenants in the local market area, their space requirements, and growth and turnover in the area
- Vacancy and rental rates in competing facilities in the local market
- Local zoning and building code requirements pertaining to construction and parking facilities

However, because of the type of tenancy attracted by incubator buildings, there cannot normally be a preset formula for the ratio of office versus warehouse space, size of units, etc.

Lease terms in incubator buildings generally run between one and five years. Roughly 60 percent of the tenants will want options for increased space, with future rentals to be determined initially by a Consumer Price Index escalator clause. Leases typically provide for a pass-through of increases in real estate taxes and insurance premiums during the lease term.

Because leases are relatively short term and a certain percentage of tenants are likely to fail, the owner must pay close attention to lease terms and leasing procedures. In addition, the owner will be responsible for external maintenance, landscaping and snow removal, and possibly security and office cleaning. Each module has a separate unit for HVAC (heating, ventilation, and air conditioning).

The tenant assumes responsibility for these utility services as well as interior alterations.

By definition, an incubator building is a speculative project; many prospective tenants may not even be in existence when the building is planned. Thus financing may be difficult and a substantial equity investment will be required. Many incubator projects today are being developed and financed in-house by insurance companies and major developers with a good track record.

[4] Industrial Parks

[a] Key Elements of Industrial Parks

Industrial parks represent one of the more significant examples of new property types in the past three decades. The key to a successful industrial park is strict lease restrictions on tenants, which permit the creation of a controlled environment providing all necessary facilities for industrial use, including utilities, streets, railroad sidings, and automobile parking. Landscaping prohibitions against front loading and outside stockpiling, and the absence of heavy industry create an attractive, nonpolluting environment, which makes this type of business development popular with local communities.

Office parks, also popular today, actually are an offshoot of industrial parks. Initially, many industrial tenants use part of the space for office purposes. The attractiveness of the planned environment drew others interested primarily in office use; developers were quick to seize the opportunity to develop parks devoted to office use only.

An industrial park is created by a developer who buys raw ground wholesale, refines it, and retails it for a profit. This process is accomplished within a framework of a preconceived plan, with minimum standards from both an aesthetic and a use viewpoint. Ideally, an industrial park should do the following:

- Encompass between 200 and 500 acres in area
- Be located at or near an access interchange of a limited-access highway, within thirty minutes by car of a major urban center
- Offer a complete utility pattern including power, sewer, water, and gas
- Include, if possible, rail facilities—a very definite positive factor for primary use or as an alternative to trucking
- Be covered by a complete set of preimposed restrictions enforceable upon all occupants, both tenants and those owning sites outright

In addition, there should be a continuing management responsibility beyond the completion of the project, either through partial ownership by the developer or by the establishment of a park association, composed of the occupants, that will continue to enforce the original restrictions.

The developer should be in a position to make a broad market offering with several options, for example, a company may (1) buy an improved site and, within present restrictions, retain its own architect and contractor; (2) retain the developer to build the complete facility and, upon completion, buy the ground and building; (3) have the developer build to the company's specifications and lease the facility on a long-term basis.

[b] Site-Selection Process

The following factors are important when selecting a site:

☐ *Location.* From a developer's or investor's point of view, the first consideration is that of location. Location far outweighs any consideration of physical site characteristics. Ideally, the site should be within twenty to thirty minutes' distance from a major urban center.

In a regional context, heavy industry has remained in the colder regions of the country, whereas the new high-technology firms concentrate in New England or California (to be near the large graduate schools in business and engineering). The Sun Belt, however, draws increasing interest as its population and industry grow. Within metropolitan areas, near-in locations will be preferred to more distant ones because of increased accessibility and lower commuting costs.

☐ *Size.* The park should be of sufficient size (at least 200 acres) to insure that the application of time, overhead expense, and marketing effort is worthwhile. A large complex enables the developer to obtain lower unit costs on such necessary site improvements as roads and water and sewer lines.

☐ *Zoning and community attitudes.* Investigation of all local zoning ordinances and government controls is essential to reveal any obstacles that would seriously affect the outcome of the development. A community's attitude toward the industrial development of its land must also be determined. Community services, such as police, hospitals, and schools, must be carefully weighed.

☐ *Labor.* The quality, as well as the quantity, of labor is an essential factor. As jobs become more highly sophisticated, the quality of labor becomes increasingly important.

☐ *Physical characteristics.* The site must be investigated for soil-bearing capacity, drainage qualities, and geometry of subdivision.

[c] Market Analysis and Financing

The best-planned industrial park is useless if the industrial community has no use or need for new facilities in the area. A competent real estate appraiser should be retained to do a market feasibility study. Bear in mind that the viability of the park may depend on its attracting a diversified range of tenants.

The initial projection should indicate precisely the cost of the raw ground. A margin of profit at least 30 percent above the total cost of the land acquisition plus improvements must be anticipated. If not, the site should be rejected, regardless of the investment already made in preliminary investigation.

The matter of financing is almost as critical as location. This type of industrial development consumes capital at an appalling rate in the early stages, and cash flow often does not start for many years after the initial investment has been made. A project that is not properly financed at the outset could be in serious trouble well before the turn around in cash flow occurs.

Ultimate rates of return can be so good, however, that proper financing is readily available on viable projects. Moreover, it is now possible to interest major lenders in taking active partnership positions and, thereby, a share in profits.

11.04 OFFICE BUILDINGS

[1] Introduction

Good location is particularly critical for office buildings because of the elements of prestige and convenience. An office building in the wrong place (for example, at a considerable distance from the central business district) may end up an inefficient warehouse. By comparison, an apartment building often can find tenants at lower rentals no matter where the building is sited.

In the case of suburban buildings, good location generally means good access to major highway arteries (and also to a regional air facility), and location within a high-income residential area where property values are stable and growing. Suburban buildings also should be in reasonable proximity to restaurants and shopping facilities, since these often are necessary in order to attract tenants.

The prestige of an office building is directly related to the quality of its tenants. Of the various types of real estate, office buildings are generally more people-intensive, have higher operating expenses as a percentage of revenues and hence require much more management. Capital expenditures may also be required as the building ages, for elevator renovation, new air-conditioning facilities, etc. The construction is much more complex than the shell space that constitutes the structure of the shopping center or industrial park.

From a financing point of view, office buildings represent excellent collateral and mortgages with high loan-to-value ratios often can be obtained. In recent years, there has been a trend toward involving major tenants in the ownership of the building; for the developer, this is a way to raise equity capital while it gives the major tenant a say in the design and construction of the building as well as a return in the form of cash flow on its investment or a preferred rental for the space it utilizes.

Tax shelter in office building investments generally is quite good since in both downtown and suburban locations, a relatively large proportion of the investment is attributable to the structure and so can be recouped via depreciation deductions.

The value of a well-maintained and well-located office building is likely to appreciate at least as fast as the rate of inflation and, during periods of tight demand, considerably faster (since considerable time is needed to create new space). On the other hand, the demand by many firms for prestige space means that new facilities often can draw tenants from existing buildings, thus creating a substantial amount of vacant space that must be re-leased. This leads, at least temporarily and sometimes permanently, to lessened cash flow and a possible decline in market value.

[2] Evaluating an Office Building

[a] Current Income and Expenses

The first step the investor will take in evaluating a proposed office building investment is to estimate the income that can be anticipated from the property. There will naturally be a difference between the income the property currently yields and the income the investor hopes to receive in the future. Consequently, the investor should distinguish among:

- *Scheduled income.* The gross rental income the property would throw off if it were fully rented at prevailing rentals.
- *Current income.* The gross rental income currently yielded by the property.
- *Projected income.* The gross rental income the investor believes he can achieve within the near future. Normally, this would be less than scheduled income, since a vacancy allowance would be provided (perhaps 5 to 10 percent), but still more than the current income.
- *Net operating income.* This represents gross rental income under either of the above assumptions minus all operating expenses.

The second step is to determine the operating expenses currently being paid and projecting these expenses into the future. The key expenses for an office building are the following:

☐ *Real estate taxes.* Current taxes normally can be ascertained from the owner's tax bills or the local tax office. In making his projections, the buyer normally will assume that these taxes will increase at a rate in line with past experience.

☐ *Payroll.* This should be a relatively low figure in a commercial building as compared, say, to a residence that provides a doorman, manned elevators, etc. Examination of the owner's payroll records will give the necessary figures. Again, payroll increases to keep pace with inflation should be assumed.

☐ *Insurance premiums.* The two principal types of insurance maintained by the owner of commercial property are fire and extended coverage and owner's liability insurance. Current quotations can be obtained from an insurance broker.

☐ *Maintenance contracts.* The building owner normally carries maintenance contracts for the elevators and heating and central air-conditioning systems. He may also provide trash pickup, although sometimes the latter is the responsibility of the tenant.

☐ *Utilities.* Electricity, gas, water, and sewer charges often will be paid by the tenant, but this is not always the case. A careful reading of all of the leases will indicate who bears the burden of these costs.

☐ *Parking-lot maintenance.* This is generally the owner's responsibility and involves periodic cleaning, maintenance, and repair of the blacktop and painting of the white lines.

☐ *Maintenance and repair.* This includes exterior painting and maintenance of the structure and the heating, lighting, and plumbing equipment. This is normally the owner's responsibility. A rule of thumb is that these costs will run about 3 percent of the scheduled gross income per year.

☐ *Replacement reserves.* Although the basic structure of the building has a long life, certain parts will wear out much more rapidly and will have to be replaced at periodic intervals (anywhere from five to twenty years). These include the roof, air-conditioning system, elevators, floor coverings, water heaters, and storefronts. Whether or not the owner maintains an actual cash reserve for these replacements, they do represent an annual bookkeeping cost that should be reflected in the financial statement. It may be wise to have an engineer or other professional examine the building for the purpose of preparing a replacement schedule.

☐ *Lease commissions.* An expense item often overlooked is the need to pay lease commissions to brokers. One rule of thumb is that 3 percent of scheduled income should cover this cost.

[b] Increasing Net Operating Income

One important step when considering an office building investment is to consider ways to boost the operating income from the property. This, of course, can be done only by increasing gross rentals or cutting down operating expenses. Every property will provide opportunities in this direction if the investor knows what to look for.

Here are some ways to increase income with a minimum of renovation or modernization expense:

☐ *Rent out management space.* The previous owner may have used a portion of the space in the building as his office. The investor should convert it to rental space and manage his property at home or in a cheaper location.

☐ *Convert the basement.* Many office buildings, particularly older structures, have large basements that have never been effectively utilized. In today's inflationary era, many businessmen who do not deal with the public would be happy to pay a low rental for such space. In addition, larger buildings can support restaurants or retail operations there. For a small initial cost, this space can contribute significantly to rental income.

☐ *Close up second entrance.* Some buildings have more than one entrance. Converting one to retail space can add to income without seriously inconveniencing tenants.

☐ *Maximize use of parking area.* Availability of parking, particularly in suburban office buildings, is a major attraction to tenants. If tenants are not presently offered parking, acquisition of adjacent or nearby space as a parking area (with a consequent increase in rentals) can pay off. If rental space already is being offered, perhaps the space can be utilized by nearby restaurants or entertainment facilities in the evening or on weekends, at a fee, when the office building tenants will not be using it.

☐ *Add escalator clause to leases.* As leases come up for renewal, the investor should be sure that a broad escalation clause (covering operating expenses as well as taxes) is included or, even better, try to tie rentals to increases in the Consumer Price Index, which permits the landlord to increase his operating profit in addition to recouping rising costs.

☐ *Renegotiate retail leases.* If any retail tenant is not utilizing all of his space, the investor should try to create space for new tenants. The present tenants probably will be glad to renegotiate their leases for terms that will enable an investor to increase his overall rental income.

Some of the ways to cut operating costs include

☐ *Automating the elevators.* This calls for a large initial outlay but can be quickly made up by the savings in payroll, always one of the top two (along with real estate taxes) expense items.

☐ *Seek real estate tax review.* Many owners do not have their property assessments reviewed, believing that any savings will be small. Over a period of years, however, the savings can add up. This is always worth at least an initial investigation.

☐ *Cleaning and maintenance.* Sometimes it is worthwhile to the investor to retain an outside cleaning service instead of using his own staff. The greater efficiency of outside specialists may more than offset the profit they expect to make.

[3] Suburban Office Buildings

Despite a decrease in demand for office space in some downtown areas, attributable perhaps to overbuilding, many suburban areas continue to experience a demand for office space, and are thus prime locations for the construction of an office building. Although the demand is not from the large national corporations seeking headquarter space, there is a significant demand from the same corporations for branches or "outposts" either on an experimental or permanent basis.

The same holds true for banks, which in many parts of the country are expanding their branches rapidly. Perhaps more important for the suburban builder is the multitude of smaller tenants, such as attorneys, accountants, and businessmen who find that their clientele is primarily in the suburbs, or for whom a downtown location is not important.

Perhaps the key attraction of suburban development is the availability of land. Consequently, the developer has a much greater choice of locations than in the city. But this makes it more important for him to compare locations carefully, checklisting the following points:

- *Trade patterns.* An office building should be near other buildings or related uses.
- *Accessibility and transport.* The building should be accessible from nearby residential areas and also from downtown, if downtown relationships will be maintained.
- *Adequate parking space.* A major motive for many people moving from the city, parking is an important amenity in the suburbs.
- *Availability of employees for tenants.* This not only means the building should be accessible to areas from which employees are drawn, but that it should be attractive for them, too, providing shopping facilities, restaurants, etc.

A developer should distinguish two main types of locations. One is the "pioneer" location, away from an established urban area. Space here is inexpensive, but depends upon future urban growth and sufficient demand by tenants for an out-of-the-way building. The other type of location is that adjacent to an already developed urban area; here, the main attraction is the availability of virtually all urban services, combined with cheaper costs and with more pleasant working conditions.

Key planning considerations for a suburban office building include

☐ *Feasibility studies.* Adequate planning includes projecting market demand and economic pro formas. If demand is small or uncertain, experts strongly recommend building a pilot office project first. If this is done, the developer should be sure to hold options on adjacent land (equal to twice the land needed for the pilot project, plus parking area) so that expansion is feasible.

☐ *Availability of labor and material.* Construction costs may vary widely in the suburbs, because materials and skilled labor may not be available. Consequently, the developer should satisfy himself in advance that no unacceptable risk of shortages exists.

☐ *Zoning.* The land either must be presently zoned for an office building, or the purchase must be made conditional upon rezoning.

☐ *Availability of utilities.* Particularly for the "pioneer" project, there should be adequate sewer, water, electrical, and fire protection facilities.

☐ *Planned parking.* Service parking should be carefully designed so that visitors will not have too far to walk. As land costs increase, we will see more decked parking, which becomes justified whenever land cost exceeds the cost of the parking structure.

☐ *Building services.* The two greatest tenant displeasures in suburban buildings are air conditioning and elevators. Thus, even in a small building, only top quality equipment should be used.

11.05 SHOPPING CENTERS

[1] Introduction

Shopping centers—integrated and self-contained multistore shopping areas—appeared in their present form following World War II and are both a cause contributing to and a result of the suburban explosion, which began at that time and which only recently is showing signs of slowing. There are now close to 20,000 shopping centers of all types in the United States, and they account for close to one half of total retail sales.

As the shopping center evolved, four types emerged, each distinctive in its own function: the neighborhood, the community, the regional, and the super regional. In all cases, a shopping center's type is determined by its major tenant or tenants; the type is based on neither site area nor square feet of the structure.

A neighborhood center provides for the sale of convenience goods (foods, drugs, and sundries) and personal services (laundry and dry cleaning, barbering, shoe repairing, etc.) for the day-to-day living needs of the immediate neighborhood. It is built around a supermarket as the principal tenant. In theory, the neighborhood center has a typical gross leasable area of 50,000 square feet. In practice, it may range in size from 30,000 to 100,000 square feet. The neighborhood center is the smallest type of shopping center.

In addition to the convenience goods and personal services of the neighborhood center, a community center provides a wider range of facilities for the sale of soft lines (wearing apparel for men, women, and children) and hard lines (hardware and appliances). The community center makes a greater variety of merchandise available—in sizes, styles, colors, and prices. It is built around a junior department store, variety store, or discount department store as the major tenant, in addition to a supermarket. It does not have a full-line department store, though it may have a strong specialty store. In theory, the typical size is 150,000 square feet of gross leasable area, but in practice it may range in size from 100,000 to 300,000 square feet. The community center is the intermediate type of center, most difficult to estimate for size and pulling power.

The regional center provides for general merchandise, apparel, furniture, and home furnishings in depth and variety, as well as a range of services and recreational facilities. It is built around one or two full-line department stores of generally not less than 100,000 square feet. In theory, a typical size for definitive purposes is 400,000 square feet of gross leasable area. The regional center is the second largest type of shopping center. As such, the regional center provides services typical of a business district yet not as extensive as those of the super regional center.

A super regional center provides for extensive variety in general merchandise, apparel, furniture, and home furnishings, as well as a variety of services and recreational facilities. It is built around at least three major department stores of generally not less than 100,000 square feet each. The super regional shopping center represents the widespread growth in shopping center usage. In theory, the typical size of a super regional center is about 750,000 square feet of gross leasable area. In practice, the size ranges to more than 1,000,000 square feet.

The key to understanding shopping centers is to remember they are merchandising ventures and must serve the merchandise needs of their markets. The success of a particular center will depend on the size of its market area, the quality of the market (i.e., stability and growth of consumer income) and the competitive position of the center.

More specifically, income potential is dependent upon tenant mix, length of leases, and lease terms. Income potential is greatest when

- Nonanchor tenants are carefully selected on the basis of their ability to achieve high sales volume and so pay percentage (overage) rents.
- Lease terms are fairly short (perhaps five years), which permits frequent adjustments of rent.
- Lease terms minimize the landlord's exposure to operating expenses through various types of expense escalation provisions in the leases.

Usually, the minimum (fixed) rentals paid by tenants in the center are sufficient to pay the landlord's basic operating expenses plus debt service on a mortgage loan. The landlord's profit comes primarily from percentage rentals that will become payable as the sales volume of the individual tenants exceeds the "floor" level set in the leases. And when leases also require the tenants to pay any increases in property taxes and other operating expenses over those incurred in a base year, the center becomes an ideal inflation hedge.

Because of the inclusion of percentage rentals in many shopping center leases, the cash flow position of the landlord improves so long as the sales volume of the center continues to grow. Because percentage rentals are usually tied to gross sales rather than net profits, rentals may increase even though the tenants' profits remain level. In addition, the high degree of debt financing and relatively low operating expenses mean that a large proportion of the cash outlay of the landlord is in the form of a fixed debt service; thus, a large portion of increased rentals flow directly to the landlord.

Well-leased regional centers pass on most of the business risk to the tenants. As noted, they can be ideal inflation hedges. Since inflation is a major factor in long-term appreciation, the well-leased regional mall has excellent long-term prospects for appreciation.

[2] Shopping Center Design

Understanding the relationship of the building pattern to the type of shopping center, and the placement of tenants within the pattern, is important not only for developers of new centers but for owners interested in expanding an existing center and changing its tenant makeup.

The major consideration in leasing space is to place the anchor tenants (the traffic generators) in such a way that customers going from one to another must pass by the smaller stores. The most-used patterns are the following:

☐ *The strip.* The simplest and earliest of the shopping center patterns, this is basically a straight line of stores tied together by a canopy over a pedestrian walk running along the storefronts. Parking space is available between the public street and the stores. Typically, the neighborhood shopping center uses this form, with two major units—usually a supermarket and a drugstore—at each end. It is important that the strip not run beyond a comfortable walking distance. About 400 feet is normal; some strips run 750 feet and more.

☐ *The L and the U.* The L is a strip pattern with one end turned, while the U has both ends turned in the same direction. The major advantage of these forms is to reduce an overlong strip. They also are more appropriate for sites that are somewhat square in shape since they make more efficient use of the land. In general, the L form is suitable for large neighborhood and smaller community centers, while the U is designed for larger community centers.

☐ *The mall.* This is the standard pattern for regional centers and is also used for community centers. Essentially, it consists of a pedestrian walk between two facing strips, with anchor tenants placed at either end (or, if there are more than two, spotted throughout the mall). Consumer traffic is generated back and forth along the walk. Most regional centers today are enclosed malls, which makes them suitable for year-round shopping regardless of weather. A common form of upgrading open-mall centers is to enclose them; this will be justified whenever the cost of doing so is offset by increased sales volume.

☐ *The cluster.* An extension of the mall, the cluster consists of a group of separate strips which together may form an X, a Y, or a dumbbell. When the center has a single key tenant, it is placed in the middle with the satellite stores surrounding it.

☐ *The specialty center.* This final category includes centers having no typical patterns, with design based upon the particular location and market area.

[3] Investing in an Existing Shopping Center

The following factors should be considered in deciding if an existing shopping center is a good investment:

☐ *Location.* A good location makes renting easier, can almost insure overages, and facilitates financing. Check that changes in growth pattern, neighborhood, or transportation facilities have not transformed a once prime location to a poor one.

☐ *Vacancy allowance.* A center fully leased to high-credit tenants may not call for any vacancy allowance in its income statement. If remaining lease terms are short, perhaps a 2 percent allowance should be made. Where sales per square foot per year are not as high as in competing centers, then a larger allowance should be made since some tenants may move when they are able. Sometimes, a buyer will apply a 5 to 10 percent allowance to space leased to local tenants to reflect the greater risk of vacancies.

☐ *Source of rentals.* A buyer should not have a hard-and-fast rule as to the percentage of rentals from blue-chip tenants (e.g., 70 percent). In many successful centers local tenants provided 50 percent or more of the income. More important factors are tenant mix, sales trends, and sales per square foot.

☐ *Percentage and overage rentals.* The question here is whether overage rentals should be given the same weight as minimum rents in the capitalization process. If the sales trend is flat or declining, some buyers will discount overages by 10 percent or more. In a very successful center, a buyer may be convinced to give extra weight to overages because they are rising year by year.

☐ *Management.* Management expense for a shopping center usually runs between 3 and 6 percent of gross income, depending on property size and the division of responsibility between owner and tenant. The operating statement for a center should reflect this expense.

☐ *Reserve for repairs.* The typical center coming on the market is between five and fifteen years old. Some provision for maintenance and repair should be made even if there is no indication of deferred maintenance. In particular, a buyer should check the quality of the center's construction and the condition of the parking area, the latter being the single greatest source of repair expense.

☐ *Real estate taxes.* The two most important considerations are the trend of tax increases and whether all leases have tax-escalation clauses. If they do not, a reserve for tax increases should be provided.

☐ *Financing.* An investor should carefully examine provisions for primary and secondary financing, and make sure that the amount necessary for refinancing is reasonably attainable and that the new debt service cost will be less or at least not exceed the existing carrying cost.

☐ *Maintenance.* One must beware of skimpy, unrealistic figures for proper daily and long-term preventative maintenance, and make sure there are sufficient reserves for roof, exteriors, parking fields, etc. Costs for employing a maintenance crew versus outside contractors should be compared.

☐ *Insurance.* The existing coverage may be inadequate, given today's soaring costs, not only for replacement values but for protection against large liability claims. Changing area conditions may mandate additional forms of protection in addition to higher renewal rates.

☐ *Utilities.* Inaccurate utility figures can greatly affect the projected cash flow. Calculate projected costs by multiplying total kilowatt hours used for the past twelve months by existing rates, and add at least 15 percent for the next year's projected rate hikes.

☐ *Tenant contributions.* The investor should check to see if this center is one in which all or a portion of specified expenses are picked up by the tenants. Today, builders are seeking protection from the tenants against all rising costs, including, in some cases, management and equipment replacement.

☐ *Expansion.* The investor should check to see if the center has additional land available for new buildings without violating parking requirements spelled out in the leases, or if existing structures can be augmented, should major tenants request it. Conversely, can land not being utilized be sold off, without seeking the approval of the mortgage holders? Usable land, located within or adjacent to a thriving center, can command a good price.

[4] The Shopping Center Lease

The shopping center lease is often viewed as the maverick of commercial leases. It differs from the ordinary lease just as the shopping center itself differs from the traditional commercial property. Furthermore, legal and tax considerations and development techniques affecting shopping centers have changed markedly within the past ten years, necessitating new approaches in the drafting of the leases between the developer-owner and his retail tenants.

Shopping center leases differ from other leases in two major aspects:

- Provisions governing the use of common areas
- Provisions establishing the relationship between all the parties in the center, not just the landlord and particular tenant

[a] Types of Tenants in a Center

The bargaining position of the shopping center tenant will vary depending on the class to which it belongs, which includes:

☐ *The major department store.* In making a lease the major tenant can dictate to the developer the essential planning of the center, the type and extent of landscaping, the conditions as to commencement of the term, and the liability for rent. Its rents are nominal or very low; indeed, the landlord frequently loses money on the major tenant. However, the tenant imparts the necessary prestige to attract shoppers and the satellite tenants, who pay much higher rents. If the center turns out badly, the major tenant normally can cut its losses since it can close up shop and vacate, being obligated to pay only the minimum rent for the remainder of the term.

☐ *The satellite (local) tenants.* These are in a far less favorable negotiating position, paying a high rent and having no say in the planning of the center. They are obligated to operate their stores continuously with "adequate" staff and stock and to do "maximum business." The right to sublet or assign is generally not given, and the obligation to pay rent continues whether the center turns out well or not.

☐ *The national credit-rated tenants.* They are usually in a better position to negotiate than the local tenants. Often occupying a small store, these tenants sell merchandise or provide services conforming to an established standard and will draw customers because of national as well as local goodwill and advertising. The national chains will want to use their own lease forms, and their success in obtaining concessions from the landlord will depend on the desirability of the particular chain for the purposes of the center (i.e., its public image and ability to generate sales) and its place in the "tenant mix." These tenants may be successful in getting an exclusive for their products or services.

[b] Key Provisions of Leases

☐ *Construction of center and store premises.* In new centers, the tenant should ask for an affirmative covenant that the landlord will build the shopping center and the building that will contain its store. The landlord, however, normally will resist this demand, as such a promise could make him liable for damages if the center is not completed for any reason.

The developer constructs the leased premises either on a turnkey or a shell-and-allowance basis. Under the turnkey arrangement, the tenant supplies the landlord with drawings for the layout and fixtures; the latter prepares the store completely (except for the trade fixtures). Under the shell-and-allowance approach, the landlord puts up a minimum shell and the tenant constructs and finishes the store, receiving an allowance from the landlord.

When the tenant is to do the work, the landlord should pay particular attention to these four items in the lease agreement:

- A detailed work letter, spelling out just what the tenant may and may not do
- Provisions for adequate insurance covering the landlord and for his indemnification in case of loss
- A compatible-labor clause (to prevent union conflicts between tenant's and landlord's workmen)

- A requirement that the tenant's workers waive the right to file mechanic's liens against the landlord's property.

☐ *Commencement of the term.* In new shopping centers, the lease becomes effective when signed, placing the tenant under all obligations other than rent. (Rent normally will begin when the tenant opens for business or thirty to ninety days after notice from the owner that the store is ready for occupancy, whichever is earlier.) The tenant should agree, if the landlord requests, to defer opening if there is to be a joint opening. The tenant will prefer that one or more of the major tenants have noncancellable leases for ten years or more and open simultaneously with it (since the major tenant is the traffic generator).

Some landlords will permit satellite tenants to examine the major tenants' leases but will then insist on a signed statement that the tenant is aware of the terms of those leases—thus avoiding any claim of implied representations by the landlord that conflict with the leases.

The landlord should have the right to cancel the lease if satisfactory financing is not obtained by him, or if he is prevented from building for causes beyond his control.

Tenants subject to seasonal slack periods should ask that their opening (and rent obligation) be deferred until their busy season commences; so should tenants who cannot obtain an adequate inventory until a later date.

☐ *Common-area charges.* Common areas should be defined and the method of determining the tenant's proportionate share of expenses should be spelled out. Although the charge is usually based on the ratio of the tenant's area to the area of all occupied space, a flat square-foot charge is sometimes used.

The tenant should insist that expenses be itemized and that capital expenditures and the landlord's office expenses be omitted. There should be a separate tax bill for the shopping area. The tenant should have the right to examine records if certified financial statements will not be supplied to him, and it should be given an annual statement showing total cost and each tenant's share.

☐ *Tax escalation.* The landlord customarily will insist that all tenants share any increases in real estate taxes on the shopping center as well as any assessments for public improvements. There are two methods for computing the real estate tax liability: (1) tenants pay all taxes; and (2) tenants pay all taxes over a stated floor. If the latter method is used, the tenant should ask that the base year be the average of the first three full years of operation to avoid a negotiated low assessment for the first year.

Tenants should also pay all tax increases because of tenant improvements. If there is a tax reduction, it will usually be credited to the tenants out of bonus rent. Tenants should also have the right to protest when taxes are too high and to apply for tax reductions.

☐ *Use clause.* The landlord will draft the lease to specifically limit the use to which each premises will be put, and where possible the particular items of merchandise to be sold will be spelled out. Sometimes the amount of space to be used for a line of goods is limited (in lieu of an outright ban). The tenant may ask that if the shopping center grows beyond a certain size, all exclusives be canceled, on the theory that there will be sufficient business for all.

☐ *Noncompetition clause.* The landlord will usually insist on a provision that the tenant may not open another store within three or five miles of the center, and not enlarge an existing store within the specified radius. Some landlords attempt to forbid advertising that mentions other locations, the shift of personnel to other stores, and referral of customers by salespeople to other locations. The measure of damages for breach of such covenants is the inclusion of "outside" gross sales for the purpose of computing a percentage rental.

☐ *Continuous operation.* The landlord will want a covenant that the tenant must conduct business six days a week and a given number of hours; will not close more than a fixed number of days; and will maintain a full staff of employees, adequate stock, and a certain amount of advertising. (Inventory-taking often must be at times the store is not normally open for business.)

☐ *Parking areas.* Landlords will try to restrict tenant and employee parking to rear lots, to restrict the spaces allotted to each tenant, and enforce these restrictions by fines. The tenant should insist on adequate lighting, free parking (via validated parking tickets) if parking is metered, and an express obligation on the landlord to maintain parking areas.

☐ *Damage and destruction by fire.* The tenant should have an assurance that the premises will be restored in the event of fire or other casualty and that rent will be abated until the premises are usable. Responsibility for minor repairs often remains with the tenant, particularly if caused through his negligence. In the case of major damage, the landlord may have the option to cancel the lease rather than repair. If the damage to the shopping center itself is extensive, the landlord may want the right to cancel leases of stores not damaged. The tenant may ask for the same right, and the tenant should have the right to cancel if the landlord does not repair within a stated period.

[5] Outlet Centers

The basic rationale for the outlet center is that significant numbers of the buying public are sufficiently interested in obtaining bargains to go out of their way—sometimes by a considerable distance—to find them. Everyone is familiar with the manufacturers' outlets located in small towns, often near the factory, which for many years have sold seconds, irregulars, and excess inventory at 50 percent or more below regular prices. Jobbers and retailers, seeing a good thing, then began opening up outlet stores in cities and suburbs. Finally, in 1972 the first major-factory outlet center opened up in Reading, Pa. Now containing over 150 outlets housed in converted factory buildings, the Reading center has become a major tourist attraction, with shoppers coming from as far as 300 miles away.

It is too early to tell whether outlet centers will become a permanent addition to the retail scene or will merely prove to be a passing phenomenon. A developer or investment group interested in this type of operation should have firm answers to three key questions before going ahead.

[a] Location

Location is crucial to the success of any shopping center, but in the case of outlet centers, some special considerations apply. These can be summed up as follows:

☐ *Inexpensive land.* Because rentals at outlet centers are low—often in the $5-$8-per-square-foot range, outlying locations are required where land and other services are relatively cheap.

☐ *Distance from regular centers.* Because manufacturers are loath to open up, or supply, off-price outlets that might compete with their regular customers, these specialty centers must keep their distance from standard retail outlets. This also dictates an out-of-the-way location.

☐ *Large trading area.* At the same time, the high volume required for the center to be profitable, as well as the fact that many consumers are not interested in discount purchases, means that the specialty center requires a large trading area. Combining this requirement with that of an out-of-the-way location means that large numbers of customers must be willing to travel dozens or even hundreds of miles to make the center a success. And if gas prices continue to rise (or supplies run short), these centers may be the first to suffer drastic declines in sales volume.

[b] Promotion

Closely related to the problem of location is that of promotion. Absent from the outlet centers are large department stores or chain operations that do a great deal of advertising. In addition, low rentals limit the amount of advertising funds available to the center itself. One approach used by many centers is to promote themselves as tourist attractions, with brochures distributed through tourist information centers and motels. In addition, billboards, TV, radio, and newspaper ads are used in urban centers within the trading area.

[c] Tenant Selection

Some elements that should be considered when selecting tenants are the following:

☐ *Tenant mix.* As with a regular center, tenant mix is very important since one bad store can spoil the traffic for the remainder. Quality must be as high as possible and discounts as deep as possible. This means prices at least 30 percent off regular retail (and preferably close to 50 percent) to overcome the usually inconvenient locations of the outlet centers (since land must be purchased cheaply).

☐ *Traffic generator.* The usual anchor tenant in an outlet center is the women's clothing store. Perhaps 25 percent of the total space should go to women's clothing since this generates the traffic for other stores.

☐ *Other tenants.* Secondary tenants in an outlet center usually are stores selling shoes and children's and men's clothing. Other possibilities are bedding and bath shops, fabric, underclothing, kitchenware, and leather-goods stores. Hard goods are being considered for some new centers. One problem with hard goods in an outlet center (which draws its customers from a large radius) is that customers cannot easily take home a refrigerator or similar large purchase.

11.06 HOSPITALITY FACILITIES

[1] Introduction

The hospitality industry—hotels and motels—with its millions of rooms for sale each day, is a major factor in the real estate market and in the economy in general. Hotel and motel chains continue to grow and now account for approximately 50 percent of all rooms. At the same time, many of the public companies (such as Sheraton and Hilton) which formerly owned most of their properties are selling off all or part of their ownership interests and concentrating in both existing and new properties on the franchising and management end. Related fees may run anywhere from 3 to 10 percent of gross revenues.

Hotels and motels are relatively speculative investments, being management-intensive and highly subject to such outside influences as competition and energy shortages. In that respect, they are like any retail business. They have one major advantage in an inflationary economy; their rates can be changed every day. But, unlike a shopping center, the investor is not passing on the primary business risk to the tenant.

Hotels and motels fall into two general categories: (1) transient facilities, and (2) destination facilities. Those in the first type usually are located on major highways or at airports and depend primarily on persons in transit from one location to another. Destination facilities, by comparison, seek guests who will remain for at least several days, perhaps to spend a vacation or attend a convention. Consequently, these destination facilities often are located in desirable resort areas or in cities that attract a large number of tourists, and they offer complete banquet, meeting room, and convention facilities.

Obtaining financing for hospitality facilities is more difficult than for many other types of real estate because of the risks that cash flow will be substantially reduced at some future date by the existence of new competition, a change in travel patterns, or the sudden unavailability of gasoline for automobile travel.

This reluctance to finance, combined with increasingly heavy costs of construction, means that equity ratios in a new facility often must equal 25 to 50 percent of total capital. Major considerations of lenders are (1) the management capability of the hospitality facility operator (this puts a premium on professional (outside) management or on investors who have had long experience with this type of property), and (2) national reservation systems, which are considered vital to high-occupancy ratios.

Since hospitality facilities are more susceptible to changes in the economic cycle than many other types of real estate, the market value of such properties also may vary over a fairly wide range. The physical structures are unique and complex, the number of employees is large, and cash control is a significant problem, all of which increase risk. In general, hotels can be big winners or big losers. Some of the risk of operation can be reduced by obtaining a major chain franchise and hiring a national management firm, but the costs significantly reduce potential residual cash flow.

[2] Outlook for Motels

[a] New Construction

The motel market in the United States remains relatively strong despite constantly rising costs due to inflation. New projects continue to be built and an active resale market exists, largely because both owners and lenders see demand growing for motel rooms for the foreseeable future.

The motel business is still primarily dominated by smaller operators who own most of the 2.3 million rooms in the United States. Given today's tight-money situation, the typical new project takes the form of a joint venture with a 50-50 split between operator and lender, with the operator taking a 3 to 5 percent management fee off the top and possibly an initial development fee as well.

The key points for the developer of a new project to remember are that

- The project's feasibility must be demonstrated and there ordinarily must be a franchise or referral affiliation.
- The proposed management must have a strong operating track record since motels are as much of a business as a real estate investment.
- The loan submission, including detailed projections of construction and overhead costs, must be more professionally done than has generally been true in the past.

Sources for financing include off-shore funds and local pension trusts, as well as large life insurance companies and other traditional sources.

[b] Financing Requirements

In today's market, a property having most or all of the following features is most likely to obtain financing:

- *A strong or growing market area.* Texas, California, and Colorado have been especially favorable in the recent past.
- *The best location.* This will hold even though a premium price must be paid for land. At one time, Holiday Inns would spend no more than $2,000 per room on land costs. Today, some firms are spending $10,000 to $12,000 or more.
- *A solid generator of room demand.* The source of demand usually consists of office or industrial buildings. Urban and airport properties in general are still regarded favorably, while roadside and resort properties normally cannot qualify.
- *Immediate cash flow.* Lenders are not willing to wait two or three years for positive cash flow to develop; instead, they expect properties to make money the first year.

[c] Resale Market

Generally, there has been a strong demand for existing motel properties. Interest on the part of foreign investors as well as by domestic institutions and pension funds has increased buyer competition faster than the rate at which properties are being put up for sale. Buyer interest is stimulated by the fact that motels still have a better cash flow than other types of real estate investments and, in addition, future appreciation seems likely for good locations.

The capitalization rate used to value motel properties varies according to location as well as the type of motel being valued—whether resort, highway-oriented, destination, or downtown. As a general rule, cash throw-off before depreciation is a multiplier ranging from six and one half to nine and one half times the free-and-clear earnings. Resort properties as a class have the highest multiplier.

One expert suggests as a guideline that for every $1,000 in room acquisition costs, the average room rate should be $1.25 to $1.65. (Varying costs of operation around the country explain the variance.) This average rate should produce a 14 to 18 percent cash-on-cash return at 72 percent occupancy.

11.07 RESTAURANTS

[1] Introduction

Food bought in restaurants represents nearly 40 percent of total food expenditures in the United States, and this percentage may well reach 50 percent in the 1990s. Two reasons for this predicted growth are (1) the growing number of two-income families in which neither spouse performs a housekeeping role, and (2) the continued aging of the population (since older people eat out more).

Restaurants are considered to be within the orbit of the real estate professional because location and site selection play a major role in the success of many of these operations, particularly fast-food outlets. At the same time, specialized management skills are crucial in a restaurant operation. Consequently, a restaurant can be viewed as a location-oriented business, i.e., one in which real estate considerations are important but far from exclusive keys to success.

Real estate investors participate in restaurant operations in one of three ways:

☐ *As landlords.* Most restaurants lease rather than buy land in order to reduce the need for equity capital. Since a free-standing restaurant (particularly a fast-food outlet) is a special-purpose property (i.e., not easily convertible to another use), it is important for the landlord to protect anticipated rentals under the lease by (1) obtaining a guarantee from a principal or other third party with adequate assets, or if this is not feasible, (2) requiring the tenant to show a feasibility study supporting the proposed venture. In addition, because of the extra risks involved with a location-oriented business, the landlord may be in a position to insist on some participation in profits (via a contingent rental) over and above the fixed rental.

☐ *As financial partners.* If a restaurant appears to be an attractive proposition, a real estate owner may contribute land, and possibly cash as well, in exchange for a partnership interest in the venture. Obviously, this means that the investor is participating fully in the risks of the operation and may lose his entire investment if it fails.

☐ *As operators.* Finally, some real estate investors take the full plunge and actually manage and operate a restaurant. In the case of a full-service restaurant, a partnership with an experienced restaurant man is usually essential, because of the special management skills required. In the case of a fast-food outlet, with its limited menu, assistance from the franchise organization, and fixed method of food preparation, success may depend as much on location and site selection as on previous restaurant experience.

[2] Types of Restaurant Operations

For anyone contemplating leasing to or investing in a restaurant, the first step is to identify the type of operation involved. Three market segments exist within the restaurant industry: (1) fast-food, (2) middle-market, and (3) specialty house. While all share some common characteristics, each is to some degree unique.

☐ *Fast-food operation.* This, the fastest growing segment of the industry, is normally characterized by the following:

- Extremely competitive market conditions
- Small profit margins
- Small capital investment required
- Limited menus
- Association with a franchisor

In this type of operation, the most important determinants for success are location and recognition factor. Also crucial is the extent to which the franchisor will provide management expertise and operational guidelines. Many of the large franchise organizations have developed highly elaborate guidelines since the typical fast-food operator is not an experienced restaurant person.

☐ *Middle-market operation.* This is the typical family restaurant that may or may not be involved with a franchisor. Distinguishing characteristics include:

- Relatively higher capital investment required
- Relatively higher payroll in relation to sales due to a greater emphasis on service
- A menu offering greater variety
- As a result of the above, a need for higher operating margins and hence higher prices

In this type of operation, the ability and experience of management are much more crucial than in a fast-food outlet.

☐ *Specialty house.* Here, a restaurant depends least on the real estate aspects and most upon management ability and a reputation for good food and service. Characteristics include:

- Significant capital investment required for building and decor
- Higher costs for food and payroll
- Concentration of business on weekends and at night (ordinarily, breakfast is not served)
- As a result, a need for higher prices and consequently, more affluent customers

An interesting presentation of the results of different types of restaurants in recent years is shown in Table 11.1. Note particularly the significant role of beverage (liquor) sales in keeping total gross profit at a high figure for both the specialty restaurant and the table service restaurant. Nevertheless, each of these had lower profit-before-occupancy costs than either the fast-food outlet or family steak house; the reason was significantly higher payroll.

TABLE 11.1 Comparison of Profit Ratios for Types of Restaurants

	Family Steak House	*Franchised Fast-Food Restaurant*	*Large Specialty Restaurant*	*Traditional Table-Service Restaurant*
Sales:				
Food	85.0%	100.0%	70.0%	90.7%
Beverages	15.0	—	30.0	9.3
Total sales	100.0%	100.0%	100.0%	100.0%
Cost of sales:				
Food	45.0%	42.0%	38.0%	35.0%
Beverages	30.0	—	23.0	28.0
Total cost of sales	43.0%	42.0%	33.5%	34.3%
Gross profit:				
Food	55.0%	58.0%	62.0%	65.0%
Beverages	70.0	—	77.0%	72.0
Total gross profit	57.0%	58.0%	66.5%	65.7%
Operating expenses:				
Payroll and related expenses	20.0%	19.0%	34.0%	38.5%
Advertising and promotion	2.0	3.0	2.5	1.5
Franchise fee	—	4.0	—	—
Other operating expenses	9.0	9.0	8.5	11.0
Total operating expenses	31.0%	35.0%	45.0%	51.0%
Profit before occupancy costs	26.0%	23.0%	21.5%	14.7%
Occupancy costs:				
Rent	—	8.0%	—	4.5%
Real estate taxes	1.0%	—	1.3%	
Depreciation	2.5	2.2	2.6	3.5
Insurance	.3	.6	.3	.3
Total occupancy costs	3.8%	10.8%	4.2%	8.3%
Profit before corporate overhead, interest and income taxes	22.2%	12.2%	17.3%	6.4%

SOURCE: E. Green, "Guide to Restaurants and Other Food Services," 1 *Mahon's Indus. Guides for Accountants and Auditors* 9 (1980).

[3] Restaurant Location

The next step in analyzing a proposed restaurant is a careful evaluation of the market. Market studies range from the intuitive judgment of a small independent to the computerized analysis and strict guidelines of the large fast-food franchisors. The point to remember is that people will travel only so far for meal service (except in the case of a restaurant with a national or international reputation). The typical study for restaurant location concentrates on demographic factors of which the following are among the most important:

- Population, classified as to sex, age, marital status, and ethnic group
- Family size and structure, type of dwellings, average rents, or mortgage payments
- Types of employment
- Income and education

A market-demand study for a full-service or "white tablecloth" restaurant cannot be approached in the same scientific fashion because this type of operation is not subject to the same kind of objective analysis. The best way to do market research in such case is to study the competition. Real estate brokers, restaurant associations and local chambers of commerce may be helpful in providing statistical data.

When a particular neighborhood or area has been selected for a restaurant, the specific site remains to be chosen. It is here that the large fast-food franchise organizations have developed highly detailed guidelines.

For example, an organization may establish disqualifiers for ruling out proposed sites; only those that have one or no disqualifications will be eligible for further study. The following disqualifiers may be used for a fast-food outlet:

- *Traffic count.* Less than 25,000 cars passing the location on a two-way street in a twenty-four-hour period.
- *Traffic flow.* Lane adjacent to store carrying traffic to work or shopping and the far lane taking traffic home (thus requiring home-bound drivers to make a left turn to reach the restaurant).
- *Visibility.* Restaurant or its sign not visible beyond 350 feet in the right lane and 500 feet in the left lane.
- *Competition.* Two national competitors within one mile with combined volumes of over $500,000 or local competitors within one mile with combined volumes of over $750,000.
- *Obstruction potential.* Possibility that future construction near the site will hamper visibility.
- *Traffic speed.* Over 40 miles per hour.
- *Poor image.* Site adjacent to a business not compatible with the restaurant's image.

Obviously, these requirements may vary widely depending on the particular type of restaurant but they offer an appropriate starting point for analysis.

[4] Return on Investment

A standard for return on investment from a restaurant operation is not easily reduced to a formula. One important reason is the crucial role of management skills in a restaurant's success; another is the always significant risk of changing public tastes and the importance of reputation. Finally, many persons go into the restaurant business because of their love of food and wine; their willingness to accept a low (or nonexistent) return on capital makes them difficult competition.

Nevertheless, Eric F. Green[5] offers some suggestions about acceptable and achievable rates of return on investment. The high risk of failure, as well as the need to replace short-lived tangible personal property, suggests an annual return on and of investment of 30 percent (which will enable the investor to recoup his investment over five years as well as realize a return on investment of 15 percent annually).

TABLE 11.2 Calculation of Return on Investment in Restaurant

	High Volume		*Low Volume*	
	Amount	*Percentage*	*Amount*	*Percentage*
Sales	$300,000	100%	$200,000	100%
Profit before occupation costs and return on investment	$60,000	20%	$44,000	22%
Less: Rent or occupation costs	30,000	10	14,000	7
Return of and on investment	$30,000	10%	$30,000	15%
Investment	$100,000			
Required annual return 30% (15% over 5 years—factor 0.2983)	$30,000			

SOURCE: E. Green, "Guide to Restaurants and Other Food Services," 1 *Mahon's Indus. Guides for Accountants and Auditors* 9 (1980).

To achieve this return, sales must be approximately three times investment. Table 11.2 shows a hypothetical financial statement; note that for the high-volume operation the profit before occupation costs and return on investment is 20 percent, approximately the mid-point of the four types of operations shown in Table 11.1. If a sales volume equal only to two times investment is achieved, profit before occupation costs must increase and rent or occupation costs must decrease in order for the same 30 percent return on investment to be achieved. This illustrates the fact that the restaurant business is one of high sales leverage; that is, once sales pass the break-even point, profit margins rise rapidly.

The restaurant business is sufficiently risky when employees and suppliers are completely honest. But the restaurant business is particularly susceptible to both underreporting of sales and misappropriation of merchandise and supplies.

[5] E. Green, "Guide to Restaurants and Other Food Services," 1 *Mahon's Indus. Guides for Accountants and Auditors* 9 (1980).

Underreporting of sales occurs when bartenders or waiters provide drink or food that is not reflected on the check. To prevent this, the serving person should not receive anything from the kitchen or bar without a record of the transfer being made. When this is not possible (as in a coffee shop), numbered checks should be used and each one should be accounted for.

In the case of merchandise and supplies, some workers do not hesitate to consume food on the premises or take it with them when they leave. Suppliers frequently seek to pass off poor quality merchandise or supply lower quantities than billed, either with or without the connivance of a restaurant employee. This type of theft or misrepresentation can be avoided only by strict internal controls including receiving and inspection procedures carried out by persons not directly responsible for purchases.

A landlord who is entitled to a contingent rental, or any investor in a restaurant operation, should insist that those actively managing the operation stay continually alert to the risk of losses from these causes.

11.08 PARKING LOTS

[1] Introduction

A national study of public and private parking facilities by the National League of Cities showed that there are more than 6 million parking spaces throughout the country. Two thirds are operated by municipalities, and one third by private operators. Not surprisingly, private parking facilities are concentrated in the central business districts (CBDs) of cities with more than 100,000 population. Of those cities, 70 percent have private facilities within the CBD, while 17 percent also have private parking facilities elsewhere in the city. For cities under 100,000, the figures are 12 percent with private lots in the CBD and 4 percent outside.

Parking facilities represent a classic interim-land use. Landowners who are hoping that the passage of time will create a demand for a high-rise apartment or office building frequently can utilize the land as a parking lot until further development is justified. Or, an investor trying to assemble several parcels into a single tract can generate income from those he owns while waiting for the others to become available.

As with most other location-oriented businesses, parking lots permit the real estate investor a choice of approaches.

☐ *Percentage lease.* The investor may lease the land to an operator who will assume all the burden and risk of running the lot. The lease may provide for a fixed rental to the landowner or, more commonly, a percentage rental based on gross income.

☐ *Outside management.* The investor can own the business but hire an operator under a management contract, paying the operator a percentage (perhaps 10 or 15 percent) of gross revenues.

☐ *Own and operate.* The investor may decide to invest his own time and run the entire operation himself.

[2] Types of Parking Facilities

Parking facilities are distinguished essentially by whether the driver parks by himself (self-service) or an attendant parks the car.

☐ *Self-service lots.* The least expensive type of parking facility is the self-service lot. The investor need make a minimum of physical improvements (blacktop, striping, and perhaps fencing). Only a single employee (cashier) is required. (Some lots that have experimented with metered parking have found a very high rate of nonpayers.)

☐ *Self-service multistory garages.* These involve a greater investment, which may be justified if the demand for parking is great enough. In this type of garage, drivers proceed up a ramp to upper floors until they find available space. Labor costs are held to a minimum, but ramps and parking spaces must be somewhat wider than in an attended garage because trained attendants are not doing the parking.

☐ *Attended lots.* Labor costs will be somewhat higher than for surface lots, but more cars can be accommodated. Most drivers probably would choose a self-service lot over an attended lot because they prefer to park their own cars and thus minimize the risk of damage.

☐ *Attended garages.* Of the four types of parking facilities, these are the most expensive and normally will be justified only in areas of highest demand.

A fifth type of parking facility is the mechanical garage, in which cars are moved up and down by elevator. These involve substantially greater investments than any of the others described.

[3] Financial Analyses

The investor considering the purchase or development of a parking facility must ask himself these questions:

- What is the potential income from the various types of parking facilities, at varying rate structures, at the particular location being considered?
- What are the expenses for the different types of facilities at the location?
- What is the total investment cost and to what degree can it be financed?

As with most other types of location-oriented businesses, figuring the initial investment and the operating expenses of a parking lot is not very difficult. The crucial projection is of gross income, which can fluctuate sharply due to such factors as new competition, and restrictions on cars entering the shopping area.

The formula for projecting gross income is as follows:

- Determine the daily turnover rate, i.e., the total number of cars parked on an average day divided by the number of parking spaces.
- Then determine the average parking rate per car.
- The result is income per space per year, the standard by which parking lot income is measured.

An investor plans a parking lot with sixty spaces; his analysis of the market indicates that on an average day 120 cars can be parked, for a turnover rate of two (i.e., on average each space is occupied twice during the day). If the average parking rate is $1, the income per space per day is $2 and the income per space per year (assuming weekday parking only) is $500. With sixty spaces, total gross income is $30,000.

The success or failure of a parking lot investment depends upon how accurately one can judge the turnover rate at different price levels. For this, the investor would be well advised to call in a specialist. For example, in business districts, the weekends may be very slow unless there are restaurants and theaters to draw people to the area. Parking lots in suburban shopping districts may be hurt severely by the opening of a new shopping center that offers free parking. In any location, new competition could severely jolt the income flow.

Total income also will be affected by decisions to charge hourly, daily, or monthly rates. Longer-term rates assure an investor of a smoother income flow, but hourly rates offer the greatest profit potential.

Most of the initial cost will be spent on land, the price of which will vary widely. Improvements (paving, fencing, lighting, signs) are the major additional expense.

Operating costs will include real estate taxes, labor costs, liability and collision insurance, utilities, and other miscellaneous expenses. These can be estimated quite accurately.

Financing may be somewhat difficult in today's tight-money market. Normally, a mortgage equal to perhaps 70 percent of total investment can be obtained, running for a term of up to ten years. The amount of debt service will depend upon the length of the loan and the interest rate. Even though parking lots are location-oriented businesses, they often are stable enough to justify fairly good loan terms.

Overall, an investor should anticipate a free-and-clear return on total investment of 10 percent a year or more. Financing might increase this by several percent. If the investor also operates the business, he should anticipate an additional return for his labor.

11.09 RECREATIONAL FACILITIES

[1] Introduction

Rising incomes, higher standards of living, and more leisure time have combined to stimulate a tremendous expansion of recreational facilities in the past two decades. In its broadest sense, recreational property ranges from the local amusement arcade to elaborate resort condominiums and second-home developments. As used here in its more limited sense, the term refers to facilities that charge an admission or membership fee and offer some form of recreational activity, for example, tennis courts, bowling alleys, golf courses, ski facilities, roller- and ice-skating rinks and the like.

The key consideration to remember when investing in a recreational facility is that it is a location-oriented business; that is, while good location is an important factor in determining the success of the operation, knowledge of the business and careful management is at least as important and probably more so. In other words, recreational facilities are primarily business operations, not real estate investments. They are of interest to real estate investors because the major investment in buildings and improvements may generate large depreciation deductions so that the business may generate tax-free cash flow plus taxable losses, which can be used to shelter outside income of the investors. However, these types of facilities often carry above-average risks, for at least two reasons.

The first reason, already noted above, is that they are management-intensive. Unless the real estate investor is prepared to devote considerable time to the business (and the expertise required), professional management will have to be retained and be rewarded either with substantial compensation or a share of ownership.

The second reason is that a locality can easily become surfeited by a particular kind of recreational facility. Too many facilities can be built to satisfy the effective demand. This frequently occurs when a particular type of activity becomes a fad—this happened with bowling in the 1960s and tennis in the 1970s—with the result that an excessive investment capital is attracted too quickly for the market to absorb. In addition, demand itself tends to be volatile. A sport or activity may be popular for a season or two but then may lose many of its followers because of its difficulty or expense. For this reason, projections for new recreational facilities should be taken with a grain of salt, particularly with respect to the projected revenue levels.

Although the risks in recreational facility investments are high, the rewards can be commensurately great. Since most of the investment normally is in "bricks and mortar," the facility can be extremely profitable once the break-even point is reached. The secret of success in such ventures is to structure them in such a way that the break-even point (in terms of usage or number of customers) is as low as possible. This means that cost must be kept under control, financial leverage should be used to the extent possible, and tax savings should be maximized. Three types of recreational facility investments are discussed below to illustrate the potentials in this type of investment.

[2] Tennis Courts

[a] In General

Tennis and other racquet-and-ball sports have experienced an incredible growth in the two past decades. According to one estimate, there were about 8 million tennis players in the United States in 1970; in 1980, the sport was played (with varying degrees of skill) by perhaps 35 million people. To this can be added perhaps 5 million or more racquetball players. The tremendous growth in popularity of these sports has been accompanied by numerous real estate investment opportunities in the development of indoor and outdoor facilities.

The U.S. Tennis Association estimated a few years ago that there were 141,000 tennis courts in the United States. Of these:

- 33 percent were in colleges and other schools
- 31 percent were in outdoor clubs and resorts

- 18 percent were municipal courts
- 11 percent were owned by private individuals
- 6 percent were in indoor clubs

Private tennis facilities fall into one of five types:

- The traditional outdoor tennis club
- The newly developed indoor club
- The indoor-outdoor combination
- The tennis resort
- The residential project with tennis facilities

Generally, the discussion that follows will deal with the indoor club or the combination facility. Indoor courts usually are of one of two types: the air-pressure-supported plastic or the prefabricated steel building.

In addition to tennis, the other popular racquet-and-ball sports include

☐ *Racquetball.* The sport appeals primarily to persons in the twenty-to-forty-year age group and is essentially the game of handball with a sawed-off tennis racquet played in a rectangular enclosed court. The smaller court (20 by 40 by 20 feet high) means that four or five racquetball courts equal one tennis court.

☐ *Squash.* As tennis once did, squash until quite recently drew its devotees primarily from the wealthy and from college and private school students (mostly in the East). It is a faster game than other racquet sports and is played on a court measuring 32 feet by 18½ feet; thus, six squash courts can fit into one tennis court.

☐ *Paddle tennis.* Originally intended as a game for children, this is the racquet sport most similar to tennis. It is played exactly as is tennis except that the dimensions of the court are one half the traditional tennis court. Easily learned and not as strenuous as other racquet sports, it appeals to people of all ages.

☐ *Platform tennis.* This is very similar to paddle tennis but is nevertheless a distinct sport. Both games are played on courts, with similar equipment, but in platform tennis the court fencing is used as a part of the play, which cannot be done in paddle tennis.

[b] Supply and Demand Factors

Tennis being the oldest and most popular of the racquet sports, guidelines to measure the effective demand for tennis facilities are the most developed. In general, the break-even occupancy point for a new indoor tennis club is around 72 to 73 percent; clubs built between 1973 and 1976 can break even in the mid-60-percent range, and clubs built earlier break even in the upper-50-percent range. These differences are due primarily to higher construction and financing costs for new courts. Since the average club is open 112 hours per week, this means that a newly built facility must sell 13 more hours per court per week to be on an even footing with a five-year-old facility.

An indoor tennis club generally will draw tennis players within fifteen minutes' driving time (about a 6-mile radius in a congested location, more where access is by a freeway or expressway). The number of players that can be attracted will depend upon three factors:

☐ *Climate.* This obviously is a crucial factor in the case of indoor clubs. Generally, indoor operations can be successful where there are approximately thirty weeks of inclement (cold or rainy) weather. Demand for air-conditioned indoor courts will also exist during very hot weather, but even at such times, many persons prefer to play outside or to engage in such outdoor activities as swimming and camping.

☐ *Income.* As a general rule, tennis court memberships come from families with annual incomes over $15,000. But this guideline should not be followed strictly since communities with lower average incomes but where the cost of living is lower may be able to support a facility. Surveys have shown that anywhere from 25 to 30 percent of such families have at least one tennis-playing member.

☐ *Competing facilities.* The effective demand for a new tennis court will depend upon the number of existing and planned facilities. These will include not only other private clubs but also municipal, school, and institutional facilities, as well as courts available at resort and residential projects.

[c] Site Considerations

In choosing a site for a tennis or similar facility, the investor should concentrate on these considerations:

☐ *Location.* The facility should be close to the market that it will serve—normally, but not always, a residential neighborhood. Since much playing is done at night, personal security is an important factor, so isolated locations are undesirable. A good site is one close to other commercial recreational uses that are noncompetitive.

☐ *Size.* Tennis clubs generally require one acre for every three courts, but this varies greatly depending upon clubhouse facilities, parking requirements, and setbacks. Other racquet facilities require substantially less land per court.

☐ *Shape.* Rectangular parcels permit the best layout of courts and normally will be required when indoor courts are to be constructed. However, outdoor courts can be built on a wide variety of shapes.

☐ *Access.* As with all commercial and recreational facilities, ease of ingress and egress is important.

☐ *Zoning.* Sport clubs generally must be located on land zoned for commercial use. However, in many suburbs an indoor club is able to obtain a conditional use or variance permitting location in a residential neighborhood.

[3] Roller-Skating Rinks

[a] In General

In the past ten to fifteen years, the roller-skating industry has experienced phenomenal growth and change. Perhaps the most significant change has been in the image of the activity—from a kid's game to an adult sport that caters to every level of society. As a result, many rinks have become architecturally advanced fun centers that can produce sufficient revenue to justify high-priced locations. Banking institutions are much more willing than formerly to provide the necessary financing. Indeed, the major problem in some parts of the country is the threat of overbuilding by investors who have not properly researched sites or market potential. Nevertheless, many attractive investment opportunities exist.

Because the choice of a site is often the most important consideration in developing a roller-skating rink, this type of operation is considered a location-oriented industry, a classification that includes such other recreational facilities as tennis courts, racquetball courts, bowling alleys, and the like. These operations are often of interest to real estate investors because of their expertise in choosing sites. However, risks are present too—most notably those of oversaturation of a market and inadequate management. Good management in a roller-skating facility is vitally important, since the activity is a promotional one that requires the maintenance of a close relationship with youth groups, church groups, schools, and other community organizations.

[b] Site Selection

As already noted, site selection for a roller-skating rink is crucial since once established, it cannot be moved and the initial investment is very large. Some feasibility studies have indicated that a commercial roller-skating rink requires an average population base of 50,000 to 75,000 people. However, other factors are sufficiently important so that a simple body count is never enough.

Of the other factors, possibly the most important is the proximity of competing roller-skating facilities. While many adults patronize rinks, it is youngsters who keep a skating center busy on weekday afternoons and evenings. Consequently, the ratio of youngsters to the neighborhood population (within a 5-mile radius) is important. In addition, consider the competition from other recreational facilities in the area, as well as the number of schools, churches, and other community groups, which are the key source of party bookings.

The impact of these other factors is such that a successful rink may be established in a rural community with as few as 15,000 to 20,000 people, while in a metropolitan area, a population base of 200,000 or more per facility may be needed to overcome the competition for the recreation dollar.

A site usually will run from one and one half to two acres of land (depending upon local zoning requirements for parking and easements). The investor should avoid the temptation to buy cheap land in an outlying area; because location is so important, paying a premium for the land (which is not likely to add much to the total investment) is worthwhile. However, location on a main thoroughfare is probably not necessary since a rink does not draw off-the-street traffic.

[c] Constructing a Rink

Costs of construction of a rink obviously will vary for any given location, depending among other things upon soil conditions, labor costs, zoning and building codes, climate conditions. In the recent past, finished rinks averaged between $12 and $17 per square foot, with $15 the most common figure. Taking a 15,000-

square-foot building as typical, construction costs would then be $225,000 to which must be added $25,000 to $40,000 for rental skate equipment. Thus, total costs (excluding land) will run anywhere from $250,000 on up.

Various types of building construction are used, the most common being the pre-engineered steel building. This creates a clear-span skating surface, is quick to erect, and may be customized with stone, brick, or paneling to give an attractive appearance.

Another substantial expense is for paving the parking area. Most rinks require one parking space per 200 square feet of building area (and even less is adequate if not much adult business is expected). Many zoning codes require one parking space per 100 square feet of building, but this generally is more than is needed by a roller-skating rink.

It is generally a good idea to consult with a firm specializing in rink construction when drawing up building plans. This type of construction is not very common, and consequently, building contractors and architects may lack specific know-how.

Rink size depends upon population base, available financing, and property limitations. Rinks are often classified as small, medium, and large. An overall building of 11,000 square feet is considered small, while 11,000 to 18,000 square feet is medium, and anything above that is large. The total space is divided between the actual skating rink and the service area. The latter usually represents 40 to 50 percent of the total area. The service area contains the snack bar, skate rental facility, and restrooms, as well as space where customers can socialize. Many experienced operators consider this social area to be a vital part of the operation.

In terms of design, the three important considerations are utility, flexibility, and appearance. The test of utility is whether traffic can flow smoothly without bottlenecks. Flexibility means the ability to expand in the event the rink is successful. (Consider that a rink has a normal life of twenty-five to fifty years, during which time the community may change significantly.) Finally, appearance is important since the attractiveness and brightness of the facility will be important in creating repeat business.

[d] Financial Analysis

A large percentage of total cost will be represented by debt service (or rental cost). Many rinks have been financed with ten-year loans; if longer terms (or longer amortization schedules) can be obtained, debt service will be lessened.

Operating costs, in general terms, may run as follows:

- Labor—20 to 25 percent
- Goods and materials—12 percent
- Taxes and licenses—2 to 6 percent
- Telephone and utilities—3 percent
- Insurance—2.5 percent

So total operating expenses may run between 39.5 and 48.5 percent of gross receipts. If debt service (or building rental) runs 15 percent of gross, total costs will range between 54.5 and 63.5 percent of gross.

General statements of income are impossible to make since so much depends upon the particular rink and its competition. About all that can be said is that an industry survey in 1976 gave the following percentage breakdown of total income:

- Admissions—45 percent
- Skate rentals—20 percent
- Snack bar—19 percent
- Equipment sales—8 percent
- Lockers—3 percent
- Game room—3 percent
- Miscellaneous—2 percent

In this survey, admission prices varied from 75 cents to $1.50 for matinees, and between $1 and $2 for evenings. Skate rentals averaged 50 to 75 cents.

A roller-skating rink is a highly leveraged business, so that once a break-even point is reached, a very large percentage of additional gross receipts will flow down to net income.

[4] Golf Courses

[a] In General

The 1980s may see a substantial upsurge in golf-course development as the game continues to grow in popularity and as more reports and planned residential developments incorporate golf courses in their basic design.

Golf courses have another advantage. They generally are regarded as a good environmental use since, in effect, they constitute a green belt in a developed area. They are particularly suitable where cluster development is possible; in one case, a developer had a 200-acre tract of land of which 150 acres became a golf course. The developer was able to obtain the highest-density zoning for the remaining 50 acres, on which he built multifamily units.

[b] Financial Analysis

Table 11.3 below shows the cost breakdown for building an 18-hole regulation-length course. Not included is the cost of land (which can vary widely), clubhouse, golf professional shop, and furnishings.

Table 11.4 below illustrates a cash-flow statement for a regulation course. These figures assume a $600,000 mortgage for twenty years at 11.5 percent constant and 10 percent annual interest. Thus, the mortgage covers the total construction cost, with the developer's equity represented by the land.

Table 11.5 below shows the free-and-clear return from operations (i.e., assuming no financing and again ignoring the land cost).

Golf-course revenues can be generated in one of three ways. On a public course, the basic revenues come from greens fees (as in Table 11.4). A developer may operate on this basis until sufficient interest has developed to support the club

TABLE 11.3 Cost Estimates of an 18-Hole Regulation-Length Golf Course

	From:	*To:*
Course construction costs, including irrigation system	$400,000	$ 850,000
Post-construction maintenance (from planting to opening)	25,000	110,000
Course-maintenance equipment	60,000	85,000
Maintenance building	25,000	100,000
Car paths, shelters, bridges, etc.	10,000	100,000
Golf-car storage	10,000	20,000
Service road	8,000	50,000
Entrance road and parking	3,500	35,000
Subtotals	$541,500	$1,350,000
Plus 10% contingency	54,150	135,000
Totals	$595,650	$1,485,000

on a private basis. In a nonequity private club, members pay an initiation fee and annual membership dues (with the public sometimes admitted at higher fees). In this type of private club, the developer controls and operates the golf course on a for-profit basis. Finally, in the membership-owned equity club, the developer sells

TABLE 11.4 Cost-Flow Statement

Assuming golf-course construction costs are $600,000 and can be 100 percent financed, a development golf-course income statement (without clubhouse operations) might look like this:

Amortization of principal, including interest at 10% annually	$ 69,000
Taxes and insurance	25,000
Golf-course maintenance (national average considering escalated costs projected 10 years)	130,000
Total golf-course operating costs	$224,000
Income: 40,000 greens fees at $7 (average)	$280,000
Profit from operation	$56,000

Note: The above profits could also be achieved by 500 members paying annual membership fees of $600; or by 300 members, plus greens fees.

TABLE 11.5 Free-and-Clear Return

Total income (Table 11.4)	$280,000
Total operating costs (taxes, insurance, and maintenance from Table 11.4)	155,000
Net operating income	$125,000
Total construction cost	$600,000
Free-and-clear return (excluding land cost)	21%

his interest at a (presumed) profit and thereafter has no further connection with the operation.

11.10 APARTMENT BUILDINGS

[1] Introduction

Apartment buildings, or apartment complexes, make up a large portion of the nation's housing stock and have always represented a significant area for real estate investors. Since apartment buildings share many features with the one-family house, this type of investment is often the next step for investors who seek a market in which they have some familiarity.

Apartment buildings fall into two well-defined groups: (1) conventionally financed buildings, which are those in which financing is provided by a private or institutional lender and the loan is not government-guaranteed, and (2) subsidized buildings, which are financed directly by government, either city, state or federal, or by a government-guaranteed loan.

There are many factors to consider when choosing an apartment building. As with other types of properties, the importance of location is critical. From the physical standpoint, the attractiveness of the property will affect rental levels, and the quality of construction will affect operating expenses. In addition, in recent years such amenities as swimming pools and tennis courts have become important features of many buildings. Finally, the mix of apartment units—for example, studio, one bedroom, or two bedroom—is important in relation to the potential demand from single persons, families with children, etc.

As discussed in 10.01, property management is certainly a key factor, particularly when the landlord provides utilities and significant amenities.

Financing is usually good for apartment properties. However, any indication of poor maintenance or a deteriorating neighborhood may discourage lenders. The lender looks primarily to the rental income stream to service the loan; by comparison, the creditworthiness of the borrower is the crucial element for one-family houses.

As a general rule, the value of any income property is a function of the cash flow it generates. For some properties, such as shopping centers, investors are willing to pay very high prices (a low capitalization rate) because of expected steady increases in cash flow. This is not true of apartment buildings because of fears that physical and functional obsolescence and possibly even rent control will put a lid on cash-flow growth. Consequently, an apartment building's prospects for appreciation will be good only if there is sound reason to believe that cash flow will rise in the future. However, a well-maintained and well-located project represents one of the more stable forms of investment and consequently is a good prospect to appreciate at least in line with the inflation rate.

Apartment buildings technically are defined as structures with five or more housing units having interior access; that is, one first enters the building before entering any individual apartment unit. A related type of residential investment is the multiplex, which is a single structure having two to eight separate housing units, each with exterior access; that is, one need not go through a central lobby to reach each unit. The most common example is the two-family house.

[2] Types of Apartment Buildings

Apartment buildings fall into two essential types: (1) garden-apartment (low-rise) projects, and (2) elevator (high-rise) buildings. The essential distinction between these two (apart from the obvious need for elevator service in the latter) is in their design and cost of construction, the two being intimately related. Garden-apartment projects usually contain from ten to twenty units per acre and normally do not exceed two stories, although they sometimes will reach three. They contain a good deal of open space, which accounts for the name. Once a building rises above the third floor, however, construction costs increase sharply because concrete and steel must now replace frame and stucco. Consequently, much higher density (units per ground space) must be created in order for the project to be economically sufficient. In other words, a high-rise building (because it costs more) must be a high-rise building (because the additional density is necessary to make the project profitable).

From an investment point of view, there are some important distinctions between garden apartments and high-rise projects. First of all, garden apartments tend to have a more favorable building-land ratio for purposes of the depreciation deduction; that is, the land represents a smaller percentage of the total cost than it does in the case of a high-rise project, which usually is in a more heavily populated and more central area. Since only the portion of total costs attributable to the building is depreciable (land not being depreciable for tax purposes), the garden-apartment owner is usually able to depreciate a larger percentage of his total costs than is the high-rise project owner.

The second difference is in the elasticity of the rent structure. In a word, rentals in a garden-apartment project are more elastic; that is, rent reductions are more likely to bring an increase in demand for space while rent increases are more likely to send people looking for alternative housing (if they can find it). By contrast, rentals in a high-rise project generally are higher from the outset (because the project is more expensive) and thus attract higher-income tenants who are less likely to be bothered by an increase, or are less likely to be attracted to the building because of a rent concession. Of course, this is not an invariable rule. When many cities had an oversupply of high-rise housing in the early 1970s, buildings were often filled rather quickly when sufficient inducements (including several months free rent or a free trip to Europe) were offered. Nevertheless, it is generally true that rent-cutting in high-rise projects in order to fill vacancies is generally not considered a very good idea, whereas even a relatively small reduction in a garden-apartment project may bring good results.

By comparison with either of these types of true apartment buildings, the multiplex (two to eight units) is more like the extension of a one-family house. Such investments are ideal for investors who intend to live in one of the units and do much of the maintenance and repair themselves; by the same token, their availability to their tenants means they will be continually bothered whenever problems arise. However, the return on investment (ROI) in this type of situation often can be quite high, both because cash outlays for management are low and because financing is often easier to obtain than on larger buildings. On the other side, the rent income tends to be more volatile than in larger buildings because a single vacancy will have a much greater impact upon the total rent roll when there are a maximum of eight tenants.

[3] How to Analyze an Apartment Building Investment

[a] Judging Demand for Apartment Units

In analyzing an investment in an apartment building, there are many factors to be considered. The investor will obviously want to know all the details of the particular apartment building he is considering, as well as the area or community in which it is situated. The investor will usually rely on general knowledge of the area in selecting a particular apartment to look at, making a more detailed study of the area after ensuring that the offering is an attractive one. The sequence of investigation is probably not too important, but many investors prefer to study the area in some detail before examining specific transactions, since the information gathered, if indicating a satisfactory investment climate, will be of value regardless of the particular investment choice made.

A good deal of information about the area will be available from public sources and community organizations, such as local chambers of commerce, but some of it may have to be gathered privately. The following is a list of things a large institutional investor-lender would need to know and how to gather the information:

☐ *Vacancy rates.* Up-to-date information is obtained regularly by sending out first-class mailings to "Occupants" at each unit address in each area. The number of vacancies in each project can be determined by counting the number of letters that are returned because the apartments are vacant, and then correlating the returns with an existing list of projects. Trends can be seen by comparing current with past figures. The lender considers 5 percent or less to be a favorable figure and generally holds off when vacancies reach a figure above 7 percent. Projects that fall in the gray area between 5 and 7 percent should be carefully scrutinized.

☐ *Absorption rate of new units.* Information can be derived from the vacancy survey, as well as from visits to projects and conversations with rental agents.

☐ *Housing-attitude survey.* Apartment dwellers are given the opportunity to provide information on such topics as the type of housing the respondent wants in his next move, how much rent he will be willing to pay, and major complaints about his present quarters.

☐ *Household formation.* Analyzing the rate of new household formations determines the need for apartments aimed at the young couple and family market.

☐ *In-migration statistics.* Newcomers, for example, may be either retired couples or corporate or military transfers. The former are looking for small apartments with specific amenities, the latter are apt to be family oriented, interested in more rooms, schools, and play areas.

☐ *Housing purchases.* A high purchase rate may mean that rental opportunities have been inadequate. Condominium and town house sales may indicate that the newcomers have been buying a nonmaintenance way of life. If so, they may be prime apartment targets.

☐ *Job market.* An increase in jobs will mean either increased family income as wives go to work, or an increase in demand as more workers (and their families) enter the area. Conversely, the housing market will be affected by unemployment and retirement figures.

☐ *Neighborhood.* The investor should be aware of possible undesirable or nuisance features nearby, which may include railroad tracks, dense traffic, noise, and nearby industry.

☐ *Transportation.* The investor should determine travel time to downtown areas, employment centers, shopping, recreation, and schools.

[b] Analyzing an Apartment Building Offering

The following are excerpts from an actual offering of an apartment building in a large southeastern city. The tables accompanying the analysis are part of the offering statement.

[i] Description of Property. Table 11.6 is a brief description of the property, which obviously emphasizes the positive features. Naturally, an investor will make his own inspection of the property and have a competent engineer or other qualified person prepare a written report. It would be helpful to have both interior and exterior plans including room sizes, layout, traffic patterns, and landscaping.

TABLE 11.6 Property Description

Number of units: 30— 20 one-bedroom, 1-bath apartments and 10 two-bedroom, 1-bath apartments

Year built: 1966

Lot size: 265 ft. × 315 ft. × 69 ft. × 230 ft.——Total 37,115 sq. ft.

Roof: Mansard perimeter, tar and gravel

Floors: Concrete under carpet

Windows: Awning type, plus two sets of large sliding glass doors per apartment for access to the terrace

Air conditioning & heating: Individual central air and heat in each apartment

Furnished: All apartments, including wall-to-wall carpet

Water & sewer: City

Off-street parking: 45 spaces

Swimming pool: 20 ft. × 36 ft. oval

[ii] Rental Income and Operating Expenses. Table 11.7 is a lease expiration table (only a portion is reproduced here). It lists each apartment, its rental and size, and indicates the date upon which the lease will expire. The prospective buyer will, at some point, confirm these figures by having his attorney read all leases to determine if rent concessions (e.g., one free month per year for the life of the lease) or other types of rent offsets exist. The amount of value of any such concessions should be applied to reduce the annual gross rental income.

The rents must fit into the market range in the area. Higher rents must be justified by what the project offers, and what the market will tolerate.

TABLE 11.7 Lease-Expiration Table

Apartment	*Rent*	*Size*	*Lease Expiration*
101	$190	1 Br.	5/74
102	195	1 Br.	2/74
103	185	1 Br.	(no lease)
104	175	1 Br.	8/73

(Others omitted)

Total of 30 apts.: $6,125 × 12 = $73,500 current annual gross rental income

More importantly, a lease-expiration schedule tells the buyer the amount of space that will become vacant in each future year. Unless the buyer is extremely optimistic about the strength of the local apartment market, he will be leery of a schedule that shows high vacancies in the near future, since this means that current rental flow is not assured.

An owner whose property is 100 percent rented will not hesitate to show gross rental income based upon full occupancy. Indeed, many brokers assume full occupancy in their flyers (offering statements), even though this is not the fact (the gross rental income is then called scheduled net).

Cautious investors normally will reduce rental income to some extent (perhaps 5 or 10 percent) to provide a cushion against future vacancies. This certainly should be done if there is a current oversupply of space in the neighborhood and any leases in the particular building will expire in the near future.

The owner must provide the purchaser not only with a list of all leases, but also with a summary of their rental provision. He should also represent that there are no side agreements with tenants that contravene the lease terms. In addition, the purchaser or his attorney should read all leases to verify this information.

Years ago, when high vacancy rates were the rule, unscrupulous landlords would "pack" a building with short-term tenants or persons paying no rent at all to give the appearance of full occupancy. While this is much less common today, it remains a possibility to be guarded against when dealing with unknown sellers. Another way for a landlord to defraud a purchaser is to enter into side agreements prior to the sale with some tenants, giving them free rent in the future in exchange for an immediate cash payment to the landlord (called milking the property).

A buyer who doubts the ethics of the seller should personally interview some or all of the tenants to verify their rent obligations. A more formal way to do this is to have the tenants execute estoppel statements, in which the tenants acknowledge their continuing obligation to pay rent pursuant to the lease terms.

Table 11.8 below lists total income and expenses "as reported by the owner." There are a variety of ways in which income statements and projections of income and expenses can be distorted. The prospective investor must, therefore, not take the owner's statement and projections at face value.

TABLE 11.8 Existing Income and Expenses as Reported by Owner

Gross Income:		
Rental income	$73,500	
Laundry room	720	
		$74,220
Operating Expenses:		
Real estate taxes	$ 9,700	
Insurance	1,500	
Utilities (gas & electric)	1,800	
Licenses	100	
Air-conditioning contract	1,080	
Maintenance	2,400	
Pool supplies	480	
Management	2,400	
Elevator contract	455	
Garbage	960	
		20,875
Net operating income		$53,345

Here are some ways in which current net operating income and projections of future income can diverge from the property's true earning power and what the purchaser can do to protect himself:

☐ *Deferred maintenance.* This is one of the most frequently encountered problems, and it refers to any inadequacies in maintaining and repairing the property. Simple examples include the failure to paint at proper intervals, periodically maintain the boiler, and inspect and repair the heating, electrical, and plumbing elements in the building. An owner may defer maintenance because he does not have the necessary cash flow to do the work or he may deliberately be seeking to show the highest possible operating income to prospective purchasers.

A thorough inspection of the property by a competent engineer is the most obvious way for a purchaser to protect himself. Experienced investors also will have developed rules of thumb concerning the percentage of rental income that should be devoted to maintenance and repair each year (e.g., 5 percent of rental income). A financial statement that shows a much smaller percentage devoted to this purpose is suspect.

☐ *Substantial capital improvements needed.* In addition to deferring necessary maintenance, the owner may have postponed needed capital improvements (causing what investors call functional depreciation). Capital improvements may be required to keep the property in efficient condition (e.g., a new roof) or may be necessary so that the building can remain competitive, for example, an apartment building may require a swimming pool and other amenities in order to avoid losing tenants to newer buildings.

Again, complete inspection of the property is a must. In addition, the purchaser should do whatever market research is necessary to ascertain what the property needs to maintain its competitive position.

☐ *Inadequate replacement reserves.* When personal property is a significant factor (as in the case of apartment buildings offering furnished units), adequate cash reserves should be maintained to replace short-lived items such as furniture and carpets. To the extent the reserves are inadequate, a new owner may be forced to invest a substantial amount of additional capital soon after he acquires title to the property.

The purchaser should deduct an amount necessary to fund the reserves to their proper level from the price he initially is willing to pay for the property.

☐ *Improper capitalization of expenses.* The first three items discussed all relate to actual inadequacies. But even when the owner has properly maintained the property, his financial records can be misleading if, in order to increase net operating income, the owner has capitalized (i.e., added to his capital account) expenditures that properly should have been deducted currently from gross rental income. In other words, by shifting actual expenditures from the operating statement to the capital account statement, an owner can present an inflated net operating income picture.

While the distinction is sometimes difficult to make in practice, the general rule is that costs that do not increase the value of the property are to be regarded as expenses rather than capital expenditures. Experienced investors, as already noted, usually have their own rule of thumb as to the percentage of gross income that should be devoted to repairs and maintenance and so will substitute this figure for the one in the owner's financial statements.

11.11 ONE-FAMILY HOUSES

[1] Introduction

Many investors, having a relatively small amount of cash and being unwilling to join with others in a syndicate, find the one-family house an ideal entry into residential investment. In addition to the fact that the initial equity required is low, one-family houses have two other definite advantages:

- Mortgage financing is often available on excellent terms (even though the investor will not live in the house).
- Relatively minor upgrading and improvement can often bring both a higher rental during the holding period and a higher profit on resale.

A particular type of one-family-house investment is the vacation home, either purchased as a straight investment or with the intention of using it part time for the personal use of the owner and part time for rental. The vacation home is subject to special tax rules, which are discussed in 11.11[3].

The physical and economic characteristics of one-family houses often produce a low periodic cash flow, with most of the total return anticipated to come from appreciation, to be realized when the property is sold. Relying on potential appreciation is justified only if property values are currently rising, the trend is expected to continue, and the subject property is well-located and constructed.

Prices of one-family houses have risen quite rapidly over the past few years, sometimes as much as one percent per month. This substantial appreciation has been one major inducement to investors to come into the residential property market. It is unlikely that appreciation can continue to substantially exceed inflation in the nation generally; however, particular markets may see higher appreciation because of local conditions.

[2] Investment Considerations

In buying a one-family house for resale, the investor must concentrate on three key considerations:

☐ *Neighborhood.* This remains the most important factor in determining home value. While large profits have been made in buying houses in "turnaround" areas, spotting the turn in a neighborhood is an extremely difficult feat. A number of separate influences must come together to upgrade a neighborhood—a number of well-maintained houses, a common desire by the residents to improve their area, and cooperation from city agencies in providing adequate fire, police, and sanitation services are just a few.

☐ *Location.* The accessibility of the residence to work, shopping, recreational, and cultural facilities is also important. Outstanding location can make up to some degree for a merely adequate neighborhood.

☐ *Cost.* Before buying the house, the investor should have a fairly accurate idea of his intended resale price. This will be based upon recent sale prices of comparable well-maintained properties in the neighborhood. To his acquisition cost, the investor must add the closing costs for both purchase and resale and any necessary renovation. The difference then should represent a reasonable profit.

Cosmetic renovation—painting, cleaning, some landscaping, and the repair of obvious faults—should always be done because the cost will be returned several times over by a higher selling price. When it comes to more substantial improvements such as new plumbing, electrical systems, or a swimming pool, the investor should think very carefully before making the investment. Outdoor improvements, in particular, may not increase the price by the amount of their cost. In addition, there is always the risk of overimproving the house in terms of its neighborhood; a residence normally will not sell for a great deal more than surrounding properties that are comparable in major respects (number of rooms, amount of land, etc.)

There are two chief dangers in this kind of investment, either of which could prove fatal. The first almost goes without saying—that is, avoid bad locations. The investor should buy a house in an area where property values are rising, which is not so terribly difficult to do, since this has been happening in many urban and most suburban areas of the country.

The second major piece of advice is to be very selective about tenants. A destructive or irresponsible tenant can wipe out profits in a fraction of the time it took to build them up. Credentials, employment, prior living situations, and landlords should all be checked. The investor should insist upon at least a month's rent as security, make sure the rental agreement allows destructive tenants to be evicted, and never let the tenant fall behind in his rent.

The investor would be wise to consider having the property managed by a real estate management firm. He should always maintain a cash reserve equal to a few months rent, which will be a cushion against unexpected repairs, increases in property taxes and energy costs, and odd months when the house goes unrented. And an investor should not get involved with this kind of investment if he is not in a position to tie up his money for at least four years. This is not a liquid investment, and if the house must be sold within a year or two, broker's commissions and other transaction costs will eat up any appreciation in value.

[3] Vacation-Home Deductions

Many people own vacation homes that are used partly for personal use and partly for rental to others (an investment use). The question arises as to how expenses are to be allocated between the personal (nondeductible) use and investment (deductible) use. Prior to the Tax Reform Act of 1976 (TRA 1976),[6] constant litigation arose between the IRS and taxpayers over this issue. The key provision of the Internal Revenue Code was Section 183 (the hobby-loss provision), which has already been discussed in 3.09[1][c]. In essence, that section limits a vacation homeowner's deductions to the amount of gross income he receives from the vacation home unless the taxpayer can establish a profit-seeking motive (e.g., by showing a profit for two out of the five preceding years).

The TRA 1976 created a new Section 280A, which provides more definitive rules as to when maintenance and upkeep expenses of vacation homes, as well as depreciation write-offs, can be taken. The fairly complex relationship between Section 183 and Section 280A can be best understood by dividing all vacation-home usages into three situations.

[a] Limited Rental Use

If the vacation home is rented for less than fifteen days during the taxable year, no deductions attributable to the rental are allowable and no income derived from the rental is includable in gross income. The entire transaction is treated as a wash. (The IRS will not bother to provide deductions or recognize income in this situation because the relative amounts are too small.)

[b] Limited Personal Use

If personal use of the vacation home is limited to not more than fourteen days during the taxable year or, if greater, not more than 10 percent of the number of days during the year that the house is rented, a deduction is permitted for the portion of the expenses allocable to rental use of the house. For example, if three fourths of the total use of the house is for rental purposes, then a deduction of three fourths of the rental-related expenses is permitted.

---

[6] Pub. L. No. 94-455, 90 Stat. 1520, 26 U.S.C.A. §§ 1 et seq.

This category is subject to the hobby-loss rules of Section 183 of the Code. Deductions are limited by Section 183 if the activity is not engaged in for profit. In this situation, a deduction is allowed for expenses that could be deducted if the activity were engaged in for profit (i.e., depreciation, insurance, and maintenance) but only to the extent these expenses do not exceed the amount of gross income derived from the activity reduced by the deductions that are allowed in any event (i.e., interest and taxes).

Rental-related expenses are deductible without limit if the vacation-home activity is engaged in for profit. A taxpayer is presumed to be engaged in an activity for profit for a taxable year if, in two or more years of the five consecutive taxable years ending with that taxable year, the activity was carried on at a profit. For purposes of this presumption, the activity is treated as being carried on for a profit in a taxable year if gross income from the activity exceeds the deductions attributable thereto that would be allowable if it were engaged in for profit.

[c] Substantial Rental and Personal Use

If too much rental use of the property is made to qualify for the rules under situation 1, and if too much personal use is made of the property to qualify for the rules under situation 2, the allowable deduction is computed as follows:

(1) Determine gross rental income received from the vacation home during the year. ......

(2) Determine total expenses that would be deductible in any event. ......

(3) Subtract line (2) from line (1). The difference sets an outside limit on the amount of the rental expense deduction that will be allowed. (If line (2) is equal to or greater than line (1), no deduction will be allowed.) ......

(4) Determine the total potential rental expenses. These may include:

Insurance ......
Depreciation ......
Maintenance ......
Utilities ......
Other ......
Total ......

(5) Determine the proportion of rental use of the vacation home. For example, if the vacation home is rented out for three months and used by the taxpayer for one month, the proportion to be used would be three fourths. ......

(6) Multiply the sum of line (4) by the fraction determined on line (5). ......

(7) The deduction allowable is the lesser of line (3) or (6). ......

Each year stands on its own in determining which set of guidelines applies. It is possible that the tax treatment of vacation-home expenses could be controlled by a different guideline each year. Section 183, however, has overriding applicability as to the existence of profit or loss during each of five consecutive years;

that is, despite the fact that Section 280A of the Code may have applied to one or more years during the five-year period, those years will still be considered in determining whether the taxpayer has realized a profit in two or more years. Presumably, profit or loss for this test is calculated without regard to any limitation on deductions. If, however, Section 280A rendered expenses nondeductible in any of the years, no further expenses may be disallowed by applying Section 183.

[d] Personal Use

Several of the calculations require a determination of the extent to which personal use of the vacation home is made. Here are the rules as to what does and does not constitute personal use.

☐ Activities that do constitute personal use of the vacation home:

- Use of the home by any of the following persons: taxpayer; taxpayer's spouse; taxpayer's brothers and sisters; taxpayer's ancestors (parents, grandparents, and so on); taxpayer's lineal descendants (children, grandchildren, etc.); and spouses of the taxpayer's lineal descendants.
- Use of the home by any individual under a reciprocal arrangement, whether or not a fair rental is charged. (E.g., *Y* lets *X* use *Y*'s vacation home in exchange for the privilege of *Y*'s using *X*'s condominium.)
- Use of the home by any other individual unless a fair rental is charged.
- If the home is owned by a partnership, estate, trust, or Subchapter S corporation, use by the partners, beneficiaries, or stockholders, as the case may be.

☐ Activities that do not constitute personal use of the vacation home:

- Time spent during the normal workday in repairing, painting, cleaning, or maintaining the vacation home.
- If the vacation home is used by an employee for the employer's convenience (i.e., the value of the lodging is excluded from the employee's gross income under Section 119 of the Code).

For purposes of applying these rules, the following types of dwelling units are treated as the equivalent of a vacation home: houses, apartments, condominiums, mobile homes, boats, similar dwelling units, and all appurtenant structures (e.g., garages).

[e] Applying Rules to Taxpayer's Advantage

The rules under Section 280A of the Code are automatic, whereas the rules of Section 183 have usually provided a guideline for the IRS in disallowing vacation-home expenses. Before Section 280A was enacted in 1976, the vacation-home owner need not have been unduly concerned with the mechanics for expense disallowance until the IRS proposed adjustments. Now, however, the taxpayer is expected to limit his deductions himself if the combination of personal and rental use places his vacation-home expenses within the purview of Section 280A. Thus, one must be aware of the new rules even before expenses are incurred.

Assume, for example, that an owner rents his vacation home for 150 days during 1980 and uses it personally for fifteen days. If the facility were to be left vacant for the remainder of the year, Section 183 would govern the deductibility of expenses. (Personal use of the home is not more than 10 percent of rental use, and both exceed fourteen days.) Assume further that the owner fails the profit-motivation test of Section 183. He still can choose to avoid imposition of Section 183. If he uses the facility himself for one additional day, the applicable guidelines for deductions would change to those of Section 280A, because sixteen days of personal use exceed 10 percent of the 150 days of rental use. Thus, by increasing his personal use, he will trigger a different deduction limitation and may actually increase his allowable deductions. Of course, this will not always be the

TABLE 11.9 Limitations on Tax Deductions for Vacation-Home Rentals

Test	*Rules of Limitations of Deductions*
• **Situation 1:** Actual rental of property is less than 15 days	The deductions attributable to such rental are not allowable, except for normal itemized deductions of a personal residence and none of the income will have to be reported for tax purposes.
• **Situation 2:** Actual rental of property is 15 days or more and personal use does not exceed the greater of 14 days or 10 percent of the actual rental days	The deductibility of expenses is not limited if profit is realized in two out of five preceding years or facts and circumstances show activity is engaged for profit (in other words, the hobby-loss tests of Section 183 must be met or the deductions will be limited).
• **Situation 3:** Actual rental of property is 15 days or more but the personal use exceeds the greater of 14 days or 10 percent of the actual rental days	The hobby-loss limitations of Section 183 apply; therefore, the rental expense deductions may not exceed the excess of the rental income over interest, taxes, and casualty losses.

case. If the expenses allocable to the rental activity, other than those otherwise allowable, are less than or equal to the deduction limitation calculated under Section 183, increased personal use will result in a lesser amount of total deductions.

11.12 CONDOMINIUMS AND COOPERATIVES

[1] Introduction

Two special forms of real estate ownership, used both for residential and business purposes, are the condominium and the cooperative housing corporation.

[a] Condominiums

The condominium concept does not derive from English common law. Rather, it dates back over 4,000 years to Roman law, from which it has become a part of the civil law followed by most countries in Western Europe and South America. Although introduced into our country as recently as 1952 (in Puerto Rico), statutes authorizing condominium ownership now have been passed by every state and the District of Columbia.

Condominium (*co-dominion*) means joint ownership and control, as distinguished from sole ownership and control. In a condominium project, each unit (e.g., apartment) is individually owned, while the common elements of the building (e.g., lobby, corridors, exterior walls) are jointly owned. While by far most condominium projects are residential, the concept has been extended to commercial, industrial, and recreational projects.

To create a condominium, the owners of the property must file a declaration of condominium (or master deed) with the local land-records office. The declaration includes a detailed description of the individual units in the property and of the common areas that may be used by all of the owners. The declaration also sets forth the percentage of ownership that attaches to each individual unit. This percentage establishes the voting rights of each unit owner and each owner's contribution to the operating expenses of the property.

Each owner of a condominium unit may sell or mortgage his unit as he sees fit. Property taxes are levied on each unit rather than on the entire project. The condominium unit owners constitute an owners' association and elect a board of directors, which is responsible for the day-to-day management of the condominium project.

Since the condominium owner owns his unit outright, he is treated as any other homeowner for tax purposes. He may deduct real estate taxes that he pays on his unit and the interest on the mortgage on his unit. If his unit is damaged by a casualty, he is entitled to a casualty-loss deduction. If he realizes a profit from the sale of his unit, he may postpone reporting the profit by purchasing a new principal residence, the same as the owner of a single-family house. And if he rents his unit to others, he will be entitled to the landlord's normal deductions for depreciation, repairs, and maintenance. In short, the condominium dweller has all the tax advantages of a homeowner as a result of his direct ownership of his unit.

[b] Cooperative Housing Corporations

The essential element of a cooperative housing corporation (cooperative) is that ownership is in a corporation, the shares of which are divided among several persons, each of whom is entitled to lease a portion of the space by virtue of his ownership interest—that is, ownership and the right to lease and use the space are inseparable. Typically, a residential building is acquired by a corporation organized as a cooperative (as distinguished from a business corporation organized for profit). Each share or specified group of shares in the corporation carries with it the right to lease and use a designated apartment. Each shareholder executes a proprietary lease with the corporation, which is similar to a standard lease and pursuant to which the tenant-owner may occupy the designated unit.

Just as with a condominium, the cooperative project is run by a board of directors. Unlike a condominium, the project has a single owner—the cooperative corporation—that may mortgage the property (thus automatically providing financing for each apartment owner). The property is a single parcel for purposes of real estate taxation and the taxes paid by the corporation are allocated among the various unit owners, as are all of the common-area and maintenance expenses of the building. Each owner then pays a monthly assessment (equivalent to rent) to cover the operation expenses and necessary repairs and replacements.

A tenant-stockholder in a cooperative corporation may deduct that part of the "rent" that he pays to the cooperative corporation that represents his proportionate share of (1) real estate taxes allowable as a deduction to the corporation paid or incurred by it on the residential property; and (2) interest allowable as a deduction to the corporation paid or incurred by it on indebtedness relating to the property. The indebtedness must have been contracted in the acquisition, construction, alteration, rehabilitation, or maintenance of the improvements or in the acquisition of the land on which the improvements are situated.[7] A tenant-stockholder's proportionate share of taxes and interest is that proportion which the stock owned by him bears to all outstanding stock including stock held by the corporation.

A tenant-stockholder may claim deductions for depreciation on his stock to the extent that it represents a proprietary lease or right of tenancy in depreciable property used by him in a trade or business or for the production of income. And stock in a cooperative may be considered a principal residence for purposes of the election to defer gain on the sale of a residence where the proceeds are invested in another principal residence.

[c] Difference Between Condominiums and Cooperatives

A significant difference between a condominium and cooperative lies in the possible "snowball" effect if an individual owner defaults. In the case of a cooperative, default by a tenant-shareholder means that his portion of real estate taxes, mortgage debt service, and common-area expense must be assumed by the remaining owners. If a number of tenant-shareholders default, the burden on the remaining owners becomes correspondingly heavier and a snowball effect may be created, causing more and more tenants to default. Precisely this kind of situation happened during the 1930s depression, causing many cooperatives to fail.

By contrast, a condominium unit owner is responsible for his own mortgage financing and real estate taxes on the unit owned. Consequently, in the event of a default by a single unit owner, only that owner's share of operating expenses (but not taxes or debt service) must be assumed by the remaining owners. As a result, a "snowball" is much less likely to occur in a condominium project—one obvious reason for the popularity of this form of ownership.

Another advantage in taking the condominium route is that the tax benefits of real estate ownership are not available to business organizations that buy cooperative units because the Internal Revenue Code provides that only individuals may deduct real estate taxes and mortgage interest attributable to ownership of a cooperative. The promoter of a condominium, therefore, is in a much better position to sell units to national corporations and other business enterprises for the housing of their executives or use by customers.

---

[7] I.R.C. § 216(a).

An important related matter is that if business organizations own space in a cooperative, the project may run afoul of the 80-20 rule, which prohibits income from other than tenant stockholders to exceed 20 percent of the project's gross income. If the 20 percent ceiling is violated, all of the tenant-stockholders lose their deductions for real estate taxes and mortgage interest. Condominiums, on the other hand, are not subject to the 80-20 rule.

Other factors that make condominiums more attractive to purchasers include:

☐ Financing for units can be negotiated on an individual basis (or the owner may choose to pay all cash).

☐ Subleases and sales of units in cooperatives are subject to the approval of the board of directors; in condominiums, the most the managing board can obtain is a right of first refusal.

☐ Tax-exempt organizations buying into a cooperative cannot take advantage of their tax-exempt status since a single real estate tax is imposed against the entire building. In the case of the condominium, where each individual unit is separately assessed and taxed, the tax-exempt organization may be able to avoid the tax (this is a matter to be determined by the particular municipality).

[2] Financing a Condominium Project

[a] In General

A common pattern of financing a new condominium is as follows:

☐ *Standby commitment.* The developer first obtains from a mortgage banker a standby commitment to take out the construction lender if the project is converted to rental or if the developer is left with a large number of condominium units unsold. The fee for the standby runs one to 2 percent a year.

☐ *Construction loan.* The developer is then able to obtain a construction loan from a real estate investment trust or commercial bank, which is equal to approximately 90 percent of total cost (including land, construction, interest, and overhead).

☐ *End (permanent) loans.* Finally, when the units are sold, the purchasers will obtain long-term loans from a savings association or insurance company (or may pay cash).

Table 11.10 illustrates a typical condominium construction loan.

A great danger in condominium construction is cost overruns that could force the lender to choose between putting up more money or seeing the loan in default. To insure against this, the construction loan balance must always be equal to the balance of the construction cost; moreover, cost estimates should continually be updated during construction. If there is any slowdown in the project, this is often a warning signal.

In order for the developer to sell condominium units, the construction lender must agree to release his lien from the units sold. Since the best units usually are the first sold, the lender must create safeguards so that a number of unsold units at the end will not mean a default on the balance of the construction loan.

TABLE 11.10 Condominium Construction Loan ($ millions)

Land cost	$0.8
Construction cost	6.2
Interest, carrying, selling, etc.	1.0
Total cost	$8.0
Potential sales price	$10.0
Construction mortgage (90% of cost = 72% of sales price)	$7.2

The formula recommended by some experts is that no apartments be released until 50 percent have been sold. At that point, 95 percent of the sales price should go to reduce the construction loan. The result is that as each unit is sold, the construction lender's exposure is reduced, as illustrated by Table 11.11.

[b] Checklist for Condominium Construction Loans

Here are the key points that a lender looks for in processing a construction loan application:

☐ *Location.* The project must be feasible for the area and be harmonious with existing or proposed development. The investor should check neighborhood trends and growth patterns, and the availability of services such as shopping, commuting, and the like.

☐ *Site evaluation.* An analysis should be made of the topography of the land, soil condition, and the location of the various improvements on the site. The local zoning and planning boards and the building department should be contacted to be sure there are no violations. For added insight, the investor should talk to local appraisers and brokers.

☐ *Layout of the building.* The area of each unit should be computed, both with and without balconies and patios, and all of the amenities that will be offered to unit owners should be listed.

☐ *Competition.* Comparable projects should be studied to see what the competition is offering and what the sales prices are. Sales prices should be analyzed

TABLE 11.11 Reduction of Construction Loan

Release clause: When 50% sold, release apartments and retain 95% of listed sales price.

50% sold: Lender retains $5.0 million @ 95% ($4.75 million)

Remaining apartments: $5.0 million value

Remaining mortgage: $2.45 million (49% loan-to-value ratio)

on a square-foot basis. Comparison shoppers should attempt to purchase units to see if deals can actually be made at the asking price. If extras are offered as inducements to buy, the comparable sales prices must be adjusted.

☐ *Carrying costs.* The maximum financing available should be determined and the constant payment that will be required under the end loans computed. Real estate taxes are estimated on the basis of a talk with a tax assessor and of comparison with taxes on recently completed condominiums. Utility costs are estimated separately for water, sewer, electricity, and fuel. Estimated costs for insurance, common-area maintenance, and the like should be added and the result will be total carrying costs. The portion that is tax deductible should be identified.

☐ *Physical analysis.* The condominium should be of better quality than a comparable rental job. This means that density should be less, apartment size should be larger, garages or covered parking should be available, storage facilities should be provided, and in general, the fixtures and finishing work should be of a higher quality.

☐ *Presale requirement.* Although presales are very difficult in today's market, if the marketability of the units seems questionable, presale commitment should be required with end-loan commitments to the purchasers confirmed.

☐ *Local condominium regulations.* A variety of local laws now affects the sale of condominium units. These cover the need for disclosures, escrow deposits, and the conditions under which these are returnable to the purchasers, recreational leases, and management contracts.

☐ *The sponsor.* The most important factor is the borrower. Lenders will not become involved with a neophyte who must be taught the business. Cost projections must be accurate and complete.

[3] Commercial and Industrial Condominiums

[a] Prospects for Commercial Condominiums

The relatively few commercial condominiums that already exist in the United States generally involve business or professional firms that

- Are in the same profession or line of business.
- Have well-defined space needs not likely to change in the future.
- Share the need for special building requirements.

Since doctors and dentists meet all of these requirements, it is not surprising that the medical condominium has been by far the most popular type. In addition, these professionals either have, or can borrow, the necessary funds to meet the equity requirement. However, many business and industry groups are likely to have similar common interests. For example, jewelers and dealers in precious stones not only do a great deal of business among themselves but have a common requirement of strict security for their place of business.

On the other hand, large corporations are not likely to enter into condominium arrangements, since they often are in a position to buy or erect their own buildings. In some cases, however, a large firm may join with another to buy a building and share it between them on a condominium basis. A notable example is a large office building in midtown Manhattan that, after failing as a rental project, was purchased jointly by the New York Telephone Company and Teachers Insurance Annuity Association. The former is using its half for its own space needs and the latter is renting out its half for income (the bulk of the rental space being taken by International Paper Corporation).

[b] Advantages for Unit Owners

The potential benefits of condominium ownership for business firms include the following:

- Common areas and facilities (such as parking fields or railway sidings) give the smaller firm advantages it could not otherwise afford
- Landlord profit is no longer an element in the operating costs of the business
- Potential drastic rent hikes and nonrenewal of leases no longer are worries to the unit owners
- The unit owner has a voice in how the building is maintained and operated
- The business firm has an equity in the property that very likely will grow in value
- Improvements added by the owner can be recaptured on resale of the unit (whereas such improvements often are a total loss when a lease expires)
- Commercial occupancy taxes on tenants imposed by some major cities can be avoided if the business firm is an owner.

One objection of business tenants to condominium ownership is that they may lose the tax savings resulting from the complete deductibility of rental payments (which, of course, are a business expense). However, all payments made by the commercial condominium owner are also deductible as business expenses. They include interest payments on a mortgage given to finance the purchase and real estate taxes (which would be deductible in any event) as well as maintenance charges and depreciation deductions. Since the basis for the depreciation deduction is the entire cost of the unit (even though only a small cash down payment is made), the resulting tax saving may compare very favorably to those realized from rent payments.

[c] Advantages of Leasing Rather Than Owning

While financial and investment considerations would seem, on balance, to favor condominium ownership over leasing for many business tenants, there are the following additional considerations:

☐ *The need to expand.* A rapidly growing business anticipating the need for additional space every few years may be well advised to stick to a series of short-term leases to protect its options, even at the cost of rising rentals for each new lease term. Or the tenant may be able to negotiate a long-term lease with options to acquire additional space in the building at specified future dates, which shifts the planning burden to the landlord rather than the tenant. In a condominium, less turnover can be anticipated so obtaining more space will be more difficult.

One solution in the condominium is a right of first refusal. This requires any unit owner desiring to sell or lease all or part of his unit to give the remaining owners the first opportunity to acquire the space.

☐ *The need to contract.* This may be a less serious problem for the condominium owner since he can lease or sell part of his space that becomes excess. By comparison, the typical commercial lease either prohibits subleasing absolutely or hedges it with many restrictions.

☐ *The need to move.* The condominium owner is, of course, entitled to sell his unit at any time and so, in theory at least, has a flexibility denied to the average tenant who must wait out the balance of his lease. As a practical matter, however, it may be difficult to sell a commercial condominium, at least until the concept becomes more popular. A tenant can retain flexibility either by short-term leases or by negotiating a cancellation clause, which may permit him to terminate the lease upon payment of a predetermined penalty.

We have been assuming that comparable space is available to both the tenant and condominium owner. This may not always be true. The mutual interests of a group of condominium users may make it possible to construct or adapt improvements in a prime location at a reasonable price that meet the precise needs of the unit buyers. Also, the prestige of the condominium arrangement may have an intangible public relations or advertising value which, though hard to measure, is quite real.

11.13 CONDOMINIUM CONVERSIONS

[1] Introduction

In the past few years, conversions have transferred many thousands of rental units into the hands of owners and it is clear that this trend will not be soon reversed; indeed, the process may well continue until a large proportion of suitable rental projects become owner-occupied. The reason is simply that both tax and economic factors make residential ownership more and more attractive to American households.

The following discussion reviews some of the considerations for an investor deciding whether or not to convert a rental project into a condominium. (The same factors usually apply to cooperative conversions as well.)

Even though there may be an overall demand for condominium units, the owner of a rental building is not likely to consider conversion unless he has one of the following reasons:

☐ *Low cash flow.* The building is showing an unsatisfactory cash flow (or is in a declining cash flow trend) because of rent control or the inability to raise rents in line with escalating costs.

☐ *Declining ROI.* Return on investment (ROI) may be dropping to an unacceptable level as equity grows through appreciation and as tax shelter runs out because of declining depreciation write-offs.

☐ *Large immediate gain.* Probably the most common reason for conversion is the opportunity to realize a substantial one-time gain. A frequently heard estimate is that the total value of condominium units in a building runs about 30 percent more than the fair market value of the building as a rental project. (In essence, this represents the difference between selling individual units at retail and selling the whole building at wholesale.) However, out of that 30 percent must come the costs of conversion, which may be substantial.

An owner who sells his building to a converter realizes capital gain but, of course, he gives up part of the ultimate profit. An owner who does his own conversion keeps the potential profit, but probably it will be taxed as ordinary income because he will be considered a dealer in real estate.

[2] Selecting a Building

The most serious mistake—because it is not curable—that a converter can make is to choose the wrong building. An investor who plans to convert a building he already owns is particularly susceptible to this mistake for obvious reasons, but even converters who first must buy a building are often tempted to sacrifice the right building in order to save on the initial acquisition cost. Here are the major factors that most specialists agree on:

☐ *Location.* Conversions can compete with new developments only on the basis of price and location. If the conversion is located in an area where new development is too costly or where land is unavailable (such as a prime downtown location or a prestigious built-up residential neighborhood), the converter will have a bit more leeway in setting his prices. At the same time, the best buildings for conversion (discussed below) often are located in the prime neighborhoods. Consequently, prime location is probably the most important requirement in choosing a building.

☐ *Quality of construction.* Of course, buyers will be more particular than renters in considering such items as building appearance, lobby, soundproofing, room size, ceiling height, etc. In addition, high-quality buildings attract high-income buyers; they, in turn, benefit more from the tax advantages of ownership and will have less trouble obtaining mortgage financing.

☐ *Size.* A number of reasons favor choosing a relatively small building with high-priced units. One reason is that the conversion process is normally much quicker, reducing the carrying charges that can be a substantial portion of total cost. Another is that smaller buildings are more manageable and often are more attractive to buyers.

☐ *Age.* Actual age of a building is not a critical factor since a long-standing but well-maintained structure may have a much shorter effective age. At the same time, older buildings may have limitations or defects that are either incurable or would require very heavy expense to correct. Examples include lack of parking (which may be unimportant in a downtown location), layout of rooms, window views (which can be important in a high-priced unit), and lack of amenities. To some extent, such defects may be overcome by benefits such as extremely high-quality construction that cannot be duplicated in today's economic climate.

☐ *Amenities.* Many new condominiums feature swimming pools, saunas, exercise facilities, large amounts of storage space, and perhaps a community recreation room. These features are seldom found in older rental buildings. A conversion does not necessarily have to offer all or most of these amenities; much will depend upon competition from other rental and condominium projects nearby. But most converters consider the cost of adding a "package" of amenities to be prohibitive and will normally not consider a conversion if these are considered necessary for a successful sellout.

☐ *Remodeling costs.* The amount the converter can afford to spend to remodel and improve the property will be determined by his feasibility study (see below). But as a general rule, a building that will require much rehabilitation, particularly to the individual apartments, is probably not a good bet for conversion. The cost of conversion not only increases the final price, but also will extend the marketing period and so increase carrying costs.

[3] Assessing the Market Potential for the Project

The next step taken by the converter is to analyze the market to see if a demand exists for units at a price that will permit a reasonable profit to be made. By one rule of thumb, a unit should sell somewhere around 120 times the monthly rent that was formerly charged. This would make the value of the building about nine or ten times the gross annual rental formerly charged. Two other general rules about price:

- Unit prices should be 20 to 30 percent lower than that for a new unit or for a comparable one-family house.
- Carrying charges (including debt service on mortgage) should not be more than rentals for comparable space.

Ultimately, of course, demand can only be determined by a marketability study. Two separate sources of demand must be investigated:

☐ *Existing tenants.* These constitute the single most important source of demand. If at least 30 percent of the present tenants are not willing to buy their units (at a 10 to 15 percent discount reflecting the absence of marketing costs), the conversion probably is not a good idea.

☐ *Outside buyers.* This market must be judged as would the market for any other project, and will include a study of competing space, both rental and condominium and whether existing or proposed.

[4] Economic Feasibility of the Project

Having projected a market for the units at a given price, the converter must next determine if the project is economically feasible, that is, whether he can buy the property, convert it, and end up with a reasonable profit. A quick rule of thumb is that, of the ultimate sales price of the units,

- 75 percent represents the initial acquisition cost,
- 15 percent represents conversion costs, and
- 10 percent represents profit.

These figures assume that the price paid for the property is equal to its fair market value as a rental project, since the final sales price of the units is calculated at the usual one-third markup over the acquisition cost. If the seller is aware of the intent to convert and raises his sales price, this may cut sharply into the converter's profit unless the deal turns out to be unusually successful.

One approach for a converter to consider is a contingent price or joint-venture agreement with the seller. For example, a minimum sales price equal to fair market value may be set, with the seller to participate in any sales proceeds above a designated floor. Or, an actual joint venture can be formed, with the owner putting up the property (and perhaps some of the cash for improvements) and the converter putting up some cash and his expertise.

In addition to the initial acquisition, significant conversion costs include

☐ *Renovation.* A rule of thumb is that renovation costs should not exceed 3 percent of total sales price. Most such costs should be spent on exterior and common areas. Many buyers will prefer to pay a somewhat lower price and do their own renovation.

☐ *Financing.* Normally, interim financing will be obtained in order to pay off the existing mortgage (unless the present lender agrees to the conversion). In any case, interest costs will be high since this is a form of construction lending. In addition, paying off the existing mortgage may involve a prepayment penalty.

☐ *Consultant fees.* These include legal fees (which can be substantial because of the documentation required and the need to comply with local statutes), engineering and architectural fees (since the building must be thoroughly examined and each unit must be identified and described), and fees for marketing and feasibility studies.

☐ *Management and marketing.* The building must continue to be operated during the conversion period. And, in addition, there will be substantial marketing costs for sales personnel, advertising, etc.

Offsetting the conversion costs will be rental income from existing tenants. A common error for converters is to assume this cash flow will be much higher than it turns out to be. Tenants who do not intend to buy will normally move out as quickly as possible and vacancies may mount sharply. This is one reason why it is important to shorten the marketing period as much as possible.

11.14 TIME-SHARING OWNERSHIP

[1] Introduction

Time-sharing ownership (TSO) is the newest variation on the condominium theme. Time-sharing is shared occupancy of improved real property where each owner has the exclusive right to use the property annually during one or more chosen time periods. TSO is particularly suited to recreational and resort areas, for second homes and vacation homes.

Resort time-sharing originated in Europe in the 1960s, fostered by circumstances similar to those existing in the United States today: sharply rising prices for second homes; energy and gasoline shortages; and escalating vacation costs as demand for resort facilities outpace supply. Time-sharing (or interval ownership) enables a middle-income family to "own a slice" of a resort offering fully furnished accommodations and full facilities. In the present market a fairly wide range of interval facilities are priced anywhere from $1,000 to $16,000, depending on the season, location, unit size and amenities.

Resort time-sharing comes in two main forms, each with several variations.

☐ *Fee simple ownership.* Here, purchasers actually buy real estate and receive title through a deed. Title insurance is obtainable and interests may be sold, leased or transferred by will. In addition, owners may deduct their share of real property taxes on their tax returns.

☐ *Right to use.* By this method the buyer obtains, instead of a property interest, a membership right to use the vacation home for a specified period of time over a certain number of years. Ownership is retained by a builder or another person, and possession reverts to the owner at the end of the contract period. Often, the contract prohibits the buyer from selling his right to use interest at a profit.

[2] State of the Time-Sharing Industry

Following the 1974 real estate depression, resort time-sharing was frequently utilized as a means of salvaging losing developments. But today it has established itself as a growth industry with solid economic underpinnings. This is clear from a series of recent studies conducted by the Resort Timesharing Council of the American Land Development Association (ALDA).

Significant results of the surveys:

☐ The occupancy rate for time-sharing resorts averages 80 percent while the average peak period for units in the sample is about 7.7 months each year, compared to 4.2 months for non-time-share units.

☐ More than 50 percent of the buyers in ownership resorts paid cash; 23 percent paid cash in right-to-use facilities. Those using financing had an excellent record of payments, with a 2.4 percent delinquency rate, and a one percent default rate, for ownership projects, and somewhat higher rates of 3.4 percent and 2.6 percent for right-to-use projects.

☐ Three out of four ownership resorts are newly constructed, whereas right-to-use facilities generally are conversions of existing structures.

☐ The typical time-share purchase is by a family with two children, having an annual income between $25,000 and $30,000, and living within 150 miles of the time-share unit, although many live more than 1,000 miles away.

[3] Potential Problems With Time-Shares

Time-sharing has its problems too. While none seem very significant at the present time, they bear watching.

☐ *Marketing and consumer protection.* Since time-sharing means that twenty-five to fifty purchasers must be found for each unit (depending upon whether one-week or two-week intervals are sold), a vigorous marketing effort must be made. While the industry has never been marked by the scandals that were common in the sales of resort homesites a few years ago, industry leaders recognize the need for full disclosure and for restraint in selling practices. Two points often made by state regulatory agencies: Buyers should have a right to rescind purchases within a specified number of days, and all sales personnel should be licensed as real estate brokers or salesmen.

☐ *Real property taxes.* In most areas, time-share units are assessed just as are full-ownership units for local property tax purposes. However, tax assessors in Colorado and Florida have recently sought to assess interval ownership units on the basis of the total sales price to all owners. This could double or triple property taxes and so cause a sharp rise in annual maintenance costs. Time-share developers are resisting strongly, arguing that the community incurs no extra costs by reason of the time-share use so that such increased taxation is patently unfair.

☐ *Community opposition.* Because adjoining property owners often regard time-share occupants as transients, continued time-share growth could arouse community opposition. However, since time-sharing almost always occurs in a resort or vacation area where the economy depends on tourism, this opposition is not likely to become significant.

☐ *Long-term maintenance.* Because of the intensive use of time-share units, and the need for maintenance by hired managers, there is clearly a risk that over the long term, time-share properties may deteriorate much more quickly than anticipated. Because the industry is so young, there is no way to know if this will become a serious problem.

[4] Time-Shares Exchange Services

Undoubtedly a major stimulus to time-share sales has been the availability of services that enable owners to exchange their vacation period for one at another resort at the same or a different time. The two leading services are Resort Condominiums International (RCI) and Interval International (II).

Both services have been very successful in arranging exchanges, but one reason has been the availability of "back-up" space, namely, unsold units at member resorts that are made available to the exchange services. As such unsold space diminishes, more and more exchanges will have to be based upon "real" trades. Since many exchange requests inevitably seek a space/time slice more favorable than the slice being offered, unfulfilled requests are bound to rise. Recognizing the potential problem, both exchange services are studying possible solutions.

11.15 PROPERTY REHABILITATION

[1] Introduction

To the profit-seeking investor, inflation provides the stimulus for efforts at rehabilitating older properties. As the costs of new construction rise higher and higher, "bricks and mortar" that are already in place should also rise in value, provided the particular property can continue to be used either for its original purpose or for a new one. Of course, "continue to be used" are the operative words. Well-constructed buildings in a neighborhood in which no sensible person wishes to live will be abandoned both by tenants and by owner even though the building may have many years of physical life remaining. But such extreme examples are, fortunately, rare. More often, well-located solidly built old properties that do badly cash-wise do so because they have been poorly managed, are in bad condition, or are in a deteriorating neighborhood that has now apparently stabilized. Upgrading these properties, even at substantial expense, may enable a speculator to reduce vacancies, increase rents, and ultimately resell the property at a large profit. In addition, significant tax shelter can be achieved. (See 3.04.)

All successful remodelers have substantial amounts of imagination and creativity, combined with a hard core of experience, knowledge, and practicality. However, there is no magic formula for making money out of the business of buying up old properties, rehabilitating them, and selling or renting them for a profit. What it takes is solid planning, thorough analysis of locations, properties, zoning, and neighborhood trends, and adequate knowledge of the market.

There are some major planning risks involved in rehabilitation that are not concerns of the new construction builder. First of all, the rehabilitator never knows precisely what he is going to find when he starts his own operation. Despite his most careful inspections, walls that seem substantial may crumble, and seemingly sound pipes may snap. He must plan for contingencies without knowing precisely what they might be.

In addition, it may be difficult, time-consuming, and sometimes impossible to empty a building of its tenants. One expert advises avoiding areas where municipal laws require the developer to relocate any tenants who are in the building. This expense can make the whole transaction unprofitable.

Although rehabilitating in marginal and fringe areas ripe for upgrading offers top opportunity for profits, the entire equity can be lost if the neighborhood decline cannot be reversed so that tenants able to pay higher rentals consider it unappealing, if not downright dangerous. Similarly, while neighborhoods next to urban renewal areas can benefit dramatically if the renewal proceeds on schedule, developers remodeling buildings near areas snagged down with government red tape have experienced marketing delays which ate up their profits.

Although these risks are substantial, they can be minimized through careful study, planning, and timing.

[2] Rehabilitating Residential Properties

[a] Choosing a Property

Although residential rehabilitation properties rarely are located in a prime neighborhood, they should be close to thriving downtown business and commercial areas, and other well-established residential neighborhoods. (In many cities, the difficulties of commuting, plus the attraction of cultural facilities, have awakened interest in living near the central core.) The neighborhood should reflect some social solidity and a history of home-ownership and pride in home maintenance. Ideally, it should be at a point where a few conversions will encourage others to upgrade their properties.

If, on the other hand, the general area is shabby and run-down, an overall urban revival should be occurring before a decision is made to invest. Neighborhoods next to urban renewal areas that are progressing well are particularly promising for these reasons:

- A renewal project frequently will decrease traffic congestion, or even reroute traffic to create parks and play areas.
- Public facilities, such as schools and recreational areas, will be improved and upgraded. Any increase in maintenance services will also upgrade the property.
- Demolition of blighted areas will operate to the investor's benefit.
- Renewal agencies often have staffs of experts who can provide assistance in planning, renovating, and complying with local building codes.

☐ *Know your market.* When analyzing potential areas and buildings, keep in mind the characteristics of the people most likely to rent or buy a remodeled unit in a particular location. Lower- and middle-income families with children require inexpensive, roomy quarters near public transportation and schools. Comfort, pleasant surroundings, and space are important qualities.

Catering to singles and couples without children is another often-profitable approach because buildings with the maximum number of studio and one-bedroom apartments often produce the highest return. Not all neighborhoods, of course, are attractive to this type of tenant. Atmosphere, convenience, and social assets should be stressed with the young employee, junior executive, and others of the swinging-singles set when planning the renting and selling strategy.

Elegance and luxury appeal to still another rehabilitation market. Run-down apartment houses have been transformed to modernistic cooperative buildings made up of triplexes, duplexes, and penthouses. Similarly, drab row houses have been transformed to charming town houses. When dealing with high-quality rehabilitation for the luxury market, the charm and grace of the old building must be retained. A great deal of old material must be salvaged, and what is new must be aged to look old. The crew must be highly trained to discover and preserve spindles, cornices, mantels, and moldings, and to carefully take material apart without destroying it.

☐ *Scatter-site or large lots?* There are, of course, advantages, particularly to the large developer, in rehabilitating blocks or groups of buildings. When a whole block or row of houses is acquired, the big impact on the area is certain to impress banks and tenant/buyers. Moreover, substantial economies can be achieved by doing much of the work on a production basis. Capital and operating costs can be substantially trimmed, for instance, by installing a single-heating/hot-water package to service several buildings. In large, singly managed developments, groups of structures can be linked together by converting interior courtyards into common exteriors, thereby increasing security and reducing building costs and maintenance. Several buildings might be serviced with a single elevator, spreading the costs over a larger number of apartments.

On the other hand, small developers may find it difficult or impossible to acquire the front money required to purchase a group of buildings and carry them over a long period. Where private interests try to acquire adjacent properties, word of their activities somehow spreads, and asking prices escalate. A selective (scatter-site) approach aims at the rehabilitation of single buildings that can be revitalized on an individual basis. Such properties are usually relatively cheap, as they are often vacant and throwing off no income. The incentive to sell is particularly great in the case of an absentee owner, or of property in an area where building codes are being strictly enforced.

☐ *Locating prospects.* Good prospects for the small investor are run-down one-family houses, or buildings that were originally one-family homes but are now rooming houses or small apartment buildings. The investor should keep an eye open for buildings that have been damaged, but not gutted, by fire. These, as well as other prospects, will be channeled by real estate brokers operating in areas ripe for rehabilitation. Tax-lien sales and auctions are also good sources, as are mortgage officers in lending institutions who know of buildings about to be foreclosed. Local attorneys may have likely properties in estates of deceased persons that they are handling. In addition, frequent cruising in blighted areas is helpful in locating vacant or condemned structures. Letters to the owners of these properties (whose names can be obtained from the city record listings) can stimulate interest in selling.

[b] Determining Feasibility

The real feasibility test in choosing a property is whether the construction costs are in line with anticipated income. The following checklist points out what may have to be done either in a one- or two-family house or an apartment building to accomplish the rehabilitation.

- Check if the walls, windows, or roof need replacement or merely repair.
- Find out if elevators, boilers, and plumbing meet local code requirements. If not, what will it take to bring them up to standards?
- How about the fire code? Do fire exits, emergency equipment, and materials meet its requirements?
- If you doubt that the electrical system is sound, get a good estimate on what it will take to repair or replace components.
- Exterior surfaces are important in attracting buyers. Check whether only a paint job is needed, or whether large-scale bricking or siding is required.
- Figure in the cost of landscaping and yard work.
- Check zoning requirements regarding parking. Buying additional land to satisfy requirements may make the whole scheme unprofitable.
- Determine how much it will cost to modernize kitchens and bathrooms. Plan on installing modern sinks, appliances, and designer-type cabinets in kitchens, and installing ceramic tiles and vanities in bathrooms to increase sales appeal.

The maximum cost for purchase plus renovation must be well below the cost of constructing a new building, since in most cases rentals or sale price cannot compete with new developments. If interested in rehabilitating structures for lower-income families, the investor should bear in mind that the finished product must be one that they can afford.

One expert recommends working backwards, from return to investment:

☐ *Selling price or rental income.* This will vary considerably, according to the market in a particular neighborhood.

☐ *Overhead marketing expense and profit.* Deduct this amount from the projected income from the operation.

☐ *Cost for rehabilitation.* Estimate the cost of doing the reconstruction and modernization. Include a contingency fund.

☐ *Purchase price.* What is left after subtracting the last two items from the first is the maximum amount the investor can afford to pay for the property. This amount should also cover legal fees, back taxes, and liens.

11.16 HISTORIC PRESERVATION

[1] Introduction

Historic property rehabilitation was given a tremendous boost by the Economic Recovery Tax Act of 1981 (ERTA 1981).[8] The new law creates a 25 percent credit for rehabilitation of certified historic structures, whether residential or nonresidential. In addition, the rehabilitation credit does not reduce the depreciable basis of certified historic structures, whereas the basis of other rehabilitated buildings must be reduced. (See 3.04[1][b].)

Tax incentives for historic preservation were first introduced by the Tax Reform Act of 1976.[9] In the years since then, more than 2,500 projects involving an investment exceeding $1.2 billion have qualified for federal tax benefits. Buildings in all fifty states, ranging from historic hotels and office buildings to factories and apartment houses have been rehabilitated.

Through 1981, 141 local ordinances and 111 local districts have been certified by the Secretary of the Interior, making historic buildings within these districts eligible for tax benefits. In the same period, listings on the National Register of Historic Places have increased from 13,500 to 24,300.

Geographically, rehabilitation projects are concentrated along the East Coast. However, significant pockets of rehabilitation are scattered across the country, from Augusta, Georgia, to Seattle, Washington (with New Orleans leading the country in number of projects undertaken).

Historic structures rehabilitated under the 1976 incentives involve myriad uses. Nearly 46 percent are residential rentals, 35 percent office or commercial

---

[8] Pub. L. No. 97-34, 95 Stat. 172, 26 U.S.C. § 128.

[9] Pub. L. No. 94-455, 90 Stat. 1520, 26 U.S.C.A. §§ 1 et seq.

space, one percent industrial, 2 percent hotels, and the remaining 16 percent mixed use. More than 13,000 new housing units have been created, 6,300 of which are for low- and moderate-income families.

Applicants using federal tax incentives tend to fall into three categories: (1) individuals with an interest in preservation who undertake relatively small, residential rental projects (between $50,000 and $150,000 total investment); (2) organizations such as law firms and banks needing additional office space (spending under $1 million); and (3) large-scale investors who, as limited partnerships, typically undertake such projects as multimillion-dollar conversions of historic mills into housing or renovations of major office buildings or hotels.

[2] What Is a Historic Building or District?

The central concept in the historic preservation program is that of a historic structure or historic district. The original historic landmarks program dates back to 1935, when the Historic Sites Act authorized the Secretary of the Interior to survey historic sites and buildings and identify those of national significance.

The idea of a National Register of districts, sites, buildings, structures and objects was contained in the National Historic Preservation Act of 1966.[10] What are the criteria used by federal and state agencies in evaluating potential entries for the National Register? They are properties or districts that either

- Are associated with events that have made a significant contribution to the broad patterns of our history.
- Are associated with the lives of persons significant in our past.
- Embody the distinctive characteristics of a type, period, or method of construction, or that represent the work of a master, or that possess high artistic values, or that represent a significant and distinguishable entity whose components may lack individual distinction.
- Have yielded, or may be likely to yield, information important in prehistory or history.

Individual properties and historic districts may be placed on the National Register only by state governments, which operate through State Historic Preservation Officers (SHPOs).

A historic district also may be designated under a state or local statute, but such a district must meet two requirements before it is considered (for rehabilitation credit purposes) the same as a historic district on the National Register. First, the local or state statute must be certified by the Secretary of the Interior as containing a satisfactory set of standards. Second, the particular historic district designated under the statute must be certified by the Secretary as one that meets the standards of the statute.[11]

---

[10] Pub. L. No. 89-665, 80 Stat. 915, 16 U.S.C.A. § 470.

[11] A volume entitled *The National Register of Historic Places,* with updated supplements, is available from the Superintendent of Documents, U.S. Government Printing Office, Washington, D.C. 20402.

[3] Requirements for the Rehabilitation Tax Credit

A rehabilitation will qualify for the historic preservation tax credit if

- The rehabilitation is of a "certified historic structure," and
- The rehabilitation itself is a "certified rehabilitation."

A certified historic structure is defined as a depreciable building that is

- Listed in the National Register;
- Located in an historic district listed in the National Register and certified by the Secretary of the Interior as being a building that contributes to the historic significance of that district; or
- Located in a historic district designated under a state or local statute provided the two certifications described above (pertaining to the statute and pertaining to the district) have been made. In addition, the building must be certified by the Secretary as being one that contributes to the historic significance of that district.

A certified rehabilitation is defined as any rehabilitation of a certified historic structure that the Secretary of the Interior has certified as being consistent with the historic character of the property itself or the district in which it is located.

The Secretary of the Interior has drawn up Standards for Rehabilitation that are used to determine if a rehabilitation should be certified.[12]

[4] How to Proceed

Suppose an investor has noticed a building that he believes might be worthy of historic structure designation. What does he do? The National Trust for Historic Preservation suggests:

☐ Start with the local preservation organization. Inquire if the building has been designated or is being considered for designation. If no such organization exists in the particular city, then try the city planning office.

☐ Find out all that is possible about the building. When was it built? For whom? Did any events important to the city's history take place there?

☐ Consider whether the building is a good example of an architectural style of the past that was popular. (The local history section of your library may be able to be of assistance.) Ask property owners in the neighborhood what they know about the building.

☐ After an investor has learned all he can about the building, he should contact his state historic preservation office to find out if it has records or other information on the building. The office can provide information as to whether it is on the National Register or whether it is likely to meet the criteria for listing.

☐ If at this point an investor is seriously considering buying the building, he should ask the SHPO for the Historic Preservation Certification application. This

---

[12] These standards and recommended rehabilitation techniques are available by writing to the Technical Preservation Services Division, National Park Service, Washington, D.C. 20240.

must be filled out to get National Park Service (NPS) approval so that the building will be eligible for the 25 percent tax credit. Part 1 of the application describes the building, its significant features, and its contribution to the district. Part 2 describes the investor's proposal for rehabilitation and the effect of his plans on both the exterior and interior of the building. The six most common features of rehabilitation programs are as follows:

- Exterior masonry cleaning
- Exterior masonry repair
- New window sashes
- New mechanical systems
- Removing interior plaster work
- Storefront alterations

[5] Case Study of Historic Preservation Rehabilitation

To illustrate the new tax incentives for certified rehabilitations of historic structures, the National Park Service (NPS) and the National Trust for Historic Preservation have prepared several hypothetical case studies. The one that is summarized below combines tax write-offs with a deductible gift of a preservation easement, with financing raised through a combination of a mortgage loan and an equity syndication.

[a] The Property

Mrs. Calinwell, a real estate investor, secures options to buy two ten-story high-rise buildings in the central business district, which has been designated a local historic district by the city council. The local ordinance itself has been certified by the NPS on behalf of the Secretary of the Interior; however, this particular district has not yet been certified.

Mrs. Calinwell first obtains a certification for the district from the NPS. This is done by a request from the city council to NPS (since such a request must come from the municipality, not from an individual). The NPS, on the basis of the application, does certify the district.

The next step for Mrs. Calinwell is to have the two buildings and the proposed rehabilitation certified. This requires preparation of Parts 1 and 2 of the Historic Preservation Certification application for each of the two buildings. The completed applications are submitted to the State Historical Property Officer and the NPS regional office. The application is approved, which means that (1) each building is a certified historic structure; and (2) each is to be subject to a certified rehabilitation.

[b] Donation of Preservation Easement

Mrs. Calinwell is informed by her attorney that she can obtain a further tax benefit by donating to the municipality a preservation easement. Such an easement limits alterations to the facades, prohibits demolition, and limits any further development of the building site. Since Mrs. Calinwell does not intend to take any of these actions, she is happy to make the donation.

The amount of the charitable deduction she may take is equal to the value of the donated easement. This in turn is the difference between the value of the two properties before and after the proposed contributions. She retains an independent appraiser who concludes that the value of the easement donation is $600,000. In arriving at this figure, the appraiser considers the following:

- Modernization and alteration of Mrs. Calinwell's two buildings would be limited because of restrictions imposed by the local historic district ordinance as well as by existing zoning.
- Nevertheless, with modern building technology, the buildings could be altered to create much more rentable floor area.

As a result, the present buildings, even with existing restrictions, do not fully use the development potential of the land. By giving up this development potential through the donated easement, Mrs. Calinwell is suffering a loss of market

TABLE 11.12 Mrs. Calinwell's High-Rise Buildings

Acquisition cost:		$1,200,000
Land	$600,000	
Buildings	600,000	
Rehabilitation costs		1,500,000
Total project costs		$2,700,000
Limited partners (120 @ $10,000)		$1,200,000
1982 ITC (25% of $1.5 million)		$375,000
1982 ITC for limited partners (98%)		$367,500
1982 deduction for easement donation for limited partners: $600,000 × 98%		$588,000
Limited partner's tax treatment (per $10,000 units):		
ITC ($367,500 ÷ 120 units)		$3,063
Easement donation deduction ($588,000 ÷ 120 units)	$4,900	
Tax savings due to easement donation ($4,900 × 50% bracket)		2,450
Total tax savings first year		$5,513
Reduction in $1.2 million basis attributable to gift of $600,000 easement:		
Adjusted basis "before" easement gift:		
Land	$600,000	
Buildings	$600,000	
Adjusted basis "after" easement gift:		
Land	$200,000	
Buildings	$400,000	

ITC = Investment tax credit

value equal to $600,000. The appraiser allocates this loss of value as follows: $400,000 to the land and $200,000 to the buildings.

The allocation between land and buildings is important because the value attributed to the buildings reduces their depreciable basis, as shown in Table 11.12.

[c] The Financing

Mrs. Calinwell plans to syndicate the two buildings in order to raise the $1.2 million of equity needed. (It is assumed that the balance of $1.5 million can be financed with a mortgage.) Table 11.12 shows the tax benefits received by the limited partners in the first year due to the investment tax credit and the easement donation deduction. (Note that 2 percent of the tax benefits are retained by the general partner, Mrs. Calinwell.) The tax benefits equal 55 percent of the equity investment.

Table 11.12 ignores any depreciation deductions. Assuming the syndicate utilizes a fifteen-year recovery period and straight-line depreciation, the total depreciation write-offs each year would be $126,667. (This represents 6.7 percent annual write-off of $1.9 million basis, consisting of the $1.5 million rehabilitation cost plus the adjusted building basis of $400,000.) Assuming 98 percent of the total write-off is available to the limited partners, each $10,000 unit would be entitled to an annual depreciation write-off of $1,034, or just over 10 percent of the original investment.

Appendix

Financing—Computation Tables

Financing—Current Trends

Cost and Price Trends

Consumer Price Indexes

Depreciation Schedules

Tax Tables: 1982

Returns on Real Estate Investment

Housing Units and Construction Activity

Demographics

TABLE 1 Growth of One Dollar: Daily Compounding, 360-Day Basis Year

Description: This table shows what a single $1 deposit will grow to in the future.

Example: At 8.00% one dollar will grow to $ 1.50 by the end of the fifth year.

YEAR	8.00%	8.10%	8.125%	8.20%	8.25%	8.30%	8.375%	8.40%	8.50%	8.60%	8.625%	8.70%
1	1.0845	1.0856	1.0859	1.0867	1.0872	1.0878	1.0886	1.0889	1.0900	1.0911	1.0914	1.0922
2	1.1761	1.1785	1.1791	1.1809	1.1821	1.1833	1.1851	1.1857	1.1881	1.1905	1.1911	1.1929
3	1.2755	1.2793	1.2803	1.2832	1.2852	1.2871	1.2901	1.2911	1.2950	1.2989	1.2999	1.3029
4	1.3832	1.3888	1.3902	1.3945	1.3973	1.4001	1.4044	1.4058	1.4115	1.4173	1.4187	1.4230
5	1.5001	1.5077	1.5096	1.5154	1.5192	1.5231	1.5289	1.5308	1.5386	1.5464	1.5483	1.5542
6	1.6268	1.6367	1.6392	1.6467	1.6517	1.6568	1.6643	1.6669	1.6770	1.6873	1.6898	1.6976
7	1.7642	1.7768	1.7799	1.7894	1.7958	1.8022	1.8118	1.8150	1.8279	1.8410	1.8442	1.8541
8	1.9133	1.9289	1.9328	1.9446	1.9525	1.9604	1.9724	1.9764	1.9924	2.0087	2.0127	2.0250
9	2.0749	2.0939	2.0987	2.1131	2.1228	2.1325	2.1471	2.1520	2.1718	2.1917	2.1967	2.2117
10	2.2502	2.2731	2.2789	2.2963	2.3080	2.3197	2.3374	2.3433	2.3672	2.3913	2.3974	2.4157
15	3.3755	3.4272	3.4402	3.4797	3.5062	3.5330	3.5735	3.5871	3.6421	3.6979	3.7120	3.7545
20	5.0634	5.1671	5.1934	5.2729	5.3267	5.3809	5.4634	5.4911	5.6036	5.7184	5.7474	5.8355
25	7.5955	7.7904	7.8399	7.9904	8.0922	8.1954	8.3527	8.4058	8.6215	8.8428	8.8990	9.0697
30	11.3937	11.7455	11.8352	12.1082	12.2937	12.4821	12.7700	12.8675	13.2648	13.6743	13.7787	14.0966

YEAR	8.75%	8.80%	8.875%	8.90%	9.00%	9.10%	9.125%	9.20%	9.25%	9.30%	9.375%	9.40%
1	1.0928	1.0933	1.0941	1.0944	1.0955	1.0966	1.0969	1.0978	1.0983	1.0989	1.0997	1.1000
2	1.1941	1.1953	1.1971	1.1978	1.2002	1.2026	1.2032	1.2051	1.2063	1.2075	1.2093	1.2100
3	1.3049	1.3069	1.3099	1.3108	1.3148	1.3188	1.3198	1.3229	1.3249	1.3269	1.3299	1.3309
4	1.4259	1.4288	1.4332	1.4346	1.4404	1.4463	1.4478	1.4522	1.4551	1.4581	1.4625	1.4640
5	1.5582	1.5621	1.5681	1.5701	1.5781	1.5861	1.5881	1.5941	1.5982	1.6022	1.6083	1.6104
6	1.7027	1.7079	1.7157	1.7183	1.7288	1.7394	1.7420	1.7500	1.7553	1.7606	1.7687	1.7714
7	1.8607	1.8673	1.8772	1.8806	1.8940	1.9074	1.9108	1.9210	1.9279	1.9347	1.9450	1.9485
8	2.0333	2.0415	2.0540	2.0581	2.0749	2.0918	2.0960	2.1088	2.1174	2.1260	2.1390	2.1433
9	2.2219	2.2320	2.2473	2.2525	2.2731	2.2939	2.2992	2.3150	2.3255	2.3362	2.3522	2.3576
10	2.4279	2.4403	2.4589	2.4651	2.4903	2.5156	2.5220	2.5413	2.5542	2.5671	2.5867	2.5933
15	3.7832	3.8121	3.8558	3.8705	3.9298	3.9900	4.0052	4.0511	4.0820	4.1132	4.1603	4.1762
20	5.8949	5.9550	6.0462	6.0769	6.2014	6.3284	6.3605	6.4580	6.5238	6.5902	6.6912	6.7252
25	9.1854	9.3025	9.4810	9.5412	9.7861	10.0373	10.1011	10.2949	10.4261	10.5591	10.7617	10.8301
30	14.3125	14.5318	14.8670	14.9805	15.4430	15.9199	16.0413	16.4114	16.6628	16.9181	17.3084	17.4405

YEAR	9.50%	9.60%	9.625%	9.70%	9.75%	9.80%	9.875%	9.90%	10.00%	10.10%	10.125%	10.20%
1	1.1011	1.1022	1.1025	1.1033	1.1039	1.1045	1.1053	1.1056	1.1067	1.1078	1.1081	1.1089
2	1.2124	1.2149	1.2155	1.2173	1.2186	1.2198	1.2217	1.2223	1.2248	1.2273	1.2279	1.2297
3	1.3350	1.3391	1.3401	1.3431	1.3452	1.3472	1.3503	1.3513	1.3554	1.3596	1.3606	1.3637
4	1.4699	1.4759	1.4774	1.4819	1.4849	1.4879	1.4925	1.4940	1.5001	1.5061	1.5077	1.5123
5	1.6186	1.6268	1.6288	1.6350	1.6392	1.6434	1.6496	1.6517	1.6601	1.6685	1.6706	1.6770
6	1.7822	1.7931	1.7958	1.8040	1.8095	1.8150	1.8233	1.8261	1.8372	1.8484	1.8512	1.8597
7	1.9624	1.9763	1.9798	1.9904	1.9975	2.0046	2.0153	2.0189	2.0332	2.0477	2.0513	2.0623
8	2.1607	2.1783	2.1828	2.1961	2.2050	2.2140	2.2275	2.2320	2.2502	2.2685	2.2731	2.2869
9	2.3792	2.4010	2.4065	2.4230	2.4341	2.4452	2.4620	2.4676	2.4902	2.5130	2.5188	2.5361
10	2.6197	2.6464	2.6531	2.6734	2.6870	2.7006	2.7212	2.7281	2.7559	2.7840	2.7911	2.8123
15	4.2402	4.3051	4.3215	4.3711	4.4044	4.4380	4.4889	4.5060	4.5751	4.6452	4.6629	4.7163
20	6.8629	7.0035	7.0391	7.1469	7.2197	7.2933	7.4050	7.4426	7.5950	7.7506	7.7900	7.9093
25	11.1080	11.3931	11.4655	11.6855	11.8345	11.9854	12.2154	12.2930	12.6085	12.9321	13.0143	13.2640
30	17.9790	18.5341	18.6755	19.1063	19.3990	19.6962	20.1506	20.3044	20.9313	21.5775	21.7422	22.2437

YEAR	10.25%	10.50%	11.00%	12.00%	13.00%	14.00%	15.00%	16.00%	17.00%	18.00%	19.00%	20.00%
1	1.1095	1.1123	1.1180	1.1294	1.1409	1.1525	1.1642	1.1761	1.1881	1.2002	1.2124	1.2247
2	1.2310	1.2372	1.2498	1.2754	1.3016	1.3282	1.3554	1.3832	1.4115	1.4404	1.4699	1.5000
3	1.3658	1.3762	1.3973	1.4404	1.4849	1.5307	1.5780	1.6267	1.6769	1.7287	1.7820	1.8371
4	1.5153	1.5308	1.5621	1.6268	1.6941	1.7641	1.8371	1.9131	1.9923	2.0747	2.1605	2.2499
5	1.6813	1.7027	1.7464	1.8372	1.9327	2.0331	2.1388	2.2500	2.3669	2.4900	2.6194	2.7555
6	1.8654	1.8939	1.9524	2.0748	2.2049	2.3432	2.4901	2.6462	2.8121	2.9884	3.1757	3.3748
7	2.0696	2.1067	2.1827	2.3432	2.5155	2.7004	2.8990	3.1121	3.3409	3.5865	3.8502	4.1332
8	2.2962	2.3433	2.4402	2.6463	2.8698	3.1122	3.3751	3.6601	3.9692	4.3044	4.6679	5.0621
9	2.5477	2.6064	2.7281	2.9886	3.2741	3.5868	3.9293	4.3046	4.7156	5.1660	5.6593	6.1997
10	2.8266	2.8992	3.0499	3.3752	3.7353	4.1337	4.5746	5.0625	5.6025	6.2000	6.8612	7.5929
15	4.7523	4.9364	5.3263	6.2009	7.2191	8.4044	9.7843	11.3906	13.2607	15.4378	17.9721	20.9224
20	7.9899	8.4052	9.3019	11.3922	13.9522	17.0873	20.9269	25.6290	31.3875	38.4396	47.0759	57.6523
25	13.4331	14.3116	16.2447	20.9295	26.9651	34.7410	44.7590	57.6652	74.2926	95.7135	123.3100	158.8621
30	22.5845	24.3683	28.3697	38.4513	52.1150	70.6336	95.7317	129.7469	175.8467	238.3241	322.9967	437.7483

Source: Thorndike Encyclopedia of Banking and Financial Tables (rev. ed. 1980)

TABLE 2 Constant Annual Percentage to Amortize Mortgage

MONTHLY PAYMENT IN ARREARS

Description: This table shows the percent of the principal amount of a loan needed each year to pay off the loan when the actual payments are monthly and are paid in arrears. Divide the percent by 12 to get the level monthly payment per $100 that includes both interest and principal.

Example: The Constant Annual Percent needed to pay off a 15%, 30 year loan if payments are made monthly and in arrears is 15.18%. Divide by 12 to get the actual monthly payment. The constant annual payment for a $50,000 loan is $7,590. The monthly payment is $632.50.

INTEREST RATE	5 yr	6 yr	7 yr	8 yr	9 yr	10 yr	11 yr	12 yr	13 yr	14 yr	15 yr	16 yr	17 yr	18 yr	19 yr	20 yr
4.00	22.10	18.78	16.41	14.63	13.25	12.15	11.26	10.51	9.88	9.35	8.88	8.48	8.12	7.81	7.53	7.28
4.25	22.24	18.92	16.55	14.77	13.40	12.30	11.40	10.66	10.03	9.49	9.03	8.63	8.28	7.96	7.68	7.44
4.50	22.38	19.05	16.69	14.91	13.54	12.44	11.55	10.81	10.18	9.65	9.18	8.78	8.43	8.12	7.84	7.60
4.75	22.51	19.19	16.83	15.05	13.68	12.59	11.69	10.95	10.33	9.80	9.34	8.94	8.59	8.28	8.01	7.76
5.00	22.65	19.33	16.97	15.20	13.83	12.73	11.84	11.10	10.48	9.95	9.49	9.10	8.75	8.44	8.17	7.92
5.25	22.79	19.47	17.11	15.34	13.97	12.88	11.99	11.25	10.63	10.11	9.65	9.26	8.91	8.60	8.33	8.09
5.50	22.93	19.61	17.25	15.48	14.12	13.03	12.14	11.41	10.79	10.26	9.81	9.42	9.07	8.77	8.50	8.26
5.75	23.07	19.75	17.39	15.63	14.26	13.18	12.29	11.56	10.94	10.42	9.97	9.58	9.24	8.94	8.67	8.43
6.00	23.20	19.89	17.54	15.77	14.41	13.33	12.45	11.72	11.10	10.58	10.13	9.74	9.40	9.10	8.84	8.60
6.25	23.34	20.03	17.68	15.92	14.56	13.48	12.60	11.87	11.26	10.74	10.29	9.91	9.57	9.27	9.01	8.78
6.50	23.48	20.18	17.82	16.07	14.71	13.63	12.75	12.03	11.42	10.90	10.46	10.07	9.74	9.44	9.18	8.95
6.75	23.63	20.32	17.97	16.22	14.86	13.78	12.91	12.19	11.58	11.07	10.62	10.24	9.91	9.62	9.36	9.13
7.00	23.77	20.46	18.12	16.37	15.01	13.94	13.07	12.35	11.74	11.23	10.79	10.41	10.08	9.79	9.54	9.31
7.25	23.91	20.61	18.26	16.52	15.16	14.09	13.22	12.51	11.91	11.40	10.96	10.58	10.25	9.97	9.71	9.49
7.50	24.05	20.75	18.41	16.67	15.32	14.25	13.38	12.67	12.07	11.56	11.13	10.75	10.43	10.14	9.89	9.67
7.75	24.19	20.90	18.56	16.82	15.47	14.41	13.54	12.83	12.24	11.73	11.30	10.93	10.61	10.32	10.08	9.86
8.00	24.34	21.04	18.71	16.97	15.63	14.56	13.70	12.99	12.40	11.90	11.47	11.10	10.78	10.50	10.26	10.04
8.25	24.48	21.19	18.86	17.12	15.78	14.72	13.87	13.16	12.57	12.07	11.65	11.28	10.96	10.69	10.44	10.23
8.50	24.62	21.34	19.01	17.28	15.94	14.88	14.03	13.33	12.74	12.24	11.82	11.46	11.14	10.87	10.63	10.42
8.75	24.77	21.49	19.16	17.43	16.10	15.04	14.19	13.49	12.91	12.42	12.00	11.64	11.33	11.06	10.82	10.61
9.00	24.92	21.64	19.31	17.59	16.26	15.21	14.36	13.66	13.08	12.59	12.18	11.82	11.51	11.24	11.01	10.80
9.25	25.06	21.78	19.46	17.74	16.42	15.37	14.52	13.83	13.25	12.77	12.36	12.00	11.70	11.43	11.20	11.00
9.50	25.21	21.93	19.62	17.90	16.58	15.53	14.69	14.00	13.43	12.95	12.54	12.18	11.88	11.62	11.39	11.19
9.75	25.35	22.09	19.77	18.06	16.74	15.70	14.86	14.17	13.60	13.12	12.72	12.37	12.07	11.81	11.58	11.39
10.00	25.50	22.24	19.93	18.21	16.90	15.86	15.03	14.35	13.78	13.30	12.90	12.56	12.26	12.00	11.78	11.59
10.25	25.65	22.39	20.08	18.37	17.06	16.03	15.20	14.52	13.96	13.48	13.08	12.74	12.45	12.20	11.98	11.78
10.50	25.80	22.54	20.24	18.53	17.23	16.20	15.37	14.69	14.14	13.67	13.27	12.93	12.64	12.39	12.17	11.99
10.75	25.95	22.69	20.39	18.69	17.39	16.37	15.54	14.87	14.31	13.85	13.46	13.12	12.84	12.59	12.37	12.19
11.00	26.10	22.85	20.55	18.86	17.56	16.54	15.72	15.05	14.50	14.03	13.64	13.31	13.03	12.79	12.57	12.39
11.25	26.25	23.00	20.71	19.02	17.72	16.71	15.89	15.23	14.68	14.22	13.83	13.51	13.23	12.98	12.78	12.60
11.50	26.40	23.15	20.87	19.18	17.89	16.88	16.07	15.40	14.86	14.41	14.02	13.70	13.42	13.18	12.98	12.80
11.75	26.55	23.31	21.03	19.34	18.06	17.05	16.24	15.58	15.04	14.59	14.21	13.89	13.62	13.39	13.18	13.01
12.00	26.70	23.47	21.19	19.51	18.23	17.22	16.42	15.77	15.23	14.78	14.41	14.09	13.82	13.59	13.39	13.22
12.25	26.85	23.62	21.35	19.67	18.40	17.40	16.60	15.95	15.42	14.97	14.60	14.29	14.02	13.79	13.60	13.43
12.50	27.00	23.78	21.51	19.84	18.57	17.57	16.78	16.13	15.60	15.16	14.80	14.49	14.22	14.00	13.80	13.64
12.75	27.16	23.94	21.67	20.01	18.74	17.75	16.96	16.32	15.79	15.36	14.99	14.68	14.42	14.20	14.01	13.85
13.00	27.31	24.09	21.84	20.17	18.91	17.92	17.14	16.50	15.98	15.55	15.19	14.88	14.63	14.41	14.22	14.06
13.25	27.46	24.25	22.00	20.34	19.08	18.10	17.32	16.69	16.17	15.74	15.39	15.09	14.83	14.62	14.44	14.28
13.50	27.62	24.41	22.16	20.51	19.26	18.28	17.50	16.87	16.36	15.94	15.58	15.29	15.04	14.83	14.65	14.49
13.75	27.77	24.57	22.33	20.68	19.43	18.46	17.68	17.06	16.55	16.13	15.78	15.49	15.25	15.04	14.86	14.71
14.00	27.93	24.73	22.49	20.85	19.61	18.64	17.87	17.25	16.75	16.33	15.99	15.70	15.45	15.25	15.08	14.93
14.25	28.08	24.89	22.66	21.02	19.78	18.82	18.05	17.44	16.94	16.53	16.19	15.90	15.66	15.46	15.29	15.15
14.50	28.24	25.05	22.83	21.19	19.96	19.00	18.24	17.63	17.14	16.73	16.39	16.11	15.87	15.68	15.51	15.36
14.75	28.40	25.22	22.99	21.37	20.14	19.18	18.43	17.82	17.33	16.93	16.60	16.32	16.09	15.89	15.72	15.59
15.00	28.55	25.38	23.16	21.54	20.31	19.37	18.62	18.02	17.53	17.13	16.80	16.53	16.30	16.11	15.94	15.81
15.25	28.71	25.54	23.33	21.71	20.49	19.55	18.80	18.21	17.73	17.33	17.01	16.74	16.51	16.32	16.16	16.03
15.50	28.87	25.71	23.50	21.89	20.67	19.73	18.99	18.40	17.93	17.53	17.21	16.95	16.72	16.54	16.38	16.25
15.75	29.03	25.87	23.67	22.06	20.85	19.92	19.19	18.60	18.12	17.74	17.42	17.16	16.94	16.76	16.60	16.48
16.00	29.19	26.04	23.84	22.24	21.04	20.11	19.38	18.79	18.33	17.94	17.63	17.37	17.16	16.98	16.83	16.70
16.25	29.35	26.20	24.01	22.42	21.22	20.29	19.57	18.99	18.53	18.15	17.84	17.58	17.37	17.20	17.05	16.93
16.50	29.51	26.37	24.18	22.59	21.40	20.48	19.76	19.19	18.73	18.36	18.05	17.80	17.59	17.42	17.27	17.15
16.75	29.67	26.53	24.35	22.77	21.58	20.67	19.96	19.39	18.93	18.56	18.26	18.01	17.81	17.64	17.50	17.38
17.00	29.83	26.70	24.53	22.95	21.77	20.86	20.15	19.59	19.14	18.77	18.47	18.23	18.03	17.86	17.72	17.61
17.25	29.99	26.87	24.70	23.13	21.95	21.05	20.35	19.79	19.34	18.98	18.69	18.45	18.25	18.08	17.95	17.84
17.50	30.15	27.04	24.88	23.31	22.14	21.24	20.54	19.99	19.55	19.19	18.90	18.66	18.47	18.31	18.17	18.06
17.75	30.31	27.21	25.05	23.49	22.33	21.43	20.74	20.19	19.75	19.40	19.11	18.88	18.69	18.53	18.40	18.29
18.00	30.48	27.37	25.23	23.67	22.51	21.63	20.94	20.39	19.96	19.61	19.33	19.10	18.91	18.76	18.63	18.52
18.25	30.64	27.54	25.40	23.86	22.70	21.82	21.14	20.60	20.17	19.82	19.55	19.32	19.13	18.98	18.86	18.76
18.50	30.80	27.71	25.58	24.04	22.89	22.01	21.34	20.80	20.38	20.04	19.76	19.54	19.36	19.21	19.09	18.99
18.75	30.97	27.89	25.76	24.22	23.08	22.21	21.54	21.01	20.59	20.25	19.98	19.76	19.58	19.44	19.32	19.22
19.00	31.13	28.06	25.93	24.41	23.27	22.41	21.74	21.21	20.80	20.47	20.20	19.98	19.81	19.67	19.55	19.45
19.25	31.30	28.23	26.11	24.59	23.46	22.60	21.94	21.42	21.01	20.68	20.42	20.21	20.03	19.89	19.78	19.69
19.50	31.46	28.40	26.29	24.78	23.65	22.80	22.14	21.63	21.22	20.90	20.64	20.43	20.26	20.12	20.01	19.92
19.75	31.63	28.57	26.47	24.96	23.84	23.00	22.34	21.84	21.43	21.11	20.86	20.65	20.49	20.35	20.24	20.16
20.00	31.80	28.75	26.65	25.15	24.04	23.20	22.55	22.04	21.65	21.33	21.08	20.88	20.72	20.58	20.48	20.39
20.25	31.96	28.92	26.83	25.34	24.23	23.39	22.75	22.25	21.86	21.55	21.30	21.10	20.94	20.82	20.71	20.63
20.50	32.13	29.10	27.01	25.52	24.42	23.59	22.96	22.46	22.08	21.77	21.53	21.33	21.17	21.05	20.95	20.86
20.75	32.30	29.27	27.20	25.71	24.62	23.80	23.16	22.68	22.29	21.99	21.75	21.56	21.40	21.28	21.18	21.10

MONTHLY PAYMENT
IN ARREARS

Description: This table shows the percent of the principal amount of a loan needed each year to pay off the loan when the actual payments are monthly and are paid in arrears. Divide the percent by 12 to get the level monthly payment per $100 that includes both interest and principal.

Example: The Constant Annual Percent needed to pay off a 15%, 30 year loan if payments are made monthly and in arrears is 15.18%. Divide by 12 to get the actual monthly payment. The constant annual payment for a $50,000 loan is $7,590. The monthly payment is $632.50.

INTEREST RATE	21 yr	22 yr	23 yr	24 yr	25 yr	26 yr	27 yr	28 yr	29 yr	30 yr	31 yr	32 yr	33 yr	34 yr	35 yr	40 yr
4.00	7.05	6.85	6.66	6.49	6.34	6.20	6.07	5.95	5.84	5.73	5.64	5.55	5.47	5.39	5.32	5.02
4.25	7.21	7.01	6.83	6.66	6.51	6.37	6.24	6.12	6.01	5.91	5.81	5.73	5.65	5.57	5.50	5.21
4.50	7.37	7.17	6.99	6.83	6.67	6.54	6.41	6.29	6.18	6.09	5.99	5.91	5.83	5.75	5.68	5.40
4.75	7.54	7.34	7.16	7.00	6.85	6.71	6.58	6.47	6.36	6.26	6.17	6.09	6.01	5.94	5.87	5.59
5.00	7.71	7.51	7.33	7.17	7.02	6.89	6.76	6.65	6.54	6.45	6.36	6.28	6.20	6.13	6.06	5.79
5.25	7.87	7.68	7.50	7.34	7.20	7.06	6.94	6.83	6.73	6.63	6.54	6.46	6.39	6.32	6.25	5.99
5.50	8.04	7.85	7.68	7.52	7.37	7.24	7.12	7.01	6.91	6.82	6.73	6.65	6.58	6.51	6.45	6.19
5.75	8.22	8.03	7.85	7.70	7.55	7.42	7.31	7.20	7.10	7.01	6.92	6.85	6.77	6.71	6.65	6.40
6.00	8.39	8.20	8.03	7.88	7.74	7.61	7.49	7.39	7.29	7.20	7.12	7.04	6.97	6.91	6.85	6.61
6.25	8.57	8.38	8.21	8.06	7.92	7.80	7.68	7.58	7.48	7.39	7.31	7.24	7.17	7.11	7.05	6.82
6.50	8.75	8.56	8.39	8.24	8.11	7.98	7.87	7.77	7.68	7.59	7.51	7.44	7.37	7.31	7.25	7.03
6.75	8.93	8.74	8.58	8.43	8.30	8.17	8.06	7.96	7.87	7.79	7.71	7.64	7.58	7.52	7.46	7.25
7.00	9.11	8.93	8.76	8.62	8.49	8.37	8.26	8.16	8.07	7.99	7.91	7.85	7.78	7.72	7.67	7.46
7.25	9.29	9.11	8.95	8.81	8.68	8.56	8.46	8.36	8.27	8.19	8.12	8.05	7.99	7.93	7.88	7.68
7.50	9.47	9.30	9.14	9.00	8.87	8.76	8.65	8.56	8.47	8.40	8.32	8.26	8.20	8.15	8.10	7.90
7.75	9.66	9.49	9.33	9.19	9.07	8.96	8.85	8.76	8.68	8.60	8.53	8.47	8.41	8.36	8.31	8.12
8.00	9.85	9.68	9.53	9.39	9.27	9.16	9.06	8.97	8.88	8.81	8.74	8.68	8.63	8.57	8.53	8.35
8.25	10.04	9.87	9.72	9.59	9.47	9.36	9.26	9.17	9.09	9.02	8.95	8.90	8.84	8.79	8.75	8.57
8.50	10.23	10.07	9.92	9.79	9.67	9.56	9.47	9.38	9.30	9.23	9.17	9.11	9.06	9.01	8.97	8.80
8.75	10.43	10.26	10.12	9.99	9.87	9.77	9.67	9.59	9.51	9.45	9.38	9.33	9.28	9.23	9.19	9.03
9.00	10.62	10.46	10.32	10.19	10.08	9.97	9.88	9.80	9.73	9.66	9.60	9.55	9.50	9.45	9.41	9.26
9.25	10.82	10.66	10.52	10.39	10.28	10.18	10.09	10.01	9.94	9.88	9.82	9.77	9.72	9.68	9.64	9.49
9.50	11.01	10.86	10.72	10.60	10.49	10.39	10.31	10.23	10.16	10.10	10.04	9.99	9.94	9.90	9.86	9.73
9.75	11.21	11.06	10.93	10.81	10.70	10.60	10.52	10.44	10.38	10.31	10.26	10.21	10.17	10.13	10.09	9.96
10.00	11.41	11.26	11.13	11.01	10.91	10.82	10.73	10.66	10.59	10.54	10.48	10.44	10.39	10.36	10.32	10.19
10.25	11.62	11.47	11.34	11.22	11.12	11.03	10.95	10.88	10.82	10.76	10.71	10.66	10.62	10.58	10.55	10.43
10.50	11.82	11.68	11.55	11.43	11.34	11.25	11.17	11.10	11.04	10.98	10.93	10.89	10.85	10.81	10.78	10.67
10.75	12.03	11.88	11.76	11.65	11.55	11.46	11.39	11.32	11.26	11.21	11.16	11.12	11.08	11.05	11.02	10.91
11.00	12.23	12.09	11.97	11.86	11.77	11.68	11.61	11.54	11.48	11.43	11.39	11.35	11.31	11.28	11.25	11.14
11.25	12.44	12.30	12.18	12.08	11.98	11.90	11.83	11.77	11.71	11.66	11.62	11.58	11.54	11.51	11.48	11.38
11.50	12.65	12.51	12.40	12.29	12.20	12.12	12.05	11.99	11.94	11.89	11.85	11.81	11.77	11.74	11.72	11.62
11.75	12.86	12.73	12.61	12.51	12.42	12.35	12.28	12.22	12.16	12.12	12.08	12.04	12.01	11.98	11.95	11.87
12.00	13.07	12.94	12.83	12.73	12.64	12.57	12.50	12.44	12.39	12.35	12.31	12.27	12.24	12.22	12.19	12.11
12.25	13.28	13.16	13.05	12.95	12.87	12.79	12.73	12.67	12.62	12.58	12.54	12.51	12.48	12.45	12.43	12.35
12.50	13.50	13.37	13.26	13.17	13.09	13.02	12.96	12.90	12.85	12.81	12.78	12.74	12.71	12.69	12.67	12.59
12.75	13.71	13.59	13.48	13.39	13.31	13.24	13.18	13.13	13.09	13.05	13.01	12.98	12.95	12.93	12.91	12.84
13.00	13.93	13.81	13.71	13.62	13.54	13.47	13.41	13.36	13.32	13.28	13.25	13.22	13.19	13.17	13.15	13.08
13.25	14.14	14.03	13.93	13.84	13.77	13.70	13.64	13.59	13.55	13.51	13.48	13.45	13.43	13.41	13.39	13.32
13.50	14.36	14.25	14.15	14.07	13.99	13.93	13.87	13.83	13.79	13.75	13.72	13.69	13.67	13.65	13.63	13.57
13.75	14.58	14.47	14.37	14.29	14.22	14.16	14.11	14.06	14.02	13.99	13.96	13.93	13.91	13.89	13.87	13.81
14.00	14.80	14.69	14.60	14.52	14.45	14.39	14.34	14.30	14.26	14.22	14.19	14.17	14.15	14.13	14.11	14.06
14.25	15.02	14.92	14.82	14.75	14.68	14.62	14.57	14.53	14.49	14.46	14.43	14.41	14.39	14.37	14.36	14.30
14.50	15.24	15.14	15.05	14.98	14.91	14.86	14.81	14.77	14.73	14.70	14.67	14.65	14.63	14.61	14.60	14.55
14.75	15.47	15.37	15.28	15.21	15.14	15.09	15.04	15.00	14.97	14.94	14.91	14.89	14.87	14.86	14.84	14.80
15.00	15.69	15.59	15.51	15.44	15.37	15.32	15.28	15.24	15.21	15.18	15.15	15.13	15.12	15.10	15.09	15.04
15.25	15.92	15.82	15.74	15.67	15.61	15.56	15.51	15.48	15.45	15.42	15.40	15.38	15.36	15.34	15.33	15.29
15.50	16.14	16.05	15.97	15.90	15.84	15.79	15.75	15.72	15.69	15.66	15.64	15.62	15.60	15.59	15.58	15.54
15.75	16.37	16.28	16.20	16.13	16.08	16.03	15.99	15.95	15.93	15.90	15.88	15.86	15.85	15.83	15.82	15.79
16.00	16.59	16.50	16.43	16.37	16.31	16.27	16.23	16.19	16.17	16.14	16.12	16.10	16.09	16.08	16.07	16.03
16.25	16.82	16.74	16.66	16.60	16.55	16.50	16.47	16.43	16.41	16.38	16.36	16.35	16.33	16.32	16.31	16.28
16.50	17.05	16.97	16.89	16.83	16.78	16.74	16.71	16.67	16.65	16.63	16.61	16.59	16.58	16.57	16.56	16.53
16.75	17.28	17.20	17.13	17.07	17.02	16.98	16.94	16.92	16.89	16.87	16.85	16.84	16.82	16.81	16.80	16.78
17.00	17.51	17.43	17.36	17.31	17.26	17.22	17.19	17.16	17.13	17.11	17.10	17.08	17.07	17.06	17.05	17.02
17.25	17.74	17.66	17.60	17.54	17.50	17.46	17.43	17.40	17.38	17.36	17.34	17.33	17.32	17.31	17.30	17.27
17.50	17.97	17.90	17.83	17.78	17.74	17.70	17.67	17.64	17.62	17.60	17.59	17.57	17.56	17.55	17.55	17.52
17.75	18.20	18.13	18.07	18.02	17.97	17.94	17.91	17.88	17.86	17.85	17.83	17.82	17.81	17.80	17.79	17.77
18.00	18.44	18.37	18.31	18.26	18.21	18.18	18.15	18.13	18.11	18.09	18.08	18.06	18.05	18.05	18.04	18.02
18.25	18.67	18.60	18.54	18.49	18.45	18.42	18.39	18.37	18.35	18.34	18.32	18.31	18.30	18.29	18.29	18.27
18.50	18.91	18.84	18.78	18.73	18.69	18.66	18.64	18.61	18.60	18.58	18.57	18.56	18.55	18.54	18.54	18.52
18.75	19.14	19.07	19.02	18.97	18.94	18.90	18.88	18.86	18.84	18.83	18.81	18.80	18.80	18.79	18.78	18.77
19.00	19.37	19.31	19.26	19.21	19.18	19.15	19.12	19.10	19.09	19.07	19.06	19.05	19.04	19.04	19.03	19.02
19.25	19.61	19.55	19.50	19.45	19.42	19.39	19.37	19.35	19.33	19.32	19.31	19.30	19.29	19.28	19.28	19.26
19.50	19.85	19.79	19.74	19.69	19.66	19.63	19.61	19.59	19.58	19.56	19.55	19.55	19.54	19.53	19.53	19.51
19.75	20.08	20.02	19.98	19.94	19.90	19.88	19.86	19.84	19.82	19.81	19.80	19.79	19.79	19.78	19.78	19.76
20.00	20.32	20.26	20.22	20.18	20.15	20.12	20.10	20.08	20.07	20.06	20.05	20.04	20.03	20.03	20.02	20.01
20.25	20.56	20.50	20.46	20.42	20.39	20.36	20.34	20.33	20.32	20.30	20.30	20.29	20.28	20.28	20.27	20.26
20.50	20.80	20.74	20.70	20.66	20.63	20.61	20.59	20.57	20.56	20.55	20.54	20.54	20.53	20.53	20.52	20.51
20.75	21.03	20.98	20.94	20.90	20.88	20.85	20.84	20.82	20.81	20.80	20.79	20.78	20.78	20.77	20.77	20.76

(continued)

TABLE 2 Constant Annual Percentage to Amortize Mortgage

(continued)

QUARTERLY PAYMENT
IN ARREARS

Description: This table shows the percent of the principal amount of a loan needed each year to pay off the loan when the actual payments are quarterly and are paid in arrears. Divide the percent by 4 to get the level quarterly payment per $100 that includes both interest and principal.

Example: The Constant Annual Percent needed to pay off a 15%, 30 year loan if payments are made quarterly and in arrears is 15.19%. Divide by 4 to get the actual quarterly payment. The constant annual payment for a $50,000 loan is $7,595. The quarterly payment is $1,898.75.

INTEREST RATE	5 yr	6 yr	7 yr	8 yr	9 yr	10 yr	11 yr	12 yr	13 yr	14 yr	15 yr	16 yr	17 yr	18 yr	19 yr	20 yr
4.00	22.17	18.83	16.45	14.67	13.29	12.19	11.29	10.54	9.91	9.37	8.90	8.50	8.14	7.83	7.54	7.29
4.25	22.31	18.97	16.60	14.82	13.43	12.33	11.43	10.69	10.06	9.52	9.06	8.65	8.30	7.98	7.70	7.45
4.50	22.45	19.12	16.74	14.96	13.58	12.48	11.58	10.84	10.21	9.67	9.21	8.81	8.45	8.14	7.86	7.61
4.75	22.59	19.26	16.88	15.10	13.72	12.63	11.73	10.99	10.36	9.82	9.36	8.96	8.61	8.30	8.02	7.78
5.00	22.73	19.40	17.02	15.25	13.87	12.77	11.88	11.14	10.51	9.98	9.52	9.12	8.77	8.46	8.19	7.94
5.25	22.87	19.54	17.17	15.39	14.02	12.92	12.03	11.29	10.67	10.14	9.68	9.28	8.93	8.63	8.35	8.11
5.50	23.02	19.69	17.31	15.54	14.17	13.07	12.18	11.44	10.82	10.29	9.84	9.44	9.10	8.79	8.52	8.28
5.75	23.16	19.83	17.46	15.69	14.32	13.22	12.34	11.60	10.98	10.45	10.00	9.61	9.26	8.96	8.69	8.45
6.00	23.30	19.97	17.61	15.84	14.47	13.38	12.49	11.75	11.14	10.61	10.16	9.77	9.43	9.13	8.86	8.62
6.25	23.45	20.12	17.75	15.98	14.62	13.53	12.64	11.91	11.30	10.78	10.33	9.94	9.60	9.30	9.03	8.80
6.50	23.59	20.27	17.90	16.13	14.77	13.68	12.80	12.07	11.46	10.94	10.49	10.10	9.77	9.47	9.21	8.98
6.75	23.74	20.41	18.05	16.28	14.92	13.84	12.96	12.23	11.62	11.10	10.66	10.27	9.94	9.64	9.38	9.15
7.00	23.88	20.56	18.20	16.44	15.08	13.99	13.12	12.39	11.78	11.27	10.83	10.44	10.11	9.82	9.56	9.33
7.25	24.03	20.71	18.35	16.59	15.23	14.15	13.28	12.55	11.95	11.44	11.00	10.62	10.29	10.00	9.74	9.51
7.50	24.17	20.86	18.50	16.74	15.38	14.31	13.44	12.72	12.11	11.60	11.17	10.79	10.46	10.17	9.92	9.70
7.75	24.32	21.00	18.65	16.89	15.54	14.47	13.60	12.88	12.28	11.77	11.34	10.96	10.64	10.35	10.10	9.88
8.00	24.47	21.15	18.80	17.05	15.70	14.63	13.76	13.05	12.45	11.94	11.51	11.14	10.82	10.54	10.29	10.07
8.25	24.62	21.30	18.95	17.20	15.86	14.79	13.92	13.21	12.62	12.12	11.69	11.32	11.00	10.72	10.47	10.26
8.50	24.76	21.45	19.11	17.36	16.01	14.95	14.09	13.38	12.79	12.29	11.86	11.50	11.18	10.90	10.66	10.45
8.75	24.91	21.61	19.26	17.52	16.17	15.11	14.25	13.55	12.96	12.46	12.04	11.68	11.36	11.09	10.85	10.64
9.00	25.06	21.76	19.42	17.67	16.34	15.28	14.42	13.72	13.13	12.64	12.22	11.86	11.55	11.28	11.04	10.83
9.25	25.21	21.91	19.57	17.83	16.50	15.44	14.59	13.89	13.31	12.82	12.40	12.04	11.73	11.46	11.23	11.02
9.50	25.36	22.06	19.73	17.99	16.66	15.61	14.76	14.06	13.48	12.99	12.58	12.23	11.92	11.65	11.42	11.22
9.75	25.51	22.22	19.88	18.15	16.82	15.77	14.93	14.23	13.66	13.17	12.76	12.41	12.11	11.85	11.62	11.42
10.00	25.66	22.37	20.04	18.31	16.99	15.94	15.10	14.41	13.83	13.35	12.95	12.60	12.30	12.04	11.81	11.62
10.25	25.82	22.52	20.20	18.47	17.15	16.11	15.27	14.58	14.01	13.54	13.13	12.79	12.49	12.23	12.01	11.82
10.50	25.97	22.68	20.36	18.64	17.32	16.28	15.44	14.76	14.19	13.72	13.32	12.98	12.68	12.43	12.21	12.02
10.75	26.12	22.84	20.52	18.80	17.48	16.45	15.61	14.94	14.37	13.90	13.50	13.17	12.88	12.62	12.41	12.22
11.00	26.27	22.99	20.68	18.96	17.65	16.62	15.79	15.11	14.55	14.09	13.69	13.36	13.07	12.82	12.61	12.42
11.25	26.43	23.15	20.84	19.13	17.82	16.79	15.96	15.29	14.74	14.27	13.88	13.55	13.27	13.02	12.81	12.63
11.50	26.58	23.31	21.00	19.29	17.99	16.96	16.14	15.47	14.92	14.46	14.07	13.74	13.46	13.22	13.01	12.83
11.75	26.74	23.47	21.16	19.46	18.16	17.14	16.32	15.65	15.11	14.65	14.27	13.94	13.66	13.42	13.22	13.04
12.00	26.89	23.62	21.32	19.62	18.33	17.31	16.50	15.84	15.29	14.84	14.46	14.14	13.86	13.63	13.42	13.25
12.25	27.05	23.78	21.49	19.79	18.50	17.49	16.68	16.02	15.48	15.03	14.65	14.33	14.06	13.83	13.63	13.46
12.50	27.20	23.94	21.65	19.96	18.67	17.66	16.86	16.20	15.67	15.22	14.85	14.53	14.26	14.04	13.84	13.67
12.75	27.36	24.10	21.81	20.13	18.84	17.84	17.04	16.39	15.86	15.41	15.04	14.73	14.47	14.24	14.05	13.88
13.00	27.52	24.26	21.98	20.30	19.02	18.02	17.22	16.57	16.05	15.61	15.24	14.93	14.67	14.45	14.26	14.10
13.25	27.67	24.43	22.14	20.47	19.19	18.19	17.40	16.76	16.24	15.80	15.44	15.13	14.88	14.66	14.47	14.31
13.50	27.83	24.59	22.31	20.64	19.37	18.37	17.59	16.95	16.43	16.00	15.64	15.34	15.08	14.87	14.68	14.53
13.75	27.99	24.75	22.48	20.81	19.54	18.55	17.77	17.14	16.62	16.19	15.84	15.54	15.29	15.08	14.90	14.74
14.00	28.15	24.91	22.65	20.98	19.72	18.74	17.96	17.33	16.81	16.39	16.04	15.75	15.50	15.29	15.11	14.96
14.25	28.31	25.08	22.81	21.15	19.90	18.92	18.14	17.52	17.01	16.59	16.24	15.95	15.71	15.50	15.33	15.18
14.50	28.47	25.24	22.98	21.33	20.07	19.10	18.33	17.71	17.21	16.79	16.45	16.16	15.92	15.71	15.54	15.40
14.75	28.63	25.41	23.15	21.50	20.25	19.28	18.52	17.90	17.40	16.99	16.65	16.37	16.13	15.93	15.76	15.62
15.00	28.79	25.57	23.32	21.68	20.43	19.47	18.71	18.10	17.60	17.19	16.86	16.58	16.34	16.14	15.98	15.84
15.25	28.95	25.74	23.49	21.85	20.61	19.65	18.90	18.29	17.80	17.39	17.06	16.79	16.55	16.36	16.20	16.06
15.50	29.11	25.91	23.67	22.03	20.80	19.84	19.09	18.48	18.00	17.60	17.27	17.00	16.77	16.58	16.42	16.28
15.75	29.28	26.07	23.84	22.21	20.98	20.03	19.28	18.68	18.20	17.80	17.48	17.21	16.98	16.80	16.64	16.51
16.00	29.44	26.24	24.01	22.38	21.16	20.21	19.47	18.88	18.40	18.01	17.69	17.42	17.20	17.01	16.86	16.73
16.25	29.60	26.41	24.10	22.56	21.34	20.40	19.66	19.07	18.60	18.21	17.90	17.63	17.42	17.23	17.08	16.96
16.50	29.76	26.58	24.36	22.74	21.53	20.59	19.86	19.27	18.80	18.42	18.11	17.85	17.63	17.46	17.31	17.18
16.75	29.93	26.75	24.53	22.92	21.71	20.78	20.05	19.47	19.01	18.63	18.32	18.06	17.85	17.68	17.53	17.41
17.00	30.09	26.92	24.71	23.10	21.90	20.97	20.25	19.67	19.21	18.84	18.53	18.28	18.07	17.90	17.76	17.64
17.25	30.26	27.09	24.88	23.28	22.08	21.16	20.44	19.87	19.42	19.04	18.74	18.49	18.29	18.12	17.98	17.86
17.50	30.42	27.26	25.06	23.46	22.27	21.36	20.64	20.07	19.62	19.25	18.96	18.71	18.51	18.35	18.21	18.09
17.75	30.59	27.43	25.24	23.65	22.46	21.55	20.84	20.28	19.83	19.47	19.17	18.93	18.73	18.57	18.43	18.32
18.00	30.76	27.60	25.41	23.83	22.65	21.74	21.04	20.48	20.04	19.68	19.39	19.15	18.95	18.79	18.66	18.55
18.25	30.92	27.77	25.59	24.01	22.84	21.94	21.24	20.68	20.24	19.89	19.60	19.37	19.18	19.02	18.89	18.78
18.50	31.09	27.95	25.77	24.20	23.03	22.13	21.44	20.89	20.45	20.10	19.82	19.59	19.40	19.25	19.12	19.02
18.75	31.26	28.12	25.95	24.38	23.22	22.33	21.64	21.09	20.66	20.32	20.04	19.81	19.63	19.47	19.35	19.25
19.00	31.43	28.29	26.13	24.57	23.41	22.52	21.84	21.30	20.87	20.53	20.26	20.03	19.85	19.70	19.58	19.48
19.25	31.59	28.47	26.31	24.75	23.60	22.72	22.04	21.51	21.08	20.75	20.47	20.25	20.08	19.93	19.81	19.71
19.50	31.76	28.64	26.49	24.94	23.79	22.92	22.24	21.72	21.30	20.96	20.69	20.48	20.30	20.16	20.04	19.95
19.75	31.93	28.82	26.67	25.13	23.99	23.12	22.45	21.92	21.51	21.18	20.92	20.70	20.53	20.39	20.28	20.18
20.00	32.10	28.99	26.85	25.32	24.18	23.32	22.65	22.13	21.72	21.40	21.14	20.93	20.76	20.62	20.51	20.42
20.25	32.27	29.17	27.04	25.51	24.37	23.52	22.86	22.34	21.94	21.62	21.36	21.15	20.99	20.85	20.74	20.65
20.50	32.44	29.35	27.22	25.70	24.57	23.72	23.06	22.55	22.15	21.83	21.58	21.38	21.21	21.08	20.97	20.89
20.75	32.61	29.52	27.40	25.88	24.76	23.92	23.27	22.76	22.37	22.05	21.80	21.60	21.44	21.31	21.21	21.12

QUARTERLY PAYMENT
IN ARREARS

Description: This table shows the percent of the principal amount of a loan needed each year to pay off the loan when the actual payments are quarterly and are paid in arrears. Divide the percent by 4 to get the level quarterly payment per $100 that includes both interest and principal.

Example: The Constant Annual Percent needed to pay off a 15%, 30 year loan if payments are made quarterly and in arrears is 15.19%. Divide by 4 to get the actual quarterly payment. The constant annual payment for a $50,000 loan is $7,595. The quarterly payment is $1,898.75.

INTEREST RATE	21 yr	22 yr	23 yr	24 yr	25 yr	26 yr	27 yr	28 yr	29 yr	30 yr	31 yr	32 yr	33 yr	34 yr	35 yr	40 yr
4.00	7.07	6.86	6.68	6.51	6.35	6.21	6.08	5.96	5.85	5.74	5.65	5.56	5.48	5.40	5.33	5.03
4.25	7.23	7.02	6.84	6.67	6.52	6.38	6.25	6.13	6.02	5.92	5.82	5.74	5.66	5.58	5.51	5.22
4.50	7.39	7.19	7.01	6.84	6.69	6.55	6.42	6.30	6.20	6.10	6.00	5.92	5.84	5.76	5.69	5.41
4.75	7.56	7.36	7.18	7.01	6.86	6.72	6.60	6.48	6.37	6.28	6.18	6.10	6.02	5.95	5.88	5.60
5.00	7.72	7.53	7.35	7.18	7.03	6.90	6.77	6.66	6.56	6.46	6.37	6.29	6.21	6.14	6.07	5.80
5.25	7.89	7.70	7.52	7.36	7.21	7.08	6.95	6.84	6.74	6.64	6.56	6.47	6.40	6.33	6.26	6.00
5.50	8.06	7.87	7.69	7.53	7.39	7.26	7.14	7.03	6.92	6.83	6.74	6.66	6.59	6.52	6.46	6.20
5.75	8.24	8.04	7.87	7.71	7.57	7.44	7.32	7.21	7.11	7.02	6.94	6.86	6.79	6.72	6.66	6.41
6.00	8.41	8.22	8.05	7.89	7.75	7.62	7.51	7.40	7.30	7.21	7.13	7.05	6.98	6.92	6.86	6.62
6.25	8.59	8.40	8.23	8.08	7.94	7.81	7.70	7.59	7.49	7.41	7.33	7.25	7.18	7.12	7.06	6.83
6.50	8.77	8.58	8.41	8.26	8.12	8.00	7.89	7.78	7.69	7.60	7.52	7.45	7.38	7.32	7.27	7.04
6.75	8.95	8.76	8.60	8.45	8.31	8.19	8.08	7.98	7.89	7.80	7.72	7.65	7.59	7.53	7.47	7.25
7.00	9.13	8.95	8.78	8.64	8.50	8.38	8.27	8.18	8.08	8.00	7.93	7.86	7.79	7.74	7.68	7.47
7.25	9.31	9.13	8.97	8.83	8.70	8.58	8.47	8.37	8.29	8.20	8.13	8.06	8.00	7.95	7.89	7.69
7.50	9.50	9.32	9.16	9.02	8.89	8.78	8.67	8.58	8.49	8.41	8.34	8.27	8.21	8.16	8.11	7.91
7.75	9.69	9.51	9.35	9.21	9.09	8.97	8.87	8.78	8.69	8.62	8.55	8.48	8.42	8.37	8.32	8.13
8.00	9.88	9.70	9.55	9.41	9.29	9.17	9.07	8.98	8.90	8.82	8.76	8.69	8.64	8.59	8.54	8.36
8.25	10.07	9.90	9.74	9.61	9.49	9.38	9.28	9.19	9.11	9.03	8.97	8.91	8.85	8.80	8.76	8.58
8.50	10.26	10.09	9.94	9.81	9.69	9.58	9.48	9.40	9.32	9.25	9.18	9.12	9.07	9.02	8.98	8.81
8.75	10.45	10.29	10.14	10.01	9.89	9.79	9.69	9.61	9.53	9.46	9.40	9.34	9.29	9.24	9.20	9.04
9.00	10.65	10.48	10.34	10.21	10.10	9.99	9.90	9.82	9.74	9.67	9.61	9.56	9.51	9.46	9.42	9.27
9.25	10.84	10.68	10.54	10.41	10.30	10.20	10.11	10.03	9.96	9.89	9.83	9.78	9.73	9.69	9.65	9.50
9.50	11.04	10.88	10.74	10.62	10.51	10.41	10.32	10.24	10.17	10.11	10.05	10.00	9.95	9.91	9.87	9.73
9.75	11.24	11.09	10.95	10.83	10.72	10.62	10.54	10.46	10.39	10.33	10.27	10.22	10.18	10.14	10.10	9.97
10.00	11.44	11.29	11.15	11.04	10.93	10.84	10.75	10.68	10.61	10.55	10.50	10.45	10.40	10.37	10.33	10.20
10.25	11.64	11.49	11.36	11.25	11.14	11.05	10.97	10.90	10.83	10.77	10.72	10.67	10.63	10.59	10.56	10.44
10.50	11.85	11.70	11.57	11.46	11.36	11.27	11.19	11.12	11.05	11.00	10.95	10.90	10.86	10.82	10.79	10.67
10.75	12.05	11.91	11.78	11.67	11.57	11.48	11.41	11.34	11.27	11.22	11.17	11.13	11.09	11.05	11.02	10.91
11.00	12.26	12.12	11.99	11.88	11.79	11.70	11.63	11.56	11.50	11.45	11.40	11.36	11.32	11.29	11.26	11.15
11.25	12.47	12.33	12.21	12.10	12.00	11.92	11.85	11.78	11.72	11.67	11.63	11.59	11.55	11.52	11.49	11.39
11.50	12.68	12.54	12.42	12.32	12.22	12.14	12.07	12.01	11.95	11.90	11.86	11.82	11.78	11.75	11.73	11.63
11.75	12.89	12.75	12.64	12.53	12.44	12.36	12.29	12.23	12.18	12.13	12.09	12.05	12.02	11.99	11.96	11.87
12.00	13.10	12.97	12.85	12.75	12.66	12.59	12.52	12.46	12.41	12.36	12.32	12.28	12.25	12.22	12.20	12.11
12.25	13.31	13.18	13.07	12.97	12.89	12.81	12.75	12.69	12.64	12.59	12.55	12.52	12.49	12.46	12.44	12.35
12.50	13.52	13.40	13.29	13.19	13.11	13.04	12.97	12.92	12.87	12.82	12.79	12.75	12.72	12.70	12.68	12.60
12.75	13.74	13.62	13.51	13.41	13.33	13.26	13.20	13.15	13.10	13.06	13.02	12.99	12.96	12.94	12.91	12.84
13.00	13.96	13.83	13.73	13.64	13.56	13.49	13.43	13.38	13.33	13.29	13.26	13.23	13.20	13.18	13.15	13.08
13.25	14.17	14.05	13.95	13.86	13.78	13.72	13.66	13.61	13.56	13.53	13.49	13.46	13.44	13.41	13.39	13.33
13.50	14.39	14.27	14.17	14.09	14.01	13.95	13.89	13.84	13.80	13.76	13.73	13.70	13.68	13.65	13.64	13.57
13.75	14.61	14.50	14.40	14.31	14.24	14.18	14.12	14.07	14.03	14.00	13.97	13.94	13.92	13.90	13.88	13.82
14.00	14.83	14.72	14.62	14.54	14.47	14.41	14.35	14.31	14.27	14.23	14.20	14.18	14.16	14.14	14.12	14.06
14.25	15.05	14.94	14.85	14.77	14.70	14.64	14.59	14.54	14.50	14.47	14.44	14.42	14.40	14.38	14.36	14.31
14.50	15.27	15.17	15.07	15.00	14.93	14.87	14.82	14.78	14.74	14.71	14.68	14.66	14.64	14.62	14.60	14.55
14.75	15.49	15.39	15.30	15.23	15.16	15.10	15.06	15.02	14.98	14.95	14.92	14.90	14.88	14.86	14.85	14.80
15.00	15.72	15.62	15.53	15.46	15.39	15.34	15.29	15.25	15.22	15.19	15.16	15.14	15.12	15.11	15.09	15.05
15.25	15.94	15.84	15.76	15.69	15.63	15.57	15.53	15.49	15.46	15.43	15.40	15.38	15.37	15.35	15.34	15.29
15.50	16.17	16.07	15.99	15.92	15.86	15.81	15.76	15.73	15.70	15.67	15.65	15.63	15.61	15.59	15.58	15.54
15.75	16.39	16.30	16.22	16.15	16.09	16.04	16.00	15.97	15.94	15.91	15.89	15.87	15.85	15.84	15.83	15.79
16.00	16.62	16.53	16.45	16.38	16.33	16.28	16.24	16.21	16.18	16.15	16.13	16.11	16.10	16.08	16.07	16.04
16.25	16.85	16.76	16.68	16.62	16.56	16.52	16.48	16.45	16.42	16.39	16.37	16.35	16.34	16.33	16.32	16.28
16.50	17.08	16.99	16.92	16.85	16.80	16.76	16.72	16.69	16.66	16.64	16.62	16.60	16.58	16.57	16.56	16.53
16.75	17.31	17.22	17.15	17.09	17.04	16.99	16.96	16.93	16.90	16.88	16.86	16.84	16.83	16.82	16.81	16.78
17.00	17.54	17.45	17.38	17.32	17.27	17.23	17.20	17.17	17.14	17.12	17.10	17.09	17.08	17.06	17.06	17.03
17.25	17.77	17.69	17.62	17.56	17.51	17.47	17.44	17.41	17.38	17.36	17.35	17.33	17.32	17.31	17.30	17.28
17.50	18.00	17.92	17.85	17.80	17.75	17.71	17.68	17.65	17.63	17.61	17.59	17.58	17.57	17.56	17.55	17.52
17.75	18.23	18.15	18.09	18.03	17.99	17.95	17.92	17.89	17.87	17.85	17.84	17.82	17.81	17.80	17.80	17.77
18.00	18.46	18.39	18.32	18.27	18.23	18.19	18.16	18.14	18.11	18.10	18.08	18.07	18.06	18.05	18.04	18.02
18.25	18.70	18.62	18.56	18.51	18.47	18.43	18.40	18.38	18.36	18.34	18.33	18.32	18.31	18.30	18.29	18.27
18.50	18.93	18.86	18.80	18.75	18.71	18.67	18.65	18.62	18.60	18.59	18.57	18.56	18.55	18.54	18.54	18.52
18.75	19.16	19.09	19.04	18.99	18.95	18.92	18.89	18.87	18.85	18.83	18.82	18.81	18.80	18.79	18.79	18.77
19.00	19.40	19.33	19.27	19.23	19.19	19.16	19.13	19.11	19.09	19.08	19.07	19.06	19.05	19.04	19.03	19.02
19.25	19.63	19.57	19.51	19.47	19.43	19.40	19.38	19.36	19.34	19.32	19.31	19.30	19.29	19.29	19.28	19.27
19.50	19.87	19.81	19.75	19.71	19.67	19.64	19.62	19.60	19.58	19.57	19.56	19.55	19.54	19.54	19.53	19.51
19.75	20.11	20.04	19.99	19.95	19.92	19.89	19.86	19.84	19.83	19.82	19.81	19.80	19.79	19.78	19.78	19.76
20.00	20.34	20.28	20.23	20.19	20.16	20.13	20.11	20.09	20.07	20.06	20.05	20.04	20.04	20.03	20.03	20.01
20.25	20.58	20.52	20.47	20.43	20.40	20.37	20.35	20.34	20.32	20.31	20.30	20.29	20.28	20.28	20.28	20.26
20.50	20.82	20.76	20.71	20.68	20.64	20.62	20.60	20.58	20.57	20.56	20.55	20.54	20.53	20.53	20.52	20.51
20.75	21.06	21.00	20.95	20.92	20.89	20.86	20.84	20.83	20.81	20.80	20.79	20.79	20.78	20.78	20.77	20.76

(continued)

TABLE 2 Constant Annual Percentage to Amortize Mortgage

(continued)

MONTHLY PAYMENT
IN ADVANCE

Description: This table shows the percent of the principal amount of a loan needed each year to pay off the loan when the actual payments are monthly and are paid in advance. Divide the percent by 12 to get the level monthly payment per $100 that includes both interest and principal.

Example: The Constant Annual Percent needed to pay off a 15%, 30 year loan if payments are made monthly and in advance is 14.99% Divide by 12 to get the actual monthly payment. The constant annual payment for a $50,000 loan is $7,495. The monthly payment is $624.59

INTEREST RATE	5 yr	6 yr	7 yr	8 yr	9 yr	10 yr	11 yr	12 yr	13 yr	14 yr	15 yr	16 yr	17 yr	18 yr	19 yr	20 yr
4.00	22.03	18.72	16.35	14.58	13.21	12.11	11.22	10.48	9.85	9.31	8.85	8.45	8.09	7.78	7.50	7.25
4.25	22.16	18.85	16.49	14.72	13.35	12.25	11.36	10.62	9.99	9.46	9.00	8.60	8.25	7.94	7.66	7.41
4.50	22.29	18.98	16.62	14.86	13.49	12.40	11.50	10.76	10.14	9.61	9.15	8.75	8.40	8.09	7.81	7.57
4.75	22.42	19.12	16.76	15.00	13.63	12.54	11.65	10.91	10.29	9.76	9.30	8.90	8.56	8.25	7.97	7.73
5.00	22.56	19.25	16.90	15.13	13.77	12.68	11.79	11.06	10.44	9.91	9.46	9.06	8.71	8.41	8.13	7.89
5.25	22.69	19.39	17.03	15.27	13.91	12.82	11.94	11.21	10.59	10.06	9.61	9.22	8.87	8.57	8.30	8.06
5.50	22.82	19.52	17.17	15.41	14.05	12.97	12.09	11.36	10.74	10.22	9.77	9.37	9.03	8.73	8.46	8.22
5.75	22.96	19.66	17.31	15.55	14.20	13.11	12.23	11.51	10.89	10.37	9.92	9.53	9.19	8.89	8.63	8.39
6.00	23.09	19.79	17.45	15.70	14.34	13.26	12.38	11.66	11.05	10.53	10.08	9.69	9.36	9.06	8.79	8.56
6.25	23.22	19.93	17.59	15.84	14.49	13.41	12.53	11.81	11.20	10.68	10.24	9.86	9.52	9.22	8.96	8.73
6.50	23.36	20.07	17.73	15.98	14.63	13.56	12.68	11.96	11.36	10.84	10.40	10.02	9.69	9.39	9.13	8.90
6.75	23.49	20.21	17.87	16.13	14.78	13.71	12.84	12.12	11.52	11.00	10.56	10.18	9.85	9.56	9.31	9.08
7.00	23.63	20.35	18.01	16.27	14.93	13.86	12.99	12.27	11.67	11.16	10.73	10.35	10.02	9.73	9.48	9.25
7.25	23.76	20.48	18.15	16.42	15.07	14.01	13.14	12.43	11.83	11.33	10.89	10.52	10.19	9.91	9.66	9.43
7.50	23.90	20.62	18.30	16.56	15.22	14.16	13.30	12.59	11.99	11.49	11.06	10.69	10.36	10.08	9.83	9.61
7.75	24.04	20.76	18.44	16.71	15.37	14.31	13.46	12.75	12.16	11.66	11.23	10.86	10.54	10.26	10.01	9.79
8.00	24.18	20.91	18.58	16.86	15.52	14.47	13.61	12.91	12.32	11.82	11.40	11.03	10.71	10.44	10.19	9.98
8.25	24.31	21.05	18.73	17.01	15.68	14.62	13.77	13.07	12.48	11.99	11.57	11.20	10.89	10.61	10.37	10.16
8.50	24.45	21.19	18.88	17.15	15.83	14.78	13.93	13.23	12.65	12.16	11.74	11.38	11.07	10.79	10.56	10.35
8.75	24.59	21.33	19.02	17.30	15.98	14.94	14.09	13.40	12.82	12.33	11.91	11.55	11.24	10.98	10.74	10.53
9.00	24.73	21.47	19.17	17.45	16.14	15.09	14.25	13.56	12.98	12.50	12.09	11.73	11.42	11.16	10.93	10.72
9.25	24.87	21.62	19.32	17.61	16.29	15.25	14.41	13.73	13.15	12.67	12.26	11.91	11.61	11.34	11.11	10.91
9.50	25.01	21.76	19.46	17.76	16.45	15.41	14.58	13.89	13.32	12.84	12.44	12.09	11.79	11.53	11.30	11.10
9.75	25.15	21.91	19.61	17.91	16.60	15.57	14.74	14.06	13.49	13.02	12.61	12.27	11.97	11.72	11.49	11.30
10.00	25.29	22.05	19.76	18.06	16.76	15.73	14.90	14.23	13.67	13.19	12.79	12.45	12.16	11.90	11.68	11.49
10.25	25.43	22.20	19.91	18.22	16.92	15.89	15.07	14.40	13.84	13.37	12.97	12.64	12.34	12.09	11.88	11.68
10.50	25.57	22.34	20.06	18.37	17.08	16.06	15.24	14.57	14.01	13.55	13.15	12.82	12.53	12.28	12.07	11.88
10.75	25.72	22.49	20.21	18.53	17.24	16.22	15.40	14.74	14.19	13.73	13.34	13.01	12.72	12.48	12.26	12.08
11.00	25.86	22.64	20.37	18.68	17.40	16.38	15.57	14.91	14.36	13.91	13.52	13.19	12.91	12.67	12.46	12.28
11.25	26.00	22.79	20.52	18.84	17.56	16.55	15.74	15.08	14.54	14.09	13.70	13.38	13.10	12.86	12.66	12.48
11.50	26.15	22.93	20.67	19.00	17.72	16.72	15.91	15.26	14.72	14.27	13.89	13.57	13.29	13.06	12.86	12.68
11.75	26.29	23.08	20.82	19.16	17.88	16.88	16.08	15.43	14.90	14.45	14.08	13.76	13.49	13.26	13.06	12.88
12.00	26.43	23.23	20.98	19.32	18.05	17.05	16.26	15.61	15.08	14.64	14.26	13.95	13.68	13.45	13.26	13.09
12.25	26.58	23.38	21.13	19.47	18.21	17.22	16.43	15.79	15.26	14.82	14.45	14.14	13.88	13.65	13.46	13.29
12.50	26.72	23.53	21.29	19.64	18.37	17.39	16.60	15.97	15.44	15.01	14.64	14.34	14.08	13.85	13.66	13.50
12.75	26.87	23.68	21.44	19.80	18.54	17.56	16.78	16.14	15.62	15.19	14.83	14.53	14.27	14.05	13.87	13.71
13.00	27.02	23.84	21.60	19.96	18.71	17.73	16.95	16.32	15.81	15.38	15.03	14.73	14.47	14.26	14.07	13.91
13.25	27.16	23.99	21.76	20.12	18.87	17.90	17.13	16.50	15.99	15.57	15.22	14.92	14.67	14.46	14.28	14.12
13.50	27.31	24.14	21.92	20.28	19.04	18.07	17.31	16.69	16.18	15.76	15.41	15.12	14.87	14.66	14.48	14.33
13.75	27.46	24.29	22.07	20.45	19.21	18.25	17.48	16.87	16.37	15.95	15.61	15.32	15.07	14.87	14.69	14.54
14.00	27.60	24.45	22.23	20.61	19.38	18.42	17.66	17.05	16.55	16.14	15.80	15.52	15.28	15.07	14.90	14.76
14.25	27.75	24.60	22.39	20.78	19.55	18.60	17.84	17.24	16.74	16.34	16.00	15.72	15.48	15.28	15.11	14.97
14.50	27.90	24.76	22.55	20.94	19.72	18.77	18.02	17.42	16.93	16.53	16.20	15.92	15.68	15.49	15.32	15.18
14.75	28.05	24.91	22.71	21.11	19.89	18.95	18.20	17.61	17.12	16.72	16.39	16.12	15.89	15.70	15.53	15.40
15.00	28.20	25.07	22.88	21.27	20.06	19.13	18.39	17.79	17.31	16.92	16.59	16.32	16.10	15.91	15.75	15.61
15.25	28.35	25.22	23.04	21.44	20.24	19.30	18.57	17.98	17.50	17.11	16.79	16.53	16.30	16.12	15.96	15.83
15.50	28.50	25.38	23.20	21.61	20.41	19.48	18.75	18.17	17.70	17.31	16.99	16.73	16.51	16.33	16.17	16.04
15.75	28.65	25.54	23.36	21.78	20.58	19.66	18.94	18.36	17.89	17.51	17.20	16.94	16.72	16.54	16.39	16.26
16.00	28.80	25.69	23.53	21.95	20.76	19.84	19.12	18.55	18.08	17.71	17.40	17.14	16.93	16.75	16.60	16.48
16.25	28.95	25.85	23.69	22.12	20.93	20.02	19.31	18.74	18.28	17.91	17.60	17.35	17.14	16.97	16.82	16.70
16.50	29.11	26.01	23.85	22.29	21.11	20.20	19.49	18.93	18.48	18.11	17.80	17.56	17.35	17.18	17.04	16.92
16.75	29.26	26.17	24.02	22.46	21.29	20.39	19.68	19.12	18.67	18.31	18.01	17.76	17.56	17.40	17.26	17.14
17.00	29.41	26.33	24.19	22.63	21.46	20.57	19.87	19.31	18.87	18.51	18.22	17.97	17.78	17.61	17.47	17.36
17.25	29.56	26.49	24.35	22.80	21.64	20.75	20.06	19.51	19.07	18.71	18.42	18.18	17.99	17.83	17.69	17.58
17.50	29.72	26.65	24.52	22.98	21.82	20.94	20.25	19.70	19.27	18.91	18.63	18.39	18.20	18.04	17.91	17.80
17.75	29.87	26.81	24.69	23.15	22.00	21.12	20.44	19.90	19.47	19.12	18.84	18.61	18.42	18.26	18.13	18.03
18.00	30.03	26.97	24.85	23.32	22.18	21.31	20.63	20.09	19.67	19.32	19.04	18.82	18.63	18.48	18.35	18.25
18.25	30.18	27.13	25.02	23.50	22.36	21.49	20.82	20.29	19.87	19.53	19.25	19.03	18.85	18.70	18.58	18.48
18.50	30.34	27.29	25.19	23.67	22.54	21.68	21.01	20.49	20.07	19.73	19.46	19.24	19.06	18.92	18.80	18.70
18.75	30.49	27.46	25.36	23.85	22.72	21.87	21.21	20.68	20.27	19.94	19.67	19.46	19.28	19.14	19.02	18.92
19.00	30.65	27.62	25.53	24.03	22.91	22.06	21.40	20.88	20.47	20.15	19.88	19.67	19.50	19.36	19.24	19.15
19.25	30.80	27.78	25.70	24.20	23.09	22.25	21.59	21.08	20.68	20.36	20.10	19.89	19.72	19.58	19.47	19.38
19.50	30.96	27.95	25.87	24.38	23.27	22.43	21.79	21.28	20.88	20.56	20.31	20.10	19.94	19.80	19.69	19.60
19.75	31.12	28.11	26.04	24.56	23.46	22.62	21.98	21.48	21.09	20.77	20.52	20.32	20.16	20.02	19.92	19.83
20.00	31.28	28.28	26.22	24.74	23.64	22.82	22.18	21.68	21.29	20.98	20.74	20.54	20.38	20.25	20.14	20.06
20.25	31.43	28.44	26.39	24.92	23.83	23.01	22.38	21.88	21.50	21.19	20.95	20.75	20.60	20.47	20.37	20.28
20.50	31.59	28.61	26.56	25.10	24.01	23.20	22.57	22.09	21.71	21.40	21.16	20.97	20.82	20.69	20.59	20.51
20.75	31.75	28.77	26.73	25.28	24.20	23.39	22.77	22.29	21.91	21.62	21.38	21.19	21.04	20.92	20.82	20.74

MONTHLY PAYMENT
IN ADVANCE

Description: This table shows the percent of the principal amount of a loan needed each year to pay off the loan when the actual payments are monthly and are paid in advance. Divide the percent by 12 to get the level monthly payment per $100 that includes both interest and principal.

Example: The Constant Annual Percent needed to pay off a 15%, 30 year loan if payments are made monthly and in advance is 14.99% Divide by 12 to get the actual monthly payment. The constant annual payment for a $50,000 loan is $7,495. The monthly payment is $624.59

INTEREST RATE	21 yr	22 yr	23 yr	24 yr	25 yr	26 yr	27 yr	28 yr	29 yr	30 yr	31 yr	32 yr	33 yr	34 yr	35 yr	40 yr
4.00	7.03	6.82	6.64	6.47	6.32	6.18	6.05	5.93	5.82	5.71	5.62	5.53	5.45	5.37	5.30	5.00
4.25	7.19	6.98	6.80	6.64	6.48	6.34	6.22	6.10	5.99	5.89	5.79	5.71	5.63	5.55	5.48	5.19
4.50	7.35	7.15	6.97	6.80	6.65	6.51	6.39	6.27	6.16	6.06	5.97	5.89	5.81	5.73	5.66	5.38
4.75	7.51	7.31	7.13	6.97	6.82	6.68	6.56	6.44	6.34	6.24	6.15	6.07	5.99	5.92	5.85	5.57
5.00	7.67	7.48	7.30	7.14	6.99	6.86	6.73	6.62	6.52	6.42	6.33	6.25	6.17	6.10	6.04	5.77
5.25	7.84	7.65	7.47	7.31	7.16	7.03	6.91	6.80	6.70	6.60	6.52	6.43	6.36	6.29	6.23	5.97
5.50	8.01	7.82	7.64	7.48	7.34	7.21	7.09	6.98	6.88	6.79	6.70	6.62	6.55	6.48	6.42	6.17
5.75	8.18	7.99	7.82	7.66	7.52	7.39	7.27	7.16	7.07	6.97	6.89	6.81	6.74	6.68	6.62	6.37
6.00	8.35	8.16	7.99	7.84	7.70	7.57	7.46	7.35	7.25	7.16	7.08	7.01	6.94	6.87	6.81	6.57
6.25	8.52	8.34	8.17	8.02	7.88	7.76	7.64	7.54	7.44	7.36	7.28	7.20	7.13	7.07	7.01	6.78
6.50	8.70	8.51	8.35	8.20	8.06	7.94	7.83	7.73	7.63	7.55	7.47	7.40	7.33	7.27	7.22	6.99
6.75	8.88	8.69	8.53	8.38	8.25	8.13	8.02	7.92	7.83	7.74	7.67	7.60	7.53	7.47	7.42	7.20
7.00	9.05	8.87	8.71	8.57	8.44	8.32	8.21	8.11	8.02	7.94	7.87	7.80	7.74	7.68	7.63	7.42
7.25	9.23	9.06	8.90	8.76	8.63	8.51	8.40	8.31	8.22	8.14	8.07	8.00	7.94	7.89	7.84	7.63
7.50	9.42	9.24	9.08	8.94	8.82	8.70	8.60	6.51	8.42	8.34	8.27	8.21	8.15	8.10	8.05	7.85
7.75	9.60	9.43	9.27	9.14	9.01	8.90	8.80	8.71	8.62	8.55	8.48	8.42	8.36	8.31	8.26	8.07
8.00	9.78	9.62	9.46	9.33	9.21	9.10	9.00	8.91	8.83	8.75	8.68	8.62	8.57	8.52	8.47	8.29
8.25	9.97	9.80	9.66	9.52	9.40	9.29	9.20	9.11	9.03	8.96	8.89	8.83	8.78	8.73	8.69	8.52
8.50	10.16	10.00	9.85	9.72	9.60	9.49	9.40	9.31	9.24	9.17	9.10	9.05	8.99	8.95	8.90	8.74
8.75	10.35	10.19	10.04	9.91	9.80	9.70	9.60	9.52	9.44	9.38	9.32	9.26	9.21	9.16	9.12	8.97
9.00	10.54	10.38	10.24	10.11	10.00	9.90	9.81	9.73	9.65	9.59	9.53	9.48	9.43	9.38	9.34	9.19
9.25	10.73	10.58	10.44	10.31	10.20	10.10	10.02	9.94	9.87	9.80	9.74	9.69	9.65	9.60	9.56	9.42
9.50	10.93	10.77	10.64	10.52	10.41	10.31	10.22	10.15	10.08	10.02	9.96	9.91	9.86	9.82	9.79	9.65
9.75	11.12	10.97	10.84	10.72	10.61	10.52	10.43	10.36	10.29	10.23	10.18	10.13	10.09	10.05	10.01	9.88
10.00	11.32	11.17	11.04	10.92	10.82	10.73	10.65	10.57	10.51	10.45	10.40	10.35	10.31	10.27	10.24	10.11
10.25	11.52	11.37	11.24	11.13	11.03	10.94	10.86	10.79	10.72	10.67	10.62	10.57	10.53	10.49	10.46	10.34
10.50	11.72	11.57	11.45	11.34	11.24	11.15	11.07	11.00	10.94	10.89	10.84	10.79	10.76	10.72	10.69	10.58
10.75	11.92	11.78	11.65	11.54	11.45	11.36	11.29	11.22	11.16	11.11	11.06	11.02	10.98	10.95	10.92	10.81
11.00	12.12	11.98	11.86	11.75	11.66	11.58	11.50	11.44	11.38	11.33	11.28	11.24	11.21	11.17	11.15	11.04
11.25	12.32	12.19	12.07	11.96	11.87	11.79	11.72	11.66	11.60	11.55	11.51	11.47	11.43	11.40	11.38	11.28
11.50	12.53	12.39	12.28	12.18	12.09	12.01	11.94	11.88	11.82	11.78	11.73	11.70	11.66	11.63	11.61	11.51
11.75	12.73	12.60	12.49	12.39	12.30	12.23	12.16	12.10	12.05	12.00	11.96	11.92	11.89	11.86	11.84	11.75
12.00	12.94	12.81	12.70	12.60	12.52	12.44	12.38	12.32	12.27	12.23	12.19	12.15	12.12	12.09	12.07	11.99
12.25	13.15	13.02	12.91	12.82	12.74	12.66	12.60	12.54	12.50	12.45	12.41	12.38	12.35	12.33	12.30	12.22
12.50	13.36	13.23	13.13	13.04	12.95	12.88	12.82	12.77	12.72	12.68	12.64	12.61	12.58	12.56	12.54	12.46
12.75	13.57	13.45	13.34	13.25	13.17	13.11	13.05	12.99	12.95	12.91	12.87	12.84	12.82	12.79	12.77	12.70
13.00	13.78	13.66	13.56	13.47	13.39	13.33	13.27	13.22	13.18	13.14	13.10	13.07	13.05	13.03	13.01	12.94
13.25	13.99	13.87	13.78	13.69	13.62	13.55	13.49	13.45	13.40	13.37	13.33	13.31	13.28	13.26	13.24	13.18
13.50	14.20	14.09	13.99	13.91	13.84	13.77	13.72	13.67	13.63	13.60	13.57	13.54	13.52	13.50	13.48	13.42
13.75	14.42	14.31	14.21	14.13	14.06	14.00	13.95	13.90	13.86	13.83	13.80	13.77	13.75	13.73	13.71	13.66
14.00	14.63	14.52	14.43	14.35	14.28	14.22	14.17	14.13	14.09	14.06	14.03	14.01	13.99	13.97	13.95	13.90
14.25	14.85	14.74	14.65	14.57	14.51	14.45	14.40	14.36	14.32	14.29	14.26	14.24	14.22	14.20	14.19	14.14
14.50	15.06	14.96	14.87	14.80	14.73	14.68	14.63	14.59	14.55	14.52	14.50	14.48	14.46	14.44	14.42	14.38
14.75	15.28	15.18	15.09	15.02	14.96	14.91	14.86	14.82	14.79	14.76	14.73	14.71	14.69	14.68	14.66	14.62
15.00	15.50	15.40	15.32	15.25	15.19	15.13	15.09	15.05	15.02	14.99	14.97	14.95	14.93	14.91	14.90	14.86
15.25	15.72	15.62	15.54	15.47	15.41	15.36	15.32	15.28	15.25	15.23	15.20	15.18	15.17	15.15	15.14	15.10
15.50	15.93	15.84	15.76	15.70	15.64	15.59	15.55	15.52	15.49	15.46	15.44	15.42	15.40	15.39	15.38	15.34
15.75	16.16	16.06	15.99	15.92	15.87	15.82	15.78	15.75	15.72	15.69	15.67	15.66	15.64	15.63	15.62	15.58
16.00	16.38	16.29	16.21	16.15	16.10	16.05	16.01	15.98	15.95	15.93	15.91	15.89	15.88	15.87	15.86	15.82
16.25	16.60	16.51	16.44	16.38	16.33	16.28	16.25	16.21	16.19	16.17	16.15	16.13	16.12	16.10	16.09	16.06
16.50	16.82	16.74	16.67	16.61	16.56	16.51	16.48	16.45	16.42	16.40	16.38	16.37	16.35	16.34	16.33	16.30
16.75	17.04	16.96	16.89	16.84	16.79	16.75	16.71	16.68	16.66	16.64	16.62	16.61	16.59	16.58	16.57	16.55
17.00	17.27	17.19	17.12	17.06	17.02	16.98	16.95	16.92	16.89	16.87	16.86	16.84	16.83	16.82	16.81	16.79
17.25	17.49	17.41	17.35	17.29	17.25	17.21	17.18	17.15	17,13	17.11	17.10	17.08	17.07	17.06	17.05	17.03
17.50	17.71	17.64	17.58	17.52	17.48	17.44	17.41	17.39	17.37	17.35	17.33	17.32	17.31	17.30	17.29	17.27
17.75	17.94	17.87	17.81	17.75	17.71	17.68	17.65	17.62	17.60	17.59	17.57	17.56	17.55	17.54	17.53	17.51
18.00	18.17	18.09	18.04	17.99	17.95	17.91	17.88	17.86	17.84	17.82	17.81	17.80	17.79	17.78	17.77	17.75
18.25	18.39	18.32	18.26	18.22	18.18	18.15	18.12	18.10	18.08	18.06	18.05	18.04	18.03	18.02	18.01	17.99
18.50	18.62	18.55	18.50	18.45	18.41	18.38	18.35	18.33	18.31	18.30	18.29	18.28	18.27	18.26	18.25	18.24
18.75	18.85	18.78	18.73	18.68	18.64	18.61	18.59	18.57	18.55	18.54	18.52	18.51	18.51	18.50	18.49	18.48
19.00	19.07	19.01	18.96	18.91	18.88	18.85	18.82	18.80	18.79	18.77	18.76	18.75	18.75	18.74	18.73	18.72
19.25	19.30	19.24	19.19	19.15	19.11	19.08	19.06	19.04	19.03	19.01	19.00	18.99	18.99	18.98	18.97	18.96
19.50	19.53	19.47	19.42	19.38	19.35	19.32	19.30	19.28	19.26	19.25	19.24	19.23	19.23	19.22	19.22	19.20
19.75	19.76	19.70	19.65	19.61	19.58	19.56	19.53	19.52	19.50	19.49	19.48	19.47	19.47	19.46	19.46	19.44
20.00	19.99	19.93	19.88	19.85	19.82	19.79	19.77	19.75	19.74	19.73	19.72	19.71	19.71	19.70	19.70	19.68
20.25	20.22	20.16	20.12	20.08	20.05	20.03	20.01	19.99	19.98	19.97	19.96	19.95	19.95	19.94	19.94	19.93
20.50	20.45	20.39	20.35	20.32	20.29	20.26	20.24	20.23	20.22	20.21	20.20	20.19	20.19	20.18	20.18	20.17
20.75	20.68	20.63	20.58	20.55	20.52	20.50	20.48	20.47	20.45	20.44	20.44	20.43	20.43	20.42	20.42	20.41

(continued)

TABLE 2 Constant Annual Percentage to Amortize Mortgage

(continued)

QUARTERLY PAYMENT
IN ADVANCE

Description: This table shows the percent of the principal amount of a loan needed each year to pay off the loan when the actual payments are quarterly and are paid in advance. Divide the percent by 4 to get the level quarterly payment per $100 that includes both interest and principal.

Example: The Constant Annual Percent needed to pay off a 15%, 30 year loan if payments are made quarterly and in advance is 14.64%. Divide by 4 to get the actual quarterly payment. The constant annual payment for a $50,000 loan is $7,320. The quarterly payment is $1,830.00.

INTEREST RATE	5 yr	6 yr	7 yr	8 yr	9 yr	10 yr	11 yr	12 yr	13 yr	14 yr	15 yr	16 yr	17 yr	18 yr	19 yr	20 yr
4.00	21.95	18.65	16.29	14.53	13.16	12.07	11.18	10.43	9.81	9.28	8.81	8.41	8.06	7.75	7.47	7.22
4.25	22.08	18.78	16.42	14.66	13.29	12.20	11.31	10.57	9.95	9.42	8.96	8.56	8.21	7.90	7.62	7.37
4.50	22.20	18.90	16.55	14.79	13.43	12.34	11.45	10.72	10.09	9.56	9.11	8.71	8.36	8.05	7.78	7.53
4.75	22.33	19.03	16.68	14.93	13.56	12.48	11.59	10.86	10.24	9.71	9.25	8.86	8.51	8.20	7.93	7.69
5.00	22.45	19.16	16.81	15.06	13.70	12.62	11.73	11.00	10.38	9.86	9.40	9.01	8.66	8.36	8.09	7.85
5.25	22.58	19.29	16.95	15.19	13.84	12.76	11.87	11.14	10.53	10.01	9.55	9.16	8.82	8.52	8.25	8.01
5.50	22.71	19.42	17.08	15.33	13.97	12.90	12.02	11.29	10.68	10.15	9.71	9.32	8.97	8.67	8.41	8.17
5.75	22.83	19.55	17.21	15.47	14.11	13.04	12.16	11.43	10.82	10.30	9.86	9.47	9.13	8.83	8.57	8.33
6.00	22.96	19.68	17.35	15.60	14.25	13.18	12.30	11.58	10.97	10.46	10.01	9.63	9.29	8.99	8.73	8.50
6.25	23.09	19.81	17.48	15.74	14.39	13.32	12.45	11.73	11.12	10.61	10.17	9.78	9.45	9.16	8.90	8.66
6.50	23.21	19.94	17.61	15.88	14.53	13.46	12.60	11.88	11.28	10.76	10.32	9.94	9.61	9.32	9.06	8.83
6.75	23.34	20.07	17.75	16.01	14.67	13.61	12.74	12.03	11.43	10.92	10.48	10.10	9.77	9.48	9.23	9.00
7.00	23.47	20.21	17.88	16.15	14.82	13.75	12.89	12.18	11.58	11.07	10.64	10.26	9.94	9.65	9.40	9.17
7.25	23.60	20.34	18.02	16.29	14.96	13.90	13.04	12.33	11.74	11.23	10.80	10.43	10.10	9.82	9.57	9.35
7.50	23.73	20.47	18.16	16.43	15.10	14.05	13.19	12.48	11.89	11.39	10.96	10.59	10.27	9.99	9.74	9.52
7.75	23.86	20.60	18.29	16.57	15.25	14.19	13.34	12.64	12.05	11.55	11.12	10.76	10.44	10.16	9.91	9.70
8.00	23.99	20.74	18.43	16.72	15.39	14.34	13.49	12.79	12.20	11.71	11.29	10.92	10.61	10.33	10.09	9.87
8.25	24.12	20.87	18.57	16.86	15.54	14.49	13.64	12.95	12.36	11.87	11.45	11.09	10.78	10.50	10.26	10.05
8.50	24.25	21.01	18.71	17.00	15.68	14.64	13.80	13.10	12.52	12.03	11.62	11.26	10.95	10.68	10.44	10.23
8.75	24.38	21.14	18.85	17.14	15.83	14.79	13.95	13.26	12.68	12.20	11.78	11.43	11.12	10.85	10.62	10.41
9.00	24.51	21.28	18.99	17.29	15.98	14.94	14.10	13.42	12.84	12.36	11.95	11.60	11.29	11.03	10.80	10.59
9.25	24.64	21.41	19.13	17.43	16.12	15.09	14.26	13.57	13.01	12.53	12.12	11.77	11.47	11.21	10.98	10.78
9.50	24.77	21.55	19.27	17.57	16.27	15.24	14.41	13.73	13.17	12.69	12.29	11.94	11.64	11.38	11.16	10.96
9.75	24.91	21.69	19.41	17.72	16.42	15.40	14.57	13.89	13.33	12.86	12.46	12.12	11.82	11.56	11.34	11.15
10.00	25.04	21.82	19.55	17.87	16.57	15.55	14.73	14.06	13.50	13.03	12.63	12.29	12.00	11.75	11.52	11.33
10.25	25.17	21.96	19.69	18.01	16.72	15.71	14.89	14.22	13.66	13.20	12.80	12.47	12.18	11.93	11.71	11.52
10.50	25.30	22.10	19.84	18.16	16.87	15.86	15.05	14.38	13.83	13.37	12.98	12.64	12.36	12.11	11.90	11.71
10.75	25.44	22.24	19.98	18.31	17.02	16.02	15.21	14.54	14.00	13.54	13.15	12.82	12.54	12.29	12.08	11.90
11.00	25.57	22.38	20.12	18.45	17.18	16.17	15.37	14.71	14.17	13.71	13.33	13.00	12.72	12.48	12.27	12.09
11.25	25.70	22.52	20.27	18.60	17.33	16.33	15.53	14.87	14.33	13.88	13.50	13.18	12.90	12.67	12.46	12.28
11.50	25.84	22.66	20.41	18.75	17.48	16.49	15.69	15.04	14.50	14.06	13.68	13.36	13.09	12.85	12.65	12.48
11.75	25.97	22.80	20.56	18.90	17.64	16.65	15.85	15.21	14.68	14.23	13.86	13.54	13.27	13.04	12.84	12.67
12.00	26.11	22.94	20.70	19.05	17.79	16.81	16.02	15.38	14.85	14.41	14.04	13.72	13.46	13.23	13.03	12.86
12.25	26.24	23.08	20.85	19.20	17.95	16.97	16.18	15.54	15.02	14.58	14.22	13.91	13.64	13.42	13.23	13.06
12.50	26.38	23.22	20.99	19.35	18.10	17.13	16.35	15.71	15.19	14.76	14.40	14.09	13.83	13.61	13.42	13.26
12.75	26.51	23.36	21.14	19.51	18.26	17.29	16.51	15.88	15.37	14.94	14.58	14.28	14.02	13.80	13.61	13.45
13.00	26.65	23.50	21.29	19.66	18.42	17.45	16.68	16.05	15.54	15.12	14.76	14.46	14.21	13.99	13.81	13.65
13.25	26.79	23.64	21.43	19.81	18.58	17.61	16.84	16.22	15.72	15.30	14.94	14.65	14.40	14.19	14.01	13.85
13.50	26.92	23.79	21.58	19.96	18.73	17.77	17.01	16.40	15.89	15.48	15.13	14.84	14.59	14.38	14.20	14.05
13.75	27.06	23.93	21.73	20.12	18.89	17.94	17.18	16.57	16.07	15.66	15.31	15.02	14.78	14.58	14.40	14.25
14.00	27.20	24.07	21.88	20.27	19.05	18.10	17.35	16.74	16.25	15.84	15.50	15.21	14.97	14.77	14.60	14.45
14.25	27.34	24.22	22.03	20.43	19.21	18.27	17.52	16.92	16.42	16.02	15.68	15.40	15.17	14.97	14.80	14.66
14.50	27.47	24.36	22.18	20.58	19.37	18.43	17.69	17.09	16.60	16.20	15.87	15.59	15.36	15.17	15.00	14.86
14.75	27.61	24.50	22.33	20.74	19.53	18.60	17.86	17.27	16.78	16.39	16.06	15.79	15.56	15.36	15.20	15.06
15.00	27.75	24.65	22.48	20.89	19.69	18.77	18.03	17.44	16.96	16.57	16.25	15.98	15.75	15.56	15.40	15.27
15.25	27.89	24.79	22.63	21.05	19.86	18.93	18.20	17.62	17.14	16.76	16.44	16.17	15.95	15.76	15.60	15.47
15.50	28.03	24.94	22.78	21.21	20.02	19.10	18.38	17.80	17.33	16.94	16.62	16.36	16.14	15.96	15.81	15.68
15.75	28.17	25.08	22.93	21.37	20.18	19.27	18.55	17.97	17.51	17.13	16.81	16.56	16.34	16.16	16.01	15.88
16.00	28.31	25.23	23.09	21.52	20.35	19.44	18.72	18.15	17.69	17.31	17.01	16.75	16.54	16.36	16.21	16.09
16.25	28.45	25.38	23.24	21.68	20.51	19.61	18.90	18.33	17.87	17.50	17.20	16.95	16.74	16.56	16.42	16.29
16.50	28.59	25.52	23.39	21.84	20.67	19.78	19.07	18.51	18.06	17.69	17.39	17.14	16.94	16.76	16.62	16.50
16.75	28.73	25.67	23.55	22.00	20.84	19.95	19.25	18.69	18.24	17.88	17.58	17.34	17.13	16.97	16.83	16.71
17.00	28.87	25.82	23.70	22.16	21.01	20.12	19.42	18.87	18.43	18.07	17.77	17.53	17.33	17.17	17.03	16.92
17.25	29.01	25.97	23.85	22.32	21.17	20.29	19.60	19.05	18.61	18.26	17.97	17.73	17.53	17.37	17.24	17.13
17.50	29.15	26.11	24.01	22.48	21.34	20.46	19.78	19.23	18.80	18.45	18.16	17.93	17.74	17.58	17.44	17.34
17.75	29.29	26.26	24.16	22.64	21.50	20.63	19.95	19.42	18.99	18.64	18.36	18.13	17.94	17.78	17.65	17.54
18.00	29.43	26.41	24.32	22.80	21.67	20.81	20.13	19.60	19.17	18.83	18.55	18.33	18.14	17.99	17.86	17.75
18.25	29.57	26.56	24.47	22.97	21.84	20.98	20.31	19.78	19.36	19.02	18.75	18.52	18.34	18.19	18.07	17.96
18.50	29.72	26.71	24.63	23.13	22.01	21.15	20.49	19.97	19.55	19.21	18.94	18.72	18.54	18.40	18.28	18.18
18.75	29.86	26.86	24.79	23.29	22.18	21.33	20.67	20.15	19.74	19.41	19.14	18.92	18.75	18.60	18.48	18.39
19.00	30.00	27.01	24.94	23.45	22.35	21.50	20.85	20.33	19.93	19.60	19.34	19.12	18.95	18.81	18.69	18.60
19.25	30.14	27.16	25.10	23.62	22.52	21.68	21.03	20.52	20.12	19.79	19.54	19.33	19.15	19.02	18.90	18.81
19.50	30.29	27.31	25.26	23.78	22.69	21.85	21.21	20.71	20.31	19.99	19.73	19.53	19.36	19.22	19.11	19.02
19.75	30.43	27.46	25.42	23.95	22.86	22.03	21.39	20.89	20.50	20.18	19.93	19.73	19.56	19.43	19.32	19.23
20.00	30.57	27.61	25.58	24.11	23.03	22.21	21.57	21.08	20.69	20.38	20.13	19.93	19.77	19.64	19.53	19.44
20.25	30.72	27.76	25.73	24.28	23.20	22.38	21.76	21.27	20.88	20.57	20.33	20.13	19.97	19.85	19.74	19.66
20.50	30.86	27.92	25.89	24.44	23.37	22.56	21.94	21.45	21.07	20.77	20.53	20.34	20.18	20.05	19.95	19.87
20.75	31.01	28.07	26.05	24.61	23.54	22.74	22.12	21.64	21.26	20.97	20.73	20.54	20.39	20.26	20.16	20.08

QUARTERLY PAYMENT
IN ADVANCE

Description: This table shows the percent of the principal amount of a loan needed each year to pay off the loan when the actual payments are quarterly and are paid in advance. Divide the percent by 4 to get the level quarterly payment per $100 that includes both interest and principal.

Example: The Constant Annual Percent needed to pay off a 15%, 30 year loan if payments are made quarterly and in advance is 14.64%. Divide by 4 to get the actual quarterly payment. The constant annual payment for a $50,000 loan is $7,320. The quarterly payment is $1,830.00.

INTEREST RATE	21 yr	22 yr	23 yr	24 yr	25 yr	26 yr	27 yr	28 yr	29 yr	30 yr	31 yr	32 yr	33 yr	34 yr	35 yr	40 yr
4.00	7.00	6.79	6.61	6.44	6.29	6.15	6.02	5.90	5.79	5.69	5.59	5.50	5.42	5.35	5.27	4.98
4.25	7.15	6.95	6.77	6.60	6.45	6.31	6.18	6.07	5.96	5.86	5.76	5.68	5.60	5.52	5.45	5.16
4.50	7.31	7.11	6.93	6.76	6.61	6.48	6.35	6.23	6.13	6.03	5.94	5.85	5.77	5.70	5.63	5.35
4.75	7.47	7.27	7.09	6.93	6.78	6.64	6.52	6.41	6.30	6.20	6.11	6.03	5.95	5.88	5.81	5.54
5.00	7.63	7.43	7.26	7.09	6.95	6.81	6.69	6.58	6.47	6.38	6.29	6.21	6.13	6.06	6.00	5.73
5.25	7.79	7.60	7.42	7.26	7.12	6.99	6.86	6.75	6.65	6.56	6.47	6.39	6.32	6.25	6.18	5.92
5.50	7.95	7.76	7.59	7.43	7.29	7.16	7.04	6.93	6.83	6.74	6.65	6.57	6.50	6.43	6.37	6.12
5.75	8.12	7.93	7.76	7.60	7.46	7.33	7.22	7.11	7.01	6.92	6.84	6.76	6.69	6.62	6.56	6.32
6.00	8.29	8.10	7.93	7.78	7.64	7.51	7.40	7.29	7.19	7.11	7.02	6.95	6.88	6.82	6.76	6.52
6.25	8.46	8.27	8.10	7.95	7.82	7.69	7.58	7.47	7.38	7.29	7.21	7.14	7.07	7.01	6.95	6.72
6.50	8.63	8.44	8.28	8.13	8.00	7.87	7.76	7.66	7.57	7.48	7.40	7.33	7.27	7.21	7.15	6.93
6.75	8.80	8.62	8.46	8.31	8.18	8.06	7.95	7.85	7.76	7.67	7.60	7.53	7.46	7.40	7.35	7.13
7.00	8.97	8.79	8.63	8.49	8.36	8.24	8.13	8.04	7.95	7.86	7.79	7.72	7.66	7.60	7.55	7.34
7.25	9.15	8.97	8.81	8.67	8.54	8.43	8.32	8.23	8.14	8.06	7.99	7.92	7.86	7.80	7.75	7.55
7.50	9.32	9.15	8.99	8.85	8.73	8.61	8.51	8.42	8.33	8.25	8.18	8.12	8.06	8.01	7.96	7.76
7.75	9.50	9.33	9.18	9.04	8.92	8.80	8.70	8.61	8.53	8.45	8.38	8.32	8.26	8.21	8.16	7.98
8.00	9.68	9.51	9.36	9.23	9.10	8.99	8.90	8.81	8.72	8.65	8.58	8.52	8.47	8.42	8.37	8.19
8.25	9.86	9.70	9.55	9.41	9.29	9.19	9.09	9.00	8.92	8.85	8.79	8.73	8.67	8.62	8.58	8.41
8.50	10.04	9.88	9.73	9.60	9.49	9.38	9.29	9.20	9.12	9.05	8.99	8.93	8.88	8.83	8.79	8.63
8.75	10.23	10.07	9.92	9.79	9.68	9.58	9.48	9.40	9.33	9.26	9.20	9.14	9.09	9.04	9.00	8.84
9.00	10.41	10.25	10.11	9.99	9.87	9.77	9.68	9.60	9.53	9.46	9.40	9.35	9.30	9.26	9.22	9.06
9.25	10.60	10.44	10.30	10.18	10.07	9.97	9.88	9.80	9.73	9.67	9.61	9.56	9.51	9.47	9.43	9.29
9.50	10.79	10.63	10.50	10.37	10.27	10.17	10.08	10.01	9.94	9.87	9.82	9.77	9.72	9.68	9.65	9.51
9.75	10.97	10.82	10.69	10.57	10.46	10.37	10.29	10.21	10.14	10.08	10.03	9.98	9.94	9.90	9.86	9.73
10.00	11.16	11.01	10.88	10.77	10.66	10.57	10.49	10.42	10.35	10.29	10.24	10.19	10.15	10.11	10.08	9.95
10.25	11.35	11.21	11.08	10.96	10.86	10.77	10.69	10.62	10.56	10.50	10.45	10.41	10.37	10.33	10.30	10.18
10.50	11.55	11.40	11.28	11.16	11.07	10.98	10.90	10.83	10.77	10.71	10.67	10.62	10.58	10.55	10.52	10.40
10.75	11.74	11.60	11.47	11.36	11.27	11.18	11.11	11.04	10.98	10.93	10.88	10.84	10.80	10.77	10.74	10.63
11.00	11.93	11.79	11.67	11.57	11.47	11.39	11.31	11.25	11.19	11.14	11.09	11.05	11.02	10.98	10.96	10.85
11.25	12.13	11.99	11.87	11.77	11.68	11.59	11.52	11.46	11.40	11.35	11.31	11.27	11.24	11.20	11.18	11.08
11.50	12.32	12.19	12.07	11.97	11.88	11.80	11.73	11.67	11.62	11.57	11.53	11.49	11.46	11.43	11.40	11.30
11.75	12.52	12.39	12.27	12.18	12.09	12.01	11.94	11.88	11.83	11.78	11.74	11.71	11.68	11.65	11.62	11.53
12.00	12.72	12.59	12.48	12.38	12.29	12.22	12.15	12.10	12.05	12.00	11.96	11.93	11.90	11.87	11.84	11.76
12.25	12.92	12.79	12.68	12.59	12.50	12.43	12.37	12.31	12.26	12.22	12.18	12.15	12.12	12.09	12.07	11.99
12.50	13.11	12.99	12.89	12.79	12.71	12.64	12.58	12.53	12.48	12.44	12.40	12.37	12.34	12.31	12.29	12.22
12.75	13.32	13.19	13.09	13.00	12.92	12.85	12.79	12.74	12.69	12.65	12.62	12.59	12.56	12.54	12.52	12.44
13.00	13.52	13.40	13.30	13.21	13.13	13.07	13.01	12.96	12.91	12.87	12.84	12.81	12.78	12.76	12.74	12.67
13.25	13.72	13.60	13.50	13.42	13.34	13.28	13.22	13.17	13.13	13.09	13.06	13.03	13.01	12.98	12.97	12.90
13.50	13.92	13.81	13.71	13.63	13.55	13.49	13.44	13.39	13.35	13.31	13.28	13.25	13.23	13.21	13.19	13.13
13.75	14.12	14.01	13.92	13.84	13.77	13.71	13.65	13.61	13.57	13.53	13.50	13.48	13.45	13.43	13.42	13.36
14.00	14.33	14.22	14.13	14.05	13.98	13.92	13.87	13.82	13.79	13.75	13.72	13.70	13.68	13.66	13.64	13.59
14.25	14.53	14.43	14.34	14.26	14.19	14.14	14.09	14.04	14.01	13.97	13.95	13.92	13.90	13.88	13.87	13.82
14.50	14.74	14.64	14.55	14.47	14.41	14.35	14.30	14.26	14.23	14.20	14.17	14.15	14.13	14.11	14.09	14.04
14.75	14.94	14.84	14.76	14.68	14.62	14.57	14.52	14.48	14.45	14.42	14.39	14.37	14.35	14.33	14.32	14.27
15.00	15.15	15.05	14.97	14.90	14.84	14.78	14.74	14.70	14.67	14.64	14.61	14.59	14.58	14.56	14.55	14.50
15.25	15.36	15.26	15.18	15.11	15.05	15.00	14.96	14.92	14.89	14.86	14.84	14.82	14.80	14.79	14.77	14.73
15.50	15.57	15.47	15.39	15.33	15.27	15.22	15.18	15.14	15.11	15.08	15.06	15.04	15.03	15.01	15.00	14.96
15.75	15.77	15.68	15.61	15.54	15.48	15.44	15.40	15.36	15.33	15.31	15.29	15.27	15.25	15.24	15.23	15.19
16.00	15.98	15.89	15.82	15.75	15.70	15.65	15.62	15.58	15.55	15.53	15.51	15.49	15.48	15.46	15.45	15.42
16.25	16.19	16.10	16.03	15.97	15.92	15.87	15.84	15.80	15.78	15.75	15.73	15.72	15.70	15.69	15.68	15.65
16.50	16.40	16.32	16.25	16.19	16.13	16.09	16.06	16.02	16.00	15.98	15.96	15.94	15.93	15.92	15.91	15.88
16.75	16.61	16.53	16.46	16.40	16.35	16.31	16.28	16.25	16.22	16.20	16.18	16.17	16.15	16.14	16.13	16.10
17.00	16.82	16.74	16.67	16.62	16.57	16.53	16.50	16.47	16.44	16.42	16.41	16.39	16.38	16.37	16.36	16.33
17.25	17.03	16.95	16.89	16.83	16.79	16.75	16.72	16.69	16.67	16.65	16.63	16.62	16.60	16.60	16.59	16.56
17.50	17.24	17.17	17.10	17.05	17.01	16.97	16.94	16.91	16.89	16.87	16.85	16.84	16.83	16.82	16.81	16.79
17.75	17.46	17.38	17.32	17.27	17.22	17.19	17.16	17.13	17.11	17.09	17.08	17.07	17.06	17.05	17.04	17.02
18.00	17.67	17.60	17.54	17.49	17.44	17.41	17.38	17.36	17.33	17.32	17.30	17.29	17.28	17.27	17.27	17.24
18.25	17.88	17.81	17.75	17.70	17.66	17.63	17.60	17.58	17.56	17.54	17.53	17.52	17.51	17.50	17.49	17.47
18.50	18.09	18.02	17.97	17.92	17.88	17.85	17.82	17.80	17.78	17.77	17.75	17.74	17.73	17.73	17.72	17.70
18.75	18.31	18.24	18.18	18.14	18.10	18.07	18.04	18.02	18.00	17.99	17.98	17.97	17.96	17.95	17.94	17.93
19.00	18.52	18.45	18.40	18.36	18.32	18.29	18.27	18.24	18.23	18.21	18.20	18.19	18.18	18.18	18.17	18.15
19.25	18.73	18.67	18.62	18.57	18.54	18.51	18.49	18.47	18.45	18.44	18.43	18.42	18.41	18.40	18.40	18.38
19.50	18.95	18.88	18.83	18.79	18.76	18.73	18.71	18.69	18.67	18.66	18.65	18.64	18.63	18.63	18.62	18.61
19.75	19.16	19.10	19.05	19.01	18.98	18.95	18.93	18.91	18.90	18.88	18.87	18.87	18.86	18.85	18.85	18.83
20.00	19.37	19.32	19.27	19.23	19.20	19.17	19.15	19.13	19.12	19.11	19.10	19.09	19.08	19.08	19.07	19.06
20.25	19.59	19.53	19.49	19.45	19.42	19.39	19.37	19.36	19.34	19.33	19.32	19.31	19.31	19.30	19.30	19.29
20.50	19.80	19.75	19.70	19.67	19.64	19.61	19.59	19.58	19.56	19.55	19.55	19.54	19.53	19.53	19.52	19.51
20.75	20.02	19.96	19.92	19.89	19.86	19.83	19.82	19.80	19.79	19.78	19.77	19.76	19.76	19.75	19.75	19.74

Source: Thorndike Encyclopedia of Banking and Financial Tables (rev. ed. 1980)

TABLE 3 Price of Mortgage to Obtain Specified Yield

8.00 %

MONTHLY PAYMENT MORTGAGE

Description: This table shows the price to pay for a mortgage at the yield rate. The yield is to maturity.

Example: The price of a 8.00%, 16 year mortgage to yield 8.00% to maturity is $100.00.

	YEARS TO MATURITY															
YIELD	1 yr	2 yr	3 yr	4 yr	5 yr	6 yr	7 yr	8 yr	9 yr	10 yr	11 yr	12 yr	13 yr	14 yr	15 yr	16 yr
0.0	104.39	108.55	112.81	117.18	121.66	126.24	130.92	135.71	140.60	145.59	150.68	155.87	161.16	166.54	172.02	177.59
1.00	103.82	107.42	111.09	114.82	118.62	122.48	126.40	130.37	134.41	138.50	142.64	146.83	151.06	155.35	159.68	164.04
2.00	103.26	106.32	109.40	112.53	115.68	118.87	122.08	125.32	128.58	131.86	135.16	138.48	141.81	145.15	148.51	151.87
3.00	102.71	105.23	107.75	110.29	112.84	115.40	117.96	120.52	123.09	125.65	128.21	130.76	133.31	135.85	138.38	140.90
4.00	102.16	104.15	106.14	108.12	110.10	112.07	114.03	115.98	117.91	119.84	121.74	123.63	125.51	127.36	129.20	131.01
4.25	102.02	103.88	105.74	107.59	109.43	111.26	113.07	114.88	116.67	118.44	120.20	121.94	123.66	125.36	127.03	128.69
4.50	101.89	103.62	105.34	107.06	108.76	110.45	112.13	113.79	115.44	117.07	118.68	120.27	121.84	123.39	124.92	126.43
4.75	101.75	103.35	104.95	106.53	108.10	109.66	111.20	112.72	114.23	115.72	117.19	118.64	120.07	121.48	122.86	124.22
5.00	101.61	103.09	104.56	106.01	107.45	108.87	110.28	111.66	113.04	114.39	115.72	117.04	118.33	119.60	120.85	122.07
5.25	101.48	102.83	104.17	105.49	106.80	108.09	109.36	110.62	111.86	113.08	114.28	115.46	116.62	117.76	118.88	119.98
5.50	101.34	102.57	103.78	104.97	106.15	107.32	108.46	109.59	110.70	111.80	112.87	113.92	114.95	115.97	116.96	117.93
5.75	101.21	102.31	103.39	104.46	105.51	106.55	107.57	108.58	109.56	110.53	111.48	112.41	113.32	114.21	115.08	115.93
6.00	101.07	102.05	103.01	103.95	104.88	105.79	106.69	107.57	108.44	109.28	110.11	110.92	111.72	112.49	113.25	113.99
6.25	100.94	101.79	102.62	103.45	104.25	105.05	105.82	106.58	107.33	108.06	108.77	109.47	110.15	110.81	111.46	112.09
6.50	100.80	101.53	102.24	102.94	103.63	104.30	104.96	105.61	106.24	106.85	107.45	108.04	108.61	109.16	109.71	110.23
6.75	100.67	101.27	101.86	102.44	103.01	103.57	104.11	104.64	105.16	105.66	106.16	106.63	107.10	107.55	107.99	108.42
7.00	100.53	101.02	101.49	101.95	102.40	102.84	103.27	103.69	104.10	104.50	104.88	105.26	105.62	105.98	106.32	106.66
7.25	100.40	100.76	101.11	101.46	101.79	102.12	102.44	102.75	103.05	103.34	103.63	103.91	104.18	104.44	104.69	104.93
7.50	100.27	100.51	100.74	100.97	101.19	101.41	101.62	101.82	102.02	102.21	102.40	102.58	102.76	102.93	103.09	103.25
7.75	100.13	100.25	100.37	100.48	100.59	100.70	100.80	100.90	101.00	101.10	101.19	101.28	101.36	101.45	101.53	101.60
8.00	100.00	100.00	100.00	100.00	100.00	100.00	100.00	100.00	100.00	100.00	100.00	100.00	100.00	100.00	100.00	100.00
8.25	99.87	99.75	99.63	99.52	99.41	99.31	99.21	99.11	99.01	98.92	98.83	98.75	98.66	98.58	98.51	98.43
8.50	99.73	99.50	99.27	99.05	98.83	98.62	98.42	98.23	98.04	97.86	97.68	97.51	97.35	97.20	97.05	96.90
8.75	99.60	99.25	98.90	98.57	98.25	97.94	97.64	97.35	97.08	96.81	96.55	96.30	96.07	95.84	95.62	95.41
9.00	99.47	99.00	98.54	98.10	97.68	97.27	96.87	96.49	96.13	95.78	95.44	95.12	94.81	94.51	94.22	93.95
9.25	99.34	98.75	98.18	97.64	97.11	96.60	96.11	95.65	95.20	94.76	94.35	93.95	93.57	93.20	92.85	92.52
9.50	99.21	98.50	97.83	97.17	96.55	95.94	95.36	94.81	94.27	93.76	93.27	92.80	92.36	91.93	91.52	91.13
9.75	99.08	98.26	97.47	96.71	95.99	95.29	94.62	93.98	93.37	92.78	92.22	91.68	91.17	90.68	90.21	89.76
10.00	98.95	98.01	97.12	96.26	95.43	94.64	93.89	93.16	92.47	91.81	91.18	90.58	90.00	89.45	88.93	88.43
10.25	98.81	97.77	96.76	95.80	94.88	94.00	93.16	92.36	91.59	90.86	90.16	89.49	88.86	88.25	87.68	87.13
10.50	98.68	97.52	96.41	95.35	94.34	93.37	92.44	91.56	90.72	89.92	89.15	88.43	87.73	87.08	86.45	85.86
10.75	98.55	97.28	96.06	94.90	93.79	92.74	91.73	90.77	89.86	88.99	88.16	87.38	86.63	85.93	85.25	84.62
11.00	98.42	97.04	95.72	94.46	93.26	92.11	91.03	89.99	89.01	88.08	87.19	86.35	85.55	84.80	84.08	83.40
11.25	98.29	96.80	95.37	94.01	92.72	91.50	90.33	89.23	88.18	87.18	86.24	85.34	84.49	83.69	82.93	82.21
11.50	98.16	96.56	95.03	93.58	92.20	90.89	89.65	88.47	87.35	86.30	85.29	84.35	83.45	82.61	81.81	81.05
11.75	98.04	96.32	94.69	93.14	91.67	90.28	88.97	87.72	86.54	85.42	84.37	83.37	82.43	81.54	80.70	79.91
12.00	97.91	96.08	94.35	92.71	91.15	89.68	88.29	86.98	85.74	84.57	83.46	82.41	81.43	80.50	79.63	78.80
12.25	97.78	95.84	94.01	92.27	90.64	89.09	87.63	86.25	84.95	83.72	82.56	81.47	80.45	79.48	78.57	77.71
12.50	97.65	95.60	93.67	91.85	90.13	88.50	86.97	85.53	84.17	82.89	81.68	80.55	79.48	78.48	77.54	76.65
12.75	97.52	95.37	93.34	91.42	89.62	87.92	86.32	84.81	83.40	82.07	80.82	79.64	78.53	77.50	76.52	75.61
13.00	97.39	95.13	93.00	91.00	89.11	87.34	85.68	84.11	82.64	81.26	79.96	78.75	77.60	76.53	75.53	74.59
13.25	97.26	94.90	92.67	90.58	88.62	86.77	85.04	83.42	81.89	80.46	79.12	77.87	76.69	75.59	74.56	73.59
13.50	97.14	94.66	92.34	90.16	88.12	86.21	84.41	82.73	81.15	79.68	78.30	77.00	75.79	74.66	73.61	72.62
13.75	97.01	94.43	92.01	89.75	87.63	85.64	83.79	82.05	80.42	78.90	77.48	76.15	74.91	73.76	72.67	71.66
14.00	96.88	94.20	91.69	89.34	87.14	85.09	83.17	81.38	79.70	78.14	76.68	75.32	74.05	72.86	71.76	70.73
14.25	96.76	93.97	91.36	88.93	86.66	84.54	82.56	80.72	79.00	77.39	75.89	74.50	73.20	71.99	70.86	69.81
14.50	96.63	93.74	91.04	88.52	86.18	83.99	81.96	80.06	78.30	76.65	75.12	73.69	72.37	71.13	69.99	68.92
14.75	96.50	93.51	90.72	88.12	85.70	83.45	81.36	79.41	77.60	75.92	74.36	72.90	71.55	70.29	69.12	68.04
15.00	96.38	93.28	90.40	87.72	85.23	82.92	80.77	78.78	76.92	75.20	73.60	72.12	70.74	69.47	68.28	67.18
15.25	96.25	93.05	90.08	87.32	84.76	82.39	80.19	78.14	76.25	74.49	72.86	71.35	69.95	68.66	67.45	66.34
15.50	96.13	92.82	89.76	86.93	84.30	81.86	79.61	77.52	75.59	73.80	72.14	70.60	69.18	67.86	66.64	65.51
15.75	96.00	92.60	89.45	86.53	83.84	81.34	79.04	76.90	74.93	73.11	71.42	69.86	68.42	67.08	65.85	64.71
16.00	95.88	92.37	89.13	86.14	83.38	80.83	78.47	76.30	74.29	72.43	70.71	69.13	67.67	66.32	65.07	63.92
16.25	95.75	92.15	88.82	85.75	82.93	80.32	77.91	75.69	73.65	71.76	70.02	68.41	66.93	65.56	64.30	63.14
16.50	95.63	91.92	88.51	85.37	82.48	79.81	77.36	75.10	73.02	71.10	69.33	67.71	66.21	64.83	63.55	62.38
16.75	95.50	91.70	88.20	84.99	82.03	79.31	76.81	74.51	72.40	70.45	68.66	67.01	65.50	64.10	62.82	61.64
17.00	95.38	91.47	87.89	84.61	81.59	78.81	76.27	73.93	71.78	69.81	68.00	66.33	64.80	63.39	62.10	60.91
17.25	95.25	91.25	87.59	84.23	81.15	78.32	75.73	73.36	71.18	69.18	67.34	65.66	64.11	62.69	61.39	60.19
17.50	95.13	91.03	87.28	83.85	80.71	77.84	75.20	72.79	70.58	68.55	66.70	65.00	63.44	62.01	60.69	59.49
17.75	95.01	90.81	86.98	83.48	80.28	77.35	74.68	72.23	69.99	67.94	66.06	64.35	62.77	61.33	60.01	58.80
18.00	94.88	90.59	86.68	83.11	79.85	76.87	74.16	71.68	69.41	67.33	65.44	63.71	62.12	60.67	59.34	58.13
18.25	94.76	90.37	86.38	82.74	79.42	76.40	73.64	71.13	68.83	66.74	64.82	63.08	61.48	60.02	58.69	57.46
18.50	94.64	90.16	86.08	82.37	79.00	75.93	73.13	70.59	68.27	66.15	64.22	62.46	60.85	59.38	58.04	56.82
18.75	94.51	89.94	85.78	82.01	78.58	75.46	72.63	70.05	67.70	65.57	63.62	61.85	60.23	58.75	57.41	56.18
19.00	94.39	89.72	85.49	81.65	78.16	75.00	72.13	69.52	67.15	64.99	63.03	61.25	59.62	58.14	56.79	55.55
20.00	93.90	88.86	84.32	80.23	76.53	73.20	70.19	67.47	65.01	62.78	60.76	58.94	57.28	55.78	54.41	53.17
25.00	91.52	84.74	78.81	73.63	69.08	65.09	61.58	58.48	55.75	53.33	51.19	49.29	47.60	46.09	44.75	43.55
30.00	89.23	80.89	73.82	67.80	62.67	58.28	54.51	51.26	48.46	46.02	43.91	42.06	40.45	39.03	37.78	36.67

8.00 %

MONTHLY PAYMENT MORTGAGE

Description: This table shows the price to pay for a mortgage at the yield rate. The yield is to maturity.

Example: The price of a 8.00%, 40 year mortgage to yield 8.00% to maturity is $100.00.

YEARS TO MATURITY

YIELD	17 yr	18 yr	19 yr	20 yr	21 yr	22 yr	23 yr	24 yr	25 yr	26 yr	27 yr	28 yr	29 yr	30 yr	35 yr	40 yr
0.0	183.24	188.99	194.83	200.75	206.75	212.83	218.99	225.23	231.54	237.93	244.39	250.91	257.50	264.16	298.31	333.75
1.00	168.45	172.89	177.37	181.88	186.41	190.97	195.56	200.17	204.80	209.44	214.10	218.77	223.45	228.13	251.61	274.98
2.00	155.23	158.60	161.97	165.34	168.71	172.07	175.42	178.76	182.09	185.41	188.72	192.00	195.27	198.52	214.41	229.61
3.00	143.41	145.89	148.37	150.82	153.25	155.66	158.05	160.42	162.76	165.07	167.36	169.61	171.84	174.04	184.56	194.23
4.00	132.80	134.57	136.31	138.03	139.72	141.39	143.03	144.64	146.22	147.78	149.30	150.80	152.26	153.70	160.41	166.37
4.25	130.32	131.93	133.52	135.08	136.61	138.12	139.60	141.05	142.47	143.87	145.23	146.57	147.88	149.16	155.11	160.35
4.50	127.91	129.37	130.80	132.21	133.59	134.95	136.28	137.58	138.86	140.11	141.32	142.52	143.68	144.82	150.08	154.66
4.75	125.56	126.88	128.17	129.44	130.68	131.89	133.08	134.24	135.38	136.49	137.57	138.63	139.66	140.66	145.29	149.29
5.00	123.28	124.46	125.61	126.74	127.85	128.93	129.99	131.02	132.03	133.01	133.97	134.90	135.80	136.69	140.73	144.20
5.25	121.05	122.10	123.13	124.13	125.11	126.07	127.00	127.91	128.80	129.66	130.50	131.32	132.11	132.88	136.39	139.38
5.50	118.88	119.81	120.71	121.60	122.46	123.30	124.12	124.91	125.69	126.44	127.17	127.88	128.57	129.23	132.26	134.81
5.75	116.76	117.58	118.37	119.14	119.89	120.62	121.33	122.02	122.68	123.33	123.96	124.57	125.16	125.74	128.32	130.48
6.00	114.71	115.41	116.09	116.75	117.40	118.02	118.63	119.22	119.79	120.34	120.88	121.40	121.90	122.39	124.57	126.37
6.25	112.70	113.29	113.87	114.44	114.98	115.51	116.02	116.52	117.00	117.47	117.91	118.35	118.77	119.17	120.98	122.47
6.50	110.74	111.24	111.72	112.19	112.64	113.08	113.50	113.91	114.31	114.69	115.06	115.42	115.76	116.09	117.56	118.76
6.75	108.84	109.24	109.63	110.01	110.37	110.72	111.06	111.39	111.71	112.02	112.31	112.59	112.87	113.13	114.30	115.24
7.00	106.98	107.29	107.59	107.89	108.17	108.44	108.70	108.96	109.20	109.44	109.66	109.88	110.09	110.29	111.18	111.89
7.25	105.17	105.40	105.62	105.83	106.03	106.23	106.42	106.60	106.78	106.95	107.11	107.27	107.42	107.56	108.19	108.70
7.50	103.40	103.55	103.69	103.83	103.96	104.09	104.21	104.33	104.44	104.55	104.65	104.75	104.85	104.94	105.34	105.66
7.75	101.68	101.75	101.82	101.89	101.95	102.01	102.07	102.13	102.18	102.23	102.28	102.33	102.38	102.42	102.61	102.76
8.00	100.00	100.00	100.00	100.00	100.00	100.00	100.00	100.00	100.00	100.00	100.00	100.00	100.00	100.00	100.00	100.00
8.25	98.36	98.29	98.23	98.17	98.11	98.05	97.99	97.94	97.89	97.84	97.80	97.75	97.71	97.67	97.50	97.36
8.50	96.76	96.63	96.51	96.38	96.27	96.16	96.05	95.95	95.85	95.76	95.67	95.59	95.51	95.43	95.10	94.85
8.75	95.21	95.01	94.83	94.65	94.48	94.32	94.17	94.02	93.88	93.74	93.62	93.50	93.38	93.27	92.80	92.44
9.00	93.69	93.43	93.19	92.97	92.75	92.54	92.34	92.15	91.97	91.80	91.64	91.48	91.33	91.19	90.60	90.14
9.25	92.20	91.90	91.61	91.33	91.06	90.81	90.57	90.34	90.13	89.92	89.72	89.54	89.36	89.19	88.48	87.94
9.50	90.75	90.40	90.06	89.73	89.43	89.13	88.86	88.59	88.34	88.10	87.87	87.66	87.46	87.26	86.45	85.83
9.75	89.34	88.94	88.55	88.18	87.84	87.51	87.19	86.89	86.61	86.34	86.09	85.85	85.62	85.41	84.50	83.82
10.00	87.96	87.51	87.08	86.68	86.29	85.92	85.58	85.25	84.94	84.64	84.36	84.10	83.85	83.61	82.62	81.88
10.25	86.61	86.12	85.65	85.21	84.79	84.39	84.01	83.65	83.31	83.00	82.69	82.41	82.14	81.88	80.82	80.03
10.50	85.30	84.76	84.26	83.78	83.33	82.90	82.49	82.11	81.74	81.40	81.08	80.77	80.49	80.22	79.08	78.25
10.75	84.01	83.44	82.90	82.39	81.91	81.45	81.02	80.61	80.22	79.86	79.52	79.19	78.89	78.61	77.41	76.54
11.00	82.76	82.15	81.58	81.04	80.52	80.04	79.58	79.15	78.75	78.37	78.01	77.67	77.35	77.05	75.81	74.90
11.25	81.53	80.89	80.29	79.72	79.18	78.67	78.19	77.74	77.32	76.92	76.54	76.19	75.86	75.55	74.26	73.33
11.50	80.34	79.67	79.03	78.43	77.87	77.34	76.84	76.37	75.93	75.52	75.13	74.76	74.42	74.10	72.76	71.81
11.75	79.17	78.47	77.81	77.18	76.60	76.05	75.53	75.04	74.59	74.16	73.76	73.38	73.02	72.69	71.33	70.35
12.00	78.03	77.30	76.61	75.96	75.36	74.79	74.25	73.75	73.28	72.84	72.43	72.04	71.68	71.34	69.94	68.95
12.25	76.91	76.15	75.44	74.78	74.15	73.57	73.01	72.50	72.01	71.56	71.14	70.74	70.37	70.02	68.60	67.59
12.50	75.82	75.04	74.31	73.62	72.98	72.37	71.81	71.28	70.79	70.32	69.89	69.48	69.11	68.75	67.31	66.29
12.75	74.75	73.95	73.20	72.49	71.83	71.22	70.64	70.10	69.59	69.12	68.68	68.27	67.88	67.52	66.06	65.03
13.00	73.71	72.89	72.12	71.39	70.72	70.09	69.50	68.95	68.43	67.95	67.50	67.09	66.70	66.33	64.85	63.82
13.25	72.69	71.85	71.06	70.32	69.63	68.99	68.39	67.83	67.31	66.82	66.37	65.94	65.55	65.18	63.69	62.65
13.50	71.70	70.83	70.03	69.28	68.58	67.92	67.31	66.74	66.21	65.72	65.26	64.83	64.43	64.06	62.56	61.52
13.75	70.72	69.84	69.02	68.26	67.55	66.88	66.26	65.69	65.15	64.65	64.19	63.75	63.35	62.98	61.47	60.43
14.00	69.77	68.87	68.04	67.26	66.54	65.87	65.24	64.66	64.12	63.61	63.14	62.71	62.30	61.93	60.41	59.37
14.25	68.84	67.93	67.08	66.29	65.56	64.88	64.25	63.66	63.11	62.60	62.13	61.69	61.29	60.91	59.39	58.35
14.50	67.93	67.00	66.14	65.35	64.61	63.92	63.28	62.69	62.13	61.62	61.15	60.71	60.30	59.92	58.40	57.36
14.75	67.03	66.10	65.23	64.42	63.67	62.98	62.34	61.74	61.18	60.67	60.19	59.75	59.34	58.96	57.44	56.41
15.00	66.16	65.21	64.34	63.52	62.77	62.07	61.42	60.82	60.26	59.74	59.26	58.82	58.41	58.03	56.51	55.48
15.25	65.31	64.35	63.46	62.64	61.88	61.18	60.52	59.92	59.36	58.84	58.36	57.92	57.51	57.13	55.61	54.59
15.50	64.47	63.50	62.61	61.78	61.01	60.31	59.65	59.04	58.48	57.96	57.48	57.04	56.63	56.25	54.74	53.72
15.75	63.65	62.68	61.77	60.94	60.17	59.46	58.80	58.19	57.63	57.11	56.63	56.18	55.77	55.39	53.89	52.87
16.00	62.85	61.87	60.96	60.12	59.35	58.63	57.97	57.36	56.80	56.28	55.80	55.35	54.94	54.56	53.07	52.06
16.25	62.07	61.08	60.16	59.32	58.54	57.82	57.16	56.55	55.99	55.47	54.99	54.54	54.14	53.76	52.27	51.27
16.50	61.30	60.30	59.38	58.54	57.76	57.04	56.37	55.76	55.20	54.68	54.20	53.76	53.35	52.97	51.49	50.50
16.75	60.55	59.54	58.62	57.77	56.99	56.27	55.61	54.99	54.43	53.91	53.43	52.99	52.59	52.21	50.73	49.75
17.00	59.81	58.80	57.88	57.02	56.24	55.52	54.85	54.24	53.68	53.16	52.69	52.25	51.84	51.47	50.00	49.02
17.25	59.09	58.08	57.15	56.29	55.51	54.79	54.12	53.51	52.95	52.43	51.96	51.52	51.12	50.74	49.29	48.32
17.50	58.38	57.37	56.44	55.58	54.79	54.07	53.41	52.80	52.24	51.72	51.25	50.81	50.41	50.04	48.59	47.63
17.75	57.69	56.67	55.74	54.88	54.09	53.37	52.71	52.10	51.54	51.03	50.56	50.12	49.72	49.36	47.92	46.97
18.00	57.01	55.99	55.06	54.20	53.41	52.69	52.03	51.42	50.86	50.35	49.88	49.45	49.05	48.69	47.26	46.32
18.25	56.35	55.32	54.39	53.53	52.74	52.02	51.36	50.76	50.20	49.69	49.22	48.79	48.40	48.04	46.62	45.69
18.50	55.70	54.67	53.73	52.88	52.09	51.37	50.71	50.11	49.56	49.05	48.58	48.15	47.76	47.40	46.00	45.07
18.75	55.06	54.03	53.09	52.24	51.45	50.73	50.08	49.48	48.92	48.42	47.96	47.53	47.14	46.78	45.39	44.47
19.00	54.43	53.40	52.47	51.61	50.83	50.11	49.46	48.86	48.31	47.81	47.35	46.92	46.54	46.18	44.80	43.89
20.00	52.05	51.02	50.09	49.24	48.46	47.75	47.11	46.52	45.98	45.49	45.04	44.63	44.26	43.91	42.57	41.70
25.00	42.47	41.51	40.64	39.86	39.16	38.53	37.96	37.44	36.97	36.55	36.16	35.81	35.49	35.20	34.09	33.37
30.00	35.70	34.83	34.06	33.37	32.75	32.20	31.70	31.26	30.85	30.49	30.16	29.86	29.59	29.35	28.41	27.81

(continued)

TABLE 3 Price of Mortgage to Obtain Specified Yield

(continued)

10.00 %

MONTHLY PAYMENT MORTGAGE

Description: This table shows the price to pay for a mortgage at the yield rate. The yield is to maturity.

Example: The price of a 10.00%, 16 year mortgage to yield 8.00% to maturity is $113.08.

YIELD	YEARS TO MATURITY 1 yr	2 yr	3 yr	4 yr	5 yr	6 yr	7 yr	8 yr	9 yr	10 yr	11 yr	12 yr	13 yr	14 yr	15 yr	16 yr
0.0	105.50	110.75	116.16	121.74	127.48	133.39	139.45	145.67	152.05	158.58	165.26	172.09	179.06	186.18	193.43	200.81
1.00	104.93	109.60	114.39	119.29	124.30	129.41	134.63	139.94	145.35	150.85	156.44	162.10	167.85	173.67	179.55	185.50
2.00	104.36	108.47	112.65	116.90	121.22	125.60	130.03	134.51	139.05	143.62	148.24	152.89	157.56	162.27	166.99	171.73
3.00	103.80	107.36	110.96	114.58	118.24	121.93	125.64	129.37	133.11	136.86	140.61	144.37	148.12	151.87	155.61	159.33
4.00	103.25	106.26	109.29	112.33	115.37	118.41	121.45	124.49	127.51	130.53	133.52	136.50	139.45	142.38	145.28	148.15
4.25	103.11	105.99	108.88	111.77	114.67	117.55	120.44	123.31	126.17	129.01	131.83	134.62	137.39	140.14	142.85	145.52
4.50	102.97	105.72	108.47	111.22	113.97	116.71	119.43	122.14	124.84	127.51	130.16	132.79	135.38	137.94	140.47	142.97
4.75	102.83	105.45	108.07	110.68	113.28	115.86	118.44	120.99	123.53	126.04	128.53	130.98	133.41	135.80	138.15	140.47
5.00	102.70	105.18	107.66	110.13	112.59	115.03	117.46	119.86	122.24	124.59	126.92	129.21	131.47	133.70	135.89	138.04
5.25	102.56	104.91	107.26	109.59	111.91	114.21	116.49	118.74	120.97	123.17	125.34	127.48	129.58	131.65	133.68	135.67
5.50	102.42	104.65	106.86	109.06	111.23	113.39	115.53	117.64	119.72	121.77	123.79	125.77	127.73	129.64	131.52	133.35
5.75	102.29	104.38	106.46	108.52	110.57	112.58	114.58	116.54	118.48	120.39	122.26	124.10	125.91	127.68	129.41	131.10
6.00	102.15	104.12	106.07	107.99	109.90	111.78	113.64	115.47	117.27	119.03	120.77	122.47	124.13	125.76	127.34	128.89
6.25	102.01	103.85	105.67	107.47	109.24	110.99	112.71	114.41	116.07	117.70	119.29	120.86	122.38	123.88	125.33	126.75
6.50	101.88	103.59	105.28	106.95	108.59	110.21	111.80	113.36	114.89	116.38	117.85	119.28	120.67	122.04	123.36	124.65
6.75	101.74	103.33	104.89	106.43	107.94	109.43	110.89	112.32	113.72	115.09	116.43	117.73	119.00	120.24	121.44	122.60
7.00	101.61	103.07	104.50	105.91	107.30	108.66	109.99	111.30	112.57	113.82	115.03	116.21	117.36	118.47	119.56	120.61
7.25	101.47	102.80	104.12	105.40	106.67	107.90	109.11	110.29	111.44	112.56	113.66	114.72	115.75	116.75	117.72	118.66
7.50	101.34	102.55	103.73	104.90	106.03	107.15	108.23	109.29	110.33	111.33	112.31	113.25	114.17	115.06	115.92	116.75
7.75	101.20	102.29	103.35	104.39	105.41	106.40	107.37	108.31	109.23	110.12	110.98	111.82	112.63	113.41	114.16	114.89
8.00	101.07	102.03	102.97	103.89	104.79	105.66	106.51	107.34	108.14	108.92	109.67	110.40	111.11	111.79	112.45	113.08
8.25	100.93	101.77	102.59	103.39	104.17	104.93	105.67	106.38	107.07	107.74	108.39	109.02	109.62	110.21	110.77	111.31
8.50	100.80	101.52	102.22	102.90	103.56	104.20	104.83	105.43	106.02	106.59	107.13	107.66	108.17	108.66	109.13	109.58
8.75	100.66	101.26	101.84	102.41	102.95	103.49	104.00	104.50	104.98	105.44	105.89	106.32	106.74	107.14	107.52	107.89
9.00	100.53	101.01	101.47	101.92	102.35	102.78	103.18	103.58	103.96	104.32	104.67	105.01	105.34	105.65	105.95	106.24
9.25	100.40	100.75	101.10	101.43	101.76	102.07	102.37	102.67	102.95	103.22	103.48	103.73	103.96	104.19	104.41	104.62
9.50	100.27	100.50	100.73	100.95	101.17	101.37	101.57	101.77	101.95	102.13	102.30	102.46	102.62	102.77	102.91	103.05
9.75	100.13	100.25	100.36	100.47	100.58	100.68	100.78	100.88	100.97	101.06	101.14	101.22	101.30	101.37	101.44	101.51
10.00	100.00	100.00	100.00	100.00	100.00	100.00	100.00	100.00	100.00	100.00	100.00	100.00	100.00	100.00	100.00	100.00
10.25	99.87	99.75	99.64	99.53	99.42	99.32	99.23	99.13	99.05	98.96	98.88	98.80	98.73	98.66	98.59	98.53
10.50	99.74	99.50	99.28	99.06	98.85	98.65	98.46	98.28	98.10	97.94	97.78	97.63	97.48	97.34	97.21	97.09
10.75	99.60	99.25	98.92	98.59	98.28	97.99	97.70	97.43	97.17	96.93	96.69	96.47	96.26	96.06	95.87	95.68
11.00	99.47	99.01	98.56	98.13	97.72	97.33	96.96	96.60	96.26	95.94	95.63	95.34	95.06	94.79	94.55	94.31
11.25	99.34	98.76	98.20	97.67	97.16	96.68	96.22	95.77	95.36	94.96	94.58	94.22	93.88	93.56	93.25	92.97
11.50	99.21	98.52	97.85	97.22	96.61	96.03	95.48	94.96	94.46	93.99	93.55	93.12	92.72	92.35	91.99	91.65
11.75	99.08	98.27	97.50	96.76	96.06	95.39	94.76	94.16	93.59	93.04	92.53	92.05	91.59	91.16	90.75	90.37
12.00	98.95	98.03	97.15	96.31	95.52	94.76	94.04	93.36	92.72	92.11	91.53	90.99	90.48	89.99	89.54	89.11
12.25	98.82	97.78	96.80	95.86	94.98	94.13	93.33	92.58	91.86	91.19	90.55	89.95	89.38	88.85	88.35	87.88
12.50	98.69	97.54	96.45	95.42	94.44	93.51	92.63	91.80	91.02	90.28	89.58	88.93	88.31	87.73	87.19	86.68
12.75	98.56	97.30	96.11	94.98	93.91	92.90	91.94	91.04	90.19	89.39	88.63	87.93	87.26	86.63	86.05	85.50
13.00	98.43	97.06	95.77	94.54	93.38	92.29	91.26	90.28	89.37	88.51	87.70	86.94	86.23	85.56	84.93	84.35
13.25	98.30	96.82	95.42	94.10	92.86	91.68	90.58	89.54	88.56	87.64	86.78	85.97	85.21	84.50	83.84	83.22
13.50	98.17	96.58	95.08	93.67	92.34	91.09	89.91	88.80	87.76	86.78	85.87	85.02	84.22	83.47	82.77	82.12
13.75	98.04	96.35	94.75	93.24	91.82	90.49	89.24	88.07	86.97	85.94	84.98	84.08	83.24	82.45	81.72	81.04
14.00	97.92	96.11	94.41	92.81	91.31	89.91	88.59	87.35	86.19	85.11	84.10	83.16	82.28	81.46	80.69	79.98
14.25	97.79	95.87	94.08	92.39	90.81	89.32	87.94	86.64	85.43	84.29	83.24	82.25	81.33	80.48	79.68	78.95
14.50	97.66	95.64	93.74	91.97	90.30	88.75	87.30	85.94	84.67	83.49	82.39	81.36	80.41	79.52	78.70	77.93
14.75	97.53	95.40	93.41	91.55	89.81	88.18	86.66	85.24	83.92	82.69	81.55	80.49	79.50	78.58	77.73	76.94
15.00	97.40	95.17	93.08	91.13	89.31	87.61	86.03	84.56	83.19	81.91	80.73	79.63	78.60	77.66	76.78	75.97
15.25	97.28	94.94	92.75	90.72	88.82	87.05	85.41	83.88	82.46	81.14	79.91	78.78	77.73	76.75	75.85	75.02
15.50	97.15	94.71	92.43	90.31	88.33	86.50	84.79	83.21	81.74	80.38	79.12	77.95	76.86	75.86	74.94	74.08
15.75	97.02	94.47	92.10	89.90	87.85	85.95	84.18	82.55	81.03	79.63	78.33	77.13	76.02	74.99	74.04	73.17
16.00	96.90	94.24	91.78	89.49	87.37	85.40	83.58	81.90	80.33	78.89	77.56	76.32	75.18	74.13	73.17	72.28
16.25	96.77	94.01	91.46	89.09	86.90	84.87	82.99	81.25	79.64	78.16	76.79	75.53	74.37	73.29	72.31	71.40
16.50	96.65	93.79	91.14	88.69	86.42	84.33	82.40	80.61	78.96	77.44	76.04	74.75	73.56	72.47	71.46	70.54
16.75	96.52	93.56	90.82	88.29	85.96	83.80	81.81	79.98	78.29	76.74	75.30	73.99	72.77	71.66	70.64	69.70
17.00	96.39	93.33	90.50	87.90	85.49	83.28	81.24	79.36	77.63	76.04	74.57	73.23	72.00	70.86	69.82	68.87
17.25	96.27	93.10	90.19	87.50	85.03	82.76	80.66	78.74	76.97	75.35	73.86	72.49	71.23	70.08	69.03	68.06
17.50	96.14	92.88	89.88	87.11	84.57	82.24	80.10	78.13	76.33	74.67	73.15	71.76	70.48	69.32	68.25	67.27
17.75	96.02	92.65	89.56	86.73	84.12	81.73	79.54	77.53	75.69	74.00	72.46	71.04	69.75	68.56	67.48	66.49
18.00	95.89	92.43	89.25	86.34	83.67	81.23	78.99	76.94	75.06	73.34	71.77	70.34	69.02	67.82	66.73	65.73
18.25	95.77	92.21	88.94	85.96	83.23	80.72	78.44	76.35	74.44	72.69	71.10	69.64	68.31	67.10	65.99	64.98
18.50	95.65	91.98	88.64	85.58	82.78	80.23	77.90	75.77	73.82	72.05	70.43	68.96	67.61	66.38	65.27	64.25
18.75	95.52	91.76	88.33	85.20	82.34	79.74	77.36	75.19	73.22	71.42	69.78	68.28	66.92	65.68	64.55	63.53
19.00	95.40	91.54	88.03	84.82	81.91	79.25	76.83	74.63	72.62	70.79	69.13	67.62	66.24	64.99	63.86	62.82
20.00	94.91	90.67	86.82	83.35	80.20	77.34	74.76	72.42	70.30	68.38	66.64	65.07	63.64	62.35	61.19	60.13
25.00	92.50	86.46	81.16	76.49	72.39	68.77	65.59	62.77	60.29	58.09	56.14	54.42	52.89	51.53	50.32	49.25
30.00	90.18	82.53	76.01	70.44	65.67	61.58	58.06	55.03	52.40	50.13	48.16	46.44	44.94	43.63	42.48	41.47

10.00 %

MONTHLY PAYMENT MORTGAGE

Description: This table shows the price to pay for a mortgage at the yield rate. The yield is to maturity.

Example: The price of a 10.00%, 40 year mortgage to yield 8.00% to maturity is $122.12.

YEARS TO MATURITY

YIELD	17 yr	18 yr	19 yr	20 yr	21 yr	22 yr	23 yr	24 yr	25 yr	26 yr	27 yr	28 yr	29 yr	30 yr	35 yr	40 yr
0.0	208.33	215.97	223.73	231.61	239.60	247.70	255.90	264.21	272.61	281.10	289.69	298.35	307.10	315.93	361.06	407.59
1.00	191.51	197.57	203.68	209.84	216.03	222.26	228.52	234.81	241.12	247.44	253.78	260.13	266.49	272.84	304.54	335.82
2.00	176.48	181.24	186.00	190.76	195.51	200.26	204.99	209.70	214.39	219.06	223.70	228.31	232.88	237.43	259.51	280.41
3.00	163.04	166.72	170.37	174.00	177.60	181.17	184.69	188.18	191.62	195.02	198.38	201.69	204.94	208.15	223.38	237.20
4.00	150.98	153.78	156.53	159.25	161.92	164.55	167.13	169.67	172.16	174.59	176.98	179.31	181.59	183.82	194.16	203.17
4.25	148.16	150.76	153.32	155.84	158.31	160.74	163.12	165.45	167.74	169.97	172.15	174.28	176.36	178.39	187.74	195.83
4.50	145.42	147.83	150.21	152.54	154.82	157.06	159.25	161.39	163.48	165.53	167.52	169.46	171.36	173.20	181.65	188.88
4.75	142.75	144.99	147.18	149.33	151.44	153.50	155.51	157.47	159.39	161.26	163.07	164.84	166.56	168.23	175.85	182.31
5.00	140.15	142.22	144.24	146.23	148.16	150.05	151.90	153.69	155.44	157.14	158.80	160.41	161.96	163.48	170.34	176.10
5.25	137.62	139.53	141.39	143.21	144.99	146.72	148.41	150.05	151.64	153.19	154.69	156.15	157.56	158.92	165.09	170.21
5.50	135.15	136.91	138.62	140.29	141.91	143.50	145.03	146.53	147.98	149.38	150.74	152.06	153.33	154.56	160.08	164.64
5.75	132.75	134.36	135.93	137.45	138.93	140.38	141.77	143.13	144.44	145.71	146.94	148.13	149.27	150.38	155.32	159.35
6.00	130.41	131.88	133.31	134.70	136.05	137.36	138.62	139.85	141.04	142.18	143.29	144.35	145.38	146.37	150.77	154.33
6.25	128.12	129.46	130.77	132.03	133.25	134.43	135.58	136.68	137.75	138.78	139.77	140.73	141.65	142.53	146.43	149.57
6.50	125.90	127.12	128.29	129.43	130.54	131.60	132.63	133.62	134.58	135.50	136.39	137.24	138.06	138.84	142.29	145.04
6.75	123.73	124.83	125.89	126.92	127.91	128.86	129.78	130.67	131.52	132.34	133.13	133.88	134.61	135.30	138.34	140.74
7.00	121.62	122.60	123.55	124.47	125.35	126.21	127.03	127.81	128.57	129.30	129.99	130.66	131.30	131.91	134.56	136.64
7.25	119.56	120.44	121.28	122.10	122.88	123.63	124.36	125.05	125.72	126.36	126.97	127.55	128.11	128.64	130.95	132.75
7.50	117.55	118.33	119.07	119.79	120.48	121.14	121.77	122.38	122.97	123.52	124.05	124.56	125.05	125.51	127.50	129.04
7.75	115.60	116.27	116.92	117.55	118.15	118.72	119.27	119.80	120.31	120.79	121.25	121.68	122.10	122.50	124.20	125.50
8.00	113.69	114.27	114.83	115.37	115.89	116.38	116.85	117.31	117.74	118.15	118.54	118.91	119.26	119.60	121.04	122.12
8.25	111.83	112.32	112.80	113.26	113.69	114.11	114.51	114.89	115.25	115.60	115.92	116.24	116.53	116.81	118.01	118.90
8.50	110.01	110.42	110.82	111.20	111.56	111.91	112.24	112.55	112.85	113.13	113.40	113.66	113.90	114.13	115.10	115.83
8.75	108.24	108.57	108.89	109.20	109.49	109.77	110.04	110.29	110.53	110.76	110.97	111.17	111.37	111.55	112.32	112.89
9.00	106.51	106.77	107.02	107.26	107.48	107.70	107.90	108.10	108.28	108.46	108.62	108.78	108.93	109.07	109.65	110.08
9.25	104.82	105.01	105.19	105.37	105.53	105.69	105.84	105.98	106.11	106.24	106.35	106.47	106.57	106.67	107.09	107.40
9.50	103.18	103.30	103.42	103.53	103.63	103.74	103.83	103.92	104.01	104.09	104.16	104.24	104.30	104.37	104.63	104.82
9.75	101.57	101.63	101.69	101.74	101.79	101.84	101.89	101.93	101.97	102.01	102.05	102.08	102.11	102.14	102.27	102.36
10.00	100.00	100.00	100.00	100.00	100.00	100.00	100.00	100.00	100.00	100.00	100.00	100.00	100.00	100.00	100.00	100.00
10.25	98.47	98.41	98.36	98.31	98.26	98.21	98.17	98.13	98.09	98.06	98.02	97.99	97.96	97.93	97.82	97.74
10.50	96.97	96.86	96.76	96.66	96.57	96.48	96.39	96.32	96.24	96.17	96.11	96.05	95.99	95.94	95.72	95.56
10.75	95.51	95.35	95.20	95.05	94.92	94.79	94.67	94.56	94.45	94.35	94.26	94.17	94.09	94.01	93.70	93.48
11.00	94.09	93.88	93.68	93.49	93.32	93.15	93.00	92.85	92.71	92.59	92.47	92.35	92.25	92.15	91.75	91.47
11.25	92.70	92.44	92.20	91.97	91.76	91.56	91.37	91.20	91.03	90.88	90.73	90.60	90.47	90.35	89.88	89.55
11.50	91.33	91.04	90.75	90.49	90.24	90.01	89.79	89.59	89.40	89.22	89.05	88.90	88.75	88.62	88.07	87.70
11.75	90.01	89.67	89.35	89.05	88.77	88.50	88.26	88.03	87.81	87.61	87.43	87.25	87.09	86.94	86.33	85.91
12.00	88.71	88.33	87.97	87.64	87.33	87.04	86.77	86.51	86.28	86.06	85.85	85.66	85.48	85.32	84.65	84.20
12.25	87.44	87.02	86.64	86.27	85.93	85.62	85.32	85.04	84.79	84.55	84.32	84.12	83.92	83.75	83.03	82.55
12.50	86.20	85.75	85.33	84.94	84.57	84.23	83.91	83.62	83.34	83.08	82.84	82.62	82.42	82.23	81.47	80.95
12.75	84.99	84.51	84.06	83.64	83.25	82.88	82.54	82.23	81.93	81.66	81.41	81.17	80.96	80.76	79.95	79.42
13.00	83.80	83.29	82.81	82.37	81.96	81.57	81.21	80.88	80.57	80.28	80.02	79.77	79.54	79.33	78.50	77.94
13.25	82.64	82.10	81.60	81.13	80.70	80.29	79.92	79.57	79.24	78.94	78.67	78.41	78.17	77.95	77.08	76.51
13.50	81.51	80.94	80.42	79.93	79.47	79.05	78.66	78.29	77.96	77.65	77.36	77.09	76.84	76.62	75.72	75.13
13.75	80.40	79.81	79.26	78.75	78.28	77.84	77.43	77.05	76.71	76.38	76.08	75.81	75.56	75.32	74.40	73.79
14.00	79.32	78.70	78.13	77.60	77.11	76.66	76.24	75.85	75.49	75.16	74.85	74.57	74.31	74.06	73.12	72.51
14.25	78.26	77.62	77.03	76.48	75.98	75.51	75.08	74.68	74.31	73.96	73.65	73.36	73.09	72.85	71.88	71.26
14.50	77.22	76.57	75.96	75.39	74.87	74.39	73.94	73.53	73.15	72.81	72.48	72.19	71.92	71.66	70.69	70.05
14.75	76.21	75.53	74.91	74.33	73.79	73.30	72.84	72.42	72.04	71.68	71.35	71.05	70.77	70.52	69.53	68.89
15.00	75.22	74.52	73.88	73.29	72.74	72.23	71.77	71.34	70.95	70.58	70.25	69.94	69.66	69.40	68.40	67.76
15.25	74.25	73.53	72.88	72.27	71.71	71.20	70.72	70.29	69.89	69.52	69.18	68.87	68.58	68.32	67.31	66.66
15.50	73.29	72.57	71.90	71.28	70.71	70.19	69.70	69.26	68.85	68.48	68.14	67.82	67.54	67.27	66.25	65.60
15.75	72.36	71.62	70.94	70.31	69.73	69.20	68.71	68.26	67.85	67.47	67.13	66.81	66.52	66.25	65.22	64.57
16.00	71.45	70.70	70.00	69.36	68.78	68.24	67.74	67.29	66.87	66.49	66.14	65.82	65.53	65.26	64.23	63.58
16.25	70.56	69.79	69.09	68.44	67.84	67.30	66.80	66.34	65.92	65.53	65.18	64.86	64.56	64.29	63.26	62.61
16.50	69.69	68.91	68.19	67.54	66.93	66.38	65.88	65.41	64.99	64.60	64.25	63.92	63.63	63.36	62.32	61.67
16.75	68.83	68.04	67.32	66.65	66.04	65.49	64.98	64.51	64.08	63.69	63.34	63.01	62.71	62.44	61.41	60.76
17.00	68.00	67.20	66.46	65.79	65.18	64.61	64.10	63.63	63.20	62.81	62.45	62.12	61.83	61.55	60.52	59.87
17.25	67.18	66.37	65.63	64.95	64.33	63.76	63.24	62.77	62.34	61.95	61.59	61.26	60.96	60.69	59.65	59.01
17.50	66.37	65.56	64.81	64.12	63.50	62.93	62.41	61.93	61.50	61.11	60.75	60.42	60.12	59.85	58.81	58.17
17.75	65.59	64.76	64.01	63.32	62.69	62.12	61.59	61.12	60.68	60.29	59.93	59.60	59.30	59.03	58.00	57.36
18.00	64.82	63.98	63.22	62.53	61.90	61.32	60.80	60.32	59.88	59.49	59.13	58.80	58.50	58.23	57.20	56.57
18.25	64.06	63.22	62.46	61.76	61.12	60.55	60.02	59.54	59.10	58.71	58.35	58.02	57.72	57.45	56.43	55.79
18.50	63.32	62.47	61.70	61.00	60.37	59.79	59.26	58.78	58.34	57.95	57.59	57.26	56.96	56.69	55.67	55.04
18.75	62.59	61.74	60.97	60.27	59.63	59.05	58.52	58.04	57.60	57.21	56.85	56.52	56.22	55.95	54.94	54.31
19.00	61.88	61.03	60.25	59.54	58.90	58.32	57.79	57.31	56.88	56.48	56.12	55.80	55.50	55.23	54.22	53.60
20.00	59.17	58.30	57.52	56.81	56.16	55.58	55.05	54.57	54.14	53.75	53.39	53.07	52.78	52.52	51.53	50.93
25.00	48.29	47.43	46.67	45.99	45.38	44.84	44.35	43.92	43.53	43.18	42.86	42.58	42.33	42.10	41.26	40.76
30.00	40.58	39.80	39.11	38.50	37.96	37.47	37.05	36.67	36.33	36.02	35.75	35.51	35.29	35.10	34.39	33.97

(continued)

TABLE 3 Price of Mortgage to Obtain Specified Yield

(continued)

12.00 %

MONTHLY PAYMENT MORTGAGE

Description: This table shows the price to pay for a mortgage at the yield rate. The yield is to maturity.

Example: The price of a 12.00%, 16 year mortgage to yield 8.00% to maturity is $126.90.

	YEARS TO MATURITY															
YIELD	1 yr	2 yr	3 yr	4 yr	5 yr	6 yr	7 yr	8 yr	9 yr	10 yr	11 yr	12 yr	13 yr	14 yr	15 yr	16 yr
0.0	106.62	112.98	119.57	126.40	133.47	140.76	148.28	156.03	163.99	172.17	180.55	189.13	197.91	206.88	216.03	225.36
1.00	106.04	111.81	117.75	123.86	130.13	136.57	143.15	149.89	156.76	163.77	170.90	178.16	185.52	192.98	200.53	208.17
2.00	105.47	110.66	115.96	121.38	126.91	132.54	138.26	144.07	149.96	155.92	161.95	168.02	174.15	180.31	186.50	192.72
3.00	104.91	109.52	114.21	118.97	123.80	128.67	133.60	138.56	143.56	148.58	153.62	158.67	163.72	168.76	173.79	178.80
4.00	104.34	108.40	112.50	116.63	120.79	124.96	129.15	133.34	137.53	141.71	145.87	150.01	154.13	158.21	162.25	166.25
4.25	104.20	108.12	112.08	116.05	120.05	124.05	128.07	132.07	136.07	140.06	144.02	147.95	151.86	155.72	159.54	163.31
4.50	104.06	107.85	111.66	115.48	119.32	123.16	127.00	130.83	134.64	138.43	142.20	145.93	149.63	153.28	156.89	160.44
4.75	103.93	107.57	111.24	114.91	118.59	122.27	125.94	129.60	133.23	136.84	140.41	143.95	147.45	150.90	154.30	157.64
5.00	103.79	107.30	110.82	114.35	117.87	121.39	124.90	128.38	131.84	135.27	138.66	142.01	145.31	148.57	151.77	154.91
5.25	103.65	107.03	110.41	113.79	117.16	120.52	123.86	127.18	130.47	133.72	136.93	140.10	143.22	146.29	149.30	152.25
5.50	103.51	106.75	110.00	113.23	116.46	119.66	122.84	126.00	129.12	132.20	135.24	138.23	141.17	144.06	146.88	149.65
5.75	103.37	106.48	109.59	112.68	115.76	118.81	121.84	124.83	127.79	130.70	133.57	136.39	139.16	141.87	144.53	147.12
6.00	103.23	106.21	109.18	112.13	115.06	117.96	120.84	123.68	126.47	129.23	131.94	134.59	137.19	139.74	142.22	144.65
6.25	103.10	105.94	108.77	111.58	114.37	117.13	119.85	122.54	125.18	127.78	130.33	132.82	135.27	137.65	139.97	142.24
6.50	102.96	105.67	108.37	111.04	113.69	116.30	118.88	121.41	123.91	126.35	128.75	131.09	133.38	135.61	137.77	139.88
6.75	102.82	105.41	107.97	110.51	113.01	115.48	117.91	120.31	122.65	124.95	127.19	129.39	131.53	133.61	135.63	137.59
7.00	102.68	105.14	107.57	109.97	112.34	114.67	116.96	119.21	121.41	123.57	125.67	127.72	129.71	131.65	133.53	135.35
7.25	102.55	104.87	107.17	109.44	111.67	113.87	116.02	118.13	120.19	122.21	124.17	126.08	127.93	129.73	131.47	133.16
7.50	102.41	104.61	106.78	108.91	111.01	113.07	115.09	117.06	118.99	120.87	122.69	124.47	126.19	127.86	129.47	131.02
7.75	102.27	104.34	106.38	108.39	110.36	112.28	114.17	116.01	117.80	119.55	121.24	122.89	124.48	126.02	127.50	128.94
8.00	102.14	104.08	105.99	107.87	109.71	111.50	113.26	114.97	116.63	118.25	119.82	121.34	122.80	124.22	125.59	126.90
8.25	102.00	103.82	105.60	107.35	109.06	110.73	112.36	113.94	115.48	116.97	118.42	119.81	121.16	122.46	123.71	124.91
8.50	101.87	103.56	105.22	106.84	108.42	109.97	111.47	112.93	114.34	115.72	117.04	118.32	119.55	120.74	121.88	122.97
8.75	101.73	103.30	104.83	106.33	107.79	109.21	110.59	111.93	113.22	114.48	115.69	116.85	117.97	119.05	120.08	121.07
9.00	101.60	103.04	104.45	105.82	107.16	108.46	109.72	110.94	112.12	113.26	114.36	115.41	116.43	117.40	118.33	119.22
9.25	101.46	102.78	104.07	105.32	106.54	107.72	108.86	109.96	111.03	112.06	113.05	114.00	114.91	115.78	116.61	117.41
9.50	101.33	102.52	103.69	104.82	105.92	106.98	108.01	109.00	109.96	110.88	111.76	112.61	113.42	114.19	114.93	115.64
9.75	101.19	102.27	103.31	104.32	105.30	106.25	107.17	108.05	108.90	109.71	110.49	111.24	111.96	112.64	113.29	113.91
10.00	101.06	102.01	102.94	103.83	104.69	105.53	106.33	107.11	107.85	108.57	109.25	109.90	110.53	111.12	111.68	112.22
10.25	100.93	101.76	102.56	103.34	104.09	104.81	105.51	106.18	106.82	107.44	108.03	108.59	109.12	109.63	110.11	110.57
10.50	100.79	101.50	102.19	102.85	103.49	104.11	104.70	105.26	105.81	106.33	106.82	107.29	107.74	108.17	108.57	108.96
10.75	100.66	101.25	101.82	102.37	102.90	103.41	103.89	104.36	104.81	105.23	105.64	106.02	106.39	106.74	107.07	107.38
11.00	100.53	101.00	101.45	101.89	102.31	102.71	103.10	103.47	103.82	104.15	104.47	104.78	105.06	105.34	105.59	105.84
11.25	100.40	100.75	101.09	101.41	101.72	102.02	102.31	102.58	102.84	103.09	103.33	103.55	103.76	103.96	104.15	104.33
11.50	100.26	100.50	100.72	100.94	101.15	101.34	101.53	101.71	101.88	102.05	102.20	102.35	102.48	102.61	102.74	102.85
11.75	100.13	100.25	100.36	100.47	100.57	100.67	100.76	100.85	100.93	101.01	101.09	101.16	101.23	101.29	101.35	101.41
12.00	100.00	100.00	100.00	100.00	100.00	100.00	100.00	100.00	100.00	100.00	100.00	100.00	100.00	100.00	100.00	100.00
12.25	99.87	99.75	99.64	99.54	99.43	99.34	99.25	99.16	99.08	99.00	98.93	98.86	98.79	98.73	98.67	98.62
12.50	99.74	99.51	99.28	99.07	98.87	98.68	98.50	98.33	98.17	98.02	97.87	97.74	97.61	97.49	97.37	97.27
12.75	99.61	99.26	98.93	98.62	98.32	98.03	97.76	97.51	97.27	97.04	96.83	96.63	96.44	96.27	96.10	95.95
13.00	99.48	99.01	98.58	98.16	97.76	97.39	97.04	96.70	96.39	96.09	95.81	95.55	95.30	95.07	94.86	94.66
13.25	99.34	98.77	98.23	97.71	97.22	96.75	96.31	95.90	95.51	95.15	94.80	94.48	94.18	93.90	93.64	93.39
13.50	99.21	98.53	97.88	97.26	96.67	96.12	95.60	95.11	94.65	94.22	93.81	93.43	93.08	92.75	92.44	92.15
13.75	99.08	98.29	97.53	96.81	96.13	95.50	94.90	94.33	93.80	93.30	92.84	92.40	92.00	91.62	91.27	90.94
14.00	98.95	98.04	97.18	96.37	95.60	94.88	94.20	93.56	92.96	92.40	91.88	91.39	90.94	90.51	90.12	89.75
14.25	98.83	97.80	96.84	95.93	95.07	94.26	93.51	92.80	92.14	91.52	90.94	90.40	89.89	89.43	88.99	88.59
14.50	98.70	97.56	96.49	95.49	94.54	93.66	92.82	92.05	91.32	90.64	90.01	89.42	88.87	88.36	87.89	87.46
14.75	98.57	97.32	96.15	95.05	94.02	93.05	92.15	91.30	90.51	89.78	89.09	88.46	87.87	87.32	86.81	86.34
15.00	98.44	97.09	95.81	94.62	93.50	92.46	91.48	90.57	89.72	88.93	88.19	87.51	86.88	86.29	85.75	85.25
15.25	98.31	96.85	95.48	94.19	92.99	91.87	90.82	89.84	88.93	88.09	87.31	86.58	85.91	85.29	84.71	84.18
15.50	98.18	96.61	95.14	93.77	92.48	91.28	90.16	89.13	88.16	87.26	86.43	85.66	84.95	84.30	83.69	83.14
15.75	98.05	96.38	94.81	93.34	91.97	90.70	89.52	88.42	87.40	86.45	85.57	84.77	84.02	83.33	82.70	82.11
16.00	97.93	96.14	94.47	92.92	91.47	90.13	88.88	87.72	86.64	85.65	84.73	83.88	83.10	82.38	81.72	81.11
16.25	97.80	95.91	94.14	92.50	90.98	89.56	88.24	87.02	85.90	84.86	83.90	83.01	82.19	81.44	80.76	80.12
16.50	97.67	95.67	93.81	92.09	90.48	88.99	87.62	86.34	85.16	84.08	83.08	82.15	81.31	80.53	79.81	79.16
16.75	97.54	95.44	93.49	91.67	89.99	88.43	87.00	85.67	84.44	83.31	82.27	81.31	80.43	79.63	78.89	78.21
17.00	97.42	95.21	93.16	91.26	89.51	87.88	86.38	85.00	83.72	82.55	81.47	80.48	79.58	78.74	77.98	77.29
17.25	97.29	94.98	92.84	90.85	89.02	87.33	85.77	84.34	83.02	81.80	80.69	79.67	78.73	77.88	77.09	76.38
17.50	97.16	94.75	92.51	90.45	88.54	86.79	85.17	83.69	82.32	81.07	79.92	78.87	77.90	77.02	76.22	75.49
17.75	97.04	94.52	92.19	90.05	88.07	86.25	84.58	83.04	81.63	80.34	79.16	78.08	77.09	76.19	75.37	74.62
18.00	96.91	94.29	91.87	89.65	87.60	85.72	83.99	82.40	80.95	79.62	78.41	77.30	76.29	75.37	74.53	73.76
18.25	96.79	94.06	91.56	89.25	87.13	85.19	83.41	81.78	80.28	78.92	77.67	76.54	75.50	74.56	73.70	72.92
18.50	96.66	93.84	91.24	88.85	86.67	84.66	82.83	81.15	79.62	78.22	76.95	75.78	74.73	73.76	72.89	72.10
18.75	96.54	93.61	90.92	88.46	86.21	84.15	82.26	80.54	78.97	77.53	76.23	75.04	73.96	72.99	72.10	71.29
19.00	96.41	93.38	90.61	88.07	85.75	83.63	81.70	79.93	78.32	76.86	75.53	74.32	73.22	72.22	71.32	70.50
20.00	95.91	92.49	89.37	86.54	83.96	81.62	79.49	77.57	75.82	74.24	72.81	71.51	70.34	69.29	68.34	67.48
25.00	93.48	88.20	83.54	79.42	75.79	72.58	69.74	67.24	65.02	63.07	61.34	59.81	58.45	57.26	56.20	55.26
30.00	91.14	84.19	78.24	73.14	68.75	64.98	61.74	58.94	56.52	54.42	52.61	51.04	49.67	48.48	47.44	46.54

12.00 %

MONTHLY PAYMENT MORTGAGE

Description: This table shows the price to pay for a mortgage at the yield rate. The yield is to maturity.

Example: The price of a 12.00%, 40 year mortgage to yield 8.00% to maturity is $145.04.

YEARS TO MATURITY

YIELD	17 yr	18 yr	19 yr	20 yr	21 yr	22 yr	23 yr	24 yr	25 yr	26 yr	27 yr	28 yr	29 yr	30 yr	35 yr	40 yr
0.0	234.85	244.50	254.31	264.26	274.35	284.58	294.92	305.39	315.97	326.65	337.43	348.30	359.26	370.30	426.53	484.08
1.00	215.89	223.67	231.52	239.42	247.37	255.35	263.37	271.41	279.46	287.53	295.61	303.68	311.75	319.80	359.76	398.84
2.00	198.95	205.19	211.43	217.66	223.87	230.07	236.24	242.38	248.49	254.55	260.56	266.53	272.44	278.29	306.57	333.03
3.00	183.79	188.75	193.66	198.54	203.36	208.14	212.85	217.51	222.10	226.62	231.07	235.45	239.75	243.98	263.88	281.72
4.00	170.20	174.09	177.93	181.70	185.41	189.05	192.62	196.12	199.54	202.88	206.14	209.33	212.43	215.45	229.36	241.30
4.25	167.02	170.68	174.28	177.81	181.28	184.67	188.00	191.24	194.42	197.51	200.52	203.46	206.32	209.09	221.79	232.58
4.50	163.93	167.37	170.74	174.04	177.28	180.44	183.53	186.55	189.49	192.35	195.13	197.83	200.46	203.01	214.59	224.33
4.75	160.92	164.14	167.30	170.39	173.41	176.35	179.22	182.02	184.74	187.38	189.95	192.44	194.85	197.19	207.74	216.53
5.00	157.99	161.01	163.96	166.84	169.65	172.39	175.06	177.65	180.16	182.60	184.97	187.26	189.47	191.61	201.22	209.15
5.25	155.14	157.96	160.72	163.40	166.02	168.56	171.04	173.43	175.76	178.01	180.18	182.29	184.32	186.27	195.02	202.16
5.50	152.36	154.99	157.57	160.07	162.50	164.86	167.15	169.37	171.51	173.58	175.58	177.51	179.37	181.16	189.11	195.53
5.75	149.65	152.11	154.50	156.83	159.09	161.28	163.39	165.44	167.42	169.32	171.16	172.93	174.63	176.26	183.48	189.25
6.00	147.01	149.30	151.53	153.69	155.78	157.81	159.76	161.65	163.47	165.22	166.90	168.52	170.07	171.56	178.11	183.29
6.25	144.44	146.57	148.64	150.64	152.58	154.45	156.25	157.99	159.66	161.27	162.81	164.29	165.70	167.06	172.98	177.63
6.50	141.93	143.91	145.83	147.68	149.47	151.20	152.86	154.45	155.99	157.46	158.87	160.21	161.50	162.74	168.09	172.26
6.75	139.49	141.32	143.10	144.81	146.46	148.05	149.57	151.04	152.44	153.78	155.07	156.30	157.47	158.59	163.42	167.15
7.00	137.10	138.80	140.44	142.02	143.54	145.00	146.39	147.73	149.02	150.24	151.41	152.53	153.60	154.61	158.96	162.29
7.25	134.78	136.35	137.86	139.31	140.70	142.04	143.32	144.54	145.71	146.83	147.89	148.91	149.87	150.78	154.70	157.66
7.50	132.52	133.96	135.35	136.68	137.96	139.18	140.34	141.46	142.52	143.53	144.50	145.41	146.28	147.11	150.62	153.25
7.75	130.31	131.64	132.91	134.12	135.29	136.40	137.46	138.48	139.44	140.36	141.23	142.05	142.84	143.58	146.72	149.05
8.00	128.16	129.37	130.53	131.64	132.70	133.71	134.67	135.59	136.46	137.29	138.07	138.81	139.52	140.18	142.98	145.04
8.25	126.06	127.16	128.22	129.23	130.19	131.10	131.97	132.80	133.58	134.33	135.03	135.69	136.32	136.92	139.40	141.22
8.50	124.01	125.01	125.97	126.88	127.75	128.57	129.35	130.10	130.80	131.46	132.09	132.69	133.25	133.77	135.98	137.57
8.75	122.02	122.92	123.78	124.60	125.38	126.12	126.82	127.48	128.11	128.70	129.26	129.79	130.28	130.75	132.69	134.08
9.00	120.07	120.88	121.65	122.38	123.08	123.73	124.36	124.95	125.50	126.03	126.52	126.99	127.43	127.84	129.54	130.74
9.25	118.17	118.89	119.57	120.22	120.84	121.42	121.97	122.49	122.99	123.45	123.88	124.29	124.67	125.03	126.51	127.55
9.50	116.31	116.95	117.55	118.13	118.67	119.18	119.66	120.12	120.55	120.95	121.33	121.69	122.02	122.33	123.60	124.50
9.75	114.50	115.06	115.59	116.09	116.56	117.00	117.42	117.82	118.19	118.54	118.86	119.17	119.46	119.72	120.81	121.57
10.00	112.73	113.21	113.67	114.10	114.51	114.89	115.25	115.59	115.90	116.20	116.48	116.74	116.98	117.21	118.13	118.77
10.25	111.00	111.41	111.80	112.17	112.51	112.84	113.14	113.42	113.69	113.94	114.18	114.39	114.60	114.79	115.55	116.08
10.50	109.32	109.66	109.98	110.29	110.57	110.84	111.09	111.33	111.55	111.75	111.95	112.13	112.29	112.45	113.07	113.50
10.75	107.67	107.95	108.21	108.46	108.69	108.90	109.11	109.30	109.47	109.64	109.79	109.93	110.07	110.19	110.69	111.02
11.00	106.07	106.28	106.48	106.67	106.85	107.02	107.18	107.32	107.46	107.59	107.70	107.81	107.92	108.01	108.39	108.64
11.25	104.50	104.65	104.80	104.94	105.07	105.19	105.30	105.41	105.51	105.60	105.68	105.76	105.84	105.90	106.17	106.35
11.50	102.96	103.06	103.16	103.25	103.33	103.41	103.48	103.55	103.62	103.67	103.73	103.78	103.83	103.87	104.04	104.15
11.75	101.46	101.51	101.56	101.60	101.64	101.68	101.72	101.75	101.78	101.81	101.84	101.86	101.88	101.90	101.98	102.04
12.00	100.00	100.00	100.00	100.00	100.00	100.00	100.00	100.00	100.00	100.00	100.00	100.00	100.00	100.00	100.00	100.00
12.25	98.57	98.52	98.48	98.44	98.40	98.36	98.33	98.30	98.27	98.25	98.22	98.20	98.18	98.16	98.09	98.04
12.50	97.17	97.08	96.99	96.91	96.84	96.77	96.71	96.65	96.59	96.54	96.50	96.45	96.42	96.38	96.24	96.15
12.75	95.81	95.67	95.55	95.43	95.32	95.22	95.13	95.05	94.97	94.89	94.83	94.76	94.71	94.66	94.45	94.32
13.00	94.47	94.30	94.13	93.98	93.84	93.72	93.60	93.49	93.38	93.29	93.20	93.13	93.05	92.99	92.73	92.56
13.25	93.16	92.95	92.75	92.57	92.40	92.25	92.10	91.97	91.85	91.74	91.63	91.54	91.45	91.37	91.06	90.87
13.50	91.89	91.64	91.41	91.20	91.00	90.82	90.65	90.50	90.36	90.23	90.11	90.00	89.89	89.80	89.45	89.23
13.75	90.64	90.36	90.10	89.85	89.63	89.43	89.24	89.06	88.90	88.76	88.62	88.50	88.39	88.28	87.89	87.64
14.00	89.42	89.10	88.81	88.55	88.30	88.07	87.86	87.67	87.49	87.33	87.18	87.05	86.93	86.81	86.38	86.11
14.25	88.22	87.88	87.56	87.27	87.00	86.75	86.52	86.31	86.12	85.95	85.79	85.64	85.51	85.38	84.92	84.63
14.50	87.05	86.68	86.34	86.02	85.73	85.46	85.22	85.00	84.79	84.60	84.43	84.27	84.13	84.00	83.50	83.20
14.75	85.91	85.51	85.14	84.81	84.50	84.21	83.95	83.71	83.49	83.29	83.11	82.94	82.79	82.65	82.13	81.81
15.00	84.79	84.37	83.98	83.62	83.29	82.99	82.71	82.46	82.23	82.02	81.83	81.65	81.49	81.35	80.80	80.47
15.25	83.70	83.25	82.84	82.46	82.11	81.80	81.51	81.24	81.00	80.78	80.58	80.40	80.23	80.08	79.51	79.17
15.50	82.63	82.16	81.72	81.33	80.97	80.64	80.33	80.06	79.81	79.58	79.37	79.18	79.01	78.85	78.26	77.91
15.75	81.58	81.09	80.64	80.22	79.85	79.50	79.19	78.90	78.64	78.40	78.19	77.99	77.81	77.65	77.05	76.69
16.00	80.55	80.04	79.57	79.14	78.75	78.40	78.07	77.78	77.51	77.26	77.04	76.84	76.66	76.49	75.87	75.51
16.25	79.55	79.02	78.53	78.09	77.69	77.32	76.98	76.68	76.40	76.15	75.92	75.72	75.53	75.36	74.73	74.36
16.50	78.56	78.01	77.51	77.06	76.64	76.26	75.92	75.61	75.32	75.07	74.83	74.62	74.43	74.26	73.62	73.24
16.75	77.60	77.03	76.52	76.05	75.62	75.24	74.89	74.57	74.28	74.01	73.78	73.56	73.37	73.19	72.54	72.16
17.00	76.65	76.07	75.55	75.07	74.63	74.23	73.87	73.55	73.25	72.99	72.74	72.52	72.33	72.15	71.49	71.11
17.25	75.73	75.14	74.60	74.11	73.66	73.25	72.89	72.56	72.26	71.98	71.74	71.52	71.32	71.14	70.47	70.08
17.50	74.82	74.22	73.67	73.16	72.71	72.30	71.93	71.59	71.28	71.01	70.76	70.53	70.33	70.15	69.48	69.09
17.75	73.94	73.32	72.75	72.25	71.78	71.36	70.99	70.64	70.33	70.05	69.80	69.58	69.37	69.19	68.51	68.12
18.00	73.07	72.44	71.86	71.35	70.88	70.45	70.07	69.72	69.41	69.13	68.87	68.64	68.44	68.25	67.57	67.18
18.25	72.21	71.57	70.99	70.47	69.99	69.56	69.17	68.82	68.51	68.22	67.96	67.73	67.53	67.34	66.66	66.26
18.50	71.38	70.73	70.14	69.61	69.12	68.69	68.30	67.94	67.62	67.34	67.08	66.85	66.64	66.45	65.77	65.37
18.75	70.56	69.90	69.30	68.76	68.28	67.84	67.44	67.08	66.76	66.47	66.21	65.98	65.77	65.58	64.90	64.51
19.00	69.76	69.09	68.49	67.94	67.45	67.00	66.60	66.25	65.92	65.63	65.37	65.14	64.93	64.74	64.05	63.66
20.00	66.70	66.01	65.38	64.81	64.31	63.85	63.44	63.08	62.75	62.46	62.19	61.96	61.74	61.56	60.87	60.49
25.00	54.43	53.70	53.05	52.48	51.97	51.52	51.12	50.76	50.45	50.17	49.93	49.71	49.52	49.34	48.74	48.41
30.00	45.75	45.06	44.46	43.93	43.46	43.05	42.70	42.38	42.10	41.86	41.64	41.45	41.29	41.14	40.62	40.34

(continued)

TABLE 3 Price of Mortgage to Obtain Specified Yield

(continued)

13.00 %

MONTHLY PAYMENT MORTGAGE

Description: This table shows the price to pay for a mortgage at the yield rate. The yield is to maturity.

Example: The price of a 13.00%, 16 year mortgage to yield 8.00% to maturity is $134.06.

	YEARS TO MATURITY															
YIELD	1 yr	2 yr	3 yr	4 yr	5 yr	6 yr	7 yr	8 yr	9 yr	10 yr	11 yr	12 yr	13 yr	14 yr	15 yr	16 yr
0.0	107.18	114.10	121.30	128.77	136.52	144.53	152.81	161.35	170.14	179.17	188.44	197.95	207.67	217.60	227.74	238.08
1.00	106.60	112.92	119.45	126.18	133.11	140.23	147.53	155.00	162.64	170.44	178.38	186.46	194.66	202.98	211.40	219.92
2.00	106.03	111.76	117.64	123.66	129.81	136.09	142.49	148.99	155.59	162.27	169.03	175.85	182.73	189.66	196.62	203.60
3.00	105.46	110.61	115.86	121.20	126.63	132.12	137.68	143.29	148.94	154.63	160.34	166.06	171.79	177.51	183.21	188.90
4.00	104.89	109.48	114.12	118.82	123.55	128.31	133.09	137.89	142.68	147.47	152.25	157.01	161.73	166.41	171.05	175.64
4.25	104.75	109.20	113.70	118.23	122.79	127.38	131.98	136.58	141.18	145.76	150.32	154.85	159.34	163.79	168.19	172.53
4.50	104.61	108.92	113.27	117.65	122.05	126.46	130.88	135.29	139.69	144.07	148.42	152.73	157.01	161.23	165.39	169.50
4.75	104.47	108.64	112.84	117.07	121.31	125.55	129.79	134.02	138.23	142.41	146.55	150.66	154.72	158.72	162.66	166.54
5.00	104.33	108.37	112.42	116.49	120.57	124.65	128.71	132.76	136.78	140.77	144.72	148.63	152.48	156.27	160.00	163.66
5.25	104.19	108.09	112.00	115.92	119.84	123.75	127.65	131.52	135.36	139.16	142.92	146.63	150.28	153.87	157.39	160.84
5.50	104.05	107.82	111.58	115.35	119.12	122.87	126.60	130.30	133.96	137.58	141.15	144.67	148.13	151.52	154.85	158.10
5.75	103.92	107.54	111.17	114.79	118.40	121.99	125.56	129.09	132.58	136.02	139.41	142.75	146.02	149.23	152.36	155.42
6.00	103.78	107.27	110.76	114.23	117.69	121.13	124.53	127.90	131.22	134.49	137.71	140.86	143.96	146.98	149.94	152.81
6.25	103.64	107.00	110.34	113.68	116.99	120.27	123.51	126.72	129.88	132.98	136.03	139.01	141.93	144.79	147.56	150.27
6.50	103.50	106.72	109.93	113.12	116.29	119.42	122.51	125.56	128.55	131.50	134.38	137.20	139.95	142.64	145.25	147.78
6.75	103.36	106.45	109.53	112.58	115.59	118.58	121.52	124.41	127.25	130.03	132.76	135.42	138.01	140.53	142.98	145.35
7.00	103.23	106.19	109.12	112.03	114.91	117.74	120.54	123.28	125.97	128.60	131.16	133.67	136.11	138.47	140.77	142.99
7.25	103.09	105.92	108.72	111.49	114.23	116.92	119.56	122.16	124.70	127.18	129.60	131.95	134.24	136.46	138.60	140.67
7.50	102.95	105.65	108.32	110.95	113.55	116.10	118.61	121.06	123.45	125.79	128.06	130.27	132.41	134.48	136.49	138.42
7.75	102.81	105.38	107.92	110.42	112.88	115.29	117.66	119.97	122.22	124.41	126.55	128.61	130.62	132.55	134.42	136.21
8.00	102.68	105.12	107.52	109.89	112.21	114.49	116.72	118.89	121.01	123.06	125.06	126.99	128.86	130.66	132.40	134.06
8.25	102.54	104.85	107.13	109.36	111.56	113.70	115.79	117.83	119.81	121.73	123.60	125.40	127.14	128.81	130.42	131.96
8.50	102.40	104.59	106.74	108.84	110.90	112.91	114.87	116.78	118.63	120.43	122.16	123.83	125.45	127.00	128.48	129.91
8.75	102.27	104.33	106.35	108.32	110.25	112.14	113.97	115.75	117.47	119.14	120.75	122.30	123.79	125.22	126.59	127.91
9.00	102.13	104.06	105.96	107.81	109.61	111.36	113.07	114.72	116.32	117.87	119.36	120.79	122.17	123.48	124.74	125.95
9.25	102.00	103.80	105.57	107.29	108.97	110.60	112.18	113.71	115.19	116.62	117.99	119.31	120.57	121.78	122.94	124.04
9.50	101.86	103.54	105.19	106.78	108.34	109.85	111.31	112.72	114.08	115.39	116.65	117.85	119.01	120.11	121.17	122.17
9.75	101.73	103.29	104.80	106.28	107.71	109.10	110.44	111.73	112.98	114.18	115.33	116.43	117.48	118.48	119.43	120.34
10.00	101.59	103.03	104.42	105.78	107.09	108.36	109.58	110.76	111.90	112.99	114.03	115.02	115.97	116.88	117.74	118.56
10.25	101.46	102.77	104.04	105.28	106.47	107.62	108.73	109.80	110.83	111.81	112.75	113.65	114.50	115.31	116.08	116.81
10.50	101.33	102.51	103.67	104.78	105.86	106.90	107.90	108.86	109.77	110.65	111.49	112.29	113.05	113.78	114.46	115.11
10.75	101.19	102.26	103.29	104.29	105.25	106.18	107.07	107.92	108.74	109.51	110.26	110.96	111.63	112.27	112.87	113.44
11.00	101.06	102.00	102.92	103.80	104.65	105.46	106.25	107.00	107.71	108.39	109.04	109.66	110.24	110.80	111.32	111.81
11.25	100.93	101.75	102.55	103.31	104.05	104.76	105.44	106.08	106.70	107.29	107.85	108.38	108.88	109.35	109.80	110.22
11.50	100.79	101.50	102.18	102.83	103.46	104.06	104.63	105.18	105.70	106.20	106.67	107.12	107.54	107.93	108.31	108.66
11.75	100.66	101.25	101.81	102.35	102.87	103.37	103.84	104.29	104.72	105.13	105.51	105.88	106.22	106.54	106.85	107.14
12.00	100.53	100.99	101.44	101.87	102.29	102.68	103.05	103.41	103.75	104.07	104.37	104.66	104.93	105.18	105.42	105.65
12.25	100.40	100.74	101.08	101.40	101.71	102.00	102.28	102.54	102.79	103.03	103.25	103.46	103.66	103.85	104.02	104.19
12.50	100.26	100.50	100.72	100.93	101.13	101.33	101.51	101.68	101.85	102.00	102.15	102.29	102.42	102.54	102.65	102.76
12.75	100.13	100.25	100.36	100.46	100.56	100.66	100.75	100.84	100.92	100.99	101.07	101.13	101.20	101.26	101.31	101.37
13.00	100.00	100.00	100.00	100.00	100.00	100.00	100.00	100.00	100.00	100.00	100.00	100.00	100.00	100.00	100.00	100.00
13.25	99.87	99.75	99.64	99.54	99.44	99.35	99.26	99.17	99.09	99.02	98.95	98.88	98.82	98.77	98.71	98.66
13.50	99.74	99.51	99.29	99.08	98.88	98.70	98.52	98.36	98.20	98.05	97.92	97.79	97.67	97.56	97.45	97.36
13.75	99.61	99.26	98.94	98.63	98.33	98.06	97.79	97.55	97.32	97.10	96.90	96.71	96.53	96.37	96.22	96.08
14.00	99.48	99.02	98.58	98.17	97.79	97.42	97.08	96.75	96.45	96.16	95.90	95.65	95.42	95.21	95.01	94.82
14.25	99.35	98.78	98.24	97.72	97.24	96.79	96.36	95.96	95.59	95.24	94.91	94.61	94.33	94.06	93.82	93.60
14.50	99.22	98.53	97.89	97.28	96.71	96.17	95.66	95.19	94.74	94.33	93.94	93.59	93.25	92.94	92.66	92.39
14.75	99.09	98.29	97.54	96.84	96.17	95.55	94.96	94.42	93.91	93.43	92.99	92.58	92.20	91.84	91.52	91.22
15.00	98.96	98.05	97.20	96.40	95.64	94.94	94.27	93.66	93.08	92.55	92.05	91.59	91.16	90.77	90.40	90.07
15.25	98.83	97.81	96.86	95.96	95.12	94.33	93.59	92.91	92.27	91.68	91.12	90.61	90.14	89.71	89.31	88.94
15.50	98.70	97.57	96.51	95.52	94.59	93.73	92.92	92.17	91.47	90.82	90.21	89.66	89.14	88.67	88.23	87.83
15.75	98.57	97.33	96.18	95.09	94.08	93.13	92.25	91.43	90.67	89.97	89.32	88.72	88.16	87.65	87.18	86.75
16.00	98.44	97.10	95.84	94.66	93.56	92.54	91.59	90.71	89.89	89.13	88.43	87.79	87.20	86.65	86.15	85.69
16.25	98.31	96.86	95.50	94.24	93.06	91.96	90.94	89.99	89.12	88.31	87.57	86.88	86.25	85.67	85.13	84.65
16.50	98.19	96.63	95.17	93.81	92.55	91.38	90.29	89.29	88.36	87.50	86.71	85.98	85.31	84.70	84.14	83.63
16.75	98.06	96.39	94.84	93.39	92.05	90.80	89.65	88.59	87.60	86.70	85.87	85.10	84.40	83.76	83.17	82.63
17.00	97.93	96.16	94.51	92.97	91.55	90.24	89.02	87.90	86.86	85.91	85.04	84.23	83.50	82.83	82.21	81.65
17.25	97.80	95.92	94.18	92.56	91.06	89.67	88.39	87.22	86.13	85.13	84.22	83.38	82.61	81.91	81.27	80.69
17.50	97.68	95.69	93.85	92.15	90.57	89.12	87.77	86.54	85.41	84.37	83.41	82.54	81.74	81.02	80.35	79.75
17.75	97.55	95.46	93.52	91.74	90.08	88.56	87.16	85.87	84.69	83.61	82.62	81.71	80.89	80.14	79.45	78.83
18.00	97.42	95.23	93.20	91.33	89.60	88.01	86.55	85.22	83.99	82.87	81.84	80.90	80.05	79.27	78.57	77.93
18.25	97.30	95.00	92.88	90.92	89.12	87.47	85.95	84.56	83.29	82.13	81.07	80.10	79.22	78.42	77.70	77.04
18.50	97.17	94.77	92.56	90.52	88.65	86.93	85.36	83.92	82.61	81.41	80.31	79.32	78.41	77.59	76.84	76.17
18.75	97.04	94.54	92.24	90.12	88.18	86.40	84.77	83.29	81.93	80.69	79.56	78.54	77.61	76.77	76.01	75.32
19.00	96.92	94.31	91.92	89.72	87.71	85.87	84.19	82.66	81.26	79.99	78.83	77.78	76.83	75.96	75.18	74.48
20.00	96.42	93.41	90.66	88.16	85.88	83.81	81.92	80.21	78.66	77.26	75.99	74.85	73.81	72.88	72.04	71.29
25.00	93.97	89.08	84.74	80.91	77.52	74.52	71.87	69.53	67.46	65.63	64.02	62.59	61.34	60.23	59.25	58.38
30.00	91.62	85.03	79.37	74.51	70.33	66.73	63.62	60.95	58.64	56.64	54.91	53.41	52.12	50.99	50.02	49.17

13.00 %

MONTHLY PAYMENT MORTGAGE

Description: This table shows the price to pay for a mortgage at the yield rate. The yield is to maturity.

Example: The price of a 13.00%, 40 year mortgage to yield 8.00% to maturity is $156.69.

	YEARS TO MATURITY															
YIELD	**17** yr	**18** yr	**19** yr	**20** yr	**21** yr	**22** yr	**23** yr	**24** yr	**25** yr	**26** yr	**27** yr	**28** yr	**29** yr	**30** yr	**35** yr	**40** yr
0.0	248.60	259.29	270.16	281.18	292.35	303.66	315.10	326.67	338.35	350.14	362.03	374.01	386.08	398.23	459.98	522.97
1.00	228.53	237.21	245.95	254.75	263.59	272.48	281.39	290.32	299.26	308.21	317.16	326.10	335.02	343.93	387.97	430.88
2.00	210.60	217.60	224.60	231.59	238.56	245.50	252.41	259.27	266.09	272.85	279.56	286.20	292.78	299.28	330.61	359.78
3.00	194.55	200.16	205.73	211.25	216.70	222.10	227.42	232.67	237.83	242.92	247.92	252.83	257.65	262.38	284.58	304.35
4.00	180.16	184.63	189.02	193.34	197.57	201.73	205.80	209.78	213.67	217.47	221.17	224.78	228.29	231.71	247.35	260.69
4.25	176.80	181.01	185.14	189.20	193.17	197.06	200.86	204.57	208.19	211.71	215.14	218.48	221.72	224.86	239.18	251.26
4.50	173.53	177.49	181.38	185.19	188.91	192.54	196.09	199.55	202.91	206.18	209.36	212.44	215.43	218.32	231.42	242.35
4.75	170.34	174.07	177.73	181.30	184.78	188.18	191.48	194.70	197.83	200.86	203.80	206.64	209.40	212.06	224.03	233.92
5.00	167.24	170.75	174.18	177.52	180.78	183.95	187.04	190.03	192.93	195.74	198.45	201.08	203.62	206.06	217.00	225.95
5.25	164.22	167.52	170.73	173.86	176.91	179.87	182.74	185.52	188.21	190.81	193.32	195.74	198.08	200.32	210.31	218.40
5.50	161.28	164.37	167.39	170.32	173.16	175.92	178.59	181.17	183.66	186.07	188.38	190.62	192.76	194.83	203.94	211.24
5.75	158.41	161.31	164.13	166.87	169.52	172.09	174.57	176.97	179.28	181.50	183.64	185.69	187.66	189.56	197.87	204.45
6.00	155.61	158.33	160.97	163.53	166.00	168.39	170.69	172.91	175.05	177.10	179.07	180.96	182.77	184.50	192.08	198.02
6.25	152.89	155.44	157.90	160.29	162.59	164.81	166.94	169.00	170.97	172.86	174.68	176.41	178.07	179.66	186.55	191.90
6.50	150.24	152.62	154.92	157.14	159.28	161.34	163.31	165.21	167.04	168.78	170.45	172.04	173.56	175.01	181.28	186.10
6.75	147.65	149.87	152.02	154.08	156.07	157.98	159.81	161.56	163.24	164.84	166.38	167.84	169.23	170.55	176.24	180.58
7.00	145.13	147.20	149.20	151.11	152.95	154.72	156.41	158.03	159.57	161.05	162.45	163.79	165.06	166.27	171.43	175.32
7.25	142.67	144.60	146.45	148.23	149.93	151.57	153.13	154.62	156.04	157.39	158.67	159.90	161.06	162.16	166.83	170.32
7.50	140.28	142.07	143.78	145.43	147.01	148.51	149.95	151.32	152.62	153.86	155.03	156.15	157.21	158.21	162.43	165.56
7.75	137.94	139.60	141.19	142.71	144.16	145.55	146.87	148.12	149.32	150.45	151.52	152.54	153.50	154.41	158.22	161.02
8.00	135.66	137.20	138.67	140.07	141.40	142.68	143.89	145.04	146.13	147.16	148.14	149.06	149.93	150.76	154.20	156.69
8.25	133.44	134.86	136.21	137.50	138.73	139.89	141.00	142.05	143.04	143.99	144.87	145.71	146.50	147:24	150.34	152.56
8.50	131.27	132.58	133.82	135.00	136.13	137.19	138.20	139.16	140.06	140.92	141.72	142.48	143.19	143.87	146.64	148.62
8.75	129.16	130.36	131.49	132.57	133.60	134.57	135.49	136.36	137.18	137.96	138.68	139.37	140.01	140.61	143.09	144.85
9.00	127.10	128.19	129.23	130.21	131.15	132.03	132.87	133.65	134.39	135.09	135.75	136.36	136.94	137.48	139.69	141.25
9.25	125.08	126.08	127.02	127.92	128.77	129.57	130.32	131.03	131.70	132.33	132.91	133.46	133.98	134.46	136.43	137.80
9.50	123.12	124.02	124.88	125.69	126.45	127.17	127.85	128.49	129.09	129.65	130.18	130.67	131.13	131.56	133.30	134.50
9.75	121.20	122.02	122.79	123.52	124.20	124.85	125.46	126.03	126.56	127.06	127.53	127.97	128.37	128.75	130.29	131.34
10.00	119.33	120.06	120.75	121.40	122.02	122.59	123.13	123.64	124.12	124.56	124.97	125.36	125.72	126.05	127.40	128.31
10.25	117.50	118.16	118.77	119.35	119.89	120.40	120.88	121.33	121.75	122.14	122.50	122.84	123.15	123.45	124.62	125.40
10.50	115.72	116.30	116.84	117.35	117.83	118.27	118.69	119.09	119.45	119.79	120.11	120.40	120.68	120.93	121.94	122.61
10.75	113.98	114.48	114.96	115.40	115.82	116.21	116.57	116.91	117.23	117.52	117.80	118.05	118.28	118.50	119.37	119.94
11.00	112.28	112.71	113.12	113.50	113.86	114.20	114.51	114.80	115.07	115.32	115.56	115.77	115.97	116.16	116.89	117.37
11.25	110.61	110.98	111.33	111.66	111.96	112.25	112.51	112.75	112.98	113.19	113.39	113.57	113.74	113.89	114.50	114.90
11.50	108.99	109.30	109.59	109.86	110.11	110.35	110.57	110.77	110.96	111.13	111.29	111.44	111.58	111.70	112.20	112.52
11.75	107.40	107.66	107.89	108.11	108.31	108.50	108.68	108.84	108.99	109.13	109.26	109.38	109.49	109.59	109.98	110.23
12.00	105.85	106.05	106.23	106.40	106.56	106.71	106.84	106.97	107.08	107.19	107.29	107.38	107.47	107.54	107.84	108.03
12.25	104.34	104.48	104.62	104.74	104.85	104.96	105.06	105.15	105.23	105.31	105.38	105.45	105.51	105.56	105.78	105.91
12.50	102.86	102.95	103.04	103.12	103.19	103.26	103.32	103.38	103.44	103.49	103.53	103.57	103.61	103.65	103.78	103.87
12.75	101.41	101.46	101.50	101.54	101.58	101.61	101.64	101.67	101.69	101.72	101.74	101.76	101.78	101.80	101.86	101.90
13.00	100.00	100.00	100.00	100.00	100.00	100.00	100.00	100.00	100.00	100.00	100.00	100.00	100.00	100.00	100.00	100.00
13.25	98.62	98.57	98.54	98.50	98.47	98.43	98.41	98.38	98.35	98.33	98.31	98.29	98.28	98.26	98.20	98.17
13.50	97.27	97.18	97.11	97.03	96.97	96.91	96.85	96.80	96.76	96.71	96.67	96.64	96.61	96.58	96.46	96.39
13.75	95.94	95.82	95.71	95.61	95.51	95.42	95.34	95.27	95.20	95.14	95.08	95.03	94.99	94.94	94.78	94.68
14.00	94.65	94.49	94.35	94.21	94.09	93.98	93.87	93.78	93.69	93.61	93.54	93.47	93.41	93.36	93.15	93.03
14.25	93.39	93.19	93.02	92.86	92.71	92.57	92.44	92.33	92.22	92.13	92.04	91.96	91.89	91.82	91.58	91.43
14.50	92.15	91.93	91.72	91.53	91.36	91.20	91.05	90.92	90.80	90.69	90.58	90.49	90.41	90.33	90.05	89.88
14.75	90.94	90.68	90.45	90.24	90.04	89.86	89.69	89.54	89.41	89.28	89.17	89.07	88.97	88.89	88.57	88.39
15.00	89.76	89.47	89.21	88.97	88.75	88.55	88.37	88.21	88.05	87.92	87.79	87.68	87.58	87.49	87.14	86.94
15.25	88.60	88.29	88.00	87.74	87.50	87.28	87.08	86.90	86.74	86.59	86.46	86.33	86.22	86.12	85.75	85.53
15.50	87.46	87.13	86.82	86.53	86.28	86.04	85.83	85.63	85.46	85.30	85.15	85.02	84.90	84.80	84.40	84.17
15.75	86.35	85.99	85.66	85.36	85.08	84.83	84.61	84.40	84.21	84.04	83.89	83.75	83.62	83.51	83.09	82.85
16.00	85.27	84.88	84.53	84.21	83.92	83.65	83.41	83.19	83.00	82.82	82.66	82.51	82.38	82.26	81.82	81.57
16.25	84.20	83.80	83.43	83.09	82.78	82.50	82.25	82.02	81.81	81.63	81.46	81.31	81.17	81.04	80.59	80.33
16.50	83.16	82.73	82.34	81.99	81.67	81.38	81.12	80.88	80.66	80.47	80.29	80.13	79.99	79.86	79.39	79.12
16.75	82.14	81.69	81.29	80.92	80.59	80.28	80.01	79.76	79.54	79.34	79.15	78.99	78.84	78.71	78.23	77.95
17.00	81.14	80.68	80.26	79.87	79.53	79.21	78.93	78.67	78.44	78.23	78.05	77.88	77.73	77.59	77.10	76.82
17.25	80.16	79.68	79.24	78.85	78.49	78.17	77.88	77.61	77.37	77.16	76.97	76.80	76.64	76.50	76.00	75.71
17.50	79.20	78.71	78.26	77.85	77.48	77.15	76.85	76.58	76.33	76.11	75.92	75.74	75.58	75.44	74.93	74.64
17.75	78.26	77.75	77.29	76.87	76.49	76.15	75.84	75.57	75.32	75.09	74.89	74.71	74.55	74.41	73.89	73.59
18.00	77.34	76.82	76.34	75.91	75.53	75.18	74.86	74.58	74.33	74.10	73.89	73.71	73.55	73.40	72.87	72.58
18.25	76.44	75.90	75.42	74.98	74.58	74.22	73.90	73.62	73.36	73.13	72.92	72.73	72.57	72.42	71.89	71.59
18.50	75.56	75.01	74.51	74.06	73.66	73.29	72.97	72.68	72.41	72.18	71.97	71.78	71.61	71.46	70.92	70.63
18.75	74.69	74.13	73.62	73.17	72.75	72.39	72.05	71.76	71.49	71.25	71.04	70.85	70.68	70.53	69.99	69.69
19.00	73.84	73.27	72.75	72.29	71.87	71.50	71.16	70.86	70.59	70.35	70.14	69.94	69.77	69.62	69.08	68.77
20.00	70.61	70.00	69.45	68.96	68.53	68.13	67.79	67.47	67.19	66.95	66.73	66.53	66.35	66.20	65.65	65.35
25.00	57.62	56.95	56.36	55.84	55.38	54.97	54.62	54.30	54.02	53.78	53.57	53.38	53.21	53.07	52.56	52.29
30.00	48.43	47.79	47.23	46.74	46.31	45.94	45.62	45.33	45.09	44.87	44.68	44.51	44.37	44.24	43.81	43.58

(continued)

TABLE 3 Price of Mortgage to Obtain Specified Yield

(continued)

14.00 %

MONTHLY PAYMENT MORTGAGE

Description: This table shows the price to pay for a mortgage at the yield rate. The yield is to maturity.

Example: The price of a 14.00%, 16 year mortgage to yield 8.00% to maturity is $141.38.

	YEARS TO MATURITY															
YIELD	1 yr	2 yr	3 yr	4 yr	5 yr	6 yr	7 yr	8 yr	9 yr	10 yr	11 yr	12 yr	13 yr	14 yr	15 yr	16 yr
0.0	107.74	115.23	123.04	131.17	139.61	148.36	157.42	166.77	176.40	186.32	196.50	206.95	217.64	228.56	239.71	251.08
1.00	107.16	114.04	121.16	128.53	136.12	143.94	151.97	160.21	168.63	177.24	186.01	194.94	204.00	213.20	222.52	231.93
2.00	106.59	112.86	119.32	125.96	132.75	139.70	146.78	153.99	161.32	168.74	176.26	183.85	191.50	199.21	206.95	214.72
3.00	106.01	111.71	117.52	123.46	129.49	135.62	141.83	148.10	154.43	160.80	167.20	173.61	180.03	186.45	192.84	199.21
4.00	105.45	110.57	115.76	121.03	126.34	131.71	137.10	142.51	147.94	153.36	158.76	164.14	169.49	174.79	180.04	185.23
4.25	105.30	110.28	115.33	120.43	125.57	130.75	135.95	141.16	146.37	151.57	156.75	161.89	166.99	172.04	177.03	181.95
4.50	105.16	110.00	114.89	119.83	124.81	129.81	134.82	139.83	144.83	149.82	154.77	159.68	164.54	169.35	174.09	178.75
4.75	105.02	109.72	114.46	119.25	124.05	128.87	133.70	138.52	143.32	148.09	152.82	157.51	162.14	166.71	171.21	175.63
5.00	104.88	109.44	114.04	118.66	123.30	127.95	132.59	137.22	141.82	146.39	150.91	155.38	159.79	164.14	168.41	172.59
5.25	104.74	109.16	113.61	118.08	122.55	127.03	131.49	135.93	140.34	144.71	149.03	153.30	157.49	161.62	165.66	169.63
5.50	104.60	108.88	113.19	117.50	121.82	126.12	130.41	134.67	138.89	143.07	147.19	151.25	155.24	159.15	162.99	166.73
5.75	104.46	108.61	112.76	116.93	121.08	125.22	129.34	133.42	137.46	141.45	145.38	149.24	153.03	156.74	160.37	163.91
6.00	104.32	108.33	112.35	116.36	120.36	124.33	128.28	132.19	136.05	139.85	143.60	147.27	150.87	154.38	157.82	161.16
6.25	104.18	108.06	111.93	115.79	119.64	123.45	127.23	130.97	134.66	138.28	141.85	145.34	148.75	152.08	155.32	158.47
6.50	104.05	107.78	111.51	115.23	118.92	122.58	126.20	129.77	133.29	136.74	140.13	143.44	146.67	149.82	152.88	155.85
6.75	103.91	107.51	111.10	114.67	118.21	121.72	125.18	128.59	131.94	135.22	138.44	141.57	144.63	147.61	150.49	153.29
7.00	103.77	107.24	110.69	114.12	117.51	120.86	124.17	127.42	130.60	133.73	136.77	139.75	142.64	145.44	148.16	150.79
7.25	103.63	106.97	110.28	113.57	116.81	120.01	123.17	126.26	129.29	132.25	135.14	137.95	140.68	143.33	145.89	148.36
7.50	103.49	106.70	109.87	113.02	116.12	119.18	122.18	125.12	128.00	130.80	133.54	136.19	138.77	141.26	143.66	145.98
7.75	103.35	106.43	109.47	112.47	115.44	118.35	121.20	123.99	126.72	129.38	131.96	134.46	136.89	139.23	141.48	143.65
8.00	103.22	106.16	109.07	111.93	114.76	117.52	120.23	122.88	125.46	127.97	130.41	132.77	135.04	137.24	139.35	141.38
8.25	103.08	105.89	108.67	111.40	114.08	116.71	119.28	121.78	124.22	126.59	128.88	131.10	133.24	135.30	137.27	139.17
8.50	102.94	105.63	108.27	110.87	113.41	115.90	118.33	120.70	123.00	125.23	127.38	129.46	131.47	133.39	135.24	137.00
8.75	102.81	105.36	107.87	110.34	112.75	115.10	117.40	119.63	121.80	123.89	125.91	127.86	129.73	131.53	133.25	134.89
9.00	102.67	105.10	107.48	109.81	112.09	114.31	116.48	118.58	120.61	122.57	124.46	126.28	128.03	129.70	131.30	132.83
9.25	102.53	104.83	107.09	109.29	111.44	113.53	115.56	117.53	119.44	121.27	123.04	124.73	126.36	127.91	129.40	130.81
9.50	102.40	104.57	106.70	108.77	110.79	112.76	114.66	116.50	118.28	119.99	121.64	123.21	124.72	126.16	127.53	128.84
9.75	102.26	104.31	106.31	108.26	110.15	111.99	113.77	115.49	117.14	118.73	120.26	121.72	123.12	124.45	125.71	126.91
10.00	102.13	104.05	105.92	107.74	109.51	111.23	112.88	114.48	116.02	117.49	118.90	120.25	121.54	122.77	123.93	125.03
10.25	101.99	103.79	105.54	107.23	108.88	110.47	112.01	113.49	114.91	116.27	117.57	118.81	120.00	121.12	122.18	123.19
10.50	101.86	103.53	105.15	106.73	108.26	109.73	111.15	112.51	113.82	115.07	116.26	117.40	118.48	119.51	120.48	121.39
10.75	101.72	103.27	104.77	106.23	107.63	108.99	110.29	111.54	112.74	113.88	114.97	116.01	116.99	117.92	118.80	119.64
11.00	101.59	103.01	104.40	105.73	107.02	108.26	109.45	110.59	111.68	112.72	113.71	114.64	115.53	116.38	117.17	117.92
11.25	101.46	102.76	104.02	105.24	106.41	107.53	108.61	109.64	110.63	111.57	112.46	113.30	114.10	114.86	115.57	116.24
11.50	101.32	102.50	103.64	104.74	105.80	106.81	107.79	108.71	109.60	110.43	111.23	111.99	112.70	113.37	114.00	114.59
11.75	101.19	102.25	103.27	104.25	105.20	106.10	106.97	107.79	108.58	109.32	110.02	110.69	111.32	111.91	112.47	112.99
12.00	101.06	102.00	102.90	103.77	104.60	105.40	106.16	106.88	107.57	108.22	108.84	109.42	109.97	110.48	110.96	111.41
12.25	100.92	101.74	102.53	103.29	104.01	104.70	105.36	105.99	106.58	107.14	107.67	108.17	108.64	109.08	109.49	109.88
12.50	100.79	101.49	102.16	102.81	103.42	104.01	104.57	105.10	105.60	106.07	106.52	106.94	107.33	107.70	108.05	108.37
12.75	100.66	101.24	101.80	102.33	102.84	103.33	103.79	104.22	104.63	105.02	105.39	105.73	106.06	106.36	106.64	106.90
13.00	100.53	100.99	101.44	101.86	102.26	102.65	103.01	103.36	103.68	103.99	104.28	104.55	104.80	105.04	105.26	105.46
13.25	100.39	100.74	101.07	101.39	101.69	101.98	102.25	102.50	102.74	102.97	103.18	103.38	103.57	103.74	103.90	104.05
13.50	100.26	100.49	100.71	100.92	101.12	101.31	101.49	101.66	101.82	101.96	102.10	102.23	102.36	102.47	102.57	102.67
13.75	100.13	100.25	100.36	100.46	100.56	100.65	100.74	100.82	100.90	100.98	101.04	101.11	101.17	101.22	101.27	101.32
14.00	100.00	100.00	100.00	100.00	100.00	100.00	100.00	100.00	100.00	100.00	100.00	100.00	100.00	100.00	100.00	100.00
14.25	99.87	99.75	99.65	99.54	99.45	99.35	99.27	99.19	99.11	99.04	98.97	98.91	98.85	98.80	98.75	98.71
14.50	99.74	99.51	99.29	99.09	98.89	98.71	98.54	98.38	98.23	98.09	97.96	97.84	97.73	97.62	97.53	97.44
14.75	99.61	99.27	98.94	98.64	98.35	98.08	97.82	97.59	97.37	97.16	96.97	96.79	96.62	96.47	96.33	96.20
15.00	99.48	99.02	98.59	98.19	97.81	97.45	97.11	96.80	96.51	96.24	95.99	95.75	95.54	95.34	95.15	94.98
15.25	99.35	98.78	98.25	97.74	97.27	96.83	96.41	96.03	95.67	95.33	95.02	94.73	94.47	94.22	94.00	93.79
15.50	99.22	98.54	97.90	97.30	96.74	96.21	95.72	95.26	94.83	94.44	94.07	93.73	93.42	93.13	92.87	92.63
15.75	99.09	98.30	97.56	96.86	96.21	95.60	95.03	94.50	94.01	93.56	93.14	92.75	92.39	92.06	91.76	91.49
16.00	98.96	98.06	97.21	96.42	95.68	94.99	94.35	93.75	93.20	92.69	92.22	91.78	91.38	91.01	90.67	90.37
16.25	98.83	97.82	96.87	95.99	95.16	94.39	93.68	93.01	92.40	91.83	91.31	90.83	90.39	89.98	89.61	89.27
16.50	98.70	97.58	96.54	95.56	94.65	93.80	93.01	92.28	91.61	90.99	90.42	89.89	89.41	88.97	88.56	88.20
16.75	98.57	97.35	96.20	95.13	94.13	93.21	92.35	91.56	90.83	90.16	89.54	88.97	88.45	87.97	87.54	87.14
17.00	98.45	97.11	95.86	94.70	93.63	92.63	91.70	90.85	90.06	89.34	88.67	88.06	87.51	87.00	86.53	86.11
17.25	98.32	96.87	95.53	94.28	93.12	92.05	91.06	90.14	89.30	88.53	87.82	87.17	86.58	86.04	85.55	85.10
17.50	98.19	96.64	95.20	93.86	92.62	91.48	90.42	89.45	88.55	87.73	86.98	86.29	85.67	85.10	84.58	84.11
17.75	98.06	96.40	94.87	93.44	92.12	90.91	89.79	88.76	87.81	86.95	86.15	85.43	84.77	84.17	83.63	83.13
18.00	97.94	96.17	94.54	93.03	91.63	90.35	89.16	88.08	87.08	86.17	85.34	84.58	83.89	83.26	82.70	82.18
18.25	97.81	95.94	94.21	92.61	91.14	89.79	88.54	87.40	86.36	85.41	84.54	83.74	83.02	82.37	81.78	81.25
18.50	97.68	95.71	93.89	92.20	90.66	89.24	87.93	86.74	85.65	84.65	83.75	82.92	82.17	81.50	80.88	80.33
18.75	97.56	95.48	93.56	91.80	90.18	88.69	87.33	86.08	84.94	83.91	82.97	82.11	81.34	80.63	80.00	79.43
19.00	97.43	95.25	93.24	91.39	89.70	88.15	86.73	85.43	84.25	83.18	82.20	81.31	80.51	79.79	79.13	78.55
20.00	96.93	94.34	91.97	89.80	87.82	86.03	84.39	82.91	81.56	80.34	79.24	78.25	77.35	76.55	75.83	75.18
25.00	94.47	89.96	85.96	82.42	79.27	76.50	74.04	71.86	69.95	68.25	66.76	65.44	64.28	63.26	62.36	61.57
30.00	92.10	85.87	80.51	75.89	71.92	68.49	65.54	62.99	60.80	58.90	57.26	55.84	54.62	53.56	52.64	51.85

14.00 %

MONTHLY PAYMENT MORTGAGE

Description: This table shows the price to pay for a mortgage at the yield rate. The yield is to maturity.

Example: The price of a 14.00%, 40 year mortgage to yield 8.00% to maturity is $168.43.

	YEARS TO MATURITY															
YIELD	**17** yr	**18** yr	**19** yr	**20** yr	**21** yr	**22** yr	**23** yr	**24** yr	**25** yr	**26** yr	**27** yr	**28** yr	**29** yr	**30** yr	**35** yr	**40** yr
0.0	262.65	274.40	286.34	298.44	310.71	323.12	335.66	348.34	361.13	374.03	387.03	400.12	413.30	426.55	493.78	562.15
1.00	241.44	251.03	260.68	270.39	280.15	289.94	299.75	309.58	319.41	329.24	339.06	348.86	358.64	368.39	416.48	463.16
2.00	222.50	230.28	238.06	245.81	253.54	261.23	268.88	276.47	284.00	291.47	298.86	306.18	313.42	320.57	354.91	386.74
3.00	205.54	211.83	218.06	224.22	230.31	236.33	242.26	248.10	253.84	259.49	265.04	270.48	275.81	281.04	305.49	327.15
4.00	190.34	195.38	200.34	205.21	209.98	214.66	219.23	223.70	228.06	232.31	236.44	240.47	244.38	248.18	265.52	280.22
4.25	186.79	191.56	196.23	200.82	205.30	209.69	213.97	218.14	222.20	226.16	230.00	233.73	237.35	240.86	256.76	270.08
4.50	183.34	187.84	192.24	196.56	200.77	204.88	208.89	212.78	216.57	220.25	223.81	227.27	230.61	233.85	248.42	260.51
4.75	179.97	184.22	188.37	192.43	196.38	200.23	203.98	207.62	211.14	214.56	217.87	221.07	224.16	227.14	240.49	251.45
5.00	176.69	180.70	184.61	188.42	192.14	195.74	199.24	202.63	205.92	209.09	212.16	215.12	217.97	220.72	232.95	242.88
5.25	173.50	177.28	180.96	184.54	188.02	191.39	194.66	197.82	200.88	203.83	206.67	209.41	212.04	214.57	225.77	234.76
5.50	170.39	173.95	177.41	180.77	184.03	187.19	190.24	193.18	196.02	198.76	201.39	203.92	206.35	208.68	218.93	227.07
5.75	167.36	170.71	173.97	177.12	180.17	183.12	185.96	188.71	191.34	193.88	196.32	198.65	200.89	203.04	212.41	219.77
6.00	164.41	167.56	170.62	173.57	176.43	179.18	181.83	184.38	186.83	189.18	191.44	193.59	195.66	197.63	206.19	212.85
6.25	161.53	164.49	167.36	170.13	172.80	175.37	177.84	180.21	182.48	184.66	186.74	188.73	190.63	192.44	200.26	206.28
6.50	158.73	161.51	164.20	166.79	169.28	171.67	173.97	176.17	178.28	180.29	182.22	184.05	185.80	187.46	194.60	200.04
6.75	156.00	158.61	161.12	163.54	165.87	168.10	170.23	172.28	174.23	176.09	177.86	179.55	181.16	182.68	189.19	194.10
7.00	153.33	155.78	158.13	160.39	162.56	164.63	166.62	168.51	170.32	172.04	173.67	175.22	176.70	178.10	184.03	188.46
7.25	150.74	153.03	155.23	157.33	159.35	161.28	163.12	164.87	166.54	168.13	169.63	171.06	172.41	173.69	179.09	183.08
7.50	148.21	150.35	152.40	154.36	156.24	158.03	159.73	161.35	162.89	164.35	165.74	167.05	168.29	169.46	174.37	177.97
7.75	145.74	147.74	149.65	151.47	153.22	154.87	156.45	157.95	159.37	160.71	161.99	163.19	164.32	165.39	169.85	173.09
8.00	143.33	145.19	146.97	148.67	150.28	151.82	153.28	154.66	155.96	157.20	158.37	159.47	160.50	161.48	165.53	168.43
8.25	140.98	142.72	144.37	145.94	147.44	148.86	150.20	151.47	152.67	153.81	154.88	155.88	156.83	157.72	161.38	163.99
8.50	138.69	140.30	141.84	143.29	144.67	145.98	147.22	148.39	149.49	150.53	151.51	152.43	153.29	154.10	157.42	159.75
8.75	136.46	137.95	139.37	140.72	141.99	143.20	144.33	145.41	146.42	147.37	148.26	149.10	149.88	150.61	153.61	155.70
9.00	134.28	135.66	136.97	138.21	139.38	140.49	141.54	142.52	143.44	144.31	145.12	145.88	146.59	147.26	149.96	151.83
9.25	132.15	133.43	134.63	135.78	136.85	137.87	138.82	139.72	140.56	141.35	142.09	142.78	143.43	144.03	146.46	148.12
9.50	130.08	131.25	132.36	133.41	134.39	135.32	136.19	137.01	137.78	138.49	139.16	139.79	140.37	140.91	143.09	144.57
9.75	128.05	129.13	130.14	131.10	132.00	132.85	133.64	134.39	135.08	135.73	136.34	136.90	137.42	137.91	139.86	141.18
10.00	126.07	127.06	127.99	128.86	129.68	130.45	131.17	131.84	132.47	133.06	133.60	134.11	134.58	135.02	136.76	137.92
10.25	124.14	125.04	125.88	126.68	127.42	128.12	128.77	129.38	129.94	130.47	130.96	131.41	131.83	132.23	133.77	134.80
10.50	122.26	123.07	123.84	124.55	125.23	125.85	126.44	126.98	127.49	127.96	128.40	128.81	129.18	129.53	130.90	131.80
10.75	120.42	121.15	121.84	122.49	123.09	123.65	124.18	124.67	125.12	125.54	125.93	126.29	126.62	126.93	128.14	128.92
11.00	118.62	119.28	119.90	120.47	121.01	121.52	121.98	122.42	122.82	123.19	123.54	123.85	124.15	124.42	125.48	126.16
11.25	116.86	117.45	118.00	118.51	118.99	119.44	119.85	120.23	120.59	120.92	121.22	121.50	121.76	121.99	122.91	123.50
11.50	115.15	115.67	116.15	116.61	117.03	117.42	117.78	118.12	118.43	118.71	118.98	119.22	119.44	119.65	120.45	120.95
11.75	113.47	113.93	114.35	114.75	115.11	115.45	115.77	116.06	116.33	116.58	116.80	117.01	117.21	117.38	118.06	118.49
12.00	111.84	112.23	112.60	112.94	113.25	113.54	113.81	114.06	114.29	114.50	114.70	114.88	115.04	115.19	115.77	116.13
12.25	110.24	110.57	110.88	111.17	111.44	111.69	111.91	112.12	112.32	112.50	112.66	112.81	112.95	113.07	113.55	113.85
12.50	108.67	108.95	109.21	109.45	109.67	109.88	110.07	110.24	110.40	110.55	110.68	110.81	110.92	111.02	111.41	111.65
12.75	107.14	107.37	107.58	107.78	107.95	108.12	108.27	108.41	108.54	108.66	108.76	108.86	108.95	109.03	109.35	109.53
13.00	105.65	105.83	105.99	106.14	106.28	106.41	106.53	106.63	106.73	106.82	106.91	106.98	107.05	107.11	107.35	107.49
13.25	104.19	104.32	104.44	104.55	104.65	104.74	104.83	104.90	104.98	105.04	105.10	105.16	105.20	105.25	105.42	105.52
13.50	102.76	102.85	102.92	102.99	103.06	103.12	103.17	103.22	103.27	103.31	103.35	103.38	103.42	103.45	103.55	103.62
13.75	101.37	101.41	101.44	101.48	101.51	101.54	101.57	101.59	101.61	101.63	101.65	101.67	101.68	101.70	101.75	101.78
14.00	100.00	100.00	100.00	100.00	100.00	100.00	100.00	100.00	100.00	100.00	100.00	100.00	100.00	100.00	100.00	100.00
14.25	98.66	98.63	98.59	98.56	98.53	98.50	98.48	98.45	98.43	98.41	98.40	98.38	98.37	98.36	98.31	98.28
14.50	97.36	97.28	97.21	97.15	97.09	97.04	96.99	96.95	96.91	96.87	96.84	96.81	96.78	96.76	96.67	96.62
14.75	96.08	95.97	95.87	95.78	95.69	95.62	95.55	95.48	95.43	95.37	95.33	95.28	95.25	95.21	95.08	95.01
15.00	94.83	94.69	94.55	94.44	94.33	94.23	94.14	94.06	93.98	93.92	93.86	93.80	93.75	93.71	93.54	93.45
15.25	93.60	93.43	93.27	93.13	93.00	92.88	92.77	92.67	92.58	92.50	92.43	92.36	92.30	92.25	92.05	91.94
15.50	92.41	92.20	92.02	91.85	91.70	91.56	91.43	91.32	91.21	91.12	91.03	90.96	90.89	90.83	90.60	90.48
15.75	91.23	91.00	90.79	90.60	90.43	90.27	90.13	90.00	89.88	89.78	89.68	89.60	89.52	89.45	89.20	89.06
16.00	90.08	89.83	89.59	89.38	89.19	89.01	88.86	88.71	88.58	88.47	88.36	88.27	88.19	88.11	87.84	87.68
16.25	88.96	88.68	88.42	88.19	87.98	87.79	87.62	87.46	87.32	87.20	87.08	86.98	86.89	86.81	86.51	86.35
16.50	87.86	87.55	87.28	87.03	86.80	86.59	86.41	86.24	86.09	85.96	85.83	85.73	85.63	85.54	85.23	85.05
16.75	86.78	86.45	86.16	85.89	85.65	85.43	85.23	85.05	84.89	84.75	84.62	84.50	84.40	84.31	83.98	83.79
17.00	85.73	85.38	85.06	84.78	84.52	84.29	84.08	83.89	83.72	83.57	83.44	83.31	83.21	83.11	82.76	82.57
17.25	84.69	84.32	83.99	83.69	83.42	83.18	82.96	82.76	82.58	82.42	82.28	82.16	82.04	81.94	81.58	81.38
17.50	83.68	83.29	82.94	82.63	82.35	82.09	81.86	81.66	81.47	81.31	81.16	81.03	80.91	80.81	80.43	80.23
17.75	82.69	82.28	81.92	81.59	81.30	81.03	80.79	80.58	80.39	80.22	80.06	79.93	79.81	79.70	79.32	79.11
18.00	81.71	81.29	80.92	80.57	80.27	79.99	79.75	79.53	79.33	79.15	79.00	78.86	78.73	78.62	78.23	78.01
18.25	80.76	80.33	79.93	79.58	79.26	78.98	78.73	78.50	78.30	78.12	77.95	77.81	77.68	77.57	77.17	76.95
18.50	79.83	79.38	78.97	78.61	78.28	77.99	77.73	77.50	77.29	77.10	76.94	76.79	76.66	76.54	76.14	75.92
18.75	78.91	78.45	78.03	77.66	77.32	77.02	76.76	76.52	76.30	76.12	75.95	75.80	75.66	75.55	75.13	74.91
19.00	78.02	77.54	77.11	76.73	76.39	76.08	75.81	75.56	75.34	75.15	74.98	74.83	74.69	74.57	74.15	73.93
20.00	74.60	74.08	73.61	73.20	72.83	72.50	72.21	71.95	71.72	71.51	71.33	71.17	71.03	70.91	70.47	70.24
25.00	60.88	60.27	59.73	59.27	58.85	58.49	58.18	57.90	57.66	57.45	57.27	57.10	56.96	56.84	56.42	56.21
30.00	51.16	50.57	50.05	49.61	49.22	48.88	48.59	48.34	48.12	47.93	47.77	47.62	47.50	47.39	47.03	46.85

(continued)

TABLE 3 Price of Mortgage to Obtain Specified Yield

(continued)

15.00 %

MONTHLY PAYMENT MORTGAGE

Description: This table shows the price to pay for a mortgage at the yield rate. The yield is to maturity.

Example: The price of a 15.00%, 16 year mortgage to yield 8.00% to maturity is $148.85.

	YEARS TO MATURITY															
YIELD	1 yr	2 yr	3 yr	4 yr	5 yr	6 yr	7 yr	8 yr	9 yr	10 yr	11 yr	12 yr	13 yr	14 yr	15 yr	16 yr
0.0	108.31	116.37	124.80	133.59	142.74	152.24	162.09	172.28	182.78	193.60	204.72	216.13	227.80	239.74	251.93	264.34
1.00	107.73	115.16	122.89	130.90	139.17	147.71	156.49	165.50	174.73	184.16	193.79	203.58	213.54	223.63	233.85	244.18
2.00	107.15	113.98	121.03	128.28	135.73	143.35	151.14	159.08	167.15	175.34	183.63	192.01	200.45	208.95	217.49	226.06
3.00	106.57	112.81	119.20	125.74	132.40	139.17	146.04	152.99	160.01	167.08	174.19	181.31	188.44	195.57	202.67	209.73
4.00	106.00	111.66	117.41	123.26	129.18	135.15	141.17	147.22	153.29	159.35	165.40	171.43	177.41	183.34	189.21	195.01
4.25	105.86	111.37	116.97	122.65	128.39	134.17	139.99	145.83	151.67	157.50	163.30	169.07	174.79	180.45	186.05	191.56
4.50	105.72	111.09	116.53	122.05	127.61	133.21	138.82	144.45	150.07	155.67	161.24	166.76	172.23	177.63	182.95	188.19
4.75	105.57	110.80	116.10	121.45	126.83	132.25	137.67	143.09	148.50	153.88	159.21	164.50	169.72	174.87	179.93	184.91
5.00	105.43	110.52	115.66	120.85	126.06	131.30	136.53	141.75	146.95	152.11	157.22	162.28	167.26	172.17	176.99	181.71
5.25	105.29	110.24	115.23	120.26	125.30	130.35	135.40	140.43	145.42	150.37	155.27	160.10	164.85	169.52	174.10	178.59
5.50	105.15	109.96	114.80	119.67	124.55	129.42	134.28	139.12	143.91	148.66	153.34	157.96	162.49	166.94	171.29	175.54
5.75	105.01	109.68	114.37	119.08	123.80	128.50	133.18	137.83	142.43	146.98	151.46	155.86	160.18	164.41	168.54	172.57
6.00	104.87	109.40	113.95	118.50	123.05	127.59	132.09	136.56	140.97	145.32	149.60	153.80	157.92	161.94	165.86	169.67
6.25	104.73	109.12	113.53	117.93	122.32	126.68	131.01	135.30	139.53	143.69	147.78	151.78	155.70	159.52	163.23	166.84
6.50	104.59	108.85	113.10	117.36	121.59	125.79	129.95	134.06	138.11	142.09	145.99	149.80	153.52	157.15	160.67	164.08
6.75	104.45	108.57	112.69	116.79	120.86	124.90	128.90	132.83	136.71	140.51	144.22	147.85	151.39	154.83	158.16	161.39
7.00	104.31	108.30	112.27	116.22	120.14	124.02	127.86	131.63	135.33	138.95	142.49	145.95	149.30	152.56	155.71	158.76
7.25	104.17	108.02	111.85	115.66	119.43	123.16	126.83	130.43	133.97	137.42	140.79	144.07	147.26	150.34	153.32	156.19
7.50	104.04	107.75	111.44	115.10	118.72	122.30	125.81	129.25	132.63	135.92	139.12	142.23	145.25	148.16	150.98	153.69
7.75	103.90	107.48	111.03	114.55	118.02	121.44	124.80	128.09	131.30	134.43	137.48	140.43	143.28	146.04	148.69	151.24
8.00	103.76	107.21	110.62	114.00	117.33	120.60	123.81	126.94	130.00	132.97	135.86	138.66	141.35	143.95	146.45	148.85
8.25	103.62	106.94	110.22	113.45	116.64	119.76	122.82	125.81	128.72	131.54	134.27	136.92	139.46	141.91	144.27	146.52
8.50	103.48	106.67	109.81	112.91	115.95	118.94	121.85	124.69	127.45	130.12	132.71	135.21	137.61	139.92	142.13	144.24
8.75	103.35	106.40	109.41	112.37	115.28	118.12	120.89	123.58	126.20	128.73	131.18	133.53	135.79	137.96	140.04	142.02
9.00	103.21	106.13	109.01	111.84	114.60	117.31	119.94	122.49	124.97	127.36	129.67	131.88	134.01	136.05	137.99	139.84
9.25	103.07	105.87	108.61	111.31	113.94	116.50	119.00	121.42	123.75	126.01	128.18	130.27	132.26	134.17	135.99	137.72
9.50	102.94	105.60	108.22	110.78	113.28	115.71	118.07	120.35	122.56	124.68	126.72	128.68	130.55	132.33	134.03	135.64
9.75	102.80	105.34	107.82	110.25	112.62	114.92	117.15	119.30	121.38	123.37	125.29	127.12	128.87	130.53	132.12	133.62
10.00	102.66	105.07	107.43	109.73	111.97	114.14	116.24	118.26	120.21	122.08	123.88	125.59	127.22	128.77	130.24	131.63
10.25	102.53	104.81	107.04	109.21	111.32	113.36	115.34	117.24	119.06	120.81	122.49	124.08	125.60	127.04	128.41	129.70
10.50	102.39	104.55	106.65	108.70	110.68	112.60	114.45	116.23	117.93	119.56	121.12	122.61	124.02	125.35	126.61	127.80
10.75	102.26	104.29	106.27	108.19	110.05	111.84	113.57	115.23	116.82	118.33	119.78	121.16	122.46	123.69	124.86	125.95
11.00	102.12	104.03	105.88	107.68	109.42	111.09	112.70	114.24	115.72	117.12	118.46	119.73	120.93	122.07	123.14	124.15
11.25	101.99	103.77	105.50	107.18	108.79	110.35	111.84	113.27	114.63	115.93	117.16	118.33	119.43	120.48	121.46	122.38
11.50	101.85	103.51	105.12	106.68	108.17	109.61	110.99	112.30	113.56	114.75	115.88	116.95	117.96	118.91	119.81	120.65
11.75	101.72	103.26	104.74	106.18	107.56	108.88	110.15	111.35	112.50	113.59	114.63	115.60	116.52	117.38	118.20	118.95
12.00	101.59	103.00	104.37	105.68	106.95	108.16	109.31	110.41	111.46	112.45	113.39	114.27	115.10	115.88	116.62	117.30
12.25	101.45	102.75	103.99	105.19	106.34	107.44	108.49	109.49	110.43	111.33	112.17	112.97	113.71	114.41	115.07	115.68
12.50	101.32	102.49	103.62	104.71	105.74	106.73	107.68	108.57	109.42	110.22	110.97	111.68	112.35	112.97	113.55	114.10
12.75	101.19	102.24	103.25	104.22	105.15	106.03	106.87	107.67	108.42	109.13	109.80	110.42	111.01	111.56	112.07	112.55
13.00	101.05	101.99	102.88	103.74	104.56	105.33	106.07	106.77	107.43	108.05	108.64	109.18	109.70	110.17	110.62	111.03
13.25	100.92	101.74	102.52	103.26	103.97	104.65	105.28	105.89	106.46	106.99	107.50	107.97	108.41	108.81	109.19	109.55
13.50	100.79	101.49	102.15	102.79	103.39	103.96	104.51	105.02	105.50	105.95	106.37	106.77	107.14	107.48	107.80	108.09
13.75	100.66	101.24	101.79	102.31	102.81	103.29	103.73	104.15	104.55	104.92	105.27	105.59	105.89	106.17	106.43	106.67
14.00	100.52	100.99	101.43	101.85	102.24	102.62	102.97	103.30	103.62	103.91	104.18	104.44	104.67	104.89	105.09	105.28
14.25	100.39	100.74	101.07	101.38	101.67	101.95	102.22	102.46	102.69	102.91	103.11	103.30	103.47	103.63	103.78	103.92
14.50	100.26	100.49	100.71	100.92	101.11	101.30	101.47	101.63	101.78	101.93	102.06	102.18	102.29	102.40	102.50	102.59
14.75	100.13	100.25	100.35	100.46	100.55	100.65	100.73	100.81	100.89	100.96	101.02	101.08	101.14	101.19	101.24	101.28
15.00	100.00	100.00	100.00	100.00	100.00	100.00	100.00	100.00	100.00	100.00	100.00	100.00	100.00	100.00	100.00	100.00
15.25	99.87	99.76	99.65	99.55	99.45	99.36	99.28	99.20	99.13	99.06	99.00	98.94	98.88	98.83	98.79	98.75
15.50	99.74	99.51	99.30	99.10	98.91	98.73	98.56	98.41	98.26	98.13	98.01	97.89	97.79	97.69	97.60	97.52
15.75	99.61	99.27	98.95	98.65	98.36	98.10	97.85	97.62	97.41	97.21	97.03	96.86	96.71	96.57	96.44	96.32
16.00	99.48	99.03	98.60	98.20	97.83	97.48	97.15	96.85	96.57	96.31	96.07	95.85	95.65	95.46	95.29	95.14
16.25	99.35	98.79	98.26	97.76	97.30	96.86	96.46	96.09	95.74	95.42	95.13	94.86	94.61	94.38	94.17	93.98
16.50	99.22	98.55	97.91	97.32	96.77	96.25	95.78	95.33	94.92	94.55	94.20	93.88	93.59	93.32	93.08	92.85
16.75	99.09	98.31	97.57	96.88	96.24	95.65	95.10	94.59	94.12	93.68	93.28	92.92	92.58	92.28	92.00	91.75
17.00	98.96	98.07	97.23	96.45	95.72	95.05	94.43	93.85	93.32	92.83	92.38	91.97	91.59	91.25	90.94	90.66
17.25	98.83	97.83	96.89	96.02	95.21	94.46	93.76	93.12	92.53	91.99	91.49	91.04	90.62	90.25	89.90	89.59
17.50	98.71	97.59	96.56	95.59	94.70	93.87	93.11	92.40	91.75	91.16	90.62	90.12	89.67	89.26	88.89	88.55
17.75	98.58	97.36	96.22	95.17	94.19	93.29	92.45	91.69	90.99	90.34	89.76	89.22	88.73	88.29	87.89	87.52
18.00	98.45	97.12	95.89	94.74	93.69	92.71	91.81	90.99	90.23	89.54	88.91	88.33	87.81	87.34	86.91	86.52
18.25	98.32	96.89	95.55	94.32	93.19	92.14	91.17	90.29	89.48	88.74	88.07	87.46	86.90	86.40	85.95	85.54
18.50	98.19	96.65	95.22	93.91	92.69	91.57	90.54	89.60	88.74	87.96	87.25	86.60	86.01	85.48	85.00	84.57
18.75	98.07	96.42	94.90	93.49	92.20	91.01	89.92	88.93	88.02	87.19	86.44	85.75	85.14	84.58	84.08	83.62
19.00	97.94	96.19	94.57	93.08	91.71	90.45	89.30	88.25	87.30	86.43	85.64	84.92	84.28	83.69	83.17	82.69
20.00	97.43	95.27	93.28	91.46	89.79	88.28	86.90	85.65	84.51	83.48	82.56	81.72	80.97	80.29	79.69	79.15
25.00	94.96	90.85	87.19	83.94	81.05	78.50	76.24	74.24	72.47	70.92	69.55	68.34	67.28	66.35	65.54	64.82
30.00	92.58	86.72	81.66	77.29	73.53	70.29	67.49	65.07	62.99	61.20	59.65	58.32	57.17	56.18	55.33	54.59

15.00 %

MONTHLY PAYMENT MORTGAGE

Description: This table shows the price to pay for a mortgage at the yield rate. The yield is to maturity.

Example: The price of a 15.00%, 40 year mortgage to yield 8.00% to maturity is $180.24.

	YEARS TO MATURITY															
YIELD	**17** yr	**18** yr	**19** yr	**20** yr	**21** yr	**22** yr	**23** yr	**24** yr	**25** yr	**26** yr	**27** yr	**28** yr	**29** yr	**30** yr	**35** yr	**40** yr
0.0	276.97	289.81	302.83	316.03	329.39	342.91	356.56	370.35	384.25	398.26	412.37	426.57	440.85	455.20	527.86	601.55
1.00	254.61	265.12	275.69	286.32	297.00	307.69	318.41	329.14	339.86	350.57	361.26	371.92	382.54	393.12	445.23	495.63
2.00	234.63	243.21	251.76	260.30	268.79	277.23	285.62	293.94	302.19	310.35	318.43	326.42	334.31	342.09	379.40	413.84
3.00	216.76	223.72	230.61	237.43	244.16	250.80	257.34	263.78	270.10	276.30	282.39	288.36	294.20	299.91	326.57	350.08
4.00	200.73	206.35	211.88	217.30	222.61	227.80	232.88	237.83	242.66	247.35	251.92	256.36	260.67	264.85	283.85	299.86
4.25	196.98	202.31	207.53	212.65	217.65	222.53	227.29	231.92	236.43	240.81	245.06	249.18	253.17	257.03	274.48	289.01
4.50	193.34	198.38	203.32	208.14	212.84	217.43	221.89	226.23	230.43	234.51	238.47	242.29	245.98	249.55	265.57	278.77
4.75	189.79	194.56	199.22	203.77	208.19	212.50	216.68	220.73	224.66	228.46	232.13	235.68	239.10	242.39	257.09	269.07
5.00	186.33	190.84	195.24	199.53	203.69	207.73	211.65	215.44	219.10	222.64	226.05	229.34	232.50	235.54	249.03	259.90
5.25	182.96	187.23	191.38	195.41	199.33	203.12	206.78	210.32	213.74	217.03	220.20	223.25	226.17	228.98	241.35	251.21
5.50	179.68	183.71	187.63	191.43	195.10	198.65	202.08	205.39	208.57	211.64	214.58	217.40	220.11	222.70	234.04	242.98
5.75	176.49	180.29	183.98	187.55	191.01	194.33	197.54	200.63	203.60	206.44	209.17	211.78	214.28	216.67	227.07	235.18
6.00	173.37	176.97	180.44	183.80	187.04	190.15	193.15	196.03	198.79	201.44	203.97	206.39	208.70	210.90	220.42	227.77
6.25	170.34	173.73	177.00	180.15	183.19	186.11	188.91	191.59	194.16	196.62	198.96	201.20	203.33	205.36	214.08	220.74
6.50	167.39	170.58	173.65	176.61	179.46	182.19	184.80	187.31	189.69	191.97	194.15	196.21	198.18	200.05	208.03	214.06
6.75	164.50	167.51	170.40	173.18	175.84	178.39	180.83	183.16	185.38	187.50	189.51	191.42	193.23	194.95	202.25	207.71
7.00	161.70	164.52	167.24	169.84	172.34	174.72	176.99	179.16	181.22	183.18	185.04	186.80	188.48	190.06	196.73	201.67
7.25	158.96	161.62	164.16	166.60	168.93	171.16	173.27	175.29	177.20	179.02	180.74	182.36	183.90	185.35	191.45	195.92
7.50	156.29	158.78	161.17	163.46	165.63	167.71	169.68	171.55	173.32	175.00	176.59	178.09	179.50	180.84	186.40	190.44
7.75	153.69	156.03	158.27	160.40	162.43	164.36	166.19	167.93	169.57	171.13	172.59	173.97	175.27	176.50	181.57	185.22
8.00	151.15	153.34	155.44	157.43	159.32	161.12	162.82	164.43	165.95	167.38	168.74	170.01	171.20	172.32	176.95	180.24
8.25	148.67	150.73	152.68	154.54	156.30	157.97	159.55	161.04	162.45	163.77	165.02	166.19	167.28	168.31	172.52	175.49
8.50	146.26	148.18	150.00	151.73	153.37	154.92	156.39	157.77	159.06	160.28	161.43	162.50	163.51	164.45	168.28	170.95
8.75	143.90	145.69	147.40	149.01	150.53	151.97	153.32	154.59	155.79	156.91	157.97	158.95	159.87	160.73	164.21	166.61
9.00	141.60	143.27	144.86	146.35	147.77	149.10	150.35	151.52	152.63	153.66	154.62	155.52	156.36	157.15	160.31	162.47
9.25	139.36	140.92	142.39	143.78	145.08	146.31	147.47	148.55	149.56	150.51	151.39	152.22	152.99	153.70	156.56	158.50
9.50	137.17	138.62	139.98	141.27	142.48	143.61	144.67	145.67	146.60	147.47	148.28	149.03	149.73	150.38	152.97	154.71
9.75	135.04	136.38	137.64	138.83	139.94	140.99	141.96	142.88	143.73	144.52	145.26	145.95	146.58	147.17	149.52	151.07
10.00	132.95	134.19	135.36	136.45	137.48	138.44	139.34	140.17	140.95	141.68	142.35	142.97	143.55	144.08	146.20	147.59
10.25	130.91	132.06	133.13	134.14	135.08	135.96	136.79	137.55	138.26	138.92	139.53	140.10	140.62	141.11	143.01	144.24
10.50	128.93	129.98	130.97	131.89	132.76	133.56	134.31	135.01	135.66	136.25	136.81	137.32	137.79	138.23	139.94	141.04
10.75	126.99	127.95	128.86	129.70	130.49	131.23	131.91	132.54	133.13	133.67	134.17	134.64	135.06	135.45	136.98	137.96
11.00	125.09	125.97	126.80	127.57	128.29	128.96	129.58	130.15	130.68	131.17	131.62	132.04	132.42	132.77	134.14	135.00
11.25	123.24	124.04	124.80	125.50	126.15	126.75	127.31	127.83	128.31	128.75	129.16	129.53	129.87	130.19	131.40	132.16
11.50	121.43	122.16	122.84	123.48	124.06	124.61	125.11	125.58	126.01	126.40	126.77	127.10	127.40	127.68	128.76	129.43
11.75	119.66	120.32	120.94	121.51	122.04	122.53	122.98	123.39	123.78	124.13	124.45	124.75	125.02	125.27	126.21	126.80
12.00	117.94	118.53	119.08	119.59	120.06	120.50	120.90	121.27	121.61	121.92	122.21	122.47	122.71	122.93	123.76	124.27
12.25	116.25	116.78	117.27	117.72	118.14	118.53	118.88	119.21	119.51	119.78	120.04	120.26	120.47	120.66	121.39	121.83
12.50	114.60	115.07	115.50	115.90	116.27	116.61	116.92	117.21	117.47	117.71	117.93	118.13	118.31	118.48	119.10	119.48
12.75	112.99	113.40	113.78	114.13	114.45	114.74	115.01	115.26	115.49	115.70	115.89	116.06	116.21	116.36	116.89	117.21
13.00	111.41	111.77	112.09	112.39	112.67	112.93	113.16	113.37	113.57	113.74	113.90	114.05	114.18	114.31	114.76	115.03
13.25	109.87	110.17	110.45	110.71	110.94	111.16	111.35	111.53	111.70	111.85	111.98	112.11	112.22	112.32	112.69	112.92
13.50	108.37	108.62	108.85	109.06	109.26	109.44	109.60	109.75	109.88	110.00	110.12	110.22	110.31	110.39	110.70	110.88
13.75	106.89	107.10	107.29	107.46	107.61	107.76	107.89	108.01	108.12	108.22	108.31	108.39	108.46	108.53	108.77	108.91
14.00	105.45	105.61	105.76	105.89	106.01	106.13	106.23	106.32	106.40	106.48	106.55	106.61	106.67	106.72	106.90	107.01
14.25	104.05	104.16	104.27	104.36	104.45	104.53	104.61	104.67	104.73	104.79	104.84	104.88	104.92	104.96	105.09	105.17
14.50	102.67	102.74	102.81	102.87	102.93	102.98	103.03	103.07	103.11	103.15	103.18	103.21	103.23	103.26	103.34	103.39
14.75	101.32	101.36	101.39	101.42	101.45	101.47	101.50	101.52	101.54	101.55	101.57	101.58	101.59	101.60	101.64	101.67
15.00	100.00	100.00	100.00	100.00	100.00	100.00	100.00	100.00	100.00	100.00	100.00	100.00	100.00	100.00	100.00	100.00
15.25	98.71	98.67	98.64	98.61	98.59	98.56	98.54	98.52	98.51	98.49	98.48	98.46	98.45	98.44	98.41	98.38
15.50	97.45	97.38	97.32	97.26	97.21	97.16	97.12	97.09	97.05	97.02	96.99	96.97	96.95	96.93	96.86	96.82
15.75	96.21	96.11	96.02	95.94	95.86	95.80	95.74	95.68	95.64	95.59	95.55	95.52	95.49	95.46	95.36	95.30
16.00	95.00	94.87	94.75	94.65	94.55	94.47	94.39	94.32	94.26	94.20	94.15	94.10	94.06	94.03	93.90	93.83
16.25	93.81	93.66	93.51	93.39	93.27	93.17	93.07	92.99	92.91	92.84	92.78	92.73	92.68	92.64	92.48	92.40
16.50	92.65	92.47	92.30	92.15	92.02	91.90	91.79	91.69	91.60	91.52	91.45	91.39	91.34	91.29	91.11	91.01
16.75	91.52	91.31	91.12	90.95	90.80	90.66	90.54	90.43	90.33	90.24	90.16	90.09	90.03	89.97	89.77	89.67
17.00	90.40	90.17	89.96	89.77	89.60	89.45	89.31	89.19	89.08	88.99	88.90	88.82	88.75	88.69	88.48	88.36
17.25	89.31	89.06	88.83	88.62	88.44	88.27	88.12	87.99	87.87	87.76	87.67	87.59	87.51	87.45	87.21	87.09
17.50	88.24	87.97	87.72	87.50	87.30	87.12	86.96	86.82	86.69	86.57	86.47	86.38	86.30	86.23	85.98	85.85
17.75	87.20	86.90	86.64	86.40	86.18	85.99	85.82	85.67	85.53	85.41	85.31	85.21	85.13	85.05	84.79	84.65
18.00	86.17	85.86	85.58	85.32	85.10	84.89	84.71	84.55	84.41	84.28	84.17	84.07	83.98	83.90	83.63	83.48
18.25	85.17	84.84	84.54	84.27	84.03	83.82	83.63	83.46	83.31	83.18	83.06	82.95	82.86	82.78	82.49	82.34
18.50	84.18	83.83	83.52	83.24	82.99	82.77	82.57	82.39	82.24	82.10	81.98	81.87	81.77	81.69	81.39	81.24
18.75	83.22	82.85	82.53	82.23	81.97	81.74	81.54	81.35	81.19	81.05	80.92	80.81	80.71	80.62	80.32	80.16
19.00	82.27	81.89	81.55	81.25	80.98	80.74	80.53	80.34	80.17	80.02	79.89	79.77	79.67	79.58	79.27	79.11
20.00	78.67	78.24	77.85	77.51	77.21	76.94	76.70	76.50	76.31	76.15	76.00	75.88	75.77	75.67	75.34	75.17
25.00	64.20	63.65	63.17	62.76	62.39	62.08	61.80	61.56	61.35	61.17	61.01	60.88	60.76	60.66	60.32	60.15
30.00	53.96	53.41	52.94	52.53	52.18	51.88	51.62	51.40	51.20	51.04	50.89	50.77	50.66	50.57	50.27	50.13

Source: Thorndike Encyclopedia of Banking and Financial Tables (rev. ed. 1980)

TABLE 4 Mortgage Markets: Terms on Conventional Home-Mortgage Loans Made, 1977–1981[1]

Period	Contract interest rate[2] (percent)	Initial fees and charges[3] (percent)	Effective rate[4] (percent)	Term to maturity (years)	Loan amount (thousands)	Purchase price (thousands)	Loan-to-price ratio (percent)	Percentage distribution of estimated number of loans by loan-to-price ratio class: 70.0 percent or less	70.1-80.0 percent	80.1-90.0 percent	Over 90.0 percent
					All Loans						
1977	8.82	1.22	9.02	26.2	36.2	49.5	75.0	NA	NA	NA	NA
1978	9.34	1.30	9.56	26.7	41.2	56.8	74.7	NA	NA	NA	NA
1979	10.60	1.51	10.87	27.4	48.3	68.0	73.5	33	43	18	7
1980	12.48	1.96	12.86	27.2	51.6	73.4	72.7	35	41	16	9
Nov	12.77	2.07	13.18	26.7	49.7	69.8	73.9	31	41	19	9
Dec	13.06	2.12	13.48	27.0	51.9	73.5	73.2	33	42	17	9
1981											
Jan	13.12	2.23	13.57	27.5	53.1	73.6	75.4	31	36	18	15
Feb	13.49	2.23	13.94	27.2	54.4	76.8	73.7	33	39	17	11
Mar	13.76	2.41	14.25	27.4	54.3	77.3	73.6	32	42	16	11
Apr	13.86	2.36	14.36	26.8	52.1	72.2	74.4	31	41	18	10
May	14.01	2.29	14.49	26.2	51.3	71.6	73.9	33	39	18	11
June	14.32	2.32	14.82	26.0	54.5	78.0	72.7	35	40	16	9
July	14.57	2.47	15.10	26.9	55.8	79.6	73.1	33	40	16	11
Aug	14.88	2.53	15.45	26.2	55.1	79.4	71.9	38	39	16	8
Sept	15.14	2.48	15.70	25.6	53.4	76.8	72.0	40	36	16	9
Oct	15.35	2.44	15.89	25.9	52.7	77.9	70.1	43	32	14	11
Nov	15.75	2.52	16.37	24.6	53.1	76.6	73.2	37	35	12	16
				Purchase of newly built homes							
1977	8.80	1.33	9.01	27.9	40.5	54.3	76.3	26	43	21	11
1978	9.30	1.39	9.54	28.0	45.9	62.6	75.3	29	42	19	11
1979	10.48	1.66	10.77	28.5	53.3	74.4	73.9	33	43	17	9
1980	12.25	2.09	12.65	28.2	59.2	83.4	73.2	34	41	16	10
Nov	12.62	2.15	13.04	27.6	56.1	77.1	75.2	27	38	25	11
Dec	12.86	2.15	13.28	28.2	63.9	90.1	72.9	37	39	14	11
1981											
Jan	12.80	2.40	13.26	29.1	63.0	87.0	75.6	29	38	17	15
Feb	13.02	2.59	13.54	29.0	65.6	90.3	75.6	31	37	18	14
Mar	13.48	2.64	14.02	28.7	64.5	90.9	73.9	32	42	16	11
Apr	13.62	2.61	14.15	28.6	64.1	88.5	74.7	30	40	18	12
May	13.56	2.60	14.10	28.5	65.5	88.9	76.7	28	34	23	16
June	14.12	2.50	14.67	27.5	66.8	94.1	72.6	33	42	16	10
July	14.14	2.73	14.72	28.3	67.9	95.2	73.9	32	40	14	14
Aug	14.60	2.98	15.27	27.2	70.3	98.1	74.7	33	38	17	11
Sept	14.69	2.75	15.29	26.6	64.8	89.1	74.4	37	35	17	12
Oct	15.04	2.86	15.65	27.4	63.5	89.2	73.0	37	33	14	16
Nov	15.68	2.52	16.38	23.4	62.7	84.5	77.3	32	30	11	27
				Purchase of previously occupied homes							
1977	8.83	1.17	9.02	25.8	34.7	47.5	75.1	27	48	20	6
1978	9.37	1.26	9.58	26.4	39.4	54.2	75.1	28	45	21	7
1979	10.66	1.45	10.92	27.1	46.3	64.6	74.0	31	43	19	6
1980	12.58	1.90	12.95	26.8	48.0	68.0	73.3	34	41	17	9
Nov	12.85	2.03	13.26	26.5	47.5	66.3	74.5	30	42	18	9
Dec	13.15	2.12	13.58	26.5	46.3	65.3	73.7	31	43	19	8
1981											
Jan	13.24	2.16	13.67	27.1	48.6	66.7	76.1	31	35	18	16
Feb	13.73	2.06	14.16	26.3	48.9	69.6	73.3	31	41	18	10
Mar	13.91	2.25	14.38	26.7	47.1	66.5	74.2	30	42	17	11
Apr	13.99	2.25	14.47	26.0	45.1	62.2	74.8	31	40	19	11
May	14.19	2.17	14.66	25.4	44.8	63.5	73.0	34	40	17	9
June	14.40	2.22	14.88	25.3	49.3	70.8	73.1	35	39	17	9
July	14.77	2.36	15.28	26.3	50.2	72.4	72.9	32	40	18	10
Aug	15.03	2.31	15.54	25.7	48.1	70.3	70.9	39	40	14	7
Sept	15.38	2.40	15.93	25.2	47.2	69.4	71.2	39	37	16	8
Oct	15.47	2.42	16.01	25.7	48.1	71.9	70.9	41	34	15	10
Nov	15.80	2.52	16.38	25.4	46.0	70.1	70.8	40	39	12	9

1. By savings and loan associations, mortgage bankers, commercial banks, and mutual savings banks.
2. Excludes the estimated cost of private (nongovernmental) mortgage insurance from the contract rate for the relatively small number of loans including such costs in the rate.
3. Includes any general or specific charges paid by the borrower, or seller, in order to obtain a loan, except those for mortgage, credit, life, or property insurance, property transfer, and title search and insurance.
4. Contract rate plus initial fees and charges amortized over 10 years, the assumed actual average life of a conventional mortgage.

Note: Data are weighted averages compiled by the FHLBB in cooperation with the Federal Deposit Insurance Corporation from data reported by a sample of the indicated types of lenders for fully amortized conventional first-mortgage loans that are both secured by and for purchase of single-family nonfarm residential properties.

TABLE 5 Security Yields and Rates: Treasury Bills, Bonds, Mortgages, 1977–1981 (percent)

Period	Short-term: U.S. Government obligations[1]			Intermediate- and long-term: Bonds and notes[1]				Mortgages		
	3-month bills	6-month bills	1-year bills	U.S. Government[2] 5-year	U.S. Government[2] 20-year	Aaa[3] State and local government	Aaa[3] corporate	FHA-insured[4]	Conventional[5] New homes	Conventional[5] Existing homes
1977	5.27	5.53	5.71	6.99	7.67	5.20	8.02	8.68	9.01	9.02
1978	7.19	7.58	7.74	8.32	8.48	5.52	8.73	9.70	9.54	9.58
1979	10.07	10.06	9.75	9.52	9.33	5.92	9.63	10.87	10.77	10.92
1980	11.43	11.36	10.89	11.48	11.39	7.86	11.94	12.29	12.65	12.95
1980										
Nov	13.73	13.50	12.66	12.83	12.44	8.71	12.97	14.47	13.04	13.26
Dec	15.49	14.64	13.23	13.25	12.49	9.44	13.21	14.08	13.28	13.58
1981										
Jan	15.02	14.08	12.62	12.77	12.29	8.98	12.81	14.23	13.26	13.67
Feb	14.79	14.05	12.99	13.41	12.98	9.46	13.35	14.79	13.54	14.16
Mar	13.36	12.81	12.28	13.41	12.94	9.50	13.33	15.04	14.02	14.38
Apr	13.69	13.45	12.79	13.99	13.46	9.78	13.88	15.91	14.15	14.47
May	16.30	15.29	14.29	14.63	13.82	9.90	14.32	16.33	14.10	14.66
June	14.73	14.09	13.22	13.95	13.20	9.86	13.75	16.31	14.67	14.88
July	14.95	14.74	13.91	14.79	13.92	10.21	14.38	16.76	14.72	15.28
Aug	15.51	15.52	14.70	15.56	14.52	11.10	14.89	17.96	15.27	15.54
Sept	14.70	14.92	14.53	15.93	15.07	11.55	15.49	18.55	15.29	15.93
Oct	13.54	13.82	13.62	15.41	15.13	12.05	15.40	17.43	15.65	16.01
Nov	10.86	11.30	11.20	13.38	13.56	11.05	14.22	15.98	16.38	16.38

1. Monthly data are averages of daily secondary market quotations, except for State and local government bonds, which are based on Thursday quotations only. Except for bills, the quotations are for a limited number of suitable issues of the indicated type, including only general obligations for State and local government bonds. For bills, averages are based on market yields quoted on a bank-discount basis.
2. Yields on most actively traded issues adjusted to constant maturities by U.S. Treasury.
3. Aaa is the highest quality rating given by Moody's Investors Service.
4. Monthly data are based on opinion reports of FHA field offices on prevailing conditions in their localities as of the first of the succeeding month. Yields are derived from secondary market prices for sec. 203, 30-year mortgages with minimum down-payment and an assumed prepayment at the end of 15 years. Gaps in monthly data are because of periods of adjustment to changes in maximum permissible contract interest rate. Data represent gross yield to the investor—i.e., the yield to the purchaser before deduction of serving costs.
5. Average effective interest rates; data prior to 1973 not completely comparable with later period due to revision in series effective January 1973.
6. Preliminary.

Note: Annual data are averages of monthly data. Figures for U.S. Government obligations are from the Board of Governors of the Federal Reserve System, for corporate and State and local government bonds from Moody's Investors Service, for FHA mortgages from the Federal Housing Administration, and for conventional mortgages from the Federal Home Loan Bank Board.

TABLE 6 Prime Rate on Short-Term Business Loans (percentage per annum)

Effective date		Rate
1980		
January	17	15.25%
February	19	15.75
	22	16.25–16.50
	29	16.75
March	4	17.25
	7	17.75
	14	18.50
	19	19.00
	28	19.50
April	2	20.00
	18	19.50
May	1	18.50–19.00
	2	18.50
	7	17.50
	16	16.50
	23	14.50
	30	14.00
June	6	13.00
	13	12.00–12.50
	20	12.00
July	7	11.50
	25	11.00
August	22	11.25%
	27	11.50
September	8	12.00
	12	12.25
	19	12.50
	26	13.00
October	1	13.50
	17	14.00
	29	14.50
November	6	15.50
	17	16.25
	21	17.00
	26	17.75
December	2	18.50
	5	19.00
	10	20.00
	16	21.00
	19	21.50
1981		
January	2	20.50
	9	20.00
February	3	19.50
	23	19.00
March	10	18.00%
	17	17.50
April	2	17.00
	24	17.50
	30	18.00
May	4	19.00
	11	19.50
	19	20.00
	22	20.50
June	3	20.00
July	8	20.50
September	15	20.00
	22	19.50
October	5	19.00
	13	18.00
November	3	17.50
	9	17.00
	17	17.00
	20	16.50
	24	16.00
December	1	15.75

1980

Month	Average rate
January	15.25%
February	15.63
March	18.31
April	19.77
May	16.57
June	12.63
July	11.48
August	11.12
September	12.23
October	13.79
November	16.06
December	20.35

1981

Month	Average rate
January	20.16%
February	19.43
March	18.05
April	17.15
May	19.61
June	20.03
July	20.39
August	20.50
September	20.08
October	18.45
November	16.84
December	15.75

TABLE 7 Monthly Department of Commerce Composite Construction Cost Indexes: 1964–1980

Year	Month												Annual index
	Jan.	Feb.	Mar.	Apr.	May	Jun	Jul	Aug	Sep	Oct	Nov	Dec	
1964	41.8	41.9	41.8	41.9	41.9	42.0	42.2	42.4	42.6	42.5	42.4	42.4	42.2
1965	42.9	43.2	43.3	43.1	43.1	43.3	43.5	43.8	44.1	44.1	44.1	44.1	43.6
1966	44.2	44.1	44.4	45.1	45.6	45.8	45.8	45.7	45.7	45.8	45.9	46.0	45.4
1967	46.1	46.3	46.3	46.3	46.5	46.8	47.1	47.3	47.5	47.7	48.0	48.2	47.1
1968	48.5	48.7	49.0	49.1	49.3	49.6	49.4	49.6	49.9	50.2	50.6	51.2	49.6
1969	51.4	51.9	52.3	52.5	52.8	52.9	53.6	53.8	54.2	54.6	54.9	55.1	53.4
1970	55.0	54.9	55.2	56.1	56.7	57.6	57.1	57.0	57.1	57.5	57.9	58.3	56.8
1971	58.1	58.9	59.4	59.5	60.0	60.5	60.5	61.2	61.2	61.4	61.9	62.5	60.5
1972	62.6	62.8	63.0	63.0	63.2	63.5	63.7	64.3	64.8	65.5	66.0	66.5	64.1
1973	66.2	66.5	67.1	68.4	68.8	69.2	69.7	70.6	71.2	71.8	72.2	72.5	69.6
1974	74.1	75.8	77.6	78.4	79.8	81.4	83.1	84.1	85.2	86.2	86.8	87.3	81.8
1975	88.4	88.7	88.9	88.8	89.1	89.2	89.2	89.1	90.0	89.7	90.0	90.5	89.3
1976	90.6	90.5	90.9	91.2	91.9	92.3	92.7	92.8	92.8	93.6	94.2	94.8	92.4
1977	95.6	96.4	97.0	97.9	98.9	99.8	99.7	100.4	101.6	102.9	104.4	105.6	100.0
1978	105.7	105.8	106.4	108.8	110.0	111.6	113.4	115.0	116.0	117.6	118.5	119.8	113.0
1979	121.3	122.7	123.9	124.3	126.7	127.3	128.8	130.6	131.3	133.3	134.3	134.8	128.7
1980	137.0	139.3	139.8	140.3	142.2	144.4	145.0	144.8	145.0	145.6	146.7	147.8	143.3

TABLE 8 Construction Cost Indexes

[1977=100]

Period	Department of Commerce composite cost index*	American Appraisal Company	"Boeckh Indexes," The American Appraisal Company, Inc.			Engineering News-Record		Environmental Protection Agency	
			Residences	Apartments, hotels, and office buildings	Commercial and factory buildings	Building	Construction	Sewers	Plant
	Annual averages								
1976	92.4	94	91.7	92.4	92.6	92.3	93.1	94.1	94.3
1977	100.0	100	100.0	100.0	100.0	100.0	100.0	100.0	100.0
1978	113.0	109	109.0	106.5	107.5	108.4	107.7	109.5	109.5
1979	128.7	118	119.0	114.7	117.1	117.8	116.5	123.2	120.4
1980	143.3	125	128.9	125.1	127.7	125.9	125.6	133.6	131.3
	Monthly indexes		Bimonthly indexes			Monthly indexes		Quarterly indexes	
1980: January	137.0	121	122.9	120.1	123.1	122.9	121.5	130.3	128.5
February	139.3	122				122.8	121.6		
March	139.8	122	123.1	121.0	123.8	124.2	122.6		
April	140.3	121				123.2	122.0	132.4	130.1
May	142.2	122	124.6	123.2	125.4	122.5	121.8		
June	144.4	125				124.3	124.1		
July	145.0	127	125.1	126.4	129.1	126.5	126.5	135.8	133.0
August	144.8	128				127.8	128.2		
September	145.0	127	127.2	129.6	132.0	128.0	128.8		
October	145.6	127				128.0	129.1	135.9	133.5
November	146.7	128	128.9	130.5	132.9	129.5	130.3		
December	147.8	128				130.7	131.0		
1981: January	149.2	129	129.7	131.1	133.9	130.5	130.9	137.2	136.2
February	149.7	129				130.6	130.9		
March	152.1	129	131.3	132.6	135.3	130.4	131.3		
April	r151.2	130				133.7	134.0	141.3	141.8
May	r150.7	132	134.4	135.4	138.1	134.5	134.8		
June	r150.3	133				134.9	136.2		
July	150.9	134	138.3	139.7	141.9	136.6	138.3		
August	150.8	134				137.2	138.8		
September			140.4	142.1	145.3	138.5	140.1		
October									
	Percent change								
Latest period 1980-81	+4	+5	+10	+10	+10	+8	+9	+7	+9

Period	Federal Highway Administration		Bureau of the Census new one family houses excluding Census lot value	Bureau of Reclamation	Turner Construction Company	Handy-Whitman Public Utility		Bell System Telephone Plant		Federal Energy Regulatory Commission Pipeline
								Telephone and telegraph		
	Structures	Composite				Bulidings	Electric light and power	Buildings	Outside plant	
	Annual averages									
1976	95.4	93.4	88.9	94	97	95	94	93.8	95.6	98
1977	100.0	100.0	100.0	100	100	100	100	100.0	100.0	100
1978	118.0	119.4	114.3	106	106	109	106	108.2	104.8	112
1979	148.1	142.6	129.3	117	118	122	116	117.3	116.0	121
1980	169.1	163.0	143.3	130	131	135	127	128.8	129.7	133
	Quarterly indexes					Semiannual indexes		Annual indexes		
1980: 1st quarter	168.0	157.9	138.0	124	126	130	122	128.8	129.7	133
2nd quarter	172.1	168.3	142.7	128	129					
3rd quarter	166.9	163.1	145.0	132	132	135	126			
4th quarter	163.8	161.8	146.8	135	135					
1981: 1st quarter	167.5	160.0	150.6	137	139	141	134			
2nd quarter	158.8	152.4	152.5	140	142					
3rd quarter				144	146					
4th quarter										
	Percent change									
Latest period 1980-81	−8	−9	+7	+9	+11	+8	+10	. . .	. . .	. . .

ʳRevised.

*An implicit price deflator, computed by the Bureau of the Census, which is the ratio of the estimate of total new construction put in place in current dollars (seasonally adjusted) to the corresponding estimate in 1977 dollars. In form, the index is a weighted harmonic mean of the deflators used for various categories of construction (and, hence, of the basic cost indexes which make up these deflators), with weights proportionate to the value-put-in-place estimates (seasonally adjusted) for these categories. Since this "implicit price deflator" is in the form of a changing weight index, it measures the combined result of cost changes as well as monthly changes in the weights of different types of construction in the current-dollar construction activity aggregate. Sources as stated.

TABLE 9 Regional Breakdown of Median and Average Prices of New Houses Sold

Period	Median sales price					Average sales price				
	United States	North-east	North Central	South	West	United States	North-east	North Central	South	West
1976	$44,200	$47,300	$44,800	$40,500	$47,200	$48,000	$50,000	$48,600	$43,800	$51,900
1977	48,800	51,600	51,500	44,100	53,500	54,200	54,800	55,200	48,100	60,700
1978	55,700	58,100	59,200	50,300	61,300	62,500	63,000	64,200	55,600	70,100
1979	62,900	65,500	63,900	57,300	69,600	71,800	71,500	73,000	63,800	82,000
1980	64,600	69,300	63,400	59,700	72,400	76,400	79,300	74,400	69,200	89,400
1980: January	63,200	61,900	66,100	60,000	69,100	72,500	71,400	74,200	65,200	83,000
February	64,800	68,400	65,400	58,900	74,500	76,600	75,700	75,800	67,500	91,300
March	62,300	61,000	62,600	58,000	70,800	71,100	72,400	69,600	64,000	85,300
April	62,800	69,800	55,400	59,300	74,600	74,100	86,000	72,800	65,500	88,400
May	63,200	66,300	62,300	58,900	71,500	73,100	70,600	73,500	67,800	86,000
June	65,400	67,600	63,400	58,600	76,100	76,300	72,300	73,300	67,600	94,000
July	64,400	68,000	63,900	59,700	70,600	76,800	77,800	79,500	69,000	88,300
August	63,200	71,200	58,300	60,200	67,900	76,500	85,700	68,800	71,600	86,200
September	68,500	73,100	67,600	61,900	73,900	80,300	83,900	76,000	75,100	89 400
October	66,100	71,200	63,200	59,300	72,000	77,700	85,000	76,200	69,300	91,300
November	67,100	67,700	65,600	64,300	71,300	82,200	82,400	79,000	76,700	94 200
December	67,200	71,400	63,900	62,300	81,800	81,500	82,900	72,700	73,400	103,100
1981: January	67,900	71,900	63,600	65,000	71,500	80,200	85,500	89,700	72,000	90,300
February	65,800	67,400	69,000	59,800	78,200	80,100	78,500	88,600	69,700	96,100
March	67,100	73,900	69,900	62,200	77,100	81,200	87,700	86,000	73,800	93,900
April[r]	68,400	83,400	74,600	59,800	73,300	82,900	86,400	94,900	74,400	92,400
May[r]	71,200	84,900	67,500	66,900	79,400	83,700	92,900	83,600	75,600	96,700
June[r]	69,200	83,800	63,800	64,700	84,100	85,300	100,900	72,100	78,300	100,000
July	70,000	79,000	61,000	65,400	79,100	83,400	94,000	71,600	76,000	96,700
August	73,900	82,800	73,700	69,300	82,200	88,400	87,300	86,700	80,600	105,400

Note: The sales price includes the land. Median and average sales prices reflect changing proportions of houses of different sizes, locations, etc., as well as any changes of houses with identical characteristics. [r] Revised.

Source: U.S. Department of Commerce, Bureau of the Census

TABLE 10 Median Monthly Rental of Completed Apartments

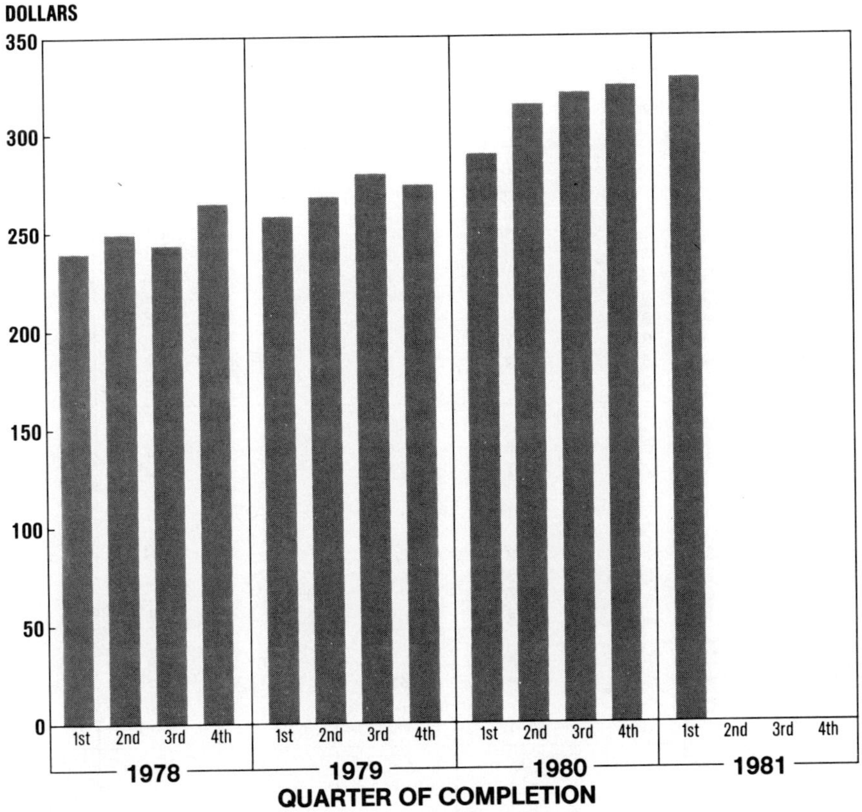

Note: Limited to buildings with five units or more in permit-issuing places.

Source: U.S. Department of Housing and Urban Development, and U.S. Department of Commerce, Bureau of the Census

TABLE 11 Percentage Lease Rates

Type of store	Michael Hirschfeld, Garrick-Aug Associates, New York, N.Y.	Brent F. Howell, Coldwell, Banker & Co., Los Angeles, Calif.	Richard F. Walker, SWD Management Corp., Jacksonville, Fla.	Kenneth R. Jensen, Green Tree Bldg. Management Co., Minneapolis, Minn.	Marvin S. Schwartz, Lewis & Fink, Cleveland, Ohio	S. G. Kartalls, Henry S. Miller Co., Dallas, Tex.	J. McGregor Dodds, Resume & Dodds, Detroit, Mich.
Art shops	8–10	6–8	6	10	6–10	6–8	6–8
Auto accessories	4–6	3–4	3–4	5	3–5	3–6	5–6
Bakeries	6–8	5–8	6	5	5–7	6–8	6–8
Barber shops	8–10	6–10	6	10	8–10	6–10	8–10
Beauty shops	8–10	5–8	5–8	10	8–10	6–10	8–10
Books and stationery	5–7	5–7	5–6	8	5–6	5–6	5–8
Bowling lanes	9–10	6–10	—	10	9–10	8–10	—
Candy	8–10	6–9	7	8	8–10	6–10	6–8
Children's clothing	6–8	5–7	6	6–8	5–6	5–7	6–8
Cocktail lounge	8–10	6–9	6–8	10	7–8	5–8	8–10
Credit clothing	6–7	—	4–6	6	4–6	5–8	4–5
Delicatessen, specialty foods	6–7	5–6	5–6	7	4–5	4–8	8–10
Department stores	2½–3	0–2	1½–3	2½–3	2–2½	2–3	2–2½
Discount stores (over 75,000 sq. ft.)	1½–2½	1–1½	1–1½	1½–2½	1–1½	1–4	1½–2
Discount stores (under 75,000 sq. ft.)	1½–2½	1–2	1½–2	2–3	1½–2½	2–4	2–4
Drug stores (chain)	2½–4	1–3	2–4	3–3½	2½–3½	2–6	3–5
Drug stores (individual)	4–6	2–5	4	5	3–5	2–6	4–6
Drug stores (prescription)	7–10	5–8	4	8–10	5–8	6–9	7–10
Dry cleaning & laundry	6–8	6–8	6–8	8	6–7	5–10	6–8
Dry cleaning & laundry (coin-operated)	10	8–10	—	10	8–10	5–10	—
Electrical appliances	3–5	3–6	4–5	4–5	2½–5	3–8	4–6
Fabrics	4–6	5–6	5–6	6	4–5	5–6	6
Florists	10–12	6–10	6	10	7–10	5–10	8–10
Florists (garden supply)	5–6	—	6	5	5–6	5–9	—
Furniture	4–5	3–5	5–6	5	4–5	4–8	3–6
Furs	6–8	4–6	—	6–8	6–8	5–7	6–8
Garage (storage)	45–55	—	—	50	40–50	40–55	50
Gas stations, cents per gallon	1½–2	0–1½	1½	2	1–2	1½–2	1–1½
Gift shops	8–10	6–10	6–8	8–10	6–10	5–10	6–8
Grocery stores (individual)	1½–3	2–3	—	2½	1¼–2	1–1½	—
Grocery stores (chain)	1–1½	1–1½	1–1½	1–2	1–1½	1–1½	1–2
Grocery stores (convenience)	—	1–3	2½	3–3½	2–3½	1–3	—
Hardware	4–6	2½–6	4–5	5–6	3–5	4–5	4–6
Hobby shops, toys	6–8	5–10	5–6	6–8	6–7	5–8	6–8
Hosiery and knit goods	8–10	7–10	7	8	6–8	5–10	6–8
Jewelry (costume)	8–10	6–10	6–8	8–10	7–10	6–10	6–8
Jewelry (exclusive)	7–8	6–10	4½–6	8	6–8	4–7	6–8
Leather goods	6–8	6–8	6	6–8	6–8	5–8	6–8
Liquors and wines	3–4	3–6	2–4	3–5	—	4–6	—
Meat markets (individual)	4–5	4–6	—	5	3–4	4–5	3–4

Type of store	Michael Hirschfeld, Garrick-Aug Associates, New York, N.Y.	Brent F. Howell, Coldwell, Banker & Co., Los Angeles, Calif.	Richard F. Walker, SWD Management Corp., Jacksonville, Fla.	Kenneth R. Jensen, Green Tree Bldg. Management Co., Minneapolis, Minn.	Marvin S. Schwartz, Lewis & Fink, Cleveland, Ohio	S. G. Kartalls, Henry S. Miller Co., Dallas, Tex.	J. McGregor Dodds, Resume & Dodds, Detroit, Mich.
Meat markets (chain)	3–4	$2^1/_2$–4	—	3–4	2–3	4–5	3–4
Men's clothing	4–6	5–7	4–6	4–6	5–6	4–6	5–6
Men's furnishings	6–8	5–7	4–6	6–8	6–8	4–6	6–8
Men's hats	7–8	—	—	8	7–8	4–6	5–7
Men's shoes	6–8	6–7	5–6	6–8	5–7	5–7	6–8
Men's shoes (volume)	6–7	4–6	6	6	4–5	4–6	5–6
Millinery	10	5–6	5–8	10	8–10	6–10	8–10
Motion-picture theaters	$12^1/_2$–15	8–12	6	10–12	7–$12^1/_2$	8–15	5–7
Office supply	5–7	4–6	5–6	5	5–7	5–7	5–7
Optical	8–10	7–10	10	8–10	8–10	8–10	8–10
Paint, wallpaper supplies	4–6	4–6	3–5	6	4–6	4–6	6
Parking lots & garages (attendant)	40–65	—	50	40–60	40–50	40–55	50–60
Parking lots & garages (nonattendant)	60–70	—	—	60–70	60–70	60–65	50
Photography	6–10	5–8	6	10	8–10	6–10	6–8
Pianos and musical instruments	4–6	3–5	4	5	4–6	5–7	6
Radio, television, hi-fi	4–6	3–7	$2^1/_2$–5	5	3–5	3–6	6
Record shops	7–9	5–6	5–6	6	5–7	4–7	6–7
Restaurants	6–10	5–7	5–6	6–7	5–7	5–10	6–10
Restaurants (with bar)	8–10	5–8	6	7–8	6–8	5–10	5–10
Shoe repair	10	—	—	8–10	10	8–10	6–8
Sporting goods	4–6	4–6	5–6	6–8	5–6	3–8	6–8
Wig shops	10–12	—	5–6	10	6–8	7–10	8–10
Women's dress shops	4–7	4–7	4–7	4–7	5–6	4–6	4–8
Women's furnishings	6–7	5–7	4–6	6	6–7	4–7	5–10
Women's shoes	8–10	6–7	4–6	5–7	5–7	6–7	6–8
5–10¢ or 25¢–$2 stores	3–5	2–4	3–4	5	3–4	4–6	5

Source: Buildings, the Construction and Building Management Journal (Dec. 1980)

TABLE 12 Lodging Industry Income and Expense Ratios (all amounts are medians and do not necessarily add to the totals shown; 1979 ratios to total sales)

	Size of property				Average rate			
	Under 150 rooms	150–299 rooms	300–600 rooms	Over 600 rooms	Group A (under $25)	Group B ($25–$35)	Group C ($35–$45)	Group D (over $45)
Rooms								
Sales	100.0%	100.0%	100.0%	100.0%	100.0%	100.0%	100.0%	100.0%
Departmental expenses:								
Payroll & related expenses	18.6	17.6	16.4	17.3	20.0	17.7	16.5	16.0
Other	6.1	5.6	7.1	7.9	5.4	5.9	7.1	7.3
Total	25.1	23.3	23.9	24.9	25.8	23.6	23.4	23.4
Departmental income	74.9	76.8	76.2	75.1	74.2	76.4	76.6	76.7
Ratio to total sales	48.6	48.8	45.6	41.0	47.8	49.2	45.1	42.9
Food & Beverage								
Sales:								
Food	70.7	70.8	72.2	72.2	71.8	71.8	71.1	70.4
Beverage	30.9	30.2	27.8	27.8	28.7	28.5	28.9	29.6
Total	100.0	100.0	100.0	100.0	100.0	100.0	100.0	100.0
Cost of Sales:								
Food	37.0	37.1	33.8	32.6	37.6	37.0	33.4	33.8
Beverage	23.0	22.5	21.9	20.4	25.3	22.5	21.4	20.8
Total	32.5	32.4	30.1	29.4	33.5	32.1	30.0	30.0
Gross profit	67.5	67.6	69.9	70.6	66.5	67.9	70.0	70.0
Public-room sales	2.1	3.0	4.0	1.4	2.3	3.1	3.1	1.9
Other income	.2	.2	.8	1.0	.1	.2	.6	1.0
Gross profit & other income	70.2	70.6	72.2	72.4	69.9	70.5	72.3	72.4
Departmental expenses:								
Payroll & related expenses	39.3	39.6	39.9	42.1	44.4	39.2	39.5	42.3
Other	12.1	12.2	11.3	1.0	12.2	12.6	10.7	11.1
Total	52.9	52.2	52.1	53.8	55.7	51.9	50.2	53.7
Departmental income	18.2	18.4	20.9	20.4	17.1	18.8	21.1	18.8
Ratio to total sales	5.9	5.4	6.5	6.7	5.3	5.8	6.7	7.3
Telephone Departmental Income	(.5)	(.4)	(.6)	(.8)	(.5)	(.4)	(.7)	(.7)
Net Income From Minor Operated Departments	(1.0)	N	N	.3	(.3)	(.1)	.1	.2
Rentals & Other Income	.4	.7	1.4	1.4	.5	.7	1.1	1.3
Gross Income	53.3	55.1	53.4	50.6	51.8	55.2	53.1	52.9

	Size of property				Average rate			
	Under 150 rooms	150–299 rooms	300–600 rooms	Over 600 rooms	Group A (under $25)	Group B ($25–$35)	Group C ($35–$45)	Group D (over $45)
Undistributed Operating Expenses								
Administrative & general:								
Payroll & related expenses	3.6	3.6	4.2	4.2	3.6	3.6	4.4	4.2
Other	8.9	7.4	7.1	5.8	9.3	7.6	7.0	6.2
Total	12.8	11.2	11.4	9.8	13.1	11.5	10.7	10.4
Marketing	5.1	5.1	4.6	4.2	6.3	5.1	4.4	4.0
Energy costs	5.7	4.9	4.0	4.5	6.4	5.2	4.2	3.5
Property operation & maintenance	5.7	5.3	5.0	5.8	6.1	5.4	4.9	4.9
Total undistributed expenses	30.0	26.8	26.3	24.3	32.2	27.7	24.6	23.0
Income Before Fixed Charges	24.7	28.8	29.8	28.4	20.7	28.0	29.2	30.0
Property taxes & insurance	2.9	3.1	3.0	2.9	2.9	3.0	3.0	2.8
Income Before Interest & Depreciation	13.7	21.2	18.5	24.4	14.8	20.4	21.0	22.5

TABLE 13 Office Rental Rates in Seventeen Major Cities (rental rates in Fall-Winter 1981)

City	Existing buildings		Buildings under construction	
	Average/Range CBD	Average/Range outside CBD	Average/Range CBD	Average/Range outside CBD
Atlanta	$14.00/11.50–16.00	$12.00/11.25–15.50	$17.00/14.50–26.00	$14.75/14.00–17.00
Baltimore	14.50/13.50–15.50	11.25/11.00–14.00	16.50/16.00–17.00	12.00/11.75–13.50
Boston	28.00/20.00–40.00	15.00/13.00–17.00	30.00/16.00–40.00	15.50/13.50–18.50
Chicago	19.00/15.00–30.00	13.50/11.50–16.00	23.00/18.75–30.00	15.00/13.00–18.00
Cleveland	15.00/13.00–17.00	12.50/10.50–16.00	19.50/18.50–21.00	13.00/11.00–16.00
Dallas	15.72/13.51–18.56	12.45/10.81–15.86	22.51/16.04–26.50	14.86/12.16–21.22
Denver	21.00/18.00–35.00	18.00/14.00–22.00	26.50/18.00–35.00	18.50/15.50–22.00
Hartford	15.00/ 9.00–18.50	13.50/ 6.50–16.00	25.00/22.50–28.00	16.00/15.00–17.00
Houston	21.00/15.00–27.00	13.30/ 9.60–17.00	25.00/18.00–40.00	15.75/ 9.60–19.00
Kansas City	11.00/10.50–12.50	11.00/10.00–15.00	N/A	12.50/11.75–16.00
Los Angeles	22.20/18.00–34.80	19.80/10.80–27.00	28.20/21.00–35.28	22.20/16.20–36.00
Miami	17.50/14.00–27.00	14.00/11.00–25.00	19.50/15.00–27.00	14.50/12.00–30.00
New York City	37.00/25.00–60.00	19.00/10.00–35.00	45.00/35.00–60.00	37.00/33.00–40.00
Philadelphia	15.50/13.50–22.00	10.25/ 9.50–17.50	18.50/16.00–25.00	15.50/14.00–17.50
Pittsburgh	19.00/15.00–25.00	13.00/ 9.00–15.00	24.00/18.00–30.00	14.00/13.00–15.00
San Francisco	35.00/30.00–40.00	N/A	35.00/30.00–40.00	N/A
Washington, D.C.	24.00/18.50–29.50	13.80/11.75–15.00	25.90/18.50–35.50	16.36/11.75–23.00
Average rate/Range Annual rate—$ per sq. ft.	$20.26/ 9.00–60.00	$13.90/ 6.50–35.00	$25.07/14.50–60.00	$16.71/ 9.60–40.00

Source: The Office Network, Inc.

TABLE 14 Consumer Price Indexes: All Urban Consumers (U.S. city average, by expenditure category)

(1967 = 100)

Group	Relative importance, December 1980	Unadjusted indexes		Unadjusted percent change to Nov. 1981 from—		Seasonally adjusted percent change from—		
		Oct. 1981	Nov. 1981	Nov. 1980	Oct. 1981	Aug. to Sept.	Sept. to Oct.	Oct. to Nov.
	Expenditure category							
All items	100.000	279.9	280.7	9.6	0.3	1.2	0.4	0.5
All items(1957-59 = 100)	-	325.5	326.5	-	-	-	-	-
Food and beverages	18.309	270.3	269.9	4.9	-.1	1.0	.2	.2
Food	17.322	277.6	277.1	4.8	-.2	1.0	.3	.2
Food at home	12.003	272.1	271.0	3.4	-.4	1.2	.1	.0
Cereals and bakery products [1]	1.507	275.0	276.3	8.0	.5	.6	.3	.5
Meats, poultry, fish, and eggs	4.047	256.4	254.2	-.3	-.9	2.1	.4	-.3
Dairy products	1.603	244.6	245.0	4.1	.2	.0	-.1	-.2
Fruits and vegetables	1.682	275.2	272.0	7.4	-1.2	1.5	-1.5	.2
Sugar and sweets	.505	359.9	359.1	-5.8	-.2	.8	.2	.3
Fats and oils	.333	268.5	262.2	6.0	-2.3	-.4	.4	-1.9
Nonalcoholic beverages	1.321	414.8	413.4	1.9	-.3	1.0	1.1	.6
Other prepared foods [1]	1.005	260.5	262.7	9.5	.8	.4	.6	.8
Food away from home	5.319	296.2	297.2	8.0	.3	.6	.7	.5
Alcoholic beverages	.987	201.4	202.3	6.0	.4	.4	-.5	.5
Housing	45.519	303.5	304.2	11.1	.2	1.3	.0	.4
Shelter	31.650	326.6	327.2	11.0	.2	1.5	-.1	.2
Rent, residential [1]	5.120	213.6	215.0	8.4	.7	.8	.8	.7
Other rental costs	.714	308.7	305.3	13.8	-1.1	3.5	.6	-.5
Homeownership	25.816	366.7	367.2	11.5	.1	1.6	-.3	.2
Home purchase [1]	10.303	272.5	270.2	1.1	-.8	.7	-.7	-.8
Financing, taxes, and insurance [1]	11.963	501.8	505.6	21.3	.8	2.8	.0	.8
Maintenance and repairs	3.550	320.8	322.8	9.7	.6	.2	-.2	.9
Maintenance and repair services	2.737	351.1	353.8	11.0	.8	.3	-.3	1.1
Maintenance and repair commodities [1]	.813	249.3	249.7	5.3	.2	-.3	.2	.2
Fuel and other utilities	6.550	330.1	329.8	15.4	-.1	1.0	-.2	1.3
Fuels	4.796	419.0	417.6	16.4	-.3	.7	-.6	1.5
Fuel oil, coal, and bottled gas [1]	1.296	672.7	676.1	19.2	.5	-.2	-.1	.5
Gas (piped) and electricity	3.500	360.6	358.3	15.4	-.6	1.0	-.8	1.9
Other utilities and public services [1]	1.754	189.4	190.7	12.8	.7	2.0	1.1	.7
Household furnishings and operation	7.319	225.6	227.2	7.7	.7	.4	.5	.6
Housefurnishings	3.935	188.7	189.4	6.3	.4	.3	.5	.3
Housekeeping supplies [1]	1.460	274.3	275.4	7.6	.4	.5	.4	.4
Housekeeping services [1]	1.924	300.5	305.2	10.5	1.6	.5	.7	1.6
Apparel and upkeep	4.854	191.5	191.3	3.5	-.1	.6	.2	-.2
Apparel commodities	4.192	182.1	181.8	2.6	-.2	.6	.1	-.4
Men's and boys' apparel	1.310	183.6	183.6	5.0	.0	.6	1.2	-.5
Women's and girls' apparel	1.541	161.2	160.6	.4	-.4	.9	-1.3	-.4
Infants' and toddlers' apparel [1]	.106	268.5	264.9	6.4	-1.3	1.1	.8	-1.3
Footwear	.635	204.2	205.4	4.5	.6	.5	.3	.5
Other apparel commodities [1]	.600	216.2	214.8	.5	-.6	-.3	1.4	-.6
Apparel services	.662	263.2	264.6	9.4	.5	.7	.3	.6

1. Not seasonally adjusted.
Note: Index applies to a month as a whole, not to any specific date.

Source: U.S. Department of Labor, Bureau of Labor Statistics

TABLE 15 Consumer Price Indexes: Urban Wage Earners and Clerical Workers (U.S. city average, by expenditure category)

(1967 = 100)

Group	Relative importance, December 1980	Unadjusted indexes		Unadjusted percent change to Nov. 1981 from—		Seasonally adjusted percent change from—		
		Oct. 1981	Nov. 1981	Nov. 1980	Oct. 1981	Aug. to Sept.	Sept. to Oct.	Oct. to Nov.
	Expenditure category							
All items	100.000	279.7	280.4	9.4	0.3	1.1	0.4	0.5
All items(1957-59 = 100)	-	325.3	326.1	-	-	-	-	-
Food and beverages	20.001	270.7	270.3	4.5	-.1	.9	.3	.3
Food	18.926	277.8	277.4	4.4	-.1	.9	.3	.3
Food at home	13.220	271.3	270.4	3.2	-.3	1.0	.2	.2
Cereals and bakery products [1]	1.671	274.0	275.5	7.3	.5	.4	.3	.5
Meats, poultry, fish, and eggs	4.498	256.0	254.0	-.1	-.8	2.1	.4	-.3
Dairy products	1.768	244.2	244.7	3.7	.2	-.5	.0	-.1
Fruits and vegetables	1.742	270.8	268.1	6.6	-1.0	1.1	-1.1	.4
Sugar and sweets	.544	360.2	359.0	-6.5	-.3	.8	-.1	.3
Fats and oils	.361	268.1	263.1	6.0	-1.9	-.7	.6	-1.3
Nonalcoholic beverages	1.514	416.0	415.2	1.8	-.2	.8	1.0	.8
Other prepared foods [1]	1.122	262.3	264.5	10.0	.8	.3	.7	.8
Food away from home	5.706	299.0	299.6	7.2	.2	.8	.7	.5
Alcoholic beverages	1.075	204.3	204.6	6.1	.1	.2	-.2	.3
Housing	42.149	303.3	303.8	11.0	.2	1.3	-.1	.4
Shelter	28.753	328.1	328.5	10.8	.1	1.5	-.1	.2
Rent, residential [1]	4.832	213.2	214.5	8.3	.6	.8	.8	.6
Other rental costs	.488	308.4	305.0	13.6	-1.1	3.4	.4	-.5
Homeownership	23.432	369.7	369.8	11.3	.0	1.7	-.3	.1
Home purchase [1]	9.064	271.4	268.6	.1	-1.0	.6	-.9	-1.0
Financing, taxes, and insurance [1]	11.204	508.3	511.9	21.0	.7	2.8	-.1	.7
Maintenance and repairs	3.164	319.2	319.8	9.9	.2	.6	.6	.6
Maintenance and repair services	2.258	354.2	354.9	12.3	.2	.6	.8	.7
Maintenance and repair commodities [1]	.906	244.0	244.5	3.8	.2	.4	.0	.2
Fuel and other utilities	6.441	330.9	330.9	15.6	.0	1.1	-.3	1.3
Fuels	4.764	418.4	417.4	16.5	-.2	.9	-.8	1.6
Fuel oil, coal, and bottled gas [1]	1.290	675.9	679.3	19.5	.5	-.1	-.2	.5
Gas (piped) and electricity	3.473	359.3	357.5	15.4	-.5	1.3	-1.0	1.9
Other utilities and public services [1]	1.677	189.8	191.0	13.0	.6	1.9	1.1	.6
Household furnishings and operation	6.955	222.2	223.6	7.4	.6	.5	.5	.5
Housefurnishings	4.010	186.6	187.3	6.2	.4	.4	.5	.3
Housekeeping supplies [1]	1.501	271.2	271.9	7.3	.3	.7	.3	.3
Housekeeping services [1]	1.443	298.9	303.9	11.5	1.7	.6	.7	1.7
Apparel and upkeep	4.853	190.6	190.5	3.9	-.1	.4	-.3	.0
Apparel commodities	4.222	181.5	181.5	3.1	.0	.3	-.5	.0
Men's and boys' apparel	1.307	182.9	183.2	4.8	.2	.6	.6	-.2
Women's and girls' apparel	1.575	162.7	162.1	1.4	-.4	.2	-1.9	-.1
Infants' and toddlers' apparel [1]	.122	281.6	274.1	7.9	-2.7	.2	.6	-2.7
Footwear	.672	204.1	206.2	5.0	1.0	.1	.2	1.0
Other apparel commodities [1]	.547	206.2	206.1	1.0	.0	.0	.1	.0
Apparel services	.631	262.1	262.3	9.3	.1	.7	.7	.2

1. Not seasonally adjusted.
Note: Index applies to a month as a whole, not to any specific date.

Source: U.S. Department of Labor, Bureau of Labor Statistics

DEPRECIATION SCHEDULES

Description: Tables 16, 17, and 18 show the annual depreciation allowance and the adjusted basis at the end of the year for straight-line depreciation. The original depreciable amount is $100.

Example: The estimated useful life of an asset is 40 years. After deducting salvage value and other adjustments, the depreciable amount is $50,000. If the straight-line method is used, the depreciable allowance for the first year is 2.5% of the depreciable amount, $1,250.

Note: The official Internal Revenue Service tables showing annual deductions using the 175% and 200% declining-balance methods of depreciation are provided at page 3-18.

TABLE 16 Fifteen-Year Straight-Line Depreciation

Year	Annual Allowance	Adjusted Basis	Year	Annual Allowance	Adjusted Basis
1	6.666667	93.333333	**8**	6.666667	46.666667
2	6.666667	86.666667	**9**	6.666667	40.000000
3	6.666667	80.000000	**10**	6.666667	33.333333
4	6.666667	73.333333	**11**	6.666667	26.666667
5	6.666667	66.666667	**12**	6.666667	20.000000
6	6.666667	60.000000	**13**	6.666667	13.333333
7	6.666667	53.333333	**14**	6.666667	6.666667
			15	6.666667	0.000000

TABLE 17 Thirty-Five-Year Straight-Line Depreciation

Year	Annual Allowance	Adjusted Basis	Year	Annual Allowance	Adjusted Basis	Year	Annual Allowance	Adjusted Basis
1	2.857143	97.142857	**13**	2.857143	62.857143	**25**	2.857143	28.571429
2	2.857143	94.285714	**14**	2.857143	60.000000	**26**	2.857143	25.714286
3	2.857143	91.428571	**15**	2.857143	57.142857	**27**	2.857143	22.857143
4	2.857143	88.571429	**16**	2.857143	54.285714	**28**	2.857143	20.000000
5	2.857143	85.714286	**17**	2.857143	51.428571	**29**	2.857143	17.142857
6	2.857143	82.857143	**18**	2.857143	48.571429	**30**	2.857143	14.285714
7	2.857143	80.000000	**19**	2.857143	45.714286	**31**	2.857143	11.428571
8	2.857143	77.142857	**20**	2.857143	42.857143	**32**	2.857143	8.571429
9	2.857143	74.285714	**21**	2.857143	40.000000	**33**	2.857143	5.714286
10	2.857143	71.428571	**22**	2.857143	37.142857	**34**	2.857143	2.857143
11	2.857143	68.571429	**23**	2.857143	34.285714	**35**	2.857143	.000000
12	2.857143	65.714286	**24**	2.857143	31.428571			

TABLE 18 Forty-Five-Year Straight-Line Depreciation

Year	Annual Allowance	Adjusted Basis	Year	Annual Allowance	Adjusted Basis	Year	Annual Allowance	Adjusted Basis
1	2.222222	97.777778	**16**	2.222222	64.444444	**31**	2.222222	31.111111
2	2.222222	95.555556	**17**	2.222222	62.222222	**32**	2.222222	28.888889
3	2.222222	93.333333	**18**	2.222222	60.000000	**33**	2.222222	26.666667
4	2.222222	91.111111	**19**	2.222222	57.777778	**34**	2.222222	24.444444
5	2.222222	88.888889	**20**	2.222222	55.555556	**35**	2.222222	22.222222
6	2.222222	86.666667	**21**	2.222222	53.333333	**36**	2.222222	20.000000
7	2.222222	84.444444	**22**	2.222222	51.111111	**37**	2.222222	17.777778
8	2.222222	82.222222	**23**	2.222222	48.888889	**38**	2.222222	15.555556
9	2.222222	80.000000	**24**	2.222222	46.666667	**39**	2.222222	13.333333
10	2.222222	77.777778	**25**	2.222222	44.444444	**40**	2.222222	11.111111
11	2.222222	75.555556	**26**	2.222222	42.222222	**41**	2.222222	8.888889
12	2.222222	73.333333	**27**	2.222222	40.000000	**42**	2.222222	6.666667
13	2.222222	71.111111	**28**	2.222222	37.777778	**43**	2.222222	4.444444
14	2.222222	68.888889	**29**	2.222222	35.555556	**44**	2.222222	2.222222
15	2.222222	66.666667	**30**	2.222222	33.333333	**45**	2.222222	0.000000

Source: Thorndike Encyclopedia of Banking and Financial Tables (rev. ed. 1980)

TAX TABLES: 1982

The Economic Recovery Tax Act of 1981, Pub. L. No. 97-34, 95 Stat. 172, 26 U.S.C. § 128, provides for a credit of 1.25% multiplied by the amount of tax imposed on individuals for taxable income earned in 1981.

The Act also provides for changes in tax rates for estates and trusts, corporations, and individuals that will decrease the amount of tax owed on income earned and gifts and transactions made after December 31, 1981. The information in Tables 19, 20, and 21 may be used for planning for income, estate, or gift taxation in 1982.

TABLE 19 Estate and Gift Tax Rates

Increase in Unified Credit and Reduction in Rates. Estate and gift taxes are unified so that a single progressive rate schedule is applied to cumulative gifts and bequests. Generally, the estate or gift tax liability is determined by first computing the gross estate or gift tax and then subtracting the unified credit to determine the amount of estate or gift tax. Under prior law, estate and gift tax rates ranged from 18% for the first $10,000 in taxable transfers to 70% on taxable transfers in excess of $5 million. The amount of the unified credit was $47,000. With a unified credit of $47,000, there was no estate or gift tax owed on transfers up to $175,625.

The Economic Recovery Tax Act of 1981 increases the unified credit as follows:

Year of death	Amount of credit	Equivalent amount
1982	$ 62,800	$225,000
1983	79,300	275,000
1984	96,300	325,000
1985	121,800	400,000
1986	155,800	500,000
1987 and thereafter	192,800	600,000

The Act reduces the top estate and gift tax rate from 70% to 65% in 1982, 60% in 1983, 55% in 1984, and 50% in 1985 and subsequent years.

TABLE 20 Corporate Tax Rates

Taxable income	Applicable rate
Up to $25,000	16%
$25,000 to $50,000	19
$50,000 to $75,000	30
$75,000 to $100,000	40
Over $100,000	46

TABLE 21 Individual Tax Rates for 1982 Income

Unmarried Individuals

If taxable income is:	*The tax is:*
Not over $2,300	No tax
Over $2,300 but not over $3,400	12% of excess over $2,300
Over $3,400 but not over $4,400	$132 plus 14% of excess over $3,400
Over $4,400 but not over $6,500	$272 plus 16% of excess over $4,400
Over $6,500 but not over $8,500	$608 plus 17% of excess over $6,500
Over $8,500 but not over $10,800	$948 plus 19% of excess over $8,500
Over $10,800 but not over $12,900	$1,385 plus 22% of excess over $10,800
Over $12,900 but not over $15,000	$1,847 plus 23% of excess over $12,900
Over $15,000 but not over $18,200	$2,330 plus 27% of excess over $15,000
Over $18,200 but not over $23,500	$3,194 plus 31% of excess over $18,200
Over $23,500 but not over $28,800	$4,837 plus 35% of excess over $23,500
Over $28,800 but not over $34,100	$6,692 plus 40% of excess over $28,800
Over $34,100 but not over $41,500	$8,812 plus 44% of excess over $34,100
Over $41,500	$12,068 plus 50% of excess over $41,500

Heads of Households

If taxable income is:	*The tax is:*
Not over $2,300	No tax
Over $2,300 but not over $4,400	12% of excess over $2,300
Over $4,400 but not over $6,500	$252 plus 14% of excess over $4,400
Over $6,500 but not over $8,700	$546 plus 16% of excess over $6,500
Over $8,700 but not over $11,800	$898 plus 20% of excess over $8,700
Over $11,800 but not over $15,000	$1,518 plus 22% of excess over $11,800
Over $15,000 but not over $18,200	$2,222 plus 23% of excess over $15,000
Over $18,200 but not over $23,500	$2,958 plus 28% of excess over $18,200
Over $23,500 but not over $28,800	$4,442 plus 32% of excess over $23,500
Over $28,800 but not over $34,100	$6,138 plus 38% of excess over $28,800
Over $34,100 but not over $44,700	$8,152 plus 41% of excess over $34,100
Over $44,700 but not over $60,600	$12,498 plus 49% of excess over $44,700
Over $60,600	$20,289 plus 50% of excess over $60,600

Married Individuals Filing Separate Returns

If taxable income is:	*The tax is:*
Not over $1,700	No tax
Over $1,700 but not over $2,750	12% of excess over $1,700
Over $2,750 but not over $3,800	$126 plus 14% of excess over $2,750
Over $3,800 but not over $5,950	$273 plus 16% of excess over $3,800
Over $5,950 but not over $8,000	$617 plus 19% of excess over $5,950
Over $8,000 but not over $10,100	$1,006 plus 22% of excess over $8,000
Over $10,100 but not over $12,300	$1,468 plus 25% of excess over $10,100
Over $12,300 but not over $14,950	$2,018 plus 29% of excess over $12,300
Over $14,950 but not over $17,600	$2,787 plus 33% of excess over $14,950
Over $17,600 but not over $22,900	$3,661 plus 39% of excess over $17,600
Over $22,900 but not over $30,000	$5,728 plus 44% of excess over $22,900
Over $30,000 but not over $42,800	$8,852 plus 49% of excess over $30,000
Over $42,800	$15,124 plus 50% of excess over $42,800

(continued)

TABLE 21 Individual Tax Rates for 1982 Income

(continued)

Married Individuals Filing Joint Returns and Surviving Spouses

If taxable income is:	*The tax is:*
Not over $3,400	No tax
Over $3,400 but not over $5,500	12% of excess over $3,400
Over $5,500 but not over $7,600	$252 plus 14% of excess over $5,500
Over $7,600 but not over $11,900	$546 plus 16% of excess over $7,600
Over $11,900 but not over $16,000	$1,234 plus 19% of excess over $11,900
Over $16,000 but not over $20,200	$2,013 plus 22% of excess over $16,000
Over $20,200 but not over $24,600	$2,937 plus 25% of excess over $20,200
Over $24,600 but not over $29,900	$4,037 plus 29% of excess over $24,600
Over $29,900 but not over $35,200	$5,574 plus 33% of excess over $29,900
Over $35,200 but not over $45,800	$7,323 plus 39% of excess over $35,200
Over $45,800 but not over $60,000	$11,457 plus 44% of excess over $45,800
Over $60,000 but not over $85,600	$17,705 plus 49% of excess over $60,000
Over $85,600	$30,249 plus 50% of excess over $85,600

Estates and Trusts

If taxable income is:	*The tax is:*
Not over $1,050	12% of taxable income
Over $1,050 but not over $2,100	$126 plus 14% of excess over $1,050
Over $2,100 but not over $4,250	$273 plus 16% of excess over $2,100
Over $4,250 but not over $6,300	$617 plus 19% of excess over $4,250
Over $6,300 but not over $8,400	$1,006 plus 22% of excess over $6,300
Over $8,400 but not over $10,600	$1,468 plus 25% of excess over $8,400
Over $10,600 but not over $13,250	$2,018 plus 29% of excess over $10,600
Over $13,250 but not over $15,900	$2,787 plus 33% of excess over $13,250
Over $15,900 but not over $21,200	$3,661 plus 39% of excess over $15,900
Over $21,200 but not over $28,300	$5,728 plus 44% of excess over $21,200
Over $28,300 but not over $41,100	$8,852 plus 49% of excess over $28,300
Over $41,100	$15,124 plus 50% of excess over $41,100

TABLE 22 Performance of Commingled Open-End Real Estate Funds

Name	Year end	Performance measure	1972	1973	1974	1975	1976	1977	1978	1979[3]	Starting date
PRISA	9/30	Net assets	119.0	236.2	497.0	655.2	681.0	762.5	855.5	1114.5	7/30/70
		Cash yield	5.4	6.4	7.6	7.2	7.5	7.5	8.7	8.7	
		Appreciation	1.0	2.5	1.1	1.4	0.6	2.5	5.2	18.4	
		Total return	6.4	8.9	8.7	8.6	8.1	10.0	13.9	27.1	
Equitable	9/30	Net assets			43.0[1]	90.0[1]	129.0[1]	202.7	377.9	841.1	8/20/73
		Cash yield			7.7	8.7	8.7	9.1	9.7	8.5	
		Appreciation			2.5	(1.1)	1.5	2.2	4.7	4.4	
		Total return			10.2	7.6	10.2	11.3	14.4	12.9	
Fund F	12/31	Net assets			73.2	99.0	115.2	132.6	165.4	198.1	9/30/73
		Cash yield			8.4	8.1	7.7	7.7	7.9	7.9	
		Appreciation			1.9	(2.1)	(0.6)	0.8	2.2	3.2	
		Total return			10.3	6.0	7.1	8.5	10.1	11.1	
Continental	9/30	Net assets	5.3	8.6	16.4	37.6	42.1	46.7	51.8	48.7	6/1/71
		Cash yield	6.4	11.0	10.3	8.3	7.0	6.5	8.6	8.2	
		Appreciation	0.0[2]	0.0[2]	0.0[2]	(2.1)	(5.9)	1.0	4.6	4.2	
		Total return	6.4	11.0	10.3	6.2	1.1	7.5	13.2	12.4	
Wachovia	6/30	Net assets	3.9	6.0	11.4	15.6	25.5	31.0	36.4	46.6	1968
		Cash yield	N/A	N/A	N/A	N/A	N/A	N/A	4.3	4.5	
		Appreciation	N/A	N/A	N/A	N/A	N/A	N/A	11.5	9.2	
		Total return	11.3	6.6	10.6	5.5	12.3	1.7	15.8	13.7	
Bank of America	6/30	Net assets					11.7	19.7	28.3	43.8	9/15/75
		Cash yield					7.4	9.7	9.3	9.4	
		Appreciation					0.0	0.0	2.8	4.6	
		Total return					7.4	9.7	12.1	13.9	
Wells Fargo	12/31	Net assets			6.2	11.7	15.4	19.9	30.7	42.9	6/30/73
		Cash yield			11.2	7.4	7.3	6.3	7.9	8.3	
		Appreciation			0.1	0.5	5.7	1.9	3.5	4.5	
		Total return			11.3	7.9	13.0	8.2	11.4	12.8	
Crocker	12/31	Net assets						5.9	14.0	38.6	11/1/76
		Cash yield						2.6	7.4	7.9	
		Appreciation						0.5	1.6	1.4	
		Total return						3.1	9.0	9.3	
First National of Boston	9/30	Net assets				1.4	7.6	10.2	18.7	33.8	8/25/75
		Cash yield				0.9	9.5	9.3	9.4	10.5	
		Appreciation				0.0	1.5	2.3	1.0	0.8	
		Total return				0.9	11.0	11.6	10.4	11.3	
Travelers	9/30	Net assets					6.4	8.3	49.6	87.7	3/15/76
		Cash yield					2.4	10.2	9.4	9.4	
		Appreciation					0.0	1.3	(2.6)	0.1	
		Total return					12.4	11.5	6.8	9.5	
Aggregate		Net assets	128.2	250.8	629.2	910.5	1033.9	1239.5	1628.3	2495.8	
Weighted average		Cash yield	5.4	6.6	7.8	7.5	7.7	7.8	8.8	8.5	
Simple average		Cash yield	5.9	8.7	9.0	6.8	8.4	7.7	8.3	8.3	
Standard deviation		Cash yield	0.7	2.3	1.5	2.7	1.7	2.2	1.5	1.5	
Weighted average		Appreciation	1.0	2.4	1.3	0.6	0.4	2.1	4.5	10.4	
Simple average		Appreciation	0.5	1.3	1.1	(0.6)	0.4	1.4	3.5	5.1	
Standard deviation		Appreciation	0.5	1.3	1.0	1.3	3.0	0.8	3.5	5.1	
Weighted average		Total return	6.6	8.9	9.1	8.1	8.2	9.7	13.3	18.9	
Simple average		Total return	8.0	8.8	10.2	6.1	9.2	8.3	11.7	13.4	
Standard deviation		Total return	2.3	1.8	0.8	2.4	3.5	3.3	2.6	4.8	

1. Approximate numbers rounded to the one million.
2. No appreciation because portfolio composed only of mortgage loans.
3. Annualized from the year-to-date data.

Source: John McMahan Associates, Inc., San Francisco, Cal.

TABLE 23 Comparison of Real Estate Returns With Returns From Bonds and Equities

	Total return					
	1951–1978			1968–1978		
	Nominal	Real	Standard deviation	Nominal	Real	Standard deviation
Real estate[1]	13.92%	10.25%	3.83%	17.97%	11.27%	1.51%
Bonds[2]	3.45	(0.22)	6.65	6.15	(0.55)	8.81
Equities[2]	11.44	7.77	18.29	4.80	(1.90)	18.40

1. Returns are for specific composite of properties including office, shopping center, and industrial property types.
2. Source: R. Ibbotson & R. Sinquefield, *Stocks, Bonds, Bills & Inflation* (1977).

Source: John McMahan Associates, Inc., San Francisco, Cal.

TABLE 24 Estimates of Housing Inventory

Tenure, race, and vacancy status	Total units 1970 No. (1,000)	Total units 1970 %	Total units 1978 No. (1,000)	Total units 1978 %	Percent average annual change 1970–1978	New units constructed 1970–1978 [1] No. (1,000)	New units constructed 1970–1978 [1] %	Units removed 1973–1978 [2] No. (1,000)	Units removed 1973–1978 [2] %
All housing units	**68,672**	**100.0**	**84,618**	**100.0**	**2.6**	**16,532**	**100.0**	**3,781**	**100.0**
All-year-round units	67,699	98.6	82,833	97.9	2.6	16,357	98.9	3,746	99.1
Occupied units	63,445	92.4	77,167	91.2	2.5	15,192	91.9	3,084	81.6
Owner-occupied [3]	39,886	58.1	50,283	59.4	2.9	10,576	64.0	1,280	33.9
White	37,005	53.9	46,076	54.5	2.8	9,870	59.7	1,141	30.2
Black	2,568	3.7	3,583	4.2	4.3	518	3.1	129	3.4
Renter-occupied [3]	23,560	34.3	26,884	31.8	1.7	4,616	27.9	1,805	47.7
White	19,601	28.5	21,588	25.5	1.2	3,980	24.1	1,303	34.5
Black	3,607	5.3	4,597	5.4	3.1	534	3.2	467	12.4
Vacant year-round	4,254	6.2	5,667	6.7	3.7	1,165	7.0	662	17.5
For sale only	501	.7	624	.7	2.8	205	1.2	44	1.2
For rent	1,666	2.4	1,545	1.8	.9	321	1.9	212	5.6
Other vacant	2,087	3.0	3,498	4.1	6.7	638	3.9	406	10.7
Vacant or seasonal [4]	973	1.4	1,785	2.1	7.9	174	1.1	34	.9

1. April 1, 1970 to October 31, 1978.
2. Removed between October 1973 and October 31, 1978 by demolition, disaster, or other means.
3. Includes races not shown separately.
4. Includes migratory.

Source: U.S. Department of Commerce, Bureau of the Census

TABLE 25 Vacancy Rates of Units for Rent or for Sale (percentages)

Rental units	1975	1977	1978	1979	Homeowner units	1975	1977	1978	1979
Total rental units	**6.0**	**5.2**	**5.0**	**5.0**	**Total homeowner units**	**1.2**	**1.2**	**1.0**	**1.1**
Inside SMSAs	6.1	5.3	5.2	5.0	Inside SMSAs	1.3	1.0	1.0	1.1
Outside SMSAs	5.7	5.2	4.5	4.9	Outside SMSAs	1.1	1.4	1.2	1.1
Northeast	4.1	5.1	4.8	4.0	Northeast	1.0	.9	.8	.9
North Central	5.7	5.1	4.8	5.1	North Central	1.0	.9	1.0	1.1
South	7.7	5.7	5.5	5.8	South	1.5	1.7	1.3	1.1
West	6.2	5.0	4.8	4.9	West	1.5	.9	1.0	1.3
Units in structure: 1 unit	3.6	3.1	3.1	3.1	Units of structure: 1 unit	1.0	.9	.9	1.0
2 or more	7.3	6.4	6.1	5.9	2 or more	5.4	5.4	3.2	3.8
5 or more	8.3	7.1	6.7	6.6	5 or more	14.4	16.3	9.2	6.1
Units with: 3 rooms or less	8.4	7.7	6.9	7.0	Units with: 3 rooms or less	3.5	5.1	3.0	4.0
4 rooms	5.8	4.7	4.8	4.6	4 rooms	2.1	2.2	1.3	1.4
5 rooms	4.6	4.6	3.8	3.9	5 rooms	1.1	1.0	1.1	1.2
6 rooms or more	3.3	2.8	3.2	3.0	6 rooms or more	1.0	.9	.9	1.0
Monthly rent: Less than $60	5.5	4.4	4.0	3.9	Value: Less than $10,000	1.4	1.2	1.5	1.8
$60–$79	5.7	5.5	5.0	3.7	$10,000–$19,999	1.0	.9	.9	.9
$80–$99	4.6	5.3	5.0	4.5	$20,000–$24,999	.9	.6	.7	.8
$100 or more	6.7	5.4	5.2	5.1	$25,000 or more	1.4	.9	.9	1.0
Year built: 1960 or later	8.3	5.6	6.0	5.8	Year built: 1960 or later	2.2	1.6	1.2	1.4
1965 or later	9.0	5.8	6.2	6.0	1965 or later	2.7	2.0	1.4	1.6
1950–1959	4.8	4.2	3.5	4.1	1940–1959	.5	.7	.6	.6
1939 or earlier	5.4	5.7	5.5	5.0	1939 or earlier	1.1	1.2	1.3	1.4
Plumbing: With all facilities	5.9	5.0	4.8	4.7	Plumbing: With all facilities	1.3	1.1	1.0	1.1
Lacking facilities	11.2	12.4	12.0	12.9	Lacking facilities	2.0	3.4	2.9	4.6

Source: U.S. Department of Commerce, U.S. Bureau of the Census

TABLE 26 Inventory of Unsold Homes

End of month	New homes for sale (in thousands of units)				
	Total	Stage of construction			As ratio of new home sold during month
		Completed	Under construction	Not started	
December					
1977	408	87	256	65	NA
1978	421	98	260	63	NA
1979	403	117	227	59	NA
1980	343	111	178	54	NA
1980					
Oct	342	108	181	53	7.7
Nov	344	110	181	53	7.3
Dec[1]	343	111	178	54	7.5
1981					
Jan	328	106	170	52	9.1
Feb	322	108	164	50	8.2
Mar	319	107	161	52	6.7
Apr	323	105	166	52	7.4
May	318	101	165	51	7.2
June	310	102	158	50	8.3
July	305	102	154	49	8.7
Aug	300	104	148	49	9.1
Sept	298	107	143	48	11.2
Oct	290	106	137	47	10.3

1. Preliminary.
Note: Detail may not add to total because of rounding.

Source: U.S. Department of Commerce, Bureau of the Census, and U.S. Department of Housing and Urban Development

TABLE 27 Rental Vacancy Rates for the United States and Major Regions

Year and quarter	United States	Northeast	North central	South	West
	New series[1,2]				
1977	5.2	5.1	5.1	5.7	5.0
1978	5.0	5.0	5.0	6.0	5.2
1979	5.4	4.5	5.7	6.1	5.3
1980	5.4	4.2	6.0	6.0	5.2
1979[1]					
1st	5.1	4.3	5.6	5.6	4.9
2nd	5.5	4.5	5.4	6.3	5.5
3rd	5.7	4.3	6.0	6.9	5.4
4th	5.4	4.9	5.8	5.6	5.5
1980[1]					
1st	5.2	4.7	5.4	5.6	5.1
2nd	5.6	4.1	6.1	6.5	5.5
3rd	5.7	4.3	6.7	6.5	5.2
4th	5.0	4.8	5.0	4.6	5.5
1981					
1st	5.2	3.7	6.2	5.8	5.0
2nd	5.0	3.7	6.1	5.1	5.0

1. Revised to include vacant, for-rent units classified as dilapidated.
2. Average of four quarters as published by Bureau of Census.

Source: U.S. Department of Commerce, Bureau of the Census

TABLE 28 Indicators of Housing Activity (thousands of units; last column, $ millions)

Period [1]	Private housing units started [2]								Private nonfarm starts financed by Government home programs		New private housing units authorized [2]	New homes sold [3,4]	New construction put in place: total residential buildings [2]
	U.S. total	Region				Type of structure							
		Northeast	North central	South	West	1 unit	2-4 units	5 units or more	FHA	VA			
1977	1,987.1	201.6	464.6	783.1	537.9	1,450.9	121.7	414.4	100.1	218.1	1,690.0	821	80,956
1978	2,020.3	200.3	451.2	823.7	545.2	1,433.3	125.0	462.0	94.4	126.8	1,800.5	818	93,424
1979	1,745.1	177.9	349.2	747.5	470.5	1,194.1	122.0	429.0	106.5	121.7	1,551.8	706	99,030
1980	1,292.2	124.5	218.1	642.7	306.0	852.2	109.5	330.5	99.5	95.5	1,181.6	530	87,261
1980													
Nov	1,550	110	316	758	366	1,019	143	388	116	110	1,355	564	95,617
Dec	1,532	126	256	812	338	971	135	426	136	110	1,235	545	98,898
1981													
Jan	1,660	163	329	887	281	993	149	518	108	101	1,228	523	100,686
Feb	1,215	93	189	666	267	791	112	312	82	95	1,165	500	99,684
Mar	1,297	130	217	684	266	838	105	354	99	87	1,153	507	96,266
Apr	1,332	123	203	695	311	897	92	343	89	93	1,186	451	95,206
May	1,158	125	172	597	264	764	106	288	71	86	1,167	478	89,719
June	1,039	98	154	545	242	688	88	263	68	73	963	402	85,971
July	1,047	151	170	493	233	704	86	257	56	74	913	408	85,340
Aug	941	108	154	467	212	606	76	259	53	69	865	350	84,699
Sept	920	128	121	476	195	646	58	216	60	54	850	313	83,831
Oct	864	103	154	318	229	508	82	274	54	59	722	360	80,844
Nov [6]	871	79	127	496	169	560	92	219	NA	54	718	NA	NA

[1] Monthly data are seasonally adjusted annual rates.
[2] Bureau of the Census, Department of Commerce; figures are based on 13,000 permit-issuing places beginning 1967, 14,000 permit-issuing places beginning 1972.
[3] Bureau of the Census, Department of Commerce.
[4] Department of Housing and Urban Development.
[5] Not available.
[6] Preliminary.

TABLE 29 New Construction Put in Place in the United States ($ millions)

Period	New construction put in place: Total	New construction put in place: Private	New construction put in place: Public	Private construction, Residential buildings (including farm housing): Total	New housing units: Total	New housing units: 1 unit structures	New housing units: 2 or more unit structures	Additions and alterations	Nonhouse-keeping
1977: January	10,134	8,017	2,116	4,353	3,402	2,794	608		72
February	10,292	8,041	2,251	4,353	3,527	2,862	665	2,530	76
March	12,083	9,545	2,539	5,354	4,376	3,613	763		78
April	13,358	10,494	2,863	6,259	4,883	4,058	825		88
May	14,831	11,525	3,305	7,164	5,568	4,617	951	4,298	84
June	16,121	12,378	3,743	7,690	6,091	5,119	972		101
July	16,298	12,618	3,680	7,970	6,420	5,434	986		87
August	17,090	13,154	3,935	8,139	6,586	5,598	989	4,284	91
September	17,062	13,096	3,965	8,015	6,571	5,641	931		85
October	16,606	12,910	3,696	7,811	6,573	5,592	981		83
November	15,815	12,484	3,331	7,434	6,345	5,421	924	3,097	76
December	14,139	11,391	2,748	6,415	5,409	4,523	886		78
1978: January	11,661	9,375	2,286	5,243	4,274	3,519	755		85
February	11,595	9,328	2,267	5,159	4,305	3,518	786	2,618	81
March	13,714	11,068	2,647	6,274	5,224	4,267	951		91
April	15,598	12,249	3,349	7,288	5,704	4,679	1,026		101
May	17,518	13,562	3,956	8,302	6,403	5,246	1,158	5,051	110
June	18,983	14,676	4,307	8,949	7,052	5,816	1,236		118
July	19,484	14,892	4,593	9,165	7,384	6,151	1,233		107
August	20,423	15,430	4,993	9,319	7,560	6,279	1,281	4,827	125
September	20,227	15,266	4,961	9,098	7,467	6,190	1,277		113
October	20,145	15,384	4,761	8,849	7,361	6,050	1,312		113
November	19,104	14,825	4,278	8,480	7,096	5,837	1,259	3,853	114
December	17,107	13,609	3,498	7,297	5,978	4,835	1,143		111

Period		New construction put in place			Private construction					
					Residential buildings (including farm housing)					
						New housing units				
		Total	Private	Public	Total	Total	1 unit structures	2 or more unit structures	Additions and alterations	Nonhousekeeping
1979:	January	14,399	11,635	2,764	6,466	5,238	4,190	1,049		115
	February	13,611	11,107	2,504	5,926	4,724	3,629	1,095	3,506	118
	March	16,021	13,030	2,991	6,931	5,475	4,238	1,237		146
	April	17,207	13,822	3,385	7,734	5,903	4,537	1,365		165
	May	19,393	15,237	4,156	8,549	6,515	5,028	1,487	5,318	172
	June	20,805	16,313	4,492	9,205	7,234	5,587	1,647		181
	July	21,527	16,702	4,824	9,441	7,550	5,923	1,627		190
	August	22,449	17,261	5,188	9,591	7,710	6,067	1,644	4,949	208
	September	22,344	17,110	5,233	9,444	7,660	6,013	1,647		209
	October	22,728	17,492	5,237	9,363	7,597	5,842	1,755		236
	November	21,110	16,568	4,542	8,837	7,107	5,428	1,679	4,463	244
	December	19,187	15,413	3,774	7,545	5,874	4,307	1,567		223
1980:	January	16,981	13,485	3,496	6,824	5,255	3,681	1,574		209
	February	16,089	12,780	3,309	6,210	4,648	3,199	1,449	4,270	222
	March	17,201	13,553	3,648	6,708	4,905	3,454	1,451		233
	April	17,992	13,908	4,083	6,883	4,764	3,282	1,481		250
	May	18,895	14,228	4,668	7,001	4,725	3,228	1,497	5,827	250
	June	19,766	14,577	5,188	6,985	4,791	3,326	1,465		263
	July	20,048	14,613	5,434	7,131	4,998	3,638	1,360		246
	August	20,500	14,978	5,522	7,560	5,415	4,024	1,391	5,586	256
	September	21,309	15,527	5,782	7,938	5,850	4,394	1,455		279
	October	21,477	16,132	5,345	8,248	6,165	4,705	1,460		259
	November	20,319	15,702	4,617	8,292	6,199	4,733	1,466	5,442	273
	December	19,696	15,413	4,283	7,480	5,424	3,998	1,426		257
1981:	January	16,882	13,190	3,693	6,623	4,920	3,569	1,352		256
	February	16,184	12,689	3,496	6,178	4,668	3,184	1,484	4,093	259
	March	18,020	14,182	3,839	6,924	5,242	3,669	1,572		288
	April	r19,254	r15,088	r4,166	r7,584	5,524	3,840	1,684		306
	May	r19,978	r15,565	r4,414	r7,883	r5,613	r4,020	1,593	5,583	318
	June	r21,297	r16,355	r4,941	r8,001	r5,810	r4,122	r1,688		r314
	July	21,603	16,563	5,039	8,051	5,697	4,177	1,520		349
	August	21,526	16,550	4,976	7,924	5,456	4,012	1,443		344

(continued)

TABLE 29 New Construction Put in Place in the United States ($ millions)

(continued)

Period	Private construction										
	Nonresidential buildings								Farm (other than residential)	Public utilities	
	Total	Industrial	Office buildings	Other commercial	Religious	Educational	Hospital and institutional	Miscellaneous nonresidential buildings		Total	Telephone and telegraph
1977: January	1,883	525	369	550	65	43	260	71			242
February	1,878	503	360	567	67	47	258	77			265
March	2,083	573	407	628	77	53	268	78			352
April	2,240	618	429	684	78	55	288	89	Monthly	Monthly	335
May	2,291	634	432	721	85	50	273	96			366
June	2,454	650	472	806	98	55	270	105	data	data	402
July	2,536	653	478	865	93	61	278	109			354
August	2,684	714	458	959	95	65	273	121	not	not	413
September	2,745	711	479	990	100	63	284	119			402
October	2,270	719	488	1,008	102	61	275	117	available	available	413
November	2,714	723	474	945	98	59	296	119	but	but	417
December	2,416	690	426	794	87	49	267	103	imputations	imputations	385
1978: January	2,138	592	431	678	68	41	242	85	included	included	296
February	2,142	598	410	694	68	38	253	82			298
March	2,464	731	439	788	83	49	272	102	in	in	427
April	2,697	772	475	891	98	57	291	113			421
May	2,863	767	511	1,019	101	66	285	116	appropriate	appropriate	440
June	3,143	902	555	1,103	108	66	285	126			520
July	3,299	1,006	581	1,110	113	72	277	141	totals.	totals.	446
August	3,458	1,079	595	1,157	119	81	283	145			530
September	3,511	1,125	613	1,156	118	74	290	135			488
October	3,658	1,158	666	1,218	128	69	298	121			548
November	3,552	1,111	667	1,157	132	64	296	125			502
December	3,368	1,152	633	1,021	112	54	277	120			504

Period	Private construction										
	Nonresidential buildings								Farm (other than residential)	Public utilities	
	Total	Industrial	Office buildings	Other commercial	Religious	Educational	Hospital and institutional	Miscellaneous nonresidential buildings		Total	Telephone and telegraph
1979: January	2,828	961	555	824	98	42	257	91			378
February	2,837	999	554	811	96	42	247	89			354
March	3,380	1,223	625	978	107	49	297	101			484
April	3,533	1,182	673	1,089	116	61	298	113			453
May	3,807	1,220	748	1,249	126	66	291	107			531
June	4,081	1,257	811	1,387	137	71	296	122	Monthly	Monthly	559
July	4,303	1,382	842	1,433	129	80	298	139			543
August	4,394	1,289	894	1,528	147	90	307	140	data	data	630
September	4,442	1,321	907	1,541	138	78	305	151	not	not	549
October	4,745	1,417	969	1,637	159	78	317	170			678
November	4,561	1,365	954	1,533	155	76	315	164	available	available	604
December	4,388	1,337	930	1,452	141	74	302	154	but	but	580
1980: January	4,016	1,111	922	1,323	134	72	312	142	imputations	imputations	484
February	3,898	1,107	945	1,227	111	66	296	147			499
March	4,054	1,127	999	1,262	124	86	303	154	included	included	557
April	4,203	1,123	1,062	1,330	135	87	326	142	in	in	593
May	4,409	1,175	1,132	1,405	129	102	311	156			564
June	4,535	1,250	1,109	1,465	132	100	327	152	appropriate	appropriate	606
July	4,479	1,154	1,124	1,475	140	111	332	143			583
August	4,522	1,138	1,164	1,481	144	115	341	138	totals.	totals.	564
September	4,547	1,165	1,180	1,430	148	120	358	147			595
October	4,664	1,129	1,245	1,484	153	115	382	157			617
November	4,570	1,132	1,210	1,426	147	107	396	154			528
December	4,536	1,228	1,228	1,320	140	95	363	162			545
1981: January	4,110	1,093	1,150	1,174	126	86	344	139			456
February	4,042	1,063	1,152	1,131	124	77	346	149			455
March	4,450	1,252	1,238	1,219	124	93	388	136			588
April	4,614	1,239	1,338	1,271	140	91	401	135			557
May	4,716	1,283	1,387	1,311	117	94	388	136			566
June	r5,073	r1,370	r1,458	r1,417	r138	r125	r423	r143			611
July	5,333	1,492	1,502	1,526	138	107	410	158			590
August	5,445	1,634	1,510	1,500	151	112	393	146			n.a.

n.a. = Not available   r = Revised

Source: U.S. Department of Commerce, Bureau of the Census

TABLE 30 New Housing Units Started: By Ownership, Type of Structure, Inside-Outside SMSAs and Geographic Region (thousands of units; because of rounding, detail may not equal total)

Period	PRIVATE AND PUBLIC HOUSING UNITS (Including farm housing)												
	Total private and public housing units	Public housing units	Private housing units										
			Total	In structures with–				Location*		Regions**			
				1 unit	2 units	3 and 4 units	5 units or more	Inside SMSA's	Outside SMSA's	North-east	North Central	South	West
1976	1,547.6	10.1	1,537.5	1,162.4	44.0	41.9	289.2	1,043.5	494.1	169.2	400.1	568.5	399.6
1977	r2,001.7	r14.6	1,987.1	1,450.9	60.7	61.0	414.4	1,377.3	609.8	201.6	464.6	783.1	537.9
1978	r2,036.1	r15.8	2,020.3	1,433.3	62.2	62.8	462.0	1,432.1	588.2	200.3	451.2	823.7	545.2
1979	r1,760.0	r14.8	1,745.1	1,194.1	56.1	65.9	429.0	1,240.6	504.6	177.9	349.2	747.5	470.5
1980	r1,312.6	r20.4	1,292.2	852.2	48.8	60.7	330.5	913.6	378.7	125.4	218.1	642.7	306.0
1980: January	r73.8	r0.8	73.1	49.3	3.7	3.4	16.7	56.2	16.9	5.6	5.6	39.7	22.2
February	r80.8	r0.9	79.9	49.9	2.5	2.8	24.8	59.9	20.0	2.5	7.7	46.6	23.1
March	r86.8	r1.7	85.1	51.7	4.1	3.7	25.5	63.9	21.2	7.4	11.8	44.6	21.3
April	r96.8	r0.5	96.2	61.5	2.7	6.6	25.4	66.3	30.0	9.7	15.0	48.4	23.2
May	r93.0	r1.3	91.7	64.9	4.0	4.4	18.4	62.0	29.7	11.9	14.8	43.9	21.0
June	r117.7	r1.4	116.4	76.9	3.3	4.2	32.0	82.0	34.4	13.2	20.8	58.0	24.4
July	r121.6	r1.4	120.1	85.6	4.0	3.7	26.9	82.6	37.5	13.0	20.3	58.9	27.9
August	r131.7	r1.8	129.9	92.0	4.5	6.9	26.5	90.6	39.3	13.9	20.9	62.5	32.6
September	r147.0	r8.7	138.3	95.0	6.4	6.6	30.3	94.3	44.0	17.1	30.6	59.6	30.9
October	r153.7	r1.0	152.7	97.5	4.9	8.0	42.2	104.8	47.9	12.1	33.3	74.4	32.8
November	r113.5	r0.6	112.9	71.2	4.3	6.6	30.7	80.9	32.0	9.6	24.4	54.2	24.7
December	r96.3	r0.4	95.9	56.6	4.5	3.7	31.1	70.1	25.8	9.2	12.8	52.0	21.9
1981: January	r85.2	r0.7	84.5	48.0	3.3	5.4	27.8	65.1	19.4	5.5	8.3	52.2	18.5
February	72.5	0.5	71.9	48.0	2.3	3.4	18.2	54.6	17.4	2.8	6.2	44.7	18.3
March	108.9	1.1	107.8	70.5	4.1	4.8	28.4	77.7	30.0	8.5	15.0	62.2	22.1
April	124.0	1.0	r123.0	r83.6	3.7	5.0	r30.7	r89.4	r33.6	r10.2	r18.5	r65.8	r28.4
May	111.2	0.7	r110.4	r74.4	r5.3	r4.9	r25.8	r78.7	r31.8	r11.7	r20.2	r53.6	r24.9
June	105.6	1.1	104.5	70.5	3.8	4.7	25.5	71.5	33.0	11.2	18.0	51.5	23.8
July													
August													
September													
October													
November													
December													
	Percent change												
Latest month 1980-81	−10	−21	−10	−8	+15	+12	−20	−13	−4	−15	−13	−11	−2
Cumulative 1980-81	+11	−22	+11	+12	+11	+12	+10	+12	+9	−1	+14	+17	+1

Period	Total	1 unit	2 to 4 units	5 units or more	Northeast	North Central	South	West
	PRIVATE HOUSING UNITS, SEASONALLY ADJUSTED ANNUAL RATE (Including farm housing)							
		In structures with–			Region**			
1978: January	1,718	1,257	104	357	124	392	704	498
February	1,738	1,235	104	399	90	437	688	523
March	2,032	1,429	125	478	168	426	876	562
April	2,197	1,517	136	544	250	477	903	567
May	2,075	1,508	94	473	196	463	876	540
June	2,070	1,430	147	493	205	475	845	545
July	2,092	1,459	136	497	215	478	835	564
August	1,996	1,425	128	443	198	420	814	564
September	1,970	1,389	110	471	237	401	820	512
October	1,981	1,384	132	465	198	424	847	512
November	2,094	1,525	144	425	186	538	838	532
December	2,044	1,460	121	463	229	409	761	645
1979: January	1,672	1,128	112	432	234	253	764	421
February	1,444	1,007	91	346	190	217	612	425
March	1,817	1,290	120	407	180	364	797	476
April	1,760	1,304	113	343	173	366	698	523
May	1,867	1,268	124	475	167	420	774	506
June	1,891	1,285	124	482	175	379	832	505
July	1,758	1,195	137	426	176	361	764	457
August	1,777	1,219	144	414	183	379	764	451
September	1,844	1,216	119	509	147	366	777	554
October	1,697	1,131	129	437	185	309	757	446
November	1,502	967	111	424	179	246	709	368
December	1,563	1,056	110	397	154	322	642	445

(continued)

TABLE 30 New Housing Units Started: By Ownership, Type of Structure, Inside-Outside SMSAs and Geographic Region

(continued)

Period		PRIVATE HOUSING UNITS, SEASONALLY ADJUSTED ANNUAL RATE (Including farm housing)							
		Total	In structures with—			Region**			
			1 unit	2 to 4 units	5 units	Northeast	North Central	South	West
1980:	January	1,389	965	119	305	165	211	675	338
	February	1,273	777	98	398	79	219	654	321
	March	1,040	628	89	323	113	168	499	260
	April	1,044	650	99	295	120	162	509	253
	May	938	651	87	200	120	128	478	212
	June	1,184	760	77	347	126	182	631	245
	July	1,277	867	83	327	124	194	669	290
	August	1,411	971	133	307	131	218	689	373
	September	1,482	1,032	140	310	180	281	665	356
	October	1,519	1,009	121	389	111	284	770	354
	November	1,550	1,019	143	388	110	316	758	366
	December	1,535	974	131	430	131	259	793	352
1981:	January	1,660	993	149	518	163	329	887	281
	February	1,215	791	112	312	93	189	666	267
	March	1,297	838	105	354	130	217	684	266
	April	[r]1,332	[r]897	[r]92	[r]343	[r]123	[r]203	[r]695	[r]311
	May	[r]1,159	[r]767	[r]108	[r]284	[r]121	[r]179	[r]599	[r]260
	June	1,032	671	90	271	100	153	543	236
	July								
	August								
	September								
	October								
	November								
	December								

* The distribution of Housing starts between units inside and units outside Standard Metropolitan Statistical Area (SMSAs) is based on the definitions published by the Office of Management and Budget in *Standard Metropolitan Statistical Areas.* Data for the period beginning January 1976 are based on the 1974 definitions as amended August 1975; data for the period January 1975-December 1975 are based on the 1967 definitions, as amended April 1974; data for the period January 1974-December 1974 are based on the 1967 definitions, as amended November 1973; data for April 1973-December 1973 are based on the 1967 definitions as amended February 1973; data for April 1968-March 1973 are based on 1967 definitions.

** Composition of regions same as for Table 35.

[r] = Revised

Source: U.S. Department of Commerce, Bureau of the Census

TABLE 31 Private Residential Real Estate Activity (thousands of units; monthly figures at seasonally adjusted annual rates, except as noted)

				1980		1981					
Item	1978	1979	1980	Nov.	Dec.	Jan.	Feb.	March	April	May	June
NEW UNITS											
Permits authorized	1,801	1,552	1,191	1,366	1,249	1,214	1,165	1,153	1,186	1,167	976
1-family	1,183	981	710	809	753	715	677	678	689	654	567
2-or-more-family	618	571	481	557	496	499	488	475	497	513	409
Started	2,020	1,745	1,292	1,550	1,535	1,660	1,215	1,297	1,332	1,159	1,032
1-family	1,433	1,194	852	1,019	974	993	791	838	897	767	671
2-or-more-family	587	551	440	531	561	667	424	459	435	392	361
Under construction, end of period [1]	1,310	1,140	896	905	915	940	938	927 r	915	901	n.a.
1-family	765	639	515	529	535	544	541	533	527	511	n.a.
2-or-more-family	546	501	382	376	381	397	397	394 r	387	390	n.a.
Completed	1,868	1,855	1,502	1,274	1,373	1,252	1,389	1,362 r	1,516	1,242	n.a.
1-family	1,369	1,286	957	819	895	903	965	880 r	955	850	n.a.
2-or-more-family	498	569	545	455	478	349	424	482	561	392	n.a.
Mobile homes shipped	276	277	222	239	261	233	256	255	265	255	n.a.
Merchant builder activity in 1-family units											
Number sold	818	709	530	560	514	523	500	507	457	493	408
Number for sale, end of period [1]	419	402	340	337	336	329	334	325	327	324	312
Price ($ thousands) [2]											
Median											
Units sold	55.8	62.7	64.9	67.1	67.2	67.9	65.8	67.1	68.4	71.8	71.6
Average											
Units sold	62.7	71.9	76.6	82.2	81.5	80.2	80.1	81.2	82.5	84.3	88.3
EXISTING UNITS (1-family)											
Number sold	3,863	3,701	2,881	2,960	2,910	2,580	2,560	2,490	2,610	2,500	2,650
Price of units sold ($ thousands) [2]											
Median	48.7	55.5	62.1	64.3	63.0	64.5	64.1	64.4	65.3	66.3	67.9
Average	55.1	64.0	72.7	74.9	74.0	76.1	75.7	76.2	77.3	78.6	80.3

1. Not at annual rates.
2. Not seasonally adjusted.

TABLE 32 Metropolitan and Nonmetropolitan Area Population by State (thousands of persons, except where percent is indicated)

Division and state	Metropolitan area population							Nonmetropolitan area population						
	Total (1,000)			Percent change		Percent of state or division		Total (1,000)			Percent change		Percent of state or division	
	1960 (Apr.)	1970 (Apr.)	1978 (July)	1960–1970	1970–1978	1970	1978	1960 (Apr.)	1970 (Apr.)	1978 (July)	1960–1970	1970–1978	1970	1978
United States	**128,005**	**149,878**	**159,134**	**17.1**	**6.2**	**73.6**	**72.9**	**51,305**	**53,424**	**58,889**	**4.1**	**10.2**	**26.4**	**20.1**
New England	**8,043**	**9,046**	**9,123**	**12.5**	**14.4**	**76.4**	**73.6**	**2,467**	**2,801**	**3,091**	**13.6**	**10.4**	**23.6**	**26.4**
Maine	233	243	249	4.1	2.5	24.4	22.8	736	751	842	2.0	12.1	75.6	77.2
New Hampshire	194	262	317	34.9	21.0	35.5	36.5	413	476	552	15.3	16.0	64.5	63.5
Vermont	—	—	—	(x)	(x)	(x)	(x)	390	445	487	14.1	9.4	100.0	100.0
Massachusetts	4,564	4,980	4,955	9.1	—.5	87.5	86.4	584	709	779	21.3	9.9	12.5	15.8
Rhode Island	786	867	860	10.3	—.8	91.3	92.2	73	83	75	13.1	—9.6	8.7	7.8
Connecticut	2,265	2,695	2,742	19.0	1.7	88.9	88.0	270	337	356	24.9	5.6	11.1	12.0
Middle Atlantic	**29,902**	**32,628**	**31,854**	**9.1**	**—2.4**	**87.7**	**86.5**	**4,267**	**4,585**	**4,971**	**7.5**	**8.4**	**12.3**	**13.5**
New York	14,968	16,290	15,686	8.8	—3.7	89.3	88.4	1,814	1,951	2,063	7.6	5.7	10.7	11.6
New Jersey	5,807	6,756	6,725	16.3	—.5	94.2	91.8	260	415	602	59.6	44.9	5.8	8.2
Pennsylvania	9,127	9,582	9,444	5.0	—1.4	81.2	80.4	2,193	2,219	2,306	1.2	3.9	18.8	19.6
East North Central	**27,949**	**31,489**	**31,903**	**12.7**	**1.3**	**77.9**	**77.4**	**8,276**	**8,774**	**9,330**	**6.0**	**6.3**	**22.1**	**22.6**
Ohio	7,745	8,596	8,562	11.0	—.4	80.7	79.7	1,962	2,061	2,187	5.1	6.1	19.3	20.3
Indiana	3,226	3,660	3,783	13.5	3.4	68.0	70.4	1,436	1,535	1,591	6.9	3.6	32.0	29.6
Illinois	8,074	9,053	9,146	12.1	1.0	81.5	81.4	2,007	2,057	2,097	2.5	1.9	18.5	18.6
Michigan	6,440	7,354	7,470	14.2	1.6	82.8	81.3	1,383	1,528	1,719	10.4	12.5	17.2	18.7
Wisconsin	2,464	2,824	2,942	14.6	4.2	63.9	62.9	1,487	1,593	1,737	7.1	9.0	36.1	37.1
West North Central	**7,470**	**8,565**	**8,951**	**14.7**	**4.5**	**52.1**	**52.6**	**7,924**	**7,762**	**8,067**	**—2.0**	**3.9**	**47.9**	**47.4**
Minnesota	2,052	2,451	2,578	19.5	5.2	64.4	64.3	1,362	1,355	1,430	—.6	5.6	35.6	35.7
Iowa	937	1,033	1,077	10.3	4.2	36.6	37.2	1,821	1,792	1,819	—1.6	1.5	63.4	62.8
Missouri	2,692	3,042	3,093	13.0	1.7	65.0	63.6	1,628	1,636	1,767	.5	8.0	35.0	36.4
North Dakota	171	196	225	14.6	14.9	21.8	34.5	462	422	427	8.7	1.2	78.2	65.5
South Dakota	157	172	194	9.4	12.9	25.8	28.1	524	495	496	—5.5	.2	74.2	71.9
Nebraska	542	637	699	17.4	9.7	42.9	44.6	869	849	867	—2.4	2.1	57.1	55.4
Kansas	920	1,035	1,086	12.5	4.9	46.0	46.3	1,259	1,214	1,262	—3.5	3.9	54.0	53.7
South Atlantic	**15,940**	**20,223**	**22,829**	**26.9**	**12.9**	**65.9**	**66.0**	**10,019**	**10,456**	**11,751**	**4.4**	**12.4**	**34.1**	**34.0**
Delaware	307	386	397	25.5	2.8	70.4	68.1	139	162	186	16.9	14.6	29.6	31.9
Maryland	2,583	3,357	3,507	29.9	4.5	85.5	84.6	518	567	636	9.6	12.1	14.5	15.4
District of Columbia	764	757	674	—1.0	—11.0	100.0	100.0	—	—	—	(x)	—	(x)	(x)
Virginia	2,423	3,074	3,374	26.9	9.8	66.1	65.5	1,531	1,577	1,774	3.0	12.5	33.9	34.5
West Virginia	681	664	671	—2.6	1.1	38.1	36.1	1,179	1,080	1,188	—8.4	10.0	61.9	63.4
North Carolina	1,870	2,285	2,523	22.2	10.4	44.9	45.2	2,686	2,799	3,054	4.2	9.1	55.1	54.8
South Carolina	1,033	1,223	1,409	18.4	15.2	47.2	48.3	1,349	1,367	1,508	1.3	10.3	52.8	51.7
Georgia	2,048	2,594	2,892	26.6	11.5	56.5	56.9	1,895	1,994	2,192	5.2	9.9	43.5	43.1
Florida	4,230	5,884	7,382	39.1	25.5	86.6	85.9	722	908	1,212	25.8	33.5	13.4	14.1
East South Central	**5,968**	**6,679**	**7,275**	**11.9**	**8.9**	**52.1**	**52.0**	**6,082**	**6,129**	**6,727**	**.8**	**9.8**	**47.9**	**48.0**
Kentucky	1,324	1,511	1,578	14.1	4.4	46.9	45.1	1,714	1,710	1,921	—.2	12.3	53.1	54.9
Tennessee	2,216	2,497	2,733	12.7	9.5	63.6	62.7	1,351	1,429	1,624	5.7	13.7	36.4	37.3
Alabama	1,987	2,129	2,320	7.1	9.0	61.8	62.0	1,280	1,316	1,422	2.8	8.1	38.2	38.0
Mississippi	441	543	644	23.0	18.6	24.5	26.8	1,737	1,674	1,760	—3.6	5.1	75.5	73.2
West South Central	**10,842**	**13,129**	**15,316**	**21.1**	**16.7**	**67.9**	**69.5**	**6,109**	**6,197**	**6,731**	**1.4**	**8.6**	**32.1**	**30.5**
Arkansas	622	734	842	18.0	14.7	38.2	38.5	1,164	1,189	1,344	2.1	13.0	61.8	61.5
Louisiana	1,985	2,262	2,505	14.0	10.7	62.1	63.1	1,272	1,382	1,462	8.6	5.7	37.9	36.9
Oklahoma	1,179	1,412	1,604	19.7	13.6	55.2	55.7	1,149	1,148	1,276	—.1	11.2	44.8	44.3
Texas	7,057	8,721	10,365	23.6	18.8	77.9	79.6	2,523	2,478	2,649	—1.8	6.9	22.1	20.4
Mountain	**3,672**	**4,951**	**6,234**	**34.8**	**25.9**	**59.7**	**60.6**	**3,183**	**3,338**	**4,059**	**4.9**	**21.6**	**40.3**	**39.4**
Montana	152	169	190	11.0	12.5	24.4	24.3	522	525	594	.6	13.1	75.6	75.7
Idaho	93	112	153	20.1	36.1	15.7	17.4	574	601	725	4.7	20.6	84.3	82.6
Wyoming	—	—	—	(x)	—	(x)	(x)	330	332	424	.7	27.4	100.0	100.0
Colorado	1,326	1,776	2,159	34.0	21.5	80.4	80.8	428	433	512	1.1	18.0	19.6	19.2
New Mexico	276	333	409	20.6	22.7	32.8	33.7	675	684	803	1.4	17.5	67.2	66.3
Arizona	929	1,323	1,755	42.4	32.7	74.5	74.6	373	453	599	21.3	32.4	25.5	25.4
Utah	683	843	1,028	23.4	21.9	79.6	78.6	207	216	280	4.3	29.4	20.4	21.4
Nevada	212	394	540	86.2	36.9	80.7	81.4	74	94	123	28.4	30.8	19.3	18.6
Pacific	**18,219**	**23,167**	**25,649**	**27.2**	**10.7**	**87.3**	**86.0**	**2,979**	**3,381**	**4,162**	**13.5**	**23.1**	**12.7**	**14.0**
Washington	2,031	2,491	2,683	22.6	7.7	73.0	71.1	822	922	1,091	12.2	18.3	27.0	28.9
Oregon	1,038	1,281	1,452	23.3	13.4	61.2	59.4	730	811	992	11.0	22.3	38.8	40.6
California	14,566	18,638	20,614	28.0	10.6	93.3	92.5	1,151	1,333	1,680	15.8	26.0	6.7	7.5
Alaska	83	126	180	52.6	42.2	41.8	44.6	143	176	223	22.9	26.5	58.2	55.4
Hawaii	500	631	720	26.0	14.1	81.9	80.3	132	139	177	5.3	27.0	18.1	19.7

— = Zero or rounds to zero x = Not applicable

Source: U.S. Department of Commerce, Bureau of the Census

TABLE 33 Marital Status by Age and Sex (as of end of 1979, in thousands of persons age 18+, except where percent is indicated)

Sex and age	Total	Single	Married	Widowed	Divorced	Percent distribution: Total	Single	Married	Widowed	Divorced
Male	**72,716**	**16,970**	**50,329**	**1,945**	**3,471**	**100.0**	**23.3**	**69.2**	**2.7**	**4.8**
18–19 years	4,017	3,813	199	—	5	100.0	94.9	5.0	—	.1
20–24 years	9,713	6,545	3,002	—	166	100.0	67.4	30.9	—	1.7
25–29 years	8,812	2,661	5,650	16	485	100.0	30.2	64.1	.2	5.5
30–34 years	7,907	1,180	6,136	16	575	100.0	14.9	77.6	.2	7.3
35–44 years	11,940	988	10,081	41	830	100.0	8.3	84.4	.3	7.0
45–54 years	11,036	761	9,447	194	633	100.0	6.9	85.6	1.8	5.7
55–64 years	9,744	510	8,449	328	458	100.0	5.2	86.7	3.4	4.7
65–74 years	6,385	358	5,188	591	248	100.0	5.6	81.3	9.3	3.9
75 years and over	3,163	154	2,178	759	71	100.0	4.9	68.9	24.0	2.2
Female	**80,629**	**13,644**	**51,181**	**10,449**	**5,355**	**100.0**	**16.9**	**63.5**	**13.0**	**6.6**
18–19 years	4,184	3,475	673	—	36	100.0	83.1	16.1	—	.9
20–24 years	10,136	5,003	4,793	15	326	100.0	49.4	47.3	.1	3.2
25–29 years	9,128	1,789	6,582	41	715	100.0	19.6	72.1	.4	7.8
30–34 years	8,206	777	6,528	66	835	100.0	9.5	79.6	.8	10.2
35–44 years	12,671	747	10,335	275	1,314	100.0	5.9	81.6	2.2	10.4
45–54 years	11,790	520	9,402	895	972	100.0	4.4	79.7	7.6	8.2
55–64 years	10,887	504	7,629	2,045	709	100.0	4.6	70.1	18.8	6.5
65–74 years	8,382	504	4,090	3,454	335	100.0	6.0	48.8	41.2	4.0
75 years and over	5,245	324	1,150	3,656	113	100.0	6.2	21.9	69.7	2.2

— = Zero or rounds to zero

TABLE 34 Population Projections by Region and State (thousands of persons)

State	Series II–A			Series II–B			Series II–C		
	1985	1990	2000	1985	1990	2000	1985	1990	2000
United States	**232,371**	**243,004**	**259,869**	**232,371**	**243,004**	**259,869**	**232,371**	**243,004**	**259,869**
New England	**13,141**	**13,703**	**14,615**	**13,070**	**13,600**	**14,449**	**13,246**	**13,867**	**14,855**
Maine	1,143	1,192	1,273	1,196	1,273	1,405	1,140	1,191	1,274
New Hampshire	939	1,007	1,121	935	1,002	1,113	881	923	991
Vermont	528	560	614	517	543	586	513	538	578
Massachuetts	6,186	6,415	6,787	6,209	6,450	6,842	6,312	6,606	7,073
Rhode Island	1,000	1,040	1,107	1,003	1,045	1,117	1,014	1,061	1,141
Connecticut	3,345	3,489	3,713	3,210	3,287	3,386	3,386	3,548	3,798
Middle Atlantic	**38,338**	**39,144**	**40,239**	**37,700**	**38,196**	**38,703**	**40,326**	**42,084**	**44,912**
New York	18,288	18,528	18,816	17,927	17,995	17,961	19,902	20,938	22,727
New Jersey	7,964	8,344	8,958	7,741	8,010	8,425	7,962	8,326	8,901
Pennsylvania	12,086	12,272	12,465	12,032	12,191	12,317	12,462	12,820	13,284
East North Central	**43,371**	**44,847**	**47,005**	**42,314**	**43,260**	**44,398**	**44,669**	**46,747**	**49,951**
Ohio	11,251	11,570	11,999	10,861	10,988	11,051	11,644	12,144	12,895
Indiana	5,621	5,804	6,069	5,481	5,595	5,731	5,778	6,038	6,441
Illinois	11,688	12,015	12,491	11,454	11,665	11,923	12,246	12,833	13,777
Michigan	9,866	10,302	10,970	9,546	9,814	10,148	10,049	10,562	11,356
Wisconsin	4,945	5,156	5,476	4,972	5,198	5,545	4,952	5,170	5,482
West North Central	**17,495**	**18,016**	**18,782**	**17,550**	**18,101**	**18,909**	**17,903**	**18,620**	**19,661**
Minnesota	4,209	4,382	4,637	4,179	4,338	4,561	4,253	4,448	4,732
Iowa	2,930	2,988	3,058	2,957	3,031	3,131	3,047	3,165	3,329
Missouri	5,051	5,226	5,506	4,985	5,129	5,346	5,055	5,223	5,469
North Dakota	631	633	631	675	698	732	699	736	791
South Dakota	676	679	679	707	724	748	743	781	839
Nebraska	1,628	1,679	1,755	1,665	1,738	1,851	1,667	1,739	1,848
Kansas	2,370	2,429	2,516	2,380	2,443	2,540	2,439	2,528	2,653
South Atlantic	**38,648**	**41,182**	**45,400**	**39,675**	**42,727**	**47,949**	**36,269**	**37,622**	**39,666**
Delaware	648	684	742	626	651	689	630	658	697
Maryland	4,721	5,048	5,612	4,637	4,928	5,436	4,489	4,683	4,964
District of Columbia	694	693	697	667	651	627	781	812	861
Virginia	5,585	5,899	6,414	5,730	6,117	6,768	5,433	5,664	6,008
West Virginia	1,837	1,869	1,912	1,907	1,973	2,076	1,908	1,971	2,071
North Carolina	6,026	6,332	6,830	6,185	6,573	7,226	5,883	6,102	6,426
South Carolina	3,164	3,346	3,644	3,261	3,494	3,893	3,097	3,241	3,472
Georgia	5,638	6,006	6,625	5,721	6,133	6,840	5,412	5,654	6,047
Florida	10,335	11,305	12,924	10,941	12,207	14,394	8,636	8,837	9,120
East South Central	**14,512**	**15,063**	**15,918**	**14,822**	**15,526**	**16,661**	**14,606**	**15,193**	**16,124**
Kentucky	3,647	3,796	4,032	3,751	3,953	4,290	3,652	3,799	4,035
Tennessee	4,552	4,755	5,085	4,592	4,816	5,183	4,463	4,612	4,827
Alabama	3,842	3,967	4,148	3,958	4,140	4,425	3,912	4,069	4,314
Mississippi	2,471	2,545	2,653	2,521	2,617	2,763	2,579	2,713	2,948
West South Central	**23,437**	**24,791**	**27,017**	**23,742**	**25,254**	**27,792**	**23,043**	**24,196**	**26,107**
Arkansas	2,292	2,390	2,545	2,353	2,479	2,690	2,256	2,336	2,463
Louisiana	4,090	4,245	4,471	4,096	4,255	4,486	4,201	4,417	4,768
Oklahoma	2,976	3,116	3,347	3,016	3,178	3,449	2,906	3,007	3,162
Texas	14,079	15,040	16,654	14,277	15,342	17,167	13,680	14,436	15,714
Mountain	**11,274**	**12,075**	**13,351**	**11,857**	**12,936**	**14,732**	**10,841**	**11,501**	**12,602**
Montana	793	821	862	843	894	977	817	859	921
Idaho	926	982	1,069	979	1,061	1,195	913	968	1,060
Wyoming	408	425	450	442	474	527	415	437	471
Colorado	3,007	3,237	3,615	3,123	3,409	3,892	2,818	2,962	3,183
New Mexico	1,262	1,322	1,409	1,361	1,466	1,636	1,305	1,395	1,545
Arizona	2,771	3,031	3,452	2,926	3,261	3,822	2,490	2,643	2,913
Utah	1,398	1,493	1,643	1,449	1,571	1,775	1,435	1,557	1,780
Nevada	709	764	851	734	800	908	648	680	729
Pacific	**32,157**	**34,184**	**37,539**	**31,641**	**33,405**	**36,277**	**31,467**	**33,172**	**35,991**
Washington	4,047	4,312	4,759	3,792	3,936	4,161	3,869	4,042	4,310
Oregon	2,610	2,781	3,066	2,610	2,781	3,070	2,446	2,533	2,655
California	24,081	25,588	28,083	23,767	25,111	27,309	23,678	24,994	27,192
Alaska	419	441	474	455	491	544	433	470	534
Hawaii	1,000	1,062	1,157	1,017	1,086	1,193	1,041	1,133	1,300

Note: All of Series II assumes 2.1 births per woman. II-A assumes 1965–1975 interstate migration patterns will continue.
II-B assumes 1970–1975 interstate migration patterns will continue.
II-C assumes no interstate migration after 1975.

Source: U.S. Department of Commerce, Bureau of the Census

TABLE 35 Components of Population Change by Region and State (thousands, except where percent is indicated)

Division and state	April 1, 1960 to April 1, 1970: Net change No.	Net change % [1]	Births	Deaths	Net total migration [2]	April 1, 1970 to July 1, 1979: Net change No.	Net change % [1]	Births	Deaths	Net total migration [2]
United States	**23,912**	**13.3**	**39,033**	**18,192**	**3,070**	**16,797**	**8.3**	**30,567**	**17,800**	**4,030**
New England	**1,338**	**12.7**	**2,169**	**1,147**	**316**	**444**	**3.7**	**1,484**	**1,042**	**2**
Maine	24	2.5	203	109	−69	103	10.4	149	98	52
New Hampshire	131	21.5	133	71	69	149	20.2	112	69	106
Vermont	55	14.1	85	45	15	49	10.9	66	40	22
Massachusetts	541	10.5	1,040	574	74	80	1.4	681	509	−92
Rhode Island	90	10.5	171	93	13	−20	−2.1	114	85	−49
Connecticut	497	19.6	537	255	214	83	2.7	361	242	−37
Middle Atlantic	**3,034**	**8.9**	**6,725**	**3,749**	**59**	**−502**	**−1.4**	**4,702**	**3,381**	**−1,823**
New York	1,458	8.7	3,361	1,852	−51	−593	−3.3	2,319	1,626	−1,287
New Jersey	1,101	18.2	1,259	645	488	161	2.2	909	617	−131
Pennsylvania	475	4.2	2,105	1,252	−378	−70	−0.6	1,473	1,138	−406
East North Central	**4,028**	**11.1**	**7,832**	**3,652**	**−153**	**1,025**	**2.5**	**5,948**	**3,418**	**−1,506**
Ohio	946	9.7	2,047	975	−126	73	0.7	1,546	908	−565
Indiana	531	11.4	1,023	475	−16	205	3.9	799	444	−150
Illinois	1,033	10.2	2,153	1,077	−43	119	1.1	1,647	986	−542
Michigan	1,052	13.4	1,754	729	27	325	3.7	1,331	705	−300
Wisconsin	466	11.8	856	395	4	302	6.8	625	375	52
West North Central	**930**	**6.0**	**3,133**	**1,604**	**−599**	**791**	**4.8**	**2,370**	**1,488**	**−91**
Minnesota	391	11.5	744	327	−26	254	6.7	546	309	16
Iowa	68	2.4	541	291	−183	77	2.7	397	263	−56
Missouri	358	8.3	857	502	2	190	4.1	670	465	−16
North Dakota	−15	−2.3	135	55	−94	39	6.3	98	51	−8
South Dakota	−14	−2.1	146	65	−94	23	3.4	107	61	−23
Nebraska	72	5.1	291	146	−73	89	6.0	226	137	—
Kansas	70	3.2	419	218	−130	120	5.3	326	202	−4
South Atlantic	**4,700**	**18.1**	**5,965**	**2,598**	**1,332**	**4,297**	**14.0**	**4,739**	**2,820**	**2,378**
Delaware	102	22.8	109	45	38	34	6.2	81	45	−2
Maryland	822	26.5	740	303	385	225	5.7	522	303	5
District of Columbia	−7	−1.0	182	89	−100	−101	−13.4	102	71	−131
Virginia	682	17.2	909	369	141	545	11.7	687	372	230
West Virginia	−116	−6.2	339	190	−265	133	7.7	268	182	47
North Carolina	526	11.5	1,032	412	−94	522	10.3	800	429	151
South Carolina	208	8.7	573	216	−149	341	13.2	459	221	103
Georgia	646	16.4	975	379	51	529	11.5	795	393	128
Florida	1,838	37.1	1,107	596	1,326	2,068	30.5	1,024	804	1,848
East South Central	**754**	**6.3**	**2,665**	**1,213**	**−698**	**1,297**	**10.1**	**2,124**	**1,202**	**375**
Kentucky	181	6.0	647	313	−153	306	9.5	523	308	91
Tennessee	357	10.0	755	353	−45	454	11.6	612	360	202
Alabama	177	5.4	729	319	−233	325	9.4	567	318	75
Mississippi	39	1.8	534	228	−267	212	9.6	421	216	7
West South Central	**2,371**	**14.0**	**4,012**	**1,599**	**−42**	**3,144**	**16.3**	**3,441**	**1,688**	**1,392**
Arkansas	137	7.7	401	193	−71	257	13.4	321	200	136
Louisiana	386	11.9	832	316	−130	373	10.2	656	317	34
Oklahoma	231	9.9	461	244	13	332	13.0	406	250	177
Texas	1,617	16.9	2,318	847	146	2,182	19.5	2,058	921	1,045
Mountain	**1,429**	**20.8**	**1,724**	**602**	**307**	**2,383**	**28.7**	**1,669**	**657**	**1,372**
Montana	20	2.9	144	66	−58	92	13.2	115	62	38
Idaho	46	6.9	146	58	−42	192	26.9	151	60	100
Wyoming	2	.7	70	28	−39	117	35.3	65	28	81
Colorado	453	25.8	401	163	215	563	25.5	379	166	350
New Mexico	65	6.8	263	68	−130	224	22.1	204	74	94
Arizona	470	36.1	365	122	228	675	38.0	368	157	464
Utah	169	18.9	245	65	−11	308	29.1	297	69	80
Nevada	203	71.3	91	31	144	213	43.6	89	41	165
Pacific	**5,328**	**25.1**	**4,808**	**2,028**	**2,547**	**3,920**	**14.8**	**4,092**	**2,103**	**1,931**
Washington	556	19.5	591	284	249	513	15.0	497	279	295
Oregon	323	18.2	346	182	159	436	20.8	319	189	305
California	4,236	27.0	3,634	1,511	2,113	2,723	13.6	3,057	1,581	1,248
Alaska	76	33.6	73	13	16	104	34.3	71	14	47
Hawaii	137	21.7	164	37	11	145	18.8	149	40	36

— = Zero or rounds to zero
1. 1960 to 1970 based on 1960 population; 1970 to 1979 based on 1970 population.
2. Comprises both net immigration from abroad and net interdivisional or interstate migration according to the area shown. Includes movements of persons in the Armed Forces.

Source: U.S. Department of Commerce, Bureau of the Census

TABLE 36 Components of Population Change by Race (thousands of persons, except as indicated)

Item	Total [1]	White	Black
April 1, **1960** to April 1, **1970**			
Population, beg. of period	179,323	158,832	18,872
Net change during period [2]	23,912	19,266	3,709
Births[3]	39,073	32,543	5,948
Deaths	18,209	15,986	2,107
Net civilian immigration	3,887	3,362	234
Population, end of period	203,235	178,098	22,581
April 1, **1970** to Jan. 1, **1979**			
Population, beg. of period	203,235	178,098	22,581
Net change during period [2]	15,809	11,106	3,080
Births	28,905	23,549	4,663
Deaths	16,837	14,768	1,944
Net civilian immigration	3,136	1,735	343
Population, end of period	219,044	189,204	25,661

Item	Total [1]	White	Black
1960 (calendar year):			
Net growth rate	16.1	15.1	22.1
Birth rate	23.9	22.7	32.9
Death rate	9.5	9.4	10.3
General fertility rate[4]	118.0	113.2	152.7
1970 (calendar year):			
Net growth rate	12.0	10.6	18.0
Birth rate	18.3	17.3	25.4
Death rate	9.4	9.4	10.0
General fertility rate[4]	87.5	83.5	114.7
1978 (calendar year):[5]			
Net growth rate	8.0	6.3	13.7
Birth rate	15.3	14.3	21.1
Death rate	8.8	9.0	8.7
General fertility rate[4]	66.5	63.1	86.5

1. Includes other races not shown separately.
2. Includes changes due to movement of Armed Forces to posts overseas and the "error of closure" (the amount necessary to make the components of change add to the net change between censuses).
3. Adjusted for underregistration.
4. Registered births per 1,000 resident females aged 15 to 44, estimated as of July 1.
5. Preliminary.

Source: U.S. Department of Commerce, Bureau of the Census

Index

[References are to sections.]

[*References are to sections.*]

[*References are to sections.*]

[*References are to sections.*]

E

[*References are to sections.*]

F

[*References are to sections.*]

G

H

[*References are to sections.*]

I

[*References are to sections.*]

J

L

[*References are to sections.*]

[*References are to sections.*]

M

[*References are to sections.*]

[*References are to sections.*]

[*References are to sections.*]

R

[*References are to sections.*]

[*References are to sections.*]

[*References are to sections.*]

[*References are to sections.*]

[*References are to sections.*]

U

V

W

Z